Jesus and Judaism

BMSEC
BAYLOR–MOHR SIEBECK
Studies in Early Christianity

Wayne Coppins and Simon Gathercole
Series Editors

ALSO AVAILABLE

Jesus and Judaism

Martin Hengel and Anna Maria Schwemer

Translated by
Wayne Coppins

BAYLOR UNIVERSITY PRESS

Mohr Siebeck

Series cover design by Natalya Balnova.

The German version of this book was published as Martin Hengel and Anna Maria Schwemer, *Jesus und das Judentum* (Tübingen: Mohr Siebeck, 2007), volume 1 of the 4-volume *Geschichte des frühen Christentums*, ISBN 978-3-16-149359-1.

This English edition is published in Germany by Mohr Siebeck under ISBN 978-3-16-158920-1.

Distributors

For all other countries
Baylor University Press
One Bear Place #97363
Waco, Texas 76798
USA

For Europe and the UK
Mohr Siebeck
Wilhelmstr. 18
72074 Tübingen
Germany

Library of Congress Cataloging-in-Publication Data
Names: Hengel, Martin, author. | Schwemer, Anna Maria, author. | Coppins, Wayne, 1975- author.
Title: Jesus and Judaism / Martin Hengel, Anna Schwemer, Wayne Coppins.
Other titles: Jesus und das Judentum. English
Description: Waco : Baylor University Press, 2019. | Originally published as: Jesus und das Judentum (Tübingen: Mohr Siebeck, 2007). | Summary: "Examines the life, deeds, and teachings of Jesus of Nazareth against the backdrop of first-century Palestine"-- Provided by publisher.
Identifiers: LCCN 2018056778 | ISBN 9781481310994 (hardcover) | ISBN 9781481311014 (pdf)
Subjects: LCSH: Jesus Christ--History of doctrines--Early church, ca. 30-600. | Jesus Christ--Messiahship--History of doctrines--Early church, ca. 30-600. | Jesus Christ--Jewishness. | Church history--Primitive and early church, ca. 30-600. | Judaism--History--Post-exilic period, 586 B.C.-210 A.D.
Classification: LCC BR198 .H4613 2019 | DDC 232.9--dc23
LC record available at https://lccn.loc.gov/2018056778

Summary of Contents

Contents

Part II
Preliminary Questions about
the Person and History of Jesus

Part III
Jesus the Galilean and John the Baptist

Part IV
Jesus' Activity and Proclamation

Part VII
The Testimony to the
Resurrection of Jesus

Editors' Preface

The Baylor–Mohr Siebeck Studies in Early Christianity series aims to facilitate increased dialogue between German and Anglophone scholarship by making recent German research available in English translation. In this way, we hope to play a role in the advancement of our common field of study. The target audience for the series is primarily scholars and graduate students, though some volumes may also be accessible to advanced undergraduates. In selecting books for the series, we will especially seek out works by leading German scholars that represent outstanding contributions in their own right and also serve as windows into the wider world of German-language scholarship.

The University of Tübingen scholars Prof. Martin Hengel (1926–2009) and Prof. Anna Maria Schwemer (1942–present) are already well-known to the English-speaking world, not least through the excellent translations of John Bowden (1935–2010). In addition to their self-authored publications, such as Martin Hengel's *Judentum und Hellenismus* (Tübingen: Mohr Siebeck, ³1988; ET = *Judaism and Hellenism*, trans. J. Bowden [Eugene: Wipf & Stock, 2003]) and Anna Maria Schwemer's *Studien zu den den frühjüdischen Prophetenlegenden* (Tübingen: Mohr Siebeck, 1995/1996), they have coauthored several important works, including *Paulus zwischen Damaskus und Antiochien* (Tübingen: Mohr Siebeck, 1998; ET = *Paul Between Damascus and Antioch*, trans. J. Bowden [Louisville: Westminster John Knox, 1997]), *Der messianische Anspruch Jesu und die Anfänge der Christologie* (Tübingen: Mohr Siebeck, 2001), *Geschichte des frühen Christentums*, vol. 1, *Jesus und das Judentum* (Tübingen: Mohr Siebeck, 2007; ET = *Jesus and Judaism*, trans. W. Coppins [Waco: Baylor University Press, 2019]), and *Geschichte des frühen Christentums*, vol. 2, *Die Urgemeinde und das Judenchristentum* (Tübingen: Mohr Siebeck, 2019). In addition to the information about her research provided at Anna Maria Schwemer's university web page, a list of her English-language publications as well as those of Martin Hengel can be found at Wayne Coppins' blog *German for Neutestamentler*. Jörg Frey has compiled a full bibliography of Martin Hengel's publications in Hengel 2010b, 557–609.

As the seventh volume in the BMSEC series, we have chosen Martin Hengel and Anna Maria Schwemer's book *Jesus and Judaism*, which represents the first volume of their history of early Christianity and the last major work completed during Prof. Hengel's lifetime. As a substantial contribution to the study of early Judaism and the historical Jesus, it is noteworthy for its rigorous methodological and historiographical reflections, its characteristically intensive engagement with the primary sources, its substantial discussion of Judaism in its own right, its incisive presentation of the form and content of Jesus' proclamation, its sustained focus on Jesus' messianic claim, and its robust analysis of Jesus' passion and the testimony to his resurrection.

With regard to the translator's divided allegiance to the source and target languages, Wayne Coppins has generally attempted to adhere closely to the German wording, while allowing for some adjustments for the sake of clarify and readability in English. In some cases, of course, communication with Anna Maria Schwemer has led to more extensive reformulations and occasionally to minor additions or subtractions vis-à-vis the German version. With regard to primary and secondary literature in foreign languages, we have sometimes provided our own translations and sometimes quoted from existing translations. In a few cases, we have modified existing English translations. For example, when quoting from the LCL translation of Josephus, we have changed the name Ananus to Annas, so that it conforms with our spelling of this name elsewhere in the volume. While great efforts have been made to add references to existing English translations of German works at many points, only a modest number of new references to secondary literature have been added in the course of translation. These have usually been marked with expressions such as "cf. now" or "see now." The following specific points of translation may be mentioned here. For the sake of precision, I have translated the term *Eiferer* with "zealous ones," *Zeloten* with "Zealots," and *zelotisch* with "zealot." The term *Persongeheimnis* has sometimes been rendered with the "secret of his person" and sometimes with the "mystery of his person"; it could also be translated with "secret identity" (for further discussion of this term, see Deines 2012a, 85). The technical term *Fortschreibung* has been translated with "updating." The word *Lohn* has sometimes been rendered with "wages" and sometimes with "reward." The terms *Annäherungen* and *Annäherungsversuche* have sometimes been translated with "attempts at historical approximation" and sometimes with "attempts to approach" or "attempts to draw near." With some reservations, I have translated *jesuanisch* with "dominical" rather than with "Jesuanic," *Bauhandwerker* and *Handwerker* with "craftsman" or "artisan" rather than with "carpenter" or "handworker," *Naherwartung* with "near expectation" rather than "imminent expectation," and *endzeitlich* with "eschatological" rather than with "end-time" or "eschatic."

For help with difficult German sentences, references to secondary literature, and transliteration, Wayne Coppins would like to thank Christoph Heilig, Jacob Cerone, Andrew Bowden, Jan Rüggemeier, Kevin Collier, and Peter J. Williams. As with previous translations, I am especially thankful to Simon Gathercole for his careful reading of the manuscript and his numerous excellent suggestions for improving it. Likewise, I am grateful to Anna Maria Schwemer for her valuable feedback on the translation as a whole and for her helpful responses to my many specific questions. Finally, thanks are due to my wife, Ingie Hovland, and my daughters, Sophia and Simone, for creating space in our life for my translation work.

Both editors wish to express their thanks to Katharina Gutekunst at Mohr Siebeck and Carey Newman at Baylor University Press for their exceptional support and guidance in the continued development of this series. Likewise, we are thankful to the many people at Baylor University Press who have given us concrete assistance and guidance along the way, especially Jenny Hunt and Cade Jarrell. Finally, a word of thanks is due to our copyeditor, John Morris, and our proofreader, Robert Hand, for their invaluable help in fine-tuning and polishing this book.

Wayne Coppins and Simon Gathercole
Athens, Georgia, and Cambridge, England
February 2019

Author's Preface to the English Edition

I am very happy that Martin Hengel's and my jointly authored book *Jesus and Judaism*, the first volume of a planned four-volume history of early Christianity, is now appearing in English.

Martin Hengel (1926–2009) would also have greatly welcomed this development and taken special delight in the publishers' courage in launching a new series with the name Baylor–Mohr Siebeck Studies in Early Christianity. I regard it as a great honor that our work was selected for this series by the editors, Wayne Coppins and Simon Gathercole, and thus found its way into the English-language sphere through the translation of Wayne Coppins.

I am especially glad that the second volume of our history of early Christianity, *Die Urgemeinde und das Judenchristentum*, has also now been completed and will be published by Mohr Siebeck in 2019. The continuation of the first volume in the second is already signaled at many points in the English translation.

In the time before the publication of *Jesus und das Judentum*, Martin Hengel said to me that I should brace myself for harsh reviews. But such reviews did not come, and they have not appeared to this day. I have consciously refrained from continuously adding supplementary material to the English translation, from taking up the most recent discussion in German scholarship, and from responding to reactions to this volume in the notes. However, Wayne Coppins has judiciously supplemented the bibliography for the English version.

Small errors and oversights were silently improved. However, I wish to make note of one addition that I regard as important. Since knowledge of the Aramaic language in the first century CE, i.e., in the time of Jesus, has improved in the last decade, and the retranslation of the Lord's Prayer into Aramaic in particular stands on a much better philological basis, I have added brief references to this in the English translation.

Martin Hengel and I consciously did not want to write a "Jesus book," and yet it became one. Since it is the first part of a multivolume history of early Christianity, our concern was not only with embedding the history of Jesus and the emergence of Christianity in the history of early Judaism, but also, especially, with the question of the continuity between the Galilean Jesus, the primitive community, and Paul. This continuity proved to be more extensive than had been assumed for a long time in German scholarship. Christianity did not first begin, as many scholars like to claim, with the Easter appearances. For this reason, the first volume of our history of early Christianity had to begin with Jesus and his social and cultural Jewish background.[1]

In our view, the key to the historical and theological understanding of the person of Jesus and the emergence of Christology lies in the messianic claim of Jesus and in Jesus' certainty that it is precisely with his activity that the kingdom of God already becomes present (Luke 11.20; 17.21). Closely connected with Jesus' messianic claim is his talk of himself as "Son" and of God as his "Father," in distinction from "our Father" as the Father of the disciples. This Father-Son relationship forms the center of Jesus' own self-understanding, his *Persongeheimnis*. In this question we can only approximate the figure of Jesus historically, but there is no reason for radical skepticism in relation to the sources. Historical work is not possible without hypotheses, but we must provide good justifications for our assumptions and at the same time remain conscious of the limits of our attempts at historical approximation.

I wish to express my heartfelt thanks to Wayne Coppins—and his helpers—for his careful and sensitive translation. He sticks closely to the German text and translates it into English with the expert knowledge of a New Testament scholar. I have great respect for his ability to translate our complicated, multiclause German sentences and the technical terms of German New Testament scholarship in a clear and comprehensible way.

Finally, I would like to express my thanks once again to the editors, Wayne Coppins and Simon Gathercole, and the publishers, Baylor University Press and Mohr Siebeck, for making it possible for our work to appear in an English version.

Anna Maria Schwemer
Tübingen, February 2019

---

[1] On this, see Martin Hengel's posthumously published retrospective on this volume (Hengel 2010c; 2013).

Authors' Preface to the German Edition

The first volume of the planned history of early Christianity contains a concise description of Judaism in the motherland between 63 BCE and 70 CE, followed by a presentation of the activity of Jesus. Christianity has its origin in Palestinian Judaism and is much more strongly shaped by this than scholars in earlier decades wanted to believe. Through his activity and fate, the Galilean Jew Jesus of Nazareth also determined the way of the church in a decisive way. Both of these conclusions emerge from our most important sources, the four Gospels, and no longer require justification. The influence of Hellenistic civilization, which had been in effect for more than three hundred years in Syria and Palestine, also did not bypass the Jewish people. The "Hellenists" who founded the Gentile mission came from Jerusalem. The message and passion of Jesus also influenced the former Pharisee Paul in a more lasting way than many scholars had long assumed.

Since the historical quest for Jesus of Nazareth has been controversial since the eighteenth century and will remain so in the future, we have placed detailed reflections on the course of research on the sources before the actual historical presentation. These reflections clarify that in this quest it can only be a matter of attempts at historical approximation, which do, to be sure, allow very clear contours of this unique figure to become visible. A special emphasis is placed on the still largely misjudged problem of the messianic claim of Jesus, without which the accounts of the Gospels cannot be understood. The ever so popular "unmessianic Jesus" never existed. This is shown by the comparison of Jesus with John the Baptist, his proclamation in authority, his deeds of power, the passion story with its accusation that he is "the king of the Jews," and the emergence of the earliest Christology, which has its ultimate foundation in Jesus' activity and way.

Both authors are jointly responsible for this volume. Anna Maria Schwemer wrote, among other things, above all chapters 3 and 4 on Judaism and chapter 12 on the poetic form of the proclamation of Jesus.

We thank the DFG, which provided the means for paying an academic research assistant for two years, as well as our friends and colleagues Helmut Merkel and Fritz Neugebauer for their reading of the manuscript and for valuable pointers. We thank Dr. Sung-Hyun Kim and Sven Wagschal for typing out the text and Monika Merkle, Prof. Dr. Anne Käfer, and Dr. Christoph Schaefer for helping to proofread the manuscript. Special thanks are due to Dr. Claus-Jürgen Thornton for his careful compilation of the indices and for proofreading the manuscript at multiple stages.

Martin Hengel
Anna Maria Schwemer
Tübingen, Germany
August 2007

Preliminary Observations

1

The Overall Temporal and Thematic Framework for a History of Early Christianity

According to the unanimous judgment of all four evangelists, the temporal starting point for a history of the beginnings of Christianity is the appearance of John the Baptist. The beginning of the public activity of Jesus is most intimately connected with his person. Despite their theological significance, the stories of birth and childhood in the first two chapters of Luke and Matthew elude a historical presentation. At most we can infer from them that Jesus was born prior to the death of King Herod (4 BCE). The evangelist Luke therefore connects his only exact chronological specification regarding the activity of Jesus with the appearance of the Baptist in a synchronism of various rulers patterned on Jer 1.1-2 (LXX), which begins with Emperor Tiberius, and places it in his fifteenth year, i.e., in 27 or 28 CE.[1] Tiberius became princeps on September 19, 14 CE. The time of his reign must be calculated from this date. There is no reason to

---

[1] Luke 3.1-2. Pontius Pilate, the prefect of Judaea (see section 3.1.3), the sons of Herod and tetrarchs Herod (Antipas) and Philip (see section 3.1.2) with exact specifications of their regions, the tetrarch Lysanias of Abiline (see Schürer 1973–1987, I: 567ff.), and the high priests Annas and Caiaphas (see section 3.1.3) are also named. Cf. also Luke 1.5, which places the birth of the Baptist (and of Jesus; see Matt 2) at the time of King Herod, as well as Luke 2.1-2, which places the birth of Jesus at the time of the tax estimate under Augustus and Cyrenius (P. Sulpicius Quirinius), the governor of Syria. To be sure, this governorship only occurred in 6 CE, when Judaea was turned into a Roman province and a census was thus carried out; see Schürer 1973–1987, I: 258–59, 399–427. The evangelist has erred here. Luke places great value on the historical anchoring of Jesus' activity in world history; cf. Acts 18.2, 12; 26.26, etc. His historical specifications are much more precise than those of educated Christian authors of the second century such as Justin (*1 Apol.* 31.3–4; *Dial.* 103.3–4) or Irenaeus, *Epid.* 74; cf. *Haer.* 2.22.4–5 with appeal to John 8.57.

fundamentally mistrust Luke here,[2] to place the appearance of the Baptist in 26 CE, and, for example, to place the death of Jesus already in the following year 27 CE.[3] Whoever fundamentally rejects the information provided in Luke 3.1-2 must entirely forgo the attempt to provide a more exact chronology of Christian beginnings. Since Pilate did not come to Palestine until the summer of 26 CE, Jesus would have been executed at the first Passover festival in which the prefect participated.[4] Against this speaks not only the passion story—Pilate shows himself to be familiar with the Jewish relations there—but also the bloody incident effected by Pilate, which is portrayed in Luke 13.1ff. If Pilate "mixed the blood of Galileans with the blood of their sacrificial animals," then the concern is probably with an event on a day of preparation for the Passover festival, when the pilgrims brought their Passover lambs to the temple for slaughter. After all, the prefects usually came to Jerusalem only for the main festivals and above all for the festival of Passover. The incident confirms the various indications in Josephus and the Gospels that this festival was always especially threatened by unrests.[5]

Thus, this first volume of our portrayal encompasses the time of the activity of the Baptist from about 27/28 CE and the time of Jesus, who was executed, according to the Synoptics, on Nisan 15, the first day of the Passover festival, presumably of the year 30 CE.[6] This means that in the case of Jesus' public activity we are dealing with a relatively short period of time of scarcely more than a year and a half to two years, from which, to be sure, unique world-historical effects resulted. From this brief period a tradition that is astonishingly detailed by ancient standards is preserved for us, in which historical recollection and later interpretation are often inseparably fused with each other. These few years and the traditions bound up with them have changed the world as no other comparable period of time in antiquity. The contents of our first volume are concentrated on this period of time. The attempt to provide a portrayal of the activity of Jesus cannot be separated without loss from a history of emerging early

---

[2] Thus, however, Lüdemann 1980, 67 and elsewhere; Schneemelcher 1981, 37–38. The late dating to 36 CE by N. Kokkinos is equally improbable (see Kokkinos 1989; 1998, 196 n. 82, 301, and elsewhere). On this, see note 231 in chapter 3.

[3] For the year of Jesus' death, see Riesner 1994, 31–52. The age specification of "ca. thirty years" in Luke 3.23 also makes a reliable impression; see, however, note 6 in chapter 11.

[4] Josephus, *J.W.* 2.169–170; *Ant.* 18.35; cf. Schürer 1973–1987, I: 383–87.

[5] See the discussion of Archelaus at the end of section 3.1.1 and section 18.3 below.

[6] For the day of Jesus' death and for the chronology, which extends for more than two years in John, see section 18.2 below. For the second volume of our history of early Christianity, see Hengel/Schwemer 2019.

Christianity. The connection to Jesus has imprinted itself upon his disciples; the whole tradition about him was handed on, shaped, and configured by them. The tradents of the oral tradition—above all Peter—were, like the evangelists later, important community members who had authority. The primitive church as well was determined to a large extent by Jesus tradition in the shaping of its life and faith. This always remained vibrant in primitive Christianity. Accordingly, in the treatment of John the Baptist and the activity and passion of Jesus, the first volume will repeatedly keep in view the later tradition history of the Jesus tradition in the primitive community. A concise presentation of the political, the social, and especially the religious conditions in Jewish Palestine, which had been restless since the time of the Maccabees, belongs, of course, in this volume. This includes especially the time of the Hasmoneans, Herod I (37–4 BCE) and his successors, and then the fate of Judaea as a Roman province from 6 CE to the outbreak of the Jewish War in 66 CE.

The forty years between the emergence of the primitive community after Easter and the destruction of Jerusalem in 70 CE can be designated as a second epoch. It is the actual time of "primitive Christianity,"[7] to which the designation "apostolic period" rightly applies,[8] for it is dominated by the reality of the first generation, whose leading men, James, the brother of the Jesus, Peter, and Paul, were executed before 70 CE.[9] The designation "apostolic period"[10] appears for the first time in Eusebius' *Ecclesiastical History* and encompasses for him the time of emergence of the writings gathered in the New Testament, which he regarded

---

[7] Cf. Schneemelcher 1981.

[8] J. Becker 1993, 12, 121. Against the criticism of Schneemelcher 1981, 7–8, a valuation in the sense of a "time of the *one*, undivided pure church" is no longer connected with this term. Schneemelcher is followed with not very convincing arguments by Alkier 1993, who wants to call into question the term/concept "primitive Christianity" altogether. In our judgment, his suggestion that it be replaced by the term/concept "early Christianity" (264–65) makes little sense. He only turns an X into a Y. "Early Christianity" basically extends to Galerius' decree of toleration in 311 CE. Therefore, in light of the subject matter, the use of appropriate terms for periods cannot be prohibited because they have sometimes been used in an improper way. That amidst all diversity in the first century there was nevertheless an awareness of the "unity" of the new faith movement is shown by texts such as 1 Cor 15.1-11; the cry "Abba" in Gal 4.6, Rom 8.16, and Mark 14.36; Paul's collection journey to Jerusalem despite endangerment (Rom 15.26ff.); and the fact that the church of the second and third centuries (without protection from the state) did not split into innumerable groups and sects. On the identity and plurality of early Christianity, cf. now also Markschies 2015, 301–45, esp. 335–45 (GV = 2007, 337–83, esp. 373–83).

[9] See further below.

[10] Eusebius, *Hist. eccl.* 3.31.6: οἱ ἀποστολικοὶ χρόνοι; we already find the adjective ἀποστολικός in Ign. *Trall.* inscr.

as authentic apostolic writings.[11] The underlying conception reaches back to the beginning of the second century CE. The apologist Justin already speaks fifteen times of the Gospels as "reminiscences of the apostles"[12] and knows that their authors were "apostles or followers of apostles," and Irenaeus regarded the great majority of the texts contained in the New Testament as apostolic writings.[13] However, one will have to qualify this traditional understanding, for, with the exception of the authentic letters of Paul, the Gospel of Mark, and perhaps the Letter of James, all New Testament writings arose after 70. They belong to the second or third generation, which means, strictly speaking, to the so-called "post-apostolic period." Thus, in the full sense of the word, the seven authentic letters of Paul are the only apostolic testimonies that we possess, for they alone have an apostolic author. James, the brother of Jesus, can perhaps be added to this, for the letter ascribed to him could originate from James himself.[14] In this second epoch, between 30 and 70 CE, only *four* apostolic figures stand out clearly from the larger number of disciples of Jesus and the early members of the community: Peter, Paul, John, and James, the brother of the Lord. With regard to their attestation in the early sources, the last two clearly take a backseat to the two mentioned first. We know *Paul* best through his seven authentic letters, the earliest Christian original testimonies, written between ca. 50 and 62 CE. With respect to the writings preserved in the New Testament, he is, from a theological perspective, the apostle par excellence. The personal and theological profile of the others is much less clearly recognizable. The later fathers of the second and third centuries therefore often simply call him ὁ ἀπόστολος.

Luke's Acts of the Apostles, which gives Paul the title of apostle exceptionally only in 14.4 and 14, together with Barnabas (otherwise he reserves this title for the twelve), devotes more than half of its narrative to Paul and makes it possible for us in the first place to grasp in rough outlines and in a very fragmentary way the history of these first decisive thirty to forty years of the new messianic movement that rapidly expanded after the activity of Jesus. Its actual goal is

---

[11] All of them except James, 3 John, 2 Peter, Jude, and Revelation.

[12] Ἀπομνημονεύματα τῶν ἀποστόλων; see *1 Apol.* 66.3; 67.3, and thirteen times between *Dial.* 100.4 and 107.1. He uses the εὐαγγέλιον—which was difficult to understand for the Gentile readers as a designation for a writing—only three times: *1 Apol.* 66.3 (plural); *Dial.* 10.2; 100.1.

[13] Justin, *Dial.* 103.8; Hengel 2008c, 34–36 with n. 99 (ET = 2000b, 20, 221–22 n. 83); cf. Irenaeus, *Haer.* 1.3.6; 5 *praefatio*.

[14] Hengel 2002, 511–48; Stuhlmacher 2018, 494ff. (GV = 1999, 59ff.). The letter can be best understood under this presupposition. For the authenticity of the letter, see now in detail Hengel/Schwemer 2019.

the presentation of the mission of Paul between Damascus (or Jerusalem) and Rome,[15] and its content could therefore be expressed with the phrase "from Jesus to Paul." Nevertheless, its title, Acts of the Apostles (πράξεις ἀποστόλων), is old. The writing—which is entirely uncommon for the first two hundred years of Christianity and which, like the Gospel, is dedicated to an otherwise unknown member of the upper stratum, Theophilus—probably was not circulated without a title.[16] The "acts" presumably refer to the two dominant figures of the work, *Paul*, the unique missionary to the Gentiles, and before him *Peter*, the speaker of the disciples in the Gospels, the first witness of the resurrection, and the leader of the twelve in Acts 1-12.[17] The divinely directed, successful activity of these two men, which in the view of the author was of decisive importance for the primitive church, is meant to be recounted in this exceptional work—with conscious sequencing and strict selection in the independent shaping of the material. The third figure, about whom we know much less, *James*, the brother of Jesus, was the leader of the primitive community in Jewish Palestine beginning approximately with the persecution of Agrippa in 42/43 CE. For Jewish Christians he became the actual head of the new eschatological movement. The very unequal weight of these three figures in the New Testament tradition can be seen in a numerical comparison: Simon Peter (or Cephas) appears in the New Testament, above all in the Gospels, ca. 180 times and Saul-Paul still about 173 times, whereas James, the brother of Jesus, appears only eleven times. This does not correspond to James' original significance, but is a sign of the one-sidedness of the traditions available to us, which points at the same time to the suppression of Palestinian Jewish Christianity. Prior to the outbreak of the Jewish War in 66/70 CE it initially played a large—indeed, perhaps the decisive—role in the young church, but it already had to recede in all four Gospels (which arose roughly between 69/70 CE and the beginning of the second century CE) and in Acts. This means that the early Christian apostolic tradition preserved for us is already largely determined by the Jewish Christian authors, who were focused on the Gentile mission, which had only a reduced interest in Palestinian Jewish Christianity, the brothers of Jesus,[18] and the activity of the circle of the twelve. This example demonstrates how one-sided our knowledge is.

[15] Cf. Rom 15.19.

[16] On this, see section 6.4.3.

[17] On this, see Hengel 2010a, 14–36 (GV = 2006b, 21–58).

[18] In the New Testament the "brothers of Jesus" appear corporately in nine texts, sometimes in a negative context; see section 8.3.

As a fourth figure we can additionally mention John, the son of Zebedee.[19] Already in Acts he has only a secondary role as the second after Peter.
Paul mentions him only once as the last of the three "pillars" in Gal 2.9 at
the apostolic council. Next to him, one would need to mention—according
to the letters of Paul and Acts—Barnabas as a fifth figure, associate of
the disciples in Jerusalem and subsequent missionary colleague of Paul
in Antioch and in southeastern Asia Minor. In the case of these first three
or five figures we are undeniably dealing with special, indeed singular
authorities, who were fundamental for the development of the earliest
church. In this connection it remains an open question whether John, the
son of Zebedee, is connected with the Johannine corpus, which has been
attributed to him since the second century.[20] The conspicuous emphasis
on these men of the first apostolic generation in our sources makes clear
how much earliest Christianity and its traditions were shaped not in the
first instance—as is often supposed—by anonymous "community tradition" but by *leading* authorities and theologically creative personalities.
For the apostolic era this can be recognized in the figure of Paul and in
his relation to the communities founded by him. But it applies, of course,
all the more to the period that grounded primitive Christianity, i.e., to the
one and a half to two years in which Jesus himself and before him John
the Baptist were active. This time of fellowship with their master, truly
decisive for Simon Peter and the more intimate circle of disciples (and
indirectly probably also for the brothers of Jesus), paved the way for all
future developments. This was too easily forgotten in earlier presentations
of the early history of Christianity, especially when scholars had it begin
only with the developments in the period after Easter—which are largely
unknown to us.[21]

The end of the apostolic period in the strict sense is therefore indicated
by the death of the three men mentioned first. All three died a martyr's
death shortly before the outbreak of the Jewish War in 66 CE: Paul and
Peter in Rome, presumably in the Neronian persecution of 64/65 CE,
and James, the brother of the Lord, ca. 62 CE in Jerusalem.[22] A note in
Papias, which is admittedly disputed, says that the two sons of Zebedee,
who were the most important disciples in the circle of the twelve after
Peter, were killed by the Jews. In the case of James, the son of Zebedee,

[19] In the Synoptics the pair of brothers James and John obtain the second most important role after Peter, admittedly far behind him.
[20] See Hengel 1993a (ET = 1989a).
[21] See section 5.1 below.
[22] If his letter that is indirectly directed against Paul is authentic, it would have arisen
ca. 60–62; cf. note 14 above.

this occurred very early, probably in 42/43 CE by Herod Agrippa I.[23] In the case of his brother John we do not know when it is supposed to have happened; perhaps while he was still in Jerusalem but probably only when he was in Asia Minor.[24] The catastrophe of the Jewish War (66–73), which led to the destruction of Jerusalem in August/September of 70 CE and through which Palestinian Christianity lost its previously dominant significance, then formed the capstone of this earliest epoch, which was apostolic in the strict sense of the word. The Gospel of Mark in 69/70 CE is an answer to this crisis. The same may also be true for a hypothetical original form of Revelation, which admittedly emerged as a complete work, according to Irenaeus, only at the end of the reign of Domitian (81–96).[25] Even the *Doppelwerk* of the physician Luke, a former traveling companion of Paul, which was composed relatively soon after the destruction of Jerusalem, approximately between 75 and 85 CE, is still entirely shaped by the situation and the events before 70 CE. It contains, together with the somewhat older Mark, the most important contribution to the history of Jesus.

This second span of time of a history of early Christianity—that of the apostolic period or of the emergence and spread of the primitive community after the activity of Jesus between ca. 30 and 70 CE—can, in turn, be divided into two periods. The first encompasses the first ca. thirteen to eighteen years and ends with the sharpening of the situation in Judaea through the persecution under Agrippa I in ca. 42–43 CE or with the apostolic council in ca. 48–49 CE,[26] which established the definitive recognition of the law-critical mission by the community in Jerusalem and Judaea and opened up the way to the worldwide mission. Until this time the primitive Christian mission was largely restricted to Palestine, Syria, and Cilicia as well as the island of Cyprus, and the regions that bordered Asia Minor and beyond this had probably only obtained a foothold in Rome.[27] These few years until 48 CE, about which we have very fragmentary information in Acts 1–15 and Gal 1 and 2, are the *actual early time of primitive Christianity in statu nascendi*, which forms the content of the second volume of our history of early Christianity. Because of the sparse indications in the sources, it is also the darkest and most disputed period of

---

[23] Acts 12.1-2.

[24] Hengel 1993a, 36, 88–92, 119 (no equivalent in ET).

[25] Irenaeus, *Haer.* 5.30.3 = Eusebius, *Hist. eccl.* 5.8.6–7. Justin already attributes the same to "John, one of the apostles of Christ," in *Dial.* 81.4 (ca. 160 CE). Domitian was murdered on September 18, 96 CE.

[26] Acts 12; Gal 2.10ff.; and Acts 15. On this, see Hengel/Schwemer 1998, 270ff., 389ff., 394 (ET = 1997, 172ff., 257ff., 260).

[27] On this, cf. Rom 1.13; 15.22 with 15.18-19 and 1 Cor 15.10; Gal 1.21; 2.1; see also Hengel/Schwemer 1998, 389–94 (ET = 1997, 257–60).

time, in which, to be sure, what is really decisive in the spread and development of its teachings has already occurred,[28] for in it the fundamental features of the Christian message were formed, which confront us in the whole New Testament and then in the second century and are already presupposed in the letters of Paul. These already include the Gentile mission, which admittedly was initially concentrated primarily on the converting of "God-fearers" on the margins of the synagogue. With regard to Christian teaching, more took place in this brief period of thirteen to eighteen years than in the centuries thereafter.[29] This applies especially to the center of the new message, Christology in its unity with soteriology. In his mission communities Paul already proclaims a high Christology entirely as a matter of course. This includes the divine dignity of the preexistent Christ, his mediation of creation, and his becoming human. The apostle must have already learned this Christology in the time of his activity in Cilicia and Syria, roughly between 36 and 48 CE. In our view, something similar also applies to aspects of the specifically Pauline Gospel, i.e., his understanding of the law, his anthropology, and his teaching on justification. According to Gal 1.11-17 he received his "gospel" through "a revelation of Christ Jesus," presumably in temporal connection with his conversion outside of Damascus—at the latest, three years after the foundational event of Jesus' death and resurrection.[30] The foundations of his gospel, which he proclaimed as the most successful missionary to the Gentiles, did not emerge only as the accidental product of later developments.

The second period of the apostolic age, encompassing ca. twenty to twenty-five years, is the era of the great missionary journeys of Paul to the interior of Asia Minor, Macedonia, Greece, the province of Asia, and, as a prisoner, to Rome, where he arrived in 60 CE and lived for two years as a prisoner.[31] Presumably he gained his freedom again and visited Spain, as he had long planned to do.[32] In that case he would have been executed after his return to Rome, during the Neronian persecution in 64/65 CE. During this whole period, however, Peter was also predominantly active outside of Judaea as a missionary, pastoral leader,

---

[28] On this, see Hengel/Schwemer 1998, 429–61 (ET = 1997, 283–310).

[29] Hengel 1983c, 30–47, 156–66 (GV = Hengel 1972b; 2006a, 27–51); Hengel 1976b (GV = 1977b = 2006a, 74–145).

[30] Hengel/Schwemer 1998 (ET = 1997); Hengel 2002, 213–39.

[31] Acts 28.30-31.

[32] Romans 15.24, 28; 1 Clem. 5.7; *Actus Vercellenses* 1 (Lipsius 1976, I: 45–46); *Canon Muratorianus* 38ff. in Schneemelcher 1991/1992, I: 42–45 (GV = 1987, 28–29). In our judgment, texts such as Mark 13.10; 14.9; Luke 24.47; and Acts 1.8 presuppose knowledge of this. It was only with the Pastoral Epistles that this tradition was partly suppressed again in favor of another journey of Paul to the east.

and organizer, and he was probably crucified in the same persecution in Rome.[33] The Jewish Christian community in Palestine was greatly shaken by the stoning of James and other leading Christians in 62 CE and by the outbreak of the Jewish War.[34] With the destruction of Jerusalem in 70 CE it ceased to play a decisive role. Its place was taken relatively quickly by the Roman community, which by then was already predominantly composed of Gentile Christians.

The third volume of our history is to encompass this second period of the apostolic era, which is dominated by the information about Paul, until the destruction of Jerusalem and first part of the "post-apostolic period" that follows it until the end of the Flavian epoch or the beginning of the time of Trajan, the Johannine corpus, 1 Clement, Ignatius, and the Pastoral Epistles, which means also the first half of the third epoch.

This third epoch can be designated with some justification as the post-apostolic epoch. In 1905 Rudolf Knopf wrote his great work—which has still not been surpassed even after more than one hundred years—*Das nachapostolische Zeitalter* (The Post-apostolic Age), with the subtitle *Geschichte der christlichen Gemeinden vom Beginn der Flavierdynastie bis zum Ende Hadrians* (History of the Christian Communities from the Beginning of the Flavian Dynasty to the End of Hadrian),[35] which means from ca. 69 CE, the beginning of the reign of Vespasian, who as the Roman commander in Judaea was acclaimed emperor by his legions, until ca. 138 CE, the year of Hadrian's death. This third span of time can also be subdivided into two periods. The first period is the time of the Flavian emperors, from Vespasian via Titus to Domitian, who was murdered in 96 CE, or until the beginning of the time of Trajan (98–117). Most of the great New Testament writings were written in this period, including all four Gospels in the temporal sequence Mark, Luke, Matthew, and John. The definitive, painful separation between synagogue and church took place in it, although the Jewish Christian element and its traditions together with the Septuagint continued to be influential also in the church of the second century. This development was accompanied by an increasingly tense relationship to Roman rule. At this same time, inner-ecclesiastical crises—the confrontation with an ethically indifferent or rigorously ascetic enthusiasm and with a docetic rejection of the true humanity of Christ—and a first

---

[33] John 21.18-19; 1 Clem. 5; Ascension of Isaiah 4.2–3; Dionysius of Corinth around 160 CE, according to Eusebius, *Hist. eccl.* 2.25.8: "They suffered martyrdom in Rome at the same time." Irenaeus, *Haer.* 3.1.1, cf. 3.3.1; cf. also Ign. *Rom.* 4.3; *Actus Vercellenses* 35–40 (Lipsius 1976, I: 88ff.); Tertullian, *Scorp.* 15.3.

[34] Josephus, *Ant.* 20.200–201; Eusebius, *Hist. eccl.* 3.5.3: the flight to Pella.

[35] Knopf 1905. He wrote this work as a thirty-year-old *Privatdozent* and died much too early (October 26, 1874–January 19, 1920).

step in the development of a fixed ecclesiastical office become visible. It is also a time in which there was a creative processing of the apostolic message. Within two and a half decades—approximately 75 to shortly after 100 CE—at least five or six major theological conceptions arose, which were very different in some respects. These are (in temporal sequence): (1) the *Doppelwerk* of Luke, his Gospel, and—with a certain temporal distance—the Acts of the Apostles between 75–85 CE, whose significance for our knowledge of the Christian primitive history, i.e., Jesus and the primitive community, cannot be estimated highly enough; (2) Hebrews, which was handed down anonymously, at about the same time;[36] (3) the Gospel of Matthew, around 90–100 CE; (4) 1 Peter, around 95–100 CE; (5) the Johannine corpus (the Gospel and three letters), which was probably published shortly after 100 CE; and (6) Revelation, which appeared at about the same time, though the extent to which, despite great differences, a certain historical connection nevertheless exists between the Johannine corpus and the Revelation of John is debated.[37] At least the earliest witnesses of the second century claimed such a connection. To us this seems not impossible. Together with the earlier seven authentic letters of Paul and the Gospel of Mark, these texts form the main content of the New Testament. First Clement and the Pauline corpus—i.e., the collection of the authentic letters of Paul and, from the inauthentic letters, Colossians, Ephesians, and 2 Thessalonians, as well as Hebrews,[38] which remained preserved for us through the fact that the unknown editor incorporated it into the Pauline corpus around 100 CE[39]—still belong to the end of this period, though not the Pastoral Epistles, which emerged even later. It was a high time of theological thinking, with the personalities of the authors now remaining in darkness, partly to the advantage of the singular apostolic authorities of the past to which they appealed and which were sometimes already named pseudepigraphically as the author of a given work. Only the *Doppelwerk* of Luke, 1 Clement, and, in our view, the

---

[36] Here we are not certain whether it is not, in fact, to be dated prior to 70 CE since the destruction of the temple is not even hinted at and 1 Clement and the collection of the letters of Paul presuppose it around 100 CE (cf. note 38 below and note 51 in chapter 6). Amidst all the great theological differences between them, Luke and Hebrews are connected by the reference to the "eye-" and "earwitnesses"; see Luke 1.2 and Heb 2.3; cf. also Acts 1.21-22 and John 15.27.

[37] Frey 1993; 2015.

[38] It could have arisen approximately between 60 and 66 and been directed to a community in the east. See note 36 above and note 51 in section 6.2.

[39] Perhaps the author of Ephesians was the editor of this collection; cf. Ephesians with Rom 16.25-27, which agrees theologically with Ephesians and probably originates from its author. In that case he showed in this letter how he wanted Paul to be understood in connection with the much older Colossians.

Johannine corpus were circulated with the name of their own author during these ca. thirty years. The third volume is to contain this period of time of a bit more than fifty years from the apostolic council to the beginning of the second century CE. In it too the theologically grounded authority of the authors, who could still regard themselves as students of the apostles, or the authoritative communities that stood behind them, such as Rome[40] or Ephesus, played a decisive role.

A certain upheaval in the second part of this third epoch—which, despite the earlier misuse of this phrase, could also be designated, *cum grano salis*, as a period of "early Catholicism"[41]—becomes evident through 1 Clement, which probably arose between 96 CE, the death of Domitian, and the early period of Trajan, around 100 CE. It is an era in which oppositions break open. The eschatological consciousness and the concomitant near expectation receded, at least in part—on the other hand, the (final version) of Revelation arose in precisely this time. There were gradual attempts to come to terms with the Roman state, whose pressure became much stronger and placed greater weight on the inner order and organization of the community, in connection with an ethos that was strict vis-à-vis the pagan environment and at the same time marked by social solidarity, and on the development of ecclesiastical offices, which were becoming traditional, as guarantors of the preservation of the ideals and authoritative apostolic tradition that was now taking form. This process climaxed in the gradual establishment of the monarchic office of bishop, which is strongly emphasized in the letters of Ignatius because it was still controversial in the communities themselves.[42] The free activity of the Spirit was increasingly controlled by officeholders and the binding to the tradition, a development that proceeded not without considerable resistance. In addition to the letters of Ignatius, examples of this can be found in the Pastoral Epistles from about the same time, in the letter of Polycarp, in the Shepherd of Hermas, in the Teaching of the Twelve Apostles, and—as a mirror image, so to speak—in the traditions about the prophetesses of Asia

---

[40] First Clement; Heb 13.24; Ign. *Rom.*, praescr.; Irenaeus, *Haer.* 3.3.2.

[41] The phrase was polemically misused for a time. Cf., for example, E. Käsemann on 2 Peter (Käsemann 1964c, 169; GV = Käsemann 1960/1964, I: 135): In his view it is "from beginning to end a document expressing an early Catholic viewpoint and is perhaps the most dubious writing in the canon." In "Paul and Early Catholicism" (Käsemann 1969c; cf. 1960/1964, II: 239–52), Käsemann admittedly takes his polemic *ad absurdum*, for he finds an abundance of early Catholic elements in the apostle himself. Schulz 1976 uses the term in an entirely unqualified way. For criticism of a questionable use of the term introduced by E. Troeltsch, see Hahn 1978; Alkier 2008 (GV = 2000); Markschies 2015, 191–92 with n. 1 (GV = 2007, 215–16 with n. 1).

[42] Chadwick 1950; 2001, 65–83 (77ff.).

Minor, to which the emerging Montanism in the second half of the second century appealed.[43]

At the same time there began, since more and more educated people found their way into the church, a new time of theological reflection and experimentation. Religious-philosophical circles developed on the margins of larger communities into theological laboratories, which, influenced by the middle Platonic *zeitgeist*, were no longer interested only in Christology, soteriology, and ethics, but also in protology and the doctrine of the soul, and which, at the same time, also began to use "scholarly" philological methods to interpret the holy texts of the Septuagint and the Gospels and letters of Paul. The ever-increasing popular-philosophical influence facilitated among them a docetic Christology, which denied the full humanity of Christ, and led to the first rudiments of "gnosticizing" formations. The term "gnosis" appears for the first time in 1 Tim 6.20 around 115 CE as a designation for a not yet clearly delineated "heresy." By contrast, Luke could still use the term αἵρεσις neutrally in the sense of "religious party." However, from the beginning of the second century "heretic" is used with the meaning "sectarian" as a polemical designation of those who deviate from the true "apostolic" faith.[44] To be sure, the various gnostic groups obtain clearer contours only in the first two books of the five-part work of Irenaeus, which, for its part, is based on a lost polemical writing of Justin.[45] The Pastoral Epistles and the seven letters of Ignatius[46] also evince the first approaches toward a monarchical episcopacy, which—presumably influenced by the model of James, the brother of the Lord—penetrated from the east into the west. The Shepherd of Hermas, which arose in Rome ca. 120–130 CE, does not yet know of such an episcopacy and also attests the continuation of an apocalyptic, Christian prophetism that is strongly Jewish in character and ethically oriented. Rome still did not have a monarchical bishop at that time; indeed, this is not yet clearly the case even in Justin around 150.[47] First Clement and the

---

[43] Cf., for example, Rev 2.20; Eusebius, *Hist. eccl.* 3.39.9; 5.17.3–4; 5.24.2. Justin, *Dial.* 82.1 (cf. Eusebius, *Hist. eccl.* 4.18.8), also still speaks of the activity of the prophetic spirit.

[44] Titus 3.10 exhorts one to avoid contact with "heretics." Second Peter 2.1 speaks of "destructive heresies." Luke still uses the term with the meaning "religious party" and views the Christians as such a party like the Sadducees and Pharisees (Acts 5.17; 15.5; 24.5, 14; 26.5; 28.22). By contrast, the term is negative in Ign. *Eph.* 6.2; Ign. *Trall.* 6.1. In the sense of bad way of thinking, teaching, see Herm. Sim. 9.23.5 [= 100.5]; Justin, *Dial.* 17.1: in Jewish eyes Christians are a αἵρεσις ἄθεος, etc.

[45] See Irenaeus, *Haer.* 4.6.2 = Eusebius, *Hist. eccl.* 4.18.9: against Marcion; cf. Justin, *1 Apol.* 26.8: "Syntagma against all heresies."

[46] Ignatius writes between 110 and 114 CE, since Trajan set out for the Parthian war in the east in the summer of 114 CE; the Pastoral Epistles were written ca. 110–120.

[47] Justin, *1 Apol.* 67.4 mentions only a presider (ὁ προεστώς) as a preacher at the Sunday worship service.

Shepherd of Hermas attest a plural leadership through presbyters there. The Didache sheds light on the life of rural south-Syrian communities, and the Epistle of Barnabas, ca. 135, on the intensification of the conflict with Judaism alongside the simultaneous adoption of a Jewish "ethical" catechism, the "teaching of the two ways," which we also encounter in the Didache. This is also the time in which the latest New Testament writings arise: the Pastoral Epistles around 115 CE, which are located temporally between Acts (ca. 80–85) and the novelistically told Acts of Paul (ca. 180); the Epistle of Jude, which may presuppose the actually authentic Epistle of James and may itself have influenced 2 Peter; and 2 Peter, which may have arisen as late as 130 CE. Second Peter is the latest text of the New Testament "canon." It is later than a whole series of works assigned to the "Apostolic Fathers." It already presupposes the collection of the letters of Paul and the fight for its proper interpretation. The emergence of the twenty-seven writings of the New Testament begins with 1 Thessalonians around 50 CE and thus encompasses about eighty years. To be sure, as a canon-like, authoritative collection of writings, which was probably used in the worship service, though still without 3 John, James, Jude, and 2 Peter, this collection appears for the first time in Irenaeus around 180, though it is necessary to stress that the apologetic and antiheretical literature prior to Irenaeus, which could have known such texts, has largely been lost. This means that the collection could be much older. The term "canon" itself surfaces only in the fourth century, and the complete closure of the New Testament corpus for the Greek church occurred much later through the *Thirty-Ninth Easter Letter* of Athanasius in 367 CE.

Thus, at the end of this third epoch stands the clear formation of a New Testament collection of writings, which comes alongside the already recognized collection of the holy books of the "Old Testament"[48] in the Greek language. For Justin the translation of the seventy, the Septuagint, encompassed all the Old Testament writings and is for him prophetic prediction of Christ throughout. A major step in the direction of a New Testament becomes clear for the first time in Marcion, who, with the purified Gospel of Luke, which had been shortened to about half its length, and the likewise purified letters of Paul (still without the Pastoral Epistles) as "apostle text," gave to his separate church, which he established, something like an absolutely binding corpus of writings.[49] Marcion already presupposes

---

[48] For the designation, see Melito's inventory of writings in Eusebius, *Hist. eccl.* 4.26.14.

[49] With his "purification" he deletes all references to the inferior "just God" (Tertullian, *Marc.* 2.29.1) of the Old Testament, which for him had no significance for the Christian faith.

a collection of four Gospels and demarcates himself from it. He needed
his own, separately authoritative Holy Scripture because he rejected the
entire Old Testament. As a countermove, the "great church" created a
more extensive apostolicon with the letters of Paul (including the Pastoral
Epistles), Acts, and the Catholic Epistles, with 1 Peter and the letters of
John, which we encounter as a corpus in Irenaeus around 180 CE as generally recognized in the church.[50] Much earlier we already find references
to the Gospels of Mark and Matthew, Revelation, and probably also to
1 John and 1 Peter in the fragments and information—which are primarily
preserved by Eusebius—about the five-volume work of Papias at the time
of Hadrian (117–138 CE), which attempted to gather older oral dominical and apostolic traditions. To be sure, the fragments of Papias already
show the considerable extent to which the oral tradition had run wild. His
contemporary Polycarp, in his letter to the Philippians, also presupposes
the Synoptic Gospel tradition, the letters of Paul, 1 Peter, and the letters of
John. Justin, about 150 CE, already knows all four Gospels and calls them
"reminiscences of the apostles." He knows that the authors were "apostles
and students of apostles," and he reports the reading of them as well as the
reading of the Old Testament writings in the worship service as a tradition that was established and assumed as a matter of course.[51] Toward the
end of this period of time the Jewish community in Judaea was destroyed
in the Bar Kokhba revolt (132–136 CE), through which law-observant
Jewish Christianity was once again severely constricted and gradually
pushed into the "Ebionite" heresy. The new Roman establishment of Aelia
Capitolina in place of Jerusalem now became a purely Gentile Christian
community.

   A fundamental change becomes visible at this time in the rise of
apologetic literature. In an analogous way to some "gnostic writings," it
breaks through the literary walls to the educated upper class. Until then
only Luke, with his *Doppelwerk*, had made an attempt in this direction.
His dedication to Theophilus had been an absolute exception; now such
literary conventions became more common. In ca. 124 or 129 CE a certain Quadratus is said to have presented the first apology to the Emperor
Hadrian, from which a small fragment is preserved only in Eusebius.[52] The
next known apologist, Aristides, wrote under Hadrian or Antoninus Pius.
Justin, whose work, despite large gaps, is preserved in its essential parts,

---

[50] The designation of 1 John as καθολικὴ ἐπιστολή probably appears in the controversy over Montanism in Asia Minor toward the end of the second century CE; see Eusebius, *Hist. eccl.* 5.18.5; and Hengel 1993a, 102 n. 18 (ET = 1989a, 162 n. 9).

[51] *First Apology* 66.3; 67.3; *Dial.* 103.8; see also note 12 above and Hengel 2008c,
34–36 with note 99 (ET = 2000b, 20, 221–22 n. 83).

[52] Eusebius, *Hist. eccl.* 4.3.

wrote at the time of Antonius Pius and Marcus Aurelius, under whom he suffered martyrdom. His two apologies probably emerged shortly after 150 CE. An increasingly marked demarcation from Judaism is also evident. Toward the end of the Bar Kokhba revolt (132–136 CE) the Epistle of Barnabas emerges. Justin places his dialogue with the Jew Trypho, who had fled to Asia Minor, at this same time, with the work itself being composed around 160 CE. A forerunner, which presumably comes from the period shortly after the Bar Kokhba revolt, is the lost dialogue of the Jewish Christian Jason with the Alexandrian Jew Papiscus by Ariston of Pella.[53] Other influential apologists are Melito of Sardis; Tatian, a student of Justin, who compiled a harmony from the four Gospels; Athenagoras; and Theophilus of Antioch, a contemporary of Irenaeus.

Parallel in time to the apologists was the composition of the — sometimes increasingly lengthy — religious-philosophical writings by educated Christian intellectuals who were condemned as "Gnostics" from the time of Irenaeus at the latest. Between 130 and 140 CE the Christian thinker Basilides in Alexandria taught a Platonizing, speculative Paulinism and also composed a sort of commentary on the Gospel tradition.[54] At almost the same time, ca. 138 CE, we find Valentinus — coming from Alexandria — in Rome as a free Christian teacher with considerable ecclesiastical influence.[55] Already a fairly long time before Marcion (ca. 144 CE) — the great religious-philosophical system-builder, who had been assigned to Christian gnosis ever since Irenaeus and Clement of Alexandria — and the apologists, the "New Testament"[56] writings, which were not yet Gnostically influenced themselves, were definitively concluded. The time of their impact and interpretation begins. In the second half of the second century CE, Heracleon, probably a student of Valentinus, composed at a high philological and philosophical level the first commentary on a whole New Testament writing, which has been preserved in fragments.[57] The large, predominantly Gnostic trove of Coptic texts from Nag Hammadi, which are often overestimated in their significance for the New Testament, illuminates the variety of the Gnostic and pseudepigraphical production, but

---

[53] Prostmeier 1998, 51–52. It seems improbable to us that Justin did not know this dialogue.

[54] Cf. W. A. Löhr 1996.

[55] On this, see Markschies 1992.

[56] The designation appears only later in Tertullian and Clement of Alexandria. Melito of Sardis (ca. 170) speaks for the first time of the "books of the Old Testament" (in Eusebius, *Hist. eccl.* 4.26.14); see note 48 above.

[57] See the brilliant investigation of Wucherpfennig 2002, which shows that Heracleon was a serious discussion partner for Origen and that he can be designated as a "heretic" only retrospectively.

contributes—due to the diffuse character of its writings—disappointingly little to the solution of the still open question of the emergence of this ecclesiastical movement and its history in the Christian early period. The most important texts are the ones that are similar to the Gospels, such as the Gospel of Thomas and the Gospel of Philip. Many of the tractates more likely belong to the third than to the second century CE. It is conspicuous that the names of the great founders of schools, such as Satornilus, Basilides, Carpocrates, Valentinus, and Ptolemy, do not appear there.

In addition to the apologetic and religious-philosophical writings, we find from the middle of the second century a rich popular literature, the apocryphal Acts of apostles, which only superficially take the Acts of the Apostles as their model and correspond much more closely to the fictive ancient novel literature. The most impactful is the *Grundschrift* of the Jewish Christian, anti-Pauline Pseudo-Clementines attributed to Clement of Rome, in which James and Peter, who fights against Simon Magus, stand in the center. To this one can add apocryphal writings according to the type of Gospel, such as the Gospel of Thomas and the Gospel of Peter or the—anti-gnostic—*Epistula Apostolorum*, which contains conversations of the risen Jesus with his disciples, a genre that is otherwise especially popular among the Gnostics, whom it seeks to combat. We must also mention the apocalypses connected with the Jewish heritage, such as the Apocalypse of Peter, the Apocalypse of Paul, the older Ascension of Isaiah, and similar revelatory writings, as well as some Jewish corpora, such as the Sibylline Oracles, the Testament of the Twelve Patriarchs, the Life of Adam and Eve, and the Lives of the Prophets, which were Christianized and further developed. The separation from Judaism did not weaken the interest in Jewish-apocalyptic writings but rather promoted it, as the numerous Christian interpolations in these writings demonstrate. It was the church of the second century, in theological centers such as Rome or Alexandria, that took up, handed down, and thus preserved the Jewish Hellenistic literature, beginning with the Septuagint (including its "apocrypha") and the works of Philo and Josephus. By contrast, the Judaism of the second century almost completely rejected this literature and only took it up again later from Christian sources.

The history of primitive Christianity in the extended sense—in other words, the history of Jesus, of the apostolic period, and of the post-apostolic age—encompasses about 100/110 years, from ca. 30 CE to ca. 130/140 CE. At the end of this period, we find the attempt to gain reassurance through the collection of oral tradition or the personal appeal to bearers of the tradition of the "beginnings"—thus in Papias and Quadratus and yet also in philosophically influenced teachers such as Basilides and Valentinus, who appealed to named students of Paul and

Peter. Amidst every emphasis on periods, the early history of Christianity proves to be a *continuous, historically fruitful continuum that is full of meaning*. Due to the fragmentary character of the preserved sources we can often present this continuity only very imperfectly. The really difficult, clearly demonstrable breaks usually come from outside and tend to have a violent character. This applies, for example, to the death of the three leading heads of the first generation as martyrs in the sixties and to the destruction of Jerusalem that followed shortly thereafter, which robbed the Jewish Christian community of its previously decisive influence and allowed Rome to become the new center of the church. The expulsion of Marcion from the community in Rome and the founding of a Marcionite counterchurch around 144 CE could also be described as a forceful act of ecclesiastical discipline, which was far-reaching, though unavoidable. The temporal boundary to ca. 100 CE, which is set through the emergence of the majority of the canonical writings,[58] was not perceived as such. Rather, the change from the second to the third generation was more likely felt in connection with the stronger grasp of the state since the time of the later Domitian and Hadrian. For much too long New Testament scholarship suffered from an overemphasis on the theologically and ecclesiastically necessary but—from a historical perspective—questionable boundary of the canon and from the idealization of the authors who alone seemed to be really theologically interesting, such as Paul and John, as representatives of true primitive Christianity. Terms that have become traditional, such as "primitive Christianity," "apostolic period," "post-apostolic period," and "early Catholicism," are indeed still usable today, but they should no longer be used in an evaluative sense.

In reality, the second century CE is fundamental for the emergence of the New Testament, for it was precisely during this time and until Irenaeus in Lyon around 180 CE and a little later until Tertullian in Carthage and Clement of Alexandria that these writings, by virtue of their content, established themselves in the church. Here it is conspicuous that neither Irenaeus nor the great literary work of Tertullian evinces an appreciable influence from New Testament apocrypha. Rather, these writings are already decisively rejected by both of them. Even for Clement the writings that are "authoritative" for the church are clearly fixed, even if he, in correspondence to the spiritual situation in Alexandria and for the sake of discussion with gnosticizing Christian philosphers of religion, also cites "doubtful" texts now and again. The three great corpora of sources for these authors, which in scope surpass everything that has otherwise

---

[58] With the exception of the Pastoral Epistles, Jude, and 2 Peter.

been preserved of Christian writings from the second and first centuries, simultaneously provide an important foundation for a concluding retrospective on the earlier time of Christian beginnings and the astonishing development of the church in the second century. After all, the theological thinking and ecclesiastical life portrayed in them go back entirely to presuppositions that were formed in the course of the first and second centuries, and to a great extent their theological conceptions must also be understood from there. They were not farther apart in time than we are from F. Schleiermacher, F. C. Baur, and A. Ritschl, with the last 150 years involving more rapid change than was the case in Greco-Roman society. Accordingly, they can form the sensible conclusion of a history of the earliest church. From then on begins, long before Constantine, the history of the church of the Roman Empire.

The fourth planned volume is meant to conclude with these three theologians and an overview of their literary work. It reaches from the beginning of the "dark age" after Ignatius to the beginnings of the third century CE.

What we experience from that temporal period of ca. 150–170 years is simultaneously little and much. It is too little to allow an even reasonably continuous history of the development of the new movement in the first and second centuries CE to become visible. Our two main sources, Luke's Acts of the Apostles and the first six books of Eusebius' *Ecclesiastical History*, are much too fragmentary for a continuous presentation of the overall connections. This applies all the more to the fragments of the five books of Hegesippus' *Hypomnemata*, to which we are especially indebted for information about Jewish Christianity and the first bishops. The attempt to present the emergence of the church can usually be carried out only in very rough lines by connecting individual points, which means only with many gaps and with the constant use of working hypotheses. However, in comparison with other religious and philosophical movements in antiquity, we know on the whole a relatively large amount about particular sections of time and people, for example, about the activity of Jesus or the Pauline mission, and above all we know an astonishing amount about particular theological conceptions, such as those of Paul, John, Ignatius, Justin, and Melito, not to mention Irenaeus, Tertullian, and Clement of Alexandria. By ancient standards the emergence of Christianity and the history of its first 150–170 years are actually excellently attested. Thanks to the Lukan *Doppelwerk* and the letters of Paul, this applies especially to the decisive first forty years up to the destruction of Jerusalem. The darkest phase is the very early ten years between 30 and 40 CE and then again the later part of the post-apostolic epoch, roughly between Ignatius and Justin. Here, however, our knowledge receives valuable supplementation through Roman sources, such as the letter of Pliny and the answer of Trajan,[59] an edict of Hadrian,[60] and the fragments of Papias and Hegesippus preserved by Eusebius. In general, Eusebius, with the first four books of his unique *Ecclesiastical History*, accompanies our entire journey. It is unfortunate that to date no church historian has been able to bring him- or herself to write a detailed, usable commentary on this foundational text.

The presentation of the theological conceptions on the basis of the individual writings is in itself the task of a theology of the New Testament and then of the early history of dogma, with the former usually being presented today as a kind of intellectual history of primitive Christianity in the form of the development of its ideas of faith and with impulses for hermeneutical implementation in the present. However, this usual division of the material into a literary history (or introduction to the New Testament), a presentation of the theology of the New Testament, and the attempt to provide a history of primitive Christianity always ran the risk of becoming one-sided, abstract, and static if it did not also keep in view the various historical situations in space and time and the acting persons and their conversation partners. Accordingly, we cannot tear apart the development of the theological thinking, the—very fragmentary—biographical, social, and political details, and the literary history. The authority of individual theological teachers, authors, founders of schools, and bishops has always been of fundamental significance. Therefore, we cannot completely eliminate the mention of these personalities, even if we usually know very little about them biographically. This is already evident from a consideration of the first six books of the *Ecclesiastical History* of Eusebius, who attempted—drawing on the large library of his teacher Pamphilus in Caesarea—to describe the first ca. 270 years of the emergence of the church and without whom a history of early Christianity could not be written at all. To be sure, in Eusebius the actual presentation of the theological thought falls short of the mark in comparison with biographical and ecclesiastical-political "facts" and the works that are quoted, extending to the listing of book titles and short surveys and quotations of literature. He is much too entangled in the evaluative scheme of orthodoxy and heresy. Over against this scheme, the presentation of the historical particularities and theological characteristics of individual writings and their authors, i.e., the main sources of our knowledge, and the profile of their ideas of faith drawn from this constitute the most important part

---

[59] Pliny the Younger, *Ep*. 10.96–97. For the Latin text with an English translation and commentary, see Williams 1990. Cf. also Walsh 2006.

[60] Justin, *1 Apol*. 68. On this, see Hengel 1996a, 358–91.

of the presentation of the early history of Christianity. Above all, the theological-christological thinking and its formation and development prove to be the actual moving force in this beginning period. They remain so also in the next centuries, as becomes evident from the great councils of the fourth and fifth centuries and the christological controversies connected with them.

2

Judaism and Early Christianity

No Christian theologian today doubts that primitive Christianity grew up in Jewish soil. This consensus becomes questionable, however, when one adds only one word—that it arose *wholly* out of Judaism. For this fundamental thesis, namely that Christianity is, viewed historically, completely a child of Judaism, contradicts a view that Hermann Gunkel formulated and that has largely established itself in New Testament scholarship via the history-of-religions school and then especially through Rudolf Bultmann and his students, namely that Christianity is a *syncretistic* religion with a variety of roots. According to this view, in addition to Judaism, there were at Christ's crib also pre-Christian, predominantly pagan gnosis, Greek and oriental mysteries, magic, astrology, pagan popular philosophy, and several other godparents.[1]

The key word "syncretism" has not advanced the understanding of Christian beginnings, as, in general, this popular label does justice neither to the Judaism in the motherland and diaspora nor to the Christian beginnings in the first century. Only certain later Gnostic currents, say, since the second third of the second century CE, such as the teaching of the Simonians or the Naassene sermon and then especially Manichaeism

---

[1] Gunkel 1903; see especially p. 88 and the conclusion on p. 95: "Christianity is a syncretistic religion"; Bultmann 1956, 156ff. (GV = 1952, 146ff.): "The Mystery Religions"; 162ff. (GV = 152ff.): "Gnosticism"; 175ff. (GV = 163ff.): "Primitive Christianity as a Syncretistic Phenomenon": "Thus Hellenistic Christianity is no unitary phenomenon, but, taken by and large, a remarkable product of syncretism. It is full of tensions and contradictions" (ET = 177, modified; GV = 165). In reality this applies equally to Judaism and basically to all significant ancient religions. Prümm 1972 presented an extensive study with the title *Gnosis an der Wurzel des Christentums? Grundlagenkritik der Entmythologisierung* (Gnosis at the Root of Christianity? Criticism of the Foundations of Demythologizing). His fundamental criticism is to a large extent accurate and was unfortunately scarcely taken notice of in his time.

in the third century CE, can be designated as religious formations that have very consciously been syncretistically configured through a mixing of religions. Early Christianity—at least in the first century CE—does not yet belong here, unless one uses the term in an overly undifferentiated and general way. For ever since the earliest beginnings Israel at first and then Judaism were exposed to *foreign religious influences* in manifold ways. Accordingly, one could *always* speak of syncretism. But in the course of history the religious identity of Judaism in attraction and rejection only increased thereby, and this applies precisely to the Hellenistic period, in which the foreign religious infiltration of the Jewish religion is said to have been the greatest. Of course, Judaism did incorporate numerous foreign influences into itself at that time, but, as already shown previously by the Babylonian exile and the Persian period, it either integrated or rejected them and through them only became stronger in its inner power. This is apparent—to mention just one example—from the attractiveness of the Greek-speaking synagogue to non-Jews and from the great number of Gentile God-fearers who gathered in the Jewish houses of prayer. We would assert this self-assured consciousness of identity for Qumran, the Pharisees, and the Jewish apocalyptic in the same way as for the literature of the Septuagint or for Philo of Alexandria. A nice example is provided by Josephus' apology *Against Apion*. The syncretistic elements, which are overemphasized by H. Gressmann in his famous essay "Die Aufgaben der Wissenschaft des nachbiblischen Judentums" (The Tasks of Scholarship on Post-biblical Judaism),[2] apply more to the pagan interest in Judaism than to Judaism itself. In comparison to their pagan environment, Judaism and early Christianity, which was still closely connected with Judaism, were precisely not syncretistic religions, unless one understands the term "syncretistic" very generally to mean foreign religious influences of any sort, in which case it becomes too general and thus empty of meaning.

We draw the following conclusion from this fundamental thesis: *What has been postulated regarding remaining "pagan influences" in early Christianity can consistently go back to Jewish mediation.* A direct, enduring influence by pagan cults or non-Jewish pagan thinking that is not mediated by way of a Jewish milieu cannot be demonstrated at any point. What one generally designates as "Hellenistic" in the New Testament usually comes from Jewish sources, which admittedly neither desired to nor were able to withdraw themselves from the religious koine of the Hellenistic period. For it was only by participating in the religious language and conceptual world of their time that they could have an attractive impact

---

[2] Gressmann 1929. On this, see Hengel/Schwemer 1998, 132–39, 251–60 (ET = 1997, 76–80, 161–67).

upon outsiders and convincingly advocate the truth of their specific message. This applies equally to the Christians later. Accordingly, in the diaspora and among its leading figures in the motherland, Judaism very rapidly accepted the Greek language, which dominated the world, including its religious terminology, in a similar way to what it had already done with Aramaic in the Babylonian exile and in the Persian period. In this regard, we must pay attention to the fact that at the time of Jesus and the apostles Eretz Israel had been under Greek influence for more than three hundred years, so that with full justification we can designate as Hellenistic the entirety of Judaism in the first and second centuries CE, which was influenced in various ways through the radiance of—and confrontation with—Hellenistic civilization. This extends even to Qumran, where Greek-pagan elements were sharply rejected in principle.[3] The word "Hellenistic" is therefore just as inadequate as "syncretistic" for making clear differentiations. Ever since the days of the Hasmoneans and Herod, Jerusalem, the world-famous pilgrimage city, possessed a Hellenistic culture with its own character.[4] There we find a Jewish Hellenism, which differed fundamentally from the Hellenism of Alexandria, for it was characterized more strongly by the letters of the Torah and by the holy land and temple and was shaped less philosophically than halakically. For a nuanced historical evaluation we need more precise labels than catchwords such as "syncretistic" and "Hellenistic" can provide. To this can be added the fact that the so-called Jewish-Hellenistic diaspora also did not form a unified whole. The Jews in Syria or Rome were under Palestinian influence to a greater extent than, say, the Jews in Alexandria and Egypt, and people thought differently in Parthian Babylon than in Latin Carthage. Further, we must consider the social differences. The Herodians and priestly and aristocratic Boethuseans in Jerusalem, and all the more the very rich family of Philo of Alexandria, were much more strongly "Hellenized," which means that they possessed a higher education than the average Jew. In the centuries around the turn of the eras, ancient Judaism was characterized by a greater richness and creativity than is usually assumed.

These Jewish foundations of the new messianic movement of primitive Christianity are connected with the fact that *the great majority of the New Testament authors were Jewish Christians*, who predominantly either came from the Palestinian motherland or had a connection to it. The latter applies especially to Paul, the earliest Christian author. Further, one would need to mention John Mark, the earliest evangelist, the unknown scribal author of the Gospel of Matthew, the author of Revelation, and

---

[3] Hengel 2003a (GV = 1988); Hengel 1996a, 258–94.
[4] On this, see Hengel 1996a, 1–90 (57–63, 71–72); Hengel 1999b, 114–56.

the author of the Johannine corpus. In our view, the author of the Fourth
Gospel and of the letters, who is probably identical with the "Elder" of
the second and third letters, came from the Jerusalem aristocracy.[5] Luke,
"the beloved physician" (Col 4.14), was probably a God-fearer before
he became a Christian and later a travel companion of Paul. Of all the
non-Jewish authors in antiquity, his *Doppelwerk*, which is unique in early
Christian literature, evinces by far the best knowledge of Judaism in both
the diaspora and the motherland. The unknown author of Hebrews must
have been a rhetorically adept Jewish Christian, who masterfully wielded
the Alexandrian art of allegorical and typological exegesis, and the author
of 1 Clement in Rome also still appears to have a close relation to the
synagogue's use of Scripture and to its liturgy. For him the Septuagint is
a large collection of models for the ordering of the church. There are not
many writings left in the New Testament that could be ascribed to "Gentile Christians" with a higher degree of probability. It stands to reason
that the—very clearly—anti-Pauline Epistle of James can hardly originate from a Gentile Christian, and something similar applies to the Epistle
of Jude, which is attributed to the brother of James. Thus, there is left
for Gentile Christians perhaps the Epistle to the Ephesians, the very late
Pastoral Epistles, the somewhat earlier 1 Peter around 100 CE, and the
much later 2 Peter, which is dependent, in turn, on the Epistle of Jude. We
must also consider that for the first twenty years or so, primitive Christianity was almost exclusively restricted to Palestine and Syria/Cilicia,
and Syria possessed the largest Jewish diaspora in the Roman Empire. It
only gradually extended to further parts of the empire, not least through
the worldwide mission program of the former Pharisee Paul of Tarsus. As
shown by the Gospels, the letters of Paul, and the Acts of the Apostles,
this Palestinian-Syrian early history, with Jerusalem as the center, deeply
shaped primitive Christianity.

In the contestation of the Jewish character of primitive Christianity,
the old latent anti-Judaism of German idealism continues to have an effect.
It said that in the course of the "upbringing of the human race" Judaism lost its religious right to existence with the emergence of Christianity.
Above all, F. C. Baur and his school, in their sharply evaluative distinction between Palestinian Jewish Christianity and the universalistic Gentile
Christianity inaugurated by Paul, showed too little understanding for the
Jewish atmosphere of the majority of the New Testament writings and
pointed scholarship in a one-sided direction for a long time.

It is, to be sure, telling that the no less apologetically oriented older
Jewish presentations of Christianity, such as those of Graetz, Perles,

[5] Hengel 1993a (ET = 1989a).

Elbogen, the early Leo Baeck, and others, gladly took up the erroneous extreme late dating of the Baur school, appealed with the old Tübingen scholars to the notorious historical unreliability and the pagan influencing of the New Testament writings, and largely denied them a historical source value that was to be taken seriously. Here it was the achievement of Light-foot, Zahn, Harnack, and Schlatter to have placed the historical guideposts in a reliable way again, and from them a German American advocate of reform such as Kaufmann Kohler and an Israelite historian such as Joseph Klausner learned to be much more cautious on this question. This rigorous destructive skepticism robs the Jewish and all the more the Christian historian of valuable pointers for their *own* respective histories, for the early history of the new messianic-universalistic movement still remains *also* a piece of Jewish history.

The rootedness of primitive Christianity in Judaism is also visible in the *fundamental significance of the Jewish holy Scriptures* for the new, eschatological-messianic movement. It pertains to their worship service as well as the formation of their teaching in all areas from Christology to ethics. In particular, the controversy with other Jewish groups was shaped by the discussion of specific texts of Scripture. This polemically conducted discussion was then continued in the early church. Since "the Scriptures" in early Christianity were understood not least as prophetic prophecies of eschatological fulfillment through the coming of the Messiah Jesus, they could be designated simply as "the (writings of the) prophets."[6] The phrase "books of the Old Testament" appears for the first time in Melito of Sardis in the second half of the second century in his letter to Onesimus and refers there to the books of the Hebrew Bible. Even though the Christian Septuagint canon was more extensive in scope than this, the Hebrew Bible—as shown by the philological work of Origen or Jerome—stood as the final authority in the background. In the development of Christology a special role was played, in addition to numerous messianically interpreted prophetic texts, especially by the "messianic psalms," since they, as Christ hymns, which were interpreted in relation to Jesus, could be sung. They presumably stimulated the spirit-effected christological hymns of the new community, as, for example, Old Testament songs were continued in Qumran.[7] Further agreements with the Qumran Essenes can be seen in the fact that both communities held the same books in the highest regard: the Psalms, Isaiah, Deuteronomy, Genesis, Exodus, the Twelve Prophets, Jeremiah, and Daniel. The high regard for these books corresponded to

---

[6] Hengel 1999b, 335–80.

[7] On this, see Hengel 1983c, 78–96 (GV = 1980b; 2006a, 185–204) and Hengel 1995, 227–91 (GV = Hengel 1987a; 2006a, 205–58).

their theological-religious content and a tendency in Palestinian Judaism. By contrast, in the diaspora, as Philo shows, the Pentateuch above all was cited. This fundamental significance of the Jewish Holy Scriptures for early Christianity grounds the unique bond between Christianity and Judaism, which—despite all tensions and conflicts—remains in force to this day. The methods for interpreting Scripture of the Judaism of that time also remained preserved in early Christianity. Above all, early Christianity is connected with interpretation in Qumran and apocalyptic Judaism by the reference to the present as the end-time (1 Cor 9.10; 10.11; Rom 4.23-24; 15.4; Heb 11.39-40; 1 Pet 1.10-12), i.e., the time of the fulfillment of the prophetic promises.

The expression *"to the Jews first . . ."*—which occurs almost stereotypically in the letters of Paul in different variations—likewise evinces the Jewish character of the new movement.[8] The "first" in Rom 1.16 is not simply "a *de facto* worthless concession to the 'chosen people'"[9] but rather points to the salvation-historical priority, which is grounded in God's promise to the fathers. It is then elucidated in Rom 9–11: Israel alone was entrusted with the "oracles of God" (τὰ λόγια τοῦ θεοῦ, Rom 3.2); Israel alone was "guarded and shut in" by the "disciplinarian until Christ" (Gal 3.23-24). We encounter a similar idea in the Gospels when Jesus' mission is initially restricted to Israel (Mark 7.24ff.; Luke 1.32-33; 2.11, 34; 24.19-21; Matt 10.5-6; 15.24; cf. Acts 1.6; John 1.41, 49, etc.). Only after the resurrection does he send the disciples to all nations. With this Israel is by no means entirely excluded from salvation; rather, it is included in this command to "make disciples of all nations" (Matt 28.19). In the Acts of the Apostles the Gentile mission also begins—against the historical reality—only relatively late (cf. Acts 10.1-11.24; 13.16-48). In reality it probably already began in Damascus (Acts 9.20ff.) with the God-fearers in the diaspora synagogues. Accordingly, in his missionary journeys later, Paul, presumably from the very beginning, seeks out precisely synagogues, until he is driven out of them. He wishes to address Jews and God-fearing Gentiles there, but he meets with a positive response especially from the latter. This phase of missionary proclamation, which was focused on Jews and God-fearers, probably lasted until the outbreak of the Jewish War in 66 CE. Only those who, like the former Tübingen school of F. C. Baur, read the Old Testament with the eyes of Marcion could criticize

---

[8] Romans 1.16; 2.9-10; cf. 3.1-2. Cf. also the front placement of the Jews in Rom 3.9, 29; 9.24; 10.12; 1 Cor 1.22-23; 9.20-21; 10.32; 12.13; Gal 3.28; cf. Col 3.11 as well as, fundamentally, Rom 9–11 and 15.8-12.

[9] Thus Lietzmann 1928, 30. It was not without reason that Marcion omitted this πρῶτον.

this state of affairs, which is relatively clear in Luke, as unhistorical. The apostle to the Gentiles is initially especially the missionary of these God-fearers in the synagogues, who were still regarded as Gentiles legally but were already familiar with the foundational Jewish teachings and with the Septuagint. Therefore, he can already presuppose knowledge of the Jewish writings and interaction with them in his mission communities and argue in such a virtuoso manner with scriptural quotations. In comparison with the great attractiveness of the Jewish synagogues in Gentile cities, also for Gentiles—we can indeed speak here of a successful Jewish religious "propaganda" among Greeks and Romans—the primitive Christians' *mission* constituted something new, for it was based on the *eschatological sending* by the risen Messiah, which fills out the period of time for repentance between exaltation and parousia, in order to prepare for his coming as judge and consummator of the world. This is a radical new move in the history of ancient Mediterranean religion, one that is grounded in the eschatological universalism of the Old Testament prophets and is without parallel in the ancient world.

On the basis of this complex state of affairs, the separation of the synagogue and the new enthusiastic-messianic Jesus movement, which took place amidst pain, *cannot be clearly assigned a fixed, let alone an early, date*. Rather, it was a long and complicated process. "Christianity," as an entirely new religion of the ancient world, did not enter the arena of history entirely without mediation. Moreover, the designation that established itself in history for this offensive, eschatological sect, *Christianoi*, which basically means "Messiah's people," was not a self-designation but rather a designation given to the movement by outsiders in Antioch (Acts 11.26). This means that this typically Latin form of a party name, which we also find in the case of the Ἡρῳδιανοί (Mark 3.6; 12.13), was common in the Greek-speaking East, but was used especially in circles that were close to Rome. In the New Testament this word form—which is foreign to Greek—Χριστιανοί = *Christiani* appears only three times[10] and always in relation to the outside. The Gentile Christian and martyr Ignatius, ca. 114 CE, first uses the word more frequently and juxtaposes Christianity, Χριστιανισμός, and Judaism, Ἰουδαϊσμός, for the first time.[11] It is telling that in Ignatius the expectation of martyrdom tied to the present has at the same time almost entirely suppressed the consideration of the near end of the world. Only then, in the first centuries of the second

---

[10] In addition to Acts 11.26, see Acts 26.28 and 1 Pet 4.16. On this, see Hengel/Schwemer 1998, 340–51 (ET = 1997, 225–30).

[11] Ignatius has the term Χριστιανισμός ca. seven times and the opposition Χριστιανισμός–Ἰουδαϊσμός four times.

century, was the parting line between mother and daughter *definitively* drawn. At almost the same time, Pliny writes to Trajan about his proceedings against the *Christiani* as a *superstitio prava et immodica*, and a little later Suetonius speaks of them as *superstitio nova et malefica*, i.e., these Roman authors regard the *Christiani* as a new, potentially dangerous religious movement. By contrast, Tacitus explicitly reports that this *exitiabilis superstitio* began in Judaea, was revived after being repressed by Pilate, and came from there to Rome. For him, the hater of Jews and Christians, it was the worst criminal form of the Jewish *superstitio*.[12]

By contrast, the Jewish designation *nôṣrîm/naṣôrāyyā/Nazōraioi* is to be derived from the origin of Jesus from the Galilean Nazareth and corresponds to a Palestinian-Jewish custom of designating bearers of more frequent names according to their origin. This Jewish "name of a party" was originally a byname of Jesus. It is telling that in the trial against Paul the prosecutor appointed by the high priest Ananias speaks of the (Jewish) "sect of the Nazoraeans,"[13] while King Agrippa II uses the word *Christianos*.[14] Thus, for the high priest, Paul is, according to Luke, a "ringleader" of an *inner-Jewish haeresis*. A little later Luke has Paul designate himself as a former adherent of the Pharisees, i.e., "of the strictest 'haeresis' of our religion."[15] In this way he accurately represents the historical state of affairs for Christians and Pharisees. Both, Pharisees and "*nôṣrîm*," are, viewed from the outside, different Jewish *haireseis* in Luke. On the Jewish side, we find an indication of the separation in the fact that the popular name *Yešûaʿ*, the short form of *Yᵉhôšûaʿ*, completely disappears in the Tannaites from about the second century CE onward, while it still appears twenty-two times in Josephus and is also still relatively frequent in the documents from the escape caves of the Bar Kokhba period. The common people reacted more slowly than the rabbinic teachers, who no longer wanted to mention the now-cursed name and returned to the original, longer form *Yᵉhôšûaʿ*. The introduction and establishment of the much-discussed "cursing of the heretics" in the Eighteen Benedictions is probably to be dated only to the early second century CE. It refers especially to the Jewish Christians. Conversely, the church, which was becoming increasingly independent, understood itself as the "true people of God," the "true Israel," and to the outside, consequently, as the "third race" or "people" alongside Greeks and Jews. The Gentile Christians, who now

---

[12] Pliny the Younger, *Ep.* 10.96.8 (trans. Williams 1990, 71): "debased and extravagant superstition"; Suetonius, *Nero* 16.2 (trans. Edwards 2000, 203): "a new and dangerous superstition"; Tacitus, *Ann.* 15.44.3 (trans. Woodman 2004, 325): "baleful superstition."

[13] Acts 24.5: ἡ τῶν Ναζωραίων αἵρεσις, cf. 24.14.

[14] Acts 26.28.

[15] Acts 26.5.

gradually became predominant, had for Judaism never belonged to "Israel" anyway.

This means, however, that the controversy—which is visible in the New Testament writings and is sometimes vehement—between the messianic sect of the *nôṣrîm*, the "people of the Nazarene," and the various Jewish groups in Judaea, i.e., Pharisees, scribes, Sadducees, priestly aristocracy, and Herodians, and then, later, with the synagogue communities in the diaspora from Syria to Rome, initially represents an *inner-Jewish family conflict*. With reference to the hard statement of Paul in 1 Thess 2.14-16, Richard L. Rubenstein, in his book *My Brother Paul*, speaks of a "family dispute" and explains that "his harshness was not unlike that of the members of the Community of the Scrolls."[16] It is an old biblical motif. We encounter the conflict of brothers already in central texts of the Old Testament: with Joseph and his brothers, with "Rebecca's children,"[17] and (paradigmatically for the course of the human history that begins with it) with the fatal outcome of the story of Cain and Abel. Even Jesus' relationship to his brothers was not without problems.[18] The thesis of the conflict between siblings even applies where, as in John, there is polemic not simply against specific groups, such as scribes and Pharisees or Herodians, but rather where "the Jews"—the leaders and speakers of the people are meant—are directly attacked in the strongest terms. What is at issue is the rejection—which is difficult to comprehend for the new, enthusiastic movement—by his and their own people of the "Messiah," "Son of God," and "king of Israel,"[19] in whom God himself came to Israel and thus to all humans. To this height of the claim corresponded the heatedness of the controversy in and with his and their own people.[20] Family conflict can result in a situation in which individual members turn against the majority of their own family and, in some circumstances, are expelled (cf. John 9.22; 12.42; 16.2). No New Testament author could have known that with the messianic movement of the *Nazoreans* or *Christianoi* a new religion would emerge with a long history alongside the Jews and against them, let alone that it would come to power in the empire centuries later. At first it was an oppressed, even a persecuted "sect." The phrase "third race" or "people" alongside Jews and Gentiles does not yet appear in the New Testament, but only in the writings of the apologists of the second century CE, first in the Preaching of Peter and in Aristides. Tertullian rejected it. After

[16] Rubenstein 1972, 115.

[17] Thus the significant title of Segal 1986, with the subtitle *Judaism and Christianity in the Roman World*.

[18] Cf. John 7.5 or Mark 3.21. See section 8.3 below.

[19] John 1.41, 49; 20.31.

[20] John 4.22; cf., however, also 8.44, 47.

all, Christians lived in the consciousness of the fulfillment of the eschatological promises of the holy Scriptures and initially by no means regarded
themselves as a new religion but rather expected the near arrival of the
kingdom of God and the concomitant return of the crucified Messiah and
Son of God Jesus of Nazareth, who rose from the dead and was exalted
to the right hand of God, i.e., the redeemer prophesied by the prophets
and the judge of the people of God and of all the nations as well.

This means that while the elements that separated the Nazoreans from
the rest of Israel were certainly enthusiastic and eschatological in character, they were nevertheless *fundamentally Jewish* in their individual
characteristics, their building blocks. The particularly divisive element,
Christology, did indeed have a Jewish character in its elements and was by
no means syncretistically riddled with pagan elements that were foreign
to Judaism. In the first—decisive—years, primitive Christian preaching
could otherwise not have been understood at all by the still predominantly
Jewish hearers in Judaea and Syria. What was new, by contrast, was the
overall conception, the apostolic witness to Christ, which Paul describes
in 1 Cor 15.1-11 as the "gospel," which is proclaimed by all the witnesses
and apostles according to 15.11 and which he presents in poetic form in
Phil 2.6-11. First Corinthians 15.3 attests that this gospel of the atoning
death and resurrection of Christ constituted the recognized foundation of
faith of primitive Christianity, namely in Judaea and in Syria as well as
in the areas of the Pauline mission around the Aegean. This new message
of faith in the crucified Messiah and Lord Jesus and of his salvific work
must have provoked offense and contradiction.[21] The polemic of individual New Testament authors from Paul via Luke and Matthew through
to John against the traditional Jewish rivals and their counterreaction
was not sharper than the polemic of the Essenes against "Ephraim" and
"Manasseh," i.e., against the Pharisees and Sadducees, even though the
theological differences with the new Messianic "sect" may have been even
greater due to its distinctive Christology and soteriology. Sharp, wounding polemic also occurs in other Jewish groups. We must not forget that
there were bloody conflicts between Pharisees and Sadducees at the time
of John Hyrcanus and Alexander Jannaeus and then between Zealots and
those who sought peace in the years before and after the outbreak of the
Jewish War, for which the ultimate motive was not social but religious
and in which the controversial eschatology also played a role. The rabbis later accused the zealous fighters before 70 CE and Bar Kokhba of
wanting to "force" the end. Would not the message of a Messiah who had
already come, who was proclaimed as a universal savior and judge in the

---

[21] First Corinthians 1.23; Gal 5.11; Phil 3.18.

present, and who was expected to return soon have had to appear—viewed phenomenologically—as an expression of dangerous eschatological impatience or as an offensive utopia?

The theme of "anti-Judaism in the New Testament," which is sometimes connected today with weighty accusations against the primitive Christian authors, has, to be sure, a relative validity with a view to the fateful *Wirkungsgeschichte* of individual texts. This, however, only began centuries later. At first the Jewish mother was indeed stronger than the unruly daughter. In the first century CE, the "church" did not persecute the "synagogue" but rather, conversely, the "synagogue" persecuted the "church" time and again. While the new movement, after its expulsion from the synagogue, was completely unprotected legally and could be persecuted—sometimes violently—by the organs of the imperial administration since the end of the first century CE, the Jewish ethnos, with its traditional religion—if we disregard the three large revolts of 66–73, 115–117, and 132–136 CE—was under the protection of the political policy of Rome, which was relatively tolerant on religious questions. With respect to the primitive Christian authors themselves, who—this still applies even to John[22]—await the near parousia of the Messiah and Son of God, the accusation of anti-Judaism is therefore *anachronistic* and bespeaks an unhistorical way of thinking that fails to recognize the historical situation of that time, which was completely different from later epochs. The young communities looked to the *near end* and the coming of the world judge and redeemer—the Jewish Messiah Jesus of Nazareth exalted to God. They, who themselves stood under the double pressure of the suspicious state authorities and the influential and self-conscious Jewish mother communities, who were understandably indignant about the enthusiastic escapades of the new—still Jewish—movement, could not know how their polemical texts would be misused centuries later. The family conflict between the primitive Christian communities and the synagogue—or, better, the various authorities of a stronger "normative Judaism"—was not more vehement than other conflicts, in which inner battles extended for three hundred years between the beginning of the Maccabean insurgence and the Bar Kokhba revolt. But the following observation also holds true: family controversies are more wounding and have more lasting effects than all others. They hurt so much because the persons involved are so close. This applies also to the later inner-Jewish and inner-ecclesiastical controversies, at bottom even still today. This conflict became so severe and was carried out so painfully because the concern was always with the *question of religious truth*, with God's *holy will*, and because this was

---

[22] Cf. John 21.22-23; 1 John 3.2-3.

taken very seriously by both sides: precisely the taking seriously of the question of truth is Old Testament-Jewish heritage.

What was most conspicuous in this conflict was that it possessed clear contours from the beginning and was focused on central religious concerns of Judaism, on questions of faith, hope, and life practice. The concern was with the relation of messianic redemption and the traditional validity of temple and Torah. The last two entities—as it were, the heart of Jewish faith until then—had already been threatened in connection with the radical Hellenistic attempt at reform under Antiochus IV Epiphanes after 175 CE, when the identity of Israel as the people of divine election and belonging was at stake. Since that time it had reacted allergically, indeed bitterly, to every real and putative attack on these goods entrusted to it by God, and for the most part demarcated itself even more strongly—at least in the motherland—from the "nations of the world," although it did not withdraw itself from every foreign influence. At that time, this was an understandable, indeed a necessary, reaction. In the new Messianic movement, in which Jesus was proclaimed as the crucified Messiah and liberator from sin and death who rose from the dead, it seemed as though these highest goods of Israel were being called into question again, though under a completely different banner than was the case two hundred years earlier. In the time of Antiochus IV, the Jewish "Hellenists" of the upper stratum strove for assimilation to the nations and the "secularization" of the temple and threatened thereby the purity of Jewish "monotheism." Now monotheism was no longer threatened. The new movement itself rejected with the utmost sharpness every form of "foreign service," i.e., polytheism and pagan libertinism. Their motives were entirely different. Now the direct salvific significance of temple and Torah became questionable, at least partially, under the banner of the dawning kingdom of God and of the messianic redemption, with them proclaiming at the same time the universal eschatological fulfillment of the promises of the fathers and the prophetic prophecies. Trust, *emunah*, and hope were placed not primarily in the holy text given to Israel at Sinai and in one's own possibility of obedient doing but in a person, who was promised by the holy Scriptures of Israel and who corresponds to God, in whom the prayer of Isa 63.19 (LXX 64.1) is, as it were, fulfilled: "O that you would rend the heavens and come down. . . ." What was said in Exod 19.11 and Ps 18.10 with respect to the "coming down" of God upon Sinai now became in the full sense "bodily" reality. God himself comes in a human being, the shoot of David promised by the prophet, at the end of time to his people. The heavenly Father sends the Son as he sends in the Jewish wisdom tradition of Sirach or Wisdom of Solomon the *Hokhma*, the divine wisdom, who inspired Israel's men of God. As the servant of God and suffering righteous one, he vicariously takes upon himself the guilt of all and absolves them through his death on the accursed wood[23]—a message that could fascinate and repel the hearers. Even the notions of "mediation" between God and humanity and "incarnation" could pick up on Old Testament-Jewish models, thus on the interpretation of Gen 1.26-27; 18.1-33; Exod 23.20-23; 24.9-11; Lev 26.11; Ps 8.5-6; 45.7-8; 89.27-28, 37; 110; Dan 7.9-14 (especially in the Septuagint version), and—not least—Isa 53.[24] The Judaism of the time also knew of—to adopt a phrase from 1 Cor 2.10—the traces of the "depths of God" (τὰ βάθη τοῦ θεοῦ), which, according to Paul, only the Spirit (which effects the apostolic witness) searches out and reveals. In later Jewish mysticism such conceptions were revived again. To be sure, still very imperfect *vestigia trinitatis* appear in this way already in the Old Testament and in the Jewish environment of the New Testament. Here, we must consider, in addition to the preexistent Wisdom or Torah, the Philonic Logos, 11QMelchizedek, the Son of Man of the parables of 1 Enoch, and the prayer of Joseph.

Thus, this new heaven-storming messianic movement of the "Nazoreans," which also claimed for itself the eschatological gift of the prophetic Spirit, could appeal to fundamental faith statements of Israel, and it did this—even in Eretz Israel—not without success. This central point of the person of the Messiah Jesus, the *mᵉšîḥā' yešûᵃ'*, "Χριστὸς Ἰησοῦς," and of the universal redemption effected by him constitutes the aspect of the enthusiastic and eschatological αἵρεσις τῶν Ναζωραίων[25] that was *actually new*, that pointed into the future, and that was thus, at the same time, what was dangerous. According to Luke, the rhetorician Tertullus, speaking on the commission of the high priest and of the San-hedrin, designates Paul, its "ringleader," with understandable anger, as "one who stirs up sedition among all Jews" (Acts 24.5). With respect to our earliest author, Paul, the new could be designated in the form of a slogan, in a somewhat exaggerated manner, with the formula "Messiah contra Torah." For this movement Moses and the law from Sinai were no longer the *mediator* between God and his chosen people but the Messiah Jesus, the bringer of the new eschatological covenant of Jer 31.31-34.[26] While Gal 3.19 still designated Moses as "mediator" of the Torah on Sinai, Jesus becomes the "mediator of the new covenant" in Hebrews,[27] and in

---

[23] Galatians 3.13; cf. Deut 21.23; 27.26; Acts 5.30; 10.39; 13.29; 1 Pet 2.24.

[24] Hengel 1976b (GV = 1977b; 2006a, 74–145); Hengel/Bailey 2004 (GV = Hengel 1996b).

[25] Acts 24.5, cf. 24.14.

[26] Cf. Jer 33.14, 25-26.

[27] Hebrews 8.6; 9.15; 12.24.

1 Timothy he becomes the "mediator between God and humans."[28] Paul can therefore call Christ "the end of the law for righteousness for everyone who believes."[29] At the same time, he no longer understands the Torah exclusively as the Jewish law, but, starting from the first commandment, as God's holy will for all humans, as a law that is active through the conscience even in the hearts of Gentiles.[30] Alongside the first commandment of the Decalogue in connection with Deut 6.4 comes the love commandment of Lev 19.18. In this focused form, which goes back already to Jesus, it serves, according to Paul, to display the absolute, culpable incapacity of the human being to fulfill God's holy will, i.e., rightly understood, it effects—salutary—knowledge of sin.[31] To be sure, such an opposition must have appeared absurd to Pharisaically educated Jews, but, oddly enough, it found—this is shown already by the stoning of Stephen, who, according to the accusation of Acts 6.13, continually "spoke words against this holy place and the law"—a not insignificant resonance, even among individual Jews in Jerusalem. This resulted in the expulsion of the Jewish Hellenists from the capital of Judaea, who then became missionaries of the new messianic message in the Syrian synagogues. Indeed, even James, the brother of the Lord, who was said to be so law-abiding, and other Jewish Christians were executed by stoning as "lawbreakers" (ὡς παρανομησάντων) by Annas II, an event that prompted even Pharisaic protest.[32]

A central hope of the new messianic and universalistic movement soon became the fulfillment of the *worldwide eschatological conversion of the nations to the one true God of Israel*, which was grounded on various prophetic promises, and of the Abrahamic promise (Gen 12.3) in the form of conversion to God's anointed one, who—this is what is distinctive—*had already come*. But how was this to happen if the Torah, as it states in the Letter of Aristeas (139), surrounded Israel vis-à-vis the nations "with unbroken palisades and iron walls" and if these walls, according to m. 'Abot 1.1, must themselves be guarded again with a fence? Even Paul can speak of this—indeed also protective—"shutting-in" function of the Torah in Gal 3.23-24 (cf. Rom 3.1-2), though only until the sending of the Son into the world, i.e., until the "coming of faith." Here a fundamental aporia in the prophetic faith of the Old Testament becomes visible. The promise for the nations could only become full reality when

---

[28] First Timothy 2.5.
[29] Romans 10.4.
[30] Romans 2.14ff.
[31] Romans 3.19-20.
[32] Acts 6–9; Josephus, *Ant.* 20.200–201.

the barriers that separated the Jewish people from the converted nations of the world who believed in the one true God were somehow nullified. This occurred in the eschatologically motivated *primitive Christian mission*, which at first was addressed primarily to the numerous God-fearers of the diaspora synagogues of Syria. This means that the eschatologically grounded "mission to the nations" could build on the attractiveness of the synagogal sermon. In this regard the expectation of the near parousia of the redeemer and the assurance of the already effective presence of the reign of God ἐν Χριστῷ, "in Christ," in growing distance to the earthly, *politically exclusive* existence of the Jewish people, created a new, eschatological-universal consciousness: "For in Christ you are all sons of God through faith. . . . There is neither Jew nor Greek, neither slave nor free, neither man nor woman, for you are all one in Christ Jesus" (Gal 3.26, 28). Or Phil 3.20: "But our citizenship (πολίτευμα) is in heaven, and from there we await as redeemer the Lord Jesus Christ. . . ." Correspondingly, in Gal 4.26 Paul says: "But the Jerusalem above (in heaven) is free, and it is our mother." According to Rev 21.1-22.5, the holy city comes down from heaven into a renewed creation (cf. Isa 65.17) and as the place of the presence of God and Christ incorporates into itself all those who believe, both Jews and Gentiles.

This new element was at the same time the extremely offensive element, for under some circumstances it could—under an eschatological claim and in Paul, the former Pharisaic scribe, with sublime theological justification—ultimately call into question the existence of Israel as exclusively chosen people, i.e., *as a political and religious entity that was fundamentally separated from the nations of the world*. This was at least an accusation made against Paul. One apparently charged him with seducing Jews to fall away "from Moses" (Acts 21.21, 28). As shown by Rom 9–11, this is not accurate for Paul in this way. For him all believers from Jews and Gentiles are chosen, and when he, according to Rom 11.26, which calls to mind m. Sanh. 10.1 ("all Israel has a share in the coming world"), on the basis of the promise to the fathers, maintains that with the coming of the Messiah *all Israel will be saved through God's grace*, then it corresponds to this that, at the end of world history, *all nations*, under the banner of the gospel, will find their way back to God, in order that *his grace alone* may triumph over all powers of evil, sin, death, and devil. In our view, here the messianic expectation of Paul was indeed realistic and concrete, but it completed itself not through one's own political action, as was the case for the Zealots, but alone through God's action at the parousia of the redeemer (Rom 11.26-27). Thus, Israel becomes for him the great *paradigm of grace*, of the free election by God, and of the "justification of the godless" (Rom 4.5), which the former Pharisee and persecutor had experienced in relation to himself. Correspondingly, the last sentence of the "dogmatic" section of Romans concludes with the lapidary statement *"For God has shut in all under disobedience in order that he may have mercy on all"* (Rom 11.32).[33] We could add: in Christ, the Messiah and Son of God, who was sent into the world for the salvation of Israel and the nations.[34] For Paul this can be followed only by hymnic praise: the *soli Deo gloria* as the only possible human answer to God's grace. Could one think of a "more Jewish" conclusion to a theological tractate than this praise, which is oriented to the Psalms: "Oh the richness of the wisdom and the knowledge of God . . . ," which ends with the words "To him be glory forever! Amen"? The paraenesis that immediately follows is then grounded in the experience of God's mercy and seeks to guide one to a thankful new life "in Christ" by leading the human as an answer to the received grace to the giving of his or her life and to the "reasonable worship" (Rom 12.1ff.). Here we can speak of a new, eschatological-universal form of the Jewish *kawwanāh* that is effected by God's Spirit.

Viewed in this way, Jesus and the worldwide movement triggered by him points to *a* historically understandable—*cum grano salis* we could also say legitimate—possibility in the development of Judaism during the late period of the Second Temple, which—based on a prophetic-apocalyptic perspective on the Old Testament tradition—took a route entirely different from the rabbinic branch, which emerged after the catastrophe of the destruction of the temple and determined the subsequent way of the Jewish people.

---

[33] It is one of the most important statements in the whole of the New Testament.

[34] Romans 15.8-12. On the hymnic praise of God, see Rom 11.33-36.

PART I
Judaism

3

Judaism under Roman Rule in the First Century BCE and CE

3.1 Judaea as a Roman Client Kingdom and as a Province[1]

The works of Josephus[2] form the only continuous historical narrative about the period of Roman rule from the subjection of Judaea by Pompey in 63 BCE and the suppression of the Jewish revolt in 66–73 CE. We can only represent these epochs by following him. But he also has gaps, precisely for the time of the prefects before Pilate, because his source, Nicolaus of Damascus, falls out from that point on.[3] Furthermore, Josephus has very clear tendencies. In *Jewish War*, which was written directly after the war in the years 75–79 CE, he likewise presents the prehistory of the war. He exonerates the people to the disadvantage of the Zealots. Likewise he exonerates the Roman administration after the banishment of Archelaus in 6 CE and the transformation of Judaea into a Roman province, admittedly in order to incriminate the last procurator, Gessius Florus, for being complicit in the catastrophe. The later, extensive presentation of this period in *Jewish Antiquities*, which he published in 93/94 CE, is for the most part more reliable and less pro-Roman. In his *Life*, an addendum to the *Antiquities*, he explicitly defends his own behavior at the beginning of the revolt in 66–67 CE, when he was a military leader in Galilee. His last work, an apology for Judaism, its very ancient religion and its laws, entitled,

---

[1] On this, see Boffo 1994; Michel/Bauernfeind 1962; Siegert 2001; Mason 2001; Gabba 1999; Goodblatt 1994; Hengel 1989c (GV = 1976c; 2011); 1996a; 1999b; 2002; 2003a (GV = 1988); 2001d; Hengel/Schwemer 1998 (ET = 1997); Klausner 1945, 129–228; Kokkinos 1998; Millar 1993; Pucci Ben Zeev 1998; Riesner 1994; Schalit 2001; Schürer 1973–1987, I–III/2; Schwartz 1990; Stern 1976–1984. Cf. now also H. Lichtenberger 2013.

[2] For editions of texts and recent literature, cf. Wandrey 2005 (GV = 1998); Rajak 2010 (GV = 2001). A complete edition is now being published by Brill (unfortunately without the Greek text): Mason 1999ff.

[3] On Nicolaus, see section 3.1.1 below.

because he was countering the attacks of the Alexandrian enemy of the Jews Apion, *Against Apion*, is not only an important source collection of Greek-Hellenistic testimonies about the Jews and ancient Judaism but also an indispensable description of Jewish interpretation of the law and customs.[4] The numbers he provides are often shaky and mistaken in scale, but they are not generally unreliable. To be sure, we receive from him a one-sided picture, but without this picture all too much in the Gospels would be historically incomprehensible. The milieu from which he comes and for which he writes is akin to that of Luke. It was a Hellenized Judaism, surrounded by a circle of Gentile sympathizers. Josephus—a nationally conscious priest from Jerusalem—belonged to the Jewish aristocracy and wrote his works as a freedman of the Flavian imperial household in Rome. In this regard it is interesting how much he, as an apologist for Judaism, let himself be influenced by Greek and Roman culture, in a similar manner to the highly educated Galilean Justus of Tiberias, with whom he competed.

Against more recent secondary literature, which wants to view Josephus above all as a rhetorician and pure propagandist, he must be taken seriously as a historian. Apart from him and Philo of Alexandria we possess only chance references from the Greco-Roman authors for this time, thus from Strabo, Tacitus, Cassius Dio, and others.[5] Above all, the philosophical exegete Philo's historical apologies *Legatio ad Gaium* and *In Flaccum* concerning the Caligula crisis and its prehistory in 38–41 CE not only portray the happenings in Alexandria and Rome but also shed light on the conditions under the Herodian rulers and prefects in Judaea and supplement the presentation of Josephus, who highly esteems these Jewish aristocrats from the diaspora.[6]

Among the Jewish writings from the Hellenistic-Roman period, the books of the Maccabees and the Psalms of Solomon, as well as more strongly legendary narratives and, last but not least, the texts discovered at Qumran, are especially informative as sources.[7] By contrast, the rabbinic reports are slanted in a deeply tendentious manner.[8] Without the corrections through Josephus it would be impossible to evaluate them due to the lack of any historical context, for they would give rise to a completely false

---

[4] On this, cf. C. Gerber 1997.

[5] See the collection of Stern 1976–1984. On Josephus' rhetorically colored picture of Herod, see now Landau 2006.

[6] Josephus, *Ant.* 18.259–260. Cf. Veltri 2011 (GV = 2003).

[7] Cf. the older description of the sources in Schürer 1973–1987, I: 17–122; III.1/2; see also Hengel 1999b, 176–92; Mittmann-Richert 2000.

[8] On J. Neusner's initially justified criticism of older research but then increasingly radical rejection of the use of rabbinic texts for the historical representation prior to 70 CE, cf. Deines 1997, 536ff.

picture. Judaism changed radically after 70 CE, and after the catastrophe the rabbis were no longer interested in a presentation of their history. They regarded their task as the halakic, legal, and haggadic, moral-theological, interpretation of Scripture.

3.1.1 On the Prehistory:
From Pompey to the Reign of Herod I (63–4 BCE)

The religious emergency under Antiochus IV Epiphanes and the successful Maccabean fight for freedom in the second century BCE were a significant watershed in the history and self-understanding of the Jewish people.[9] Due to the decline of the Seleucid Kingdom and its gradual dissolution, the small Judaea under the leadership of the Maccabean freedom fighters was able to gain its political independence in a decades-long, vicissitudinous revolt after more than four hundred years of foreign rule and extend its sphere of rule so far that it approached the Old Testament ideal of the land of the twelve tribes in around 100 CE. From the beginning an alliance with Rome was meant to ensure the success of this fight for freedom.[10] After his victory over Nicanor[11] in the spring of 161 BCE, Judas Maccabeus had sent an embassy to Rome, which made an alliance of peace and arms with the Roman senate.[12] The alliance was directed against the Seleucid ruler Demetrius I, as can be inferred from the simultaneous writing to him, to whom the threatening accusation of the senate applied:

> Why have you made your yoke heavy on our friends and allies the Jews? If now they appeal again for help against you, we will defend their rights and fight you on sea and on land.[13]

---

[9] For the Hellenistic reform in Judaism and the religious emergency under Antiochus IV Epiphanes, which provoked the revolt, see Bickerman 1937; Hengel 2003a (GV = 1988). On the religious repercussions of the persecution, the martyrdoms, and the resurrection hope as well as the emergence of religious parties, see chapter 4.

[10] The Roman Republic had already conquered the Seleucid ruler Antiochus III at the battle of Magnesia (190 BCE), and the peace agreement of Apamea that followed (188 BCE) completed his defeat, for the Seleucid lost every claim to Greece and Asia Minor and had to produce a massive sum as war reparations, which put a heavy burden on the finances of the state and presumably led to increased taxes also in Palestine. Antiochus IV Epiphanes (see below) grew up as a hostage in Rome.

[11] Cf. 1 Macc 7.43ff.

[12] First Maccabees 8.17–30; cf. 2 Macc 4.11.

[13] First Maccabees 8.31–32 (NRSV); cf. 1 Macc 12.1–4; 14.16–19. For the problem of the authenticity of the documents, see Schürer 1973–1987, I: 171–73; cf. further Justin, *Epitome of Pompeius Trogus* 36.3.9; Pompeius Trogus dates the "freedom" in the time of Demetrius I: *A Demetrio cum descivissent, amicitia Romanorum petita primi omnium*

The treaty of the Romans with the people of the Jews stood on a bronze tablet in Rome, and the Jerusalemites received a copy.[14] In the self-understanding of the Jewish population it guaranteed above all the freedom from the Seleucid "yoke" and not so much the recognition of the hegemony of Rome, for at that time the Romans were still far away. To be sure, after the victorious conflict with Antiochus III (192–188 BCE), they already showed a lively interest in the events in Syria and intervened multiple times against the Seleucids. At the time of his victorious second campaign in Egypt, Antiochus IV was already forced to withdraw and to renounce his claims to Egypt by the Roman commander Popillius Laenas on the basis of a resolution of the senate.[15]

About one hundred years later Syria became a Roman province through the end of the Seleucid Kingdom,[16] and the Jewish Hasmonean state in Palestine came under Roman overlordship as an adjunct of Syria. After the decisive subjugation of Mithridates VI in 66 BCE, Pompey conquered Tigranes in Armenia and "liberated" the Hellenistic Seleucid heartland of Syria, Cilicia, and Phoenicia, which Tigranes had occupied. He sent his general Scaurus into southern Syria to put things in order there. When Scaurus came to Damascus, two lieutenants, Lollius and Metellus, had already liberated the Hellenistic polis from the rule of the Nabataeans. Scaurus therefore continued on to Judaea, where the two sons of the Hasmonean high priest-king Alexander Jannaeus (103–76 BCE) and the queen Alexandra Salome (76–67 BCE) were fighting to inherit the kingship after her death. At her accession to the reign, Alexandra had already appointed the older Hyrcanus II as high priest and had allied herself at the same time with the previously anti-Hasmonean Pharisees and their adherents. While she was still living, she had also marked out Hyrcanus to inherit the kingship,[17] but she increasingly had

---

ex Orientalibus libertatem acceperunt, facile tunc Romanis de alieno largientibus. "On revolting from Demetrius and soliciting the favour of the Romans, they were the first of all the eastern peoples that regained their liberty, the Romans then readily bestowing what was not their own" (text and translation in Stern 1976–1984, I: 336, 338).

[14] Cf. Josephus, *Ant.* 12.415–419. Josephus emphasizes that this was the first treaty between Romans and Jews. According to 1 Macc 8.22, by contrast, bronze tablets came to Jerusalem. For the debate over the authenticity of the treaty in 1 Maccabees, see Schürer 1973–1987, I: 171ff.

[15] On this, see the more detailed discussion in Schürer 1973–1987, I: 151–52, 171. These events were attentively observed in Judaea. See Dan 11.30.

[16] Through Pompey in 64 BCE, officially in 58 BCE. In 27 BCE it became a province of Caesar through Augustus and was under a legate. On this, see Millar 1993, 31: "the 'provinces of Caesar' were the military areas. . . . Syria . . . was a military area, and one in which at all times comparatively large military forces were stationed."

[17] Josephus, *J.W.* 1.120.

to confront the striving for power of her younger son, Aristobulus II, who relied on the previous adherents of his father—the Sadducean aristocracy. After Salome's death, an open war broke out between the brothers. Hyrcanus II was defeated by Aristobulus II and removed from the throne. However, the ambitious aristocrat and Idumaean magnate Antipater,[18] who had control over the administration of Judaized Idumaea and had become the political advisor of the incapable Hyrcanus II, appealed in his name to the Nabataeans for support[19] and besieged together with them the Jerusalem temple mount, which was held by Aristobulus II. The fight was so embittered that during this siege a charismatic miracle worker, Onias, known from rabbinic texts as Honi the Circle-Drawer, was stoned by an enraged crowd because he refused to curse Aristobulus and petitioned God not to let the plans of the fighting brothers succeed.[20] Both men, Hyrcanus and Aristobulus, then sought to win the Roman general Scaurus for their party. Scaurus favored Aristobulus so that he could subject the army of Hyrcanus and Antipater to a crushing defeat. When Pompey arrived in Damascus in 64 BCE, the brothers presented their respective claims before him.

> Here he (Pompey) heard the case of the Jews and their leaders, Hyrcanus and Aristobulus, who were quarrelling with one another, while the nation (ἔθνος) was against them both and asked not to be ruled by a king, saying that it was the custom of their country to obey the priests of the God who was venerated by them, but that these two, who were descended from the priests, were seeking to change their form of government in order that they might become a nation of slaves.[21]

The delegation of the people, presumably headed by the Pharisees, fundamentally rejected the rule by kings—which already existed since Alexander Jannaeus or his brother Aristobulus I (104–103 BCE)—as not in

---

[18] Josephus, *J.W.* 1.123: "An Idumaean by race, his ancestry, wealth, and other advantages put him in the front rank of his nation." For Antipater and his family, who originally came from Ashkalon and whose father already managed Idumaea under Jannaeus and Alexandra Salome, see Kokkinos 1998, 94–139. The father of Antipater presumably converted to Judaism during the forced Judaizing of Idumaea by John Hyrcanus (135–104 BCE). Josephus' source for all these events is above all Nicolaus of Damascus; cf. below.

[19] Antipas himself was married to a Nabataean woman; see note 71 below.

[20] Josephus, *Ant.* 14.22–24. For the rabbinic traditions, see Schürer 1973–1987, I: 235 n. 6; cf. Vermes 1973, 69ff.

[21] Josephus, *Ant.* 14.41 (trans. R. Marcus, LCL, 409); on this, see the parallel account of Diodorus Siculus 40.2 (text in Stern 1976–1984, I: 185ff.). Cf. Hengel/Deines 1996, 458 n. 181 (ET = 1995, 53 n. 130), who refer to the Pharisaic standpoint of this delegation.

keeping with the Jewish law.[22] Pompey did not discuss this 'referendum,' but he admonished them to peace and warned Aristobulus against revolt and against apostasy from Rome, i.e., the representative of Rome regarded himself—self-evidently—as the master of the East, which now had to be newly ordered by Rome.[23] He took Aristobulus captive when his adherents were willing neither to pay the promised amounts nor to hand over Jerusalem. The adherents of Aristobulus entrenched themselves again in the temple, while Hyrcanus gave over the city and the royal palace to Pompey.[24] After a two-and-a-half-month siege, Pompey stormed the temple, at which time many priests, who were carrying out their service, were killed,[25] and entered the interior of the sanctuary, though without plundering it:

> Of all the calamities of that time none so deeply affected the nation as the exposure to alien eyes of the Holy Place, hitherto screened from view Pompey indeed, along with his staff, penetrated to the sanctuary, entry to which was permitted to none but the high priest, and beheld what it contained: the candelabrum and lamps, the table, the vessels for libation and censers . . . and the store of sacred money amounting to two thousand talents. However, he touched neither these nor any other of the sacred treasures.[26]

Pompey confirmed Hyrcanus only as high priest and not as ethnarch or king and subjected the land to tribute—in a short time ten thousand talents

---

[22] Whether they appealed here to the treaty of alliance made with the people (ἔθνος) of the Jews and the Roman senate from 161 BCE (see the *senatus consultum* in 1 Macc 8.23–30; cf. 2 Macc 4.11; cf. Josephus, *Ant.* 12.415–419, on this, see note 14 above) and therefore wanted to place themselves under Roman protection is not recognizable from the report in *Jewish Antiquities*. Josephus omits the delegation of the people in the shorter report in *Jewish War*. The account of Diodorus Siculus (see note 21) is clearer here and mentions the treaty of alliance with the senate.

[23] This also supports the view that the treaty of alliance and support with Rome had not been forgotten. Cf. 1 Macc 12.1, 3–4 (the high priest Jonathan and the people renew the treaty with Rome); 1 Macc 14.16ff. (Rome renews the treaty with the high priest Simon); Josephus, *Ant.* 13.260–266 (renewal of the treaty with the Jewish δῆμος—in 132 BCE or, with less probability, in 105 BCE); 14.247ff. (renewal of the treaty to the advantage of the Jewish ἔθνος and the high priest John Hyrcanus).

[24] Josephus, *J.W.* 1.142ff.; *Ant.* 14.59.

[25] Josephus, *J.W.* 1.150 (trans. H. St. J. Thackeray, LCL, 71): "Then it was that many of the priests, seeing the enemy advancing sword in hand, calmly continued their sacred ministrations, and were butchered in the act of pouring libations and burning incense; putting the worship of the Deity above their own preservation." Cf. *Ant.* 14.65–68.

[26] Josephus, *J.W.* 1.152–153 (trans. H. St. J. Thackeray, LCL, 71); cf. Strabo 16.40 (in Josephus, *Ant.* 14.71ff.; Stern 1976–1984, I: 276); Tacitus, *Hist.* 5.9.

had to be paid. He also separated off all the Hellenistic cities that had been conquered in the Hasmonean period; handed them over again, as "free cities," to their former inhabitants,[27] some of whom had been driven out; and joined them to the province of Syria. Pompey took Aristobulus and his family, as well as numerous prisoners of war,[28] with him to Rome, where Aristobulus was led in the triumphal procession of Pompey.[29] Josephus blames both brothers along with their fraternal war for this misfortune of Jerusalem, the profanation of the temple, the loss of freedom, and the subjection under Rome.

> For this misfortune which befell Jerusalem Hyrcanus and Aristobulus were responsible, because of their dissension. For we lost our freedom and became subject to the Romans.[30]

The Psalms of Solomon — composed in the early Herodian period — lament these events from a Pharisaic perspective:

> 2.1ff.: In his arrogance the sinner (Pompey) broke down towering walls with the battering ram, . . . foreign peoples ascended your altar, with their shoes they trampled it down in arrogance, because the sons of Jerusalem had defiled the sanctuary of the Lord . . . through lawless acts had profaned.
> 17.11–12: The lawless one (Pompey) stripped our land of its inhabitants . . . , sent them to the west, and made the leaders of the people an object of ridicule.

Pompey received the just punishment for his wickedness (Pss. Sol. 2.26–27), but the Hasmoneans were also punished for their misdeeds, for

---

[27] Josephus, *Ant.* 14.75–76 mentions Gadara, Hippos, Scythopolis, Pella, Dion, Samaria, Marisa, Ashdod, Jamnia, Arethusa, and the coastal towns of Gaza, Joppa, Dora, and Straton's Tower. Pss. Sol. 17.14–18 refers to the merciless collection of this tribute in Jerusalem and to the tax evasion of the "pious" in the wilderness; for the "anachoresis" in Judaea, cf. note 330 below.

[28] These were not least priests and Levites who had defended the temple and maintained the cult until the penetration of the Romans. They formed the heart of the Jewish diaspora in Rome. For their descendants as freedpersons in Rome, see Philo, *Legat.* 155–156; for returning emigrants, cf. the Theodotus inscription in chapter 4 below (note 160). Cf. also Pss. Sol. 17.11–12.

[29] For the triumph of Pompey, cf. Diodorus Siculus 40.4 (Stern 1976–1984, I: 188–89); Pliny the Elder, *Nat.* 7.98 (Stern 1976–1984, I: 483–84); Appian, *Mithridatica* 117.571ff., 576ff. (Stern 1976–1984, II: 182–83). Pss. Sol. 17.12 mentions the mocking of the Jewish rulers.

[30] Josephus, *Ant.* 14.77 (trans. R. Marcus, LCL, 487).

they seized the kingly "diadem" due to their arrogance and "made desolate David's throne" (Pss. Sol. 17.5–6):

> But you, O God, will crush them and take their seed from the earth, by having a man who is foreign (ἀλλότριον) to our race rise against them. According to their sins, you will repay them, O God . . . (Pss. Sol. 17.7–8)

The Psalms of Solomon regard the subsequent assumption of power and the actions of the "half-Jew" of Idumaean origin Herod—he is the one who is meant by "the foreigner"[31]—against the Hasmoneans as the just punishment of God, who "is faithful in all his judgments" (17.10).

The Roman rule of the late republic was primarily interested in an effective—indeed excessive—taxation of the new province and, besides this, in strengthening the Hellenistic cities and their culture, which, after the Roman-promoted fall of the Seleucids, had become threatened by the oriental "barbarians," Parthians, Armenians, Nabataeans, and Jews. At the same time, due to the growing Parthian danger, the Romans desired a pacification of the new province of Syria, which had become splintered through the collapse of the Seleucid kingdom. Therefore, in ca. 57 BCE Gabinius divided the Jewish rump state into five *synodoi*, i.e., administrative districts, with Jerusalem and Jericho as seats of *synhedria* in Judaea, Amathus in Peraea, Adora in Idumaea, and Sepphoris in Galilea, to ensure stability and order and the regulated collection of the tribute.[32] At the same time, the land received an "aristocratic" constitution,[33] as was also common elsewhere in the subjected provinces of the Romans, for in the new Roman client state Hyrcanus II initially stood at the head only as high priest, whereas the administration and the judicature were in the hands of the leading local families.[34] Alexander, the son of Aristobulus II, who was already able to escape from captivity on the way to Rome; Aristobulus himself, after he had fled from Rome; and, later, his son Antigonus all continued to assert their claim to the throne and to the high priesthood, with the support of a large group of adherents among the people in each case.

---

[31] Cf. As. Mos. 6.2; Josephus, *Ant.* 14.403: ἡμιουδαῖος (on this, cf. note 71 below). For the Pharisaic conviction that the reign of Herod was the just punishment of God, see note 54 below.

[32] Cf. Cicero, *Prov. cons.* 5.10 (text and commentary in Stern 1976–1984, I: 202ff.); Cassius Dio 39.56.5–6 (text in Stern 1976–1984, II: 354–55). Cf. Gabba 1999, 98–99: "The arrangement imposed by Gabinius was ineffective, and must have lasted quite a short time. In 56 BCE Aristobulus himself, having escaped from Rome, gathered many followers and tried yet another revolt, once again crushed by Gabinius." Cf. further Gabba 1999, 100.

[33] Josephus, *Ant.* 14.91; cf. *Ant.* 11.111.

[34] Schürer 1973–1987, I: 184–98; cf. also Goodblatt 1994, 30, 110–11.

They ensured that the constant unrests in Judaea—which had difficulty bearing the loss of its independence—did not cease.[35] The Roman legates in Syria, who had three legions at their disposal—though these were stationed in northern Syria because of the Parthian danger—had to attack them in multiple campaigns.[36] With a clearly pro-Roman—realistic—attitude, Antipater and Hyrcanus attempted to retain their power. The high priest appears not to have protested even when Crassus, to finance his Parthian campaign, plundered the temple in 54 CE, and the master of the temple treasury, with great diplomacy, was even able to rescue the temple curtains.[37] The fear that the Romans would destroy the city and temple, as the Babylonians had once done, or desecrate the latter, as Antiochus IV had done, probably grew latently among the population after the encroachments of Pompey and Crassus, which were to be followed by others.[38] Due to the defeat of Crassus at Carrhae (53 BCE) and the invasion of the Parthians in Syria, instances of open unrest broke out again in Galilee, which Cassius Longinus put down.[39] After the death of Pompey, Hyrcanus and Antipater supported Julius Caesar in his difficult situation during his Egyptian campaign (48–47 BCE) with fifteen hundred Jewish auxiliary troops[40] and brought over the Egyptian Jews to Caesar's side. Caesar appears for this reason to have especially favored the Jews in his sphere of power.

The division into five *synodoi* or *synhedria* by Gabinius had not facilitated the pacification of the land[41] and was therefore repealed by Caesar in 47 BCE in connection with a reorganization of the region. Hyrcanus and Antipater were fittingly rewarded for their support in the

---

[35] Josephus, *Ant.* 14.93: "Many Jews had attached themselves to Aristobulus because of his old glory and because they always had joy in revolutionary activity." Cf. *Ant.* 14.100ff.: Aristobulus' son Alexander comes to power for a second time, forces many Jews to "fall away," and marches through the land with a great army, killing every Roman. Gabinius conquers him at Tabor, and ten thousand (μύριοι—a typically exaggerated number specification) Jews lose their lives.

[36] Josephus, *Ant.* 14.82–88, 92–97, 101–102, 120.

[37] Josephus, *J.W.* 1.179; *Ant.* 14.105–109.

[38] Cf. the mention of the eschatological destruction of the temple in the Life of Habakkuk in the Lives of the Prophets (12.11): "And concerning the end of the temple he prophesied: 'it will occur by a people from the west.'" According to this writing, the prophet Jonah had prophesied the eschatological destruction of Jerusalem (10.8). Cf. Josephus, *J.W.* 6.300–309; John 11.48; Mark 13.2.

[39] Josephus, *J.W.* 1.180; *Ant.* 14.119–120.

[40] Josephus, *J.W.* 1.187 and *Ant.* 14.128, 139, gives the number three thousand. In *Ant.* 16.52 (in the speech of Nicolaus of Damascus before Agrippa) the number is two thousand; in the decree of Caesar quoted by Josephus in *Ant.* 14.193, however, the number is fifteen hundred, which is presumably more accurate. On this, cf. Pucci Ben Zeev 1998, 40, 48–49.

[41] See note 32 above.

Egyptian campaign. Hyrcanus was named ethnarch of the Jews, and his descendants were also to retain this office. Moreover, the hereditary office of high priest was confirmed to him.[42] Antipater received not only Roman citizenship and personal freedom from taxation but also the authority to rule in whatever form he regarded to be correct. This made him the actual master in the land.[43] The Jews were exempted from military service both in Judaea and in Asia Minor,[44] and were to live according to their traditional customs, i.e., to keep the Sabbath and to collect the temple tax and transfer it to Jerusalem. Moreover, Caesar granted a remission of taxation in Judaea,[45] and in addition to Joppa, the most important harbor of the land, he also gave back the Hasmonean property to Hyrcanus.[46] However, when Herod was appointed as king by Octavian and Mark Antony in 40 CE, the arrangements for Hyrcanus and his children were already nullified or transferred to Herod and his family.[47]

Josephus quotes these Roman decrees in such an unusually detailed manner until Claudius' edict to the Alexandrians and the letter of Petronius to the Palestinian port city Dora, which guaranteed the Jewish rights again after the Caligula crisis,[48] in order to convince his Jewish compatriots in Judaea and the diaspora toward the end of the first century CE that they were protected by these decrees—even after the First Jewish War—if they behaved loyally toward Roman rule. At the same time, however, it was also an admonition to the Romans that they not depart from

---

[42] Josephus, *Ant.* 14.194–195, 196, 199, 210. Pucci Ben Zeev 1998 provides an extensive commentary on the documents (letters of Caesar from 47–44 BCE and relevant *senatus consulta*, which Josephus quotes in *Ant.* 14 and 16). She rightly stresses the importance of these documents (373): "Along with Polybius, Appian and not many others, and along with his Jewish predecessors, Ezra and the authors of the books of the Maccabees, Josephus is one of the few ancient historians who quotes the text of documents. In spite of his apologetic bias in choosing them, in spite of his lack of attention to their content, and in spite of the fact that they are not original documents but copies (and often copies of copies) already translated into Greek, there is no doubt that his quotations constitute an enormous contribution to our knowledge of Jewish rights. More than that: they provide us with almost all the information available concerning Jewish rights in the first century BCE and in the first century CE."

[43] Josephus, *Ant.* 14.143; cf. *J.W.* 1.194, 199–200.

[44] Josephus, *Ant.* 14.227, 228. In Judaea this was connected with the exemption from providing winter quarters for Roman troops.

[45] Josephus, *Ant.* 14.201.

[46] Josephus, *Ant.* 14.202–210. On this, see Pucci Ben Zeev 1998, 80–92; Gabba 1999, 100–101.

[47] With this was connected the privilege of being admitted to the senate and of receiving an answer within ten days (Josephus, *Ant.* 14.210). Cf. the quick hearing of Herod before the senate, which took only seven days to appoint him king (*Ant.* 14.387). See Kokkinos 1988, 98–99.

[48] On this, see the excursus below in section 3.1.4.

their previous good tradition.[49] It was his firm conviction—as Philo of Alexandria had already held before him—that precisely the Pax Romana propagated by Augustus and his successors guaranteed the free exercise of the Jewish cult.[50] This view of the political situation of Judaea was indeed realistic.

Antipater first appointed his two sons as strategists, i.e., as military and civil commanders: Phasael in Jerusalem and the younger Herod in Galilee. This gave Herod the opportunity for his first heroic action in 47 BCE.[51] The "robber captain" Hezekiah maintained a private army with which he carried out raids in southern Syria. Herod captured him and his adherents and had them executed. The fact that Hezekiah[52] could not have been a simple "robber" is evident also from the aftermath in Jerusalem, for not only did the representatives of the priestly and lay aristocracy, the leading Jews, demand that Hyrcanus call Herod to account, since only the high priest and his Sanhedrin had the right to carry out capital punishment, but the mothers of those killed by Herod pressed the high priest daily in the Jerusalem temple that he must bring Herod before the court. Hyrcanus gave in, but let Herod—at the wish of the Roman governor—escape.[53] The trial itself degenerated into a farce because of the cowardice of the members of the Sanhedrin in the face of the self-confident appearance of Herod with his armed bodyguard. Only the Pharisee Samaias took the floor, blamed the members of the counsel, and announced to them the future rule and

---

[49] The emperor Domitian (81–96 CE) collected with intensified cruelty the *fiscus Iudaicus*, the two-drachma tax, which all the Jews had to pay to the temple of Jupiter Capitolinus after the destruction of the Jerusalem temple and the end of the Jewish War (Suetonius, *Dom.* 12), and punished Romans who converted to Judaism (Cassius Dio 67.14.2); cf. Schürer 1973–1987, III: 122–23, and note 177 in chapter 4 below.

[50] Cf. Kehne 2007 (GV = 2000). See especially Agrippa's speech that urged for peace at the beginning of the revolt in 66 CE (Josephus, *J.W.* 2.345–401). See further note 375 below. This knowledge also plays a role for Paul in Rom 13; see Hengel/Schwemer 1998, 95–96 (ET = 1997, 60). It is a presupposition of the primitive Christian worldwide mission.

[51] Josephus, *J.W.* 1.204–211; *Ant.* 14.159–160, 184.

[52] On Hezekiah and his dynasty, see Hengel 1989c, 313–24 (GV = 1976c, 319–24); Freyne 1998, 211–16; Gabba 1999, 101; cf. notes 208, 299, and 386 below. For the designation "robber" for all enemies of the Roman rule in Josephus and not only for bandits, see Hengel 1989c, 24–46 (GV = 1976c, 25–47); Schürer 1973–1987, I: 441; II: 600, 604. Hezekiah was apparently a powerful anti-Roman partisan of Aristobulus, who assailed Gentile areas from Galilee. His son Judas played a role later in the uprisings after the death of Herod I in 4 BCE, and he is probably the same person as the founder of the zealot freedom movement, Judas the Galilean. After the time of this Hezekiah, Josephus calls insurgents against Herod and the Romans "robbers" almost stereotypically. In this respect he follows his source Nicolaus of Damascus.

[53] Josephus, *Ant.* 14.170, 177ff. Herod fled to Damascus, but he was then appointed as prefect over the Decapolis and Samaria by the Roman governor. With this he obtained an official Roman office.

revenge of Herod. Because of their sins they could not escape him.[54] Hezekiah himself must have belonged to the nationally conscious aristocracy.

Herod's rise to power was initially due to the influence of his father, Antipater, and later more and more to his military, political, and economic gifts, his unscrupulous will to power, and his consistent loyalty to the respective Roman commanders. When Cassius demanded a tribute of seven hundred talents, Herod in Galilee was the first to bring together the amount that was required of him.[55] The unrests did not cease, because Antigonus, the son of Aristobulus II, gathered an army, but Herod conquered him in Galilee.[56]

After the victory at Philippi, Mark Antony took over rule in the East. He named Herod and his brother Phasael tetrarchs and had the Jewish embassy in Tyre, who had made accusations against Herod, executed (41 BCE).[57] Herod had successfully survived the change of party from Cassius, one of the murderers of Caesar, to Antony, but the Parthian attack in Judaea in spring 40 BCE changed the game.[58] He had to flee. The Parthians plundered Jerusalem as well as the surrounding land, and they destroyed Marisa, which had once been the main city of Idumaea and was the home city of Herod. They captured Hyrcanus II and Phasael. With their support Antigonus became high priest and king (40–37 CE). He had his uncle Hyrcanus' ears cut off so that he could never again hold the office of high priest. Phasael died.[59] Herod had previously safely brought his assets to an unknown location in the south, presumably in the powerful Hellenistic city of Ashkalon, which was never Jewish.[60] He rescued his adherents and his whole family, above all his fiancée Mariamne—the granddaughter

[54] Josephus, *Ant.* 14.171–176. Later it was also Samaias who opened the doors of Jerusalem to Herod when he besieged it with Sossius (cf. *Ant.* 15.3–4). This passage has no parallel in *Jewish War*. The dramatic depiction probably goes back to Nicolaus of Damascus, whom Josephus follows for his detailed story of Herod (*Ant.* 14–17). Cf. note 31 above on Pss. Sol. 17.5–8, 11; As. Mos. 6.2.

[55] Josephus, *J.W.* 1.220–221; *Ant.* 14.274. According to *J.W.* 1.225; *Ant.* 14.280, Cassius promised Herod that he would make him king of Judaea because of his extraordinary competency when he defeated Octavian and Antony. But Cassius and Brutus lost the battle at Philippi in 42 BCE and died there.

[56] Josephus, *Ant.* 14.297ff.

[57] Josephus, *Ant.* 14.326, 327ff.

[58] Josephus, *J.W.* 1.248–273; *Ant.* 14.330–369.

[59] Josephus, *J.W.* 1.270ff.; *Ant.* 14.366–369. He took his own life or attempted to do so and was later poisoned by a physician of Antigonus. Elsewhere, however, Josephus says that Phasael was killed by the Parthians (*J.W.* 1.484 [on this, see the commentary in Michel/Bauernfeind 1962, I: 421 n. 233]; 2.46; 5.162; *Ant.* 14.379; 17.257). In the work of Julius Africanus the information of Justus of Tiberias has been preserved, according to which Phasael fell in the battle against the Parthians; on this, see Kokkinos 1998, 159.

[60] Cf. Kokkinos 1998, 100 n. 58.

of Hyrcanus—in the fortress of Masada, which was regarded as unconquerable, and fled via Nabataea and Egypt to Rome in 40 BCE. Octavian and Mark Antony received him in a friendly manner and helped him. At the recommendation of Antony the senate named Herod king, because he seemed to be the right man to represent the Roman interests in the Parthian War and to fight against Antigonus, who had been installed by the Parthians.[61] From now on a king of Judaea could only be appointed by Rome.[62]

The Parthians had already laid waste to part of the land, and the population suffered even more during the three years of fighting between Herod and Antigonus. Because he had only inadequate support from Roman troops at the start, Herod initially focused on breaking the resistance of the "robbers" in Galilee, i.e., the adherents of Antigonus, who preferred to die rather than to become "slaves" under Herod.[63] Herod and the Roman general Sossius, who was tasked with supporting him, finally took Jerusalem in 37 CE after a three-month siege, exactly twenty-six years after it was conquered by Pompey, and it was only with difficulty that Herod was able to hinder excesses when the city was plundered by the Roman soldiers. Antigonus, mocked by Sossius as "Antigone," was led in chains to Antioch and beheaded by Mark Antony at the wish of Herod.[64]

For his description of the rise and reign of Herod Josephus extensively uses in *Jewish Antiquities* the presentation of Nicolaus of Damascus, a close friend of the king and an eyewitness, as well as the memoirs of Herod, and yet also an anti-Herodian priestly source, which he allows to shape his judgment about the king more strongly, for he reasoned that Nicolaus, who lived at the court of the king, must have flattered Herod.[65] Nicolaus had brought up

---

[61] Josephus, *Ant.* 14.384ff.: Herod expected that the young Hasmonean Aristobulus, grandson of Hyrcanus II, would be named king.

[62] For the accusation that Jesus declared himself to be king of the Jews, which was brought against him before Pilate, cf. Schwemer 2001c, 155, and sections 20.2.2 and 21.1.2.

[63] Josephus, *J.W.* 1.303–313; *Ant.* 14.413–430. Josephus presumably owes the more dramatic depiction of the destruction of the "robbers" in the caves of Arbela in *Jewish Antiquities* (14.429: θάνατον πρὸ δουλείας ὑπομένων) to Nicolaus of Damascus (or the memoirs of Herod?), who stresses that the king himself was present and, despite the taunts that the last of the heroes hurled against him, offered him his hand and a free retreat.

[64] Josephus, *J.W.* 1.353; *Ant.* 14.465–488. For the mocking of Antigonus, cf. Hengel 1984c, 50. For the execution of Antigonus, see *J.W.* 1.357; *Ant.* 14.489–491; Strabo (in Josephus, *Ant.* 5.9–10); Cassius Dio 49.22.3ff. (text in Stern 1976–1984, II: 359ff.): Antony had Antigonus bound to a pole (σταυρός) and flogged—a punishment that no other king had to endure at the hands of the Romans—before he was killed. Similarly Plutarch, *Ant.* 36.4 (text in Stern 1976–1984, I: 568). On this, see sections 21.1.3 and 21.2 for the execution of Jesus as "king of the Jews."

[65] Josephus, *Ant.* 16.184; cf. 14.9; according to 15.174 Josephus also used the memoirs of Herod.

the children of Mark Antony and Cleopatra and presumably came to Herod
shortly after the battle of Actium, the suicide of Antony and Cleopatra, and
the dissolution of their court. He would not have spent so many years at the
court and, finally, have collaborated in the regulation of Herod's will if Herod
had been only a primitive oriental despot. Stemming from a noble family of
Damascus, Nicolaus was not simply a historian and diplomat of rank but the
leading polymath of his time. In his philosophical views he followed Aristotle and also advocated his encyclopedic educational ideal. Herod studied the
philosophers with him, but the king had a far greater interest in historiography.[66] Nicolaus began his history of the world, in 144 books, in Jerusalem,
and he also composed his portrayal of Augustus at the instigation of Herod.
Josephus could draw on this history of the world until the unrests following
the death of Herod in Palestine and the disputes surrounding his will.[67] The
fact that this great scholar stayed for many years in Jerusalem also reveals
the "Hellenization" of the upper class in the Jewish capital. He must have
possessed an extensive library there.

After the conquest of Jerusalem, Herod had forty-five members of the
Sanhedrin and adherents of Antigonus from the rich Sadducean aristocracy killed and confiscated their assets.[68] While the siege of Jerusalem
was still going on, he had his wedding with Mariamne, the granddaughter of Hyrcanus II and Aristobulus, in Samaria. This union with a Hasmonean wife served to legitimate him dynastically and politically—as
the timing of the wedding shortly before the conquering of Jerusalem
betrays—and was probably sought after not only by Hyrcanus but also
already by Antipater.[69] The marriage admittedly brought neither the
hoped-for strengthening of the legal position of king nor the goodwill of

---

[66] Nicolaus of Damascus, FGrH 90, F 135 (in Stern 1976–1984, I: 248–50); on this,
cf. Kokkinos 1998, 124.

[67] For Nicolaus, cf. in detail Wacholder 1962; Hengel 1996a, 60–63 and elsewhere;
Hengel 1999b, 141ff. and elsewhere; see 460 index, s.v. "Nikolaus"; for the significance
of Nicolaus as an eyewitness, cf. Millar 1993, 41: "in the modern historiography of the
Roman Imperial system at this formative stage the contemporary evidence of Nicolaus has
hardly played the role that it should."

[68] Josephus, *J.W.* 1.358; *Ant.* 15.5–6.

[69] Josephus, *Ant.* 14.300, 467; *J.W.* 1.344: he allowed the wedding to take place during
the siege. Mariamne's father was Alexander, the son of Aristobulus I. Her mother, Alexandra, the daughter of Hyrcanus II, had promised Herod the girl when he was general in
Galilee. The brother of Herod, Pheroas, later married the younger sister of Mariamne, but
she died around 20 BCE; cf. Kokkinos 1998, 211; against Schalit 2001, 66, who argued that
Herod married for love and saw the political motivations only on the side of Hyrcanus and
of Marriamne's mother, Alexandra.

the people,[70] for the rivalry and enmity between the new dynasty and the old dynasty—which could look back upon a history that had lasted for more than one hundred years and had sometimes been glorious—led to constant intrigues at the kingly court, at which the sister of Herod, Salome, had a special position of power. In the eyes of the Hasmoneans, Herod, as a former private person of Idumaean origin, remained—despite the conversion of his Idumaean grandfather to Judaism—a "half-Jew" and not of equal birth.[71] With this marriage Herod himself established the root of "his domestic misfortune,"[72] for his jealousy and the resistance of the beautiful, proud woman—who did not forgive him for the murder of her brother and grandfather but rather openly accused him and whose hatred for the king must have been just as great as his passionate love for her—led to the execution of Mariamne in 29 BCE.[73]

With a total of ten marriages and an 'oriental' harem, which included boys, Herod demonstrated his power and his wealth.[74] Initially he only had his sons whom he had begotten with Mariamne be raised in Rome, in preparation for the succession, but later he also did so for the sons of the Samaritan Malthace. In his family politics he relied on the dynastic strengthening through marriages to relatives among the descendants of Hyrcanus II and his family. In the case of his sister and daughters, he

---

[70] Josephus, *Ant.* 20.248 (trans. L. H. Feldman, LCL, 521): "Herod married Aristobulus' sister Mariamme, hoping to capture the goodwill of the people for himself, thanks to their recollection of Hyrcanus."

[71] The mother of Herod was "Arabian," i.e., Nabataean. His father belonged to the Idumaeans, who had been converted to Judaism for two generations. This means that from a legal perspective Herod was, like his father Antipater, a Jew. Cf. further Josephus, *J.W.* 1.313; *Ant.* 14.430, 489; cf. *J.W.* 1.478. Antigonus already mocked Herod as a half-Jew (Josephus, *Ant.* 14.403); Josephus, who was proud of his own priestly and Hasmonean descent, shared this viewpoint; cf. *Ant.* 14.403; 17.192. By contast, vis-à-vis the Jewish and non-Jewish world of his time, Herod placed value on being regarded as a Jew. Nicolaus of Damascus reconstructed for him a family tree, which traced back his descent to Jewish ancestors in the Babylonian exile (Josephus, *Ant.* 14.9), which Josephus, as a priest, saw through, of course, as a lie. Cf. Hengel 1996a, 63; Kokkinos 1998, 101–2. In opposition to him, one appealed to Deut 17.15: "You are not permitted to put a foreigner, who is not your brother, over you." Cf. m. Soṭah 7.8 on Agrippa I; Schürer 1973–1987, I: 447; and note 277 below.

[72] Josephus, *J.W.* 1.431, 665: ἐν δὲ τοῖς κατ' οἶκον ἀτυχέστατος (presumably following Nicolaus of Damascus).

[73] Josephus, *Ant.* 15.229ff. The specifiation given in *J.W.* 1.441–444 is corrected by Josephus in *Ant.* 15.87.

[74] Polygamy was permitted to the king according to Jewish law (cf. Josephus, *J.W.* 1.477; m. Sanh. 2.4: he is permitted to have eighteen wives); it was rejected by the Essenes (CD IV 21; V 2–6; 11QT 57.17ff.). No other member of his family, however, had (simultaneously) as many wives as Herod; on this, see Kokkinos 1998, 143ff., 211, 244–45.

placed value on marrying according to Jewish law.[75] He rejected suiters who were not willing to be circumcised.[76] The struggle of his sons for the succession, in a court full of hatred and intrigue, overshadows the last years of his reign. Against the advice of Nicolaus he had the two sons of the Hasmonean Mariamne strangled in Sebaste, after he, following years of mutual suspicions and reconciliations, thought he had found her guilty of conspiracy and of a plan to murder him.[77] His oldest son, Antipater, who was behind these intrigues and could not wait for the natural death of his father, died five days before the king. He was executed because he had wanted to poison his father.[78]

At the beginning of his reign, the enmity and covetousness of Cleopatra caused Herod difficulties. In addition to the Decapolis and the Palestinian coastal strips, she would have liked to incorporate Judaea and Nabataea into her kingdom and thus reestablish the Ptolemaic kingdom of the third century BCE in Palestine, but Antony did not entirely yield to her wishes. Still, among other things, in 34 BCE she obtained a choice slice of Herod's, the balsam plantations at Jericho, for which Herod had to pay the considerable sum of two hundred talents each year.[79]

Since he came from a nonpriestly family, Herod could not unite the two highest offices in his person. In order to disempower the Hasmoneans and their retinue in the priesthood, he appointed Hananel (37–36 BCE) from Babylon—he was presumably of Zadokite descent—as high priest,[80] which met with hefty opposition from his mother-in-law Alexandra[81] and his wife, who asserted the hereditary claims of Mariamne's brother to this office and conspired with Cleopatra. Herod presumably yielded to this

---

[75] Later this also remained the custom with the Herodian rulers; cf. Hengel/Schwemer 1998, 120 n. 494 (ET = 1997, 71, 365 n. 376).

[76] Kokkinos 1998, 182ff., wrongly assumes a rejection of Syllaeus (Josephus, *Ant.* 16.225) for political reasons. The religious reasons, which Josephus adduces, are displaced. But Josephus has no reason to do this in relation to his Gentile readers. The sister of Herod, Salome, could hope to be queen in Nabataea through this marriage. For the relationship between Jews and Nabataeans, see Hengel 2002, 193ff.

[77] Nicolaus (FGrH II, A 90, F 136; Stern 1976–1984, I: 251–52); Josephus, *J.W.* 1.513–551; *Ant.* 16.300–394; Kokkinos 1998, 214–15; for Sebaste, see the subsequent discussion in the present section of this volume.

[78] Josephus, *J.W.* 1.661–664; *Ant.* 17.182–187; cf. Schalit 2001, 642; Kokkinos 1998, 501 index, s.v. "Antipater II."

[79] Josephus, *J.W.* 1.360–362; *Ant.* 15.79, 95–96, 106–107. For the gifts of Antony to Cleopatra, cf. Schalit 2001, 772–81; see further Gabba 1999, 114: already for this reason Herod probably readily changed sides and crossed over to Octavian after the battle of Actium.

[80] Josephus, *Ant.* 15.22, 34, 39ff., 56.

[81] Herod then had Alexandra, daughter of Hyrcanus II, executed in 28 BCE. Josephus, *Ant.* 15.251.

pressure after a year as a political calculation, since he must have discerned that such a radical, sudden change, as long as there was a legitimate candidate from the Hasmonean family, would produce more difficulties than benefits for him. He appointed Aristobulus, the brother of Mariamne, as high priest, but then had the young man, who was just seventeen years old, drowned in a feigned swimming accident, after his first public appearance at the festival of tabernacles had evoked enthusiastic acclamation from the people.[82] In the new occupation of the office, he again circumvented the Palestinian priestly aristocracy and appointed Jesus, son of Phiabi, from Alexandria.[83] Altogether Herod appointed seven high priests and later favored the rich clan of Boethus, who also came from Alexandria and was likewise presumably of Zadokite descent.[84] The first high priest from this family was Simon, son of Boethus, who became Herod's father-in-law through Herod's marriage to his daughter, the second Mariamne.[85] With this consciously anti-Hasmonean policy with respect to the occupation of the highest Jewish political-religious office, Herod broke with the hereditary succession and lifelong administration of the office, which, after the chaos of the Maccabean struggle for freedom, had become a matter of course also with the new family of the Hasmoneans.[86] The high priestly families themselves regarded every one of their members who had held office as high priest for life; hence the plural ἀρχιερεῖς in Josephus and in the Gospels and Acts. In the time that followed four rich families pushed through to the top and competed with one another.[87] However, the judicial murder of Hyrcanus II reveals how uncertain the situation was at the outset. Before Herod departed for Rhodes in 30 BCE, in order to pay his respects to Octavian[88] as the victor of Actium, he had Hyrcanus II

---

[82] Josephus, *J.W.* 1.437; *Ant.* 15.53–56. Cf. Kokkinos 1998, 212. Josephus uses βαπτίζεσθαι for "drown." On this and on John the Baptist, cf. section 9.3.

[83] Josephus, *Ant.* 15.322. On his dynasty, cf. notes 226 and 370 below. This Alexandrian priestly family may have been connected with the Zadokite-Oniadic priesthood of the temple of Leontopolis, which was founded by Onias IV, who had fled to Egypt; see Schürer 1973–1987, I: 168; III: 47–48, 145–47. In that case Herod would have brought an opponent of the Hasmoneans as high priest to Jerusalem.

[84] All the brothers of the second Mariamne appear to have served as high priests; cf. Kokkinos 1998, 218. For the legendary wealth of this family, see Hengel 1996a, 25 and elsewhere; see the index in Hengel 1999b, 454, s.v. "Boëthos." For the clan of Boethus, cf. notes 226 and 267 below.

[85] Josephus, *Ant.* 15.320–322; 17.78; 18.109; 19.297. According to Josephus, Simon obtained this office because Herod wanted to marry the beautiful daughter.

[86] Cf. Schalit 2001, 312. The controversy between Hyrcanus and Aristobulus and the removal of Hyrcanus by Antigonus constituted exceptions—analogously to the demise of the Oniads.

[87] Cf. note 226 below.

[88] He took the byname Augustus in 27 CE.

executed—he was accused of conspiring with the Nabataeans—at the age of seventy-one, for although Hyrcanus could no longer be considered for the high priestly office because of his mutilation, from the Jewish perspective he was still legally entitled to the kingship.[89]

Augustus, who had already supported the installation of Herod as client king, confirmed him after Actium as king of Judaea, strengthened his position in the following year, and gave Jericho back to Herod as well as the Hellenistic cities that had once been "liberated" by Pompey, namely Gadara, Hippos, Samaria, and the coastal cities Gaza, Anthedon, Joppa, and Straton's Tower,[90] which thus came under the rule of a Jewish king again, though one who valued Hellenistic civilization.

Herod refounded Samaria under the name Sebaste, in honor of the emperor, with a predominantly Gentile population which he settled there, and in the course of time he lavishly fitted it out.[91] From Sebaste and Caesarea he drew his most faithful troops alongside the soldiers from Cilicia and Asia Minor. Because he did not have to fear a rebellion among the population and among the soldiers in this non-Jewish city, he later had the sons of Mariamne executed there.[92]

With his refounding of Straton's Tower as Caesarea (Maritima) in 22 BCE[93] he connected a magnificent harbor complex, one of the largest in all antiquity, secured by breakwaters, piers, and mighty light towers, which were dedicated to Drusus and Tiberius, the sons of Livia, the wife of Augustus.[94] In the center of the city he erected a temple of Augustus and Roma. As a whole the individual dedications in the building program to

[89] Josephus, *J.W.* 1.433–434, 437; cf. *Ant.* 15.164. Josephus says that Hyrcanus was eighty-one years old at that time (*Ant.* 15.178), but his parents did not marry until 103 BCE, so he could only have been a bit older than seventy.

[90] Josephus, *J.W.* 1.396; *Ant.* 15.217. Cf. the difficulties of Herod with the Gadarenes, who accused him before Augustus because of his "cruelty"; see Josephus, *Ant.* 15.351–358. It is for this reason that Augustus later took it away from Archelaus and placed it, as an important place of the Decapolis, under the governor of Syria (*Ant.* 17.320).

[91] Josephus, *J.W.* 1.403; *Ant.* 15.292–298.

[92] Cf. note 77 above. Josephus, *J.W.* 1.551; for the protest of the veteran soldier Tiro against the execution, which Tiro himself and other soldiers had to pay for with death, see Josephus, *J.W.* 1.544ff., 550; *Ant.* 16.375ff.

[93] The city was founded by the Phoenicians. It received its new name in honor of Augustus. The building of the harbor lasted twelve years; see Josephus, *J.W.* 1.408–415; *Ant.* 15.331–341. For the palace of Herod (which the prefects and procurators later used as a "praetorium"), the temple of Augustus, the theater, the stadion, and the hippodrome, cf. Broshi 1999, 16–18; Netzer 2006, 94–118.

[94] Josephus, *J.W.* 1.412; *Ant.* 15.336 mentions the Tower of Drusus as the largest. Pilate renovated the tower, dedicated to Tiberius, as can be inferred from the inscription, which was later installed secondarily in the theater. For the reconstruction of the inscription, see the convincing reading of Alföldy 1999, 106–7:

the family of the emperor are related to one another.[95] The secure harbor was meant to open his kingdom to world trade, to secure easy access for the festival pilgrims from the diaspora, and in this way to promote the land economically.[96] In Caesarea Herod introduced quadrennial musical and athletic competitions according to the Greek model as well as gladiatorial games and animal spectacles according to the Roman model.[97] In its structure, his own palace also corresponded to the need for representation of a Roman-Hellenistic king.[98] It was not surprising that the Roman prefects, later Agrippa I, and the procurators thereafter chose this city for their residence and lived in the former palace of Herod as "praetorium"[99] and not in the religiously strict Jerusalem, where too many legal restrictions had to be observed. Caesarea was predominantly settled by Hellenized Syrians,[100] but it had a significant, self-confident Jewish minority, and the portion of Samaritans was also not small. It must have been a pleasure to live in this beautiful new city, but the Jewish population felt disadvantaged

---

[NAUTÍ]S TIBERIÉUM
[– PO]NTIUS PÌLATUS
[PRAEF]ECTUS IUDAE[A]E
[REF]É[CIT]

For the sailors Pontius Pilate,
the prefect of Judaea,
rebuilt the Tiberieum.

The inscription is unusually arranged because both the "beneficiaries" and the "object of the foundation" are named before the founding prefect. Pilate presumably wanted to demonstrate his loyalty to the emperor (idem, 106). Already under Herod the entire complex of the harbor and the city with their dedications expressed that "the security of the seafaring and the concomitant prosperity of the kingdom . . . was due the emperorship" (idem, 102). On this, cf. the acclamation of the sailors from Alexandria in relation to Augustus (Suetonius, *Aug.* 98.2).

[95] On the colossal statue of Augustus, which was "not inferior to Olympian Zeus, which served for its model, and on another of Rome, rivalling that of Hera at Argos" (Josephus, *J.W.* 1.414, trans. H. St. J. Thackeray, LCL, 197), see also Millar 1993, 355.

[96] On the economic benefits, cf. Gabba 1999, 122–23.

[97] Josephus, *Ant.* 16.137–138; *J.W.* 1.415.

[98] For the excavation reports, cf. A. Lichtenberger 1999, 122ff.; Netzer 2006, 106–12. Herod the Great presumably 'commuted' between Caesarea and Jerusalem to a greater extent than the later rulers in the land.

[99] Cf. Acts 23.35 (perhaps also Phil 1.13) for the imprisonment of Paul in the "praetorium of Herod" in Caesarea. Cf. also Millar 1993, 69. The evangelist Philip chose the predominantly Gentile Caesarea as voluntary place of residence and presumably founded a community there. Peter converted the centurion Cornelius and his family there (Acts 8.40; 10; 21.8).

[100] Josephus, *J.W.* 2.266, speaks of "Syrians," though they probably referred to themselves as "Greeks."

from the beginning, for they were not granted the same citizenship rights as the "Greeks." Their synagogue was located on a portion of land whose point of access was in Gentile possession, and the Jewish community was not able to expand the plot. This led to difficult conflicts, which, according to Josephus, sparked off the Jewish War in 66 CE.[101] Herod and later his sons Antipas and Philip were the first and in this time the only rulers in the East who came to the fore with the refounding of cities in the Greco-Roman style. The orientation to Rome and the imperial house is revealed by the names Caesarea, Sebaste, and later Autocratoris, Tiberias, Julias, and Caesarea Philippi.[102]

In Jerusalem Herod built a theater, a stadium, and an amphitheater but—in contrast to the Hellenistic Jewish aristocrats at the time of Antiochus IV, around 175 BCE—no gymnasium with ephebia.[103] Herod's building program included the expansion of the Hasmonean fortresses and palaces and other new establishments. He reinforced the fortress in the northwest of the Jerusalem temple area and gave it the name Antonia, expanded the Hasmonean palaces in Jerusalem and Jericho, and restored fortresses such as Masada and Machaerus.[104] This building politics not only served his own security and glory and the urbanization of the land but also employed day laborers, landless farmers, and craftsmen for decades. Since these constructions of Herod began especially in the years after 24 BCE, they could have been a reaction to the famine and the epidemics in 25–24 BCE, when the king had to buy grain in Egypt from his own resources in order to prevent the worst.[105] Josephus describes numerous building projects of the king, including many outside his land. The latter were meant to strengthen his influence in the cities in the east of the kingdom.[106] The archaeological discoveries confirm this information about the

---

[101] Josephus, *J.W.* 2.266–270, 284–292. In this context the rich Jews in Caesarea claimed that the city was theirs, for its founder was said to be a Jewish king (*J.W.* 2.266). On *isopoliteia*, cf. Kasher 1990, 260ff. Cf. also section 3.1.7 below.

[102] Cf. Millar 1993, 354–55; Horbury 1999, 157.

[103] Josephus, *Ant.* 15.267–279. Since these innovations also encountered resistance, he yielded to some extent and had the images of humans removed again. He appears to have forgone gymnasium and ephebia because of the events under the high priest Jason after 175 BCE, at the time of the Hellenistic reform. On this, cf. Hengel 1999b, 145. By contrast, Herod furnished the Gentile cities of Tripolis, Damascus, and Ptolemais with gymnasia (Josephus, *J.W.* 1.422).

[104] For the building program of Herod and the more recent archaeological excavations, see also Roller 1998; Netzer 1999; A. Lichtenberger 1999; Netzer 2006, passim.

[105] Thus also Gabba 1999, 122 n. 135. Cf. Josephus, *Ant.* 15.299–316.

[106] Josephus, *J.W.* 1.401–428; he notes especially cities in Syria, Asia Minor, and Greece, where many Jews lived (such as Cos, Rhodes, etc.). He also showed himself to be a benefactor of the "whole oikumene" as the sponsor of the Olympic Games (*J.W.* 1.426–427).

incredible building extravagance of the king, which even surpassed the constructions of Augustus in Rome.

At the southern border of Galilee, in the large plain, Herod founded the "city of horses" Gaba, where he settled veterans from his army.[107] In 23 BCE he received from Augustus the regions of Trachonitis, Batanaea, and Auranitis east of the Jordan, classic robber regions, which Herod secured also for the pilgrims from Babylon on their way to Jerusalem through the settlement of Jewish military settlers from Babylon in the Batanaea.[108] At the time of his visit in Syria in 20 BCE, Augustus also handed over to Herod the territory of Zenodorus: Ulatha and Paneas with their surrounding land. He evidently thought that the region between the Trachonitis and Galilee would be better held under control by the Jewish king—due to his own interest in maintaining tranquility in this region—than by the Roman legate in distant Antioch.[109]

This gain in land strengthened Herod's position. He was the most important client king in the east of the Roman Empire. His wealth must have been immense. For a long time his family had possessed estates in Idumaea. His father, Antipater, had considerable resources at his disposal, and he increased them further as financial manager of Hyrcanus II. The confiscation of the assets and estates of his opponents after the conquering of Jerusalem likewise brought in a fair amount,[110] and he was able to increase his assets further through the ownership of the royal domains of the Hasmoneans and through the earnings of the copper mines in Cyprus and the taxes from Syrian cities.[111] In any case, he trusted that he could carry out his largest building project with his own resources[112]—the glori-

---

[107] Josephus, *J.W.* 3.36; *Ant.* 15.294; cf. *Life* 118–119, where he writes about the grain reserves of Queen Berenice, sister of Agrippa II, in the "villages" at Beth Shearim.

[108] Josephus, *Ant.* 17.23–31.

[109] Josephus, *J.W.* 1.400; *Ant.* 15.359–360. For the conflict of Herod with the Nabataeans in 12–9 BCE, who supported the bands of robbers in the Trachonitis (Josephus, *Ant.* 16.271–299, 335–355), see Millar 1993, 40–41. The Romans did not intervene militarily themselves. Afterwards, Herod settled a colony of three thousand Idumaeans and Jewish cavalrymen from Babylon in the Trachonitis in order to secure the region.

[110] Even though the "gifts" of Herod to Mark Anthony at this time were considerable (Josephus, *J.W.* 1.358; *Ant.* 15.5, 75).

[111] On this, see Schalit 2001, 257–62; Gabba 1999, 118–24.

[112] Josephus, *Ant.* 15.380; 17.162. In later years the temple treasury was, to be sure, also drawn upon; cf. Josephus, *Ant.* 20.220. Donations and contributions such as the Gate of Nicanor by a rich Jew from Alexandria were famous. The restoration of the temple of (Hadad-)Zeus in Damascus was entirely financed from resources of the temple treasury and from donations (SEG 2 [1924], nr. 828; 829; 830; 832); on this, see Hengel/Schwemer 1998, 99 (no equivalent in ET, i.e., 1997, 61).

ous renovation and expansion of the Jerusalem temple (20–19 BCE), which Herod, according to Josephus, announced to the people with a speech:

> I think I have, by the will of God, brought the Jewish nation to such a state of prosperity as it has never known before. . . . But since, by the will of God, I am now ruler and there continues to be a long period of peace and an abundance of wealth and great revenues, and—what is of most importance—the Romans, who are, so to speak, the masters of the world, are (my) loyal friends, I will try to remedy the oversight caused by the necessity and subjection of that earlier time, and by this act of piety make full return to God for the gift of this kingdom.[113]

The building of the temple belonged from of old to the obligations of the king. By rededicating the inner sanctuary on the day of his coronation Herod acted like a Hellenistic monarch and underlined at the same time his legitimacy as successor to Solomon.[114] When Herod mentions his reign, peace, and prosperity as presuppositions, he calls to mind among his people Solomon's building of the temple and, at the same time, forges a connection to the Roman program of the Pax Augusta and to the "piety" of the princeps.[115] While a time of peace of not even two decades may

---

[113] Josephus, *Ant.* 15.383, 387 (trans. R. Marcus, LCL, 185, 187–88). Here too the source is probably Nicolaus of Damascus.

[114] Josephus, *Ant.* 15.421, 423: "The temple itself was built by the priests in a year and six months, and all the people were filled with joy and offered thanks to God, first of all for the speed (of the work) and next for the king's zeal, and as they celebrated they acclaimed the restoration. . . . And it so happened that the day on which the work of the temple was completed coincided with that of the king's accession, which they were accustomed to celebrate, and because of the double occasion the festival was a very glorious one indeed." On this, see Horbury 1991, 113, who also notes that it is not by chance that Josephus has placed the prophecy of the Essene Menahem, who announced the kingly dignity of Herod, directly before the resolution of Herod for the reconstruction of the temple (Josephus, *Ant.* 15.373–379).

[115] On the motif of peace, cf. the era of internal peace that begins with the principate of Augustus (30/27 BCE), the "Pax Augusta," which replaced the time of the civil wars. The *Ara Pacis Augustae* in Rome was then "praised" on the basis of the senate resolution of July 4, 13 BCE; cf. Höcker 2002 (GV = 1996). For the connection of the Pax Augusta with Herodian Judaism, see Horbury 1999, 157: "There was first peace after the *civilia bella* also in Judaea under Herod—as in Rome . . . under the *princeps*. Further, a Herodian loyal to the king could claim that as Rome conquered the external enemies, above all the Parthians, so Herod conquered Parthians and Arabians. . . . Finally, we must consider that just like Augustus, so also Herod in Judaea was a proponent of *eusebeia*, primarily as builder of temples for Augustus and Rome but also for the God of Israel." Horbury shows how this program of Vergil is celebrated with allusion to Herod (*palmae Idumaeae*, cf. the discussion of "Idumaea" as a designation

appear short today, it was palpable for the subjects of Herod after the preceding continuous unrests and civil wars ever since the time of Alexander Jannaeus, indeed ever since the time of the desecration of the temple by Antiochus IV, and to many it could appear as an unexpected gift from God.[116] Herod demonstrated his victory over the enemies and the inaugurated time of peace by placing "barbarian" spoils and plundered weapons from the war with the Nabataeans around the temple building.[117] His victories were signs of divine help. Officially the whole renovation required only nine and a half years, while the actual temple building was already finished after one and a half years.[118] However, building continued on the huge pillar hall of the outer court (of the Gentiles), and this work was not

---

for Palestine later in this section). Cf. further Horbury 1991, 103–49. For the positive impact of the Pax Romana, see Hengel 1999b, 140–41, 144. See also the encomium to Augustus in Philo, *Legat.* 144–145 (trans. F. H. Colson, LCL, 73), which praises his ending of the civil wars: "the whole human race exhausted by mutual slaughter was on the verge of utter destruction, had it not been for one man and leader Augustus whom men fitly call the averter of evil (ἀλεξίκακον, cf. Homer, *Il.* 10.20). This is the Caesar who calmed the torrential storms on every side, who healed the pestilences common to Greeks and barbarians, pestilences which descending from the south and the east coursed to the west and north sowing the seeds of calamity over the places and waters which lay between." The names of the synagogues in Rome also demonstrate the loyal behavior and the thankfulness in relation to the rulers of the Augustan time. The Jewish inscriptions in the city (from the third and fourth century) mention most frequently—eight times—the synagogue of the Augustesians, which probably goes back to freedpersons of Augustus; see Noy 1995, 539–40, index; cf. the respective commentary. But the synagogue of the Agrippesians (after Marcus V. Agrippa, the friend and son-in-law of Augustus) is attested at least three times, as is the synagogue of the Vernaclesians ("the one born at the place"?) and the synagogue of the Volumnesiens (derived from Volumnius, the procurator of Syria in 8 BCE).

[116] This may apply at least for the urban population. Cf. Alexandra Salome: while she ruled only nine years, her reign remained a golden time of peace in Pharisaic-Rabbinic memory. On this, see Schürer 1973–1987, I: 231–32; Hengel 1984c. Cf. section 4.3.2 for her relationship to the Pharisees.

[117] Josephus, *Ant.* 15.402: σκῦλα βαρβαρικά; in this year Augustus had regained the weapons and Roman standards from the Parthians; cf. Horbury 1991, 109: "it is likely that 'barbarian spoils' are meant to recall the Herodian Jewish contribution to this vaunted achievement of the Augustan peace." At the same time, with his victory over the Arabians/Nabataeans Herod had outdone the Hasmoneans. Cf. the 'last words' of Herod (Josephus, *Ant.* 17.162): "In the 125 years of their rule the Hasmoneans were not able to accomplish such a thing to the glory of God." The placement of weapons in the Jerusalem temple corresponded to the Solomonian example. The Septuagint addition to 1 Kgs 14.26 mentions the golden spears that David had conquered and that were kept in the sanctuary; in Josephus, *Ant.* 8.259, they are golden shields made by Solomon and conquered golden quivers of David, which were taken by Shishak in the plundering of the temple.

[118] Cf. note 114 above. During this time it is said to have rained only at night (Josephus, *Ant.* 15.425; cf. Sifra, Behuq 1.1; Wayiqra Rabbah 35.10; b. Taʿan 23a).

completed until 62–64 CE, with some things remaining uncompleted, as shown by the excavations.[119]

In this building project Herod showed scrupulous concern for the Jewish purity regulations. Thus, only priests, who were correspondingly trained in a craft, worked in the innermost part of the temple, and the king avoided entering this area himself. The Greek warning inscriptions, which forbade non-Jews to enter the inner area of the temple with the threat of capital punishment, are also signs of the king's respect for the Torah with regard to the purity of the sanctuary.[120] The large substructures with which the plateau on the temple mount was expanded could also be completed by other workers. Among others, even craftsmen and architects from Greece and Rome were employed, both in the work on the outer court and in the construction of the city and palace.[121] Herod renovated the old, second temple and enlarged it, while also creating something new. The actual *naos* remained small. The priestly court, the court of the Israelites, and the court of the women did not take on colossal exterior measurements, but the court of the Gentiles was disproportionally expanded. Its outer dimensions were 315 meters in the north, 470 meters in the east, 280 meters in the south, and 488 meters in the west. The ideal dimensions of a square[122] could not be obtained on the site of the Temple Mount, but by means of mounds and supporting walls a large platform for the huge forecourt was obtained, which was intended for the crowds of pilgrims from Palestine and the diaspora at the major pilgrimage festivals. The forecourt thus became the "agora" of Jerusalem and was on its eastern side "the portico of Solomon," the place of the preaching of Jesus and of the apostles.[123] The magnificent renovation of the Jerusalem sanctuary became a model for the renovation of the temple of Zeus in Damascus and of the temple of Bel in Palmyra, with the Jerusalem temple far surpassing the others, which were renovated shortly thereafter, in its outer dimensions due to the forecourts. It was thought to be the largest

---

[119] John 2.20 speaks of a building time of forty-six years, i.e., into the time of Jesus; Mark 13.1 praises the splendor of the building. Cf. further Bahat 1999; Netzer 2006, 137–78.

[120] The Romans abided by this rule in times of peace; see Josephus, *J.W.* 6.125–126. For the discovery of two inscription tablets, see Boffo 1994, 283–90 nr. 32.

[121] We know of a Jewish architect through his Aramaic ossuary inscription; see Beyer 1984, 344: "Simon, the Temple Builder."

[122] Cf. Ezek 40.47; 42.16-20; 45.2: a square plot of 500 × 500 cubits; the Temple Scroll from Qumran (36–38.11; 38.12–40.5; 40.5–45.6) specifies the outer extent of the inner court at 300 × 300 cubits, the middle court at 508 × 508 cubits, and the outer court at ca. 1640 × 1640 cubits; on this, see the German translation and commentary of J. Maier 1978b, 25–49, 67–72, 99–102 = fig. 2 (p. 126) (= J. Maier 1997); cf. Steudel 2001, 70–71, 74–91.

[123] John 10.23; Acts 3.11; 5.12; see section 18.3.

single temple in all of antiquity.[124] The Herodian temple made Jerusalem famous. It was praised by Pliny the Elder, and even the Baylonian Talmud still states: "Whoever has never seen the building of Herod has never seen a beautiful building in his life."[125]

Herod renovated the tomb of David in Jerusalem, which was traced back to a foundation by Solomon, and erected a tomb monument.[126] While this has been interpreted as an "atoning monument," it was presumably built by Herod to honor the founder of the city, as a sort of Jewish *heroon*, which called to mind the old glorious past.[127] The formidable enclosing wall that Herod erected in Hebron over the graves of the patriarchs in the Cave of Machpelah was also probably intended to make the pilgrimage there even more attractive to the pilgrims and attest the piety of the king. After all, Abraham and Isaac were the common ancestors of Esau/Edom and Jacob/Israel. Josephus mentions the tombs but does not indicate that the *ḥaram* was erected by Herod, just as he says nothing about Herod's building measures in the Abraham sanctuary in Mamre.[128]

Like Hyrcanus II, Herod, as protector and benefactor, advocated for the Jews in the diaspora. The widely disseminated Jewish diaspora increased

---

[124] On this, cf. Hengel/Schwemer 1998, 98–99 (no equivalent in ET, i.e., 1997, 61); Ådna 1999, 32–71 (the Egyptian-Hellenistic Caesarion as architectonic model for the temple expansion); Netzer 2006, 275–76: the *stoa basileia* on the southside of the temple was built by Herod for the reception of guests and pilgrims. It was not used for the imperial cult.

[125] b. Baba Batra 4a; b. Sukkah 51b. Cf. Mark 13.1: the disciples say to Jesus: ἴδε ποταποὶ λιθοι καὶ ποταπαὶ οἰκοδομαί. Luke loves the temple more than the other evangelists (on this, see also sections 3.1.7 and 6.4.3). He has his Gospel begin (1.18-23) and end (24.53) in the temple. His narrative of the birth and childhood of Jesus recounts the presentation of Jesus in the temple (2.22-38) and the stay of the twelve-year-old Jesus in the house of his "Father" (2.49) for instruction among the scribal teachers (2.42-49). While the person of the king in b. B. Bat. 3b is evaluated negatively, no shadow falls upon the temple, and the name of the king as builder is explicitly mentioned. On this, see Horbury 1991, 115–18. Cf. Pliny the Elder, *Nat.* 5.70 (Stern 1976–1984, I: 469): ... *Hierosolyma longe clarissima urbium Orientis non Iudaeae modo* (Jerusalem, by far the most famous city of the East, not only of Judaea).

[126] Lives of the Prophets 1.7; see Schwemer 1995/1996, I: 146–52.

[127] In Acts 2.29 Peter will not by chance recall to the memory of the festival pilgrims the tomb of David. For ἱλαστήριον μνῆμα, the atoning monument of Herod, see Josephus, *Ant.* 16.182–183: Herod is said to have atoned for his tomb sacrilege with this monument. Nicolaus of Damascus did not mention this incident. According to Liv. Pro. 23.1–2, the blood guilt for the murder of the prophet Zechariah, the son of Jehoiada (2 Chr 24.20-21), continued to lie unatoned upon the house of David. Therefore, signs announce the end of the temple cult. Cf. Schwemer 1995/1996, II: 283–321. Mittmann-Richert 2000, 162, 167–68, therefore connects the mention of the atoning monument in Josephus with the murder of Zechariah, the son of Jehoiada.

[128] Josephus, *J.W.* 4.531ff.: πάνυ καλῆς μαρμάρου καὶ φιλοτίμως εἰργασμένα. Cf. Keel/Küchler/Uehlinger 1982, 688–91, 701–2.

his unique importance in the entire Roman Empire, but especially in the eastern provinces and in Rome itself. Josephus reports about this in the context of Herod's journey with Agrippa to Asia Minor and Greece, after Agrippa had previously visited Jerusalem and made an offering in the temple.[129] In his commission in Ionia, Nicolaus of Damascus delivered a long speech before Agrippa in support of the Jews there, in which he praised the benefits of the Roman rule of the world and the loyalty of the Jews in Palestine and in the diaspora, but not least also the loyalty of the king and of his father Antipater.[130] The buildings of Herod in Gentile cities contributed not only to the honor of the imperial house but also to the reputation of the Jewish minorities in the diaspora and their patron in Jerusalem, for example the theater in Damascus and the grand boulevard in Antioch on the Orontes. The fame of Herod as *euergetes* was probably intended to benefit the especially numerous Jewish inhabitants here, who had such a "philanthropic" leader.[131]

It was not only with his building politics that the king brought a "blossoming of Hellenism"[132] in Roman guise for his land. In his court lived, in addition to Nicolaus of Damascus, other intellectuals with a Greek education. The promotion of scholarship and art made an impact through the long reign of the king upon the knowledge of the Greek language and the education of the upper and middle classes; reached—as shown by the numerous Greek (and some Latin) ossuary inscriptions[133]—broader strata

---

[129] Josephus, *Ant.* 16.12ff., 55 in 15 BCE; cf., by contrast, the affirmation of Augustus, when his grandson Caesar Caius, the son of Agrippa, demonstrated his reverence neither to the Apis in Egypt nor to the Jerusalem temple (Suetonius, *Aug.* 93; in Stern 1976–1984, II: 110–11).

[130] Josephus, *Ant.* 16.27–61; 16.27–28 (trans. R. Marcus, LCL, 219): "It was also at this time, when they were in Ionia, that a great multitude of Jews, who lived in its cities, took advantage of their opportunity to speak out freely, and came to them and told them of the mistreatment which they had suffered in not being allowed to observe their own laws and in being forced to appear in court on their holy days because of the inconsiderateness of the examining judges. And they told how they had been deprived of the monies sent as offerings to Jerusalem and of being forced to participate in military service and civic duties and to spend their sacred monies for these things, although they had been exempted from these duties because the Romans had always permitted them to live in accordance with their own laws." On this, cf. Schalit 2001, 426ff.; here Josephus quotes verbatim the presentation of Nicolaus with some of his own additions; cf. Pucci Ben Zeev 1998 390–91. On Hyrcanus II, cf. the previous discussion in this section.

[131] Cf. Horbury 1991, 120–21, 135.

[132] For the high point of the Hellenistic influence under Herod, see Hengel 1996a, 1–90 (63).

[133] In and around Jerusalem about 40 percent of these inscriptions are composed in Greek. The inscriptions primarily come from the time between Herod I and the destruction of the Jerusalem temple in 70 CE.

of the population; and provided an additional incentive for the return of diaspora Jews. The Theodotus synagogue in Jerusalem, which was built in or soon after his reign, owes its founding to a priest who returned from Roman 'exile,' was completed by his grandson (?) Theodotus, son of Vettenus, and served the study of the law and, additionally, as a place of lodging for pilgrims.[134] Jerusalem became attractive to diaspora Jews. They came, like Hillel, from Mesopotamia and yet also from the Greek-speaking West. The pilgrimages also brought considerable prosperity to Jerusalem, which can be seen, for example, in the private buildings from the Herodian period. This affected large portions of the urban population, which tended to be more peaceful and pro-Roman than the simple population of the land, which had to bear a high burden of taxes and duties.

The Hellenistic-Roman character of Jerusalem during the long reign of the king did not only reach the upper class but extended also to the broader strata of the population. If the Romans had more strongly supported this upper class and, especially after the death of Agrippa I (in spring 44 CE), had let the Herodian dynasty in Jerusalem and in the Jewish heartland come to power instead of increasingly entrusting the political leadership to procurators who were insensitive to the Jewish religious sensibilities, then the First Jewish War, in which members of the upper class, such as Annas II and Josephus,[135] also joined the revolt in an act of "national despair," would hardly have occurred. The radical Zealots would not have been able to prevail in their fight for freedom, which was proclaimed according to the model of the Maccabees. Jerusalem would not have been destroyed, and under the rule of Herodian client kings, who were descended from the Hasmoneans on their mother's side, the benefits of the Pax Romana could also have persuaded the "pious."[136] A Jewish-Hellenistic culture, one that was entirely its own, would have developed, and perhaps a more liberal, "reformed" Judaism would have become a world religion[137] and not the eschatological and messianic movement of the Christians.

Josephus, who was born in Jerusalem, is known to us as an advocate of the Jewish priestly aristocracy, which was educated in Hebrew and Greek.

---

[134] CIJ 2.1404. Cf. Schürer 1973–1987, II: 425; Kloppenborg Verbin 2000, 243–80 (lit); Hengel 1996a, 171–95; 1999b, 437 (index: CIJ 2.1404); Hengel 2002, 34, 61. The patronymic "Vettenus" suggests a freedman of the *gens Vettia*. For the inscription, see also Boffo 1994, 274–82 nr. 31. This synagogue is presumably identical with the synagogue of the "Freedmen" in Acts 6.9. For the plurality of synagogues in Jerusalem, see Acts 24.12.

[135] On this, see his commentary in *Ant.* 20.257; on this, see section 3.1.7.

[136] On this, see Hengel 1996a, 63, and the discussion at the beginning of this section.

[137] Philo of Alexandria hopes for this. See *Mos.* 2.41–44; *Praem.* 152.

Paul comes from the diaspora and is a representative of the middle class, who received his Pharisaic-scribal scriptural education in Jerusalem.[138]

Herod led Palestine to economic and cultural blossoming. In the later time period, he was no longer drawn into larger military conflicts.[139] The last Roman civil war between Mark Antony and Octavian bypassed his land. His own large assets are documented in his will. Twice he granted a remission of taxes. In his coinage he refrained from using pictorial representations[140] of humans and animals out of consideration for the Jewish prohibition of images.[141] However, he was and remained hated by large portions of his people. It was probably for this reason that he had the Jewish population spied upon, in order to nip disturbances in the bud.[142] The perfidious murder of the young high priest Aristobulus, the last of the Hasmonean family, could not be forgotten, nor could the killing of his Hasmonean wife Mariamne and of his sons born from her as well as the numerous other political murders that he—in this respect a true oriental despot—committed in the interest of preserving his power.[143] He let burglars—against Jewish law—be sold as slaves into foreign lands as a punishment, which gave them no prospect of manumission after seven years. This had a more severe effect upon the lower classes.[144] He gave confiscated estates to his favorites. The large estate economy that he promoted caused independent small farmers to sink to the status of dispossessed tenants—the Israelite ideal was, by contrast, the small farmer.[145]

---

[138] On this, see Hengel 1991a (GV = 1991b; 2002, 68–184).

[139] For his conflicts with the Nabataeans he drew on himself the wrath of Augustus, but Nicolaus mediated (Nicolaus, FGrH II, A 90, F 136; text and commentary in Stern 1976–1984, I: 250, 255–56; Josephus, *Ant.* 16.271ff., 286–299).

[140] Josephus, *Ant.* 15.365; 16.64.

[141] A telling exception is the "Tyrian shekel," the currency in the Jerusalem temple with which the temple tax (cf. Matt 17.24) also had to be paid. This coin, which was minted in Tyre, bore the head of Melqart-Heracles on one side and the Ptolemaic eagle on the other side. On this, see Mildenberg 1998, 171–72: "the typical tetradrachma and didrachma constituted the only stable, available, and neutral large silver currency because the Seleucid and Roman overlords only granted the Hasmoneans and Herodians the right to mint bronze secondary coins. . . . Prior to the Jewish War, the economic laws were what counted, and one was far removed from ideological scruples. With the beginning of the war, however, there was a turnabout: it was of decisive importance for the insurrectionists that they created their own silver money." For the coins of the revolt, see section 3.1.7.

[142] Josephus, *J.W.* 1.570, 573; *Ant.* 15.285–289, 366–367.

[143] Josephus, *Ant.* 15.9–10 (a quotation from Strabo).

[144] Josephus, *Ant.* 16.1–5. Cf. Schalit 2001, 231–51, who assumes that Herod did not merely take action against simple thieves, but also proceeded in this way against rebellious robbers.

[145] Cf. Hengel 1989c, 323–24 (GV = 1976c, 329–30). For the large estate economy in the parables of Jesus, see section 18.4.

The pagan temples, which he had built primarily in non-Jewish regions in honor of Augustus, stood in opposition to the Jewish laws. His excuse that he had to do this to honor the emperor and because of the good relationship to Rome was not accepted,[146] although this very thing corresponded to the reality and to his position as a Roman client king, for a *rex socius et amicus populi Romani* was entirely dependent on Rome—and in this time that meant on the personal goodwill of the emperor. His entire reign was a constant balancing act between the Roman power and the Jewish population, which was largely hostile to him. He had disempowered the Sadducean nobility at the very beginning of his reign, and his relationship to the Pharisees was shaky. At first he relied on them and promoted them, but when he had solidified his position around 20/19 BCE and had, after the visit of the emperor, required his subjects to swear an oath of loyalty to himself and to Augustus, the scholars Pollion and Sameas, as well as other Pharisees, refused to do so. Out of consideration for these scholars he did not punish their refusal of the oath,[147] nor that of the Essenes, whom Herod appears to have always treated with respect.[148] By contrast, according to the presentation that Josephus takes over from Nicolaus of Damascus about this same event, Herod imposed a penalty, which, to the great irritation of Herod, his sister-in-law, the wife of Pheroas, paid for six thousand Pharisees.[149] Even the episode of the eagle in the temple is presumably connected with the increasing Pharisaic opposition to the king. Shortly before Herod, who was suffering from cancer, died, two Jerusalem scholars thought that it was an opportune time to tear down the unlawful golden eagle with which Herod had adorned the temple building. When forty students complied with the exhortation, they were seized, and the king had them burnt alive, after they had defiantly hurled against him at the trial as a confession:

> We believe that it is less important to observe your decrees than the laws that Moses wrote as God prompted and taught him, and left behind. And with pleasure we shall endure death or whatever punishment you may

---

[146] Josephus, *Ant.* 15.328ff.

[147] Josephus, *Ant.* 15.370–371. Here Josephus uses a source that is hostile to Herod.

[148] The Essene Menahem is said to have prophesied the future rule as a schoolchild and after this accession to power to have specified the length of his reign with twenty, indeed with more than thirty years. "From then on Herod held all Essenes in honor" (Josephus, *Ant.* 15.373–378)—this is probably scarcely an indication of their political influence upon Herod. His positive attitude toward the Essenes is more likely connected with the fact that he regarded them as politically unthreatening and that they were the opponents of the ruling priestly aristocracy and of the Pharisees.

[149] Josephus, *Ant.* 17.42. Cf. chapter 4 for a more detailed discussion of this problem.

inflict on us because we shall be conscious that death walks with us not because of any wrongdoing on our part but because of our devotion to piety.[150]

The last years of Herod fell under an unlucky star and not only because of the fight for the succession. The "zealous ones," whom Josephus lets speak here, announce the emergence of the zealot "fourth party" of Judas the Galilean.[151] But the riots that broke out immediately after Herod's death show the skill and political responsibility with which he, despite all personal cruelty and capriciousness, helped his land to peace and relative prosperity under Roman overlordship, i.e., after about one hundred years of constant wars and after the decade-long civil war. The upper class that rose with the help of Herod—especially the new high priestly families—profited from this to a greater extent, of course, than the lower class, which complained that he compelled them to constant forced labor.[152] The judgment of Joseph Klausner—"the Maccabbeans built up a Jewish Palestine: The Herodian kings destroyed it"[153]—is understandable in the mouth of a fervent Zionist at the beginning of the twentieth century, who had to defend the Hasmoneans against widespread criticism in the scholarship of that time, which sometimes had an anti-Jewish slant, but it is scarcely tenable in a neutral consideration of the events in the time of the Herodian and Hasmonean rule. The Hasmonean rule led to fraternal strife, civil war, and the intervention of Rome, whereas Herod brought peace that lasted for more than thirty years. Therefore, Abraham Schalit opposed Klausner's dictum with good reasons.[154] In the defense of his constantly threatened power Herod was not more cruel than Alexander Jannaeus, and on his path to rule he did not proceed against his opponents in a different way than, say, Augustus.[155] To be sure, he ruled his land with an iron fist, and the court intrigues in the struggle for the succession and

---

[150] Josephus, *Ant.* 17.149–159 (159; trans. R. Marcus, LCL, 445); cf. *J.W.* 1.648–653.

[151] For the martyrs of the Maccabean period and their love for the law, cf. the excursus at the end of section 4.4. For the "zeal" of the zealot martyrs, see Hengel 1989c, 59–76, 146–228 (GV = 1976c, 61–79, 154–234). See further chapter 4 below.

[152] Josephus, *Ant.* 15.366: ἐπιτάττων δ' ἀεὶ γίνεσθαι πρὸς τοῖς πόνοις.

[153] Klausner 1945, 135; cf. the even more personally reproachful statement against Herod on p. 137: "But all that the Maccabeans built up was destroyed by the Romans and by Herod 'the Great,' who, by the help of the Romans, sat on the throne of Judaea."

[154] Schalit 2001, xxv–xxvi (preface).

[155] Unlike Alexander Jannaeus, Herod, according to our sources (which may leave much unsaid), did not allow anyone to suffer long torments on the cross in executions. He may have consciously distanced himself from the Hasmoneans in this way. Augustus is said to have had three hundred senators and equestrians slaughtered at the altar of Caesar like sacrificial animals (Suetonius, *Aug.* 14).

the execution of three of his sons, especially of the two sons of the Hasmonean Mariamne, could have led to the legend of the murder of the children in Bethlehem.[156] On the whole Herod was presumably more popular and well-liked in the diaspora. This is shown by the torches that the Roman Jews set up on the "day of Herod."[157] Nevertheless, after his death, the Jewish population in Rome supported the demands of the emissaries of the people for direct rule by Rome and the removal of the sons of Herod (see below, with note 165).

None of his predecessors or successors so easily challenges Herod for the appellation "the Great"—Agrippa I and Agrippa II then adopted it as a title. This applies to his politics of peace, which in the situation of that time could be reached only with the Romans and not outwardly with the Parthians or inwardly with those who were zealous for the law, and especially to his building of the temple, which, in contrast to his person, always remained in good memory.[158] For the judgment of pagan contemporaries about Herod I, the wordplay of Augustus handed down in Macrobius—that it is better to be the pig (ὗς) than the son (υἱός) of Herod—is usually quoted as a sign of his cruelty.[159] Aside from Nicolaus of Damascus, only a few witnesses about Herod have been preserved from non-Jewish, Roman and Greek authors.[160] Therefore, one should not ignore the role that "Idumaea" has as a designation for Palestine in Roman literature. It can also be understood with reference to the high estimation of the oriental barbarian ruler in the Hellenistic style from the Roman perspective.[161]

---

[156] Matthew 2.16-18. The report that Herod had numerous noble Jews kept in the stadium in Jericho, who were to be murdered at his death, so that the whole land would grieve, may be an exaggerated, half-legendary report (Josephus, *J.W.* 1.659–660, 666; *Ant.* 17.180–181, 193).

[157] Persius, *Sat.* 5.179–184 (Stern 1976–1984, I: 436–37). For the problem of whether the custom refers simply to the Sabbath or to Herod or his descendants, see Horbury 1991.

[158] For the appraisal of Herod, cf. Schalit 2001, xxv–xxvi; cf. also D. R. Schwartz's preface to the second edition of this work, vi–xix; Schürer 1973–1987, I: 294ff.; Hengel 1996a, 55–63.

[159] Macrobius, *Saturn.* 2.4.11 (Stern 1976–1984, II: 665–66).

[160] Cf. Pliny the Elder, *Nat.* 5.70 (Stern 1976–1984, I: 469; quoted above in note 125). Against his usual tendency, which is influenced by Nicolaus of Damascus, Josephus, *Ant.* 16.150–159, enters into critical dialogue with the predominantly positive image that "others" made of Herod. His ambivalent nature is said to have been θηριώδης (i.e., beastly, i.e., tyrannical), his benefactions are said to have arisen, in truth, from his thirst for fame, but the Jewish people love what is right (τὸ δίκαιον) and not fame (δόξαν). With this he expresses his own opinion.

[161] Cf. Vergil, *Georg.* 3.12ff. (Stern 1976–1984, I: 316–17). On this, see Horbury 1991; see further the aftereffect in Lucan, *Pharsalia* 216 (Stern 1976–1984, I: 438–40); Valerius Flaccus, *Argonautica* 1.12 (Stern 1976–1984, I: 504); Silius Italicus, *Punica* 3.600 (Stern 1976–1984, I: 507); Statius, *Silvae* 1.6.13; 3.2.138; 5.2.139 (Stern 1976–1984, I:

Herod died shortly before the Passover festival in 4 BCE after a thirty-three-year reign in the land. In his definitive final will, which was also read right after his death, he appointed Archelaus, the son of the Samaritan Malthace, as king over Judaea, Idumaea, and Samaria. His full brother Antipas received Galilee and Peraea, and their half-brother Philip obtained the predominantly Gentile regions of Gaulanitis, Trachonitis, and Batanaea. Herod's sister Salome received the coastal cities of Jamnia, Ashdod, and Phasaelis, and Herod bequeathed great sums to Augustus.[162] The people immediately presented demands to Archelaus for a remission of taxes and the release of prisoners, and Archelaus gave in to these requests.[163] However, a bloodbath occurred at the Passover festival, for Archelaus had a great number of demonstrators, with the aid of his entire army, including the cavalry, killed in the temple area.[164] We are dealing here with an aftermath of the eagle episode, for as a quid pro quo the members and friends of the people executed by Herod first demanded that Archelaus punish those honored by Herod, a demand that Archelaus was not, of course, willing to grant. At the Passover festival the protest became much more intense due to the number of festival pilgrims. Archelaus therefore feared an insurrection and brutally proceeded against the pilgrims in the forecourt.

The will, however, first had to be confirmed and put into effect by the emperor. Archelaus therefore traveled to Rome, supported by Herod's friend Nicolaus of Damascus, who now became his advisor. At the same time or a little later, his brothers, Antipas and Philip, as well as Salome and other relatives, also went to Rome. A delegation of fifty men who represented the interests of the people followed later. They presented complaints against the rule of Herod and Archelaus and were supported by eight thousand Jewish inhabitants of Rome.[165] They had traveled to Rome with the permission of Varus, who was the governor of Syria at that time, and thought that it would be a better solution to the political problems if they were placed under the direct rule of Rome, as the delegation to Pompey (64 BCE) in Damascus had already advocated earlier. In their view, the unrest following the death of Herod and the murder of so many innocent people by Archelaus demonstrated the inability of these "tyrants" to bring peace to the land:

516–20); Martial, *Epigr.* 2.2.5; 10.50.1 (Stern 1976–1984, I: 523, 527); Juvenal, *Sat.* 8.160 (Stern 1976–1984, II: 102); Aelian, *Nat. an.* 6.17 (Stern 1976–1984, II: 408–9).

[162] Josephus, *J.W.* 1.668–669; *Ant.* 17.188–192. Salome bequeathed her territory to Livia.

[163] Josephus, *J.W.* 2.4; *Ant.* 17.204–205.

[164] Josephus, *J.W.* 2.5–13, 30; *Ant.* 17.213–218.

[165] Josephus, *J.W.* 2.80–92; *Ant.* 17.300–301, 304–314.

They implored the Romans to take pity on the relics of Judaea and not to fling what remained of it to those who were savagely rending it in pieces, but to unite their country to Syria and to entrust the administration to governors from among themselves. The Jews would then show that, calumniated though they now were as factious and always at war, they knew how to obey equitable rulers.[166]

Thus, there was still a strong national, anti-Herodian party in Palestine, which favored a high priestly leadership under a Roman governor and which was supported by many Jews in Rome. The Roman Jews showed through this their especially close connection with Judaea, which went back to those who had once been deported by Pompey. Presumably the Jewish delegation spoke for the Sadducean priestly aristocracy and the majority of the Pharisees. Augustus heard all the parties and ultimately confirmed Herod's will with some changes. Archelaus was not named king and had to relinquish the Hellenistic cities of Gaza, Gadara, and Hippos, which were added to the province of Syria. Antipas and Philip received the title of tetrarch.[167]

While these proceedings took place in Rome, further disturbances broke out in Palestine.[168] In Jerusalem crowds of pilgrims at the festival of weeks protested against the seizing of Herod's assets by Sabinus, the financial administrator (ἐπίτροπος = procurator) of the province of Syria, and especially against his attack on the temple, when he wanted to force his way into the temple treasury with military force.[169] Thus, in only fifty days the temple was profaned for a second time, for on Passover Archelaus had, after all, caused a bloodbath among the festival pilgrims (see above with note 164). In defense of the temple the armed pilgrims shut in Sabinus with his legions in Jerusalem. In Galilee Judas, the son of the "robber captain" Hezekiah, broke into the royal palace in Sepphoris, plundered the arsenal of weapons, and armed his followers. In *Jewish War* Josephus says that Judas attacked all those who strove after the rulership. In *Jewish Antiquities* he follows Nicolaus of Damascus: it is said that Judas himself sought the kingship.[170] In Peraea,

---

[166] Josephus, *J.W.* 2.90–92 (trans. H. St. J. Thackeray, LCL, 357).

[167] Josephus, *J.W.* 2.93–100; *Ant.* 17.317–323. Luke 3.1, 19; 9.7 = Matt 14.1; cf. Acts 12.1 and note 81 in chapter 9. Gadara and Hippos became cofounders of the Decapolis; see A. Lichtenberger 2003, 6–20, 27–28, 83–84.

[168] Josephus, *J.W.* 2.55–79; *Ant.* 17.250–298.

[169] Josephus, *J.W.* 2.49–50 (the soldiers robbed four hundred talents); *Ant.* 17.261–264 (a great portion of the temple treasure was stolen by soldiers; Sabinus openly seized only four hundred talents).

[170] Josephus, *J.W.* 2.56; *Ant.* 17.272.

Simon, a "slave" (δοῦλος)[171] of Herod, put the diadem on his head and with his followers destroyed the royal palaces in Jericho and Ammatha. Gratus, the commander of the Herodian troops, was able to conquer and behead Simon with the help of Roman reinforcements.[172] Athronges, a former shepherd like David of old, is said to have been distinguished, like Simon, already by his notable size and strength and likewise to have made a claim to the kingship. Together with his four brothers he made Judaea unsafe. They engaged in battles with the royal and Roman troops. At Emmaus they were able to ambush a Roman centurion and his supply convoy. It took a fairly long time before these revolutionaries, some of whom were presumably political messianic pretenders, were conquered.[173] Josephus states:

> And so Judaea was filled with brigandage. Anyone might make himself king as the head of a band of rebels whom he fell in with, and then would press on to the destruction of the community.[174]

Varus suppressed the revolts by moving into the land with three legions and additional auxiliary troops from Ptolemais as well as those of the Nabataean king Aretas IV. He burned down Sepphoris in Galilee and sold the inhabitants into slavery, and proceeded in the same way with Emmaus. Jerusalem was spared, for the inhabitants received Varus and credibly assured him that they had been besieged by the insurrectionists together with the Romans. Varus had two thousand of the chief culprits crucified in the vicinity of Jerusalem and sent the "ringleaders" to Rome to be sentenced by the emperor.[175]

The revolt had been sparked off by the two desecrations of the temple. The unrests primarily took place in the country. Jerusalem was drawn in through the armed festival pilgrims, for the urban population remained relatively peaceable. In the open land the insurgents proceeded against the Hellenistic-Roman luxury constructions of Herod for religious reasons, for in their view these buildings contravened the law. The prevailing social

---

[171] This need not necessarily mean "king" but could also designate an officeholder of Herod in Peraea; see Kokkinos 1998, 227 n. 79.

[172] Josephus, *Ant.* 17.273–277.

[173] Josephus, *J.W.* 2.63ff.; *Ant.* 17.278–284. The messianic claims are contested but unmistakable; cf. Hengel 1989c, 327ff. (GV = 1976c, 334ff.).

[174] Josephus, *Ant.* 17.285 (trans. R. Marcus, LCL, 305; cf. *J.W.* 2.65). Josephus presumably takes this passage and the terminology from Nicolaus of Damascus; see Hengel 1989c, 41 (GV = 1976c, 42).

[175] Josephus, *J.W.* 2.73; *Ant.* 17.293. For the military specifications, cf. Millar 1993, 41–42. The numbers may—as often with Josephus—be exaggerated.

tension can be seen especially in the fact that the poorer classes attached themselves to the self-appointed messianic pretenders. Their emergence, in turn, reveals the excessive excitement of the messianic near expectation, a legacy of the Maccabean period. At the same time, these pretenders did not pursue a unified concept, neither religiously nor strategically.[176] Rather, we are dealing here with an emotional reaction of the common people of the land to the severe rule of Herod and to the abuses of Archelaus and the Romans. The disturbances had social and religious causes, which can hardly be separated in the Judaea of the first century BCE and CE. The economic situation of the simple population in Syria and Egypt was probably more difficult than in Judaea, but we do not hear of comparable disturbances there.

3.1.2 The Sons of Herod

Little is known about the reign of Archelaus (4 BCE–6 CE), since the main source of Josephus, Nicolaus of Damascus, breaks off with him. Immediately after his return from Rome as ethnarch, he got even with his opponents and the insurrectionists.[177] The parable of the talents in the Lukan version presumably alludes to Archelaus. The nobleman who goes out of the land in order to obtain the kingship, after whom the citizens send a delegation demanding that he should not be king, and who exercises bloody revenge after his return, corresponds best with Archelaus in its concrete details. It shows how well Luke was informed about the details of Jewish history in Palestine.[178] The ethnarch accused the high priest Joazar, son of Boethus, with conspiracy, removed him, and appointed first Eleazar, of the family of Boethus, as high priest and then Jesus, son of Sethi, who was presumably a brother of Annas.[179] He minted his own coins under the dynastic name Herod. This explains why his brother Antipas and his nephew Agrippa I likewise obtained the popular name Herod in the New Testament. He rebuilt the winter palace in Jericho, which had been destroyed by Simon, and founded Archeleis to the north of it. Due to his mismanagement and cruelty, he was already deposed by Augustus after more than nine years and banished to Vienna in Gaul when a delegation from Judaea and a delegation from Samaria brought an action against him before the emperor.[180]

---

[176] Hengel 1989c, 328–30 (GV = 1976c, 335–36).

[177] Josephus, *J.W.* 2.64, 111; cf. *Ant.* 17.339, 342.

[178] Luke 19.12-27. The negative evaluation of Archelaus appears also in Matt 2.22.

[179] Josephus, *Ant.* 17.339, 341; cf. 20.249, 251; on this, see Kokkinos 1998, 226 n. 78.

[180] Josephus, *J.W.* 2.111ff.; *Ant.* 17.342–348; in *Life* 5 Josephus mentions the tenth year of the reign of Archelaus. It appears telling that Archelaus named his only refounding after himself and not, as his brothers did, in honor of the emperor.

In Josephus we learn little about Philip[181]—who ruled over the area of Trachonitis, Auranitis, Batanaea, and Paneas to the east of the Jordan and of the sea of Gennesaret, which was predominantly inhabited by non-Jews—but what we do learn is only positive. The tetrarch took care of his land by not living abroad and by traveling through his small kingdom instead. In doing so he brought his judgment seat with him and administered justice, thereby exercising his duties as a ruler in an exemplary fashion. He did not become entangled in military conflicts. He could, without having to fear opposition from his predominantly Gentile subjects, mint coins with his own image and with the image of the emperor, and he was the first Jewish ruler to represent a woman, Livia/Julia, on coins.[182] He refounded Paneas as Caesarea (Philippi), and later he elevated Bethsaida to the city of Julia, which was named after the wife of Augustus and mother of Tiberius, Livia/Julia. Philip was much loved. His Gentile subjects erected statues in honor of him.[183] Children were also named after him, including Jewish children such as Philip, the disciple of Jesus, from Bethsaida.[184] When he died without children in 34 CE, after a fairly long reign, his region was initially added to the province of Syria. However, boundary disputes between Antipas and the Nabataean king Aretas IV arose over his former territory.[185]

The picture that we have of Antipas, the territorial sovereign of Jesus, who ruled over Galilee and Peraea, is not quite so positive.[186] He built up the destroyed Sepphoris as the capital of Galilee, where Herod I had already possessed a royal palace with an arsenal of weapons and which had suffered badly in the campaign of Varus. This "jewel of all Galilee" was located only a few kilometers from Nazareth, the hometown of the family of Jesus. Antipas named it Autocratoris in honor of Augustus. He probably erected a predecessor building of the large theater that has

---

[181] In the synchronism of Luke 3.1, Luke mentions him as the tetrarch of Iturea and Trachonitis.

[182] Strickert 2002.

[183] For the inscription in Siʿa/Seeia and others, see Kokkinos 1998, 239.

[184] John 1.44; 12.21. He is always named as the fifth person in lists of the twelve (Mark 3.18; Luke 6.14; Matt 10.3; Acts 1.13). Whether the "evangelist" Philip (Acts 6.5), who missionized in Samaria and later in Ashdod and Caesarea (Acts 8.26-40; 21.8-9), was named after this ruler is uncertain. Another example is the leader of the Jewish cavalry from Babylon and general of Agrippa II, Philip, son of Jakimos, whom Josephus often mentions, especially in the *Life*. In any case, the name remained common in the region of Philip for centuries; see Kokkinos 1998, 240.

[185] On this, see below.

[186] He ruled from 4 BCE to 39 CE. Cf. in detail Hoehner 1972; Kokkinos 1998, 229–35; Jensen 2006.

been excavated there but he did not build a pagan temple.[187] In Peraea he refounded Bethramphtha as Julias. Presumably he received, like his brother Philip, the dynastic name "Herod" in 6 CE, when Archelaus was deposed.[188] In 19/20 CE he founded Tiberias as a Hellenistic city, among other reasons, to demonstrate his good relationship to the emperor and to promote the Hellenization of Galilee and the economy, as a new capital city—beautifully situated on the Lake of Gennesaret in the vicinity of hot springs—through a *synoikismos*. Since the city was built on an old graveyard, he had to compel some of the new inhabitants to settle or court them with benefactions such as manumission and bestowals of houses and farmland. Josephus speaks of a population that is very mixed socially, but they must have been predominantly Galilean Jews, whose upper stratum spoke Greek, to which a minority of Gentiles were added.[189] The city obtained a constitution according to the Greek model with a city council of six hundred members, an archon, and a governing body of ten leading men, the *dekaprotoi*.[190] With the royal palace, theater, and stadium it was meant to compete with Jerusalem—Jesus criticized the display of splendor at the court in connection with his verdict about John the Baptist.[191] The absence of a pagan temple documents the predominantly Jewish character of the city, as does the erection of a large synagogue, which bore the name *proseuche*, as the synagogues in the diaspora, and with its multiple-aisle basilica it competed with the famous synagogue in Alexandria. It was the Galilean counterpart to the temple in Jerusalem, which had been so gloriously renovated by his father.[192] Herod Antipas' coins had

[187] Josephus, *Ant.* 18.27: πρόσχημα τοῦ Γαλιλαίου παντός; cf. *J.W.* 2.68; *Ant.* 17.289. On the theater, cf. Freyne 2000, 69, who does not entirely rule out the possibility that it was built by Antipas; for the later dating, see Netzer/Weiss 1994, 19, for whom it was built in the second half of the first century CE or, even more likely, after the First Jewish War; see likewise Meyers/Meyers 1997, 530; Chancey 2002, 74–75; Reed 2000, 119–20. Jensen 2006, 154ff., points now to the imminent appearance of the concluding excavation reports, whose results support the view that there were two phases of the theater and that the smaller, older complex goes back to Antipas.

[188] Strabo, *Geogr.* 16.2.46 (Stern 1976–1984, I: 299; cf. the commentary on p. 311) thinks that Antipas and Philip only narrowly escaped banishment in 6 CE.

[189] Josephus, *Ant.* 18.36–38. According to Josephus, *Life* 67, the Gentile minority was killed by radical Zealots at the beginning of the revolt.

[190] For the βουλή, see Josephus, *J.W.* 2.641; *Life* 169, 284, 300, 313, 381; for its ἄρχων, see *J.W.* 2.599; *Life* 134, 271, 278, 294. For the δέκα πρῶτοι, see *J.W.* 2.639; *Life* 296.

[191] Luke 7.25; on this, cf. section 81 with note 22.

[192] Josephus, *Life* 277, 280, 293; cf. t. Sukkah 4.6 for the massive double stoa in Alexandria. On this, see further Hengel 1996a, 65–66, 171–95; a concise overview is provided in Siegert 2001, 174–75. It is also mentioned in the Talmudic literature; see Jastrow 1903, I: 303–4. When Jensen 2006, 138, stresses that it is never explicitly stated that the building

images only of plant motifs and not humans or animals.[193] However, in the inner part of his palace he did not forgo representations of animals. Due to these images, the palace was burned down by zealot Jews at the beginning of the First Jewish War.[194] On the other hand, he could stand up for the religious interests of the Jews, for when Pilate set up dedicated shields—presumably with offensive inscriptions—in his palace in Jerusalem, Antipas, with three brothers, lodged a complaint against him and ultimately succeeded in getting the emperor to order Pilate to remove them from the holy city.[195] Like his father, Antipas pursued economic improvement, trade, and urbanization.[196] Galilee and Peraea experienced a relatively peaceful period, but the social tensions continued. Antipas regarded religious renewal movements with suspicion. He had John the Baptist executed because he regarded his criticism as politically dangerous and feared unrest.[197] He wanted to get Jesus out of the land.[198] Although Jesus, as far as we know, was not publicly active in cities such as Sepphoris and Tiberias (presumably because he wanted to avoid a run-in with Antipas or because he rejected these "Hellenistic" cities), he nevertheless had relationships with members of the court. Thus, the wife of the administrator Chuza supported him from her assets because she had been healed by him.[199] The relationship of Antipas to the emperor Tiberius remained free of strain. By contrast, his marriage to his sister-in-law was unwise, for it contradicted the law[200] and harmed his relationship with his neighbor, the

---

of stadium, baths, and the large synagogue go back to Antipas and suggests that they could also have been built by Agrippa I, who possessed the city for five years, or by Agrippa II, who had the city under his control for not much longer, he underestimates Antipas as city founder.

[193] Cf. Jensen 2006, 203–17, 297–300. For the founding coins of Tiberias and Jesus' critique of Antipas, see section 8.1.

[194] Josephus, *Life* 65–67.

[195] Philo, *Legat.* 299–300. The sons of Herod were inferior to kings in nothing. According to Luke 23.12, Antipas and Pilate became friends, although they had previously been opponents, because Pilate had the courtesy to send Jesus first to his territorial sovereign as the correct authority. The conflict between Antipas and Pilate probably refers to the episode of the shields. Cf. also section 21.1.1.

[196] On this, see Freyne 2000, 45–113; Jensen 2006, 242–51; cf. section 8.1.

[197] On this, see section 9.1.1.

[198] Cf. the advice of the Pharisees and Herodians that Jesus should leave the land because Antipas was seeking to kill him in Luke 13.31ff. Since Jesus sends them back to Antipas ("tell that fox . . ."), they probably came from him. On this, see section 11.3.

[199] Luke 8.2-3. On this, see section 7.1. Cf. the table companion (σύντροφος) Manaen/Menahem of Antipas, who appears in Acts 13.1 in the list of the Christian "prophets and teachers" in Antioch on the Orontes. See section 8.1.

[200] He had married the wife of his brother while his brother was still alive. Cf. the criticism of John the Baptist; on this, see section 9.2.

Nabataean king Aretas IV. Antipas had presumably already been married to Aretas' daughter by his father in order to improve political relations. When Antipas gave a promise of marriage to his sister-in-law Herodias, Aretas' daughter fled to her father. This event already lay at some remove in the past when a military confrontation arose as a result of border disputes over an area that had previously belonged to Philip after his death in 36 CE, which resulted in the destruction of Antipas' army by Aretas. This defeat was regarded by the people as a just punishment for the execution of John the Baptist.[201] Since Tiberius sided with Antipas, the Roman legate and Syrian governor Vitellius[202] was expected to carry out a punitive action against the Nabataean king. This, however, was left undone because Tiberius died on March 16, 37 CE. Antipas ran into problems with Tiberius' successor, Caligula, because his ambitious wife, Herodias, could not bear to see her husband remain inactive when her brother and nephew of Antipas, Agrippa I, received the territory of Philip together with the title of king and traveled with her husband to Rome to petition Caligula that he also receive the title of king. They were not successful. Agrippa foiled their plans by slandering Antipas before Caligula, who let himself be convinced by him. Antipas had to go into exile in Gaul, and his wife followed him.[203]

3.1.3 The Prefects (6–41 CE)

After Archelaus was deposed in 6 CE, his territory became a Roman province of the third class under a prefect from the equestrian class,[204] who was endowed with military authority that extended to the issuing of sentences of capital punishment for provincials and Roman citizens[205] but

---

[201] Josephus, *Ant.* 18.109–115, 116–119. Cf. Hengel/Schwemer 1998, 182 (ET = 1997, 111).

[202] Vitellius had deposed Pilate and Caiaphas in the previous year. On this, see the concluding paragraphs of section 3.1.3 below.

[203] Josephus, *J.W.* 2.181ff.; *Ant.* 18.240–255.

[204] For the many-sided title *praefectus*, see Eck 2007 (GV = 2001). For the classification of the provinces, see Strabo, *Geogr.* 17.3.35; cf. Schürer 1973–1987, I: 357–58; Millar 1993, 44–45. The office designation *praefectus* is secured by the Pilate inscription (cf. note 94 above) from Caesarea Maritima, which was secondarily installed in the theater and originally documented the renovation of the light tower in the harbor, which was dedicated to Tiberius; on this, see Alföldy 1999. Josephus and Tacitus anachronistically speak of ἐπίτροπος, *procurator*. With the reconversion of Judaea into a province under Claudius in 44 CE, the title *procurator* replaced the earlier title *praefectus*. Egypt as a "private" *dominium* of Augustus and coastal regions such as Raetia, Noricum, and Mauretania were also under a prefect from the *ordo equester*.

[205] Josephus, *J.W.* 2.117: μέχρι τοῦ κτείνειν. Cf. section 20.2.1.

who was subordinate to the governor in Syria. The high priests and their family members stood at the head of the Jewish aristocracy. As the local authority utilized by the Romans, they now had much more influence on politics than they had under Herod. The highest court was their Sanhedrin, in whose changing composition the lay aristocracy and the scribal Torah jurists played a certain role alongside the ruling priestly aristocrats.[206]

The governor in Syria, Quirinius, initially had a census carried out in the whole province (including the new territories of Judaea, Samaria, and Idumaea), which was used to estimate the number and the assets of the population for the collection of the head tax and land tax.[207] This led again to unrests, for Judas the Galilean, the son of Hezekiah, stepped forth in Judaea with a prophetic speech of reproach and claimed that Jews were not permitted to pay taxes to the Romans and that they must not let themselves be enslaved.[208]

> . . . Judas who . . . induced multitudes of Jews to refuse to enroll themselves when Quirinius was sent as censor to Judaea.[209]

However, on the basis of the urgent warning and persuasion of the high priest Joazar, son of Boethus, the majority let themselves be counted. As shown by Mark 12.13-17, the question of the payment of tax to the emperor remained controversial and retained its religious and political significance. Primitive Christianity never rejected this payment, as the answer of Jesus shows. It is demanded in the later New Testament letters. From the beginning the Jesus movement was not a *political* protest movement against

---

[206] Josephus, *Ant.* 20.251; cf. Goodblatt 1994, 27ff., 215–16 (on the function of the high priest as "nominal leader of the nation"); 108–30 (on the discussion about the Sanhedrin, the Jerusalem βουλή, and of the Jerusalemites in Josephus and the New Testament).

[207] Josephus, *J.W.* 2.117–118; *Ant.* 18.1. Luke 2.1ff. places this census in the time of Herod's reign. Luke probably took over this error from his source, the legendary story of Jesus' birth and childhood. On this, cf. the excursus in Schürer 1973–1987, I: 399–427; on the inscriptional documentation of the carrying out of the census in Syrian Apameia in 6/7 CE (*iussu Quirini censum egi Apameae civitatis millium homin[um] civium*), see Boffo 1994, 182–203 nr. 23. Cf. also Millar 1993, 46–47, who rightly emphasizes that the protest of Judas the Galilean was more strongly directed against the collaborators than against the Romans and has a parallel in the unrests in Galilee when Augustus carried out a census in a province for the first time in 27 BCE. On the religious condemnation of the census, see Hengel 1989c, 140–44 (GV = 1976c 143–49). On questions pertaining to administration, see Cotton 1999.

[208] Josephus, *J.W.* 2.118; *Ant.* 18.4–10. Judas is probably the same person as Judas, the son of Hezekiah, who instigated the unrest in Sepphoris in Galilee.

[209] Josephus, *J.W.* 7.253 (trans. H. St. J. Thackeray, LCL, 577); cf. *Ant.* 18.4–9.

Rome.[210] According to Acts 5.37, Judas the Galilean died a violent death, and his followers were dispersed.[211] Together with the Pharisee Zadok he had founded a distinct "freedom party," to which Josephus does not assign a name, but which probably gave itself the religious designation "zealous ones," i.e., Zealots. They came from the radical wing of the Pharisees, rebelled with their zeal for the uniqueness of God and his law against Roman rule, and, with their fanatical striving for "freedom," triggered the First Jewish War with its catastrophic consequences. Their model was the violent zeal of the priest Phinehas for the law (Num 25) and the successful revolt of the Maccabees.[212] It is certain that their action was eschatologically motivated, for the Roman rule as the "fourth kingdom" according to Dan 7 was opposed to God's rule and was to be removed by it.

Josephus reports very little about the early prefects. They resided from the beginning in Caesarea Maritima in the former palace of Herod[213] but came to Jerusalem at the time of the high festivals. They took over the five non-Jewish cohorts of about six hundred men—which were recruited from Palestine—as auxiliary troops, which were previously at the disposal of Archelaus and Herod, as well as cavalry and garrisons in the Herodian fortresses. Only the governor of Syria on the Parthian border had Roman legions at his command.[214] This means that the occupying forces were relatively small and tended to be hostile to Jews. When there were greater unrests the governor of Syria had to intervene with his legions. The administrative task of the prefects included especially the collection of taxes. The land and head taxes were paid directly to the Romans—in the form of payment in kind for the ground tax and as a payment of money for the head tax

---

[210] Cf. Luke 20.20-26 and 23.2; Matt 22.15-22; Rom 13.6-7; 1 Pet 2.13-19; cf. John 18.36; see note 59 in chapter 6 and section 21.3.

[211] Acts 5.37 placed this revolt after the revolt of Theudas; on this problem, cf. Barrett 1994/1998, I: 294ff. Mason 2003, 273–83, 291–93, and elsewhere has taken up the old hypothesis that Luke knew the writings of Josephus and that the error can be explained on this basis. The only *particula veri* of this assumption is that Josephus and Luke write for a similar milieu—Luke for the "most honorable Theophilos" (whoever may lie behind this eponym "lover of God") and Josephus for Epaphroditus, perhaps the rich freedman of Nero, who was his secretary (*a libellis*) and was banished and executed by Domitian in 95 CE. This is connected with the dating of *Jewish Antiquites*, *Life*, and *Against Apion*. Both are addressed with κράτιστε. Cf. Hengel/Schwemer 1998, 116 (no equivalent in the ET, i.e., 1997, 69); see further, note 175 in chapter 6.

[212] On Judas and the program of the Zealots, cf. Josephus, *Ant.* 18.4ff., 23–25; *J.W.* 2.433–434, 651; 4.160, 302ff. On the whole, see Hengel 1989c (GV = 1976c); cf. further, section 4.1.

[213] Schürer 1973–1987, I: 361.

[214] Josephus, *Ant.* 17.355; 18.2; cf. Tacitus, *Ann.* 12.23.1 (text in Stern 1976–1984, II: 75–76). See further Schürer 1973–1987, I: 360, 362–66. Millar 1993, 44–45. In Jerusalem a cohort was always stationed in the Antonia; cf. Schürer 1973–1987, I: 366.

or property tax. Other taxes were collected by tax farmers.[215] The tax burden was probably not lower than under Herod but also not higher than in other Roman provinces. It was increased by the religious dues for the temple.[216] Further, the construction of streets and aqueducts belonged to their tasks, as well as the dispensation of justice, in which they worked together with local authorities, while especially reserving for themselves the jurisdiction of capital punishment. The high priests were now appointed by the Roman prefects, and the high priestly robes—which had been kept since Hyrcanus in the royal fortress and accordingly by Herod I in the Antonia—now passed as a matter of course to the power of disposition of the prefects with the occupation of the fortress, so that they were handed over by the prefects to the priests at each of the high festivals until Vitellius did away with this custom at the request of the Jews and gave over the high priestly vestments into the hands of the priesthood.[217] Right after the completion of the census, Quirinius deposed the high priest Joazar from the family of Boethus, who was in office for a second time (cf. section 3.1.2 above), despite the fact that he had done him a valuable service, because Joazar had made himself unpopular among the people with his pro-Roman attitude, and he appointed Annas I son of Sethi (6–15 CE) in his place.[218] This Annas was the head of the most influential and most powerful high priestly family, who—being nationally conscious and Sadducean in orientation—knew how to exercise their influence with the Roman overlords and the successors of Herod I up to the fateful year of 66 CE.[219]

> It is said that the elder Annas was extremely fortunate. For he had five sons, all of whom, after he himself had previously enjoyed the office for a very long period, became high priests of God—a thing that had never happened to any other of our high priests.[220]

---

[215] On the tax farming system, cf. Herrenbrück 1990. On the census, cf. Cotton 1999.

[216] Tacitus, *Ann.* 2.42.5, recounts that the province of Judaea petitioned Emperor Tiberius in 17 CE for a reduction of taxes: "the provinces of Syria and Judaea, exhausted by their burdens, begged a diminution of taxation" (trans. Woodman 2004, 61; cf. Stern 1976–1984, II: 67–68). Vitellius reduced the dues of produce at the Jerusalem market during his visit in 36 CE (Josephus, *Ant.* 18.90).

[217] Josephus, *Ant.* 18.90–95. Schwartz 1990, 64, hypothesdizes that Vitellius proceeded in this way because there was no prefect appointed by the emperor at this time. The custom itself probably goes back to Herod. Presumably this transfer was connected in each case with a corresponding payment, at least under the prefects and procurators.

[218] Josephus, *Ant.* 18.3, 26. On this, cf. Hengel 1989c, 140, 330 (GV = 1976c, 143, 337).

[219] The exclusively Aramaic-Hebrew ossuary inscriptions, which have been preserved for members of this family, support such a relatively "nationally conscious" orientation; cf. Hengel 1999b, 325ff.

[220] Josephus, *Ant.* 20.198 (trans. L. H. Feldman, LCL, 495, modified).

Accordingly, Annas is mentioned both in the synchronism of Luke 3.2 as well as in Acts 4.6 and in the passion narrative of John as the head of this family, whose members were the leaders of the party of the Sadducees.[221] To these five sons of Annas I can be added his son-in-law Caiaphas, the high priest in the passion story of Jesus.[222] The house of Annas proved to be especially hostile to Christians also later.

Little is known about the early prefects. During the time of *Coponius* the Samaritans desecrated the Jerusalem temple at the festival of Passover with human bones. After that the priests took care to ensure that the temple area was more secure. The event demonstrates the hatred between the two people groups.[223] Coponius was followed by Marcus Ambivulus (9–12 CE), Annius Rufus (12–15 CE), and Valerius Gratus (15–26 CE),[224] about whom we learn in Josephus nothing more than the approximate lengths of their time in office and which high priests they appointed and deposed. Gratus initially changed the high priests yearly, deposed Annas I, appointed Ishmael, son of Phiabi (15–16 CE), then Eleazar, son of Annas I (16–17 CE), then Simon, son of Camith (17–18 CE). He had a better understanding with Joseph Caiaphas (18–36 CE), or else Caiaphas was rich enough to pay the high yearly bribes, and he left him in office.[225] Although the high priests often changed under the Roman prefects, they had more power than under Herod I. To be sure, their strength lay much more in the clan and its riches than in the individual family members. The preeminence of the family of Annas also becomes clear under the Roman prefects and procurators. It held a singular position of power between 6 and 66 CE (especially until 41 CE), presumably because in comparison with others its members had a better understanding of how to bring about a balance between the Roman overlords and the goodwill of the people.[226]

---

[221] Cf. Acts 5.17; on this, cf. Hengel 1999b, 325. See also chapter 4.

[222] On this, see section 19.2. We learn he is the son-in-law of Annas only from John 18.13.

[223] Josephus, *Ant.* 18.29–30. L. H. Feldman, the editor and translator of the volume for the LCL, postulates a gap in the text (Feldman 1965, 27 n. c). It is perhaps for this reason that we learn nothing about the reaction of the prefect.

[224] Josephus, *Ant.* 18.31–35.

[225] Josephus, *Ant.* 18.34. Of all the high priests Caiaphas was in office the longest.

[226] On the power of the four high priestly families (Phiabi, Boethus, Annas, and Kamith) and their place in the Sanhedrin as the highest court, cf. Schürer 1973–1987, II: 215, 232–33. On Annas and Caiaphas, cf. Hengel 1999b, 322–34. See especially also the mocking song about these familes from the turbulent time before the outbreak of the Jewish War (b. Pesaḥ 57a; trans. H. Freedman in Epstein 1938, 285):

Woe is me because of the house of Boethus; woe is me because of their staves!
Woe is me because of the house of Ḥanin, woe is me because of their whisperings!
Woe is me because of the house of Ḳathros, woe is me because of their pens!

It is first with Pontius Pilate (26–26 CE), who was closer to him in time, that Josephus provides a more detailed report. His portrayal is supplemented by the remarks of Philo. Presumably severe conflicts first took place under Pilate, which Pilate himself provoked due to his disdain for the Jewish people. For this reason the reports about him in Josephus and Philo are more detailed. After all, Josephus writes with the goal of explaining the Jewish revolt against Rome with respect to its causes. Philo, in turn, was concerned to shed light on the prehistory of the pogroms in Alexandria and the Caligula crisis. Probably at the beginning of his prefecture, Pilate had his soldiers secretly bring Roman standards with medallion busts of the emperor, which could be regarded as idols by the Jews, into Jerusalem. A great crowd of leading Jews peacefully protested before Pilate against this violation of the law for many days in Caesarea and requested that the images be removed. He ultimately threatened them with his soldiers but then yielded in view of their readiness to die.[227] Philo recounts a similar, later incident. According to him, Pilate had consecrated shields without images but probably with inscriptions set up in the palace in Jerusalem in honor of Tiberius and only removed them at the direct command of the emperor. Four sons of Herod, the Herodian family, and the leading body of the people had appealed first to Pilate against this violation of the Jewish laws (πάτρια ἔθη), saying that it did not correspond to the will of Tiberius to incite the people to revolt. Stubborn by nature, inflexible, and full of disdain for the Jews, Pilate reacted only when the Jewish complaint had success with the emperor.[228] When Pilate used money from the temple treasury for the improvement or expansion of an aqueduct to Jerusalem, this also met with strong protest among the people, which he suppressed.[229] We can no longer determine with certainty when Pilate "mixed the blood of the Galileans with their sacrifices" (only a Passover

---

Woe is me because of the house of Ishmael the son of Phabi, woe is me because of their
  fists!
For they are High Priests and their sons are [Temple] treasurers
and their sons-in-law are trustees and their servants beat people with staves.

[227] Josephus, *J.W.* 2.169–174; *Ant.* 18.55–59: "Pilate, astonished at the strength of their devotion to the laws, straightaway removed the images from Jerusalem and brought them back to Caesarea" (*Ant.* 18.59; trans. L. H. Feldman, LCL, 45, 47). According to Eusebius, *Dem. ev.* 8.2.122–123, not only Philo but also Josephus reported that Pilate set up the standards in the temple.

[228] Philo, *Legat.* 299–305; cf. section 3.1.2 above. In this context Philo also mentions the bribabilty and other bad character traits of Pilate. For his behavior in the trial of Jesus, see section 21.1.2. The formula *dei filius*, which is also found on the denarii of the emperor, may have played a role in the case of the medallions and inscriptions. See section 3.1.2 above.

[229] Josephus, *J.W.* 2.175ff.; *Ant.* 18.60ff.

festival can be in view). However, the concern must be with an incident that took place before the Passover of Jesus' death in 30 CE.[230] The trial of Jesus, which Mark portrays most reliably, presents the prefect as already quite familiar with Jewish customs und practices and reveals his disdain for his Jewish subjects as well as his simultaneous collusion with Joseph Caiaphas.[231] The Testimonium Flavianum—which is admittedly preserved only with Christian interpolations but which has certainly not been 'improved' in a Christian way at this point but accords with Josephus' language elsewhere—corresponds exactly to the specifications of Mark (15.1):

> At the denunciation (ἐνδείξει) of the most distinguished men among us Pilate condemned him to be crucified. . . .[232]

It is all the more conspicuous that the sources never report that Pilate and his successors persecuted the young messianic movement that proceeded from Jesus. Pilate never transferred the office of high priest to another person during his time in office, and he was deposed by Vitellius at almost the same time as Caiaphas, which certainly means that the two harmonized well, in fact too well, with each other. The brutal military action of Pilate against Samaritan adherents of a prophet, who wanted to show them the hidden holy temple vessels of Moses on Mount Gerazim,[233] ultimately led

---

[230] Luke 13.1; on this, cf. section 1 and section 8.1.

[231] All attempts to date the execution of Jesus in the beginning of Pilate's rule appear doubtful for this reason. However, the late dating to 36 CE in Kokkinos 1998, 196 n. 82, 301, and elsewhere is also unlikely; cf. already Kokkinos 1989. The execution of John the Baptist need not have occurred only in 35 CE, right before the military conflict between Antipas and Aretas IV. It is clear from Josephus, *Ant.* 18.116–119, that we are dealing with an addendum. The opinion of the people understood the defeat of Antipas in 36 CE as a punishment for his judicial murder of the Baptist in ca. 29 CE. Although about eight years lay between the execution of James, the brother of the Lord, and the destruction of Jerusalem, the Jewish Christian legend understood the latter as a direct consequence of the former (Hegesippus in Eusebius, *Hist. eccl.* 2.23.18: καὶ εὐθὺς Οὐεσπασιανὸς πολιορκεῖ αὐτούς). Luke already hints at it, and Matthew clearly explains the destruction as a punishment for the crucifixion of Jesus. Cf. especially the sound arguments for the dating of the crucifixion by Riesner 1994, 37–38, against the late dating of Kokkinos. On the date of Jesus' death, see also section 11.1.

[232] Josephus, *Ant.* 18.64. On the translation, cf. also L. H. Feldman, LCL, 51: "When Pilate, upon hearing him accused by men of the highest standing among us, had condemned him to be crucified. . . ." On this much-discussed passage and the various hypotheses regarding its reworking, cf. Theissen/Merz 1998, 64–74 (GV = 1997, 74–82), and Bardet 2002. See further, note 58 in chapter 6.

[233] Instead of the Davidic Messiah the Samaritans expected an eschatological prophet on the basis of Deut 18.15ff.; see note 120 in chapter 4.

to his downfall. Tiberius usually left Roman officials in office for a long time in the provinces. As justification for this policy he is said to have quoted Aesop's fable of the flies. During the time of his reign he sent two prefects, Gratus and Pilate, to Judaea. However, with this incident, to which distinguished Samaritans also fell victim, Pilate appears to have finally gone too far. He was deposed by Vitellius and sent to Rome to give an account of his action.[234]

After that, Vitellius entrusted one of those close to him, Marcellus, with the administration of Judaea (ἐπιμελητής), and Maryllus, who is also otherwise unknown, is said to have received the military responsibility (ἱππάρχης) from Caligula.[235]

3.1.4 Agrippa I (41–44 CE)

Soon after his accession to power Gaius Caligula appointed Agrippa, his personal friend and the grandson of Herod I and of the Hasmonean Mariamne, to be king over the whole former area of Herod Philip and perhaps already over the tetrarchy of Lysanias (37 CE).[236] After the exile of Herod Antipas (39 CE) Agrippa also received the territory of his uncle, and finally, after the murder of Caligula on January 24, 41 CE, he was given almost the entire kingdom of his grandfather by Emperor Claudius (41 CE) as

---

[234] Josephus, *Ant*. 18.85–89. The Acts of Pilate recount legendary material about his subsequent fate. Cf. Schürer 1973–1987, I: 387. Justin, *1 Apol*. 35.9 and 48.3, already refers to alleged "acts of Pilate," which could inform the emperors addressed in the Apology, i.e., Antonius Pius, Marcus Aurelius, and Lucius Verus. See also Schneemelcher 1991/1992, I: 444ff. (GV = 1987, 395ff.); Ehrman/Pleše 2011, 491–567. The legend begins already in Matthew, who—against Jewish accusations—begins, with corresponding polemic, to whitewash Pilate. Inter alia he has the wife of Pilate intervene on behalf of Jesus (Matt 27.19). For the tendency of Pilate to be friendly to Jesus in the Apocrypha, see Bauer 1967b, 188–98.

[235] Josephus, *Ant*. 18.89, 237. The form of the name is handed down in the manuscripts of Josephus as Μάρκελλος and Μάρυλλος or Μάριλλος, whereas a Roman would more likely be named Marullus. It is debated whether the same person is in view. Cf. Kokkinos 1998, 284, against Schwartz 1990, 62–66. Philo, *Legat*. 199, mentions Herennius Capito as the tax collector of all Judaea, who enriched himself there in an intolerable manner. According to Josephus, Capito was, however, the rich tax collector only of Jamnia, i.e., the former area of Salome, which Salome had bequeathed to Livia. Cf. note 241 below on Capito and Agrippa.

[236] Josephus, *Ant*. 18.237; cf. Philo, *Flacc*. 25 (trans. Van der Horst 2003, 58): "The emperor Gaius gave Agrippa, the grandson of king Herod, as his kingdom a third of his grandfather's inheritance, of which Philip the tetrarch, his paternal uncle, used to enjoy the usufruct." Cf. *Flacc*. 40 (trans. Van der Horst 2003, 61) the title "king," "friend of Caesar," and "honored by the Senate of Rome with praetorian insignia." On this, see Van der Horst 2003, 114ff., 131–32.

thanks for his successful mediation efforts between senate and praetorians.[237] Under Claudius he called himself "the great" on coins and inscriptions, a title that he had received from the Roman senate and that Josephus likewise gives to him.[238] On the inscriptions of his son, Agrippa II, he appears as "friend of the emperor" and "friend of the Romans."[239] The rule of Agrippa I (41–44 CE) interrupted the sequence of prefects in Judaea.[240]

Caligula's appointment of Agrippa I as the successor to Philip already evoked astonishment and jealousy.[241] When Agrippa, on his journey through his area of rule, arrived in Alexandria in the summer of 38 CE, the Alexandrian rabble mocked the new Jewish king with the shout "Marin," "our Lord" in Syriac (that is, Aramaic), and with a royal mime for the amusement of the people in the theater.[242] A little later there was a desecration of synagogues by the erection of statues of the emperor and a bloody pogrom, unrests that also had an impact on Palestine. The imperial cult appeared to the rabble as a proven method for venting its hatred of the Jewish population. This also applies to the Palestinian Jamnia, after

---

[237] Josephus, *Ant.* 19.274–275; *J.W.* 2.215–216. The pact between Agrippa and the emperor, senate, and people of Rome mentioned here is presented in the form of a handshake on coins. See Meshorer 1990–1991, 123 nr. 10–10a; cf. 124 nr. 11–11a; 14–14a; see also Kokkinos 1998, 297–98. For ὁμόνοια, "concord," between Jews and Romans, cf. the accusation of Titus, which Josephus, *J.W.* 6.216 puts in his mouth shortly before the destruction of the temple: He is said to have offered the Jews peace and independence, "but they preferred sedition (στάσις) to concord (ὁμόνοια)."

[238] Βασιλεὺς μέγας. Meshorer 1990–1991, 124 nr. 11–11a; 12; Josephus, *Ant.* 17.28; 18.110, 142; 20.104; cf. further Schwartz 1990, 136.

[239] See note 357 below.

[240] Cf. Schwartz 1990, passim; Kokkinos 1998, 271–304.

[241] Cf. Josephus, *Ant.* 18.239. For the reaction of his sister Herodias, cf. the end of section 3.1.2. After the death of his mother, Berenice, a niece of Herod, Agrippa—having grown up in Rome—determinedly worked toward the goal of obtaining a rule that was appropriate to his origin and toward the regulation of his financial problems through a regular income, for which reason he spent the years of his youth in Rome at the imperial court and lived as a great extravagant lord as long as his assets permitted. At the beginning of the thirties he went, without means, to Palestine, accumulated great debts there, and failed in his attempts to gain political influence. He fled from his creditor Herennius Capito (see note 235 above) via Alexandria toward Rome. In 36 CE he arrived, furnished with a credit from the alabarch Alexander, the brother of Philo. Tiberius no longer thought anything of his ambitions. Agrippa had to back his successor, Caligula, for which reason Tiberius imprisoned him. Caligula freed him from the prison and immediately thereafter placed the royal diadem on his head. See Josephus, *Ant.* 18.143–237, and note 236 above.

[242] Philo, *Flacc.* 34, 36–39, 41. Cf. Van der Horst 2003, 128–33; Hengel/Schwemer 1998, 198–99 (1997, 120–21) on the addressing of Agrippa as "Lord." See further the mocking of Jesus by the anti-Jewish band of soldiers eight years earlier. On this, see note 45 in chapter 21. For the designation, cf. the primitive Christian cry of prayer *maranatha* in 1 Cor 16.22 and Did. 10.6; on this, see note 61 in chapter 19.

an altar of the emperor was destroyed there,[243] and presumably also to Antioch on the Orontes.[244] The reaction of the emperor to these incidents brought Palestine to the brink of war.

The Caligula Crisis (38–41 CE)

Herod I had already had a temple in honor of the emperor with the statues of Augustus and Roma erected in Caesarea Maritima and a temple of Augustus in Sebaste,[245] but Jerusalem itself and the predominantly Jewish areas of his kingdom remained free from the public imperial cult with its manifestations in images. Until the outbreak of the First Jewish War two lambs and a bull were sacrificed—at the cost of the emperor (thus Philo) or of the people (thus Josephus)—for the well-being of the ruler and of the Roman people.[246] The discontinuance of this sacrifice by the Jewish priesthood was regarded as an official declaration of war, for with the sacrifice for the emperor in Jerusalem the Jews demonstrated their loyalty to the emperor himself and to Rome. The sacrifice for the well-being of the emperor rather than for the emperor himself as god was not an exception in the early imperial period, not even in Greece and Egypt. The imperial cult was regulated locally and not centrally prescribed.[247] The prayer for the respective imperial house had been a given in the Jewish synagogues of the diaspora already since the Persian period. The Jewish, aniconic cult could be described neutrally from the Roman perspective, and could even be praised as exemplary by some philosophical

---

[243] The conflict in Jamnia was incited by the tax collector Herennius Capito, who harbored a hatred for Agrippa I because the latter did not want to pay him his debts and who portrayed this incident in an exaggerated way to Caligula in a letter. See Philo, *Legat.* 199–202. Josephus, *Ant.* 18.257–260, mentions the Alexandrian enemy of the Jews Apion's accusations before Caligula: "these people alone scorned to honor him with statues and to swear by his name" (258; trans. L. H. Feldman, LCL, 153, 155).

[244] Cf. Hengel/Schwemer 1998, 277–86 (ET = 1997, 181–83).

[245] See section 3.1.1.

[246] Josephus, *J.W.* 2.197; *Ag. Ap.* 2.77–78, 196–197; Philo, *Legat.* 157, 232, 317. The difference in the specifications may be due to the fact that the two emphasize different aspects. In reality the costs were raised from the taxes: see Schürer 1973–1987, II: 312; Pucci Ben Zeev 1998, 472. Sacrifices for the king are mentioned already in Ezra 6.9-10 and Aristeas 45. The synagogue inscriptions from Egypt attest their erection in honor of the Ptolemies. See Horbury/Noy 1992, 19–20 nr. 13 (Alexandria, first century BCE); 35 nr. 22 (Schedia, third century BCE); 40ff. nr. 24 and 25 (second century BCE) and elsewhere; cf. also Pucci Ben Zeev 1998, 479.

[247] See the attestations in Pucci Ben Zeev 1998, 474–81: "The imperial cult constituted an act of homage more than an act of worship" (476).

intellectuals.[248] Augustus and Tiberius had tended to reject and restrict the imperial cult, whereas Caligula demanded during his lifetime that he be recognized as god in a way that was especially unbearable for his Jewish subjects:

He not only said but he believed that he was a god (θεός).[249]

After the incidents in Antioch and Jamnia, in the summer of 39 CE Caligula gave the command to erect a colossal statue in the Jerusalem temple and to transform the temple into a sanctuary of Διὸς Ἐπιφανοῦς ... Νέου Γαίου, of "Gaius who has appeared as new Zeus."[250] For the Jews this intention evoked the religious emergency and time of horror under Antiochus IV Epiphanes and the fear—which had been smoldering since they were conquered by Pompey and which was repeatedly confirmed through new incidents—that the Romans would desecrate the temple and destroy Jerusalem. Caligula entasked the governor of Syria, Petronius, with carrying out this endeavor with half of the troops that were stationed at the Euphrates.[251] Petronius was not happy about this task and sought to play for time, but occupied with his troops the winter quarters in Ptolemais before the gates of Galilee.[252] He had artists in Sidon begin the production of the statue and first informed the

[248] Cf. Varro's praise (first century BCE) of the aniconic worship of the Jewish God: Fragment 18 (handed down in Augustine, *Civ.* 4.31; cf. Stern 1976–1984, I: 209; Cardauns 1976, 22).

[249] Philo, *Legat.* 162; cf. Josephus, *J.W.* 2.184; *Ant.* 18.256; for Roman criticism of the paranoid behavior of the Caesar, see Suetonius, *Cal.* 19: Caligula bridged the Gulf of Baiae with a ship's bridge, which he secured with a layer of earth and built out like the Via Appia, upon which he traveled back and forth, i.e., as a god he made the sea traversable. He had famous statues of gods brought to Rome and put his head on them and let himself be praised and honored with daily offerings of "flamingos, peacocks, black grouse, different breeds of guinea-hens, and pheasants" (*Cal.* 22; trans. Edwards 2000, 147). At night he invited the moon goddess to his bed, and in the daytime he held private conversations with Jupiter (*Cal.* 22).

[250] Philo, *Legat.* 346. Cf. note 256 below. This event found no direct expression in the early Christian sources; see Hengel/Schwemer 1998, 276ff. (ET = 1997, 180ff.); on the anti-Jewish unrest in Antioch in this time, see idem, 281–84 (ET = 183–86). The thesis—reaching back to Wellhausen—that Mark 13 is a "leaflet" from this time has little plausibility. The text points to the expectation regarding the Antichrist at the time of the Jewish War; cf. also 2 Thess 2.5-12. It may, however, be the case that the Caligula episode furthered the development of the "motif of the enemy of God," which goes back already to Antiochus IV, in Judaism and primitive Christianity.

[251] Philo, *Legat.* 188, 198, 207; cf. Josephus, *Ant.* 18.262: many auxiliary troops and two legions.

[252] Philo, *Legat.* 213: Petronius carefully set the matter in motion. In doing so he respected the exemption of Judaea from providing winter quarters; on this, see note 44 above. However, with the choice of the winter quarters in Ptolemais he kept himself ready.

leading body of the Jewish aristocracy of the emperor's order.[253] The inhabitants of Jerusalem, indeed of the whole land, went to Petronius in Ptolemais in
the spring of 40 CE, when Petronius was to march into Judaea at the command
of the emperor, and declared their readiness to die rather than to allow this
wickedness. Only after their death could the command be carried out.[254] Philo
hypothesizes that Petronius was sympathetic to the Jewish "philosophy" or
at least that he had obtained some knowledge about the religion of a considerable portion of his subjects, for he let the work on the statue proceed only
slowly, while quickly asking the emperor by letter for an extension of time,
for the harvest would first have to be gathered, so that the province would be
prepared for Caligula's visit in connection with his journey to Egypt, which
was planned for the next year.[255] However, the emperor demanded that his
command be carried out quickly and thus that his statue be completed.

Agrippa, who had presumably been staying in Rome since the fall of
39 CE and knew nothing about the order of the emperor or of the correspondence between Caligula and Petronius, first learned about this when he met
with the emperor in September of 40 CE—together with the information that
he too had personally fallen into disfavor due to the Jewish refusal to erect
a statue of Zeus in the Jerusalem temple.[256] Philo's portrayal of Agrippa's
shock is dramatic but is not incredible as the presentation of a contemporary
eyewitness.[257] By contrast, the wording of Agrippa's diplomatic letter to the
emperor was surely much more cautious than the long letter of petition that
Philo ascribes to him.[258] Agrippa probably appealed to the respect of Augustus
and Tiberius vis-à-vis the Jewish cult to the emperor as a model and regarded
himself as protector of the temple. However, he certainly would not have
been so blundering as to protest to Caligula that he himself was a descendant

---

See Josephus, *Ant*. 18.262–263: in the spring Caligula gave the order to begin the campaign
(πολεμεῖν) if the resistance did not cease.

[253] Philo, *Legat*. 222ff.

[254] Philo, *Legat*. 225–242; 236: ἀποθανόντων τὸ ἐπίταγμα γενέσθω.

[255] Philo, *Legat*. 245–253. For the answer of the emperor, see *Legat*. 254–260.

[256] According to Philo, *Legat*. 265 (trans. F. H. Colson, LCL, 135): Caligula accused
Agrippa: "your excellent and worthy fellow-citizens, who alone of every race of men do
not acknowledge Gaius as a god, appear to be courting even death by their recalcitrance.
When I ordered a statue of Zeus to be set up in the temple they marshalled their whole
population and issued forth from the city and country nominally to make a petition but
actually to counteract my orders."

[257] Philo, as the leader of the Alexandrian-Jewish delegation in 39/40 CE, stayed in
Rome and Puteoli and describes the events in *Legatio ad Gaium*. On this, see Schürer
1973–1987, III/2: 816.

[258] Philo, *Legat*. 276–329. While Agrippa did not want to lose his rule or the goodwill
of the emperor, in order not to completely lose his claims to Judaea he had to represent the
interests of all Jews in the Jerusalem temple and its special cult.

of priests and kings (through his grandmother Mariamne he was descended from the Hasmoneans, which legitimated him from the Jewish side) and that the temple in Jerusalem, from of old without an image of god, was the temple of the one true God. Likewise, Agrippa would hardly have made an indirect demand on behalf of the Jewish people for Roman citizenship and direct freedom and remission of taxes.[259] The fact that Agrippa—like Philo and the Alexandrian-Jewish delegation—only learned of Caligula's command at so late a point is surprising and probably connected with Caligula's campaign in Gaul and Germany. Caligula spent the winter of 39/40 CE in Lyon and, after various militarily senseless operations, returned to Rome with a "small triumph" on August 31, 40 CE.[260] In any case, Agrippa met the megalomaniac emperor after his return in September 40 CE and got Caligula to rescind his order and send a corresponding letter to Petronius.[261] Caligula, however, quickly backpedaled from this goodwill when he read Petronius' report of his actions in Tiberias. In late summer, Petronius had gone to Tiberias in Agrippa's capital, where he conferred with the representatives of Agrippa and his relatives in order to avoid a war.[262] The opposition of the population remained so unwavering that they refused to sow the seed in the fall. Petronius promised to give a report to the emperor and withdrew to Antioch with the troops stationed in Ptolemais. The emperor responded by ordering Petronius to commit suicide, but Petronius received the news of the death of the emperor—who was murdered on January 24, 41 CE—before he received his sentence of death.[263] The intervention of Agrippa did not have definitive success. What was decisive was the sagaciousness of Petronius, who deployed no troops, although he met with opposition from the Jewish masses, who were not entirely unarmed—as Josephus does not grow weary of stressing.[264]

---

[259] Thus, however, Philo, *Legat.* 287, 290, who thus attributes his own wishes to Agrippa.

[260] Cassius Dio 59.24.1 says that Agrippa was with Caligula in the winter of 39/40 CE. Kokkinos 1998, 285 n. 74, therefore assumes that Agrippa accompanied Caligula to Gaul and Germany as one of the *amici* whom Suetonius, *Cal.* 45.1, mentions and that the epigram of Philippus of Thessalonica refers to the hospitality during this campaign (Stern 1976–1984, I: 375–76). All this, however, remains very uncertain. Josephus, *Ant.* 18.289–297, assumes that Agrippa was staying in Rome.

[261] Philo, *Legat.* 333–334; Josephus, *Ant.* 18.301–302.

[262] Josephus, *Ant.* 18.273–288; *J.W.* 2.193–202.

[263] Josephus, *Ant.* 18.304–309. Cf. *J.W.* 2.203.

[264] Cf. Tacitus, *Hist.* 5.9.2 (trans. C. H. Moore, LCL, 191): *sub Tiberio quies; dein iussi a C. Caesare effigiem eius in templo locare arma potius sumpsere, quem motum Caesaris mors diremit* ("Under Tiberius all was quiet. Then, when Caligula ardered the Jews to set up his statue in their temple, they chose rather to resort to arms, but the emperor's death put an end to their uprising"). Cf. *Ann.* 12.54.1. On this, see the commentary of Stern 1976–1984, II: 51. See further Josephus, *Ant.* 18.302.

If Petronius had not acted so wisely, the First Jewish War would have already occurred in 40 CE and not only in 66 CE. This crisis, which shook not only Palestine but also the Jewish diaspora, came to an end only with the murder of Caligula and the peacemaking measures of Claudius.[265]

When Agrippa returned in the early summer of 41 CE to his area of rule, which had been considerably expanded by Claudius, he especially had to make efforts to stabilize the conditions. He first held a triumphal entry into Jerusalem, offered sacrifices, and dedicated the golden chain that he had received from Caligula in 37 CE as a dedicatory gift in the temple.[266] He deposed Theophilus, the son of Annas, as high priest and appointed Simon Kantheras from the house of Boethus. This may have occurred already in 38 CE. In this case, Caligula had already appointed him as protector of the temple at that time. In any case, he initially favored the house of Boethus and thus took the policy of his grandfather Herod I as a model.[267] He demonstrated his "love" to the Jerusalemites with a remission of taxes, and when youths in Dora desecrated the synagogue with an image of the emperor, as the protector of the Jewish diaspora he immediately lodged a complaint with Petronius, who correspondingly reprimanded the population of Dora.[268]

[265] On the edicts of Claudius (*CPJ* nr. 153; Josephus, *Ant.* 19.280–285 and 286–291), cf. Schürer 1973–1987, I: 398.

[266] This dedicatory gift was probably regarded as analogous to the "barbarian weapons" that Herod allowed to be affixed in the temple (see note 117 in this chapter). In that case it served, so to speak, as a sign of victory over the ungodly emperor. There is no reason, as Schwartz 1990, 12/17, 32, 68–69, assumes, to move this dedication forward to 38 CE. See also Kokkinos 1998, 282–83, who regards the dedication of the chain as a "compensation" for the attempted sacrilege of the emperor. On the pagan foundation inscription from el Mushennef in the Auranitis, which gives thanks for Agrippa's favorable return from Rome (OGIS nr. 418: ὑπὲρ σωτηρίας κυρίου βασιλέως Ἀγρίππα . . .) and gives an account of the erection of a temple of Zeus-Apollo due to an oath, see Hengel/Schwemer 1998, 199 (ET = 1997, 120–21, 394 n. 634).

[267] Cf. note 54 above. Josephus, *Ant.* 19.297–298. Josephus emphasizes that the family of Boethus thus reached again the same high number as the high priest Simon, son of Onias, with his three sons. These three sons were Onias III, Jesus-Jason (see note 103 above), and Onias-Menelaus, the last Zadokite Oniads who held the office of high priest in Jerusalem (cf. *Ant.* 12.237–240). Jason and Menelaus were the Hellenistic reformers who sparked off the crisis under Antiochus IV. Presumably the family of Boethus went back to the son of Onias III, Onias IV, who had to flee to Egypt (*Ant.* 12.387) and erected a temple of YHWH there (cf. note 83 above). Theophilus was appointed by Vitellius in 37 CE (*Ant.* 18.123). His name appears on an ossuary inscription. See Rahmani 1994, 258–59 nr. 871: "*Yoḥana*, daughter of *Yoḥanan*, son of *Thophlos*, the priest." On his son *Yoḥanan*/John, see Acts 4.6. If Agrippa already became the protector of the temple in 38 CE, we can already assume the appointment of Simon Kantheras in this year; cf. Hengel 1999b, 328; Hengel/Schwemer 1998, 377–78 (ET = 1997, 249). The literary separations of Schwartz 1990, 11–38, are not necessary for this assumption.

[268] Josephus, *Ant.* 19.299–311.

Agrippa, who was, after all, a descendant of the Hasmoneans, was intent on maintaining equilibrium and peace in his area of rule. This also applies to the rival high priestly clans, whom he kept under control through a policy of *divide et impera*. Thus, in place of Simon Kantheras he soon reappointed a member of the family of Annas, Matthias, son of Annas, and shortly before his death in 44 CE he appointed a member of the clan of Boethus again, Elionaeus, son of Kantheras.[269]

The execution of James, son of Zebedee, and the imprisonment of Peter mentioned in Acts 12.1-19 probably fall within this period of time (festival of Passover in 43 CE), when the highest office was held by a member of the family of Annas, which was more nationally conscious than the family of Boethus,[270] which came from Alexandria. According to Luke, Agrippa "mistreated" some members of the primitive community and had the Zebedaid killed with the sword. When he saw that this pleased the 'Jews,' he also had Peter arrested, but wanted to postpone his execution to the time after the festival of the Passover and the weeks of unleavened bread that followed it. The proceedings of Agrippa against leading members of the primitive community in Jerusalem probably scarcely resulted from his own interests. Otherwise, he would have persecuted the Christians more insistently and not simply ended the proceeding with the execution of the guards after the flight of Peter.[271] According to the picture that Josephus—probably following a biographical source—paints of the reign of Agrippa, this reign was characterized by moderation,[272] by the wish to do a favor for his subjects—whether Jews or Gentiles—when he could, and by the careful concern to maintain equilibrium between the parties. As we have already emphasized, this included the fact that he furnished the two most powerful high priestly families with the highest office in an alternating manner. The primitive community in Jerusalem was especially a thorn in the side of the family of Annas. Caiaphas, the son-in-law of Annas, was the high priest in office, whom Jesus provoked

---

[269] Josephus, *Ant.* 19.313–316; for the appointment of Elionaeus, see *Ant.* 19.342.

[270] On this, see Hengel 1999b, 149, 322–44. Cf. note 219 above.

[271] Schwartz 1990, 122ff., postulates political reasons: the Zebedaids are said to have stood near to the Zealots. Riesner 1994, 109–10, sees the reasons for the persecution in the king's own messianic claims and the beginning of the Gentile mission. He dates the persecution too early, to the Passover festival in 41 CE, when Agrippa could not yet even have been in the land. Moreover, in that case one would have to hear of another action of Agrippa against the Christians. On this, see Hengel/Schwemer 1998, 369–83 (ET = 1997, 244–57). The persecution under Agrippa I and the flight of Peter signified a deep caesura in the history of the primitive community. On this, see Hengel 2010a, 10, 77 (GV = 2006b, 15, 125); Schwemer 2005.

[272] As an example of this kingly moderation, Josephus, *Ant.* 19.332–334, adduces his behavior toward a scribe who questioned Agrippa's pure Jewish descent or his ritual purity and demanded that he be excluded from visiting the temple.

with his "blasphemy"[273] at the hearing and who handed him over to Pilate for execution. The depictions of the hearing in Acts 4.5ff. and 5.17-18 and the execution of James, the brother of the Lord, by Annas II in ca. 62 CE provide further evidence of the lasting hatred of this high-priestly clan in particular.[274] Therefore, it is likely that with his action against the primitive community Agrippa wanted to do a favor for the clan of Annas and at the same time paid attention to the reaction of the Jerusalemites. He probably no more regarded these enthusiasts as politically dangerous than the Roman prefects and procurators, none of whom thought it necessary to proceed against the Christians in Palestine in the period between 30 and 66 CE.[275] Roman rule was challenged by different, zealot groups. The Christians did not take part in the First Jewish War. At the outbreak of the war in 66 CE, the primitive community fled to Pella. Only after the war are the "relatives of the Lord," like other Jews, said to have become suspicious in the eyes of the Romans due to their Davidic descent.[276]

Both the biographical sources of Josephus and the later rabbinic literature[277] praise the Jewish piety of the king. Caligula also marvels at Agrippa's superstitious concern for the Jerusalem sanctuary. To be sure, this must be

---

[273] Mark 14.60–64; cf. Schwemer 2001c, 149–50, with reference to the legal principle (in Josephus, *Ag. Ap.* 2.194): "Any who disobey him, will pay the penalty as for impiety (ἀσεβῶν) toward God himself" (trans. H. St. J. Thackeray, LCL, 371), which was probably derived from Exod 22.28; cf. Acts 23.5.

[274] On this, see Hengel/Schwemer 1998, 379–80 (ET = 1997, 250–51) and, section 19.1 with note 18. On Annas II as leading Sadducee, see chapter 4 below. By contrast, the martyrdom of Stephen (ca. 32 CE) and the expulsion of the "Hellenists" from Jerusalem probably did not go back to direct persecution by Caiaphas but were more likely the result of the conflict in the Greek-speaking synagogues of Jerusalem, which were protected by the high priest. On this, see Hengel 2002, 1–67 (38–39). The high priest did not have the right to impose capital punishment, nor did his power extend to Damascus for him to be able to bring undesirable persons to Jerusalem. The concrete events that Luke portrays suggest mob justice in a Jerusalem synagogue community. The interrogation by the high priest himself (which can easily be removed from the context) is a typical Lukan exaggeration. See Hengel/Schwemer 2019.

[275] Cf. 1 Thess 2.14; Acts also speaks only of persecutions at the hands of Jews. Cf. also Mark 13.9; Luke 12.11-12; 21.12; Matt 10.17; 23.34. Too little consideration is given to this fact in current scholarship. It also sheds light on the trial of Jesus; see section 21.3.

[276] Eusebius, *Hist. eccl.* 3.12: a persecution is said to have taken place against "relatives of the Lord" when Vespasian, after the victory over the insurgents, had all the descendants of David tracked down.

[277] m. Sotah 7.8; y. Sotah 7.7(8), 22a: "Agrippa the King stood up and received it and read it standing up, and sages praised him on that account. And when he came to the verse, *You may not put a foreigner over you, who is not your brother* (Dt. 17:15), his tears ran down from his eyes. They said to him, 'Do not be afraid, Agrippa, you are our brother, you are our brother, you are our brother!'" (trans. Neusner 1988, 459; cf. Hüttenmeister 1998, 181).

evaluated not so much as a sign of his personal piety but as an indication of his consideration for the various parties and his recognition that the erection of an image of the emperor in the Jerusalem sanctuary would transgress the limits of tolerance and make a Jewish revolt against Rome unavoidable. He scarcely had an interest in Pharisaic purity regulations, but he fulfilled his political-religious duties in a conscientious and conspicuous manner.[278]

Following the model of his grandfather, Agrippa was active as a builder in the Hellenistic cities with their Jewish diaspora. Thus, he is said to have especially favored Berytos (Beirut), which had already been dealt with generously by his grandfather and had become a Roman colony in 15 CE.[279] On the other hand, he wanted to strengthen the solidarity of the client rulers in the east of the Roman Empire, some of whom were related to the Herodian house, in order to enlarge his own political influence in this way, and he invited these rulers to a meeting in his residence in Tiberias. Josephus mentions Antiochus of Commagene, Sampsigeramus of Emesa, Cotys of Armenia Minor, Polemon of Pontus, and Polemon's brother Herod of Chalcis. However, this awakened the suspicion of the Roman governor in Syria, Marsus, who did not think that such a meeting of minds corresponded to Roman interests.[280] He came to Tiberias and made an abrupt end of the illustrious gathering. Previously, Marsus had already denounced Agrippa before the emperor for building a "third wall" in Jerusalem.[281]

After a rule of about thirty years over almost the whole territory of his grandfather, Agrippa I died completely unexpectedly at the age of only fifty-four in Caesarea Maritima.[282] According to Acts 12.20-23 the cities of Sidon and Tyre had asked him for an audience and for peace, for he was—for an unspecified reason—so angry with them that he had blocked them from food deliveries—for example, grain from Galilee. Appearing with much splendor, he let himself be flattered by the people: there speaks from him "the voice of a god, not of a man" (12.22), as a consequence of which—thus the Lukan version—the angel of God struck him with a deadly illness, so that he died quickly, being eaten by worms in his living body. Josephus provides a similar portrayal of the end of Agrippa.

---

[278] Josephus, *Ant.* 19.331; on Caligula, see Philo, *Legat.* 268. On this, see Hengel/Schwemer 1998, 377 (ET = 1997, 248–49).

[279] Josephus, *Ant.* 19.335–377. Cf. also the building inscription of his children Berenice and Agrippa II; on this, see note 357 below.

[280] Josephus, *Ant.* 19.338–341.

[281] Josephus, *Ant.* 19.326–327. These walls were intended to secure the north side of the city, where Jerusalem had no natural protection by rocky hillsides. Josephus, *J.W.* 2.218–219 says that if this wall had been completed, the Romans would not have been able to take Jerusalem. Its construction was discontinued because of the premature death of Agrippa.

[282] Josephus, *J.W.* 2.219; *Ant.* 19.343, 350ff. The exact point in time of Agrippa's death can no longer be determined because Josephus fails to give the name of the emperor for whose σωτηρία the games took place. He presumably died in the winter/spring of 44 CE.

Games in honor of "Caesar," rather than a fight with Sidon and Tyre, are said to have been the occasion for the fact that Agrippa appeared in a robe woven completely from silver, which shone in the morning sun, so that the "flatterers" called him a god.[283] Since the king did not reject the flattery, he was seized by an illness, from which he—deeply regretting his hybris—died. His subjects gave little thanks to Agrippa for his benefactions. His non-Jewish troops, recruited from Caesarea and Sebaste, set up statues of his daughters in brothels.[284] The Jewish subjects reacted to his death after a short reign with the story—preserved in Luke and Josephus—that he tolerated the ruler cult as flattery and for precisely this reason died the agonizing death of an enemy of God.[285]

Agrippa left a son, Agrippa (II), whom he had long intended to be his successor, as is evident from his coinage, and who was brought up in Rome—as was already the case for his father and for the sons of Herod.[286] However, since Agrippa II was only seventeen years old at that time, Claudius, against his original intention and on the advice of his freedmen and friends, did not appoint him as the heir of the kingdom of his father but instead sent Cuspius Fadus as procurator to Judaea and to the whole former kingdom.[287] This was, as soon became evident, a fateful political error. The Herodian politics of equilibrium with Rome alongside the simultaneous preservation of Jewish religious identity and of "national interests" would have been the only

---

[283] Josephus, *Ant.* 19.345: φωνὰς ἀνεβόων, θεὸν προσαγορεύοντες, εὐμενής τε εἴης, ἐπιλέγοντες, εἰ καὶ μέχρι νῦν ὡς ἄνθρωπον ἐφοβήθημεν, ἀλλὰ τοὐντεῦθεν κρείττονά σε θνητῆς φύσεως ὁμολογοῦμεν. Cf. Klauck 2003b, 251–67, who rightly opposes Mason's hypothesis that Luke uses Josephus as a source (256–57). In reality we are dealing with a popular narrative from oral tradition. Josephus and Luke supplement each other here. The sickness portrayed in Acts 12.23 is the divine punishment for the enemy of God; see Barrett 1994/1998, I: 591–92.

[284] According to Josephus, *Ant.* 19.356ff., it is the whole population of these cities. That Agrippa I erected statues of his daughters in "Gentile" Caesarea at all is one of the indications of his "liberal" stance, which hardly corresponded to the Pharisaic strictness with regard to the law. Claudius wanted to have the anti-Jewish troops punitively relocated to Pontus because of this incident; see Josephus, *Ant.* 19.364ff. Cf. section 3.1.5 below.

[285] Acts 12.22-23; Josephus, *Ant.* 19.345–350, also refers, however, to the great grief of the people with fasting and prayer for the dying king (349). On this, see now Schwemer 2016. For the torturous death of the enemy of God, cf. Antiochus IV (2 Macc 9.5–28); Judas (Matt 27.5; Acts 1.18; further intensified in Papias with the motifs of pus, stench, and worms; see Fragment III.2 in Lindemann/Paulsen 1992, 294); Herod I (Josephus, *J.W.* 1.656ff.; *Ant.* 17.168ff.); Titus (tormented to death by a mosquito according to a Jewish legend; see b. Giṭ. 56b); cf. also Lactantius, *De mortibus persecutorum*.

[286] On the coins, cf. the overview in Schürer 1973–1987, I: 471 n. 1; Meshorer 1967, 138–41 and 141–51; 1982, II: 250–58; Kokkinos 1998, 286. In a letter that Josephus ascribes to Claudius, the emperor designates him as "my friend Agrippa, whom I have brought up and now have with me" (*Ant.* 20.12; trans. L. H. Feldman, LCL, 395).

[287] Josephus, *Ant.* 19.360–363. Cf. section 3.1.1 for this decision, which was fateful for the subsequent fate of Palestine.

traversable way to integrate the Jewish people in the motherland into Roman rule. The constantly changing procurators, some of whom were imperial freedmen and favorites, were not up to this task. Agrippa II, as successor to his father and king of Judaea, would have been able to prevent the outbreak of the First Jewish War.

3.1.5 The Time of the Procurators (44–66 CE)

Judaea was now a province again, at whose head stood procurators from the equestrian class or imperial freedmen. Cuspius Fadus (44–46 CE) first settled the open conflict which had broken out between Jews in Peraea and the city of Philadelphia because of border controversies and condemned an "arch-brigand," who had made Idumaea unsecure, to death, so that

> from then on all Judaea was purged of robber-bands thanks to the prudent concern displayed by Fadus.[288]

Likewise, at the beginning of his time in office he demanded that the high priestly robe be kept in the Antonia again under Roman custody, but allowed a Jewish embassy to present this question to the emperor for his decision. With reference to the opinion of the young Agrippa (II), Claudius specified that the regulation made by Vitellius should be upheld.[289] Herod, king of Chalcis, received the right to appoint the high priests. Thus, succeeding his brother Agrippa I, he was appointed protector of the temple.[290]

The "pseudo-prophet" Theudas arose under Fadus. He led a great crowd of people with their possessions to the Jordan with the promise that the river would part and the miracle of the entry under Joshua would be repeated in the opposite direction. This is the first trek into the wilderness under an eschatological prophet[291] that we hear about. Fadus prevented this "exodus" and sent his cavalry—the followers of Theudas died in the battle or were taken captive. Fadus had the head of Theudas brought to Jerusalem as a trophy.[292] Josephus designates him as a γόης,[293] but consciously

---

[288] Josephus, *Ant.* 20.5 (trans. L. H. Feldman, LCL, 393).

[289] Josephus, *Ant.* 20.6–14.

[290] Josephus, *Ant.* 20.15–16.

[291] Cf., however, the significance of Isa 40.3 for John the Baptist. See section 9.1.2.1. Cf. also 1QS VIII 14. On this, see note 36 in chapter 9.

[292] Josephus, *Ant.* 20.97ff. On this, cf. the excursus on eschatological prophets in this section.

[293] "Scoundrel, deceiver, magician, deceptive miracle worker"; the *terminus technicus* occurs for the first time in *Jewish Antiquities*; cf. Hengel 1989c, 229–33 (GV = 1976c, 235–36, 238–39), on Theudas and on the trek into the wilderness.

avoids mentioning that his adherents were, of course, armed. In the speech of Gamaliel, Theudas appears in a historically incorrect sequence before Judas the Galilean (Acts 5.36-37) as a prophetic-messianic pretender, and the popular movements sparked off by them are compared with that of Jesus.[294]

In *Jewish War*, Josephus gives a good testimony regarding both Fadus and his successor Tiberius Julius Alexander (46–48 CE),

> who by abstaining from all interference with the customs of the country kept the nation at peace.[295]

The fact that it could only have been a time of relative tranquility—in a similar way as in the sweeping judgment of Tacitus: *sub Tiberio quies*—in comparison to the preceeding and following crises is evident from the more detailed report in *Jewish Antiquities*. For Tiberius Alexander—son of the alabarch Alexander and nephew of Philo and thus from the high aristocracy of Alexandria,[296] who had become an apostate for the sake of a promising military-political career[297]—his time in office in Judaea was a short interlude.[298] He had two sons of Judas the Galilean, James and Simon, crucified. Josephus does not discuss the specific circumstances, but this was surely intended to serve the "tranquility" of the people and scotch the political machinations of the "Fourth Party," which had been stoked by a severe supply crisis in Palestine that made food products more expensive and severely affected the poorer strata of the population.[299] Through the purchase of grain in Egypt and figs in Cyprus, the pious queen Helena of Adiabene (which belonged to the Parthian Empire), who had converted to Judaism with her son Izates, alleviated the "great famine," which had already begun under Fadus and lasted for quite some time[300] and which

---

[294] Cf. Hengel 1989c, 230 n. 8 (GV = 1976c, 236 n. 4).

[295] Josephus, *J.W.* 2.220 (trans. H. St. J. Thackeray, LCL, 409).

[296] He was the son of the Jewish Rothschild of his time. His family possessed not only Roman citizenship but also equestrian status. His father managed the assets of Antonia Minor, the mother of Claudius (Josephus, *Ant.* 19.276). Berenice, the sister of Agrippa II, married his brother Marcus, who died early. On both of them, see Sullivan 1978.

[297] Josephus, *Ant.* 20.100: τοῖς γὰρ πατρίοις οὐκ ἐνέμεινεν οὗτος ἔθεσιν.

[298] On his career path, cf. Tacitus, *Ann.* 15.28.3 (Stern 1976–1984, II: 86–87) and elsewhere. On this, cf. Schürer 1973–1987, I: 457–58 n. 8; III/2: 815 n. 14.

[299] Josephus, *Ant.* 20.102; cf. Hengel 1989c, 259–60, 332, 345–46 (GV = 1976c, 265, 338, 352–53, 356); for the dynasty of Judas the Galilean, see notes 52, 208, and 335 in this chapter.

[300] Josephus, *Ant.* 20.101: μέγαν λιμόν, which means "great price increase"; cf. *Ant.* 20.51–52; *Ant.* 3.320–321. On the supply crises under Claudius, cf. Riesner 1994, 112–19; Hengel/Schwemer 1998, 365–69 (ET = 1997, 240–44). For the "conversion" of the royal

also affected the Christian communities in Judaea and especially the community in Jerusalem.[301]

Already under Cumanus (48–52 CE) the Romans got what was coming to them for Claudius' decision not to punitively relocate the anti-Jewish auxiliary troops, who had enlisted in Caesarea and Sebaste, to Pontus but rather to leave them in the land at their request.[302] A soldier who was posted on the roof of the porticoes surrounding the forecourt provoked the pilgrims in the temple with an obscene gesture at the festival of Passover. The procurator did not appease the crowd with an immediate punishment of this "blasphemy" but as stones flew had a reinforcement of troops march in, so that the fleeing participants in the festival trampled on one another in the narrow temple gates and steps and in the streets of the city.[303] In the next incident the procurator acted in a very different way: "revolutionary" Zealots had attacked and robbed an imperial slave, who was presumably transporting duties, in the vicinity of Beth Horon. One of the soldiers, who had been sent to carry out a punitive action in the surrounding villages, where the insurgents had found support, had torn a Torah scroll there and burnt it. This time Cumanus reacted immediately to the Jewish complaint by executing the guilty man because of the sacrilege.[304] The extent to which the boldness of the Zealots had increased in the meantime became evident when a Galilean festival pilgrim was murdered in a neighboring Samaritan town, Ginai/Gema (today's Jenin).[305] Since Cumanus did not punish the guilty ones, they made a call to arms and, under the leadership of zealot guerillas Eleazar ben Dinai[306] and Alexander, destroyed Samaritan villages. Cumanus attacked with his forces and captured many. The leaders of the people, having rushed there from Jerusalem, continually begged the rebellious population in

---

house of Adiabene, cf. Hengel/Schwemer 1998, 108–9 (ET = 1997, 64). Helena was buried in Jerusalem in a magnificent tomb, which Pausanias (8.16.5) mentions and which can still be seen today.

[301] Acts 11.28ff.: the λιμὸς μεγάλη announced by the prophet Agabus leads to a relief action of the "disciples" in Antioch for the "brothers in Judaea." On this, see Hengel/Schwemer 2019.

[302] Cf. note 284 above.

[303] Josephus, *J.W.* 2.224–227; *Ant.* 20.108–112.

[304] Josephus, *J.W.* 2.228–231; *Ant.* 20.113–117. Roman law was implacable in the case of the crime of sacrilege. The destruction of a Torah scroll was just as weighty as the destruction of images of gods or of a temple.

[305] Josephus, *J.W.* 2.232–246; in *Ant.* 20.118–136 several pilgrims were killed; cf. Hengel 1989c, 346ff. (GV = 1976c, 353ff.). See also section 8.1 with note 20.

[306] Josephus, *Ant.* 20.121; in the Mishnah (m. Sotah 9.9) this ben Dinai is regarded as a great murderer; in Midrash Shir HaShirim 2.18, by contrast, he is a man who wanted to liberate Israel. On his imprisonment through Felix, see note 315 below.

"sackcloth and ashes" to put down the weapons and managed to get the people to return home and the "robbers" to withdraw to their hiding places in the Jewish wilderness. As during the Caligula crisis, the province had come again to the brink of war. The consequence of these incidents was an increasing destabilization.

> Many (of the Jews), however, turned to brigandage, because they had no fear of punishment (from that quarter) and predatory raids took place throughout the whole country, together with revolts on the part of audacious people.[307]

The Samaritans asked the governor in Syria, Ummius Quadratus, to punish the Jews. He conducted a hearing in Samaria and had some of the main guilty people, both Samaritans and Jews, crucified. In Judaea he took even more vigorous measures. He had Jewish rebels executed immediately; the high priest Ananias, son of Nedebai, and the captain of the temple, Ananus (Annas), he sent in chains to Rome. However, Cumanus, with his military tribune Celer, the commander of a cohort, and Samaritan nobles, also had to give an account before Claudius. Claudius decided in favor of the Jews, on behalf of whom Agrippa II had once again spoken.[308] Cumanus was exiled, the Samaritans were executed, and, at the order of the emperor, Celer was brought back to Jerusalem, driven in an public spectacle through the city, and finally beheaded.[309] Roman rule attempted to be impartial and to reestablish equilibrium by strict action against abuses, but it had not been dealt a good hand of cards in this regard. After Herod of Chalcis (ca. 48/49 CE) had died, Agrippa II received the rule over the area of his uncle Herod in the territory of Lebanon and his privilege of appointing the high priests as protector of the temple.[310] In 53 CE Claudius gave him the title of king and the territory of the former tetrarchy of Philip. Roman procurators, however, continued to rule over the Jewish heartland of Judaea and (the larger portion of) Galilee, Idumaea, Peraea, and Samaria.[311]

---

[307] Josephus, *J.W.* 2.238 (trans. Hengel 1989c, 347; GV = 1976c, 354); cf. *Ant.* 20.124.

[308] Josephus, *Ant.* 20.135; cf. the beginning of this section.

[309] Josephus, *J.W.* 2.246; *Ant.* 20.136. Josephus does not explain why Celer was punished in such a disgraceful manner. He was presumably the leader of the cohort responsible for the security of the temple during the festival at which the insurrection began, which had committed special cruelties against the Jews.

[310] See in detail notes 360–61 below.

[311] On this, cf. section 3.1.6.

Cumanus was followed by Antonius Felix (52–59 CE),[312] an imperial freedman and brother of Pallas, who was a powerful figure at the court of Claudius.[313] He was presumably appointed at the request of the high priest Jonathan. Under him

> In Judaea matters were constantly going from bad to worse. For the country was again infested with bands of brigands and imposters who deceived the mob.[314]

"Robbers" and "deceivers" are used to speak of the religious-political instigators of unrest across their full spectrum from plain bandits, via moderate and radical Zealots, to eschatological prophets, which now appear more frequently. Eleazar ben Dinai was a popular Zealot leader who was able to survive for twenty years in the hiding places and caves of the Jewish wilderness and who presumably took over the leadership of the radical resistance movement after the crucifixion of the sons of Judas the Galilean by Tiberius Alexander. Felix lured this "robber captain" to Caesarea with the assurance of freedom from punishment and then had him transported to Rome in chains.[315] The eyewitness Josephus illustrates the growing support for the Zealots among the Jewish rural population with the statement

> Of the brigands whom he crucified, and of the common people who were convicted of complicity with them and punished by him, the number was incalculable.[316]

Rather than being deterred by the brutal punitive actions and numerous crucifixions, they were strengthened in their hatred for the Romans and increasingly pressed onto the side of the anti-Roman "freedom movement."

---

[312] Felix married the sister of Agrippa II, Drusilla, after he had persuaded her through the Jewish magician Atomus to leave her husband, King Azizos of Emesa, who had converted to Judaism, a "transgression of the law" by Drusilla, which Josephus reproaches; see *Ant.* 20.142–143; cf. Tacitus, *Hist.* 5.9; Suetonius, *Claud.* 28. See also Acts 24.24-26 and note 336 below.

[313] Claudius left the administration of the empire largely to his freedmen.

[314] Josephus, *Ant.* 20.160. On the character of Felix, cf. Tacitus, *Hist.* 5.9: *per omnem saevitiam ac libidinem ius regium servili ingenio exercuit* ("through every cruelty and lust he exercised the power of a king with the instincts of a slave"; see Stern 1976–1984, II: 21, 29); similarly *Ann.* 12.54 (Stern 1976–1984, II: 76–77; on this, see the commentary on 78–82).

[315] Josephus, *Ant.* 20.161. On this, see Hengel 1989c, 349–51 (GV = 1976c, 356–57). He is mentioned by Josephus and in the Talmudic literature. See note 306 above.

[316] Josephus, *J.W.* 2.253; cf. *Ant.* 20.160.

At the end of his time in office Felix appears to have given up on the pacification of the land through continual fighting against the radical instigators of unrest together with their sympathizers and supporters. On the contrary, via a bribed middleman he himself now made use of the Sicarii to have the former high priest Jonathan, son of Annas, murdered, who possessed good relations with Rome and had criticized Felix's conducting of his office.[317] Radical Zealots had now adopted a new tactic. They no longer did away with their opponents only in the country but now also in Jerusalem, where they mixed themselves, "daggers under their clothing," among the festival pilgrims, and could carry out their murders in secret and without punishment in the midst of crowds of people even in the temple area.[318]

EXCURSUS
Eschatological Prophets

At the same time, under Felix and his successors there was a further increase of "false" prophets, who led their droves into the wilderness, for

there God would give to them miraculous signs that announce freedom.[319]

While the hands of these deceivers of the people were clean, since they did not stain them with murder, they made no less a contribution to the destruction of Jerusalem than the Sicarii. In accordance with the apocalyptic notion that the last things will occur as the first things,[320] they led their followers to the east over the Jordan into the wilderness, as the Israelites, led by Moses,

---

[317] Josephus, *J.W.* 2.256; *Ant.* 20.163–164. On this, see Hengel 1989c, 351–52 (GV = 1976c, 357–58); contrast Gabba 1999, 145.

[318] The Greek σικάριοι is a Latinism (*sicarius*; see Georges 2003, II: 2650: "assassin, bandit") and is derived from the weapon *sica*, "dagger." It is not an originally Jewish designation for a group and is used by Josephus, in *Jewish War*, especially for the followers of Judas the Galilean. Josephus, *J.W.* 2.254ff. (trans. H. St. J. Thackeray, LCL, 423): ". . . a new species of banditti was springing up in Jerusalem, the so-called *sicarii*, who committed murders in broad daylight in the heart of the city. The festivals were their special seasons, when they would mingle with the crowd, carrying short daggers concealed under their clothing, with which they stabbed their enemies. . . . The panic created was more alarming than the calamity itself; every one, as on the battlefield, hourly expecting death." Cf. the explanation of the word *sica* in *Ant.* 20.186. On this, see Hengel 1989c, 46–47 (GV = 1976c, 47–48 and elsewhere).

[319] Josephus, *J.W.* 2.259; cf. *Ant.* 20.167–168.

[320] Barnabas 6.13: "And the Lord says: 'Behold, I make the last things as the first" (trans. Holmes 2002). On the rabbinic principle "as the first redeemer (Moses), so the last redeemer (the Messiah)" (Qohelet Rabbah 1.28 and elsewhere), cf. Jeremias 1967c (GV = 1942, 864–65).

had trekked out of slavery in Egypt through the Reed Sea into the wilderness. The last zealot defenders of the upper city in Jerusalem also wanted to make this "trek into the wilderness" when Titus exhorted them to surrender after the destruction of the temple in 70 CE:

> To this they replied that they could not accept a pledge from him, having sworn never to do so; but they asked permission to pass through his line of circumvallation with their wives and children, undertaking to retire to the desert and to leave the city to him.[321]

The hope that the eschatological salvation would dawn in the wilderness was given by Old Testament prophecy and had already been a living hope again for some time.[322] Josephus is careful to reproduce the promises of these prophets in direct speech. He only emphasizes their announcements: that the crowds of people in the wilderness would see the τέρατα καὶ σημεῖα, the signs and wonders, of the wilderness trek of Israel as signs of the dawning freedom.

A writing that more likely reflects the Pharisaic expectations for the end-time and not directly the zealot hopes, the Lives of the Prophets, preserves for us such eschatological predictions from the time before 70 CE, which had grown from the Old Testament prophecy and were attributed to the Old Testament prophets. According to the Life of Jeremiah, the people will flee to Sinai in the end-time before the enemy of the end and there, after the "first resurrection" of the ark of the covenant, will receive the law again from Moses and Aaron. As he once prophesied the downfall to Nineveh, the prophet Jonah promises that Jerusalem will also be leveled by its enemies.[323] In the Life of the prophet Zechariah, Zechariah not only knew of the rebuilding of the temple after the exile but also that this temple would be destroyed by a people from the west, i.e., the Romans, but that the new temple would then be revealed at Sinai, where Moses had already erected the first sanctuary.[324]

---

[321] Josephus, *J.W.* 6.351; cf. 366 on the oath not to surrender oneself; on this, see Hengel 1989c, 254–55 (GV = 1976c, 260–61). The defenders of Masada had contacts with Jerusalem; cf. note 391 in this chapter. The Romans granted free passage to those who occupied Machaerus—presumably into the wilderness (Josephus, *J.W.* 7.205–206).

[322] Cf. the discussion of Theudas at the beginning of section 3.1.5. The Samaritan prophet who wanted to find the temple vessels on Gerizim is an analogous case (see note 120 in chapter 4). Cf. also the quotation of Isa 40.3 in 1QS VIII 14 and on John the Baptist in section 9.1.2.1. See further Hengel 1989c, 230–37, 249–55 (GV = 1976c, 236–43, 255–61), on the different reasons for the withdrawal into the wilderness since the time of the Maccabees.

[323] Lives of the Prophets 10.8. On the sign of Jonah in Luke 11.29; 19.42-44; Matt 12.39; 16.4, cf. Mittmann-Richert 2000, 169–70.

[324] The Life of the prophet Zechariah ben Jehoiada (cf. 2 Chr 24.21) evaluates the fate of the Second Temple in a correspondingly negative way. The murder of the prophet

The Lives of the Prophets do not reckon with the appearance of new prophets, but the catastrophes of the end-time break in, as the prophets once predicted. The leaders of the people in the end-time will again be Moses, "the chosen of God" (Liv. Pro. 2.11), Aaron, and Jeremiah. The Messiah plays a subordinate military role here. He will only bring an end to the rule of the Ptolemies.[325]

The new prophets—who arose before and in the First Jewish War in the tension-filled decades that were filled with eschatological hopes, when the zeal for the law, the struggle against all pagan uncleanness, and the hatred of the Roman-pagan foreign rule continued to increase—can, in some cases, be clearly assigned to the type of the Moses *redivivus* in fulfillment of Deut 18.15. This is the case for the Samaritan prophet in 35/36 CE, against whose followers Pilate took action,[326] and for Theudas, whose endeavor Fadus had crushed.[327] Additional prophets enticed crowds of people into the wilderness with similar promises in the fifties. The expectation of *freedom* from the Roman yoke and the rejection of the Roman overlordship connected these prophetic movements with the Zealots, and for precisely this reason the procurators also took action against them. Zealot freedom fighters could withdraw with their followers for decades into inaccessible rock caves in the Jewish wilderness. This is why, for example, Felix was only able to capture Eleazar ben Dinai through deceit. The attempt of an exodus of the people that was analogous to the model of the exodus under the leadership of Moses would have to disturb the order of the province. Therefore, here too the procurators felt compelled to intervene militarily. The Markan "apocalypse" around 69/70 warns against being led astray by "pseudo-Messiahs" and "false-prophets," who "produce signs and wonders to lead astray the elect," which Matthew then supplements with the warning "Even if they say to you, behold (the Messiah) is in the wilderness, do not go out; behold in the wilderness caves (ταμείοις), do not believe (it)."[328] This warning appears to be a recollection of the fate of those people who let themselves be convinced by these prophets and deceivers of the people that in the wilderness

they would show them unmistakable marvels and signs that would be wrought in harmony with God's design. Many were, in fact, persuaded and

---

continues to weigh on the house of David and on the temple, where this murder took place. Therefore the divinatorial power of the priesthood fails in every respect.

[325] On the Lives of the Prophets, see Schwemer 1995/1996; 1997.

[326] See note 120 in chapter 4.

[327] Cf. note 292 above.

[328] Mark 13.22; Matt 24.26; cf. Hengel 1989c, 232 (GV = 1976c, 238); Hengel 2002, 406 n. 385.

paid the penalty of their folly; for they were brought before Felix and he punished them.[329]

Felix had the followers of these prophets executed, for with their often-armed exoduses they revolted against Rome and withdrew from their obligations as Roman subjects, namely their work and with it their payment of taxes.[330] The "Egyptian," i.e., a Jew from the Egyptian diaspora, was such an impressive and initially successful figure that he—like Judas the Galilean and Theudas—is mentioned not only by Josephus but also explicitly by Luke.

A still worse blow was dealt at the Jews by the Egyptian false prophet. A charlatan, who had gained for himself the reputation of a prophet, this man appeared in the country, collected a following of about thirty thousand dupes, and led them by a circuitous route from the desert to the mount called the mount of Olives. From there he proposed to force an entrance into Jerusalem and, after overpowering the Roman garrison, to set himself up as a tyrant of the people.[331]

Further details are contained in the parallel account in *Jewish Antiquities*. This Egyptian declared that at his command the walls of Jerusalem would fall—as had once been the case with the walls of Jericho. The numbers are somewhat more realistic here. Felix came ahead of this Messianic pretender with infantry and cavalry, killed four hundred of his followers, and captured two hundred. The Egyptian himself was able to flee, for which reason his sudden return was expected.[332] In *Jewish War*, by contrast, Josephus stresses that "the whole people" participated in the defense, which is entirely improbable and betrays the apologetic tendency of the historian. Presumably, this specification was restricted to the influential portion of the Jerusalem population, which derived great advantages from the Pax Romana, for this alone guaranteed the importance of Jerusalem as an international pilgrim city and the prosperity that was obtained thereby. Those who were deceived to fall away from Rome by the "false prophets" could easily be destroyed, while the "robbers," i.e., the zealot guerillas, continued to incite the people to war against Rome and destroyed the villages that opposed them.[333] Even Luke alludes to

---

[329] Josephus, *Ant.* 20.168.

[330] Cf. Schwartz 1992, 29–43 (35). On "anachoresis," cf. Hengel 1989c, 33–34, 249–50 (GV = 1976c, 34, 255).

[331] Josephus, *J.W.* 2.261–262 (trans. H. St. J. Thackeray, LCL, 425). The number is exaggerated.

[332] Josephus, *Ant.* 20.172: ἀφανὴς ἐγένετο; this could be interpreted with reference to a miraculous translation and with reference to his coming again.

[333] Josephus, *Ant.* 20.172.

this event, which threw the city into agitation. After the Roman soldiers of the Antonia had rescued Paul from the threatening mob justice of the crowd, the commander of the cohort of the city, Claudius Lysias, surprised at his knowledge of Greek, asked the apostle in Acts 21.38: "Then you are not the Egyptian who led four thousand Sicarii into the wilderness?"

Since Pompey's conquest, when many priests died or were enslaved, not only the Jewish violators of the law but also Roman abuses threatened the temple, which gave rise to the expectation of the eschatological redemption in the wilderness. But as they concentrated on the wilderness, so the eschatological hopes continued to concentrate also on the sanctuary in Jerusalem, above all in the time of the revolt, when the temple unexpectedly fell quickly into zealot hands.[334] After its destruction by the Romans, the eschatological hope was oriented again to the wilderness.[335]

Felix's delaying tactics in the trial of Paul cast a revealing light upon his dispensation of justice. According to Luke, he does not let himself be impressed by the accusations of the high priest Ananias and his rhetorician Tertullus. By contrast, he is not uninterested in the person of the accused, whom he hears multiple times (also in the presence of his wife Drusilla), while regarding him and the "sect" of the Christians, as his predecessors since Pilate already had, as politically harmless. However, he continues to keep him in custody in the hope of receiving a sizable bribe and eventually hands him over—because this hope proves to be deceptive—as a prisoner to his successor Festus.[336] The young Josephus, as the leader of a Jewish embassy to Rome in 63/64 CE, was able, with the support of Poppaea, the pro-Jewish wife of Nero, to secure the release of some priests whom Felix had arrested "for small and far-fetched reasons" and had sent to Rome in order to give an account of themselves before the emperor.[337]

Near the end of Felix's time in office unrests broke out in Caesarea Maritima. A controversy over citizenship rights arose between the Jewish

---

[334] Hengel 1989c, 240–45 (GV = 1976c, 246–51).

[335] Josephus, *J.W.* 6.351 (see the beginning of this excursus). However, the hope for the rebuilding of the temple by no means died out. In the legend of the zealot messianic pretender Menahem ben Hezekiah (see section 3.1.7 below) the sentence "If the temple was destroyed for his sake, it will be rebuilt for his sake" stands at the center. Cf. Schwemer 1994; Himmelfarb 2002.

[336] Acts 24.1-27. Luke characterizes the married couple in Acts 24.24-25 (see note 312 above): it is said that Paul spoke with them about righteousness, (sexual) self-control, and the future judgment.

[337] Josephus, *Life* 13–16. Presumably these priests, whose piety Josephus emphasizes, had failed to make Felix more gracious through bribes. Their offense is not explained. Like Jonathan, they probably criticized the way Felix carried out his office. For the translation, see Siegert 2001, 27, 29.

and the "Syrian," i.e., pagan-Hellenistic inhabitants.[338] Stones flew once again and Felix intervened in favor of the "Syrians" and allowed Jewish houses to be plundered. However, at the request of the moderate and aristocratic Jewish inhabitants he called off the action of the military. Later, when his successor Festus had already taken office, a Jewish embassy attempted to complain about the action of Felix before Nero. The emperor, however, reacted with the denial of equal citizenship rights for the Jews, which is said to have been a cause for the outbreak of the war.[339]

Porcius Festus (59–ca. 62 CE) found Judaea in very bad condition. It was full of "Sicarii,"[340] who even dared to burn down larger villages if the inhabitants were not willing to support their fight against the Roman overlords.

> Festus . . . proceeded to attack the principal plague of the country: he captured large numbers of the brigands and put not a few to death.[341]

However, he also intervened militarily against a "false prophet" and his followers, to whom the false prophet had promised salvation (σωτη-ρία) from the evil conditions of the present if they followed him into the wilderness.[342]

After multiple hearings, to which he had also drawn Agrippa II and his sister Berenice as experts in Jewish-religious questions, the procurator sent Paul—who, after he had already waited on his trial for two years as a prisoner in Caesarea, now appealed to Caesar—to Rome in the autumn of 59 CE.[343] After only two years Festus died in the province.

His successor was Albinus (62–64 CE). However, before Albinus arrived in the province, the high priest and leading Sadducee Annas II, the youngest son of Annas I (whom we know from the passion narrative), used the vacancy of the seat and had James, the brother of the Lord, and other leading Jewish Christians stoned as lawbreakers.[344] Against this usurpation of authority—the high priest and the advisory council, the Sanhedrin,

---

[338] Josephus, *Ant.* 20.173: ἰσοπολιτεία. There were similar tensions in Alexandria and in Antioch. Cf. Hengel/Schwemer 1998, 287ff. (ET = 1997, 186ff.).

[339] Josephus, *Ant.* 20.182ff. Schürer 1973–1987, I: 467, by contrast, partly follows the presentation in *J.W.* 2.270–271, 284.

[340] Josephus, *Ant.* 20.186. On this, cf. note 318 above.

[341] Josephus, *J.W.* 2.271 (trans. H. St. J. Thackeray, LCL, 429).

[342] Josephus, *Ant.* 20.188.

[343] Acts 25.1–27.1. For the dating of the change from Felix to Festus, see Meshorer 1982, II: 183. Cf. Reiser 2000, 472, on the departure of Paul in 59 CE. For the course of the ship journey, see Reiser 2001a.

[344] Josephus, *Ant.* 20.200: ὡς παρανομησάντων. On this, see Hengel 2002, 551–57.

which was called by him contrary to the law, did not have the authority
of capital punishment[345]—Pharisees protested before Agrippa II and sent
a delegation to Alexandria to meet Albinus, which informed him about
this incident. The new procurator reacted with indignation. For this reason
Annas II was deposed by Agrippa after only three months in office.[346] He
continued, however, to be politically influential as a former high priest and
head of the Sadducean party.

Albinus is said to have continued the corrupt politics of Felix. While
the latter had let himself be bribed in secret, Albinus openly extorted
money whenever he could get it:

> "there was no form of villainy which he omitted to practice. Not only did
> he, in his official capacity, steal and plunder private property and bur-
> den the whole nation with extraordinary taxes, but he accepted ransoms
> from their relatives on behalf of those who had been imprisoned for rob-
> bery by the local councils or by former prosecutors; and the only persons
> left in gaol as malefactors were those who failed to pay the price."[347]

However, a prophet of disaster, who announced the downfall of the
city and of the temple with loud cries four years prior to the beginning of
the First Jewish War, had been released again by Albinus, after a flogging,
as a madman. This narrative is an important analogy for the understanding of the trial of Jesus.[348] Albinus is said to have accepted bribes from
both parties, the Zealots and those who were committed to peace. The
former high priest Ananias son of Nebedeus likewise secured his position
of power with "gifts" to Albinus and to the officiating high priest Jesus,
son of Damneus.[349] The high priestly families profited from the general
breakdown of law and order, for they had their slaves take the tithes from
the threshing floor, which belonged to the poorer priests, and at the same
time maintained private gangs that they used to fight among one another.[350]

---

[345] On this, see 20.2.1 for discussion of this question with regard to the trial of Jesus.

[346] Josephus, *Ant.* 20.197–203. The οἱ περὶ τοῦ νόμου ἀκριβεῖς (201) were evidently
anti-Sadducean Pharisees.

[347] Josephus, *J.W.* 2.272–273 (trans. H. St. J. Thackeray, LCL, 429, 431).

[348] Josephus, *J.W.* 6.305. On this, cf. section 19.2 on the trial of Jesus before Pilate.

[349] Ananias was appointed by Herod of Chalcis and was in office ca. 47–59 CE (Josephus, *Ant.* 20.103, 131; cf. *J.W.* 2.243). He was the high priest who conducted the accusation against Paul (Acts 23.2ff.). He was murdered by the Zealots at the very beginning
of the revolt (Josephus, *J.W.* 2.429, 441). For his trial in Rome before Claudius, see the
previous discussion in this section. For his notable career, see Kokkinos 1998, 324 n. 201.

[350] Josephus, *Ant.* 20.180–181 (already under Felix); 20.206–207, 213 (under Albinus). By contrast, *J.W.* 2.274ff. mentions only zealot "brigand chiefs." See the satirical
song against the leading high priestly families in note 226 above.

Ananias, son of Nebedeus, held the upper hand due to his wealth, but members of the Herodian family were also active as "gang leaders," for they surrounded themselves with strong bodyguards.[351] When "Sicarii" abducted the secretary of the captain of the temple Eleazar, who was himself a son of the high priest Ananias, they were able to obtain from Albinus the release of ten imprisoned Zealots.[352]

As a "farewell gift" to the population of the province, Albinus emptied the prisons by condemning the prisoners who were clearly guilty of death, while releasing all others for a corresponding sum of (bribery) money:

> Thus the prison was cleared of inmates and the land was infested with brigands.[353]

Gessius Florus (64–66 CE) proved to be the straw that broke the camel's back. In comparison with him Albinus was a benefactor, an ἀγαθώτατος. Since his wife was friends with the empress Poppaea, no one dared to protest against him in Rome. He plundered entire cities and made common cause with brigands as long as they shared the plunder with him. With reference to him the rhetorically intensifying accusation of Josephus reaches its high point:

> Certainly his avarice brought desolation upon all the cities, and caused many to desert their ancestral haunts and seek refuge in foreign provinces.[354]

This also brought an end to the return from the diaspora, which had begun during the time of peace under Herod I. Josephus stresses in an exaggerated manner the greed of the procurators in order to emphasize and explain why the radicals were able to gain the upper hand, so that even well-to-do members of the upper stratum, who were previously loyal to Rome, joined the fight for freedom (on *J.W.* 2.308, see below). In this way he attempts to exonerate his own people. On the basis of a prophetic oracle, the primitive Jerusalem community also migrated at that time—either before or during the outbreak of the war—to Pella, a Hellenistic city in the Jordan Plain, which the rebels were not able to conquer.[355]

---

[351] Josephus, *Ant.* 20.214: Costobar and Saul.

[352] Josephus, *Ant.* 20.208ff.; cf. Hengel 1989c, 353–54 (GV = 1976c, 360).

[353] Josephus, *Ant.* 20.215 (trans. L. H. Feldman, LCL, 503).

[354] Josephus, *J.W.* 2.279 (trans. H. St. J. Thackeray, LCL, 433); *Ant.* 20.252–257; Schürer 1973–1987, I: 470; cf. Schröder 1996, 63–64.

[355] Eusebius, *Hist. eccl.* 3.5.2–3: (3). Cf. Schürer 1973–1987, I: 498. There is no reason for doubting this information, which probably comes from the apologist Ariston of Pella around 140 CE. On this, see in greater detail Hengel/Schwemer 2019.

3.1.6 Agrippa II (52–92/93 CE)

Like his father, Agrippa II held, in addition to the title of king, the byname the "great" and was likewise a loyal "friend of Caesar"[356] and "friend of Rome."[357] He was raised in Rome and stayed at the court of Claudius at the death of his father.[358] When his uncle Herod of Chalcis died (ca. 48/49 CE), he received his kingdom, but in 51/52 he was in Rome again when the case of Cumanus was tried.[359] This inheritance was connected with supervision of the Jerusalem temple,[360] i.e., he had, like his uncle before him, the right to appoint and depose the high priests and to authorize construction works on the temple. This control over the temple gave him a close relationship to Jerusalem, for through it he could involve himself in the inner issues of the province of Judaea[361] and at the same time regard himself as the representative of the interests of all the Jews. In the twelfth year of his reign (52/53 CE), Claudius gave him, in place of Chalcis, a much more important region, which encompassed the former tetrarchy of Philip and of Lysanias,[362] and it was at the latest during this time that Agrippa came to the east for good. From Nero he additionally received the rich Galilean cities of Tiberias and Tarichaea (= Magdala) on the Lake of Gennesaret as well as the strategically significant Gamla in the Gaulanitis and Julias in Peraea.[363]

While his relationship with Felix was probably rather cool,[364] in 59 CE he traveled with his sister to welcome Festus to Caesarea, where they also had the opportunity to take part in an examination of Paul.[365] It was pre-

---

[356] Cf. Josephus, *Life* 33; see further the next note.

[357] Josephus, *Life* 408. The inscription OGIS nr. 419 contains his full title (Boffo 1994, 334–37 nr. 40): Ἐπὶ βασιλέως μεγάλου Ἀγρίππα Φιλοκαίσαρος Εὐσεβοῦς καὶ Φιλορωμ[ί]ου, τοῦ ἐκ βασιλέως μεγάλου Ἀγρίππα Φιλοκαίσαρος Εὐσεβοῦς καὶ [Φι]λορωμαίου . . . ; on μέγας in OGIS nr. 420, 422, 425 and elsewhere, cf. Boffo 1994, 336 n. 9. On the use of the title κύριος for Agrippa I and Agrippa II in OGIS nr. 418, OGIS nr. 425, and elsewhere, see Hengel/Schwemer 1998, 199 (ET = 1997, 120–21, 394 n. 634–35); cf. further the excursus on Agrippa II in Schürer 1973–1987, I: 471–83; Kokkinos 1998, 317–40.

[358] Cf. note 286 in this chapter on Josephus, *Ant.* 20.9–12; on his Greek education, which he, like all the members of the Herodian house, possessed, see Josephus, *Life* 359.

[359] On this, see section 3.1.5.

[360] Josephus, *Ant.* 20.15–16, 222.

[361] Cf. Kokkinos 1998, 319.

[362] Josephus, *Ant.* 20.138; cf. *J.W.* 2.421.

[363] Josephus, *Ant.* 20.159; cf. *J.W.* 2.252.

[364] Cf. Josephus, *Ant.* 20.143: the sisters Drusilla (married to Felix) and Berenice, who long held a position of power at the court of their unmarried brother Agrippa II, did not get along with each other.

[365] Acts 25.13-27; 26.1-32. Agrippa II and Berenice appeared at the hearing μετὰ πολλῆς φαντασίας (25.23), i.e., with a great retinue. Cf. also note 343 in this chapter.

sumably not only due to the curiosity of the king and as a result of a gesture of the politeness of the procurator that they did so, for Agrippa II
was, after all, the protector of the temple, where Paul had been saved from
the mob justice of an incensed crowd only through the intervention of the
Roman commander of the Antonia. He was accused of bringing a Gentile
into the temple in violation of the law. Charged by the temple aristocracy
before Felix and Festus with sacrilege, he appealed to Caesar in order to
avoid being sentenced in Jerusalem.

Agrippa II remained unmarried and childless. His sister Berenice
lived with him after the death of her uncle and husband Herod of Chalcis.
In order to avoid the rumor that she had an incestuous relationship with her
brother, she married King Polemon of Cilicia around 64 CE, but she soon
left him again, for we find her in Jerusalem at the beginning of the revolt
and then as mistress at the side of the much younger Titus.[366] The two ultimately had to refrain from marrying for political reasons.[367]

In Jerusalem Agrippa II possessed, in addition to property,[368] above
all the Hasmonean-Herodian palace, which he expanded in such a manner
that from his dining room he had an open view of the inner temple precincts and in this way could reinforce his oversight of the temple. This led
to controversy with the priesthood, who blocked the view of the king with
a high wall and at the same time made it impossible for the Roman guard
posts — which were set up during the festivals on the western portico — to
look into the temple courts. Festus was no less enraged than Agrippa II. He
ordered that the wall be torn down, but then granted the petition of the high
priesthood, who sent a delegation led by the high priest Ishmael ben Phiabi
and Helcias, the treasurer of the temple. Due to the advocacy of his wife
Poppaea, who was a sympathizer with the Jewish religion, Nero decided
in favor of the priesthood.[369]

---

[366] Josephus, *Ant.* 20.145–146; *J.W.* 2.310–314 (on this, see section 3.1.7 below);
Juvenal, *Sat.* 6.156–160; she becomes Titus' lover in 70 CE; see Tacitus, *Hist.* 2.2. On
Berenice, cf. Stern 1976–1984, I: 514 (commentary on Quintilian, *Inst.* 4.1.19); Schürer
1973–1987, I: 474; Kokkinos 1998, 329–30.

[367] Suetonius, *Tit.* 7.1: *insignem reginae Berenices amorem, cui etiam nuptias pol-
licitus ferebatur* ("his extraordinary love for the Queen Berenice, to whom he is said to
have even promised marriage"); 7.2: *Berenicen statim ab urbe dimisit invitus invitam* ("He
immediately sent Berenice away from Rome, against his and her will"). Cf. Cassius Dio
65.15.4.

[368] Cf. the "vineyard of Agrippa" in 4 Bar. 3.14, in which, at the behest of the prophet
Jeremiah, Abimelech, outside of the city, may "oversleep" its destruction.

[369] In *Ant.* 20.189–196 Josephus calls her θεοσεβής, cf. *Life* 16. Poppaea kept Ishmael ben Phiabi and Helcias as hostages at her court. Ishmael was later beheaded at the
outbreak of the First Jewish War in Cyrene. *J.W.* 6.114. Cf. Kokkinos 1998, 201.

In about 59 CE Agrippa II had appointed Ishmael ben Phiabi as high priest (ca. 59–61 CE), then, two years later, Joseph Kabi (ca. 61–62 CE), son of the high priest Simon, then Annas II (ca. 62 CE for three months), who was followed by Jesus, son of Damneus (ca. 62–63 CE), who was, in turn, replaced by Jesus, son of Gamaliel (ca. 63–64 CE). The last high priest before the outbreak of the war was Matthias, son of Theophilus (ca. 65 CE).[370] Agrippa II was apparently not interested in social questions, for he did not intervene against the robbery of the poorer priests by the former high priest Ananias, but when Annas II had James, the brother of Jesus, and some other Christians stoned he reacted immediately. With this action he did a favor for the party of the Pharisees, which was outraged over the execution of the law-observant James, and at the same time preempted an intervention of the new procurator, who could have sent Annas II, indeed even as a prisoner, to Rome.[371]

Just as Agrippa II had upset the priesthood with his comfortable viewing place over the temple precincts, so he snubbed them with privileges that he granted to the Levites. The latter were now permitted, just like the priests, to wear white linen clothes and received more independence in the liturgy of the psalmnody, an offense against the "ancestral laws," which Josephus, as a priest, reprimands and specifies as one of the reasons for the destruction of the temple.[372] He rejected the proposal to tear down a temple portico of the outer forecourt from the Hasmonean period—the "portico of Solomon," which is also known from the New Testament—and to replace it with a more magnificent new construction as a way of providing ongoing employment for the people who were working on the construction of the temple, and he instead had the streets of Jerusalem paved with marble.[373] Agrippa II enlarged his capital city of Caesarea Philippi and refounded it as Neronias. Like his father and grandfather, he was active as a builder and benefactor in the Syrian cities. The Roman colony of Beirut received another theater and numerous statues, including copies of famous older

[370] He incorporated in rapid sequence the families of Phiabi (Ishmael), Kamith (Joseph), Boethus (Jesus, son of Gamaliel), and the clan of Annas twice (Annas II and Theophilus), after he had initially left the powerful Ananias, son of Nebedeus, in office. For the affiliation of the high priestly families, see Schürer 1973–1987, II: 231–32, 234. For the yearly sequence of high priests, see the reference in John 11.49. It did not, however, apply to Caiaphas.

[371] Cf. the case of Ananias, mentioned in section 3.1.5.

[372] Josephus, *Ant.* 20.216–218. Josephus does not provide more exact details about this liturgical reform. He says only that the singers recited the psalms (ὕμνοι) from memory. On the temple singers, see also m. Mid. 2.5; m. Tamid 5.6; 7.4.

[373] Josephus, *Ant.* 20.219–222. Cf. Acts 3.11; John 10.23: place of the teaching of Jesus and of the apostles.

works, as well as annual games with generous gifts of grain and oil to the population, which evoked the envy of his Jewish subjects in Palestine.[374]

During the Jewish revolt against Rome in 66–73 CE Agrippa II always placed himself on the side of the Romans. His troops fought together with those of Vespasian and Titus against the Jewish insurgents. Josephus places a speech in his mouth at the beginning of the revolt, which begins and ends with the key word "peace."[375] He has Agrippa praise the benefits of the Pax Romana and recall to memory the history of the people. Even though this speech is designed by Josephus and reflects in retrospect the catastrophe of the destruction of the temple, it probably does in fact correspond to Agrippa's intention. The two men knew each other personally, and Josephus proudly mentions that he received sixty-two letters from the king, which confirmed, in his view, the reliability of his historical presentation.[376]

Agrippa presumably died in 92/93 or 100 CE.[377] He was the last of the Herodian Jewish kings, and his domain was added to the province of Syria.

3.1.7 The First Jewish War (66–73 CE)

At the end of *Jewish Antiquities* Josephus discusses again in retrospect the causes of the outbreak of the revolt and at the same time justifies his own participation. The war appears here as a suicidal act of desperation:

> It was Florus who constrained us to take up war with the Romans, for we preferred to perish together rather than by degrees.[378]

---

[374] Josephus, *Ant.* 20.212 speaks of μῖσος, hate. On the buildings of Herod I and Agrippa I in Beirut, see Josephus, *J.W.* 1.422; *Ant.* 19.335ff.; on the Latin (!) inscription in the Roman colony of Beirut (AE 1928 nr. 82), which attests the renovation of the buildings of her grandfather by "Regina Berenice" and Agrippa II, see Boffo 1994, 338–42 nr. 41.

[375] Josephus, *J.W.* 2.345, 401. On this, see section 3.1.7 below.

[376] Josephus, *Life* 364–367; cf. 362 (trans. H. St. J. Thackeray, LCL, 133, 135): "To many others also I immediately presented my *History*, some of whom had taken part in the war, such as King Agrippa and certain of his relatives."

[377] For the late dating, see Kokkinos 1998, 396–400; cf., against this, Schürer 1973–1987, I: 473 n. 8; in detail Mason 2001, xv–xix.

[378] *Antiquities* 20.257 (trans. L. H. Feldman, LCL, 525), which corresponds to Tacitus, *Hist.* 5.10.1 (trans. C. H. Moore, LCL, 193): *duravit tamen patientia Iudaeis usque ad Gessium Florum procuratorem* ("Still the Jews' patience lasted until Gessius Florus became procurator"). Cf. the commentary in Stern 1976–1984, II: 53ff. In books 18–20 of *Jewish Antiquities* Josephus firmly advocates the Jewish standpoint, which differs significantly from the standpoint of *Jewish War*, which had been written on the commission of Vespasian and Titus.

The first cause of the open outbreak of the war was an incident that took place in Caesarea Maritima—where the situation was already extremely tense ever since the decision of Nero that was unfavorable to the Jews—in 66 CE, when the synagogue was desecrated by a pagan bird offering. The local equestrian commander was not able to bring an end to the unrest, and the Jewish population fled from the city. The rich, moderate Jews, who had already attempted previously to gain Florus' favor with a "gift" of eight talents, went to him in Sebaste and petitioned him—with the wealthy tax farmer John at the head of them—for help, but he had them arrested. In order to collect the missing taxes, Florus at the same time confiscated seventeen talents from the temple treasury—an amount that was not unbearable in itself[379]—which gave rise to unrest in Jerusalem. Here he did not hear again the arguments of the pro-Roman aristocratic leaders of the people but allowed the city to be plundered and had peaceful inhabitants, including women and children, killed.

> The calamity was aggravated by the unprecedented character of the Romans' cruelty. For Florus ventured that day to do what none had ever done before, namely to scourge before his tribunal and nail to the cross men of equestrian rank, men who, if Jews by birth, were at least invested with that Roman dignity.[380]

These aristocratic Jews were, as Roman citizens, presumably on account of their great assets, elevated to equestrian status and came either from Jerusalem or from Caesarea. It is possible that they were returning emigrants from Rome or Alexandria. The tax farmer John probably belonged to them. They were members of that wealthy stratum, which was in itself pro-Roman and which had promoted the Hellenization and Romanization of Palestine against the radical powers. Even when Berenice, the sister of Agrippa II, petitioned Florus for moderation, she achieved nothing and only brought her own life into danger.[381] In the end, the high priests initially managed once again to mediate and to calm the people, but Florus had more troops brought in with the purpose of penetrating the temple area and establishing a connection to the occupying forces in the Antonia.

---

[379] Cf. Matt 18.24.

[380] Josephus, *J.W.* 2.308 (trans. H. St. J. Thackeray, LCL, 443). Cf. Hengel 1977a, 26; see further the accusation against Piso in a resolution of the senate, recorded in an inscription, which charges him with having a centurion, who was a Roman citizen, crucified in Antioch (copy A of the inscription, column II, line 51–52; copy B, column I, line 42); see Eck/Caballos/Gómez 1996, 13, 26, 42–43, 170: "A Roman citizen was only crucified in exceptional cases."

[381] Josephus, *J.W.* 2.309–314.

However, the "people" resisted and from the roofs bombarded the soldiers, who were not able to advance in the narrow streets because of the crowds of people. The insurgents tore down the porticos that connected the Antonia with the temple in order to make it impossible for Florus to access the temple treasury. Florus withdrew to Caesarea with the troops that in Jerusalem had so violently proceeded against and plundered the population. The leaders of the city and Berenice informed Cestius Gallus, the governor of Syria, of the events by letter, and Florus, in turn, complained before him about the deterioration of the province.[382] Cestius Gallus, however, did not intervene militarily but sent only his legate Neapolitanus to Jerusalem to evaluate the situation. He met with Agrippa II, who was returning from Alexandria, in Jerusalem, after they had already spoken with the high priests about the situation.[383]

With his speech (see the end of section 3.1.6) Agrippa attempted to calm the tempers on all sides and warned that an armed national uprising against the procurator and a refusal to pay taxes would inevitably lead to a hopeless war against Rome. The well-to-do quickly gathered at least a portion of the missing taxes, but the outrage about the Florus' regiment continued. Agrippa II did not, however, allow a delegation of the people to be sent to Nero in order to present these grievances against Florus before Nero, and he also refused to protest against Florus in Rome himself.[384] Finally, Agrippa II was banished from the city by the majority of its population.[385]

Menahem ben Judah ben Hezekiah, a son (or grandson) of Judas the Galilean and (great-)grandson of the "robber captain" Hezekiah, surprisingly succeeded in capturing the Masada fortress on the Dead Sea, in slaughtering the Roman occupying forces, and in arming his followers from the arsenal there. He entered into Jerusalem "as a king."[386] At the same time, a younger, leading member of the priestly aristocracy, the captain of the temple Eleazar, who was supported by the numerous poorer priests, succeeded, against the will of the other high priests, in bringing about the discontinuation of the sacrifice for the emperor:

> Another incident occurred at the same time in the Temple. Eleazar, son of Ananias the high-priest, a very daring youth, then holding the positon of captain, persuaded those who officiated in the Temple services to

[382] Josephus, *J.W.* 2.333.

[383] Josephus, *J.W.* 2.334–335, 338–339.

[384] Josephus, *J.W.* 2.342ff.—presumably also because of Florus' wife's friendship with the empress Poppaea (see the end of section 3.1.5).

[385] Josephus, *J.W.* 2.406–407.

[386] Josephus, *J.W.* 2.408, 433–434. He presumably made messianic claims.

accept no gift or sacrifice from a foreigner. This action laid the foundation of the war with the Romans; for the sacrifices offered on behalf of
that nation and the emperor were in consequence rejected. The chief
priests and the notables earnestly besought them not to abandon the
customary offering for their rulers, but the priests remained obdurate.
Their numbers gave them great confidence, supported as they were by
the stalwarts of the revolutionary party; but they relied above all on the
authority of the captain Eleazar.[387]

At the request of the party of peace, Agrippa II sent two thousand cavalry
from the Babylonian-Jewish military colony in Hauran, in Batanaea, and
in Trachonitis out of concern

> for the rebels and for the nation against which they were rising in arms,
> anxious that the Romans should not lose the Jews nor the Jews their
> Temple and mother city, conscious, moreover, that he had nothing to
> gain from this disorder.[388]

The civil war, however, continued. The insurgents also fought against the
Jewish troops of Agrippa II and burned down the house of Ananias, who
was especially hated for his wealth, and the palace of the king. They also

> carried their combustibles to the public archives, eager to destroy the
> money-lenders' bonds and to prevent the recovery of debts.[389]

Here it becomes clear that the revolt possessed a strong social component.
It was also a rebellion of the poorer strata and of the youth against the
Jerusalem aristocracy, which had been predominant up to then. Menahem
granted the Jewish troops of the king free passage, whereas the Roman
soldiers fled into the towers of Herod's fortress. He had the high priest
Ananias, the head of the pro-Roman party within the high priesthood, and
his brother Ezechias executed, but he himself, when he appeared for prayer
in "royal clothing" in the temple accompanied by "armed Zealots,"[390] was

---

[387] Josephus, *J.W.* 2.409–410 (trans. H. St. J. Thackeray, LCL, 483, 485). For the significance of the sacrifice for the well-being of the emperor, cf. notes 426–27 below.

[388] Josephus, *J.W.* 2.421 (trans. H. St. J. Thackeray, LCL, 487, 489).

[389] Josephus, *J.W.* 2.427. At the same time, it appears to have been a family conflict
between father, the high priest Ananias, and son.

[390] Josephus, *J.W.* 2.444. This first mention of the "Zealots"—τοὺς ζηλωτάς in
absolute usage with article and without genitive attribute designates the "zealous ones
(for the law)"—shows that "zealous ones" was presumably already a designation of honor
for the movement that proceeded from Judas the Galilean, although Josephus uses this

seized and killed via torture by the temple captain Eleazar, the ringleader of the priestly insurgents who had control of the temple, and by his followers. There was obviously a deep division among the anti-Roman troops already at the beginning of the revolt.

Under the leadership of his relative Eleazar son of Yair, the other followers of Menahem were able to escape to the fortress of Masada at the Dead Sea, which was regarded as impregnable. In this way they lost all military influence upon the further course of the revolt.[391] The Roman soldiers, who had withdrawn into the towers of Herod's fortress and had been promised free passage, were murdered except for their leader, the centurion Metilius, who promised "to turn Jew, and even to be circumcised."[392]

These events at the beginning of the revolt cast a revealing light upon its causes, which had political, social, and, above all, religious aspects. Of all the peoples who were subjected by Rome for a significant period of time, the Jews in the motherland (66–73/74 and 132–136 and 115–117 CE also in Egypt, Cyrenica, and on Cyprus) fought most fiercely against Roman rule. This cannot primarily be explained "sociologically." The maladministration of the procurators, especially since Felix, and the increasing inconsideration of the last one, Florus, toward the religious views of Judaism, which extended to taking money from the temple treasury and the incident in the synagogue in Caesarea Maritima, led at the end to an open revolt of the people. They no longer wanted to continue to expose the purity of the temple and the free practice of religion according to the regulations of the Torah to pagan capriciousness in a defenseless manner. Therefore, it was regarded as necessary to take up arms according to the example of Phineas, the prophet Elijah, and

---

religious designation later for a priestly insurgent party, which stood rather in opposition to the "Sicarii" in Masada and to other insurgent groups. The Greek use of ζηλωτής in a neutral sense to mean "followers" always requires a genitive attribute. The religious absolute meaning "zealous ones" appears only in Jewish and Christian sources; cf. 4 Macc 18.12; Luke 6.15 = Acts 1.13 and in the names of parties in Josephus. See Hengel 1989c, 382–83, 388–404 (GV = 1976c, 390, 395–412 and elsewhere).

[391] Josephus, *J.W.* 2.447. In Masada numerous coins of the revolt were found and tithes and the priestly shares were paid. This means that there must have been continued relations with Jerusalem. The discovery of scrolls also supports contacts with the Qumran Essenes. Masada was the last fortress that the Romans conquered, in 73/74 CE. Those who occupied it killed themselves before the Roman soldiers penetrated into the fortress (*J.W.* 7.389–401). Josephus (*J.W.* 7.320–388) has Eleazar deliver a final speech that shows sympathy and understanding for the zealot freedom fighters. On the upper-class, educated women, relatives of Eleazar, as witnesses of this event, see Ilan 1996.

[392] Josephus, *J.W.* 2.454 (trans. H. St. J. Thackeray, LCL, 499). All this also took place on a Sabbath (2.456).

the freedom fighters of the Maccabees in "zeal" for God and his law.[393] The refusal to pay taxes and the rejection of Roman foreign rule, which now found concrete expression in the discontinuation of the sacrifice for the emperor, together with the cry for freedom and the sole reign of God, already belonged to the program of Judas the Galilean. The burning of the records of debts and the execution of the high priest Ananias shed light on the social situation, for the tensions between poor and rich, which were intensified through the unrests in the land, brought increasingly large portions of the common population, especially in the country, including the poorer priests, over to the side of the insurgents. The murder of the messianic pretender Menahem by the party of the priestly insurgent group around Eleazar, son of Ananias,[394] shows that the insurgent movement was already divided when it began and at the same time points to the *messianic* driving force, for what spurred the insurgents on to war the most (τὸ δ᾿ ἐπᾶραν αὐτοὺς μάλιστα πρὸς τὸν πόλεμον) was an "ambiguous oracle,"

> likewise found in their sacred scriptures, to the effect that at that time one from their country would become ruler· of the world. This they understood to mean someone of their own race, and many of their wise men went astray in their interpretation of it. The oracle, however, in reality signified the sovereignty of Vespasian, who was proclaimed Emperor on Jewish soil.[395]

Josephus and the Roman historians Tacitus and Suetonius interpreted this oracle as applying to Vespasian, who as Roman commander in Judaea was acclaimed as emperor by his legions in 69 CE. However, since this oracle, the Balaam oracle of Num 24, had inspired the insurgents from the very beginning, it was probably applied to Menahem and, later in the war, to Simon bar Giora, as it was also then applied to Bar Kokhba in the revolt under Hadrian.[396] The rabbinic literature has handed down the legend of

---

[393] On these connections, see Hengel 1989c, passim (GV = 1976c, passim). On this, cf. now also Schwemer 2013.

[394] He probably also wanted to avenge the killing of his father.

[395] Josephus, *J.W.* 6.312–313 (trans. H. St. J. Thackeray, LCL, 467). Cf. Tacitus, *Hist.* 5.13.2 (Stern 1976–1984, II: 23 and the commentary on pages 61–62); Suetonius, *Vesp.* 4.5; 5.6–7; cf. also Cassius Dio 64.9.1; 65.1.2–4, on a similar pagan oracle on Mount Carmel. In the Jewish perspective Num 24.17-24 is presumably in view: "A star will arise out of Jacob," but Dan 7.13-14; 9.27 may also have played a role. See Hengel 1989c, 237–44 (GV = 1976c, 243–49).

[396] The revolt under Trajan (115–117 CE) in Egypt and Cyrenaica also stood under the leadership of a messianic pretender, the "king" Lukuas. Cf. Hengel 1996a: 314–43;

the Messiah Menahem and remembered him in an altered form with many variants.[397] It is possible that the revolt, like the revolt of Bar Kokhba, could have—initially—taken a different course if Menahem had been able to keep his position at its head and been able to unite the various groups that were prepared to revolt.

In the fall of 66 CE Cestius Gallus led the twelve legions, considerably strengthened by Syrian and Nabataean auxiliary troops, with siege engines against Jerusalem. In the line of approach and provisioning of his troops he allowed himself to be advised by Agrippa II. He pitched camp in the northeast of the city, on Mount Scopus. He succeeded in conquering the northern suburban area but did not think he would be able to besiege the city and its temple mount and chose to withdraw.[398] This was disastrous for his army, which was attacked from all sides in the steep pass of Beth Horon and decimated to such an extent that Cestius Gallus only escaped by cunning with the rest of his legion to Antipatris in the coastal region. He must have died soon after the defeat—perhaps by committing suicide.[399] In Josephus' view, Cestius Gallus could easily have succeeded in bringing Jerusalem into Roman hands again, and in hindsight he regards his retreat as one of the causes of the self-destruction of the city by the civil war within the walls and of its overthrow and complete destruction by Titus.[400]

The victory over Cestius Gallus was celebrated as a great success[401] and led to the hope that the hated Romans could be driven for good from the land and conquered:

Horbury 1996. Cf. also Schwemer 2011. Bar Kokhba was a messianic name of honor, "Son of a Star" (Num 24.17; see note 393). His actual name was Simon bar Kosiba.

[397] Schwemer 1994. Cf. also the excursus on eschatological prophets in section 3.1.5.

[398] Cf. Gabba 1999, 158.

[399] Tacitus, *Hist.* 5.10.1: *fato aut taedio occidit* ("he died either of natural causes or from weariness of life"). Famous national victories were won at the steep place of Beth Horon: Josh 10.10-11; 1 Sam 14.31; Judas Maccabeus also won his first victory there: 1 Macc 3.16, 24; 7.39; cf. Hengel 1989c, 284 (GV = 1976c, 290); Hengel 1983a, 174 (ET = Hengel 1983c, 117, 120, 205 n. 118). In the first century CE it was a dangerous pass where attacks by robbers could easily succeed (*J.W.* 2.228; *Ant.* 20.113; this explains the strong military accompaniment that Paul received on the way from Jerusalem to Caesarea, Acts 23.23-24, 31-32). It belonged to the places at which a pious Jew in a later time spoke a blessing "in memory of the miracles of God" (b. Ber. 54a; cf. m. Ber. 9.1).

[400] *Jewish War* 2.531–532, 539–540 (trans. H. St. J. Thackeray, LCL, 381): "Had he but persisted for a while with the siege, he would have forthwith taken the city; but God, I suppose, because of those miscreants, had already turned away even from His sanctuary and ordained that that day should not see the end of the war" (2.539).

[401] Josephus, *J.W.* 2.554: laden with booty and singing psalms, the victors entered into Jerusalem.

> This reverse of Cestius proved disastrous for our whole nation; for those
> who were bent on war were thereby still more elated and, having once
> defeated the Romans, hoped to continue victorious to the end.[402]

In the eyes of the radicals this surprising success appeared to be a prelude
to the eschatological final battle and to confirm that God was fighting on
the side of the Jews.[403] Presumably it was also the reason that moderates
such as Annas II and Josephus joined the revolt and organized it, so that
the radical Zealots did not come to power.[404] At the same time, the Jewish
victory over a Roman legion awakened the surrounding pagan population's fear of the insurgents. The inhabitants of the Hellenistic cities in
Palestine and Syria

> proceeded to lay hands on and kill, with their wives and children, the
> Jewish residents among them, without the slightest ground of complaint;
> for they had neither entertained any ideas of revolt from Rome nor har-
> boured any enmity or designs against the Syrians.[405]

The rather moderate "high priests and Pharisees" initially took over the
military organization in Jerusalem by forming a sort of "revolutionary
council"[406] and by attempting to form, from the various "bandits and insurrectionists," a national Jewish army, which had not existed since the time
of the Hasmoneans, with paid troops. Eleazar, son of Ananias, was sent
for this purpose to Idumaea, and Josephus was sent to Galilee with two

---

[402] Josephus, *Life* 24 (trans. H. St. J. Thackeray, LCL, 11). Cf. *J.W.* 2.540–555.

[403] For the idea of the divine *summachia*, cf. Hengel 1989c, 147, 176, 222ff., 243,
249, 272–73, 285, 287, 303, 306 (GV = 1976c, 470 index, s.v. "Eingreifen Gottes"). For-
ays against pagan cities such as Ashkalon, which were made following the model of the
Maccabees, were quickly abandoned after the first failures. See Hengel 1989c, 284–85
(GV = 1976c, 290–91).

[404] Millar 1993, 366, notes the turn of the previously rather pro-Roman upper stratum
to the insurgents, which is difficult to explain. Cf. also Gabba 1999, 158, on the reasons for
the participation of the leaders of the people. Subsequent to his removal from office, the
priestly-Sadducean Annas II, who was also characterized by national pride, was presumably hostile to Agrippa II and the procurators. Josephus had gone to Rome in 63/64 CE
in order to liberate priests who were especially faithful to the law from Roman imprisonment. They had already been imprisoned by Felix "on a slight and trifling charge" and
sent to Rome to be held accountable (*Life* 11–16 [13], trans. H. St. J. Thackeray, LCL, 7).
Moreover, Agrippa II was a poor peacemaker, for unlike his father, he did not know how to
exercise his oversight of the temple without protest from the priesthood. Cf. section 3.1.6.

[405] Josephus, *Life* 25 (trans. H. St. J. Thackeray, LCL, 11); cf. *J.W.* 2.457–480, 559ff.;
7.361–369. Cf. Hengel/Schwemer 1998, 83, 95 (ET = 1997, 52, 60).

[406] Josephus, *J.W.* 2.562–565, mentions Joseph, son of Gorion, and the former high
priest Annas II at the head, but they were soon ousted by Eleazar, son of Simon.

other priests in order to gather an army and to prepare the region for the expected attack of the Romans.[407]

In Galilee three parties fought and plotted against one another, namely the radical Zealots under the leadership of John of Gischala, those who remained loyal to King Agrippa II, and the moderate insurgents, at the head of which Josephus placed himself, who as a member of the rich upper stratum was always under suspicion—like this stratum as a whole—of actually being a secret partisan of Rome. The image of the unrests in Galilee in the sixties, which Josephus sketches as an eyewitness in *Jewish War* and in his *Life*, makes clear that the Gospels describe the activity of Jesus in the comparably calm time under Herod Antipas. The safe "itinerant life" of Jesus and his disciples in the Galilean villages, at the Lake of Gennesaret, in the region of Tyre, of the Decapolis, and of the villages of Caesarea Philippi would no longer have been possible in this way in the later time, when the Jewish-pagan hostilities poisoned the climate.[408] Here Mark, around 70, reports about events from an earlier, much quieter time.[409]

Nero sent the experienced Vespasian, who was in Greece, as supreme commander of an army of three legions and additional auxiliary troops to Judaea and made this into an independent province.[410] As expected, from Ptolemais Vespasian initially conquered Galilee in the spring of 67 CE. Sepphoris refused to participate in the revolt and remained loyal to Rome. Here the catastrophe under Varus may have had an effect. After Jotapata was conquered, Josephus passed over—initially as a captive—to the Roman side. When he was captured, he had announced the future rule of the world to Vespasian with reference to his priestly gift of prophecy.[411] Tiberias surrendered without a fight, Tarichaea (= Magdala), Gamla in the Gaulanitis, and the fortress on Mount Tabor were conquered. After the fall of Gischala, which surrendered, the Zealot leader John and his followers

---

[407] Josephus, *Life* 29: "they dispatched me with two other priests, Joazar and Judas, men of excellent character, to induce the disaffected to lay down their arms and to impress upon them the desirability of reserving these for the picked men of the nation. The latter, such was the policy determined on, were to have their weapons constantly in readiness for future contingencies, but should wait and see what action the Romans would take" (trans. H. St. J. Thackeray, LCL, 13; cf. Siegert 2001, 35 and the commentary on page 35 n. 43).

[408] Cf. also Millar 1993, 342; Freyne 2000, 187.

[409] With the exception of Mark 13; cf. "*sub Tiberio quies*"; on this, see note 264 above.

[410] Josephus, *J.W.* 3.69–70, exaggerates, stating: a total of sixty thousand men "without the train of servants," who were likewise equipped for war and could be deployed in battle.

[411] Josephus, *J.W.* 3.399–402; cf. 4.622–629 on the release of Josephus after Vespasian was acclaimed as Caesar by the troops. In rabbinic literature this prophecy is attributed to Yohanan ben Zakkai (Ekha Rabbah 1.13).

managed to flee to Jerusalem around the end of the year. Here he established a "reign of terror," supported by the radical wing of the predominantly priestly Zealots and the others who fled from the regions ruled by the Romans, which "came from the land into the city."[412] These came to Jerusalem not only because it was a fortified city but also and especially in the trust that city and temple were impregnable due to divine protection. The miracle that had taken place during the siege by Sennacherib was now expected to an even greater extent as a result of an eschatological mentality. The pro-Roman and moderate upper stratum, composed of the lay nobility and the high priestly families, were further disempowered, and prominent people were murdered or thrown into prison.[413] Phanni (Phineas), son of Samuel, was specified as new high priest by lot—a judgment of God, as it were. He was not from any of the high priestly families that had come to power with Herod I but from came from the common priesthood. According to rabbinic information he is said to have been a stonemason.[414] This meant, after the discontinuation of the sacrifice for the emperor, a second "cleansing of the temple," so to speak, by the Zealots who were shut up in the temple and who called the people in the temple to arms. However, Idumaeans came to the aid of the Zealots in the temple. They were called by John of Gischala and proceeded against the leading members of the high priestly clan with the charge that these leaders wanted to hand over the city to the Romans.[415] Among other things, they murdered Annas II and threw his corpse over the city wall, where it lay unburied. In the verdict of Josephus,

> the capture of the city began with the death of Annas; and . . . the overthrow of the walls and the downfall of the Jewish state dated from the day on which the Jews beheld their high priest, the captain of their salvation, butchered in the heart of Jerusalem . . . In a word, had Annas lived, they would undoubtedly . . . have arranged terms.[416]

Josephus comments on the horrific end of Annas II first as a priest from a theological perspective—which provides an important reference to the

[412] Josephus, *J.W.* 4.138; cf. 4.121ff. Cf. the warning not to flee into the city in Luke 21.20-24; Mark 13.14-19 portrays the events in a very unrealistic way from Rome.

[413] Josephus, *J.W.* 4.135–146.

[414] Josephus, *J.W.* 4.147–150, 153–157; t. Yoma 1.6 (Zuckermandel 1880, 180); cf. Hengel 1989c, 176 n. 154; 219–20 (GV = 1976c, 181 n. 2; 224ff.).

[415] Josephus, *J.W.* 4.226, 229, 245, 273, 347.

[416] *Jewish War* 4.316–318, 321 (trans. H. St. J. Thackeray, LCL, 95, modified).

religious significance of the high priestly office[417] — and then as a political figure and historian. His appraisal of the situation does not appear so incorrect at all; at any price the radical Zealots wanted to hinder such an "equilibrium / terms of peace."

Despite the continuing confusion of the civil war and the struggles for power, Jerusalem and the parts of Judaea that were not initially conquered by the Romans constituted a "free" state for four years. This freedom is documented by the coins of the rebellion. For the first time since the beginning of Roman rule Jews minted not only small change but also silver coins (from the silver available in the temple treasury) minted with proud inscriptions composed in Palaeo-Hebrew and no longer in Greek, as had been common since Herod I. The regained sovereignty was celebrated by the coin legends "shekel of Israel," "Jerusalem is holy," and "the holy Jerusalem," which points to the city cleansed of foreigners and the special divine protection. They replaced the previous temple currency, the Tyrian tetradrachma and didrachma, on which Melqart-Heracles — stylized as Alexander the Great — and the Ptolemaic eagle were displayed.[418] The less valuable bronze coins announced the "freedom of Zion" and the "redemption of Zion."

Jerusalem owed these years of 'freedom' to the cautious strategy of Vespasian, who — in light of the unrest in the empire, which was already becoming visible in 68 CE — delayed the siege of the capital city[419] and within a year and a half conquered the greatest portion of the rest of the land with the exception of Jerusalem, its immediate surroundings, and the fortresses of Herodion, of Masada in the south, and of Machaerus in the east. In the 'year of the three emperors,' i.e., 69 CE,[420] after the

---

[417] On the function of the high priest as ἡγεμὼν τῆς ἰδίας σωτηρίας in *J.W.* 4.318, cf. Heb 2.10: the true high priest, Christ, is the ἀρχηγὸς τῆς σωτηρίας. Josephus regards Annas II, although he was only in office for three months, as a legitimate high priest and leader of the people (cf. *Ant.* 20.251: τὴν δὲ προστασίαν τοῦ ἔθνους οἱ ἀρχιερεῖς ἐπεπίστευντο; ever since the beginning of the rule of the Roman prefects and procurators the high priest had stood at the head of the people). On προστασία, cf. Goodblatt 1994, 27ff., 215–16; Hengel 2003a, II: 324 index (GV = 1988, 687 index).

[418] On this, see Mildenberg 1998, 170–75; cf. note 141 in this chapter. The new images on the coins with a cup (cf. "cup of salvation" in Ps 116.13) on the front and a pomegranate on the back were also intended to distinguish these coins clearly from all predecessors. Cf. the images in Mildenberg 1998, 362–63, table LI. On the coin legends, cf. Schürer 1973–1987, I: 605–6.

[419] Josephus, *J.W.* 4.366 (trans. H. St. J. Thackeray, LCL, 107): "The Roman generals, regarding the dissension in the enemy's ranks as a godsend, were all eager to march against the capital, and urged Vespasian, as commander-in-chief, to take this course."

[420] In the intervening time it came to civil war and multiple changes of emperors in the Roman west. Galba, the successor to Nero, was murdered by Otho, and Otho was

assassination of Nero (June 9, 68 CE), he completely discontinued actions of war and desisted from the planned siege of Jerusalem.[421] Vespasian profited during this time from the civil war which prevailed in Jerusalem, for insurgents fled into the city from the regions that were threatened or had been conquered by him and fought with one another for the power. The commander himself said:

> If I stay put, I will have to deal with fewer (enemies), since they are exhausting themselves in their civil war. . . .[422]

Vespasian was acclaimed as emperor by the troops in 69 CE in Alexandria and in Caesarea Maritima—in agreement with the prefect of Egypt Tiberius Alexander and the governor in Syria Lucinius Mucianus—and waited in Alexandria until the summer of 70 CE for the victorious march of his troops into the West to Italy and Rome.[423] In spring of 70 CE he sent his son Titus with a reinforced army to Jerusalem to conquer the city and end the war.

Three insurgent parties fought with one another in Jerusalem. A powerful opponent of John of Gischala[424] arose in Simon bar Giora, the son of a proselyte. During the ceasefire he had initially ruled Judaea and Idumaea with his zealot followers. He had been driven back by Annas II, but then

---

conquered by Vitellius, the commander of the legions at the border of the Rhine. The Gospel of Mark, which emerged in Rome (in 69/70), refers to the Roman civil war in Mark 13.7-8.

[421] Josephus, *J.W.* 4.491. Cf. 4.550–555: on June 23, 68, Vespasian set out from Caesarea on a campaign to Judaea and Idumaea, at the end of which "every fortress being now subdued except Herodion, Masada, and Machaerus, which were held by the brigands, Jerusalem was henceforth the one objective before the Romans" (4.555; trans. H. St. J. Thackeray, LCL, 165). Cf. *J.W.* 4.588ff.: after his return to Caesarea, Vespasian learned of the turmoil in Rome and of the appointment of Vitellius. After this he planned his own rise.

[422] Josephus, *J.W.* 4.369. Among other things the insurgents destroyed the reserves of grain in their fratricidal war. On this, cf. Hengel 1989c, 50, 66, 367, 394–95 (GV = 1976c, 401–2 and 470 index).

[423] Tacitus, *Hist.* 2.79.1, mentions the proclamation of Vespasian to autocrator in Egypt; Josephus, *J.W.* 4.592–621, mentions the proclamation in Caesarea; cf. Schürer 1973–1987, I: 500; Millar 1993, 73ff.; Eck 2010, 334–37 (GV = 2003, 126). Vespasian became the ruler of the East. The Flavian propaganda worked for this change of dynasty not only with the oracle from the orient (Tacitus, *Hist.* 5.13.2), which was probably identical to the prophecy of Balaam for Josephus, but also with the miracles of Vespasian in the temple of Serapis in Alexandria; cf. Tacitus, *Hist.* 4.81.1–3; Suetonius, *Vesp.* 7.2–3. Cf. note 395 above.

[424] On his 'tyranny,' before which many Jerusalemites fled to the Romans, cf. Josephus, *J.W.* 4.389–397.

came to Jerusalem at the invitation of the high priest Matthias in the spring of 69 CE.[425]

> Haughtily consenting to be their master, he entered as one who was to rid the city of the Zealots, acclaimed by the people as their saviour (σωτήρ) and protector (κηδεμών); but, once admitted with his forces, his sole concern was to secure his own authority.[426]

Like Menahem, Simon was a political messianic pretender. He held—now allied with the Idumaeans—the upper city and occupied a great portion of the lower city, whereas John of Gischala had to withdraw into the area of the temple with his Galileans.[427] Eleazar, son of Simon, and his predominantly priestly followers, whom Josephus usually calls "the Zealots,"[428] split away for a time from the group around John of Gischala,[429] so that there was a "three-front war," in which the population suffered the most.[430] This bloody strife (ἔρις) was brought to an end only by the siege of Titus in the spring of 70 CE.[431]

---

[425] Josephus, *J.W.* 4.573–577; 5.527–533. He is said to have ended the tyranny of John of Gischala, of the priestly Zealots, and of the Idumaeans.

[426] Josephus, *J.W.* 4.575–576 (trans. H. St. J. Thackeray, LCL, 171). The bronze shekels with the inscription "Year 4" and "For the Redemption of Zion" were presumably minted by Simon; see Hengel 1989c, 297 (GV = 1976c, 303). His messianic ambitions are suggested also by his end: after the destruction of the temple and the conquest of Jerusalem by the Romans, he appeared suddenly in the temple area in royal garments from the underground passages and surrendered himself to the Romans. On his end, see note 439 in this chapter.

[427] Josephus, *J.W.* 4.577–584.

[428] Cf. note 390 in this chapter.

[429] Josephus, *J.W.* 5.5ff.: He had already brought his "Zealots" into the temple area at the beginning of the revolt.

[430] Josephus, *J.W.* 5.2: στάσιν . . . τριμερῆ (cf. 5.21); 5.14–20, 27: "the people, like some huge carcase, was torn in pieces" (27; trans. H. St. J. Thackeray, LCL, 209). Cf. Tacitus, *Hist.* 5.12.3–4: *Tres duces . . . : extrema et latissima moenium Simo, mediam urbem Ioannes [quem et Bargioram vocabant], templum Eleazarus firmaverat. . . . Mox Ioannes, missis per speciem sacrificandi qui Eleazarum manumque eius obtruncarent, templo potitur. Ita in duas factions civitas discessit, donec propinquantibus Romanis bellum externum concordiam pareret* ("There were three generals . . . : the outermost and largest circuit of the walls was held by Simon, the middle of the city by John, and the temple was guarded by Eleazar. . . . Then John got possession of the temple by sending a party under pretence of offering sacrifice, to slay Eleazar and his troops. So the citizens were divided into two factions until, at the approach of the Romans, foreign war producd concord") (trans. C.H. Moore, LCL, 197; see also the text, translation, and commentary in Stern 1976–1984, II: 23, 30-31, 59).

[431] Josephus, *J.W.* 5.71–74. Cf. 5.98–105: even during the siege John and Simon fought against each other again.

Until the conquering of the temple, zealot prophets reinforced the unshakable assurance that the sanctuary was impregnable and that God would deliver them.[432] They were opposed by prophets of doom such as Jesus, son of Ananias, who had announced his oracles of woe in the city without interruption for "seven years and seven months," until he was struck by a projectile at the beginning of the siege.[433] Josephus, a brilliant opportunist who had in the meantime become a Jewish advisor of Titus, also regarded himself to be a prophetic warner, as the prophet Jeremiah had once been, and sought to bring the insurgents in the city to their senses:[434]

> Thus it was that the wretched people were deluded at the time by charlatans and pretended messengers of the deity; while they neither heeded nor believed in the manifest portents that foretold the coming desolation.[435]

Thus it happened that—when the temple was already burning—the Roman troops came upon a group of six thousand, whom a prophet had led into the temple, for

> God commanded them to go up to the temple court, to receive there the tokens of their deliverance.[436]

This prophet presumably appealed to Dan 9.27. After all, the Romans had penetrated into the temple court after a siege of three months, and the daily sacrifice had been discontinued.[437] It was also no accident that Titus—probably based on a pointer from his "advisor" Josephus—gave the command to make the final attack on the sanctuary on the tenth of Ab, i.e., the day on which the first temple was destroyed.[438] As the most

---

[432] Josephus, *J.W.* 6.286: "Numerous prophets, indeed, were at this period suborned by the tyrants (i.e., John of Gischala and Simon bar Giora [M.H./A.M.S.]) to delude the people, by bidding them await help from God, in order that desertions might be checked and that those who were above fear and precaution might be encouraged by hope." See the discussion earlier in this section.

[433] Josephus, *J.W.* 6.300–309. For Albinus' treatment of him, cf. note 348 above. For his significance for the trial of Jesus, see section 19.2.

[434] On his speech in *J.W.* 5.362–419, cf. Hengel 1989c, 241–42 (GV = 1976c, 247–48).

[435] Josephus, *J.W.* 6.288 (trans. H. St. J. Thackeray, LCL, 459, 461).

[436] Josephus, *J.W.* 6.285. The number is again a typical exaggeration.

[437] Josephus, *J.W.* 6.93–94; on this, see Hengel 1989c, 242–43 (GV = 1976c, 248–49).

[438] Cf. Hengel 1989c, 243 (GV = 1976c, 249). Even though Josephus repeatedly gives assurance that Titus wanted to preserve the temple, it was surely destroyed at the command of Titus (and Vespasian); cf. the closing of the Jewish temple in Leontopolis in Egypt at the command of Vespasian (Josephus, *J.W.* 7.421). See also Sulpicius Severus, *Chronica*

important leader, Simon bar Giora was 'ritually' executed following the triumphal procession of the victors Vespasian and Titus in Rome.[439] John of Gischala remained in Roman imprisonment for life.

The early Christians viewed the catastrophe of 70 CE as the fulfillment of Jesus' prophecy about the temple (Mark 13.1-2). The Synoptic apocalypse in Mark 13 reflects the eschatological expectations shortly before the destruction of the temple, whereas Luke and Matthew look back upon it. Luke, who probably writes his Gospel soon after the catastrophe, is deeply affected by it personally and depicts the individual events in a detailed and substantially correct way.[440]

2.30.7 (trans. Goodrich 2015, 158): "other men and Titus himself advised that the temple should be destroyed at once; in this way, the religion of the Jews and Christians would be more thoroughly destroyed. Clearly, these religions, although opposed to one another, had nevertheless evolved from the same founders. Christianity had sprung from the Jews; with the root destroyed, the branch would more easily wither." On this, see Hengel 2002, 418–19.

[439] The form of his self-surrender to the Romans attests his messianic claim (Josephus, *J.W.* 7.26–36), as does his execution (Josephus, *J.W.* 7.118, 154). Cf. Hengel 1989c, 297–98 (GV = 1976c, 303–4). Bringmann 2005, 258, portrays a distorted picture.

[440] Cf. Hengel 2008c, 324–31 (ET = 2000b, 189–94).

4

The Jewish Religious Parties in Palestine

Pharisees, Essenes, Sadducees, Zealots,

Samaritans, and Other Groups[1]

4.1 The Jewish Parties in Josephus' Catalogues of Sects and Their Parallels

A concise survey of the history of Judaea must also discuss the meaning of the religious parties for the historical development and would remain unintelligible without a presentation of Pharisees, Sadducees, Essenes, and Samaritans, as well as of the Zealots, who were already spoken of in detail. In antiquity religion and the state were not separated. Especially in Judaism—whose inner constitution Josephus rightly calls not only an "aristocracy," with the high priest at its head,[2] but also a "theocracy"[3]— politics and religion, interpretation of the law, and striving for the power to establish these among the people were inseparably connected with each other.

Josephus portrays on multiple occasions the fundamental tripartite division of the Jewish religious parties, which he describes and distinguishes doctrinally for his Roman-Greek readership according to an older model as philosophical schools of thought (αἱρέσεις):[4]

---

[1] On this, cf. Böhm 1999; Deines 1997; 2001a; Dexinger 1992; Frey 1999; Hengel 1989c (GV = 1976c); Hengel/Deines 1996 (ET = 1995); Lichtenberger/Lange 1997; Meier 1994, 289–613; Saldarini 2000; Stemberger 1991; 1999; Qimron/Strugnell 1994; VanderKam 2010.

[2] *Antiquities* 20.251.

[3] *Against Apion* 2.165. This is the ideal constitution, which Moses gave to the Israelites, and corresponds for Josephus to the βασιλεία τοῦ θεοῦ, the central notion of the "(royal) rule of God," which is understood in a very different way in the proclamation of Jesus.

[4] Josephus, *J.W.* 2.119 (trans. H. St. J. Thackeray, LCL, 369). Nicolaus of Damascus presumably already designated the Jewish religious parties as αἱρέσεις, for Josephus, *Ant.* 13.171ff., probably uses Nicolaus as a source. Cf. note 24 in this chapter. See also Philo, *Hypoth.*

Jewish philosophy, in fact, takes three forms. The followers of the first school are called Pharisees,[5] of the second Sadducees,[6] of the third Essenes.[7] The Essenes have a reputation for cultivating peculiar sanctity.

In *Jewish War* Josephus—following a source[8]—comments in particular detail about the strict asceticism of the Essenes, who live in ritual purity and community of goods[9] in a group association, for which there are rules for admission and behavior and in which the priests have the leadership, and about their teaching of the immortality of the soul and regarding "fate," i.e., divine determinism.[10] He distinguishes a group that despises marriage

---

(Eusebius, *Praep. ev.* 8.11). The earliest Greek authors, Theophrastus, Clearchus of Soli as a student of Aristotle, and Megathenes, the Seleucid envoy in India, describe the Jews positively as "philosophers"; cf. Hengel 2003a, I: 255–61 (GV = 1988, 464–73). Correspondingly, the Jewish religious philosopher Aristobulus (ca. 170 BCE) justifies changing "Zeus" to "God" in his Aratus quotation with the claim that "all philosophers agree that one must have holy terms for God. Our school (αἵρεσις) is rightly most concerned with this. For the whole establishment of our law is oriented to piety, righteousness, self-control, the remaining goods that correspond to truth" (Eusebius, *Praep. ev.* 12.12.6-8). A few sentences earlier (and elsewhere), he assumes as a given that the Greek philosophers Pythagoras, Socrates, and Plato sometimes followed the older Moses, whose "school" he himself represents. Luke also calls Sadducees, Pharisees, and Jewish Christians (Nazoreans) αἱρέσεις (Acts 5.17; 15.5; 24.5 etc.).

[5] Probably "the separated ones"; see Deines 2000, 740.

[6] Deines 2001b, 1204 (ET = 2008, 858): "The Greek name *Saddukaioi* . . . presumably goes back to Zadok, the chief priest at the time of David"; it was believed that "the high priestly dignity was hereditary in his family into the second century BCE."

[7] "Pious ones"; the Greek name is probably the translation of Aramaic *ḥassaya* (corresponding to Hebrew *ḥasîd*) and was a designation given by others; the Qumran Essenes themselves called themselves *yaḥad* ("oneness/community") or "(the new) covenant"; cf. 1QS passim; CD VI 19; VIII 21; XIX 33; XX 12, and elsewhere. Philo, *Prob.* 75 (cf. also *Hypoth.* 11.1), rightly refers for the derivation of the name to the Greek equivalent ὁσιότης and ὅσιος. The Aramaic name of Qumran "fortress of the pious" (*msd ḥsdyn*) is attested on a papyrus (Murabb'at 45.6; Benoit/Milik/de Vaux 1961 = DJD IIa). See also 4QLevi[b]ar = 213a frag. 3/4 line 6: "the name of the pious (*šm ḥsyh*) will not be blotted out" = Brook et al. 1996, 22 (DJD 22: Qumran Cave 4, XVII, 3); on this, see the commentary on p. 35 with reference to the Syriac-Aramaic *ḥasyāh*; on this, see Brockelmann 1928, 245.

[8] The frame in 2.119 and 2.162–163 reveals this, although Josephus does not specify a source. Cf. Deines 2001a, 475 n. 110. Isser 1999, 569, assumes, following M. Smith, that Josephus and Hippolytus used a common source, which mentioned the Samaritans as a third 'sect'; Josephus, it is said, deleted this and replaced it with the account of the Essenes. See Hengel 1989c, 70–73 (GV = 1976c, 73–76).

[9] On this, see Klauck 1989.

[10] Josephus, *J.W.* 2.120–161. Priests speak the prayer before and after the meals, which are eaten in ritual purity. The morning prayer in the direction of the sun is meant to remind the educated reader of Socrates (Plato, *Symp.* 220d 4–5); cf. the morning prayer in 4Q408, which praises God, who has created the morning as a sign of light. On strict determinism as a striking feature of the Essenes, cf. VanderKam 2010, 102–4, 137–38, 155; Lichtenberger/Lange 1997 (lit). It has a certain parallel in the teaching on predestination in Paul and John.

from those Essenes who regard it as necessary for the sake of offspring, and mentions that members of this party live in all the larger cities of the land.[11] There must have been a significant settlement of the Essenes in Jerusalem, which could not have been without influence on the religious and spiritual life of the city.[12] They took pains over "the written works of the ancients," especially over secret, additional revelatory writings. The spectacular, unique discovery of writings (among other things, remains of more than nine hundred scrolls) in the Essene settlement of Qumran, on the northwest side of the Dead Sea, has confirmed and expanded the picture sketched by Josephus and by other ancient authors such as Philo and Pliny in a surprising way, while also raising many new questions.[13] It is significant that Josephus presents his portrayal of the Jewish religious parties in a certain *interpretatio graeca*, in order to make them understandable for his Greek-Roman readers.

In the case of the Pharisees, Josephus emphasizes that they are the "first (i.e., most significant) school of thought"[14] and that they distinguish themselves by the particular "exactness"[15] of their interpretation of the law. In terms of teaching, they differ from the Essenes through the fact that they

> attribute everything to Fate and to God; they hold that to act rightly or otherwise rests, indeed, for the most part with men, but that in each action Fate co-operates.

In their view, every soul is immortal, but only the souls of the good go into another body at the end of time, whereas the souls of the wicked are punished in the underworld.[16]

---

[11] Josephus, *J.W.* 2.124 (trans. H. St. J. Thackeray, LCL, 371): "They occupy no one city, but settle in large numbers in every town." On the problem of "celibacy," see the excursus at the end of section 4.4.

[12] Josephus mentions the Essene gate (*J.W.* 5.145), which was located at the southwest wall of the city; cf. Hengel 2002, 136; see in detail Riesner 1998, 2–30.

[13] For the ancient accounts of the Essenes, see Adam/Burchard 1972.

[14] πρώτη αἵρεσις: *J.W.* 2.162; cf. *Life* 10. This means that they are for him the most influential group, which fully agrees with the New Testament accounts.

[15] ἀκρίβεια: *J.W.* 2.162–163; *Ant.* 17.41; 19.332; *Life* 191; ἀκριβοῦν: *J.W.* 1.648; cf. 1.108; he also characterizes it as ἀκριβής: *J.W.* 1.110; *Ant.* 20.201. Cf. Acts 22.3; 26.5.

[16] Josephus, *J.W.* 2.163 (trans. H. St. J. Thackeray, LCL, 235). On the term for fate εἱμαρμένη in Josephus, which corresponds to the divine providence (cf. Pss. Sol. 9.4), cf. Schürer 1973–1987, II: 393ff. It is only with reference to the Pharisees that Josephus mentions the "bodily" resurrection in a form that is understandable for his Greek-Roman readers (cf. also *Ag. Ap.* 2.218). The synergy of divine predestination and free will appears in Josephus' theology of history (on this, see note 43 in this chapter), in Pss. Sol. (14.8 and elsewhere), as Deuteronomic heritage and also still in the maxim of Akiba (m. 'Abot 3.19): "Everything is foreseen, but free choice is given." On the topic of freedom of the

By contrast, the Sadducees completely denied the idea of predetermination by fate, for God could not do evil at all, and

> man has the free choice of good or evil, and . . . it rests with each man's will whether he follows the one or the other.[17]

They did not want to know anything of a continued life of souls after death. Thus, they fundamentally denied the notion of the resurrection of the dead, which had been especially furthered by the martyrdoms in the religious emergency under Antiochus IV.[18]

In accord with an ancient consensus, it was also a given for Josephus that "philosophical teaching" included the practice of life that was appropriate to it. Since not all the members of the Jewish people are members or partisans of these "schools," Josephus describes not only their behavior in relation to one another but also their outward influence in relation to their compatriots. The Essenes, more than all other Jews, are bound together by special love,[19] but they separate themselves from the rest of the people through their strict initiation rites and purity regulations. They form a closed association. No outsider has access to their shared activities. A 'novice' is only accepted into the meal fellowship after a three-year period of testing and after committing himself by oaths.[20] The Pharisees are also closely connected with one another, but also strive for unanimity for the benefit of the whole community,[21] i.e., they want to draw the entire people

---

will, see Hengel 2003a, I: 120, 126, 140, 148 (GV = 1988, 221–22, 232–33, 254ff., 268, 294, 420ff.); G. Maier 1971. For the Pharisaic belief in the resurrection, see Hengel 2001a, 139–72 = KS IV, 406–39. The presentation of Josephus corresponds to his *interpretatio graeca*. See also Tacitus, *Hist.* 5.5.3 (trans. C. H. Moore, LCL, 183): *animosque proelio aut suppliciis peremptorum aeternos putant: hinc generandi amor et mortis contemptus* ("they believe that the souls of those who are killed in battle or by the executioner are immortal: hence comes their passion for begetting children and their scorn of death").

[17] Josephus, *J.W.* 2.164–165 (trans. H. St. J. Thackeray, LCL, 387).

[18] Cf. Mark 12.18-27 parr.; Acts 23.6-9.

[19] Josephus, *J.W.* 2.119: φιλάλληλοι δὲ . . . τῶν ἄλλων πλέον.

[20] Josephus, *J.W.* 2.137–142. This is why older scholarship regarded the Essenes as an order of monks and after the discovery of the settlement in Qumran initially viewed it as a sort of "monastery." Cf., e.g., Lietzmann 1999, I: 22 (24): "The Essenes are a proper order of monks, which established its monastery in the cities and especially in the villages of Palestine." Others discovered parallels to the Pythagoreans. See Hengel 2003a, I: 243–47 (GV = 1988, 445–53); Hengel 1996a, 258–94. See further VanderKam 2010, 114ff.

[21] Josephus, *J.W.* 2.166: Φαρισαῖοι . . . φιλάλληλοί τε καὶ τὴν εἰς τὸ κοινὸν ὁμόνοιαν ἀσκοῦντες ("The Pharisees are affectionate to each other and cultivate harmonious relations with the community"; trans. H. St. J. Thackeray, LCL, 387). With τὸ κοινόν he designates the entirety of all citizens, the nation, the authorities, and the people of a community, not the association; see Rengstorf 1973–1983, II: 509.

to their understanding of the Torah. By contrast, the aristocratic-priestly Sadducees are as brusque in their interaction with one another and with their compatriots as one is with foreigners.[22] This corresponds to the typical arrogance of aristocrats.

In the two "catalogues of sects" in the *Jewish Antiquities* Josephus supplements this picture of the spiritual elite and adds some material, especially in the second one, on the Pharisees and Sadducees.[23] He gives an account of this tripartite division of the "philosophical schools" at the right place historically—and not due to literary posturing—in connection with special situations of crisis: once at the accession to power of the Maccabee Jonathan as high priest[24] and then (as in *Jewish War*) in the context of the emergence of the "Fourth Party," which was called into life by Judas the Galilean around 6 CE, when Judas called upon the inhabitants of Judaea in the context of the census to refuse to pay taxes to the Romans.[25] While Josephus emphasizes in *Jewish War* that this Judas was a scribe with very distinctive views, "whose school of thought resembles the other parties in nothing,"[26] he expresses himself in a more nuanced manner ca. fifteen years later in *Jewish Antiquities*: Judas of Gamla in the Gaulanitis is said to have called into life this "Fourth Party," which agreed entirely in its teachings with the Pharisees, but differed from all the rest through an unrestrained love for freedom, which recognized God alone as Lord,[27] and whose revolutionary "innovation and upheaval" especially attracted the youth and led to the revolt against Rome and to the catastrophe of the First Jewish War.[28] This means that they can be regarded as the revolutionary wing of the Pharisaic party of the people. Josephus prefers to use the religiously based party name "Zealots"—which he does not mention here—for the radical priestly insurgents in the

---

[22] *Jewish War* 2.166.

[23] *Antiquities* 13.171–173; cf. 18.11–22.

[24] *Antiquities* 13.171–173 around 153–152 BCE; Nicolaus of Damascus is presumably his source here. The historical point in time is rightly chosen and is confirmed by CD. See section 4.3.2 below. Cf. Saldarini 2000, 119; against Stemberger 1991, 91, who asserts that "Josephus simply inserted an atemporal note redactionally."

[25] On this, see section 3.1.3.

[26] *Jewish War* 2.118. He designates him and his son Menahem (on him, see section 3.1.7) as σοφιστής.

[27] *Antiquities* 18.23: ἡγεμόνα καὶ δεσπότην. Cf. *J.W.* 2.118. On this, see section 3.1.3.

[28] *Antiquities* 18.4–10, 23. On the "program" of Judas, cf. Hengel 1989c, 90–145 (GV = 1976c, 93–150) and section 3.1.3. On the division of the Pharisees in 6 CE or before the outbreak of the war, see Hengel 1989c, 200–206, 402–4 (GV = 1976c, 204–11, 409–10).

First Jewish War.[29] Josephus makes this "Fourth Party" responsible for the radicalization—which led to the catastrophe—of the "zeal" for the law in the fight against the superior power of Rome, whose present rule of the world is included, in his view, within God's providence. For him, as for broad circles of Judaism and early Christianity, Rome is the fourth kingdom of Dan 2 and 7 and possesses its power only until the time determined by God. Therefore, in his view, the Zealots rebel against God's will when they want to force the end to come. Josephus interprets the religious-social component in their revolt against their own upper stratum and against Rome in a one-sided manner as greed and desire to kill. However, prior to the ritually performed mass suicide at the fortress of Masada, he effectively places a final "swan song," which is—ultimately—marked by sympathy, in the mouth of the leader Eleazar ben Yair, who was probably a grandson of Judas the Galilean.[30]

He distinguishes the Pharisees, in turn, from the Sadducees and Essenes. They appeal in their interpretation of the law and in their practice to their "tradition of the fathers," which adapts the law to historical situations, whereas the Sadducees adhere to the conservative and literal interpretation of the law, that is, to the stricter interpretation:

> the Pharisees had passed on to the people certain regulations handed down by former generations and not recorded in the Laws of Moses, for which reason they are rejected by the Sadducean group (γένος), who hold that only those regulations should be considered valid which were written down (in Scripture), and that those which had been handed down by former generations need not be observed. And concerning these matters the two parties came to have controversies and serious differences, the Sadducees having the confidence of the wealthy alone but no following among the populace, while the Pharisees have the support of the masses.[31]

---

[29] Cf. note 390 in chapter 3. On this, see Hengel 1989c, 388–404 (GV = 1976c, 395–412). For Josephus the followers of Judas the Galilean and the "Sicarii" who proceeded from him are not worthy of this name of honor, which is based on the high priest and son of Aaron Phineas (cf. Num 25).

[30] *Jewish War* 7.320–388; cf., by contrast, 7.262–274; on this, see note 391 in chapter 3.

[31] *Antiquities* 13.297–298 (trans. R. Marcus, LCL, 377); Pharisees: νόμιμά τινα παρέδοσαν τῷ δήμῳ . . . ἐκ πατέρων διαδοχῆς; Sadducees: τὰ δ' ἐκ παραδόσεως τῶν πατέρων μὴ τηρεῖν. On the problem of the oral and written Torah, cf. Hengel/Deines 1996, esp. 426–27 (ET = 1995, esp. 30–31). For the polemic of Jesus against the Pharisaic παράδοσις τῶν πατέρων, see Mark 7.8-13 = Matt 15.3-6.

Josephus portrays here the basic conflict of the two most important parties between the time of the Hasmoneans and 70 CE. The Pharisees have success because they are turned to the people with the goal of training them in the proper obedience vis-à-vis the law. With Josephus the New Testament and the later rabbis, as heirs of the Pharisees, regard this adherence to and handing down of extra-biblical "tradition of the fathers" as the characteristic feature of Pharisaic teaching.[32] Later Josephus emphasizes again the fundamental readiness of the Pharisees to defend this tradition also with force, and the success that they have among the people on the basis of their teaching, entirely in contrast to the Sadducees:

> The Pharisees simplify their standard of living, making no concession to luxury. They follow the guidance of that which their doctrine (ὁ λόγος) has selected and transmitted (παρέδωκεν) as good, attaching the chief importance to the observance of those commandments which it has seen fit to dictate to them. They show respect and deference to their elders, nor do they rashly presume to contradict their proposals . . . the good souls receive an easy passage to a new life. Because of these views they are, as a matter of fact, extremely influential among the townsfolk; and *all prayers and sacred rites of divine worship* are performed according to their exposition. This is the great tribute that the inhabitants of the cities, by practicing the highest ideals both in their way of living and in their discourse, have paid to the excellence of the Pharisees.[33]

According to Josephus, the success of the Pharisees is due, in addition to their exactness in the interpretation of the law, especially to their "doctrine of souls," which had discovered, in correspondence to the spirit of the Hellenistic time, the salvation of the individual. Temple cult and Pharisaic piety belong together here, for the law regulates the divinely desired performance of the cult in the temple. The placement of the prayers before the sacrifices can presumably be viewed also as a pointer to the synagogue worship services.[34]

> The doctrine (ὁ λόγος) of the Sadducees holds that the soul perishes along with the body. They own no observance of any sort apart from the laws;[35] in fact, they reckon it a virtue to debate with the teachers of the path of wisdom that they pursue. There are but few men to whom

---

[32] Mark 7.3, 5, 8-13; m. ʾAbot 1.1ff.

[33] Josephus, *Ant.* 18.12–15 (trans. L. H. Feldman, LCL, 11, 13; our emphasis).

[34] Cf. Hengel/Deines 1996, 430 n. 101 (ET = 1995, 33 n. 86).

[35] On this, cf. Schröder 1996, 114ff.

this doctrine has been made known, but these are men of the highest standing. They accomplish practically nothing, however. For whenever they assume some office, though they submit unwillingly and perforce, yet submit they do to the formulas of the Pharisees, since otherwise the masses would not tolerate them.[36]

The "highest standing" pertains to the aristocracy, in the first instance to the priestly aristocracy and—with lesser influence—to the lay aristocracy of large estate holders, mostly former Hasmonean military leaders and influential heads of clans. The small number of followers and the relative lack of influence of this party is a consequence of the collapse of Hasmonean rule. They were persecuted by Herod and regained a certain—political—power only under the Roman prefects in Jerusalem and in the temple. Their direct influence upon the people was not very large.[37] With regard to the Essenes, Josephus adds what he had passed over in his long report on the sects in *Jewish War*, for example that they send only votive offerings to the Jerusalem temple, whereas they do not sacrifice there but rather have their own rites. This distance vis-à-vis the temple is confirmed also by the Qumran writings.[38]

In his autobiography—an apologetic appendix to *Jewish Antiquities*, where Josephus defends himself[39] against a competitor, Justus of Tiberias, especially because of his participation in the Jewish revolt at the beginning of the war, and adds or corrects some background to the events that were communicated in rather summary form in *Jewish War*—Josephus reports that he passed through the three schools himself in order to be able to "choose the best,"[40] while also attaching himself in youthful enthusiasm to an ascetic Bannus, who lived by the Jordan and chastened himself not only through special asceticism with regard to food and clothing but also

---

[36] *Antiquities* 18.16–17 (trans. L. H. Feldman, LCL, 15, 17, modified).

[37] Cf. Acts 4.1; 5.17. Josephus rarely mentions the party affiliation of persons. Annas II is designated once as a Sadducee (*Ant.* 20.199). But the rabbinic accounts confirm the picture in Acts; cf. Stern 1987, 610ff.

[38] The account of the Essenes in Josephus, *Ant.* 18, has such clear points of contact with the discussion in Philo that the agreements are best explained by the assumption that the two of them used a similar source or that Josephus directly relied on Philo; cf. Schürer 1973–1987, II: 562. Philo, *Prob.* 75, and Josephus, *Ant.* 18.18–22, mention the number four thousand, the rejection of animal sacrifice, agriculture as the predominant work, and the rejection of slavery; all this is lacking in *J.W.* 2.119–161.

[39] Mason 2003, 121–31, opposes this older consensus of scholarship. According to Mason, Josephus, following rhetorical convention, presents a sketch of his own character in *Life*. Cf. the introduction to his commentary (Mason 2001, xlviiiff.) The apologetic character of *Life* in the late period of Domitian, is, however, clear.

[40] *Life* 10: οὕτως γὰρ ᾠόμην αἱρήσεσθαι τὴν ἀρίστην; cf. *Life* 10–12.

through ritual washings.[41] After the course of his three-year study he turned to a public career path at the age of nineteen and chose the "best party," i.e., that of the Pharisees. For Josephus, following a party involves personal "choice" (αἵρεσις) and the decision of the individual, which demonstrates at the same time the appropriateness of the designation "choice" for the respective parties[42] and also reveals once more the importance of the Pharisees. In Josephus their party appears as the most influential group in religious and political questions from the time of Salome Alexandra (see section 3.1.1), and the Zealots formed their "extreme left wing," which was close to the nationally oriented school of Shammai, from the time of Judas the Galilean.

The self-confident portrayal of Josephus regarding his education and his following of the Pharisees has not only been called into question in scholarship[43] but also criticized as a collecting point for everyday

---

[41] He may have been an earlier representative of the daily baptizers, hemerobaptists, mentioned in later "catalogues of sects." On this, see Rudolph 1999. He forms a parallel of sorts to John the Baptist; see section 9.3.

[42] LSJ, s.v. αἵρεσις: "system of philosophic principles, or those who profess such principles, sect, school." On the Christians as a Jewish αἵρεσις, cf. Acts 24.5, 14; 28.22. On the shift of meaning of the term, cf. note 44 in chapter 1. The translation of πολιτεύμαι is difficult. According to *Life* 258, 262 it more likely has the nuance of "to exercise an official office." Josephus was probably consecrated to be a priest at nineteen years of age. One need not think here of a proper joining of a party, for the Pharisees formed an open association. Whether one was a Pharisee was decided by one's relation to the law (cf. Phil 3.5-6) and one's way of life. Josephus' interpretation of the law is Pharisaic; cf. Hengel/ Deines 1996, 435 n. 113 (no equivalent in the ET).

[43] Siegert 2001, 163 (so also Mason and Saldarini 2000, 118 etc.): "A proper belonging of Josephus to the Pharisees, which he never mentions elsewhere, is . . . to be called into question . . . in light of (his) . . . widely critical presentation of Pharisees. . . . Only to the extent that he wanted to exercise political influence . . . did he orient himself to the Pharisaic partner." Thus it is said that Josephus gave his sympathy to the Essenes, in his heart he is said to have remained an aristocratic Sadducee and, like them, followed the Pharisees in his public career only out of 'opportunism.' However, as Josephus presents the three parties in terms of their teaching, he belonged to those who let divine providence and free will work together; cf., for example, *J.W.* 6.310 (trans. H. St. J. Thackeray, LCL, 467): "Reflecting on these things one will find that God has a care for men, and by all kinds of premonitory signs shows His people the way of salvation, while they owe their destruction to the folly and calamities of their own choosing." With this Josephus explains not only the destruction of the Jerusalem temple; this view, which is Deuteronomistic in terms of its origin, determines his theology of history as that of the Psalms of Solomon (see section 3.1.1 and note 16 in this chapter). His high estimation of the book of Daniel, with its apocalyptic worldview, which the Sadducees firmly rejected, and other observations also reveal a stance that is indeed Pharisaic. When, in addition to a member of the high priestly families, three Pharisees belonged to the group of four sent from Jerusalem (*Life* 189–207), who supported John of Gischala and intended to remove Josephus as commander in Galilee, then this not only confirms the well-known rivalry among the leaders of the revolt from

topoi.[44] However, he remains—even in light of the discoveries from Qumran (see section 4.2)—the most important "eyewitness" for the New Testament period, and one should not underestimate his intimate knowledge of the Jewish religious parties in view of the seemingly stereotypical specifications in the catalogue of sects, for it is in this way that they achieve an understandable form for his readers. Besides Paul, who says "with regard to the law a Pharisee"[45] in relation to his pre-Christian outlook, Josephus is the only ancient author still known to us who assigns himself to this party. Both Paul and Josephus indicate that what is primarily characteristic for the designation "Pharisee" is an intensive attachment to the law, which is interpreted according to the oral tradition of the fathers. This "ancestral tradition" makes it possible to adapt the interpretation of the regulations of the law to the respective circumstances and demands of the time.[46]

Josephus has been criticized for describing the Jewish religious parties in such a Greek guise.[47] But why should he, after the catastrophe of 70 CE, suddenly break with the tried and tested form of introducing these parties to a Gentile readership?[48] Josephus, like Philo and the early Jewish

---

the beginning but also shows how divided the Pharisaic party was at the beginning of the revolt, when Shammites fought bloodily. Family bonds, old friendships, and political inclination carried more weight here than pure "party affiliation." Moreover, Josephus with his "maneuverings" was suspected of leaning toward the Romans or wanting to seize power in Jerusalem. On the division of the Pharisees right before the outbreak of the war, see Hengel 1989c, 200–206, 402–4 (GV = 1976c, 204–11, 409–10). On the radical, anti-foreigner eighteen halakhot of the school of Shammai that led to the discontinuation of the sacrifice for the emperor, see Hengel 1989c, 358ff. (GV = 1976c, 365ff.).

[44] Thus Mason 2003, 39: "it brims with rhetorical commonplaces"; cf. Mason 2001, 21.

[45] Phil 3:5-6: κατὰ νόμον Φαρισαῖος κατὰ ζῆλος διώκων τὴν ἐκκλησίαν. Cf. Gal 1.13-14; Acts 22.3. On this, see Hengel 2002, 68–192 (130ff.).

[46] Deines 2001a, 492–93. The "prosbul" (proviso) of Hillel (m. Giṭ. 4.3; m. Šebu. 10.3–7; b. Giṭ. 36a–b) is the most well-known example of how the biblical law is reinterpreted in order to preserve its meaning among other conditions (here the change to monetary transactions). With this proviso introduced into the certified document in court, a moneylender could prevent his loan from being lost in the year of the Sabbath with the remission of debts. The alternative would have been the fundamental refusal to give loans, with catastrophic social consequences.

[47] Cf. Lietzmann 1999, I: 20 (22): "On multiple occasions Josephus takes pleasure in telling his readers about the 'philosophical schools' of the Jews and puts forth all sorts of things about Pharisees and Sadducees, which taste like philosophy, but are suitable for impeding the understanding of the real opposition."

[48] In the diaspora (and probably also in Rome) the worship in the synagogues with prayer, reading of Scripture, and predominantly ethical preaching was regarded as a philosophical meeting and had an attractive impact as such. Pagan cults did not have anything comparable to offer. Philo proceeds in the same way in his description of the Essenes as model students of Moses and true philosophers (Philo, *Prob.*). See also his apology for Judaism *Hypothetica* (Fragment apud Eusebius, *Praep. ev.* 8.11.1–18). Philo explains the behavior of the Roman governor in Syria, Petronius, during the Caligula crisis by stating

'apologists,'[49] takes up this positively regarded, attractive side of Judaism when he describes the religious parties of his people as philosophical schools comparable to the Stoics and the Pythagoreans.[50] Moreover, every educated reader was aware that the Greek philosophical schools were also politically active. These philosophical schools were also not concerned with mere abstract theory, but especially with the proper, ethical way of living.

He does not coordinate the ascetic Bannus with any of the 'philosophical' elites, but he also does not say that Bannus guided him into the Pharisaic school. We also hear nothing from him about the relationship of John the Baptist and Jesus of Nazareth to the parties. Only in his account of Annas II, whom he explicitly designates as a Sadducee here, and in the execution of James, the brother of the Lord, is it recognizable that it must have been above all Pharisees who reacted with outrage to the judicial murder of James and other Jewish Christians.[51]

When Josephus speaks of concrete incidents (see section 4.3 below), we learn more precisely that the controversies within the Jewish parties, the reasons why they insisted on differentiation, were based in their different interpretations of the 'Mosaic law.'

The Jewish parties are basically reduced to two in the Synoptic Gospels. In Mark the opponents of Jesus in Galilee are above all Pharisees: once in combination with the Herodians—i.e., partisans of the ruler Herod

---

that he was probably not entirely without knowledge of the Jewish "philosophy"; cf. note 255 in chapter 3.

[49] They turned Abraham and Moses into philosophers, lawgivers, and founders of a religion, who were older than the Greeks, who took their wisdom from them; cf., for example, Artapanos, Aristobulus, Letter of Aristeas, and then Philo (especially in his *Life of Moses*) and Josephus (for example, *Ant.* 1.158–159; *Ag. Ap.* 2.154). Cf. Hengel 1996a, 210–11, 241–42, 250: "The certainty of the greater antiquity of their own religion or of the dependence of the Greek thinkers on Moses and Abraham was able to strengthen the trust in the truth and superiority of their own faith and attract pagan sympathizers." In Ps.-Clem. Hom. 4–6 a Jewish apology from the second century is preserved (4.8.1; 4.13.3: ὁ δὲ . . . Ἰουδαίων λόγος εὐσεβέστατός ἐστιν). These views also radiated into the motherland.

[50] Josephus, *Life* 12: Pharisees = Stoics; *Ant.* 15.371: Essenes = Pythagoreans; he classifies the Sadducees neither with the Epicurians nor with the Cynics. While he does not mention the Cynics at all, he designates the Epicureans as deniers of divine providence and guidance of the world (*Ant.* 10.278ff.), which he views as refuted by the prophecies of Daniel. In Jerusalem Alexander lets himself be convinced by the book of Daniel that victory over the Persians is granted to him (*Ant.* 11.337). Therefore, among the Jews an Epicurean view of God exists just as little as an atheistic one (*Ag. Ap.* 2.180–181). Nevertheless, his description of the Sadducees calls the Epicureans to mind. Philo of Alexandria follows a similar tendency as Josephus when he sings the praises of the Jewish Therapeutai, a group related to the Essenes that was located near Lake Mareotis in Lower Egypt, and of the Essenes in Palestine; see Philo, *Contempl.*; *Prob.*; *Hypoth.* 11.1–18.

[51] *Antiquities* 20.199–203; cf. note 346 in chapter 3 and section 20.2.2.

Antipas—and once with scribes who come from Jerusalem (Mark 3.6; 7.1). Mark distinguishes more clearly between Pharisees and scribes than Matthew later, but he regards the latter to be the leading group of the Pharisees, who are committed to the study of the law. Thus, we may be dealing with "ideal scenes" in which what is typical is portrayed, because Jesus' behavior elicits Pharisaic protest. Emphasis is placed on Jesus' closeness to sinners and his forgiveness of sins,[52] his nonascetic way of life, his freedom vis-à-vis Pharisaic purity practices such as the washing of the hands before eating,[53] and the conflicts due to his healings on the Sabbath.[54] In a historically appropriate way, the Sadducees appear only in Jerusalem. Their controversy dialogue with Jesus pertains to the question of the resurrection.[55] This means that ideal scenes can very well have a historical background. There are multiple references to the tripartite group of high priests, elders, and scribes as opponents of Jesus in the Markan passion narrative. They form the leadership of the Jewish aristocracy in the Sanhedrin, which consisted of the officiating high priest with members of the high priestly families, the elders as the lay nobility, and the scribes as the legal specialists. They send some Pharisees and Herodians to Jesus with the catch question of whether one may pay taxes to the emperor.[56] In the passion narrative, the hierarchs, as the politically powerful leadership group, are not coordinated *expressis verbis* to the religious parties.[57] In his Gospel and in Acts Luke makes further specifications that show that he has knowledge of reliable tradition and, in some cases, unique details. We learn only from him that Jesus accepts the hospitality of Pharisees, and controversial questions regarding ritual purity are discussed in the conversation at the table. At the same time, in 12.1 he retains the warning against the "leaven of the Pharisees."[58] This Pharisaic interest in Jesus in Luke emphasizes—even more than in the Markan account—the attentiveness of the Pharisees to the people. Among other things, it may be connected with their shared eschatological expectation. The family of Jesus probably came from a Pharisaic milieu (see section 8.3). The bitter opponents of

---

[52] Mark 2.16; Luke 7.36-50; cf. 5.21, 30; 15.2.

[53] Mark 7.1-5; Luke 11.37-38.

[54] Mark 2.23-24, 27-28 parr.; 3.1-6 parr. Cf. Doering 1999, 398–478.

[55] Mark 12.18-27 parr. Cf. Acts 23.8. See section 18.4.

[56] Mark 12.13-17 parr.; cf. already 3.6. In the actual trial against Jesus the Pharisees are no longer mentioned.

[57] On this, cf. section 19.2.

[58] Luke 7.36-39; 11.37-54; 14.1-6; 12.1; cf. Mark 8.15. The interpretation of their teaching and education on the law, which penetrates everything as leaven, as "hypocrisy," in 12.1 is a Lukan addition; Mark 8.15 warns Jesus against the leaven of Herod (Antipas); Matt 16.6 adds in addition the Sadducees, about whom he no longer has a proper notion; see note 70 in chapter 18.

the apostles and of the primitive community in Jerusalem are for about thirty-five years the Sadducean hierarchs, whereas the Pharisaic school head Gamaliel acted more cautiously and with a wait-and-see attitude.[59]

Around 150 CE Justin mentions Sadducees, Genists, Merists, Galileans, Hellenians, Pharisees, and Baptists as Jewish sects.[60] In this enigmatic list he starts from the number seven. Independent of him, Hegesippus, around 170, speaks multiple times of seven parties that are said to have existed within the Jewish people at the time of Jesus and lists Essenes, Galileans, Hemerobaptists, Masbotheans, Samaritans, Sadducees, and Pharisees.[61] Hegesippus and Justin probably use "Galileans" to designate the inhabitants of Galilee and not the Zealots, the followers of Judas the Galilean.[62] Day-baptizers and Masbotheans are baptist sects; in Justin they are summarized under the term "Baptists." Justin, who comes from Neapolis in Samaria, does not view the Samaritans as a Jewish religious party but rather regards them as cousins, who, like the Jews, worship the true God and expect the Messiah, and who, like them, do not believe in Jesus and are in danger of allowing themselves to be led astray by false teachers such as Simon Magus.[63] In any case, an even greater diversity in Palestinian Judaism is visible in these obscure early Christian texts than is mediated to us in Josephus' account of the parties.

The attestations about the Jewish parties at the time of Jesus in the rabbinic literature mostly come from the Tannaitic period, i.e., from the second century CE. Thus, they appear to be not so far removed in time. However, the recollections of that time are subject to an inner censorship, which has reshaped them.[64] Nevertheless, characteristic features of the Sadducees surface in the discussions between Sadduceans/Boetheans and the "wise"

---

[59] Acts 4.1-23; 5.17-42. On this, see section 19.1.

[60] *Dialogue* 80.4; οἱ γενισταί—appear to be attested only here; Isidore of Seville (*Etymologiae* 8.4.8) explains οἱ μερισταί as *meristae appellati eo quod separent scripturas, non credentes omnibus prophetis, dicentes aliis et aliis spiritibus illos prophetasse*.

[61] Eusebius, *Hist. eccl.* 4.22.7. Cf. Hippolytus, *Haer.* 9.18–30 (does not, however, mention the 'baptist sects'); Ps.-Clem. Rec. 1.53–54; Const. ap. 6.61; Epiphanius, *Ancoratus* 13.3–15; *Pan.* 16.1ff.; 19.1–6; 53.1–9. On the Samaritans, see Pummer 2002.

[62] A different position is still advocated in Hengel 1989c, 58ff. (GV = 1976c, 59ff.); on the Christians as "Galileans" in Epictetus (*Diatr.* 4.7.6), cf. note 87 in chapter 6 and Hengel 2004c, 106–10.

[63] *First Apol.* 53.3–7. Cf. Pummer 2002, 27; on his origin, see Justin, *1 Apol.* 1.1; on Simon Magus and the Samaritans, see *1 Apol.* 26.3.

[64] Cf. Stemberger 1999, 437ff. on the controversy between Sadducees (Boetheans) and Pharisees in rabbinic literature. On the rabbinic censorship, which reshaped the haggadic material more strongly than the halakic, cf. Hengel 2002, 133ff., 145ff., and elsewhere. In addition, the general term *mînîm*, the "heretic," which included especially also the Jewish Christians, also appeared.

over questions of the law and the regulations on ritual purity,[65] which we learn about in Josephus only in general form. Thus he describes the Sadducees as "more heartless than all other Jews,"[66] and indirectly signals that this is to be attributed to their strict, conservative criminal law in capital processes. The scroll of fasting—a calendar with national holidays—lists the fourth Tammuz (June/July) as a festival day on which one may not fast: "On the fourth Tammuz the book of the regulations (presumably a Sadducean criminal law book) was removed."[67]

By contrast, the abstract "ideal" criminal law of the Mishnah appears to attribute a more humane stance to the Sadducees in some cases: Whoever has born false witness may only be stoned if a judgment of death was carried out on the basis of this witness. The "wise" as heirs of the Pharisees, however, impose the judgment (of death) over the false witnesses as soon as he has pronounced his false witness.[68] The (Pharisaic) opinion of the wise appears only superficially as "more heartless," for it is meant to more effectively protect the innocent person who is being accused. In another case as well, the Pharisaic-rabbinic interpretation of the law appears stricter at first glance. According to Sadducean opinion, the master is responsible for the deeds of his slaves and not only for the harm that his animal has caused. By contrast, the Pharisees regard the master to be only responsible for his animal, whereas they regard the slaves as accountable human beings with their own free will. The Sadducean stance corresponds to the conservative, rich aristocrats, estate holders, who possess their slaves like animals and precisely for this reason are fully responsible for them.[69]

The religious motivation for the Sadducees' stance of rejection vis-à-vis the teaching of the resurrection of the dead and the reward in judgment in

---

[65] The didactic letter 4QMMT from Qumran (on this, see below) shows that such controversies were already conducted in the middle of the second century BCE.

[66] *Ant.* 20.199; cf. *Ant.* 13.294.

[67] Megillat Ta'anit 12; cf. Beyer 1984, 356. The festival day more likely refers to an event at the time of Alexandra Salome than to an event at the beginning of the First Jewish War; Stemberger 1999, 437, leaves the question open. The scroll of fasts lists festival days that recall events from the Maccabean revolt until the beginning of the Jewish War; for their Pharisaic character, cf. Beyer 1984, 356; Deines 2001a, 484ff. The perspective of the festival list is rigorously nationalistic and anti-Sadducean, a document of the radical wing of the Pharisees, i.e., the Shammites and Zealots.

[68] m. Makkot 1.6. The stance of the wise corresponds to the model of Daniel in the Susanna narrative. On the Sadducee–Pharisee controversy in rabbinic literature, cf. Instone-Brewer 1992, 88–118.

[69] m. Yadayim 4.7. Cf. Stemberger 1999, 437.

the beyond (cf. Isa 66.5-6, 14-15) might appear in the note of Antigonus of Sokho (ca. 180 CE) in m. 'Abot 1.3:

> Do not be like servants who serve the master under the condition of receiving a reward but be like servants who serve the master not under the condition of receiving a reward. And may the fear of God be over you.

In 'Abot R. Nat. A 5 this saying is later continued and quoted for the beginning of the Sadducean movement.[70] Here the conflict does not emerge over the contestation of the idea of reward in Antigonus, but a quarrel arises only "over the denial of the beyond and the resurrection."[71] In the rabbinic tradition as well, the Sadducees continue to be characterized by their rejection of the resurrection and by their wealth. In the second recension Zadok and Boethus become students of Antigonus and not separated from him by three generations.[72] The legendary line of tradition, which makes "Zadok" and "Boethus" into a pair, truncates historical recollection in personalized form. Moreover, it remains uncertain whether the saying of Antigonus reflects the religious earnestness of the Sadducees in the first century CE or from an earlier time.[73] At any rate, it calls to mind Ecclesiastes' sapiential admonition to fear God, its exhortation to proper joy in life in the thought of death.[74] In 'Abot of Rabbi Nathan a lingering echo of

---

[70] "Antigonus of Sokkho had two students, who learned his words. And they taught (them) to students, and (these) students (taught them again) to students. They stood up and tested and said . . . Alone, had our Fathers known that there was another world and (that) there was a resurrection of the dead, they would not have spoken in this way. They stood up and separated themselves from the Torah, and from them there spread two sects, the Sadducees and the Boethoseans; the Sadducees were named after Zadok, the Boethoseans were named after Boethus. And they used silver vessels and golden vessels all their lives. For they were (admittedly) not haughty toward them (i.e., the Pharisees); but the Sadducees say: It is among the Pharisees a tradition that they chasten themselves in this world, and in the coming world they have nothing." According to m. 'Abot 1.4 the legitimate (Pharisaic) line of tradition goes via the student of Antigonus Jose ben Joezer and Jose ben Jochanan. Cf. also Schremer 1997.

[71] Avemarie 1996, 366.

[72] 'Abot R. Nat. B 10 (Schechter 1887, 26). On this, see Avemarie 1996, 367–68. In this way the emergence of the party of the Sadducees in the Maccabean period, portrayed with typical rabbinic reshaping, would come near the temporal approximation obtained through Josephus and the Qumran texts.

[73] Cf. Stemberger 1999, 441, who refers to the parallel in Ps.-Clem. Rec, 1.54. The Sadducees deny the resurrection *dicentes non esse dignum ut quasi sub mercede proposita colatur deus* ("saying that it is not appropriate for God to be worshiped as if for promised pay"; trans. F. S. Jones 1995, 87).

[74] Cf. Gese 1996, 93, 97: "Kohelet positively regards the limitation of human knowing in principle as the . . . basis of the fear of God. . . . The knowledge of the limit enables joyfulness." Hengel 2003a, I: 128 (GV = 1988, 236): "When Sadduceans and Boethusians

Sadducean theology could have been preserved, which—as Ecclesiastes and Sirach show—does not end in pure skepticism, let alone atheism, but rather takes seriously human knowledge in its limitations.[75]

In our view, Josephus does indeed provide a materially appropriate reproduction of the situation of the parties in the catalogue of the sects and in his *Life*. His picture corresponds to an astonishing degree to the picture in the New Testament and in the early rabbinic literature. Thus, alongside the rich sources made accessible by the Dead Sea scrolls, it rightly remains the main witness for the picture of the parties in the first century CE, which is supplemented by the New Testament, individual apocrypha and pseudepigrapha, archaeological discoveries, and rabbinic accounts, whereas the later Christian catalogues of sects in Justin, Hegesippus, and Epiphanius remain enigmatic to some extent.

4.2 The Modification of the Picture of the Parties through the Discoveries from Qumran

The discoveries at Qumran have confirmed the basic tripartite division of Josephus. Under the cover names "Judah," "Ephraim," and "Manasseh," the Nahum commentary mentions the Qumran Essenes, the Pharisees, and the Sadducees.[76] The simple people stand under the influence of "Ephraim" and is therefore designated by the Pesher with the phrase

---

were associated with later generations of the pupils of Antigonus, defending the enjoyment of life because they were without hope for the coming world, historical accuracy may have been strained, but justification was certainly present."

[75] Since the literary witnesses with a Sadducean "tendency"—apart from Ecclesiastes, Sirach (with qualifications, i.e., without the later additions), and 1 Maccabees—are so rare, the corresponding grave inscriptions obtain special weight. The Aramaic and Greek inscriptions in the Jerusalem tomb of Jason, a rich priestly family tomb from the time around 100 BCE, which was looted by Herod I, speak the same language. In Greek "Rejoice, you living, brothers, and drink together, no one is immortal"; in Aramaic the fourfold wish of peace is conspicuous (שלם). Cf. Hengel 2003a, I: 60, 124; II: 150 n. 754 (GV = 1988, 112, 228, 412 n. 688); Horbury 1994b, 43: "The agreement on the finality of death between the majority of the inscriptions (in Egypt) and the Greek Ecclesiasticus . . . suggests that a broadly Sadducaic position on death was influential among Jews in both Egypt and Judaea in the late Ptolemaic and early Roman periods." This may apply especially to the priestly aristocracy of the Oniads at the temple of Leontopolis. For the reconstruction of the Tomb of Jason inscription, see Avigad 1967; Beyer 1984, 328–29; Puech 1983, 492ff.; on the discussion, cf. Park 2000, 29–30, 67–72, 96–97. It is not without reason that Paul cites Isa 22.13 in 1 Cor 15.32; cf. Eccl 9.5.7 as well as 2.24; 3.12ff., 22; 5.17; 8.15.

[76] With "Ephraim" and "Manasseh" the names of the disloyal northern tribes are used for the opponents. "Judaea" serves as their self-designation. "Israel" means the whole people. Cf. CD, on this, see section 4.3.2. On the problem of this interpretation, cf. Stemberger 1991, 104–5; Deines 2001a, 476–77.

"simple ones of Ephraim." They let themselves be led astray by the ones who "seek after smooth things," i.e., by the Pharisaic teachers, who interpret the Torah "hypocritically" in a "smooth" way that lightens the specifications of the law.[77] In the present "Judah" has no influence on "the simple ones of Ephraim" and is, on the face of it, completely defeated by the Pharisees, but in the future

> when the glory of Judah is revealed, the simple ones of Ephraim will flee from their assembly and leave those who mislead them and will join [the entirety of Is]rael.[78]

At that time the counsel of those who "seek after smooth things" will perish. Then the "simple ones" will allow themselves to be guided by the Essenes.[79] Also the aristocratic party of the Sadducees, "the great ones of Manasseh, the nobles," who possess "warriors and heroes of war"—that is, who have control of the military power—will lose the rule over Israel at the end of time:

> His women, his infants, and his children will go into captivity, his heroes and his nobles [will fall] by the sword.[80]

Numerous allusions to contemporary history in this interpretation of the book of Nahum make it probable that the Pesher reflects the situation after the appearance of the Romans under Pompey—they are called *kittim*—and the plundering of the temple by Crassus and looks back to the past under Demetrius III Eucaerus, Alexander Jannaeus—he is called Angry Lion—and Queen Alexandra Salome. The bitter controversy is

---

[77] 4QpNah Frag. 3–4 II, 8: "[Its] interpretation concerns those who mislead Ephraim, who through deceptive teaching . . . mislead many, kings, princes, priests, and people together with proselytes. . . ." Cf. III, 3: "Its interpretation concerns those who seek after smooth things (*dôrše ha-ḥᵃlaqôt*), whose evil deeds will be exposed to all Israel in the final time." "*Dôrše ha-ḥᵃlaqôt*" is a wordplay with allusion to Isa 30.10; Dan 11.32ff. and presumably stands in place of *dôrše ha-hᵃlakhôt*, those seeking (lightened) *halakhot*. Cf. 4QpIsaᶜ Frag. 23 10; 4QpNah Frag. 3–4 III, 3.7; 4QMidrEschat IX 12, 13: "They are the congregation of those who seek after sm[ooth] things, who seek to to destroy [the men of the congregation] through their jealousy and through [their] hostility . . ." (text and translation after Steudel 2001, 205; cf. García Martínez / Tigchelaar 1997/1998, I: 365); see further Flusser 1981, 127ff.; Deines 2001a, 476–77.

[78] 4QpNah Frag. 3–4 III, 4–5. Cf. the different reconstruction and translation in García Martínez / Tigchelaar 1997/1998, I: 339.

[79] Deines 2001a, 476 n. 114: "To teach the 'simple' and to join . . . them together in the יחד is the expressed purpose of the Qumran-community (see 11QPs 18:3–4 . . .)."

[80] 4QpNah Frag. 3–4 IV, 4.

conducted especially with the powerful Pharisees, whose influence upon the people with respect to questions of the law is regarded as especially dangerous in the eyes of the Qumran Essenes. Because the law possesses a soteriological function, in the fact that it regulates the cult and the life of persons, its scrupulous interpretation is vital.[81] The Nahum Pesher and other Essene texts as well as Josephus and the Gospels forbid underplaying the importance of the Pharisees in the first century BCE and CE.

The most important discovery from Qumran for the early history of the Jewish parties (4QMMT) is a didactic letter that is halakic, i.e., concerned with the ritual law on the basis of the interpretation of Pentateuch, Prophets, and Psalms (an early attestation for the canon), behind which stands the authority of the Teacher of Righteousness and which is presumably aimed at the Maccabean Jonathan, before he became high priest.[82] It likewise confirms the fundamental "tripartite division" of Josephus and also grants—without "Greek guise"—insight into the inner conflicts in the middle of the second century BCE. The author of the letter writes "we" and directs his presentation of the ritual law—for which twenty-two controversial cases are provided, which are primarily related to ritual impurity and sacrifice—at a group, which is addressed with "you [pl]" (or "you [sg]" and "your people"). The views of a third group—they are called "they"—are rejected. The letter seeks to win the agreement of the group addressed with "you [pl]" to its own position in the interpretation of the law and—in contrast to later Pesher texts on the question of parties—does not contain sharp polemic.[83] Initially an agreement had been hoped for. However, the senders stress, in an unmistakable manner,

> we have separated ourselves from the mass of the people and from all its impurity,[84]

because, in their priestly perspective, the holiness of Israel, Jerusalem, and the temple is violated by false rites in the temple service and by

---

[81] Deines 2001a, 493.

[82] 4Q171 IV 7–9; Qimron/Strugnell 1994, 117–21; cf. A. Lange in Lichtenberger/Lange 1997, 53–54: "MMT is . . . a letter of priestly circles to a Hasmonean ruler" (54). Qimron/Strugnell 1994, 121, dates it in the years 159–152 BCE.

[83] Cf. the conclusion of the writing, which stresses: "We have seen that you have wisdom and knowledge of the Torah. Consider all these things and seek him that he may strengthen your will . . ." (C 27–32); Qimron/Strugnell 1994, 62–63. For the translation, cf. also J. Maier 1995–1996, II: 375–76.

[84] C 7–8; Qimron/Strugnell 1994, 58–59, cf. 133. Here we have the first attestation for פרש, prš, with the meaning "to separate oneself from the people"; it is not yet established as a party designation for the Pharisees. The later Essene terminology "turned aside from the way of the people" (סור) takes up biblical language.

illegitimate marriages. A few years earlier, at the end of 164 BCE, after the crisis triggered by the Hellenistic reformers, the temple had been purified and rededicated by Judas Maccabeus. At this time rites were also introduced, against which this writing protests. The author strictly insists that the ritual commandments must be kept in agreement with the literal sense of Scripture and condemns all attempts to adapt the performance of the law to the demands of the time. In this regard, the "we" and the "you [pl]" groups advocate the later Sadducean position in the interpretation of the law, whereas the view of the party rejected with the designation "they" corresponds to the Pharisaic perspective.[85] Thus, 4QMMT shows that later discussions in the Mishnah were already being carried out in the middle of the second century BCE.

In one of the six manuscripts a calendar that follows a solar calendar of 364 days is placed before this foundational document. The different calendars preserved in Qumran sometimes present in parallel the solar calendar of 364 days and the lunar calendar of 354 days, together with the arrangements for acting priests, for which a six-year comprehensive cycle is then obtained. They designate the months with cardinal numbers and not—as is the case for the priesthood in Jerusalem—with the month names of Nisan to Adar, which correspond to the Seleucidian calendar. This "Qumranite" calendar avoids movable feasts and serves to sanctify the Sabbath in a special way, for in this calendar no annual festival can fall on a Sabbath, and ritual festival obligations and Sabbath rest do not conflict with each other. Such an ideal calendar also serves to ensure complete correspondence to the heavenly order with the worship service of the angels.[86]

In questions of ritual purity (and secondarily in the question of the correct calendar) the pious in Qumran were not willing to make any compromises. Therefore, they separated themselves from the majority of the people and from the cult in the Jerusalem temple. They understood themselves as "a holy house for Israel and the foundation of the holy of holies for Aaron," as a temple of people, in order "to atone for the land" and in the wilderness to prepare a way for God through the study of the law in the last time before the imminently expected final judgment and eschatological

---

[85] For discussion, cf. Qimron/Strugnell 1994, 116–17; Deines 2001a, 463–74.

[86] Qimron/Strugnell 1994, 203. First Enoch and Jubilees also follow the calendar of 364 days. It is likewise followed by the description of the worship service in community with the angels in the Songs of the Sabbath Sacrifice, which—even if it arose in Hasidic, pre-Essene circles—was held in special esteem in Qumran. In the case of the calendars handed down by the Qumran Essenes we are presumably dealing with older priestly calendars that were changed in the Jerusalem temple during the Hellenistic reform in connection with the Seleucid cultic calendar (Dan 7.25; 1 Macc 1.45–47, 59; 2 Macc 6.7); cf. VanderKam 1981. On this, see further Albani 1997.

salvation for the members of the *yaḥad*, to which also "Israel" will then have joined itself.[87] While the Essenes overintensify their requirements for purity, so that they could be practiced by only a (small) portion of the people, and for precisely this reason had to separate themselves from the Jerusalem temple, which was unclean for them, the Pharisees wanted to be a holiness movement for the whole people and land. The requirements for holiness were prescribed by the Torah for all Israel and for the land that God had given to Israel. For precisely this reason, the Pharisees insisted on a graded extension of the purity specifications, but they did not simply want to transfer general priestly regulations and prerogatives to all Jews in Eretz Israel.[88]

Points of contact with the Sadducees exist not only in the Essene interpretation of the law, for in Qumran there are also biblical manuscripts in Palaeo-Hebrew script, which allow one to infer the influence of Sadducean scribal scholarship.[89] In general the "library" preserved in the caves of Qumran has massively enriched our knowledge about ancient Palestinian Judaism. Apart from the aforementioned writings, it contains, among other things, all the texts of the books later canonized as the Old Testament (with the exception of Esther), along with apocrypha and pseudepigrapha as well as other texts that were not composed by the Qumran Essenes but were received by them, such as the Temple Scroll, in which God speaks in the first person and which presents the plan for an ideal Jerusalem temple and a systematic updating of the laws of Deuteronomy, and the War Scroll, a regulation for the eschatological battle of the sons of light against the sons of darkness. Using older sources in Qumran, these writings were revised and updated in the sense of the group's own ideology. There are, however, also (collections of) psalms, some of which were previously unknown, and liturgies, such as the Songs of the Sabbath Sacrifice, which in the form of praise describe the heavenly worship service of the angels and presumably go back to Hasidic-mystical circles. Thus, in addition to the genuinely Qumranic texts—such as community rules,

---

[87] 1QS VIII 5.14 (trans. García Martínez / Tigchelaar 1997/1998, I: 89). The designation *yaḥad* implies, as in Hellenistic associations, a voluntarily joined community; see note 125 in this chapter and Hengel 1996a, 271–75. For the rejection of the Jerusalem temple cult as unclean, cf. CD XI 17–21; 1QS IX 3ff. and elsewhere; the priestly self-understanding finds expression especially in the rules of the sect. Isaiah 40.3 is quoted in 1QS VIII 14; for the conception of the "temple of humans" in the Midrash on Eschatology (4Q174), see section 4.5.

[88] Cf. Hengel/Deines 1996, 446–49: They "wanted . . . to derive the graded purity prescribed for the whole people from Scripture and tradition and live it out as models" (448; ET = 1995, 47).

[89] Tov 1996.

psalms, and prayers, fragments of calendars and priestly orders, and the earliest commentaries on the Psalter and on the books of the prophets, the so-called pesharim, in which the holy Scriptures are allegorically interpreted in relation to their own community in the last days and in relation to the end-time—this "library" also contains works that are not "sectarian products" but provide information about the eschatological expectations of broader circles, to which we will return at a later point.

The discoveries from Qumran have confirmed the basic tripartite division of the major Jewish parties of Josephus. However, they have shown at the same time that while they are not incorrect, the different opinions specified by Josephus as criteria of party membership—on the one hand, about divine providence and free will, and, on the other hand, about the fate of the dead—do not represent the origin of the controversy that led to disagreement. What was decisive were halakic questions of purity, of the cult, and of the understanding of Scripture. In both *Jewish War* and in *Jewish Antiquities* Josephus provides a "philosophical" description of the parties, in which he presupposes a broad consensus of the Jewish self-understanding and avoids discussing the controversy over the proper interpretation of the law and the eschatological hopes of the people, which would have been incomprehensible for his non-Jewish readers.[90] For political reasons already, he could not discuss in Rome the urgent Jewish eschatological expectation. That he was familiar with it, indeed that he himself basically shared it, is shown by his conspicuous high estimation of the book of Daniel. Like Luke, at approximately the same time, he was an opponent of a self-destructive near expectation only on the basis of painful historical experience.

4.3 On the History of the Parties

4.3.1 On the Samaritan Schism

More recent excavations on the holy mountain of the Samaritans, Mount Gerizim, appear to have shed more light into the darkness of the emergence

---

[90] Qimron/Strugnell 1994, 175–76: "From MMT we learn the reasons for the schism. . . . Josephus gives the impression that the sects were primarily divided over theological questions. . . . He was concerned to produce an explanation that would make sense to his Greek (and Roman) readers. But the fact that only matters of practice are mentioned in MMT confirms the view that it was not dogma, but law that was apt to produce lasting schisms in Judaism." The question is whether "dogma" and "law" can be separated in this way, for the view that only the literal understanding of the "law" corresponds to God's undistorted will is itself "dogma." This also applies to the ordering of the cult determined by the solar calendar. The threat of judgment is also "dogma."

of the Samaritan religious community.[91] The excavators assume that there was a sanctuary there, which was built at the time of Nehemiah and that continued older Yahwistic traditions.[92] In the fourth and third century BCE this temple was expanded into a sanctuary, which was surrounded with a formidable temenos wall, on the main peak in the center of a Hellenistic city. They were both destroyed toward the end of the second century CE.[93] Already the Davidide Zerubbabel and the high priest Joshua are said to have rejected the rebuilding of the Jerusalem temple with the support of the upper stratum, who had been deported by the Assyrians from the land of the two rivers to Samaria and had accepted the Yahweh faith, which provoked the indignation of the "people of the land."[94] The rivalries between Jerusalem and Samaria were probably intensified when Nehemiah became the Persian governor of Judaea. The controversy between him and the Persian governor of Samaria, Sanballat I, had initially led, due to political competition, to the building of the aforementioned Yahweh temple on Mount Gerizim.[95] This was not built according to the Jerusalem model. However, there is no reason to regard doctrinal, halakic, or liturgical differences as the original cause of the schism, for the cult on Mount Gerizim also corresponded to the ritual requirements of the Pentateuch.[96] At the same time, the marriage law given by Nehemiah, which was intended to serve the religious restitution of Judaea, was directed against the clan of the "Horonite" Sanballat (I), whose son-in-law came from the Jerusalem high priestly family,[97] and against the clan

---

[91] On the present-day terminology, which uses "Samaritans" to designate the Yahweh-believing religious community, whose cultic center is Mount Gerizim and who have monotheism, Pentateuch, and observance of the law in common with the Jewish adherents of Zion, see Dexinger 1992, 83, 100 (and passim), who also makes a distinction between "proto-Samaritans" and "Samaritans" after the destruction of the temple on Mount Gerizim; Böhm 1999, 7–8; Pummer 2002, 2; Zangenberg 2008 (GV = 2001).

[92] Naveh/Magen 1997, 10*; cf. Magen 2000; Stern/Magen 2002; Na'aman 2004, 816 (ET = 2012).

[93] Cf. Naveh/Magen 1997; for the conquering by John Hyrcanus, see note 113 below.

[94] Ezra 4.1-5. Cf. Dexinger 1992, 96–100: "with עם הארץ the nondeported Israelites of the northern kingdom (are) meant. . . . The legitimate rejection of the syncretistic colonists of the north . . . is silently transferred to the Yahweh-believing portion of the population . . . = proto-Samaritans" (99–100).

[95] Cf. Albertz 1997, II: 589; Frey 1999, 185: ". . . we may conclude, that . . . in the present case of temple rivalry, the political interests on both sides seem to have provided the most important reasons for the establishment of the Samaritan sanctuary." On Sanballat, see note 97 below.

[96] Frey 1999, 185: "we have no reason to think that doctrinal, halakic, or liturgical differences were the basic motivation for the Samaritans' cultic separation."

[97] Nehemiah 13.28-29: "And one of the sons of Jehoiada, son of the high priest Eliashib, was the son-in-law of Sanballat the Horonite; I chased him away from me. Remember

of the "Ammonite" Tobias.[98] These two clans wanted to strengthen their influence in Jerusalem by marrying into the high priestly family and into the aristocracy and, against the corresponding hope of the Jewish aristocracy, with this politics of marriage to promote the unity and well-being of the whole nation. With the Samaritan upper stratum the Yahweh-believing population in the territory of Samaria was simultaneously excluded from the Jerusalem cult, which necessitated the building of a Yahweh temple on Mount Gerizim.[99]

Josephus consistently follows the anti-Samaritan polemic of the Jews, which was common in the first century. He dates the first temple construction on Mount Gerizim and the conflict with the priesthood more than one hundred years later under Sanballat II, shortly before the time of Alexander the Great,[100] and connects this with a schism within the Jewish priesthood, triggered by a "mixed marriage."[101]

During the reign of Darius III (336–330 BCE), Manasseh, the brother of the high priest Jaddua, married Nicaso, the daughter of the governor Sanballat (III) of Samaria. Sanballat is said to have promised that good relationships with Jerusalem would result from this marriage.[102] But the elders in Jerusalem required that Manasseh either get divorced from his

---

them, O my God, because they have defiled the priesthood, the covenant of the priests and the Levites" (NRSV). The Manasseh tradition goes back to this son-in-law. Sanballat I, the Persian governor of Samaria, was an Israelite. His family probably belonged to the people who returned from exile under Zerubbabel, who colonized the east-Jordan land. Nehemiah calls him "Horonite," because he came from Hauran. Sanballat was Yahweh-believing and gave his sons Yahweh-phoric names; on this, see Mittmann 2000, 17–28. For Josephus this Sanballat is identical with his descendant Sanballat III, whom he dates under Darius III and for whom he is a (half-)pagan "Cuthite" (cf. 2 Kgs 17.24); according to him, the Samaritans come from these Cuthites (*Ant.* 11.302). In the portrayal of the dissolution of mixed marriages under Ezra (*Ant.* 11.145–153) he follows the presentation of 1(3) Ezra and thus avoids coming into difficulties with his late placement of Sanballat.

[98] Nehemiah 6.1ff.; 13.4, 7. The Tobiads, whom we encounter again in Ptolemaic time (see Hengel 2003a, I: 267–69; GV = 1988, 487–89), were also "Israelites," as shown by the Yahweh-phoric name *tôbiyyā*/Τωβίας. Tobias was the governor of Ammon appointed by the Persians. Later the Tobiads were Ptolemaic and Seleucid "liege lords."

[99] On this, see Frey 1999, 185.

[100] Josephus, *Ant.* 11.321–322. For the analysis of the sources and traditions used by Josephus in *Ant.* 11.302–347, cf. Dexinger 1992, 102–27.

[101] Josephus, *Ant.* 11.302–324. For the interpretation of 2 Kgs 17, where the Cuthites are named among the people deported to north Israel by the Assyrians, in the time of early Judaism, cf. Böhm 1999, 105–33.

[102] *Antiquities* 11.302–303. Note the Greek names. The recently discovered coins of "Shomron" and the seal impressions of the Samaritan documents of Wadi ed-Dāliyeh demonstrate already prior to Alexander a considerable "Hellenistic" cultural influence, dependent on the Phoenician metropolises, in the city. On this, see Pummer 2002, 187; Meshorer/ Qedar 1991. On the seal impressions, see Leith 1997. The latter already had a completely

wife or surrender his high priestly rights. Manasseh turned to his father-in-law, who promised him the high priesthood in the temple that was to be erected on Mount Gerizim following the Jerusalem model. But it was not only Manasseh who was married to a Samaritan woman:

> But as many priests and Israelites were involved in such marriages, great was the confusion which seized the people of Jerusalem. For all these deserted to Manassēs, and Sanaballetēs supplied them with money and with land for cultivation and assigned them places wherein to dwell, in every way seeking to win favour for his son-in-law.[103]

"Unlike in Neh 13.28 the concern in the Manasseh tradition is . . . not with the problem of mixed marriages as such but with the readiness of some Jerusalem priestly groups to be in charge of a temple outside of Jerusalem."[104] In Josephus' account of the temple on Mount Gerizim different events have merged into one. The temple from the Persian time and the expansions to a large temple district under Antiochus III become a single temple erected under Alexander the Great. Like the miraculous events at Alexander's visit in Jerusalem and his reverence for the high priest Jaddua, which are recounted by Josephus in this context, the accounts of the founding of the temple on Mount Gerizim and of Alexander's inquiries about whether the Samaritans were really Jews are painted over in a strongly legendary manner. Through later sources we know that Alexander destroyed Samaria in 331 BCE because of a revolt and replaced it with a Macedonian military colony. Shechem and the temple city on Mount Gerizim thus became the main places of the Samaritans.[105] By contrast, from then on Samaria itself was a pagan city, and—apart from the short interruption in the Hasmonean period—this also remained the case under Roman rule.

Josephus' note that the temple on Mount Gerizim outlasted Alexander's short reign and that the priest city "Shechem" was a place of refuge for the Jerusalem person (priest?) who was accused of having eaten something unclean, of violating the Sabbath, or of having done something

---

Hellenistic character prior to Alexander, even more than the coins, which also show a Persian influence in part. On this, see Hengel 2001e, 14–16.

[103] Josephus, *Ant.* 11.312 (trans. R. Marcus, LCL, 465). We find a late echo of the mixed-marriage problem in 4 Bar. 8.1–9, which reckons with the eschatological conversion of the Samaritans and their 'homecoming' to Zion (see *OTP* II, 414–25; cf. Schaller 1998, 743–47). In Mart. Isa. 3.1–12 they are not viewed so positively. The opponent of Isaiah is a Samaritan named Belkira/Malkira. On this, see Van der Horst 2006, 140–44.

[104] Dexinger 1992, 126–27.

[105] Hengel 1980c, 8–9 (GV = Hengel 1976a, 19–20).

else against the law reflects the continuing rivalry.[106] However, the first Jerusalem priests who supported the Yahweh cult on Mount Gerizim by no means understood themselves as apostate, and there was also not a "definitive break."[107]

The Torah of Moses and the life according to the law remained in common. The changes in the Samaritan Pentateuch represent a later development,[108] and the controversy about which mountain God should be worshipped on is still discussed in the Gospel of John.[109] As the two inscriptions from the Samaritan diaspora synagogue in Delos attest,[110] the Samaritans designate themselves as

Israelites who bring offerings to the holy temple on Hargarizin.

The debate in the Egyptian diaspora between Jews and Samaritans over the age of the respective temples appears to have lasted for quite some

[106] Josephus, *Ant.* 11.346–347.

[107] Albertz 1997, II: 589: "endgültigen Bruch."

[108] Several fragments of texts from Qumran (4QPaleoExᵃ; 4Q158 frag. 6–8; 4Q175 1–8) likewise contain expansions in the Decalogue following Exod 20.17; in common is especially the expansion with Deut 18.18 ("I will raise up for them a prophet like you . . ."), which attests the expectation—which is characteristic of Samaritan eschatology—of a Moses *redivivus* as the eschatological savior also for Judaea. The stronger emphasis on Mount Gerizim through the insertion of Deut 27.2b-3a, 4-7 as tenth commandment presumably took place in the Samaritan Pentateuch only after the destruction by Hyrcanus, just as this happened, conversely, with the (Jewish) placement of Mount Gerizim in the vicinity of Gilgal (Deut 11.30). The commonalities between the Qumran fragments and the Samaritan Pentateuch attest the continuing close connection in the third and second centuries BCE. The later changes reflect the conflicts after the Hasmonean conquest. Cf. Böhm 1999, 80, 313–16.

[109] John 4.20. On the Jewish polemic, cf. Tob 1.4-8; Sir 50.26: "the foolish people that dwell in Shechem"; Jubilees 30.5ff.; Testament of Levi 5–7; Liv. Pro. 5.2: Hosea, the prophet of the northern kingdom, refers the disloyal Samaritans (cf. Hos 14.1) to their transgression of the obligations adopted with Josh 24.25ff. See Schwemer 1995/1996, II: 11–19; Van der Horst 2006, 140–44.

[110] Bruneau 1982, 462–74, 483–84, dates one of them to 250–175 BCE and the other to 150–50 BCE. The Samaritan author of Pseudo-Eupolemos, Frag. 1.15 (Eusebius, *Praep. ev.* 9.17.5–6; Holladay 1983, 172), recounts the hospitable reception of Abraham by Melchizidek in the city in the temple of Hargazin, which in translation means "Mountain of the Highest." Ἀργαριζιν is written as one word in the Samaritan literature; cf. Holladay 1983, 183 n. 21. During the "religious emergency" under Antiochus IV, the Samaritans, with their designation the "hospitable Zeus" (Ζεὺς ξένιος: 2 Macc 6.2) for the highest God and the preservation of the traditional cult, remained loyal to the regulations of the Mosaic law, entirely differently from the radical Hellenistic reformers in Jerusalem; on this, see Hengel 2001e, 16.

time[111] and also to have been acrimoniously conducted with regard to the respectively legitimate succession of the high priestly office.[112]

No wonder the Hasmoneans, in the 'restitution' of the state to a unity that encompassed the whole territory of the twelve-tribe people, wanted to bring an end to this "competition temple" as quickly as possible. The city with its temple, which was presumably named Hagarizim after the mountain, was destroyed by John Hyrcanus and was never able to be rebuilt by Samaritans.[113] Hyrcanus also leveled the priestly city Shechem. Samaria was taken after a one-year siege.[114] Thus, Hyrcanus destroyed not only the Hellenistic-pagan Samaria but also the cult centers of the Samaritan religious community in order to establish the Jerusalem monopoly of the cult and his dynasty's legitimation claim to the high priestly office.[115] The Hasmonean conquest had serious consequences, but it led neither to a crisis of identity for the Samaritans nor to their attachment to the Jerusalem temple. However, it also did not result in a complete break, as the analogous religious developments demonstrate.[116] The marriage of Herod I with the Samaritan Malthace and the appointment of her sons as successors (see section 3.1.1) more likely promoted again the violent outbreak of religious tensions in the first century. We have already refered to the nightly defilement of the Jerusalem temple with bones of the dead by Samaritans[117] and the later military conflicts between Jews and Samaritans on account of the murder of one or several Galilean festival pilgrims.[118] The fact that these Jerusalem pilgrims were not appreciated and welcomed by Samaritans is understandable after the Hasmonean destruction of their

---

[111] Josephus, *Ant.* 12.10, speaks of στάσεις and says that they fought with each other over the question of where the offerings should be sent.

[112] Josephus, *Ant.* 13.74–79: Ptolemaios Philometer (180–145 BCE) decided the controversy in favor of the Jews. The speakers of the Samaritans and their followers were condemned to death.

[113] Josephus, *J.W.* 1.62–63; *Ant.* 13.254ff. Josephus dates these conquests to ca. 128 BCE. According to the archaeological investigations, we must date them later, to ca. 107 CE. Cf. also Megillat Ta'anit 22.

[114] Josephus, *J.W.* 1.64; *Ant.* 13.281. For the liberation by Pompey and the refounding by Herod as "Sebaste," see note 91 in chapter 3. On the history of Samaria, cf. also Böhm 1999, 46–54. The place that succeeded Shechem was presumably the Sychar mentioned in John 4.5; cf. Hengel 1999b, 300–8; Böhm 1999, 90–93.

[115] Cf. Böhm 1999, 84.

[116] On the *miqva'ot*, the structures for ritual baths of immersions, cf. Böhm 1999, 82–83.

[117] Josephus, *Ant.* 18.29–30, dates the incident under Coponius (6–8 CE). On this, see note 223 in chapter 3.

[118] Josephus, *J.W.* 2.232–246; *Ant.* 20.118 speaks, by contrast, of many pilgrims. On this incident, cf. note 305 in chapter 3.

sanctuary.[119] We find a pointer to this in the narrative of the rejection of Jesus and his disciples in a Samaritan village in Luke 9.51-56, "because he was on the way to Jerusalem" (v. 53).

The Samaritans also allowed themselves to be infected by the apocalyptic fever. The trek to Mount Gerizim under the leadership of a prophet in 35/36 CE, in order to find the temple vessels of Moses, probably did not serve only to prove the legitimacy of this mountain vis-à-vis Mount Zion. Once again we know of this incident only through the tendentious presentation of Josephus, but the emphasis on the promise of Deut 18.18-22 in the Samaritan Pentateuch makes it likely that this prophet regarded himself as Moses *redivivus*, i.e., as the Samaritan 'Messiah.'[120]

The Samaritans participated in the revolt against Rome, and a liturgical text with "Hagarizim" in Samaritan script was found on the fortress of Masada.[121]

The confusion of Samaritans and Sadducees among the church fathers led to a persistently held view that the Sadducees also regarded only the Pentateuch as holy Scripture.[122] The Samaritan Simon Magus, who was baptized by Philip and who was reprimanded because of his erroneous belief by Peter (a conflict whose outcome Luke leaves open),[123] became a heresiarch in the course of the second century CE. Justin states that he came from Gitta and notes that "almost all Samaritans honor him as the first God." Irenaeus traces back all Christian Gnostic false teaching to Simon; he is regarded as the teacher of the Gnostic Menander, who came from the Samaritan village of Kapparetaia and whose student Satornil is said to have been active in Antioch. Christian gnostics of the second century presumably appealed to Simon as well as to other negative figures.[124]

---

[119] Luke 9.51-53; John 4.9; cf. Josephus, *J.W.* 2.232; *Ant.* 20.118; *Life* 145, 241, 268ff., 317ff. On this, see Böhm 1999, 216ff.

[120] On the political connections, see the end of section 3.1.3. The term "Taheb," the "Restorer" as Samaritan Messiah, is only attested much later, but the Samaritan Decalogue expansion with Deut 18.18 and 27.4-7 connects the eschatological "Prophet like Moses" and Mount Gerizim (on the Samaritan messianic expectation, cf. also John 4.25 and Justin, *1 Apol.* 53.6); on this, see Böhm 1999, 81. The Samaritans had to reject the Davidic Messiah just as much as the temple on Zion. Deuteronomy 18.15-22 also plays a certain role in Qumran. See J. Zimmermann 1998, 314–15, 332–42, 476ff., and 512 index.

[121] Josephus, *J.W.* 3.307–315. Cf. Talmon 1997; Hengel 2001e, 16.

[122] Thus Böhm 1999, 78, with reference to J. Maier 1988, 216.

[123] Acts 8.9-13, 18-24. On this, see Avemarie 2002b, 51–54, 243–54, and elsewhere.

[124] Justin, *Dial.* 120.6; *1 Apol.* 26.2; 56.2; Irenaeus, *Haer.* 1.23.1–4. Irenaeus makes Simon the anti-apostolic founding father of the gnostic heresy. Cf. Hengel 1997b, 212ff. (ET = 2012a, 505ff.); K. Beyschlag 1974. See also Hengel/Schwemer 2019.

4.3.2 On the History of the Essenes, Pharisees, and Sadducees

As Wellhausen had already observed, the emergence of the Jewish parties is located in the context of the Hellenization of Palestinian Judaism and of the concomitantly "emerging *individualism*. . . , which found expression as *personal decision* for a specific form of piety."[125]

Josephus presupposes the existence of the three parties in the middle of the second century BCE. At the time of Jonathan Maccabeus (the time after his victory over Demetrius II is in view, ca. 146 BCE), Josephus says that

> there were three schools of thought among the Jews, which held different opinions concerning human affairs.[126]

Their emergence is located in connection with the rapid collapse of the anti-Hellenistic front, which had sustained the Maccabean revolt. This chronology is confirmed by the Essene Damascus Document:

> And at the period of wrath, three hundred and ninety years after having delivered them up into the hand of Nebuchadnezzar, king of Babylon, he visited them and caused to sprout from Israel and from Aaron a shoot of the planting, in order to possess his land. . . . And they realised their iniquity and knew that they were guilty {men}; but they were like blind persons and like those who grope for a path over twenty years. And God appraised their deeds . . . and raised up for them a Teacher of Righteousness, in order to direct them in the path of his heart.[127]

According to the Essene reckoning of time, with the number 390 we come to the year 170 BCE, to the time of the "Hellenistic reform" and of the following religious emergency under Antiochus IV.[128] In this

---

[125] Deines 1997, 47, 546 (quotation and emphasis by Roland Deines); cf. Hengel 1996a, 79–80, 159, 168, 270, 308; on the phenomenon, see Nock 1933. The Essenes are also an "association," which the members voluntarily join on the basis of personal "repentance"; see note 87 above. The membership can be applied for only by adults (1QS V 1.10; 1QSa I 6ff.). On the other side, this voluntary decision is traced back to God's election, which is understood deterministically. Here, there exists an analogy to Paul and John.

[126] *Antiquities* 13.171: αἱρέσεις.

[127] CD I 5–11 (trans. García Martínez / Tigchelaar 1997/1998, I: 551; cf. Lohse 1971b, 67). Cf. Hengel 2003a, I: 175ff., 179–80 (GV = 1988, 319ff., 327–28).

[128] With this we come — independently of Josephus but in agreement with him — to a dating of the "schism." Cf. also section 4.5 for the dating. The "reform" began with the accession to the reign of Antiochus IV in 175 BCE. The actual persecution with the desecration of the temple and the revolt of Judas Maccabeus began in 167 BCE.

crisis the religious repentance movement of the Hasidim offered resistance to the Hellenistic foreign infiltration and supported the struggle for freedom under the leadership of Judas Maccabeus.[129] After ca. twenty years, the repentance movement[130] split with the emergence of a priest, the prophetic-charismatic Teacher of Righteousness, to whom God had "opened all the secrets of the words of his servants, the prophets," into the Essene-Qumranic group under his priestly leadership and into the Pharisees—under the leadership of the "Man of the Lie," who is excluded from the "counsel of the community"[131]—who initially remained allied with the Maccabees. Essenes and Pharisees possess a common root in this "community of the pious," the Hasidim. The Teacher of Righteousness was of Zadokite lineage, i.e., he came from the old, legitimate high priestly dynasty of the Zadokites, who had lost power through the reformers at the time of Antiochus IV, but we unfortunately do not learn his proper name in any of the sources.[132] The "Teacher Hymns" contained in the Hodayot reflect the difficult conflicts with opponents but also his consciousness of been chosen by God:

> . . . so that I became a trap for offenders, but a medicine for all who turn away from offence. . . . But you have set me like a banner for the elect of justice, like a knowledgeable mediator of secret wonders.

> You have established me (for priestly service) for your covenant, and I will cling to your truth [. . .] You made me a father for the sons of kindness. . . .

> I give [you] thanks, [Lord], because you have taught me in your truth, you have made me know your wonderful mysteries. . . .[133]

---

[129] First Maccabees 2.42: συναγωγὴ Ἀσιδαίων; cf. 7.13; 2 Macc 14.6; cf. the "wise" in Dan 11.33ff. On this, cf. Hengel 2003a, I: 175–210 (GV = 1988, 319–81); Hengel 1996a, 165–70; Kampen 1988, 45–150. Cf. also the derivation of Ἐσσαῖοι or Ἐσσῆνοι from Aramaic *ḥsyh* in note 7 above.

[130] 1QpHab VII 3–5 interprets Hab 2.2 with reference to the Teacher of Righteousness. On his person, see G. Jeremias 1963.

[131] 4QPs^a 37 (4Q171) IV 14; IV 18–19. The "Groningen hypothesis" advocates a different hypothesis: the pious in Qumran split off from the Essenes and thus became a subgroup of the Essenes. Cf. García Martínez / Van der Woude 1989/1990; on this, see J. Maier 1995–1996, III: 21.

[132] 4QpPs^a 37 II 18; III 15; IV 8: The "Wicked Priest," who is presumably to be identified with the high priest Jonathan, sought to kill him. Here, there is also mention of the "torah" that the Teacher of Righteousness had sent to the Wicked Priest, which probably corresponds to 4QMMT. Cf. the presentation of the discussion in VanderKam 2010, 127–33.

[133] 1QH^a X 8–9.13; XV 19–20, 26–27 (trans. García Martínez / Tigchelaar 1997/1998, I: 161, 162, 179). On the numbering and demarcation of Teacher Hymns, see A. Lange in

In light of the irenic writing 4QMMT, it is unlikely that he wanted to establish himself in Jerusalem as high priest (let alone that he held the office after Alcimus 159–152 BCE) and was displaced by the Maccabean Jonathan of the priestly order of Joarib, who was appointed high priest by Alexander Balas for political-military reasons and designated "Wicked Priest" in the commentary on Ps 37. The sharp polemic against the Pharisees in the Qumran writings can be explained by both their mutual nearness and their opposing solutions to the problem of how the true Israel that was well-pleasing to God was to come into existence. The Essenes achieved the divinely desired holiness in the elite separation from all impurity in their community, in the *yaḥad*. The Pharisees, by contrast, regarded themselves as a holiness movement for the whole people. This earned them the Essene accusation of "seeking after smooth things," for a capacity to compromise, as it was exhibited by the Pharisees, could appear only as "deception" to them. The Essenes had in common with the Sadducees the conservative, literal interpretation of the law. Analogously to the Samaritan "schism," these new factions had their origin above all in divisions within the priesthood as the religious-political "hereditary nobility" of the Jewish people. Even though the Pharisees in the first century CE appear as a renewal movement that was predominantly carried by laypeople, though it had numerous followers in the simple priesthood, they nevertheless had—in addition to their Hasidic heritage—priestly-scribal roots.[134]

A break between Pharisees and Hasmoneans already occurs under John Hyrcanus. The conflict was triggered by doubt regarding the legitimacy of his holding of the office of high priest, since his mother was a Seleucid prisoner of war for a time, and the question of whether such an attack on the high priest represented a blasphemy that must be punished by death (so the Sadducean view) or only with fetters and blows (thus the Pharisees). Hyrcanus allied himself thereafter with the Sadducees and abrogated new legal regulations that he had introduced together with the Pharisees.[135] After this there was a civil war, which intensified under Alex-

---

Lichtenberger/Lange 1997, 64. In the Habakkuk Pesher this Teacher becomes the "exegete of the prophets par excellence" (Steudel 1994, 204).

[134] Schaper 1999 traces back the Pharisees somewhat one-sidedly to the Levites. This may apply in the first instance for the scribes; however, at least some of the Pharisaic early figures, such as Jose ben Joezer, the uncle of Alcimus/Jacimus, were priests (m. ʾAbot 1.4). Cf. Deines 2001a, 494ff. with note 183. On the Pharisees as a movement that was predominantly composed of laypersons, cf. Hengel 1999b, 63–64.

[135] Josephus, *Ant.* 13.288–298. Stemberger 1991, 98–103, regards the account about Hyrcanus' break with the Pharisees to be historically doubtful and suggests that the break occurred only under Alexander Jannaeus. This skepticism, however, is unjustified; see Hengel/Deines 1996, 462ff. (ET = 1995, 55ff.); even the Rabbinic tradition records that Hyrcanus fell away from the Torah at the end of his reign. The problem of blasphemy

ander Jannaeus, who had eight hundred Pharisees, whom Demetrius III called on for help against him, crucified.[136] But on his deathbed Jannaeus advised his wife to seek reconciliation with the Pharisees, for they had great influence upon the people.[137] Alexandra Salome comes to power through the support of the Pharisees, who then execute bloody vengeance on their opponents, for "while she had the title of sovereign, the Pharisees had the power."[138] She also reintroduces the Pharisaic laws "in accordance with the tradition of the fathers," which her father-in-law Hyrcanus had abrogated.[139] For this change of power we have as continuous sources the one-sided presentation of Josephus, which is based on Nicolaus of Damascus. To this can be added individual comments in the Qumran texts and in rabbinic literature. The Nahum commentary castigates both parties for these events,[140] but likewise fails to mention the names of the Jewish opponents. It is only with the rabbinic sources that the change of power is traced back to Simeon ben Shetach:

> And the world was desolate until Simeon ben Shetach came and the Torah returned to its former significance.[141]

During the reign of Salome Alexandra the Pharisees held the majority in the Sanhedrin and thus the jurisdiction of capital punishment, even though the weak Hyrcanus II presided. The tractate 'Abot attributes to ben Shetach and his companion Yehuda ben Tabai maxims that call for careful

---

against the high priest also appears in the trial of Jesus; see note 33 in chapter 20 and section 20.2.2.

[136] Josephus, *Ant.* 13.380–383. After this, eight thousand opponents of Jannaeus fled into exile.

[137] Josephus, *Ant.* 13.401: δύνασθαι δὲ πολὺ παρὰ τοῖς Ἰουδαίοις τούτους. John Hyrcanus already wanted to appoint his widow as his successor, but he was not successful. The short account of *J.W.* says nothing about this advice of Jannaeus to his wife. In that text she initiates this coalition on her own accord.

[138] Josephus, *Ant.* 13.409 (trans. R. Marcus, LCL, 433); cf. 410–411; *J.W.* 1.110–113. For a very critical analysis of the presentation of the queen in Josephus, see now Ilan 2006.

[139] Josephus, *Ant.* 13.408; cf. Megillat Taʿanit 24: "On the twenty-eighth of Tebet (ca. 76/75 BCE) the Sanhedrin (ruled by Pharisees) took its seat for judgment."

[140] 4QpNah frag. 3–4 I, 2–8. The "Angry Lion" Jannaeus is reprimanded for hanging men alive on wood, i.e., for crucifying them. During the rule of those "who seek after smooth things" war and civil war will not cease, but "they will certainly stumble over the counsel of their guilt" (II 4–10). According to 11QT 64.13–18, crucifixion was the punishment for traitors to the country.

[141] b. Qidd. 66a; on this, see Hengel 1984c, 38. With reference to Levine, Stemberger 1991, 106, criticizes the attempt "to fill out the silence of Josephus with rabbinic material about Simeon ben Shetach." He does not discuss the arguments of Hengel.

administration of justice.[142] However, in the "coup" the leading Pharisees appear to have proceeded ruthlessly against their opponents, who never really recovered from this defeat. In the rabbinic tradition, these events from the early Pharisaic period have only been preserved in polemical encryption.[143]

Initially the opposition party of the Sadducean nobility, only under the leadership of Alexandra's younger son Aristobulus, could complain before the queen that they were being slaughtered like livestock. But they created an equilibrium by leaving the Pharisees in Jerusalem in their position of power, but entrusting a series of fortresses to the nobility. In this way they ended the civil war and ruled in peace, a peace that was transfigured in rabbinic literature, because it was at that time that "the Torah came to its (Pharisaic) significance."[144]

The Pharisees could obtain full political power only in the nine years under Alexandra Salome. At the same time, however, the sources never suggest that their legal regulations were rescinded. At least to some extent, they also continued to determine the halakah of the Jerusalem cult. In Josephus the Essene interest in the political processes is limited to dynastic prophecies.[145] These Essenes are mentioned by name in contrast to the Pharisaic leaders of the early time. Sameas and Pollion (= Shemaiah and Abtalion) constitute an exception here, whom Josephus, following his source Nicolaus, mentions twice in connection with the rise of Herod I. They initially welcomed his rule. After all, he proceeded against the royal

---

[142] m. 'Abot 1.8: Yehuda ben Tabai demands that judges must be impartial in their judgments. "Simeon ben Shetach says: Question the witnesses thoroughly. However, be careful in your words, so that do not learn to lie from them."

[143] Hengel 1984c, 54ff. and passim. The Sadducean party was damaged further by the struggle for power between Hyrcanus II and Aristobulus, and then by Herod I, who disempowered and decimated them again and replaced them with the new high priestly family of the Boethusians. On the fate of one such priest, cf. the tomb inscription of Abba in note 150 below.

[144] Cf. b. Qidd. 66a. Josephus, *Ant.* 13.411–418, 432 (trans. R. Marcus, LCL, 432): ἐν εἰρήνῃ τὸ ἔθνος διεφύλαξεν ("she had kept the nation at peace").

[145] Josephus, *Ant.* 13.311–313: the Essene Judas is said to have predicted the murder of Antigonus by his brother Aristobulus I. This murder—engineered by Aristobulus' wife Alexandra Salome (?)—paved the way for Alexander Jannaeus' rule (13.308, 320), who then married Alexandra. Cf. further the prophecies for Herod; see note 147 in chapter 3. By contrast, not only the commentaries on the prophets occupied themselves with the events; a calendar fragment mentions Aemilius Scaurus, a high priest, and the names Jochanan and Shalomzion = Alexandra (4Q324a + b). A prayer for King Jonathan (Alexander Jannaus?) has even been preserved; see 4Q448; on this, see Eshel/Eshel/Yardeni 1992. However, in view of the dramatic Jewish history in the second and first century BCE, the historical allusions and mentioning of names are, considering the great number of Qumran texts, small and often encrypted. They evince the Essene distance from politics.

party and the Sadducean nobility. However, at the latest, they came into conflict with Herod when they refused to take the oath. Again a woman came to the support of the Pharisees, for the wife of the brother of Herod Pheroas paid the fine for six thousand Pharisees who refused to take the oath, while the king accepted the Essene refusal of the oath without a fine.[146] Pharisees, who had access to the court and its harem, announced to the wife of Pheroas toward the end of the rule of Herod that her descendants would receive the (messianic) royal throne, and they promised one of her eunuchs that he would become capable of begetting children when this future miracle worker began his reign. The messianic undertones are unmistakable.[147] Nicolaus of Damascus, to whom Josephus owes this story, states with bitterness regarding this:

> There was also a group of Jews priding itself on its adherence to ancestral custom and claiming to observe the laws . . . , and by these men, called Pharisees, the women (of the court) were ruled. These men were able to help the king greatly because of their foresight, and yet they were obviously intent on combating and injuring him.[148]

Not only Alexandra Salome but also the wife of Pheroas favored the Pharisees; indeed, according to Josephus, the whole harem of the king was influenced by them.[149] Herod had the Pharisees who were involved and their followers executed. The representatives of the parties that interfered in the controversies over the succession at the court were opposed by the scribes and their followers in the episode involving the eagle, which demonstrates the spectrum of the Pharisees—they were united, at least in the later time, in their hatred for the king. The Sadducees were no longer able to exercise influence under Herod, for he decimated them at the beginning of his reign as partisans of the Hasmoneans and abased them with the appointment of Ananel from Babylon and of the families of Boethus and

---

[146] On the refusal to take the oath, see notes 47–49 in chapter 3 as well as the discussion in the main text there.

[147] Josephus, *Ant.* 17.42–45. The wife of Pheroa was presumably of Davidic descent; cf. Kokkinos 1998, 173. On the eschatological hope for eunuchs, cf. Isa 56.4-5; Acts 8.26-40. Josephus takes this report, which is unfavorable for some (!) Pharisees, because he shares in this case the judgment of Nicolaus. The Pharisee-critical tradition at individual points is consistently determined by his source Nicolaus of Damascus.

[148] Josephus, *Ant.* 17.41 (trans. R. Marcus, LCL, 391): οἷς ὑπῆκτο ἡ γυναικωνῖτις, Φαρισαῖοι καλοῦνται. The Pharisees are characterized as προμηθεῖς, which is usually translated with "possessing the gift of prophecy," because in 17.43 there is talk of their "foreknowledge"; here, however, προμηθεῖς means "wise, prudent, far-seeing."

[149] We will need to return to the question of why women in particular attached themselves to the Pharisees. See the excursus at the end of section 4.4.

Phiabi (from Egypt) to the highest religious office.[150] It was only under the prefects that high priests who belonged to the Palestinian priestly nobility were appointed. In terms of doctrine, including questions of the ritual law, the high priests who came from Egypt agreed with the party of the Sadducees, which is why the Boethusians are largely identified with Sadducees in rabbinic literature.

Josephus is silent about the most famous Pharisaic teachers of this time, Hillel and Shammai. In 66 CE the conflict between their schools led to the bloody establishment of the eighteen halakhot, severe anti-Gentile specifications by the Shammaites against the Hillites. The Pharisaic goal of "unity for the benefit of the community" was missed by far not only by the emergence of the "fourth party," which probably grew out of the radical left wing of the Pharisees and was close to the Shammaites.[151] In the same way the Sadducean priestly aristocracy was divided when the temple captain Eleazar made himself an ally of the Sicarii. The Hillelites, which included the family of Gamaliel, formed the moderate wing, which was more open to the world. Around 80–90 CE Gamaliel II, the son of Simon and grandson of Gamaliel I, became the 'successor' to Yohanan ben Zakkai as the leader of the influential school of intellectuals in Yavneh/ Jamnia, which became the intellectual center of the Jewish renewal after the destruction of Jerusalem.[152] After the catastrophe, the consolidation under Pharisaic-scribal leadership began in the "period of Yavneh" and the foundation for rabbinic Judaism was laid. This renewal in Yavneh also affected the collection of older legal specifications and the changes to the law that had become necessary in the time without the temple. These moves were intended to overcome the dangerous split into "two *torot*" in the schools of Hillel and Shammai and were then summarized in the

[150] A Palaeo-Hebrew tomb inscription (around the turn of the century) from Jerusalem attests the fate of an exiled priest: "I, Abba, son of the priest Eleaz(ar), the son of Aaron the Elder, I, Abba the abased and expelled, who was born in Jerusalem, migrated to Babylon and brought Mattatthy(a), the son of Judah (to Jerusalem)—and I buried him in the cave, which I had bought through a purchase agreement" (trans. after Beyer 1984, 347).

[151] Cf. Josephus, *J.W.* 2.166; on this, see note 21 in this chapter. On the eighteen halakhot, see Hengel 1989c, 200ff., 359–64, 401–2 (GV = 1976c, 204ff., 365–71, 409–10). Cf. the Pharisaic opponents of Josephus (*Life* 197ff.); the controversies over questions of the law between Beth Hillel and Beth Shammai are also discussed after 70 CE, but usually decided in favor of the "liberal" Beth Hillel.

[152] Gamaliel I is mentioned as the teacher of the apostle Paul in Acts 5.34-39 and 22.3. Josephus, *Life* 190–194, mentions his son as the leader of the Pharisees. On Yohanan ben Zakkai, Gamaliel II, and other significant early rabbinic teachers and their houses of teaching, see Schürer 1973–1987, II: 367–74.

corpus of the Mishnah around 200 CE.[153] The incorporation of the so-called "heretic blessing," the *birkat ha-mînîm*, into the twelfth benediction of the Eighteen Benedictions also occurred in the decades after 70 CE. It is directed against all deviants (*mînîm*), but not least against Jewish Christians.[154] The introduction of ordination and the introduction of the title "rabbi" were also innovations. The change in self-understanding is also reflected in the chains of tradition in ʾAbot and ʾAbot of Rabbi Nathan: Yohanan ben Zakkai is connected, on the one hand, with the Pharisaic tradition, and, at the same time, he becomes the eye of the needle, for all rabbinic scribal scholarship is traced back to him.[155] The Gospel of Matthew is located between 90 and 100 CE, as Matt 23 demonstrates, in the bitter conflict with the Judaism that was renewing itself under Pharisaic leadership.[156] The instability of the situation becomes clear in the Bar Kokhba revolt (132–136 CE), where a leader with such fame as Akiba greeted Simon Bar Kosiba as the Messiah and "Son of a Star" promised in Num 24, as "Bar Kokhba."[157] Only at the turn from the second to the third century were the successors of Gamaliel able with Yehuda *han-nāśîʾ* — the first "patriarch" under whom the Mishnah was redacted — to establish themselves definitively at the head and to obtain full recognition by the Roman rule.

4.4 On the Social Significance of the Parties

In the first century CE the spiritual leaders of the Pharisees were scribes, and the members of this party were mostly laypeople. The priestly element receded somewhat, although members of the priestly class did indeed attach themselves to the Pharisaic school.[158] The schools for scholars were located in Jerusalem. It was there that the 'establishment' of all the parties met. There it was possible to study their different schools of thought as

---

[153] Cf. Strack/Stemberger 1996, 2 (GV= Stemberger 1992, 12): "A reorganization of Jewish self-government developed only gradually from Yabneh, the new centre of religious learning. There, soon after 70, Yoḥanan ben Zakkai began to gather around himself Jewish scholars primarily from Pharisaic and scribal circles, but also from other important groups of contemporary Judaism. From these early beginnings there slowly developed a new Jewish leadership of Palestine, able to guide Judaism through a period without Temple and state: viz., the patriarchate with its school and its court in continuation of the Sanhedrin of Temple times." On this, see also Hengel/Deines 1996, 437 (ET = 1995, 40).

[154] On this, cf. Carleton Paget 1999, 772–73.

[155] Strack/Stemberger 1996, 4–6 (GV = Stemberger 1992, 14–15).

[156] Hengel 2008c, 336–38 (ET = 2000b, 197–98); H.-J. Becker 1990, 45–51 and elsewhere.

[157] y. Taʿanit 4.8 68d, see Hengel 1996a, 344–50 (348ff.), 379–91.

[158] Cf. Josephus, *Life* 12, 197–198.

can be seen with reference to the example of Paul and Josephus and also of John of Gischala, Yohanan ben Zakkai, and others.

With the ascent of the Pharisees under Alexandra Salome changes in the religious customs of Palestine begin, which can be documented archaeologically. In the palace of the Hasmoneans in Jericho a synagogue was discovered, which served the staff and members of the court.[159] Other synagogues, which were built before 70 CE, were located in Gamla, Magdala, Masada, and Herodion. These archaeological discoveries agree with the literary pointers in Josephus and in the Gospels. In Jerusalem the synagogues mentioned by Luke are documented by the Theodotus inscription. The establishment of the synagogue as an institution of the Jewish community is attested for the first time in the Egyptian diaspora toward the end of the third century BCE, where the synagogue was originally called (place of) prayer (προσευχή), but it was introduced in Palestine only after the territorial expansions of the Hasmonean state and receives there the common-sounding designation *bet hak-keneset*, which means (place) of assembly, in Greek συναγωγή.[160] The driving power behind this development was not the priests, who more likely feared that it would compete with the temple, but rather the Pharisees, in whose interest it was to instruct broad strata of the population in the law and in the commandments. The introduction of the synagogue in the motherland is connected with the growth of the power of the Pharisees in the late Hasmonean period and Herodian period. The weekly reading of the Scripture and the interpretation of the commandments on the Sabbath served to provide the knowledge that was necessary for it to be even possible to keep the commandments and rites, whose observance was intended to sanctify and purify the people. Priests spoke the concluding blessing as in the temple when they were present, but, in contrast to

[159] Netzer 1999. A ritual bath is said to have been located in the vicinity. As in other synagogues, here too a dining room is also said to have been attached to the large assembly room. On the discussion concerning the identification, see Claussen 2002, 185–86.

[160] The Jerusalem temple was meant to continue to be a "place of prayer" (cf. Isa 56.7). On the revealing exception in Tiberias, see note 192 in chapter 3. Cf. the Theodotus inscription: "Theodotus, son of Vettenos, priest and synagogue leader (ἀ[ρ]χισυναγωγός), son of a synagogue leader, grandson of a synagogue leader, built the synagogue (συναγωγ[ή]ν) for the reading of the law and for the teaching of the commandments and shelter and side rooms and the water installations for lodging for those from abroad, who require these establishments. His father and the elders and Simonides founded the synagogue" (Boffo 1994, 274–82 nr. 31; see also note 134 in chapter 3). On the basis of the dating of the inscription in the first century CE the founding of the synagogue points to the time of Herod I and probably goes back to returnees from Rome or Italy, freedpersons (*liberti*) of the *gens Vettia*; cf. Acts 6.9. On this, see Hengel 1996a, 20, 24–25; 2002, 1–67 (34–35). On the Galilean synagogues in the Gospels, see the end of section 11.2 with notes 39–45.

the Essene assemblies, their participation was not necessary.[161] More-over, since the middle of the first century BCE we find widespread ritual baths, *miqvot*, often in the vicinity of synagogues or of oil presses, which corresponded to Pharisaic purity needs and stipulations. The Essenes in Qumran had possession of especially impressive *miqvot*, supported by a cleverly devised, 'modern' water system. The change of the burial customs — the secondary burial in stone boxes for bones, ossuaries that were often inscribed with names by family members — can also be best explained with reference to the Pharisaic hope in the resurrection of indi-viduals.[162] Moreover, the emergence of stone vessels for "water for the Jewish purification" also speaks in favor of the establishment of Phari-saic purity practices.[163] In contrast to clay vessels, stone vessels — for example in cases of death — could not take on ritual impurity and there-fore did not have to be destroyed.

EXCURSUS

Priesthood and Temple Service

The organization of the priesthood at the Second Temple goes back into the late Persian period. One became a priest by birth. Therefore it was impor-tant to keep family trees meticulously and when priests were getting mar-ried to pay attention to the pure Israelite descent of the wife in each case. Since these, however, were not restricted to women of priestly descent, there was no complete demarcation vis-à-vis the rest of the people. The priests alone had the right to present the offering in the temple, to enter into the

---

[161] Cf. Hengel 1996a, 171–95, 428ff.

[162] Rahmani 1994, 53: "The concept of *ossilegium* was apparently based on the ideas of personal and individual physical resurrection propagated by Ḥassidim in the second cen-tury BCE"; on the floral adornments, cf. Figueras 1983; Deines 1993. The aforementioned ossuary inscription of Johanna, granddaughter of the high priest Theophilus, betrays again something of the influence of Pharisaic piety upon women. The so-called tomb of Caiaphas scarcely represents the family tomb of our Caiaphas; cf. Horbury 1994a.

[163] John 2.6; on this, see Deines 1993, passim. Contrast Doering 1999, 511: "The con-nection that Deines sees between the discovery of stone vessels and Phariseeism remains suggestive," for stone vessels have also been found in Qumran and in the "Bar Kokhba caves." He isolates the stone vessels from the emergence of synagogues, *miqvot*, and ossu-aries. The question, however, is why these objects, together with synagogues, began to spread only in the Herodian period. Phariseeism established itself among the people under Herod. For the Essenes, who were even more rigorously concerned with ritual purity, stone vessels were all the more practical.

actual sanctuary[164] and represent Israel before its God. Bodily defects made the priests unqualified for cultic service, but did not exclude them from the income due to the priesthood.[165] When he was about seventeen–twenty years of age, the young priest was introduced into his office and consecrated according to the prescriptions of the Torah in a seven-day ceremony: through a bath of purification, investiture with the holy garments, a series of offerings, sprinkling with blood and oil. "His hands were filled" as a sign of his future duties. In order to involve all the priests in the cult there was a system of rotation in which the twenty four priestly orders took turns.[166] In this regard the prestige of the individual priestly orders was different. Josephus, for example, stresses that he came from the first order, Joarib, to which the Hasmoneans also belonged.[167]

The twenty-four orders of service of the Levites were subordinated to the priests in the temple cult. They were subdivided into the classes of the singers and of the temple guards. Like the priests, they formed a "caste" based on birth and descent, but they could also take wives for themselves from the people.[168]

Until Antiochus IV the high priestly office was in possession of the family of the Oniads, who were credited with Zadokite descent, then the Hasmoneans, who came from the minor clergy. The hereditary character had lapsed since Herod and the prefects, and the holders of the highest office were appointed with a certain arbitrariness and sometimes in rapid succession from leading priestly families. The investiture and anointing of the high

---

[164] Older traditions survived only at Passover. Here the father of each family sacrificed, whereas the priests collected the blood and poured it on the altar.

[165] Leviticus 21.21-22.; Philo, *Spec*.1.81–82, 117; Josephus, *Ant.* 3.278; *J.W.* 5.228; m. Zebaḥ 12.1; m. Menaḥ 12.10. According to the respective disability, the priests could receive their byname; among the ancestors of Josephus we find "Simon the stutterer" and "Matthias the hunchback." In rabbinic literature there is mention of a high priest "Joseph, son of the Mute." Cf. Schürer 1973–1987, II: 229, 243 n. 21.

[166] First Chronicles 24.7-18; on this, cf. the calendar with mishmarot from Qumran in García Martínez / Tigchelaar 1997/1998, II: 679–707.

[167] Josephus, *Life* 1–2. According to Luke 1.5, the father of John the Baptist belonged to the eighth order of Abia, and his mother belonged to the "daughters of Aaron," i.e., she was of priestly descent. For the discussion about whether it was only with the Hasmoneans that "Joarib" attained to the head in 1 Chr 24.7-18, see Schürer 1973–1987, II: 250.

[168] Cf. 1 Chr 25. The singing of psalms with instrumental music accompanied the daily offering and the festival worship services (Schürer 1973–1987, II: 289–90). The twenty-four orders of the temple guards were responsible for the opening and closing of the gates and for guarding them as well as for controlling access to the various spheres of purity. On the warning inscriptions, which forbade Gentiles from entering the inner courts of the temple, see Boffo 1994, 283–90 nr. 32. On the early history of the Levites, see Schaper 2000. On the conflicts between priests and Levites, see note 372 in chapter 3.

priests took place in the prescribed form in the temple.[169] Through this consecration he obtained special purity and holiness. In the sacrificial worship service he participated in Sabbaths and festivals. He alone was legitimated and obligated to enter once each year on the great Day of Atonement into the Holy of Holies of the temple, where he presented incense offerings and performed the blood ritual.[170] In the second place stood the captain of the temple, στρατῆγος τοῦ ἱεροῦ, the commander of the "temple police," who played a role in the arrest of Jesus. He was responsible for maintaining order in the temple area. The sons of the high priest functioned as temple strategists. The office of the master of the temple treasury, who oversaw the finances, the holy vessels, and the costly priestly garments, was also in the hands of high priestly family members.[171]

The priestly orders started their weekly service on the Sabbath. The departing order performed the morning worship service, the arriving order performed the evening worship service. They were accompanied by the correspondingly changing Levites and staff, the lay representatives of the people, who came from the hometowns of the respective priestly families.

After the bath in the early morning, the priests drew lots for the various works: cleansing the burnt-offer altar of ashes, slaughtering, preparation of the grain and wine offering, bringing wood, bringing offering pieces to the altar, as well as tending to the incense altar and maintaining the seven-armed menorah in the front part of the temple house. The most important part of their service was the daily burnt offering (*tamid*) in the morning and in the evening, in which a year-old lamb was burnt with grain and drink offerings on the altar before the temple house, accompanied by the singing of the Levites. The people, praying in the forecourt, participated in the celebration, and it was dismissed with a blessing at the end by the five priests who had provided their service in the inner part of the temple house.[172] Above all the

[169] Leviticus 8.1-36; 21.10ff.; Exod 28.2-39, 41 par.

[170] According to Lev 16 he was obligated to participate in the sacrificial worship service only on this day. Josephus, *J.W.* 5.230–237, speaks of his participation also in the Sabbaths and the great festivals. On the Day of Atonement he wore a simple, archaic linen garment (Lev 16.4; Josephus, *J.W.* 5.236; m. Yoma 3.7); cf. m. Yoma in detail for the seven-day preparation of the high priest, the appointment of a replacement, and the special rites.

[171] On the στρατηγός, see Acts 4.1; 5.24, 26; Josephus, *Ant.* 20.131; *J.W.* 2.409; on the γαζοφύλαξ, see Josephus, *Ant.* 11.136; 14.106–107 (τῶν χρημάτων φύλαξ ἱερεύς); 20.194. On the γαζοφύλακες who were subordinate to him, see Josephus, *Ant.* 15.408; 18.93. Small gifts were also welcome in the "offering box" (γαζοφυλάκιον; see Mark 12.41-44); cf. Schürer 1973–1987, II: 277–84.

[172] Exodus 29.38-42; Num 28.3-8. This daily offering is portrayed in an especially impressive way in the Mishnah tractate Tamid. On the drawing of lots as a judgment of God, cf. Acts 1.26.

tamid sacrifice was connected with the idea of cultic atonement, but "the whole sacrificial system serves to atone and finds its meaning in the atoning function of the sacrifice itself."[173] On the Sabbath the sacrificial gifts were doubled and the bread of the presence was changed out. At the great feasts the sacrificial gifts encompassed a fourfold in addition to their own respective rites. Moreover, we must not forget the daily burnt offering, consisting of two lambs and a bull, in the name of the emperor.[174] The priests obtained the skins of the animals from these burnt offerings.

In addition to these collective regular offerings, there were much more numerous private offerings and meal offerings, which were obligatory or voluntary.[175]

All the priests and a large portion of the population of the motherland came to Jerusalem for the three great pilgrimage festivals, the Passover with the Weeks of Unleavened Bread, the Festival of Weeks fifty days later, and the festival cycle in the fall (with New Year, Day of Atonement, and the Festival of Booths). But many pilgrims also came from the diaspora in the east and west. To the originally agrarian festivals the pilgrims brought their first fruits in festive processions, the priests' portion and their tithe as payment in kind, or, if they came from farther away, in the form of money.[176] Since the time of the Hasmoneans, the most significant regular income of the sanctuary was the temple tax of half of a Tyrian shekel or two drachmas, which was used to finance the Tamid sacrifice and many other things. It was obligatory for all adult Jews, and the diaspora communities also sent their payments of this tax to Jerusalem.[177] In addition, there were donations and votive offerings for the temple.

---

[173] Gese 1981, 103 (GV = 1977, 94). Cf. Janowski 1982.

[174] Philo, *Legat*. 157, 232, 317. In contrast to the Pharisees the Essenes rejected the sacrifice of Gentiles (Qimron/Strugnell 1994, 149–50); for the discontinuance of the sacrifice for the emperor as a declaration of war in 66 CE, see Josephus, *J.W.* 2.409–417; cf. the excursus on the Caligula crisis in chapter 3.

[175] Philo, *Spec*. 1.168; Josephus, *Ant*. 3.224. Schürer 1973–1987, II: 268, 295–96, 308: "Needless to say, the numerous private offerings formed the bulk of the sacrifices" (296). Cf. the regulations for sin, guilt, and community offerings in Lev 3–7. The flesh of sin and guilt offerings was permitted to be eaten only by priests. The slaughtered offerings or thank offerings were community meals, in which the officiating priests received the breast and the right shoulder of the animal, which they could eat with their families, while the people who had brought the sacrifice ate the other parts.

[176] On this, see Schürer 1973–1987, II: 262ff. Cf. Josephus, *Life* 80: the Galileans were happy to give their contributions to him as a priest (cf. also *Life* 63).

[177] Matthew 17.24; Josephus, *Ant*. 18.312; *J.W.* 7.218. Roman rule guaranteed the secure transfer of this tax from the diaspora. After 70 CE the temple tax had to be paid by all Jews as *fiscus Iudaicus* to the temple of Jupiter Capitolinus in Rome.

The high priestly families owed their prosperity to their constant income from the temple cult. Moreover, they were rich landowners.[178] In contrast to this, the majority of the lower priests and the Levites were in danger of impoverishment, since they profited much less from the offerings and duties. These simple rural priests often had only a small land holding, and others had to earn their livelihood as craftsmen and tradesmen.[179] It was probably much more common for these simple priests to join the Pharisees and then the Zealots than for the priestly aristocracy, which had economic and political control of the temple. The criticism of this aristocracy was also widespread, not least among the lower clergy, and was strongest among the Essenes, who were headed by priests and who rejected the official cult as impure.

EXCURSUS

The Relationship of Women to the Religious Parties

Following Nicolaus, Josephus describes the influence of the Pharisees on the overly "pious" Queen Alexandra Salome negatively, and yet he casts a revealing light on the relationship of this party on women and its self-understanding as a lay movement. It was not only Alexandra who supported the Pharisees. The wife of Herod's brother Pheroas, Queen Helena of Adiabene, and other noble, rich women demonstrated their sympathy for this party, although they did not come from this milieu in terms of their background. What made it attractive for women? Josephus (or Nicolaus of Damascus) ascribes it, when he discusses it at all, to the natural weakness of their gender, which tended to exessive piety. Tal Ilan thinks that the reason was that they formed an opposition party,[180] but they were this only vis-à-vis Jannaeus and against the later Herod. When women are emphasized in early Jewish literature, then it is

---

[178] Josephus is an example of this (*Life* 422). In the Sadducean view, the produce of the fourth year (Lev 19.23ff.) and the second tithe was to be given to the priesthood, whereas Pharisaic-rabbinic interpretation entrusted it to the owners to consume in Jerusalem. Cf. Qimron/Strugnell 1994, 164–65.

[179] Josephus, *Ant.* 15.390: Herod equipped one thousand priests with priestly garments so that they could work on the building of the temple, i.e., they did not even possess the linen garments that were necessary for their priestly service. The king then had them trained as craftsmen. Cf. further t. Yoma 1.6 (Zuckermandel 1880, 180). On the difficult social tensions, especially in the years before the Jewish War, see note 350 in chapter 3.

[180] Cf. Ilan 1999, 37: "The Pharisees were an opposition party during most of the Second Temple period; this may be the reason why women supported them." On p. 79 she also refers to the women who accompanied the zealot messianic pretender Simon bar Giora (Josephus, *J.W.* 4.505) and to the military significance that his wife must have had (*J.W.* 4.538).

because of their piety. One need call to mind only the mother who preferred to be martyred than to leave her sons uncircumcised, the heroic mother with her seven sons in 2 Macc 7 and 4 Maccabees. Esther, Judith, and Susanna are purely literary figures, but they are praised by (proto-)Pharisaic authors because of their piety. The individualizing of piety at this time made it possible also for women to make a decision for the religious party that attracted them the most. In the case of the Pharisees this occurred through material support when the women were rich and in general through the observance of their purity regulations.[181] When it was necessary to join a group, they did this too. The Qumran Essenes, who in themselves took a position of distance toward marriage, had a married portion and women members. However, the view that there is even mention of a female scribe and that women are called elders alongside men, and not, for example, only as the older generation, is probably a feminist exaggeration.[182] After the young man became a member of the *yaḥad* at the age of twenty, he was permitted to marry. His wife obtained in this case the obligation to speak against him before the court in the community in the case of offenses against the law and the right to be heard. Loyalty in relation to the "sect" was higher than marital loyalty. In the case of the Qumran Essenes, belonging in the "covenant" was no longer given through birth but through voluntary entrance into it. Therefore, they called themselves the "new covenant," as promised by Jer 31.31. Such an entrance was also possible for women (presumably via marriage).[183] The lack of marriage among the Essenes is not based on their alleged misogyny but on their strict asceticism for reasons of ritual purity and their intense near expectation of the end events.[184]

4.5 Eschatology and Messianic Expectation

The emergence of apocalyptic eschatological expectation can be traced in the late updating of the prophetic books (especially Isa 24–27, 66; Zech 9.9-10; 12; 14; Malachi and elsewhere) and of the Psalter in connection

[181] See the later assurance that (almost) all the Sadducean women kept the purity regulations of the Pharisees: b. Nid. 33b; cf. m. Nid. 4.2.

[182] Following E. M. Schuller, Ilan 1999, 39–40, interprets 4Q274 frag. 1 I, 7; 4Q502 in this perspective in a manner that is not really convincing. Cf., however, by contrast, the women among the Therapeutai (see Philo, *Contempl.* 32–33, 68, 83, 87–88).

[183] 1QSa I 9–11; cf. CD XVI 10ff.; see Ilan 1999, 40ff. (here also on the graves of women in Qumran). On the self-designation, see note 7 in this chapter.

[184] They are accused of misogyny by Josephus, *J.W.* 2.121; *Ant.* 18.21; cf. Philo, *Hypoth.* 11.14–15; Pliny the Elder, *Nat.* 5.17: *sine ulla femina, omni venere abdicata* ("without women, renouncing all sexual desire"). On early Jewish "encratites," cf. Schwemer 1995/1996, I: 309–12.

with a sapientially characterized overall perspective on the world and its history. The messianic expectation is also sometimes reflected in the translation of the Septuagint, for example in the Psalter.[185] The earliest preserved apocalypses place Enoch (Gen 5.21-24) as the prophetic wise person of the primordial time at the center. The Book of Watchers (1 En. 1–36) arose around the middle of the third century BCE. It portrays its "eschatological discourse" as a revelation that was given to him through his translation into heaven:

> And Enoch, the blessed and righteous man of the Lord, took up (this parable) while his eyes were open and he saw, and said, "(This is) a holy vision from the heaven which the angels showed me: and I heard from them everything. . . . I look not for this generation but for the distant one that is coming. I speak about the elect ones and concerning them." And I took up with a parable (saying), "The God of the universe, the Holy Great One, will come forth from his dwelling. And from there he will march upon Mount Sinai and appear in his camp emerging from heaven with a mighty power. . . . And there shall be a judgment upon all, (including) the righteous. And to all the righteous he will grant peace. He will preserve the elect, and kindness shall be upon them. They all belong to God . . . and the light of God shall shine unto them. Behold, he will arrive with ten million of the holy ones in order to execute judgment upon all. He will destroy the wicked ones and censure all flesh on account of everything that they have done, that which the sinners and the wicked ones committed against him."[186]

The final judgment leads to the destruction of all evil and to the everlasting blessedness of the righteous. It has its correspondence in the primordial time. Therefore God appears, as he did then, upon Mount Sinai. Prophetic and sapiential traditions are combined to form a universal perspective on primordial time and end-time, on the emergence of evil and its destruction in the end-time. Wisdom and eschatology may no longer be separated starting with the late Persian–early Hellenistic time. This applies also to the Jesus tradition. The Book of Watchers marks the beginning of the

---

[185] This updating begins in the time of Alexander in the second half of the fourth century BCE and takes up universal messianic aspects. Cf. Gese 1991; Steck 1991; Janowski 1997, 65–66; Schaper 1995; Hengel 2003a, I: 175–210, esp. 203ff. (GV = 1988, 319–81, esp. 371ff.): "The wise men acquired prophetic features, and the prophets became inspired wise men" (ET = 206; GV = 375, italics in original); Hengel 1999b, 1–71 (15ff., 20ff., 44ff.). Cf. Schwemer 2001b, 176–82.

[186] First Enoch 1.2–9 (trans. E. Isaac, *OTP* I: 13–14; cf. Uhlig 1984, 507–10). The passage is quoted in the New Testament in Jude 14–15 alongside other allusions to Enoch.

great apocalyptic writings in Judaism, which, as with the book of Daniel around 165 BCE, the Sibylline Oracles, the Parables of Enoch, through to 4 Ezra and 2 Baruch at the beginning of the second century CE, increasingly connect to the expectation of final judgment and eschatological salvation also the expectation of God's messianic authorized agent and representative.

In his chapter "Religious and Intellectual Conditions" Joseph Klausner writes:

> The whole nation looked forward to the coming of the Messiah: but the degree of expectation was not the same with all. The sect of the Zealots was the most enthusiastic. . . . Least bound up with the belief were the Sadducees.[187]

Long before the discoveries at Qumran decisively enriched our picture of the Jewish messianic expectations, for Klausner the "mystical and moral messianic belief of the Essenes was nearest that of Jesus." By contrast, for Klausner the Pharisees had developed their belief in the Messiah into "a political and a spiritual ideal."

The eschatological expectations of the Essenes are now well documented. Originally they reckoned that the end would come during the lifetime of the "Teacher of Righteousness." Analogously to the book of Daniel, they started from the ten Jubilees and placed the announcement of the end by Melchizedek(-Michael), the divine authorized agent and redeemer of the people of God, in the years 121–114 BCE and its arrival in 72 CE.[188] According to CD XX 13–15, the end comes forty years after the death of the "Teacher." Because these times elapse, another intensive investigation of the Scripture—as already in Daniel—begins, which has found expression in the Pesher interpretation. The community understood itself as the eschatological Israel, which lived in the last time of the purification—indeed, the end-time has already broken in; the phrase "last days" is used for this.[189] At numerous points the community is designated as temple. In the Midrash on Eschatology (4Q174) it forms a "temple of

---

[187] Klausner 1945, 201. For the next two quotations, see idem, 201–2.

[188] 11QMelch II 6–7: "And liberty will be proclaimed for them, to free them from [the debt of] all their iniquities. And this [wil]l [happen] in the first week of the jubilee which follows the ni[ne] jubilees. And the d[ay of aton]ement is the e[nd of] the tenth [ju]bilee" (trans. García Martínez / Tigchelaar 1997/1998, II: 1207; cf. Steudel 2001, 179, and the commentary on 105–6 n. 6–7). On Michael, see Dan 12.1ff.

[189] On this, see Steudel 1994, 161–64, 197, 202–7. Zimmermann 1998, 105–6: "The concern is . . . both with the future leading to the end and with the eschatologically defined present of the community."

humans," in which "works of thanks" are presented as incense offerings. This "human temple" probably represents the 'eschatological' interim temple, which will be replaced by the future true temple, which is promised in 2 Sam 7.10-11 and Exod 15.17b-18:

> *2* This (refers to) the house which [he will establish] for [him] in the last days, as it is written in the book of *3* [Moses: *Exod 15:17-18* «The temple of] YHWH your hands will est[a]blish. YHWH shall reign for ever and ever». . . . *5* «Y[HW]H [shall reign for] ever». He will appear over it for ever; foreigners shall not again lay it waste, as they laid waste, in the past, *6* the tem[ple of I]srael on account of their sins. And he commanded to build for himself a temple of man, to offer him in it, *7* before him, the works of thanksgiving. . . . *10* [And] YHWH [de]clares to you that *2 Sam 7:12-14* «he will build you a house. I will raise up your seed after you and establish the throne of his kingdom *11* [for ev]er. I will be a father to him and he will be a son to me.» This (refers to the) «branch of David», who will arise with the Interpreter of the law who *12* [will rise up] in Zi[on in] the [l]ast days.[190]

The interpretation brings together in a narrow space the eschatological themes: eschatological temple,[191] realization of the kingdom of God,[192] Davidic and priestly-prophetic Messiah. Just as in the Pharisaic Psalms of Solomon (especially chapter 17), reign of God and of the Messiah do not

[190] 4Q174 frag. 1i, 21, 2–12 (trans. García Martínez / Tigchelaar 1997/1998, I: 353); cf. Zimmermann 1998, 102. On the community as temple, cf. 1QS VIII–IX. Against D. Dimant, Steudel 1994, 166–67, thinks that in 4Q174 III 1–13 (= 4Q174 frag. 1i, 21,1–13) there is not talk of three temples (the defiled Jerusalem temple, the temple of people, and the eschatological temple, which already exists in heaven) but that the temple of people is the eschatological temple. Cf. against this Zimmermann 1998, 109: "More likely is probably . . . the suggestion by Dimant that the temple as building (lines 2–4) must be distinguished from the Qumran community . . . (lines 6–7)." On the designation of the Davidic Messiah as "shoot of David," cf. Jer 23.5; 33.15; Zech 3.8; 6.12. The motif of the eschatological temple, which is identified with the new community of salvation, also appears with many variations in Paul (1 Cor 3.8-17), Eph 2.20-22, and 1 Pet 2.4ff. upon a christological foundation. The "temple cleansing" by Jesus (Mark 11.15-17 parr.) and his temple saying in the trial (Mark 14.58 parr.) also have a messianic-eschatological background. See the end of section 18.3 and section 20.2.2.

[191] On this, cf. Temple Scroll, New Jerusalem, War Scroll. See Schiffman 1999, 279–80: "the sectarians expected that the present-day Temple from which they abstained because of ritual disagreements would eventually be replaced by a perfect structure of divine creation." In addition, they studied and revised among others older works such as Jubilees, the Aramaic Testament of Levi, and the sources of the Temple Scroll.

[192] Heavenly temple and kingdom of God constitute central themes in the Songs of the Sabbath Sacrifice from Qumran. On this, see note 86 in this chapter.

form an opposition among the Qumran Essenes. Alongside the warlike-kingly Messiah, who is admittedly not designated as *māšiᵃḥ* ("anointed") but as *nāśî* (leader/"prince")—thus thirty-seven times in Ezekiel—a priestly-prophetic Messiah is expected, as in the (presumably Essene) Testament of the Twelve Patriarchs.[193] In 4Q175 (Testimonia) the expectation of a prophet like Moses (Deut 18.15-18) is added.[194] We can read off the development of the *terminus technicus* "Messiah" from the texts from Qumran. Alongside the Old Testament "anointed one" of the past, the expected eschatological figures also receive the predicate "anointed one," which initially may have been understood primarily as a statement of function and not as a "title of majesty" from the start.[195] As in the Gospels later, the title "anointed one" does not necessarily have to be mentioned by name, since the Scriptures from Moses to Daniel could provide a whole series of equivalent "titles."

The Midrash on Eschatology (4Q174) is preserved in very fragmentary form, but, through the quotation of Dan 12 with the saving intervention of the "prince of light" Michael, reference is made to the final battle (IV 3–9), which is described in detail in the War Scroll. The end comes on the "Day of Vengeance" and with "God's battle," which the Sons of Light conduct against the Sons of Darkness in the War Scroll.[196]

> [And th]is a time of salvation for the nation of God and a period of rule for all the men of his lot, and of everlasting destruction for all the lot of Belial . . . the rule of the Kittim will come to an end, wickedness having been defeated, with no remnant remaining, and there will be no escape for [any of the sons] of darkness.[197]

---

[193] 4Q174 is a genuine Qumranic text. On the various aspects of the Messianic expectation in the Dead Sea Scrolls, see Zimmermann 1998, passim.

[194] See Zimmermann 1998, 428ff., on 4Q175 and 512 index. Cf. Schwemer 2001b, 165–230, and the end of section 4.3.1 above.

[195] Cf. 11QMelch II 18, where the "one anointed by the Spirit" (cf. Isa 61.1ff.) is identical with the "messenger of joy" from Isa 52.7 and may refer to the Teacher of Righteousness.

[196] 1QM VII 5; IX, 5; XV 3. Cf. Hengel 1989c, 271–90 (GV = 1976c, 277–96).

[197] 1QM I 5–9 at the beginning of the War Scroll (trans. García Martínez / Tigchelaar 1997/1998, I: 113). This was revised in Qumran, and this passage explains (a) the Essene's readiness to be martyred in the Jewish revolt, which was praised by Josephus (*J.W.* 2.152–153), (b) the Essene John as general, and (c) the destruction of the settlement in Qumran by the *kittim* in 68 CE. The *kittim* are the Greeks/Macedonians and later the Romans.

After the final war has been decided . . . a new kind of communion with God and the angels will begin,[198]

and the restoration of the "glory" of Adam is awaited.

Talk of the resurrection of the dead is relatively rare in the Qumran texts, which may be connected with the fact that the conclusion of a scroll is usually not preserved. At any rate, Isaiah and Daniel were intensively interpreted in Qumran, the book of Jubilees was studied,[199] and they took up an Ezekiel apocryphon, which interprets Ezek 37.1-14 eschatologically,[200] and above all a psalm in which there is talk of the Messiah and where it states:

> Then he (God) will heal the pierced, and he will make the dead alive, and he will proclaim good news to the poor.[201]

The conceptions presumably developed in the course of the two-hundred-year history of the Qumran Essenes. For the tradition handed down by Josephus that the Essenes, "in agreement with the sons of the Greeks," think that the souls of the good receive a place blown on by the zephyr beyond the ocean, one could think of the Book of Parables (1 En. 37–71).[202] The Book of Parables was not found in Qumran; it may have been a text

---

[198] VanderKam 2010, 146. On אדם כבוד, cf. 1QS IV 23; 1QH XVII 15; CD III 20. On Jesus as new Adam in Mark's temptation story, see section 10.2.

[199] Unfortunately, just five lines are fragmentarily preserved on Jubilees 23.30–31 in 4Q176. The text is also unclear in the Ethiopic translation. Presumably there is talk of the intermediate state, in which the bones rest in the earth, but the spirit already rejoices with God, and of the end-time, in which "the Lord (will) heal his slaves, and they will arise."

[200] 4Q385 (Deutero-Ezekiel) frag. 2, 7–8: "a great crowd of people will arise and praise Yahweh Sebaoth, who [revived them]." The sign of the bending down and straightening up of a tree (a widespread tree prodigy in antiquity) must be interpreted in relation to the messianic change of ruler. Eschatological resurrection of the dead and arrival of the Messiah belong together. For the effective history of Ezek 37, cf. Hengel 2001a, 151ff.

[201] 4Q521 frag. 2 II, 12; H. Lichtenberger 2001, 85: "If 4Q521 were a text composed by the Qumran-Essene community, it would be the only certain witness to the belief of the Qumran Essenes in the resurrection, more precisely, in the making alive of the dead." Zimmermann 1998, 343–89, provides a detailed interpretation. Due to the affinity with the Beatitudes, Luke 4.18-21, Luke 7.18-23, and Pss. Sol. 17, it is probably the case that 4Q521 was a widely read psalm; see Schwemer 2001b, 210–11. On the relation to the proclamation of Jesus, see the end of section 10.5.

[202] Josephus, *J.W.* 2.155. Their eschatological battle was directed at Zion. Josephus, writing in Rome, may have thought that the eschatological Zion was something like the island of the blessed for the Greeks. It could also be an *interpretatio graeca*, which he took from a source. According to Hippolytus, *Haer.* 9.27.1, the Essenes know of a holding place for the souls of the righteous, which corresponds to the Greek "islands of the blessed," before the bodily resurrection and the final judgment. Cf. further Hengel 2001a, 170.

of a special group from the time between Herod and the destruction of Jerusalem (37 BCE–70 CE).

> . . . in those days the earth will give back what is entrusted to it, and the underworld will give back what it has received. . . .[203]

The earth gives back the bodies, the underworld the souls, so that the righteous can inhabit the new earth. After the final judgment, the everlasting blessedness climaxes in the messianic banquet in the eschatological temple, in which God "dwells" over the righteous, after they have received the "garment of glory," i.e., the resurrection body:

> The Lord of Spirits (= God) will dwell over them, and with that Son of Man they will eat and lie down (to rest) and rise up forever and ever. . . . And this will be your garment: the garment of life from the Lord of Spirits; your garments will not become old, and your glory will not pass away.[204]

In Palestinian Judaism the Greek notion of the immortality of the soul, which is connected solely to the individual and is emphatically incorporeal, does not establish itself, but rather the notion of a bodily resurrection, because it alone "made possible at all . . . the real eschatological restitution of the whole people of God as a unity in the reign of God (and, when applicable, this simultaneously means also of his anointed one)."[205] Moreover, the fulfillment of the promise of land and the gathering of the "dispersed" of Israel required the bodily resurrection. The martyrdoms of the early Maccabean period let grow the hope for the resurrection of individuals and for the restitution of the people through God's new creation in the promised land.

Through their shared Hasidic heritage, Essenes and Pharisees were closely related in their "haggadah," more precisely in their eschatology.

The originally collective hope—aimed at the whole people of God—that those who "rest in dust will rise" is first found in the small apocalypse of Isa 26.19 and then in Dan 12.1-2. The writings that are closely related to the Pharisees—such as 2 Maccabees, the Psalms of Solomon, and yet also the Testament of the Twelve Patriarchs, which is more likely "Essene" in character—speak very openly of the hope in the bodily

---

[203] First Enoch 51.1ff. On this, cf. further chapter 22.

[204] First Enoch 62.14–16; cf. Rev 21.1-4, 23-27; 22.1-5. On the meal with the Son of Man / Messiah in Jesus and in early Christianity, see section 13.2.

[205] Hengel 2001a, 150 (= Hengel 2006a, 417).

resurrection.[206] On his deathbed, the patriarch Judah also teaches his sons about the order of rank at the resurrection; he and his brothers will then be rulers over the tribes of Israel.

In early Judaism, messianic expectations were varied but not chaotic. Three basic lines can be identified. The kingly anointed one from the tribe of David, the priestly anointed one "from Aaron," and the eschatological anointed prophet according to Deut 18.15-18 were expected.[207] When scholars have previously readily reduced the messianic expectations in pre-Christian Judaism to a minimum, they have usually given too little attention to the Septuagint as the earliest commentary on the prophetic texts.[208] The Qumran discoveries have demonstrated that the Jewish term "anointed one" was variable and not restricted to concept of a kingly Davidide. Moreover, the problem of the "multiplicity of approaches," which tends to vary and combine motifs and titles without surrendering the connection to the same subject matter and which contradicts our analytically separating approach, has been inadequately perceived.

The messianic expectations in the Parables of 1 Enoch are the closest parallel to the early Christian expectations both temporally and in terms of substance. However, this work cannot be clearly assigned to one of the three parties but rather points to the variety and overlaps in the eschatological notions of the various groups. The mythical world of the Old Testament Jewish expectations regarding the future was much richer and multifarious than the earlier main sources of Josephus and early rabbinic literature let one suspect. The fact that we cannot always clearly classify this variety demonstrates once again the fragmentary character of our knowledge about Judaism in the time before 70 CE, even after the Qumran discoveries. Unique figures such as Bannus, the Baptist movement, and the eschatological prophets who led their crowds into the wilderness can be assigned neither to the Essenes nor to the Pharisees. Something similar can be said about the Parables of 1 Enoch. There were three basic streams but many variations. In addition to messianic expectations, there were theocratic expectations, which could also be combined with each other, as in Pss. Sol. 17. The intensification of the controversies over the "zeal for the law" is clearly recognizable in the Jewish "sects" that proceeded from the Zealots, which gripped priests and laypeople and in the

---

[206] Testament of Simeon 4.2, 7a; T. Levi 18; T. Jud. 25.1: "rise to life"; 25.4: "and those who died in sorrow will rise in joy . . . and those who died for the Lord's sake will be raised to life." This shows the close relationship between martyrdoms and hope in the resurrection in the same way as the 'classic' attestations in Dan 12.1ff.; 2 Macc 7. On this, cf. now Elledge 2006a; 2006b; 2006c.

[207] See Schwemer 2001b.

[208] On this, see already Schaper 1995, passim; Horbury 1998a.

end divided the people in a disastrous way. This very zeal for the law then also led to a deterioration of the situation of the Jewish Christians in Jerusalem with the Agrippa persecution in ca. 43 CE and the flight of Peter (and other leading disciples) and to the strengthening of the wing of the new messianic movement that was rigorously loyal to the law. From then on it could assert itself in the holy city, led by James the Just, the brother of Jesus, only through its pronounced observance of the Torah.[209]

---

[209] On this, see Hengel/Schwemer 2019.

PART II
Preliminary Questions about the Person and History of Jesus

·

5

On the Quest for Jesus of Nazareth

5.1 The Necessary Incorporation of the Person of Jesus into a History of Early Christianity

Especially in Germany it was long disputed whether a history of early Christianity was permitted to contain a presentation of the activity of Jesus and of his passion, since the church began only with Easter and the proclamation of the "kerygma" of the death and resurrection of Jesus. *In favor of this view*, it could be said that the primitive church itself told this very history of Jesus in the form of the four Gospels as the foundation of their message, i.e., of the "gospel,"[1] and regarded this as the most important written witness of their faith already in the middle of the second century in Justin, so that it was read aloud in the worship service.[2] For the apologist Justin this is an assumed custom that has been practiced for quite some time. The founding of the church was connected with the whole activity of Jesus. *Against it* stands the objection that these texts were all written in the light of the experience of Easter, that the Gospels introduced the post-Easter Christology into the "life of Jesus" (i.e., already presuppose the existence of the church and its kerygma), and that the disciples did not really understand Jesus' message prior to Easter according to these same Gospels. In their own ways both Mark and John emphasize this incomprehension of the disciples.[3] Jesus' activity and fate belong therefore still in a presentation of contemporary Judaism. Hans Conzelmann thus begins his outline of primitive Christianity with a preliminary defensive observation:

---

[1] Mark 1.1; 14.9.

[2] *First Apology* 67.3; cf. 66.3. Prior to Justin, the apologist Aristides had already urged the emperor Hadrian to read the "evangelical writings." On this, see Hengel 2008c, 107 n. 312 (ET = 2000b, 247 n. 241).

[3] Mark 8.14-21, 32-33; 9.9, 19, 32; 10.32 etc.; John 2.22; 12.16; 14.26; 16.13; 20.9. See section 17.3.2.

Jesus' life and teaching are the *presupposition* of church history. The presentation of them does not belong *in* it, but *prior to* it. The history of the church begins after the death of Jesus. She was founded by the appearance of the resurrected One, regardless of how the historian may explain these.[4]

In this way he walks in the footsteps of his teacher Rudolf Bultmann, who introduced his *Theology of the New Testament* with the sentence "*The message of Jesus* is a presupposition for the theology of the New Testament rather than a part of that theology itself."[5]

This sharp division between the Jewish preconditions, to which the person of Jesus belonged, and the beginnings of the church or the New Testament ideas of faith themselves is questionable in light of the *primitive Christian self-understanding* and in light of the history of Judaism.

The Synoptic evangelists trace the *new beginning to the prophetic preaching of repentance of John the Baptist and the baptism of Jesus in the Jordan*, which was understood as the induction of the Son of God Jesus into his "messianic task." The Gospel of John presupposes the Synoptic account and turns the Baptist into the first witness of the incarnate Son of God. After Jesus' baptism his public activity begins, which then leads immediately to the calling of the first disciples. By contrast, the stories of Jesus' childhood in Luke 1 and 2 and Matt 1 and 2 are prehistory; Mark and John can forgo them. With this beginning the Gospels reproduce an uncontested consensus in the primitive church. The name John the Baptist appears in all four Gospels no less than eighty times.[6] Should we take leave of this primitive Christian consensus?

With regard to a theology of the New Testament, one would need to ask whether the later faith of the disciples in the resurrection of the crucified Messiah Jesus as God's salvific act did not possess its materially necessary antecedent in a linkage to Jesus' activity in word and deed, with this linkage including the *belief in his messianic sending* as the proclaimer

---

[4] Conzelmann 1973b, 7, Conzelmann's emphasis (GV = 1971, 1). A similar position is taken by Schneemelcher 1981. In his idiosyncratic *Geschichte des frühen Christentums*, F. Vouga also does not go into further detail about the question of Jesus but understands the history of early Christianity as "evolution of a deterministic chaos" (Vouga 1994, § 3.2, pp. 13–19) and begins with 1 Cor 15.3-7 (pp. 23ff.). Wedderburn 2004, 16–17, begins his presentation with the Easter appearances and ends with the year 70 CE because he wishes to provide a concise introduction for students.

[5] Bultmann 2007, I: 3 (GV = 1984, 1); on this, see note 10 in this chapter.

[6] Cf. also Acts 1.5, 22; 10.37; 11.16; 13.24-25; 18.25; 19.3-4. See also the frequent mention of it in Justin, *Dial.* 49.3–7; 50.2–3; 51.1–3; 52.3; 84.4; 88.2–3, 6–7. On the Baptist and Jesus, see sections 10.1–10.3.

of the kingdom of God, and this means also in his *unique authority*, which determined his entire activity down to his way to the cross. After all, the passion of Jesus is directly connected with his confession to this God-given messianic authority. Can we really exclude the history of Jesus from a history of the early church? It is only because Easter confirmed pre-Easter experiences and memories that the Gospels came to be written at all.

In addition to being grounded in the Easter event—whose form and significance is, precisely for the scholarship that presents itself as markedly critical, so difficult to grasp today and therefore contested—is not the church also already previously grounded *in the calling of the disciples by Jesus himself*? Could one not say that it is not the—artificially isolated—later events but rather the *messianic sending* of Jesus that provides the ultimate foundation of the Christian faith? After all, this is what prompted Jesus to call twelve disciples, and this is what brings him in the end—as the entire process demonstrates—to the cross and what proves itself true in his resurrection according to the opinion of the community of disciples. In our view, the notion that Jesus became "Messiah" only via the resurrection through the faith of the primitive community and entirely against his original intention is an untenable hypothesis, which is opposed by the early Christian texts.[7] Even though the catastrophe of the arrest and execution of Jesus led to a fundamental crisis of faith, to the flight of the disciples, and to denial, which was overcome by the appearances of the risen one, we must pay attention to the fact that the risen one "was seen" first by the disciples who were called by him and *that they recognized him as their master Jesus.*[8] The appearance to the persecutor Saul, who had been unbelieving up to then, is a special case, which becomes possible only on the basis of the initial appearances to Peter and the "twelve." This means that the people whom Jesus encountered first were not people who were unknown but rather those whom he himself had called into his *discipleship*. After all, in the actual, literal sense, a person could follow initially only the earthly Christ and not the Christ exalted to the right hand of God.[9] Thus, Easter confirms pre-Easter experience.

The content of Jesus' teaching cannot simply be defined with Bultmann as "pure Judaism, pure prophetism."[10] Rather, ever since his baptism

---

[7] On this, see Hengel/Schwemer 2001; Hengel 1995, esp. 1–72, and chapter 17. Cf. now also Deines 2012a, esp. 82–87; 2012b.

[8] First Corinthians 15.3-4; cf. 9.1-2; Luke 24; Matt 28; John 20-21; and the speeches of Acts. On this, see section 22.2.

[9] Hengel 1981b, 86 (GV = 1968b, 97; 2007b, 133).

[10] Bultmann 1933–1965, I: 265. Bultmann alludes here to the well-known statement of Wellhausen 1987, 102: "Jesus was not a Christian but a Jew." He "proclaims no new faith but teaches [his hearers] to do the will of God." "Pure prophetism" is, of course, a

by John, he was, in our view, the messianic pretender called by God, whose activity brings the beginning of the new,[11] that is, of the *eschatological fulfillment*, which the primitive church, according to its self-understanding as the eschatological people of God composed of Jews and Gentiles, distinguished from the "old covenant." A logion of Jesus, Luke 16.16, very clearly emphasizes this: "The law and the prophets reach until John. From then on the kingdom of God is proclaimed. . . ." For Jesus John the Baptist is at the same time the greatest and last prophet. With him the time of "law and prophets" comes to an end. To this, however, Jesus adds: "but the smaller one in the kingdom of God is greater than he."[12] This means that *for the primitive community—looking back—the radical new already begins with Jesus'—messianic—activity in word and deed*,[13] the dawning of the kingdom of God, which is inseparably connected with his person and his unique authority. After Easter it continues to be proclaimed by the disciples with his own words as the reign of the crucified Jesus of Nazareth, who has been exalted to God's right hand. It is not least Jesus' message of the presence of the fatherly love of God, his interpretation of the true will of God, and his eschatological outlook that shape the proclamation of the church and the formation of their life and hope also after Easter. For precisely this reason Jesus' words were remembered and, after the end of the first generation, Gospels were composed that recounted the messianic activity of Jesus and not heavenly presentations of the Christ enthroned at the right hand of God.[14] We can no more separate Jesus' words and deeds from the church than we can imagine a plant without roots.

The term "presupposition," which Bultmann and Conzelmann use, is misleading. There were many important presuppositions of the church of the New Testament theology: the Old Testament collection of Scriptures with Torah, Prophets, and Psalms, and yet also also the Greek Septuagint, apocalyptic and Hellenistic Judaism, Pharisaism, the Essenes of Qumran, and the imperial Roman peace, without which there could not have been a Gentile mission. In contrast to this plurality of "presuppositions," of which Palestinian Judaism is the most important, the New Testament sources

---

historically incomprehensible, idealizing, modern category. Jesus can be compared to the Old Testament prophets only to a limited degree. See already Mark 8.28-29. "Pure Judaism" also remains incomprehensible.

[11] Mark 1.14-15.

[12] Luke 7.28 = Matt 11.11; see section 10.8.

[13] Cf. Mark 1.27; 2.21-22; Luke 5.36-38; John 13.34; see also Mark 14.24-25 parr.; 1 Cor 11.25; 2 Cor 3.6ff.; 5.17; Heb 8.8; 9.15.

[14] Only Revelation constitutes an exception here, but it consciously encodes Jesus as the slaughtered sacrificial lamb (Rev 5.6-10; in total ἀρνίον appears twenty-nine times in Revelation).

speak of only one—decisive—"presupposition": the activity of John the Baptist as the prophetic "Elijah *redivivus*" or as the first witness of Jesus. Accordingly, following the Gospels, a history of earliest Christianity must begin with the activity of the Baptist and attempt to deal with the whole activity of Jesus, including his passion and the emergence of the resurrection tradition. Without them, this history remains a torso. Jesus' activity and suffering do not simply form the "presupposition" but are the root and foundation—we could also say, *the historical and theological origin* of early Christianity. The two cannot be separated, just as the resurrection of Jesus cannot be separated from his passion.

The presupposition thesis, which basically goes back to Wellhausen and was upheld by Bultmann, to some extent also against the protest of many of his students,[15] points to an erroneous development of New Testament scholarship in Germany. To be sure, this protest of the students against the master received the one-sided form of a special, allegedly hermeneutically shaped Jesus scholarship, and was propagated by James M. Robinson as *A New Quest of the Historical Jesus*.[16] It appealed to distinctive, indeed unique characteristics of his activity, such as the turning of God's love to sinners, his "call to freedom,"[17] and his radicalization of the will of God and of grace, which were said to point to—Bultmann had already approved the terminology—an "implicit Christology." Their results were not so new and also questionable insofar as they inadequately perceived the basic *Jewish* foundations of the activity of Jesus and his intensive connection to the Old Testament texts and continued to deny the *messianic claim*, which is unmistakable in our view.[18]

5.2 The Problem

If the presentation of Jesus must be a part of a history of earliest Christianity, there arises the question of its methods and content. Since the Enlightenment theology of the second half of the eighteenth century—and especially since the *Wolfenbüttel Fragments* published by Lessing in 1774–1778 from a larger work of the Hamburg orientalist Hermann Samuel Reimarus (1694–1768), who was influenced by English deism—this question has been posed *critically*. Reimarus regarded Jesus and his disciples

---

[15] E. Käsemann, E. Fuchs, H. Braun, G. Bornkamm, and G. Ebeling. See the dispute with them in Bultmann 1964 (GV = 1965; 1967b).

[16] J. M. Robinson 1959.

[17] Käsemann 1972 (ET = 1969b).

[18] On the more recent history of research, see Lüdemann 2000c, 121–79, 285–349. Theissen/Merz 1998, 7–8 (GV = 1997, 26–27). Cf. further the discussion in section 5.2 below.

as a national Jewish-messianic movement with theocratic political aims. The new faith is said to have finally established itself with the aid of the deception of the disciples. In a radical manner the young Tübingen *Stifts-repetent* (tutor) David Friedrich Strauss took up again the Jesus question in his epoch-making *Life of Jesus* (1835/36), a book whose effects were like those of an earthquake.[19]

The quest for the "history of Jesus" has been continually and often heatedly debated in the past two hundred and thirty years since Lessing and Reimarus. In part, it was and still is answered in extremely diverse ways. While one gets the impression that historically serious scholarship strives for a certain basic consensus, the divisions and prejudices remain substantial even in the present. There is agreement that we can write neither a life of Jesus nor a continuous history of early Christianity.[20] We possess only fragments, which are, to be sure, impressive, indeed unique. The attempt of many theologians of the nineteenth century to build a load-bearing Christology upon the presentation of such a life of Jesus collapsed with this.

A typical example of such an attempt can be found in the work of Bernhard Weiss (1827–1918), the first holder of the New Testament chair in Berlin,[21] which was founded in 1876 and goes back to Schleiermacher. In his autobiography Weiss writes the following about his two-volume life of Jesus, which was published in 1882:[22]

---

[19] Strauss 1835/1836 (ET = 1892). On this, see Kümmel 1972, 89ff., 120ff. (GV = 1970, 105ff., 147ff.). On Reimarus, see Schulte 1997. On Strauss, see T. K. Kuhn 2001. On both, see Schweitzer 2000, 14-26, 74-109 (GV = Schweitzer 1913, 14–26, 79–123).

[20] This skepticism basically goes back to D. F. Strauss and was covered over far too much by A. Schweitzer's own picture of Jesus. Cf., for example, the judgments of J. Wellhausen, W. Bousset, W. Wrede, and systematic theologians such as M. Kähler and W. Herrmann, the teacher of K. Barth and R. Bultmann. In his habilitation, A. von Harnack already defended in 1874 the thesis *vita Jesu scribi nequit* ("a *life of Jesus* cannot be written"); see Zahn-Harnack 1951, 46, and in affirmation Loofs 1916, 128 n. 1, in connection with his criticism of the Jesus book of P.Wernle. See also note 73 in this chapter.

[21] Kupisch 1957. His predecessor August Twesten, who had succeeded Schleiermacher in Berlin, had still read philosophy, dogmatics, and New Testament exegesis. Schleiermacher himself regarded his New Testament lectures as an especially important focus of his teaching. Cf. Nowak 2001, 237–46: "In the spectrum of the theological disciplines Schleiermacher dealt most often with the New Testament" (237).

[22] B. Weiss 1882. An older, comparable work is Hase 1891 (see pp. vii: preface to the second edition), which extended to 774 pages. The author saw no reason to make *fundamental* changes to his lecture, which he had presented for the first time in Tübingen in 1823/24 and had allowed to be published in 1875 after one hundred semesters and repeated revisions; cf. pp. 768–69. See also W. Beyschlag 1893 (XLVIII + 482 pages); 1897 (482 pages). He dedicated his opus magnum to "my devoted students from sixty five semesters." With such works the "life of Jesus" genre was "exhausted" in the truest sense of the word.

In none of my works have I worked with such inner involvement.

He was all the more disappointed by the result:

> The reviews state only either that I am too liberal and heretical or that I am too conservative and orthodox. No one has discussed my detailed investigations about the laws, according to which historical and unhistorical are mixed in the tradition, and my criticism of the sources based upon that, no one has discussed my attempt to present the dramatic movement of the life of Jesus. The critic cloaks himself in the mantle of a noble-minded skepticism and rejects my expositions as arbitrary combinations.[23]

This professor's lament becomes more understandable through Albert Schweitzer's harsh criticism that the author even surpasses the liberals in his psychologizing arbitrariness that explains everything, while he, like the conservatives, is said to cover up all oppositions, "difficulties and stumbling-blocks with the mantle of Christian charity which he has woven out of the most plausible of the traditional sophistries."[24] Ironically, Schweitzer then adds: "As a dialectical performance . . . his Life of Jesus rivals in importance any except Schleiermacher's."[25] This example may be typical for the aporia of a life of Jesus scholarship that sought—in the seventy years between the destructive criticism of David Friedrich Strauss[26]

While they were united in their opposition to D. F. Strauss, these authors heavily criticized one another.

[23] B. Weiss 1927, 179, 181–82. He continues with the self-satisfied sentence "Nevertheless, the book has made its way to a fourth edition and has even been translated into English."

[24] Schweitzer 2000, 185 (GV = 1913, 216). The first edition of Schweitzer's work already appeared in 1906 with the title *Von Reimarus zu Wrede*. On his own psychologizing attempt at reconstruction, see Schweitzer 1914 (GV = 1956).

[25] Schweitzer 2000, 185 (GV = 1913, 216). Schleiermacher still firmly believed in the historical originality of the Gospel of John and its priority vis-à-vis the Synoptics and attempted to defend this in his life of Jesus lecture of 1832, which was not published until long after his death in 1864 (GV = Schleiermacher 1864; ET = 1975). D. F. Strauss immediately answered with a sharp critique, which bore the revealing title *The Christ of Faith and the Jesus of History: A Critique of Schleiermacher's Life of Jesus* (GV = Strauss 1865; ET = 1977); see Schweitzer 2000, 56–90 (GV = 1913, 59–68). With Schleiermacher and against Strauss and Schweitzer, Loofs 1916 still vainly attempted to defend the historical value of the Fourth Gospel in comparison with the Synoptics.

[26] In the third edition Strauss 1838/1839 revised his radical criticism and portrayed a "more positive" picture of Jesus in the sense of a religious genius, but he later retracted this concession to his opponents. See also note 27 below for his popular presentation of the "Life of Jesus Adapted for the German People" (Strauss 1864).

and its swansong through the well-known work of Albert Schweitzer—to
ground the truth of the Christian faith through the religious self-
consciousness of Jesus, which was to be determined historically.

Let us make this fundamental problem clear from the start: The Christian faith can never be adequately "grounded" in its claim to truth by the
results of historical research, which rest on the reconstruction of past matters, even if they are the most impressive portraits of Jesus, but can at best
be elucidated or illustrated by having the attempt at historical understanding come alongside faith. Thus, our theme belongs in the wide field of the
fides quaerens intellectum or specifically of a *fides quaerens veritatem his-
toricam*. For only God himself can ground true faith in the sense of *fiducia*,
i.e., trust, namely, by addressing us with his word, through which Christ
encounters us and overcomes our self-serving heart. We cannot regress
and lose this old, early Christian and reformational insight, which the dialectical theology of Karl Barth (and also of Rudolf Bultmann) attempted
to bring to light again. The alternative would be entirely to forgo the question about the truth of faith, since this truth is something different than
the research results of our historical search for truth, which are always
relative, are based on analysis and reconstruction, and therefore must be
rechecked again and again. Accordingly, we must decisively contradict
D. F. Strauss when he, looking back at his life's work—which was ultimately destructive in every question of historical truth—and in the dispute
with Schleiermacher, opined that "the decisive battle of Christian theology
has to be fought out in the field of the life of Jesus."[27] This is not the case.

----

[27] Strauss 1872, 47 (ET = 1873, 53). Cf. Strauss 1864, 5: "The thought of a life of
Jesus is the snare in which the theology of our time must be caught and in which it must
come to ruin. As soon as anyone proceeded seriously with the biographical treatment, it
was all over for the ecclesiastical Christ. If one wanted, conversely, to hold onto this Christ,
then one had to forgo the biographical treatment." Martin Kähler and Rudolf Bultmann
could have made similar statements. As the liberal K. von Hase, who bitterly opposed
Strauss, indicated (Hase 1891, 768), the orthodox Lutheran Hengstenberg enthusiastically
affirmed Strauss at this point (on this, see also Schweitzer 1913, 108–9; 2000, 98–99).
According to Hase: "a cowardly counsel, which basically vindicated Strauss." Strauss, to
be sure, continues: "it (has been) the solution of the more recent time to deny everything
(*sic!*) as foreign which was not human and natural. If Christ is still to have any meaning
at all for this time, then he had to have been such a person who could be captured biographically; thus the attempt had to be made to treat his life on the same footing, according to the same pragmatism, as other great men." In this way Strauss precisely does not
do justice to the secret of the person of Jesus and of his activity—we almost wish to say:
of his activity, which is without analogies. As his popular book shows, he ends up with a
"biography" of Jesus that is at bottom extremely banal. Cf. A. Schweitzer's verdict on the
popular liberal presentations of Jesus by Strauss and others: "They had to transpose a way
of envisaging the world which belonged to a hero and a dreamer to the plane of thought
of a rational bourgeois religion" (Schweitzer 2000, 179; GV = 1913, 207). For Schweitzer

It was a sham fight in which both parties, the radical critics as well as the historicizing conservatives and liberal defenders, were in the wrong.

At the same time, the historical question of the human being Jesus of Nazareth and the beginnings of the Christian faith is of fundamental interest for every educated person and not only for Christians, let alone only for theologians, for through his short activity and his passion, the carpenter from Nazareth has moved world history like no one else.[28] However, the Christian also wants to know more about the origin of his or her faith so that he can better understand it in its genesis and can advocate it publicly against innumerable absurd hypotheses. This applies in the same way to a history of early Christianity, at whose beginning stands the Nazarene. This inquiry into Jesus' person and his analogy-less "*Wirkungsgeschichte*" by means of historical methods is indeed a "profane" activity and in no way bound to an ideological confession. It will, however, hardly succeed if the historian who "inquires" does not have a certain amount of positive interest in his object of inquiry and regards the content of the Gospels from the outset as pure fiction or as utter nonsense. In this way he would produce only distorted pictures. On the other hand, it is lamentable that in the twentieth century there have scarcely been any ancient historians of distinction who have still occupied themselves with Jesus and early Christianity.[29] In the quest for the "historical Jesus" the historians — to our disadvantage — have left the theologians alone. Theologians, of course, are themselves to blame for this, for they have detached the object of their investigations much too much from the consensus of ancient historical scholarship and have not uncommonly given the impression that they have lost contact with this research.

In retrospect, one wishes to say — despite all the fundamental errors of the "life-of-Jesus scholarship" between David Friedrich Strauss (1835) and Albert Schweitzer (1906) — that this must have been a happy time because, with relatively minor variants, one could basically choose between two "pictures of Jesus": the liberal picture of Jesus that proceeded from the

---

Strauss' *Leben Jesu für das deutsche Volk bearbeitet* (Life of Jesus Adapted for the German People), which, in contrast to the epoch-making text of 1835/1836, eliminated again the eschatological-messianic element with respect to Jesus, represented a step backwards (2000, 90, 168-69; GV = 1913, 97, 193) in an "arbitrary spiritualization of the Synoptic Jesus" (2000, 175; GV = 1913, 198: "gewaltätige Vergeistigung der synoptischen Jesus"), which, despite all differences, connected him with Schleiermacher's posthumously published life of Jesus lecture, which appeared in the same year.

[28] Gogarten 1948, 25: "For almost two thousand years the figure of Jesus has been the obligating and consecrating guiding image of Western humanity. Without it and the power going forth from it the history of these two thousand years simply could not be imagined."

[29] See note 68 below.

Synoptics and the conservative picture of Jesus that harmonized all four Gospels. Standing between the two, the mediating theology of Bernhard Weiss quoted above, which attempted — with the aid of psychologizing criticism and harmonizing apologetic — to reconcile the irreconcilable, had sought out the third — most thankless — possibility. It foundered on Scylla *and* Charybdis.

The radical consequences drawn by Bruno Bauer went far beyond D. F. Strauss. He declared the Gospels to be completely unhistorical and traced them back to a "creative primitive evangelist" in the vein of Mark. Not only Jesus as a person, but the whole of primitive Christianity, including the letters of Paul, were declared by him to be fiction and traced back to the spiritual milieu of the time of the early Roman Empire, as we encounter it, for example, in the writings of Josephus, Philo, and Seneca.[30] In the last 150 years the attempt to demonstrate the nonhistoricity of Jesus and other primitive Christian figures has been made time and again, but again and again it has only demonstrated the authors' inability to deal with ancient sources in a critical manner and to think in historical categories. Here the wish has usually been the father of the thought.[31] But even if no reasonable historian doubts the historicity of the person of Jesus any longer, one still encounters a far-reaching skepticism regarding the possibility of a historical inquiry, not infrequently for "theological" reasons. We will constantly have to enter into debate with this skepticism. The radical, destructive criticism has often arisen from the heads of theologians who have lost the ground of historical reality under their feet. Historical common sense already speaks against them.

Appealing to an eyewitness, Karl von Hase recounts:

> At the court ball in Weimar at the time of the Erfurt congress Napoleon stated against Wieland that Jesus may have never lived. The chancellor

---

[30] On this, see A. Schweitzer, who, despite fundamental rejection, sometimes also discusses Bruno Bauer's criticism in a positive way (1913, 9–10, 141–61; 652 index; 2000, 10–11, 124–142, 555 index). On Bruno Bauer's person and work, see Mehlhausen 1980; 2007 (GV = 1998). His criticism deeply influenced K. Marx and F. Engels and then the later official view of the Soviet Union about Jesus and primitive Christianity. On this, see the Soviet "scholar of religion" Lencman (Lenzmann) 1974. Cf., for example, the introduction (p. 5): "The most important thing (of the question of primitive Christianity) . . . consists in the fact that its scientific answer undermines the most important foundation of the ecclesiastical ideology by unmasking the myth about the divine origin of Christianity and exposing the material roots of the emergence and victory of the most influential of the three so-called world religions."

[31] On this, see the overview in Windisch 1929/1930. Drews 1909 was especially influential. A more recent, but no less abstruse, attempt can be found in Wells 1986. See also Loofs 1916 and his dispute with W. B. Smith and A. Drews; see the index and pages 3–31.

Müller, who was there, assured me that Napoleon only threw this out in order to hear what the German intellectual would say to it. Wieland answered: in this way it could easily be claimed after a thousand years that Napoleon never lived and that the battle of Jena was never fought. The Emperor said: très bien! and walked on smiling.[32]

Today, about three generations after the concluding phase of the life of Jesus literature introduced by A. Schweitzer and after a constantly advancing refinement[33] of our methods, the situation has become, in comparison to the end of the nineteenth century, more complicated and unwieldy. It was not least the history-of-religions scholarship, especially in the sphere of early Judaism, which intensified the situation, for it increased our knowledge of the history of that time. Thus, the son of Bernhard Weiss, Johannes Weiss, discovered in a new way the apocalyptic-eschatological character of Jesus' preaching of the kingdom of God, which could no longer be understood, as it was in the dominant Ritschl school, in the sense of an ethical-religious, inner-historical advancement and thereby became alienating for modern thought. His revolutionary book appeared in 1892, ten years after the life of Jesus of his father, who, as his autobiography shows, was not very happy about the theological development of his son. While Johannes Weiss retracted somewhat the sharpness of his revolutionary theses later, they continued to have effects in the history-of-religions school, and there especially on Albert Schweitzer, whose picture of Jesus was entirely based upon the near expectation of Jesus and the revelation of the secret of his messiahship. Rudolf Bultmann took over the apocalyptic near expectation of Jesus, but, in an intensification of Wrede's view, denied the messianic self-consciousness of Jesus. Since Jesus could speak not only of the near future but also of the presence of the kingdom of God in his activity, this point has remained disputed up to the present day.[34]

---

[32] Hase 1891, 11. The denial of the existence of Jesus goes back to Volney 1791 (ET = 1796; 1828) and Dupuis 1794 (ET = 1984); see Schmid 1958.

[33] It is tempting to speak in the meantime also of an "overrefinement," which no longer takes us further but rather leads to dead ends.

[34] J. Weiss 1892; 1900 (second edition); 1964 (third edition and appendix "with important selections from the first edition"). The same year (1892) saw the publication of the second, expanded edition of W. Baldensperger's *Das Selbstbewußtsein Jesu im Lichte der messianischen Hoffnungen seiner Zeit* (Baldensperger 1892). Already D. F. Strauss and F. C. Overbeck had pointed to the shape of the preaching of Jesus, which was alien because of its eschatological character. In the preface to the second edition, Weiss 1900 stresses that "the first edition of this writing emerged as the result of a personal conflict that oppressed me." For "early on I was already unsettled by the clear sense that Ritschl's notion of the kingdom of God and the identically named idea in the proclamation of Jesus are two very different things." "Further studies convinced me that the actual roots of Ritschl are located

Rabbinic and Aramaic scholarship brought further advancements — and new problems. Inspired in part by Jewish scholars, it could point to numerous linguistic and material parallels between the Gospels (especially Matthew) and the Talmudic literature or the Aramaic translations of the Old Testament, the Targums. A high point for this branch of research is reached with the monumental commentary of the pastor Paul Billerbeck, which despite some criticism made the rabbinic texts fruitful for the understanding of the Gospels in a manner that is unsurpassed up to the present.[35]

This *reconnecting of Jesus to Judaism* created, of course, new controversies. What gave rise to debate was not simply the fact that Jesus' Jewishness was not entirely undisputed — some continued to dream of an un-Jewish Jesus or of a Jesus who made a fundamental break with his Judaism (which was identified with legalism)[36] — but even more strongly the question: *which Judaism?* Let us highlight some more recent examples:

In 1967 Georg Strecker, in a sharp critique of the quest for the historical Jesus, started from four different, mutually contradictory *Jewish pictures of Jesus*, namely, the apocalyptic-messianic type, which was already postulated by Reimarus; the nonapocalyptic teacher of wisdom; the proponent of a radical ethic, which summoned the individual to a decision; and the socially motivated revolutionary. In view of this, he says that the historian too "is compelled to far-reaching skepticism with respect to the possibilities of recognizing the historical phenomenon of Jesus."[37] Here one would have to ask whether we do justice to the complexity of the phenomena through such a strict division, which separates what belongs together as mutual contradictory "types." Can a figure such as Jesus be captured in a single type, which has been preformed by the modern interpreter? With a view to Judaism during the time of Jesus, could not each of these contain a *particula veri* and at the same time be false if taken in isolation? In a completely different way, D. J. Harrington, twenty years later, listed

---

in Kant and in Enlightenment theology." For the appraisal of J. Weiss, see Schweitzer 2000, 198ff. (GV = 1913, 232ff.); cf. also 202–20 (GV = 236–59) for the heated disputes among the theologians after the writings of Baldensperger and Weiss. On Weiss and Schweitzer, cf. now also Carleton Paget 2017.

[35] Strack/Billerbeck 1922 (1055 pages); 1924 (867 pages); 1926 (857 pages); 1928 (1323 pages). No commentary illuminated New Testament scholarship in the first half of the twentieth century as much as that of Billerbeck (= Bill.). For sixteen years he bore the actual burden of this unimaginable work. Alongside it we must mention above all the works of G. Dalman, i.e., Dalman 1930 (= 1965); 1922. To these may be added Dalman's great works on Palestine, i.e., Dalman 1967 [1919]; 1928–1942; 2001.

[36] See note 46 below.

[37] Strecker 1969 = 1979, 159–82 (quotation on p. 174).

seven different pictures of Jesus[38] which were presented in English and American Jesus books between 1967 and 1988:

1. the political revolutionary,[39]
2. the magician,[40]
3. the Galilean charismatic,[41]
4. the Galilean rabbi,[42]
5. the Essene,
6. the Hillelite or proto-Pharisee,[43] and
7. the eschatological prophet.[44]

These differences refer historically exclusively "to the different Jewish backgrounds" against which the authors "have chosen to locate their image of the historical Jesus."[45] This means that the portraits vary according to the respective staffages that are built around the enigmatic figure of Jesus, with these scenarios being determined by selection of texts and thus always also by the subjective, guiding interest of the author. This means, however, that the approach of modern Jesus authors in this point is actually not *so* far removed from the interpretive eclecticism of the evangelists, for already in the selection of the traditions for their "Jesus biographies" they also already allowed themselves to be determined, among other things, also by their theological tendencies. With respect to all of these attempts, what is to be evaluated positively is the fact that in contrast to German scholarship on Jesus in the past, Jesus is at any rate taken seriously as a *Jew*. There is no longer talk of a supposedly non-Jewish origin of Jesus, of a fundamental opposition to Judaism, or of an overcoming of Judaism.[46]

[38] In the presidential address of the Catholic Biblical Association in 1986, published as Harrington 1987; cf. also Harrington 1983, quoted in Crossan 1991, xxvii–xxviii. Cf. now the selected list on Jesus literature between 1991 and 2003 in Bauckham 2017, 3.

[39] Brandon 1967.

[40] Smith 1978. A striking variant to this book is the presentation of Jesus as a Palestinian shaman, who came somewhat too late. See R. Finne in the *Forschungsbeilage* of the FAZ nr. 48 from February 26, 1992, on Bystrina 1991. The reviewer, R. Finne, notes in conclusion: "Even though the figure of Jesus may appear 'more primitive' and thus more interesting—it does not become more authentic thereby." Kollmann 1996; 2000 also considers shamanic influences. On the criticism of this unsharp use of terminology, see also W. Klein 2012 (GV = 2004).

[41] Vermes 1973.

[42] Chilton 1984.

[43] Falk 1985.

[44] Sanders 1985; 1993.

[45] Crossan 1991, XXVII; Harrington 1983, 36.

[46] Repulsive examples are Grundmann 1941; Hirsch 1939, appendix 158–65: The Bloodline of Jesus; cf. also Seeberg 1918. Seeberg claimed that Mary was a Galilean

This emphasis on the Jewish origin of Jesus corresponds to the "third quest" for the historical Jesus, which has been especially prominent in America. Typical of this is the title of the extremely thorough, monumental work of John P. Meier, *A Marginal Jew: Rethinking the Historical Jesus*.[47] Expressions such as "new quest" or "third quest" easily give the impression of changing fashions.[48] The discovery of Jesus as a Jew is much older. First, while it is true that the Judaism of Jesus was often not understood and appreciated in the whole of the nineteenth century, in our view it was also never doubted by theologians who are to be taken seriously. Secondly, the discovery of the Jew Jesus is closely connected with the bringing home of Jesus into Judaism, for which Joseph Klausner's impressive Jesus book[49] constitutes a milestone.[50]

The fact that the number of pictures of Jesus could be increased arbitrarily is demonstrated by John Bowden,[51] who focuses his survey on European scholarship since A. Schweitzer's masterwork. In the section titled "The Kaleidoscopic Christ" he mentions, as a mere selection, ten such pictures, from Lord Beaverbrook's "Divine Propagandist" to Jesus Christ Superstar, and it would probably be possible to extend the list much further without much effort. Sometimes one no longer knows whether in these attempts one is dealing with a real portrait or only with a caricature or even with a mere wished-for image or mirror of the various authors. More recent "postmodern" mirror images of this sort are John Dominic Crossan's "peasant Jewish cynic,"[52] Burton L. Mack's "Jewish Socrates," and Robert W. Funk's work with the pretentious title *Honest to Jesus*.[53] Funk is also one of the inaugurators of the "Jesus Seminar," in which the

---

non-Jew. This whole nonsense goes back not least to Houston Stewart Chamberlain 1899, a widely read son-in-law of Richard Wagner who was influential in a fateful way. See, by contrast, the critical observation of Bill. I: v. With a very different tendency, but one that was no less antisemitic, Ernst Haeckel advocated a non-Jewish Jesus. On this, see Deines 2007a.

[47] Meier 1991; 1994; 2001; 2009; 2016.

[48] See also what is said about the "New Quest" at the end of section 5.1.

[49] Klausner 1945. See also section 17.2.

[50] On this, see Lindeskog 1973; 1986, esp. 29–42.

[51] Bowden 1988, 57–58.

[52] Crossan 1991; cf. the closing words on 421–22.

[53] See the advertisement text of HarperCollins Publishers, San Francisco, 1992, AAR/SBL Annual Meeting, p. 158 on Mack 1993: "reveals a Jewish Socrates mythologized in the New Testament Christ"; cf., by contrast, already Strauss 1873 (GV = 1872, 73): "A Socrates, with his purely reasonable method of teaching, would not have fascinated the Galilean mind at that time." Whoever wants to earn money with a Jesus book must present himself as a "revealer" as far as possible and connect his wished-for images of Jesus with new revelations. On the book of R. W. Funk 1996, see the subtitle, *Jesus for a New Millennium*.

authenticity of the sayings of Jesus was judged by the votes of the members and only 18 percent were acknowledged as authentic. Among others, all the apocalyptic-eschatological sayings and thus all the expressions of judgment were rejected. Thus, the work of this seminar—which is dedicated to Galileo Galilei, Thomas Jefferson, and D. F. Strauss—provides a 'truly progressive, politically correct picture of Jesus.' It no longer has much to do with the historical reality.[54]

In this wax figure cabinet of recent pictures of Jesus only a single one may no longer be mentioned, but is to be kept at a distance whenever possible: Jesus as the *Christos*, the Messiah of Israel, i.e., the picture of Jesus of the earliest community and of the oldest witnesses, although he is called this in all the New Testament texts, with the exception of 3 John.[55] John Bowden rightly refers to the famous sentences of Albert Schweitzer:

> Thus each successive epoch of theology found its own thoughts in Jesus; that was, indeed, the only way in which it could make him live. But it was not only each epoch that found its reflection in Jesus; each individual created Jesus in accordance with his own character. There is no historical task which so reveals a man's true self as the writing of a Life of Jesus.[56]

Schweitzer, however, goes one step further:

> No vital force comes into the figure unless a man breathes into it all the hate or all the love of which he is capable. The stronger the love, or the stronger the hate, the more lifelike is the figure whch is produced.[57]

According to A. Schweitzer, Hermann Samuel Reimarus, the deist of the eighteenth century,[58] was such a "hater" that he made Jesus and above all his disciples into Jewish enthusiasts or deceivers, and in a certain

---

[54] Funk/Hoover/Jesus Seminar 1997. On the same basis there appeared as a supplement Funk/Jesus Seminar 1988 (*The Acts of Jesus*) with the narrative tradition treated in the same way. The crowning finale is the summary of the putative authentic pieces as "The Gospel of Jesus" (Funk/Jesus Seminar 1999). One is reminded of the methods of Marcion in the production of his Gospel (of Luke).

[55] According to Morgenthaler 1958, 107, 156, Jesus occurs 905 times, Christ 529 times. According to Aland 1983, the two occur together 222 times. On the problem, see Hengel/Schwemer 2001, passim.

[56] Bowden 1988, 85; cf. 207 = Schweitzer 2000, 6 (GV = 1913, 4). In 1969 Martin Hengel began his inaugural lecture in Erlangen with this famous sentence: Hengel 1971b (GV = 1970; 2007b, 217).

[57] Schweitzer 2000, 6 (GV = 1913, 4).

[58] See note 19 above.

way this also applies to D. F. Strauss, who wanted to strip Jesus of his superhuman-divine glory. For him, the dignity that primitive Christianity imposed upon Jesus was, in accordance with Hegelian philosophy, to apply to humanity as a whole. Schweitzer, however, stumbles upon a false path when he says:

> It is not the most orderly narratives, those which conscientiously weave in every detail of the text, that have advanced the study of the subject, but precisely the eccentric ones, those that take the greatest liberty with the text.[59]

He no longer observed the deterioration of a certain kind of Jesus literature in the twentieth century, since he concluded the second edition of his "history of Jesus scholarship" in 1913 and basically let the topic rest until his death. At the same time, according to him, "the critical study of the life of Jesus," which moves fitfully forward in this way, was "a school of honesty for theology." His additional statement that

> the world had never seen before, and will never see again, a struggle for truth so full of pain and renunciation as that which the Lives of Jesus of the last hundred years contain[60]

sounds a bit too much like literary rhetoric. Was the struggle over the question of the law between Paul and the primitive church or at the time of the reformation fought out with less "pain and renunciation," and is this not also the case for many other spheres of the spiritual struggle for the "truth of the gospel"?

One certainly cannot repeat this pathos-filled judgment for the scholarship of the twentieth century. With this Schweitzer had given far too much of a green light to the subjective freedom, indeed arbitrariness, of the respective authors. Already his own conception, which connected Jesus' way biographically entirely to the unveiling of the Markan messianic secret and thus did not itself shy away from novelistic characteristics, should provide a warning for us here. Something similar applies to the radical skepticism of his opponent William Wrede, which Wrede recanted with regard to his doubting of Jesus' messianic claim in a letter to Harnack just two years before his death.[61] With his work Schweitzer

---

[59] Schweitzer 2000, 10 (GV = 1913, 9).

[60] Schweitzer 2000, 7, 10 (GV = 1913, 5, 9).

[61] Rollmann/Zager 2001. On this, see Hengel/Schwemer 2001, IX, 17–34 (ET = Hengel 1995, 15–32). See also notes 3, 44, and 95 in chapter 17. In his *Lehrbuch der*

also concludes an epoch, namely the epoch of the *life* of Jesus research; and what may have been true of it can lead one astray today. Therefore, instead of the motivation by "love" and "hate" described by Schweitzer, what would be needed is, thus, the consciously critical distance of the historian, who knows that in the quest for the activity of Jesus in Jewish Galilee in 30 CE, he moves in an entirely different world that is foreign to him, that his sources (as is usually the case in antiquity) possess a different angle of vision and are, therefore, "problematic," and that he, subordinating all his own theological or emancipatory wishes, must ask about the historical *truth*, about what impact Jesus had upon his contemporaries at that time and about what they remembered—even though he can grasp this only in a very limited way, by way of approximation, in graded degrees of probability and in a fragmentary manner.

In some points there is a basic consensus today, which has stood the test for more than one hundred years. With respect to the "Synoptics," Luke and Matthew are literarily dependent upon the older Mark, which emerged shortly before or after 70 CE. They take up Mark to a great extent and owe the course of their narrative to it. Since Harnack, the material that the two larger Gospels have in common against Mark, which consists primarily of sayings of Jesus (logia), has often been ascribed to *a single* "sayings source" (Q).[62] This source, however, remains a hypothesis, which can no longer be reconstructed, since the much later Matthew also used Luke. Due to the large amount of special material in Matthew and Luke alone, we must already reckon with multiple "sayings sources."[63] By contrast, today there is far-reaching agreement that John, who is wholly shaped by the independent Christology of the author, contributes only relatively little to a secure knowledge about Jesus' activity. The opposition to the Synoptics is too large; it can no longer be bridged in a harmonizing manner. This problem was an issue for the early church from the second century onward, i.e., basically from the beginning.[64] Our most important sources are therefore Mark—whose historical value is not undisputed—and the

---

Dogmengeschichte (Harnack 1909, 68 n. 1 and 74 n. 1), Harnack had sharply rejected Wrede's basic thesis ("Wrede's brave but methodologically untenable and ultimately unusable book") but partly accepted his Mark criticism: the Gospel is said to be "a diffuse conglomerate of traditions of very different value" (Harnack 1909, 68 n. 1). The Bultmann school then greatly overvalued the significance of Wrede's book. For a certain time it almost became a New Testament "cult book."

[62] Harnack 1907.

[63] Cf. the πολλοί in Luke 1.1. On this, see Hengel 2012b (GV = 2007a) and Hengel 2008c, 274–356 (ET = 2000b, 169–207).

[64] On this, see Merkel 1971; Hengel 1993a, 26ff. (ET = 1989a, 5ff.); Hengel 2008c, 38ff. (ET = 2000b, 21ff.).

sayings tradition, which here means again especially the Gospel of Luke. Matthew follows only in the third place. With respect to the messianic consciousness of Jesus, the Fourth Gospel, despite its questionable historical value, always stands in the background as a historically unresolved, indeed insoluble problem.[65]

To be sure, if the attempt at a presentation of the reality of Jesus were primarily a mirror of a person's own subjectivity and wishes, then it would be justified to adopt the radically negative, basically ahistorical stance that repudiates the historical question about the human being Jesus and withdraws—as Martin Kähler once did and his many imitators have subsequently done—into the "storm-free zone" of the "biblical historical Christ" (whatever one is meant to understand by that).[66] With his sharply formulated demand—which continues to have a lasting impact decades later, indeed, basically up to the present day—Kähler also claimed to "to set up a warning sign before allegedly presuppositionless historical research when it ceases to do real research and turns instead to a fanciful reshaping of the data." For it "what is usually happening is that the image of Jesus is being refracted through the spirit of these gentlemen themselves."[67] That even Schweitzer and many of his predecessors succumbed to this danger is beyond question. However, even modern portraits of Jesus appear to validate this old warning from more than 125 years ago (1892), although we ourselves can acknowledge neither the prohibition of Kähler nor his demand for a "storm-free zone," because these attempts at historical approximation neither seek to suppress or to replace the Christ of faith, nor ought they to do so. The foundation of the Christian faith is the "apostolic witness" in the New Testament, which is a witness that speaks for itself.

---

[65] On this, see Hengel 1993a, 322–23 (ET = 1989a, 132–33).

[66] Kähler 1953 (reprint of the first edition of 1882; "more important reformulations of the second edition [have been] recorded in the notes" [12]). The phrase "storm-free zone" occurs twice in the second edition (1896, II: 201–2 = 1953, 78–79 n. a; there is no equivalent in the English translation, i.e., Kähler 1988). On the older discussion of Kähler's writing, see Scholz 1899. On the later criticism, see Michel 1955 (= 1986, 135–47), who, in turn, formulates too one-sidedly again: "The discipleship of Jesus, the faith in the risen one and in the one who is present to the community are only possible if one takes the entire burden of the historical conflict upon oneself" (360 = 146). Who is able to take *this* burden *really* in an adequate manner upon him- or herself? We can only attempt again and again to do justice to it—to some extent—with our limited means with regard to the difficult situation of the sources and the controversial research.

[67] Kähler 1988, 57, modified (GV = Kähler 1953, 29–30). The last sentence, which is emphasized by the author in the German version, alludes to a well-known Faust quotation. Cf. Schlatter 1995 (GV = 1905, 229–50; 1969, 134–50) on a theology that "gives its historical novels titles like *Life of Jesus* or *New Testament Theology*" (ET = 216; GV = 230–31; 139), and on "the profane, modern manufacture of conjectures" (ET = 224; GV = 249; 149).

The question is whether there are not ways that avoid extreme subjectivism, which leads to free expressionistic or to politically correct portraits, and take up the *particulae veri* of individual pictures of Jesus, while using a sober assessing historical method on the whole, which is a given in scholarship on ancient history and which excludes a general radical skepticism. It is deeply lamentable that apart from Eduard Meyer and Joseph Klausner, no major ancient historians have intensively occupied themselves with the first beginnings of Christianity.[68] This may be connected to the fact that we New Testament scholars have buried the access to the sources to such an extent with our — often very hypothetical — secondary literature[69] that no "foreigner" dares to approach them any longer. Both works — that of J. Klausner, whose Jesus book was published in Hebrew in 1922 in Jerusalem,[70] and that of Eduard Meyer[71] — were not treated seriously enough by the New Testament scholars at the time and are precisely for this reason still worth reading.[72]

---

[68] Cf. also the popular presentation of Grant 1977 and the independent, interesting essay of Millar 1990. Schweitzer 2000, 7 (GV = 1913, 6), already pointed to this problem for the nineteenth century: "For the problem of the life of Jesus has no analogy in the field of history. No historical school has ever laid down canons for the investigation of this problem, no professional historian has ever lent his aid to theology in dealing with it. Every ordinary method of historical investigation proves inadequate to the complexity of the conditions. The standards of ordinary historical science are inadequate here, its methods not immediately applicable." We are not willing to agree with these two sentences in their generalization. We call to mind just the problem of Socrates or the sayings of Heraclitus.

[69] The criticism also frequently operates with hypotheses that can scarcely be justified. This is shown not only by D. F. Strauss, by the Tübingen school of his teacher F. C. Baur, and by William Wrede as well as by Dibelius' and Bultmann's much praised foundational investigations on form criticism (on this, see section 7.1) and all the more by many products of the most recent Jesus literature; see, e.g., the works discussed earlier in this section.

[70] On this, see note 49 above.

[71] Meyer 1921; 1962.

[72] The damning criticism of Schmidt 1921, which was written in the midst of the elation of the newly discovered form criticism, did an injustice to the work of Meyer (119): "Thus the content of the book is a failure." In reality E. Meyer was *entirely justified* in "ascribing far too much" to the authorial "intention of the primitive Christian authors," especially of Mark, which form criticism neglected (120). The progress of scholarship has confirmed Meyer here. On this, see, e.g., the verdict of the ancient philologist Zuntz 1984a, 222: "Whoever seeks to understand the second Gospel in this 'unitary' meaning may soon find himself enriched through the knowledge of a masterwork of astonishing originality." See also Zuntz 1984b, 47–71, on his early dating to 40 CE, which appears too optimistic to us. Cf. the verdict of W. Schadewaldt 1985 (ET = 1982), which goes in a similar direction and likewise comes from the pen of a famous ancient philologist. The radical, thoroughgoing form criticism has led us into an unhistorical dead end. Too much was sacrificed to a new fashion at that time. Their verdicts were often, indeed usually, not determined by the "form" of the tradition but by the content on the basis of the personal judgment of the critic.

The insight that we cannot sketch a life of Jesus, indeed that we cannot even sketch a picture of Jesus that does not have internal contradictions, is not a discovery that arrived only with the emergence of form criticism. We find it, sometimes expressed in a pointed manner, already in D. F. Strauss and in some "liberal" authors of the nineteenth century. It is absolutely necessary to uphold this insight.[73] It is therefore all the more conspicuous that the successful book of Crossan claims again to present *The Life of a Mediterranean Jewish Peasant*. Perhaps this occurred in the service of promoting better sales. This is suggested by the self-confident blurb: "The first comprehensive determination of who Jesus was, what he did, what he said."

Even the relationship of the Jew Jesus to his own people can no longer be specified in a simple way. We do not know him or the diverse Judaism—today one often speaks within the framework of a fashionable pluralism of "Judaisms"—at the turn of the century with enough precision to do so. For, on the one hand, he does not "relate" to Judaism as a foreigner: "Jesus was not a Christian but a Jew," says Wellhausen tersely.[74] We could even say that he did not "relate" to Judaism but lived and acted exclusively in it.[75] And yet the Jewish historian Joseph Klausner, the founder of a seri-

---

The criticism of Dibelius 1921 underestimates the significance of the evangelists as authors and as tradents. See also section 7.1.

[73] On D. F. Strauss, see Ziegler 1908, 605–6, and Strauss 1873, 87–88 (GV = 1872, 76–77): "The evangelists have overlaid the picture of his life with so thick a coat of supernatural colouring . . . that the natural colours cannot now be restored. . . . He who has once been deified has irretrievably lost his manhood. It is an idle notion that by any kind of operation we could restore *a natural and harmonious picture of a life and of a human being* from sources of information which, like the Gospels, have been adapted to suit a supernatural being, and distorted, moreover, by parties whose conceptions and interests conflicted with each other's" (our emphasis). On this, see the Strauss quotation in note 27 above and K. Barth 2001, 550–51 (GV = 1947, 511–12); see already the insight of the young Harnack in 1874 (see note 20 above) or of Hausrath 1908, I, X: "A hundred hypotheses are suggested but what is the objective truth? . . . Our sources are neither abundant enough nor sufficiently clear to write a life of Jesus according to the demands of the scholarship of history." Cf. Jülicher 1906, 72; at a later time, even Holtzmann 1907, VI, expressed himself with caution. This applies all the more to the old master of historical criticism J. Wellhausen, who speaks of "inadequate fragments" (Wellhausen 1987, 103). The question, however, is whether our modern notions about a "natural and coherent picture of a human being and his life" are the measure of all things and thus also applicable to the activity of the Galilean. Such "life pictures" that are satisfying to us often cannot be written any longer for influential figures of antiquity. The argument of Strauss suffers—no differently from his liberal and conservative opponents—from a *petitio principii*.

[74] Wellhausen 1987, 102; see note 10 in this chapter. Bultmann repeatedly took up this thesis but evaluated it incorrectly in terms of substance: the whole of primitive Christianity was Jewish. It rests on an alternative that is false for the early period of the first century.

[75] See the fitting title of Charlesworth 1988: *Jesus within Judaism*.

ous Jewish research on Jesus, could write the sentence "in spite of all this, there was in him something out of which arose 'non-Judaism.'"[76]

In what follows, with constant comparisons with the texts of the Gospels, our concern will be — quite modestly — to secure traces and to discern and trace basic lines and contours (one could almost say: in the manner of a woodcut), even though we do not have a coherent, absolutely clear picture of his personality and course of life and more questions remain open than can be answered. In some cases it is a matter of neglected traces that have been missed by a widespread skepticism. The contours, too, are not always familiar to us but may appear foreign, even alienating. In his last work, *Der alte und der neue Glaube* (1872), D. F. Strauss correctly perceived an essential point within the boundaries that were given to him as an opponent of the Christian faith:

> Above all, I must have a distinct, definite conception of him in whom I am to believe, whom I am to imitate as an exemplar of moral excellence. A being of which I can only catch fitful glimpses, which remains obscure to me in essential respects, may, it is true, interest me as a problem for scientific investigation, but it must remain ineffectual as regards practical influence on my life. But *a being with distinct features, capable of affording a definite conception, is only to be found in the Christ of faith.*

This for him means

> of legend, and there, of course, only by the votary who is willing to take into the bargain all the impossibilities, all the contradictions contained in the picture: the Jesus of history, of science, is only a problem; but a *problem* cannot be an object of faith, or a pattern by which to shape our lives.[77]

With this he puts his finger on the great error of the "liberal" Christology of the nineteenth century, which proceeded from Schleiermacher and was oriented far too much to the reconstruction of a "historical Jesus." To be sure, we must add that Strauss, according to his own self-evaluation, did

---

[76] Klausner 1945, 413; cf. also the introduction (9): "Had there not been in Jesus' teaching something contrary to the 'world-outlook' of Israel, there could never have arisen out of it a new teaching so irreconcilable with the spirit of Judaism: *ex nihilo nihil fit.*" On this, see Mussner 1987, 137ff. We can, however, ask whether Klausner's modern notion of Judaism, which is nationalistic or Zionistic in character, really corresponds entirely to the Judaism at the turn of the century and its diversity of thought. However, his critical remarks are justified. Cf. also Bockmuehl 1994, 103–24.

[77] Strauss 1873, 90–91 (modified), our emphasis (GV = 1872, 79).

not primarily want to be a historian: "I am not a historian; with me every-thing has proceeded from dogmatic . . . concerns."[78] He had a "dogmatic interest" in destroying the traditional picture of Jesus. At the end of his life he was scarcely interested any longer in the contours of the historical fig-ure of Jesus, which were still—by ancient standards—very clear. For him Jesus was only still a "problem" and no longer a person. The destructive analyst, filled by the pathos of belief in progress, had suppressed the retro-spective, conscientiously comparative, reconstructive historian of the time of his work as a tutor. To be sure, his radical criticism vis-à-vis the naïve optimism precisely also of the "progressive" and "liberal" theologians was necessary and in a certain way salutary at that time.

The result of our historical attempts at reconstruction or, better, approximation (which are necessarily fragmentary due to the situation of the sources) should and can for this reason—we wish to stress this point once again—never, ever become the foundation or "object of faith."[79] This is always only the *real* Jesus Christ, as the incarnate Son of God who has been "exalted to the right hand of God," and never the product of our his-torical strivings. Such a faith, however, is grounded on the whole apostolic witness, which is handed down to us in the New Testament, including the Fourth Gospel—which is to a great extent consciously and idiosyncrati-cally unhistorical—and the epistolary literature! One could also say: Only the encounter with the "Christ of faith" in the preaching of the apostles bestows the assurance of faith. Precisely this, however, must be rejected as "legend" and "myth" according to Strauss. Our attempt at historical approximation initially consciously postpones a theological development of this "Christ of faith." We then encounter him in the primitive commu-nity. The attempt must demonstrate that in the quest for the development of Christology what becomes visible already with Jesus himself is not "merely a problem" but rather "contours" that are indeed *clear*. It could be that in the activity of Jesus that extends to his passion, characteristics become visible that lead with an inner consistency to the "Christ of faith."

---

[78] Letter of July 22, 1846 (cited from Barth 2001, 529; GV = 1947, 492).
[79] Strauss 1873, 91, modified (GV = 1872, 79); on this, see Ziegler 1908, II: 683–84.

6

The Sources[1]

6.1 On the Situation of the Sources

We must now, as it were, plunge into the ancient world, leave the present with all our wishes and questions behind us, and first ask about the *sources*. Here it is A. Schweitzer again who makes us aware of a fact that is often overlooked, namely

> that there are few characters of antiquity about whom we possess so much indubitably historical information, of whom we have so many authentic discourses. The position is much less favorable, for instance in the case of Socrates, for he is pictured to us by literary men who exercised their creative ability upon the portrait. Jesus stands much more immediately before us, because he was depicted by simple Christians without literary gifts.[2]

We must qualify this optimism with respect to the words "undoubtedly" and "literarily ungifted Christians." The literary-critical perspective, which is flourishing today and which revels in the discovery of rhetorical and narrative strategies, has resulted in a greater desire than ever to regard the authors of the Gospels as literarily adept authors, who sometimes work with sophisticated techniches and an understanding of the art of dramatic presentation that carried to an extreme. Radical historical skeptics even turn them into authors of novelistic fictions. Forgotten is the time about a hundred years earlier when such an influential scholar as Martin

---

[1] Cf. Aufhauser 1925; Klausner 1945, 17–70; Trilling 1966, 51ff.; Meier 1991, 56–111; Theissen/Merz 1998, 17–124 (GV = 1997, 35–124); Van Voorst 2001; Dunn 2003b, 141–42.

[2] Schweitzer 2000, 7 (GV = 1913, 6).

Dibelius, at the beginning of his *Formgeschichte des Evangeliums*, wrote in an — apparently — programmatic way:[3]

> The composers are only to the smallest extent authors. They are principally collectors, vehicles of tradition, editors

while

> St. Luke more than the other synoptics shows the strongest literary character. Thereby it can be estimated in how lowly a degree after all St. Matthew and St. Mark may pass as authors.

For more than a generation this thesis dominated and misled the market of New Testament exegesis in Germany. The truth probably lies between the extremes, i.e., Mark and Matthew — in our view already through oral presentation as teachers, which ultimately stands behind all the Gospels — were also "more eloquent" than the fathers of form criticism wanted to acknowledge in their joy of discovery. All four Gospels reach a high degree of theological reflection, which need not mean that the historical tradition was largely suppressed by the theological tendency that shaped them. This clearly occurs only with the Fourth Gospel, which goes its own way. But even here one would need to ask: Is it not, in fact, likely that primitive Christianity — including John at the end of the first century — would have taken over theologically essential basic ideas largely from the activity and way of Jesus himself? This question will accompany us through this entire volume.

A. Schweitzer, however, is right. This is shown not only by a comparison of the Synoptics' picture of Jesus with the Socrates of the Platonic Dialogues, with the *Memorabilia* of Xenophon, or with the fragments of Aeschines and other "Socratics,"[4] but also with later

---

[3] Dibelius 1971, 3 (GV = 1919; 1933, 2–3). Cf. Bultmann 1963, 2–4, 338–51 (GV = 1995, 3–4, 362–76): "Mark is not sufficiently master of his material to be able to venture on a systematic construction (*Gliederung*) himself" (ET = 350; GV = 375). In reality Mark is very carefully structured. On K. L. Schmidt's largely unjustified criticism of Eduard Meyer and on the very different judgment of ancient philologists such as Wolfgang Schadewaldt and Günther Zuntz, see note 72 in chapter 5.

[4] Döring 1984. See also Gigon 1979, 63–64: "The chronicle as list of names and facts, on the one hand, and the anecdote, on the other hand, are (around the end of the fifth century BCE) . . . the two only original forms of historical tradition. The biography as the presentation of a self-enclosed and meaningful course of life only appears a few generations after the death of Socrates in Greek literature." Gigon reaches the judgment "that the quest for the personality and work of the historical Socrates is practically entirely unanswerable because everywhere we encounter only Socrates literature and never Socrates biography"

ancient biographies from the pens of Plutarch, Lucian,[5] Arrian, and Philostratus.[6]

To this we can add the fact that even in the case of ancient personalities, who were incomparably "more powerful" than the craftsman from Nazareth, our historical-biographical source situation is likewise not unproblematic, even though we know more historical details about them. The earliest continuous presentation of *Alexander* by a historian that is preserved as a work is that of Diodorus Siculus, who wrote at the time of the early Augustus, nearly three hundred years after Alexander. The most important Greek biographer of Alexander, Arrian, wrote ca. 450 years later, and Plutarch ca. 400 years later. The most important Latin biographer, Curtius Rufus, was probably a contemporary of Arrian in the middle of the second century CE or even later. Of course, they had, in turn, numerous older sources at their disposal. However, only quotations and excerpts are preserved from the historians who were contemporary with Alexander, and there are sometimes extreme deviations between them in their evaluation of the world conqueror. Moreover, precisely these sources show that the formation of legends around Alexander already began in his lifetime.[7] They extend in many languages and branches into the Middle Ages. Robin

---

(16). Instead, he seeks to trace back from the Socrates literature to the creator of this literature, i.e., what "is graspable for us is not Socrates as a historical teacher of his students but Socrates as a central object of a philosophical literature" (16). Nevertheless, for him too the "trial and (. . . the) execution of Socrates in 399 . . . stands beyond all doubt" (21). Another example would be the great rabbinic teachers since Hillel, about which we have an abundance of individual traditions of halakic and haggadic character, which cannot, however, be combined into a whole "biographically." On this, see Bacher 1903; 1890 and the investigations of J. Neusner on individual teachers such as Yohanan ben Zakkai, Eliezer ben Hyrcanus, etc. See also Neusner 1971.

[5] Here one would neet to point especially to Lucian's *Demonax*.

[6] Here, however, we must note that his *Life of Apollonius of Tyana* has much more novelistic than biographical traits and in this respect is precisely not comparable to the Synoptic Gospels. On this, see now Schirren 2005b. In our view, Philostratus' presentation is a sort of philosophical "anti-Gospel," composed at the wish of the empress Julia Domna after her death in 217, at a time when Christianity gained considerable influence. At the turn from the third to the fourth century CE, Hierocles followed in his footsteps in directly polemical form. See Eusebius, *Contra Hieroclem* (Des Places / Forrat 1986).

[7] A compilation and English translation of the fragments of the thirty-six early Alexander historians (FGrH 117–152) can be found in C. A. J. Robinson 1953/1963, I: 1: "Of the five extant historians whose complete accounts of Alexander survive, Arrian is the best by far." On the person and work of Arrian, see Wirth 1964; Heucke 2003 (GV = 1997). He lived between approximately 85/90–170 CE and wrote, among other works, a history of Alexander in seven books, in which he endeavored primarily to use the works of eyewitnesses as sources. On the formation of legends, see Meyer 1962, 54ff., 159 (against Wellhausen). Hengel 1984a, 17–18 with notes 70–74. On the question of miracles, see section 16.4.

Lane Fox begins his large biography on Alexander with the observation that we cannot write a biography of any personality in antiquity, except of Augustine, Cicero, and perhaps the emperor Julian, from which figures we possess many letters or other autobiographical witnesses. However, he then writes a book with 568 pages about his hero with the revealing qualification "This book is a search, not a story."[8] This statement would also need to stand over every serious presentation of Jesus and over every history of early Christianity.

Let us examine yet another example, which is extremely different from Jesus and comes from a closer point in time. *Augustus* was certainly the most politically influential ruler in antiquity. He died in 14 CE after fifty-seven years of political activity. Luke 2.1 consciously connects his person with the birth of Jesus.[9] If we disregard the autobiographical inscription of the *Res gestae divi Augusti*, preserved in fragmentary form in three places,[10] which very succinctly recounts his own achievements, then the first biographical presentation that has been preserved in full for us, by Suetonius, who wrote very selective biographies of emperors between ca. 119 and 121, was written more than one hundred years after the death of Augustus.[11] The *Annals* of Tacitus, which originated a short time earlier, deal only with the very last period of the emperor in their first book.[12] Appian (ca. 100–180?) describes only the civil war. Only the early time of Octavian up to 44 BCE is preserved from the contemporary biography of Nicolaus of Damascus, the intimate of Herod in Jerusalem (ca. 64 BCE–10 CE).[13] The most detailed presentation of his reign is handed down to us in the Roman history of Cassius Dio Cocceianus,[14] which arose in the first decades of the third century CE. Signs, dreams, and miracles already play an important role in Suetonius and even more in Cassius Dio. The only preserved historical presentation of a contemporary is the very succinct historical outline of Velleius Paterculus, who,

---

[8] Lane Fox 1973, 11. In the preface to Lane Fox 2006, he objects to authors who "adopt a confident tone," clarifies that the concern is with "a search," and indicates that a full picture of the life of Alexander is not possible.

[9] On this, see the affirmative comment of Melito of Sardis ca. 160 CE in Eusebius, *Hist. eccl.* 4.26.7–8.

[10] Volkmann 1969; text, translation, and commentary can be found in Weber 1974.

[11] Sallmann 2008 (GV = 2001). As secretary to Trajan (from ca. 114 CE) and Hadrian (until 121 CE) he had—*a studiis, a bibliothecis*, and finally, *ab epistulis*—access to the imperial archive with entirely personal testimonies of Augustus.

[12] He wanted to write a work on the time of Augustus, but he did not get to it (*Ann.* 3.24.3).

[13] FGrH 90, F 125–130. On his person, see the discussion in section 3.1.1 with notes 65–67.

[14] Books 46–56 (43 BCE–14 CE).

having been born ca. 20 BCE, wrote at the time of Tiberius.[15] Through these examples from the entirely different sphere of politics, it becomes clear that even the tradition about the greatest ruler figures of antiquity is fragmentary, i.e., dependent on the chance preservation of sources. We must, of coure, add that in addition to the texts of these biographers and historians about Alexander and Augustus, which are often preserved only in fragmentary form, we find other pointers through inscriptions, coins, and above all in the contemporary and later literature.[16] This especially applies to the first Roman principate, which radically changed the empire.

But even with respect to such an entirely different figure as Jesus of Nazareth, we have, in addition to the four Gospels, also the New Testament epistles, Acts, and Revelation, as well as the whole early Christian literature with corresponding pointers, which sometimes have, of course, very different historical value. Here one would need to mention the diverse "apocryphal" Gospel-like texts that emerged since the second century, beginning with the Gospel of Thomas, which is largely overvalued today, and with the numerous Jesus logia of unknown origin.[17]

If one considers that Jesus was not a successful world ruler known by all, but an initially completely obscure Galilean craftsman who was active for a very short time, and if one takes into account the fact that the earliest preserved literary pointers begin with Paul ca. twenty years after the crucifixion of Jesus and the first "Jesus biographies" start with Mark ca. forty years after this same event, then the broad and early tradition—measured by ancient standards—does indeed appear quite conspicuous, even though it is supposed to have a predominantly nonauthentic, legendary character. It is an indication of the extent to which this simple Jew from a Galilean village must already have made an impact upon his contemporaries in Jewish Palestine and soon also outside of this area. By the time of Claudius and Nero at the latest, he also unsettled the Roman world. The frequently heard accusation that no Greek or Roman historian before the end of the first or the beginning of the second century mentioned Jesus and his movement

[15] He treats the fifty-seven years from the murder of Caesar in 44 BCE to the death of Augustus in 14 CE in sixty-six short chapters, 2.59–124 (Hellegouarc'h 1982). Alongside this, reference could additionally be made to Pompeius Trogus' history of the Mediterranean region in forty-four books, but it is preserved only in a concise epitome of Justinus from the third century, which mentions Augustus relatively rarely and only with a view to the provinces.

[16] See, e.g., Ehrenberg/Jones 1949 and Mattingly 1983. For literature, see Cicero, Horace, Ovid, Propertius, Tibullus, etc. The large biography of Augustus by Bleicken 1998 (ET = 2016) concisely specifies the sources for the individual chapters in the notes.

[17] See the extensive collection of Resch 1906; Jeremias 1965; critically Hofius 1978; 1991; 2012. In his letter to bishop Soter of Rome in 170 CE, Dionysius of Corinth already lamented the various forgery attempts of "writings of the Lord," Eusebius, *Hist. eccl.* 4.23.12.

demonstrates only the critic's ignorance of the situation of the ancient sources. Between 30 and 120 CE there are no historians preserved for us who could have written about Christ and the Christians, except for Josephus, Tacitus, and Suetonius—and they do so!

With respect to the history of ancient religion and intellectual history the intensive reporting about Jesus is actually quite astonishing. Despite the relatively short time of his activity, we have more *comparatively early* traditions about him than about most great thinkers of antiquity. For Muhammad, who died in 632 CE, we have only *one* much later biography, which goes back to Ibn Ishaq (died in 768). His work itself was lost, but it was edited by even later authors, especially by Ibn Hisham (died 834), two hundred and twelve years after the *Hijra*, and then by Bukhari, the author of the oldest collection of Hadith, in 870. All later presentations are based on this.[18]

The closest parallel already stands itself entirely in the Christian tradition. The most recent sensational discoveries include the Cologne Mani-Codex. It contains a Life of Mani (216–276), which is partly presented in the first person. It was composed in the first third of the fourth century, and the names of the guarantors of the tradition are mentioned. In this way there arose an "almost seamless biography," which is reminiscent of Tatian's harmony of the Gospels, except that in the Mani-Codex the specification of the source is never lacking.[19] However, for this (as later probably also for Muhammad) the Christian tradition itself constitutes again a model of sorts. Mani (and Muhammad) understood themselves to be continuers and completers of the work of Jesus, as the "seal of the prophets,"[20] and their activities, and this means also their "biographies," presuppose the Gospels in one way or another.

---

[18] Muhammad was born around 570. He died in 632, only six years before Jerusalem was conquered by the Muslims. For the problem, see Paret 1957: "The basic stock of the factually secured traditional material (can)not be dated back before the first half of the eighth century." This means it is about a hundred years later than the "historical Muhammad." To be sure, an abundance of tradition bearers are mentioned in the biography of Muhammad. One will recall the efforts of a Papias. From Muhammad's migration to Medina in 622 Islam increasingly became a political-religious movement that was extremely successful militarily. The difference from the early history of Christianity before Constantine could not be greater. This is forgotten by many today.

[19] Henrichs/Koenen 1988, xv–xvi.

[20] Cf. Colpe 1990, 15ff., 227ff. The concept first appears in Pseudo-Tertullian, *Adv. Jud.* 8.12, who designates Jesus as *signaculum omnium prophetarum* in connection with Dan 9.24-27.

6.2 Early Christian Testimonies to Jesus Outside of the Gospels[21]

If we examine the primitive Christian literary testimony to Jesus, then it begins for us ca. twenty years after his crucifixion with an outsider and former opponent, Paul. He wrote his first letter that is known to us to the newly founded community in Thessalonika, in which he speaks of the death and resurrection of Jesus and of saving faith in this Jesus as the Messiah, Lord, and Son of God, who will preserve one from God's coming judgment of wrath.[22] Paul quotes an apocalyptic "word of the Lord" about his parousia and emphasizes that the Lord comes "as a thief in the night."[23] Both call to mind apocalyptic sayings of Jesus in the Synoptics and probably go back to Jesus tradition.[24] In a number of the authentic letters of Paul, which were written in the following decade, we find pointers to the human being Jesus—in the mention of Jesus' birth through a (Jewish) woman, his placement under the Mosaic law (Gal 4.4); in his descent from Judaism (Rom 9.5), more precisely from the lineage of David (Rom 1.3), the son of Jesse (Rom 15.12);[25] in his messianic service to Israel, his own people (Rom 9.3ff.; 15.8);[26] and, above all, in his death on the cross. In 1 Corinthians there are two references to authoritative sayings of the Lord, i.e., to statements of Jesus. One is concerned with the prohibition of divorce and remarriage after divorce[27] and the other with the command that those who proclaim the gospel should live from their work of proclamation, which points to the Synoptic tradition of the sending out of the twelve disciples.[28] Mere allusions to sayings of the Synoptic tradition without indications that the concern is with a "word of the Lord" occur much more often, among others, multiple times in the paraenesis of Rom 12.9-21; 13.8ff., and in 1 Cor 13.2. What is fundamental for Paul is also the invocation of God as "Father," Ἀββα, as a sign of being a child of God, which goes back to Jesus' address to God in prayer and probably also contains

---

[21] Koester 1957; Trilling 1966; Dungan 1971; Fjärstedt 1974; Stuhlmacher 1991 (GV = 1983); Riesner 1988, see index, s.v. "Paulus, Jesus-Überlieferung"; Theissen/Merz 1998, 17–24, 37–59 (GV = 1997, 35–41, 51–69); Wenham 1995; Hengel 2004d.

[22] First Thessalonians 4.14; cf. 5.10; 1.10. On the topic of Jesus tradition in Paul, cf. Riesner 1997; see in detail Wenham 1995; Häusser 2006.

[23] First Thessalonians 4.15-17; 5.2; cf. Luke 12.39; Matt 24.30 parr.; 24.43; Rev 3.3; 16.15. On the "words of the Lord," see Hengel 2008c, 112–20, 223ff. (ET = 2000b, 61–65, 131ff.). See section 6.6.

[24] On this, see Hengel 2002, 346ff.

[25] Cf. Isa 11.10; Matt 1.5-6; Luke 3.32.

[26] Cf. Mark 10.45 = Matt 20.28; cf. Luke 22.27; Isa 53.10ff.

[27] First Corinthians 7.10-11.

[28] First Corinthians 9.14; cf. Luke 10.7 = Matt 10.10b: "The worker is worthy of his wages." See section 11.7.

an indirect pointer to the Lord's Prayer, which begins with this address. This Aramaic acclamation, as well as the Maranatha, demonstrates Paul's connection with the primitive Jerusalem community.[29] That Paul, when he founded communities, *recounted* the story of the passion and presupposed knowledge of it in his communities emerges from 1 Cor 15.3-8 with the "chronological" enumeration of death, burial, resurrection, and appearances in temporal[30] succession and from the account of Jesus' last meal with his disciples in 1 Cor 11.23ff. With the quotation of the Lord's Supper paradosis—"the Lord Jesus, in the night in which he was betrayed (or handed over), took bread, gave thanks, broke it, and said . . ."—Paul not only points to his introduction of the Lord's Supper[31] when he founded the community in Corinth but also to his telling of the story of the passion in its temporal-historical course. It contains a concrete date, in all probability the night of Passover.[32] Thus, in Paul we can infer a chronological connection of three days, beginning with the last meal of Jesus on the night of Passover via the betrayal, the crucifixion, and the burial through to the morning of Easter.[33] For without this temporal background the community would understand neither this text, of which Paul wants to remind them, nor his talk of the "word of the cross" in 1 Cor 1.18, nor a formulation such as what we find in 1 Cor 5.7-8, where he writes: "for our Passover lamb has been slaughtered, Christ. Therefore let us celebrate not with leaven . . . but with the unleavened bread. . . ." In this way he mentions in passing what is well-known in Corinth, i.e., there too it was known that Jesus was crucified in Jerusalem at a Passover festival; after all, Passover lambs could not be slaughtered elsewhere. The "rulers of this age" (1 Cor 2.8), who crucified Christ because they did not recognize his divine dignity ($\delta\delta\xi\alpha$), also refer in the first place to the political powers, such as Pilate and the high priests, who were, in turn, themselves henchmen of demonic powers. In 1 Thess 2.14-15 it is, in an emotionally charged Pauline text, "the Jews" who "killed Jesus and the prophets and persecuted us."

---

[29] Rom 8.15-16; Gal 4.5-6; see also section 13.2 with note 58. On this, see Hengel 2004a. Cf. now Frey 2016.

[30] On this, see Hengel 2001a.

[31] On the formulation, see 1 Cor 11.20: κυριακὸν δεῖπνον.

[32] Cf. 1 Cor 5.6ff. and Luke 22.8, 14-15: Is he perhaps indirectly alluding to the event of Luke 22.3; John 13.2, 27 with 1 Cor 5.5? Cf. also 1 Cor 6.1, 9-10 and Luke 22.28-30. On this, see Hengel 2004d.

[33] The phrase ἐν τῇ νυκτὶ ᾗ παρεδίδετο (1 Cor 11.23) points in the first instance to the nighttime betrayal of Judas. At the same time the "handing over" by God (Rom 4.25; 8.32; cf. Isa 53.6, 12) lies in the background. Due to the clear specification of time we can relate the παρεδίδετο to the whole passion. It extended over the following day to the "ninth hour" (Mark 15.33). The special offense is "the betrayal" by Jesus' own disciple. This temporal sequence corresponds basically to 1 Cor 15.3-5.

The often repeated argument that Paul knew very little or no Jesus tradition, indeed that he did not want to know of it because he was not interested in it, since he proclaimed only the "kerygma" of the crucified and risen Kyrios, is misleading and based on the misuse—which is common among theologians—of the *argumentum e silentio*, for in the few situation-specific letters that have been preserved for us, more or less by chance, he no longer had to discuss things that were long known in the community. In his letters, we learn about the way in which he founded his communities at best in short marginal notes.[34] The temporally structured account of Jesus' activity, death, and resurrection belongs in the community-founding preaching (1 Cor 15.1-8), which is almost entirely unknown to us. It is absurd to believe that the apostle (and the other missionaries to the Gentiles) could have proclaimed a crucified Jew and state criminal[35] from remote Galilee as Messiah, Son of God, and Savior of the world, without telling his Jewish and Gentile hearers about the life, activity, and death of this Jesus and the concomitant fulfillment of the prophetic promises.[36] When, according to 1 Cor 2.2, Paul, in Corinth, wants to know nothing except Jesus Christ crucified, this self-evidently includes the report about Jesus' passion and death. Without telling the passion story, "the word of the cross" (ὁ λόγος τοῦ σταυροῦ, 1 Cor 1.18) could not be proclaimed in a comprehensible manner at all! Something similar applies to the "gospel" in 1 Cor 15.3-4, which he proclaimed or, better, recounted as first and foremost (ἐν πρώτοις); for what underlies this text, in most abbreviated formulaic form, is a—christologically interpreted—narrative. In Corinth, as in every other newly founded community, people probably asked Paul searching questions about these events. The preaching of the crucified and risen Christ, who was not merely a mythical, heavenly figure, but precisely as the crucified Messiah, the Χριστὸς ἐσταυρωμέ-νος,[37] was a concrete human person—to be sure of absolutely singular, divine rank (Phil 2.6-9)—who suffered a brutal and shameful, abhorrent death, also includes statements about his person, activity, and fate. One should not impute any docetism to Paul as if he did not take seriously the humanity of Jesus. It is no longer permissible to cite 2 Cor 5.16 in this context. The concern there is not with Christ "according to the flesh" (κατὰ σάρκα) in the sense of the human being Jesus,[38] i.e., with the κατὰ

---

[34] First Thessalonians 1.6, 9; 2.1-2; 1 Cor 1.16; 2.1-5; Phil 4.15.

[35] Cf. 1 Cor 2.8 as well as Tacitus *Ann.* 15.44.3 (see note 71 below).

[36] First Corinthians 15.3-4; cf. Rom 1.1-4; 9.4-5; 1 Cor 10.1-11; Gal 3.13-14, etc.

[37] First Corinthians 1.23; 2.2; Gal 3.1. On the repelling character of crucifixion, see section 21.2.

[38] Thus Rom 9:5: ἐξ ὧν (this means Israel) ὁ Χριστὸς ὁ κατὰ σάρκα. Note the post-placement of γενομένου ἐκ σπέρματος Δαυὶδ κατὰ σάρκα in Rom 1.3. Romans 1.3 is

σάρκα the concern is not with an attribute of Christ but with the fact that Paul as a persecutor had once known Christ "in a fleshly way"—to clarify the meaning of the adverbial phrase, one could also say: had "failed to know" him.[39] Paul was probably reproached for this time and again. After all, for the letter writer, these events lay only ca. two decades in the past. A sizable number of eyewitnesses were still around. In 1 Cor 15.6 he speaks of an appearance of Jesus before about "five hundred brothers at once, of whom the majority are alive until today." Paul knew the leading disciples of Jesus personally. He mentions Cephas-Peter[40] ten times and James, Jesus' brother, four times, and John, "the twelve," and "the brothers of the Lord" twice in each case.[41] In Galatia and Corinth it was known exactly who these people were. Paul must have reported in relatively great detail about them, otherwise there could not, for example, have been a "Cephas party" in Corinth. Presumably, Cephas-Peter had also visited the community in Corinth after it was founded by the apostle to the Gentiles and had made a strong impression there.[42] Is it plausible that Paul spoke in many

---

also a positive statement, as is Rom 4.1 on Abraham. Both sentences are not meaningless for him!

[39] Second Corinthians 5.16: εἰ καὶ ἐγνώκαμεν κατὰ σάρκα Χριστόν. Even R. Bultmann concedes that the adverbial meaning is "more probable," but then obscures this clear pointer with an absurd reversal: "for a 'Christ regarded in the manner of the flesh' is just what a 'Christ after the flesh' is" (Bultmann 2007, I: 238–39; GV = 1984b, 239). See already Bultmann 1933–1965, I: 185, 259: "The old controversy over whether 'according to the flesh' belongs to 'Christ' or to 'if we have known' is unimportant" (185). In this context Paul precisely does not mean a "human personality," which "is past," but rather a deeply sinful knowing of Jesus, which takes offense at the crucified Messiah. Jesus was, after all, not transformed from a human being into a God. He is for Paul already the preexistent one who has become human and as the crucified one the exalted Son of God and Messiah (Gal 4.4; 1 Cor 8.6; Phil 2.6ff.); how could the humanity of Jesus be unimportant to him! On this, see Hengel 2002, 261–301. The christological deficit of Bultmann becomes visible here. Althaus 1959, 35–36 (GV = 1963, 20), rightly rejects this misuse of 2 Cor 5.16. On the adverbial use of in 2 Corinthians, see 1.17; 10.2. Even Theissen/Merz 1998, 95 (GV = 1997, 100), want to continue to see a devaluation of the appeal back to the historical Jesus in 2 Cor 5.16. This false interpretation apparently cannot be eradicated. Against it, see now Grässer 2002, 220–21, against Bultmann and Schweitzer: "The identity of the exalted Lord and the earthly Jesus alone, which is a given for the apostle, already fends off this false use of our verse." Behind the sentence stands a real accusation against Paul, which the apostle decisively rejects. It could come from the circle that proclaims another Jesus and another gospel according to 2 Cor 11.4, i.e., presumably emissaries of the Peter mission. See Hengel 2010a, 71–72, 74–75 (GV = 2006b, 116–17, 121–22).

[40] Both names, the Aramaic and the Greek, are known to him; cf. Gal 2.8. This means that he probably also knew about the circumstances of the emergence of this name. Presumably he alludes to this in 1 Cor 3.11; see Hengel 2010a, 16ff. (GV = 2006b, 25ff.).

[41] First Corinthians 9.5; 15.6-7. Cf. Gal 1 and 2.

[42] The "Cephas party" in 1 Cor 1.12 would be best explained in this way. See also Dionysius of Corinth in his letter to Soter of Rome around 170 CE in Eusebius, *Hist. eccl.*

ways about Cephas, James, and the other disciples but said nothing about the human being Jesus?

We must assume that Cephas-Peter—the apostle for the mission to the Jews and, after the conflict in Antioch (Gal 2.11ff.), also an opponent of Paul—as former speaker of the disciples of Jesus and eyewitness had access to a much greater extent of Jesus tradition, being superior to Paul in this respect, and that this was one of the reasons that he was estimated more highly by the opponents of Paul in Corinth. The Cephas party in Corinth was not concerned with the question of the law, as F. C. Baur and his school thought, but more likely with the relation to Christ,[43] with regard to which the "Cephas adherents" devalued Paul vis-à-vis the Jerusalem apostles, and here especially vis-à-vis Cephas-Peter, with the rationale that he had not been a real disciple of Jesus and eyewitness. Nevertheless, Paul *most certainly* did not entirely forgo the use of narratives and traditions about Jesus when he founded his communities. Otherwise, when he founded new communities it would not have been possible at all to proclaim Jesus as the crucified one, hanged on the accursed wood,[44] who removed the law's condemning judgment, to his hearers.

The mission sermons before Jews and Gentiles in Acts also contain a—compact and rudimentary—narration of the activity, death, and resurrection of Jesus, closely connected with the Old Testament demonstration from Scripture.[45] Behind this stands a certain, situationally necessary scheme, which still determines the structure of the Gospel of Mark, where the emphasis lies on the passion. The speeches in Acts are configured by the author according to older models, as they were common in the mission preaching before Jews and Gentiles. Here, the well-known admission of Thucydides regarding the difficulty of the exact reproduction of speeches

---

2.25.8: "Both began the planting (1 Cor 3.6ff.) in our city Corinth." On this, see now Hengel 2010a, 16ff., 23ff., 35, 66–73 (GV = 2006b, 25ff., 37ff., 56, 106–18).

[43] Cf. 1 Cor 1.12-13; 2 Cor 10.7; 11.23.

[44] Galatians 3.13; cf. Luke in Acts 5.30; 10.39; 13.29 and in addition Deut 21.23.

[45] Since Luke had provided a detailed presentation in the Gospel, he could spare himself more extensive remarks in the short sermons of Acts. It is all the more astonishing how much he reports about Jesus there. In the decades before his work he and other missionaries probably preached in a similar way. This finds most detailed expression in the sermon of Peter before Cornelius, his family, and his friends (Cornelius forms a parallel to Theophilus, Luke 1.3). Acts 10.24, 34-43; cf. also Peter in Jerusalem at Pentecost 2.22-23 and 3.13ff.; 4.10; 5.30-31. In the speeches before the Jews he presupposes the activity of Jesus in accord with the situation and places the passion and resurrection at the center; a much greater role is played by the proof from Scripture here. See also the reference to the eyewitness status of the disciples in 2.32; 4.20. On Paul, see 13.23-31. The center of gravity lies here on the fulfillment of the promises to the fathers and on the passion. On the problem, see Hengel 2012b (GV = 2007a).

from memory has rightly been pointed out: he says that he formulated them "in the way I thought each would have said what was especially required in the given situation,"[46] though Luke has considerably abbreviated these speech formations for reasons of space. It is interesting that in the speeches and dialogues in Acts he takes it for granted that the activity and fate of Jesus was generally known in Judaea, even in the case of Cornelius and his circle of friends[47] and with regard to King Agrippa II. These events did not "take place in a corner."[48] He accurately reproduces the historical reality here.

The actual *enigma of the Pauline preaching*, which we cannot, after all, know directly—occasional letters, where everything has to be expressed in extreme brevity and mere intimations, are something different from a free oral lecture that has been practiced for decades[49]—is how, already shortly after Easter, when numerous eyewitnesses were still living, the crucified Galilean Jesus of Nazareth could be proclaimed as the one exalted to the right hand of God, indeed even as preexistent mediator of creation. This development is unique in the history of ancient religion. The second question is whether this almost explosive development of Christology has some sort of point of reference in the activity of Jesus or whether it completely contradicts it. Whoever is able to believe the latter may do so. We do not believe it.[50]

The tendency to make occasional allusions to well-known Jesus tradition, which is already visible in Paul, continues in later letters. Hebrews[51] alludes to the proclamation of Jesus and to his hearers, who passed on his message "to us," and mentions the miracles connected with it (2.3-4). The unknown author thus shows himself to be (like Mark and Luke) a member of the second generation. The opening sentence of the letter, which

---

[46] Thucydides, *Hist*. 1.22.1 (trans. Lattimore 1998, 13).

[47] Acts 10.37: ὑμεῖς οἴδατε τὸ γενόμενον ῥῆμα καθ᾽ ὅλης τῆς Ἰουδαίας.

[48] Acts 26.26. The ἐν γωνίᾳ may hold true for the view of Rome but not for Judaea and Syria.

[49] Luke provides an example in Acts 20.7ff. Cf. 13.16-41 and 19.9 for the lectures of the apostle in the school of Tyrannus of Ephesus, which he rented, with the interesting "novelistic" addition of Codex D.

[50] On this, see Hengel/Schwemer 2001. Cf. also Hengel 2002, 240–60. See further chapter 17 and Hengel 1995, esp. 1–72. Cf. now also Deines 2012b; 2012a.

[51] Hebrews emerged ca. 75–85 or ca. 60–66 CE, before 1 Clement, which uses it (this was already recognized by Eusebius, *Hist. eccl.* 3.38.1) and prior to the collection of the Pauline letters, which took it up. With Bickerman 1986, 336–49 (338), who refers, with Theodoret of Cyr, to 13.10, we regard the date before the destruction of Jerusalem as more likely. The collector of the Pauline letters probably took it up into his collection as a traditional, recognized writing, perhaps because he knew that the letter stemmed from a male or female student of Paul; see Harnack 1900.

states that God, after he had formerly spoken in various ways through the prophets, "has spoken to us at the end of these days through his Son," includes the proclamation of the earthly Jesus as a matter of course. The same applies to Heb 12.2, where Jesus is designated as the "originator and perfecter of the faith," who "endured the cross and despised its shame." The *auctor ad Hebraeos* mentions both Jesus' intense trial in view of his approaching death, i.e., the Gethsemane scene (5.7), and his death outside of the gate of Jerusalem (13.12). He too had knowledge of the passion story.

Toward the end of the first century 1 Clement, which knows Hebrews, appeals multiple times to sayings of the Kyrios, which are related to the Synoptic tradition.[52] These presumably come from the catechetically fixed oral community paraenesis, but they could also already presuppose knowledge of a written Gospel, for example, of the Gospel of Mark. The Epistle of James contains—without reference to the origin—paraenetic Jesus tradition at multiple points, sometimes in ancient, pre-Matthean form.[53] Something similar applies to the letters of Ignatius, who knows the account of the baptism of Jesus by John from the Gospel of Matthew, mentions Pontius Pilate three times and the tetrarch Herod (Antipas) once, knows of the nailing up of the crucified one, and recounts a resurrection story with Peter and the disciples.[54] When 1 Tim 6.13, at about the same time as Ignatius, speaks of the "good confession" that Jesus "testified" before Pontius Pilate, he alludes to Jesus' confession of his messianic task before the Roman prefect, perhaps already in the expanded tradition that also stands behind the Fourth Gospel.[55] It is conspicuous that Ignatius and the Pastoral Epistles know the double name Pontius Pilate, which we

---

[52] First Clement 13.1–7; on this, cf. Luke 6.31, 36-38; Matt 5.7; 6.12, 14; 7.1, 12; see further Pol. *Phil.* 2.3, and Clement of Alexandria, *Strom.* 2.91; 1 Clem. 46.7–8; cf. Mark 14.21 and 9.42; Luke 17.1-2; Matt 26.24; 18.6-7; 1 Clem. 24.5; cf. Mark 4.3 parr.; see also the quotation of Isa 29.13 in 1 Clem. 24.5, which is related to Mark 7.6 (Matt 15.8). See Hagner 1973.

[53] See, e.g., Hartin 1991. Burchard 2000, 17–18: "Whoever puts a premium on the content of Jesus tradition . . . should reckon James among the sources of Jesus research" (18). On the dating, see note 22 in chapter 1. See also Hengel 2002, 511–48, which considers the authenticity of the letter as anti-Pauline polemic. In that case its emergence would have to be located between 60 and 62 CE.

[54] Ignatius, *To the Ephesians* 11.1 = Matt 3.7; Ign. *Smyrn.* 1.1 = Matt 3.15; Ign. *Pol.* 2.2 = Matt 10.16; Ign. *Eph.* 14.2 = Matt 12.33; Pontius Pilatus: Ign. *Magn.* 11.1; Ign. *Trall.* 9.1; Pontius Pilatus, the tetrarch Herod (cf. Luke 3.1; 23.6ff.), and nailing: Ign. *Smyrn.* 1.1–2; appearance of the risen one: Ign. *Smyrn.* 3.1; cf. Luke 24.39-43 and Acts 1.4; 10.41. Presumably he already knew—as the Pastoral Epistles also did—the Lukan work.

[55] John 18.29-19.19; on the key word μαρτυρεῖν, see 18.37. On this, see Stettler 1998, 118–22.

only encounter elsewhere in Luke 3.1,[56] Acts 4.27, and Matt 27.2, with it
being possible that Matthew found the name in Luke.

In the letters of the New Testament and of the Apostolic Fathers, traces
of an oral stream of tradition become visible, more or less by chance,
alongside the Gospels, before and after them, which can be documented
far into the second century. It becomes increasingly mixed with traditions
from the written Gospels and—as shown by the work of Papias around
130 and the "apocryphal" Gospels, for example the Gospel of Thomas
and the Gospel of Peter—gradually runs wild.[57]

6.3 Extra-Christian Testimonies[58]

Due to the fact that for the Roman authorities primitive Christianity was
initially a peculiar Jewish sect of enthusiasts from a remote province,[59] in
which one only gradually smelled danger, it is understandable that it only
appears at the margins in the Jewish and pagan Greco-Roman sources of
the first and second centuries CE that have been preserved for us. There
were other things to talk about. Nevertheless, a comparison with other
personalities of the ancient world, which have left no written testimonies of their own, shows that the historicity of Jesus is astonishingly well
attested. If ever since the radical tendency criticism of the previous century, for example in the work of Bruno Bauer and extending to Augstein's
Jesus-Menschensohn,[60] the historicity of Jesus has time and again been

---

[56] There, as in Ign. *Smyrn.* 1.1–2, together with the tetrarch Herod. On the latter, see
Luke 3.19; 9.7; Acts 13.1; and (taken over from Luke) Matt 14.1.

[57] On this, see Hengel 2008c, 103–34, 197–238 (ET = 2000b, 57–73, 116–41). On the
Gospel of Thomas, see Schröter 1997.

[58] On the *Testimonium Flavianum*, see Eisler 1929/1930; Feldman 1965, 48–49;
Schneemelcher 1991/1992, I: 436–37 (GV = 1990, 387–88); Bammel 1986, 186ff. (with
only three small changes); Feldman 1984, 679–703, 951–52; Theissen/Merz 1998, 64–74
(GV = 1997, 74–82); Bardet 2002; Mason 2017. On the other witnesses, see Aufhauser
1925; Windisch 1929/1930; Klausner 1945, 17–70; Theissen/Merz 1998, 63–91 (GV =
1997, 73–99); Hengel 2002, 418–26; Hengel 2004c.

[59] In Judaea the Romans rightly regarded them as not dangerous politically. For this
reason Pilate and his successors did not persecute them, in contrast to the Sadducean leaders of the people. It is only at the beginning of the second century that we hear of Roman
authorities persecuting Christians in Judaea; see Eusebius, *Hist. eccl.* 3.32.1–3, according
to Hegesippus: the martyrdom of Bishop Simeon of Jerusalem under a Proconsul Atticus,
who was in office in Judaea ca. 99/100–102/103 CE; cf. Schürer 1973–1987, I: 516. Eliezer
ben Hyrcanus is said to have been summoned before the Roman authorities around 90 CE
because he was suspected of being a Jewish Christian. See note 102 below.

[60] On Augstein 1971 (ET = 1977), see Hengel 1972a (= 2007b, 306–15), and on the
revised edition (Augstein 1999), see Hengel 2001b (= 2007b, 316–22). Augstein considerably softens his thesis in the revised edition.

entirely or halfheartedly doubted, then this indicates only a complete lack of historical-critical thinking. In the controversy about Jesus some like to claim that we possess, after all, only Christian—i.e., thoroughly tendentious and therefore unreliable—witnesses. This overlooks the fact that in the first 150 years of Christianity[61] there are, by ancient standards, a considerable number of very diverse non-Christian witnesses. John Bowden's judgment "that their information could easily be written on a postcard and they do not tell us anything of substantial interest"[62] is thus somewhat too one-sided.

In his *Jewish Antiquities* ('Ιουδαϊκὴ ἀρχαιολογία), whose twenty books reach from the creation of the world (Gen 1.1) to the time right before the outbreak of the Jewish War, the Jewish historian, Jerusalem priest, and imperial freedman Josephus[63] mentions the person of Jesus twice. In the last book, *Ant.* 20.200, he gives an account of the execution of James, the brother "of the so-called Christ." The high priest Annas II (the son of the Annas of the passion story) is said to have had James, together with a larger number of Jewish Christians, condemned to death by stoning as "lawbreakers."[64] With the neutral formula Josephus refers back to his earlier mention of Jesus in the context of his presentation of the activity of Pilate, the *Testimonium Flavianum*,[65] which is admittedly controversial, since it has been regarded as a forgery. Today, after detailed linguistic analyses, there is a tendency to accept that an originally rather negative characterization of Jesus in Josephus was changed by a Christian scribe into a positive one through a light retouching of the passage, which means that the fundamental content is authentic. Attempts have repeatedly been made to reconstruct the original form by means of few changes. For example, this has now been attempted again by Gerd Theissen, following W. Bienert and R. Eisler.[66] The originality of such a note about Jesus in Josephus is supported by a number of arguments. Above all, this view is supported by the fact that Josephus' report about Jesus,[67] reflecting a historically accurate placement, follows two reports about Jewish unrests at the time of Pilate.[68] In this way Jesus appears as an instigator

---

[61] On the comparable time frame, see section 6.1.

[62] Bowden 1988.

[63] On his person and work, see chapter 3.

[64] Ca. 62 CE; Hengel 2002, 551ff.; cf. section 3.1.5.

[65] Josephus, *Ant.* 18.63–64.

[66] See section 3.1.3 with note 232. Cf. also Van Voorst 2001, 103–4.

[67] *Antiquities* 18.63–64.

[68] *Antiquities* 18.55–62: the Roman standards with medallion busts of the emperor at the entrance of the cohorts into the Antonia and the use of the temple treasure for the restoration of the water system of Jerusalem. This is followed by religious deceptions by priests

of unrest. Beyond this, the Christian "corrections" can be easily removed.
R. Eisler postulates that an originally negative σοφιστὴς ἀνήρ was turned
into a σοφὸς ἀνήρ, and an ἀπηγάγετο, "he led astray," was changed into
a positive ἐπηγάγετο. Josephus is said to have portrayed Jesus originally
as a misleader of the people. Other formulations remained unchanged,
such as the reference to his "extraordinary deeds" (παράδοξα ἔργα), his
activity as a teacher (διδάσκαλος ἀνθρώπων), and especially the decisive statement "and when Pilate had condemned him to crucifixion at the
accusation of our leaders, his earlier followers did not cease." Something
similar holds true for the concluding sentence: "Until today this tribe (τὸ
φῦλον) of Christianoi has not ceased to exist." The agreement with the
style of Josephus supports the authenticity of this basic content. The fact
that Josephus says only a little about Jesus and the Christians is not surprising. He is also silent about the Essene Teacher of Righteousness and
about the most famous early Pharisaic teachers, Simeon ben Shetach, Hillel, Shammai, and Yohanan ben Zakkai.[69]

Around 116/117 CE Tacitus[70] describes, with deep contempt for their
"baleful superstition," the persecution of the *"Chrestiani"* by Nero in Rome
in 64 CE. In this context he also discusses the founder of this superstition.

> The source of the name was Christus, on whom, during the command
> of Tiberius, reprisal had been inflicted by the procurator Pontius Pila-
> tus; and though the baleful superstition had been stifled for the moment,
> there was now another outbreak, not only across Judaea, the origin of
> the malignancy, but also across the City, where everything frightful or
> shameful, of whatever provenance, converges and is celebrated.[71]

Tacitus, as a Roman proconsul under Trajan (112 CE) in the province of
Asia, presumably got to know Christians and conducted trials against

---

of Isis and two Jews in Rome (18.65ff.) with the crucifixion of the guilty (18.79) and the
unrests in Samaria, which led to the removal of Pilate (18.85–87).

[69] He mentions only a leading Pharisee Sameas from the early time of Herod
(*Ant.* 14.172–176) and his student Pollion (15.3–4, 370; see section 3.1.1 with notes 54
and 147). Gamaliel, the most famous scribe in the second fourth of the first century and
teacher of Paul (Acts 22.3; cf. 5.34), is also mentioned only as the father of his son Simeon
(*J.W.* 4.159 and *Life* 190). Josephus says nothing about his importance. On this, see note
152 in chapter 4.

[70] Tacitus, *Ann.* 15.44 (trans. Woodman 2004, 325).

[71] Tacitus, *Ann.* 15.44.3 (trans. Woodman 2004, 325): *Auctor nominis eius Christus
Tiberio imperitante per procuratorem Pontium Pilatum supplicio adfectus erat; repres-
saque in praesens exitiabilis superstitio rursum erumpebat, non modo per Iudaeam, origi-
nem eius mali, sed per urbem etiam, quo cuncta undique atrocia aut pudenda confluent
celebranturque.*

them. He regards them as "criminals who deserve the ultimate exemplary treatment."[72] At about the same time, his friend Pliny the Younger in Bithynia/Pontus also persecuted the Christians there. Like Josephus, Tacitus presupposes the reality of the execution of Jesus as a given, and he knows that it took place in Judaea under the procurator Pontius Pilate. Unfortunately, in the Annals we are missing not only books 7–10, the time from the death of Tiberius (March 16, 37 CE) until the middle of the reign of Claudius (until ca. 47 CE), but also the majority of the fifth book, on the years from 29 CE to the autumn of 31 CE. It is possible that Tacitus had provided a brief report about the death of Jesus and perhaps also about the Christians there and that this report was so negative that these parts of his work were not handed down. According to Sulpicius Severus, who used as a source the *Histories*, which have been lost with the exception of books 1–5, Titus is said to have advocated the destruction of the temple in the council of war, because in this way with the Jews the Christians would also be eradicated.[73]

Shortly before, ca. 110/111 CE, Pliny the Younger wrote the famous *Letter to Trajan*.[74] He does not discuss the origin of the sect but stresses only that in the interrogations in the trials of Christians he had learned that they assembled before dawn on a certain day in order to sing hymns to Christ as to a god.[75] He himself demanded from the offenders that they sacrifice to the gods and curse this Christ.[76] In the letter it is presupposed as a given that the emperor knows who this Christ was. The cursing of this crucified criminal corresponded to the national interest and was also a sign that the offender had broken with this "depraved and extravagant superstition."[77]

A short time after Tacitus, Suetonius[78] also mentions the Neronian persecution of Christians, but he does not speak about the founder of

---

[72] Tacitus, *Ann.* 15.44.5 (trans. Woodman 2004, 326): *sontes et novissima exempla meritos*. Cf. Schwemer 2001c, 134ff.

[73] Sulpicius Severus, *Chronica* 2.30.6–7; on this, see Stern 1976–1984, II: 64ff. with commentary. Here the question is whether the reference to the Christians goes back to Tacitus or was added by the Christian author. The latter need not necessarily be the case. After all, the Christians later regarded the destruction of the temple more as something positive than as punishment for the Jews. On this, cf. Hengel 2002, 418ff.

[74] Pliny the Younger, *Ep.* 10.96. For the Latin text with an English translation and commentary, see Williams 1990. Cf. also Walsh 2006.

[75] Pliny the Younger, *Ep.* 10.96.7: *carmenque Christo quasi deo dicere*.

[76] Pliny the Younger, *Ep.* 10.96.5: *maledicerent Christo*; Bar Kokhba requires the same thing from the Jewish Christians in Justin, *1 Apol.* 31.6.

[77] Pliny the younger, *Ep.* 10.96.8 (trans. Williams 1990, 71): *superstitionem pravam, immodicam*.

[78] Suetonius, *Nero* 16.3.

"this new and dangerous superstition."[79] However, it is very likely that he already mentioned him previously in his account of Claudius. Claudius is said to have expelled the Jews, who fomented constant unrests at the instigation of a certain Chrestus.[80] Since Christ was an unintelligible name for Greek ears,[81] Greek hearers understood it—because of the itacism in which ἦτα was pronounced as ἰῶτα—in the sense of *Chrēstus*,[82] a popular slave name. In *Ann.* 15.44.2, Tacitus therefore writes *Chrestiani*.[83] Tertullian, *Apol.* 3.5, also confirms this misinterpretation. Suetonius' note about Claudius probably alludes to unrests in the Jewish synagogue communities in Rome around 47/49 CE, which were caused by the penetration of the message about Christ and, as Luke testifies in Acts 18.2, led to the expulsion of the troublemakers. All these reports also present us with the historical basic problem of Christology. *How could* a Jewish criminal who was executed on a cross become a god? How did this "skandalon"[84] for Jews, Greeks, and Romans come to be?

In the middle of the second century, we learn from the pen of Lucian about the "sophist" crucified in Palestine and the laws given by him,[85] while on multiple occasions the physician Galen juxtaposes Moses and Christ as teachers, who both demand faith for their teachings. Beyond this, he stresses the ethical life and the Christians' despising of death.[86] Both here and there we encounter Christ as an authoritative teacher. An earlier witness is that of Epictetus (ca. 50–130), who, in his *Diatribes*

---

[79] Suetonius, *Nero* 16.3 (trans. Edwards 2000, 203): *superstitio nova ac malefica*. *Maleficus* can also mean magical.

[80] Suetonius, *Claud.* 25.3, cf. Acts 18.2; on this, see in detail Riesner 1994, 139–80, and Botermann 1996.

[81] In Greek outside of the Septuagint and related texts the verbal adjective was known in the sense of "spreadable, spread on, rubbed with ointment" or the substantive in the neuter "ointment, tool for spreading." Grundmann 1973, 485 (ET = 1974, 495); cf. LSJ, 2007; see also 1170: νεόχριστος/ον, "newly plastered." It was completely unknown as a designation of a person in the sense of "the anointed one." On this, see note 34 in chapter 22.

[82] "The good one, the useful one, the upright one."

[83] Tacitus, *Ann.* 15.44.2; perhaps with light irony: the people called those who were hated on account of crimes (*propter flagitia invisos*) *Chrestiani*, i.e., 'followers of an upright one.' On the title and name Christ, see Hengel 2002, 240–61; on the "*Christianoi*," see Hengel/Schwemer 1998, 340–51 (ET = 1997, 225–30).

[84] Cf. 1 Cor 1.23; cf. Gal 5.11; 6.12; Phil 3.18-19.

[85] Lucian, *Peregr.* 11–13, 16. Presumably he also alludes to the passion story in the portrayal of the suicide of Peregrinus Proteus in Olympia (167 CE). Peregrinus himself became a Christian and community leader for a time in Palestine and Syria, interpreted the books of the Christians (this probably especially means the Gospels), and let himself be cared for by them in prison. By contrast, *Alexander the False Prophet* designates the Christians as ἄθεοι (Lucian, *Alex.* 25.38). Lucian also appears to know of Christian miracles in his *Philopseudes*.

[86] Den Boer 1965, 12; Walzer 1949; Hengel 2004c, 101–2.

mediated through Arrian, speaks of the "Galileans," among whom madness or custom rather than reason effects freedom from the fear of death. This indicates that he knew that the Christians went back to a Galilean and his Galilean disciples.[87] According to Origen, *Cels.* 4.51, the philosopher Numenius (second half of the second century CE), who had an interest, among other things, in Jewish traditions and the Septuagint, also recounted and allegorically interpreted a story about Jesus, though without mentioning Jesus' name. Finally, scholarship has given far too little consideration to the real or fictive Jewish authority of Celsus[88] in his writing against the Christians around 170 CE. He not only knows all the Gospels,[89] but also presupposes something like a Jewish "anti-Gospel," which knows of the divorcing of Jesus' mother because of adultery with the soldier Panthera,[90] presents Jesus as a robber captain, and recounts his magical arts, which he is said to have learned in Egypt. We are dealing here with traditions whose first traces are intimated in Matthew[91] and which we encounter much later in fancifully developed form in the Toledot Yeshu.[92] These diverse non-Christian splinters of information already point to some fundamental basic lines. Even if we possessed only these, they could take up several columns in an encyclopedia such as Pauly-Wissowa.

Another, less-known witness is the letter of Mara bar Serapion, which is preserved in Syriac. To be sure, it can scarcely be dated before the second half of the second century CE, since no earlier Syriac literature can be documented.[93] If it is based on a Greek text, then it could be older. In it the author writes to his son—presumably in connection with the suffering of the population of Samosata when the Commagane was occupied by Vespasian in 72 CE—and mentions the Jews, who suffered devastation and expulsion because they killed their wise king, just as the Athenians were punished for the death of Socrates. Socrates is said to have continued to

---

[87] Epictetus, *Diatr.* 4.7.6; Hengel 2004c, 106ff. On the μανία, cf. Justin, *1 Apol.* 13.4, and the accusations of *amentia* in Pliny the Younger, *Ep.* 10.96.4, and the ψιλὴ παράταξις in Marcus Aurelius 11.32. On the "Galileans," see Mark 14.70 = Luke 22.59 = Matt 26.69; cf. Luke 23.6; Matt 26.71; Acts 1.11; 2.7; see also section 11.1.

[88] Cf. Bammel 1986, 265–83; on Celsus and the Jesus tradition, see Cook 2000, 26–31.

[89] The Jew Trypho also knows of the teachings of the Christians about Jesus. Indeed, he has read the Gospel of Matthew (and here especially the Sermon on the Mount) (Justin, *Dial.* 10.2) and is impressed by its rigorous, unfulfillable demands.

[90] Origen, *Cels.* 1.32–33, 69. For further attestations, see note 53 in chapter 8.

[91] Matthew 2.15; 28.11-15; cf. also Tertullian, *Spect.* 30.5–6.

[92] Origenes, *Cels.* 1.28–2.79; on this, see Bader 1940, 52–84. Horbury 1998b, 162–75; see now the fundamental study of Cook 2000, 17–102. On the Toledot Yeshu, see Krauss 1977 [1902]; Schlichting 1982. On Jesus in Talmudic literature, see below.

[93] It begins only with Tatian's Diatessaron and Bardaisan; see Baumstark 1922; Brock 2012 (GV = 2004).

live through Plato and "the wise king of the Jews because of the new law that he gave." The letter is written by a Stoic who has a positive stance toward Christianity.[94]

According to the Christian polymath and chronographer Julius Africanus, the librarian of the emperor Alexander Severus, the Samaritan (?) freedman of Tiberius, Thallos, in his history of the world, is said to have explained the darkness at the crucifixion of Jesus, which was effected by a miracle, in a natural way as a solar eclipse. Since this identification is based on a conjecture in Josephus, however, it is scarcely viable.[95] Phlegon of Tralles, a historian and freedman of Hadrian (117–138 CE) with an interest in miracle stories, presumably identified this darkness with the eclipse that took place on November 24, 29 CE, i.e., in the fifteenth year of Tiberius. Moreover, according to Origen, he appears—in a confused way—to have recounted fulfilled predictions of Jesus about Peter (or of Peter),[96] while a generation later Celsus recounts only the miracles of Jesus and ascribes them to his magical arts. Phlegon could thus be the first pagan who had knowledge of statements of the Gospels. His contemporary, the famous rhetorician M. Cornelius Fronto, the tutor of Marcus Aurelius, also proceeded with hideous accusations against the Christians and in doing so probably included their founder.[97]

---

[94] Cureton 1855, 43; Aufhauser 1925, 2.5–11; cf. Theissen/Merz 1998, 76–79 (GV = 1997, 84–86), who date the letter too early. Cf. now also Merz/Tieleman 2012. The expulsion of the Jews from their home could also refer to the consequences of the Bar Kokhba revolt in 132–136 CE. The "new law" points to Matthew and the apologists. Theissen/Merz 1998, 79 (GV = 1997, 85), rightly stress a "clear *external* perspective in his assessment of Jesus and Christianity" (authors' emphasis).

[95] FGrH 256 F 1 = Mosshammer 1984, 391, and Josephus, *Ant.* 18.167: conjecture Hudson Θάλλος instead of ἄλλος Σαμαρεύς, affirmed by Windisch 1929/1930, 285ff.; Theissen/Merz 1998, 84 (GV = 1997, 91). By contrast, the commentary of Jacoby (FGrH, pp. 635ff.) is rightly critical of this conjecture. According to Origen, *Cels.* 2.33, 59, and others (see FGrH 257, F 16), the solar eclipse was also reported by Phlegon, who probably knew Luke 23.44. On this, see Hengel 2004c, 110–15.

[96] *Cels.* 2.14 = FGrH 257, F 15d: "In the thirteenth or fourteenth book of Chronicles . . . he allowed Christ the foreknowledge (πρόγνωσιν) about certain future events; he admittedly confused (συγχυθείς) things that concerned Peter with such that related to Christ, but he attests that the word spoken by Jesus literally came to pass." It is presumably the earliest reference of a pagan author to a text of the Gospels; cf. Mark 8.31ff.; Mark 14.29-30; John 13.36ff.; 21.18ff. According to Photius, *Bibl.* 97.1–5 (FGrH 257 T 3), he was a dreadful hack writer who was primarily interested in sensational oracles. In his milieu the Gospels could also attract attention. It is possible that he reported about the passion of Jesus or the martyrdom of Peter. On this, see Hengel 2004c, 110–15.

[97] Minucius Felix, *Oct.* 9.6; 31.2 (Fronto was born roughly between 100 and 110 CE in African Cirta). The first Christian philosophers of religion and apologists arose at the same time and bore witness to the interest of the educated in the new religion. The polemical writing of Celsus was probably an answer to them.

A completely different category are the relatively numerous—admittedly not uncontroversial and sometimes garbled in the details—*Talmudic* witnesses to Jesus, whose oldest tradition could likewise reach back to the end of the first or the beginning of the second century CE.[98] We mention just the most important examples. They are all understandably bluntly anti-Christian. Jesus appears as an "unperson," whose name one readily expresses with other words. As the authority of Celsus claimed, he is said to be the illegitimate son of Mary, with his father being a certain Panthera.[99] According to an old tradition (Baraita) from the Babylonian Talmud,[100] "Jesus, the *nôṣrî*,[101] was condemned by a Jewish court and stoned and hanged on the eve of the Passover festival . . . for practicing magic and for deceiving and leading astray Israel." Five disciples of Jesus, Matthai, Naqaj, Neṣer, Buni, and Thoda, are also said to have been executed. The famous and idiosyncratic early rabbinic teacher Eliezer ben Hyrcanus is said to have been accused of being a Jewish Christian by the Roman authority around 90 CE, since he had positive contact with Jewish Christians earlier, especially with a Jacob of Sikhnin,[102] and, among other things, positively evaluated an interpretation of the law of Jesus ben Panthera.[103] From a somewhat later time, around 100 CE, comes the report that a famous rabbi preferred to let his nephew, who had been bitten by a snake, die than to allow a (different?) charismatic Jewish Christian, Jacob of Kefar Sama, heal the wounded one in the name of "Jesus ben

---

[98] Strack 1910; Klausner 1945, 17–54. By contrast, J. Maier 1978a judges negatively and thus apologetically and without genuine historical understanding of these singular texts. See now the fundamental study of Schäfer 2007. See in greater detail Hengel/Schwemer 2019.

[99] See the previous discussion in this section and section 8.3 on the family of Jesus. On the name Panthera, see also Celsus (see note 90 above) and notes 52–53 in section 8.3.

[100] b. Sanh. 43a; Strack 1910, 18* § 1a and 43–44* § 13. On this, see Schäfer 2007, 63–74.

[101] *Nôṣrîm* was the conventional Jewish designation for Christians, derived from Jesus' place of origin, Nazareth. Schaeder 1967 (GV = 1942). See section 8.2.

[102] Klausner 1945, 40–42, postulates here (wrongly) James, the brother of the Lord; however, the concern could be with a later relative of the Lord. Hegesippus mentions a James as Jesus' great nephew and grandson of Jesus' brother Judas (according to a fragment from the church history of Philip of Side; text in Preuschen 1905, 111, line 17), who, due to his testimony before Domitian together with his brother Zoker, was highly regarded among the Jewish Christians in Galilee. Cf. Eusebius, *Hist. eccl.* 3.20.1–6; 3.32.5–6. See the end of section 8.3 on Jesus' family.

[103] t. Ḥul. 2.24; b. Avod. Zar. 17a; Strack 1910, 23–24* § 4. According to the Babli, this Jacob introduces the Jesus halakah with the formula "Thus Jesus the *nôṣrî* (Tosefta: *ben Panṭerî*) taught me." The event is said to have taken place at the upper marketplace in Sepphoris.

Panthera."[104] The—wiser—wife of Eliezer ben Hyrcanus, Imma Shalom, the sister of R. Gamaliel II, who between 90 and 110 CE was the highest scribal authority and head of the academy of Yavneh, is said, together with her brother, to have convicted a (Jewish Christian) "philosopher," who appealed to Matt 5.17, of accepting bribes.[105] While these narratives about well-known early rabbinic teachers may be legendary in character, they nevertheless give us, starting from a bitter enmity, insight into the sometimes initially still ambivalent relationship of individual Tannaitic teachers to Jewish Christianity and to Jesus himself.

These chance, predominantly polemical extra-Christian reports about Jesus and early Christianity *in themselves already make certain the historicity of Jesus*. He appears as a controversial Jewish teacher who was executed by Pontius Pilate for crimes against the Roman state or as a false prophet and deceiver and who founded a publicly dangerous sect that was well-known to all sides. The polemic—which is still heard today—that the Jesus tradition involves falsifications of earlier Christian circles already founders on the diverse character of these non-Christian traditions, which were originally more abundant but have largely been lost because they were not handed down by Christians. This applies, for example, also to the imperial decrees against Christians.[106] We must consider how little interest the ancient world initially had in the events in remote Galilee or Judaea. Moreover, we must remember that for more than two hundred years intellectual circles readily kept silent about the existence of Christians. This also applies to the Talmudic tradition. The most important author of a Roman history in Greek, Cassius Dio (ca. 200–230), also never mentions the Christians, who already played a large role in his time, but alludes to them only indirectly. Thus when, in a speech of Maecenas, he has the emperor Augustus give the exhortation to proceed violently against subversive new deities.[107] But such phenomena are often encountered in the ancient world. The founder of the Jewish freedom movement, Judas the Galilean, is mentioned only by Josephus and Acts and not at all in the other ancient and Talmudic texts. The preserved Roman sources are also silent about the Jewish leader in the revolt of 132–136 CE, who unsettled the

---

[104] t. Ḥul. 2.22–23; Strack 1910, 21* § 3; cf. y. Šabb. 14.4; Strack 1910, 45* § 19.

[105] b. Šabb. 116a/b; Strack 1910 19*ff. § 2.

[106] According to Lactantius, *Inst.* 5.11.19, Domitius Ulpianus collected the *rescripta principum nefaria* against the Christians at the beginning of the third century CE in the seventh book of his work *De officio proconsulis*.

[107] Cassius Dio, *Historia Romana* 52.36.1–3: He should force (ἀνάγκαζε) his subjects to revere the "divine power (τὸ θεῖον) according to the ancestral tradition" and to fend off the spread "of new divinities" (καινά τινα δαιμόνια), since these threatened the state.

Roman Empire for more than three years. We know his name, Simon bar Kosiba or Kokhba, only from Christian (Justin and Eusebius) and Talmudic sources, from coins of the revolt, and now through original documents from the discoveries of scrolls in the wilderness of Judaea.[108] We must view the scattered early pagan and Jewish reports about Jesus against the background of the situation of our sources, which are fragmentary and accidental as is commonly the case for ancient history. The situation with regard to the Galilean craftsman from Nazareth and his movement is astonishingly good.

6.4 The Synoptic Gospels[109]

If then the attestation of Jesus and the Christians is not so bad by ancient standards, then the question of the trustworthiness of our main sources remains. Can one with a good conscience still call the Synoptic Gospels reliable texts? Here too D. F. Strauss, allegedly in the interest of a "purely historical consideration . . . of the primitive history of Christianity," raises his critical voice. In 1872, two years before his death, he writes in his concluding "confession":

> No modern theologian, who is also a scholar, now considers any of the four Gospels to be the work of its pretended author, or in fact to be by an apostle or the colleague of an apostle. The first three Gospels, as well as the Acts, pass for doctrinal compilations of the beginning of the second century after Christ, the fourth, since Baur's epoch-making investigation, as a dogmatising composition of the middle of the same century.[110]

However, this self-confidence of the radical Tübingen school and its certainty of victory were unfounded. It had fundamentally missed the mark about the time of emergence of the four Gospels, which is located between ca. 70 and 100/110 CE, i.e., only ca. forty–seventy/eighty years after the activity of Jesus. And scholars such as A. Ritschl, H. J. Holtzmann, A. von Harnack, M. Dibelius, and H. Lietzmann, who had for quite some time no longer thought in such a radical manner as the Tübingen scholars—to say nothing of Bishop J. B. Lightfoot, T. Zahn, and A. Schlatter—can

---

[108] Schäfer 1981; Mildenberg 1984; Hengel 1996a, 344–50 and 379–91.

[109] Kümmel 1975 (GV = 1983); Vielhauer 1975; Hengel 1983b (ET = 1985b, 31–63); 1984a; 1984b (all three studies can be found together in 2007b, 430–567, and in English translation in 1985b); 1987c (= 1999b, 219–92); 2008c (ET = 2000b); Schnelle 2002 (ET = 1998).

[110] Strauss 1873, 46 (GV = 1872, 41). Cf. by contrast the judgment of Justin, *Dial.* 103.8.

hardly be denied their scholarly status. Precisely on this decisive point, the question of dating and authorship, hypercriticism has come to a dead end. The two earliest Gospels, the Gospel according to Mark and the Gospel according to Luke, which are not yet ascribed to apostles, stem, in our view, from the authors whose names they bear. In the second century, they would have been ascribed to apostolic authors, i.e., to a Peter and a Paul. Non-apostolic authors of Gospels had become impossible after Matthew and John, for which reason the pseudepigrapha then accumulate.

Despite its late dating of the Gospels in general, the Baur school, in accord with early church tradition, maintained the priority of Matthew, which toward the end of the nineteenth century was advocated almost only by very conservative scholars such as T. Zahn and A. Schlatter and which has hardly any supporters today. It is generally acknowledged that Mark is the oldest Gospel and Luke and Matthew are literarily dependent upon it to a considerable extent. Also John presupposes at least Mark and Luke.[111] In all the individual questions, however, there is an unbroken diversity of opinions also in the present. This applies both to the question of the authors, their background and dating, and—apart from the use of the Gospel of Mark—to their sources, their relation to Judaism, and their theological placement in general. In what follows, we can attempt only to present and ground our own view.

6.4.1 Mark

Mark undisputedly stands in the first position today. It arose in the uncertain time of the civil war, shortly before the overthrow of Jerusalem by Titus in August/September 70 CE. Jerusalem was not yet destroyed. Its destruction was admittedly expected, though not by the Romans but by the Antichrist (cf. Mark 13.14), who was identified with Nero *redivivus*; with him begins the last eschatological tribulation before the parousia of the Son of Man.[112] Josephus attests that in the outbreak of the

---

[111] On the Gospels' titles and their authors, see Hengel 1984b (ET = 1985b, 64–84); Hengel 2008c (ET = 2000b). Time and again there are of course attempts by scholars to rehash the old theses of Baur. They have not, however, been able to stand up. On the much-discussed Synoptic problem, see the more recent introductions to the New Testament, for example, Jülicher/Fascher 1931, 274–370; Kümmel 1975, 38–151 (GV = 1983, 13–120); Vielhauer 1975, 263–80; Holladay 2005, 41–268: a thorough presentation of the whole problem. Cf. also Goodacre 2002. For the relationship between John and the Synoptics, cf. Frey 2013.

[112] Mark 13.14-23; see Hengel 1984a, 21–43 (ET = 1985b, 13–28). Nero was murdered on June 19, 68 CE. This marked the beginning of the Roman civil war, which lasted for more than eighteen months. On the Nero *redivivus* motif and the Antichrist motif, see

Jewish revolt "many, foreseeing the impending disasters, made open lamentations. . . . In short, the city before the coming of the Romans wore the appearance of a place doomed to destruction."[113] The numerous Latinisms[114]—which are conspicuous in a Greek writing and only comparable with the Shepherd of Hermas—as well as the complete ignorance of the true military proceedings in Judaea between 66 and 70 CE point to an origination in Rome, where people were no longer well informed about the true events in the rebellious province, especially after the outbreak of the civil war in 68 and in the year of the three emperors in 69.[115] The origin in Rome is indirectly attested by Ireneaus in his report on the Gospels, which is composed from a Roman perspective and probably came from the archive of the Roman community. He is materially correct in his emphasis that the Gospel arose only after the death of Peter and Paul, who died in connection with the Neronic persecution in 64/65 CE.[116] A little later the Roman origin is attested *expressis verbis* by Clement of Alexandria and the earliest Gospel prologue.[117] It is very likely that we owe to this Gospel the title "Gospel according to" (Εὐαγγέλιον κατά) plus author name, which became common for the four canonical Gospels and for later apocryphal Gospels and which represents an absolute *novum*. The impetus for this uncommon book title was given by Mark 1.1, "Beginning of the gospel of Jesus Christ" (Ἀρχὴ τοῦ εὐαγγελίου Ἰησοῦ Χριστοῦ) and the seven redactional occurrences of the word "gospel" in the work. Mark 1.1 and especially 14.9 show that proclamation of the gospel and narration of the story of Jesus are identical for the evangelist. Since three of the Gospels—Mark, Matthew, and John[118]—were written especially for the reading in the worship service, they required (like the books of the Septuagint) a title from the moment of their circulation in the communities, for the hearers had to

---

Jenks 1991, though he places the Nero *redivivus* motif too late and the deutero-Pauline text 2 Thess 2.1-17 too early. Mark 13 and this text supplement each other.

[113] Josephus, *J.W.* 2.649–650 (trans. H. St. J. Thackeray, LCL, 571); cf. Mark 13.1-2. Cf. the flight of the Christians to Pella due to a prophetic saying (Eusebius, *Hist. eccl.* 3.5.3).

[114] Dschulnigg 1986, 265–68; Hengel 1984a, 43ff. (ET = 1985b, 28ff.); 1969 (= 2007b, 177–93); 2008c, 141–42 (ET = 2000b, 78–79, 258–59).

[115] A few years later Luke is much better informed.

[116] Irenaeus, *Haer.* 3.1.1. Thornton 1991, 10–54. On the death of Peter and Paul, see 1 Clem. 5; Dionysius of Corinth according to Eusebius, *Hist. eccl.* 2.25.8, and Tertullian, *Scorp.* 15.3. On this, see Lietzmann 1927; Hengel 2008c, 120ff., 141–96 (ET = 2000b, 65ff., 78–115); Hengel 2010a (GV = 2006b), index, s.v. "martyr/martyrdom."

[117] Eusebius, *Hist. eccl.* 2.15.1–2, and with some divergences *Hist. eccl.* 6.14.5–7, from the lost *Hypotyposes*.

[118] Only Luke, as the prologue shows, is a special case. On this, see Hengel 2012b (GV = 2007a).

be told, after all, which writing was being read. If the Gospels had been circulated anonymously, then—as is the case with many apocrypha—a variety of titles would have necessarily arisen, for in the communities they would have received different titles ad hoc. The Gospel titles, however, are completely unified in their attestation in the early period from the second to the fourth century CE. We find the title with John (and, in addition, once with Luke) on the two Bodmer papyri P[66] and P[75] around 200. The Gospel titles of the *Vetus Latina*, the old Latin translation, also go back to the second century CE. For Irenaeus, Clement of Alexandria, and Tertullian toward the end of the second century CE, they are taken entirely as a given. This means, however, that the author specifications of all the Gospels have to be taken seriously and must be explained. We cannot dismiss them as secondary additions, for a later unified emergence cannot be sensibly explained.[119]

The author Mark was certainly not an anonymous Gentile Christian, as many people like to claim today, but a Greek- and Aramaic-speaking Jewish Christian from Palestine who is well informed about the land and its customs, especially about Jerusalem, and there is no adequate reason to doubt his identification with the John Mark of the book of Acts.[120] The same applies to the much-discussed note of Papias—who owes this to John the "elder" and whose content therefore reaches far into the first century CE—which says Mark was the interpreter of Peter, so that his Gospel is based upon Petrine tradition. This is wrongly rejected as an apologetic legend. The tradition is supported by the following reasons:[121]

1. In this note Mark is more criticized than defended as an author, for it is said that his Gospel does not possess the correct (chronological and thematic) order and is not based on eyewitness testimony but rather provides an unordered tradition at second hand. The student of John, Papias, probably measures the second Gospel by the standard of the fourth. Independently of the Papias note, we also

[119] On this, see Hengel 1984b (ET = 1985b, 64–84); Hengel 2008c, 141–84 (ET = 2000b, 78–106). See also Mutschler 2006, 249–54, 264–65, 273–74, and 623 index, s.v. "Evangelienüberschrift." Cf. now also Gathercole 2018.

[120] Acts 12.12, 35; 15.37, 39; Phlm 24; Col 4.10; 2 Tim 4.11; 1 Pet 5.13. Cf. Lietzmann 1999, I: 35. See also Hengel 1983b, 244–45 (ET = 1985b, 50–53); Hengel 2008c, 143–45 with notes 412–18 (ET = 2000b, 260–61 n. 324–30). The Gospel title shows Mark to be a well-known personality and authority. The community knew who he was.

[121] Hengel 1993a, 76–95 (ET = 1989a, 16–23); Hengel 2008c, 120–26 (ET = 2000b, 65–68, 253–54 n. 274–84); Hengel 2010a, 12, 37–38, 46, 103 (GV = 2006b, 19, 60, 74, 167). A different view is advocated—not very convincingly, to be sure—by Heckel 1999, 219–65. See further Bauckham 2017, 202–39 ("Papias on Mark and Matthew").

encounter the student relation between Mark and Peter in 1 Pet 5.13, a text that arose around 100 CE, likewise in Rome.

2. In the Gospel Peter plays the dominant role as a disciple, in a very conspicuous way at the beginning, in the middle, and at the end, i.e., his person fundamentally defines the thought-out structure of the work. In his relatively short Gospel, Mark mentions Peter twenty-five times, i.e., as often as Matthew, which is 70 percent longer and for which the authority of Peter is likewise important (Matt 16.17-19). By contrast, John and James, the sons of Zebedee, are mentioned only ten times and almost always together with Peter. Moreover, Peter always stands at the head of the list of disciples and is, with one exception, the only one mentioned by name as a dialogue partner of Jesus among the disciples.[122] The *inclusio* connected with his name is unique. In 1.16 he is the first disciple, who is named immediately after the public appearance of Jesus (and he is mentioned twice for emphasis), and he is the last disciple mentioned in 16.7—in an unnecessary way. The angel commands the women: "tell his disciples and Peter."[123] The name of Simon Peter is thus consciously placed at the beginning and the end. We regard this as a clear signature for the specification of the disciple to whom the author knows himself to be obligated.[124]

3. This knowledge of the authority of Peter, which lies behind the second Gospel, was also a reason for the fact that Luke, for whom Mark was the most important author among the "many" sources (Luke 1.1), and, after him, the unknown author of the Gospel of Matthew took over the outline of Mark for their "Jesus biographies." Here, the author of Matthew, a self-conscious theological teacher, let himself be guided by Mark in an astonishing way. He not only takes over—apart from a few rearrangements and certain shortenings—its structure and material but also about 80 percent

---

[122] Hengel 2008c, 148–50 (ET = 2000b, 83–84); Hengel 2010a, 25–26 (GV = 2006b, 40–41). Only in Mark 9.38 does John address Jesus. On the lists of disciples, see Bauckham 2017, 93–113.

[123] This point is not considered in the more recent commentaries and studies. It could additionally be an indirect reference to the first appearance to Peter, but only for those who knew about it. Mark himself gives no indication of this. On this, cf. now Bauckham 2017, 155–82 ("The Petrine Perspective in Mark").

[124] Hengel 2008c, 146–47 (ET = 2000b, 82). The second signature is the mysterious text of 14.51–52, which would be most intelligible if the author, Mark, referred to himself thereby. These two signatures cannot be explained from the Gospel. See the end of section 20.1.

of its wording—and even with Luke it is about 65 percent.[125] Mark is an authority for Matthew and Luke because it is based on Petrine tradition.

The second Gospel, the first continuous narrative account of Jesus' activity from the appearance of John the Baptist to the discovery of the empty tomb, was not written by an insignificant anonymous person but by a well-known teacher in the primitive church who possessed authority himself and could appeal to an even greater authority. Only in this way can its influence in the earliest time be explained, although it was then quickly displaced by the First Gospel in the second century, which produced in more perfect form what the church needed and gave the appearance of being apostolic in origin with the title "The Gospel According to Matthew." John, which was even somewhat later, also presupposes Mark. From now on the apostle-student Mark had to recede behind these Gospels, but the authority of Peter connected with him—which, in addition to the testimony of Papias, is attested in the second century also by Justin, Irenaeus (or the Roman archive), and Clement of Alexandria[126]—prevented his Gospel, although it was almost entirely incorporated by Matthew, from being lost, as presumably occurred with the older sayings collection associated with the name of Matthew.[127] Of the approximately twenty-eight pre-Constantinian Gospel fragments on papyrus in Nestle-Aland,[128] fifteen contain John, eleven contain Matthew, and six contain Luke, whereas *only two contain Mark*, namely the composite codex (*Sammelcodex*) P[45] with all four Gospels and the Acts of the Apostles, along with P.Oxy 83 5345. It seems like a miracle that Mark remained preserved. Apparently, in the course of the second century, the later Gospels of Matthew and John,

---

[125] See Kümmel 1975, 57 (GV = 1983, 30): "In sections common to Mt and/or Lk there are 10,650 words of Mark, 8,189 of which are in both other Gospels (7,040 in Lk and 7,678 in Mt). In the material that is common to all three, Mt and Lk have extensive congruence with Mk" (following S. de Solages). According to the reckoning of Morgenthaler 1958, the percentage of Mark in Matthew is even greater and the amount in Luke smaller: 8,555 or 6,737 of 11,078.

[126] Justin, *Dial.* 106.3; Irenaeus, *Haer.* 3.1.1; Clement of Alexandria apud Eusebius, *Hist. eccl.* 2.15.1–2 and 6.14.5ff., cf. 1 Pet 5.13. On the Roman archive, see Thornton 1991, 29, 45, 48–55.

[127] See notes 149 and 156 below.

[128] NA[27], 684–90. Presumably, the large communties such as Rome, Ephesus, Antioch, and Alexandria already afforded themselves at any early date—i.e., already in the first decades of the second century—a collection of all four Gospels. Irenaeus presupposes it as a given, and it is already given in Justin with his ἀπομνημονεύματα τῶν ἀποστόλων (see *1 Apol.* 66.3; 67.3; and especially *Dial.* 103.8; 106.1–107.1 and elsewhere).

which were ascribed to apostles, were esteemed more highly than the earlier Gospels of the apostle-students Mark and Luke.[129]

The error of the life-of-Jesus scholarship of the nineteenth century through to A. Schweitzer was that it believed that the dependence on Petrine tradition was a guarantee of "historical" reliability and that Mark contained a temporally sequential biographical narrative of Jesus' activity over the course of about one year. The "eyewitnesses," which—as the prologue of Luke demonstrates[130]—certainly played a large role, were conceived of in a way that was too modern. However, as form criticism and redaction criticism have shown, Mark does not provide the kind of historical-biographical account that modern historians would wish for. Rather, he writes a *kerygmatic biography of Jesus*, i.e., he narrates the story of Jesus as a preacher in a paradigmatic way as "gospel." If he, as some like to ascribe to him, created a new literary genre, then it is this form of "*kerygmatic* biography." The preaching character of his work finds expression in a structure that is, for theological reasons, configured dramaturgically and determined by his Christology and the extent to which this structure is thought out extends even to its details. However, he does not write—as is often claimed today—religious fiction. Rather, he largely reworks "tradition"—one could also say, "memory" that is selected and shaped according to theological and missionary aspects—including in the so-called "redactional" summaries and framing pieces. For what reasonable exegete would want to doubt that Jesus first wandered through Galilee, preaching and healing; called fishermen at the Lake of Gennesaret; attracted crowds so that they followed him; disputed with scribes and Pharisees; taught the disciples whom he had called; and in the end was crucified in Jerusalem? The—rough—outline of his Gospel is accurate in substance. At the beginning stands the activity of the Baptist and Jesus' baptism. This is followed by an activity of some length in Galilee with its center in Capernaum. Starting in chapter 5 he also sometimes crosses over into the Gentile area surrounding Galilee. Only with 10.1 do we then find him in Judaea and Peraea. With 11.1 the last week in Jerusalem begins, which, starting in chapter 14, culminates in the passion of Jesus. The passion is his theological goal. One could say that Mark's account becomes "gospel" in the strict sense only through the actual "passion story" in Mark 14.1–16.8. However, viewed geographically, he writes—which is correct historically—an overwhelmingly Galilean Gospel. The disciples

---

[129] On the *Wirkungsgeschichte* of Matthew and John in the second century in comparison with the other Gospels, see also Byrskog 2000; Massaux 1950; Köhler 1987; Hengel 1993a (ET = 1989a); Hengel 2008c (ET = 2000b); and Nagel 2000.

[130] Luke 1.2; cf. 1 Cor 15.5 and Heb 2.3. On this, see Hengel 2012b (GV = 2007a).

also come from Galilee,[131] above all their speaker Simon Peter: "Truly, you belong to them, for you also are a Galilean."[132] This is all the more conspicuous since Galilee no longer plays a role in the primitive Christian sources outside the Gospels. Luke and John already restrict its significance vis-à-vis Jerusalem, and Acts mentions it only three times, two of which look back to the Jesus movement.[133] It also has a very small significance in the pagan literature. Are we to believe that this geographically so uncommonly structured account of Mark, which decisively influenced the later reports, has nothing to do with history?

Furthermore, would it be naïve to believe that Mark writes without any consciousness of the temporal distance from Jesus, without any "historical consciousness," and only discusses the problems of his present? His understanding of "history" must not be measured by our modern, critical understanding. The temporal distance from the past Jesus event, which amounts, after all, to only ca. forty years—a manageable period of time—clearly emerges at numerous points.[134] He knows that the situation of Jesus and of his disciples in Galilee, as he presents it, was not simply identical with the situation of the communities that he wants to address in the critical time of the Jewish War and of the Roman civil war. Already for him the time of Jesus, which lay in the past and to which he consciously restricted himself, is unique and decisive. Salvation was grounded in it—and not in the threatening present.[135] He leads his hearers into the immediate present of the community with its difficult turbulences only at individual points, for example in Mark 2.20 and 9.1, in the compressed "church history" in 13.5-13, and in 14.9.[136] Moreover, it never becomes visible that he rejects other Christologies, let alone "heresies." We encounter this only in the later Matthew, when he warns against

---

[131] An exception is perhaps Judas Iscariot (see note 144 in chapter 11 and section 19.2 with note 49).

[132] Mark 14.69-70. Matthew, who writes in geographical proximity of Galilee (see note 194 below), adds, with knowledge of the subject matter, "for your language betrays you" (Matt 26.73). Cf. Acts 1.11; 2.7; 10.37. On the geographical knowledge of Mark, which is often wrongly contested, see Lang 1978; Hengel 1983a, esp. note 19 (ET = 1983c, 193 n. 19). See also section 8.1 on Galilee. We must not forget that maps were very rare at that time and the few that existed (for example, for the military) were not good.

[133] Once in Acts 9.31 on the peace that the Christian Jews in Judaea, Galilee, and Samaria had around 36 CE before the persecution of Agrippa, and additionally in 10.37; 13.31, where Luke emphasizes the Galilean origin. On the whole, see Hengel/Schwemer 2019.

[134] See Roloff 1970, which is still fundamental, as well as Roloff 1969; Lemcio 1991. Cf. also Hengel 1984a (ET = 1985b, 1–30).

[135] See the discussion of the term "Gospel" earlier in this section.

[136] See Hengel 1984a (ET = 1985b, 1–30).

false prophets,[137] and even more strongly in the Johannine corpus.[138] Mark wants to show to the communities in which his work is read aloud in the worship service (cf. 13.14) who Jesus really was (and is),[139] what their salvation is based upon,[140] and which consequences are to be drawn from it.[141] Nor should we—and this likewise applies to the other Gospels—ascribe his work simply to a certain "community." We know nothing about *the* "Markan community." Mark did not write his—revolutionary—work for his personal individual community. After all, it is very doubtful whether there was such a community, for as an "apostle-student" he was surely a much-traveled man. Rather, as the first "evangelist" he presumably wrote in Rome for the whole church.[142] His Gospel is not a collective product either, but rather the work of an authoritative teacher, behind whom stands, in turn, an older surpassing authority. Since such a new creation does not simply appear out of nothing, it may have had a prehistory and, as Herder already perceived, been tested and developed in the oral presentation in the worship service.[143] Primitive Christianity was a dynamic missionary movement in which—as in antiquity in general—oral, not written, communication stood at the center. Moreover, someone who expects the near end has more important things to do than to produce and cite literature. This is why we encounter so few "Gospel quotations" prior to Marcion and Justin. The first and second generations were determined by the oral word, which was living and yet also sticking in the memory. To some extent, this even still applies, as Papias shows, to the first half of the second century CE. Even later the word that was read and interpreted in the worship service and the catechetical oral teaching continued to mutually enrich each other.[144] Therefore, in his study of the Gospel tradition, S. Byrskog speaks in the context of the oral history of antiquity of the phenomenon of "re-oralization."[145] Far into the second century, the Gospels were

---

[137] Matthew 7.15; cf. the doubling of the Markan *Vorlage* of 13.22 in Matt 24.11, 24. In Mark we are dealing with an eschatological prophecy for the time of the messianic woes.

[138] Hengel 1993a, 467 index, s.v. "Doketismus" (no subject index in Hengel 1989a).

[139] Cf. the question after the stilling of the storm in Mark 4.41: τίς ἄρα οὗτός ἐστιν;

[140] Cf. Mark 1.11; 2.5, 19; 8.31; 9.7; 10.45; 14.22-24.

[141] Cf. Mark 8.29-30, 34.

[142] Mark 13.10; 14.9; on this, see Hengel 2008c, 167ff., 184ff. (ET = 2000b, 96ff., 106ff.); Bauckham 1998, 49–70. Only later, after he had written his Gospel in Rome, was he made the first bishop in Alexandria: Eusebius, *Hist. eccl.* 2.24; cf. 2.16.

[143] Hengel 2008c, 167–68 with note 487 (ET = 2000b, 96, 296 n. 397); Hengel 1983b, 256 n. 78 (ET = 1985b, 52, 157 n. 78).

[144] Papias according to Eusebius, *Hist. eccl.* 3.39.4: The preference for the φωνὴ ζῶσα καὶ μένουσα.

[145] Byrskog 2000, 138ff., 254–55; see also p. 384 index, s.v. "orality–re-oralization."

not so much cited exactly as they were quoted from memory, having been 'catechetically processed.'

Whether Mark already relied on written sources remains unclear and is controversial. He may have drawn upon an older passion narrative. This is suggested by 1 Cor 11.23ff., a text which shows that Paul already possessed a related passion tradition more than twenty years earlier, though it was still oral. The extent to which Mark used his own or someone else's notes for this and the extent to which the alleged pre-Markan "collections" come from others or were compiled by Mark himself also remain open. One's own notes could also be designated as a "source." What seems certain is that the authority of the evangelist in this truly epochal work, which created a new influential literary genre, is connected with the authority of Peter. Only five to six years lay between the composition of his work in Rome in ca. 69/70 CE and the martyrdom of Peter at the same location. This means that the figure of Peter, the martyr and most important propagator of Jesus tradition in the West, together with his surpassing authority, was still immediately present for most communities. The situation changed only in the Gospel of John, which emerged ca. thirty years later. In the Fourth Gospel the mysterious Beloved Disciple becomes the competitor of Peter. Nevertheless, there too Peter still appears prominently at decisive points.[146] One does not at all need to insert a plurality of written sources, anonymous tradents, and creative communities between Jesus and Mark. Here there has been much speculation and little demonstration. By contrast, notwithstanding all the ways that it is bound to tradition, the oldest evangelist's own theological and authorial achievement in this venture to write a "Gospel of Jesus Christ, the Son of God" as a continuous narrative from the appearance of the Baptist to the flight of the women from the tomb must be estimated all the more highly.

The fact that his Gospel chiefly contains what largely recedes in the older sayings collection, which is then reworked by Luke and Matthew, namely the passion story, miracle stories, biographical anecdotes, and controversy dialogues, suggests that he knew this stream of tradition—or corresponding collections of texts—and eclectically participated in it, but now consciously added the *story* of Jesus—which had become necessary after the death of the decisive first generation—*as a narrating, kerygmatically determined complement*, which culminated in the passion.

---

[146] E.g., John 1.41-44; 6.68; 13.6-11, 36ff.; 21.15-19 and elsewhere. Cf. Hengel 1993a, 210–19 (ET = 1989a, 76–80); Hengel 2010a, 154 index, s.v. "Disciple, Beloved" (GV = 2006b, 252 index, s.v., "Lieblingsjünger").

Ernest Best expresses in a convincing way the dialectic between Mark's own theological shaping and his faithfulness to tradition in his Gospel as follows:

> In the way in which he has placed the tradition in his total context, supplying audience, place, time, and sequence and in the summaries . . . he has been quite obviously creative. But in the way in which he has preserved the material which existed before him he has been conservative. . . . Mark appears to have had a positive respect for the material he used; this is not to say that he was attempting to write "history."[147]

This last sentence must be made more precise: 'history,' certainly not in the modern sense, but indeed in the form of a historical narration—oriented to the Old Testament episodic style—of the salvific activity of Jesus from the baptism of John to the climax of the crucifixion and the testimony to the resurrection by the *angelus interpres* to the women. We are dealing with a narrative that contains the whole message of salvation and therefore can—indeed must—be called εὐαγγέλιον, a term that not only Paul but, in our view, also Peter, the teacher of Mark, had used as the quintessence of his proclamation.[148]

6.4.2 The Sayings Tradition

The sayings tradition is the most important source for Jesus' proclamation, but it does not as such form a demonstrable literary unity. We can infer it only in a very fragmentary way from Luke and Matthew, at first from the material that is common to them that goes beyond Mark and then also from the "special material" of Luke and Matthew, which is largely to be assigned to it. This means, however, that we know neither its exact wording nor its various parts and forms nor its exact scope as a whole. Accordingly, almost all the questions connected with it are contested in scholarship.

---

[147] Best 1985, 128.

[148] Cf. Acts 15.7; 1 Pet 4.17; cf. Hengel 2008c 141–96 (ET = 2000b 78–115). On the whole problem, see the fundamental study of Byrskog 2000. E.-M. Becker 2006 has attempted to show that Mark is a historiographical work that is comparable to the great works of Hellenistic-Roman historians and arose in Syria as a reaction to the First Jewish War. A critical evaluation of Becker's untenable thesis has already been given by Backhaus 2006. Bauckham 2017, 118, has now rightly pointed out again that in terms of social status and style, the preserved historiographical works of antiquity have a completely different niveau than the Gospels.

Up to now scholars have usually assumed *a single* written "source" used by Luke and Matthew for the common material that goes beyond Mark. This has been abbreviated with the letter Q and connected with numerous hypotheses, such as hypotheses about multiple redactional layers with divergent theologies or about "communities" of Q with different Christologies. These hypotheses are largely built upon sand.[149] From the very beginning it was observed that the agreements between the texts assigned to Q in Luke and Matthew sometimes differed greatly, so that it was necessary to reckon with different forms of the sources Q^{Lk} and Q^{Mt}. Moreover, the reworking of Q in the two Gospels seemed to be fundamentally different. Whereas Matthew chiefly distributed this "Q material" in five large thematic blocks of discourse — sometimes mixed with the discourse tradition of Mark and his own special material — throughout his Gospel, while strongly shaping these speeches with his own theology at the same time (chapters 5–7; 10; 13; 18; 23–25), on the whole Luke appears to have preserved this sayings tradition much better in terms of order and wording. It extends there from the preaching of the Baptist in Luke 3 to the apocalyptic discourse on the coming of the Son of Man in Luke 17 and especially occurs, together with special material, in the two large "insertions" that interrupt the narrative thread of Mark in Luke.[150] This rightly led to the assumption that Q was not a self-enclosed literary unit in the strict sense but more likely to be an open collection whose form could no longer be adequately determined, especially since it was circulated in different versions. Thus, all attempts to discern redactional layers and a gradual development of the source and its theology become doubtful.

[149] The synopsis of Robinson/Hoffmann/Kloppenborg 2000, which is the product of long, painstaking work, is certainly useful in various ways, but as a construction of Q it brings with it the danger of an uncritical use. It would have been sufficient to designate the common passages; thus in exemplary form in Neirynck 1988; cf. also Robinson/Vaage/Daniels 1985. Now there is a danger that this artificially established text (Robinson/Hoffmann/Kloppenborg 2000) will be cited like the text of Nestle-Aland and create the impression of a certainty that in no way exists. The more recent investigation of Casey 2002 assumes old Aramaic sources, which were available to Luke and Matthew in different Greek translations. This means that Q was, in this view, no longer a unified single source in its secondary Greek form. Mark is said to have already used an older Aramaic source. The Q hypothesis is much more complex and complicated than is generally assumed. In this respect Casey comes closer to the reality than the Q hypothesis in the far too simple way in which it is often envisaged today. In any case, we must reckon with various sayings sources that were lost — not least because of their fragmentary, provisional character.

[150] Luke 6.20–8.3; 9.51–18.14; see section 11.3. The smaller block was inserted between Mark 3.19 and 20 and the larger one between Mark 9.50 and 10.1.

Its content consists predominantly of compositions of sayings, individual sayings, and parables of sapiential-ethical and prophetic-apocalyptic character, with it not being possible to make a strict distinction between the two. A demarcation of the Q material from the rich special material that is peculiar to the two Gospels of Luke and Matthew remains unclear, for we must, after all, always reckon with the fact that one of the evangelists took over material from this source while the other evangelist did not.[151] The Gospels could not exceed a certain length and the evangelists were therefore forced to select and shorten. Matthew in particular does this energetically, while he often gives preference to Mark because of the authority of Peter standing behind him. To this can be added the fact that the common material assigned to Q contains not only sayings and other redactional pieces but also some narratives such as the centurion of Capernaum and the temptation story, which, are, in our view, wrongly assigned to Q. Thus, it is entirely unproven that it is really a matter of only one "source." In addition to Mark, Luke has certainly drawn on several other sources.[152] We must also assume something similar with such a judicious author as Matthew. This would suggest that both used several collections of sayings, with it being possible that it may have partly involved strongly altered versions of an older, originally Aramaic collection. Since the Gospel of Luke, who writes roughly between 75 and 80 CE, is ca. ten–fifteen years older than Matthew, who presupposes the new constitution of Judaism in Palestine under Pharisaic leadership in the school of Yavneh (from ca. 90 CE) and, as Matt 23 shows, stands in sharp conflict with it,[153] we must assume that Matthew knew the work of the *auctor ad Theophilum* and partly copied it. This is especially suggested in those pieces in which Luke and Matthew agree in their wording. On the other hand, in a whole series of texts of the Lukan special material we can easily explain why the self-confident, anonymous Jewish Christian scribe did not take over this material from Luke, the student of Paul, since they did not fit his historical-theological concept. In others the *Vorlage* appears so completely different that we can no longer speak of *one* source.[154] Another advantage of this hypothesis that

---

[151] They proceed similarly even for the Mark material that was fundamental for them.

[152] Cf. the πολλοί in the prologue 1.1, which is indeed to be taken seriously and does not refer only to Mark and Q.

[153] Cf. Hengel 2008c, 336ff. (ET = 2000b, 196ff.) and section 6.4.4.

[154] On the omission, see, e.g., Luke 15.8-32; 16.1-31; 17.10-19; 18.1-14, etc. The assumption of different *Vorlagen* applies, for example, to the texts for which a "Paulinizing tendency" can be assumed in Luke and, further, to the Samaritan texts due to Matt 10.5 etc. The parable in Matt 18.12-14 stands in a completely different context and is changed so much that we can ask whether Matthew had it from a completely different source than Luke 15.3-7; cf. also Matt 25.14-30 with Luke 19.11-27 and Matt 22.1-14 with Luke 14.15-24.

Matthew knew Luke is that the disturbing, thus far unresolved problem of the so-called "minor agreements"—i.e., the not so few texts in which Luke and Matthew agree against Mark in Markan material—disappears. Here Matthew corrects or supplements from Luke the account of Mark, whom he predominantly follows.[155]

An enigmatic sentence in Papias—which, like the report about the emergence of the Gospel of Mark, probably goes back to the presbyter John, i.e., to a figure of the first century CE—could point to the origins of the written sayings tradition: "Matthew compiled in the Hebrew (i.e., Aramaic) language the sayings (of the Lord), and each translated them as he was able."[156] This sentence cannot possibly refer to our Greek Gospel of Matthew, which emerged roughly between 90 and 100 CE and is already an apostolic "pseudepigraphon," but probably points instead to an old Aramaic collection of sayings (and anecdotes) of Jesus, which may originate from the Jerusalem community as the early center of Palestinian Jewish Christianity and which were then translated by various primitive Christian missionaries, according to their respective abilities, into Greek. A tax collector must have been able to write; in the case of the other disciples this was not certain. This *could* explain the existence of different divergent sayings *collections*, which were used by Luke and later also by Matthew and much later *perhaps* also still in the Gospel of Thomas. After all, the appeal of the "sayings of the Lord" extends far into the second century.[157] Since, however, we must often assume that Matthew also makes recourse to Luke in the sayings tradition, these versions can no longer be reconstructed. *Luke thus becomes the main source of the proclamation of Jesus that is fragmentarily preserved in the sayings tradition.*

It is also reasonable that the Gospels composed by "students of the apostles," i.e., Mark and Luke, are older than the Gospels ascribed to an apostle,

---

[155] Hengel 2008c, 274–353 (ET = 2000b, 169–207). Thus, Matt 22.35 takes over a polemical introduction to the question of the greatest commandment from Luke 10.25 (νομικός and [ἐκ]πειράζων αὐτόν) because he cannot agree with the positive portrayal of the scribe in Mark 12.28. Cf. also in Matt 26.68 = Luke 22.64 the addition against Mark; or Matt 26.75 = Luke 22.62 against Mark 14.72: καὶ ἐξελθὼν ἔξω ἔκλαυσεν πικρῶς; see section 6.4.4. Dobschütz 1928, 345ff., already saw the problem. It is peculiar that despite the minor agreements there have been so few references to the probability of a certain dependence of Matthew upon Luke. Wilke 1838, 685–93, had already postulated such a dependence; see Hengel 2008c, 275–76 n. 814 (ET = 2000b, 303–4 n. 663). Zahn 1922, 19, who believed in the priority of the Aramaic Matthew, assumed that the Greek translator around 90 CE used Mark and Luke. From more recent times, see Huggins 1992 and Aurelius 2001. Faith in the traditional Q hypothesis is still very great.

[156] Eusebius, *Hist. eccl.* 3.39.16: Ματθαῖος μὲν οὖν Ἑβραΐδι διαλέκτῳ τὰ λόγια συνετάξατο, ἡρμήνευσεν δ' αὐτά ὡς ἦν δυνατὸς ἕκαστος.

[157] Hengel 2008c, 112–20, 223–37 (ET = 2000b, 61–65, 131–40).

i.e., Matthew and John. The First Gospel may have received its author's name from the author of the first Aramaic collection of sayings of Jesus. After it, in the second century, Gospels or Gospel-like writings were usually assigned only to authors with apostolic authority.[158]

On the whole the language of the sayings tradition is a proper, Semitizing Koine Greek. Nothing stands in the way of the assumption of an Aramaic linguistic background. It would be enough for the translator, copier, and ultimately the "final redactor" of Luke to have clothed the sayings of Jesus and stories in a passable Greek linguistic form. On the other hand, in the sayings of Jesus Luke took greater care to preserve the wording than he did with the narrative material, and Matthew even made repeated attempts to imitate or recreate individual typical linguistic forms of the proclamation of Jesus, including the parallelismus membrorum.

What must be rejected is the hypothesis — which is popular today — that only a sapiential-paraenetic collection of sayings stood at the beginning, which was then augmented later by secondary prophetic-apocalyptic sayings. Here the wish is the father of the idea. For it thereby removes what is offensive for modern people in the proclamation of Jesus and pushes it onto the later community: a humane "Galilean Cynic" or "Jewish Socrates" emerges, who is more congenial.[159] Placing it in a supposed genre of the λόγοι σοφῶν, which reaches from the old oriental wisdom to the Byzantine gnomologia,[160] is also as historically illuminating (or also meaningless) as the specification of the Mishnah as a legal collection between the Code of Hammurabi and the *Corpus Iuris Civilis* of Justinian. In reality it is precisely not the collection of the sayings of just any "wise person" (among many) but the unique collection of the sayings of the one eschatological "wise person" *par excellence*, i.e., of the Son of Man — Messiah Jesus.[161] A comparison with Ecclesiastes, Sirach, or Proverbs shows that, despite some formal parallels, in their radicality many sayings of Jesus contradict the universal and practical wisdom of the ancient orient, which arises out of empirical life experience. It is the eschatology or the connection to the kingdom of God that gives the sayings tradition its incisiveness and

---

[158] The alternative was that the Gospels were later ascribed also to certain ethnic or Jewish Christian groups: of the Egyptians, of the Hebrews, of the Ebionites, etc. But this remained the exception. The supposed "Gospel according to Basilides" (Origen, *Hom. Luc.* [Rauer 1959 = Merkel 1978, 8 line 38]) is probably a polemical designation of Origen for a collection of Gospel texts of Basilides and not a real title. We can only put forth speculations about this.

[159] Thus in Crossan and in the American Q scholarship. On Mack, see note 53 in chapter 5.

[160] On this, see, e.g., J. M. Robinson 1971.

[161] See Hengel 2001c, 18–131 (ET = 1995, 73–117).

provocative sharpness, a sharpness that is based—in a similar manner as
with the Baptist—on the apocalyptic background of the activity of Jesus.
God's reign is dawning and his judgment stands before the door. Therefore, the often sharply pointed antithetical parallelism predominates in his
sayings. We can infer the motif for such collections from Pss. Sol. 17.43,
where it says of the Messiah as the bringer of the kingdom of God (17.3):

> *His words* will be purer than the finest gold, the best. He will judge the
> peoples in the assemblies, the tribes of the sanctified. *His words* will be
> as the words of the holy ones, among sanctified peoples. (trans. R. B.
> Wright, *OTP* II: 668; emphasis added)

Such *words of the Messiah* therefore had to be kept and handed down as
firmly fixed and binding teaching.[162] One could also say with all three
Synoptics: "Heaven and earth will pass away but my words will not pass
away."[163] That the passion story is almost completely lacking in the sayings tradition could perhaps be connected with the fact that it already
existed in a pre-Markan form—belonging to an entirely different, narrative genre—and that Jesus had hardly spoken *expressis verbis* in Galilee of a future suffering. The pointer to the passion is, however, also not
completely lacking here. Thus, in Luke 14.27 = Matt 10.38 Jesus calls for
cross-bearing discipleship, and he speaks clearly of his death and of the
trials connected with it in Luke 12.50.[164]

We also regard as improbable the view that this tradition complex
is largely the product of Jewish Christian prophets in Palestine,[165] who
speak in the name of the exalted Lord. Primitive Christian prophets usually speak as they are moved by the Spirit.[166] The "exalted one," who, at
the right hand of God, speaks from heaven, also never appears *expressis
verbis* in the sayings tradition. Moreover, clear community situations from
a later time are scarcely visible in this strand of tradition.[167] In contrast to

[162] Cf. Matt 28.20; 11.29: μάθετε ἀπ᾽ ἐμοῦ; Acts 2.42; 4.20; 10.36-37, etc. On the
poetic-didactic form of the preaching of Jesus, see chapter 12.

[163] Mark 13.31 = Luke 21.33 = Matt 24.35; cf. from the sayings tradition Luke 16.17
and Matt 5.18, where the Lukan version is certainly the more original. Here the concern is
with the law, which admittedly must make space for the new, the kingdom of God.

[164] Matthew has omitted the saying, perhaps because he found it offensive, and formed
a saying of Jesus that fit in his mission discourse (10.34-36; cf. Luke 12.49-52). Cf. also
Luke 13.31-33. See section 11.3.

[165] This frequently advocated view has been refuted especially by Neugebauer 1962.

[166] Cf. Acts 11.28; 13.2; 21.10-11; Rev 14.13; cf. 1 Cor 12.8; 14.1, 29ff.

[167] The frequently expressed view that the early Christians put Spirit-inspired prophetic sayings as instructions of the exalted Lord into the mouth of the earthly Jesus later
is usually not justified. After all, the exalted one was in the Spirit-inspired words of the

Mark, this sayings tradition contains precisely no clear reference to the resurrection and exaltation of Christ! Together with pieces from the rich special material of Luke, which likewise probably comes from it, it forms the most important source for the proclamation of Jesus.

6.4.3 Luke

It is a stroke of luck that the second Gospel author known to us, Luke, due to his higher education, in the interests of his addressee, and led by Hellenistic and Jewish models, attempted to write a *historical* biography in the ancient sense. To this we can add Acts, which was unique for the church until Eusebius' *Ecclesiastical History*. We cannot thank Luke enough for his *Doppelwerk*, which belongs together in terms of subject matter (cf. Acts 1.1). To be sure, Franz Overbeck designated Luke's attempt to write an early Christian "mission history" oriented to Peter and Paul as "tactlessness on a global scale,"[168] because Luke, the "beloved physician" and companion of Paul,[169] as the first literarily educated author, was far ahead of the primitive Christianity of his time and thus contradicted Overbeck's ideal of a naïve unfalsified originality. Failing to recognize the theological and literary achievement of Luke, more recent exegetes have prematurely agreed with the judgment of Overbeck, which was directed against

---

prophet in every worship service—as Paul portrays it, for example, in 1 Cor 14—that is, constantly present. In the ever new presence of Spirit in the worship service, the prophetic words precisely did not need to be recorded and handed down but were spontaneously expressed in every new situation. Moreover, the preserved Spirit sayings in Acts and Revelation show that there was indeed a distinction drawn between the Spirit and the earthly Jesus—who was withdrawn from the community. The prophet Agabus does not say to Paul: "Jesus said this" but "the Holy Spirit says this." Rev 2.7 says: "The one who has hears, let him hear what the Spirit is saying to the community"; 14.13: "Indeed, the Spirit says: they will rest from their labors. . . ." Also, the Paraclete sayings in the Farewell Discourses in John distinguish clearly between Jesus and the Spirit. The fact that individual words of the exalted one have entered into the Synoptic tradition is rather the exception. They are easily recognizable through their christological context; cf. from the special material Matt 18.20 and on this m. 'Abot 3.2, a saying of R. Haninah ben Teradion, the martyr of the Bar Kokhba persecution: "When two sit (with each other) and words of the Torah are between them, then the shekinah dwells among them."

[168] Overbeck 1963 [1919], 78.

[169] Colossians 4.14; Phlm 24. Elsewhere it appears only in the late text of 2 Tim 4.11, where knowledge of Acts is presupposed; cf. 2 Tim 3.11 with Acts 13 and 14; see further 2 Tim 2.5 with Acts 16.1-2. Through the conspicuous praise of Mark in 2 Tim 4.11 Pseudo-Paul remedies again the break in Acts 13.13 and 15.38. On the person of Luke, see Hengel/Schwemer 1998, 9–40 (ET = 1997, 6–21). On Luke the physician, see L. Alexander 1993, 176ff., and Weissenrieder 2003, 330–46, 374: "It is attested only of Luke in diverse traditions that he was active as a physician."

Harnack's predilection[170] for the *auctor ad Theophilum*. In reality Luke performed a massive service for the church. He first preserved for us the most important parts of the proclamation of Jesus, inspired Matthew to follow him, and, beyond this, made visible the historical connection of the primitive community with the Pauline mission in Acts. The concern of Luke is then taken up again by the apologists and the fathers of the second and third century until Eusebius. As an author of the second generation he appeals to older sources in the prologue. The "many" to whom he appeals include in the first place Mark, which is based, in turn, on the paradosis of the "eyewitness and servant of the word" Peter, and then probably on multiple "collections of sayings," his special source on the passion story, and a *Vorlage* to the legendary prehistory, which is Jewish Christian in character. The traditions of women, beginning with the mother of Jesus, play a special role in Luke.[171] Both works, the Gospel and Acts, show that he undertook careful research and developed a sense for archaic traditions, if one may use this word with reference to the relatively short period of time of ca. fifty years between Jesus and Luke's present.

The *Doppelwerk* probably emerged between 75 and 85 CE, with a certain period of time lying between the Gospel and Acts, despite their inner connection.[172] There are multiple reasons that prevent one from dating it much later:

First, in the Gospel Luke still stands, as no other New Testament author, under the immediate impression of the destruction of Jerusalem. The catastrophe, which he portrays more concretely than all the other Gospels and which especially moves him, who loves Jerusalem and the temple,[173] cannot lie too far in the past. Secondly, he still writes in a time

---

[170] See his still fundamental works Harnack 1906; 1908. In contrast to the ultimately fruitless critical philosophy (*Kritizismus*) of Overbeck Harnack accurately specified the historical place of the Lukan *Doppelwerk*. The significance of Harnack as an investigator of the New Testament should be again be recognized anew; on this, see Markschies 2001. On more recent research on Acts, see Grässer 2001 and Hengel 2001f.

[171] On this, see Hengel 2012b (GV = 2007a). Cf. Luke 8.2-3; 10.38-42; 24.6-10. Luke uses the key word γυνή in the Gospel forty-one times, Matthew only twenty-nine times, Mark sixteen times, and John seventeen times; Luke uses χήρα nine times, Mark three times, and Matthew and John not at all. On this, see in detail Bauckham 2002, 47–76, 110–65, 279–83, and elsewhere.

[172] This results from the opposition of Luke 24 and Acts 1.1-11. On the dating of the Gospel and Acts, see Hengel 2008c, 320–50 (ET = 2000b, 187–205). Matthew is much later (see note 176 and notes 188–90 in this chapter).

[173] This is already a characteristic of a special material tradition and may be connected with the tendency of tradition guarantors who significantly influenced him. What is special about him is that he was influenced by very different sides, by Paul *and* by the Jerusalem tradition.

of relative tolerance from the Roman authorities, as it can be presupposed for the earlier Flavian period. The author hopes that higher Roman magistrates and members of the upper stratum will also turn to the Gospel and that the Christian proclamation will be tolerated.[174] There is still no sign of the oppression of sympathizers of the Jewish and Christian faith in the upper stratum by the late Domitian and the persecutions at the time of Trajan. The "high-born Theophilus" belongs himself to the upper stratum and presumably gave both works their title and cared for their dissemination. The meaningful name could be a code name. The address points to a person of higher standing, possibly of the equestrian rank.[175] Moreover, the picture that Luke provides of the community and above all of Judaism is completely oriented to the conditions in Palestine before 70 CE, about which he is astonishingly well informed. He writes in a milieu similar to what know from Josephus. All this would hardly have been possible any longer in ca. 90 or 100 CE. The recovery and development of Judaism after 70 CE until the rabbinate, which is fundamental for the understanding of Matthew, is not yet visible in Luke;[176] his Gospel is composed too early for this. Finally, if Matthew had been known to him, he would surely have used this impressive work with its large speeches, which would have given his Gospel a much different form. A dependence of Luke on Matthew, which is sometimes still advocated, is therefore impossible.

Luke's regard for his addressees is also visible in his theological tendency. After the catastrophe triggered by the near expectation in Jewish messianism, we can understand only too well his reserve toward all eschatological fever, which had also seized Christians to some extent. It is evidence of historical ignorance when he is reproached for this. The regard for the recipient also explains his outward reserve toward an explicitly expressed theology of atonement and of the cross, although he emphasizes

---

[174] On the destruction of Jerusalem, see Hengel 2008c, 324–31 (ET = 2000b, 189–94); on the "upper stratum," see Acts 8.26-40; 10; 13.7-12; 18.12-16; 23.25ff.; 24.24ff.; 26.30ff.; 28.31.

[175] The analogous address to the equestrian procurators Felix and Festus in Acts 23.26; 24.3; 26.25 is no accident. In Egypt the equestrian prefects and governors of the subprovinces, the *epistrategoi*, were addressed in this way. Cf. also the dedication of Josephus to Epaphroditus, the rich freedman of Nero, *Ag. Ap.* 1.1; cf. 2.1, who, according to *Ant.* 1.8, had compelled him to write the *Antiquities*, which Josephus dedicated to him according to *Life* 430, and who, as a "special lover of the truth," also cared for the dissemination of the book among like-minded people: *Ag. Ap.* 2.296. The address κράτιστε appears elsewhere in early Christian literature only in Diognetus, which makes a subtle allusion to Luke 1.1.

[176] Cf., for example, the polemic in Matt 23 and the fact that Matthew puts the address "Rabbi," which frequently appears in his Markan *Vorlage*, only in the mouth of the betrayer Judas (26.25, 49). His use of language presupposes the ordination of the scribes and the reservation of the title "Rabbi" primarily for them (23.7ff.). This scarcely occurred before 90 CE. On this, see section 11.4.

the necessity of suffering for the sake of faith, and Jesus' death and resurrection viewed together play the central soteriological role. This can be seen, for example, in the repeated ὑπὲρ ὑμῶν (Luke 22.19-20), in his portrayal of the Lord's Supper beyond Paul (1 Cor 11.24-25) and Mark (14.22-24), and the emphatic ἔδει παθεῖν τὸν Χριστόν (Luke 24.26) must also be understood on the basis of the suffering of the servant of God.[177] On the other side, we find a strong striving for harmonizing, which is connected with his apologetic interests and tends to leave conflicts unmentioned. Thus, he takes leave of Peter with his "Paulinizing" speech in Acts 15.7-11 and can pass over his conflict with Paul (Gal 2.11ff.). Moreover, he emphasizes, like no other evangelist, the love of God for sinners, indeed in Luke 5.8ff.; 15; and 18.9-14 the "justification of the ungodly." In the last-mentioned parable it becomes clear that, despite all "divergences," which show him to be a theologically independent thinker, he was a student and traveling companion of Paul. To be sure, through his contact with the Jerusalem community (see Acts 21) and his stay in Jewish Palestine, together with his special interest in the Jesus tradition, he distanced himself a bit from Paul theologically and through the critical ecclesial situation after 70 CE consciously became a counterbalancing "mediating theologian."[178] He therefore knew himself to be obligated to Paul *and* Peter, although in Acts the missionary Paul does dominate the field in the end.

6.4.4 Matthew

The rigorous and self-confident author of the first Gospel, an unknown Christian scribe, could no longer ignore the ca. ten-to-fifteen-years-older Gospel of Luke as the work of a student of Paul. As the scaffolding of his theological work, which is planned down to the last detail, he preferred not Luke but Mark, which was connected with Peter, since the authority of the "rock-man" was also fundamental for him. He alone gives the name *Kephā'*-Petros a unique ecclesiological interpretation (16.16-19). To be sure, his Petrine traditions that go beyond the Markan *Vorlage* largely have a secondary character.[179] In addition to Mark and Luke he also has access to a sayings tradition, which is available to him partly in written form. For this reason in the case of the speech material, it is usually difficult to decide whether he draws from the Lukan *Vorlage* or directly from

---

[177] Cf. Luke 9.22; 13.33-34; 17.25; 22.37 = Isa 53.12, cf. Acts 8.32-33 = Isa 53.7ff.; Luke 24.44; on this, see Mittmann-Richert 2008.

[178] Hengel/Schwemer 1998, 15–18, 23–24, 35 (ET = 1997, 9–11, no equivalent, 18); Hengel 2001f; Hengel 2012b (GV = 2007a); Hengel 2010a, 77ff. (GV = 2006b, 126ff.).

[179] Matthew 14.28-29; 16.17-19; 17.24; cf. also 15.15; 18.21. On this, see Hengel 2010a (GV = 2006b).

one of his own "sayings sources" or from both. For example, the "Sermon on the Mount," which is much more extensive than Luke's Sermon on the Plain,[180] may be based on a special "source," which arose from the catechetical instruction.[181] The speech material of the special material could also originate from his specific sayings tradition. The prehistory of Matt 1 and 2 and his resurrection account,[182] which goes beyond Mark, also point to distinctive—oral?—sources. At the same time, both texts display strong shaping by the Matthean theology. It is characterized by a Christology that presents Jesus as Messianic savior and teacher, who as Son of David "fulfills" not only the whole Scripture (5.17ff.) but through his activity and death also brings the "righteousness" required by God,[183] liberates the true people of God from the power of sin,[184] and obligates one to missionary service and to the doing of the true will of God, which Jesus himself interprets.[185] Therefore, more than all the other evangelists he places God's threatening judgment in the foreground.[186] It is his picture of Jesus that has shaped the understanding of Jesus as an ethical teacher and strict judge through to modern times. Nevertheless, his clear soteriology should not be overlooked in favor of a moralizing interpretation. Amidst all loyalty to tradition, he is superior to Mark and Luke in systematic and tradition-shaping power, whereas they were the more vivid storytellers. Above all, for reasons of space, he often shortens the texts of the Markan *Vorlage* and deletes novelistic features.

Together with the Gospel of John, his work is, at the temporal end of the New Testament, a signpost that powerfully points the way into the

---

[180] Matthew 5.1-2; 13.52; 28.20.

[181] Cf. Matt 5–7 with Luke 6.20-49, partly with a similar sequence. As an older text, Luke's Sermon on the Plain could form a point of departure for this.

[182] Matthew 28.8-20. In the prehistory it is conspicuous how strongly he places the "righteous" (1.19) "adoptive father" Joseph in the foreground—in contrast to Luke, who concentrates wholly on the mother of Jesus in chapters 1 and 2. Matt 1 and 2 appear as a partly corrective complement to the prehistory of Luke. The same also applies to his shorter resurrection account. Both the prehistory (1.18ff.) and the legend of the tomb guards (27.62-66; 28.4, 11-15) presuppose anti-Christian Jewish Jesus legends, which have points of contact with the account of the Jewish informant in Celsus; see notes 88–91 above.

[183] Matthew 3.15; 5.6, 20.

[184] Matthew 1.21; 20.28; 26.28.

[185] Matthew 5.13ff.; 28.18ff.; cf. 7.12, 21-22; 9.13 and 12.7 (= Hos 6.6); 22.39-40; 25.40.

[186] Cf. Luke 13.28 and the threat saying that is multiplied sixfold in Matthew: 8.12; 13.42, 50; 22.13; 24.51; 25.30. Matthew loves such repetitions of formulas; see Dobschütz 1928, 339–42. He regards the author perhaps in an overly bold manner as "the Jewish Christian who has gone through the school of the rabbis," indeed as the "converted Jewish rabbi" (343). At the time of Matthew, the "rabbinate" was only *in statu nascendi*.

future for the emerging church.[187] The conspicuous 'minor agreements' between Luke and Matthew are explained for us by Matthew's familiarity with Luke. Similarly, we must assume a theologically distanced knowledge in John of the older Synoptic Gospels, especially of Mark and Luke, which makes comprehensible certain parallels in wording. By contrast, it remains uncertain whether John knew the later Gospel of Matthew. These two Gospels are relatively close to each other in time.

Concerning the dating of the First Gospel, the transformation of the Pharisees into the absolutely dominant religious group in Palestine Judaism under the leadership of the scribes, i.e., the consolidation of the newly emerging rabbinate in Yavneh via the influence of R. Gamaliel II, is already presupposed in it.[188] By contrast, the other groups, Sadducees and Herodians, have become insignificant. The opponents of Jesus are understood stereoptyptically as the unity of "scribes and Pharisees,"[189] and one feels that the evangelist, as a (Jewish) Christian scribe (13.52), stands in intensive conflict with them. This, together with the fact that in Matthew, in comparison with Luke, the destruction of Jerusalem recedes again through the larger temporal distance and the restoration of Judaism in Palestine and the fact that in his language and conceptions, Matthew comes into contact most of all with the rabbinic tradition, points to a later time of emergence, roughly between 90 and 100 CE. It is no accident that with regard to the old Jesus tradition, the rich special material of Luke is much more fruitful than that of Matthew, whose expansions are, at least in some cases, legendary,[190] though he too possesses valuable special material traditions, especially in the parables: thus in Matt 13 the Parable of the Tares, the Parable of the Hidden Treasure, the Parable of the Pearl, and

---

[187] On the theology and christological soteriology of Matthew and especially on his understanding of δικαιοσύνη and νόμος, see now the fundamental study of Deines 2004.

[188] On this, see Luke 11.39-52, the *Vorlage* of his polemic against the scribes and Pharisees in Matt 23. On this, see H.-J. Becker 1990 and Hengel 2008c, 333ff. (ET = 2000b, 195ff.). The catastrophe of 70 CE also lies much further in the past than is the case for Luke. In a comparable way we find this one-sided emphasis on the Pharisees as representatives of the "Jews" who are hostile to Jesus in the latest Gospel, i.e., John.

[189] Matthew uses this formula in a stereotypical manner ten times. In his somewhat larger Gospel, Luke has this sequence only three times. The scribes are the leading group of the Pharisees.

[190] Cf., for example, in the passion story Matt 26.51-54; 27.3-10, 19, 24-25. We find here the first impulses of a developing Pilate legend: 27.51b-53, 62-66; 28.2-4, 11-15. His Petrine traditions, which are additional vis-à-vis Mark, are probably also legendary. See also note 186 above for his conception of judgment. Dobschütz 1928, 347, hypothesizes a date between 90 and 110 CE or around 100 CE. 110 CE is probably too late since Ign. *Eph.* 11.1 presupposes Matt 3.7 and Ign. *Smyrn.* 1.1 presupposes Matt 3.15. 90–100 CE is probably accurate. By contrast, Dobschütz correctly dates Luke in the time between 70 and 90 CE or around 80 CE.

the Parable of the Net, in ch. 18 the Parable of the Unforgiving Servant, in ch. 20 the Parable of the Laborers in the Vineyard, and in ch. 21 the Parable of the Ten Virgins and the Parable of the Last Judgment.[191] Correspondingly, the sayings tradition is more frequently preserved in an older form and order in Luke than in Matthew. Conversely, in Matthew the ecclesiasticalization is advanced and the community discipline is more developed. Matthew alone features rudiments of a community order. Only in Matthew are there two occurrences of ἐκκλησία, which is otherwise foreign to the Gospels.[192] Old Jesus tradition also occurs in the special material of his parables and in the Sermon on the Mount. Moreover, it is reasonable that the first "pseudepigraphical" Gospel ascribed to an apostle emerged later than the writings of students of apostles like Mark and Luke. Following him, the second century will primarily have apostles as Gospel authors. The unknown author and Jewish Christian scribe[193] in one of the Hellenistic cities of southern Syria or in Palestine itself[194] presumably adopted the name of the apostle Matthew—which appears twice with the byname "the tax collector" only in him and thus takes the place of the tax collector Levi of the Markan *Vorlage*[195]—because he was regarded as the collector of the oldest sayings tradition. This could explain the note in Papias,[196] which was already quoted above, that Matthew composed the sayings in Hebrew, which means in Aramaic. In our view, the oldest Aramaic sayings collection was connected with the name of this authority from the circle of the twelve, who is not otherwise prominent. In that case, we would also be dealing here not simply with "anonymous" Jesus tradition but with traditions behind which a disciple of Jesus stood. It was the markedly Jewish Christian character of the First Gospel together with the clear presentation of Jesus as teacher, indeed as new lawgiver in the large speeches (see

---

[191] E.g., Matt 13.24-30, 44-50; 18.23-35; 20.1-16; 21.18-21; 25.1-13, 31-46.

[192] Matthew 16.18 in the rock saying to Peter and 18.17 in his instruction on community discipline. In Mark the term does not yet appear. Luke does not introduce it in Acts until 5.11, but then uses it frequently, i.e., twenty-nine times. This means that Luke still distinguishes more clearly between the time of Jesus and the time of the community. The Trinitarian baptism command and the sending of the disciples at the end in Matt 28.19-20 also point to a later emergence. On the topic of discipline, see the great discourse on the community in Matt 18.

[193] Matthew 13.52. Presumably he received his scribal schooling originally in a Jewish academy; see note 186 above. Thus, he has—as the first volume of Billerbeck indicates—the most rabbinic parallels. On this, see Hengel 1987c (= Hengel 1999b, 219–92).

[194] Matthew 4.24-25 is the only passage that connects Syria with the activity of Jesus. This is not a coincidence.

[195] Matthew 9.9; 10.3. By contrast, Mark 3.18; Luke 6.15; Acts 1.13 mention only the name Matthew among the twelve without the addition ὁ τελώνης.

[196] Eusebius, *Hist. eccl.* 3.39.16. On this, see section 6.4.2 with note 156.

above all 5.17-48) and the claim of an apostolic origin that has gave the impression that Matthew was the oldest Gospel ever since the second century CE and into the present.

6.5 John[197]

The Gospel of John, which comes into consideration only in a qualified sense as a source for the Jesus tradition, is completely different in nature. For in the Fourth Gospel the "supremacy" of the idiosyncratic author's Christology has reshaped or suppressed the historical reality. In the ecclesiastical tradition, ever since the Valentinian Ptolemy and then again since Irenaeus, it is ascribed to John the son of Zebedee, i.e., to the apostle from the circle of the twelve.[198] The real authorship—according to 21.24-25, the enigmatic, unnamed Beloved Disciple is said to have written the whole thing—is, after all, intentionally veiled in the added chapter, for he is also not identified in John 21.2. Behind it stands, in our view, a surpassing theological teacher, John of Ephesus, who is identical with the "presbyter John" and "disciple of the Lord" in Papias, Irenaeus, and Polycrates of Ephesus in his letter to Victor of Rome around 190 CE.[199] This corresponds to the introduction of the second and third Johannine letters: ὁ πρεσβύτερος.

Papias mentions this "presbyter John" multiple times as his most important tradent. He was presumably a very young eyewitness and follower of Jesus from the Jerusalem aristocracy and a student of John the son of Zebedee.[200] It is therefore possible that in the Gospel, which his students edited (21.24), the two men, John the son of Zebedee and John the Elder, fused into one person.[201] The author, i.e., "John the Elder," writes his Gospel in clear opposition to the Synoptic tradition of a

---

[197] Dodd 1963; Brown 1966/1970, I: xliff.; Hengel 1993a (ET = 1989a); Nagel 2000; Theissen/Merz 1998, 33ff. (GV = 1997, 49ff.); Thyen 2005; Hill 2006. See now also Frey 2018b; 2018a.

[198] On this and what follows, see Hengel 1993a, 18ff., 37–38 (ET = 1989a, 3ff., 8–9); Justin, *Dial.* 81.4, mentions the apostle John as the author of Revelation. The origin from the son of Zebedee was still forcefully advocated by Schleiermacher (see note 25 in chapter 5) and Loofs 1916.

[199] Eusebius, *Hist. eccl.* 3.39.4. In Irenaeus and Polycrates of Ephesus he is also still stereotypically called "disciple of the Lord" or "the one who lay on the chest of the Lord" and not apostle.

[200] Cf. John 18.15; Hengel 1993a, 321ff. (ET = 1989a, 131ff.). On the Beloved Disciple, see also 13.23ff.; 19.26ff., 35; 20.2-8; 21.7ff., 20-34.

[201] Hengel 1993a, 313–20 (ET = 1989a, 124–31).

Petrine character, which he knows only too well (in oral and written form)[202] and which is for him is no longer sufficient to adequately present the true nature and way of the incarnate Son of God. It is understandable that Schleiermacher and his like-minded contemporaries, who wanted to make the uniquely and archetypically "constant intensity of God-consciousness" of Jesus the foundation of faith, based themselves precisely on the Gospel of John against the Synoptics and regarded John as the truest portrayal of Jesus. Under the hammer of D. F. Strauss this hypothesis was broken.[203] Here too a final uncertainty remains, such as in the question: How are we to place the authoritative saying about the unique, revelation-determining unity of Father and Son in Luke 10.22 (= Matt 11.27) from the sayings tradition?[204] It could have something like a bridge function to the Fourth Gospel. Even Rudolf Bultmann expressed in 1925 the bold speculation

> that the activity and the proclamation of Jesus may stand much more strongly in the context of the gnostic-Baptist movement, out of which the Gospel of John must be understood, than can be recognized from the Synoptic tradition. The primitive community, from which the Synoptic tradition originates, . . . may represent a Judaising reaction phenomenon, for which . . . Peter may be made responsible.[205]

Even if one disbelieves it, viewed historically the enigma of the Gospel of John remains an open, indeed unanswerable question. One should not of course speak of a "re-Judaizing" of the primitive community in the Synoptics. The Jesus movement was Jewish through and through, and the author of the Fourth Gospel is also a Jewish Christian. The recently revived hypothesis that the Fourth Gospel is older than the Synoptics[206] is erroneous. It is clearly the latest of the four Gospels. This was already known by the early church since Irenaeus and Clement of Alexandria, who are dependent here on older tradition.[207] The Fourth Gospel, which is written

---

[202] He certainly knows Mark and Luke. He uses and criticizes them. Beyond this, he is familiar with the oral tradition. On the use of this, see Theobald 2002.

[203] See note 25 in chapter 5.

[204] For an attempt at interpretation, see section 17.4.2.

[205] Bultmann 1925, 144 (= 1967a, 102).

[206] Thus J. A. T. Robinson 1985; Berger 1997.

[207] Irenaeus, *Haer.* 3.1.1; Clement of Alexandria apud Eusebius, *Hist. eccl.* 6.14.7 according to book 6 of the *Hypotyposes*: τὸν μέντοι Ἰωάννην ἔσχατον . . . πνεύματι θεοφορηθέντα πνευματικὸν ποιῆσαι εὐαγγέλιον. Cf. also the Gospel prologues and the Canon Muratori in Aland 2005, 549, 554–55, and Eusebius, *Hist. eccl.* 3.24.5–13, a text that attempts to harmonize the contradictions between the Synoptics and that goes back, at least partly, to an older source. On this, see Hill 1998, who all too optimistically

from the geographical perspective of Jerusalem, may correct the Synoptic tradition in individual points, for example in the view that the length of the activity of Jesus was longer than only a year, although the specification of the Fourth Gospel, which speaks of ca. two to three years, is again too long.[208] Moreover, one could consider the possibility that there was a "Baptist" period of transition before the public appearance of Jesus in Galilee, since Jesus obtained his first disciples from the circle of the Baptist, indeed that initially Jesus himself may have baptized, that the conflict that led in the end to his death in Jerusalem was more sustained and longer than Mark reports, and that certain details from John's passion story must also be taken seriously.[209] But all of this remains relatively uncertain. For on the whole the historical value of John recedes behind Mark, the sayings tradition, and the special material of Luke and of Matthew. We can only rarely rely on him *alone* and must justify doing so in each case. This is especially clear in the sharply pronounced high Christology of the Fourth Gospel, which presupposes the Christology of Paul. Despite all his great independence, he nevertheless also stands on the shoulders of Paul.[210] One receives the impression that John has very consciously—much more strongly than the Synoptics—retrojected the picture of the exalted Lord onto the earthly Jesus. John's own christological configuration of the Jesus tradition and older traditions are sometimes combined in the Gospel of John so seamlessly that we can hardly distinguish between tradition and interpretation.[211] His hieratic style is completely uniform so that D. F. Strauss could speak of the "seamless robe" of Christ.[212] It forbids us from adopting the still popular source hypotheses and separations of redactional layers. The prehistory of the Gospel—which is undoubtedly complicated in terms of tradition history and source criticism—and of the impressive teacher and his circle that stood behind it can no longer be reconstructed. We can make only more or less uncertain speculations about this. The theological

---

hypothesizes Papias. We would sooner hypothesize Origen or Clement of Alexandria. See also Merkel 1971.

[208] John reckons with at least three Passover festivals: 2.13, 23; 6.4; 11.55 (12.1; 13.1). See section 9.1 and section 11.1.

[209] On the historical details, see Hengel 1999a; still fundamental Dodd 1963.

[210] Hengel 1993a, 160, 299 (ET = 1989a, 50, 120); cf. Wellhausen 1908, 121: "John depends on Paul." He advocates a clear "*solus Christus, sola fide, sola gratia.*" Parts of the primitive community and Paul may, however, have been theologically closer than is often assumed. On this, see 1 Cor 15.11 and the *abba* cry of the Pauline communities.

[211] Theobald 2002 especially strives after this. In Luke 10.16 Luke indicates in the mission discourse that the disciples of Jesus could already speak theologically in their own responsibility and also regard themselves as the voice of their Lord; see note 172 in chapter 11. I owe this reference to F. Neugebauer.

[212] Hengel 1993a, 9 n. 1; cf. 226–52 (ET = 1989a, 1, 136 n. 1; cf. 84–94). See now also Thyen 2005.

language of the evangelist (and letter writer) is thus identical with the language of Jesus in the Gospel. In the Fourth Gospel Jesus proclaims himself as the preexistent Son of God sent into the world. Whoever sees him, sees the Father.[213] This speech form of the "revelatory discourses" differs fundamentally from the sayings and parables of the Synoptics, although in John too the older forms of the sayings and parables still sometimes shimmer through. To be sure, they have usually melted into the text. Also, of the seven selected miracles of Jesus, four are not reported by the Synoptics. For John they are "signs" that express the divine dignity of Jesus and do not go back to a separate literary source but rather come from oral tradition (or from Mark) and are an integral component of the Gospel. They point beyond themselves and seek to lead one to the central "sign," the resurrection of Jesus. The evangelist obtains the great freedom in the presentation of the self-proclamation of Jesus by stressing that the disciples did not or did not adequately understand Jesus' words and signs before Easter and only the Spirit as gift of the risen one, the "Paraclete" promised in the Farewell Discourses, will "teach," "remind," and "lead" them "into all truth."[214]

6.6 Apocryphal Gospels and Agrapha[215]

In comparison with our main sources, the four canonical Gospels, and here especially the first three, the Synoptics, the apocryphal Gospel texts and fragments have only secondary importance for an attempt to approach the historical Jesus. With regard to the actual "history and teaching of Jesus," they are by no means of equal value to the Synoptics. The latter are also clearly the oldest witnesses. This applies also to the so-called agrapha, the noncanonical sayings of Jesus, which we find in individual later New Testament manuscripts, in Patristic texts, indeed even in Islamic texts,[216] as well as to the texts from Nag Hammadi, with the possible exception of

---

[213] John 14.9. There are about twenty-seven formulaic references to the sending of the Son by the Father.

[214] On the σημεῖα, cf. John 2.18-22. On the miracles reported only by John, see 2.1-10; 5.2-9; 9.1-12; 11.1-44a. On the Paraclete, see 14.26; 16.13ff., cf. 14.16; 15.26; 16.7ff.; see also 20.22. On the miracles, see the excursus in section 16.4.

[215] Resch 1906; Theissen/Merz 1998, 33–62 (GV = 1997, 48–72); Schneemelcher 1991/1992 (GV = 1990); Klauck 2002 (ET = 2003a), which is at present the best German presentation of the problem. Cf. now also Ehrman/Pleše 2011; Markschies/Schröter 2012; Bockmuehl 2017. On the reworking of older sayings of the Lord in the Fourth Gospel, see Theobald 2002. Theobald speaks of "creative updating of the sayings of Jesus" (41).

[216] On the "agrapha," see Klauck 2003a, 6–21 (GV = 2002, 16–34). We already find individual texts in the New Testament. A typical case is Acts 20.35 in Paul's speech in Miletus. But 1 Thess 4.15ff. could also be reckoned to this. Other additions are found

the Gospel of Thomas. There may be individual sayings in the agrapha that possibly go back to Jesus. But this can hardly be made really probable.[217] With this we emphatically gainsay the currently popular attempts to find—or better, invent—new extra- and pre-Synoptic sources.

A typical example is the "source wizardry" of J. D. Crossan.[218] With an almost divinatory gift, paired with historical recklessness, he postulates eight Gospel-like sources from the first "stratum," i.e., from the time between 30 and 60 CE, including the *Urschrift* of the Gospel of Thomas and Papyrus Egerton 2, both of which are said to come from the 50s CE; two apocryphal papyrus fragments[219] from the third and fourth century, which clearly turn out to be secondary vis-à-vis Mark; the so-called Gospel of Hebrews,[220] from which we possess only seven quotations from the church fathers and is likewise said to have arisen already in the fifties CE in Egypt; a collection of miracles supposedly common to John and Mark; and an apocalyptic scenario that is said to stand behind Matt 24 and Did. 16.[221] The last "source," a so-called "Cross Gospel"—which is reworked in the Gospel of Peter and again said to have been written "in the fifties . . . possibly at Sepphoris in Galilee" and which supposedly represents the only source for the passion stories of the canonical Gospels[222]—is a pure phantasmagoria. In the Gospel of Peter, of which we possess a larger fragment from the passion story, the leading disciple of Jesus speaks in the first person. This does not happen in any of the older Gospels.[223] In reality it represents an anti-Jewish, fanciful-miraculous work from the middle of the second century, which already uses all four

---

in Gospel manuscripts such as Codex D on Matt 20.28; Luke 6.4; 22.28, etc. The Islamic texts, which urgently require a monographic study, are found in Asín y Palacios 1919/1926.

[217] See the critical judgment of Hofius 1978; cf. also Hofius 1991; 2012. On the Coptic library of Nag Hammadi, see J. M. Robinson 1988; Schenke/Bethge/Kaiser 2001/2003.

[218] Crossan 1991, 427–34.

[219] On P. Egerton, see Klauck 2003a, 23–26 (GV = 2002, 36–40). On P. Vindob. G 2325, third century CE = Van Haelst 1978, nr. 589, cf. Mark 14.26-30: the text form of the logion is clearly secondary vis-à-vis Mark. On P.Oxy 10.1224, fourth century CE = Van Haelst 1978, nr. 587, cf. Mark 2.16-17; Matt 5.44; Mark 9.40; on this, see Schneemelcher 1991/1992, I: 113–14 (GV = 1990, 85–86); text in Aland 2005, 63, 84, 248. This text is also secondary vis-à-vis Mark 2.16-17; Luke 6.26 (Matt 5.44); and Mark 9.40.

[220] On the problem of Jewish Christian Gospels, see Klauck 2003a, 36–54 (GV = 2002, 53–76): they extend into the Middle Ages. On the Gospel of the Hebrews, see 55–62. See also Frey 2003.

[221] The Didache knows, for its part, Matthew. See Köhler 1987, 19–55 (51ff., 55).

[222] Cf. also Crossan 1988.

[223] Cf., by contrast, 2 Pet 1.16-18 or the Infancy Gospel of Thomas; see Schneemelcher 1991/1992, I: 392 (GV = 1990, 353).

Gospels.[224] This wondrous multiplication of Gospels by Crossan continues in the second "stratum" between 60 and 80 CE. Five other apocryphal Gospels supposedly fall in this time: the Gospel of the Egyptians, the "Secret Gospel of Mark" discovered by Morton Smith (which we regard as a tendentious forgery),[225] P.Oxy 5.840,[226] the second stratum of the Gospel of Thomas, a dialogue collection, which is inserted into the Dialogue of the Savior from Nag Hammadi,[227] and the semeia source, which supposedly underlies the Fourth Gospel.[228] Alongside these fourteen newly dated Gospel-like source writings from the time between ca. 60–80 CE stand as "canonical texts" only the authentic letters of Paul, Colossians, the Sayings Source, and the Gospel of Mark. No wonder that such a flood of "new sources" inspired the author to write an entirely new "life of Jesus" extending to nearly five hundred pages.

We do well to be more modest. The Gospel of Thomas is divided today into 114 sayings. More than half of these are composed in the Synoptic style. The others consist of "Gnostic" sayings. It arose in its Greek original form in a long process, which was concluded around the middle of the second century CE. The oldest Greek papyrus fragment must be dated to around 200 CE. The Coptic translation, which is strongly influenced by the Sahidic Gospel text, comes only from the fourth century CE. Vis-à-vis the Synoptic parallels the logia of the Gospel of Thomas clearly display a further developed form with a strongly standardized, dehistoricized, de-Judaized character, which has been "purified" from all eschatological features, sometimes in connection with an ascetically colored *interpretatio gnostica*, to which the introduction "these are the hidden sayings that the living Jesus spoke" already corresponds. Precisely these features make the Gospel of Thomas so popular among some scholars. It is certainly the early Christian writing that comes closest to the modern

---

[224] Mara 1973; Klauck 2003a, 82–88 (GV = 2002, 110–18); Hengel 2008c, 22–38 (ET = 2000b, 12–20). Ab circa 130 the Peter apocrypha accumulate; see 2 Peter, Preaching of Peter, Apocalypse of Peter, Gospel of Peter, and in the second half of the second century the *Urschriften* of the Acts of Peter and of the Pseudo-Clementines.

[225] Smith 1973; Merkel 1974; Merkel 1990 (lit); Ehrman 2003, 68–89; Carlson 2005. Cf. now also Burke 2013.

[226] Fourth/fifth century = Van Haelst 1978, nr. 585; Schneemelcher 1991/1992, I: 92–94 (GV = 1990, 81–82).

[227] In our view, this is a very late gnostic text, which possibly emerged only in the third century and presupposes a developed Gnosticism.

[228] Its existence is entirely hypothetical; see Hengel 1993a, 246–48 (ET = 1989a, 91–92); the stylistic unity of the Fourth Gospel militates against it. With Overbeck one could speak of a "scholars' homunculus."

esoteric.[229] In the non-Synoptic logia, which among other things contain previously unknown parables, we can assume authenticity in one case or another. It is, however, difficult to justify this satisfactory in detail. It scarcely enlarges our knowledge about the historical Jesus. The work is interesting for the later post-Synoptic shaping of the Jesus tradition in a milieu that is typical for tendencies of the second century CE:

> More is expected of the Gospel of Thomas than the text can in fact pro-
> vide, when it is claimed that its testimony to the tradition about Jesus
> is equal or even superior to that of the synoptics. If we free it from
> this intolerable burden, we ourselves are free to discover the wealth of
> insights which its logia offer us.[230]

The early apocryphal Gospels are interesting witnesses with regard to the theological experimental, gnosticizing or popular Christianity of the second century. For our attempts to approach Jesus historically, however, we must forgo them and content ourselves with the Synoptic texts as the one fundamental main source. We have no better sources.

---

[229] Text with translation: Bethge 2005; Ehrman/Pleše 2011, 303–49; Gathercole 2014. Greek fragments, which are questionable in part, also in Lührmann 2000, 106–31 (P.Oxy 1.654.655). Fieger 1991, 1–6 (6): "As the analysis of this single logion will show . . . we are not dealing with an independent Gospel tradition that is independent from the canonical Gospels. . . . The Gospel of Thomas also does not make recourse to the Sayings Source Q, for almost always when traces of redactional work of individual evangelists can be identified with certainty, a knowledge of these redactional changes can also be identified in the Gospel of Thomas." See already Schrage 1964, 8: "In fact, it will become evident . . . in the individual analysis that the possibility of a tradition that is independent of the Synoptics cannot be excluded in the one case or the other, but otherwise Thomas primarily does not go back to a tradition stratum lying before and behind our Gospel." Cf. now also Goodacre 2012; Gathercole 2012; Bockmuehl 2017, 170–75. Due to the fact that the oldest Greek text, P.Oxy 1, is to be dated around 200 CE, Klauck 2003a, 107–22 (GV = 2002, 142–62), decides on an origin ca. 120–140 in Syria. See further Schröter 1997. Vis-à-vis this state of affairs the remarks of Crossan and Koester 1990, 81–113, represent a step backwards. It is completely senseless to assume with Crossan 1991, 427, on the basis of logion 12 (for the sake of James, the brother of the Lord, heaven and earth were created), an origin before his stoning in 62 CE under the aegis of James in Jerusalem. One should not expect such megalomania of James. Matthew 16.16ff. was also probably not formulated during the lifetime of Peter, i.e., before 64 CE. Matthew only originated ca. 90–100 CE. See Hengel 2010a, 14–28 (GV = 2006b, 21–44).

[230] Klauck 2003a, 122 (GV = 2002, 162).

7

The Historical Quest

7.1 Jesus Biography, Oral Tradition, Eyewitness Testimony, Authority, and Textualization[1]

In not a few studies on the Gospels one can read that they—perhaps with the exception of Luke—did not aim to be historical narratives let alone biographies but rather pure witnesses of faith and means of proclamation, so that for this reason the question of their historical content also misses their intention. The consequence of this opinion—which is connected with the criticism of the liberal Jesus scholarship of the nineteenth century and the newly discovered form criticism—was that the protestant Synoptic exegesis from about 1920 has suffered in part from an acute loss of history and investigated the Synoptic texts only with a view to the respective theologies of their authors in a redaction-critical kerygmatic way or, after the rise of linguistically oriented "literary criticism" in the seventies, with a view to their narrative strategies. The flood of redaction-critical or now literary-critical studies in recent decades has its basis here. In reality, however, all three Synoptic Gospels seek to narrate an event that lies in the temporal past, i.e., the history of Jesus, which does, of course, have fundamental significance for the present of the authors, for what is narrated therein was already εὐαγγέλιον for Mark. All of them, even John, are indeed conscious of the difference between the time of Jesus and the later time of the community.[2] Both Mark and John emphasize that the disciples before Easter did not really understand Jesus' activity, dignity, and way.

---

[1] Jeremias 1970, 1ff. (GV = 1979, 13ff.); Roloff 1970; Hengel 1971a, 323ff. (= Hengel 2007b, 289–305); Hengel 1980a (GV = 1984d); Hengel 1983b (ET = 1985b, 31–63); Stanton 1974; Byrskog 2000; Dunn 2003a. On the following text, see the somewhat expanded English version in Hengel 2005; on eyewitness testimony, cf. now Bauckham 2017.

[2] See chapter 5.

The Gospels do not present an atemporal cult myth but rather basically pick up the Old Testament narrative of the "great acts of God"[3] toward his people Israel, which were outdone, indeed completed, in the activity and death of Jesus, because Israel's history has reached its divinely intended fulfillment and its goal in them.[4] Here Jesus and his work appear as the incomparably greatest and concluding act of God, as "eschatological event," but in space and time, i.e., in Galilee and Judaea at the time of John the Baptist, Pilate, and Herod Antipas, and at the same time as the beginning of the end of history. In the Gospels history and eschatological expectation are not experienced as an absolute opposition. One could speak, with a certain justification, of a—one-time—goal-oriented "end-history," which had to be *narrated*.

Thus, while it is true that from a modern standpoint the Gospels are not biographies, *they can, by contrast, indeed be compared with ancient biographies and were understood in this way also in antiquity*. Even in Plutarch, the most significant ancient biography, one sometimes seeks in vain for a true chronological ordering of the material, and in Suetonius this is the norm. Even where sayings and anecdotes are placed in a series, there is no discussion of the psychological development of the hero. Rather, from the beginning the hero corresponds to a firmly defined picture. What stands in the foreground is neither the process of becoming nor the completeness but rather the ideal typical. Every part has the whole in view. Plutarch has at least two biographies that could be designated as "passion narratives with extended introductions."[5] Lucian's *Demonax* is an ancient biography that consists of anecdotes and often polemical sayings but concludes with the self-determined death of the hero and seeks to present this hero as a model. It portrays a cynic philosopher from Cyprus (ca. 70–170) who lived in Athens, was highly regarded there, and died in old age through a refusal to eat.[6]

From the beginning the motivation of the collection and passing down of the Synoptic tradition was to record the unique words and deeds of the Messiah Jesus extending to his atoning death on the cross and the miracle of his resurrection for the missionary preaching and the catechetical and

---

[3] Cf. Acts 2.11: τὰ μεγαλεῖα τοῦ θεοῦ. LXX: Deut 11.2; Ps 71(LXX: 70).19; 106(LXX: 105).21; Sir 18.4; 33(LXX: 36).7.

[4] Mark 1.14-15: πεπλήρωται ὁ καιρός. Cf. Luke 16.16; Gal 4.4.

[5] In *Cato the Younger* (95–46 BCE), chapters 58–73 address the last stay in Utica in ca. 47/46 BCE. In *Eumenes* (362/61–316 BCE), chapters 10–18 are focused on the last four-year defensive battle against Antigonus. On the formulation, see Kähler 1988, 80 n. 11 (GV = 1953, 59–60 n. 1: "*Passionsgeschichten mit ausführlicher Einleitung*").

[6] On this, see K. Funk 1907; Cancik 1984.

paraenetic instruction of the community, the memorial celebration of the Lord's Supper, and the dialogical controversy with outsiders.

Jesus and his immediate disciples left no written testimonies that have been preserved for us. The ascriptions of Gospels to authors from the circle of the twelve are not historical. This applies to Matthew, to John, the son of Zebedee, and to the later "apocryphal" Gospels. The "sayings," which Matthew, according to Papias, is said to have written down "in the Hebrew (that is, Aramaic) language," were still not a Gospel and have not been preserved for us. A special case is "John the Elder," whom Papias and the tradition of Asia Minor designate as a "disciple of the Lord" and who was identified from the beginning of the second century with John, the son of Zebedee. But this Jerusalem figure did not belong to the closest circle of the disciples of Jesus, and in the picture that he sketches of Jesus, the historical figure of Jesus is outshone by the majesty of the Son, who is equal with God and has been exalted to the Father. This means that even the claim to eyewitness testimony does not yet mean "historical" reliability.[7] Even an eyewitness could, on the basis of his deeper christological insight established through Easter and the experience of the Spirit, sketch a picture of Jesus that, by our standards, no longer corresponds to "historical reality."

This lack of extremely early literary witnesses is very understandable. Whoever expects the end of the "old, evil world" to come relatively soon was not interested in a literary processing of history for posterity.[8] It is therefore no accident that the literary portrayal of the story of Jesus begins only with Mark after the death of the great witnesses of the first generation in the sixties. Collections of sayings of Jesus could be several decades older, but they were not self-contained literary works but rather texts in notebook form,[9] which were open to expansions, i.e., texts whose histories of emergence we can no longer determine. Scholarship has invested much too much fantasy here. At best we can hypothesize on the basis of the Papias note that the oldest Aramaic prototype of these collections was connected with the name of the tax collector Matthew.[10]

On the other hand, Jesus' words and deeds made a massive impact already during his lifetime. The "Twelve" sent out by Jesus already disseminated his message, and the leaders of the people regarded this as so

---

[7] See section 6.5 on John and what is said about Peter in section 6.4.1. Cf. also the caricature of gullible "eyewitnesses" in Lucian, *Philopseudes* and in *Peregr.* 39–40. Lucian shows knowledge of Christian tradition here; cf. 13–16. On fictive eyewitnesses, see below. On the problem, see Bauckham 2017.

[8] Scribal apocalyptic authors, such as the unknown author of Daniel or the John of Revelation, constitute an exception. The Jerusalem primitive community was precisely not a "scribal" apocalyptic movement.

[9] On this, see Sato 1988.

[10] Papias apud Eusebius, *Hist. eccl.* 3.39.16. On this, see section 6.4.2 and the end of section 6.4.4.

dangerous that they quickly and decisively rendered him harmless in conjunction with the Roman prefect. This impact also included the fact that his hearers disseminated his words and deeds already back then.[11] That this occurred even in the case of his opponents is shown by "the Pharisees and some of the scribes" who, according to Mark 7.1ff., came down from Jerusalem to Galilee in order to sound out the Jesus movement, and by the "false witnesses" in the trial of Jesus.[12] The evangelists rightly emphasize the lasting impact of Jesus upon the people. It is a presupposition for the relatively rapid spread of the Jesus movement after Easter also outside of Galilee, for example in Jerusalem itself, including the emergence of the community of the Hellenists there, as Luke portrays this in Acts 2–6.

After Easter the missionaries in the motherland and especially in the Greek-speaking diaspora needed concrete information about the "words and deeds of the Lord,"[13] i.e., the main components of his activity for their community-founding sermon, for in the form of narration they had to testify to their hearers about what this crucified Messiah who was exalted by God had said and done. One can just as little call for belief in a wordless and deedless savior, in a mere bearer of a name and title, than for trust in an anonymous crucified man. They proclaimed a message that was too offensive—"a stumbling block to Jews and foolishness to Greeks" (1 Cor 1.23)—for them to be able to recount nothing definite about this Jesus, especially since they were energetically opposed by their adversaries. Missionary preaching was only possible argumentatively, and this included the words and deeds of Jesus. Arguments centered—this is still evident from Justin's *Dialogue with Trypho* and from the Jewish informant of Celsus—not only on Old Testament "prophecies" but also very concretely on the person of Jesus, on the claim that he was not a deceiver, magician, or possessed person, for example. This is why Justin had to make recourse to the "reminiscences of the apostles." This means, however, that the proclaimed Jesus was more than a mere mathematical point. He could not be restricted only to a historical crucifixion and a mythical resurrection and exaltation, for he could not be reduced simply to the ominous "that

---

[11] Cf. Mark 1.45; 3.8; Matt 4.24-25; 9.26; 14.1; Luke 4.14, 37; 6.17-18; and elsewhere.

[12] Mark 14.56ff. = Matt 26.60ff. On the problem, see Schürmann 1968b.

[13] On the expression, see Papias according to Eusebius, *Hist. eccl.* 3.39.15: τὰ ὑπὸ τοῦ κυρίου ἢ λεχθέντα ἢ πραχθέντα; cf. Acts 1.1; Polybius 2.56.10 on the task of a historian: τῶν δὲ πραχθέντων καὶ ῥηθέντων κατ᾽ ἀλήθειαν αὐτῶν μνημονεύειν πάμπαν; Josephus, *Ag. Ap.* 1.55: Josephus praises himself as an eyewitness of the Jewish War: τῶν λεχθέντων ἢ πραχθέντων οὐδ᾽ ὁτιοῦν ἀγνοήσας. Gellius, *Noctes Atticae* 14.3.5, calls the *Memorabilia* of Xenophon *dictorum atque factorum Socratis commentariis*; cf. Quintilian, *Inst.* 9.2.59; Tacitus, *Ann.* 3.65.1; Petronius, *Sat.* 1.3: *omnia dicta factaque*. We are dealing with an expression that is common among historians and rhetoricians.

of his coming" of Rudolf Bultmann.[14] Without the narration of Jesus tradition, which then found expression in the oldest Gospels, the formulaic "kerygma" would have been incomprehensible for the church from the very beginning. If he was to be proclaimed, the crucified Messiah Jesus of Nazareth would at the same time have had to be "potrayed before one's eyes,"[15] i.e., made present through vivid narration. Thus, all four Gospels *necessarily* tell a story, with Mark and Luke being closest to the historical reality. That relatively little of this appears in the letters is connected with the fact that these are largely occasional writings that address specific problems in the community and with the fact that narration plays a secondary role in the epistolary genre. The community-founding sermon is preserved in the letters only in traces and in extremely abbreviated form.[16] This means, however, that the primitive Christian emissaries were dependent on *memories* of Jesus from the beginning, and at first indeed *also* on their own experience with him. However, at the same time, people began to exchange such memories and presumably soon began to record them in more or less free note form for personal use—thus basic forms of the passion story as

[14] The phrase appears in Bultmann 1971, 252, on John 5.19: "for his proclamation can only be the proclamation of the single fact of his coming, of the coming which is the eschatological event" (GV = Bultmann 1950, 189: "daß seine Verkündigung nur das eine Wort vom Daß seines Gekommenseins als dem eschatologischen Geschehen sein kann"). It does not even hold true for the Fourth Gospel, which reports not a few "facts" about Jesus. See Bultmann 1961, 117 (GV = 1948b, 148); cf. 1964, 21–23 (GV = 1965, 9–10; 1967b, 449–50), though there we find the telling qualification "that the proficiency of the 'discipline of introduction,' and hence the historical-critical analysis of the Synoptic Gospels which inquires into the objectively ascertainable history of Jesus, suffices only to corroborate the 'that' which the kerygma maintains in the face of a possible skepticism regarding Jesus' historicity, and to illustrate it with a degree of possibility" (ET = 25–26; GV = 13–14; 454). The addition "What it cannot do, however, is to produce evidence that the historical continuity between Jesus and the kerygma is a material agreement" (ET = 25–26; GV = 13–14 and 454–55) rests on a fundamental error. The "material agreement" is grounded for primitive Christianity in the personal identity of the human being Jesus (as the incarnate Son of God), who was crucified in Jerusalem, with the exalted Lord, which also included his entire "prophetic-Messianic" activity. *For the sake of this identity and continuity, which was fundamental for the primitive community, they had to narrate the 'gospel' as 'story of Jesus' and write Gospels.* Bultmann could not understand this connection, because he ultimately regarded Christology only as a mythical speculation based on the delay of the parousia, which basically disturbed his existential interpretation. See already Bultmann 1933–1965, I: 265: "Not the what but the that of his (this means Jesus', M.H./A.M.S.) proclamation is what is decisive." Can one really separate the two? Bultmann is rightly criticized by Käsemann 1969a, 43–47, 52–53 (GV = 1960/1964, II: 49–52, 57), and Strecker 1969, 470.

[15] Galatians 3.1: as the crucified one, to be sure. This, however, also includes what leads to crucifixion: cf. 1 Cor 2; 11.23-24; and 15.3ff. See Hengel 2004d.

[16] See section 6.2.

well as a variety of sayings and deeds of Jesus. The question is how much the kerygmatic ecclesiastical use and their own changing theological and political interests transformed the tradition in the selection and oral presentation. The changes—especially the shortenings and simplifications—were considerable here. From the abundance of material that was available at the beginning the majority has been lost.

Form criticism, which emerged with the end of the First World War, attempted to grasp this oral tradition before it came to be fixed in writing. Inspired by the Old Testament scholar Hermann Gunkel and folklore studies, form criticism was concerned—in the footsteps of Herder—to work out, by means of an analysis of the Synoptic Gospels, the forms of the preliterary tradition and its development and to infer from this its setting in the life of the community and often also its secondary emergence. It was now no longer the apostles, prophets, or teachers, who encounter the community as an authority, but rather the community itself as a creative collective, which not only shaped the tradition but often created it anew. The frequently used imprecise term *Gemeindebildung* (formation or invention of the community) now became dominant in Gospel criticism, although it usually says little about what is actually decisive, namely *when, where, and why* a tradition was "formed." Here the "hypothesis" of an origin with Jesus is simply replaced by the hypothesis of a post-Easter fiction, which is said to satisfy the "needs of the community."[17] At bottom the entire Jesus tradition could, of course, be designated as *Gemeindebildung*, for it was by members of the community that this was kept in memory, translated into Greek, formed, and proclaimed freshly again and again into new situations. One ought either to define this vague term when it is first used or refrain from using it. The stark opposition 'authentic Jesus tradition / *Gemeindebildung*' overly simplifies the complexity of the matter. It is as misleading as the antithesis between "facticity" and "fictionality," which is popular today. Both are present in every narrative. Even pure "fiction" is based in some way on the observation of facts.

The starting point was—according to the protagonist Martin Dibelius—the view that in the case of the Synoptic Gospels we are dealing with *Klein-Literatur* (popular or unsophisticated literature), in which "the personality of the author recedes into the background," a literature that is largely compiled from anonymous "*Sammelgut*" (collected or traditional

---

[17] It is curious that we do not possess a community logion that lets the problem of the circumcision-free mission preaching vis-à-vis the Gentiles be decided by a saying of Jesus. Circumcision, which soon becomes so controversial, is mentioned only in relation to John the Baptist and Jesus (Luke 1.59; 2.1). One did not produce logia of Jesus according to "need."

material), which originally presented itself in small units and was shaped and expanded in the collective of the community according to "form-building laws."[18] Rudolf Bultmann analyzed all this material and divided it in the oral tradition according to his "forms,"[19] though his often radical decisions about genuineness were based not so much on the form but rather on the content, such as when he explained almost all the narrative material, especially all the miracle stories, which he ascribed to the "Hellenistic community," and almost all the controversy dialogues as unhistorical, as well as all sayings in which Jesus refers to his sending in the first person. His approach shows that he largely makes evaluative judgments, which testify to the "prejudgment" of the interpreter.

Here the narrative material was judged much more critically than the sayings tradition, which is more consistent in its phrasing in the Synoptic comparison. On the other hand, despite the variable form of narration, conspicuous experiences stick better in one's memory than the wording of proclamation that is heard, unless this was repeated a number of times, which was probable for the preaching of Jesus. It is incomprehensible that the event that must have most deeply imprinted itself upon the memory, the passion story, fell victim to the knife of criticism, with the exception of some paltry remains.[20] This new *radical point of view* met with an enthusiastic response in Germany after the First World War, and even more so after the Second World War in Germany for the following reasons:

1. Because it corresponded through the emphasis on the sermon and the worship service in the formation of the material to the dialectic Word of God theology, which was especially interested in the proclamatory character of the primitive Christian tradition.
2. Because through this the liberal life-of-Jesus research of the nineteenth century, which in part had misunderstood the Gospels as "biographies" in the modern sense and sought to build its "modern" Christology on the picture of Jesus gained through historical reconstruction, was also led *ad absurdum*. To the extent that theological thinking has again turned in a positive way to the

---

[18] Dibelius 1919, 1–4 = 1933, 1–8 (ET = Dibelius 1971, 1–8). Cf. Dibelius 1922, 129. See also Bultmann 1934b, 29–30 (GV = 1966, 20; 1933–1965, IV: 12), and the heading of § 4 (1934b, 32; 1966, 22): "The Laws Governing Popular Narrative and Tradition." On this, see below with notes 38–40.

[19] Bultmann 1963 (GV = 1921; 1931; 1995).

[20] On this, see Hengel/Schwemer 2001, 45–63, 133–63 (ET = Hengel 1995, 41–58, no equivalent).

nineteenth century since the 1980s, historical Jesus research has gained in interest once again.[21]

3. In the footsteps of Wellhausen and Wrede, K. L. Schmidt in particular had, prior to Bultmann and Dibelius, demonstrated the unhistorical character of the redactional framework in Mark, which made, according to this perspective, every attempt to write a life of Jesus impossible.[22] With corresponding sharpness he criticized the ancient historian E. Meyer's attempt to write a portrayal of Jesus on the basis of the oldest Gospel according to Mark.[23]

4. Because there stands behind this a certain disinterest—which is connected with dialectical theology and is obvious in Bultmann—in all historical realities, which, as objectifying *bruta facta* that are to hand, are supposedly not relevant theologically, reinforced by the endeavor to demonstrate one's own "scholarliness" by means of the most radical criticism and to avoid every historical question that somehow appears apologetic.[24]

In itself the form-critical question could become fruitful for the exegesis of the Synoptic texts, for through it the development and shaping of the individual units became more transparent. Thus, in his monograph on the parables of Jesus and in his presentation of the proclamation of

---

[21] A typical example is the excellent *Lehrbuch* of Theissen/Merz 1998 (GV = 1997). Gerd Theissen, a student of the radical critic Philip Vielhauer, who revised for many years the supplement to Bultmann's *Geschichte der synoptischen Tradition*, appears to have experienced a certain "conversion." See also his inspiring preliminary studies under the title *Lokalkolorit und Zeitgeschichte in den Evangelien. Ein Beitrag zur Geschichte der synoptischen Tradition* (Theissen 1989b; ET = 1992: *The Gospels in Context: Social and Political History in the Synoptic Tradition*), in which the *volte face* is clearly prepared. On the nineteenth century, see section 5.2.

[22] Schmidt 1919. On the one hand, the observations of K. L. Schmidt must largely be affirmed: "But on the whole there is no life of Jesus in the sense of a developing life story, no chronological outline of the story of Jesus, but only individual stories, pericopes, which are placed in a framework" (317). On the other side he must also concede that in Mark's introductions to the pericopes "the remains of an itinerary are still present" (317). Unfortunately, Schmidt does not inquire further about where Mark has acquired the geographical and other numerous historical details from his framework and the "summary supports" connected with it. "Memory" or "tradition" is in play in a free manner also in the "framework." Moreover, the "rough framework" in Mark is indeed accurate historically: see point 4 in section 6.4.1.

[23] On this, see note 72 in chapter 5.

[24] On the rejection of "objectifying thinking" in general in favor of the "existentialist historicality," see Hengel 2002, 413ff. Kähler 1896, 105–6 (= 1953, 43; there is no equivalent in Kähler 1988) already polemicized against the "*bruta facta* obtained by historical scholarship, which would lie as a dead stone at the beginning of the development of Christianity." Here the meaning of historical research is misunderstood and distorted.

Jesus, Joachim Jeremias made rich use of it,[25] since with its aid the emergence of the Synoptic texts could time and again be better analyzed. What was questionable, however, was the establishment of it as absolute and the attempt to make negative judgments about the genuineness of large parts of the Synoptic tradition solely on the basis of form-critical observations, judgments which often gave the impression of decrees rather than insights gained by historical-philological arguments.

Since then more recent literary-critical research has demonstrated that the Gospels were precisely not "only to the smallest extent authors" and "principally collectors, vehicles of tradition, and editors."[26] Through the shaping of the material Mark is already a dramatic storyteller who argues theologically. To be sure, it would be just as false to turn him, as some like to do currently, into the author of the first "Jesus novel."

As we have said previously, Mark does not only seek to proclaim the gospel through his narration of the *story of Jesus*. With his new, revolutionary work he steps forth *as an authority who was already known in the church* and was also recognized as such by the communities who used his Gospel. Therefore, from the very beginning this Gospel was not circulated anonymously. Thus, just as the Old Testament writings all had titles, which were specified before they were read in the worship service (after all, the hearers had to know what text was being read), so too there were titles for the new writings of the community of the Messiah Jesus.[27] The title pointed to the authority of the author. The genuine letters of Paul (the only certain written witnesses before Mark), above all Galatians and 1 Corinthians, and Acts stress the prominent position of the individual apostles and teachers. They were also the tradents and shapers of the Jesus tradition, to whom the communities looked,[28] especially Cephas-Peter.[29]

---

[25] Jeremias 1972, 23–114 (GV = 1998, 19–115); Jeremias 1970 (GV = 1979).

[26] Dibelius 1971, 3 (GV = 1919; 1933, 2). On Mark as a brilliant narrator, see the evaluation of the ancient philologist Gunter Zuntz (Zuntz 1984a, 222): "a masterwork of astonishing originality"—in contrast to the form-critical school's verdict that he is a "mere compiler." Zuntz also estimates the historical value of the Gospel as not small and dates it very early, already around 40 CE: see Zuntz 1984b. W. Schadewaldt 1985 (GV = 1982) also came to a similar conclusion; on this, see the biographical introduction of Maria Schadewaldt (M. Schadewaldt 1985; GV = 1982).

[27] On the Old Testament, cf. Mark 1.2 (with incorrect prophet name); 7.6; 12.35; Luke 3.4; 4.17; 20.42; 24.44; Acts 1.20; 8.28; 13.33; Matt 3.3, etc. Writings without titles were not usable in the worship service. On this, see Hengel 1984b (ET = 1985b, 64–84); Hengel 2008c, 71–95 (ET = 2000b, 38–54).

[28] First Cor 1.12; 9.1ff.; 15.1-11; Gal 1 and 2.

[29] On this, see Bultmann's own judgment (quoted in section 6.5 above). On Cephas in Paul, see Hengel 2010a, 48–79 (GV = 2006b, 78–129).

Individual passages in the letters[30] show how much the past of the last twenty–twenty-five years and the person of the great authorities were present in the communities. Are we to believe that this did not also apply to the "history of Jesus"? The importance of a tradition was dependent not least on the authority of the tradents or of the author. This fundamental problem was overlooked in form criticism.

The weakness of Bultmann's position was made clear by his form-critical comrade-in-arms Martin Dibelius in two reviews:

> It must be stated with all due emphasis that Bultmann's skepticism in all questions of historicality is not necessarily connected with form-critical standards but with his conception of the nature of the primitive Christian community as well as with his emphasis on the difference between Palestinian and Hellenistic Christianity.

One could also point here to the receding of "high Christology," which is already important in Paul.

Precisely this difference, indeed opposition, has been strongly relativized in the past decades. The Hellenistic community has—as Acts 6 demonstrates—its origin in Jerusalem, and the numerous tradents such as Mark, Barnabas, Philip, Paul, and others could be called "Graeco-Palestinians," who had connections to both communities or stood between them. Here, as Dibelius rightly emphasized, the differences of the communities are

> less important for the form-critical line of questioning. For the Gospels demonstrate in the clearest possible way how little the influence of more recent theological ideas upon the material of the Gospels was at bottom; otherwise Kyrios-faith and sacramental theology would have had to have made themselves felt much more strongly.[31]

---

[30] One need only think of Gal 1.15ff. and 2.1ff., 11ff.; 1 Cor 1.12ff.; 9.1ff.; 15.1-11; cf. also the individual names listed in Rom 16.

[31] Dibelius 1932, 1109 on Bultmann 1931; see also Dibelius 1922 on Bultmann 1921. Dibelius' protest is directed, among other things, against the "transgression of the limits of pure form-critical method" and against the radical skepticism in questions of genuineness, behind which stands an "unrestricted subjectivism," "which rests on a lack of congenial empathy (*Einfühlung*)." The capacity to make historical decisions was never Bultmann's strength. This is also evident in his criticism of H. Lietzmann's *Geschichte der Alten Kirche* (Bultmann 1934a; 1939; reprinted in 2002, 293–99, 377–84). Lietzmann has been proved to be historically correct in most of the places where Bultmann criticized him.

This means that the Synoptic Gospels, which emerged between ca. 70 and 100 CE, have—in comparison with the roughly simultaneous theological development (Ephesians, Hebrews, 1 Peter, 1 Clement, Pastoral Epistles, Letters of Ignatius)—a strikingly "conservative" character, which is still oriented to Jewish Palestine, whether they arose in Rome (Mark), perhaps in Greece (Luke),[32] or in southern Syria or Palestine (Matthew).

It is typical of this that in Mark (and the lists of disciples that depend on him), James, the son of Zebedee, who was executed by Agrippa I in 43 CE, always stands in the first position before his brother John,[33] who outlived him, despite the fact that he no longer had any significance for the community afterward. It is first Luke who changes the order in three places, while retaining the old Markan order in other texts.[34] For him John, the son of Zebedee, who probably outlived his brother James for quite some time, had obtained significance as a tradent, a feature that is confirmed by Gal 2.9, where John is mentioned, after James the brother of the Lord and Cephas-Peter, as the last of the three "pillars." The fact that, conversely, the Palestinian community itself—which from precisely this persecution by Agrippa I until the stoning of James, the brother of the Lord, in 62 CE had stood under the latter's leadership—no longer had influence on the Synoptic tradition since the beginning of the 40s CE can be seen in the fact that James and the other brothers of Jesus play no positive role in the Gospels. The evangelists knew that they had not yet belonged to his followers at the time of Jesus.[35]

To be sure, we can say that the whole Synoptic tradition, as it is available to us in the Greek language, obtained its final literary form only in the Greek-speaking communities. This, however, does not yet entail a judgment about the historicity of the traditions. Dibelius points here to a concession of Bultmann:

[32] Thus the oldest Gospel prologue; see Aland 2005, 549; cf. Jülicher/Fascher 1931, 312.

[33] Acts 12.1-2. See the excursus on the Caligula crisis in section 3.1.4; cf. Mark 10.35.

[34] Mark 1.19, 29; 3.17; 5.37; 9.2; 10.35, 41; 13.3; 14.33; Matthew mentions the two brothers only three times with their full names; he speaks three times of the "sons" of Zebedee. There are adjustments of order in Luke 8.51; 9.28; Acts 1.13; cf. 12.2; the old order is found in Luke 5.10; 6.14; 9.54. In Acts he places John next to Peter in 3.1-4.11; 8.14ff. He lets James recede; cf., however, 12.1-2.

[35] Mark 6.3 = Matt 13.55: in the first position of the four brothers of Jesus. See section 8.3. Cf. also the negative reference in John 7.5. See further Acts 1.14; 12.17; 15.13; 21.17: Luke got to know him on Paul's journey to Jerusalem. He is made prominent only with Gos. Thom. 12. On this, see Hengel 2002, 557ff.

The individual controversy dialogues may not be historical reports of particular incidents in the life of Jesus, but the general character of his life is rightly portrayed in them, *on the basis of historical recollection.*[36]

The reviewer states with regard to this that this judgment would also have to apply of course "in relation to other groups of material," and explicitly mentions the miracle stories.[37] Beyond this, one would especially need to mention the passion story. Here, we must go even further than Dibelius and say that the sort of *general* judgments that Bultmann makes, in an aversion to the concreteness and contingency of historical processes, are usually misleading. The problem is that we, due to a lack of comparable statements in the sources, cannot prove the historicity of individual events and that there is too much maneuvering room for personal judgments. This makes it all the more important to ask about their plausibility or probability. This presupposes, among other things, a good knowledge of the Judaism of the time and its social and political environment, an area in which Bultmann and his students were not very interested.

A misjudgment that misled form-critical research from the beginning was the claim that there were clear "laws" of the oral (and written) community tradition,[38] which must also have determined the history of the synoptic tradition. Against this E. Fascher had already protested.[39] E. P. Sanders does so in a succinct manner:

[36] Bultmann 1963, 50, our emphasis (GV = 1995, 52). Bultmann continues, "And just as such recollections were preserved in connection with certain places . . . without the localization of a particular dialogue being necessarily historical, so is the Tradition also capable of using *recollections that are otherwise historical*, e.g. in the statement about the attitude of the relatives to Jesus in Mk. 3.31 . . . or about his intercourse with the tax-gatherers" (our emphasis). Apart from the fact that here "is . . . capable of using" ought to be replaced with "must have used," this *memory* depends not on the anonymous collective of communities, since this knew nothing, after all, about Jewish Palestine, but on the eye-witnesses and authoritative tradents.

[37] On the miracle stories, see section 16.1.

[38] See already Schmidt 2002, 40–41 (GV = 1923, 88–89; Schmidt 1981, 79), with appeal to W. Bousset. Cf. further Dibelius 1933, 1ff. (ET = 1971, 1ff.), and Bultmann 1921, 2–4, who judges somewhat more cautiously in Bultmann 1931, 1–8, but makes judgments that are all the more definitive.

[39] Fascher 1924, 25, 84, 94, 142ff., 225: ". . . but one will not be able to say that Bultmann has clearly worked out 'the laws of tradition'—as he calls them in the introduction (Bultmann 1921, 3)—and presented them as fruit of the analysis. He speaks of all kinds of motives that have had an influence on the material but they are not 'the laws of tradition.' In the places where he speaks of laws . . . one has rather the impression that one has before one a recipe of the analyst" (143). Unfortunately, Bultmann does not take into account the criticism of Fascher in his second edition (Bultmann 1931). See also Schneider 1962, 406. Later, Güttgemanns 1979, 214, objected to the possibility of establishing "the specific details of a regular process that can be applied form-*critically* [i.e., with respect to

There are no hard and fast laws of the development of the Synoptic tradition. On all counts the tradition developed in opposite directions. It became both longer and shorter, both more and less detailed, and both more and less Semitic. . . . For this reason, dogmatic statements that a certain characteristic proves a certain passage to be earlier than another are never justified. . . . For this reason, we must always give room for human differences and be alert to the editorial tendencies of each particular writer.[40]

This means that form-critical judgments in the sphere of the preliterary tradition remain very uncertain. We stand on relatively firm ground only when we can compare texts. The fact that "we must always give room for human differences" also already applies of course to the primitive Christian teachers and tradents of the oral tradition. In their case we are dealing not so much with an event that is one-sidedly collective and governed by laws but rather with a relatively free event that is bound to persons and connected with the theological competency—and this means authority—of the tradents as eyewitnesses and teachers.

Another factor that has been neglected in form criticism is therefore *personal memory that is bound to an individual*, memory that can retain what has been seen and heard for decades. It is closely connected with the reports of "eyewitnesses."[41] The individual initially has memory for

---

the historical development of forms, form*geschichtlichen*] in every case" (Güttgemanns' emphasis; GV = 1970, 152–53: "aber keine Aufstellung einer in allen Fällen anzuwendenden form*geschichtlichen* Gesetzesmäßigkeit" [Güttgemanns' emphasis]). The approach of Bultmann's radical criticism was questionable from the very beginning, both for methodological reasons and because a false picture of primitive Christianity stood behind it. See Bultmann 1963, 5 (our emphasis; GV = 1995, 6): "Dibelius can no more get a clear idea of the motives of the life of the community without first making some inquiry about forms, than I, in my analysis can dispense with a provisional *picture of the primitive community and its history, which has to be turned into a clear and articulated picture in the course of my inquiries*." This is a fateful *petitio principii*, through which his misleading view of primitive Christianity is hardened all the more: "Hence an essential part of my inquiry concerns *the one chief problem* of primitive Christianity, the relationship of the primitive Palestinian and Hellenistic Christianity" (idem, our emphasis). He has specified precisely this relationship in a—fundamentally—false way. For criticism of Bultmann's method, see also the detailed analyses of Baasland 1992.

[40] Sanders 1969, 272 (Sanders' emphasis). Affirmed by Theissen 1983, 174–75 (GV = 1974, 175–76), who therefore speaks only of "tendencies of the tradition."

[41] Luke 1.2: καθὼς παρέδοσαν ἡμῖν οἱ ἀπ᾽ ἀρχῆς αὐτόπται καὶ ὑπηρέται γενόμενοι τοῦ λόγου. On the significance of autopsy for ancient doctors, see L. Alexander 1993, 34–41; for the historical convention, see Hengel/Schwemer 1998, 20–21 (no equivalent in ET); on the prologue and eyewitness testimony, see Hengel 2012b (GV = 2007a); Bauckham 2017. See also Hengel 2005.

himself, with the consequence that many "individuals" then "exchange memories" and can thus supplement and control their "treasure of memories." One often knows, even after many years, from whom one has heard a certain anecdote (for example about a scholar). Without writing them down, one can "save" such anecdotes and preserve them for a lifetime, though the wording can change slightly in the narration with the point remaining the same. The names of tradents can also remain in the memory.[42] In Mark there are multiple references to individual names as possible guarantors of memory, such as Simon of Cyrene, the father of Alexander and Rufus, who were apparently still known to the Roman community at the time of Mark.[43] By contrast, Luke and Matthew omit the names of the two sons. Other figures are Joseph of Arimathea, the healed blind man Bartimaeus in Jericho, and the leader of the synagogue Jairus in Capernaum.[44] The few names that Mark mentions, in addition to the twelve, primarily in connection with the passion of Jesus, point to this decisive point. Here we should not forget the women who are mentioned by name. Mary Magdalene usually stands at the head in the lists of women. This shows her significance, which can be compared only with that of Peter.[45] When the other names of women vary in Luke and Matthew, this could be connected with disputes over their "authority" as guarantors of tradition. Where the disciples fail, they and others enter in.[46] This fact already makes it impossible to

[42] Widespread are, for example, characteristic anecdotes about Adolf Schlatter (1852–1938). They invite a collection due to their originality. From the University of Berlin of the 1920s one could hear "apophthegmata" of Elias Bickermann, who was born in 1898, came to Berlin in 1921, and died in 1981. By contrast, he never spoke about his youth in St. Petersburg and the horrible time between 1917 and his emigration in 1921! See Hengel 2004b. The New Testament scholar O. Bauerfeind (1879–1972) told an anecdote about the late F. C. Baur (1792–1860). He heard it from his teacher Eduard von der Goltz, and he, in turn, from his father, Hermann (1835–1906), who had attended Baur's lectures on Revelation. He is said to have commented with respect to the number 666 in Rev 13.17-18: "And Hengstenberg in Berlin says that's me." We could recount not a few anecdotes that reach back eighty to a hundred years and are based on controlled oral tradition.

[43] Mark 15.21; cf. Rom 16.13; see section 21.2.

[44] Mark 10.46ff.; Matt 20.30 (cf. 9.27) makes two anonymous blind men out of this. Luke 18.35 also drops the name; cf. also Luke 10.38ff.; 19.1-10. On Joseph of Arimathea, see Mark 15.43. On Jairus, see Mark 5.22 = Luke 8.41. Matthew 9.18 omits the name and title. This could be connected with his "anti-synagogal aversion." Thus, names need not always be additions. They can also eliminated in the simplification of the tradition. On the problem of eyewitnesses, memory, and narrative, see Byrskog 2000.

[45] Hengel 1963.

[46] See Mark 15.40. The fact that the names of the women vary somewhat shows only that there was a larger circle in which certain claims were then made later. Above all, one may regard Joanna, the wife of the Herodian finance minister Chuza, in Luke as a tradent (8.3; 24.10). On this, see Bauckham 2002, 110–13, 186–94, and elsewhere.

regard Mark's passion story as pure fiction.[47] One is not permitted to speak in general of novelistic embellishment with respect to the mentioning of names. On the contrary, the tradition has a tendency to cause names to disappear.[48] Here the phenomenon of oral history, which is in line with the situation of the disciples of Jesus and of the primitive community, should be drawn upon more strongly for the understanding of the Jesus tradition.[49] The—Synoptic—Gospels are not primarily literary fiction. Rather, they claim to present real events of the past in the form of "stories" about the words and deeds of Jesus. This is ultimately based on eyewitness testimony, even if it was reshaped time and again for the purpose of missionary proclamation and teaching in the worship service.[50] The figure of Damis in Philostratus' novelistic *Life of Apollonius of Tyana* shows, conversely, that an invented eyewitness plays a central role as a guarantor of tradition in a literary fiction. In our view, Philostratus knew the Gospels and composed his work as a presentation of the true Greek philosophical religion against the growing influence of the Christians (see note 6 in chapter 6). Perhaps in his work the fictive Damis is meant to take the place of the disciples and Peter, who were, by contrast, not fictions.

However, these objections against a skepticism that is at bottom inimical to history secure for us *no real "historical certainty"* in individual cases. This can hardly exist in this milieu of tradition. Only very little can really be "conclusively proved."[51] Precisely the investigations of the 'oral history'—which usually extend over three generations, i.e., a period of time, which is still significantly less than the ca. forty–seventy years between the reported events and the Synoptic Gospels—have demonstrated that oral traditions based on memory are also often erroneous, even in the case of eyewitnesses. Without the control of a calendar, these usually cannot retain larger chronological connections, but, in a similar manner as the Gospels, retain and rework individual episodes and concise scenes, anecdotes, parables, and short blocks of sayings. This already applies to our own memory, which often fails us when we want to assign a precise date to earlier experiences. Thus, the framework of the Gospels,

---

[47] On this, see Schwemer 2001c, 153–62.

[48] Thus, in Matthew and Luke in some cases. See note 44 above.

[49] On this, see Henige 1982; Vansina 1985; and Ungern-Sternberg/Reinau 1988. This last work includes the important demarcation "This does not include the investigation of the preserved epics . . . portrayed conditions . . . nor—despite overlaps in individual cases—the broad field of the relations and interactions between orality and literature" (1–2 n. 1).

[50] On this, see Byrskog 2000.

[51] The requirement to "conclusively prove" something appears far too often in New Testament literature and indicates a deficient historical awareness of the problem. We must often be content with substantiated, plausible hypotheses.

into which everything is integrated, *must* often be secondary; this, however, does not mean that it is *always* unhistorical.[52] The summarizing frame narratives, for example in Mark and Luke, could indeed contain valuable facts and characteristics.[53] Moreover, the so-called ideal scenes could point to a real event by summarizing different similar events in a paradigmatic scene.

The gap between the Aramaic mother tongue of Jesus and the Greek Gospels constitutes another problem. Since nonliterary, basic knowledge of Greek, i.e., bilingualism and trilingualism, was relatively widespread in Jewish Palestine, including Galilee,[54] and a Greek-speaking community established itself already in Jerusalem soon after Easter, we can assume that this linguistic transformation began early. The spread of the new movement into the Greek-speaking cities of Palestine, Phoenicia, and Syria also occurred rapidly and was only possible because missionary emissaries proclaimed their message in the Greek language. We already find them around ca. 32/33 CE in Damascus. Presumably a portion of the earliest disciples of Jesus were bilingual and could therefore also proclaim in simple Greek what one had heard and seen. This may have applied already to Cephas-Peter, Andrew, Philip,[55] and John. Mark, who had a better literary education in Jerusalem than the Galilean fishermen, also belonged in this milieu.[56]

The kerygmatic purpose, apologetic interests, and development of christological thought over a more extended period of time of multiple decades also determined the selection and formation of the reliable traditional material, which gradually became smaller. In this process differences must have arisen, and secondary material could have entered in. It involved a certain difference whether a Gospel was written in southern Syria on the border of Palestine, as with Matthew, or in Rome, as with Mark, and whether the community was predominantly Jewish Christian or Gentile Christian. This makes the *agreement* of the Synoptic Gospels, which arose in very different locations and in a period of time of

---

[52] See, e.g., Merchal 1988 and Wirk 1988. See also note 6 on Lucian in this chapter.

[53] We also encounter this in many summaries in Acts.

[54] Aramaic, Hebrew as religious language, and Greek. In some cases Latin would also be spoken. Thus, probably in the case of Paul as a Roman citizen who not only desires to travel to Rome but also to Spain. On the linguistic situation in Palestine, see Hengel 2003a, I: 58–61, 103–6 (GV = 1988, 108–14, 191–95); Hengel 1996a, 1–90.

[55] Cf. John 12.20ff.: Greek festival pilgrims come to Philip in Jerusalem and want to see Jesus. He tells Andrew and the two go to Jesus with this wish. For John the first step to the mission among non-Jews is indicated here, as already in chapter 4.

[56] Hengel 2002, 1–67; Hengel/Schwemer 1998, 43–60 (ET = 1997, 24–35). See also Hengel/Schwemer 2019.

ca. twenty–thirty years, all the more striking. It shows that on the whole the Jesus tradition was handled in a careful manner, even in the case of Matthew, the Synoptic author with the clearest theological profile, after 90 CE. Despite all his individual creative activity, he often largely preserved the wording of his often heavily abbreviated Markan material. His handling of Luke and the material from the sayings tradition is similar. It was this conservative stance in conjunction with the geographical proximity to Palestine, the Jewish-rabbinic character, the strong Jewish Christian influence, and the incorrectly interpreted tradition about the "Hebrew" Matthew that gave the—later, pseudepigraphic—First Gospel a seemingly greater authenticity vis-à-vis the other Gospels in antiquity and also in modern research until the end of the nineteenth century.

Finally, the wishes, questions, and impetuses of the *hearers* (more than the readers) also had an influence on the shaping of the Gospels and the tradition that preceded them. The primitive Christian worship services included discussions and the posing of questions.[57] Thus, in his account, Luke certainly caters to the expectations of the "most excellent Theophilus" and his circle, not least by passing over uncomfortable material in silence, while Mark in Rome may still be shaped by the experience of the Neronic persecution, where we first hear of the crucifixion of Christians. Moreover, the upheavals of the Roman civil war have influenced him. By contrast, Matthew is in conflict with the reinvigorated synagogue in Palestine, just as John is a bit later in Asia Minor. In opposition to a predominantly "formalistic" approach, we should endeavor—more than has been done previously—to place the Gospels and their traditions as precisely as possible in time and space and to be prepared to take note of clear indications such as the Latinisms in Mark, Luke's unsettlement by the destruction of the temple, and Matthew's controversy with rabbinic teachers.[58]

To us it also appears significant that the authors of the Gospels were *teachers with authority who were already older* and not neophytes, let alone unknown Gentile Christians. They did not gaze spellbound at their own restricted present and the acute problems of their respective communities but rather surveyed a larger period of time. As such, they each sought in their own way to express the fundamental salvific event that occurred forty to seventy years earlier. In doing so they presumably also introduced the experiences of their missionary and teaching activity, which extended over decades.

---

[57] First Corinthians 14.29ff., 35; cf. Acts 19.9; 20.7.
[58] On Mark, see Hengel 1984a (ET = 1985b, 1–30). On Matthew and Luke, see Hengel 2008c, 320–53 (ET = 186–207).

On the other hand, *our possibilities for reconstruction remain limited.* Droysen, in his *Historik*, already objected to the erroneous notion that we could "provide an image of this or that past time."

> For it could be only a picture of fantasy, since that which would have to be portrayed is no longer available but can exist only in our *imagination*.

The task of the historian

> can only consist in understanding the memories and traditions, the remains and monuments of a past in such a way that from the materials that are still available to us we seek to understand through investigation what the ones thus . . . acting . . . desired. . . . From the material, which always contains gaps, we seek to understand them, their desires and their actions, the conditions of their desires, and the effects of their actions.[59]

Precisely this is also the—limited—task of the quest for Jesus and his community of disciples as historical figures from two thousand years ago. In another context Droysen stresses in a similar way that

> "the objective facts . . . in their reality are not at all available to our research. . . . What happens is *understood and unified* as a connected event, as a complex of cause and effect, of purpose and implementation, in short, as a fact, only through the *apprehension*, and the same details could be apprehended differently by others, they could be combined by others with different causes or effects or purposes."

Therefore, it applies that "all sources, however good or bad they may be," are "*apprehensions* of events,"[60] irrespective of whether they were written down by an eyewitness or only at a later time. This applies also to our own memory. Accordingly, historical research must *always also be critical research*, which knows that it does not have direct access to the events and must take the "apprehensions" of the oldest authors as its point of departure. The fundamental polemic against the historical-critical method does not know what historical knowing is. It therefore

---

[59] Droysen 1972, 26 (our emphasis). For Droysen's significance for New Testament scholarship, cf. now also Schröter 2013, 10–13, 22–27, 30–31, 408 index (GV = 2007, 11–14, 24–29, 33–34, 431 index).

[60] Droysen 1972, 133–34 (our emphasis). The way in which precisely theologians who seem critical speak—pejoratively—of "objective historical facts" or *bruta facta* shows that they have not yet really understood the subject-bound character of historical "apprehensions."

also cannot perceive the *reality of salvation history*, which is tied to faith. With good reason Droysen warns against reading more out of the sources than they can say, because these can, after all, never reproduce the entire real event but always only certain (to be sure, often important) excerpts in the form of conceptions. In the same way he warns against an overestimation of *eyewitness testimony*, since an eyewitness also bears in him/herself only a apprehension of an event, and finally against a false "objective" understanding of facticity in which the knowing and reporting subject is eliminated.[61]

Since we do not possess any direct self-testimonies from Jesus but only information about *how he impacted others*, what they heard from his mouth and observed from his actions, direct access to his thinking and self-understanding is barred to us. We can at best put forth speculations about this. The psychologizing access to the "secret of his person" is closed to us. We cannot grasp the real "inner life of Jesus" (W. Herrmann), the "constant strength of his God-consciousness" (Schleiermacher), with the methods of history. We encounter only fragmentary witnesses mediated by third parties about his message (including his statements about himself), activity, and suffering.[62] His *messianic claim of authority*,[63] which is so controversial in scholarship, can likewise be inferred only through the external witnesses. Accordingly, one should be cautious when making statements about Jesus' self-*consciousness*. For this reason, every attempt at "Jesus psychology" must founder. Innumerable questions, which the curious historian would like to address to him, remain unanswerable. The "unanswered questions," of which John Bowden speaks, remain our fate.[64] At the same time, what is handed down to us in the refraction of the Synoptic Gospels is so fascinatingly impressive that we cannot evade the question: What sort of man must he have been: τίς ἄρα οὗτός ἐστιν (Mark 4.41)?

---

[61] Droysen 1972, 133–34. On the wrongly suppressed term "salvation history," see Hengel 2003c (GV = 2009; 2010b, 1–33). A biblical theology that is worthy of this name cannot forgo the subject matter that stands behind this term. On eyewitness testimony, see the discussion in section 7.1 with note 7.

[62] Trocmé 1971 (ET = 1973) therefore gave his Jesus book the nice title *Jésus de Nazareth, vu par les témoins de sa vie.*

[63] Hengel/Schwemer 2001, passim.

[64] See the title of his book: *Jesus: The Unanswered Questions* (Bowden 1988).

7.2 The Criteria for the Quest for the Way,
Word, and Activity of Jesus[65]

D. F. Strauss underlines his previously mentioned skepticism (see note 73 in section 5.2) regarding a historical quest for Jesus that could lead to satisfying results with the addition:

> To check these, we ought to have information concerning the same life, compiled from a purely natural and common-sense point of view; and in this case we are not in possession of such.[66]

The question arises of whether there are not criteria for a historical control of the tradition, even though the Enlightenment thinker Strauss' wish for "information . . . composed from a natural-rational perspective" cannot be fulfilled, namely because such "as wished for" information is relatively rare in antiquity (and more generally) and because in the later Strauss the "natural and common-sense point of view" has a one-sidedly personal, enlightened-materialistic character.

Much reflection has been devoted to the criteria in the last hundred years. An entire monograph could be devoted to this topic, as Gerd Theissen and Dagmar Winter have done.[67] Here, the concern can only be with preliminary remarks, especially since the criteria prove their usability only in the carrying out of historical work and not in abstract considerations. We must not confuse them with strict means of proof. They have only argumentative character in attempts to approach the person of Jesus. One should understand them rather as aids for making decisions in controversial questions. They are not conclusive proofs for the authenticity of Jesus' words and deeds but "criteria of plausibility" for distinguishing between grades of probability. Already in his dissertation, the great Theodor Mommsen, who was certainly no historical skeptic, advocated the thesis *historiam totam esse hypotheticam* (all history is hypothetical).[68] This is something that we should never forget.

Here we must first start from the oldest sources that have been preserved for us: Mark, the sayings tradition in Luke (and to some extent in Matthew) and the few pointers in the genuine letters of Paul. What is concordantly attested in these sources probably has its origin with Jesus

---

[65] Theissen/Winter 2002 (GV = 1997).

[66] Strauss 1873, 88 (GV = 1872, 77).

[67] Theissen/Winter 2002 (GV = 1997).

[68] Mommsen 1843, thesis 9: *Niebuhrii cum splendorem tum errores in eo positos esse, ut historiam totam esse hypotheticam sive ignoraret sive negaret.*

himself. Here, it can be a matter of such different traditions as the crucifixion of the "Messiah" Jesus as "King of the Jews" in Jerusalem, the last supper, the betrayal by a disciple, the prohibition against the remarriage of divorcees, the sending out of the disciples, Jesus' turning to sinners, and the prayer cry "Abba."[69]

This argument is further strengthened when traditions appear in different *genres* that are nevertheless specific to the proclamation of Jesus, such as speech compositions, individual sayings, parables, controversy dialogues, and then again in the narrative tradition. Here one would need to mention Jesus' nearness to and difference from the Baptist; the call of the disciples; his friendship with tax collectors and sinners as well as his controversies with Pharisees, scribes, and the leading priests in Jerusalem; the concentration of the will of God on the concrete act of loving one's neighbor; the requirement to be prepared to forgive; God's loving turning to the lost; his threat of judgment; the power of trusting faith; and above all his special authority in connection with the enigmatic talk of the Son of Man and his proclamation of the kingdom of God, in which he could speak both of the presence and of the very near future of the reign of God.

Another criterion is the *Jewish-Palestinian* and even more so the *Galilean coloring* of a tradition. The Greek-speaking Jesus tradition must have left the Jewish-Palestinian sphere relatively early, for the legally strict Jewish Christianity, which evaluated the Gentile mission critically and increasingly gained influence after the persecution by Agrippa I (ca. 43 CE), plays a certain role—in relation to the past time of Jesus—only in the latest Synoptic Gospel, Matthew.[70] In contrast to Peter and the sons of Zebedee, James and the other relatives of the Lord are completely absent as authorities.[71] On the other hand, one also cannot demonstrate clear types of Gentile Christian teachings and rites in the Synoptic material. The active Gentile mission appears in the missionary commands of the resurrection story and in the Synoptic apocalypses[72] but scarcely in the Synoptic narrative tradition. There, we instead find restraint.[73] The developed high Christology with preexistence and mediation of creation, references

---

[69] See section 6.2.

[70] Cf. Matt 10.5-6, 23; 15.24; 23.2-3 and, by contrast, 28.18ff.

[71] The brothers of Jesus are mentioned by name only in Mark 6.3 = Matt 13.55-56. Acts 1.14 speaks only in general of "the mother and the brothers of Jesus." John 7.2-5 points to their unbelief. See also section 22.1 with notes 46–48.

[72] Luke 24.47; Acts 1.8; John 20.21, cf. 17.20-21 and 21.16-17; Mark 13.10 parr.; 14.9 par.

[73] Cf. Mark 7.24-30 = Matt 15.21-28 (24); Matt 10.5-6, 23, cf. 5.47; 6.7; 18.17; John 4.22.

to *Christian* baptism,[74] a developed ecclesiology, mention of later offices, and a massive turning by Jesus to non-Jews are lacking. This is all the more conspicuous since the center of gravity of the primitive Christian movement quickly shifted from rural areas into the cities. Jerusalem, Damascus, Caesarea, the Phoenician cities, Antioch and Tarsus, indeed even Rome, are stations that were already reached in the first ten to fifteen years and became decisive for subsequent development, whereas Galilee soon disappears in Acts and does not appear at all in the epistles.[75] Therefore, when we encounter traditions with a rural Galilean character, sometimes even with concrete specifications of place, we are near the original event. In the diaspora one was no longer interested in Galilean villages such as Chorazin, Bethsaida, Nain, Magdala, and Capernaum or in the countryside or lake of Gennesaret. The parables also primarily reflect a Galilean-rural milieu. With the help of the parables of Jesus and with Josephus and the Talmudic reports as sources, a small social history of Galilee could be written.[76] The evangelists look back, with an awareness of a geographical-temporal distance, to the beginnings in Galilee. This remote Jewish small province no longer had significance for their present. Gentile Christians were no longer interested in it.[77]

In this connection we must also mention *linguistic arguments*, which have been worked out especially by Gustaf Dalman and his student Joachim Jeremias.[78] This includes the traditional Jewish-Palestinian linguistic form of the *parallelismus membrorum*, which is already dismantled to some extent by the "Hellenist" Luke. Here emphasis must be placed on the sharply pointed antithetical parallelism. Moreover, we must mention conspicuous linguistic forms such as the phrase ἀμὴν λέγω ὑμῖν, which is without analogy,[79] and the frequent talk of the Son of Man or of "this

---

[74] Apart from Matt 28.19-20; cf., by contrast, John 3.22; 4.1-2. See note 72 in chapter 9.

[75] Acts 1.11; 2.7; 9.31, cf. already Gal 1.22 and 1 Thess 2.14: here Galilee may be contained in Ἰουδαία. See note 8 in chapter 11. Cf. also Hengel/Schwemer 1998, 52–54 (ET = 1997, 30–31, 337 n. 130).

[76] On this, see the important works of S. Freyne and now Chancey 2002. Cf. also the large study of Dalman 1967, which is still worth reading, and the thorough social-historical investigation of Kloppenborg 2006.

[77] Cf. Acts 10.37: ἀρξάμενος ἀπὸ τῆς Γαλιλαίας. Using a term coined by Theissen/Winter 2002, 177ff. (GV = 1997, 180ff.), we could speak here of "The Plausibility of Historical Context" (179ff.; GV = 183ff.).

[78] Dalman 1898; 1965 (ET = 1902); 1922; Jeremias 1970, 1–37 (GV = 1979, 13–46). In our judgment, Jeremias' book remains the best book on the proclamation of Jesus. See in detail chapter 12 in the present volume.

[79] It appears not in original Jewish but only in later Christian texts or additions. The longer version A of the Testament of Abraham, which places the formula in the mouth of God in relation to Michael as a message to Abraham in 8.7, and in 18.10 and 20.2 places

generation." Here we are close to the individual language of Jesus, pre-cisely because it could also be imitated, as Matthew shows. The lexical Aramaisms,[80] which are exceptional in a work of Greek literature, must be mentioned here. We can regard the names *Cephas*, *Boanerges*, and exhor-tations such as *ṭālîtā' qûm* or *effata* (Aramaic: *'eppataḥ*), and the prayer address *Abba* as *verba ipsissima*, precisely because—with the exception of *Abba*—they possess no direct kerygmatic deeper meaning in their Ara-maic form, whereas they do accurately illustrate the original milieu of the activity of Jesus.

As a methodological probe, from which one can advance to other Jesus tradition, it is necessary to mention the criterion of "underivability" or "dissimililarity," which is mentioned most frequently and repeatedly discussed.[81] It was stressed especially by P. W. Schmiedel (1851–1935), who referred to the model of the profane historian:

> When a profane historian finds before him a historical document which testifies to the worship of a hero unknown to other sources, he attaches first and foremost importance to those features which cannot be deduced merely from the fact of this worship, and he does so on the simple and sufficient ground that they would not be found in this source unless the author had met with them as fixed data of tradition. The same fundamen-tal principle may safely be applied in the case of the gospels, for they also are all . . . written by worshippers of Jesus.

This criterion is said to be independent of the source from which the text that is to be evaluated comes.[82] This means that if a Jesus tradition runs counter to—or is at least independent of—the post-Easter primitive Chris-tian devotion to Jesus and thus the tendencies that lead to the emergence of the Christology (or to primitive Christian convictions in general), then

---

the double formula ἀμὴν ἀμὴν λέγω σοι in the mouth of death in relation to Abraham, is a Christian expanded version with many later additions in contrast to version B, where the formula is still completely absent. See Denis 1970, 36.

[80] On this, see Rüger 1984, 73–84; Beyer 1984, 130, 673; Hengel 2004a.

[81] On the concept, see Gnilka 1990, 29–30 with reference to M. Lehmann 1970, 174–86. See also Lentzen-Deis 1974, who speaks here of "criteria for exclusion," and Mussner 1974, 132. On the criteria of underivability, see also Merkel 1991, 131ff n. 75 (with additional literature) and now, in detail, Theissen/Winter 2002 (GV = 1997).

[82] Schmiedel 1901, 1872. Cf. Heitmüller 1912, 361: "We must take as a basis the material that runs counter to or at least does not entirely correspond to, for example, the primitive community's faith, theology, customs, and cult. We may have absolute trust in such pieces." On this, see Loofs 1916, 123ff., who rightly stresses the limits of this rule. On Schmiedel, see Theissen/Winter 2002, 58, 81ff., 340 index (GV = 1997, 60, 83ff., 345 index).

this speaks in favor of its originality in a special way, for it goes against the slope of the development of the tradition. This criterion can be helpful in the scrutiny of individual traditions and can serve as a probe for connecting statements of the Synoptic traditions with Jesus.

Rudolf Bultmann and Ernst Käsemann, who formulated the matter with even sharper clarity, added to the *contradiction* to primitive Christian views also the *contradiction* to *the Judaism of the time*. Käsemann starts—and in this respect he is entirely a student of Bultmann—from the view that that through critical research "the historical credibility of the Synoptic tradition has become doubtful all along the line" and that "we are still short of one essential requisite for the identification of the authentic Jesus material, namely, a conspectus of the very earliest stage of primitive Christianity; and also there is an almost complete lack of satisfactory and water-tight criteria for this material." Then, however, he grants that "in only one case do we have more or less safe ground under our feet: when there are no grounds either for deriving a tradition from Judaism or for ascribing it to primitive Christianity, and especially when Jewish Christianity has mitigated or modified the received tradition, as having found it too bold for its taste."[83] One cannot, of course, separate Judaism and primitive Christianity in this way. Our knowledge of the diverse streams in the Judaism of Palestine of that time—we ought to have become fully conscious of this through the rich discoveries at Qumran—are very fragmentary and accidental. What do we know—apart from the Gospels—about the religious views of the Galilean rural population between the turn of the century and 70 CE? Jesus was a Jew and lived in an environment that was Jewish through and through. Accordingly, in our attempts at historical approximation it is sufficient to pay attention to the differences between the Jesus tradition and clear tendencies of the post-Easter community of disciples and of the primitive church that emerged from it, whose leading heads were likewise Jewish until around the end of the first century CE.

By contrast, Käsemann's last sentence is significant and already played an important role in the old liberal research, namely that Jewish Christianity "has mitigated or modified" offensive statements and modes of behavior of Jesus "as . . . too bold." Here we strike upon another criterion, which makes more precise the criterion of "dissimilarity."

---

[83] Käsemann 1964b, 36–37, modified (GV = 1954, 144; 1964a, 205). On this, cf. the justified criticism of Jeremias 1970, 2 (GV = 1979, 14): "Indeed, it has to be said that the way in which the 'criterion of dissimilarity' is often used today as a password (*Schibboleth*) is a serious source of error. It foreshortens and distorts the historical situation, because it overlooks the continuity between Jesus and Judaism." On this, see also Theissen/Winter 2002, 67ff., 179ff. (GV = 1997, 69ff., 183ff.).

Schmiedel already referred to the significance of texts that were reshaped or suppressed because of their *offensiveness*. Here one could, for example, mention Mark 3.21 regarding the conflict of Jesus with his family.[84] It is eliminated in Luke and Matthew, as is the healing of Jesus by seemingly "magic" practices, for example through spit or special touching of the sick organs, as this is still recounted in Mark.[85] In Matthew, who otherwise largely follows the work of Mark, which is "authoritative" for him, Jesus heals only through the word. The portrayal of Jesus' trial in Gethsemane is also softened in Matthew and removed in John. Other statements are also mitigated, such as the statement that Jesus could not[86] heal in Nazareth due to the unbelief of his fellow citizens and relatives and his reaction in Mark 10.18 in the scene about the "rich man," who addresses Jesus as "good teacher," which he rejects because God alone is good. In general, on the basis of the Synoptic comparison—it is fortunate that Mark remained preserved—we can probably say that texts which are more abstract, more strongly reshaped theologically, and christologically further developed must be understood as secondary stages of processing. This becomes evident especially in a comparison between the Synoptic and the Johannine tradition.

While the "criterion of dissimilarity" may be a *point of departure* for the investigative probe, on its own it yields only intermittent and therefore completely inadequate results. A figure such as Jesus, who during his lifetime sparked off a people's movement, which spread rapidly—in altered form—after his passion, i.e., the end of his direct activity, in Judaea and Syria, cannot primarily be specified negatively. In the interplay of all criteria a coherent web of interconnected Jesus traditions must be created, through which the contours of his conspicuous—indeed, in some ways "analogy-less"—activity become more perceptible and also makes it possible to adequately explain the astonishing post-Easter developments in the Jesus community, especially the emergence of Christology.[87] Here we could speak of the criterion of *coherence*.

While we can affirm Käsemann's claim that "we can no longer assume the general reliability of the Synoptic tradition about Jesus," the consequence that he draws from this is erroneous:

---

[84] On this, see also Bultmann 1963, 50 (GV = 1995, 52), which is quoted in note 36 above. See also section 8.3 with notes 78–80.

[85] Mark 7.33-34; 8.22-26. See also section 16.3.

[86] Mark 6.5; see section 8.3 with note 71.

[87] On this, see Neugebauer 1972, 11–12, 16, and his dispute with the radical theses of Vielhauer.

With the work of the form critics as a basis, our questioning has sharp-
ened and widened until the obligation now laid upon us is to investigate
and make credible not the possible unauthenticity of the individual unit
of material, but, on the contrary, its genuineness. The issue today is not
whether criticism is right, but where it is to stop.[88]

Here the possibility of form criticism is overestimated. Käsemann himself must acknowledge its failure at the decisive point, since, as a formal
instrument, it "is concerned with the *Sitz-im-Leben* of narrative forms and
not with what we may call historical individuality."[89] But what especially
matters is the historical distinctiveness of Jesus and of his witnesses. This
means that form criticism leaves us in the lurch with respect to the basic
question τίς ἄρα οὗτός ἐστιν (Mark 4.41), for it inquires in a purely
formal manner about the form of the oral tradition, and it remains problematic whether it can really convincingly determine a "setting in life" for
the formation of pieces of tradition that goes beyond the trivial assignment
to the worship service of the community or the missionary preaching.
The Gospels precisely do not "offer us primarily the primitive Christian
kerygma, and individual words and deeds of Jesus only as they are embedded in it,"[90] but the two are fused together in such a way that here one
scarcely makes progress with the prejudgment of "primary" and "secondary" alone. In historical and genetic terms, it could, conversely, be said: At
the beginning there was an abundance of memories and traditions about
Jesus, whereas the clearly defined kerygma was developed only incremen-
tally after Easter and appears in formulaic abbreviated form especially in
the epistolary literature. We also have long passages, for example in the
sayings tradition or in the special material of Luke, where, on the face
of it, one can find little of the post-Easter kerygma. For example, what
can one discover *expressis verbis* of the—christological—kerygma in the
complex of Luke 16.1-31? With the possible exception of 16.16, could not
this whole chapter also come from a Jewish outsider? And does not the

---

[88] Käsemann 1964b, 34–35, modified (GV = Käsemann 1964a, 142; Käsemann
1960/1964, I: 204); cf. idem: "Only radical criticism can therefore do justice to the situation with which we are faced whether we like it or not, to the questions of principle which it
raises and to the tasks which its sets us. By 'radical' in this context I naturally do not mean
an uncontrolled passion for any and every extreme position, but a single-minded openness
to the problems posed by the facts." This is, to be sure, never 'radical,' but possible only
as materially appropriate, historically convincing, plausible "criticism." According to our
feeling for language, we would designate rather the fateful and widespread "uncontrolled
passion for any and every extreme position" as "radical."

[89] Käsemann 1964b, 35 (GV = 1964a, 143; 1960/1964, I: 204).

[90] Käsemann 1964b, 34 (GV = 1964a, 143; 1960/1964, I: 204).

conclusion in 16.29ff—"They have Moses and the prophets, to whom they ought to listen. . . . If they do not do this, then neither will they obey if someone should rise from the dead"—appear rather to contradict the Christian kerygma?

In reality, we must examine and make credible both the arguments for and against "the genuineness of the individual unit of material." In such a weighing of arguments it is not uncommon that one scarcely gets beyond degrees of probability or must stop with a *non liquet*. It is also not a matter of the "limits" or "right of criticism," for this weighing is already historical-critical. After all, ϰρίνειν means "to evaluate." Therefore, all historical judgments that are convincingly grounded—irrespective of whether they are *pro* or *contra* the genuineness of a tradition—are "critical." By contrast, we must be careful with the concept of "proof." A real proof[91] of a historical phenomenon can be produced only on the basis of evidence, which is often not to be found in the desired manner in the relatively foreign and fortuitously preserved ancient texts. For primitive Christianity, archaeological sources such as inscriptions, papyrus documents, and coins, which lead us to direct evidence, are extremely rare (see, however, note 22 in chapter 8). Accordingly, in the quest for Jesus we are primarily dealing with literary sources that in their "authenticity" are handed down only through later manuscripts and that emerged ca. forty–seventy years after the reported events. Even though their manuscript attestation is better than in any other textual corpus in antiquity and some reaches back into the second century CE, what remains in the end is nevertheless only the debate about the individual traditions whose genuineness is under discussion.

Time and again what is decisive is *the weight of the historical-philological arguments in both directions*. Here the "radical criticism" has often made things too easy for itself in its argumentation, so that one gets the impression that what is at work in it is wishes and whims or with Käsemann "the uncontrolled passion for any and every extreme position," perhaps because this is regarded as scholarly. Not only the contested authenticity of traditions must be justified but also their later emergence in "the community." But what do we know about the individual primitive Christian communities between 30 and 100 CE and their relationship to the Jesus tradition?

Perhaps both sides, "conservative" and "radical" critics, need to be more *modest* and acknowledge that they both often work with hypotheses

---

[91] Today some like to speak of "conclusive proof" and overlook the fact that often this can be produced only with great difficult in the sphere of antiquity because of the fragmentary sources.

that can be grounded only in a limited way. To a certain extent, New Testament scholarship is always a "scholarship of hypotheses," since it possesses only a relatively small textual basis—680 pages in Nestle-Aland—with which countless hypotheses are linked, a fact that is connected with the massive *Wirkungsgeschichte* and significance of the canonical texts. Here, in our attempt at historical approximation, we are, due to the rather positive situation of the sources—again, measured by ancient standards—indeed convinced that on the whole we obtain *clear contours* of the person of Jesus, his activity in word and deed and his suffering, because our oldest sources, i.e., Mark, the sayings tradition, and the selected special material of Luke and Matthew often agree in an astonishing way here and thus yield a plausible overall picture, which precisely cannot be explained on the basis of the very different religious or social needs of the later community and its "kerygma." All the attempts since Strauss of an ultimately anti-historical criticism, which is itself "dogmatically biased," to eliminate the deep imprint that the oldest sources have received through the living memory of Jesus with the help of the hypothesis of an uninhibitedly creative "community" have at bottom failed. Despite every contestation by "radical skeptics" or "fundamentalists," the task of a historical approach to Jesus and the earliest community will retain its validity and its necessity.

PART III
Jesus the Galilean and John the Baptist

8

Jesus the Galilean

8.1 Galilee and the Galileans[1]

Jesus was a Galilean Jew, and this also applies to the circle of his earliest followers. In order to understand them, we must take a look at their homeland. Its significance was not uncontroversial, but a broad consensus has now established itself here. Walter Bauer[2] had advocated the view that remote Galilee, which was enclosed by the regions of "Hellenistic" cities, was especially open to syncretistic-pagan influences. His hypothesis was taken up by Schmithals[3] and others and grounded with the phrase "Galilee of the Gentiles" in Isa 8.23.[4] Even more erroneous was the view that remnants of the Indo-European people were in Galilee and that Jesus was not of Semitic descent, which was advocated by certain well-known theologians in the Third Reich.[5] In reality there was, after the destruction of the Northern Kingdom by the Assyrians in 722, always an Israelite minority in Galilee, which knew itself to be connected with the temple in Jerusalem and professed to being Jewish in the post-Exilic time.

---

[1] Bauer 1967b, 91–108 (= 1927); Alt 1953 (against Bauer); Bill. I: 153–89; Dalman 1967, 3–12; Freyne 1998; 1988; 2000; Bösen 1998; Theissen 1992 (GV = Theissen 1989b); Reed 2000; Chancey 2002; Dunn 2003b, 293–311, 315–23. Ostmeyer 2005 rightly opposes a one-sidedly negative social-historical presentation of Galilee; see now Kloppenborg 2006.

[2] Bauer 1967b, 91–108 (= 1927).

[3] Schmithals 1963. In his view, the primitive community was not in Jerusalem but arose "in syncretistically permeated" Galilee of the Gentiles (25–26 n.1). Moreover, according to Schmithals, this is also where the "lawless Christianity" is to be sought, which Paul persecuted "in the vicinity of Damascus." Against such speculations, which have also been taken up in the United States, see now J. L. Reed, M. A. Chancey, and J. D. G. Dunn.

[4] Cf. Matt 4.15. The saying in Isaiah refers to the Galilee already separated from Israel of the Assyrian time just before 720 BCE, the end of the Northern Kingdom.

[5] On this, see note 46 in chapter 5.

The situation of these Galilean Jews was especially exposed because they were separated from the Jewish heartland by Samaria, and the Samaritans, as "heretical" Jews, were hostile to the religious community in Jerusalem. Moreover, Galilee was ca. 100–130 kilometers north of the Jewish metropolis, entirely in the economic and cultural sphere of influence of the Phoenician-Hellenistic cities of Tyre and Sidon on the coast. The Jewish peasants not only felt exploited by these pagan trade cities; they also had to fight against non-Jewish, more strongly Hellenized neighbors[6] for the preservation of their national traditions and their religion. For precisely this reason they were not "syncretists" but conservative Jewish "nationalists" to a greater extent than, for example, the majority of the urban population of Jerusalem, which profited from the Pax Romana. In Galilee we encounter a typical borderland situation with strong ethnic-religious self-assertion, indeed to some extent hatred of foreigners. When the Hasmonean Aristobulus, and after him Alexander Jannaeus, from about 100 BCE conquered Galilee and the Gaulanitis, which was located to the east of the Lake of Gennesaret, the land, which was populated to a smaller extent by a Jewish minority but predominantly by Gentiles, became a self-enclosed Jewish settlement zone through the forced circumcision or expulsion of the Gentile Itureans and Canaaneans and the purposeful settlement policy of the Hasmoneans.[7]

It remained, however, surrounded by pagan urban areas, since Pompey, after conquering Jerusalem in 63 BCE, reestablished the Hellenistic cities in Palestine and in the area east of the Jordan. The important fortress of Scythopolis (the old Beth-Shean) was located in the south between the Jordan Valley and the Plain of Megiddo. It was connected especially with the cult of Dionysus. In the Plain of Megiddo, Herod established the city of horses Gaba, a military colony and fortress, which had the purpose of watching over the recalcitrant Galilee. As an important port of export, the Phoenician Ptolemais-Akko was located in the west on the sea. Under the Ptolemies and Seleucids it had been the capital of the province "Syria and Phoenicia" or Coile-Syria. Militarily it constituted the key to the Galilean hill country, indeed to all Judaea. Time and again the Romans

---

[6] Mark 7.26 speaks of the pagan supplicant in the region of Tyre as a Ἑλληνίς Συροφοινίκισσα, Matthew of a γυνὴ Χαναναία. Mark writes from a Roman perspective and Matthew from a Jewish-Palestinian standpoint.

[7] On the new Jewish settlements, see Freyne 2000, 60, 67–68, 128, 177–82: "Hasmonean colonization from the south . . . (would seem) as the most likely hypothesis for explaining the dominant Jewish element in first-century Galilee" (179); cf. 247. To some extent this may have involved military settlements, which explains the strong Hasmonean support in the province.

marched from here to there.[8] Farther to the northwest were the great urban areas of Tyre and Sidon, which directly bordered Galilee. In the north at the sources of the Jordan under Hermon lay Paneas, which Herod's son Philip made into his capital and renamed Caesarea Philippi.[9] The Hellenistic city Hippos was located on the eastern shore of the lake of Gennesaret, and the fortress of Gadara in the southeast above the Jarmuk Valley, which, like Hippos and Scythopolis, belonged to the band of ten cities, the so-called Decapolis.

Galilee itself, divided into the northern, hilly Upper Galilee and the southern, fertile Lower Galilee, was, by contrast, a purely rural area in which there were initially no real "cities" with Greek civil rights. A third portion of the land was the hot Jordan Valley and the western coast of the Galilean sea (two hundred meters under mean sea level). The extent of the province was ca. fifty kilometers in the north-south direction and ca. thirty-five-forty kilometers from west to east. Ca. three hundred inhabitants lived on ca. sixteen hundred square kilometers. To be sure, this small, remote region inhabited by "barbarians" is mentioned only rarely by Greek and Roman authors of antiquity.[10] We are, however, conspicuously well informed about it through Josephus, who, after the outbreak of the Jewish War in 66, was appointed commander of the rebels by the Jerusalem "rebel administration" there and became a Roman prisoner of war in 67 CE after the capture of Jotapata by Vespasian. According to Josephus,[11] it had 204 cities and villages, i.e., it was relatively densely populated. However, Josephus' statement in *Jewish War* 3.43 that the smallest place had at least fifteen thousand inhabitants is one of his many exaggerations, which is meant to highlight his own significance as captain of the province. In the first century, the only place that would merit the designation "city" in the Greek sense, Sepphoris, only ca. five kilometers northwest of Nazareth, was laid waste by Varus in 4 BCE because of an attempted rebellion, and the inhabitants were sold into slavery. Herod Antipas rebuilt it as the capital. The second city of Galilee, Tiberias on the Lake of Genneseret, was a new foundation of Antipas in honor of the emperor, built from 17 to 22 CE, and later became his residence. Through a forced "*synoikismos*" he gave it a mixed Jewish-pagan population in

---

[8] 4 BCE Varus; 39 CE Petronius; 66 CE Cestius Gallus; 67 Vespasian. See the end of section 3.1.1, the excursus on the Caligula crisis in section 3.1.4, and section 3.1.7.

[9] Mark 8.27 = Matt 16.13: Καισαρεία . . . Φιλίππου. On this, see section 17.3.3.

[10] On this, see the index in Stern 1976–1984, III: 121–22.

[11] Josephus, *Life* 235. In *Life* he describes, especially in an apologetic way, his activity as commander of the rebels in Galilee. The picture which Josephus gives of Galilee is now supplemented by the results of archaeology; on this, see S. Freyne and the most recent fundamental works of Chancey 2002 and Reed 2000.

which Jews were, however, clearly predominant. Among the rural population this founding, which was equipped with Hellenistic civic rights, was
frowned upon. It was said that Antipas built it upon a graveyard and that
the place was therefore ritually unclean. Neither city plays a role in the
Gospels. Sepphoris is not mentioned in the Gospels at all and Tiberias only
in John at the margins.[12] Jesus apparently avoided the Hellenistic cities.
When cities from neighboring pagan regions are mentioned—Caesarea
Philippi, Tyre, and Sidon—then in Mark it is only said that he stayed in the
territories of the cities and not in the polis itself.[13]

The opposition between land and city was much more strongly marked
in antiquity than we can imagine today. Landowners, who lived from the
leasing of their domains, merchants, and artisans lived in the larger cities,
where there were schools and all kinds of educational possibilities and
places of entertainment. The educated city dwellers looked down on the
uneducated, simple peasants with great disdain. For a landless tenant or
small farmer it was often only with difficulty that he fed himself and his
large family outside in the open land, since he had to pay high leases and
taxes. It was even worse for the day laborers, who had to enter into service
as casual laborers.[14] To be sure, in Josephus Galilee appears to be an economically prosperous land through its much higher rainfall in comparison
with the Jewish hill country and through its mild climate and the hard work
of its inhabitants, but this ideal picture is one-sided. Even after the Hasmonean conquest and forced Judaizing, and all the more through the politics
of Herod the Great (40–4 BCE), a large part of Galilee remained "the
land of the king" in possession of the respective territorial sovereign. In
the time of Jesus this meant crown land of Herod Antipas and later of the
Roman emperor. In addition, there were a good number of large estate
owners, some of whom had received their property in return for their
services for the territorial sovereign. The stationary farmers worked the
crown land and domains on a hereditary lease for correspondingly high
dues of up to 30 or even 50 percent of what they produced. The social
milieu of Galilee—with its large domains and landowners or land manag-
ers, its tenant farmers, small farmers, day laborers, and slaves, with debt
bondage and moneylenders, who lent with interest—is constantly present
in the parables of Jesus, including the concomitant situations of social conflict. Thus, the parable of the wicked tenants in Mark 12.1ff., for example,

---

[12] John 6.23: boats come from Tiberias; cf. also 6.1; 21.1 on the designation of the
lake. On both cities, see Schürer 1973–1987, II: 172–76 and 178–82.

[13] Thus κῶμαι (Mark 8.27) or ὅρια (7.24, 31).

[14] Cf. Matt 20.1-15.

involves an extreme social situation of conflict.[15] A nonlocal landowner has a vineyard set up by tenants who refuse to deliver the lease share of the first yield to the slaves who are sent. They kill the son who is sent last so that they can obtain possession of the vineyard themselves. That Jesus possessed relations to the leading strata of Galilee can be seen in the fact that Luke mentions among his female followers, who support him and his disciples "out of their assets," a certain Joanna, the wife of the ἐπίτροπος of Herod (Antipas), i.e., a "manager of the assets" of the tetrarch. Among the Jewish Christian "prophets" in Antioch appears Menahem (Μαναήν), an earlier friend (σύντροφος) of the territorial sovereign (Acts 13.1). The leader of the synagogue Jairus and the royal official or centurion in Capernaum likewise fit well in this milieu.[16] The influence of the Jesus movement also extended to the Galilean upper stratum.

Through its borderland situation and through the social opposition between city and land the Galileans were neither demonstrably influenced by "syncretistic Syrian Hellenism" nor inclined in a special way to collaboration with their pagan neighbors. Since Judaea was conquered by Pompey in 63 BCE they showed themselves time and again to be freedom-loving Jews who were prepared to fight to the last against foreign oppressors. When Herod landed in Ptolemais in 39 BCE, it was precisely the Galileans who put up the toughest resistance. In 66/67 CE the Galileans were also the only ones, apart from Jerusalem, who heroically defended themselves to the point of collective suicide in different small, poorly fortified cities such as Jotapata or Gamla in the Gaulanitis.[17] Not only Judas, the founder of the Zealot movement in connection with the transformation of Judaea into a Roman province in 6 BCE,[18] came from Galilee

---

[15] Hengel 1968a. On large state owners at the time of Jesus, see the examples in idem, 19ff.; Kloppenborg 2006. See also section 17.4.2.

[16] Luke 8.3; cf. Luke 24.10; Acts 13.1; on the "tetrarch," see Luke 3.1, 19; 9.7, and note 81 in chapter 9. The ἐπίτροπος corresponds to the Latin *procurator*; see also Matt 20.8. It can, however, also refer to a political office. Josephus likes to designate the equestrian governor in Judaea as ἐπίτροπος: *J.W.* 2.117 (Coponius); 169 (Pilate); 220 (Cuspius Fadus); 247 (Felix), etc. In reality, prior to Claudius they bore the title *praefectus*; see note 204 in chapter 3. On Jairus, see Mark 5.22 = Luke 8.41. Matthew 9.18 omits the—in our view original—name and speaks of an ἄρχων. On the centurion, see Luke 7.2ff., who makes him into a God-fearer, for whom the "elders" of Capernaum advocate with the words "he loves our people and he himself built us our synagogue." Matt 8.5ff. shortens the Lukan account. According to John 4.46 he is not an officer but an administrator of Antipas (βασιλικός). On σύντροφος, see Bauer/Aland/Aland 1988, 1587.

[17] See section 3.1.7. They could be compared to the Sicarii in Masada. On Jotapata, see Josephus, *J.W.* 3.336–339, 361–391; on Gamla, see *J.W.* 4.78–83; on Masada, see *J.W.* 7.389–406.

[18] On this, see Hengel 1989c, index, s.v. "Galilee," "Judas the Galilean," "John of Gischala" (GV = Hengel 1976c, index, s.v. "Galiläa," "Judas Galiläus," and "Johannes

or Gaulanitis, which bordered it in the east, but also John of Gischala, the most important leader—alongside Simon bar Giora—of the defenders of Jerusalem in 70 CE, was a Galilean. With his Galilean retinue he helped the radicals to victory against the moderate freedom party in Jerusalem. It is understandable that the Jerusalem upper stratum was mistrustful in relation to Galilean demagogues and eschatological enthusiasts and sometimes reacted in an allergic manner.[19] That incidents also occurred under Antipas and the rule of procurators amidst the easily inflammable unrest of the Galileans is shown by Luke 13.1-2, where there is talk of the Galileans whom Pilate had slaughtered at the forecourt of the temple together with their sacrificial animals (they were presumably Passover lambs), and by Josephus' account of the consequences of the murder of a Galilean festival pilgrim when he was passing through Samaritan Ginea[20] in the middle of the 40s CE. This murder provoked border fights between Jews and Samaritans, which in the end almost led to open war with Rome.

The fact that Herod Antipas, the son of King Herod the Great and the Samaritan Malthace, was, despite his not unskillful politics, not very beloved among the rural population had not so much social as religious reasons. His lifestyle was too permissive. According to Mark, conflict with the Baptist emerged over his unlawful marriage to Herodias. According to Josephus, he had the Baptist executed in the fortress of Machaerus, far from Galilee, because he feared the prophetic preacher's influence upon the masses. In Mark this occurs in connection with an oriental court intrigue; after the death of the Baptist, he is unsettled by the activity of Jesus.[21]

To the penetrating mind of Gerd Theissen we owe the interpretation of a parabolic saying of Jesus from the speech about the Baptist in Luke 7.24-25 = Matt 11.7-8:

What did you go into the wilderness to see,
a reed that is blown by the wind,
a person man dressed in luxurious garments?
Behold, those who wear luxurious garments, are in royal palaces.

He draws attention to the fact that the symbol of a reed and the name of the tetrarch appear on the first coins of Tiberias, the new capital city

---

von Gischala") as well as Acts 5.37 and Luke 2.1: Luke, to be sure, places the census at the wrong point in time.

[19] See section 3.1.3. See also the discussion below with note 26.

[20] Today's Jenin, an Arabian, conflict-rich, northern border town. Cf. *J.W.* 2.232 = *Ant.* 20.118. In *J.W.* there is only one victim. In *Ant.* there are several. Such contradictions are not infrequent in Josephus.

[21] See sections 3.1.2 and 9.2.

founded by Antipas, which was unpopular among the people and which is not mentioned in the Synoptics.[22] The "reed ($\varkappa\acute{\alpha}\lambda\alpha\mu\varsigma$) that is blown by the wind," is best explained as a pejorative reference to the opportunistic ruler. We are probably dealing with a popular derisive nickname based on this coin.[23] Through this the *parallelismus membrorum* with people in luxurious garments who live in royal palaces becomes meaningful. We have here a rare case in which a saying of Jesus becomes comprehensible through an archaeological discovery, the first coins of Tiberias. Here Jesus juxtaposes the last and greatest prophet, John, with his murderer, "the wavering reed" Herod Antipas. Every hearer knew who was meant.

Nevertheless, the land under his time of rule seems to have lived in—relative—peace, which benefited the common people. Antipas further attempted, through the founding of the cities of Sepphoris and Tiberias, to open up Galilee to Hellenistic-Roman culture. Presumably, the rural population scarcely thanked him for this. In any case, the rule of the Jewish ruler was more adroit than that of the Roman prefect of the caliber of a Pilate or later of a Cumanus, Felix, Albinus, or Florus. However, Antipas also had to be concerned for the security of his reign. This is why he had John the Baptist executed, and he probably also sought to kill Jesus.[24] In 38 CE he was denounced before Caligula by his nephew and brother-in-law Agrippa I, who said that he had hidden weapons in order to prepare a war of revenge against the Nabataeans, and he was banished to Lyons in Gaul.[25] His brother Archelaus had already suffered a similar fate as ethnarch of Judaea and Samaria under Augustus in 6 CE.

It also belonged to the opposition between city and land that the cultivated population in Jerusalem looked down on the uneducated rustic Galileans from the north with a mixture of haughtiness and mistrust. In rabbinic times, when Galilee had become the center of Judaism, there was still mockery of its dialect, which confused *ḥᵃmor*, the donkey for riding, *ḥᵃmar*, the wine for drinking, *'ᵃmar*, the wool for clothing, and *'immar*, the lamb for slaughtering, because they could not distinguish between the different gutturals.[26] It demonstrates knowledge of the Palestinian conditions when Peter, according to Matthew, is betrayed by his dialect in the

[22] Theissen 1992, 26–42 (GV = Theissen 1989b, 26–43). Meshorer 1967, 133 nr. 63–65. Year 24 = 19/20 CE. Cf. pl. IX.

[23] On the negative picture, cf. Isa 36.6; 4 Reigns 18.21: τὴν ῥάβδον τὴν καλαμίνην, on which one cannot support oneself but which pierces the hand instead. Cf. also Luke 13.31-32, where Jesus designates Herod Antipas as "fox."

[24] Mark 6.14, 17-29 parr.; Luke 13.31ff.; see section 11.3.

[25] Josephus, *Ant.* 18.247ff. See the end of section 3.1.2.

[26] Bill. I: 156–57. b. ʿErub. 53b (Baraita); cf. b. Meg. 24b; b. Ber. 32a; b. ʿErub. 53a: "Because the Galileans are not careful about their language, their teaching is not valid."

court of the high priest.[27] While the Galilean rural population was filled with national zeal for the law and loyalty to the Jewish faith, it behaved rather conservatively toward innovations, especially if they came from Jerusalem. For this reason, before 70 CE, the influence of Pharisaism and its oral interpretation of the law was less in Galilee than in Judaea and in Jerusalem. Essenes would scarcely have been found there, which is why they are not mentioned in the Gospels. The Copper Scroll from Cave 3 at Qumran tellingly contains no place that belongs to Galilee with a fair amount of certainty.[28] According to a later legend, Yohanan ben Zakkai, the famous contemporary of Jesus and Paul, is said to have stayed for twenty years in Arav in Galilee before the destruction of the temple, and during the entire time there he is said to have received only two questions about the—Pharisaic—Sabbath halakah. He therefore is said to have uttered the curse: "Oh Galilee, you despise the Torah, you will soon fall victim to the oppressors."[29] The rabbinic Torah casuistry was too abstract and subtle for the rural population there. On the other hand, it was a Galilean who stood closer to Pharisaism who reproached King Izates of Adiabene on the Tigris that it was by no means sufficient to accept only the Jewish faith; rather, despite all the political risks, he had to let himself be circumcised.[30] One may by no means interpret the disinterest of the Galileans in certain parts of the Pharisaic halakah as laxness toward the law and the faith of the fathers. Rather, their national conservatism and their border location probably made them especially receptive to eschatological and messianic expectation of the end. Thus, it is not surprising that both the message of the Baptist and the preaching of Jesus fell on fruitful soil there. The supposition—which is expressed time and again in the older literature—that the esoteric Enoch-apocalyptic and the Son of Man expectation portrayed in the Parables of 1 Enoch (ch. 37–71) was especially widespread in Galilee in contrast to the hope for a Davidic Messiah has no basis in the sources. Precisely because we know so little about Galilee before 70 CE, the temptation to put forth unjustifiable hypotheses was especially great. This also applies to the hypothesis of a Galilean origin of

---

[27] Matt 26.73; cf. Mark 14.70.

[28] Wolters 1996; García Martínez / Tigchelaar 1997/1998, I: 232–39.

[29] y. Šabb. 16.8, 15d; cf. Luke 10.13. Only after 70 CE, and even more after the Bar Kokhba revolt in 132–136 CE, which led to the destruction of the Jewish community in Judaea, did Galilee become the main area of Palestinian Judaism.

[30] Josephus, *Ant.* 20.43–45. At the same time, the scribes from distant Jerusalem seem to have possessed a certain prestige. This can be seen in the success of the predominantly Pharisaic embassy from Jerusalem in Galilee according to Josephus, *Life* 190–203. See Hengel/Deines 1996, 475–76 (ET = 1995, 66-67).

the sayings source and of a Galilean Jesus tradition that is free of Christology (see section 6.4.2).

8.2 Nazareth

If his origin from remote Galilee was already not very flattering for Jesus among Jews and Greeks, this was all the more true for the connection with his entirely insignificant home village of Nazareth,[31] which is not mentioned in the Old Testament, Josephus, or the Talmud. Some have therefore hypothesized that Jesus' origin from the place of Nazareth was derived only secondarily from the designation Ναζωραῖος,[32] which is alleged to be a designation for a pre-Christian Baptist sect, which is said to have called itself *naṣôrayyā*, i.e., "keepers."[33] By contrast, in Jewish-rabbinic texts Jesus is designated as *Yešûaʿ han-nôṣrî* and the Christians therefore as *han-nôṣrîm*, which more likely points to the name of a place. This is attested in all four Gospels and then in the Christian tradition, including Eusebius' *Onomastikon*.[34] Moreover, Nazareth (*nṣrt*) is now also attested by a synagogue inscription of the third century CE from Caesarea, in which the hometowns of the twenty-four priestly orders in Galilee after the Bar Kokhba revolt are listed. The Jewish writer Eleazar ha-Kalir from the seventh century CE confirms this tradition. Here Nazareth is listed as the residence of the priestly order Ha-Pizzez (1 Chr 24.15).[35] The origin of Jesus from the insignificant Galilean village on the southwestern border of Galilee cannot be seriously called into doubt. Someone inventing a tradition would have sought out a more well-known place. According to Julius Africanus,[36] relatives of the Lord still lived

---

[31] On the spellings of the place-name, see Bauer/Aland/Aland 1988, 1077. Luke 4.16 and Matt 4.13, which depends on it, have the Aramaic spelling Ναζαρά.

[32] Thus, above all Matt 2.23; 26.71; John 18.5, 7; Mark has Ναζαρηνός four times. Luke has both: he has Ναζαρηνός in Luke 4.34; 24.19 and Ναζωραῖος in Luke 18.37 and seven times in Acts. On the problem, see Schaeder 1967 (GV = 1942) and Bauer/Aland/Aland 1988, 1077; Dalman 1967, 115–25; Rüger 1981.

[33] There are no attestations for such a Jewish pre-Christian Baptist sect. According to Acts 24.5, before Felix the rhetorician Tertullus accused Paul as πρωτοστάτην . . . τῆς τῶν Ναζωραίων αἱρέσεως, i.e., of the Christians.

[34] Klostermann 1904, 138 lines 24–25: Ναζαρέθ (Matt 2.23). ὅθεν ὁ Χριστὸς Ναζωραῖος ἐκλήθη, καὶ Ναζαρηνοὶ τὸ παλαιὸν ἡμεῖς οἱ νῦν Χριστιανοί. This is followed by an exact geographical description of the village.

[35] Avi-Yonah 1962; Rüger 1981, 257–58. The relocation of priestly families to Galilee was a consequence of the destruction of the temple or of the Bar Kokhba revolt; Dalman 1967, 65ff.

[36] *Epistula ad Aristides* apud Eusebius, *Hist. eccl.* 1.7.14: beginning of the third century CE.

there later in the second century CE. By contrast, in the fourth century CE, Epiphanius designates it as a purely Jewish place.[37] The fact that the origin of Jesus from Galilean Nazareth presented considerable difficulties in later controversies with Jewish dialogue partners is shown by the birth stories in Luke and Matthew, where the birth of Jesus, under different presuppositions, is moved to Bethlehem, in order to fulfill the prophecy of Mic 5.1. Here we must pay attention to the fact that even in Luke and Matthew, the salvation-historically grounded birth in Bethlehem could not suppress his origin from Nazareth; rather, it is explained in respectively different ways.[38] The situation in John is similar. The objection of Nathanael—"Can anything good come from Nazareth?"[39]—and that of the Jews—"Does the Messiah come from Galilee? Does not the Scripture say that the Messiah comes from the lineage of David and from Bethlehem, the village where David lived?"[40]—show the weight that the argument of a "nonbiblical" origin of Jesus from Galilee possessed among the Jewish opponents also at a later time. The earliest sources, Mark and the sayings tradition, and yet also John, do not let themselves be impressed by this. Apart from the four chapters of Matt 1 and 2 and Luke 1 and 2, the origin from Bethlehem (and the virgin birth) plays no role in the New Testament. By contrast, the descent from the line of David is significant from the beginning onward.[41]

It is peculiar that Nazareth and its broader surroundings no longer possess significant weight as the place of the activity of Jesus. Only Luke

[37] Epiphanius, *Pan.* 30.11.7: the information is, however, questionable due to the context.

[38] In the Lukan account Mary and Joseph live in Nazareth and are compelled to go to Bethlehem only by the census of Augustus, since Joseph was a Davidide (Luke 2.1-4). In Matthew they both reside in Bethlehem and are forced to flee to Egypt by King Herod's murder attempt in the first place ca. two years after the birth of Jesus. After the death of the king they settle by divine command in Galilean Nazareth, since Herod's son Archelaus had become ruler of Judaea (Matt 2.22). Matthew is not bothered very much by the fact that Archelaus' brother Herod (Antipas) is the ruler in Galilee. He is not as historically well informed as Luke and regards the whole event as an act of scriptural fulfillment (2.23). The scriptural basis for the fulfillment quotation remains unclear. It could refer to the divinely consecrated "Nazarite" in Judg 13.5 (LXX: ἡγιασμένον ναζιραῖον) or—with greater probability—to the "shoot" (MT: *neṣer*) in Isa 11.1.

[39] John 1.46.

[40] John 7.40ff.; cf. 52.

[41] See section 8.4. Bethlehem is also lacking in the Apostolic Fathers. It first crops up again frequently in Justin: *1 Apol.* 34.1; *Dial.* 78.1–8; 102.2; 103.3. It plays an important role in the proof from Scripture. For Justin, who cites Matthew and Luke most frequently, the birth stories of the two Gospels are a central component of the Christian message. In the dispute with Trypho the virgin birth and Isa 7.14 are at the center at multiple points. On this, see Hengel 1999b, 347–52. On the virgin birth, see also Ign. *Smyrn.* 1.1. Here Ignatius presupposes knowledge of Luke and Matthew.

mentions (on one occasion) the town of Nain,[42] which was located ca. ten kilometers to the southeast. John mentions Cana four times, which lay about seven kilometers to the northeast, whereas he mentions Nazareth only in Philip's introduction of Jesus to Nathaniel, which provokes Nathanael's rejection.[43] Mark and Matthew recount only Jesus' rejection in his hometown. Luke places this scene, which he has expanded, in a biographically deft way at the beginning of Jesus' activity.[44] All four Gospels agree in locating the focal point of the public activity of Jesus in Capernaum on the northwest shore of the Lake of Gennesaret, precisely at the opposite end of the province as the last larger place before the border to the tetrarchy of Philip on the Jordan and therefore the seat of a military unit and a customs office.[45] Jesus presumably chose this region because he found his first followers there. The few place-names that the Gospels mentions pile up in this small area. Capernaum is mentioned sixteen times, Bethsaida seven times, Chorazin two times, and Gennesaret and the mysterious Dalmanutha once. This last place may be a very early miswriting of Magdala, a place which is referred to in the byname of Jesus' disciple Mary Magdalene.[46] Matthew and John resolve the tension between the hometown of Jesus and the region of his public activity, from which his first disciples also come, through the reference to a relocation of Jesus to Capernaum.[47] Mark and Luke have him appear there in the synagogue;[48] he is "at home" there.[49] This means, however, that the activity of Jesus in Galilee had a clearly defined geographical center, even though he was active as an itinerant teacher. This suggests that his public activity probably did not extend over several years but was relatively short.

---

[42] Luke 7.11: the place-name is an original component of the narrative.

[43] Cana: John 2.1, 11; 4.46; 21.2; Nazareth: 1.45-46. See also section 11.5.

[44] Mark 6.1-6; Matt 13.53-58; Luke 4.16-30.

[45] Nazareth appears eleven times in the Gospels and once in Acts—primarily as the place of the origin of Jesus—i.e., more infrequently than Capernaum. Josephus mentions Capernaum as a κώμη in *Life* 403 (unchanged spelling). In *J.W.* 3.519 it appears as a rich region. The Synoptics designate it multiple times as πόλις. See also the two attestations in Midrash Qohelet (Bill. I: 159–60). Cf. M. Fischer 2001. On Jesus' activity in Galilee, see section 11.2.

[46] Mark 8.10. On this, see the apparatus in NA[26] and Jeremias 1966a, 87–90. Reed 2000, 82–93 (on the population density in the villages); 182ff. See further Dunn 2003b, 317ff.

[47] Matthew 4.13; John 2.12: here together with his mother, his brothers, and disciples. However, he is said to have stayed there only briefly and then gone to Jerusalem for the Passover. Cf. also the move to Jerusalem after Easter in Acts 1.13-14.

[48] Mark 1.21 = Luke 4.31.

[49] Mark 2.1: ἐν οἴκῳ; cf. 3.20; 9.33. The house of Peter may be in view: Mark 1.29ff. parr.

8.3 The Family of Jesus[50]

The earliest Gospel according to Mark has, like the latest Gospel according
to John, no story of Jesus' childhood. Since both are interested only in the
"messianic activity" of Jesus, their accounts of Jesus begin only with John
the Baptist.[51] In the introduction of Jesus immediately before his baptism
by John, Mark mentions only the place of origin *"Jesus from Nazareth in
Galilee."*[52] Here, there is not yet any mention of his family and his previous occupation. In contrast to Luke and Matthew, he initially has no interest in more detailed biographical narratives. Only the portrayal of Jesus'
failed activity in the synagogue of his hometown in Mark 6.1-6 gives the
evangelist an occasion to mention fundamental information about Jesus
and his family, which shows that Mark was not only a "kerygmatic storyteller" but also could concisely and precisely provide information in a
"biographical" way.

For Mark this restraint has theological reasons and cannot simply
be attributed to ignorance. For him the prehistory of Jesus is secondary,
for it does not yet belong to the "gospel" for him. *He wants to report
as good news (1.1) only Jesus' messianic activity and suffering*. On the
other hand, he knows that his hearers and readers nevertheless want to
learn or be reminded of some key life data. The basic information about
Jesus was usually already known to the hearers in the worship service.
Since he does not want to waste a single word, Mark says only that Jesus
came into his "hometown" (πατρίς) in 6.1. After all, he had already men-
tioned the name of the place in 1.9. It is also conspicuous that he calls
Jesus only the son of Mary, and his father Joseph does not appear in the
Gospel of Mark. To be sure, one may not explain this with the claim that
Jesus was the illegitimate child of a Roman soldier named Panthera, as
Celsus and the Talmudic sources claimed,[53] nor with the suggestion that

---

[50] Zahn 1900, 225–63; Roloff 1970, 159ff.; Oberlinner 1975; Hengel 1985a (= 2002,
549-82); Bauckham 1990; Meier 1991, 313–32.

[51] See chapters 9 and 10.

[52] Mark 1.9: ἦλθεν Ἰησοῦς ἀπὸ Ναζαρὲτ Γαλιλαίας. Matthew 3.13 omits Nazareth
and says only that Jesus comes from Galilee to the Jordan. Luke 3.21 forgoes any specification of origin. Both Gospels have already informed their readers about this in the prehistory. John 1.29ff. does not even mention the baptism, though it presupposes it (1.32) and
teaches about Jesus' origin in 1.45-46.

[53] Origen, *Cels.* 1.28–29, 32–33, 69: This "Jew," i.e., the "Jewish" informant of Celsus, is a rhetorical fiction according to Origen. Nevertheless, Celsus must have been extensively informed about the Jewish polemic against Jesus in the second century CE. He
knows from these Jewish sources that the mother of Jesus, a very poor Jew, was sent away
by her betrothed, a carpenter, because of adultery (μοιχεία) with a soldier Πανθήρα, and
that, wandering around, she bore the child in secret. Jesus is said to have then emigrated to

Mark wants to allude indirectly to the virgin birth here. After all, it is the inhabitants of Nazareth who call Jesus this according to Mark. The Jewish historian Tal Ilan has investigated the not infrequent cases in which Jews are named in connection with the names of their mothers, and in some cases reaches the conclusion "that this was, most likely, due to the greater prominence of the mother or the mother's pedigree."[54] For Mark the mother of Jesus, who with her sons was later a member of the community, was certainly "of greater importance."[55] This is still clear in Luke and John, who refer with emphasis to the mother of Jesus. Only Matthew, who knew the Gospel of Luke, seeks to balance out this one-sidedness by placing special emphasis in his prehistory on Joseph as a caring "righteous man" who acts according to God's instruction.[56] Presumably the father died relatively early,[57] so that the mother was the family head for quite some time. This would also mean that Jesus, as the eldest son, would have had to contribute already early on to the support of the family with many

---

Egypt due to poverty, where he successfully learned the art of sorcery. Celsus relies here on a Jewish, oral or written "anti-Gospel," which is presupposed already in the Gospel of Matthew. The name of the father *Panterā* (or *Panderā*) appears multiple times in rabbinic literature: cf. t. Ḥul. 2.22–24. Strack 1910, § 3–5, p. 2–4 (*21–26*). In Greek authors since Epiphanius, *Pan.* 78.7 (Strack 1910, 10*ff.), the name Πάνθηρ occurs as a byname or name in the genealogy. Zahn 1900, 266ff., seeks to trace this name back to Hegesippus. On the whole, see now Schäfer 2007 on the Talmudic reports. An illegitimate origin of Jesus has been advocated again by Lüdemann 2000a, 40, 120–24, 687–88 (GV = 2000b, 60–62, 879–80). The mention of the large family with four brothers and an unspecified number of (at least two) sisters (Mark 6.3) already speaks against this view. Πάνθηρ is presumably a corruption of παρθένος by metathesis; cf. Isa 7.14, the main supporting verse for the virgin birth from the Septuagint over which, as shown by Justin's *Dialogus cum Tryphone*, there was heated debate with Jews; see Hengel 1999b, 347–52.

[54] Ilan 1992, 44. Tal Ilan considers whether this form of the name could be connected with the socially higher background of Mary (according to Luke 1.5, 36, 39ff., she is the συγγενίς of Elisabeth, the daughter of a priest [cf. note 31 in this chapter], and according to later Christian tradition, for example in the Protevangelium Jacobi, she is, after all, of Aaronic origin); see now with additional attestations, Ilan 2006, 250–58.

[55] Cf. Acts 1.14; John 2.12; 19.27.

[56] Matt 1.18-25; 2.13-23. In our view, Matthew does this in conscious opposition or at least as a supplement to the report of Luke.

[57] In his somewhat confused radical skepticism Oberlinner 1975, 73–78, overlooks the fact that the evangelists write in a Jewish and ancient milieu where the person of the father is usually of the greatest significance. The fact that Mark 6.3 is formulated so uncommonly is best explained on the basis of historical reasons. Cf. also 267ff. and 282: the New Testament never speaks *expressis verbis* of a "veneration" of Mary as "mother of the Lord." The only attestation for ἡ μήτηρ τοῦ κυρίου μου is the question of Elisabeth (Luke 1.43) and has not so much Mariological as christological significance. If Joseph had still been alive, why would he not be mentioned as "(adoptive) father of the Lord"? The alternative of a divorce of Joseph and Mary appears even less plausible, for the sons and daughter are all mentioned, after all, in connection with the mother.

children through his handwork, especially since he remained unmarried. This would also make especially comprehensible the family's agitation over his "going crazy."[58] The decisive statement, which is extremely valuable historically, is Mark 6.3, the astonished question of the inhabitants of Nazareth: "Is this not the craftsman, the son of Mary and brother of James, Joses, Judas, and Simeon, and do not his sisters live here with us?" The four brothers of Jesus with their names—which were frequent in the Judaism of the time—are oriented to the patriarchs and Maccabee brothers. For this reason one may presuppose a relatively legally strict, "nationally conscious" family, which was probably influenced by Pharisaic spirit.[59]

The name *Yešûᵃ'*, which the eldest son received,[60] a short form of *Yehôšûᵃ'* (YHWH helps/saves), also points in this direction. *Yehôšûᵃ'* (in the Septuagint Ἰησοῦς) was the "prophetic" successor to Moses and victorious leader of Israel in the taking of the land. As shown especially by Josephus, ossuary inscriptions, ostraca, and papyri, the name *Yešûᵃ'* was extraordinarily popular in Palestinian Judaism for national reasons between the time of the Maccabees and the beginning of the second century. Then the use of the name suddenly breaks off. It became a taboo word. Among the rabbis it is completely lacking. Here *Yehôšûᵃ'* replaced the short form once again.[61]

This naming of the sons in the family of Joseph and Mary in connection with the obvious validity of the Pharisaic eschatology for Jesus and the primitive community explains why Pharisees and their scribes belonged to their dialogue partners. The subsequently attested strictness with respect to the law of the most important, first-named brother James—who received for this reason the byname "the just" and against

---

[58] Mark 3.21; see note 78 below.

[59] It is only the later church tradition with Jerome that turns the brothers into "cousins" of Jesus; in the second century they are said, according to the Gospel of Peter (Origen, *Comm. Matt.* 10.17; see Aland 2005, 196) and the Protevangelium Jacobi, to stem from an earlier marriage of Joseph.

[60] According to Luke 2.7 Jesus is the "first-born son." Luke also knows about the existence of the brothers of Jesus (Luke 8.19-21; Acts 1.14), but consciously lets them recede entirely. In the case of James (Acts 12.17; 15.13; 21.18) he stresses his significance but does not say that he is the brother of Jesus. According to Luke 1.31, the naming took place upon the instruction of the angel Gabriel to Mary; according to Matt 1.21, the "angel of the Lord" gives a command to Joseph and explains the name soteriologically: "for he will save (σώσει) his people from their sins." The name already contains the soteriological task of Jesus.

[61] Ilan 2002, 126–33, counts 103 instances. We still find it in the Bar Kokhba documents. On the rabbis, see Bill. VI: 67–71.

whose execution by the high priest Annas II around 62 CE Pharisees energetically protested—would also fit with this.[62]

Mark presupposes that the four names of the brothers of Jesus are
known in the community, and names them because of their subsequent
significance for the Jewish Christian community; the sisters who live in
Nazareth remain anonymous. Only the legends since Epiphanius give
them names.[63] The fact that the Nazarenes in Mark 6.3 stress that "they
live here with us" suggests that Mark assumes that they are married in
Nazareth, while in the case of Mary and the brothers it remains unclear
whether Nazareth is still their place of residence. With the move of his
mother and brothers to Capernaum John at least knows more here,[64] while
Matthew speaks only of Jesus moving there.[65] This could be connected
with the difficulties that the family had due to Jesus' activity in Nazareth. Perhaps they followed him to Capernaum later, despite the tensions
that existed between Jesus and them, in order to reintegrate him into the
family unit.

The rejection of Jesus by his fellow villagers in Mark 6.1-6 is meant
to demonstrate that those who stand most closely to him, indeed who are
related to him, do not want to acknowledge his sending and place themselves on a level with him. The questions "Whence does he have these
things? And what is this for a wisdom, which is given to him?" are
consciously formulated in an ambivalent way.[66] In his answer—which
is often traced back to a proverb, but which cannot be documented
elsewhere—Jesus compares himself, only here in Mark, to a prophet,
who—one is reminded of Jeremiah and the men of Anathoth[67]—is rejected
in his hometown.

The sharp statement that "because of their unbelief," he "could do
no miracle there" (Mark 6.5-6) is conspicuous. This speaks, as does the
exact information about the family, for the authenticity of the narrative.
In novelistically expanded, dramatized form, Luke 4.16-30 reports that
Jesus proclaims the fulfillment of Isa 61.1-2 in the synagogue worship
service and decisively rejects the demand of the doubting hearers that

---

[62] Josephus, *Ant.* 20.200ff. Hengel 2002, 549–77.

[63] Blinzler 1967, 35ff. Bauckham 1990, 37–44.

[64] John 2.12.

[65] Matthew 4.13; cf. Luke 4.16, 30-31.

[66] Mark 6.2. Luke has emphasized the special wisdom of the boy Jesus in the impressive special material narrative about the twelve-year-old Jesus in the temple: 2.41-51
(46-47) and, in addition, the frame of 2.40 and 52 with the reference to the growing σοφία
of the young Jesus.

[67] Mark 6.4; Jer 11.21-23; cf. 1.1 and note 78 below. On the 'proverb,' see note 28 in
chapter 16.

he heal, as in Capernaum, also in Nazareth. The consequence is the first endangerment of the life of Jesus. The indignant Nazarenes sought to throw him down a steep cliff, "but he passed through their midst."[68] This already signals the end and goal of his way as servant of God and Messiah.[69] In the distinctive scene, Luke presupposes the Markan account and additional traditions, but shapes the whole into a new narrative, which has fundamental significance for him. It is one of those many examples in which "tradition" and theological "redaction" can no longer be separated.[70] Even for Mark himself, his own formulation of Jesus' inability (οὐκ ἐδύνατο) to do a miracle appears to have been too sharp, so that he weakened it again with the addition that Jesus did, after all, heal a few sick people by laying his hands on them. Matthew turns this "not being able" into a punishment and removes thereby the offense: "He did not do many miracles because of their unbelief."[71] Matthew also makes an apologetic change vis-à-vis the Markan *Vorlage* in the specification of the occupation: "Is this not the son of the craftsman? Is not his mother called Mary . . . ?" (Matt 13.55). In this way he introduces the lacking father, to whom he had assigned greater value in his prehistory than Luke, who more strongly emphasizes the role of the mother. At the same time, he ascribes to the father the occupation of Jesus, which probably appeared inappropriate for the Son of God.[72]

The *family of Jesus*, to which Mark 6.3 (and Matt 13.55 in dependence on it) point with singular extensiveness within the New Testament, played a dominant role in the later Palestinian-Jewish Christian community.[73] This is especially the case for James. He became the head of the Jerusalem community after the persecution under Agrippa I in ca. 42/43 CE

---

[68] Luke 4.30.

[69] On this, see Mittmann-Richert 2008. On this typically Johannine formulation, see at the beginning of the activity of Jesus John 2.4; cf. 7.30; 8.20; 12.23; 17.1. Luke too places the way of Jesus under the mystery of his suffering from the beginning onward; cf. Luke 2.7b, 34-35.

[70] Cf. Luke 22.53; Mark 14.41; John 2.4; 13.1; 17.1.

[71] Mark 6.5; cf. Matt 13.58. By contrast, the statement of the Markan version appears in Tatian's Gospel harmony (see Ephrem of Nisibis' commentary on the Diatessaron [ed. Leloir 1966, 210]) embedded in the Lukan narrative; on this, see Bauer 1967b, 361ff.

[72] Matthew 13.55; on the text-critical problem, see Oberlinner 1975, 268ff. As so often, the text of Matthew has influenced the later tradition of the text of Mark. On the importance of Joseph in Matthew in contrast to the other Gospels and especially to Luke, see Hengel 2008c, 341ff. (ET = 2000b, 199ff.). Matthew mentions him seven times, Luke five, John two, and Mark not at all. Presumably, Matthew already knew of the slurs about the origin of Jesus, which we then encounter in the Jew of Celsus; for this reason he places special emphasis on the role of the "righteous" Joseph (1.18ff.); on this, see note 53 above.

[73] According to 1 Cor 9.5, the brothers of Jesus were married. On their leading role, see Hegesippus apud Eusebius, *Hist. eccl.* 3.32.6.

and remained so until he was stoned in 62 CE. His successor, after the destruction of the city, is said to have been a relative of Jesus, Symeon, son of Clopas, who is said to have suffered martyrdom in 107 CE.[74] The later church tradition turns James into the first bishop in Jerusalem,[75] and also later the relatives of the Lord, the so-called δεσπόσυνοι,[76] appear to have held a special place of honor in Jewish Christian communities, which continued to have an effect until far into the second century CE. In his ecclesiastical history, Gregory Bar Hebraeus recounts that in Seleucia on the Tigris there were still in the third century CE three successive bishops who claimed descent from Joseph the carpenter: Abris, Abraham, and Jacob (James).[77]

This later significance of the brothers and relatives of Jesus stands in a peculiar opposition to the aforementioned *conflict of Jesus with his family members* in all four Gospels. Mark not only provides the most precise information about Jesus' origin, occupation, and siblings, but also recounts in brief form this disturbance, which is again a sign of his—relative—reliability. Thus, the rejection of Jesus by the relatives and acquaintances in Nazareth is only a companion piece to the previously portrayed dramatic conflict with his family. Here we initially encounter the short note in Mark 3.21, which shows that Mark knows more than he says and which is deleted—due to its offensiveness—by Luke and Matthew:

> And when his family members heard, they went out to seize him. For they said: He has lost his mind.[78]

One could imagine that from Nazareth they sought him in Capernaum. After his return from John the Baptist he became a different person. Apparently the family of Jesus wanted to bring Jesus back again "into their care" and "not to be brought into further disgrace" by him. After

---

[74] Eusebius, *Hist. eccl.* 3.11, following Hegesippus, refers to Luke 24.18; John 19.25; cf. *Hist. eccl.* 3.32. In the legendary martyr accounts he reaches the legendary age of Moses of 120 years. Eusebius dates it in the year 107 CE; however, the proconsul Atticus under whom Symeon died, is set somewhat earlier; see note 59 in chapter 6. On the persecution under Agrippa I, see Hengel/Schwemer 2019.

[75] Hengel 2002, 549–82. The church tradition since Clement of Alexandria makes him the first bishop of the church in general, who was appointed by all twelve apostles. See also Hengel 2010a, 9–10 (GV = 2006b, 13–14).

[76] Julius Africanus, *Ep. ad Aristid.* 5 (= Eusebius, *Hist. eccl.* 1.7.14).

[77] Zahn 1900, 295–96.

[78] Καὶ ἀκούσαντες οἱ παρ᾽ αὐτοῦ ἐξῆλθον κρατῆσαι αὐτόν ἔλεγον γὰρ ὅτι ἐξέστη. The prophet Jeremiah (12.6, cf. 9.3) also bitterly laments about his "brothers and family members."

all, the sharp rejection in Nazareth must have affected the entire family.[79] Mark 3.21 is the starting point for the scene 3.31-35, in which Jesus refuses his closest family members, mother and brothers, who want to speak with him, and designates his hearers, who sit around him in the house, as true "mother and brothers."[80] Like many of the narratives in Mark, this can be designated as an ideal scene, which is dramaturgically and kergymatically shaped. Nevertheless, due to its extremely offensive character for a Palestinian Jew, who regarded the fourth commandment as the most important after the first, and due to the leading role of the brothers of Jesus in the later community, it is certainly not an invention but rather goes back, just like the Nazareth scene, to real events. This is confirmed by an exchange of words from the Lukan special material (Luke 11.27-28):[81] In response to an ascription of blessedness to the mother of Jesus by a woman from the crowd, Jesus answers: "Blessed rather are those who hear the word of God and keep it." Between the two episodes involving the family of Jesus in 3.21 and 3.31ff. Mark has inserted with narrative skill the even sharper judgment of the scribes who had come down from Jerusalem to Galilee. They accuse Jesus of being in league with the ruler of the demon Beelzebul, i.e., with Satan himself (3.22-30). The two accusations, that of the family and that of the scribes, complement each other. The rejection of Jesus proceeds from the most important authorities for the Jews, namely one's own family

[79] Pesch 1984a, 212; Gnilka 1978/1979, II: 148, stresses, on the one hand, rightly that "the judgment 'he is out of his mind' . . . must not be weakened," but then claims that it has captured no historical memory but rather is to be appraised theologically. "The activity of the revealer strikes upon incomprehension, which includes even his family." Here, on the one hand, the opposition between "historical memory" and "theological appraisal" is senseless, for in Mark *everything* is, of course, "theologically appraised" through selection and arrangement of the material; on the other hand, the explanation that "the activity of the Revealer strikes upon misunderstanding" is a commonplace, which weakens the most extreme offensiveness of this text. It does not fit in the later community situation, in which the mother of Jesus was esteemed and the brothers were highly regarded. Cf. Acts 1.14; 1 Cor 9.5. Moreover, one should not designate the Markan Jesus as "Revealer." This sounds like *interpretatio gnostica*.

[80] Parallels: Luke 8.19-21; Matt 12.46-50. According to the Gospel of Hebrews the *mater Domini et fratres eius* exhort Jesus to let himself be baptized with them. Jesus initially rejects this due to his sinlessness. Cited by Jerome, *Pelag.* 3.2; see Aland 2005, 27.

[81] Luke 11.27-28; see also section 11.5. For the early fathers Irenaeus, Tertullian, and Origen Mary was not yet "free from error" and "sinless"; on this, see Bauer 1967b, 18–20. According to Origen, *Hom. Luc.* (Rauer 1959, 105ff.) on Luke 2.35, Mary, like the disciples of Jesus, has doubts about her son. He therefore died also for her sins. Tertullian, *Carn. Chr.* 7 and *Marc.* 4.19.6–13, argues against Apelles and Marcion (who invoke his question in Matt 12.48 against the reality of the humanity of Jesus) that at that time the brothers and mother of Jesus did not really believe in him "but sought to keep him from his work," so that he had to rebuff them.

and the religious leaders of the people. Before 70 CE Jerusalem was the center of scribal learning and thus of the religious authorities in Palestinian Judaism.[82]

The fact that Jesus' activity as teacher and miracle worker was—initially—rejected by his brothers is attested independently of the Synoptic tradition by John 7.5.[83] Statements of Jesus from the sayings tradition also confirm his critical stance toward familial ties: for example, when Jesus, in a way that runs counter to Jewish notions of piety, prohibits a potential follower from first burying his own father[84] or the radical saying about discipleship in Luke 14.26[85] and the logion of Luke 12.51-53 (= Matt 10.34-36) with the quotation from Mic 7.6 about the strife within one's own family in connection with Jesus' confession that he has come to bring division, which Matthew concludes with a sentence that is probably oriented to the Hebrew text: "The enemies of a person will be the members of his household." Jesus himself carried out what he requires of his followers, i.e., the break with their family members.[86]

On the other hand, it is telling that after the death of Jesus and the resurrection appearances—one of which was, after all, also bestowed on Jesus' brother James—the family of Jesus completely joined the new messianic movement, indeed, played a fundamental role in it.[87] In the case of the disciples—despite the temporary separation—the family bonds also remained stable in the long run. According to Paul, "the rest of the apostles, the brothers of the Lord and Cephas" (i.e., Peter) were all married.[88]

The fact that in all four Gospels—in contrast to the emphasis on Peter and to a lesser extent on the sons of Zebedee in the Synoptics or on Philip and Thomas in John[89]—the brothers of Jesus play no positive

---

[82] Cf. Mark 7.1. See also the end of section 4.3.

[83] Cf. also the abrupt rebuff of the communication of his mother in John 2.4: "Leave me in peace, woman!"; on this, see Bauer 1933, 44–45.

[84] Matthew 8.21-22 = Luke 9.59-60; cf. 61-62. This prohibition goes far beyond YHWH's prohibition of Ezekiel from lamenting his wife (Ezek 24.15-27), a sign act that is meant to point to the downfall of Jerusalem. With Jesus the concern is with the radical freedom for the kingdom of God; see section 10.7.

[85] Cf. Matt 10.37 and Mark 10.29 = Matt 19.29 = Luke 18.29.

[86] Luke 12.51-53 = Matt 10.34-36. Matthew gives the quotation a clearer form. With his more extensive version, Luke appears to be more original. Cf. Mark 13.12 = Matt 10.21. On discipleship and family, see Hengel 1981b (GV = 1968b; 2007b, 40–138) and section 11.4.

[87] Cf. Acts 1.14; 1 Cor 15.7; Gal 1.19; 2.9, 12.

[88] Cf. Mark 1.29ff.; 1 Cor 9.5; see Hengel 2010a, 103–16 (GV = 2006b, 166–89).

[89] For Mark and John we could also mention Andrew, the brother of Simon Peter: Mark 1.16, 29; 3.18; 13.3; John 1.40, 44; 6.8; 12.22.

role in the time of his public activity points to old tradition. Despite their future leadership role in the Jerusalem community, the picture of them is not retouched. James, the brother of the Lord, is stressed in a conspicuous way only in the later apocryphal Gospel of the Hebrews and the Gospel of Thomas from the second century CE.[90] This evident reserve of the older gospel tradition stemming from Jewish Palestine vis-à-vis the family of Jesus and especially his brothers rests on the historical recollection that Jesus himself, probably on the basis of his messianic sending, had broken with his family and that his brothers had rejected this sending or understood it a different way than Jesus. What Jesus himself carried out, however, he also demanded from others. In our view, the fact that Mark, the first "biographer" of Jesus, provides in his work a whole series of reliable basic information about Jesus' geographical origin, family, occupation, and family conflicts rules out from the outset the view that he primarily recounts "theological fictions" therein. He could be dependent here on Petrine tradition.

8.4 The Son of David

Among other things, Hegesippus also attests that Davidic descent was ascribed to the family of Jesus in Jewish Palestine.[91] This agrees with a broad New Testament tradition. Already Paul cites corresponding confessional statements in Romans, which go back to the beginnings of Christology in the primitive community.[92] Mark placed the designation υἱὸς Δαυίδ as an address to Jesus twice in the mouth of blind Bartimaeus.[93] All the more it plays a prominent role in Matthew. It appears eight times there and three times in Luke.[94] The descent from David dominates the prehistory in both Gospels. Above all, however, Luke 3 and Matt 1 introduce

---

[90] Gos. Thom. 12: For James' sake heaven and earth have been created; Gospel of Hebrews according to Jerome, *Vir. ill.* 2 (Aland 2005, 507; Ehrman/Pleše 2011, 219): James is the first witness of the resurrection; on this, see Hengel 2002, 549–82. Zahn 1900, 277 n. 1, believes that a piece of information attributed to Severian of Gabbala, which mentions James as a third witness of the empty tomb alongside the two disciples of John 20.2-10, likewise goes back to the Gospel of the Hebrews.

[91] Apud Eusebius, *Hist. eccl.* 3.19–20 (cf. chapter 12). According to this text, "heretics" are said to have denounced descendants of Judas, the brother of the Lord, as descendants of David before the Roman authorities. See section 8.5.

[92] Rom 1.3: γενόμενος ἐκ σπέρματος Δαυὶδ κατὰ σάρκα; cf. the citation of Isa 11.10 LXX in 15.12 and Rom 9.5.

[93] Mark 10.47-48 (cf. Luke 18.38-39): υἱὲ Δαυὶδ Ἰησοῦ, ἐλέησόν με and υἱὲ Δαυὶδ ἐλέησόν με; cf. Matt 20.30-31: two blind men call out twice with the addition κύριε. Mark 10.51 has for this still the emphasized Aramaic ῥαββουνί.

[94] On this, see now Deines 2004, 469–500.

two artificial[95] genealogies, which trace back the family of Jesus to David. These genealogies, which deviate already with the father of Joseph, run in different directions and contradict each other. Matthew has the official royal line from David to Jechoniah, which probably represents a correction of the unordinary genealogy in Luke,[96] whereas Luke has a peculiar secondary line, which is basically unexplainable.[97] In the aforementioned testimony of Hegesippus from ca. 170 CE this early witness reports about two great nephews of Jesus, James and Zoker, grandchildren of his brother Jude, who was brought to Rome before Emperor Domitian, a piece of information that certainly has a historical background.[98] We possess a whole series of rabbinic indications that Jewish families at the time also derived their family tree from David and other great figures of the Old Testament.[99] An ossuary from Jerusalem from ca. 70 CE has the inscription *'l by(t) dwd*, "belonging to the house (= family) of David."[100] For example, according to Phil 3.5, Paul appeals, entirely as a matter of course, to his descent from the tribe of Benjamin. These different indications make it likely that the family of Jesus already traced itself back to David with its genealogy. The peculiar version of the genealogy in Luke may be the older of the two.[101] Matthew's genealogy, which follows the royal line, shows itself to be a scribal construction from the Septuagint, which is erroneous for the sake of the consistency of the 3 × 14 scheme.[102] The harmonization of the two genealogies already presented the early church with

---

[95] Matthew 3 × 14; Luke 7 × 11 names.

[96] Matt 1.1-16 starting from Abraham. He ends with Joseph, the son of Jacob (in Luke 3.23 of Eli). Joseph is called "son of David" in Matt 1.20. The "kingship" of Jesus is emphasized in Matthew vis-à-vis the Markan *Vorlage* and Luke: Matt 1.1-16 (6-13); 2.2ff.; 21.5; 22.7; 25.34, 40, etc. Something similar applies to John 1.49; 12.13, 15; 18.33ff.; 19.14ff. and elsewhere, though here his status as Son of David is only hinted at in 7.42.

[97] Luke 3.23-38. In opposite order, starting from Jesus and his (apparent) father Joseph and ending with Adam or God himself as Adam's creator. Between Jesus and Nathan, the son of David (2 Sam 5.14; 1 Chr 3.5), Luke has 6 × 7 names, whereas Matthew with the royal line has 2 × 14, with three kings being omitted between Joram and Uzziah and with Jechoniah being counted twice. On further discrepancies, see Luz 1989, 104–13; 2007, 79–88 (GV = Luz 2002, 128–31); Bauer 1967b, 21–29: They have had a massive influence on the textual tradition. Tatian resolves the difficulty by omitting the genealogy in the Diatessaron, and the Gospel of the Ebionites proceeds similarly according to Epiphanius, *Pan*. 30.14.

[98] Eusebius, *Hist. eccl*. 3.20. The names are omitted by Eusebius, but occur in fragments of the church history of Philip of Side; see Zahn 1900, 239ff.; Preuschen 1905, 111; Bauckham 1990, 97–106.

[99] Cf. Jeremias 1969a, 284ff. (GV = 1969b, 318ff.).

[100] Flusser 1986; Rahmani 1994, nr. 430 p. 173–74.

[101] On this, see the detailed investigation in Bauckham 1990, 315–73.

[102] See notes 96–97 above.

unresolvable difficulties. The learned Julius Africanus, librarian of the emperor Alexander Severus (222–235) and friend of Origen,[103] sought to remove the contradiction through the hypothesis of a levirate marriage.[104] The ancestry of Mary has been derived—sometimes even in more recent times—both from David and from Aaron.[105] However, in the early church, the Davidic ancestry established itself in her case too, even though Luke leaves this question unanswered. Here the early church speculation possessed a wide field in which it could expand itself further.

In a few cases we also find a rejection of Jesus' Davidic sonship, such as in the anti-Jewish Epistle of Barnabas with an appeal to Ps 110.1.[106] However, this is the rare exception that proves the rule. By contrast, neither Jesus' question to the scribes in Mark 12.35-37 parr. nor John 7.40-43 ought to be interpreted in this anti-Davidic way. In Mark Jesus points to a paradox, which the scribes do not understand, and John too demonstrates only the ignorance of the people[107] with regard to the true dignity and divine origin of Jesus. There is no real reason to doubt that in the family of Jesus the tradition of its descent from David was alive and well. The genealogy in Luke could originate from there, but it too gives the impression of being a construction. This is shown by the insertion of the unfitting names "Zorobabel" and "Salathiel."[108] Despite all open—indeed unanswerable—questions, Albert Schweitzer's statement may contain a *particula veri*: "Hitherto the view has been that it was the primitive community which made the Lord into the Son of David because it held him to be the Messiah. It is time to consider seriously whether it was not rather Jesus who held himself to be the Messiah because he was descended from David."[109] In any case, with the tradition of Jesus' Davidic sonship we are dealing with a fundamental conviction of primitive Christianity.[110]

---

[103] Ca. 160–240 CE. On his person, see Broscio 1998, 408–9; Winkelmann 2002. He was probably born in Aelia Capitolina, the former Jerusalem.

[104] Eusebius, *Hist. eccl.* 1.7.2–10; on this, see Merkel 1971, 125ff., 132ff.

[105] Cf. in Luke 1.36 her kinship with the daughter of a priest, Elisabeth, the mother of the Baptist (1.5). Origen and Ephrem combatted this view; see Bauer 1967b, 8–17.

[106] Barnabus 12.10-11. On this, see Prostmeier 1999, 445ff. In our view, the polemic is directed against Jewish Christians who appeal against the notion of preexistence and incarnation to the mere sonship of David of Jesus. See also Irenaeus, *Haer.* 4.33.4; 5.1, 3.

[107] John 7.40: The question comes from hearers of Jesus ἐκ τοῦ ὄχλου.

[108] Luke 3.27; cf. 1 Chr 3.18-19 LXX; Ezra 3.2; 5.2 and 1 Esdras 4.13; 5.5, 47 LXX.

[109] Schweitzer 2000, 319 (GV = 1913, 395).

[110] Cf. also Acts 2.30; 13.23; 2 Tim 2.8; Rev 5.5; 22.16; Ign. *Eph.* 18.2; 20.2 and elsewhere.

8.5 The Occupation and Social Background of Jesus

In connection with the scene in Mark 6.1-6, which is significant for Jesus' biographical data, we also learn about his occupation. He is a "craftsman" in the comprehensive sense,[111] i.e., one who can work with wood, clay, stone, indeed sometimes even with metal, i.e., carpenter, mason, woodworker, and metalworker in one. He thus possessed an occupation that required great skilled craftsmanship. Nevertheless, artisans did not have a high standing in the social hierarchy of antiquity. Justin reports from an apocryphal source that when Jesus came for baptism at the Jordan he "appeared, as the Scriptures proclaim, unsightly (ἀειδής)[112] and was thought to be a carpenter; for he produced the works of a carpenter . . . plows and yokes."[113] Celsus mockingly connected Jesus' occupation as a carpenter with his crucifixion.[114] The Athenian orator Secundus (first century CE) was mocked by his contemporaries as "wooden nail" because he was the son of a carpenter (τέκτονος παῖς), and his student Herod Atticus ridiculed him with a satirical verse.[115]

Jesus came not from the lowest stratum of the landless day laborers and tenants but from the artisan class, i.e., from the simple middle stratum, which predominantly determined the social fabric of early Christianity in the next two centuries.

According to the report of Hegesippus, the aforementioned two great nephews of Jesus, whom Domitian had brought to Rome since they were politically suspicious as Davidides, belong to the same social milieu. They were questioned by the emperor and indicated that they possessed a farm of thirty-nine plethras (= ca. ten hectares) with a tax value of nine thousand denarii, which they worked together and for which they paid their taxes. As proof they showed him the calluses on their hands, and the emperor, full of contempt, sent them home as poor people.[116] In a corresponding way, the opponent of Christianity Celsus mocked the primitive background of Jesus and his disciples. Moreover, he speaks

---

[111] Mark 6.3: τέκτων. The Hebrew equivalent is *ḥoreš/ḥārāš*; Aramaic: *naggār*. Cf. 2 Sam 5.11 and 1 Kgs 7.14: artisans who work with wood, stone, and ore.

[112] Cf. Isa 53.3 LXX.

[113] *Dial.* 88.8.

[114] On Celsus, see Origen, *Cels.* 6.36.

[115] Philostratus, *Lives of the Sophists*, p. 544 (Wright 1922).

[116] The wrath of the emperor is directed not against the Christians as such but especially against the senatorial nobility. On Hegesippus, see Eusebius, *Hist. eccl.* 3.20.1–6; 3.32.5; cf. section 8.4.

contemptuously of "wool workers, cobblers, and fullers,"[117] who appeared as teachers and dominated the social picture of the Christian communities. On the other hand, it is conspicuous that Luke and John are silent about Jesus' occupation as a craftsman, and Matthew speaks only of his father as a "craftsman."[118]

Even though a skilled craftsman in a Galilean village had an orderly, relatively secure income, in the eyes of the ancient world he was nevertheless regarded as uneducated and uncultured. Mark has not retouched the picture of Jesus with respect to this point, although it did not correspond to the "missionary needs" of the later community. The general skepticism with which Mark 6.1-6 has been considered in the work of influential scholars is an indication of how much the feeling for the historical reality of life has been lost here.[119] It could be asked whether Jesus (and his brother James) received a light whiff of "Greek culture" in the nearby polis of Sepphoris. Revealingly, the Jewish inhabitants of this polis, which was refounded by Antipas after its destruction by Varus in 4 BCE, did not join the revolt in 66 CE but rather remained loyal to Rome and requested Roman protection against their own compatriots.[120] This points to a certain "Hellenistic" influence. Jesus presumably also spoke some Greek. This is presupposed in the Gospels, for example in the conversations with Pilate, the centurion in Capernaum, the Syrophoenician woman,[121] and in the case of the "Greeks."[122] In Mark Jesus' mother tongue is clearly Aramaic. This too goes back to the oldest tradition.[123] All the more, we can probably assume knowledge of Greek on the part of his brother James.[124] This was indispensable for the long-standing leader of the Jerusalem primitive community. Jesus may also have worked with his father on the rebuilding of the nearby Sepphoris

---

[117] Origen, *Cels.* 3.55; cf. 1.28: The mother of Jesus is said to have earned her livelihood in a toilsome manner as a "spinner." Jesus himself is said to have emigrated to Egypt due to his poverty and to have worked initially as a day laborer (μσθαρνήσας).

[118] Matthew 13.55: τοῦ τέκτονος υἱός. See note 72 above.

[119] On this, see Bultmann 1963, 31–32 (GV = 1995, 30–31) and Bultmann/Theissen/Vielhauer 1971, 25–26. The double verse P.Oxy 1.30–35 (1.9–14) = Gos. Thom. 31 (Aland 2005, 50) has been formed from Mark 6.4-5 under the influence of Luke 4.23. It is clearly secondary and certainly not the basis of the Markan narrative. See note 229 in chapter 6. Cf. Klauck 2003a, 117–18 (GV = Klauck 2000, 156–57).

[120] Josephus, *J.W.* 3.30ff.; *Life* 30ff. and elsewhere. On the history of the city, see Schürer 1973–1987, II: 172–76. See section 3.1.2.

[121] Ἑλληνίς: Mark 7.26.

[122] John 7.35; 12.20.

[123] This is already shown by the conspicuously numerous and correct lexical Aramaisms.

[124] Hengel 2002, 511–48.

by Antipas, which could have dragged on into the second decade of the turn of the eras. To be sure, the view that Jesus was taught and "enlightened" by Cynic itinerant philosophers there is too far-fetched.[125] In a predominantly Jewish city Cynic teachers would hardly have found a fruitful sphere of activity, and in Galilean villages they would have encountered only incomprehension, indeed enmity.

---

[125] This thesis is advocated above all by Downing 1992, 115–68; see especially 143ff.: Jesus and Cynics in Galilee in the twenties CE. Certain parallels in subject matter in the sayings tradition do not demonstrate historical dependence.

9

John the Baptist[1]

The peculiar fact that three Gospels begin their presentation not with Jesus but with John the Baptist has been too little appreciated in recent scholarship. Luke even strengthens this tendency by introducing his work with the promise of the birth of the Baptist and artificially interweaving his birth story with that of Jesus. Only Matthew begins with the genealogy and a shorter account of Jesus' childhood (chapters 1–2), but then has a relatively extensive account of the Baptist follow (chapter 3). Apparently, the earliest Christians already had the impression that despite all large, indeed growing, differences, despite all tensions between Baptist groups and the Jesus community, the Baptist and Jesus belonged inseparably together. John was the "forerunner" of Jesus. He is the actual "presupposition" (on this, see section 5.1) of the messianic movement that proceeded from Jesus. Accordingly, we must begin with him.

9.1 The Sources on John the Baptist and the Comparison of Their Contents

9.1.1 Josephus

Our only reports about the Baptist (and his disciples) that are to be taken seriously historically are found in the Gospels, Acts, and Josephus. The later accounts from the apocrypha—for example from the Gospel of the Hebrews or the Pseudo-Clementines—presuppose these reports.[2] This

---

[1] Bauer 1967b, 101–9; Wink 1968; Böcher 1988; Ernst 1989a; Backhaus 1991; Webb 1991; Rengstorf 1968 (GV = 1959); Oepke 1964 (GV = 1933); Meier 1994, 19–233; Tilly 1994; Theissen/Merz 1998, 196–213 (GV = 1997, 184–98); J. E. Taylor 1997; Dunn 2003b, 348–71. Cf. now also Allison 2010, 204–20.

[2] On this, see Bauer 1967b, 101–15.

means that we have no direct access to the Baptist tradition but only texts that interpret him from an early Christian perspective or from that of a Jewish-Hellenistic historian. Despite these fragmentary and "tendentious" reports, it is peculiar that the historicity of the Baptist has been questioned less than that of Jesus.

Josephus[3] reports about him in connection with the defeat of Herod Antipas in his battle against the Nabataean king Aretas IV in 36 CE. The people regarded this defeat as God's punishment for the execution of John the Baptist.[4] He is said to have been a "good man" (ἀγαθὸς ἀνήρ), who demanded from his compatriots "righteous behavior among one another and piety toward God" as a presupposition for the baptism performed by him.[5] This does not bring "forgiveness of sins" but serves only the "consecration of the body," after "the soul has previously been cleansed." Because the crowds flocked to him and were moved by his preaching, Herod feared his influence on the masses could lead to a rebellion (στά-σις). In order to forestall this, he had him captured, taken to the fortress of Machaerus in Peraea on the border with the Nabataean kingdom, and executed there.

Josephus differs from the New Testament reports in his censuring of the prophetic-apocalyptic character of the preaching of the Baptist in favor of its ethical content[6] and, even more so, in his emphasis on the tetrarch's fear of the Baptist's political influence upon the people, indeed of a revolt. However, the denial of the eschatological expectation which had such vibrancy in Jewish Palestine at the time, as well as the emphasis on the danger of political unrests, is a consistent tendency in his historical work. He views John from a perspective that the New Testament presentations supplement. What is conspicuous is his decisive rejection of the motif of the forgiveness of sins through John's baptism. Here he appears to oppose

---

[3] Josephus, *Ant.* 18.116–119.

[4] Josephus, *Ant.* 18.116: Ἰωάννου τοῦ ἐπικαλουμένου βαπτιστοῦ. The conspicuous byname occurs only in Josephus, Mark, Luke, and Matthew. See note 15 below. On Antipas, see section 3.1.2.

[5] Josephus, *Ant.* 18.117: βαπτισμός. In the New Testament it occurs in the plural for ritual purification in Mark 7.4; Heb 9.10; only in Heb 6.2 could the atypical plural point to baptism. Otherwise we consistently find βάπτισμα in early Christian linguistic usage; see note 88 in chapter 10.

[6] Josephus knows, of course, about the eschatological expectation. Indeed, he probably shared it in a moderated version; see *Ant.* 4.114–117: the Balaam oracle; 10.276–277, 280: the prophecy of Daniel and in general the high estimation of the book of Daniel; *J.W.* 6.312–313: messianic prophecies and on this, Hengel 1989c, 237ff. (GV = 1976c, 243ff.). He could, however, not write openly about it in Rome. He related the prophecy that is said to have sparked off the Jewish War as χρησμὸς ἀμφίβολος to Vespasian. On this, see section 3.1.7.

opinions that he probably heard in Rome, where he writes. In this case the concern could be with Christian baptism or with an interpretation of the baptism of John by Baptists.[7] After all, the earliest extant account of the Baptist, i.e., the account of the Gospel of Mark, emerged shortly before 70 in Rome, and the Fourth Sibyl, which was composed in Italy soon after the eruption of Vesuvius in 79 CE, speaks, likewise in an eschatological context, of a purification of the body "in ever flowing rivers," in connection with a call to repentance, prayer of repentance, forgiveness of sins, and impending judgment of fire.[8]

On fundamental points, however, the report of Josephus agrees with the primitive Christian sources. This applies to the uncommon byname "the Baptist," ὁ βαπτιστής — a word that surfaces for the first time in the Gospels and in Josephus and points to a fundamental difference between the baptism of John and the daily immersion baths for ritual purification in Judaism, which were performed by the individuals themselves.[9] The agreement also involves his ethical preaching and the fact that the baptism is meant to be accepted by God,[10] the mass movement triggered by him, the high estimation of him among the people, and the execution by Herod Antipas on account of political fears. Thus, the note on the Baptist of the Jewish priest from Jerusalem, who was an imperial freedman in Rome and contemporary witness, has "no less of a claim to historical appreciation than the biblical reports."[11]

---

[7] Cf. Mark 1.4 = Luke 3.3; Acts 2.38; Rom 6.3, etc.

[8] Cf. Mark 1.4; 4 Sib 165–168. On the dating of the Fourth Sibyl, cf. the eruption of Vesuvius in 79 CE and the expectation of Nero *redivivus* in 4 Sib 130–140. On this, see Lichtenberger 1987, 39–40. The criticism of Backhaus 1991, 305–6, is scarcely understandable. The eschatological reference does point to a singular event, the Christian influence in the Fourth Sibyl that he postulates is unlikely on chronological grounds, and nothing points to a Christian interpolation. Jewish proselyte baptism was not yet common practice around 79 CE. It is first attested in the Mishnah. On the later wandering of the adherent of a Baptist sect, which combines forgiveness of sins and baptism, to Rome and his propaganda there, see Alcibiades at the beginning of the third century CE apud Hippolytus, *Haer.* 3.13.1–6. He appealed to an older Elkesaitic revelation from the third year of Trajan (100/101 CE). Cf. also Tacitus, *Ann.* 15.44.3 (trans. Woodman 2004): Rome as the place *quo cuncta undique atrocia aut pudenda confluent celebranturque* ("where everything frightful or shameful, of whatever provence, converges and is celebrated"); or Juvenal, *Sat.* 3.62: *iam pridem Syrus in Tiberim defluxit Orontes* ("for a long time already the Syrian Orontes has flowed into the Tiber").

[9] On this, see section 9.3.

[10] Josephus, *Ant.* 18.117: καὶ τὴν βάπτισιν ἀποδεκτὴν αὐτῷ (scil.θεῷ) φανεῖσθαι.

[11] Backhaus 1991, 268. Josephus was born around 37/38 CE and finished his *Jewish Antiquities* around 93/94 CE.

9.1.2 The Gospels and the Baptist

9.1.2.1 Mark

The earliest and shortest reference to the Baptist that we possess is from Mark, right before 70 CE. For him the Baptist's activity and the baptism of Jesus are the "beginning of the gospel of Jesus Christ, the Son of God,"[12] which means that John and his activity already belong in the gospel as its ἀρχή. The scriptural quotation that follows the opening sentence[13] is meant to prove that the eschatological fulfillment of the prophetic promises in Jesus Christ (1.1) has already begun with the activity of John the Baptist as the last prophet.[14] He is identical with the "messenger," who is "to prepare the way of the Lord," and the "voice of one who calls in the wilderness" announced by Isaiah is the voice of the Baptist,[15] who appears in "the wilderness," i.e., the desert of the lower Jordan Valley, and proclaims there—with this the decisive key phrase occurs—the "baptism of repentance for the forgiveness of sins."[16]

There follows the—exaggerated—portrayal of the success of his baptism proclamation: "all Judaea and all the inhabitants of Jerusalem went out to him, let themselves be baptized by him in the Jordan, and confessed their sins" (Mark 1.5). After this fundamental information and a short reference to his conspicuous clothing and uncommon diet,[17] Mark immediately turns to the Baptist's "messianic proclamation" about the stronger one, who comes after him,[18] and thus paves the way for the baptism of "Jesus from Nazareth in Galilee," which immediately follows.[19]

---

[12] Mark 1.1: Ἀρχὴ τοῦ εὐαγγελίου Ἰησοῦ Χριστοῦ. . . . On this, see Hengel 2008c, 281–83 and 363 index to Mark 1.1 (ET = 2000b, 172–74 and 328 index to Mark 1.1); Klauck 1997. On this, cf. the two occurrences of ἀρξάμενος in Acts 1.22; 10.37 and the detailed description in a Lukan sermon of Paul in Acts 13.24-25.

[13] Mark 1.2-3 from Mal 3.1; Exod 23.20; Isa 40.3 LXX. Mark erroneously ascribes the whole quotation to Isaiah. Luke produces the Isaiah quotation in expanded form. Matthew shortens it and thereby corrects it.

[14] Mark 9.11-12 = Matt 17.10-11; Luke 16.16; Matt 11.12ff., cf. Mark 11.32 parr.

[15] Mark 1.4: ὁ βαπτίζων: substantival participle; cf. 6.14, 24. In 6.25 and 8.28 Mark has βαπτιστής, which is what Matthew and Luke consistently use. John avoids the substantive. In the Gospel of John the Baptist no longer has any "title" of his own. He is—like the evangelist (John 19.35; 21.24)—only a "witness" to Jesus: 1.6-8, 15, 19-34.

[16] Mark 1.4: κηρύσσων βάπτισμα μετανοίας εἰς ἄφεσιν ἁμαρτιῶν. Luke 3.3 takes over the formula in its entirety. Matthew omits "for the forgiveness of sins"; on this, see note 103 below.

[17] Mark 1.6; see note 123 below.

[18] Mark 1.7-8; see section 9.1.2.2.

[19] Mark 1.9-11; see chapter 10.

Beyond this, Mark has only a few pointers. In 1.14 he stresses that Jesus appeared publicly and preached the "gospel of God" only after the "handing over" of the Baptist, i.e., after he was taken into custody by Herod Antipas. The forerunner must make room for the fulfiller. The execution of the Baptist is recounted later in the style of a dramatic oriental court history or history of intrigue.[20] In this way Mark fills the gap between the sending out of the disciples by Jesus and their return.[21] In the descent from the mountain of transfiguration in Mark 9.11-13 Jesus then designates the Baptist as "Elijah *redivivus*" and as forerunner with respect to his own way of suffering. In the final confrontation in Jerusalem, Jesus reacts to the highest Jewish authorities' question about his authority in the "temple cleansing" with a counterquestion about the origin of "the baptism of John," whether it was based on God's command or human caprice. The leaders of the people evade the question because they fear the negative reaction of the crowd, "who all regarded John really as a prophet."[22] Together with the double pointer that the people in Galilee regarded Jesus, after the violent death of the Baptist, among other options, also as John the Baptist raised from the dead,[23] these reports are an indication of how close Mark regarded the connection between the Baptist movement and the Jesus movement. This must already go back to the primitive community, indeed, we can assume that Jesus himself already pointed to this positive connection. The later distance, which becomes apparent especially in Matthew and John,[24] is still lacking in Mark. Only the question of the disciples of the Baptist and of the Pharisees about why the disciples of Jesus, in contrast to them, do not fast[25]—which Jesus answers with the reference to the messianic festive joy over the presence of the bridegroom—points to something fundamentally new,[26] which Jesus brings and which may not be mixed with the old without harm. His answer basically corresponds to the announcement of the Messiah–Son of Man as the coming "stronger one" by John himself.[27]

---

[20] Mark 6.17-29 = Matt 14.3-12.

[21] Mark 6.6b-13 and 30-31.

[22] Mark 11.27-33 = Luke 20.1-8 = Matt 21.23-27. Luke and Matthew have multiple "minor agreements" against Mark, which show that Matthew also looked at Luke (see section 6.4.2).

[23] In Mark 6.14-16 this belief is also attributed to Herod himself. In v. 15 it is a widespread view in general, as in v. 14b: ἔλεγον "people were saying"; cf. 8.28.

[24] See the discussion of this point in sections 9.1.2.2, 9.1.2.3, and 10.1.

[25] Mark 2.18-20 = Luke 5.33-35 = Matt 9.14-15.

[26] See the drastic parable about the opposition between old and new that follows in Mark 2.21-22 parr.

[27] Mark 1.7-8 parr.

9.1.2.2 Luke and Matthew

In Luke we find additional information about the Baptist. Thus, he is the only one who provides information about the family background of John in his prehistory, where he connects the birth of the Baptist closely to Jesus, who is about the same age, in chapter 1. His parents are a priestly couple. The father, Zechariah, comes from the division of Abijah, the eighth of the twenty-four priestly classes, which respectively served in the temple for a week each year, with their functions being determined daily[28] by the drawing of lots.[29] His father is in the process of carrying out the incense offering in the temple when the messenger of God Gabriel announces the miracle of the birth of a son.[30]

His mother Elisabeth is also said to be of Aaronite descent. The place of origin of the Baptist was in the Judaean hill country; Jerusalem was primarily reserved for the leading priestly families.[31] Luke's legendary story of John's birth, like the story about his death in Mark, probably goes back to Baptist tradition and was presumably mediated to Luke by Jewish Christians. Here we must assume that after the death of the Baptist at least a part of the Baptist movement attached itself to Jesus or to the post-Easter community. This attachment is a presupposition for the preservation of traditions about the Baptist and of the positive picture of the Baptist in the primitive community. Like the entire prehistory in general, the story of John's birth was massively shaped by the evangelist, who shows himself to be a gifted storyteller here. Nevertheless, it contains features that ascribe a value of his own to the Baptist, which hardly go back to Christian tradition, for example, that from the womb onward he was a bearer of the Spirit and Nazarite,[32] and that he himself, "in the spirit and power of Elijah," prepares for the coming of God.[33] The concluding statement, "and

---

[28] Luke 1.5; cf. 1 Chr 24.7-19 (10); Neh 12.4, 17, see Bill. II: 54–68; on the drawing of lots, see 57ff.; on the carrying out of the incense offering, which was held in special esteem, see 71ff.; on the legends about the visions in the temple, see Schwemer 1995/1996, II: 308–15. The list of these priestly divisions and the calendar of their obligations of service play a large role in Qumran; see note 166 in chapter 4.

[29] Luke 1.9: κατὰ τὰ ἔθος τῆς ἱερατείας ἔλαχε τοῦ θυμᾶσαι. On the drawing of lots for the priestly functions and the priestly classes, see Bill. II: 57ff., and on the incense offering, see 71–77. Luke is astonishingly well informed about the procedures in the temple. Cf. Acts 1.26 on the decision by lot as the verdict of God in the election of Matthias.

[30] Luke 1.5ff.: Zechariah and John are common priestly names.

[31] Luke 1.65: ἐν ὅλῃ τῇ ὀρεινῇ τῆς Ἰουδαίας; cf. 39: Mary, the mother of Jesus, visits her relative Elisabeth there; see note 54 in chapter 8.

[32] Luke 1.15; cf. 7.33 parr. and 1.44.

[33] Luke 1.16-17; cf. Mal 3.23-24; Sir 48.10. Between 9.36 and 9.37 Luke omits the direct identification of the Baptist with the Elijah *redivivus* in Mark 9.11-13 = Matt 17.10-13

he was in the wilderness until the day of his commission for Israel," Luke 1.80, makes a bridge to the historical specification of time and the appearance of the Baptist in 3.1ff., which is portrayed in prophetic style.[34] Here we should not read in the idea that John stayed with the Essenes of Qumran in the wilderness on the Dead Sea after the early death of his parents.[35] What is fundamental is the fact that Luke, who begins his narrative with a revelation in the temple, has the account end with the stay of the hero in the wilderness. This refers to the quotation from Isa 40.3-5 in Luke 3.4ff. and points at the same time to a far-reaching change. The son of a priest, who is actually destined for service in the temple, turns to a new eschatological service in the wilderness, which is oriented to the future.[36]

Luke and Matthew introduce in almost identical wording a striking example of the Baptist's preaching of repentance in the form of a prophetic reproach, which threatens not the surrounding Gentiles but rather Israel with judgment:[37] "Brood of vipers! Who has given you the assurance that you could escape the coming judgment?" Only "true fruits of repentance" can still save. Trust in descent from Abraham is self-deception. "The axe is already laid at the roots of the trees"; it can strike at any moment.[38] "Whoever does not produce fruit is cut down and thrown into the fire." The impending judgment is a judgment of destruction. The threat of judgment common to Luke and Matthew is usually ascribed to the hypothetical source Q. Since every demonstrable narrative context is lacking here

---

(cf. Matt 11.14) and reduces it to the promise of the angel in Luke 1.17. By contrast, John 1.25 denies any connection. In comparison with Luke 1.13-17 the Benedictus more likely reflects a Christian influence; cf. 1.67-69, especially if in v. 78 the future ἐπισκέψεται is to be read with the most important ancient witnesses instead of the aorist ἐπεσκέψατο. On this, see Mittmann-Richert 1996, 46–47 and elsewhere.

[34] Cf. Jer 1.1 LXX and elsewhere. See note 1 in chapter 1.

[35] The main establishment of the Essenes was, after all, not in Qumran—the physical structures there are much too small. Rather, they lived in communities in the larger cities of Judaea, which probably means not least in Jerusalem itself: Josephus, *J.W.* 2.124; Philo, *Hypoth.* 11.1 (Eusebius, *Praep. ev.* 8.11.1). In *Prob.* 76 Philo suggests that they lived in communities at the outskirts of cities, separated from the corrupt world; see also 1QS VIII 13–16. John taught orally; scribal activity and scriptural study are not mentioned anywhere. They had central importance for the Essenes.

[36] The quotation of Isa 40.3-5 in Luke 3.4ff. (cf. Mark 1.3 = Matt 3.3 and Luke 7.27 = Matt 11.10), which characterizes the Baptist as "one who calls in the wilderness," has an entirely different meaning than in 1QS VIII 14–15, where it is related to the members of the Essene community, who are exhorted: "In the wilderness prepare the way of the Lord," which is then related again to the "study of the Torah" of Moses.

[37] Luke 3.7-9 = Matt 3.7-10. We could also translate this phrase with "devil's brood"; see Gen 3.1, 13; Rev 12.9, 15; 20.2.

[38] This means that the basis also is destroyed, cf. Ezek 17.9; Mal 3.19; Hos 9.16; Amos 2.9. The roots can no longer sprout anew as in Isa 6.13; 11.1; Job 14.7-8. We owe this reference to F. Neugebauer.

for Q[39] and Luke certainly has the more original version, we must assume that Matthew is dependent upon Luke here, but has changed the introduction. While according to Luke, in correspondence with the context, the crowd that seeks to be baptized by John is addressed by him as "brood of vipers," Matthew reduces the addressee to the leaders of the people, the "Pharisees and Sadducees." They are addressed and not the people who seek to be baptized. In order to establish a closer connection between the proclamation of the Baptist and Jesus, Matthew places this sharp address of the Baptist two more times in the mouth of Jesus, once against the Pharisees and scribes and once against the Pharisees, who accuse him of being in league with Beelzebul.[40] This means that for Matthew the enemies of Jesus are already those of the Baptist, and his proclamation of judgment corresponds to that of Jesus. Matthew also places the saying about the tree without fruit that is cut down in the Sermon on the Mount.[41] Conversely, he already puts the summary of the message of Jesus in the mouth of John the Baptist: "Repent, for the kingdom of heaven is near."[42] Thus, for Matthew the Baptist's preaching of repentance is identical in substance with that of Jesus; a fundamental difference emerges only in the turning of salvation, the "forgiveness of sins."[43]

By contrast, in Luke we also find as special material concrete ethical admonitions, which answer the alarmed question of the hearers "what should we do?": "Let the one who has two tunics give to the one who has none, and let the one who has food do the same." Tax collectors, toll collectors, and even soldiers—here the soldiers of the Jewish tetrarchs Antipas and Philip would have to be in view—receive practical instructions in response to their questions.[44] These have a counterpart in the ethical preaching of the Baptist in Josephus. The evil is sought not in foreign rule; it is one's own interpersonal behavior that must be changed!

Luke returns to the Baptist later in the large discourse of Jesus about the Baptist. "The people *and the tax collectors* acknowledged God to be just and let themselves be baptized by John" in contrast to the Pharisees

---

[39] The Critical Edition of Q (Robinson/Hoffmann/Kloppenborg 2000, 4–21) shows no verifiable meaningful connection of this entirely hypothetical source. Matthew 3.5 probably took over the formula ἡ περίχωρος (τοῦ Ἰορδάνου) from Luke 3.3. Luke has the saying multiple times: 4.14, 37; 7.17; 8.37; Acts 14.6; Matthew has it only once more: 14.35; cf. also Mark 1.28. Matthew is dependent on Luke here.

[40] Matthew 23.33; 12.34.

[41] Matthew 7.19.

[42] Matthew 3.2 and Jesus in 4.17; cf. Mark 1.15.

[43] See notes 49–50 below.

[44] Luke 3.10-14. On the question of the hearers, cf. Acts 2.37; 16.30; 22.10: Lukan stylization.

and scribes.[45] Matthew, who found the tax collector motif in connection with the Baptist twice in Luke,[46] did not want to pass over it entirely and thus later adds to Jesus' question about the origin of the baptism of John the parable of the two sons with the conclusion: "The tax collectors and prostitutes," in contrast to the Jerusalem authorities, will receive access to the kingdom of God, for they believed John, who preached "the way of righteousness," while the leaders of the people, although they had sought him out,[47] refused to obey him.[48]

For Matthew the Baptist's preaching of repentance and Jesus' announcement of the kingdom of God lie very close to each other. Both teach the "way of righteousness." However, with respect to the dignity of Christ and the salvation brought by him, the difference is clear. While Mark and Luke report without misgivings that John proclaimed the "baptism of repentance *for the forgiveness of sins*,"[49] Matthew omits this decisive sentence, moves the phrase "for the forgiveness of sins" to his account of the Last Supper, and thus supplements the saying about the cup of his Markan *Vorlage*.[50] While John, like Jesus, proclaims the impending dawning of the kingdom of God understood as judgment and calls for repentance,[51] he cannot bring the actual salvation, which resides in the forgiveness of sins. This is only mediated through Christ's death and Christian baptism with the trinitarian formula.[52] For Matthew the Baptist proclaims only an immersion in the Jordan and the confession of sins as a sign of repentance.[53]

---

[45] Luke 7.29-30: ἐδικαίωσαν τὸν θεόν; the two verses are presumably formulated by Luke. He uses the verb δικαιόω six more times, ἀθετέω five times, and the noun βουλή ten times.

[46] Luke 3.12-13; 7.29.

[47] Matthew 21.32: ὑμεῖς δὲ ἰδόντες . . . ; cf. 3.7 about the Baptist: Ἰδὼν δὲ πολλοὺς τῶν Φαρισαίων καὶ Σαδδουκαίων.

[48] Matthew 21.28-32. The whole is probably formulated by Matthew and probably also presupposes knowledge of Luke 15.11-32; 7.29-30; and 7.39.

[49] Mark 1.4 = Luke 3.3; see note 16 above. In 3.6 Matthew speaks only with Mark 1.5 of a confession of sin by the people. Luke omits this motif, but introduces it in the Benedictus (1.77) and in the sending by the risen one in 24.47; cf. Acts 2.38; 5.31; 10.43; 13.38; 26.18: the servant of God brings forgiveness of sins; see Mittmann-Richert 2008.

[50] Matthew 26.28: τὸ περὶ πολλῶν ἐκχυννόμενον εἰς ἄφεσιν ἁμαρτιῶν. Cf., by contrast, Mark 14.24: τὸ ἐκχυννόμενον ὑπὲρ πολλῶν.

[51] Matt 3.2; cf. 4.17 and Mark 1.15.

[52] Cf. the command to baptize in Matt 28.19-20, which is unique in the Gospels, and the soteriological interpretation of the name of Jesus in 1.21: αὐτὸς γὰρ σώσει τὸν λαὸν αὐτοῦ ἀπὸ τῶν ἁμαρτιῶν αὐτῶν.

[53] Matthew 3.11: βαπτίζω ἐν ὕδατι εἰς μετάνοιαν is a qualifying addition to his Lukan *Vorlage* (Luke 3.16).

His activity is meant to effectively prepare for the salvation that Jesus first brings because he alone "can fulfill all righteousness."[54]

Between admonition and reference to the coming judge Luke inserts a reaction of the people in 3.15-16, which Matthew cannot take over, because he has placed his focus on the opponents of Jesus. Full of expectation, the crowd considers whether John could not be the Messiah. At the time when Luke wrote his Gospel—ca. 75–80 CE—Baptist circles may have regarded John as a messianic figure.[55] Vis-à-vis this misunderstanding, the Baptist points to the coming stronger one, in relation to whom he is not worthy to loosen the strap of his sandals, i.e., to perform the lowest service of a slave.[56] This disjunction has its counterpart in the fundamental difference between John and the presence of the messianic fulfillment in Jesus' activity according to Jesus' speech about the Baptist.[57]

The stronger one baptizes not with water but "with the Holy Spirit and fire." Here, the phrase "with the Holy Spirit" may be an inserted *interpretatio christiana*,[58] for the "fire baptism" probably originally meant the judgment of fire already announced by the prophets, which the coming stronger one will carry out according to John. As the farmer on the threshing floor with his winnowing fork separates the wheat from the chaff, which is burned,[59] he will make a separation among the people. The judge brings the truth and deception of their life to light. The motif of the fire of judgment, which appears in Luke only in the preaching of the Baptist, is then put into the mouth of Jesus in various ways in Matthew. Starting from the preaching of the Baptist it becomes typical for Matthew's theology of judgment, which understands this as "eternal fire (of punishment)."[60]

---

[54] Matthew 3.15; cf. 5.6, 10, 17, 20, and on this, Deines 2004 passim.

[55] Ca. two decades later, in John 1.19-27, the Baptist explicitly rejects such claims vis-à-vis a delegation from Jerusalem. See section 9.1.2.3. Cf. also Ps.-Clem. Rec. 1.60.1: *unus ex discipulis Iohannis adfirmabat Christum Iohannem fuisse et non Iesum* ("one of the disciples of John affirmed that the Messiah was John and not Jesus"); cf. 1.54.8.

[56] Luke 3.16, partly taken over from Mark 1.7. Matthew 3.11 speaks somewhat more reservedly of the mere removal or carrying away (βαστάζειν) of the sandals. His less drastic version is not original and not an indication of the existence of Q. Between Matt 3.7-10 and 11 there is also a break in the addressees. The two occurrences of ὑμᾶς in v. 11 refer no longer to the leaders of the people but to the people. They let themselves be baptized. This means that the later Matthew is thematically dependent here upon the older Lukan version.

[57] Luke 7.28 = Matt 11.11; on this, see section 10.8.

[58] On this, see Acts 2.38; 11.16; cf. 10.44-46; 19.2-6. On the relationship between baptism and Spirit in the primitive community, see Avemarie 2002b.

[59] Luke 3.17 = Matt 3.12; cf. Luke 3.9 = Matt 3.10.

[60] Matthew 5.22; 7.19 = 3.10; 13.40ff., 50; 18.8-9 and 25.41: τὸ πῦρ τὸ αἰώνιον; cf. Mark 9.43: τὸ πῦρ τὸ ἄσβεστον; cf. the preaching of the Baptist in Mark 3.12 = Luke 3.17 and John 15.6. The fire (Luke 12.49) refers not to the fire of judgment but to the entire

The judge announced by the Baptist cannot be God himself. The picture of the loosening of the sandals would fit just as little here as the comparative "the stronger one" and the talk of his "coming after him." God is incommensurable and does not wear sandals. Rather, the concern must be with his authorized one, the coming Son of Man–Messiah,[61] who carries out the judgment as God's representative but is at the same time a salvific figure as the savior of the pious. This suggests the conclusion that the Baptist really understood himself as "forerunner" of the Son of Man–Messiah and that the primitive Christian interpretation of his person as Elijah *redivivus* can indeed go back to John himself.[62] With this the question of the claim of Jesus also becomes pressing, because Jesus appears after him, knows himself to be very closely connected with John, and yet distinguishes himself fundamentally from him. The function of the Baptist becomes comprehensible only through the question of his relation to Jesus, and, conversely, the Baptist already casts a light on Jesus' messianic claim.

9.1.2.3 John

The Fourth Gospel presupposes knowledge of Mark and Luke,[63] but contradicts them at decisive points, for the Baptist no longer has an independent function for John. According to his statements to the Jewish authorities who interrogate him, he is neither Elijah nor the eschatological prophet of Deut 18.15.[64] Rather, he is sent by God[65] only to be active as the *first witness* to Christ, the incarnate Son of God, "who comes after him" and yet "was before him."[66] Even his baptizing activity serves only to point to Christ, the Spirit-baptizer. It is two disciples of the Baptist who through

---

messianic activity of Jesus under the banner of the kingdom of God; see section 17.3.1. On this, see Lang 1969, 936ff., 942-44 (GV = 1959, 935ff., 941).

[61] Cf. Dan 7.13-14; on the Son of Man, see section 17.4.1; Luke 1.17 (on this, see note 33 above).

[62] Mark 9.11-13 = Matt 17.10-12; Matt 11.4. Cf. Mal 3.19-20, 22; Sir 48.10. The location of his baptism at the Jordan, whence Elijah was taken up in a fiery chariot, and his clothing also speak for this. Cf. Schwemer 1995/1996, II: 245–46; Öhler 1997, 31–110, comes to the following conclusion (107): "John the Baptist (understood) his activity as fulfillment of the Elijah promise." See note 13 above and note 119 below.

[63] Cf. John 1.26-27 = Mark 1.7-8 and Luke 3.16. Without knowledge of the Synoptic Baptist tradition the account of the Fourth Gospel becomes incomprehensible.

[64] John 1.19-20; 3.28.

[65] John 1.6; 3.28: ὅτι ἀπεσταλμένος εἰμὶ ἔμπροσθεν ἐκείνου; cf. Mark 1.2; Exod 23.20; Mal 3.1 and Luke 7.27 = Matt 11.10.

[66] See the accumulation of the key words μαρτυρία and μαρτυρεῖν in John 1.7, 15, 19, 32, 34; 3.26, 32, 33; cf. 5.33, 36ff.: Jesus has, however, a greater witness than that of John, namely the witness of his Father. On the ὀπίσω μου ἐρχόμενος, see 1.15, 27, 30; it is dependent on Mark 1.7 = Matt 3.11.

his witness become the first followers of Jesus.[67] And yet his account does contain pointers that are worthy of consideration historically.

He informs us geographically about places where John baptized: "in Bethany, beyond the Jordan," that is, in Peraea on the east side of the Jordan, which belonged to Herod Antipas' sphere of rule.[68] Since this place was no longer identifiable for Origen, he advocated the reading Bethabara.[69] In addition, there appears an "Aenon near Salem," whose location is uncertain.[70]

The Fourth Gospel contradicts the Synoptics with respect to the temporal relationship between the arrest of John and the beginning of Jesus' public activity. According to Mark and Luke, Jesus is active in Galilee only after the arrest of the Baptist.[71] According to John, the activities of the two overlap temporally. Jesus draws disciples to him as the Messiah testified to by John and performs miracles, indeed, he baptizes, namely in Judaea, and he is more successful therein than the Baptist.[72] John 3.24 corrects the Synoptics explicitly: "John was not yet thrown into prison." Correspondingly, the chronology is also expanded. At least three Passover festivals occur in the activity of Jesus, i.e., it lasts for more than two years.[73]

From this some have drawn the inference that Jesus himself was originally a disciple of the Baptist and then appeared as a competitor to the Baptist, but then abandoned his baptizing activity after the Baptist's arrest.

---

[67] John 1.33-37, for "he must increase but I must decrease" (3.30).

[68] John 1.28; cf. 10.40.

[69] Thus a series of later manuscripts. Bethabara lies on the western shore of the Jordan ca. six kilometers north of the mouth and is certainly incorrect. The location of Bethany on the Jordan is unknown. On the traditions about the place of the baptism, cf. Keel/Küchler/Uehlinger 1982, 527–31; Meier 1994, 88–89 n. 123.

[70] John 3.23: the later localization to the south of Scythopolis on the border with Samaria and not directly at the Jordan is hardly accurate. Perhaps a symbolic meaning also lies behind the place-names: "source" and "salvation." John has a whole series of interesting historical and geographical details relating to Jewish Palestine at the time of Jesus, which we do not find in this way in the other Gospels; see Hengel 1999b, 293–334.

[71] Mark 1.14 = Matt 4.12; in 3.19-20 Luke places this communication as the concluding point after his account of the proclamation of the Baptist still prior to the baptism of Jesus.

[72] John 3.22, 26; 4.1: βαπτίζει. This is corrected in 4.2: "not Jesus himself but his disciples baptize." The latter could be a correcting addition or a very old gloss; the textual tradition, however, is flawless. In Acts 10.48 Peter also has the baptism of Cornelius performed by coworkers. Paul baptizes himself only rarely: 1 Cor 1.14-17. In the case of huge crowds, the Baptist probably already baptized with the help of his disciples in some cases; see note 103 below.

[73] John 2.13, 23; 6.4; 11.55; 12.1; 13.1 and elsewhere. The church fathers reckoned with two to four years. See note 6 in chapter 11.

Such speculations remain uncertain.[74] The narrative of the Fourth Gospel has in view later tensions between the Palestinian community and the disciples of the Baptist. The Johannine Baptist, in relation to his disciples, grants absolute priority to Jesus as the true bringer of salvation, "who comes from above": "He must increase, but I must decrease."[75] The Johannine interpretation of the Baptist thus contradicts the account in Luke (and Matthew) of the Baptist's doubting question to Jesus from prison about whether he is the "coming one."[76] For the Gospel of John, as a witness to Jesus' sending and dignity, the Baptist can no longer show any uncertainty. On the one hand, it is indeed possible that Jesus appeared on the scene already some time before the arrest of the Baptist, though presumably not in "Judaea" (John 3.22) but rather in Galilee. By contrast, it is unlikely that he was first a "disciple" of the Baptist in the strict sense for an extended period of time and then became his "rival." If this were the case, traces of a break between teacher and student would have had to become visible. This, however, is not the case in the oldest sources, i.e., Mark and the Lukan special material. By contrast, in John the tensions with the later Baptist community are evident.[77]

According to John 1.35-40, the witness of the Baptist led the first disciples to Jesus, namely an unknown figure[78] and Andrew, who bears witness to the Messiah Jesus to his brother Simon and brings him to Jesus.[79] Here it is not, as in the Synoptics, fishermen on the shore of the Lake of Gennesaret who are called away from their work into discipleship; rather, disciples of the Baptist find their way to the Messiah through their master.

Obviously, there is no question that Jesus was deeply impressed by the message and person of the Baptist. Otherwise, he would not have let himself be baptized by him or spoken so positively about him later. Moreover, the close connection between Baptist movement and Jesus movement is firmly anchored in the tradition. Accordingly, it is probable that adherents of the closest circle of disciples were initially close to the Baptist. The information about the calling of the disciples by Jesus himself in the

---

[74] "Call and calling seize him in the sphere of the Baptist but not as though he were chosen by the Baptist": Neugebauer 1986, 3.

[75] John 3.30. Cf. the reserved appraisal of him by Jesus as mere "burning oil lamp" in 5.35; cf. 1.8.

[76] Luke 7.18ff. = Matt 11.2ff.: here too Matthew appears largely dependent on Luke.

[77] John 3.22-27; the picture in the answer of the Baptist in 3.29 probably alludes to Mark 2.19; on this, see Hengel 2000a, 260–63. Mark 2.18-19 and Luke 7.33-34 = Matt 11.18-19 indicate a difference but not a break.

[78] John 1.37ff.: this anonymous figure is probably meant to point already to the anonymous Beloved Disciple; cf. also 18.15; on this, see Hengel 1993a, 216, 313ff. (ET = 1989a, 78–79, 124ff.).

[79] John 1.40-42. See section 11.5 on the calling of the disciples.

Synoptics and the account of John cannot, however, be reconciled in a harmonizing way. The Fourth Gospel has configured his tradition too much on the basis of his christological interest for one to be able to reconstruct the original events from his consciously deviating account.

What must be upheld, however, is the paramount importance of the Baptist and the movement that proceeded from him not only for the primitive community but already for the closest circle of disciples and for Jesus himself. This becomes evident in the fact that the baptism "in the name of Jesus" for the forgiveness of sins, which was quickly introduced after Easter by the primitive community as a rite of initiation, is directly dependent on the baptism of John. Thus, it is plausible that initial contacts between Jesus and leading members of his later circle of Twelve already took place in the environment of the Baptist.

9.2 The Death of the Baptist

John no longer recounts the death of the Baptist. He presupposes it and is content to hint at it.[80] Luke, the historian, gives more precise information. He concludes his account (3.19-20) prior to the narrative of the baptism of Jesus: The tetrarch[81] Herod has the Baptist imprisoned because John had criticized him because of his marriage "with Herodias, the wife of his brother and because of all his (other) evil deeds."[82] Later the miraculous activity of Jesus brings the ruler into terrors of conscience,[83] since some claimed that the Baptist, whom he had caused to be beheaded, had risen from the dead.[84] The consequence is that he desires to see this miracle worker, which occurs according to Luke in the passion story.[85] For the

---

[80] Thus in the combination of John 3.24, 30: "John was not yet thrown into prison" and "He must increase but I must decrease." See also 5.35: "He was a burning oil lamp" (but this has gone out); cf. 1.8.

[81] Only Luke speaks multiple times in a historically correct manner of "tetrarchs," a title that Augustus had given the sons of Herod because he wanted to avoid the title of king (see section 3.1.1 with note 167): Luke 3.1, 19; 9.7; Acts 13.1. Mark 6.14 calls Herod in a popular manner βασιλεύς. In the parallel in Matt 14.1 the title was presumably taken over from Luke 9.7, for in the following narrative Matthew, following Mark, inconsistently calls Herod βασιλεύς: Matt 14.9 = Mark 6.22, 25-26.

[82] Luke 3.19-20; cf. Mark 6.17-18 = Matt 14.3-4. Following Mark, Luke 9.9 concisely recounts the beheading of John as a self-incrimination of Herod in one sentence.

[83] Cf. Luke 9.7: διηπόρει; cf. Mark 6.20.

[84] Mark 6.14-16; Luke 9.7-9.

[85] Luke 23.6-12; cf. 13.31-32. Luke has more to report about Herod Antipas than do the other evangelists, including valuable individual traditions: Luke 3.1, 19; 8.3; 13.31: He seeks also to kill Jesus, see section 11.3; Acts 13.1. On the passion story, see the conspicuous special tradition in 23.7-12, 15. Ignatius, *To the Smyrneans* 1.2 brings together Pontius Pilate and the tetrarch Herod (Luke 3.1; 23.7ff.) with respect to the crucifixion of Jesus. He

first 'Christian historian,' with this all that is necessary has been said. In 3.21-22 the narrative thread is immediately led back again to Jesus and his baptism. In the work that is dedicated to the illustrious Theophilus, there is no room for the gruesome oriental court intrigue that leads to the beheading of the Baptist.

Already in Mark, who recounts his death in dramatic detail, it appears as a foreign body, and he has trouble incorporating it into his Gospel in a sensible way.[86] Matthew therefore rigorously shortens the account and joins it at the end with Jesus by having the disciples of the Baptist come to Jesus after the burial of his corpse in order to tell him. Thus, they are led through the death of the Baptist to Jesus.[87] Both evangelists, Mark and Matthew, make the fate of the "Elijah *redivivus*" John a sign of Jesus' way of suffering.[88] In the Markan narrative John attacks Herod in the style of prophetic criticism because he has married Herodias, the wife of his brother Philip, in contravention of the commandment of the law: "It is not lawful for you to have the wife of your brother."[89] However, Herod fears this "just and holy man," whereas Herodias desires to kill him. At the birthday celebration of the tetrarch in the circle of his powerful ones, Herod, moved by the dance of the daughter of Herodias,[90] promises to fulfill any wish. She asks, at the prompting of her mother, for the head of John the Baptist, and Herod must reluctantly give the command to behead him.

To be sure, some discrepancies emerge from the comparison with the account of Josephus. Herodias,[91] a niece of Antipas, was not married to the tetrarch Philip, whose territory bordered Galilee to the west,[92] but

---

appears to have known the Gospel of Luke; cf. also Ign. *Smyrn.* 3.2. In Gos. Pet. 1–2 Herod has Jesus crucified; cf. Ascen. Isa. 11.19: The "sons of Israel" hand over Jesus "to the king" (= Herod Antipas) for crucifixion. On this, see Norelli 1995, 575–80.

[86] Mark 6.17-29 = Matt 14.3-12. With 14.2 Matthew builds on 11.2, where the imprisoned Baptist sends disciples to Jesus who ask him the Messiah question.

[87] Mark 6.14-29 fills with the account the gap between the sending out and the return of the disciples. While Herod gets rid of the Baptist Jesus' message is carried variously through the land. Matthew 14.1-12 has it follow upon the rejection of Jesus in Nazareth.

[88] Mark 9.12-13 and even more clearly Matt 17.11-13.

[89] Mark 6.18, cf. Lev 18.16; 20.21. Beyond this the concern is with a case of adultery. See also Nathan and David in 2 Sam 12.1-12. We could also refer to the relationship of Ahab and Jezebel to Elijah; 1 Kgs 18.16ff.; 19.1ff.

[90] We learn her name, Salome, only through Josephus, *Ant.* 18.136. According to him, she married the already aged tetrarch Philip, who died in 33/34 CE: *Ant.* 18.137; cf. 18.106–108. Mark has confused the family relationships.

[91] Herodias was daughter of Aristobulus (a half-brother of Herod Antipas), who was executed by Herod, and granddaughter of the Hasmonean Mariamne and sister of Agrippa I. See section 3.1.2 and the end of the present section.

[92] Cf. Luke 3.1; as a correction the 'historian' omits the name of Philip in 3.19 and speaks in a materially correct way only of "his brother."

rather to a half-brother of the tetrarch, who lived in Rome as a private person. The ambitious Herodias desired to become the wife of a ruler and ousted the first spouse of Antipas, a daughter of the Nabataean king Aretas IV, who, being indignant, returned to her father. This gave rise to strife between Antipas and Aretas, which led ca. seven or eight years later, after the death of Philip,[93] to war over his inheritance and to the defeat of Antipas, which the people viewed as God's punishment for the execution of the Baptist.[94]

According to Josephus, John was imprisoned and killed in the fortress of Machaerus on the southwestern border of Peraea, high above the Dead Sea. In the presentation of Mark the impression that one gets is rather that the birthday celebration of the tetrarch took place in Galilee, although no location is mentioned.[95] It is common to the accounts of Josephus and the Synoptics that the Baptist, after some time of imprisonment, was killed at the command of Antipas and that this was a consequence of his prophetic criticism—in Josephus because of his influence on the people, in the Synoptics because of his accusation against the tetrarch. Another shared feature is the *fear* of the ruler, though admittedly with different justifications. According to Josephus, he fears that a revolt will be sparked off by the Baptist's influence upon the people. According to Mark, "the king"—in contrast to Herodias, who desires to destroy the bothersome preacher of repentance—shies away from killing the man of God, who brings him into terrors of conscience, and reluctantly gives the command to execute him. According to Matthew, he fears the people, who regard John as a prophet.[96]

A peculiar agreement also emerges in the characterization of Herodias and Herod in Mark and Josephus. She is ambitious, strong-willed, and proud, whereas Herod is more of a wavering, weak character.[97] The

---

[93] Ca. 33/36 CE; see Josephus, *Ant.* 18.106–108 and section 3.1.2.

[94] Josephus, *Ant.* 18.110–111, 136, 148. Perhaps Paul's stay in Arabia (Gal 1.17) was ended by this war; cf. also 2 Cor 11.32-33; see Hengel/Schwemer 1998, 208ff. (ET = 1997, 127ff.).

[95] According to Mark 6.21, among others "the first men of Galilee" are gathered.

[96] Josephus, *Ant.* 18.118: δείσας Ἡρώδης. Mark 6.20: ἐφοβεῖτο τὸν Ἰωάννην, εἰδὼς αὐτὸν ἄνδρα δίκαιον καὶ ἅγιον; Matt 14.5: ἐφοβήθη τὸν ὄχλον. Matthew deletes the hesitation of the "king" and that he liked to hear John. In Matthew Herod also desires to kill the Baptist and not only Herodias. The motif of fear before the people surfaces again in similar formulations in the controversy dialogues in Jerusalem with a view to the Baptist and the preaching of Jesus: Mark 11.32 = Matt 21.26 = Luke 20.6; cf. Mark 12.12 = Matt 21.46 = Luke 20.19; Luke 22.2; cf. Mark 14.1–2 = Matt 26.5.

[97] Josephus, *Ant.* 18.110–111, 136, 240–255. She turns out to be a kindred sister of the no less ambitious Agrippa, whom Caligula appointed king and successor to Philip. Cf. Luke 7.24 = Matt 11.7, where Jesus characterizes Antipas as a "reed"; see section 8.1 with notes 22–23.

dramatic account in Mark is certainly not the work of the evangelist but rather comes from the popular Baptist tradition. It cannot be regarded as pure fiction.

9.3 On the History-of-Religions Background of John the Baptist

The figure of the Baptist does not fit very well in the picture of Palestinian Judaism prior to 70 CE with the temple, the priesthood, and the different "religious parties," as it is handed down to us, for example, in Josephus. His activity remains enigmatic in many respects. In him we see how fragmentary our knowledge about the time of the rule of the prefects and tetrarchs is. It is also peculiar that Josephus portrays him positively in contrast to other "charismatic" figures of that time, such as the Samaritan prophet Theudas or the unnamed Egyptian, who likewise sparked off mass movements and were killed.[98] This may be an indication that John, like Jesus, did not preach violent political revolution. On the other hand, there can be no doubt that the basic motivation for his activity was the expectation of the radical change that the impending dawning of the kingdom of God had to bring with it. Matthew is materially correct when he introduces John's proclamation with the statement that Mark and he himself put into the mouth of Jesus: "Repent, for the kingdom of God is near."[99] Even though Josephus—as in his historical work in general—almost completely censors the eschatological expectation of his people for apologetic and political reasons, the Baptist was, like almost no other, a proponent of such an expectation.

All the more conspicuous are his many *unique* characteristics. This applies, first, to the byname "the Baptist,"[100] ὁ βαπτίζων or ὁ βαπτιστής.[101] The immersion baths required by the law for the establishment of ritual purity had surpassing importance in the temple-oriented piety of the Judaism of that time in Eretz Israel. It had to be constantly repeated after every more serious ritual "defilement" and before every entry into the temple. For the priests serving in the temple—but also for the Essenes,

---

[98] The Samaritans: *Ant.* 18.85–87; Theudas: *Ant.* 20.97–98; cf. Acts 5.36; the Egyptian: *J.W.* 2.261–263; *Ant.* 20.169–172; cf. Acts 21.38. On the problem, see Hengel 1989c, 229–33 (GV = 1976c, 235–39). See section 3.15 and the excursus on eschatological prophets there.

[99] Matt 3.2; 4.17: Jesus; 10.7: the disciples, cf. Mark 1.15; Luke 10.9; see section 9.1.2.2. The perfect verb ἤγγικεν can also be translated in a present manner: "The kingdom of God is here"; thus probably in Mark 1.15; see note 11 in section 13.1.

[100] On Josephus, see note 4 in this chapter.

[101] On ὁ βαπτίζων, see especially Mark 1.4; 6.14; βαπτιστής: 6.25; 8.28; see note 15 above.

who had distanced themselves from the official temple—this occurred daily and many times when necessary. Each person had to perform this "immersion" for themselves. It was not tied to any liturgical form, and it required no "baptizer."[102] By contrast, the baptism proclaimed by John—like Christian baptism later—occurred only once and was tied to the presence of a second person, namely a baptizer. It cannot be derived from the later baptism of proselytes, for this was introduced into Judaism only in the decades after the end of the temple—presumably under Christian influence—and even in it there is no need for a "baptizer." It replaced only the first immersion bath proscribed for proselytes before the sacrifice in the temple. By contrast, Mark 1.5 makes clear that the baptism of John was connected with the person of the "Baptist": the many who came to him "were baptized *by him* in the Jordan, confessing their sins." The confession of sins is thus an expression of repentance (μετάνοια) and a presupposition of the forgiveness of sins.[103] We might hypothesize that after a collective confession of sin, the Baptist pronounced the forgiveness of sins of the persons baptized, which was sealed by an immersion in the water of the Jordan. That such a rite at the command of a prophet could bring salvation in the case of deadly sickness is shown by the example of the Syrian commander Naaman, who was healed from leprosy on the basis of an instruction of Elijah through seven immersions in the Jordan River.[104] Beyond this, cleansing through water and forgiveness of sins in

[102] On βαπτίζεσθαι with a middle meaning "to immerse oneself," see 2 Kgs 5.14 LXX about Naaman. Cf. Jdt 12.7-9; Sir 34.25: βαπτιζόμενος as purification of impurity from contact with the dead through immersion. This ritual "immersion" prescribed in the Torah occurred according to specific legally regulated outer presuppositions; on this, see the Mishnah tractate Miqvaot; cf. Strack/Stemberger 1996, 132 (GV = Stemberger 1992, 122); Deines 1993, 319–20 index, s.v. "corpse uncleanness," "Miqwaot."

[103] See also Matt 3.6. In 3.2 Matthew does not take over the phrase βάπτισμα μετανοίας εἰς ἄφεσιν ἁμαρτιῶν from Mark 1.4 but puts in the mouth of the Baptist the imperative of Jesus from Mark 1.15, i.e., μετανοεῖτε, and the reference to the nearness of the kingdom of God. On the confession of sins and forgiveness, see 2 Sam 12.13: "David said to Nathan: 'I have sinned against YHWH.' Nathan answered: 'Thus YHWH has forgiven you your sins.'" Cf. Ps 51; Luke 5.8-10; Acts 19.18; James 5.15-16. On the confession of sins of the high priest and of the individual Israelites on the great Day of Atonement, see Bill. I: 113–14. Mark 1.5: ἐβαπτίζοντο ὑπ' αὐτοῦ does not exclude the collaboration of the disciples in the baptism of masses of people; see note 72 above.

[104] Second Kings 5.14: "He immersed himself seven times in the Jordan . . . and his body was restored like the body of a small child, and he was cleansed." MT: *yiṭbol*. The verb *ṭābal* = βαπτίζεσθαι appears only here in the Old Testament. Cf. also 2 Kgs 6.1-7: the disciples of the prophet Elijah build new dwellings for themselves on the Jordan, where the miracle of the floating axe takes place. That the Jordan water was already regarded in the Mishnah as unsuitable for purification in the case of more severe ritual impurity (m. Parah 8.10—see Rengstorf 1968, 612; GV = 1959, 612) may be a rabbinic

the eschatological context appear in prophetic sayings.[105] While we have references to Jewish or Jewish Christian "baptizers" from the second to fourth centuries in Justin, Hippolytus, Epiphanius, and others,[106] there is doubt concerning how far they can really be traced back into the first half of the first century CE and whether they can be directly connected with the movement of John the Baptist. The Mandaean Baptist traditions, which were often drawn upon previously, should be left aside. They are influenced by the Nestorian baptism rite and are much later. A direct historical connection to John the Baptist and his disciples cannot be demonstrated in them.

We could designate as a contemporary "parallel" the ascetic Bannus, whom the seventeen-year-old Josephus sought out and with whom he probably spent three years.[107] He lived in the wilderness and only from

---

reaction to the preferencing of the Jordan in Jewish baptismal sects. In 4 Bar. 6.23 (25) the Jordan is the place of the testing of the exiles returning from Babylon. The idea is continued in 8.2-3, where God exhorts Jeremiah: "Get up, you and the people, and come to the Jordan; and you will say to the people, 'Let him who desires the Lord leave the works of Babylon behind'" (trans. S. E. Robinson, *OTP* 2: 423). After this the people cross over the river. The interpretation of these two texts is controversial; see Schaller 1998, 736–37, 743–44. Israel passed through the Jordan as the eastern border of the Promised Land before the occupation of the land (Josh 3). Whoever sought "to prepare the way of the Lord in the wilderness" (Isa 40.3; see note 36 above) had to cross over it in the opposite direction, such as the pseudo-prophet Theudas with his followers in ca. 44 CE (Josephus, *Ant.* 20.97–98; cf. Acts 5.36). In LAE 6–8 the Jordan is the place of a forty-day fast of repentance by Adam, who stands up to his neck in water. Through this he wanted to receive again access to paradise. In all these cases the Jordan is connected with a *"rite de passage."* There appears to have been a soteriological Jordan typology in the first century. For precisely this reason the Jordan could no longer have religious meaning as a place of purification for the rabbis later.

[105] Isaiah 4.4; Ezek 36.25; Zech 13.1; cf. Ps 51.9; Isa 44.3 and on this Num 8.7; 19.9-22. In the river proceeding from the temple in Ezek 47.3 LXX there is talk of a ὕδωρ ἀφέσεως ("water of emptying"), which flows to the east into the Dead Sea, which becomes a freshwater area with many fish, and to Galilee and Arabia. It is later interpreted with reference to Christian baptism. Cf. Peterson 1959, 327.

[106] Justin, *Dial.* 80.4 lists, among other things, βαπτισταί. Hegesippus apud Eusebius, *Hist. eccl.* 4.22.7, mentons different Jewish groups, including, in addition to "Masbothei" (derived from Aramaic root ṣb' [immerse, baptize]), above all "Hemerobaptists," who immersed daily; on this, see t. Yad. 2.20 (line 684) ṭwbly šḥryn, who take an immersion bath every morning before they speak the name of God in the *Shᵉmaʿ*; see also Const. ap. 6.6.5 (F. X. Funk 1964, 315). Ps.-Clem. Hom. 2.23.1 even designates John as ἡμεροβαπτιστής; the most important of his thirty-six disciples is said to have been the Samaritan Simon Magus (!). See also Epiphanius, *Pan.* 17 (Holl/Bergermann/Collatz 2013, 214-15); 19.5.7 (223): allegedly one of the six Jewish "sects" before 70 CE. We cannot obtain reliable material from these reports. On this, see Thomas 1935, 33-45.

[107] Josephus, *Life* 11; on this, see Siegert 2001, 26–27. He probably sought him out time and again during this period of time.

"foods that grew of themselves," wore only "clothing made from (the bark of) trees," and "bathed day and night often in cold water for the sake of purity."

If Josephus stayed with him for a longer period of time (presumably intermittently) in order—beyond the knowledge of the three known Jewish religious parties, i.e., Pharisees, Sadducees, and Essenes—to learn rigorous self-discipline and to gather additional religious experiences, then Bannus must also have had other students. The parallels to the Baptist lie in the stark asceticism with regard to food and clothing and in the life in the "wilderness" (ἐρημία) but not in the practice of immersion baptism. According to everything that we know of the Judaism of the first century CE, "*the baptism in the Jordan can be understood only as the direct and personal work of John the Baptist.*"[108] This can be seen in the byname "the Baptist," which appears for the first time with him. It points to an active proclamation of baptism and a baptizing action in the transitive sense, in which the crowd was exhorted to be baptized as a sign of their repentance, with the "Baptist" playing an essential role, for example by demanding a confession of sins and speaking a formula of absolution. The entire event was presumably understood as an eschatological "sealing"[109] with a view to God's impending judgment of wrath and the coming Son of Man–Messiah as judge of the world. In relation to this one-time act we could speak with A. Schweitzer of an "*eschatological sacrament.*" It is not merely a symbol of the forgiveness of sins but a "being marked for salvation,"[110] which does not, to be sure, become effective simply *ex opere operato* but must lead as a consequence to an ethical behavior that produces "fruits that are worthy of repentance."[111]

In view of the coming judge and of God's wrath, the mere appeal to being children of Abraham is no longer applicable: "God is able from these stones to raise up children for Abraham." Is this meant to signal that God can turn also to non-Israelites?[112] Here a motif is sounded that reap-

[108] Rengstorf 1968, 614, modified (our emphasis; GV = 1959, 614).

[109] On sealing as divine activity or marking of the people of God, see Fitzer 1964, 946–54 (ET = 1971, 946–53). In rabbinic Judaism it refers to circumcision. In early Christianity it refers, since the Shepherd of Hermas, to baptism (Similitudes 9.16.4 [= 93.4]: ἡ σφραγὶς ... τὸ ὕδωρ ἐστίν: "they descend into the water and come up alive"). In 4 Bar 6.23 (cf. 8.2-3) the testing of the exiles "with the water of the Jordan" is the "sign of the great seal," see note 104 above. According to Pss. Sol. 15.6, the righteous bear τὸ σημεῖον τοῦ θεοῦ . . . εἰς σωτηρίαν. Cf. v. 9 and already Ezek 9.4, 6: the preserving σημεῖον on the forehead.

[110] Schweitzer 1968, 76 (GV = 1967, 83). On the phrase "eschatological sacrament," see also Schweitzer 2000, 339ff. (GV = 1913, 422ff.), and Schweitzer 1998, 88, 149.

[111] Luke 3.8 (cf. Matt 3.8): ποιήσατε οὖν καρποὺς ἀξίους τῆς μετανοίας.

[112] Luke 3.8-9 = Matt 3.9-10; see also notes 37–38 above. This could be a wordplay: bānîm / bᵉnayya–ʾᵃbānîm / ʾabnayyā.

pears in Jesus and Paul[113] but plays a role already in the prophetic texts of the Old Testament: God is sovereign in his judging and electing activity.[114] Yet another feature is significant: *The activity of the Baptist presupposes a conflict with the temple cult and the priestly aristocracy that dominated it.* After all, the forgiveness of guilt was tied to cultic institutions in Judaism. This applies especially to the high priestly rite on the great Day of Atonement but also in general to all kinds of offerings through which it is possible for "an Israelite sinner to be freed from his sphere of sin at the sanctuary,"[115] in which the effectiveness of the offering had to be connected with the will to repentance or to restitution. For the Baptist, as in Qumran, in apocalyptic texts, and in primitive Christianity, all humans, even Israel itself, are "involved in iniquities, and are full of sins and burdened with transgressions" and must therefore fear God's judgment.[116] As in Qumran the overcoming of the power of sin, which separates from God, demands repentance, entrance into the community of salvation, and perfect observance of the law, but occurs without connection to the official cult in Jerusalem, so the Baptist proclaims salvation through repentance, baptism in the Jordan with forgiveness of sins, and the fruit of a new obedience in light of the impending judgment. For the son of the priest from the order of Abijah the cult apparently no longer played a significant role, and broad masses of people trusted his preaching of repentance more than the official sacrificial system in Jerusalem and let themselves be baptized by John in the Jordan and have forgiveness pronounced to them, whereas the religious leaders of the people rejected him. In this regard he could build upon the old connection between prophetic criticism of the cult and ethical exhortation.

He probably derived his message and the concomitant practice of baptism from a special, God-given prophetic-eschatological authority. Luke thus introduces him in the manner of an Old Testament prophet (3.1-2): "In the fifteenth year of the reign of Tiberius . . . the word of the Lord came to John, the son of Zechariah. . . ." That he was a prophet was, in contrast to the Jerusalem authorities, the conviction of the crowds and in a pointed way also the view of Jesus and the primitive community.[117] Here he appeared as the last prophet. A parallel to this is—admittedly in a very different context—the gathering of the Qumran community through the Teacher of Righteousness in the second century BCE. This suggests

---

[113] Cf. Luke 13.28 = Matt 8.11-12; Luke 19.9; John 8.39-40; Rom 4; Gal 3.6-9.

[114] Cf. Exod 32.9-10; Amos 9.7-10; Jer 2.9-25; 8.4-13.

[115] Koch 1980, 317 (GV = Koch 1977, 867–68).

[116] Fourth Ezra 7.68ff. (trans. B. Metzger, *OTP* 1: 539; cf. J. Schreiner 1984, 351); similarly, 7.46, 48; 8.35. See further Rom 3.9-20, 23.

[117] Mark 11.27-33 = Luke 20.1-8 = Matt 21.23-27; see sections 5.1 and 10.8.

the speculation that not only the primitive community and Jesus but also John himself understood his activity in the light of the last word of the prophetic books:[118]

Behold, I am sending to you Elijah, the prophet,
Before the great and awesome day of YHWH comes.
Behold, I am sending my messenger,
that he may prepare the way before me.

To this can be added the later interpretation:[119]

About you (Elijah) it is written,
you are ready at the appointed time
to calm the wrath before it burns.

In the various Qumran fragments we also find allusions that point to a lively eschatological expectation concerning Elijah.[120] The authority with which John appears and the impact of his eschatological preaching upon the people would best be explained on the basis of a connection with the expectation of the Elijah *redivivus*. This applies all the more since in the early Jewish haggadah Elijah was elevated as a priestly figure.[121]

The peculiar *clothing* of the Baptist (Mark 1.6) also points in this direction. The closest parallel is the garb of Elijah: "a man with a garment of hair and a leather belt."[122] The special food, i.e., "locusts and

---

[118] Mal 3.23 [ET = 4.5] and 3.1.

[119] Sirach 48.10. On Elijah, see Jeremias 1964b, 936 (GV = 1935, 938): Thus, "more worthy of consideration is the thesis that the Baptist thought of himself as the returning Elijah" with reference to Klausner 1945, 243ff. While Jeremias rejects this supposition with reference to John 1.21, 25, this text, which openly contradicts the Synoptics, is clearly secondary. See section 9.1.2.3 above. By contrast, Luke 1.16-17 already indicates that the Baptist tradition places Elijah in relation to their master; see note 33 above.

[120] Zimmermann 1998, 532 index, s.v. "Elijah," and 517 index, s.v. "Mal 3.23." Cf. esp. 4Q558 (pp. 413–15) and 4Q521 fr. 2 III, 2 (pp. 366–69).

[121] Bill. IV: 462, 781–82, 789ff.; Hengel 1989c, 162–71 (GV = 1976c, 167–75) on his identification with Phineas, the son of Aaron, as heavenly high priest; cf. the next note. On Elijah as priest and eschatological judge in the Lives of the Prophets, see Schwemer 1995/1996, II: 227–32, 241–46.

[122] Second Kings 1.8; cf. the mantle of Elijah in 1 Kgs 19.13, 19; 2 Kgs 2.8, 13-14. This is not simply the garment of a prophet, Zech 13.4, but his unique, potent clothing. See the agreement of 2 Kgs 1.8 LXX with Mark 1.6 = Matt 3.4 and on this, Davies/Allison 1988/1991/1998, I: 295–96. The Baptist appeared not as any old prophet or nameless 'herald in the wilderness.' His activity was connected from the beginning with Old Testament–apocalyptic associations. See also Hengel 1981b, 36 n. 71 (GV = 1968b, 39 n. 71; Hengel 2007b, 76 n. 124). One should not overlook the fact that in the first century

wild honey,"[123] is, for one thing, an expression of radical carelessness and needlessness, which contents itself with what God's creation affords in the "wilderness" without human intervention.[124] At the same time, the stark ascetic stance was a sign of a permanent mindset of repentance. The Baptist set a conspicuously good example here. For the disciples of the Baptist frequent fasting was therefore significant, which led to a question being posed to Jesus.[125] It is telling that Luke omits the reference to the strange clothing and food of the Baptist because it could have a rather repelling effect upon Theophilus. He contents himself with Jesus' reference to the radical ascetic in 7.33, which Matt 11.18 further intensifies.

With regard to the baptism in the Jordan for the forgiveness of sins we must consider the fact that the Greek βάπτειν and its intensivum βαπτί-ζειν has, among other senses, also the negative meaning "sink," "drown," "be flooded."[126] This applies very occasionally to the Septuagint and especially to Josephus.[127] Without parallel, however, is the formula βάπτισμα βαπτισθῆναι, which we find in the mouth of Jesus in Mark 10.38 and Luke 12.50, in the unusual meaning to suffer "destruction," "baptism of death," with the substantive βάπτισμα appearing for the first time in primitive Christian linguistic usage. The earliest attestations are Rom 6.4 and

---

Elijah could be understood as high priest of the end-time; see Jeremias 1964b, 932–34 (GV = 1935, 934–35), and Hengel 1989c, 162–68 (GV = 1976c, 167–72).

[123] Mark 1.6 = Matt 3.4; on this, see Davies/Allison 1988/1991/1998, I: 296–97. On the offense, see Luke 7.33 = Matt 11.18. On the renunciation of wine from childhood onward, as with Nazirites, see Luke 1.15. In his fundamental study, Kelhoffer 2005, 10ff., points to the difference between Mark 1.6c and Matt 2.4c. In Mark there exists the possibility that John also eats other food (ἦν . . . ἐσθίων), whereas Matthew speaks of his nourishment (τροφή). Cf. also the difference between Luke 7.33 and Matt 11.18.

[124] On Elijah, see 1 Kgs 17.3-4; 19.4-8. See further the example of Bannus in Josephus, *Life* 11: τροφὴν δὲ τὴν αὐτομάτως φυομένην. For the Jewish Christian encratism of the second century the "locusts" became offensive since they were not vegetarian. According to Epiphanius, *Pan.* 30.13.7–8, the Gospel of the Ebionites apparently replaces them with a "cake in oil" (ἐγκρίς instead of ἀκρίς). The Diatessaron spoke therefore of "milk and mountain honey"; see Bauer 1967b, 102–3; Davies/Allison 1988/1991/1998, I: 296–97.

[125] Mark 2.18ff. = Luke 5.33ff. = Matt 9.14ff.; cf. Luke 7.33. In Mark the disciples of the Baptist and Pharisees pose the question, in Luke the Pharisees and scribes following the preceding discussion in 5.30, in Matthew only the disciples of the Baptist. Luke and Matthew wanted to avoid a common action of disciples of the Baptist and Pharisees.

[126] LSJ, 305–6. On this, see the attestations in Bauer/Aland/Aland 1988, 265–66, under βαπτίζω.

[127] Cf., e.g., Isa 21.4: ἡ ἀνομία με βαπτίζει ("The lawlessness drowns or soaks me"); Job 9.31 Aquila: ἐν διαφθορᾷ βαπτίσεις με; Ps 9.16, see Field 1875, ad loc.: ἄλλος: ἐβαπτίσθησαν (["the nations"] sink); Ps 68.5, ad loc. Symmachus. On Josephus, see *J.W.* 1.437: Herod has his brother-in-law, the young high priest Aristobulus III, drowned by Gauls of his bodyguard in the swimming pool in Jericho; 2.556; 3.368, 423, 525, 527; *Ant.* 9.212; *Life* 15: the sinking of Josephus' ship in the Adriatic.

Col 2.12, where in both cases the motif of being buried or of death occurs in connection with the substantive.[128]

It is peculiar that this formula βάπτισμα βαπτισθῆναι in the sense of the "baptism of death" appears only in the mouth of Jesus. Could it go back to Baptist usage and mean that through the baptism in the Jordan the sinful human has "sunk"? This would give the baptism of John a deep sense and explain why it was continued by Christians after Easter, now "in the name of Jesus."

---

[128] The middle Hebrew or Aramaic equivalent would be *ṭᵉbîlāh* or *ṭᵉbîlûtā/ṭibbûlā'*; see Jastrow 1903, I: 516–17, 529: dipping, immersion, bathing.

10

Jesus and His Forerunner

10.1 The Baptism of Jesus

A fundamental piece of tradition, which later caused difficulties and is therefore original, is the baptism of Jesus by John. It is handed down to us in Mark 1.9-11 and in Matt 3.13, 16-17, which is dependent on the Markan passage. By contrast, Luke 3.21-22 has only a short account of the baptism, which is set off from the activity of the Baptist through the reference to his arrest. Although primitive Christianity postulated the messianic sinlessness of Jesus from the very beginning,[1] the Synoptics held fast to the fact of Jesus' baptism. They were, however, aware of the theological difficulty of this event. In order to reduce the offense, Luke omits the figure of the Baptist and writes: "When Jesus had been baptized and was praying."[2] Matthew not only deleted the reference that the baptism occurred "for the forgiveness of sins," but also added 3.14-15,[3] a dialogue of Jesus with the Baptist in which the latter initially rejects the wish of Jesus with the rationale that he, John, would need to be baptized by Jesus. He consents only when Jesus explains that "it is fitting for us to fulfill all righteousness (i.e., the whole salvific will of God)."[4] While the Gospel of John passes over the narrative of the baptism of Jesus,

---

[1] The problem that this baptism occurred for the forgiveness of sins and presupposed a confession of sins does not disturb Mark; cf., however, Paul, 2 Cor 5.21; Rom 8.3-4, on the sinlessness of Jesus. Jesus' sinlessness was from the beginning a foundation of the Christology.

[2] Luke 3.21: Ἰησοῦ βαπτισθέντος καὶ προσευχομένου and omits the ὑπὸ Ἰωάννου of Mark 1.9. In Matt 3.13 Jesus comes to the Baptist "in order to be baptized by him."

[3] This scene is further intensified in the Gospel of the Ebionites; see Epiphanius, *Pan.* 30.13.7–8 = Aland 2005, 27.

[4] On the theological significance of Matt 3.15 for the Gospel of Matthew, see Deines 2004, passim.

it presupposes the event, and in the apocryphal Gospel of the Hebrews Jesus rejects the exhortation of his mother and brother to let themselves be baptized together, with the words "What have I sinned that I should go to be baptized by him . . . ?"[5]

For Mark the baptism of Jesus is also his consecration as Messiah. Right after the immersion Jesus receives the Spirit of God and is addressed by God himself. He alone sees that the heavens split[6] and the Spirit of God "as a dove" descends upon him (εἰς αὐτον). At the same time, a voice from heaven rings out: "You are my beloved son, with you I am well pleased."[7] Here the address of Jesus as Son of God is with Ps 2.7 an expression of messianic election. It is connected with the saying about the servant of God in Isa 42.1: "Behold, my servant, . . . my chosen one, in whom my soul delights. I have put my Spirit on him." As the Son, God's anointed one,[8] and God's servant, Jesus is the *Spirit-bearer par excellence*. The exemplary, unsurpassable gifting with the Spirit applies in Judaism both to the "royal" and to the "prophetic" anointed one. It would be false to construct an antithesis here.[9] The fact this unusual narrative was preserved—indeed possesses the prominent significance of the opening to the activity of Jesus—is connected with the fact that it—by analogy to the callings of the prophets in the Old Testament—was understood as the calling of Jesus into his messianic office. This means that the baptism narrative

---

[5] John 1.32-34; Jerome, *Pelag*. 3.2 = Aland 2005, 27.

[6] Mark 1.10: εἶδεν σχιζομένους τοὺς οὐρανούς. Luke 3.21 has for this ἀνεῳχθῆ-ναι, cf. Isa 64.1: ἐὰν ἀνοίξῃς τὸν οὐρανόν, and Matt 3.16 is dependent on Luke. The same applies to βαπτισθείς/βαπτισθέντος and ἐπ' αὐτόν against Mark, who has εἰς αὐτόν.

[7] Mark 1.11: cf. Ps 2.7 and Isa 42.1; on this, see 44.2. Codex D and other Western witnesses bring into Luke 3.22 the whole verse of Ps 2.7, as does Justin, *Dial*. 88.8; 103.6. According to Epiphanius, *Pan*. 30.13.7–8, the Gospel of the Ebionites combines Ps 2.7 and Isa 42.1; see Aland 2005, 27. On the Messiah as paradigmatic bearer of the Spirit of God, see also Isa 11.1-5; 61.1ff. Justin, *Dial*. 88.3, two Old Latin manuscripts in Matt 3.15, the Gospel of the Ebionites according to Epiphanius, and the Diatessaron recount an additional light phenomenon at the baptism; see Bauer 1967b, 134ff. Bauer also discusses the early Christian and gnostic reflection on the baptism of Jesus, which already caused the early church quite a headache (110–14).

[8] On the sonship of God of the Davidic king, which in Judaism was related to the Messiah, see Ps 2; Ps 89; 2 Sam 7, also Mark 1.1: Ἰησοῦ Χριστοῦ υἱοῦ θεοῦ and again in Mark 14.61; on this, see Hengel 1976b (GV = 1977b; 2006a, 74–145); on the son of God in Qumran, see Zimmermann 1998, 540 index, s.v. "Sohn Gottes."

[9] Cf. 1 Sam 10.1ff.; Isa 11.2: "On him will rest the Spirit of the Lord" (ἀναπαύσεται ἐπ' αὐτόν; cf. Luke 3.22 = Matt 3.16 and John 1.32: ἔμεινεν ἐπ' αὐτόν); Isa 61.1; cf. 42.1; 44.2 and above all the *mšyḥ hrwḥ*, the "Spirit-anointed" in 11QMelch II 1; on this, see Zimmermann 1998, 389–412 (391ff., 410–11), who appeals to the "messenger of joy" of Isa 52.7 and to Daniel (9.26 or 12.4), behind which Isa 61.1-2 stands, a text that is also significant for Jesus; see the end of section 10.5 below.

recounts the visionary call through which Jesus experiences his election by God and is designated for his messianic task. "Before Jesus called others he himself was called."[10] The deliberate restriction of the event to Jesus through the "he saw" and the address following Ps 2.7 "You are . . ." in Mark means that *this event affected Jesus alone and the others perceived nothing*. It therefore already falls within the framework of the "Messianic secret."[11] It is not a big step to postulate that Jesus really had a visionary call experience at his baptism by John, which gave his life a completely new direction. With the baptism of Jesus in the Jordan the foundation is laid for his public "messianic" activity. Traces of such visionary experiences of Jesus or of the closest circle of disciples are found in the saying of Jesus in Luke 10.18, the narrative of the walking on the sea (Mark 6.49-50), the transfiguration story (9.2ff.), and perhaps also in the temptation story.[12] The Jesus tradition of the primitive community, which we encounter for the first time in Mark, knew that Jesus' prophetic-messianic activity had its origin here. Therefore, despite the difficulties bound up with it, it did not suppress the baptism of Jesus by John. In itself Mark could have recounted a commissioning of Jesus right before 1.15 without reference to the baptism by John. The Gospel would lack nothing without the prehistory of the activity of the Baptist. But the weight of this event and the significance of John for Jesus and primitive Christianity were too great. It was neither possible nor desirable to pass over his activity as the ἀρχὴ τοῦ εὐαγγελίου Ἰησοῦ Χριστοῦ (Mark 1.1).

[10] Neugebauer 1986, 2. This view is opposed by Hahn 2002, I: 51: "The narrative of the baptism . . . cannot be evaluated as a 'call experience' of Jesus. The account of Jesus' baptism is in its different versions much too strongly shaped over christologically. . . . At the same time we must affirm that the baptism of Jesus by John was the presupposition of his own activity."

[11] Only in the second sounding forth of the voice from heaven in Mark 9.7 ("*This is* . . .") do the disciples also hear it. Matthew already turns the "you" into a "this" in 3.17, so that all those present are addressed. While Luke 3.22 retains the pronoun "you," the descent of the Spirit in "bodily form as a dove" presupposes that it is seen by all. According to John 1.32ff., the Baptist sees "the Spirit as a dove from heaven descend and remain on him (i.e., Jesus)" and hears God's witness "this is the one who baptizes with the Holy Spirit." Through this he himself can testify to Jesus as "God's lamb" (1.29, 36) and as the "chosen one of God" (1.34: ὁ ἐκλεκτός; on the discussion of this *varia lectio*, see Metzger 1975, 200).

[12] Luke 4.1-13; Matt 4.1-11; cf. Mark 1.12-13 on the animals and on the service of the angels to the hungry Jesus.

10.2 Jesus' Activity in Galilee, the Temptation Story, and His Separation from the Baptist

Between the baptism of Jesus and the beginning of his public activity in Galilee lies, according to Mark 1.14, the arrest of the Baptist by Herod Antipas. Through this Mark wants to make a fundamental distinction between the concluded activity of the forerunner and the activity of the Messiah.[13] As a transition he had previously inserted the forty-day temptation of Jesus in the "desolate place" or wilderness. The Spirit he has just received "drives" him there. In Mark the notion of the "new" Adam may lie in the background. In the wilderness he brings about peace among animals, rejects the temptation by Satan, and is miraculously provided for by the angels.[14] This motif is continued in the Gospel. The Son of Man (and of God) overcomes the demons, sickness, and death; forgives sins; feeds hungry people; restores the disrupted creation order of marriage; and proclaims, indeed embodies, God's presence. The call into the messianic service begins with a superhuman testing, which is configured according to biblical models. Luke and Matthew followed Mark with this scheme but recount the temptation in greater detail.[15] Here too, Matthew is presumably influenced by Luke.[16] On account of their theologically configured narrative structure, these temptation accounts can no longer be investigated with a view to determining a "historical core." Perhaps another visionary experience of Jesus stood here at the beginning of his activity.

---

[13] See section 9.1.2.3. Luke makes an even sharper distinction: 3.19-20: arrest; vv. 21-22: baptism of Jesus; 4.1-13: temptation; 4.14: return to Galilee "in the power of the Spirit." Matthew recounts the arrest of the Baptist only after the temptation in 4.12-13; Jesus withdraws after that to Galilee, leaves Nazareth, and dwells in Capernaum. See section 8.2.

[14] Mark 1.12-13. The strong verb "drive" is used eleven times by Mark for the casting out of demons; in Gen 3.24 it describes the banishment from paradise; see Bauer/Aland/Aland 1988, 477: "cast out, drive out in a more or less violent way." For Judaism the wilderness is not only the place of divine revelation as with Moses and Israel on Sinai but also of the powers that are hostile to God. Luke 11.24 = Matt 12.43; Lev 16.10; Tob 8.3; Tg. Yer. I Dtn 37.10; b. Sukkah 52b; see Kittel 1964, 657 n. 1 (GV = 1935, 655 n. 1); Davies/Allison 1988/1991/1998, I: 154. On the motif of the "new Adam," see Pesch 1984a, 95–96, with rich Jewish attestations. On the peace with and among animals, see Dochhorn 2005, 304–5. See also Ps 8.5-7; Isa 11.6-9; Heb 2.5-8; 1 Cor 15.45, and section 17.4.1 on the Son of Man.

[15] Cf. Luke 4.1-13 = Matt 4.1-11; on this, see Heb 4.15. See also Neugebauer 1986.

[16] See Hengel 2008c, 296 (ET = 2000b, 182). The Lukan version is clearly the more original one. It has—in accordance with Jewish expectation—its high point in the authentication miracle of the Son of God Messiah on the pinnacle of the temple before the people. Matthew changes the order and places the temptation of world rule at the end. This corresponds to his conclusion in 28.18 and forms a contrasting inclusion to this. A motive for Luke to have changed the Matthean order is not identifiable.

A withdrawal into solitude after his baptism would also be quite conceivable. The account reflects the specification of the way of the one authorized by God. The forty days with fasting correspond to Moses' time of revelation on Sinai and Elijah's journey to the mountain of revelation.[17] The temptation story, shaped by Old Testament quotations and allusions, is artfully composed and evinces the dualism that Jesus shares with large parts of Judaism and primitive Christianity. The key word "test" occurs several other times in the Synoptics in connection with opponents who seek to entrap Jesus.[18] In the small farewell discourse in Luke 22.28ff. Jesus says that the twelve "persevered with me in my trials," and he therefore promises them a share in the meal in the kingdom.[19] The subject itself occurs again in Gethsemane. This is why Luke, at the end, has the pointer "The devil departed from him until an opportune time" (Luke 4.13). In his temptation story Matthew strengthens the parallels to the passion and resurrection of Jesus.[20] By contrast, in John there is no longer room for a temptation of Jesus.[21] The Lukan narrative also shows clear signs of the critical conflict of the Jewish Christian community with political messianism in Jewish Palestine, which flourished ever since the death of Herod in 4 BCE and the appearance of Judas the Galilean in the tax census in 6 CE and became even stronger after the death of King Agrippa I in 44 CE. The devil demands that Jesus solve the problems of the world—to turn stones into bread and thus overcome hunger, indeed, to take over the rule of the world and show himself to Israel as *Messias diabolicus* from the pinnacle of the temple through a demonstration miracle. "Bread and games" rule the world.

In John[22] we have references to Jesus and the Baptist being active for some time alongside each other and, additionally, to the first disciples coming from the circle of the Baptist and changing over to Jesus. It is possible that John has inserted the opposition between the baptizing activity of the Baptist community and that of the Christians into his contradictory

---

[17] Exodus 24.18; Elijah in 1 Kgs 19.5-8 with the angel motif; Gen 7.12: the duration of the flood; Acts 1.3: time of revelation of the risen one; on the fasting of Moses, see Exod 34.28; Deut 9.9; Bill. I: 150–51.

[18] Mark 8.11; 10.2; 12.15; Luke 10.25 and elsewhere; cf. 1 Cor 10.9.

[19] Luke 22.28: Ὑμεῖς δέ ἐστε οἱ διαμεμενηκότες μετ᾽ ἐμοῦ ἐν τοῖς πειρασμοῖς μου.

[20] For Matthew it is significant in the passion story that Jesus rejects all miraculous self-help there: Matt 26.53; cf. also the mocking scene in 27.40, where he adds vis-à-vis Mark: εἰ υἱὸς εἶ τοῦ θεοῦ. See by contrast the demonstration of his divine power in the commissioning commandment in 28.19-20.

[21] It is only hinted at and reversed in John 12.27ff. In Gethsemane the arrest immediately follows in 18.1ff.

[22] John 1.35ff. and 3.22ff.; 4.1-2.

presentation.[23] It remains, however, probable that disciples of Jesus, such as Andrew,[24] but also others, came from the Baptist's circle of disciples. Jesus' call-vision at the baptism and his marked independence vis-à-vis the Baptist speak against the view that Jesus himself was a disciple of the Baptist for an extended period of time.[25] But we can no longer penetrate this transitional time between the baptism in the Jordan and Jesus' activity in Galilee. It is possible that there was a time of self-reflection and self-testing here before the first public appearance about which we have only hints. This period of time probably was not too extensive, just as in general neither the activity of the Baptist nor that of Jesus could have lasted for an overly long period of time. Both provoked deadly conflict.[26]

The fundamental difference between Jesus and the Baptist becomes clear in his activity in Galilee, which Mark describes from 1.15 onward. John moves this more strongly toward Judaea, but with the Synoptics one will scarcely be able to doubt the center of gravity in Galilee, especially since John 1.43ff. and 2.1-12 also recount an initial activity of Jesus there, though John then recounts various journeys to the great festivals in Jerusalem.[27] That Jesus visited festivals in Jerusalem on multiple occasions is suggested by the fact that according to Mark[28] he had friends in Bethany, with whom he stayed overnight, and that he was not unknown in the holy city.

10.3 Commonalities and Differences between Jesus and the Preaching of the Baptist: The Call for Repentance Addressed to Israel and the Nearness of the Judgment[29]

All four evangelists connect Jesus in the closest way with the Baptist, irrespective of whether he appears as the last eschatological prophet, as Elijah *redivivus*, forerunner and martyr (as in the Synoptics), or as the first witness (as in John). Matthew even places in his mouth the same message

---

[23] Cf. 3.22 and 4.1-2. Here the hand of a student and corrector could perhaps become visible; cf. the "we" in John 21.24. The addition points to discussions in the Johannine school.

[24] John 1.40. See the end of section 9.1 and section 11.4.

[25] On this, see Ernst 1989b, which is somewhat too sharp in its emphasis. See also the statement of F. Neugebauer in note 74 in chapter 9.

[26] See the discussion of this point at the end of section 10.4 and in section 11.1.

[27] John 2.13: Passover; 5.1: an unnamed festival, presumably Sukkot; 6.4: Passover in Galilee (not in Jerusalem); 7.2: Sukkot; 10.22: Hanukkah; 11.55 and elsewhere: Passover connected with Jesus' death.

[28] Mark 11.11-12; 14.3; cf. 11.3; 14.13ff. Jesus shows himself to be familiar with the Jerusalem conditions. See the end of section 11.1 and section 18.2.

[29] Reiser 1997 (GV = 1990); Gregg 2005.

with which he—shortening his Markan *Vorlage*—summarizes Jesus' proclamation: "Repent, for the kingdom of God is near."[30]

Mark provides a more detailed formulation: "The time is fulfilled and the kingdom of God is very near. Repent and believe the good news!"[31] According to Mark 1.14, this is "*God's* good news" (εὐαγγέλιον τοῦ θεοῦ) because Jesus speaks and acts in God's place, because in him God himself comes to his people. With the exhortation "repent!" (μετανοεῖτε) Jesus follows, according to the Synoptics, in the footsteps of the Baptist. Like the Baptist, Jesus turns to the whole Jewish people. Like the Baptist, Jesus ignited a popular movement, and indeed, we must assume that many who were seized by the Baptist's preaching of repentance subsequently turned (with the Baptist's imprisonment and murder) to Jesus or later to the post-Easter Jesus movement. The Baptist's preaching of repentance effectively paved the way for Jesus' message. A comparison between the two figures is difficult, however, since we have much less information about the Baptist. We know about his proclamation only in extremely abbreviated—Christian—form and through the few pointers in Josephus. Nevertheless, such a comparison remains sensible since, despite the restricted nature of the source material, commonalities and differences emerge in a relatively clear manner.

In the following points a—limited—agreement becomes visible:

With Jesus the concern is also with (1) the "nearness of God," which radically changes everything, (2) the eschatological restitution of the true people of God, with the external privileges of Israel being able to be called into question, (3) deeds of obedience as genuine fruits of repentance, and (4) the impending reality of judgment. To be sure, with Jesus the preaching of repentance and judgment—in contrast to what we know of the Baptist—is completely enveloped by the good news of the boundless love of God for the lost sinner. A linguistic observation is also significant. Apart from Mark 1.15 and the proclamation of the disciples sent out by Jesus in 6.12, the verb μετανοεῖν and the substantive μετάνοια no longer occur in connection with Jesus in Mark.[32] In the material common to Luke and Matthew it appears—apart from places where it appears in connection with the Baptist—only two more

---

[30] Matthew 3.2, with the same wording as a saying of Jesus in 4.17, the *Vorlage* is Mark 1.15; cf. also the proclamation of the disciples in Matt 10.7 = Luke 10.9. On the whole subject, see section 9.1.2.2. In a consistent manner, Irenaeus turns him, who is more than a prophet (Matt 11.9 = Luke 7.26), into the first apostle: *Haer*. 3.1.1.4.

[31] Mark 1.15: πεπλήρωται ὁ καιρὸς καὶ ἤγγικεν ἡ βασιλεία τοῦ θεοῦ· μετανοεῖτε καὶ πιστεύετε ἐν τῷ εὐαγγελίῳ. On πιστεύειν ἐν, cf. Exod 14.31 (MT). We could ask whether the perfect ἤγγικεν could not be translated with "the kingdom of God is here"; cf. Mark 14.42: "See, my betrayer is here" and on this, see note 11 in chapter 13.

[32] We find it only for the description of the baptism of John in the Jordan.

times in the reproach and threat of judgment vis-à-vis the Galilean cities and this generation.[33] In comparison, πιστεύειν and πίστις are already much more frequent in the Synoptics. Thus, the call for faith appears to have played a greater role for Jesus than the traditional concept of repentance, which comes from the prophetic preaching of the Old Testament.[34] On the other hand, Luke, in his special material, shows a certain predilection for the word group μετανοεῖν/μετάνοια and sometimes adds it to his *Vorlagen*.[35] He may have found it more frequently in his special material, with a special accent being placed on it there, namely the emphasis on the joy in heaven over the sinner who repents.[36] His predilection for the word group may be connected with his theology of mission, for this tendency is continued in Acts.[37] Paul also uses this word group only in a very reserved manner in contrast to πίστις and πιστεύειν.[38] Luke esteems even more the verb εὐαγγελίζεσθαι, with which he, summarizing, can also use once to designate the preaching of the Baptist.[39] For Mark, by contrast, the substantive εὐαγγέλιον is the quintessence of the new good news of Jesus (and later of the Jesus community), which bestows "faith," i.e., trusting obedience. Thus, the emphasis is placed differently with Jesus than with the Baptist. The following points are significant for them both, though in different ways.

Since the time of the Maccabees, the eschatological atmosphere in connection with the expectation of the—relatively—near dawning of the kingdom of God or of the messianic time[40] was widespread in broad circles of the Jewish population in the motherland and in weakened form also in the diaspora. This "apocalyptic hope" is not only a basic theme

---

[33] Luke 10.13; 11.32 = Matt 11.21; 12.41. On this, see Sanders 1985, 106ff.

[34] See also section 16.2 on the miracle tradition.

[35] Luke 5.32; 11.32; cf. 17.3-4. He has the verb in the mouth of Jesus nine times, Mark once, Matthew four times; Acts uses it five times. Luke has the noun μετάνοια five times in the Gospel and six times in Acts. Mark has it once and Matthew twice. John completely avoids the verb and noun. In addition, Luke loves the word ἐπιστρέφειν, which is the predominant translation of *šûb/hešîb* in the Septuagint: Luke 1.16-17; 22.32; Acts 3.19; 9.35 and elsewhere.

[36] Luke 15.7, 10; see the discussion of Luke 15 at the end of this section.

[37] Repentance and faith become almost identical in Luke; for him both are not achievements to be performed but the gift of God, a fundamental idea that already applies to the proclamation of Jesus. See Mittmann-Richert 2008.

[38] Verb: 2 Cor 12.21; noun: Rom 2.4; 2 Cor 7.9-10.

[39] Luke 3.18; cf. also the angel to Zechariah in 1.19. Luke uses it fifteen times in the Gospel and twenty-one times in Acts, altogether more frequently than the genuine letters of Paul. By contrast, the noun εὐαγγέλιον is completely absent in the Gospel. We find it only in Acts in the mouth of Peter (15.7) and Paul (20.24). In Mark only Jesus and his disciples proclaim the εὐαγγέλιον: 1.14-15; 8.35; 10.29; 13.10; 14.9, probably redactional in each case. He is followed, in weakened form, by Matt 4.23; 9.35; 24.14: τὸ εὐαγγέλιον τῆς βασιλείας. And only in 26.13: τὸ εὐαγγέλιον τοῦτο: Here the written Gospel could be meant. The verb εὐαγγελίζεσθαι is lacking in Mark. Matthew has it only once in the allusion to Isa 61.1 in Matt 11.5 = Luke 7.22 from the sayings tradition.

[40] The two are connected: see Dan 7.13; Pss. Sol. 17-18 and the end of section 13.1.

for the emergence of primitive Christianity.[41] It applies to large Jewish groups such as the Pharisees before 70 CE, the Essenes, and the anti-Roman insurgent movement. The strongest indication of it is the high estimation of the book of Daniel in these movements. Only the "conservative" Sadducean aristocracy completely rejected it. Its expectations often had a strong political component, such as the violent liberation from the yoke of foreign rule, but this did not have to stand at the center. With the Baptist and with Jesus it does not become visible in the sources handed down to us. Both have in common an intensive relationship to the pressing "nearness" of God or of his eschatological authorized representative. However, while the Baptist proclaims this representative as the judge who stands before the door, Jesus sees God's reign itself at work already in his own "messianic" activity and is certain of its near consummation "in power."[42] The hearers of his message who are open to it can already perceive its effects in the present.

Through the kingdom of God the Baptist and Jesus expect the restitution of the true people of God promised by the prophets and therefore are oriented toward all Israel. Neither establishes an exclusive community of a "holy remnant," such as the Essenes of Qumran. Nor can we yet speak of a "church." To be sure, Jesus paves the way for its emergence. The community of disciples constituted by Easter presupposes the—messianic—activity of Jesus and is unthinkable without it. It appeals just as much to Jesus' unique words and deeds as to Jesus' death and resurrection. The two constitute a unity, otherwise the Gospels could not have emerged.[43] The fact that Jesus selected from the multitude of disciples twelve persons[44] expresses his claim on the whole twelve-tribe people of God. The Baptist also attracts disciples, who presumably also act as helpers in the baptism of masses of people. The points of contact with non-Jews are still occasional with Jesus and evince a certain distance.[45] He seeks no contact with Gentiles but rather avoids it. He can, however, present Gentiles and Samaritans as models[46] because the old salvific privileges of Israel are no longer taken for granted. Similarly, John the Baptist also says that physical descent from Abraham no longer applies without the

---

[41] On this, see Hengel 1996a, 314–43; Hengel 2002, 302–417.

[42] Mark 9.1; on this, see in greater detail section 13.5.

[43] See section 5.1.

[44] Mark 3.16-19. On this, see section 11.6.

[45] It is conspicuous that these contacts play such a small role in the Gospels. Mark 7.24ff.: the Syrophoenician woman; Luke 7.1-10: the centurion of Capernaum. John 12.20 is, like John 4.4-42, a pointer to the Jewish Christian "Hellenists," who become active soon after Easter. Cf. also Matt 10.5; see section 11.3.

[46] See the end of section 11.3 and section 14.4.

fruits of repentance.[47] In distinction from the Baptist, Jesus points to his deeds, which are "signs" of the kingdom of God that is already dawning with his activity.

The fact that Jesus, like the Baptist, demands the "good fruit of repentance"[48] can be seen in the parable of the unfruitful fig tree in Luke 13.6-9 (special material). The gardener petitions the owner, who wants to cut it down, for a final extension of time: "I will dig around it and dung it; if it then produces no fruit, cut it down." This means, now is the last grace period. Where fruits are not produced, judgment awaits. To be sure, in Jesus' preaching of repentance there also appears a reevaluation of a traditional ideal of piety, which distinguishes him from the Baptist. He demands renunciation of all pious self-regard and every reliance on merit and reward. The repentance of only one sinner is also reason for joy among humans. Therefore, the meals of Jesus with tax collectors and sinners, which are so offensive, are meals of joy, which are comparable to the celebration of the return of the lost son (Luke 15.23ff.). The Father in his boundless goodness accepts the sinner. There is no trace of this in the tradition about the Baptist preserved for us. Rather, with him and his disciples a disposition of repentance is connected with strict asceticism.[49]

An important component of the proclamation of both is the threat of impending divine judgment as the other side of the nearness of God. Each person will have to give an account of their life before the Son of Man. To be sure, in the proclamation of Jesus according to Mark and Luke, the motif of judgment recedes relatively in terms of its extent. Only with Matthew is it considerably increased, indeed multiplied, in accord with his theology, with him taking up again motifs from the preaching of the Baptist (see section 10.6 below).

10.4 Jesus' Activity as Itinerant Preacher and the *Stabilitas Loci* of John at the Jordan

The form of their activity is fundamentally different. The Baptist was active in the wilderness-like Jordan Plain on the east side in Peraea,[50] probably at a fixed place right by the river, for he required flowing water, and the popular movement that he called into life resulted in a larger number of people coming down to him at the Jordan from the whole of Jewish

---

[47] Luke 3.8 = Matt 3.9; see section 9.3 with notes 11–12.

[48] Matt 3.10 in comparison with 7.19.

[49] Mark 1.6 parr.; 2.18 parr.; Luke 7.33 par.; see the end of section 9.3.

[50] To this corresponds his imprisonment in Machaerus in south Peraea near the Nabataean border according to Josephus, *Ant.* 18.119; see section 9.2.

Palestine over an extended period of time. Apart from the two specifications of place in John,[51] we hear nothing about peregrinations of the Baptist himself. After all, he was bound to a well-known place of baptism; the people had to know where he was to be found. Jesus' sphere of activity was more limited. He too certainly had all Israel in view, but according to Mark, he restricted himself initially to Galilee. The northwestern corner of the Lake of Gennesaret with the main location of Capernaum served as his point of departure. He made journeys on the lake and moved from village to village in his home province. Later, he even crossed over its borders into pagan territory. At the end stands Jerusalem and the journey there. By contrast, nothing is reported about peregrinations throughout Judaea, not even in John.[52] Jesus too certainly attracts many people, but initially scarcely to the extent that the Baptist did.[53]

One receives through this the impression that the radius of Jesus' geographical radiance was, despite the itinerant nature of his activity, more likely less than that of the Baptist with his *stabilitas loci* on the Jordan. After all, Josephus' account of the Baptist also presupposes a lasting impact in the whole of Jewish Palestine. This suggests again that the time of the public activity of Jesus (despite the divergent presentation in John) was a shorter one than that of the Baptist. The Markan account makes it somewhat meteoric: a rapid burst of light and then the sudden end. In this regard Mark comes closest to the historical reality, even though we cannot regard him as a historical and geographical guide. The tradition of the sending out of the twelve, which has a distinctive rigorous and unrealistic character,[54] especially in the sayings tradition common to Luke and Matthew, represents a continuation of this tendency, which seeks out the

---

[51] John 1.28; 3.23; cf. 10.40.

[52] The reports in John 3.22 and 4.3 are obscure; 10.40 and 11.54 are to be understood as flight from Jerusalem and has a certain parallel in the withdrawing of Jesus into the borderlands outside of Galilee in Mark. Mark reports only in 3.7 that Jesus also had people come to him from Judaea and in 10.1 (= Matt 19.1) that he went on the way to Jerusalem to Judaea. Luke has a much larger travel account, but with few concrete place-names: 9.51–19.27. Only a Samaritan village at the beginning (9.52) and twice the city Jericho (18.35; 19.1) are mentioned. On the whole, see chapter 11.

[53] Mark 3.7-8 portrays the activity of Jesus in an exaggerated way when he writes of a "large crowd from Galilee, Judaea, Jerusalem, Idumaea, from beyond the Jordan and the regions around Tyre and Sidon." Here he may also have in view the successes of the post-Easter mission. Matthew increases this further when he includes all Syria in 4.24 (probably a pointer to the provenance of the evangelist) and in 4.25 the Gentile Decapolis. While Mark speaks only once of a crowd from Judaea, Luke repeats this information in 4.44; 5.17; 6.17; 7.17. He already shifts the center of gravity of the activity of Jesus more toward Judaea, with John augmenting this tendency. Thus, there is an inclination to amplify the reach and "missionary" activity of Jesus.

[54] Luke 10.3-12; cf. Matt 10.7-15.

hearers in their hometowns and does not, as was the case with the Baptist, have them come to himself at a specific location in order to perform there the "eschatological sacrament" of baptism in the Jordan.

10.5 The Miracle Worker and the Question of the Baptist

While John 10.41 explicitly states that "John did no sign," and the Synoptics and Josephus also do not portray him as a miracle worker,[55] Jesus' activity as healer and miracle worker, alongside his proclamation, is constitutive for the entire Jesus tradition. This must have been regarded as a characteristic feature of his activity, which continued in the primitive Christian miracle tradition. The woes against the Galilean places of his activity,[56] which scarcely differ in their sharpness from the Baptist's preaching of judgment, point to this. This is a feature which clearly distinguishes him from the Baptist. By contrast, in Jesus' activity in Galilee we no longer find any "sacramental" actions such as the baptism of John. His special authority shows itself in sensational healings of sick people and other "deeds of power." For him they are signs of the present dawning of the kingdom of God, of the turning of God to the poorest of the poor as the eschatological fulfillment of prophetic promises,[57] the expression of victory over the powers of evil.[58] While the Baptist promises the forgiveness of sins only as a consequence of the baptism of repentance, Jesus can himself pronounce forgiveness to the lame man in a unique authority. He dared, in the words of Ernst Fuchs, "to act in the place of God,"[59] a behavior that could appear as blasphemy to the onlookers. All this is an expression of the authority of Jesus that could only be understood as messianic, with which he announced the coming of God, which was already effectual in the present. It corresponds to this that Jesus was maligned as a magician in the Talmudic witnesses and in Celsus.[60] According to Mark 3.22,[61] he is accused of driving out demons with the help of Beelzebul, the chief devil. In John 8.48 he is called a Samaritan who is possessed by

---

[55] At best such an activity could be inferred from Luke 1.17a: "And he will go before him in the spirit and power of Elijah." In Mark 6.14 miracles are performed only by Jesus as John "raised from the dead."

[56] Luke 10.13-14 = Matt 11.21-22. On this, see sections 11.1, 12.12 with note 66, and section 16.1.

[57] Cf. Isa 35.2-5; 58.6; 61.1; 4Q521 and the discussion below.

[58] Luke 11.20 = Matt 12.28; see section 13.6 with notes 136–38.

[59] Mark 2.9. Fuchs 1965, 156: Jesus' "behavior, however, is neither that of a prophet nor of a wisdom teacher but rather the behavior of a person who dares to act in the place of God."

[60] On the image of Jesus as a magician, see Smith 1978; on this, see Bühner 1983.

[61] Cf. Luke 11.15 = Matt 9.34 and 12.24.

a demon. The opponents of Jesus denounce his activity, which announces God's coming to the outcasts, in polemical reversal as an epiphany of the devil. By contrast, no miracles are ascribed to John the Baptist, though his rigorous asceticism is interpreted as "possession."[62] According to our sources, the Elijah *redivivus*, who issues the call to repentance in the face of God's impending judgment of wrath, is, in contrast to the prophet Elijah and his student Elisha, not a miracle worker. Josephus, too, portrays him only as an ethical preacher, whereas with Jesus he emphasizes his "wonderful works" (παράδοξα ἔργα).[63] This difference is also confirmed by the question of the Baptist.[64] The imprisoned John is said to have sent disciples to Jesus with the question: "Are you the coming one or should we expect another?" The 'coming one' (ἐρχόμενος) refers to the announcement in the preaching of the Baptist: "there comes one who is stronger than I."[65] The answer of Jesus (Luke 11.18ff.; Matt 11.2ff.) reads:

> Go and announce to John what you have seen and heard:
> Blind see, lame walk, lepers become cleansed,
> deaf hear, dead persons rise, and *to the poor good news is preached*.
> But blessed is the one who does not take offense at me.

This entire scene, as well as the following speech of Jesus about the Baptist, prohibits the assumption that Jesus was a disciple of the Baptist for an extended period of time. It signals, despite his high esteem for John, a certain distance.[66]

The answer of Jesus echoes a series of Isaianic texts.[67] A much-discussed messianic text from Cave 4 of Qumran reads as follows:[68]

---

[62] John 10.41; on the accusation against the Baptist, see Luke 7.33 = Matt 11.18: δαιμόνιον ἔχει.

[63] Josephus, *Ant.* 18.63, 117–118; see section 9.1.1 and chapter 16.

[64] Luke 7.18ff. = Matt 11.2ff.

[65] See section 9.1.2.1 with note 27 and the end of section 9.1.2.2 on Mark 1.8 = Luke 3.16 = Matt 3.11; cf. also Mark 11.9 and Ps 118.25-26; Hab 2.3; on this, see Brunson 2003, 112–13, 121–22.

[66] See section 9.1.2.1 and section 10.1.

[67] The most conspicuous are Isa 29.18-19; 35.5-6; 26.19 and especially 61.1-2; cf. also Luke 4.17-19 and Mark 7.37 = Matt 15.31.

[68] 4Q521 frag. 2 II (trans. García Martínez / Tigchelaar 1997/1998, II: 1045, our emphasis); on this, see Zimmermann 1998, 343–89. The exhortation to "heaven and earth," i.e., the whole creation, introduces in Isa 1.2 the speech of God mediated through the prophet and in Deut 32.1 the "Song of Moses," in which God himself, in closing, speaks through Moses to his people.

1 [For the heav]ens and the earth will listen to *his anointed one*,[69]
2 [and all th]at is in them will not turn away from the precepts of the
holy ones.
3 Strengthen yourselves, you who are seeking the Lord, in his service!
4 Will you not in this encounter the Lord,
all those who hope in their heart?
5 For the Lord will consider the pious,
and call the *righteous* by name,[70]
6 and his *spirit* will hover[71] over *the poor*,
and he will renew the faithful with his strength.
7 For he will honour the pious
upon the throne of an eternal *kingdom*,[72]
8 freeing *prisoners*,
giving sight to the *blind*,
straightening out the twis[ted.][73]
9 And for[e]ver shall I cling [to those who h]ope, and in his mercy [. . .]
10 and the fru[it of . . .] . . . not be delayed.
11 And the Lord will perform *marvelous* acts such as have not existed,
just as he sa[id]
12 [for] he will *heal the badly wounded*
and *will make the dead live*,
he will proclaim good news to the poor,[74]
13 and [. . .] . . . [. . .] he will lead the [. . .] . . .[75]
and enrich *the hungry*.

The agreements between this text and Jesus' answer to the Baptist are
conspicuous. To some extent the same Old Testament texts stand behind

---

[69] *Yšm ʿw lmšḥw*: it is very likely that the singular must be read here. Defective writing in the case of the plural with suffix is very rare in the Qumran texts. The plural "his
anointed ones" in the sense of "his prophets" would also not make good sense given the
eschatological context.
[70] Cf. Isa 43.1; 45.3.
[71] *Trḥp*; cf. Gen 1.2 and Deut 32.11; Matt 5.3; Luke 6.20.
[72] *Mlkwt ʿd*; cf. Luke 22.30; Matt 19.28, see note 120 in chapter 11.
[73] Psalm 146.7-8; cf. Isa 61.1c and Matt 11.28; Luke 4.18.
[74] Isaiah 61.1.
[75] Cf. Zimmermann 1998, 347 (our emphasis), who follows Puech's supplementation:
"13 . . . (Elend)e wird er (*satt machen*), Vertriebene wird er führen—und *Hunger(nde?)*
reich machen"; ET = "13 . . . (miserabl)e he will (*make sated*), (expell)ed he will lead—and
hunger(ing ones?) he will make rich."

them.[76] Beyond this, the motif of "freeing"[77] is related to Jesus' healings of demons, the "hungry" to the feeding narratives and the messianic meal, and the exhortation to "hope" to the fulfillment of the promises and to the parousia parables.[78] Moreover, the participation of the faithful in the eternal kingdom of God (line 7) is a central motif of the proclamation of Jesus. The fact that after the reference to the universal effect of the message of the anointed one, God himself appears as the actor from line 5 onward does not tell against the "messianic" character of this unique text, which, like no other text from Qumran, illuminates the eschatological activity of Jesus: *God acts through his authorized representative for his people.*[79] The relation to the Beatitudes and to Jesus' inaugural sermon in Nazareth on Isa 61.1-2 according to Luke 4.17-21 is also conspicuous. By contrast, the text is separated by a ditch from the elements of the proclamation of the Baptist known to us.[80] Therefore, illuminated by 4Q521, probably the most important contemporary parallel to it, Jesus' answer to the question of the Baptist can be understood only as a "messianic text." It contains not only an implicit Christology but rather a Christology that is already explicit to some extent.

10.6 The Love of God for the Sinner

The climax of this listing "to the poor good news is preached"[81] points at the same time to the decisive difference between the proclamation of Jesus and of the Baptist. The Baptist announces the impending judgment and calls for repentance and its fruits. For Jesus threat and warning are not in the first instance typical—although with him, too, these are certainly not absent.[82] What is typical, however, is the proclamation of the nearness, indeed the presence of salvation, the promise of the merciful love of God for the poor and lost. In a striking way he addresses the "lost sheep of the

---

[76] Isaiah 26.19: resurrection of the dead; 35.5: healing of the blind; 61.1: proclamation of salvation in relation to the poor.

[77] Cf. Isa 61.1. On the influence of this text, see also 11QMelch II 18ff. and Luke 4.17-21.

[78] Cf. Luke 12.45; Matt 24.48; 25.5; cf. also Hab 2.3: *lo ʾyᵉ ʾaḥer.*

[79] In Isa 61.1-2 the Spirit-anointed of the Lord acts, while in lines 5 and 12 of 4Q521 God himself appears to be the proclaimer of the good news vis-à-vis the poor.

[80] Luke 6.20ff. and Matt 5.3-11.

[81] Luke 7.22 (cf. 4.18) = Matt 11.5: πτωχοὶ εὐαγγελίζονται, Isa 61.1 and 4Q521 frag. II 2, line 12. This is a strong Semitism. The Aramaic passive of *beśar* has the meaning "to receive the good news." See Levy 1867, 103.

[82] See section 10.3.

house of Israel,"[83] which means marginalized people, "tax collectors and sinners,"[84] as in the first beatitude according to Luke 6.20: "Blessed are the poor, *to you belongs* the kingdom of God."[85] This is said in the present tense. The future appears only in the two following macarisms of those who hunger and who mourn. The πτωχοί[86] are the socially poor, the sick, people who are despised and excluded because of their sin, and yet also the hated tax collectors, i.e., the "marginalized groups" of the Galilean population. To them he proclaims salvation, without tying it, as the Baptist did, to conditions that are first to be fulfilled. He does not say: "Blessed are you poor if you repent." Rather, he knows that this promise of salvation can transform human beings. The indicative, the effective presence of the dawning kingdom of God that is already active in Jesus' person, grounds the imperative and not vice versa.

Good examples can be found especially in the Lukan special material, for example in the story about the chief tax collector Zacchaeus in Jericho[87] or about the woman who is a great sinner.[88] For this reason, he is—in a completely different way from the Baptist, who is criticized for his radical asceticism—defamed by the pious because of his friendship with sinners.[89] The behavior of the father in the parable of the lost son is foundational. He hurries to meet the son, whom he sees coming from afar, and embraces and kisses him before the son can say even a word! The shepherd seeks out the lost sheep until he finds it, and the woman the lost denarius. This means the Father, in Jesus, seeks out the sinner and not vice versa. The sinner can repent only through the fact that he experiences that the Father loves him. And there is joy in heaven over such finding of the lost.[90] The return of the lost son is celebrated as a feast of joy.[91]

---

[83] Matthew 10.6; 15.24. With this phrasing, which is only used by him, the evangelist interprets in a fitting way the entire activity of Jesus; cf. also Mark 6.34 = Matt 9.36 and Luke 15.4.

[84] Mark 2.15-16 = Luke 5.30 = Matt 9.10-11; Luke 7.34 = Matt 11.19.

[85] Μακάριοι οἱ πτωχοί, ὅτι ὑμετέρα ἐστὶν ἡ βασιλεία τοῦ θεοῦ. Cf. also Matt 5.3.

[86] Here we could call to mind the fact that the "poor" (ʾebionîm and ʿanāwîm) is also used as a self-designation by the Qumran Essenes. The primitive community in Jerusalem and later the Jewish Christians adopted this designation. On this, see Hengel/Schwemer 2019.

[87] Luke 19.1-10.

[88] Luke 7.36-50; cf. also the secondarily inserted pericope of the woman taken in adultery in John 8.1-11.

[89] Cf. Matt 11.18-19 = Luke 7.33-34. See section 10.7.

[90] Luke 15.7, 10.

[91] Luke 15.22-25.

The path from Jesus to Paul passes especially through the Lukan Jesus tradition, which is historically reliable.[92] It is only with Matthew, by contrast, that the message of Jesus is brought closer again to that of the Baptist, namely through his emphasis on judgment and condemnation, which multiplies sixfold the singular threat of judgment of the sayings tradition "there will be weeping and gnashing of teeth there."[93] The long-dominant portrayal of Jesus according to the picture that Matthew gave to him had to lead to a one-sided understanding of his message, which was related to the preaching of the Baptist.

10.7 The Disciples and the Call to Freedom and Joy[94]

A difference also emerges from the calling of the disciples to follow Jesus. Like the rabbis, the Baptist received disciples who came to him in order to learn from him and probably also to imitate his ascetic way of life. As a sign of their attitude of repentance they fasted as did the Pharisees.[95] By contrast, with Jesus—as with the callings of the Old Testament prophets—the initiative proceeded not from the disciples but from Jesus himself. The calling also means election. He calls *individuals* from their occupations and families to follow him. In a similar way ever since Elisha and Amos, God called the prophets of the old covenant out of their daily life. The follower had to share with Jesus the freedom from family and the lack of possessions.[96] Those who were called were to announce the dawning reign of God—like Jesus—in word and deed.[97]

Regarding the Baptist we do not hear that he sent out his disciples as messengers. This would contradict his practice of baptism. Although he is a priest, he also does not travel, like Jesus, up to the great festivals, but the crowds come down from all parts of Jewish Palestine to him at the Jordan.

With this we come to another difference from the Baptist. While the Baptist and his disciples lived as rigorous ascetics, with Jesus we do not find any special emphasis on ascetic characteristics. The freedom from

---

[92] Luke was the travel companion of Paul; see the discussions in chapters 1 and 2 and section 6.4.3.

[93] Luke 13.28 = Matt 8.12; 13.42, 50; 22.13; 24.51; 25.30. See the end of section 10.3 and section 14.4.

[94] Hengel 1981b (GV = Hengel 1968b).

[95] See notes 25 and 125 in chapter 9.

[96] The special emphasis on cross-discipleship in Mark could be connected to the fact that in Rome, where the Gospel arose, Nero had numerous Christians crucified a few years earlier (64 CE). Tacitus, *Ann.* 15.44.4: *aut crucibus adfixi atque flammati.*

[97] Mark 1.17 = Matt 4.19; cf. Luke 5.10; on this, see Hengel 1981b, 76–78 (GV = 1968b, 85–86; 2007b, 122–33). See also section 11.5.

familial bonds, which he placed on himself and required also from his followers, is not an end in itself and is not grounded, as in Qumran, by the demand for continuous ritual purity but rather is motivated by the freedom for the service of the announcement of the kingdom of God. While he, like the Baptist and Paul later, started no family, marriage is neither depreciated nor prohibited, as it was later among the radical encratic and gnostic ascetics in the second century CE.[98] For this reason he knows no dietary asceticism. He lets himself be invited to peasant weddings, where celebrations lasted for days, until the wine ran short.[99] Likewise, he goes to banquets of the hated tax collectors and is promptly reviled by his opponents as a "glutton and winebibber," as "a friend of tax collectors and sinners," whereas the Baptist is defamed as "a man possessed" because of his radical food asceticism.[100] At the same time, however, he also accepts invitations from Pharisees.[101]

He also shows the same freedom toward traditional prejudices in his relation to women. It is not only male disciples but also individual women who are in his following. Galilean women, to some extent from his relatives, also accompany him in the last journey to Jerusalem and become eyewitnesses of the crucifixion and of the empty tomb.[102] In the tradition about the Baptist they appear only at the margins, for example in Matt 21.31 (αἱ πόρναι). That they, too, were baptized can be inferred only from plerophoric specifications such as Mark 1.5 or Luke 3.7. The Baptist and his disciples had the starkly ascetic way of life in common with the Essenes and in a attenuated way with the Pharisees. It distinguished them, however, from Jesus and his followers. Jesus' answer to the question about fasting in Mark 2.18-19 points to the radically new, which separates the time of the Baptist from the time of Jesus. It is the difference between the announcement of the coming, purely future salvation and the

---

[98] On the marriage of Peter, cf. Mark 1.29-31 = Luke 4.38-39 = Matt 8.14-15; 1 Cor 9.5. On this, see Hengel 2010a, 103–34 (GV = 2006b, 167–220). On the radical requirement of celibacy in the second century CE and a corresponding interpretation of the Gospel texts, see Bauer 1967b, 323–28. For example, sy^s and Ephraim, in dependence on Tatian, turn the seven-year marriage of Anna in Luke 2.36 into seven days; see NA^{27}, ad loc.

[99] Cf. John 2.1-10; on this, see Bauer 1967b, 316–22; in Bill. I: 505ff. we can read about the high-spirited character of such weddings: the celebration lasted for seven days, the wine flowed in streams. It is telling that such a miracle was ascribed to Jesus; on this, see Hengel 2007b, 568–600 (ET = 1995, 293–331).

[100] Luke 7.33-34 = Matt 11.18-19. All these texts later presented difficulties for interpreters who were inclined toward a stricter asceticism.

[101] Luke 7.36ff.; 11.37ff.; 14.1ff. Matthew suppresses this motif.

[102] Mark 15.40-41 = Matt 27.55-56; cf. Luke 23.49, 55-56; 24.1-11, 22. In Luke the circle of women appears to be larger than in Mark. They also are to have known about his passion predictions; cf. Luke 24.6-8. On the relatives of Jesus, see John 19.25.

proclamation of the now dawning salvation: "How can the wedding guests fast as long as the groom is among them?" In the parables the metaphor of the wedding is Jesus' expression for the kingdom of God itself. The groom is the one who brings it. The answer of Jesus thus points to the externally hidden claim of the kingdom of God in his activity. There is no longer room here for ascetic practices of repentance.

10.8 The Baptist as the Last Prophet and the Messianic Authority of Jesus

It is peculiar that despite this distinction between the activity of the Baptist and of Jesus, which is to some extent fundamental, Jesus himself and the primitive community later could sketch such a positive picture of the Baptist. At least in individual points the difference between Jesus and the Baptist appears to be hardly any less sharp than the difference between Jesus and the Pharisees.[103] One thing has also become clear: The popular summary of Jesus and the Baptist under the umbrella term of the (eschatological) *prophet*,[104] with the Baptist appearing more as a prophet of judgment and Jesus as a prophet of salvation, overlooks *the fundamental qualitative distinction* that separates the two. The key to the appropriate distinction is to be sought in Jesus' proclamation itself, for example in Luke 16.16: "The law and the prophets go until John, from then on the kingdom of God is proclaimed and everyone presses with violence into it (καὶ πᾶς εἰς αὐτὴν βιάζεται)." With the second part of the sentence Luke has presumably interpreted a text that is difficult to interpret from the sayings tradition, which Matthew may preserve in its original form: "from the days of John the Baptist until now the kingdom of God suffers violence, and violent men seize it to themselves."[105] This debated verse is to be interpreted not negatively with reference to the Zealots or other opponents of Jesus but rather in a positive way. The "violent ones" (βιασταί) are those who behave like the one who finds the treasure in the field or like the merchant with the pearl in the parable.[106] They are those who put everything on the line for the sake of the kingdom of God and in the discipleship of Jesus, who risk everything in order to win the *one* thing. What is decisive, however, is the first part of the Lukan sentence: The time of "law and prophets" reaches

---

[103] Cf. Mark 2.18 parr.; in Luke 5.33 the disciples of the Baptist, like the students of the Pharisees, connect fasting with prayer. According to Luke 11.1, the Baptist teaches his disciples to pray.

[104] Cf., for example, J. Becker 1972.

[105] Matthew 11.12: Ἀπὸ δὲ τῶν ἡμερῶν Ἰωάννου τοῦ βαπτιστοῦ ἕως ἄρτι ἡ βασιλεία τῶν οὐρανῶν βιάζεται καὶ βιασταὶ ἁρπάζουσιν αὐτήν.

[106] Matthew 13.44ff. See section 13.2 with note 52.

only until John. Then the radically new begins, i.e., the time of the kingdom of God that commences with Jesus' activity. The Matthean parallel in
11.13—"all the prophets and the law have prophesied until John"—also
shows that here Jesus assigns the Baptist still to the law and the prophets.
When Jesus, in his speech about the Baptist, characterizes him at the same
time as "more than a prophet"[107] and stresses that none of those born from
women is greater than he, then he regards him as an eschatological figure,
who surpasses all earlier prophets. The second part of the sentence in Luke
7.28 = Matt 11.11b shows the difference: "but the 'smaller one' in the kingdom of God is greater than he." With this Jesus presumably means himself
as the younger one, who comes after John and was baptized by him. Looking back on the prophetic era, the Baptist is the last and the greatest, but
now, with the dawning kingdom of God, new, entirely different standards
apply. The parallel to Jesus' answer to the question of the Baptist—"Are
you the one who is to come . . . ?"—as well as the question from the Baptist's disciples about fasting is obvious.[108] If the Baptist as Elijah *redivivus*
is greater than all earlier prophets, the series of which he concludes, then
Jesus himself is—this conclusion appears unavoidable to us—the *messianic* consummator.[109] Only in his messianic claim, which transcends all
prophetic models, does Jesus' proclamation—precisely in comparison with
the Baptist—gain its meaningful unity. With this we come to the actual key
to the activity of Jesus, which German exegesis since William Wrede has
admittedly all too often lost—it must be said, carelessly.[110]

After the appearance of the Baptist, there was basically no more room
for another eschatological prophet. If Jesus likewise appeared as such a
prophet, he would actually have had to reject the Baptist as a proclaimer of
half-truths or of falsehood. He does not, however, do this but rather praises
him, defends him and his baptism, and places him—in full consciousness
of the difference—at his side. Indeed, he turns the defamatory judgment
that the opponents make about the Baptist and him into a paradigm of their
childish foolishness and understands himself with the Baptist as representatives of divine Wisdom.[111] This close, indeed unique connection of the
Baptist with Jesus, despite all differences, is best explained by two factors:

---

[107] Luke 7.26 = Matt 11.9: περισσότερον προφήτου.

[108] See section 5.1.

[109] On this, see Neugebauer 1986, 1: "If it were possible to formalize Messiahhood in
the extreme, one would have to say: Messiah is the one after whom another is no longer
expected. This would correspond to the question, which later comes to Jesus from the Baptist: Are you the coming one or should we expect another (Matt 11.3 par.)?"

[110] On this, see the beginning of section 17.1 and sections 17.3.1 and 17.3.2.

[111] Luke 7.31-35; cf. Matt 11.16-19; on this, see Hengel 2001c, 88–91 (ET = 1995,
80–83).

first, that Jesus already regarded the Baptist as the last prophet in Israel *before* the dawning of the time of salvation, that is, as his forerunner and as Elijah *redivivus*,[112] and secondly, that he understood himself to be the one in whom the promises of the prophets were fulfilled. Hence also the opposition between the kingdom of God and the Baptist. Hence his answer to the question of the Baptist in which he points to the fulfillment of the promises of Isaiah in his healing miracles and which culminates in the quotation from Isa 61.1: "and to the poor the good news is proclaimed."[113] Here in his good news, which brings "liberation" to the poor, lies the decisive difference from the Baptist, who with a call to repentance and baptism in the Jordan prepared for the coming of the "stronger one." They are connected by the fact that their message makes a final eschatological claim, whereas the content of this message and their behavior distinguish them. At the same time, it is clear that we cannot today go back to a time before Johannes Weiss and Albert Schweitzer and thereby reshape Jesus into a noneschatological wisdom teacher, let alone a "Jewish Socrates" or "Galilean Cynic." The question, of course, is how and why he proclaimed *the coming of the kingdom of God* as the center of his message. When Conzelmann, in his article "Jesus Christ" in the third edition of *Religion in Geschichte und Gegenwart* (RGG), writes that "the concepts of prophet and rabbi designate only partial aspects and precisely not the core of the matter,"[114] we will gladly agree with him. However, when he continues: "Jesus understands himself as the *final* herald. His place is unique since after him nothing more 'comes' except God himself," then we must object: Did not the Baptist already understand himself in this way, and did not Jesus himself, according to Mark and the sayings tradition, also interpret the Baptist in this way?[115] What constitutes, then, the—certainly fundamental—difference from the Baptist? After all, there can hardly be two "unique" final heralds alongside each other or in succession, who are, in the view of Jesus and the primitive community, closely related to each other. Our attempt to approach Jesus historically is focused here on the relationship of the Galilean itinerant preacher to John the Baptist. Here, three thematic circles are significant: the proclamation of the kingdom of God with its ethical content, his activity as miracle worker, and the special *messianic* character of his message.[116]

---

[112] Mark 9.13 = Matt 17.12; 11.14; cf. Luke 1.17; see note 33 in chapter 9.

[113] See note 81 in section 10.6 above. See also section 13.2 and elsewhere.

[114] Conzelmann 1959, 633 (Conzelmann's emphasis; ET = 1973a, 50). On this, see Hengel 2001d, 31ff. (ET = 1995, 29ff.).

[115] When John 1.6-8, 15, 19, 32; 3.23-36 (cf. 5.33ff.) makes the Baptist the first witness to Jesus, he only leads the Synoptic tradition to its ultimate conclusion.

[116] On this, see chapters 13–17.

PART IV
Jesus' Activity and Proclamation

11

On the Geographical-Historical Framework of the Activity of Jesus

11.1 Galilee as the Starting Point of the Activity of Jesus and the Question of the Chronology of Jesus[1]

Since J. Wellhausen, W. Wrede, and then especially K. L. Schmidt shattered the long-recognized, seemingly historically valid "biographical framework" of the Gospel of Mark, it has been taken for granted that we can no longer write a biography of Jesus. This is certainly to be affirmed if by biography we understand a chronologically sequential presentation of a human life or of a decisive phase of life through which the inner and outer development of the hero, the consequences of his deeds and thus also his fate, are explained.[2]

The narrative of Mark—upon which Luke and Matthew build—with its visit to Jerusalem for the Passover of his death and an activity of Jesus that lasted about one year, rests in this unilinear form on a construction that simplifies the historical reality. This was already recognized in the early church. With reference to a tradition of the "Presbyter" John, Papias therefore writes that Mark reported the deeds and words of Jesus οὐ μὲν τάξει, not in the right (temporal) order. The structure of the Fourth Gospel, which knew the Gospel of Mark, contradicts this not only in its Christology and presentation of the proclamation of Jesus, but also in its chronology. We have already pointed out multiple times that according to the Gospel of John, Jesus' activity extended over three Passover festivals,[3] i.e., over more than two years. According to Eusebius and the

---

[1] Conzelmann 1973a (GV = 1959); Freyne 1988; 2000.

[2] On this, see section 7.1 with note 22.

[3] (1) John 2.13, 23; (2) 6.4; (3) 11.55; 12.1; 13.1 and elsewhere. On the difficult problem of the Passover festival in John, see Bauer 1967b, 279ff. John 5.1 was controversial,

later fathers, it lasted almost four years. John is said to have "delivered afterward" the report of the earlier years before the arrest of the Baptist, which was passed over by the Synoptics. According to John, Jesus travels also at least three times from Galilee to Jerusalem, and his last stay in Jerusalem basically lasts from the festival of booths in October via the festival of Hanukkah in December with two interruptions forced by threats to his person[4] to the Passover of his death.[5] However, in our view, it is doubtful whether this radical correction of the Synoptic chronology is more accurate historically.

We can no longer specify with exactness the time of the public activity of Jesus. The period of about one year in Mark[6] is probably somewhat too short. For example, we can probably presuppose several trips to Jerusalem since he was—also according to Mark—known there. John

---

where Irenaeus, *Haer.* 2.22.3, interpreted ἑορτή as Passover, whereas Origen rejected this identification. The Roman Presbyter Gaius considered the chronological disagreement between John and the Synoptics to be so weighty that he, toward the end of the second century, regarded the Fourth Gospel as a forgery of the arch-heretic Cerinthus; see Hengel 1993a, 26–27 (ET = 1989a, 5–6). On Papias, see Eusebius, *Hist. eccl.* 3.39.15. See also section 6.5.

[4] John 10.39–11.16 and 11.53-57. On the early church, see Schmidt 1919, 1ff.; Merkel 1971, 147ff.; Merkel 1978, 19ff.; Eusebius, *Hist. eccl.* 3.24.8–13: John is said to contain τὰ πρῶτα τῶν τοῦ Χριστοῦ πράξεων (3.24.13).

[5] John 7.2–11.55; on the two interruptions, see 10.40-41: Jesus withdraws to Peraea, where John baptized, and 11.54: according to Ephraim near the wilderness; on this, see Soggin 1972, 420–21 nr. 2.

[6] This can also be inferred only indirectly, for example through the reference to the ripe grainfields in Mark 2.23 parr. The time of the grain harvest fell in the time between the Passover festival and the festival of weeks. The duration of the activity of Jesus caused some confusion already in the early church from the beginning onward; see Bauer 1967b, 279–310. At that time advocates of a one-year activity and advocates of a duration that lasted more than a year were already juxtaposed. According to Clement of Alexandria (*Strom.* 1.146) the followers of Basilides, and according to Irenaeus (*Haer.* 1.3.3; 1.20.1; 1.22.1, 3, 5) the Valentinians, advocated a period of about one year, with the latter appealing to "the favorable year of the Lord" mentioned in Luke 4.19 (Bauer 1967b, 381–82). Due to the significance of the number twelve, they placed value on the twelve-month preaching of Jesus. Other advocates of a one-year period were the docetists in Hippolytus, the Allogoi of Epiphanius, who rejected John and therefore knew only one Passover, as well as the Pseudo-Clementines, Clement of Alexandria, Tertullian, Julius Africanus, Lactantius, and others. Even the view of Origen appears not to have been uniform here. The Johannine interpretation of at least two or three to four years is followed by authors influenced by John, such as Tatian in his Diatessaron and Melito, frag. VI (Perler 1966, 266: ἐν τῇ τριετίᾳ μετὰ τὸ βάπτισμα). By contrast, on the basis of John 8.57 (see note 10 below), Irenaeus assumes a much longer lifetime of Jesus of forty–fifty years (*Haer.* 2.22.6), although Jesus, according to Luke 3.23, was said to have been thirty years old at his baptism. According to *Epid.* 74 he was condemned to death jointly by Herod, the king of the Jews, and Pilate, the procurator of Emperor Claudius (!).

may have possessed more extensive traditions here, but they have been so transformed through his christological narrative interest that we can no longer get behind them. He sought to present with all due sharpness the controversy of Jesus with his Jewish opponents in Jerusalem, which concerned the truth of his divine claim and his oneness with the Father. He was less interested in Galilee and the Galileans. Luke occupies something of an intermediate position with his unusually long travel narrative, which he has begin with the rejection in a Samaritan village.[7] Already early on in his report of Jesus' activity he recounts that Jesus preached "in the synagogues of Judaea," although he has him appear on the Lake of Gennesaret right after this, where he calls Peter.[8] Luke 5.17 and 6.17 emphasize that the crowd streamed to him from all over Judaea and that the news of his miraculous activity circulated "in all Judaea and the surrounding (i.e., predominantly Gentile) area" (Luke 7.17). This means that Luke expands the Galilean activity in the south, while leaving the reader in the dark about the concrete geography. On the other hand, on multiple occasions he explicitly stresses, even beyond Mark and Matthew, the Galilean origin of Jesus and his disciples.[9] Apparently, he is concerned to uphold the Galilean origin of Jesus and his movement as well as his activity within all Judaea. In substance he is not entirely wrong, for after Easter Galilee plays no role in the early Christian texts outside of the Gospels. The historian Luke is also the only one who refers to the age of Jesus at the beginning of his activity. At that time he is said to have been "about thirty years old." This specification has Old Testament models in Josephus and David and must not be misunderstood as an exact specification of age.[10]

On the whole we wish, amidst all caution, to emphasize three points:

---

[7] Luke 9.51-19.27. On the Samaritan village, see 9.52-56 and section 11.3 with note 67.

[8] Luke 4.44; cf., however, 4.14, 31: Galilee. See also note 53 in chapter 10. Here Luke may mean the expanded "Judaea," which includes Galilee. On the calling of Peter, see 5.1-11.

[9] Luke 1.26; 2.4, 39; 4.14; 22.59; 23.49, 55; 24.6; Acts 1.11; 2.7 and the formulaic ἀρξάμενος ἀπὸ τῆς Γαλιλαίας in Luke 23.5 and Acts 10.37. In general Luke was somewhat familiar with the geography of Judaea, above all of the coastal region. By contrast, he does not know Galilee. See Hengel 1983a (ET = 1983c, 87–132, 190–210) and Böhm 1999. In Mark 14.70 = Matt 26.69 Peter is designated as a Galilean in the high priestly palace before the denial.

[10] Luke 3.23: καὶ αὐτὸς ἦν Ἰησοῦς ἀρχόμενος ὡσεὶ ἐτῶν τριάκοντα; cf. Gen 41.46: Joseph before Pharaoh; 2 Sam 5.4: "David was thirty years old when he became king." If Jesus was born a few years before the death of King Herod, who died in 4 BCE, he had already passed the age of thirty: see Matt 2.3, 7, 16, 19; Luke 1.5. However, such specifications of time and age consistently have relatively small value. In John 8.57 "the Jews" charge Jesus that he "is not yet fifty years old" but claims to have seen Abraham. On the importance of this text for Irenaeus, see note 6 above.

1. With Mark and against John, the greater portion of Jesus' activity, in terms of time, took place in Galilee and in the directly adjacent regions and not in Judaea or Jerusalem. In any case, Galilee is the starting point and center of gravity of his activity. In Acts, in Epictetus, and especially in Julian the Apostate the Christians are called Γαλιλαῖοι; Jesus himself is "the Galilean."[11]

2. With John against Mark, Jesus, like every pious Palestinian Jew, traveled to Jerusalem several times a year to festivals. This is shown by the Bethany tradition[12] and by the Samaritan traditions in Luke and John,[13] which also point to a journey of Jesus through Samaria. Thus, Jesus could have visited Jerusalem with his disciples already a year before the Passover of his death for the Passover festival and then later for the festival of booths.

3. The time of Jesus' activity was relatively short—at least one year, perhaps a year and a half, but probably not two full years. The date of his death was presumably Nisan 15, i.e., the first day of the Passover festival in 30 CE. If, in accordance with Luke 3.1-2, the Baptist appeared in the fifteenth year of the emperor Tiberius, toward the end of 27 CE or the beginning of 28 CE, and was killed after being imprisoned for some time in the first half of 29 CE,[14] then Jesus' public activity could have begun toward the end of 28 CE. In the case of these hypothetical specifications of time, we assume that both the Baptist and Jesus after him made such a provocative impression on the political and religious rulers that neither was granted all that much time. At least after the execution of the Baptist, Jesus must also have reckoned with the sacrifice of his own life. This alone already makes it unlikely that his public activity lasted for more than two or up to three years, as could be inferred from John. The extent to which there were times of preparation and transition remains unclear.

This time of one year or one and a half years of Jesus' public activity is basically the most fulfilled time in all of world history. No comparably short span of time from the life of a person has given rise to such effects that span centuries and continents, although this did not take place in one of the world centers of that time or even in the circles of the leading

---

[11] Acts 1.11; 2.7; cf. Matt 26.69. On this, see Hengel 2004c, 106ff. See also note 62 in chapter 4.

[12] Mark 11.11; 14.3 (it is presupposed that Jesus is already well-known there); cf. 14.12-15, 32; John 11.1ff.

[13] Luke 9.52; 17.16; John 4.4ff.

[14] In Jesus' question about the origin of the baptism of John in Mark 11.30ff. the death of the Baptist does not appear to be already years in the past. On the chronology of Jesus, see Riesner 1994, 31–52, though he argues with John for 14 Nisan in 30 CE as the date of Jesus' death. See also note 231 in chapter 3.

stratum of the Roman empire but rather among the Jewish people, which was so despised by the Greco-Roman upper stratum.

11.2 Places and Ways of Jesus in Galilee

The question is whether we can, beyond these few specifications about the framework of the history of Jesus, identify individual *fixed points*. This is possible only here and there. We have already pointed this out in connection with Galilee.[15] Such a geographic point is the activity of Jesus on the northwestern corner of the Lake of Gennesaret, which is bordered by the three places of Capernaum, Chorazin, and Bethsaida in a triangle whose sides are five to six kilometers long: Capernaum on the shore of the lake, Chorazin to the north of it in the mountains, and Bethsaida to the east at the mouth of the Jordan, which belonged already to Philip's territory. There at Bethsaida he had founded—probably around 30 CE—the polis of Julia, which was named after (Livia) Julia Augusta, the wife of Augustus and mother of Tiberius, but which did not obtain greater significance. Jesus' sharp woe sayings against these three places, where so many "demonstrations of divine powers" (δυνάμεις) took place,[16] suggest that they constituted the starting point of his activity. They no longer played any role for the later community, and their mention in the sayings tradition is not sufficient to designate "Q" as a source of the Galilean Jesus communities.[17] Jesus' first disciples also came from this region. According to John 1.44, Philip and the pair of brothers Simon Peter and Andrew come from Bethsaida. Andrew and Philip stand out here because of their Greek names.[18] According to John 12.20-21, it is precisely the two of them who are addressed by the Greeks who want to see Jesus. John presupposes as a given that they speak Greek. We find other references in Mark 8.22ff., the narrative about the blind man from Bethsaida, and between the narrative of the feeding and walking on water in Mark 6.45. It is the only place beyond the border of Galilee that—in addition to the Galilean Capernaum

---

[15] See sections 8.1 and 8.2.

[16] Luke 10.13ff. = Matt 11.21ff. On the place, see Schürer 1973–1987, I: 171–72, and the report of Arav 1999, 79–80, 85–86. The inhabitants' way of life was simple. There is little sign of "Hellenistic civilization." See also Hengel 2010a, 12–23, 40–41 (GV = 2006b, 19–20, 65–66).

[17] Except for Chorazin the two other places of Capernaum and Bethsaida are mentioned more frequently in Mark. The sayings tradition, just like Mark, points back to the Galilean activity of Jesus and not to the post-Easter Galilean communities. See also the end of section 8.1.

[18] Philip could have been named after his territorial sovereign, the tetrarch Philip. On this, cf. note 184 in chapter 3.

and Nazareth—appears in all four Gospels. It is possible that Simon Peter moved to Capernaum after his marriage. In Mark 1.21, 29-30 Jesus heals Simon Peter's mother-in-law of a fever there, and his house also appears to have been available to Jesus as a base. After his move to Capernaum (Matt 4.13; John 2.12), Matt 9.1 calls it his "own city" (τὴν ἰδίαν πόλιν). At the beginning of the second century CE, a rabbinic report[19] still designates Capernaum as a disreputable place of residence of Jewish Christians, in Hebrew *mînîm*, sectarians, who bewitched a student of a scholar so that he rode a donkey on the Sabbath and had to be sent away to Babylon by his uncle because of this scandal. The excavations under a Byzantine octagonal church have brought to light a pre-Constantinian house church, which is said to reach back into the second century CE. Whether this is the house of Peter admittedly remains even more uncertain than the question of the tomb of Peter under Saint Peter's Basilica in Rome.[20]

In addition to the aforementioned three places, from Galilee there is mention of the villages Nain (*nā'îm* = lovely), Luke 7.11ff.; Cana, John 2.1ff.,[21] Genesareth, Mark 6.53, and perhaps Magdala,[22] Mark 8.10, ca. five kilometers southwest of Capernaum. The newly founded polis of Tiberias appears only in John 6.1, 23 and 21.1 in connection with the lake and the boat miracle.

The narrative of the exorcism in an urban region inhabited by non-Jews on the eastern shore of the Lake of Gennesaret constitutes a difficult problem. According to the best textual witnesses, Mark 5.1 and Luke 8.26 write about "the territory of the Gerasenes," which is geographically impossible, since Gerasa, which belongs to the Decapolis, lies ca. fifty kilometers to the southeast of the lake in East Jordan. Matt 8.28 therefore speaks of the "territory of the Gadarenes."[23] This also cannot be accurate, since Gadara, which is likewise a well-known city of the Decapolis, though it is only ca. ten kilometers away from the southern end of the lake, does not border the lake with its city area. The only Gentile polis on the southern shore of the lake was Hippos Susitha.[24] Thus, as a correction,

---

[19] Midrash Qohelet Rabbah 1.8; Bill. I: 159.

[20] Reed 2000, 142–43, 158; Claussen 2002, 181; Hengel 2010a, 106–7 (GV = 2006b, 172–73).

[21] Cf. John 4.46; according to 21.2 it was the hometown of Nathanael. On the Galilean places, see the end of section 8.2.

[22] See note 76 in chapter 7. Mark has the mysterious designation Dalmanutha. Matthew has Magadan. Seybold 2000 suspects the salmon estuary two kilometers north of Magdala.

[23] Mark 5.1 = Luke 8.26: εἰς τὴν χώραν τῶν Γερασηνῶν (Matt 8.28: τῶν Γαδαρηνῶν), Mark: א* B D latt sa; Luke: P[75] B D latt sy[hmg]; Matthew: B C Θ al sy[s.p.h].

[24] On Gerasa, Gadara, and Hippos, see Schürer 1973–1987, II: 130–36, 149–55.

Origen advocated the reading "Gergesenes" (Γεργεσηνῶν) and spoke of an "old city" with a rocky cliff on the lake, while Eusebius calls Gergasa a "village on a mountain on the Lake of Tiberias."[25]

Apart from the starting point Capernaum, the majority of these specifications of place have been preserved by chance. Outside of the motherland, geographical details from Galilee were no longer important. This is why one also did not novelistically invent additional place-names, even in the "apocryphal" Gospels of the second century. The Gospels are equally reserved here and therefore reliable as is the case with personal names.

A conspicuous role for the Galilean activity of Jesus is played by the Lake of Gennesaret in all the Gospels but most strongly in Mark, who mentions it between 1.16 and 7.31 a total of seventeen times as "Sea of Galilea."[26] This un-Greek designation of an inland lake as a sea is biblical linguistic usage.[27] Here Matthew follows completely the Markan specification, while John calls the lake "Sea of Tiberias" after the new capital, which only he mentions.[28] By contrast, like Josephus, the Greek Luke uses only λίμνη, inland lake, once with the more specific characterization Γεννησαρέτ, but much more rarely than Mark and Matthew.[29] This conspicuous emphasis on the "Galilean Sea" in Mark and Matthew in the presentation of the activity of Jesus in his home province may be connected with the fact that the former fisherman Peter stands behind the second Gospel as guarantor, who is also a fundamental authority for Matthew. The first scene after the "prologue," Mark 1.14-15, begins by having

---

[25] Origen, *Comm. Jo* 7.41 §§ 208–211 (Blanc 1992, 288–89); Eusebius, *Onom.* (Klostermann 1904, 74). On this, see Zahn 1920, 760–64; Dalman 1967, 190–93. The fact that the reading Γεργεσηνων, which predominates later in the manuscripts, is older than the critical remarks of Origen can be seen in the fact that it already appears in old textual witnesses, thus in Luke 8.26 in א and Θ and in Mark 5.1 among others in sy⁵ and in Ephrem's commentary on the Diatessaron: "au pays des Gergézéniens" (trans. Leloir 1966, 97). It must therefore remain open whether it was not already Mark (and following him Luke) who confused the name of the unknown village of Gergesa with the well-known Gerasa or whether Mark did not, in fact, originally have ΓΕΡΓΕΣΗΝΩΝ and a very early copyist changed this to ΓΕΡΑΣΗΝΩΝ. In Matt 8.28 א has ΓΑΖΑΡΗΝΩΝ. See also Klostermann 1971, 47: The conjecture "Gergesa" is older than Origen.

[26] In Mark 1.16 he introduces it before the calling of the first disciples as θάλασσα τῆς Γαλιλαίας and repeats this designation when it is last mentioned in 7.31.

[27] Num 34.11 (in connection with the eastern border of Israel): *yām kinneret*: θάλασσα Χενέρεθ; cf. in v. 12 the "salt sea": θάλασσα ἡ ἁλυκή (Num 34.3; Deut 3.17; Josh 15.2, 5).

[28] John 21.1: τῆς θαλάσσης τῆς Τιβεριάδος; cf. 6.1: τῆς θαλάσσης τῆς Γαλιλαίας τῆς Τιβεριάδος. John concentrates the reference to the sea entirely on chapter 6. On the city itself, see 6.23 and section 3.1.2.

[29] Luke 5.1-2; 8.22-23, 33. On Josephus, see the concordance of Rengstorf 1973–1983, s.v. λίμνη.

Jesus go along "the shore of the Galilean Sea"[30] and call into discipleship the brother pairs Simon and Andrew and James and John, who are working as fishermen.[31] Later he withdraws from the crowd that is pressing upon him, which has come from the whole land of Israel and the neighboring regions, with his disciples to the beach and asks the disciples "that they keep ready for him a boat because of the crowd, lest they crush him."[32] Finally, he teaches the crowd from the boat, while the crowd on the beach listens to his speech "in parables."[33]

On multiple occasions he also crosses the lake, which is at most twelve kilometers wide,[34] from west to east and vice versa.[35] Through his cry "be silent, hush" he banishes a dangerous storm triggered by sudden winds from the west.[36] Indeed, around the third watch of the night, he is said to have surprised his disciples during a stormy wind by walking on the lake, so that they regarded him as a ghost and cried out from fear until he calmed them and came up to them into the boat. Matthew intensifies the miracle by having Peter, at the call of Jesus, come to him upon the waves, then sink in fear and doubt, but then be saved by Jesus.[37] "The whole northern half of the lake basin (becomes) a large scene of his story."[38] Clear traces of memories of disciples can also become visible in "summary reports," ideal scenes, and miracle narratives.

A completely different site of the activity of Jesus, which Luke emphasizes the most, is the Galilean synagogues as places of his teaching,

---

[30] Mark 1.16: Παράγων παρὰ τὴν θάλασσαν; cf. the similar phrasing in 2.13 (ἐξῆλθεν πάλιν παρὰ τὴν θάλασσαν) in the calling of the tax collector Levi, in 4.1 (ἤρξατο διδάσκειν παρὰ τὴν θάλασσαν), and 5.21 (ἦν παρὰ τὴν θάλασσαν).

[31] Mark 1.16-20 = Matt 4.18-22; Luke 5.1-11; cf. also Matt 17.27.

[32] Mark 3.7-9 (special material).

[33] Mark 4.1-2 = Matt 13.1-3; cf. Luke 5.1-3.

[34] On this, see W. E. Gerber 1966, 1751: the lake has an area of 170 square kilometers and is 21 kilometers long.

[35] Mark 4.35ff. parr.; 5.1, 21; cf. 6.32-33, 45ff.; 8.10, 14 par.

[36] Mark 4.35-41 = Luke 8.22-25 = Matt 8.23-27; on this, see Dalman 1967, 196–98.

[37] Mark 6.45-52 = Matt 14.22-33; cf. John 6.16-21. A comparison shows how such miracle narratives developed further and how they are theologically configured. While Mark 6.52 reproaches the fear of the disciples when Jesus appears as incomprehension and "hardness of heart," Matthew concludes the narrative with the *proskynesis* of the passengers of the boat and the confession to Jesus as "Son of God." John, by contrast, lets them, who were previously ca. twenty-five/thirty stadia (ca. four–five kilometers) from the shore, suddenly come to their goal in a miraculous way (6.21). Luke passes over the narrative in favor of his travel narrative. Here we can ask whether the original narrative was influenced by a report of an appearance of the risen one; cf. John 21.4, 7. It is also possible that it is based on a disciple's visionary experience.

[38] Dalman 1967, 196.

especially the synagogue in his main base of Capernaum[39] but also the one in his hometown of Nazareth.[40] Following Jesus' first appearance in Capernaum, Mark reports very generally: "And he went around, preached in their synagogues in all Galilee, and cast out demons."[41] Such summarizing redactional specifications are indeed to be taken seriously historically. This is already shown by the conflict resulting from healings on the Sabbath in synagogues, which is reported on multiple occasions.[42] The synagogue first found entrance in Eretz Israel in the first century CE in the Herodian period. Previously the danger of competition with the temple did not allow this institution in the motherland. There it was not given the name "place of prayer" (προσευχή) as in the diaspora, where such places are already attested by inscriptions in Ptolemaic Egypt toward the end of the third century BCE.[43] The Palestinian Jewish designation was consciously the neutral, indeed profane "house of assembly."[44] If one disregards the glorious basilica that Herod Antipas built in Tiberias, the early Galilean synagogues of the first century must have been simple, unadorned "houses of assembly," as they have been discovered, for example, in Gamla in the Golan. In Capernaum there lies under the remains of the great synagogal basilica from the fourth/fifth century CE the basalt floor of an older structure, which presumably belongs to the synagogue of the first century.[45] The descriptions of Jesus' activity in the synagogues of Galilee show him to be

---

[39] Mark 1.21ff., 29 par.

[40] Mark 6.2 = Matt 13.54; cf. Luke 4.16-30.

[41] Mark 1.39 = Matt 4.23; cf. Luke 4.15. After the lack of success in Nazareth, Luke replaces "the synagogues of Galilee" with "of Judaea" (4.44; see also note 8 above) and thus extends Jesus' activity to the whole of Jewish Palestine.

[42] Mark 3.1-6 parr.; Luke 13.10-17; cf. Mark 1.21ff. par. and Luke 14.1-6; see section 13.3.

[43] According to Isa 56.7 the temple was the true "house of prayer" (*bêt tefillāh* = οἶκος προσευχῆς); cf. Mark 11.17-18; see section 4.4 and Hengel 1996a, 171–95.

[44] *Bêt (ha)keneset* = (οἶκος) συναγωγῆς; see Jastrow 1903, I: 650; in Greek shortened as συναγωγή. The word already appears frequently in the Septuagint as a translation of *'ēdāh*, the assembly of Israel. From the beginning ἐκκλησία = *qāhāl* was a primitive Christian eschatological counterterm to it, though it admittedly does not (yet) occur in the Gospels with the exception of Matthew (16.18; 18.17); see Hengel/Schwemer 2019.

[45] On the Palestinian synagogues prior to 70 CE, see Claussen 2002, 168–91. On Gamla in particular, see idem, 168ff., where it says that the structure "(was) erected from the beginning as a building for assembly" and that the identification as synagogue is certain. See also idem, 180–81 on Capernaum. The synagogue is only ca. thirty-five meters away from the octagonal memorial church over the "house of Peter": "In Mark 1.29 the evangelist gives precisely this impression of nearby buildings" (idem, 181). Petrine tradition probably stands behind the whole Capernaum report in Mark 1.21-39. See also idem, 181–82, on the possibility of an old synagogue in Chorazin. On the building of synagogues in Palestine, see Milson 2007. For a discussion of the synagogue and synagogue stone discovered in Magdala, see now Aviam 2018; Aviam/Bauckham 2018. The majority of

a charismatic teacher and healer with singular authority. The hearers "were deeply moved (ἐξεπλήσσοντο) by his teaching, for he taught them as one who possessed authority and not as the scribes."[46]

11.3 Jesus in a Gentile Area, in Samaria, and His Way to the Passion[47]

A decisive historical date for Jesus' activity was evidently the violent action of Herod Antipas against the Baptist, presumably in the first half of 29 CE. After all, according to Mark 1.14 and Luke 3.19-20, Jesus begins his public preaching only after the arrest of John; according to John 3.22ff., however, the activity of the two overlaps. Here John may have rightly corrected Mark. Jesus probably did not appear as late as the Synoptic Gospels present it. The violent death of John after a certain time of imprisonment marked a turning point in his activity, for after the murder of the forerunner the mistrustful territorial ruler Antipas cast his eye also on the peculiar new itinerant preacher Jesus, who, in a similar way as the Baptist, attracted the people in an alarming way and was active not, like the Baptist, in distant Peraea but in his main territory of Galilee itself. In Luke 13.31-32 (special material) Pharisees warn Jesus: "Go away and disappear from here, for Herod wants to kill you!" He answers:

> Go and tell this fox: Look, I drive out demons and perform healings today and tomorrow, and on the third day I will be completed.

The metaphor of the cunning fox in the mouth of Jesus fits with that of the wavering reed.[48] Luke thus expresses Jesus' certainty that—in contrast to the Baptist—his territorial ruler cannot harm him. He fulfills his God-given eschatological task. This consists in "casting out demons and healings," which conspicuously stand in the place of his proclamation of the kingdom of God because they caused a sensation and also made the tetrarch curious (Luke 9.7-8; 23.8). In accordance with God's will, his

---

known synagogues come from late Roman-Byzantine time and are often influenced by church construction.

[46] Mark 1.22. Matthew 7.28-29 places this sentence at the end of the Sermon on the Mount. Cf. Luke 4.32 and Mark 1.27: διδαχὴ κατ᾽ ἐξουσίαν. On the authority of Jesus, see also section 11.4.

[47] Jeremias 1970, 258ff. (GV = 1979, 264ff.); Bayer 1986; Wilckens 2002–2005, I/2: 2–18.

[48] Luke 7.24-25; see section 8.1 with notes 22–23.

journeying ends only in Jerusalem, the place of the martyrdoms of the Old Testament prophets.[49]

Mark also reports the interest of Herod—whom he calls not tetrarch but, following popular convention, "king" (βασιλεύς)—in Jesus and, after this, recounts the martyrdom of the Baptist.[50] In Mark this is followed by references to Jesus' travel outside of the borders of Galilee—the urban areas of Tyre and Sidon in the west and north and the Decapolis in the east and southeast are mentioned[51]—and in the area of Bethsaida,[52] which belonged already to the Gaulanitis, i.e., to the territory of Philip. This escape beyond the borders of Galilee to entirely or predominantly Gentile areas is not an invention of Mark. It is best explained by the view that after the death of the Baptist Jesus wanted to withdraw from his territorial ruler's hostile aims toward him. By contrast, this crossing over from Jewish Galilee to predominantly Gentile areas scarcely has something to do with the later Gentile mission. The readers outside of Palestine knew too little about the geographical relations in and around Galilee to be able to produce such a connection. The only exception is the possessed man of Gerasa/Gergesa whom Jesus bars from joining him and instead instructs to tell his family members what "the Lord has done," upon which he proclaimed in the Decapolis the deed of Jesus so that "all marveled."[53] By contrast, the Gentile inhabitants of the place exhort Jesus to leave their area,[54] so that he returns by boat over the lake to Capernaum. Here an indirect pointer to the later Gentile mission could be present.

---

[49] Luke 13.33: what is decisive is the δεῖ με . . . πορεύεσθαι. While the logion is stylized by Luke, it contains elements that are clearly traditional. On the martyrdoms of the prophets, see Luke 13.34 = Matt 23.37; Luke 11.47ff. = Matt 23.29ff.; cf. 1 Thess 2.14-15; Acts 7.52.

[50] Mark 6.14-29. Matthew, following Luke, designates Herod as tetrarch in 14.1. In 14.8 he calls him, in dependence on Mark, βασιλεύς.

[51] Mark 7.24, 31: Jesus leaves the urban area of Tyre and comes (via the area of Sidon) to the Galilean sea right through (or in the middle of) the area of the Decapolis. According to Josephus, *Ant.* 18.153, the large area of Damascus, which belonged to the Decapolis, on the Anti-Lebanon bordered that of Sidon. Hippos on the eastern shore of the Lake of Gennesaret was also a member of the league of ten cities. Thus, Jesus would have wandered around Galilee in a great arc. Mark was not such an ignorant person regarding geography as hypercritical scholarship has wanted to present him. Cf. Hengel 1983a, 150–51 (ET = 1983c, 98–99, 193 n. 19).

[52] Mark 6.45; 8.22. The fishing village Bethsaida was predominantly Jewish. By contrast, Julias, like Tiberias, more likely possessed a mixed population. See section 3.1.2.

[53] Mark 5.18-20 = Luke 8.38-39. Matthew omits this sentence since in his work Jesus consciously concentrates on the proclamation to the Jews. On the place of the action, see note 25 above.

[54] Mark 5.17 = Luke 8.37 = Matt 8.34.

Such geographical notes demonstrate again that with respect to the framework of his Gospel, Mark was not entirely uninformed but rather processed historical tradition therein. According to Mark 8.22, Jesus heals a blind man in Bethsaida and then in 8.27 journeys again—accompanied by his disciples—to the north "into the villages of Caesarea Philippi," i.e., into the municipal area of the capital of the territory of Philip at the foot of Mount Hermon.[55] As already previously in Galilee and Phoenicia, he apparently avoids the larger cities—in sharp contrast to the tendency of the later primitive Christian missionaries. It is telling that Mark, around 70 CE, contrary to the development of the last twenty years since the apostolic council, does not yet speak of a clearly visible preparation of the Gentile mission by Jesus.[56] After all, according to 7.27, Jesus abruptly rejected the petition of the Syrophoenician woman in the "region of Tyre":[57] "Let the children be filled to satisfaction first. For it is not good to take the children's bread and throw it to the dogs." In Mark too, Jesus' activity is concentrated on his own people. Matthew further intensified this motif later. Jesus is sent only "to the lost sheep of the house of Israel."[58] When he sends them out, he also prohibits the disciples from going into "a city of the Samaritans and on the way to the Gentiles."[59] According to Matthew, only the risen one sends the eleven "to all nations," so that they make them into disciples.[60] By contrast, Luke and even more strongly John relate a turning of Jesus to the Samaritan "heretics."[61]

The crossing over to a non-Jewish region, which occurs multiple times according to Mark, is not simply a construction of Mark but rather has historical causes, which Mark expresses in his own popular way. Herod

[55] After the specification of the place as Caesarea Philippi (Mark 8.27), Mark 9.2 has Jesus climb a "high mountain" with three disciples (cf. 9.9). Here one could think of Mount Hermon as a mountain between heaven and earth with a revelatory function (1 En. 6.4–6; cf. 13.7; 2 En. 18.4).

[56] This appears first in the future prediction in Mark 13.10 and at the beginning of the passion story in 14.9.

[57] Mark 7.24: εἰς τὰ ὅρια Τύρου, i.e., to the west of Galilee. Matthew 15.21 adds schematically: καὶ Σιδῶνος, cf. Mark 7.31. According to Mark 3.8 a crowd of people already comes to him from Tyre and Sidon. Since both cities possessed large Jewish communities, it remains unclear whether Mark, as in 5.18ff., means Gentiles. Cf. also the saying of Jesus in Luke 10.13-14 = Matt 11.21-22: This means that Jesus did not do any miracles in the Gentile cities.

[58] Matthew 10.6 and 15.24 (special material).

[59] Matthew 10.5.

[60] Matthew 28.19; cf. 24.14 and 26.13 following the predictions of Jesus in Mark 13.10 and 14.9.

[61] Luke 9.52ff.; 17.16; cf. 10.33 and 17.11; John 4.4-42. See also Acts 8.5, where Philip does precisely what Matt 10.5 prohibits. On this, see Böhm 1999 and Hengel/Schwemer 2019.

Antipas, who takes note of Jesus, regards him as John *redivivus*: "John whom I beheaded has risen!"[62] This means that the violent death of the Baptist casts its shadow on the way of Jesus. Here it is conspicuous that in this escape to a predominantly Gentile region, Mark says nothing about a public preaching to the people. It begins again only in the vicinity of a Galilean region.[63] While the geographical specifications may be fuzzy in Mark, who did not know maps as we do, there are nevertheless indications in his work that point to a *crisis* that was budding already in Galilee. Jesus encounters resistance and opposition. This also includes the scene at Caesarea Philippi. No "crowd"—which is still spoken of only in 8.1-9—follows him there but only his disciples (8.27).[64] It is not by chance that Mark connected here Peter's confession of Jesus as the Messiah in the name of the twelve with the first announcement of the passion formulated by him. The manner of presentation corresponds to his woodcut-like style and is shaped by the theological dramaturgy of his Gospel. It reaches an initial climax here. This, however, does not exclude historical and geographical knowledge.

According to the hypothesis of A. Schweitzer and R. Otto, the execution of "his forerunner" prompted Jesus, as suffering servant of God, to set upon the path of sacrifice to Jerusalem. This would be plausible. However, it cannot be adequately grounded for the Galilean period; to be sure, the opposite cannot be either. In any case, after the execution of the Baptist, Jesus must have seriously reckoned with the possibility of his death. The continuation of his aforementioned answer to the Pharisees' warning about Herod Antipas in Luke 13.32-33 also corresponds with this: "Thus, I must travel around today and tomorrow and the day after, for it is impossible for a prophet to die except for in Jerusalem." Jesus did not blindly stagger into death as an unworldly enthusiast. Against this speak statements such as Jesus' question to the Zebedees in Mark 10:38: "Can you drink the cup that I drink and be baptized with the baptism with which I am baptized?" and the saying of Luke 12.50: "I must be baptized with a baptism, and how impatient I am until it is finally accomplished." The reference to the

---

[62] Mark 6.16 par.; contrast Luke 9.9; see note 31 in chapter 9.

[63] Cf. e.g. Mark 8.1ff.

[64] Mark 8.27-33. The Markan hardening theory (4.10-12, 33-34), which is based on Isa 6.9 and which the evangelist connects with the interpretation of Jesus' speech in parables as incomprehensible enigmatic speech, reflects this opposition, which also finds expression for him in the Beelzebul accusation of the scribes from Jerusalem and in his family's lack of understanding (Mark 3.21-34). On this, see section 16.1 with notes 43 and 47.

suffering of the Son of Man in Mark 9.31 probably also belongs originally in this context.[65]

Thus, we must probably assume that Jesus, in his last journey to Jerusalem for the Passover festival, where he sought to summon the whole people to a decision for God's reign, firmly reckoned on the fact that he would be arrested and executed. It is controversial whether and how he connected a soteriological interpretation to this. At any rate, we possess two clear statements of Jesus that point to this at prominent places, both in Mark, which Matthew took over from him.

The first is Mark 10.45: "The Son of Man did not come to be served but to serve and give his life as a ransom for many," and the second is Jesus' actions at the Last Supper in Mark 14.22ff.[66] It is not unlikely that he understood his violent death, which he basically provoked himself at the end, as an atoning sacrifice for his people, whose leaders had rejected him and his message. In any case, the disciples understood and proclaimed his way—upon which they did, after all, accompany him until Gethsemane—in this sense later.

In contrast to Mark, who does not mention Samaria and the Samaritans, and Matthew, who mentions this region between Galilee and Judaea only once, i.e., when Jesus prohibits his disciples from entering a Samaritan city,[67] Luke and John recount experiences of Jesus in Samaritan territory. On the first station of the Lukan travel narrative, when Jesus "set his face to Jerusalem," the inhabitants of a Samaritan village refuse to receive the Jewish pilgrims to Jerusalem. James and John, the "sons of thunder" (Mark 3.17), exhort him "to let fire fall from heaven," but he sharply rebuffs them. A widespread reading adds to the exhortation of the sons of Zebedee: "as Elijah did." It could go back to Marcion, who thus characterizes the two disciples as foolish adherents of the Jewish "just God." The same applies to the negative answer of Jesus, which is handed down only in late manuscripts: "Do you not know of what spirit you are? The Son of Man has not come to destroy but to save."[68]

---

[65] We follow here Jeremias 1966a, 209–29; 1970, 281–99 (GV = 1979, 267–84). See section 17.4.1.3.

[66] Cf. the more strongly "Hellenized version" in 1 Tim 2.6 and the saying about Jesus as servant in the Lukan farewell discourse in 22.27 and in Rom 15.8. On this, see in detail Stuhlmacher 2018, 139–40, 147–64 (GV = 1992, 120–22, 127–43); see section 14.3. On the Last Supper, see the end of section 19.4.

[67] Matthew 10.5: . . . εἰς πόλιν Σαμαριτῶν μὴ εἰσέλθητε; cf. by contrast Luke 9.52: πορευθέντες εἰσῆλθον εἰς κώμην Σαμαριτῶν and Philip in Acts 8.5: κατελθὼν εἰς [τὴν] πόλιν τῆς Σαμαρείας.

[68] Luke 9.52-56 (special material). Cf. on Elijah the quotation from 2 Kgs 1.10, 12. According to Sir 48.1 Elijah was a "prophet like fire." On the dependence of the secondarily added parts of the text in vv. 55/56 on Marcion, see Harnack 1960, 204* (no equivalent

In the second half of the "travel narrative" Luke speaks of Jesus, with his disciples, going "right through Samaria and Galilee" or "between" the two regions in the direction of Jerusalem and healing ten lepers in a village, of whom one was a Samaritan.[69] Luke gives no further thought to the exact travel route. He becomes geographically concrete again only in 18.31ff., where he announces to the twelve for the last time that he is going up to Jerusalem to suffer there. Right after this he approaches—as the last leg of the journey—Jericho.[70] In opposition to Mark and Matthew, Luke says nothing about Jesus traveling through Peraea, beyond the Jordan, to the south.[71] Rather, he is concerned—correctly historically—to bring Jesus into a positive relationship with the Samaritans. In addition, in 17.11 he mentions Samaria as an introduction to the following healing of ten lepers, which has its climax in the fact that only one of the healed persons, the Samaritan, i.e., a "foreigner,"[72] returns in order to thank Jesus and pay homage to him. This has its counterpart in the exemplary behavior of the merciful Samaritan in Luke 10.30-37, who—in contrast to the representatives of the religious "hereditary nobility," a priest and a Levite—saves a person who had been attacked and injured by robbers, despite the concomitant life-threatening danger in the wilderness between Jerusalem and Jericho. By contrast, John recounts a journey of Jesus with his disciples in the opposite direction from Judaea via Samaria to Galilee and Jesus' encounter with a Samaritan woman at the well of Jacob near the holy mountain Gerizim in Sychar/Askar, which at that time was presumably the Samaritans' capital city, whose inhabitants confess Jesus as the "savior of the world" at the end as a consequence of this encounter. In this way the evangelist transforms the dramatically narrated scene, which displays familiarity with local conditions, into a paradigm for the later universal mission of the church to all nations.[73] For Luke too, the portrayal of the Samaritan mission of the "Hellenist" Philip and thereafter of Peter and John in Acts 8 is a preparation for the proclamation of the new message of salvation to non-Jews. Perhaps Jesus himself, against the presentation

---

in Harnack 1990). The aversion of the Samaritans toward the Galilean Jerusalem pilgrims could lead to severe conflicts; see section 3.1.5 with notes 305–9.

[69] Luke 17.11. On the unusual phrase, see now in detail Böhm 1999, 260–63, 271–74. One probably cannot assume for Luke an exact knowledge of the borders between Samaria and Galilee. Between the two territories lay the Plain of Jezreel, and it was not clear to whom it belonged. On Luke as "geographer," see Hengel 1983a (1983c, 87–132, 190–210).

[70] Luke 18.35 = Mark 10.46. On the announcements of suffering, see Luke 9.22 = Mark 8.31 = Matt 16.21 and in Luke also 9.31; 17.25.

[71] Mark 10.1 = Matt 19.1.

[72] Luke 17.16: καὶ αὐτὸς ἦν Σαμαρίτης; 17.18: ὁ ἀλλογενὴς οὗτος.

[73] John 4.4-42. On this, see Hengel 1999b, 297–308.

of Matthew, already reckoned the Samaritans among the "lost sheep of the house of Israel."[74] One may therefore assume that the Hellenists and the Jerusalem primitive community with the Samaritan mission, which was very unusual for Jews, could build on a behavior of Jesus and were convinced that they were acting in accordance with the intention of Jesus.

Luke thus resumes the geographical thread of the journey of Jesus to Jerusalem, which is given by Mark, only with the third passion prediction[75] and after this has Jesus, against Mark, already heal a blind man before his entrance into Jericho so that he can focus the stay in the city on Jesus' encounter with the "chief tax collector" Zacchaeus, which is theologically significant for him.[76] For the Synoptics, with the entrance of Jesus into Jerusalem from the west via Bethphage, Bethany, and the Mount of Olives, we reach the beginning of the last controversy and thus the passion story in the broadest sense.[77]

Viewed as a whole, a reconstruction of the places and journeys of Jesus is possible only in broad strokes—only as an attempt at historical approximation, so to speak. A harmonization with the frequently contradictory specifications in John, which sometimes sound astonishingly exact but can scarcely be integrated into a historically convincing framework, is just as impossible as in the case of the chronology. Against John one probably must also place the geographical and chronological center of gravity of Jesus' activity in Galilee and not extend its duration too long.

---

[74] Matt 10.6; 15.24; Matthew uses this logion, which is only handed down in his Gospel, in the sense of a demarcation from Gentiles and Samaritans; cf. also Mark 6.34 = Matt 9.36.

[75] Luke 18.31ff. = Mark 10.32ff. = Matt 20.17ff.

[76] Luke 18.35-43 = Mark 10.46-52; in Matt 20.29-34 there are two blind men. The name Bartimaeus is handed down only by Mark. Luke already omits it. On Zacchaeus, see Luke 19.1-10 (special material).

[77] Mark 11.1ff. = Luke 19.28ff. = Matt 21.1ff. The fact that Mark (and in dependence on him Luke) has Bethany follow after Bethphage is geographical carelessness, from which one is not permitted to infer that the evangelist has a complete lack of knowledge and therefore could not be a Jerusalemite. Mark narratively introduces Bethany here, which was located 2.8 kilometers east of Jerusalem behind the Mount of Olives, because it had significance for him as the place where Jesus spent the night before the Passover. Jesus must have had a "base" there from earlier visits; see Mark 11.1-2; 14.3; cf. also Luke 24.50; John 11.1ff.; 12.1-11. Matthew makes a correction by omitting the place. John's account of the entrance has a completely distinctive character. He transforms it into an "official reception" (*Einholung*) of Jesus by the Jerusalem population: 12.18; see section 18.1.

11.4 Jesus as Teacher and Lord

The Gospels uniformly portray Jesus as teacher during the entire time of his activity until the last meal with his disciples, which is connected with his farewell discourse in Luke and John. The places and circumstances of his teaching are varied and stereotyped at the same time: on a level plain, in the wilderness, on a mountain, on the lakeshore and from a boat, in a private house, on a peregrination, at banquets, and finally in the temple area. His hearers are the crowds (the Greek term ὄχλος appears 148 times in the Gospels) and his disciples as well as individuals in dialogues.

In contrast to Paul, we hear nothing about a scribal education. It is his messianic "gift" with the fullness of the Spirit of God since the Baptism by John—one could also say: his authorization as Son of God—that makes him *ex officio* the teacher for the evangelists. Only Luke reports, influenced by the form-schemes of ancient biography, that the twelve-year-old Jesus in the temple already "astounded" the scribes "with his sharpness of mind and his answers" (2.46-47).

Mark, by contrast, stresses right after the calling of the first disciples that on the sabbath in the synagogue of Capernaum the hearers were deeply impressed by Jesus' teaching, "for he taught them as one who possesses authority and not as the scribes" (1.22). A little later, after an exorcism, he further intensifies this: "and they were astonished and discussed among one another and said: What is this? A new teaching in authority; he commands also the unclean spirits and they obey him!" (1.27). Matthew very skillfully takes over the Markan evaluation of the teaching from 1.22 and places it at the end of the Sermon on the Mount (7.28). Now, however, it is no longer the hearers in the synagogue but the "crowds" (ὄχλοι) who are impressed.[78] In all the Gospels Jesus possesses unlimited, unsurpassed teaching authority vis-à-vis the crowd, the disciples, and individual persons. For this reason, looking back, he commands in his anti-rabbinic polemic in Matt 23.8: "One . . . is your teacher (διδάσκαλος), but you are all brothers," and reinforces this again in 23.10, where he specifies the name of the *one* teacher: "Christ."

---

[78] Mark 1.22: καὶ ἐξεπλήσσοντο ἐπὶ τῇ αὐτοῦ ἦν γὰρ διδάσκων αὐτοὺς ὡς ἐξουσίαν ἔχων καὶ οὐχ ὡς οἱ γραμματεῖς. Cf. Luke 4.32: . . . ὅτι ἐν ἐξουσίᾳ ἦν ὁ λόγος αὐτοῦ. Mark 1.27: καὶ ἐθαμβήθησαν ἅπαντες ὥστε συζητεῖν πρὸς ἑαυτοὺς λέγοντας, Τί ἐστιν τοῦτο; Διδαχὴ καινὴ κατ' ἐξουσίαν . . . ; cf. Luke 4.36: the whole scene of 4.31-37, which is taken over from Mark, stands in clear contrast to the immediately preceding inaugural sermon in the synagogue in Nazareth, which causes offense. Jesus' message as teacher has a double effect. It can unsettle and harden people. The Christian scribe Matthew restricts in 7.28 the criticism to the Jewish scribes by adding a αὐτῶν. Later manuscripts add "and the Pharisees."

Despite its fragmentary character, the Synoptic sayings tradition—if we compare it with the contemporary Essene and Pharisaic traditions—can indeed be designated in large parts as "new teaching with authority." With corresponding frequency, we encounter the verbs διδάσκειν and κηρύσσειν in the Gospels. Here, it is conspicuous that Mark, the oldest and shortest Gospel, which hands down to us only a relatively small amount of Jesus' teaching, emphasizes both words the most. By contrast, unlike with Paul in Acts, there is no mention of a διαλέγεσθαι of Jesus.[79]

Due to his special teaching authority, Jesus seems like a new John the Baptist or an Elijah *redivivus* or like one of the ancient prophets (Mark 8.28 parr.; Matt 6.14 par.) to the simple people, who did not know his true—messianic—dignity.

The teaching authority of Jesus corresponds to the respectful Aramaic address "rabbi," which we encounter three times in Mark and seven times in John—here as a conscious archaism. In all the evangelists, however, the Greek διδάσκαλος is more frequent, usually as an address in the vocative. Only John constitutes a certain exception here. Luke, who consistently avoids Aramaic terms, also uses the versatile word ἐπιστάτης, master, always in the vocative. It more strongly expresses authority and appears more often than διδάσκαλος in the Septuagint. At the time of Jesus and of Mark, however, "rabbi" is not yet a fixed title for ordained scribes. It only becomes this through the academy of Gamaliel II in Yavneh around 90 CE. By contrast, Matthew, who writes around this time, presupposes this meaning. Therefore, in Matt 23.7-8 he rejects the designation "rabbi" for Christians and uses this address only in the mouth of the betrayer Judas in relation to Jesus (26.25, 49) in order to discredit him. The intensive form "*rabbûnî*," which John translates with διδάσκαλε, occurs in a prominent scene in Mark (10.51) and in John (20.16), while Luke (18.41) and Matthew (20.33; cf. 9.28) have κύριε. The meaning "Lord" is suggested for this form by the fact that numerous rabbinic prayer texts use

---

[79] In Mark, between 1.21 and 14.49 fifteen of the seventeen attestations of διδάσκειν refer to Jesus, one to the disciples, and one to the scribes. Luke likewise has seventeen attestations. Matthew has fourteen and John has nine. With κηρύσσειν the ratio shifts. Of the fourteen attestations in Mark only four refer to Jesus, two to the Baptist, two to the disciples who have been sent out, two to healed people, and two to the post-Easter mission. Luke and Matthew have nine attestations each, whereas John has none. The fact that the latter term more strongly dominates the post-Easter mission is shown by a comparison with the genuine letters of Paul, which use κηρύσσειν sixteen times and διδάσκειν only eight times. For Jesus Mark also uses the simple (τὸν λόγον) λαλεῖν, which is much more frequent in the other evangelists and especially in John. Luke also loves the verb εὐαγγελίζεσθαι, which is especially dependent on Isa 61. On διαλέγεσθαι, see only Mark 9.34, where the disciples discuss "who is the greatest," and by contrast the Lukan Paul in Acts 17.2, 17; 18.4; 19.8-9; 20.7, 9; 24.9, 12.

ribbôn (*rabbûn*) as an address to God. ῥαββι, derived from *rab*, great, can already possess the connotation "lord" as an address to superiors by subordinates; the predominant translation "teacher" was not the only possibility. It is a sign of the relative historical reliability of the second Gospel that he restricts the vocative κύριε to the address of the Greek-speaking Syrophoenician woman (Mark 7.28), while διδάσκαλε (ten times) and ῥαββί are otherwise predominant in his work. In the three later Gospels κύριε is much more frequently applied to Jesus. Matthew, by contrast, puts διδάσκαλε only in the mouths of outsiders, while κύριε is reserved for the disciples. Presumably Jesus was also addressed with the Aramaic *mārî*, my lord. Soon after Easter the prayer address *māranā' tā'* may have developed from it. The earthly *mārî* had become a heavenly "Lord."[80]

11.5 The Calling of Disciples and the Followership of Jesus

For all four Gospels Jesus' first appearance and the obtaining of disciples belong inseparably together. His activity as teacher includes his immediate calling of "students"[81] to follow him. This is even more important for the evangelist than the fact that Jesus attracts "crowds."[82] The disciples form the foundation of the primitive church, not the fickle crowd. Mark and, in dependence on him, Matthew have the calling of the first disciples directly follow as the next scene the news of the public appearance of Jesus in Galilee after the arrest of the Baptist. For them there is no activity of Jesus without disciples.[83] He goes along the shore of the "Galilean Sea," encounters Simon and Andrew, his brother, as they cast out their

---

[80] On ῥαββί/ῥαββουνί, see Dalman 1965, I: 266–80; Bill. I: 916–17; Lohse 1968 (GV = 1959); Heinemann 1977, 204–17. On the connection with Lord/κύριος, see Foerster 1924, 233: "Thus we can trace the primitive Christian linguistic use of kyrios, with respect to the subject matter and the word, back into the Synoptics." See also Foerster 1966 (GV = 1938); Hengel 1981b, 42–44 (GV = 1968b, 46–48; 2007b, 84–86); Hengel/Schwemer 1998, 169ff., 194–204, 416ff. (ET = 1997, 102ff., 120–23, 275ff.); Hengel 2004a, 168–70; Hurtado 2003, 108–18.

[81] The word μαθηταί (*talmîdîm/talmîdayyā*) occurs 262 times in the New Testament. It occurs 46 times in Mark, 37 times in Luke, 73 times in Matthew, 78 times in John, and 28 times in Acts. However, it no longer appears in the epistolary literature. With very few exceptions (Mark 2.18 parr.: of the Baptist and of the Pharisees; cf. also Luke 7.18-19; 11.1; Matt 14.12; John 3.25) it always refers to the disciples of Jesus or in Acts to the Christians. The difference between the narrative writings and the argumentative epistolary literature, which is conditioned by form and tradition, becomes visible here.

[82] ὄχλος, often also plural ὄχλοι. This term likewise occurs especially in the Gospels, Acts, and 4 times in Revelation, appearing 174 times in total. The word occurs in the plural as a loanword ('*ôkhlôsîn*) relatively often in the Talmudic literature and in the Targumim. See Krauss 1964, II: 18–19.

[83] Mark 1.16-20 = Matt 4.18-22; cf. Mark 1.14-15 = Matt 4.13-17.

nets, and calls out to them: "Come, after me, I will make you become fishers of people!"[84] As Elisha at Elijah's call to follow him breaks off from plowing, so both brothers leave their nets and follow him, and something similar happens with a second brother pair, James and John. Here Mark explicitly stresses that they left their father Zebedee with the day laborers in the boat and followed Jesus. For Mark and Matthew this is basically the beginning of the community of Jesus. Accordingly, at the end of the First Gospel we find in Matt 29.19 the commissioning of the twelve "to make disciples of all nations" (μαθητεύσατε), to baptize them, and to teach Jesus' commandments. By contrast, Luke, after a brief pointer to Jesus' successful appearance in Galilee (Luke 4.14-15), has his activity begin with his appearance in his hometown,[85] which is recounted in detail and defined messianically through the quotation of Isa 61.1-2. It ends with an attack on his life and thus also points to the end of his way. Only then does Luke report—now following the narrative thread of Mark—that Jesus preaches in Capernaum[86] and performs healings. Among other things he enters there the "house of Simon" and heals his mother-in-law. In Luke the place of "Simon and his companions" is taken by the crowd, which pursues him.[87] This means that through the healings of Jesus, he, as a skilled storyteller, psychologically prepares for the calling of the first disciples, and here especially of Simon (Peter), which occurs suddenly in Mark (and Matthew). At the same time he places the abrupt rejection at Nazareth in a clear contrast to the successes in Capernaum,[88] which climax in the winning of Simon and of the two sons of Zebedee. By contrast, he can forgo Simon's brother Andrew. He places Simon at the very center and recounts a miraculous catch of fish, a motif that appears also in John 21.1-14 as a resurrection narrative.[89] As a consequence of this,

---

[84] Mark 1.17 = Matt 4.19; on the δεῦτε ὀπίσω μου, cf. 2 Kgs 6.19 LXX. On the whole, see Hengel 1981b, 76ff. (GV = 1968b, 85ff.; 2007b, 122ff.). On the "callings at the sea," see Böttrich 2001, 51–59. On the model of Elijah-Elisha, see 1 Kgs 19.19-21 and Mark 1.20 parr.

[85] Luke 4.14-30: Luke mentions only here the Aramaic place-name Nazara, a designation that Matthew takes over from Luke and that appears only in these two texts. It is unfounded to postulate here a remnant of the sayings source. This is done, however, by Robinson/Hoffmann/Kloppenborg 2000, 42.

[86] Luke, however, already has Jesus in Nazareth refer to his successful healings in Capernaum in 4.23. The Nazarenes have heard of the Jesus-praising φήμη that spreads in Galilee (4.14-15).

[87] Luke 4.31-44; cf. Mark 1.21-39.

[88] They are anticipated in 4.23: "What we heard that it happened in Capernaum, do also here in your hometown!"

[89] Luke 5.1-11; cf. also Gos. Pet. 60; unfortunately, the text breaks off here.

Simon Peter[90] throws himself before his feet in dismay: "Depart from me, for I am a sinful man!" Jesus answers: "Fear not, from now on you shall catch people."[91] After this, Simon and the two sons of Zebedee leave their boats and follow him. In his effort to compose a coherent "historically" congruous report and on the basis of his special material tradition, Luke has radically reshaped his Markan *Vorlage*, connected it with a miracle, and turned it into a narrative in which the conversion and calling of the most important disciple in the Gospel coincide (as with Paul in Acts). In this way, Simon (Peter) is characterized—in a good Pauline way—as a "justified sinner."[92] At the same time, with this scene the evangelist creates a powerful contrast to the rejection of Jesus in his hometown. The followers of Jesus are his true family. It is telling that Luke does not mention Nazareth again and mentions Jesus' family in the Gospel only once more in a negative way.[93]

The Fourth Gospel proceeds in an entirely different way. Here it is the witness of the Baptist that leads the first two disciples to Jesus so that they follow him.[94] We are dealing here with an unknown disciple, probably the beloved disciple,[95] and with the brother of Simon, Andrew. To his brother Andrew confesses: "We have found the Messiah," and he leads Simon to Jesus, who gives him the name Cephas, which was later translated with Πέτρος, "Man of Rock."[96] This is followed by the calling of Philip and of

---

[90] Luke 5.8. In contrast to Mark he lets the double name appear already here. He narrates the giving of the name only in 6.14 in parallel to Mark 3.16.

[91] Luke 5.10: ἀπὸ τοῦ νῦν ἀνθρώπους ἔσῃ ζωγρῶν. Luke may have found this phrasing in his source, which is restricted by the singular to the calling of Simon. He differs in this regard clearly in this regard from the calling formula in Mark 1.17 = Matt 4.19.

[92] Cf. also Luke 15.20ff.; 18.13-14; 19.5-6; 22.31-32. In the subsequently added chapter John 21.1-19 this scene of conversion and calling is transformed into an encounter with the risen one. John knew the Gospel of Luke. In our view, such texts and similar ones precisely in the special material (e.g., Luke 7.36-50; 15; 17.7-10; 18.9-14; 19.1-10; 23.43) show that the evangelist is a student of Paul.

[93] Luke 8.19ff. = Mark 3.31-35; Matt 12.46-50. On the mother of Jesus, cf. also Luke 11.27-28. It is only in Acts 1.14 that the family of Jesus appears again with the disciples in Jerusalem.

[94] John 1.29, 35ff.; cf. 1.37: καὶ ἠκολούθησαν τῷ Ἰησου and v. 39.

[95] On this, see Hengel 1993a, 216–17, 314–15 (ET = 1989a, 78–79, 124ff.), and John 18.15.

[96] John 1.41-42. The Aramaic Cephas (*kêfā* ⸴ rock, stone; see Jastrow 1903, I: 634–35) occurs otherwise only in the letters of Paul: 1 Cor 1.12; 3.22; 9.5; 15.8; Gal 1.18; 2.9, 11, 14. The later apocryphal tradition sometimes makes Cephas into a disciple who is distinct from Peter and who is said to have belonged to the seventy: see Bauer 1967b, 416 and 419; thus, e.g., Clement of Alexandria according to Eusebius, *Hist. eccl.* 1.12.2. In this way the offense of Gal 2.19ff. was softened. See also Lipsius 1976 (Supplement), 211 index. On the meaning of the byname, see Böttrich 2001, 42–46; Hengel 2010a, 14–28 (GV = 2006b, 21–44). Cf. now also Bockmuehl 2010, 148–57.

the otherwise unknown Nathanael.[97] Here too it is impossible to harmonize the Synoptic call narratives with John. It may be that the first disciples
of Jesus found their way to him through the Baptist movement and that
the beginning of his activity lay—contrary to the Synoptic account—in the
time before the arrest of the Baptist.[98] However, it is unlikely that Jesus
himself was active and performed baptisms in the Judaean region of the
Jordan with his disciples in a competition of sorts with the Baptist.[99]

By contrast, it is clear that the initiative for the calling of the disciples proceeded from Jesus. They did not—as was the case with the rabbis
later—become students by their own decision. Rather, he called them out
of their occupations and families into his following. This is confirmed by
other reports in Mark and by the sayings tradition. Thus, to the tax collector Levi, son of Alphaeus, at his tax booth, probably in the border town of
Capernaum, he issues the irresistible summons "follow me": "and he rose
and followed him."[100] At the end Jesus also demands the renunciation of
his possessions and discipleship from the anonymous rich man who asks
Jesus how he can "inherit eternal life."[101] Because of his "many possessions" he cannot comply with Jesus' exhortation. In the discussion that
follows Mark has Peter say: "Behold, we have left everything and followed you," and Jesus answers with a promise: "Amen, I say to you: No
one has left house or brothers or sisters or father or mother or children or
field for my sake and for the sake of the gospel, who does not receive in
this time houses, brothers, and sisters . . . with persecutions, and in the
coming age eternal life." This ideal scene shows how a saying of Jesus has
been combined with the later community situation, for instance after the
Neronic persecution.[102] We encounter a rougher, probably original version
in the sayings tradition according to Luke: Vis-à-vis the crowd that goes
with him, Jesus says: "If anyone comes to me and does not hate father and
mother, wife and children . . . , and even his own life, he cannot be my disciple. Whoever does not carry his cross and go behind me cannot be my

---

[97] John 1.43-51. On Nathanael, cf. also 21.2.

[98] Mark 1.14 = Matt 4.12; cf. Luke 3.19-20 and, in contrast, John 3.24.

[99] John 3.22-4.1.

[100] Mark 2.14 = Luke 5.27-28; cf. Matt 9.9, which replaces the name Levi with Matthew (cf. Matt 10.3) and thus makes a disciple from the circle of the twelve into a tax
collector. Presumably the unknown author of Matthew knows himself to be dependent on
this tax collector Matthew in a special way. The author gives to the Gospel his name; see
section 6.44 with notes 95–96.

[101] Mark 10.17-22; cf. Luke 18.18-23 (in Luke the petitioner is an ἄρχων, i.e., probably a noble council member) and Matt 19.16-22, who speaks of a "young man" (νεανί-
σκος; v. 22).

[102] Mark 10.23-30 = Matt 19.23-29 = Luke 18.24-30.

disciple."[103] Those who are called into discipleship are to be completely free to share the uncertain, indeed endangered life of Jesus, to "follow after" him, the itinerant preacher in the strict sense of the word, even to the point of giving up their own lives and thus to place themselves entirely in the service of the dawning kingdom of God.

Luke has the double parable of the plan to build a "tower" (πύργος), i.e., a fortress or palatial building, and of a military campaign against a powerful enemy follow, which both need to be well considered, with regard to whether one has the means to successfully carry them out, and closes with the conclusion: "Thus, none of you who does not renounce all that he possesses can be my disciple."[104] Matthew puts the saying about discipleship from the sayings tradition in Jesus' mission discourse and at the same time interprets the phrase "and does not hate" (οὐ μισεῖ), which sounds offensive to Greek ears, christologically: "Whoever loves father or mother more than me is not worthy of me."[105] It is understandable that Jesus' rigorous demand could bring controversy into families (including his own) and divide them.[106] Mark 13.12 parr. interprets this division, which could sometimes lead to deadly denunciation, as a sign of the eschatological tribulation before the end.

In three framed discipleship statements from the sayings tradition that belong together thematically Jesus underscores the daunting unconditionality of the demand of discipleship. He points out his homelessness to someone who wants to follow him everywhere. In contrast to foxes and birds "the Son of Man has no place to lay his head." He requires a direct break with piety and ethos from another, whom he calls to discipleship but who wants first to fulfill the self-evident obligatory commandment to bury his father. Jesus abruptly rejects his request: "Let the dead bury their dead; but you go and proclaim the kingdom of God!" Luke also hands down a similar third episode in which someone wants to follow Jesus but first to say farewell to his family—as Elisha did when he was called by Elijah. In contrast to Elijah, Jesus also rejects this request: "No one who puts his

---

[103] Luke 14.25-27. According to 1 Cor 9.5, the marriage of Peter (cf. Mark 1.29-30 parr.) remained in existence and the other apostles were also married. In contrast to Luke, Mark 10.29 and Matt 19.29; 10.37 omit the reference to the wife. See section 14.3 with notes 49–50.

[104] Luke 14.28-33 (special material). On πύργος, see Spicq 1978, II: 774–77.

[105] Matthew 10.37. The Hebrew *śanē'* can be understood as "explicit antonym to 'love'" (Lipiński 2004, 164; GV = 1993, 828) and with reference to a wife can also mean "spurn, neglect." The saying about bearing the cross (10.38) is also formulated analogously. The threefold οὐκ ἔστιν μου ἄξιος reinforces at the same time the christological connection. Matthew could have poured the Lukan text into a catechetically striking form.

[106] Luke 12.52-53 and Matt 10.35. The free allusion to Mic 7.6 is replaced in Matthew by a quotation that is oriented to the Masoretic text.

hand to the plow and looks back is fit for the kingdom of God."[107] Here it becomes clear that Jesus understands discipleship as service to the dawning kingdom of God, in relation to which everything, even family bonds and elementary demands of piety, must take a backseat. He calls persons to this service as God does the prophets of the Old Testament,[108] i.e., the calling of followers is an expression of his messianic authority in which he dares to act as God himself.[109]

11.6 The Appointment of the Twelve

Jesus spoke these callings in relation to individuals, probably because he had in view a special task for them. This means that his "followers" must be distinguished from the changing crowd, which time and again also gathered to him in order to hear him but then returned again to their hometowns.[110] We do not know how large the circle of those who were personally called by Jesus into his following was. Since names turn up here that do not belong to the circle of the twelve, such as the tax collector Levi or Nathanael, who is mentioned only by John, and there is also talk of anonymous followers, their circle was probably much larger and also somewhat fluctuating. Alongside the sending out of the twelve, which he takes over from Mark, Luke therefore recounts a sending of the seventy-two, which probably comes from the sayings tradition. It calls to mind the seventy and two elders from Num 11.16ff., 26ff., who receive the Spirit, but it could also point indirectly to the sending to the seventy-two nations.[111] Jesus is accompanied by a larger number of Galileans to Jerusalem, and Luke speaks before Pentecost of ca. 120 adherents of Jesus in the city, including the eleven disciples and the brothers and mother of

---

[107] Luke 9.57-62. In accord with his tendency to shorten, Matt 8.18-22, perhaps dependent on Luke, hands down only the first two episodes and makes the first petitioner a scribe because they required the *stabilitas loci* of the teacher. On Elijah and Elisha, see 1 Kgs 19.19-21. On the whole, see Hengel 1981b, passim (GV = 1968b; 2007b, 40–138).

[108] Hengel 1981b, 72–73, 82–83 (GV = 1968b, 81–82, 92; 2007b, 118–19, 129–30); cf. Exod 3.10; Judg 6.14; Amos 7.15; Jer 1.5, etc.

[109] Hengel 1981b, 67–73 (GV = 1968b, 74–82; 2007b, 112–19). See also section 13.6.

[110] Cf. Mark 5.19; 6.45; 8.2-3.

[111] Luke 10.1. The reading seventy-two is definitely to be preferred as *lectio difficilior* and due to its ancient attestation over seventy. It is found in P[75] B D and in the Old Latin and Old Syriac tradition. Luke, who does not like duplications, certainly did not invent them. Cf. also the seventy-two translators of the Septuagint according to the Letter of Aristeas, six from each tribe, who carry out this work for the benefit of all people who seek the divine truth.

Jesus.[112] According to Mark, Jesus, in a special act, calls from a larger number twelve men to himself as the more intimate circle of his followers, i.e., he appoints them as *"the twelve"* almost as to an "office."[113] While Mark inserts this "appointment of the twelve" as a contrast between the first resolution to kill Jesus of the Pharisees and Sadducees and the break with the family and the Beelzebul accusation,[114] Luke places it before the Sermon on the Plain, which is addressed in the first instance to the disciples.[115] Both evangelists emphasize the thronging of the crowd, which forces Jesus to look around for coworkers.[116] Mark grounds the choice in a twofold way. The twelve are to have fellowship with him and share their life with him, but Jesus will also send them out to proclaim the message of the dawning kingdom and, having been authorized by him, to cast out demons. Mark then recounts the sending out of the twelve later, in 6.7ff., after the rejection of Jesus in his hometown and before the execution of the Baptist. The spread of the new message of the kingdom of God connected with Jesus can be stopped neither by the people of Nazareth nor by Herod Antipas.[117] By contrast, Matthew places the appointment of the twelve disciples as "messengers" (ἀπόστολοι)—a term that he takes over from Luke 6.13—at the beginning of his large mission discourse in chapter 10. From then on the teaching of the crowd recedes more and more and the instruction of the disciples is placed in the foreground. John, by contrast, mentions the "twelve" only twice at the margins. Moreover, his disciple

---

[112] Acts 1.15. While this number is 10 × 12, i.e., a very general number, it points to a larger crowd of followers.

[113] Mark 3.13-15: ἀναβαίνει εἰς τὸ ὄρος καὶ προσκαλεῖται οὓς ἤθελεν αὐτὸς ... καὶ ἐποίησεν δώδεκα. The mountain as a place of revelation and nearness to God calls to mind Exod 24.9, 15; cf. also Mark 6.46; 9.2ff. Luke takes over the motif of the mountain in 6.12 and interprets in a materially correct manner in 6.13: Jesus chooses twelve from his disciples. The whole event is an event of revelation. Corresponding to his understanding of apostles, Luke then adds: "whom he called apostles." In Mark 3.14 this οὓς καὶ ἀποστόλους ὠνόμασεν is, despite its strong attestation, an early addition. By contrast, Mark has the designation οἱ ἀπόστολοι in 6.30 in the account of the return of the twelve. This means he already identified the "twelve" with the "apostles." Here we may be dealing with old Jerusalem tradition; see section 22.1 and Hengel/Schwemer 2019. On the problem, see Böttrich 2001, 59–63; Frey 2004; 2005, 203–4.

[114] Mark 3.6ff., 20-35.

[115] In Luke 6.12ff. he recounts Jesus' prolonged nightly prayer "on the mountain," which is followed by the choosing of the twelve from the larger number of disciples at the beginning of the day. With them he descends into the valley (6.17). There they are pursued by a "large crowd" of disciples and people who are healed. In v. 20 Jesus looks "at his disciples" and addresses them with three macarisms in vv. 20b-22. Luke has embroidered his Markan Vorlage with vibrant colors here.

[116] Mark 3.7-9, 20; Luke 6.17-19.

[117] Mark 6.7-12, 30; cf. 6.1-6 and 6.14-29.

names agree only partially with the list of the twelve. Here too he goes his own way, which cannot be placed historically.[118]

On the whole Mark has reported in a way that is indeed appropriate here. The call of individual disciples into the followership precedes the appointment of the "twelve" as a special act. It points to the growth of the Jesus movement in Galilee and has symbolic importance as a messianic sign act, for it points to the fact that Jesus' eschatological message and his activity as healer and exorcist are aimed at the twelve-tribe people, i.e., at all Israel. His activity at the Passover of his death in Jerusalem also corresponds to this. He wants to win the "twelve-tribe people"[119] for God's inbreaking reign. The sending out of the twelve in Galilee, which took place later, also has symbolic significance. A logion that is offensive to the modern "enlightened" interpretation of Jesus confirms this claim. In the small farewell discourse after the Last Supper the Lukan Jesus says to his disciples:

> "You are those who have persisted with me in my trials (πειρασμοῖς).
> Thus, I confer upon you the kingdom, as my Father conferred it upon me,
> that you may eat and drink at my table in my kingdom and sit on twelve
> thrones and judge the twelve tribes of Israel."[120]

This logion, which fits well in the tradition of Jesus' Last Supper with the twelve,[121] underlines the eschatological and messianic character of the appointment of the twelve, which certainly did not originate as an event

---

[118] John 6.67, 70-71; 20.24. In 21.2 he mentions seven disciples with Peter and Thomas at the head, then Nathanael, the two sons of Zebedee, and two unnamed disciples, so that the Beloved Disciple as author cannot be identified (21.24). Otherwise, we find in the Gospel the Beloved Disciple, Andrew, Philip, Judas Iscariot, and the "other" disciple Judas (14.22). On the disciple lists in John and others, see Hengel 1993a, 80ff. and 313ff. (ET = 1989a, 17ff. and 124ff.).

[119] On the term, see Acts 26.7; 1 Clem. 55.6. The close connection between the twelve tribes and the twelve disciples becomes clear in Rev 21.12, 14. See also James 1.1; Rev 7.5-8.

[120] Luke 22.28-30. Matthew 19.28 inserts the last part of the logion into the Markan *Vorlage* of the speech about the reward of discipleship and connects it with the judgment of the Son of Man on the "throne of glory"; see Matt 25.31-32; 16.27; on this, cf. Dan 7.9-22; 1 Cor 6.2ff.; Rev 20.4ff. In our view, Matthew took over the unusual logion from Luke. A place in Q is very unlikely. On the theological significance of this text in Luke, see Mittmann-Richert 2008.

[121] Cf. the beginning of the Passover meal in Mark 14.17: καὶ ὀψίας γενομένης ἔρχεται μετὰ τῶν δώδεκα = Matt 26.20; Luke 22.14: καὶ οἱ ἀπόστολοι σὺν αὐτῷ. On the meal in the kingdom of God, see Mark 14.25 = Matt 26.29 with the addition μεθ' ὑμῶν. See section 13.2 with note 45 and section 17.4.1 with note 163.

in the primitive community.[122] The "conferring"[123] has here the sense of a participation of the twelve in the judging function of God. The formulation οἱ δώδεκα occurs not only in all the Gospels and with special emphasis in Mark but also in the resurrection confession of 1 Cor 15.5, in Acts 6.2, and in Rev 21.14.[124] The designation of the betrayer Judas as "one of the twelve" is formulaic. The disgrace that one of the circle of the most intimate companions "handed over" the master to the temple authorities was not suppressed but recorded in this formula.[125] Within the circle of the twelve there was still the smaller group of the three most intimate companions, who were called first according to Mark: Peter and James and John, the two sons of Zebedee; Andrew sometimes joined them as a fourth.[126] The three played a leading role later also in the primitive community behind Peter, while only John is mentioned in Acts as second man beside Peter,[127] since John, the son of Zebedee, was presumably executed by Herod Agrippa I in 42/43 CE.[128]

It is no accident that Peter stands at the head in all the larger and smaller "catalogues of disciples" of the Gospels and Acts.[129] He must have possessed a prominent role among the disciples of Jesus, so that he could appear as their speaker, in a role that was further reinforced through the first vision of the risen one and that continued in Acts. This conspicuous role of Simon Peter is already visible in Paul in 1 Corinthians and Galatians. Cephas-Peter is the figure from the primitive community whom Paul mentions most frequently in his letters, ten times in total. This is certainly also connected with the fact that he became the most important mediator of the Jesus tradition for the West from Syria to Rome, indeed

---

[122] On this, see, for example, the criticism—which is actually uncritical in many points—of Klein 1961 and the even more fanciful Schmithals 1961, 56–76. This view is rightly opposed by Meier 2001, 126–97.

[123] διατίθεμαι–διέθετο; cf. Josephus, *Ant.* 13.407: τὴν βασιλείαν διέθετο, is closely connected with the notion of a testamentary disposition and the term διαθήκη; see Bauer/Aland/Aland 1988, 381. On the participation in the judging function of God, see Dan 7.9-10; Rev 20.4; 1 Cor 6.2.

[124] Mark, the oldest Gospel, uses οἱ δώδεκα most frequently, ten times in total: 3.14; 4.10; 6.7; 9.35; 10.32; 11.11; 14.10, 17, 20, 43.

[125] Mark 14.10 = Matt 26.14; cf. Luke 22.3; Mark 14.43 = Luke 22.47 = Matt 26.14. On this, see section 19.2 with notes 45–49.

[126] Mark 1.16-19 parr. (with Andrew); 5.37 par.; 9.2 parr.; 13.3 (with Andrew); 14.33 par.

[127] Acts 3.1ff., 11; 4.13, 19; 8.14.

[128] Acts 12.1-2; cf. 1.13; see section 22.1 with note 27.

[129] Cf. also 1 Cor 15.5. An exception is Gal 2.9: here Cephas-Peter had to give way to James, the brother of the Lord. In 1 Cor 1.12 we have a reversal: the climax stands at the end. Correspondingly, in catalogues of women, Mary Magdalene stands at the head. On the problem, see Hengel 1963, 249ff.

for the Christians in the whole Roman Empire, and with the fact not only that his student Mark wrote the first Gospel but also Luke and especially Matthew—in a correct way historically—carried forward this tradition of his paramount importance. This can still be seen clearly even in John and Paul.[130]

To be sure, the various references to controversies over rank among the disciples show that the question of authority played a role among them from the beginning.[131] It becomes clear in the sons of Zebedee's request for the places of honor in the kingdom of God at the right and left of Christ "in his glory."[132] The Markan Jesus points them to their future martyrdom. The Fourth Evangelist, by contrast, gives the Beloved Disciple the place at the side of Jesus and places him as decisive witness under the cross. In this way he disputes the clear leadership role of Peter, without denying his special task; indeed, the Johannine Jesus foretells his martyrdom to him.[133]

Apart from small differences in the sequence and some additions, the list of the disciple names is almost identical in all the Synoptic witnesses. A lapse into into unresolvable difficulties only arose in the later "apocryphal" tradition, especially with the attempt to integrate Nathanael and Levi into the circle of the twelve or a Cephas as another disciple who was distinct from Peter.[134] The only real opposition consists in the fact that Mark, who is followed by Matthew, has Thaddaeus[135] in the tenth posi-

---

[130] On this, see Hengel 2010a, passim (GV = 2006b, passim).

[131] Luke 22.24: Ἐγένετο δὲ καὶ φιλονεικία ἐν αὐτοῖς, τὸ τίς αὐτῶν δοκεῖ εἶναι μείζων; cf. Mark 9.33-34 = Luke 9.46; Matt 18.1; 23.11; John 13.12-17. The early Christian epistolary literature from Paul to 1 Clement shows that this human/all-too-human question continued to have effects in the whole of primitive Christianity.

[132] Mark 10.35-45 = Matt 20.20-28: there the petition is made by the mother, who for Matt 27.56 appears to be identical with the Salome of Mark 15.40.

[133] See already the postponement of his calling (in contrast to Mark; see section 11.5) in John 1.35-42. See also John 13.6-38; 18.15-18, 25-27; 19.25-27; 20.3-10 and the whole of chapter 21: see there the distinctive commission "feed my sheep" in 21.15-17 and on his martyrdom especially 21.18-19 and 13.36. On the whole, see Hengel 1993a, 475 index, s.v. "Petrus" (no subject index in Hengel 1989a).

[134] On this, see Bauer 1967b, 415–21.

[135] In Mark 3.18 Codex D and some Old Latin witnesses have the uncommon name Λεββαῖος instead of Θαδδαῖος; in Matt 10.3 this reading is also attested by Origen. The mixed form Λεββαῖος ὁ ἐπικληθεὶς Θαδδαῖος is attested only in Matthew in later uncials and in the Byzantine text. The earliest uncials ℵ, B, some minuscules, and the Coptic and overwhelming number of the Latin manuscripts read, however, the simple Θαδδαῖος; on this, see Ilan 2002, 284: "This form appears to be an Aramaization of the name Θεοδόσιος or Θεόδοτος or Θεόδωρος." It corresponds, for example, to Θευδᾶς in Acts 5.36; Josephus, *Ant.* 20.97–98; see Ilan 2002, 286 s.v. Θεόδωρος. In the list of the five disciples in b. Sanh. 43a, a disciple appears with the name *twdh*. The name Λεββαῖος, which thus far has not received a satisfactory explanation (see Luz 2001, n. 1: "The matter remains puzzling"; GV = 1985–2002, II: 82 n. 1), probably comes from the infelicitous correction

tion, whereas Luke 6.16 and Acts 1.13 speak of Judas, (son of) James.[136] Since Judas was, next to Simon, the most common name in Judaea and a second Judas also fit badly in the circle of the twelve, Mark 3.18 and Matt 10.3 may have handed down his Graecising byname Thaddaeus. The other possibility would be a later change in the circle of the twelve. It is conspicuous, however, that no names of person who were significant in the primitive community were inserted, such as the names of the two election candidates from Acts 1.23ff., Matthias and Joseph Barsabbas. This points to the age and relative reliability of the lists. Correspondingly, apart from Peter and the sons of Zebedee (and at a certain distance Andrew), the other disciple names in the Synoptics no longer play a role in Acts and in the primitive Christian epistolary literature. They appear to have possessed an importance only in the early time of the primitive community, for example in the twelve or so years until the persecution of Agrippa. Luke identifies the twelve with the circle of the apostles.[137] In reality this circle was, as shown by 1 Cor 15.3-8; 9.1ff. and Gal 1.15ff., much larger. John places some weight on the names Philip and Thomas.[138] In the First Gospel Matthew becomes the tax collector, replacing the name Levi from the Markan *Vorlage*,[139] and gives to the Gospel the first "apostolic" author name.[140] The great time of the other apostle names and adventures begins only from the second half of the second century CE with the "apocryphal" Gospels, Acts of apostles, and related literature.[141] "Simon the Cananaean,"[142] who occupies the eleventh position in Mark and Matthew, is in Luke called "Simon the Zealot," which is materially correct. He may have been a Galilean who originally stood near to the zealot movement.[143] Judas Iscariot

---

of an early scribe, who wanted to bring into the list of disciples the disciple name Λευίς in Mark 2.14; cf. Luke 5.27 in a Greek form that corresponded to a Θαδδαῖος; see Ilan 2002, 182 s.v. "Levi nr. 8."

[136] Cf. John 14.22: Ἰούδας οὐχ ὁ Ἰσκαριώτης. On this, see now Bauckham 2017, 101–2.

[137] Luke 6.13; cf. 17.5; 22.14; 24.10; Acts 1.26; cf. also 2.37. Only as exceptions do Paul and Barnabas receive the title "apostle" in Acts 14.4, 14. In this respect Luke represents a view of the Jerusalem primitive community. See Hengel/Schwemer 2019.

[138] Philip: 1.43-46; 6.5ff.; 12.21-22; 14.8; Thomas: 11.16; 14.5; 20.24-28.

[139] Matthew 9.9; cf. Mark 2.14.

[140] Matthew 10.3; cf. Mark 3.18, there without "the tax collector."

[141] Bauer 1967b, 415–51: the coworkers of Jesus. On the apostle lists, see Bauer/Hornschuh 1966 (GV = 1964). Lipsius 1976, passim; Klauck 2008 (GV = 2005). A comparison shows that Peter apocrypha are the most common by far vis-à-vis other apostle names. On the later Petrine tradition, see Froehlich 1996; Hengel 2010a, 26–27, 30, 106ff. (GV = 2006b, 42–43, 48, 206ff.).

[142] Mark 3.18 = Matt 10.4.

[143] Luke 6.15 in the ninth position: Σίμωνα τὸν καλούμενον ζηλωτήν, Acts 1.3: Σίμων ὁ ζηλωτής; on this, see Hengel 1989c, 59ff., 69ff. (GV = 1976c, 61ff., 72ff.); ὁ ζηλωτής renders the Aramaic *qan 'ānā'*, *status absolutus* of *qan 'ān*, a variant of *qannay*,

stands at the end of the list, in Mark with the addition "who handed him over" and in Luke with "who became the betrayer."[144]

Finally, it is conspicuous that Jesus, according to Mark, gives bynames to three important disciples. In the case of Simon Mark hands down only the Greek version Πέτρος. We learn of the original Aramaic form Κηφᾶς (*kêfā'*) in the meaning "rock, stone" only through Paul, who prefers this form, and through John.[145] We do not know the occasion at which Jesus gave Simon this designation. While John connects this with his calling, for Matthew the renaming is a consequence of the confession of Jesus as the Messiah from the mouth of the first disciple, to which Jesus is said to have answered:

> Blessed are you, Simon Bar Yona, for flesh and blood have not revealed this to you but my Father in heaven. And I say to you: You are Peter and on this rock I will build my church, and the gates of the kingdom of the dead will not overcome it. I will give to you the keys of the kingdom of heaven and what you bind on earth will be bound in heaven and what you loose on earth will be loosed in heaven![146]

Matthew, who beyond his Markan *Vorlage* also introduces some secondary Petrine tradition elsewhere,[147] has here handed down a saying that has received its final form through him but that probably goes back with its traditions in part to the primitive community. It is meant to emphasize the authority of the first disciple to be called, first witness of the resurrection, and speaker of the "twelve apostles." Since in the Synoptics the term ἐκκλησία occurs only here in Matt 16.18 and in the community discourse

---

zealous one. The model of this zeal was Phineas: Hengel 1989c, 147ff., 156ff. (GV = 1976c, 152ff., 160ff.). The absolute use of the word is uncommon in Greek. It corresponds, however, to Jewish usage; see 4 Macc 18.12 and the party of the "Zealots" in Josephus starting in *Ant.* 2.444.

[144] Mark 3.19; cf. Matt 10.4; Luke 6.16. The byname Ἰσκαριώθ (Mark and Luke) or Ἰσκαριώτης (Matthew) is often interpreted as a designation of origin of his father Simon according to a reading in John 6.71 and 12.4 ἀπὸ Καρυώτου: "the man from Qeriyyot" ('*îš q^eriyyôt*), cf. Josh 15.25 in southern Judaea; cf. m. 'Abot 1.4: Jose ben Joezer is '*îš ṣ^erēdāh* (1 Kgs 11.26) and in 1.5 Jose ben Jochanan is '*îš Yerûšālaim*; further examples in Dalman 1965, I: 41–42; Dalman 1922, 26. However, the interpretation remains uncertain, as is all the more the case for all other attempts at interpretation. Limbeck 1995 overlooks the numerous attestations of '*îš* with place-names produced by Dalman.

[145] First Cor 1.12; 3.22; 9.5; 15.5; Gal 1.18; 2.9-14. Paul has Πέτρος only in Gal 2.7-8, perhaps because he quotes here the "official" agreement from memory. In our view Paul alludes to the meaning of the name *Cephas-Petros* with θεμέλιος in 1 Cor 3.11.

[146] Matt 16.17-19 (special material). On this, see Luz 2001, 353–77 (GV = 1985–2002, II: 450–83); Hengel 2010a, 1–36 (GV = 2006b, 1–58).

[147] Matthew 14.28ff.; 17.24ff.; 18.21-22.

in 18.17 in connection with church discipline, and since in 18.18 the say-ing about binding and loosening, i.e., the authority to forgive sins within the community,[148] is given to all the disciples, on the whole a post-Easter origin is likely.[149] The Gospel of Thomas hands down later an analogous saying of Jesus about this brother James, which transcends all human cri-teria.[150] The time and reason for this unusual naming of Simon can there-fore no longer be clearly determined. However, a post-Easter emergence of the byname can be ruled out. Cephas-Peter rapidly suppressed the com-mon name Simon. Because Jesus gave him this name, after Easter it early on became a name of honor for the leading disciple in Jerusalem. The designation of the two sons of Zebedee as "Sons of Thunder" probably represents more a designation of human characteristics. It is handed down only by Mark and does not play a role any longer elsewhere.[151]

11.7 The Tradition of the Sending Out of Disciples

All three Synoptic Gospels hand down the tradition that Jesus—while still in Galilee[152]—sent out the twelve disciples in order to preach and to heal. Indeed, according to Mark and Matthew, they were appointed as a group in the first place for the purpose of sending them out.[153] Mark has the shortest account, though in terms of tradition history it is more likely secondary.[154] Luke has two narratives. From Mark he has the sending out of the twelve and then—while already on the long way to Jerusalem—from the sayings tradition the sending out of the seventy-two,[155] which for him is already meant to signal the post-Easter sending out to the nations of the world. He has integrated his tradition that is independent of Mark into this second mission discourse. As a parting farewell to Galilee, Jesus' woe sayings

---

[148] Cf. also John 20.23 and the decisive action of Paul in 1 Cor 5.3ff., 12-13.

[149] The reference to the "gates of the kingdom of the dead" may point to the martyr-dom of Peter in the Neronian persecution; see Hengel 2010a, 5–7 (GV = 2006b, 9–10). John 21.18-19 and 13.36 also allude to Peter's martyrdom.

[150] Gospel of Thomas 12: After Jesus' departure the disciples are "to go to James the Just for whose sake heaven and earth came to be."

[151] Mark 3.17 (special material): Βοανηϱές = υἱοὶ βϱοντῆς, cf. Justin, *Dial.* 106.3: In his "reminiscences" (i.e., in the Gospel of Mark) Peter is said to have recounted this naming. On the Aramaic form of the name, see Rüger 1984, 75–76: *bᵉnê rᵉgeš*. The *shwa* mobile could be rendered with οα; see Strabo 16.2.44: *mᵉṣādā* = Μοασάδα. On the char-acterization of the sons of Zebedee, cf. Luke 9.54 (special material); Mark 10.35 par.

[152] Mark 6.7ff. = Matt 10.1, 5ff.; Luke 9.1ff. The long journey to Jerusalem begins only in 9.51ff.

[153] Mark 3.14; Matt 10.1ff.; see section 11.6.

[154] Mark 6.6b-13.

[155] Luke 9.1-6; 10.1-12; on this, see note 111 above.

about the three Galilean places that were focal points of his previous activity stand at the end of this discourse.[156] Matthew, by contrast, has joined
together the Markan *Vorlage* with its list of disciples and his own sayings tradition to form his second great discourse after the Sermon on the
Mount.[157] This discourse opens up the view to the post-Easter mission and
persecution of the disciples and promises divine reward to those who fear-
lessly confess and follow.

The concise presentation of Mark places the conferring on the disciples
of the authority to perform exorcisms in the foreground and recounts their
preaching of repentance, their casting out of demons, and their healings
through anointing with oil.[158] In the twofold narrative of Luke and in Matthew they proclaim the same message as Jesus himself: "The kingdom of
God has come to you."[159] The behavioral obligations that Jesus places on
those who are sent out are peculiar. They are to forgo everything that would
actually be self-evident for itinerant messengers insofar as it grants them
security and subsistence. According to Mark, they are permitted at least to
possess a staff and sandals, while the sayings tradition forbids even this.[160]
Moreover, they are also prohibited from taking "bread, travel bag, money in
their belt, and two garments." While they are on their way, they are not permitted to greet anyone. However, when they enter a house, their greeting of
peace has an almost physically real effect. It rests upon the one who is "a son
of peace," whereas it returns to the disciples in the case of the "unworthy."[161]
To the reality of the blessing corresponds the command that if one is rejected
in a place one should "shake off the dust of it from one's feet." Whoever
rejects the offer of salvation judges themselves. The fate of such a place will
be worse on the day of judgment than the fate of Sodom and Gomorrah.[162]
If one receives the messengers of Jesus in a house, then, according to Luke,

---

[156] Luke 10.13-15; cf. Matt 11.20-24; see section 11.2 with note 16.

[157] Matthew 10.1-42. Here too a partial dependence on Luke cannot be entirely
excluded; cf., e.g., against Mark in Luke 9.2; Matt 10.7-8 and Luke 9.5; Matt 10.14.

[158] Mark 6.7, 12-13; cf. already the anticipation in 3.14 in the appointment of the
twelve. On the anointing with oil of the sick, see James 5.14; cf. also Luke 10.34.

[159] Luke 10.9: ἤγγικεν ἐφ' ὑμᾶς ἡ βασιλεία τοῦ θεοῦ, repeated in 10.11; cf. 9.2:
κηρύσσειν τὴν βασιλείαν τοῦ θεοῦ καὶ ἰᾶσθαι. Matthew 10.7 repeats almost word for
word Matt 4.17 and the message of the Baptist in 3.2.

[160] Mark 6.8-9; cf., by contrast, Luke 10.4 and Matt 10.10, which directly
contradict Mark.

[161] Luke 10.4-6; cf. Matt 10.11-13.

[162] Matt 10.14-15 = Mark 6.11; Luke 9.5 and 10.10ff.; cf. Matt 11.24. This threat
calls to mind Jesus' announcement of judgment on the three Galilean places Chorazin,
Bethsaida, and Capernaum; see section 10.5 with note 56. For the shaking off of dust, see
Acts 13.51. There the concern is with a sign act of primitive Christian missionaries, which
goes back to the Jesus saying.

they are to eat what one gives them, i.e., without asking about the purity commandments. The worker for "God's harvest"[163] is "worthy of his wages."[164] We can regard these puzzling instructions to the disciples who are sent out neither as later rules of behavior for charismatic itinerant missionaries nor as dominical in their entirety. As is so often the case, memory and post-Easter configuration have fused into a unity that can hardly be taken apart again. The Markan alleviations, which allow staff and sandals, show that Jesus' rigorous commandment later appeared no longer practicable. The two sendings in Luke are an attempt to do justice to the diverging traditions, with Luke 10 also not speaking *expressis verbis* of the Gentile mission. Precisely the severe, unrealistic character of these commandments points to a single demonstrative act of sending by Jesus in Galilee, which, being temporally and spatially limited, must be understood, like the appointment of the twelve, as a messianic sign act and which illuminates the "charismatic-enthusiastic" character of the activity of Jesus. The pressing nearness, indeed presence, of the inbreaking kingdom of God, to which the victorious battle against the demonic powers that enslave humans also belongs, grounds this seemingly unusual event of the sending out of the twelve with its severe instructions, which sound entirely unrealistic.

Luke has Jesus answer the enthusiastic return of the twelve — "Lord, even the demons are subject to us in your name" — with a visionary confession:

> I saw Satan fall like lightning from heaven. Behold, I have given you authority to tread on snakes and scorpions and over all the power of the enemy, and he will not harm you in any way. However, do not rejoice that the spirits are subject to you but rejoice that your names are written in heaven.[165]

The notion of "treading on snakes and scorpions" calls to mind Gen 3.15 and points to the overcoming of the power of Satan, who led astray the first human pair to disobedience and thus brought all misery into the world. The messengers of Jesus receive at the same time the promise of eternal

---

[163] Luke 10.2 = Matt 9.37.

[164] Luke 10.7 = Matt 10.10b; cf. in 1 Cor 9.14 the commandment of the Lord that the proclaimers of the gospel are to live from the gospel and 1 Tim 5.18. A proverb presumably lies behind this.

[165] Luke 10.17-20 (special material). On the fall of Satan, cf. John 12.31 and Rev 12.7ff. Rusam 2004 questions the authenticity because it is a single saying. It is said to be a Lukan explication of older Jesus tradition. This apocalyptic saying, however, does not fit Luke enough. Moreover, the baptism and probably also the tradition of the temptation and transfiguration speak against the claim that no visionary experiences of Jesus are handed down.

fellowship with God, from which Adam and Eve were excluded after the fall.[166] These words of the Lukan special material reflect an assurance of victory, which far surpasses that of a traditional prophet and which can be explained only with reference to Jesus' enthusiastically messianic confidence in God about the arrival of the kingdom in his activity. It determines the calling of the twelve as well as their sending out. In the authority peculiar to him he could transform them from followers into *fellow campaigners* for God's kingdom and the victory over Satan or to harvesters of God: "The harvest is great but the workers are few. Ask the Lord of the harvest to send out workers into his harvest."[167] This last saying shows the connection between Jesus tradition and post-Easter mission, which could make recourse to the sending out of the disciples by Jesus.[168] The "harvest" was originally an eschatological metaphor[169] and was related to the βασιλεία that was present in Jesus' activity. Its later missionary use is then found in John. The missionaries are to bring in the harvest of the seed sown by Jesus.[170] In a similar form the motif appears in the parable of the workers in the vineyard in connection with the question of the just wage.[171] Luke places a saying, which is frequently varied in the later tradition, at the end of the mission discourse:

> The one who hears you hears me, and the one who rejects you rejects me.
> But the one who rejects me rejects the one who sent me.[172]

The message of the dawning of the kingdom of God, which those who were sent out proclaimed, is none other than Jesus' message. In our view, their sending out already presupposes the first formation, indeed, in order to be able to pass on *his* message, a learning by heart of the key statements of

---

[166] Cf. Gen 3.23-24; Ps 91.13; Mark 3.22-27 parr., especially Luke 11.20; on this, see section 13.6 with notes 136–42.

[167] Luke 10.2 = Matt 9.37: in our view Matthew took it over from Luke and combined it narratively in a very skilled way with Mark 6.34 (= Matt 9.36). It fits well with the very pronounced Lukan mission theology.

[168] On this, see Hengel 1971/1972, 33–34.

[169] Mark 4.29; Matt 13.30; cf. 2 Cor 9.6; Gal 6.8-9.

[170] John 4.35-38; cf. also Paul in 1 Cor 3.6-9.

[171] Matthew 20.1-15; cf. also Luke 10.7 = Matt 10.10b.

[172] Luke 10.16; cf. Matt 10.40, where the logion, through the key word δέχεσθαι, is adjusted to the sending out tradition (Mark 6.11; cf. Luke 9.5) and to the logion in Matt 18.5 = Luke 9.48 = Mark 9.37 (cf. John 13.20 and Ign. *Eph.* 6.1). It is unlikely that Luke in his *Vorlage* replaced his typical Lukan word δέχεσθαι (sixteen occurrences in the Gospel and eight in Acts) with ἀθετεῖν, which is rare for him (only in Luke 7.30). As so often, the reconstruction attempt of Robinson/Hoffmann/Kloppenborg 2000, 188, on Q 10.16 is flawed. See also note 57 in chapter 12.

the proclamation of Jesus.[173] At the same time, the eschatological mediator role of Jesus between the God of Israel who sends him and the "community" of followers and disciples who are taken into service for the kingdom of God by him and thus a piece of *continuity* between Jesus' action and the later primitive church after Israel becomes visible.

Presumably Jesus already called the "messengers" his *šᵉlîḥîn* or *šᵉlîḥîm* (Greek ἀπόστολοι), an Aramaic or Hebrew term, behind which stands a principle of the Semitic-Jewish messenger: "The one sent (*šālûᵃḥ*) by a man is as the man himself,"[174] i.e., he represents the one who sends him within the framework of the authority conferred to him fully and legally. To be sure, a post-Easter reshaping through the missionary situation of the community becomes visible, especially in the Matthean version.[175] The originality of a basic content of the tradition, which is not yet alleviated as in Mark, is supported by the fact that these rigorous instructions were no longer applicable for the later primitive Christian missionary practice in this form. Rather, they point to a relatively short, symbolic action, which is connected with the eschatological and messianic "enthusiasm" of Jesus. What the Didache writes about the itinerant "prophets" (and "apostles")[176] later, at the beginning of the second century, has a fundamentally different character. Another argument is that what stands at the center in this sending out is solely the kingdom of God and the victory over the demons, while every thematic *christological* statement, which could point to the time after Easter, is avoided in the early tradition of the sending out.[177] All the more the question arises: Who is able, against all the older prophetic tradition, not only to appoint the twelve as messengers of the kingdom of God but also to send them out with eschatologically grounded authority and to proclaim the dawning of the kingdom of God with the destruction of the power of Satan? As was already the case with the comparison of Jesus to John the Baptist, Jesus' call to discipleship, his appointment of the twelve, and their distinctive, one-time, symbolic sending out place us before the question of the messianic authority of Jesus.

---

[173] On the problem, see Schürmann 1968b; Riesner 1988, 453–75; Byrskog 2000, 104–5, 162–65. Cf. note 2 in chapter 12.

[174] m. Berakhot 5.5: *šᵉlûḥô šel 'ādām kᵉmôtô*; on this, see Rengstorf 1965, 415 (GV = 1933, 415–16). This clear connection should never have been questioned.

[175] Thus, e.g., precisely in Matt 10.40-41, where after the δέχεσθαι of the disciples there follows as a special tradition that of the prophets and of the righteous and the promise of corresponding reward. The Jewish Christian "prophets" and "righteous" are thus in view here. The saying points to that milieu in which James, the brother of the Lord, held the predicate "the Just." On this, see note 62 in chapter 8. See also Hengel/Schwemer 2019.

[176] "Apostles" could be a secondary addition. See Hengel/Schwemer 2019.

[177] This is not hinted at until the concluding sentence of Luke 10.16 and above all in Matt 10.40-42 (cf. Mark 9.41).

12

The Poetic Form of the
Proclamation of Jesus

We do not know the presentations of Jesus' public teaching and his private instruction of the disciples in their original oral long form[1] but only in the way that his hearers remembered them—here above all his closest followers—and in the way that the disciples handed down his proclamation, in turn, in their preaching. His teaching has survived especially as collections of individual traditions in the form of short, honed aphorisms, gnomic utterances, and sayings in the framework of narrated scenes and of controversy dialogues. But it is also as somewhat longer parallel double strophes, strings of sayings grouped together, as short comparisons, parabolic sayings, developed parables, and detailed example stories that they were remembered and initially handed down at the beginning in oral form. Here we must not imagine Jesus as 'teacher' and his disciples as 'students' simply in analogy to the exclusive academies of rabbinic jurisprudence and scribal learning or to the schools of Hellenistic cities, such that Jesus would, for example, have had his disciples learn his sayings by heart through constant repetition and testing of what was learned.[2] The message

---

[1] On this, cf. the end of this section with note 13. Contrast the proud "lament" of Apuleius of Madaura, *Flor.* 9.9–10 (Helm 1977, 176–78), that his speeches were immediately taken down and read, so that he could no longer improve them for the written publication and therefore must already especially exert himself in the presentation. The pseudo-Philonic synagogue sermons *De Jona* and *De Sampsone*, edited by F. Siegert, are probably synagogue sermons that were actually delivered and written down in shorthand. See Siegert 1992, 7–8, 38–39. Casey 2002, 48–49, hypothesizes that hearers of Jesus could also have made notes on wax tablets. On this, see the end of section 12.1 with notes 44–46. This, however, was presumably the exception, for how many Galilean hearers could write?

[2] Riesner 1988; Baum 2004 tend in this direction. Rather than scholastic memorization, the comparison with early Jewish wisdom is suggested, which was not only publicly taught in schools and at the marketplaces but also—precisely among the upper class—fostered at meals and above all at symposia in private settings. Here instruction in didactic poetry and sayings and songs played an important role. On this, see Krüger 2000, 30ff. Jesus is

of the dawning kingdom contradicted a strict pedagogically oriented "school education." Moreover, Jesus spoke in his own name and in his own authority, in contrast to the later rabbinic scholars, who appealed to the authority of their teachers.[3] But even "without drawing too tight a parallel to the Hellenistic and rabbinic memory techniques, we can assume that Jesus of Nazareth rhetorically configured fundamental insights and repeatedly them again in appropriate situations."[4] He called the closest circle of followers into discipleship and sent these disciples out so that they would proclaim his message of the nearness or dawning of the kingdom of God and perform miracles of healing. What the teacher and master said to the crowd at the shore of the lake or taught in the synagogues, communicated to disciples at table conversation and en route from one place to another, or said in response to his opponents as persuasive argumentation imprinted itself on the memory of his hearers due to the impact of his person and due to the pithiness and pictorial character of his manner of speaking.[5] It is the uniqueness of Jesus' teaching authority that has a tradition-building impact. Within the Synoptic tradition, Jesus directly exhorts his hearers to "learn" from him only in the special material in Matt 11.29: "Take my yoke upon you and learn from me, for I am kind and humble in heart." But "here too Jesus is issuing a call to discipleship and not to 'learning' in a scholastic sense."[6] As personified Wisdom he invites his hearers to take his yoke, i.e., his interpretation of the law. All can learn from his example

---

reviled as a "glutton and winebibber" (Luke 7.34) because of such meals, for example with tax collectors and sinners. In the case of the twelve, their sending out by Jesus may have prompted them to memorize the wording of sayings and parables. On religious learning, see now especially the studies of Byrskog 2005 and Merkel 2005.

[3] P. S. Alexander 1991, 183, emphasizes with a certain justification: "The rabbinic schools can be used to throw some light on the teaching tradition within the early Church." He underestimates, however, the extent of the tradition that can be traced back to Jesus. Jesus was, however, also not an itinerant singer and did not compose epics. Thus, the comparison with Homeric rhapsodists or Yugoslavian folk singers and their oral rendering of epics is not very instructive. We cannot simply make inferences from Yugoslavian folklore to the Jesus tradition. The passing down of the Jesus tradition played a disproportionately large and important role in the communities. Contrast now again Mournet 2005, 135–36, with reference to the well-known studies of Lord.

[4] Dormeyer 1993, 67 with reference to H. Schürmann and B. Gerhardsson.

[5] Cf. Riesner 1988, 359ff.; Dunn 2003b, 557; Byrskog 2000 (on the importance of the eyewitnesses); on this, see also Baum 2004.

[6] Hengel 2001c, 97–98, quotation on 98 (ET = 1995, 88–89; no equivalent quotation in the English translation). The parallels in Sir 6.24ff.; 24.19-23; 51.34 display, despite all formal similarity, also a large difference. The polemical orientation becomes visible in comparison with Luke 11.46 and Matt 23.4. Cf. the taking up within the paraenesis of 1 Clem. 13.1–4: μάλιστα μεμνημένοι τῶν λόγων τοῦ κυρίου Ἰησοῦ, οὓς ἐλάλησεν διδάσκων ἐπιείκειαν καὶ μακροθυμίαν . . . ; see also Acts 20.35b.

what it means to be humble and kind.[7] Jesus stresses that what matters is not merely hearing and taking note of his words but rather acting and living according to them.[8]

The disciples remembered Jesus as "messianic teacher of wisdom" because his teaching was confirmed precisely also through the experience of cross and resurrection and thus appeared uniquely unforgettable and worthy of note,[9] due both to its distinctive style and its extraordinary content.

Jesus could summarize his proclamation in meshalim, aphorisms, which he presumably used among other things at the beginning and end of his respective speeches or sections of speeches or in controversy dialogues.[10] Likewise, parables often occur at the beginning and end of speeches, such as in an early Jewish sermon.[11] Such "key statements" as well as artificial compositions of sayings, grouped by key words and themes, were handed down in the phase of the oral tradition, collected soon after Easter in the sayings tradition also in written form, and finally joined together again by the evangelists according to thematic arrangements into longer speeches, for example in Mark in a chapter on parables and in the eschatological discourse. Matthew configured his large speeches in the most impressive manner. They allow one to discern—most clearly in the Sermon on the Mount—that they have been consciously compiled for the missionary

[7] Cf. Matt 5.5; 21.5; on this, see Luz 2001, 174 (GV = 1985–2002, II: 221). Cf. also the words of the Messiah in Pss. Sol. 17.36, 43. See section 6.4.2 with note 162.

[8] Luke 6.46; Matthew chooses the double parable that follows in Luke 6.47-49 as the conclusion of the Sermon on the Mount (7.24-27). On this, cf. section 12.3 with note 99.

[9] Cf. Dunn 2003b, 698: "memorable." Justin accordingly calls the Gospels the ἀπο-μνημονεύματα τῶν ἀποστόλων about fifteen times; in *Dial.* 106.3 he probably speaks of the Gospel of Mark as the "reminiscences" of Peter; cf. Hengel 1984b, 34 (ET = 1985b, 75–76); Hengel 2008c, 35 n. 102 (ET = 2000b, 222 n. 85); Byrskog 2000, 276, with reference to Luise Abramowski.

[10] Comparable are the sayings gathered in the Old Testament wisdom books or the sayings of Pseudo-Phocylides from the Jewish Greek-speaking diaspora or the sayings of the early Jewish teachers collected in Pirkei ʾAbot, which usually contains only one saying per teacher. In the old lists (1.1–2.8) three sayings are initially attributed to the famous Akiba (1.13–14). "Rabbi" Judah ha-Nasi also has three and Hillel five (2.5–8).

[11] The Pseudo-Philonic sermon *De Jona* ends with several comparisons in a speech of God, in which the last comparison with the toil of the farmer in the planting and watering of trees calls to mind the parable in Luke 13.6-9, the Baptist's parabolic saying about the axe that is already laid at the root, and the Qumranic parable 4Q302 frag. 2 II (on this, see section 12.3 with note 105). It ends with the sentence "For one cuts down a tree that is useless; but if it produces fruits, then one lets it stand." On this, see the translation of Siegert 1980, 46ff.; and the commentary in Siegert 1992, 214–15. Cf. also the "Aesopic" parable at the end of Lucian's dialogue *Hermotimos*. For the description of the rabbinic use of parables in Jerome, see further section 12.3 with note 98.

and catechetical use of the teachers in the communities.[12] Moreover, not a few variants have arisen in the details and double traditions, presumably through the fact that the proclamation of Jesus took place orally and was initially also handed down in oral form, i.e., through the fact that rather than there being, for example, a foundational document (*Urkunde*) written by him or one of his disciples at the beginning, his proclamation was shaped by the oral preaching of the disciples before it was committed to writing.[13]

12.1 *Parallelismus Membrorum*, Rhetoric, and the Problem of Retroversion into Aramaic

In antiquity no one could successfully appear publicly as a speaker and teacher without 'rhetoric,' i.e., without shaped speech. In this regard, prose speech also had 'poetic form.'[14] In antiquity no speaker could forgo the 'art of speaking' if he wanted to convince his hearers.

The special poetic form of the proclamation of Jesus is closely connected with his Aramaic mother tongue and the rules of Semitic poetry. This is determined especially by the parallelism of statements, the *parallelismus membrorum*, a kind of thought-rhyme that we have not only in the Old Testament psalms, in sayings in the prophets, and in older and more recent Jewish wisdom sayings but also in elevated Hebrew and Aramaic prose.[15] Moreover, in this, free prose discourse and stylized rhythmic language could merge into each other.[16] The elements of Semitic poetry—parallelism, rhythm, paronomasia, alliteration, and assonance—fell in the Greco-Roman world under the subject of rhetoric. They were discussed there

---

[12] Deines 2004, 446: "The Sermon on the Mount contains . . . a missionary discipleship ethic and belongs as a whole to the category of mission- and commission discourse."

[13] On this, see Dunn 2003a. Baum 2004, 16, goes even further. He wrongly assumes that Matthew and Luke "drew the common material not from a written source but from an oral tradition." Luke is already dependent on written sources (1.1), and Matthew, in turn, is also dependent on Luke in part.

[14] For the significance of artistic prose in the Greco-Roman world, see Dihle 2008 (GV = 2001).

[15] There is a distinction between synonymous, antithetical, synthetic, and climactic parallelism. Antithetical parallelism appears to be the most common in the sayings of Jesus in the Synoptics; see the listing of Jeremias 1970, 14–20 (GV = 1979, 24–30).

[16] Seybold 2011 (GV = 2003a); 2003b, 55ff. An example of the imitation of the parallelism of Old Testament prose in an early Jewish writing in the Greek language is Joseph and Aseneth, where this stylistic device is used extensively. In order to rank Aseneth as ancestress of all proselytes in the circle of the (mothers of the) patriarchs, the style of the Genesis narrative is imitated.

and not in the sphere of poetry.[17] Free speech belonged also in the Semitic sphere to 'prose,' but it also used "of course other formal elements ranging from rhythmic sequences and word plays to parallelisms and chiastic structures."[18] Parallelism and chiasm are the typical characteristics of Hebrew poetry in the psalms and songs and in the proverbial literature in the wisdom books and in the prophetic books of the Old Testament. The Greek translation of the Septuagint retained the *parallelismus membrorum*. Indeed, the translator could sometimes even 'improve' it by making materially appropriate additions and imitating Hebrew poetry through rhythmic prose.[19] The same phenomenon can be observed in the translation of the early Jewish wisdom writings, such as in Jesus Sirach or Proverbs. In the Aramaic portions of Daniel the Greek translation faithfully reflects the transition from the prose narrative to poetic doxological passages composed in *parallelismus membrorum*.[20] It applies to the Semitic linguistic sphere, to the Greek linguistic sphere, and more broadly that "sentences formed in parallel are in poetry and prose a widespread . . . means of effectively expressing clarifications or oppositions."[21] Greco-Roman rhetoric was likewise familiar with repetition—gemination as a strict *parallelismus* with equally long cola—as a stylistic form in sophisticated, artful speech, especially in Asianic rhetoric. Here, this stylistic device likewise serves to make what is said memorable.[22] This is why the Synoptics—sometimes

---

[17] On this, see Fitzmyer 1997, I: 16.

[18] Seybold 2003b, 56.

[19] Cf. Wifstrand 2005, 127–28: "The interest of the Hellenized Jews in Greek rhetorical form can also be seen in the Septuagint translation itself. It happens . . . that the material parallelisms in many sayings of Proverbs in the Greek translation are emphasized by a formal parallelism not found in the original." The Septuagint refrained, however, from putting it into Greek meter. Josephus speaks twice of Hebrew hexameter. In *Ant.* 2.346 he designates the Song of Moses in Exod 15 as an encomium to God in hexameter. In *Ant.* 4.303 the concern is with the Song of Moses (Deut 32), which shows that the Hebrew long verse (in double three-beat line 3 + 3) could be regarded as corresponding to the hexameter of Greek epic. Augustine, *Doctr. chr.* 4.116, points out that, in his prologue to the translation of the book of Job, Jerome mentions Hebrew meters (*exametri versus sunt, dactilo spondeoque currentes*; B. Fischer 1983, 731), which he does not translate.

[20] Cf., for example, Dan 2.23; on this, see Segert 1984, 1441.

[21] Blass/Debrunner/Rehkopf 1984, 420, § 489. Cf., for example, the regular gnomic parallelisms in Arrian's reproduction of Epictetus' moral teaching. On the difference between "Hebrew parallelism" as a "parallelism of thought" and the "national Greek" as a "parallelism of form," see already Norden 1958, 816–17. See further especially Wifstrand 2005, 111–32, who demonstrates the difference with reference to the Passover homily of Melito of Sardis.

[22] Quintilian, *Inst.* 8.5.18–19: the saying increases in impact through doubling; antitheses and comparisons are nice. Cicero, *Orator* 84–85: only very strict Atticists avoid parallel members of a sentence, consonance of endings, and repetition for emphasis. Paul, too, does not forgo such stylistic devices in his letters. He uses parallelism especially often

even developing further Jesus' manner of formulating[23]—usually retained and did not shorten the *parallelismus* for the handing down of his proclamation. In this regard Mark and Luke are usually closer to dominical speech than Matthew, who smooths out the Greek style, makes improvements, and 'rhetoricizes' it with additional literary ornamentation, which is an indication that Matthew was composed later.

While Jesus taught in Aramaic, the tradition of his proclamation has led to the fact that with the exception of a few Aramaic words and expressions we only know it in Greek translation. These words and expressions are preserved in the original language especially in Mark: "Abba" (Mark 14.36; cf. Rom 8.15; Gal 4.6), ταλιθα κουμ (Mark 5.41), εφφαθα (Mark 7.34), and the last words of Jesus on the cross, ελωι ελωι λεμα σαβαχθανι (Mark 15.34).[24] The sayings of Jesus were translated into Greek relatively early, presumably by the Greek-speaking part of the community in Jerusalem. These Hellenists needed the teaching of Jesus in their own mother tongue, but the first translations by followers probably must be assumed already during the lifetime of Jesus.[25] The numerous Semitisms in the sayings speak in favor of such early faithful translations. Moreover, in the sayings and speeches of Jesus in the Synoptic tradition we can clearly discern in the Greek translation the Semitic *parallelismus membrorum* and the formation of strophes as well as the forms of macarisms, woes, and *ṭôb* sayings, and other similar features.[26] However, paronomasia and alliteration can at best

---

in paraenetic passages, and in the high points of his discussions he changes to rhythmic "hymnic" form. Segert 1984, 1457, refers in addition to 1 Cor 13. Reiser 2001b, 74–75, mentions 1 Cor 15.42-44 as an example. On the other hand, Paul does not retain the Semitic linguistic form in his reproduction of sayings of the Lord and does not imitate it. He keeps to the wording only in the direct quotation of the Lord's Supper paradosis (1 Cor 11.24-25); cf. Schröter 2013, 84 (GV = 2004, 65; 2007, 93).

[23] Matthew does not take over some parallelisms from his Markan text, and Luke can also shorten (e.g., Luke 11.17). On the other hand, Matthew strengthens the "literary ornamentation." Petersen 2001, 313–31, shows that Matthew, for example in the beatitudes, takes over stylistic devices such as "the fourfold anaphora and the fourfold asyndeton μακάριοι (5.3, 4, 6, 11), the threefold synthetic *parallelismus* and the threefold ellipsis around μακάριοι (5.3, 4, 6, 11), and, finally, . . . the threefold internal-anaphora ὅτι (5.3, 4, 6)," but, on the other side, increases this adopted stylistic device and has "created additional 'literary ornamentation'" (325). Moreover, we can see that Matthew utilizes "*conscious* rhetorical stylistic devices" (325), for example, when he changes direct statements in Luke into rhetorical questions (Luke 12.22-32 = Matt 6.25-34). Is he attempting to imitate Jesus' style of speech in Greek linguistic form?

[24] Cf. Rüger 1978; Schwemer 1998; on this, see further section 16.3 with notes 73–76. To this can be added Aramaic names; see Mark 3.17ff.; 10.46, sometimes with translation. Cf. now Schattner-Riesner 2015.

[25] Cf. Reiser 2001b, 161; Hengel 2001c, 84 (ET = 1995, 76).

[26] The Gospel of John also appears to be written in this Semitizing Greek with parallelisms, for which reason Burney 1925 and others reckon with a translation from Aramaic.

be imitated in Greek. Like rhythm and rhyme, they can only be identified in the retroversion into Aramaic.[27]

EXCURSUS

On Retroversion into Aramaic

While there are many different attempts at retranslations into Aramaic, such a task, even in the present, is possible with some probability at best in individual cases for longer sequences of text—the experts disagree even in the case of the Lord's Prayer. Although it appears advisable to abandon the Aramaic reconstruction of *ipsissima verba*, it is also not desirable to stop with the postulate of an *ipsissima intentio*.[28] When C. F. Burney, following Gustaf Dalman, retranslated the words of Jesus into Aramaic, he certainly lamented the fact that witnesses for the Aramaic that was spoken in first century Galilee were lacking, but still used quite uninhibitedly the much later Aramaic of the Palestinian Talmud and of the midrashim for his retroversion. He described, like others before him, the *parallelismus*[29] and stressed the frequency of "antithetic parallelism" in Jesus' sayings. He discovered rhythmic forms analogous to the Old Testament prophetic and wisdom sayings and made observations on end rhymes.[30]

Matthew Black and Joachim Jeremias took up, corrected, and developed further Burney's observations. Black especially gathered examples of alliteration, assonance, and paronomasia. However, he warned against false certainty in the case of retroversions:

Burney also translated the sayings of Jesus of the Gospel of John into Aramaic. He saw the difference from the Synoptic Gospels only in the different circle of addressees—that of the Johannine Jesus is said to have been educated rabbinic intellectuals. Rightly opposed by Segert 1984, 1454: "The way in which these parallelistic thetic and antithetic relationships are expressed in John's Gospel differs in many instances from the parallelistic style in the synoptic gospels. While the parallelism in Semitic or Semitizing tradition is based on the semantic synonymity or antonymity of the words used in these structures, in John's gospel the antithesis is frequently expressed by the use of negative particles."

[27] Segert 1984, 1437, 1439, 1445: "The rhythmical and phonetic devices—alliteration, rhyme, paronomasia—can be observed only in retranslations into Aramaic or Hebrew." Cf. 1448.

[28] On the *ipsissima intentio*, cf. Hahn 2002, I: 40, with reference to Thüsing; cf. further Theissen/Winter 2002, 197–201 (GV = 1997, 201–5). Cf. now Frey 2016.

[29] Burney 1925, 71–72: antithetical parallelism can most often be observed as in the wisdom literature of the Old Testament. On the history of research, see in detail Meynet 1998, 44–166.

[30] Burney 1925, 71–90, 100–46, 147–75. In the Synoptic tradition he often wrongly regarded the shortened polished formulations of Matthew as originally dominical.

In the reconstruction into Aramaic . . . no claim can be made to finality or
absolute certainty in any single instance of a reconstructed original. Where
we are dealing, however, with common words and expressions, there exists
a high degree of probability that we have the original *Urlaut*.[31]

Here too we can only speak of attempts at historical approximation.

Building on Burney and Dalman, Joachim Jeremias emphasized the significance of antithetical parallelism and rhythm, took up observations of Black
on paronomasia, and described the phenomena of hyperbole and paradox so
that he could then pass over to the characteristics of the *ipsissima vox*, which is
also for him not identical with the *ipsissima verba*: parables, enigmatic sayings,
kingdom of God, Amen sayings, and the use of "Abba."[32] In order to identify
the rhythm he retranslated into Aramaic, relying especially on the Palestinian-
Syriac lectionary due to a lack of sources that were closer in time. The use of
two-beat lines signaled "*central ideas*" of the message of Jesus,[33] whereas the
four-beat is said to be the rhythm for "the *instruction of disciples*."[34] According to Jeremias, the three-beat, which is common for mashal in Old Testament
wisdom literature and which corresponds to the iambic trimeter in Greek gnomic poetry, is the most common rhythm in the sayings of Jesus, which made it
easier retain in the memory.[35] Jeremias observed that the rhythm of the lament,
the kīnā meter $(3 + 2)$, "serves above all to express *strong inner emotion*";
"the accumulation of rhythms" is said to point to a "distinctive characteristic
of Jesus," to demonstrate the Semitic background, and also to provide "an
important pointer to the antiquity of the tradition."[36]

In comparison with the numerous Jesus sayings and the small remains of
the proclamation of John the Baptist, we have knowledge of only a very small

[31] Black 1967, 185.

[32] Jeremias 1970, 8–37 (GV = 1979, 19–46).

[33] Jeremias 1970, 22 (GV = 1979, 32). However, Jeremias also reckons with "double
two-beat lines" and "a sequence of two-beat lines" (ET = 21; GV = 31). In our view, all his
examples belong rather to "four-beat lines"; thus, especially, Luke 7.22-23 = Matt 11.5-6,
where we must probably assume the rhythm $2 + 2, 2 + 2, 2 + 2, 2 + 2 + 2$. On this, cf. the
translation into Aramaic by Casey 2002, 105, though he refrains as a matter of principle
from information about rhythm.

[34] Jeremias 1970, 23 (GV = 1979, 33). Cf. The saying ascribed to R. Akiba in t. *Meg*
4(3).16 (Zuckermandel 1880, 226; cf. Neusner 2002, I: 648), which is preserved in the
rhythm $4 + 4$ or $2 + 2, 2 + 2, 2 + 2, 2 + 2$: "Show (honor to the dead), so that one (also)
shows (it) to you! Accompany (the dead), so that one (also) accompanies you! Hold lamentations, so that one (also) laments you! Bury (others), so that one (also) buries you!" This is
a chain saying. Similar is the rhythm in the saying of Eliezer ben Hyrcanus (m. Soṭah 9.15);
on this, cf. the Aramaic sayings assembled by Beyer 1984, 360–61.

[35] Jeremias 1970, 25 (GV = 1979, 35): "the three-beat line . . . serves *to drive home
important sayings and maxims*" (Jeremias' emphasis).

[36] Jeremias 1970, 26–27 (GV = 1979, 36–37).

number of Aramaic sayings—whether they are handed down anonymously
or attributed to specific persons—that belong in the first century until the
second century CE. However, these allow us to clearly recognize that they
are composed in the *parallelismus membrorum* and rhythmically, and we can
also easily identify paronomasia, alliteration, and other features of this kind.
The "three-beat line" is likewise used in one of the few examples of a longer
'prophet saying' in Aramaic from the time of early Judaism. This saying is
an oracle about the destruction of the Jerusalem temple, which could be relatively old, even though it is handed down only in the David Apocalypse of
Hekhalot Rabbati.[37] The Qina occurs in the prophecy of disaster ascribed to
Samuel the Small.

> Simeon and Ishmael for the sword and his associates for execution
> and the remaining people for spoils,
> and great afflictions will take place in the near future.[38]

Josephus hands down the prophecy of disaster of Jesus ben Ananias as a
word-for-word quotation in Greek. Here too we can identify, when one
retranslates into Aramaic, rhythm, paronomasia, and rhyme. However, the
retroversion in this case is much easier to produce than in the case of the sayings of Jesus.[39] While the yield from such Aramaic texts is small, one should
not—as often occurs—entirely ignore them. They are closer to the Jesus tradition than the description of the beauty of Sarah in the Genesis Apocryphon

---

[37] On this, see Schwemer 1991b, 329–33, 345ff.: presumably an early reaction to the
destruction of the temple. Boustan 2005, 224, wishes to date this oracle later.

[38] t. Soṭah 13.4 (Zuckermandel 1880, 319); the rhythm is 3 + 2, 3, 3 + 2; on the text
and translation, cf. also Beyer 1984, 362; Neusner 2002, I: 886.

[39] If we retranslate these prophetic sayings (*J.W.* 6.301, 304, 306, 309)—which are
very simple formally and in terms of vocabulary—into Aramaic, one observes the transition from a double two-beat to a three-beat and from a double three beat to a simple three
beat (2 + 2, 3, 3 + 3, 3). We are dealing with a two-strophic oracle. Every strophe is formed
with a tricolon. In addition, Josephus (trans. H. St. J. Thackeray, LCL, 463, 465, 467)
quotes simple woes over Jerusalem:

A voice from the east,
a voice from the west,
a voice from the four winds;
a voice against Jerusalem and the sanctuary,
a voice against the bridegroom and the bride,
a voice against all the people. (6.301)

Woe to Jerusalem! (6.304, 306)

Woe once more to the city and to the people and to the temple! (6.309)

from Qumran, which is adduced as a "poetic" parallel to the language of Jesus.[40]

Retroversions of sayings of Jesus remain problematic from today's standpoint since we, despite the discoveries at Qumran, know too little about the Aramaic in the first century BCE and CE, and we lack sources precisely for the Aramaic spoken in Galilee at that time.[41] Moreover, the vocalization is largely not certain enough for us always to be able to clearly determine the rhythm. The situation has been decisively improved through the Qumran discoveries and the Aramaic ossuary inscriptions. Above all, some earlier errors in word usage can be corrected. However, different answers continue to be given by the experts regarding the question of which texts can be drawn on for the Galilean dialect of Jesus.[42] At present we still lack clear Aramaic attestations from the time of Jesus and the earliest church even for well-known expressions in the New Testament such as "*Abba*" and "*maranatha*," which have simply been transliterated into Greek.[43]

To avoid the errors of his predecessors,[44] M. Casey took a different path in recent years. He did not simply retranslate individual sayings of Jesus into Aramaic but reconstructed the sources of Mark and Q as Aramaic pieces of text from the first century CE. In doing so he did not aim to offer a simple retroversion but to take account of the situation in Galilee at that time. Moreover, he assumes that the disciples could have made notes on wax tablets, for eyewitnesses must have written these notations, which are so close to the event.[45] According to Casey, the evangelist then expanded and modified these notes. Mark is said to have been composed around 40 CE and to still stand very near to the teaching of Jesus. To some extent, Luke and Matthew are said to have used different translations. Despite the sharp objections of Casey against the approach of the older Aramaic specialists, the observations of

---

[40] Thus, for example, Riesner 1988, 404; cf. 399. Distichic and tristichic Aramaic poetry is also found in 11QPs 155. This, however, is a Hebrew psalm (on the text, cf. García Martínez / Tigchelaar 1997/1998, II: 1176).

[41] It differed from the Judaean, at least in the pronunciation; see Matt 26.73. Casey 1998, 90, regards this as no serious difference, for it is said to have affected at most the pronunciation of the gutturals. Cf. Casey 2002, 36–39. Cf. now Schattner-Rieser 2015.

[42] Cf. Fitzmyer 1971; 1979; 1997. Cf. also Beyer 1984, 54, 62, who points especially to the significance for pronunciation of the Galilean place-names attested in Greek texts and assigns the middle-Aramaic inscriptions and Palestinian rabbinic literature to the Galilean dialect; cf. also Beyer 1994. Contrast Casey 2002.

[43] On this, see Hengel 2004a.

[44] Casey is sharply critical of these scholars. He says that they found too many wordplays and parallelisms. Burney is especially criticized for even reckoning with end rhyme. He expresses himself with somewhat greater respect only with regard to Matthew Black (Casey 1998, 31; 2002, 9–12, 21, 24).

[45] Casey 2002, 48–49.

Burney, Black, and Jeremias, in particular, continue to remain fundamental for the search for the *ipsissima vox* of Jesus. By contrast, Casey's hypotheses appear relatively speculative.[46]

12.2 Wisdom Sayings and Prophetic Sayings

The riches of the linguistic forms in Jesus' sayings are repeatedly praised.[47] We do not possess such a variegated tradition from any other Jewish teacher of this time.[48]

He uses synonymous parallelism. For example:

Nothing is hidden that will not become manifest,
nor secret that will not become known and public.[49]

As an example of the very common antithetical parallelism (with chiasm and anaphora), we can mention:

Whoever wishes to save his life will lose it;
and whoever loses his life for my sake . . . will save it.[50]

However, synthetic parallelism is memorably expressed in a enigmatic double saying:

[46] Cf. Dunn 2003b, 225–26; Reiser 2001b, 64 n. 84, on the Greek of Mark and his criticism of Casey.

[47] Theissen 2003a, 347: "Even if we are uncertain in the case of individual sayings, whether they really come from Jesus or not, we are astonishingly certain that we know the form language of his proclamation—thus the unique combination of literary (oral) forms, topoi, and structures, which is connected with Jesus. If we demonstrated a single exemplar as authentic in the case of every form of the Jesus tradition, we have demonstrated the whole genre for Jesus. . . . Although we are uncertain whether we can identify in detail the *parole* of Jesus, we know his *langue* very well. We know that Jesus used parables and parabolic sayings, woes and macarisms, maxims and admonitions. For all forms there are parallels in the rest of Judaism. Its combination, however, is unique."

[48] Küchler 1979 counts 108 aphorisms. Aune 1991, 242–58, lists 167 "aphorisms" from the canonical and later early Christian literature. Dormeyer 1993, 74–75, who does not restrict himself to the aphorisms, reckons with "about 170 wisdom sayings . . . , which are scattered over the Synoptics." On the number of the parables, see note 97 in section 12.3. However, the high numbers arise for the aphorisms through the fact that often double sayings or three- or four-part sayings are counted in an atomizing manner in their individual elements. We should not splinter sayings of Jesus too much. Through this they sometimes lose their originality.

[49] Luke 8.17; cf. Mark 4.22; Matt 10.26; on this, Burney 1925, 65.

[50] Mark 8.35; on this, see Burney 1925, 84–85.

I came to cast fire on the earth,
and how I wish that it were aleady set on fire.
I must be baptized with a baptism,
and how impatient I am until it is finally accomplished.[51]

In Luke this is followed by an antithetical verse as a third parallelismus:

Do you believe that I have come to give peace on the earth?
No, I say to you, but rather division.[52]

The three concise dominical beatitudes in the Lukan Sermon on the Plain, which have their counterpart in the woes, are likewise synthetic parallelisms. In the Sermon on the Mount, Matthew develops them into a long series in the form of strophes without woes.[53] In Luke and Matthew, the command to love one's enemies is configured in an especially impressive manner through synthetic parallelisms and also forms the head of the series of antitheses in Matthew.[54]

Burney uses the phrase "step parallelism" to describe the linking with anadiplosis, doubling or anaphora, which, especially when the last word is repeated, gives rise to a closer chiastic parallelism:

Do not think that I have come to abolish the law and the prophets,
I came not to abolish (them), but rather to fulfill (them).[55]

Matthew very readily uses this form of doubling, which is also favored by John. Presumably, this verse is at least redactionally shaped by Matthew, if it should go back to a genuine saying of Jesus.[56] We find this stylistic form more clearly and probably authentically in Luke 10.16:

---

[51] Luke 12.49-50. The figura etymologica βάπτισμα βαπτισθῆναι expresses Jesus' premonition of death and also occurs in Mark 10.38-39. On its significance for the baptism of John, see the end of section 9.3.

[52] Luke 12.51; Matt 10.34 represents a more perfect parallelism; cf. Burney 1925, 90. On this, see further section 17.2 with note 24.

[53] Luke 6.20-26 (v. 22 is not authentic but probably an expansive addition that is related to the situation of the primitive community); Matt 5.3-12; on this, see the stylistic analysis of Petersen 2001, 135–57. Cf. also the elaboration of the — dominical — woes against Pharisees and experts in the law from Luke 11.42-52 in Matt 23.2-39.

[54] Luke 6.32ff.; Matt 5.46-47; on this, see Petersen 2001, 220ff., 224ff., who describes the Greek stylistic figures. On the antitheses, see section 14.5.

[55] Matthew 5.17; Burney 1925, 90–96; cf. Deines 2004, 257–87.

[56] Cf. Luz 1989, 257, 264; 2007, 211, 217 (GV = Luz 2002, 229, 235); Deines 2004, 257–87.

The one who listens to you, listens to me,
and the one who spurns you, spurns me,
but the one who spurns me, spurns the one who sent me.[57]

Jesus loved parallelismus and "connected his sapiential language of forms with prophetic genres."[58] We find numerous sayings that correspond to Old Testament prophetic genres or modify them.[59] Sapiential and prophetic sayings do not form an opposition in the Jesus tradition, and it is difficult to demarcate them from each other.[60] The early 'scriptural prophets' of the Old Testament already used not only prophetic 'basic forms.' Among other things, they used ways of speaking that originally had their "setting" in wisdom or in the cult.[61] The I sayings of Jesus, and here especially the Amen sayings, outdo the prophetic messenger formula and bring to expression his messianic claim and his teaching authority.[62] In the sayings tradition, the "'sapiential' instructions" of Jesus also have "a markedly eschatological character."[63] We can best make clear how closely sapiential and prophetic sayings also belong together thematically in Jesus with reference to the double saying about the Queen of Sheba and the Ninevites:[64]

The queen of the south will rise up (in the judgment)
against the men of this generation and will condemn them.

---

[57] The Lukan version appears to be older and more original than Matt 10.40-42, where Luke 10.16 in adjustment to Mark 9.37 is taken up and where there is also reflection on the reward that the person who receives a prophet or righteous person obtains and where one is admonished to hospitality. In this way the Matthean version becomes a community rule for the primitive Christian itinerant missionaries. On this, see section 11.7 with notes 172–77.

[58] Theissen 2004, 47. On pp. 47–48 Theissen identifies sapiential, prophetic, and royal motifs in the sayings tradition. This points to the fact that in relation to Jesus' claim one cannot simply separate sapiential, prophetic, and messianic features.

[59] For the demonstration of the prophetic "micro-genres," from the prophetic announcement, the salvation saying, doom saying, reproach, macarism, and woes to the prophetic-sapiential admonitions in the sayings tradition, see Sato 1988. I sayings and Amen sayings vary the prophetic messenger saying and replace it. Cf. section 17.2 with notes 31–35.

[60] Cf. Hengel 2001c, 86 (ET = 1995, 78).

[61] Cf. Westermann 1964 (ET = 1991).

[62] On this, see section 17.2.

[63] Schröter 1997, 469.

[64] Luke 11.31-32 = Matt 12.41-42. Matthew rearranges secondarily because he attaches the double saying to the rejection of the request for a sign with the reference to Jonah and strengthens the parallelism by writing ἐν κρίσει μετὰ τῆς γενεᾶς ταύτης in every strophe, making use of the same form and sequence. He more strongly adjusts it to the formal Greek parallelism.

For she came from the ends of the earth to hear the wisdom of Solomon,
and behold, here is more than Solomon!

The men of Nineveh will stand up in the judgment
Against this generation and condem it.
For they repented at the preaching of Jonah,
And behold, here is more than Jonah!

With the two-part prophetic saying of judgment against "this generation,"
which is almost entirely parallel in form, Jesus condemns the rejection of
his message by his contemporaries and stresses as with a refrain that his
wisdom surpasses that of the most famous wise person (1 Kgs 5.9-14) and
his preaching that of the most successful prophetic preacher of repentance.

A somewhat more complicated parallel formation of strophes with end
stress can be observed in Luke 17.26-30 (cf., differently, Matt 24.37ff.):

And just as it happened in the days of Noah,
so it will be in the days of the Son of Man:
They were eating, they were drinking,
they were marrying, they were letting themselves be married,
until the day when Noah entered the ark
and the flood came and destroyed them all.

In the same way, just as it happened in the days of Lot:
They were eating, they were drinking,
they were buying, they were selling,
they were planting, they were building,
but on the day when Lot went out of Sodom,
it rained fire and brimstone from heaven
and destroyed them all.
exactly the same thing will be on the day
on which the Son of Man is revealed!

In both cases the strophe formation lends additional weight to the announcement of judgment.[65] A two-member structure can also be observed in the
woe sayings concerning the places of Jesus' activity:[66]

---

[65] On this, see Manson 1963, 54ff., who was the first to observe this strophe formation.
The concise portrayal of the daily events demonstrates an observer versed in sapiential poetry.

[66] Luke 10.13-15; Matt 11.21-24 presents a complete *parallelismus* of the strophes,
compares Capernaum with Sodom, and gives this strophe the end stress. Here Matthew
might have preserved the original form.

Woe to you, Chorazin, woe to you, Bethsaida,
for if there had occurred in Tyre and Sidon the miracles
which took place among you,
they would have long sat in sackcloth and ashes
and would have repented.
Surely, it will be more bearable for Tyre and Sidon in the judgment than
for you.

And you, Capernaum,
will you ascend to heaven?
Into the underworld you will descend.

However, double strophes do not occur exclusively in the announcements
of judgment. In the exhortation "not to worry," among other things, two
strophic comparisons correspond to each other.[67]

Consider the ravens,
for they do not sow, nor do they reap,
they have no storeroom nor barn,
but God feeds them.
Of how much more value are you are than the birds? . . .

Consider the lilies, how they grow,
they do not toil nor do they spin.
I say to you, not even Solomon in all his glory
was clothed as one of these.
But if God clothes the grass of the field,
which exists today and tomorrow is thrown in the oven,
in this way,
how much more you, you of little faith?

Such a two-member structure is also evident in the structure of the Lord's
Prayer, both in the Lukan and in the Matthean versions:

[67] Luke 12.24, 27-28 = Matt 6.26, 28ff. On this, cf. section 13.3 with notes 81–82.

Luke 11.2-4	Matt 6.9-13
Father!	Our Father in heaven!
Hallowed be your name!	Hallowed be your name!
Your kingdom come!	Your kingdom come!
	Your will be done!
	On earth as in heaven.
Give us every day our bread for tomorrow!	Give us today our bread for tomorrow!
And forgive us our sins,	And forgive us our debts,
as we also forgive our debtors!	As we also have forgiven our debtors!
And let us not fall into temptation!	And let us not fall into temptation, but deliver us from evil!

In Luke the original address of God with "Abba" has been preserved in the Greek vocative. To the two you petitions in Luke correspond three we petitions, which is supplemented in accord with the structure in Matthew, so that three petitions now symmetrically correspond to one another respectively. Even though different attempts have been made to reconstruct the Aramaic version, we can recognize a 2 + 2 rhythm in the parallel petitions. The suffixes mean the end rhyme can be heard and is still reflected in the Greek translations.[68] Both evangelists communicate the prayer in the form that was common in their circle of influence.[69]

Luke 10.21-22 = Matt 11.25-27 (the *Jubelruf*)—which is likewise a prayer[70]—in Luke and in expanded form in Matthew appears quite interesting already from a purely formal point of view.[71]

I praise you, Father, Lord of heaven and earth,
  because you have hidden these things from the wise and intelligent,
  but have revealed them to the simple ones.

[68] Cf. the retroversion of Matt 6.9-13 in Burney 1925, 113, 161, and its correction in Jeremias 1970, 193–203, esp. 196 (GV = 1979, 188–96, esp. 191), who regards the Lukan form as more original. Grelot 1984 retranslates both versions. He deviates from Jeremias especially in the bread petition. Philonenko 2002, 69ff., regards the third petition of Matthew as original and reckons with a Lukan omission. A short history of research is provided by H. Löhr 2003, 29–40. Cf. now the retroversion and the correction of the earlier reconstructions by Schattner-Rieser 2015.

[69] For a more detailed discussion, see the end of section 13.2 with notes 60 and 61.

[70] Alongside the Lord's Prayer, the prayer in Gethsemane, Mark 15.34 par. (= Ps 22.2), and Luke 23.46 (= Ps 31.6), it is the only prayer of Jesus handed down in the Synoptics. Luke 23.34 is lacking in many old manuscripts.

[71] Luke 10.21-22; Matt 11.25-30.

Yes, Father, for such was your good pleasure.
All things have been handed over to me by my Father;
  and no one knows who the Son is except the Father
  and no one knows who the Father is except the Son
and anyone to whom the Son wishes to reveal it.

To this Matthew adds:

Come to me all you who labor and have to bear heavy burdens.
  I will give you rest.
    Take my yoke upon you and learn from me;
    for I am kind and lowly of heart;
  thus you will find rest for your souls.
For my yoke is easy and my load is light.

In Luke we can identify two strophes that are connected, being chiastically connected to each other. We know of such multiple chiasmuses from the hymns and psalms in Qumran. Such an 'onion structure' can also be observed there, as well as in the Magnificat and Benedictus. In our view, there is nothing against tracing back this poetic praise of the turning of God the Father to the simple ones ultimately to Jesus. The earliest Christology had its basis not only in implicit references to the dignity and authority that Jesus claimed for himself. The continuation with the praise of the unique relationship of Father and Son is configured in an analogous manner formally and is often designated as a post-Easter commentary, although it has a very distinctive character.[72] But why should it not go back to a saying of Jesus, for example in the form of a comparison? Matthew continues with a piece of sapiential verse from his special material, which calls to mind Jesus Sirach. For the evangelist Jesus and God's wisdom become one here, and he formulates what he is saying very carefully. The form of the critique of the law in this text, however, speaks for a dominical origin of the tradition and fits with his turning to sinners and tax collectors.[73]

---

[72] Luz 2001, 164–65 (GV = 1985–2002, II: 209); contrast Jeremias 1970, 56ff. (GV = 1979, 63ff.), who emphasizes the Semitic character of the language and traces back the logion to a parabolic saying of Jesus; cf. section 17.4.2. Philonenko 2002, 13–15, 110, regards Matt 11.25-30 as a unit that is very close to the Lord's Prayer.

[73] Hengel 2001c, 97ff. (ET = 1995, 88ff.); Deines 2004, 262, 400, 404, 652, and elsewhere.

Jesus' answer to the question of the Baptist, which portrays via allusions to Isaianic texts the messianic time with a word of salvation and which climaxes in a macarism, is rhythmically configured.[74]

Double-membered with a parable about playing children and its following interpretation, which is again kept in strict parallel, Luke 7.31-35 = Matt 11.16-19 portrays the rejection of the Baptist as a crazy ascetic and the insulting of Jesus as "glutton" and "winebibber" by his contemporaries.[75] The concluding statement in Luke 7.35 forms the climax and praises, analogously to the macarism in 7.23, the fact that Wisdom is justified by all her children, i.e., by the Baptist, Jesus, and the tax collectors and sinners mentioned right before.[76]

While such pointed sentences, which make clear Jesus' claim to be the messianic envoy of "Wisdom," may have been spoken in the more intimate circle of disciples, Jesus often also addressed a broader range of hearers. He did not primarily teach only his disciples but directed his instruction to a larger circle of adherents, sympathizers to whom his ethical admonitions applied.[77] The Lukan Sermon on the Plain and the Sermon on the Mount are stylized as teaching proclamations addressed to disciples *and* crowds. In relation to the disciples and the wider circle of adherents Jesus preferred to use, among other things, the "traditional teaching device of the mashal saying or maxim," i.e., the proverb, which already determined the style of the "teaching" in Old Testament and early Jewish wisdom. From long ago the "artfully stylized mashal verse" served "primarily the capacity for retention and preservation."[78]

The number of the proverbial sayings of Jesus that have been handed down is alone already very astonishing.[79] Although Mark takes up relatively little sayings tradition, in his Gospel too the range of the mashal extends from short antithetical verses to multimembered sayings. The double saying in synthetic parallelism is formed from two antithetical statements:

---

[74] Luke 7.22-23 = Matt 11.5-6; Jeremias 1970, 21 (GV = 1979, 31); see further section 10.5.

[75] On this, see section 10.7 and note 182 in chapter 17.

[76] Matthew 11.19 speaks of the "works of wisdom," because he identifies Jesus and Wisdom. By contrast, Luke 7.35 can indeed go back to Jesus.

[77] On this, cf. Zeller 2004, 194–95.

[78] Seybold 2003b, 294–95. Cf. already note 35 above.

[79] The fact that Jesus used proverbs and coined such himself was so familiar that in Acts 20.35 the Lukan Paul quotes the Greek saying "It is more blessed to give than to receive" as a saying of the Lord; cf. 1 Clem. 2.1; Did. 1.5. On the numbers, see note 48 above.

It is not the healthy who need a doctor
but the sick.
I have not come to call the righteous
but sinners. (Mark 2.17)

The widespread proverbial saying about the doctor with the juxtaposition of healthy and sick is doubled in the controversy dialogue with an ἦλθον saying. Only the doubling with the I saying turns the doctor saying into a typically dominical statement. The sapiential aphorism obtains depth through the 'prophetic' messenger saying about the task of Jesus.[80]

An antithetical verse is used in connection with a justification, which can stand in synthetic or climactic parallelism to it, in Mark 2.27-28. The pointed antithesis in v. 27, with chiastic word placement, is very likely an authentic saying of Jesus:

The Sabbath was made for the sake of the human[81]
and not the human for the Sabbath.

But in the case of the consequence that is drawn from this in Mark,

Therefore, the Son of Man is Lord also over the Sabbath (Mark 2.28)

there is controversy over whether it belongs with v. 27 and whether it is authentic. However, this saying, as other Son of Man sayings, can indeed stem from Jesus. Luke and Matthew communicate only this consequence as an important christological statement and forgo the antithetical parallelism with its creation-theological argumentation, which probably already for Luke no longer appeared necessary for the grounding of Jesus' sovereignty over the Sabbath commandment.[82]

Mark 7.15 formulates the annulment of the difference between clean and unclean in a fundamental way with two parallel antithetical statements:[83]

---

[80] On this, see section 17.2: "The I Sayings of Jesus."

[81] ἐγένετο must be understood as *passivum divinum*, which represents a peculiarity of the language of Jesus. It refers to the creator.

[82] Luke 6.5; Matt 12.8. Luz 2001, 179–80 (GV = 1985–2002, II: 229) says that none of the various explanations for the omission of Mark 2.27 are satisfactory. See, however, Doering 1999, 422–23, who argues with good reasons for the possibility of an original belonging together of v. 27 and v. 28: as the Sabbath based on God's creation was made for the human (generic), so it also serves now the individual human, i.e., me. On the rabbinic parallels, see Bill. I: 623–24; II: 5. On the Son of Man question, see section 17.4.1.1.

[83] Paschen 1970, 177: the rhythm can be determined in the retranslation into Aramaic.

Nothing which comes from outside into the human makes him unclean but
that which comes out of the human is what makes the human unclean.

Matt 15.11 shortens, smooths out, and weakens this pointed formulation.
Paul alludes to this saying of the Lord in terms of content (Rom 14.14).
The concise, antithetically formulated saying "The spirit is willing but the
flesh is weak" serves as a rationale for the admonition

Watch and pray in order that you not fall into temptation. (Mark 14.38)

Two paradoxical antithetic stichoi are joined to a synthetical parallelism with anaphora and epiphora in Mark 10.43-44:

For whoever wants to be great among you shall be your servant;
and whoever wants to be first among you shall be slave of all.

The opposition calls to mind the saying about eschatological reversal of
the first and the last[84] and forms as a rule for the disciples the middle of the
series of sayings about ruling and serving, which climaxes in the ransom
saying.[85]

In Mark we also find a numerical saying (*Zahlenspruch*) in an Amen
saying[86] with the announcement to Peter:

Amen I say to you, in this night you will, before the cock crows twice,
deny me three times. (Mark 14.30)

The series of sayings in Mark 9.42-50 configures the sharp warning
against actions that give "offense," which hinder entrance into the kingdom of God, with a fivefold repetition of καλόν ἐστιν, "it is better," in
the form of conditional *ṭôb* sayings.[87] The compilation may stem from the
evangelist, but the three sayings are dominical: at the beginning a saying with "whoever" stresses the seriousness of judgment ("whoever gives
offense to one of these small ones who believe, it would be better for him
if a millstone were hanged around his neck and he be thrown into the
sea"). This is followed by a three-membered synonymous parallelism: it is

---

[84] Luke 13.30 in antithetical chiasm: καὶ ἰδοὺ εἰσιν ἔσχατοι οἳ ἔσονται πρῶτοι καὶ
εἰσὶν πρῶτοι οἳ ἔσονται ἔσχατοι; cf. Matt 19.30; 20.16.

[85] On the dominical origin of the series of sayings, cf. Wischmeyer 1999.

[86] On the Amen sayings, see section 17.2 with notes 31–35.

[87] The *ṭôb* saying is a subgenre of the proverb in the Old Testament, which is introduced by *ṭôb* (= good/better). Mark retains the Semitism with comparative meaning. The
parallels sometimes have συμφέρει.

better for one to cut off or rip out hand, foot, and eye as entities that lead astray than intact to land in the fire of hell.[88] The concluding proverbial-, parabolic- and admonition saying—which again uses the form of the conditional *ṭôb* saying, in which καλόν is again to be understood comparatively as "better"—warns the disciples against becoming "saltless." They are to be salted with a view to the future judgment of fire and to share salt among one another (the picture of mutual fellowship is derived from the table fellowship) and to keep peace.[89]

We find chiasms, a wordplay with "Son of Man" and "man," woe saying, and a following *ṭôb* saying sporadically in Jesus' announcement about his betrayer (Mark 14.21), in which Mark (or the tradition available to him) imitates the master language of Jesus and which is formulated in such a polished manner that Matthew takes it over without improvements:

The Son of Man goes as it is written about him;
but woe to that man through whom the Son of Man is betrayed,
it would have been better for that man if he had not been born.[90]

Typical forms of Jesus' formation of sayings were not first taken up and developed by Matthew. Mark and Luke also already proceed in this way. Through this the problem arises that it is not always easy to distinguish between the "master prophecy" and sayings that were configured by later tradents, who still remembered his manner of speaking, for the purpose of reporting about him.[91]

---

[88] The parallel in Matt 5.29-30 shows that the concern is with sexual sin. The "foot" makes good sense as a euphemism in this context (see Koehler/Baumgartner/Stamm/Ben-Ḥayyim 2004, 1106 A 4a) and is retained in Matt 18.6-9 following the Markan text. Bultmann 1963, 86 (GV = 1995, 90), regards this statement about the foot as a secondary expansion. A comparison of the stylistic devices in Mark and Matthew is offered by Petersen 2001, 197–202. He identifies in Mark hyperbole, personification, anaphora, and epiphora.

[89] On the metaphor of salt for discipleship, see Deines 2004, 201–17.

[90] Pesch 1984b, 352, refers for the conspicuously numerous Semitisms here and in the more immediate context to Black 1967, 58, 105, 117, 128, 302. He regards v. 21, however, as "scarcely authentic." Cf. also Hampel 1990, 248: "Mark has redactionally embellished Mark 9.31 in 14.21b with a view to the death of Judas." Luke shortens and omits the *ṭôb* saying, whereas Matthew follows Mark. In Matt 18.6-9 Matthew redactionally inserts a woe into the Markan series of *ṭôb* sayings.

[91] Cf. the optimistic answer of Theissen/Winter 2002, 237 (GV = 1997, 245): "the sayings tradition . . . was handed on by Jesus' followers. . . . There is thus a good chance that the sayings of Jesus were transmitted by them in the sense and spirit Jesus himself had intended them."

12.3 The Parables of Jesus

The parables are regarded as the actual center of the proclamation of Jesus,[92] and according to the general consensus of scholarship they have "almost without exception . . . a genuine core that goes back to Jesus himself."[93] Terminologically the Synoptics, like Palestinian Judaism, do not make a strict distinction between sayings and parables. Both can be called παραβολή.[94] This broad meaning corresponds to the Hebrew "*māšāl*," Aramaic "*mātāl/mᵉtal/matlā*'," of which we have already spoken, a term that was used in the Old Testament for carefully formulated texts of very different genres,[95] ranging from proverb, riddle, and maxim to parable and allegorical story, indeed to apocalyptic-prophetic eschatological discourse.[96] Both forms of the proclamation of Jesus merge into one another and cannot be strictly separated. The short comparison and the parabolic saying can also be classified as "proverbial saying." However, by compiling collections

---

[92] Hahn 2002, I: 67ff.: "Even if one does not characterize, as Jüngel tends to do, all the speeches of Jesus, according to their nature, as parabolic speech, we can nevertheless probably say that the parable speech stands at the center" (69). Theissen/Merz 1998, 316, 347 (GV = 1997, 285, 317), discuss the parables under the heading "Jesus as Poet," whereas his sayings are dealt with under the heading "Jesus as Teacher." In both cases he is both!

[93] Jülicher 1979, I: 11. Scholarship has followed his judgment almost without exception. See now, however, Meier 2016.

[94] Mark begins and closes his parable chapter programatially with the pointer that Jesus taught the crowds many things in parables; Luke and Matthew follow him. On the "proverb," cf. Mark 7.17; Matt 15.15; Luke 4.23; 6.39. For "parable," instead of παραβολή, John uses παροιμία "proverb," "concealing speech." Josephus uses παραβολή only in *Ant*. 8.44 for the parables and fables of Solomon in connection with 1(3) Kings 5.12 (LXX); in this text he calls parabolic sayings εἰκόνες "(speech) images." Jeremias 1972, 20 (GV = 1998, 16): The *māšāl* designates "figurative forms of speech of every kind." With reference to Gerhardsson 1988, Gerhardsson 1991, 266, has suggested that we should call the parables of the Synoptics "narrative meshalim."

[95] On this, see Koehler/Baumgartner/Stamm/Ben-Ḥayyim 2004, 611–12. In the Old Testament the verb has the meaning "to make a saying, parable, to say a mocking verse" and in the niphal "to be equated," "to be equal"; in the hiphil "to compare with (*lᵉ*)," hitpael "to become equal"; as a noun: "saying," "proverbial saying," "wisdom saying," "taunting song." In the common Semitic background stands the meaning "compare" or "resemble." See also Jastrow 1903, I: 855: "to speak metaphorically," "to compare, to give an illustration," or "a truth substantiated by an illustration, wise saying; fable, allegory; example; mashal"; cf. 862 on Aramaic *mᵉtal*. In Ezek 21.5 [ET = 20.49] the prophet is a *mᵉmaššel* for the people, one who always speaks in "riddle sayings" (LXX: παραβολή ἐστιν). In Mark 4.11b, 33-34, this one-sided materially inappropriate notion stands in the background. See also section 16.1 with notes 43–47.

[96] In 1 En. 1.2–3 for Aramaic מתלוה׳ in 4Q201 (García Martínez / Tigchelaar 1997/1998, I: 398–99 translate "his oracles") the Greek translation with παραβολή is attested.

of parables at certain points, the Synoptics show that they recognized and distinguished the forms.

Just as a singular abundance of forms of sayings of Jesus is handed down, so the number of parables that are attributed to him is likewise extraordinary. Mark conveys only a small selection from the abundance (cf. Mark 4.2, 33). If one also reckons to this the parables common to Luke and Matthew from the sayings tradition and their respective special material, one comes to more than forty.[97] Luke has taken up the most parables. At the same time, this evangelist is not only the best teller of parables but also our most important source for the proclamation of Jesus.

Like fables in antiquity, parables were probably originally a purely oral genre. For what purpose did one tell parables in ancient Palestine? A remark by Jerome appears instructive, although it describes the situation more than three hundred years after Jesus:

> It is customary in Syria, and even more so in Palestine, to join parables to all of one's words. In this way, by comparisons and examples, hearers can grasp what cannot be grasped by simple commands.[98]

According to the observation of Jerome, parables, like the *māšāl* verse, support the memory and are used at the end of speeches in order to impress once more upon the hearers what was said. Thus, Mark, Luke, and Matthew already have Jesus conclude his speeches with parables with astonishing frequency.[99] The aforementioned synagogue sermon *De Jona* also ends with a parable.[100] It is not unlikely that Jesus himself placed parables at the end of speeches and disbanded his hearers with a text for reflecting on what was heard. In any case, he remained in memory as the one who spoke of the kingdom of God in parables.[101] Jerome certainly thinks of the rabbinic teachers of his time and their frequent use of parables, which

---

[97] The Johannine parables and pictorial speeches have a different character. Jeremias 1972, 247–48 (GV = 1998, 7 and 242), counts forty-one parables. Klauck 1992, 843, says that depending on one's definition one counts up to one hundred parables. Rose 2003, 450, lists forty-three. Jülicher 1979, I: 28, observes in relation to this point: "Scarcely two books in which the same number of parables is obtained." On the number of "wisdom sayings" of Jesus, see note 48 above.

[98] Jerome, *Comm. Matt.* 18.23 (trans. Scheck 2008, 213; cf. Hurst/Adriaen 1969, 163); cf. Reiser 2001b, 145.

[99] Mark 13.34-35 (doorkeeper); Luke 6.47ff. = Matt 7.24-27 (house construction); Matt 18.23-25 (unforgiving servant); Matt 25.31-45 (judgment of the world); Luke 19.12-27 (entrusted minas); Luke 21.29ff. places the parable of the fig tree (cf. Mark 13.28-29; Matt 24.32-33) at the end of the eschatological discourse.

[100] See note 11 above.

[101] Cf. also Dunn 2003b, 385.

have found expression in the rabbinic literature.[102] By contrast, parable, fable, and example story appear relatively infrequently in the Old Testament and in the early Jewish writings. We find them, however, at significant points in the stories of the prophets and the books of the prophets of the Old Testament,[103] and they also belong to sapiential instruction.[104] Only a single parable appears to be preserved from the library in Qumran. It is thematically related to Luke 13.6-9, Jesus' parable of the unfruitful fig tree, to the parables of growth, and to the *mashal* about the good tree and the good fruits:

> Understand this, wise ones: if a man has a good tree that towers up to the heaven . . . [. . .] for the . . . of the lands, and it produces juicy fruit . . . early and late rains, . . . in heat and in thirst; does not he l[ove] it [. . .] . . . and he watches it [. . .] . . . to enlarge the foliage [. . . .] from its shoot to multiply [. . .] and its branches.[105]

Unfortunately, the text is fragmentary, and we can no longer reconstruct which teaching is to be made accessible to the wise and which form the parable as a whole had. In any case, it is directed not to uneducated persons but to the wise elite. Apparently, teaching in parables was not pleasing to the Qumran Essenes. They were probably too popular for them. They preferred the "clear text." They interpreted texts from the prophets

---

[102] In the early rabbinic literature ca. five thousand parables and fables have been counted; see the collection of Thoma/Lauer/Ernst 1986–1996. Theissen/Merz 1998, 317–18 (GV = 1997, 286) point to early Tannaitic attestations and similar themes. Jeremias 1972, 12 (GV = 1998, 8), reckons with the dependence of the rabbis on Jesus; his parables are said to be "something entirely new." Cf. Dunn 2003b, 698.

[103] Second Samuel 12.1-14 ("Nathan parable"); 14.1-11; 1 Kgs 20.35-40; Isa 5.1-7 (Song of the Vineyard); 28.23-29 (parable of the work of the farmer); fables: Judg 9.8-15; 2 Kgs 14.9-10; cf. also Ezek 17.3-10; 19.2-9, 10-14; 21.1-5; 24.3-5.

[104] Cf. the fable of the ants in Prov 6.6-10; more important is Eccl 9.13ff.: "I have also seen this example of wisdom under the sun, and it seemed important to me. There was a little city with few people in it. A great king came against it and besieged it, building great siegeworks against it. Now there was found in it a poor, wise man, and he by his wisdom delivered the city. Yet no one remembered that poor man" (NRSV; cf. Krüger 2000, 313). The common topos of the rich and laughing heir (Luke 12.16-21: the rich farmer) is also found in Sir 11.(16)18-19: "One becomes rich through diligence and self-denial, and the reward allotted to him is this: when he says, 'I have found rest, and now I shall feast on my goods!' he does not know how long it will be until he leaves them to others and dies" (NRSV).

[105] 4Q302 frag. 2 II (trans. García Martínez / Tigchelaar 1997/1998, II: 667). Perhaps it belongs to the widespread narratives about fruitful and unfruitful trees; on this, see already Ahiqar 73 (English translation by J. M. Lindenberger in *OTP* 2, 506). On the parallel in the Syriac Ahiqar, see Küchler 1979, 392; cf. 357. Cf. Matt 7.16-20 = Luke 6.43-44.

and psalms in the pesharim allegorically with reference to the present. This, too, fundamentally distinguished them from Jesus and his way of teaching.

Jesus did not invent the parabolic teaching form, but such an abundance of parables ascribed to a single teacher is very uncommon in the early Jewish sphere. In the rabbinic literature they then become a popular genre, which primarily illuminates the relationship of God to people, especially to Israel. As an established metaphor there is talk of God as "king" and of his "slaves," but the rural occupational world, day laborers, and estate owners also serve the comparison and "wages" is, as in the parables of Jesus, a religious metaphor.[106] Thus, the closest parallels to the New Testament parables occur in rabbinic literature, though, in contrast to Jesus, this literature often uses the animal fable. Thus, Rabbi Akiba is already said to have grounded his Torah obedience, which led him to martyrdom, in a fox fable.[107]

The Aesopic fable, originally a child of the ancient orient, had long been cherished among the Greeks. It is not restricted to animal and plant fables; the wise or foolish behavior of human beings is thematized time and again. Fable collections and compositions in verse continued to remain popular in Greco-Roman times and were compiled anew. We can also increasingly discern their influence on early Judaism.[108] With his disparaging remark about the use of small stories and fables in the speech of professional rhetoricians, with which only peasants and the simpleminded can be impressed, Quintilian gives us an indirect pointer to the simple audience of Jesus in Galilee. He really wanted to win over fishermen and peasants.[109] Quintilian has a higher estimation of the power of dem-

---

[106] Hezser 1990, 189–90: "Although the Rabbinic parables are literarily attested only much later than the parables of Jesus," a comparison between them and the parables of Jesus is indeed appropriate, "for . . . the formal characteristics of the genre 'parable' remained relatively constant; . . . the same motifs and images are found both in the New Testament and in the rabbinic parables of the most different provenance. A comparison of the parables with regard to the selection and use of specific metaphors and the associations connected with them can clarify the peculiar character of the respective teller of parables or his special intention."

[107] b. Ber. 61b.

[108] Josephus, *Ant.* 18.170–178, quotes the fable about the wounded man and the flies in the mouth of the emperor Tiberius. He is said to have used this to explain the long time of office of his prefects and procurators; see the end of section 3.1.3. Jesus' comparison of Herod Antipas to a fox (Luke 13.32) could point to knowledge of the fox fables, which were widespread in antiquity and also attested later in Judaism (cf. the previous note).

[109] Quintilian, *Inst.* 5.11, 19; among others he adduces as an example Menenius Agrippa's use of the Aesopean fable of the stomach and the members, to which Paul also alludes (1 Cor 12.14-26). The quotation of Aesopean fables was popular in speeches and was expected from orators; cf., for example, Dio of Prusa, *Orationes* 12.7 (*Olympic Discourse;*

onstration of the example story (παραβολή) and of the parabolic saying (εἰκών), with it being necessary, however, for the speaker to attend strictly to the fitting similarity.[110]

Modern parable scholarship begins with Adolf Jülicher's monumental work.[111] He not only took the field against allegorical interpretation, which remained common into his time, stressed the didactic purpose of the pictorial narrative and the orientation to a goal as the point of comparison, the *tertium comparationis*, in the parable, and distinguished, probably as the first to do so, between the source domain and the target domain, but he also—as cited above—recognized its significance for capturing the authentic proclamation of Jesus. The one-sided emphases of the liberal theologian Jülicher, who highlighted general ethical and religious truths as the content of the parables but could also say that the parables are addressed not "to the understanding that draws regular conclusions . . . but to the whole person,"[112] have been criticized and corrected by subsequent scholars. Fiebig had already pointed to the rabbinic parables as parallels.[113] The fact that Jülicher failed to recognize the eschatological character of the dominical parables has been so strongly criticized that we sometimes fail to mention how much we owe to him. Rudolf Bultmann took over from Jülicher the distinction between similitudes or undeveloped parables (*Gleichnisse*) and narrative parables (*Parabeln*) and the confidence to penetrate to the core of the Jesus tradition, but regarded the criterion for genuineness in the "distinctive eschatological temper."[114] Joachim Jeremias[115] also stressed "the eschatological import" (19/15) and investigated—building on Cadoux and especially on Dodd's successful attempt "to place the parables in the setting of the life of Jesus" (21/17)— the rules according to which the parables were reshaped in the primitive community. In order to penetrate to the proclamation of Jesus, he pointed, also here, to the necessity of retranslation into Aramaic (25/21). However, above all: "the parables of Jesus are not . . . literary productions . . . but each of them was uttered in an actual situation of the life of Jesus" (21/17).

---

on this, see the edition with commentary of Klauck 2000, 48–49; 108, 113, 165, 176); see further *Orationes* 72.13 (edited by Arnim 1962, II: 187–88); Lucian, *Hermot.* 84 (edited and translated by Möllendorf 2000, 136–37).

[110] Quintilian, Inst. 5.11.23–27. These principles of rhetoric go back to Aristotle.

[111] Jülicher 1979; on the history of scholarship, see Klauck 1994; Theissen/Merz 1998, 318 (GV = 1997, 287).

[112] Jülicher 1979, I: 162; quoted by Jüngel 1979, 102, as a "fortunate . . . inconsistency" of Jülicher.

[113] Fiebig 1912; on this, Fiebig 1904; 1929.

[114] Bultmann 1963, 205 (GV = 1995, 222: "*die spezifisch eschatologische Stimmung*").

[115] Jeremias 1972 (GV = 1998).

Therefore, his program is called: "The Return to Jesus from the Primitive Church" (23/19), in order to present "The Message of the Parables of Jesus" (115/115).[116] Eberhard Jüngel protested against such a historicizing interpretation of the parables in his dissertation. He viewed the parables as a language event: "The basileia comes to expression in the parable as parable."[117] For him it is not the comparison but the metaphor that underlies the pictorial language of the parables. Therefore, Julicher's distinction between source domain and target domain is just as unnecessary as the search for the *tertium comparationis*. Hans-Joseph Klauck turned to the problem of allegory and allegorization, which had been long neglected under the influence of Jülicher.[118] The correction of the exaggerated historical apologetic through the investigation of the realia, on which the parables build, is also significant. The social-historical approach has proven to be very useful for illuminating the historical connections.[119] In a different way one attempts today to understand the parables not only as "autonomous works of art" but through the analysis of their narrative intention and their historical context to describe them as parables told by Jesus and in their function in the Gospels.[120]

Ever since Jülicher the traditional division of the forms, following ancient example, distinguishes the parabolic saying from the similitude (*Gleichnis*) and the parable (*Parabel*). Despite some protests, this general distinction has stood the test of time, and there is, in our view, no reason to abandon it.

The concise parabolic saying and the comparison: A simple comparison is Matt 10.16: "Be as wise as serpents and innocent as doves." The parabolic sayings rest on metaphors and are closely related with the proverb "Where the carrion is, there the vultures will gather" (Matt 24.28). A

---

[116] Jeremias 1972, foreword: "Only the Son of Man and his word can invest our message with full authority" (GV = Jeremias 1998, preface to the sixth edition: "Niemand als der Menschensohn selbst und Sein Wort kann unserer Verkündigung Vollmacht geben"). He attempted to defend apologetically the historical foundations of faith.

[117] Jüngel 1979, 118–19, 135–36 (with emphasis in Jüngel; we must take note of the parallelism); on Hahn's objection, cf. note 92 above. Related is the hermeneutical understanding in E. Fuchs and H. Weder. On the continuation of the literary-critical approach in R. W. Funk, D. O. Via, and others, cf. Harnisch 1995; Theissen/Merz 1998, 321–22 (GV = 1997, 289–90).

[118] Klauck 1986 [1978]; Jülicher lacked the "distinction between allegory as text-producing, poetic-rhetorical procedure and allegoresis as text-interpretive, exegetical-hermeneutical method" (Klauck 1994, 202).

[119] Hengel 1968a; Freyne 2000.

[120] Cf. the survey of research in Theissen/Merz 1998, 322–23 (GV = 1997, 290–91); Erlemann 1999, 57–58. An exemplary consideration of the various aspects is found in Avemarie 2002a (= 2013, 453–72).

nice double parabolic saying with synonymous parallelism—which Matt 7.16b, in a rhetorically even more effective manner, puts in the form of a question—is Luke 6.44b:

> From thistles one does not pick figs,
> and from a thornbush one does not harvest grapes.

A series of three parabolic sayings occurs in Mark 2.19, 21-22: bridegroom and fasting, a new patch on an old garment, and new wine in old wineskins are not compatible. If one translates them into Aramaic, these parabolic sayings are joined with one another with alliteration: *ḥātān* is the bridegroom, new is *ḥādāš*. The three *ṭôb* sayings in Mark 9.43-48 cited above also form a group of parabolic sayings that belong together.

Similitudes (*Gleichnisse*) and parables (*Parabeln*) differ from parabolic sayings (*Bildworten*) through the extensiveness of the pictorial narrative. When they aim to present a target domain pictorially through a daily event, they are usually recounted in the present. They follow the rules of the art of popular storytelling: "brevity," "law of the scenic duality" (i.e., usually only two persons or groups are respectively depicted as acting), "unilinear narrative," "repetition," and "breaking off the narrative after the punchline."[121] Examples of very concise similitudes are, among others, the similitudes of the the seed growing secretly and of the mustard seed in Mark 4, the similitude of the leaven in Luke and Matthew, and the similitudes of the treasure in the field and of the pearl in the special material of Matthew. They are very close to the parabolic saying and the comparison. The event consists in a contrast. The portrayal is concise. The number of persons is limited (usually to two actors). The more extensive similitudes are narrated more dramatically, which are defined more specifically as parables and example stories. For their action, double, triple, or even fourfold repetitions are typical, which are then climactically intensified. The persons stand in contrast to each other, such as the rich man and the poor Lazarus, or form a "constellation of characters" in the form of a "dramatic triangle,"[122] such as the portrayal of the father in the parable of the lost son in his behavior toward the younger and the older son. The alternation in the direct speech likewise forms an intensification. In the Lukan parables we also find the interior monologue. The concern is always with fictive stories, also in the case of example stories, though these could call to mind real people and events, as in the case of the nobleman who journeys to

---

[121] Bultmann 1963, 187–92 (GV = 1995, 203–8); Theissen/Merz 1998, 331 (GV = 1997, 298).
[122] Harnisch 1995, 78–79.

a distant land to obtain the rule over his kingdom and brutally avenges himself against his enemies after his return (Luke 19.12-27), which could cause the hearers to think of Herod's son Archelaus.

In order to put special emphasis on the genre, Jesus is often specifically presented as a teller of parables by the evangelists: "He told them a parable . . ."[123] The introductions are variable, but there are two basic forms. The first form is the "nominative beginning," in which the introductory formula is lacking. It is used in the Old Testament, in early Jewish parables, and in ancient fables and fairy tales and occurs most often in Luke (especially in his parables and example stories).[124] In lightly modified form it appears as a question in the formula τίς ἐξ ὑμῶν; "who of you . . . ?"[125] The dative beginning as the second basic form contains the comparison formula, which is known from the rabbinic literature. Here the parables begin with: "A parable. To a . . ." (= *māšāl lᵉ*), which represents a short form of: "I will tell you a parable. With what can a subject matter be compared? It is the case with it as with a . . ."[126] This comparison formula refers to the whole parable. Accordingly, we must not translate "The kingdom of God is like a merchant . . ." but rather "It is the case with the kingdom of God as with a merchant, who. . . ."[127] Mark 4.30-31 uses the long form of the dative beginning with a *parallelismus membrorum* for the introduction of the parable of the mustard seed:

How shall we compare the kingdom of God? Or in which parable shall we grasp it? (It is the case with it) as with. . . .[128]

Characteristic for the dative beginning is the comparison particle "as," which corresponds to the Aramaic *lᵉ*. Mark uses this simple beginning with ὡς three times, and Luke uses it six times. Luke uses ὅμοιος "similar to" nine times in various cases, as does Matthew. In addition, they use ὁμοιόω, which in Mark appears only in 4.30, more frequently. Luke uses

---

[123] Cf. Mark 3.23; 4.2 parr.; 12.1; 13.28; beyond this eight times in Matthew and nine times in Luke.

[124] Cf. Mark 4.3 parr.; 12.1 parr.; Luke 7.41: "A money lender had two debtors . . ."; Luke 10.30: "A man went from Jerusalem to Jericho . . ."; 12.16: "The land of a rich man had a good crop . . ."; 13.6: "a certain one had a fig tree . . ."; 14.16: "A man gave a great banquet . . ."; 15.11: "A man had two sons . . ."; 16.1: "A rich man had a manager . . ."; 16.19: "A man, however, was rich . . ."; 18.2, 10; 19.12; see further Gos. Thom. 9; 63–65.

[125] Luke 11.5 (petitioning friend); 15.4 (lost sheep); cf. 14.28; 17.7.

[126] On this, see Jeremias 1972, 100–3 (GV = 1998, 99–102).

[127] Cf. Jeremias 1972, 100–2 (GV = 1998, 100–1); Theissen/Merz 1998, 330 (GV = 1997, 297).

[128] Mark 4.30-31: πῶς ὁμοιώσωμεν τὴν βασιλείαν τοῦ θεοῦ ἢ ἐν τίνι αὐτὴν παραβολῇ θῶμεν; ὡς . . . ; cf. Luke 13.20. Jeremias identifies five forms of the dative beginning.

it three times and Matthew seven times. Matthew has standardized his usage to the greatest extent, specifying the topic of the kingdom of God in the dative beginning fourteen times.[129] With this emphatic connection of parable and kingdom of God he is probably correct. Placing a theological emphasis, he imitates here, as so often, Jesus' language.

That the parables of Jesus do not *all* have the kingdom of God *directly* as their topic is shown by the parable of the playing children for the behavior of "this generation" (Luke 7.31-32 = Matt 11.16-17), which rejects Jesus' preaching of the kingdom of God, and by the double parable of building a house, which juxtaposes the respective actions of the wise and foolish hearers of the teaching of Jesus at the end of the Sermon on the Plain and Sermon on the Mount. Indirectly these comparisons and parables do indeed have something to do with the kingdom of God insofar as they thematize its rejection.

The double sayings have their counterpart in the double parables. The parable of the lost son has a double climax and also an elegant ring composition. However, since Luke himself loves ring composition with mirroring correspondences and the contrast between beginning and end, it remains uncertain whether Jesus himself recounted in precisely this way. Luke uses this stylistic device when he makes special effort in the telling of a story.[130]

At the *conclusion* of the parable we sometimes find an *epimythium*, a generalizing summary, analogous to the *fabula docet*. This is a part of the genre in the fable, but in the parables of Jesus such conclusions show themselves to be secondary.[131] The abrupt breaking off right after the punchline is characteristic of their original form. This can be seen with particular clarity, for example, in the parable of the workers in the vineyard. The saying "Thus, the last will be first and the first last" (Matt 20.16) takes up an element from the preceeding parable (v. 8b) but does not fit the actual narrative intention of the dominical parable, in which the concern is with the appropriate reaction of the person to God's free grace.

The *originality* of the parables of Jesus has been no less praised than that of his sayings. They have—even though we can repeatedly recognize for their "stock metaphors" the conventions of ancient Jewish metaphoricism—a completely distinctive coloring. That it is the case with the βασιλεία τοῦ θεοῦ as with a tiny mustard seed (Mark 4.30ff. parr.) or with the leaven of a woman (Luke 13.20-21 = Matt 13.33) seems

---

[129] Matthew 13.31, 33, 44, 45, 47; 20.1: ὁμοία ἐστὶν ἡ βασιλεία τῶν οὐρανῶν...;
Matt 13.24; 18.23; 22.2; 25.1: ὡμοιώθη/ὁμοιωθήσεται ἡ βασιλεία τῶν οὐρανῶν....
[130] Cf. Luke 24.13-34; Acts 8.26-40; 9.1-30.
[131] See the demonstration in Jeremias 1972, 110–13 (GV = 1998, 109–12).

extraordinary; they are bold metaphors. In this way, these contrast parables already stress the contrast between the inconspicuous beginning and the establishment of the kingdom of God with power by the choice of images. The fitting choice of metaphors,[132] the persuasive and disarming clarity of the narrative, and the consonance with the sayings and behavior of Jesus are an important argument for the authenticity of the parables. Within the Synoptic tradition we can also see how some bold strokes were weakened. Thus, Matthew changes the dominical parable of the the seed growing secretly (Mark 4.26-29) into the parable of the "tares," which the enemy scatters among the wheat, which fits better in the missionary and ecclesiastical situation of his time (Matt 13.24-30). Instead of a nobleman (ἄνθρωπός τις) as in Luke, a king invites people to the "great supper" in Matthew (Matt 22.2-14; Luke 14.16-24). The conclusion with the man without a wedding garment disturbs the logic of the story, and the impending judgment is likewise typical for Matthew. Perhaps he joined two different parables together here? Finally, the pictorial speeches in the Gospel of John continue Jesus' recounting of parables in a completely distinctive way in order to stress their christological revelatory character.

---

[132] Cf. Quintilian, *Inst.* 5.11.26: *solent tamen fallere similitudinum species, ideoque adhibendum est eis iudicium* ("nevertheless, the appearance of a similarity readily deceives, and therefore we must proceed critically in this regard"); see also Aristotle, *Poet.* 22 (1459a).

13

*Jesus' Proclamation of
the Kingdom of God*[1]

13.1 The Presence or Futurity of the Kingdom?
The False Alternative

Here we can make recourse to what has already been said.[2] After a long time of flawed interpretations of the phrase βασιλεία τοῦ θεοῦ—which is central for the proclamation of Jesus—we are especially indebted to Johannes Weiss and Albert Schweitzer for an interpretation that materially advanced our understanding of the subject matter. They broke with the idealistic-innerworldly interpretation, which was dominant in the last quarter of the nineteenth century, in the school of Albrecht Ritschl (1822–1889). It was, however, also advocated by conservatives and mediating theologians such as the father of J. Weiss, Bernhard Weiss, who wanted to view the "kingdom of God on earth" as a highly "religious moral entity," which "in accordance with its nature does not come to be through the one-off action of the establishment of the expected kingdom but by a gradual development,"[3] i.e., in the history of the church, which is identical with the process of the religious education of the human race or of moral

---

[1] J. Weiss 1892; 1900; 1964 (ET = 1971); Kümmel 1961 (GV = 1956); Schweitzer 1906; 1913 (ET = 2000); Schnackenburg 1965; Jeremias 1970 (GV = 1979); Hengel 1989c, 91–110 (GV = 1976c, 95–114); Schürmann 1983; Camponovo 1984; Sanders 1985; Hengel 1987c; 1999b, 275–79 (on kingdom of God and God's name in the Lord's Prayer); Merklein 1989; Hengel/Schwemer 1991, 1–19; Merkel 1991; Meier 1994, 289–506; Grappe 2001; Dunn 2003b, 383–487. Cf. now also Allison 2010, 164–203; Schröter 2014, 121–37.

[2] See sections 4.5 and 5.2.

[3] B. Weiss 1885, 51, on the parables of contrast. On the whole, see section 5.2 with note 34.

advancement.[4] In contrast to this view, J. Weiss and A. Schweitzer recognized the apocalyptic-eschatological sense of the phrase—the "mythological" sense, so to speak, and that means one that appears foreign to us. The starting point was the summary of the proclamation of Jesus in Mark, which has already been mentioned on multiple occasions:

> The time is fulfilled, and *the kingdom of God has come near* (or *is here*). Repent and believe the good news![5]

According to the sayings tradition, after their sending out, the disciples—in accord with Jesus' instruction—also proclaimed God's dawning reign in the same way.[6]

However, the controversy over the understanding of the phrase βασιλεία τοῦ θεοῦ in the proclamation of Jesus was not yet decided with this insight. Rather, after this it first obtained its real sharpness.

In his lecture two years after the appearance of the epoch-making study of Johannes Weiss and the controversy that it ignited,[7] William Wrede drew attention to a fundamental problem of Jesus' proclamation of the kingdom of God:

> Jesus never provided instruction about what he understood by the kingdom of God. He never said to his disciples that his view of the kingdom of God was different than the common view. Everywhere one gets the impression that he uses a familiar word in the same sense in which one generally understood it.[8]

---

[4] This break with the new Protestant ideas of progress was strengthened through the theological crisis that found expression after the end of World War I in the Dialectical Theology founded by Karl Barth, through which concepts such as "eschatology," "eschatological" moved to the center in a new understanding related to the present: "If Christianity be not altogether thoroughgoing eschatology, there remains in it no relationship whatsoever with Christ" (Barth 1953, 314, on Rom 8.24-25; GV = 1922, 298: "*Christentum, das nicht ganz und gar und restlos Eschatologie, hat mit Christus ganz und gar und restlos nichts zu tun*"); on this, see Hengel 2002, 312ff.

[5] Mark 1.15; cf. Luke 10.9, 11; Matt 3.2 (John the Baptist); 4.17; 10.7; see section 10.3 and note 11 below.

[6] Luke 10.9, 11: ἤγγικεν (ἐφ᾽ ὑμᾶς) ἡ βασιλεία τοῦ θεοῦ; cf. Matt 10.7 and in Matthew even in the mouth of the Baptist in 3.2; see section 9.1.2.2.

[7] J. Weiss 1892; 1900; 1964 (ET = 1971). Bousset's *Jesu Predigt in ihrem Gegensatz zum Judentum* (Jesus' Preaching in Its Opposition to Judaism) appeared in this same year (Bousset 1892). At that time, J. Weiss was twenty-nine, W. Bousset twenty-seven, and W. Wrede thirty-three years old. To the fathers they must have appeared as "theological revolutionaries."

[8] Wrede 1907b, 88; see, however, the qualification of the editor A. Wrede (Wrede 1907c, vii). Cf. Heitmüller 1913, 142: "Jesus himself nowhere gives an explicit explanation of the concept, how he uses it. He uses it as an entity that is known to his hearers."

Wrede says this with regard to the discussion initiated by J. Weiss and gives this his approval:

> According to this Jewish view, the kingdom is future and entirely future, indeed a goal of longing.

Therefore he consistently infers from this:

> Not the kingdom but the nearness of the kingdom is the content of the gospel. One must believe in this gospel in order to properly prepare for it. The necessary preparation is called repentance. For with the kingdom comes the judgment.[9]

This view established itself with small variants especially through the monumental work of Albert Schweitzer and later through Rudolf Bultmann in large portions of scholarship extending to E. P. Sanders. It has, of course, also sometimes been energetically opposed,[10] and especially today there has again been an increase in voices that, in a no less thoroughgoing manner than the "thoroughgoing eschatology" of Albert Schweitzer, demand a radical reference to the present in the proclamation of Jesus and seek to eliminate every future statement as a later "community formation." Above all, American Q scholarship has this tendency. Both parties can appeal in this regard to the thematic summary of the proclamation of Jesus according to Mark 1.15: πεπλήρωται ὁ καιρὸς καὶ ἤγγικεν ἡ βασιλεία τοῦ θεοῦ. For this can be interpreted in two ways. The present form reads: "The time is fulfilled, and the kingdom of God is here." The future possibility reads: ". . . and the kingdom of God is (temporally) near." Perhaps this ambivalence of Mark, who formulated this programmatic statement, is consciously intended. In 14.42 it occurs again in the last saying of Jesus to his disciples: "Rise, let us go. Behold, my betrayer is here (or very near)."[11]

---

[9] Wrede 1907c, 91, 96.

[10] On this, see the fundamental monograph of Grappe 2001; see further the survey of research in Merkel 1991, 120ff., which includes the important older literature. On E. P. Sanders, see Sanders 1985, 123–56: "Jesus expected the kingdom in the near future. . . . Thus we cannot shift the normal expectations of Jewish restoration theology to the periphery"; 1993, 169–204.

[11] Mark 14.42: Ἐγείρεσθε ἄγωμεν· ἰδοὺ ὁ παραδιδούς με ἤγγικεν = Matt 26.46. For the present interpretation, cf. Luke 10.9: ἤγγικεν ἐφ' ὑμᾶς ἡ βασιλεία τοῦ θεοῦ, Luke 21.8, where the false Messiahs say: ὁ καιρὸς ἤγγικεν, and Luke 11.20 = Matt 12.28: ἔφθασεν ἐφ' ὑμᾶς ἡ βασιλεία τοῦ θεοῦ. By contrast, the formula is to be understood in a future sense in Matt 3.2; 4.17; 10.7. Paul also uses ἤγγικεν in this future sense in Rom 13.12 (ἡ δὲ ἡμέρα ἤγγικεν); cf. James 5.8 and 1 Pet 4.7. Wrede 1907c, 97ff., resolutely

In opposition to a view that is also widespread today, the formulation the "kingdom of God" is neither conspicuously frequent in the Judaism of that time nor exclusively related to the future. By contrast, independent of the abstract noun "kingdom" (*malkût*/*malkûtā*/βασιλεία), the subject matter itself, i.e., God's universal kingdom or reign, is of absolutely fundamental significance for the Jewish faith.[12] It finds expression already through the Hebrew designation for God *'ᵃdonāy*, 'Lord,' which as *Qᵉrê* takes the place of the Tetragrammaton, and through the Greek equivalent in the Septuagint, κύριος. The concern is with the fact that YHWH, the God of Israel, shows himself to be without qualification the only *Lord and King* vis-à-vis the world created by him and its history. The two terms are interchangeable. The most frequent forms of address to God in prayer in Judaism are "Lord of the world" and "King of the world."[13] The concern of the kingdom of God basically finds expression most clearly through the *Shᵉma'*, which is recited twice per day by every pious person.

> Hear O Israel, YHWH is our God, YHWH alone, and you shall love YHWH, your God, with all your whole heart, with all your soul and with all your strength.

The kingdom of God becomes present where this confession, together with the demand connected with it, becomes an unqualified reality. At the Reed Sea after YHWH's miraculous act of liberation, Israel had acknowledged its God's claim to rule: "YHWH reigns as king for ever and ever" (Exod 15.18). The YHWH-King Psalms proclaim God's universal reign as king and creator "from the very beginning" and celebrate the dawning and presence of his reign in the cult.[14] This, his eternal kingdom, is called

---

rejects the present interpretation, but must then nevertheless concede, on account of Matt 12.28 = Luke 11.20, that in Jesus' victorious battle against Satan "the concern is with the *presence of the future superworldly kingdom*" (99; Wrede's emphasis). See also note 139 below.

[12] On this, see Camponovo 1984; for supplementation and corrections, see Hengel/ Schwemer 1991, 1–19, and the individual contributions on Judaism.

[13] Dalman 1965, I: 141ff., provides attestations for this in diverse variations. On "Lord of the World," *ribbônô šel 'ôlām*, see Heinemann 1977, 318 index, s.v. "Kingship of God" and *ribbônô šel 'ôlām*, etc. Already in the Old Testament God is designated as "king" more than forty times (Seybold 1984, 946–50; ET = Seybold/Fabry 1997). The designation of the highest God as "Lord" and "King" has its parallels in the Semitic environment.

[14] On the later future interpretation of the present for the verb *yimlōk* in Exod 15.18 in Mekhilta Exodus and the consequences for Israel that arise from this, see Ego 1991: "God's victory over the hostile Egyptians grounds his kingship, but it is only in the future that this obtains universal character and is acknowledged in the whole world. For the present the kingdom of God is restricted to Israel" (281). It is defined by the "realization of the

to mind by a liturgical formula that is known to all Jews in the motherland. When in the daily cult in the temple the high priest or his representative openly pronounced the Tetragrammaton YHWH in the speaking of the Aaronic blessing, the priests and Levites recited: "Praised be *the glorious name of his kingdom* for ever and ever."[15] Through this loudly recited *b^erākhā,* the speaking of the name of God by the high priest was drowned out. Thus, it appeared, so to speak, as the embodiment of God's ruling power. The same is acknowledged in the obedience toward the commandments of the Torah, especially the daily recitation, morning and night, of the *Sh^ema' Yiśrā'ēl,* which was framed by prayers. Whoever corresponds to it "takes the yoke of the kingdom (of God) upon himself."[16] The cultic significance of the term *malkût/melek* in the heavenly worship service, in which the community of Qumran already participated now, becomes clear in the Songs of the Sabbath Sacrifice from cave 4, where both terms constantly appear.[17]

Viewed in this way, the future universal reign of God was a special, important aspect—which becomes visible in later biblical prophecy, in connection with the return from exile in Mic 4.7, and then above all with the Maccabean Revolt, for instance in the book of Daniel—of the fundamental reign of God over his people, the whole creation, and world history. Since the violent rule of the godless world powers who were oppressing Israel and the disobedience of the people of God made visible the fact that the claim of God's rule was not fully acknowledged, Israel receives the promise that God's kingdom will establish itself without restriction in the near future and that the pious will have a share in it. In the later biblical prophecy of Zech 14.9 from the third century BCE—"and YHWH will be king over the whole earth. On that day YHWH will be the only one and his name the only one"—this hope is articulated and at the same time its close connection with the first commandment and Deut 6.4-5 becomes apparent.

This future realization of the kingdom of God, which is still rejected in the present, is made a topic in individual Jewish apocalyptic texts, especially in the book of Daniel, for example in chapters 2 and 7, in Qumran, and in Pss. Sol. 17 and 18, but also in later Jewish texts such as the

---

uniqueness of God in the keeping of the commandments and in the rejection of all idolatry" (282). On the YHWH-King Psalms, cf. Janowski 1989.

[15] m. Yoma 3.8; 4.1–2; 6.2; cf. m. Ber. 1.2; t. Ta'an. 1.11ff.: *bārûkh šēm k^ebôd malkûtô le 'ôlām wā'ead.* On this, see Hengel/Schwemer 1991, 2–3, 415 index, and T. Lehnardt 1991.

[16] On this, see Bill. I: 172ff., 176–77 (k–m).

[17] Newsom 1985, see index on p. 424 on *mlk/mlkwt;* cf. Charlesworth/Newsom 1999. On the concept of God, see Schwemer 1991a, 116ff.

Qaddish.[18] In the Qumran text 11QMelch it occurs through the heavenly redeemer Michael-Melchizedek, in Dan 7 it is realized in connection with the coming of that mysterious figure who is like "a (son of) man" on the clouds of heaven, who embodies the true people of God and to whom God confers his authority. In Dan 12.1ff. it is mediated through the saving intervention of the prince of light Michael[19] and in Pss. Sol. 17 through the Davidic Messiah. It would therefore be wrongheaded to want to see a fundamental opposition between the kingdom of God and a heavenly or earthly redeemer figure who is authorized by God, let alone to deny a close connection between kingdom of God and eschatological redeemer. In Pss. Sol. 17 the hope in God as the redeemer of Israel[20] and in the establishment of his enduring kingdom over all nations is addressed,[21] and then there is prayer for the coming of the Messiah-King from the tribe of David and the realization of his kingdom.[22] At the conclusion, however, God is invoked again as "Kyrios" and "our King."[23] Recently texts from Qumran have substantially expanded our source basis precisely at this point and thus our knowledge about the diverse Jewish eschatological expectations. Here we can mention merely the "messianic" text 4Q521 quoted above.[24]

Already in view of this indissoluble connection between God's eternally existing and therefore also always present reign and its expected future universal establishment, sometimes through his anointed, it is not surprising when we also encounter statements about the present and future of the kingdom of God in the Synoptic sayings of Jesus—to be sure, in a very distinctive form. And we must guard ourselves against dissolving this tension that becomes visible here in a one-sided manner by setting aside or

[18] Cf. also Mic 4.6-8: "And YHWH will be king over them on Mount Zion from now until eternity. . . . And you . . . daughter Zion, to you shall come and return the former rule, the kingship of daughter Jerusalem"; on this, see Pitre 2005, 141ff. The YHWH-King Psalms were also interpreted eschatologically around the turn of the era. On the prayers, see A. Lehnardt 2002.

[19] 11QMelch (11Q13); on this, see Zimmermann 1998, 389–412; cf. Dan 12.1ff.; see also section 16.1 with note 24. In column II line 16 the confession of the messenger of joy in Isa 52.7: "Your God (*ᵉlōhāyik*) has become king (*mālak*)" is related to Melchizedek-Michael and not to God himself.

[20] Psalms of Solomon 17.3a: ἐλπιοῦμεν ἐπὶ τὸν θεὸν σωτῆρα ἡμῶν.

[21] Psalms of Solomon 17.3c: ἡ βασιλεία τοῦ θεοῦ ἡμῶν εἰς τὸν αἰῶνα ἐπὶ τὰ ἔθνη ἐν κρίσει.

[22] Psalms of Solomon 17.21: Ἰδέ κύριε, καὶ ἀνάστησον αὐτοῖς τὸν βασιλέα αὐτῶν υἱὸν Δαυιδ . . . , 17.32: . . . καὶ βασιλεὺς αὐτῶν χριστὸς κυρίου. The text that has been handed down has χριστὸς κύριος, cf. Lam 4.20 LXX. In both cases we are dealing with an *emendatio christiana*; cf. Pss. Sol. 18.5-7. On the problem, see also Hengel/Schwemer 1991, 8ff.

[23] Psalms of Solomon 17.46; cf. v. 21.

[24] See section 10.5 with note 68 and Zimmermann 1998, passim.

reinterpreting either the future or present statements, depending on one's theological inclination, as "community formations."

However, with reference to the already discussed question of the relationship between Jesus and the Baptist, perhaps it can, nevertheless, be said in advance that in contrast to the Baptist, with Jesus the presence of salvation comes more strongly to the fore in his activity than the futurity of the threatening, impending judgment. This dialectic between the present and future of salvation, which emerges in the proclamation of Jesus, also determines the whole post-Easter community via Paul to the Johannine corpus and Revelation, though the emphasis can be placed differently in each case. The starting point is the certainty *that in Jesus the Messiah has come and the kingdom of God is at work through him.* This certainty has its beginning in Jesus'—messianic—activity in word and deed.

13.2 The Kingdom of God That Is in the Process of Realization

Wilhelm Heitmüller, the teacher of R. Bultmann, also followed the results of Albert Schweitzer in his popular Jesus book, which appeared in 1913. God himself will bring about his reign in the near future in a miraculous way and bring an end to all anti-God powers. Therefore "the kingdom of God" does not, for example, mean "an innerworldly fellowship that is realized by human action." He is therefore skeptical toward those texts that speak "of the kingdom as a present one." However, at the end he must, nevertheless, concede that

> We may not, over-cautiously, say . . . that the kingdom was thought of by Jesus *only* as future. In a few texts of reliable tradition there crops up, though rather suddenly, the notion *that it has already begun to realize itself in the present.*[25]

At the end of his parables book, J. Jeremias speaks of the fact that all the parables of Jesus are filled with "the certainty of an eschatology that is in the process of realization.'" "The hour of fulfillment is here . . . the year of God's favor has dawned."[26] These formulations of exegetes who are more inclined to emphasize the futurity show that in the controversy here—as

---

[25] Heitmüller 1913, 143 (our emphasis); the number of texts is, however, by no means "few." Cf. Merkel 1991, 127; cf. also his quotations from R. Bultmann and E. Käsemann on pp. 129–30.

[26] Jeremias 1998, 227 (ET = 1972, 230), following a suggestion by E. Haenchen. On this, see also Dodd 1963, 447 n. 1, on the formulation "which I like, but cannot translate into English." The "year of God's favor" refers to the quotation of Isa 61.2 in Luke 4.18 in Jesus' inaugural sermon in Nazareth.

so often in the interpretation of the New Testament—we are dealing with *a false alternative*. The still controversial question of whether the *main emphasis* in Jesus' proclamation of the kingdom of God lies more on the present or on the near future overlooks the fact that depending on the intention of the individual sayings and parables and the situation that they address, the one or the other aspect can predominate.

We have already pointed out that Jesus' activity differs from the Baptist, whose preaching of the impending *dies irae* teaches one to fear, in the motif of *joy*: "Can the wedding guests fast while the bridegroom is with them?"[27] The parabolic saying has a clear "messianic" undertone. At the end of the three parables of the lost sheep, the lost denarius, and the lost son we likewise find this great joy, which intensifies to celebration with friends, neighbors, and servants.[28] It corresponds to the joy upon finding the treasure in the field and the unique pearl.[29] Jesus' proclamation is therefore in Luke a εὐαγγελίζεσθαι, in Mark (and in weakened form in Matthew) εὐαγγέλιον, i.e., glad tidings, comparable to the one anointed by the Spirit in Isa 61.1, who is sent by God to the poor and imprisoned to bring the good news of liberation.[30] For this reason, he calls the poor blessed, because the kingdom of God belongs to them.[31] Blessed, therefore, are the disciples who hear his message and see his deeds.

> For (amen) I say to you, many prophets and kings wanted to see what you see and did not see and to hear what you hear and did not hear.[32]

When Jesus, in Luke 11.28, calls blessed those "who hear the word of God and keep it," he refers with this not to the interpretive word of the scribes but to his own message, i.e., the seed that he sows so that it produces

---

[27] Mark 2.19; cf. Matt 9.15; Luke 5.34 and—in the mouth of the Baptist—John 3.29.

[28] Luke 15.6-7, 9-10, 23-32.

[29] Matthew 13.44-46 (special material).

[30] Isaiah 61.1 LXX: εὐαγγελίσασθαι πτωχοῖς ἀπέσταλκέν με is quoted in Luke 4.18; cf. Luke 7.22 = Matt 11.5 and the beatitudes in Matt 5.2ff. = Luke 6.20ff. On this, see Hengel 1999b, 219–92, esp. 243ff. (= 1987c). Luke in particular loves the verb (see section 10.3 with note 39), behind which stands the Hebrew *biśśar* of the prophetic promises and of the Psalms, which the Septuagint translates with εὐαγγελίζεσθαι; in addition to Isa. 61.1, see also 40.9; 52.7; 60.6; Joel 3.5; Nah 2.1; Ps 40(LXX 39).10; 68 (67).12; 96(95).2. Cf. also the delivery of the message of victory to David in 2 Sam 18.19-31.

[31] Luke 6.20: ὅτι ὑμετέρα ἐστιν ἡ βασιλεία τοῦ θεοῦ; cf. Matt 5.3.

[32] Luke 10.24 = Matt 13.17, given special emphasis by Matthew as Amen saying. In accord with his theology (13.43, 49; 25.37, 46) he also replaces "kings" with "righteous persons." After all, most Old Testament kings were not distinguished by pious expectation. What is meant is models like David, Josiah, and Hezekiah.

fruit.[33] A decisive sign of the fulfillment of the promises and the liberation of the prisoners lies in the fact that God through Jesus pronounces the *forgiveness of their sins* to individual people in concrete situations without any sacred ritual[34] and thus brings back the lost sons and daughters of his people into the house of the Father.[35] To be sure, whoever rejects the self-experienced forgiveness of infinite guilt through one's own mercilessness and irreconcilability will, as the parable of the unforgiving servant shows, experience God as a just judge.[36] The rejection of the message of the goodness of God that is now becoming manifest in the activity of Jesus likewise excludes one from the near future salvation. Thus, *judgment* appears to be a consequence of rejecting God's turn to human beings, his goodness that transcends all human conceptions, which is now already recognizable in Jesus' presence. Jesus' offensive table fellowship with "tax collectors and sinners" in festive meals is an expression of joy over the fact that God has received these lost members of his people. At the same time, these meals, as well as the narratives of the miraculous feedings, may also be a pointer to the spectacular eschatological feast in the consummated kingdom of God.[37]

This picture of the eschatological banquet is probably the most important metaphor of Jesus for the description of the future time of salvation. It comes from a world in which for many hunger was a daily guest:

Blessed (are) the poor,
for yours is the kingdom of God.
Blessed those who hunger now,
for you shall be sated! (Luke 6.20-21)

The motif also appears in the Isaianic apocalypse as the coronation banquet for the king YHWH on Zion[38] and applies to Israel and the nations who will assemble there. Already there it had the conquering of death as a presupposition.[39] Otherwise, in contrast to apocalyptic literature, Jesus is

---

[33] On this, see Mark 4.3ff. = Luke 8.5ff. = Matt 13.3ff.

[34] See section 10.5.

[35] Mark 2.10 = Luke 5.24 = Matt 9.6; cf. Luke 7.48; after Easter the forgiveness of sins is connected with Jesus' death; cf. Matt 26.28. His atoning death bestows upon believers the certainty of forgiveness, and this means also of fellowship with God. See section 14.4.

[36] Matthew 18.23-35; cf. also 7.1ff. and Luke 6.36-38, 41-42.

[37] Mark 2.15ff. = Luke 5.29ff. = Matt 9.10ff.; cf. Luke 19.5; Luke 7.34 = Matt 11.19. A further development is the formula in the parable of the talents in Matt 25.23: εἴσελθε εἰς τὴν χαρὰν τοῦ κυρίου σου. Cf. 1 Pet 1.8.

[38] Isaiah 24.23; 25.6ff.; cf. 55.1-5.

[39] Isaiah 25.8; cf. 26.19 (on this, see Hengel 2001a, 153ff.); see also Rev 19.7; 21.4; 1 En. 62.14: the meal "of the righteous and chosen ones" with that "Son of Man"; cf. 45.6;

very reserved in relation to all elaborating portrayals of what is to come. Like the parables of the sower and harvest in Mark 4 and Mark 13, the parable of the great supper connects Jesus' presence with God's future.[40] As so often, here too the older Lukan version is the more original. In Matthew a king[41] invites people to a wedding banquet for his son. In Luke it is only a nobleman.[42] The Lukan version thus fits better in the Galilean milieu. Matthew's version is christologically and ecclesiastically reworked and very unfittingly inserts a judgment parable about a guest who does not possess a "wedding garment" and is therefore "thrown out into the outermost darkness."[43] The time of the activity of Jesus is the time of invitation. Since this invitation is rejected by those who were addressed first, the Lord of the banquet invites the poor, the disabled, and, finally, the strangers from the paths and byways.[44] The close connection between present table fellowship and the future banquet in the consummated kingdom of God also occurs in the presentation of Jesus' Last Supper with his disciples, which concludes with a vista of the future:

> Amen, I say to you that I will no longer drink from the fruit of the vine until that day on which I drink it anew in the kingdom of God.[45]

This means that primitive Christianity and already Jesus himself did indeed imagine the future kingdom with earthly, millennialist features. One will become sated in it, drink wine, and laugh, indeed dance for joy.[46] In a

---

2 En. 42.5; 2 Bar. 29.4–8; Bill. IV: 1146–47, 1154–65; cf. Dunn 2003b, 394 n. 64; 425–28; Schwemer 2004, 199ff. In Jewish apocalyptic literature the meal does not appear to have the central significance that it has in the Synoptics. However, the common meal is also understood as an anticipation of the eschatological banquet among the Essenes; see Grappe 2004; cf. further S. Schreiner 2004, 344, 348, who refers to the relatively early passage in m. 'Abot 4.16, which uses this metaphor. The following saying is attributed to R. Jacob ben Kurshai (Tanna of the fourth generation): "The world is like an antechamber of the world to come. Prepare yourself in the antechamber so that you can enter into the banquet hall (*ṭraqlin = triclinium*)."

[40] Luke 14.15-24 = Matt 22.1-14; cf. Luke 14.7-14; Mark 14.25 parr.; Rev 3.20; 19.9.

[41] Matthew 22.2: ἄνθρωπος βασιλεύς. The king is a stock metaphor for God in the numerous rabbinic king parables.

[42] Luke 14.16: ἄνθρωπός τις. V. 21: ὁ οἰκοδεσπότης. On this, cf. section 12.3.

[43] Matthew 22.11-14; cf. also v. 10: The slave who is sent out gathers "bad and good"; cf. the parable of the wheat and the tares in Matt 13.24-30.

[44] Luke 14.15-24 = Matt 22.1-14. Here we have two largely differing versions.

[45] Mark 14.25 = Matt 26.29 (with the addition "with you"); cf. Luke 13.28-29 = Matt 8.11-12. On the Last Supper, see section 17.4.1 with note 163. This eschatological reference occurs also in modified form in the Pauline version in 1 Cor 11.26: ἄχρι οὗ ἔλθῃ.

[46] Luke 6.21: γελάσετε, 23: χάρητε ἐν ἐκείνῃ ἡμέρᾳ καὶ σκιρτήσατε . . . ; cf. Luke 15.25 and Mal 3.20 (LXX). In rabbinic literature God himself can appear as "leader of

society in which hunger, hardship, and death were daily experiences, these promises had fundamental significance. Even in Paul we sometimes find millennialist features, and in the second century the millennialist realism of Revelation, as shown by Papias, Justin, Melito, Irenaeus, and Tertullian, was predominant in the church.[47]

The indissoluble connection between Jesus' activity and the consummation expected in the near future becomes visible in the contrast parables addressed above, in the parables of the sower,[48] of the the seed growing secretly,[49] of the mustard seed, and of the leaven.[50] Like the overwhelming majority of the Synoptic parables they metaphorically express *one specific, fundamental aspect* of the kingdom of God. They highlight the external, conspicuous opposition between the inconspicuous beginning of the kingdom in Jesus' activity, which was contested and characterized by failures, and the suddenly occurring miraculous consummation, and also, at the same time, the *certainty of the unbroken inner connection* between Jesus' work and the fullness that is to be expected.[51]

While the parables of contrast connect present and future, the parables of the treasure in the field and of the pearl concentrate on the present moment of finding and the overwhelming joy that it triggers, which effects the decision of "now or never."[52] The farmer who finds the treasure and the merchant who finds the pearl could be compared, in their rigorous decision, to the βιασταί, the "violent ones," who "seize"—now or never—"the kingdom of God."[53] The fact that the kingdom "belongs to the children" and that one "must receive it as a child," trustingly,

---

the dance" at the dance in the future world; see Bill. IV: 1154; S. Schreiner 2004, 350–51, refers to the summary of rabbinic conceptions of the meal of the righteous in Otiot de Rabbi Akiba: the righteous will, among other things, recline at table in paradise and God himself will dance at the meal.

[47] Hengel 2002, 355, 364–65. It remained so in the west—in contrast to the Platonizing east—until the fourth century CE. See note 111 below. The intellectuals opposed the all too realistic expectations with the pointer that "not as this world is the coming world . . ." (b. Ber. 17a); on this, see S. Schreiner 2004, 347, 368, 371.

[48] Mark 4.3-9 = Luke 8.5-8 = Matt 13.3-9; cf. Gos. Thom. 9.

[49] Mark 4.26-29.

[50] Mark 4.30-32 = Luke 13.18-19 = Matt 13.31-32; Luke 13.20-21 = Matt 13.33; cf. Gos. Thom. 96. Matthew 13.24-30, the parable of the wheat and the tares, is an ecclesiological development of an older parable by Matthew; see the end of section 12.3.

[51] Mark 4.32; cf. Luke 13.19 = Matt 13.32; cf. Ezek 17.23; 31.6; Dan 4.10-12, 18-20 (LXX and Theodotion).

[52] Matthew 13.44-46; cf. as counterexample Mark 10.21. On this, see Jeremias 1972, 200–2 (GV = 1998, 199–200): "The key-words are . . . ἀπὸ τῆς χαρᾶς (v. 44)," i.e., that "great joy, surpassing all measure."

[53] Matthew 11.12; see section 10.8 with note 105.

enthusiastically, and without any reckoning, in order to "enter" is also said with a view to the present hearers.[54]

Thus, to his simple Galilean audience, predominantly of farmers, fishermen, and artisans, Jesus portrays in the accessible form of the *māšāl*, of the parabolic saying, and of the parable, using examples that came from their lifeworld, the eschatological realization of the kingdom of God, which is already symbolically prepared for in his activity in word and deed, indeed which really "occurs," and which points at the same time to its miraculous consummation in the near future. Although Jesus, too, lived of course in the mythical and apocalyptic world of the Jewish Galilean rural population with their belief in miracles, angels and demons, their dualism, and their bizarre notions of the future, in him all impatient reckoning, all detailed apocalyptic fantasy and esoteric curiosity, recede, indeed, he directly rejects these.[55] The concern is solely with the unmerited "visitation," with the restitution of his people, indeed of all humans, through God's fatherly love, which forgives guilt and bestows new life that conforms to God, because only "the good tree can produce good fruits."[56]

The specification of the kingdom of God as the "epiphany" of the *goodness of the Father* which calls all Israel becomes visible in the peculiar fact that despite the frequent phrase the "kingdom of God," Jesus, against the common Jewish custom, hardly ever speaks of God as Lord and King[57] but addresses him in a familiar way as *'abbā'*, "(dear) Father," and authorizes his disciples to pray to God with this address. Thus, Mark has him begin his prayer in Gethsemane with the address "Abba, Father, all things are possible for you, let this cup pass me by . . ."[58] This familiar designation of God became so important to the earliest post-Easter community and its first messengers from the circle of the "Hellenists" that they brought the familiar Aramaic prayer address *'abbā'*, which was uncommon in the Judaism of the time, as a cry of the "freedom of the sons of God" even into the Gentile Christian, Greek-speaking mission communities.[59] In the community in Rome, which Paul had not founded, he presupposes the use

[54] Mark 10.14-15 = Luke 18.16-17 = Matt 19.14 and 18.3; cf. Gos. Thom. 22.

[55] Luke 17.20-21; 19.11; cf. Mark 13.5 parr.; 13.28-32 parr.

[56] Luke 6.43-44 = Matt 7.16ff.; cf. Mark 11.13, 20-21; Luke 13.6ff. Here we strike upon a metaphoricism that later gains fundamental significance for Paul, cf. Rom 6.21-22; Gal 5.22.

[57] Matthew 5.35: Jerusalem as the πόλις . . . τοῦ μεγάλου βασιλέως falls completely out of the framework of the linguistic usage of the Gospels. We can ask here whether this is not typical Matthean diction; cf. the parables in 18.23ff. and 22.1ff.; see K. W. Müller 1991, 27. See also the expanded version of the Lord's Prayer in Matt 6.9 and note 60 below. On Luke 10.21 = Matt 11.25-26, see note 61 below.

[58] Mark 14.36: Ἀββα, ὁ πατήρ; Luke 22.42 has the vocative πάτερ; Matt 26.39 has πάτερ μου. Cf. Luke 10.21-22 par.

[59] Romans 8.15ff.; Gal 4.5-6. See Hengel 2004a; see chapter 15 with note 26.

of this address of God as just as much of a given as in his own communities, for example in Galatia. The whole of primitive Christian theology could basically be summarized with this formula. It is one of the many pointers to the continuity between Jesus, the primitive church, and the Gentile Christian mission communities and may also be connected, among other things, with the use of the Lord's Prayer in all the communities. The prayer that Jesus taught his disciples began in its original Lukan form with the mere vocative πάτεϱ, i.e., in the language of Jesus with "Abba." The Matthean version "Our Father in Heaven" adjusts itself to the familiar Jewish prayer language, which we encounter since the beginning of the second century CE in rabbinic texts.[60] The present and future of salvation are most closely connected in this prayer. The only exception, where the designation "Lord" also appears, is Jesus' cry of joy:

> I praise you *Father, Lord of heaven and earth*, because you have hidden these things from the wise and intelligent but have revealed them to the simple ones. Yes, *Father*, for such was your good pleasure.[61]

Jesus' invitation into the kingdom of God is heard by the simple, uneducated people, for God shows himself to be their Father in opening their ears, in contrast to the hardening of the influential religious and political representatives of the people. This applied already to Jesus' activity in Galilee and points already there to an emerging crisis.[62] Behind it stands the idea of God's free election, which was already significant in Qumran and later played a central role in Paul and John.

13.3 God's Reign and God's Commandment

Jesus' "ethical" preaching also stands entirely under the banner of the "kingdom of God that is in the process of realization" and is only comprehensible from this perspective. One should not speak of an "ethic of Jesus" as an independent entity that can be separated from his overall message.

---

[60] Luke 11.2; Matt 6.9 adjusts to the widespread prayer address *'ābînû/'ābikhām šebaš-šāmayim*, which is more distant. On the Matthean-rabbinic formula, see Heinemann 1977, 150, 190, and Bill. I: 393ff. The request of a disciple in Luke 11.1—"Teach us to pray as John taught his disciples"—could indicate that Jesus formulated this prayer in distinction from the Baptist prayers. See fundamentally Jeremias 1966a, 1–67; cf. also Philonenko 2002 and Hengel 2004a.

[61] Luke 10.21 = Matt 11.25-26, which are almost identical in wording. The cry of prayer can easily be translated back into Hebrew or Aramaic; see Jeremias 1970, 24 (GV = 1979, 33). On the form of this prayer of thanks, see also section 12.2 with note 70.

[62] Cf. Mark 2.17; Matt 22.1ff. = Luke 14.16ff.; see also John 7.48-49.

The Lord's Prayer[63] already demonstrates that the first petition, i.e., the hallowing of the name of God (and according to the expanded version of Matthew also the third petition for the realization of the will of God) is indissolubly connected with the coming of the kingdom. Where this occurs through God's miracle, and this means where Jesus' message is heard and finds believing obedience, it can for the persons affected already become present. In this twofold (or threefold) petition God himself is the acting person. Only he can reveal his holiness[64] and cause his kingdom to come. Only he can bring it about that his holy will really come about. The first petition of the Lord's Prayer involves a *passivum divinum*, which refers, on the one hand, to the final establishment of the kingdom of God, but at the same time already applies to the present. The second petition for the "coming of the kingdom" is therefore also not to be understood exclusively in a future sense. God, as Father, wants already here and now to be confessed and loved as the *one*, and he proclaims this through Jesus' words and deeds. Mark 12.28ff. correspondingly connects the text of the *Shema' Yiśrā'ēl*, the confession to the *one* LORD and God,[65] with the double love command of love of God and love of neighbor, which stands over all other commandments.[66]

Since God as creator and preserver of the world shows his goodness without preconditions in relation to all humans, "lets his sun rise over evil and good and lets it rain over righteous and unrighteous,"[67] in the realization of his reign he calls those who let themselves be invited by Jesus also to radical renunciation of violence and love of enemies: "Become merciful as your father is merciful."[68] They are to behave toward their fellow humans, including their enemies, as God does to his creatures, including

---

[63] On this, see Jeremias 1970, 198 (GV = 1979, 192); Philonenko 2002, 44ff., 51ff. Cf. now Frey 2016.

[64] Procksch/Kuhn 1964, 111 (GV = 1933, 113): "The logical *subject* of *sanctifying* is *God alone* and not man" (Procksch's emphasis added from the German version), with reference to Ezek 20.41; 38.16. Cf. Ezek 36.22-28: God will hallow his name, lead back the exiles, purify his people, give to it a new heart and his Spirit, so that they can keep his commandments and live in the land. On this, see Meier 1994, 296–97; Pitre 2005, 140ff.

[65] Mark 12.29: = *'ᵃdonāy 'āḥād*. See Deut 6.4 and on this, cf. the introduction of Exod 20.2; Deut 5.6.

[66] Cf. Mark 12.28-32 and the independent tradition of Luke 10.25-28 with the interpretation in Matt 22.34-40 and its rabbinic-sounding formulation, according to which Matthew regards the double commandment as the summary of the whole Scripture. Since Matthew can no longer concede that a scribe is praised by Jesus, he takes over from Luke 10.25-28 the νομικός, who tests Jesus (πειράζων αὐτόν, Matt 22.35). See further the Golden Rule in Luke 6.31 and its interpretation in Matt 7.12.

[67] Matthew 5.45, cf. Luke 6.35.

[68] Luke 6.36; on the meaning of the word, see section 14.2 with note 25. Cf. also Matt 5.48, which replaces the Lukan οἰκτίρμων with τέλειος, which Matthew also inserts into the narrative of the "rich young man" in 19.21.

sinners, whom he seeks out and wants to lead to repentance, i.e., to acceptance of the forgiveness of their guilt and to a new life.

The *Torah* is measured and interpreted with reference to this basic demand, which is grounded by the behavior of the Father. Jesus was, as a Galilean Jew, certainly not an ostentatious breaker of the law. Nevertheless, where specific demands of the Torah given to Israel on Sinai and conventions of the casuistic teaching tradition grounded by it stood in opposition to the love commandment or the call of the kingdom of God, they had to recede. This resulted in the conflicts, as is shown by the narratives about healings on the Sabbath[69] and the controversy dialogue triggered by the disciples plucking heads of grain.[70] Jesus' appeal in this context to David, who ate the bread of the presence consecrated to YHWH,[71] which only the consecrated priests in the temple were permitted to eat, is an indirect pointer to his messianic authority. We must view in this context not only the controversy over the boundaries of the Sabbath commandment,[72] which were probably not infrequent, but also Jesus' call to individual persons to follow him and to leave their families, indeed for the kingdom of God's sake to disregard the piety that belongs to the fourth commandment,[73] i.e., actions through which he consciously provoked his hearers. Something similar applies to his distance vis-à-vis the purity commandments. Thus, he can express the principle "Nothing which enters from outside into the human can make him unclean but what comes out of the person, this is what makes the human unclean,"[74] for it reveals the content of his heart. "For out of the abundance of the heart the mouth speaks."[75] It is no accident that the whole problem of the ritual laws largely recedes in the Gospel tradition. It appears in the Gospel of John, though here for entirely different, christological reasons.[76] Circumcision plays no role at all,[77] and the question of purity, which was so fundamental for the

---

[69] Mark 3.1-6 = Luke 6.6-11 = Matt 12.9-14; Luke 13.14-17; 14.1-6; John 5.9-16; 9.14-17.

[70] Mark 2.23-28 = Luke 6.1-5 and Matt 12.1-8 with the additional reference to the priests in the temple and the quotation of Hos 6.6; cf. also 1 Sam 15.22.

[71] First Samuel 21.2-7.

[72] No pressing community problems are addressed any longer in the Gospels here. Rather, the whole epistolary literature shows that in the predominantly Gentile Christian communities the hallowing of the Sabbath was no longer a pressing problem. The hallowing of the Sabbath and discussions about it point back to Jesus' behavior in the motherland.

[73] See the end of section 11.5.

[74] Mark 7.15 = Matt 15.11, cf. Luke 10.8. On the form, see section 12.2 with note 83.

[75] Luke 6.45; Matt 12.34b, cf. 35-37.

[76] John 2.6; 3.25; 4.9; 13.8-10; 15.3; 18.28; 19.31.

[77] It appears only in connection with the circumcision of Jesus in Luke 2.21-22 and as an argumentation aid in John 7.22-23. This is conspicuous since it is a major point of

Judaism of the time, plays only a relatively small role.[78] With a view to the nearness of God, which changes everything, the whole sphere of the ritual law, which—as 4QMMT, the letter of the Teacher of Righteousness to the Wicked Priest, now shows—shaped and divided the Jewish religious parties,[79] became secondary. This ritual disinterest also forbids one from constructing an overly close connection between the messianic prophet Jesus from Galilee and Essenes in Judaea, who had a priestly character and a strict orientation to ritual purity.[80]

God's arrival will reestablish the original, good order of creation, which was destroyed by the fall of the first human couple. Whoever earnestly seeks the kingdom of God stands no longer under the curse and the slavery of worry.[81] The sapiential form of argumentation in the artful composition of sayings about not worrying with the reference to the (unclean) ravens,[82] whom God feeds in a wonderful way, and the lilies in the field, whom God clothes in an extremely opulent way, must not prevent us from seeing that with the rigorous rejection of all worrying Jesus contradicts the material provision and life wisdom called for by traditional wisdom.[83] God himself, as creator and preserver, cares for his creatures. No sparrow, which is of such little value that one sells five for two *assēs*, is forgotten by God. Indeed, all the hairs on a human's head are counted.[84]

For the sake of the reestablishment of God's creation, stipulations of the Torah can also be called into question. Thus, the sending away of a man's wife through a letter of divorce is a concession of Moses to the "hard-heartedness" of Israel. What remains decisive for God's good order

controversy in Acts and in the letters of Paul. The Gospel tradition of the Synoptics is presumably older for the most part than the controversies described in Acts 10; 11.1-18; 15 and Gal 2.

[78] Jesus does not show concern about becoming ritually unclean through the contact with the woman with a flow of blood; see Mark 5.25-34. He does, however, command the leper, whom he likewise touches (1.41) despite his uncleanness, to show himself to the priest (1.44) and perform the ritual of purification with a bird offering, which is required according to Lev 14.2ff. See, however, the priority of reconciliation with the personal opponent over the bringing of an offering in Matt 5.23-24.

[79] Cf. Qimron/Strugnell 1994. See the end of section 4.2 with note 90.

[80] See Hengel 2003b (ET = Hengel 2012d).

[81] Luke 12.22-31 = Matt 6.25-33, cf. Gen 3.17-19.

[82] Luke 12.24: τοὺς κόρακας is more original than the version in Matt 6.26, which has τὰ πετεινὰ τοῦ οὐρανοῦ. Jesus speaks concretely of birds and flowers. On the uncleanness of the raven, see Lev 11.15 = Deut 14.14. See, however, also Ps 147.9 and Job 38.41: God's care for the ravens. On the form of the didactic composition, see section 12.2 with note 67.

[83] The precautionary ants: Prov 6.6-11; cf. 30.25.

[84] Luke 12.6-7 = Matt 10.29-31; cf. Matt 5.36.

is: "From the beginning of the creation God made them male and female."[85] "Therefore a man will leave his father and mother and cleave to his wife, and the two will become one flesh."[86] Thus, the conclusion can only be: "What therefore God has joined together, let no human separate."[87]

It is probably not necessary to stress explicitly that these "instructions for true life" in light of the presence of the goodness of the Father in his creation do not represent a temporally restricted "interim ethic" until the real dawning of the kingdom of God as Albert Schweitzer postulated[88] but rather express the one true and original will of God from the beginning, which with his coming will finally obtain unrestricted validity in accord with the *shᵉma'* (Deut 6.4-5) or the first commandment. The "ought" (*Sollen*) must become a new "is" (*Sein*) in a renewed creation.[89]

13.4 The Parables of the Kingdom of God[90]

Basically, the whole proclamation of Jesus, i.e., including his parabolic speech, is ultimately oriented to the kingdom of God, even in places where the phrase does not appear *expressis verbis*. However, in Mark,[91] in the sayings tradition,[92] and above all in the Matthean special material,[93] we find parables that begin multiple times with similar introductory formulas[94] that directly refer to the βασιλεία τοῦ θεοῦ. The Hebrew or Aramaic basic form has the meaning "with the *kingdom of God* the case is as with a

---

[85] Mark 10.2-12 = Matt 19.3-9; Gen 1.27; 5.2 LXX.

[86] Genesis 2.24 LXX; in both cases, as also otherwise, Mark quotes the Septuagint, i.e., the biblical text that was familiar to the Roman community.

[87] Mark 10.9 = Matt 19.6; cf. Luke 16.18 = Matt 5.32-33; 1 Cor 7.10ff. In addition, contrary to the commandments of the Torah, Mark 10.12 speaks also of a wife giving her "husband the sack" (Bauer/Aland/Aland 1988, 193) and marrying another. This presupposes Roman legal circumstances and not Jewish-Palestinian ones. Matthew omits this sentence. Luke 16.18 corrects it. Cf., however, 1 Cor 7.10. Matthew 19.9 and 5.32 allow divorce in the case of "the infidelity of the wife" (πορνεία); see Bauer/Aland/Aland 1988, 1389. Jesus' rigorous prohibition was no longer able to be carried out in practice.

[88] See, for example, Schweitzer 2000, 485 (GV = 1913, 640); Schweitzer 1998, 420, 592: "An interim ethic that comes alongside the law, which . . . in the judgment warrants entrance into the kingdom."

[89] On this, see chapter 14: "The Will of God" and 14.1: "Hearing, Doing, and Being."

[90] On the forms of the parables, see section 12.3.

[91] Mark 4.26, 30-31. Dative beginning in 4.30-31 with preceding question. On this, see section 12.3 with notes 126–29.

[92] Matthew 13.33 = Luke 13.20-21.

[93] Matthew 13.24, 44-45, 47; 20.1. Matthew sometimes shows a tendency to imitate linguistic forms of Jesus. It is conspicuous that Matthew usually has the dative beginning and no example of the nominative beginning. In Luke the opposite is rather the case.

[94] The basic form is ὁμοία ἐστιν ἡ βασιλεία τοῦ θεοῦ ὡς. . . . See section 12.3 with notes 128–29.

person who sowed a field . . ." or ". . . with leaven, which . . ." or ". . . with a treasure, which. . . ."[95] This means that the kingdom of God is compared as a whole with a lively event, a real occurrence, and not only with a person or an object.

As already stated, here, depending on the content, the futurity or the presence of the kingdom can be more strongly emphasized. Thus, for example, the futurity is evident in the parable of the net and the parable of the tares in the Matthean special material. The coming judgment brings the great separation.[96] While both correspond in a special way to the theology of the evangelist and are edited by him, in a preform they could very well go back to Jesus.[97]

We have already referred to the "contrast parables" of the sower, of the seed growing secretly, of the mustard seed, and of the leaven.[98] Both the present and the future aspect of the kingdom of God become visible in them. They are dominated by the contrast between the inconspicuous, even hopeless beginning in the present of the activity of Jesus, in which God's reign is already reality in the scattered seed, and the miraculous abundance of the near completion. The activity of Jesus and the full dawning of the kingdom correspond as beginning and end, sowing and harvest. In the contrast, the continuity also becomes visible. In the parable of the seed growing secretly Jesus shows that the kingdom is not dependent on human, for example zealot, activity: "By itself the earth brings forth fruit."[99] The *malkût* comes after the sowing without help from the farmer, like the harvest when the grain is ripe, solely through God's miracle.

To be sure, some parables of the kingdom of God also stress the spontaneous effect of the preaching of Jesus that is related wholly to the present moment, such as the narrative of the treasure in the field and the parable of the pearl. The plowman sees the treasure discovered by him already now and the merchant sees the pearl as a reality right before his eyes; it is no future delusion. Therefore, without delay they must now decide to risk all their possessions. Both do so without hesitation; overcome by joy over

---

[95] Matthew 13.24, 33, 44. On the form, see section 12.3.

[96] Matthew 13.47-50, 36-43.

[97] The parable of the tares in the field could be a development of the parable of the the seed growing secretly in Mark 4.26-29; see note 50 above. Luke and Matthew do not take over this undoubtedly authentic parable because it is, in comparison with other seed parables, too simple and therefore appears to be superfluous. The parables in the Matthean special material deal relatively often with the motif of judgment and evince a stronger redactional shaping in multiple cases, e.g., Matt 18.23-35; 25.1-13, 31-46; see also the comparison of Matt 22.1-14 with Luke 14.16-24 and Matt 25.14-30 with Luke 19.12-27.

[98] See section 13.2 with notes 48–51.

[99] Mark 4.28: αὐτομάτη ἡ γῆ καρποφορεῖ.

what they have found, they cannot act otherwise.[100] Rational consideration is not excluded here. It occurs in the parable of the unjust steward, who unexpectedly must give an account and provides for himself in a shrewd manner,[101] and in the double parable of the building of a tower and the approaching enemy,[102] which warn, with a view to Jesus' call to discipleship, against the self-overestimation that leads to the wrong decision.

This means that everything is *now* at stake. *Now* Jesus' call is issued as an invitation. *Now* the kingdom of God seeks to be gained. What is in view is the ἁρπάζειν of the βιασταί in Matt 11.12. Seized by the message of Jesus, one must act on it quickly, resolutely, and with all due consideration. "Whoever seeks to preserve his life will lose it, but whoever loses it for my sake will gain it."[103] For "whoever puts the hand to the plow and looks back is not fit for the kingdom of God."[104]

13.5 The Futurity of the Kingdom

We encounter the futurity of the kingdom, as has previously been pointed out, in the second petition of the Lord's Prayer, Luke 11.2 = Matt 6.10: ἐλθέτω ἡ βασιλεία σου. The disciples can ask for this "coming in power"[105] only from God. Unlike the Zealots or individual rabbinic teachers later, they do not think that they can influence this coming through their own activity or perfect obedience, for example in the case of the Sabbath commandment, let alone that they can "force" the end itself to come or hasten it.[106] To be sure, this coming is not only restricted to the ultimate coming "in power." The *malkût* can also come to the individual, when he, called by Jesus, follows him and places himself in the service of the dawning kingdom of God. This means that there is also a direct connection to the present here.

---

[100] See section 13.2 with notes 52–53.

[101] Luke 16.1-8 (special material).

[102] Luke 14.28-32 (special material).

[103] Matt 10.39; 16.25; Luke 17.33.

[104] Luke 9.62 (special material).

[105] Mark 9.1: . . . ἕως ἴδωσιν τὴν βασιλείαν τοῦ θεοῦ ἐληλυθυῖαν ἐν δυνάμει. Luke omits this decisive ἔρχεσθαι ἐν δυνάμει. In Luke Jesus addresses not only the disciples but "all" (9.23) and relates the kingdom of God to the time of the church after Easter; on this, see Schürmann 1984, 550ff. Matthew 16.28 speaks, by contrast, of the coming of the Son of Man "in his kingdom"; cf. v. 27 and 25.31.

[106] Hengel 1989c, 122ff. (GV = 1976c, 127ff.). Individual rabbis warned against wanting to "force" the end that was firmly fixed by God through violent revolt against the world power "as in the days of (Eleazar ben) Dinai" (see section 3.1.5 with notes 306 and 315) or of "ben Kosiba." All who attempted this came to grief (Hengel 1989c, 124; GV = 1976c, 129).

Every apocalyptic reckoning in advance is also impossible: "The kingdom comes not with (calculable) observation of external signs";[107] not even the Son knows the hour, "but only the Father."[108] Above all, the metaphor beloved in the parables of the joyful banquet in the kingdom of God looks in the first instance into the future. At the end of the Last Supper Jesus speaks directly to his disciples about this and refers them here to an event that lies on the other side of his approaching death.[109]

Rather than being restricted only to the followers of Jesus and Israel, this meal is a universal occasion: "And they will come from east and west, from north and south and recline at the table in the kingdom of God."[110] This picture, in connection, for example, with the reference to the drinking of wine, shows at the same time that God's kingdom is a reality and not a spiritualistic home of souls. Jesus assumes—like his Pharisaic contemporaries and in contrast to the Sadducees—the resurrection of the body. That the founding of families and procreation cease follows from the fact that the consequences of humanity's fall through sin are overcome. Death has finally lost its power. The original fellowship with God is reestablished. The realistic eschatology of early Christianity with its millennialist characteristics basically goes back to Jesus.[111]

This reference to the future also finds expression in the formula "to enter into the kingdom of God," which is sometimes exchangeable with "to enter into (eternal) life" or "to inherit life."[112] In the Greek-speaking mission communities the speech form of "eternal life" gradually displaced that of the kingdom of God. While Paul can also still speak in a formulaic manner of the fact that grave sinners "cannot inherit the kingdom of God,"[113] talk of "eternal life" is now much more predominant. This is even

---

[107] Luke 17.20: οὐκ . . . μετά παρατηρήσεως. For details about such signs, see the Lives of the Prophets, which ascribe such "predictions" to a great number of Old Testament prophets, with these sometimes being similar to the series of prodigies in the Sibylline Oracles and Josephus as well as in Luke. Prieur 1996, 255–56, by contrast, regards the rejection of "observations of possible signs" as the false solution, claiming that the concern is only with the "rejection of the opinion that 'the coming . . . of the kingdom of God must . . . be recognizable by clearly discernible phenomena" (with reference to Baltz 1994, 35; GV = 1982, 82). In our opinion, this is imagined in a much too modern-abstract manner.

[108] Mark 13.32 = Matt 24.36; cf. Acts 1.6-7.

[109] Mark 14.25; on this, cf. note 45 above.

[110] Luke 13.29; cf. Matt 8.11.

[111] Mark 12.18-25; cf. Gen 2.17, 25; 3.6-7 and 3.19-24. The founding of families took place only after the fall in Gen 4.1ff. and leads to fratricide. On the eschatological realism, see also Rev 19.2; 22.2 and note 47 above.

[112] Cf. Mark 9.43-47 = Matt 18.8-9; Mark 10.17 = Luke 18.18 = Matt 19.16, cf. Luke 10.25.

[113] First Corinthians 6.9-10; Gal 5.21: grave sinners; 1 Cor 15.50: flesh and blood.

more the case for the Fourth Evangelist.[114] Thus, the future kingdom of God appears in the Synoptics and with Jesus himself[115] as the renewed, salvific creation of God and the fellowship with him, into which one is received or, alternatively, must remain outside of. Here too we can see a continuity in substance between the preaching of Jesus, the proclamation of the primitive community, and the faith of the predominantly Gentile Christian mission communities.[116] The older Lukan form of the beatitudes at the beginning of the Sermon on the Plain, Luke 6.20ff., understands it as a present *and* future gift of salvation: "Blessed (you), the poor, *for to you belongs the kingdom of God*," i.e., already now. By contrast, the future character is clearly emphasized in the tension between present and future in the two beatitudes that follow: "Blessed, those who now hunger, for you will become sated; blessed, those who now mourn, for you will laugh."[117] Through the clear promise "the kingdom of God is yours," it is, for believers, as God's gift, already now present and certain. Jesus' promise creates unbreakable certainty of salvation. The expanded eight (or nine) macarisms of Matthew have a similar structure that encompasses present and future.[118]

The dawning corresponds to apocalyptic expectation. Together with the kingdom the Son of Man becomes manifest as judge and bringer of salvation.[119] He comes unexpectedly and suddenly like lightning, as the flood in the days of Noah, as the fire over Sodom and Gomorrah.[120] One can neither escape nor safeguard oneself against this event: when it comes

---

[114] In John the βασιλεία appears only two times (3.3, 5; cf. also the kingdom of Christ in 18.36), whereas ζωή appears thirty-six times and thirteen times in the Johannine Epistles. Paul has the βασιλεία of God or of Christ only eight times, whereas ζωή appears twenty-six times in the genuine letters.

[115] Mark 9.47: εἰσελθεῖν εἰς τὴν βασιλείαν τοῦ θεοῦ, cf. 10.23-25 = Luke 18.24-25 = Matt 19.23-24; cf. also Matt 5.20; 7.21; 18.3; see further Matt 25.34: κληρονομήσατε τὴν . . . βασιλείαν or "inheriting" the kingdom of God, Mark 10.17, cf. 9.43, 45.

[116] Luke 13.28. Matthew 8.11-12 places this saying in the story of the centurion of Capernaum and makes this a paradigm for the Gentile mission and against the old Israel: "The sons of the βασιλεία will be cast out into the outer darkness."

[117] Luke 6.20: ὅτι ὑμετέρα ἐστὶν ἡ βασιλεία τοῦ θεοῦ. It does not say ἔσται. Marcion generalizes. He removes in this way the character as address and the eschatological tension, turns the ὑμετέρα into an αὐτῶν, and omits the two occurrences of νῦν in v. 21: see Harnack 1960, *191–92 (no equivalent in Harnack 1990).

[118] Matthew 5.3-11. Here v. 11 is a detailed explanation of the eighth beatitude in v. 10. The first and eighth correspond through the categorical promise: ὅτι αὐτῶν ἐστιν ἡ βασιλεία τῶν οὐρανῶν. Vv. 4-9 have, after the macarism of the present form of existence, the promise in the future.

[119] Mark 8.38; 9.1; 13.26-27 parr.

[120] Luke 17.24ff.

it is ubiquitous.[121] By contrast, the present that precedes it, in which with Jesus' activity the βασιλεία is not recognized and is at work in a hidden way, appears as the time of the offering of salvation, of the invitation to faith and discipleship and yet also of testing, of crisis, and of separating out.

Jesus' proclamation of the kingdom is new especially in two points:

First, it is new in the speech form of the "coming of the kingdom of God" or of "entering into the kingdom of God" or "inheriting" it, which does not have any real parallels in Judaism. We can see here the creative power of Jesus' language, which we also encounter in the parables. The apocalyptic Judaism of the time and especially the later rabbis usually speaks in this connection of the "coming age" in contrast to "this age"[122] — a formula that turns up only occasionally in the Gospels.[123] Conversely, the phrase "kingdom of God" appears *expressis verbis* relatively rarely in the Jewish-apocalyptic texts. This means that Jesus can speak of the βασιλεία as of a clearly defined entity, of a "sphere of rule" or kingdom, into which one can go or come, in which one can have a share, and yet also which, as in the Lord's Prayer, is to come to us and is now already effectual.

Secondly, it is new with respect to the people to whom access to the kingdom is promised. It applies above all to the poor and religious déclassés, extending to the "dregs of society," demoniacs, lepers, sick persons, flagrant sinners, tax collectors, and prostitutes. This is why Jesus is also defamed as "friend of tax collectors and sinners."[124] The strict First Gospel underlines this after the parable of the two sons. In contrast to the religious leaders in Jerusalem, the tax collectors and prostitutes will enter the kingdom of God,[125] for they believed the message of the Baptist.

With his message of the "kingdom" Jesus turns in the first instance to the rural population of Galilee, the *'am hā-'āreṣ*, who were regarded as religiously uneducated. According to the opinion of the Pharisees in John 7.49, "this crowd, who does not know the law, is accursed."[126] For

---

[121] Luke 17.34ff. On this, see Hengel 2002, 399–410.

[122] ὁ αἰὼν ὁ ἐρχόμενος or ὁ μέλλων: '*ôlām hab-bā*'; the counterpart is ὁ αἰὼν οὗτος: '*ôlām haz-zeh*.

[123] Mark 10.30 = Luke 18.30; Luke 16.8 (special material); 20.34 (addition of Luke); Matt 12.32. It is also lacking in Paul. He speaks only — usually in a disparaging way — of "this age" (Rom 12.2; 1 Cor 1.20; 2.6-8 and elsewhere).

[124] Luke 7.34 = Matt 11.19; cf. Mark 2.16 parr.

[125] Matthew 21.31: προάγουσιν ὑμᾶς εἰς τὴν βασιλείαν τοῦ θεοῦ. Cf. Luke 7.29-30.

[126] This statement is preceded in John 7.40ff. by a division among the crowd with different opinions about Jesus. The Pharisees react to this with the verdict (7.48): "Has any of the leaders of the people or of the Pharisees believed in him?" ὁ ὄχλος οὗτος ὁ μὴ γινώσκων τὸν νόμον ἐπάρατοί εἰσιν. With this polemical formulation (like Matthew)

Jesus the crowd is "like sheep who do not have a shepherd."[127] In addition, Matthew emphasizes twice that Jesus has been sent only "to the lost sheep of the house of Israel."[128] Jesus has this *'am hā-'āreṣ* in mind in the Beatitudes and with his reference to the simple ones in the prayer of thanks in Luke 10.21. The related saying "whoever does not receive the kingdom of God as a child will not enter it" must also be understood from this standpoint.[129] It is children who may be certain of the βασιλεία. Therefore, one should not turn them away but bring them to him so that he may touch them as a blessing.[130]

"Entering into the kingdom of God" and, what is identical to it, acquittal in the judgment are tied to one's stance toward Jesus and his message, to meeting it with trust and not taking offense at it. "I say to you, whoever confesses me before humans, the Son of Man will also confess him before the angels of God."[131] Accordingly, Jesus' answer to the Baptist applies in general: "Blessed is the one who does not take offense at me."[132]

13.6 Kingdom of God and Jesus' Messianic Authority

That this coming of God, his kingdom, occurs already as signs in the activity of Jesus and leads all apocalyptic reckonings *ad absurdum* is shown by Jesus' answer to the Pharisees' question of when this kingdom will (finally) come:

> The kingdom of God comes not with observation (of signs), also one will not say: "it is there" or "it is here" but *it is in the midst of you.*[133]

This much-discussed saying can best be explained in a sensible way through the reference to Jesus himself. In his person it is present already now in the midst of the questioners (and it is only that they do not see it).[134]

John probably already presupposes here the stance of the Pharisees, who obtained spiritual rule in Judaea after 70 CE.

[127] Mark 6.34 = Matt 9.36.

[128] Matthew 15.24; cf. Matt 10.6.

[129] Mark 10.15 = Luke 18.17. Matthew 18.3 is a further development: "If you do not repent and become as children, you will not enter the kingdom of heaven."

[130] Mark 10.13-16; Luke 18.15-16; cf. Matt 19.13-14. On this, see Heckel 2002, 53–59.

[131] Luke 12.8 and, in dependence on him and with theological corrections, Matt 10.32 (see note 176 in chapter 17); cf. also Mark 8.38 = Luke 9.26.

[132] Luke 7.23 = Matt 11.6. See section 12.2 with note 74.

[133] Luke 17.20-21.

[134] Luke 17.21: ἰδοὺ γὰρ ἡ βασιλεία τοῦ θεοῦ ἐντὸς ὑμῶν ἐστιν. The future interpretation "it will *suddenly* be in your midst," which has been popular since Wrede, can

The accusation against the hearers who can predict the weather on the basis of observation goes in a similar direction:

> Hypocrites, you know how to judge the appearance of earth and heaven. Why can you not judge this (present) time?[135]

Jesus' activity here and now is the decisive καιρός. It must be recognized. All observing and calculating speculations about the future, which were widespread at the time of Jesus in Jewish Palestine on the basis of the enigmatic temporal specifications of the Daniel apocalypse, are pointless. Everything depends on understanding that the salvation promised by God can be heard and seen in his words and deeds *now*. The presence of salvation is expressed most impressively in the well-known polemical saying of Jesus addressed against the Pharisaic accusation of being in league with the devil. This is a key text for understanding the activity of Jesus:

> But if I cast out the demons by Beelzebul, by what do your pupils cast them out? Therefore, they will be your judges! If, however, I cast out the

---

hardly be obtained from the text. There are three possible translations of ἐντὸς ὑμῶν, a phrase that is attested only here in the New Testament. The first option—"it is in your inside"—corresponds to the normal Greek usage. It is attested already in Gos. Thom. 3 and 113 and in the Gospel of Mary, then very frequently in the church fathers, where it primarily justifies the spiritual, not millennialist, view of the kingdom of God, and is still familiar today through Luther's translation "inwendig in euch" (inside in you), i.e., in your hearts. However, it fits with neither the proclamation of Jesus nor with Luke. The second possibility—"it is in your sphere, it stands at your disposal"—has been chosen since Tertullian, *Marc.* 4.35, until recent commentaries, but appears less likely as an answer of Jesus to the Pharisees in Luke. The third interpretive possibility—that in the activity of Jesus in word and deed it is present "among you"—corresponds to Luke 11.20 par. and the answer of Jesus to the question of the Baptist (Luke 7.22 = Matt 11.5). It appears to be linguistically unusual but not impossible, for Aquila reproduces Exod 17.7; 34.9 "in our midst" with ἐντὸς ἡμῶν, while the Septuagint writes ἐν ἡμῖν and Symmachus ἐν μέσῳ; cf. also Aquila in Exod 34.9, which has ἐντὸς ἡμῶν for "in our midst." Euthymius Zigabenus (PG 129, Sp. 1045, 1048) mentions this interpretation. Wolff and Bengel favored it and it was supported by de Wette and others in the nineteenth century. Today the majority of exegetes support this solution. See Bauer/Aland/Aland 1988, 544; Wolter 2016/2017, II: 302–4. See in detail Meier 1994, 423–30, 477–83, and 483 n. 144 for a plausible reconstruction of the saying of Jesus and its retranslation into Aramaic. The peculiar ἐντὸς ὑμῶν probably goes back to a pre-Lukan translation of the Aramaic saying of Jesus. Cf. further Schwemer 2009.

[135] Luke 12.56: τὸν καιρὸν δὲ τοῦτον. The parallel in Matt 16.2-3, from ὀψίας to τὰ δὲ σημεῖα τῶν καιρῶν οὐ δύνασθε (διακρίνειν), is lacking in the oldest manuscripts (cf. also Gos. Thom. 91). It is probably dependent on Luke, but expresses the christological interpretation even more clearly and must have already entered into the Matthean text at an early point.

demons by *the finger of God*,[136] then the kingdom of God has come to you.[137]

"The finger of God" is an expression of the omnipotence of God present in the actions of Jesus,[138] which as signs of the now dawning kingdom prepare an end for the tyranny of the anti-God powers that enslave human beings. E. P. Sanders regards as original only the first part of the answer of Jesus with the counterquestion of how in that case their own exorcists cast out demons. This, however, would be a banality. The actual punchline is in the second saying, which Sanders wishes to delete in order to save his hypothesis that Jesus had a purely future expectation. But such an exclusively future kingdom of God hope would contradict the statements of the Synoptic sources and rob the proclamation of Jesus of its conspicuous distinctiveness, which in this point tends rather to run counter to apocalyptic eschatology and is continued in primitive Christianity through the tension between the presence of salvation and the consummation of salvation.[139] The healings and exorcisms of Jesus, through which the demonic powers that torment and disgrace humans as God's creation are conquered,[140] are visible manifestations of the kingdom of God that is already being "realized" now. The immediately following dramatic saying about the "stronger one" who conquers the "strong one" and robs him of his booty calls to mind the announcement of the "stronger one" by the Baptist,[141] illuminates our saying of Jesus, and shows that it has "messianic" character.[142]

The closest material parallel is Jesus' answer to the Baptist, which we have already mentioned at several points. He does not simply answer it affirmatively, but his actions, to which he points, i.e., the miracles of healing and his proclamation of the good news to the poor, which are

---

[136] Luke 11.20: ἐν δακτύλῳ θεοῦ. Matthew 12.28 interprets theologically: ἐν πνεύματι θεοῦ. The conspicuous formulation of Luke is surely more original.

[137] Luke 11.19-20 = Matt 12.27-28: . . . ἄρα ἔφθασεν ἐφ' ὑμᾶς ἡ βασιλεία τοῦ θεοῦ.

[138] The metaphor comes from Exod 8.15. The Egyptian magicians must concede the superiority of the punitive miracle performed by Moses. These lead, however, to further hardening.

[139] Sanders 1985, 137–41 and 417 index; and against this view Merkel 1991, 123–24, 127–28, 137, 142–44. Cf. Luke 10.9: ἤγγικεν ἐφ' ὑμᾶς ἡ βασιλεία τοῦ θεοῦ; see notes 5–6 above. On this, see Hengel 1997a (= 2007b, 644–63); Van der Horst 1997. See also the judgment of Wrede in note 11 above.

[140] Cf. also Luke 10.17-20.

[141] Mark 1.7 = Luke 3.16 = Matt 3.11.

[142] Luke 11.21-22; cf. Matt 12.29 = Mark 3.27; Gos. Thom. 35.

perceptible to all,[143] speak for themselves. He really is "the coming one." Jesus' exhortation to the disciples of the Baptist—"go and proclaim to John what you have seen and heard"—points to the concrete perception of facts. The conclusion, which we have already quoted multiple times, "Blessed is the one who does not take offense at me," applies also to the accusation of being in league with the devil. The two texts, which are quite different in content, mutually interpret each other.

Here, two further questions arise: first, the question of Jesus' "deeds of power" and their relation to his eschatological activity, and, second, the question of the *authority* of the eschatological activity of Jesus—one could also say of his *messianic claim*.

At the same time, it must be conceded that Jesus' preaching of the kingdom of God, in form and content, as well as his behavior largely lie outside the framework of what is recounted to us about other Jewish teachers, miracle workers, and prophets in his time and after him. As a Galilean "teacher and miracle worker" he is entirely *sui generis* and cannot be placed in fixed, preexisting history-of-religions schemata. This applies with regard to the contemporary picture of prophets and teachers as well as for the expectation of a political and messianic liberator.

---

[143] Luke 7.22: πορευθέντες ἀπαγγείλατε Ἰωάννῃ ἃ εἴδετε καὶ ἠκούσατε; see section 10.5. On "seeing and hearing," cf. Luke 10.23 = Matt 13.16; see, by contrast, John 20.29.

14

The Will of God[1]

According to the longer, expanded Matthean version of the Lord's Prayer, the second petition about the coming of the kingdom in 6.10 is followed by a third: "Your will be done on earth as it is in heaven."[2] Here we are dealing with an interpretation, which fittingly supplements the first petition for the hallowing of the name of God and the second petition. Where God reveals his holiness and where therefore the kingdom can dawn, his will is also done. The nearness, indeed, the arrival of the kingdom also reveals the true will of God in order to realize it now also on the earth.[3] As we have already said previously,[4] the holy will of God, which is to establish itself in the whole creation—i.e., Jesus' ethics in the usual problematic terminology—is determined without qualification by the one fundamental theme of his proclamation, the kingdom of God.

14.1 Hearing, Doing, and Being

Since the Enlightenment, many have wanted to understand Jesus as one who brings a new, truly humane moral philosophy. Continuing an early Christian understanding, which is attested for example in the early fathers and

---

[1] Jeremias 1970, 203ff. (GV = 1979, 197ff.); Schrage 1988, 13–115 (GV = 1982, 21–119); Hengel 1978 (= 2007b, 352–74); Hengel 1981c; Hengel 1982b (= 2007b, 375–90); Strecker 1984; Hengel 1987c (= 1999b, 219–92); Wenham 1995; Deines 2004.

[2] Matthew 6.10: γενηθήτω τὸ θέλημά σου ὡς ἐν οὐρανῷ καὶ ἐπὶ γῆς. The connection to the prayer of Jesus in Gethsemane in Mark 14.36, which begins with "Abba" and ends with οὐ τί ἐγὼ θέλω ἀλλὰ τί σύ, in which Mark, in our view, presupposes the Matthean addition to the third petition, is conspicuous. On this point, cf. now Frey 2016.

[3] Cf. 1 Macc 3.60 and Hengel 1999b, 278ff.

[4] See section 13.3.

especially in Justin, he appears as new lawgiver[5] and perfect model at the same time. According to the so-called Kantian motto "only the good will is really good," Luke 17.21 (ἡ βασιλεία τοῦ θεοῦ ἐντὸς ὑμῶν ἐστιν) has been interpreted in connection with Luther's translation "the kingdom of God is inside of you" with reference to the inner ethical attitude of the human being.[6] The absoluteness of the concrete demands of Jesus is thereby reshaped and defused as a "*Gesinnungsethik*" (ethic of attitude or intention). In reality, however, this saying is concerned with the presence of the kingdom of God in the person of Jesus. Since Jesus' demand—for example in the Sermon on the Mount—was thought to be in reality unfulfillable, it was believed that what mattered was not so much the actual deed as the right attitude. This is sharply contradicted by Jesus' demand for action. Thus, in Luke at the end of the Sermon on the Plain: "Why do you call me Lord, Lord, and do not *do* what I say to you?"[7] This is followed by the concluding parable:[8]

> Everyone who comes to me and hears my words and *does them* is like a person building a house who digs deep and lays the foundation on the rock . . . but the one who *hears and does not do* them is like a person who build a house on soil without a foundation. . . .

In response to the macarism on the mother of Jesus, Jesus answers with a correction: "Blessed rather (are) those who *hear and keep* the word of God." The "word of God" is his message about the inbreaking kingdom and the concomitant interpretation of the divine will.[9] To this corresponds the rejection of the mother and siblings of Jesus and the reference to the circle of his hearers: "Behold, my mother and my brothers. For whoever does the will of God is my brother, sister, mother."[10]

---

[5] On Christ as "new lawgiver," see Justin, *Dial.* 12.2; 14.3; 18.3; cf. Origen, *Cels.* 2.1–7. On the "new law" of Christ, see Barn 2.6; Justin, *Dial.* 11.4; 12.3; 122.5; Tertullian, *Praescr.* 13.4; *Marc.* 4.1.4: *per novam legem evangelii.*

[6] See section 13.6 with note 134.

[7] Luke 6.46. Corresponding to the situation of the church at his time, Matthew then further elaborates the saying in 7.21-23; cf. already Mal 1.6: "If I am the Lord, where is the fear of me?" On the unfulfillability of the demands of the "gospel," see already the verdict of the Jewish discussion partner Trypho in Justin, *Dial.* 10.2: μηδένα δύνασθαι φυλάξαι αὐτά.

[8] Luke 6.47ff.; cf. Matt 7.24ff. Here, with the opposition between rock and sand, Matthew could have preserved the more original version; see Jeremias 1972, 194 n. 4 (GV = 1998, 193 n. 4).

[9] Luke 11.27-28 (special material); see section 13.2 with note 33.

[10] Mark 3.34-35 = Matt 12.49-50. Luke 8.21 simplifies: "My mother and brothers are those who hear and do the word of God." Jesus' word is clearly identified here with God's word.

On the other hand, Jesus knows that if the eye as "the light of the body . . . [is] clear," the "whole body [is] full of light," whereas the "evil eye" darkens the whole body.[11] In the same way, he can say:

> For no good tree produces bad fruit and no bad tree produces good fruit,
> for every tree is known by its own fruit; after all, one does not gather figs
> from thistles nor does one harvest figs from a thornbush. (Luke 6.43-44)

This theme of producing fruit is already sounded by the Baptist, but it also connects Jesus with Paul, for whom the indicative of the salvation-creating being in Christ is the presupposition for the imperative.[12] Being grounds doing:

> The good person brings forth from the good treasure of the heart good,
> the evil person from the evil (of his heart) evil, for from the abundance
> of his heart the mouth overflows.[13]

Accordingly, in clear distance from the food prohibitions of the ritual law, what defiles the human being is not unclean food "but that which comes out of the human being."[14] In Mark, Jesus, at the request of the disciples, interprets this saying, which is understandable in itself:[15] "For from the interior of the human heart come evil thoughts, sexual immorality, theft, murder. . . ." The evangelist has a long vice catalogue follow, as we also find them in Paul. Here, we are reminded of statements of the apostle about the works of the flesh and the fruit of the Spirit in Gal 5.19-23. The general judgment that pertains to the listening disciples also sounds almost Pauline:

> If you, who are evil (πονηροί), know how to give good gifts to your children, how much more will the Father from heaven give the Holy Spirit to those who ask him? (Luke 11.13; cf. Matt 7.11)

---

[11] Luke 11.34-36; cf. Matt 6.22-23. On the underlying physiological conception that the "light rays go out from the eye," see Bovon 2013, 147–48 (GV = 1996, 210). On the interpretation of this difficult text, see Bovon 2013, 144–51 (GV = 1996, 206–16).

[12] Luke 6.43-44 = Matt 7.16ff. On the Baptist, see section 9.1.2.2 with notes 36–38. Matthew connects this saying with the warning against false prophets. Cf. Rom 6.22; Gal 5.22; Phil 1.11.

[13] Luke 6.45.

[14] Mark 7.15: τὰ ἐκ τοῦ ἀνθρώπου ἐκπορευόμενά ἐστιν τὰ κοινοῦντα τὸν ἄνθρωπον; cf. Matt 15.11, which in a materially appropriate manner adds ἐκ τοῦ στόματος. See also section 13.3 with note 74.

[15] Mark 7.17 = Matt 15.15: τὴν παραβολὴν ταύτην. In Matthew Peter asks him to explain the parable.

When the apostle speaks of the "law of Christ" in Gal 6.2, he might pick up on Jesus' proclamation of obedient doing, upon which his paraenesis is dependent in much.[16]

14.2 The Double Love Command[17]

In contrast to the ethical understanding that is common among us, for Jesus the norm of action is based not on autonomous, rational insight that is grounded in an *exclusively* rationalistic way but on God's will and commandment, as it was given to Israel in Torah and Prophets. This does not exclude rational insight, but such insight stands under rather than over God's will.

> He has told you, O mortal, what is good; and what does the Lord require of you but to do justice, and to love kindness, and to walk humbly with your God? (Mic 6.8, NRSV)

The "ethical" demand of Jesus or, better, the commandment that corresponds to God's claim to rule is grounded "heteronomously," or, more precisely, theocratically. In this he shows himself to be a Jewish teacher. Fundamental for him is also the *double love command*, which can, after all, be traced back to the Torah. The exhortation to love God is found in Deut 6.4-5 as the beginning of the Jewish confession of faith in the *one* God of Israel, the *Sh*[e]*ma' Yiśrā'ēl* ("Hear Israel . . ."), the fundamental significance of which we have already pointed out multiple times:

> You shall love YHWH,[18] your God, from your whole heart, from your whole soul, and from your whole power.[19]

This commandment is basically a deepening interpretation of the first commandment of Exod 20.2-3 (Deut 5.6-7): "I am YHWH, your God, who brought you out of Egypt, the house of slavery. You shall have no other gods besides me!"

---

[16] Cf. also 1 Cor 9.21: μὴ ὤν ἄνομος θεοῦ ἀλλ' ἔννομος Χριστοῦ. On Paul and the commandments of Jesus, especially the love commandment, see Wenham 1995, 215–41, 255–71.

[17] Nissen 1974; Schrage 1988, 68ff. (1982, 69ff.); Theissen 1989a, 160ff.

[18] This reads in the *Q*[e]*rê 'adonāy*, LXX κύριος = the Lord.

[19] The command for total devotion to God and love for him appears multiple times in the Deuteronomic tradition; cf. also Deut 10.12-22; 11.1, 13-14, 22; 13.4; 19.9; cf. also the concluding sentence of Solomon's prayer on the occasion of the consecration of the temple in 1 Kgs 8.61.

The command to love one's neighbor occurs in Lev 19.18:

> You shall not take vengeance nor bear a grudge against the sons of your
> people, but you shall love your neighbor as yourself. I am YHWH.[20]

It clearly emerges from the antithetical parallelism that "nearest"[21] initially
meant only the fellow member of the people of Israel. In Lev 19.34, however, love of the foreigner is also demanded,[22] i.e., at the time of Jesus,
for the "proselyte," the Gentile convert to Judaism.[23] The fact that Jesus
breaks open this restriction in a universal way is shown by his interpretation of the love command in the Sermon on the Plain in Luke, which Matthew has brought into the sixth antithesis:

> Love your enemies,
> do good to those who hate you,
> bless those who curse you,
> pray for those who mistreat you.[24]

The grounding indicative for this resides in God's own behavior: "Be merciful as your Father is also merciful to you" (Luke 6.36). In Aramaic the
verb *r*ᵉ*ḥem* means in the first instance "love."[25] Accordingly, it could also be
translated "You shall love (your neighbor) as your Father loves (you)!" In
accord with his theology, Matthew turns "be merciful" into "be perfect."[26]
It thus becomes comprehensible that Jesus was already able to summarize
the commandments of love of God and love of neighbor in a double commandment and designate this as the decisive commandment. Mark has the
scribe ask: "Which is the first commandment of all?" Jesus answers with
Deut 6.4-5, has Lev 19.18 follow as "second," and adds: "There is no other

---

[20] Cf. already Lev 19.15-17.

[21] Hebrew: *rea'*, LXX: πλησίον.

[22] Hebrew *ger*, LXX: προσήλυτος. On this, see Bauer/Aland/Aland 1988, 1431, and
the explanation in Philo, *Spec.* 1.51.

[23] On the problem, see Nissen 1974.

[24] Luke 6.27-28; cf. Matt 5.44.

[25] Jastrow 1903, II: 1467, in the peal and pael: "1) to love (Heb. אהב)" with על "to
have compassion on, pity" is only a secondary meaning; see also Sokoloff 2002, 521:
to like, love, have mercy.

[26] Luke 6.36: Γίνεσθε οἰκτίρμονες καθὼς καὶ ὁ πατὴρ ὑμῶν οἰκτίρμων ἐστίν;
Matt 5.48: Ἔσεσθε οὖν ὑμεῖς τέλειοι ὡς ὁ πατὴρ ὑμῶν ὁ οὐράνιος τέλειός ἐστιν. On
the specific Matthean use of τέλειος, see also the rich young man in 19.21. See also section
13.3 with note 68.

commandment greater than these,"[27] i.e., the whole Torah is concentrated on this double commandment of love and must be measured by it. To the πρώτη ἐντολή Matthew adds a μεγάλη, which corresponds to the rabbinic manner of expression. The same applies to his concluding sentence: "on these two commandments hang the whole law and prophets."[28] In this way the widespread view of the equal value of all 613 commandments and prohibitions of the Torah is annulled; at the same time the discussions of Jesus with the Pharisaic scribes about the Sabbath halakah, the purity regulations, and divorce can be explained on this basis. Love, *'aḥᵃbāh*, for God and the neighbor, a word that the Septuagint already consistently translates with ἀγάπη,[29] has priority over everything else.

This one central double commandment is grounded in God's behavior. Because the creator loves, upholds, and saves his creatures, human beings, with complete devotion, he can also demand selfless, devoted, and saving love from them. In practicing such love one only passes on to one's fellow human what one has received. Such a theocentric grounding of the imperative through the indicative of the free, electing love of God is encountered to some extent already within the Old Testament in the Deuteronomistic theology and in Jeremiah,[30] and it runs through the whole of primitive Christianity via Paul through to John, for example in John 13.34: "A new commandment I give to you that you love one another as I have loved you." In James, Lev 19.18, as the "royal law" (James 2.8), is identical with the "perfect law of freedom" (James 1.25). The later rabbinic interpretation

---

[27] Mark 12.28-31; in the Lukan parallel from the special material in 10.25ff. Jesus is tested by a "scholar of the law" (νομικός) with the question "What must I do to inherit eternal life?" Matt 22.34ff. follows the Markan version, but takes over the negative presentation of the νομικός as tester of Jesus from Luke. In contrast to Mark, for him a Pharisaic scribe can no longer be evaluated positively. He therefore follows the negative version of Luke in this point.

[28] Matthew 22.38, 40; on this, see Bill. I: 907–8. See there the statements of R. Akiba on Lev 19.18: "this is a great (general) principle in the Torah," and of Ben Azzai and Bar Kappara; cf. also Hengel 1999b, 282–87.

[29] Alongside this, ἀγάπησις also appears sporadically. The very common verb *'āheb* "to love" is almost always translated with ἀγαπᾶν. Ἔρως appears only twice in the book of Proverbs. The verb ἐρᾶσθαι only occurs three times, of which two are as a translation of *'āheb*. The theological language of Jesus and of earliest Christianity is that of the Hebrew Bible and, dependent on this, of the Septuagint.

[30] Deuteronomy 7.7-8: "Not because of your number has YHWH ... chosen you from all the nations—you are, after all, the smallest among the nations, but *because YHWH loved you*"; cf. Jer 31.3: "With everlasting *love* I have loved you; therefore in goodness I have preserved you"; cf. 31.20.

knows the idea that in the "works of love" one is meant to imitate God's action toward Israel and the patriarchs.[31]

The Golden Rule in itself is very widespread in the ancient world. The positive version, which appears in Sermon on the Plain of Luke and in the Sermon on the Mount of Matthew, is closely related to the command to love one's neighbor. In Luke's Sermon on the Plain this rule therefore stands between the command to refrain from violence and the composition of sayings about loving one's enemies:[32] "And thus, as you wish that people do to you, so you ought to do to them." Matthew places the text as a conclusion in the last part of the Sermon on the Mount before the concluding admonitions in 7.13-27. He regards it, as he does the double love command, as the summary of the law and prophets.[33] In the rabbinic tradition love command and Golden Rule can become almost interchangeable. Statements about their central significance are attributed to great teachers such as Hillel and R. Akiba.[34] A. Dihle also points to their inner connection: the two rules "stress—though in different ways—the mutuality in interpersonal interaction."[35] The primitive community, which compiled the core statements of the ethical proclamation of Jesus in a catechism-like manner in the "Sermon on the Plain,"[36] regarded this, in a way, as the new "messianic Torah," the "law of the kingdom of God," which is ultimately a "law of grace." In Matthew, this Lukan "catechism of the will of God," which stems from the sayings tradition, is expanded, on the foundation of the righteousness[37] fulfilled by Jesus, to the "Sermon on the Mount."[38]

14.3 Humility and Service, Discipleship and Reward

The great disturbance in God's good creation (Gen 1.31) enters through the fact that the first human couple disregarded his command and believed

[31] Hengel 1981b, 9 n. 21, 18 n. 9, 27 n. 39 (GV = 1968b, 10 n. 26, 21 n. 9, 30 n. 39; 2007b, 48 n. 28, 58 n. 57, 67 n. 89).

[32] Luke 6.31; cf. Matt 7.12. On this, see Dihle 1962; 1981.

[33] Cf. Matt 22.40. The introduction to the Sermon on the Mount in 5.17-20 must also be understood with reference to these two texts. We are dealing here with fundamental statements of the evangelist about the validity of the law. On the interpretation, Deines 2004, 710 (index on Matt 7.12).

[34] On this, see Hengel 1999b, 282–87.

[35] Dihle 1962, 110. The two rules have grown together already in Sir 31.15 (Hebrew text and LXX).

[36] Luke 6.20-49. The designation "Sermon on the Plain" comes from τόπος πεδινός in 6.17.

[37] Matthew 3.15; 5.6, 10, 20.

[38] Matthew 5.1-7.27. Hengel 1999b, 219-92; Deines 2004, passim.

the deceptive words of the serpent: "You will be like God. . . ."[39] According to Luke and Matthew, Jesus rejects the deceiver's offer to give him "all the kingdoms of the circle of the earth" with their "power and glory" with the word of Scripture: "You shall worship the Lord, your God and serve him alone."[40] The primordial sin consists in human delusions of grandeur, which disregards God's command and makes oneself absolute. According to the primitive Christian testimony, Jesus, by contrast, takes the path of the servant of God assigned to him by the Father:

> for the Son of Man did not come
> to be served
> but to serve
> and to give his life as a ransom for many.[41]

This saying may belong in the context of Jesus' Last Supper with his disciples, where, according to Luke, Jesus, in a small farewell speech, sharply rejects a controversy over rank between the disciples about the question "who of them is the greatest":[42]

> The kings of the nations exercise lordship over them, and their rulers let themselves be called benefactors. But not so you, but let the greatest among you become as the smallest[43] and the leader as the servant. . . .
> But I am in your midst as a servant.[44]

Mark brings in a related text with the same motif after the two sons of Zebedee, James and John, ask to receive, when Jesus comes "in his glory,"[45] the respective places of honor "at his right and his left," which arouses the indignation of their fellow disciples. Jesus concludes his admonition here with a two-liner—"whoever . . . among you wants to be great, let him be your servant, and whoever . . . among you wants to be the first, let him be the slave of all"—and with reference to his service

---

[39] Genesis 3.5ff.

[40] Luke 4.5-8: καὶ αὐτῷ μόνῳ λατρεύσεις = Matt 4.8-10; see section 10.2.

[41] Mark 10.45 = Matt 20.28: οὐκ ἦλθεν διακονηθῆναι ἀλλὰ διακονῆσαι; on this, see Jeremias 1966a, 216–29; Stuhlmacher 2018, 139ff., 147–50, 162ff. (GV = 1992, 120ff., 127–30, 140ff.). See also note 46 below.

[42] Luke 22.24ff.

[43] Literally: ὡς ὁ νεώτερος, on this Bauer/Aland/Aland 1988, 1085, 2β, on Luke 22.26.

[44] Luke 22.27: ἐγὼ δὲ ἐν μέσῳ ὑμῶν εἰμι ὡς ὁ διακονῶν; cf. John 13.12-17.

[45] Mark 10.37: ἐν τῇ δόξῃ σου, Matt 20.21: ἐν τῇ βασιλείᾳ σου. In the Matthean parallel in 20.20 it is no longer the pair of brothers but rather their mother who asks the question.

as servant of God and the giving of his life as a "ransom for many."[46] This unique serving of Jesus, which nullifies the fateful disaster of the fall of Gen 3, is meant to determine the whole existence of the disciples as followers. Grounded christologically and in a post-Easter manner, Paul expresses this in the introductory context to the Philippians hymn: "Let the same mind be in you that was in Christ Jesus."[47] To be sure, questions of rank played a considerable, human/all-too-human role in the circle of disciples and in the primitive community.[48] Here, however, the concern is with more than only a moral attitude, which could be described with the concept of "renunciation of status." Serving becomes the quintessence of what it means to follow Jesus, which also includes readiness for renunciation and suffering, even to the point of martyrdom. Mark expresses this in a text that he places right after the sharp rebuff of Peter following the announcement of suffering, in which there is—as so often in Mark—a fusion of Jesus tradition and community paraenesis.

> If anyone wishes to come after me, let him deny himself and take up his cross and follow me. For whoever wishes to save his life will lose it, but whoever will lose his life for my sake and the gospel's will save it. For what does it profit a person to gain the whole world but forfeit his life?[49]

> Whoever does not bear his own cross and come after me is not able to be my disciple.[50]

According to the second passion prediction, in which the disciples' complete incomprehension becomes apparent,[51] Mark recounts a scene in

---

[46] Mark 10.35-45 = Matt 20.20-28, on this, cf. Rom 15.8: Jesus as διάκονος περιτο- μῆς, who for the sake of the truth of the will of God brings to fulfillment the promises of the fathers, and the phrase μορφὴν δούλου λαβών in Phil 2.7. A more strongly "Graecised" version appears in the creed-like text 1 Tim 2.6a.

[47] Philippians 2.5, cf. 2.3-4; Rom 12.3, 10; 15.3; 2 Cor 8.9; Gal 5.26.

[48] Cf., for example, the bitter controversy over the καυχᾶσθαι in Paul and his opponents in 1 and 2 Corinthians, Galatians, and Romans.

[49] Mark 8.34-36 = Luke 9.23-25 = Matt 16.24-26. Luke adds to the saying about suffering discipleship a generalizing καθ᾽ ἡμέραν. With his version Mark probably alludes to the Neronic persecution in Rome, which only lies ca. five to six years in the past and where there is first talk of the crucifixion of Christians; see Tacitus, *Ann.* 15.44.4: *aut crucibus adfixi atque flammati* ("fixed to crosses and made flammable"; trans. Woodman 2004, 326). See also Mark 15.21: Simon of Cyrene, who carries Jesus' cross. The motif of "cross-bearing" in connection with the readiness for radical renunciation of all life goods also occurs in the sayings tradition: Luke 14.25-27, shortened in Matt 10.37-38. This also refutes the claim that the sayings tradition (or Q) does not know the passion tradition.

[50] Luke 14.27; Matt 10.38: "is not worthy of me." Cf. note 49.

[51] Mark 9.30-32.

which the concern is again basically with self-denial in the discipleship of Jesus.[52] "On the way" (ἐν τῇ ὁδῷ) with Jesus the disciples gave thought to a question that moved them greatly; but when asked what they were discussing, they became silent in shame, for they had been discussing "who was the greatest" (τίς μείζων). Then Jesus calls the twelve together and gives them an instruction, which he repeats with a more detailed justification a little later in connection with the offense-evoking question of the sons of Zebedee:[53] "If anyone wishes to be first, he must become last of all and servant of all" (9.35). He next places a child in the middle and takes it into his arms, which means, he places it before the eyes of the disciples as "an example for the smallest and most despised person" who is in the discipleship of Jesus: "Whoever receives one of such children receives me" (9.37). This means that Jesus identifies himself with them.[54] In 18.3-4 Matthew adds in a materially sensible manner the saying of Jesus about "receiving the kingdom of God like a child," which he has taken over from Mark 10.15. In Luke there follows as a conclusion of the pericope: "For the one who . . . is the smallest among all of you, he is great." Against this background it becomes understandable that the primitive community and probably already Jesus could designate his followers as μιϰροί, as "small people."[55] To this corresponds the designation νήπιοι, the simple ones, for the recipients of the revelation of the Father in Jesus' "cry of joy" (*Jubelruf*).[56] Right after this the Matthean Jesus calls "all who are weary and carrying heavy burdens" to himself, in order that they may learn from him, who describes himself as "gentle and humble of heart."[57] Here too the evangelists are concerned with the service of the servant of God. The promise that the kingdom of God belongs to the children and that they will be received "as a child" (ὡς παιδίον) points in a similar direction.[58]

The individual saying "But many first will be last and many last will be first" probably stands in connection with the *final judgment*. The consummation of the kingdom of God brings a radical reversal of the human

[52] Mark 9.33-37, cf. Luke 9.46-48 and Matt 18.1-5.

[53] Mark 10.41-44. See the beginning of the present section.

[54] Cf. Klostermann 1971, 94. Matthew also employs this linguistic usage, since for him it is typically dominical, also in 10.42; 18.10, 14. On this, see Michel 1967 (GV = 1942).

[55] Mark 9.42 = Luke 17.2 = Matt 18.6; cf. also the "little flock" in Luke 12.32.

[56] Luke 10.21 = Matt 11.25, cf. the quotation from Ps 8.3 in Matt 21.16. See also the discussion in section 12.2.

[57] Matthew 11.28: Δεῦτε πρός με πάντες οἱ κοπιῶντες καὶ πεφορτισμένοι, v. 29: ὅτι πραΰς εἰμι καὶ ταπεινὸς τῇ καρδία. On the key word πραΰς, see also the quotation of Zech 9.9 at Jesus' entry into Jerusalem according to Matt 21.5. Cf. the invitation of Wisdom in Sir 6.28 LXX; 51.23-27.

[58] Mark 10.15 = Luke 18.17, cf. Matt 19.13-15; see the end of section 13.5 with notes 129–30.

ordering of value in the old age, and it is necessary to align onself with it already now.[59] It sounds peculiarly profane when Jesus says that when invited to a banquet one should not seek the place of honor near the host, lest another be moved forward and one be sent to the last place, but should instead choose the lowest place so that the host can seek out a more honorable place for the guest at the meal.[60] The attached individual saying "For everyone who exalts himself will be lowered and the one who lowers himself will be exalted"[61] and the context that follows point to an originally eschatological connection with the meal in the kingdom of God.[62]

Here the motif of reward crops up. It is not passed over in the proclamation of Jesus. God is righteous and rewards service, discipleship, and readiness for sacrifice. In this question, Jesus stands, as so often, in the Old Testament Jewish tradition. Thus, Peter, after Jesus' emphatic warning against riches, points to the radical following of his call to discipleship: "Behold, we have left everything and followed you." At this Jesus promises to everyone who has left possessions and family for his sake a "hundredfold reward" and the regaining of what one had left "already in this time" and "in the coming age eternal life."[63] To be sure, with respect to the key word "reward" ($\mu\iota\sigma\theta\acute{o}\varsigma$) there is a telling difference between the evangelists. Mark has it only once: "Whoever gives you a cup to drink because you belong to the Messiah ($\acute{o}\tau\iota\ X\rho\iota\sigma\tauo\hat{\upsilon}\ \acute{\epsilon}\sigma\tau\epsilon$)—truly I say to you: he will not lose his reward."[64] Luke includes the reference to reward twice formulaically from the sayings tradition in the Sermon on the Plain. Thus, in the fourth macarism: "when people hate, exclude, and revile you . . .": "behold, your reward will be great in heaven,"[65] and again in connection with the command to love one's enemies.[66] Matthew, by contrast, has the

---

[59] Mark 10.31 = Matt 19.30, cf. 20.16; Luke 13.30; cf. also Mark 9.35; Gos. Thom. 4; Barn 6.13.

[60] Luke 14.7-11 (special material), cf. the addition in Codex D (and Φ it sy^c+hmg) to Matt 20.28, which probably grew from an apocryphal Gospel or from the Diatessaron.

[61] Luke 14.11, cf. 18.14; Matt 23.12 and 18.4.

[62] See Luke 14.12-14 (special material) and the parable of the great supper in 14.15-24.

[63] Mark 10.28-30 = Luke 18.28-30 = Matt 19.27-29, which from Luke 22.30 inserts the saying that the twelve will judge the twelve tribes. Mark probably thinks that the disciple in the fellowship with Jesus and the believers in the community of Christ receives back many times what he gave up "for the sake of Jesus and the gospel," but adds—presumably as a reference to the Neronic persecution—$\mu\epsilon\tau\grave{\alpha}\ \delta\iota\omega\gamma\mu\hat{\omega}\nu$, which is omitted again by Luke and Matthew.

[64] Mark 9.41. The saying could, as the Matthean parallel in 10.42, stem from the sending out tradition.

[65] Luke 6.23: $\acute{o}\ \mu\iota\sigma\theta\grave{o}\varsigma\ \acute{\upsilon}\mu\hat{\omega}\nu\ \pi o\lambda\grave{\upsilon}\varsigma\ \acute{\epsilon}\nu\ \tau\hat{\omega}\ o\grave{\upsilon}\rho\alpha\nu\hat{\omega}$; cf. Matt 5.12.

[66] Luke 6.35: $\kappa\alpha\grave{\iota}\ \acute{\epsilon}\sigma\tau\alpha\iota\ \acute{o}\ \mu\iota\sigma\theta\grave{o}\varsigma\ \acute{\upsilon}\mu\hat{\omega}\nu\ \pi o\lambda\acute{\upsilon}\varsigma$ = Matt 5.46. Luke 10.7 sounds like a proverb: "The worker is worthy of his wages," but refers not to the "heavenly reward" but to the support of the missionary. Matthew 10.10 therefore turns the $\mu\iota\sigma\theta o\hat{\upsilon}$ into $\tau\rho o\phi\hat{\eta}\varsigma$.

word ten times, with particular frequency in the Sermon on the Mount, there twice analogously to the Lukan parallels, and additionally in the catechetically shaped text about the wrong and right almsgiving, prayer, and fasting, in which the ostentatious practice of piety, which seeks to make an impression on those watching, falls stereotypically under the verdict: "They have forfeited their reward,"[67] and three times in the mission discourse.[68] In these attestations it becomes clear how sayings of Jesus are adjusted to concrete community situations.

The parable of the laborers in the vineyard is unique.[69] The kingdom of God is like a householder who, early in the morning, hires workers for his vineyard with the—very good—daily wage of a denarius per day. He does this also at the third, sixth, ninth, indeed even at the eleventh hour, i.e., in the afternoon around five o'clock, ca. one hour before the end of work. In the evening he has his manager pay them all the same wage of one denarius, beginning with the last person hired. Understandably, this evokes the protest of those who labored for the whole day. The owner rebuffs the protest in a friendly yet decisive manner: "Friend, I do you no wrong. Did we not agree on a denarius? Take your wage and go! I want to give this last person as much as I gave you you. Am I not permitted to do what I want with what is mine? Or is your eye evil (i.e., envious) *because I am so generous?*" The wage refers to the share in the kingdom of God, which is not measured by the largeness of the achievement but which all his workers receive in the same way through God's free goodness. The parable interpretation therefore speaks with good justification of a "gracious reward" (*Gnadenlohn*).[70] The conflict with the ones who protest calls to mind the dialogue of the father with the indignant brother in the parable of the lost son.[71] In both stories of Jesus the concern is with the turning of God's free grace. As is already the case in 19.30,[72] Matt 20.16, which is dependent on the uncommon mode of payment of the wage, is attached by the evangelist and gives to the parable a one-sided orientation. The concern is not with "first and last" but with the goodness of God.

A parable from the Lukan special material, which is likewise to be understood against the background of the rural milieu of Galilee, also

---

[67] Matthew 5.12, 46; 6.1-2, 5, 16 three times ἀπέχουσιν τὸν μισθὸν αὐτῶν; 10.4-5 (cf. Mark 9.41); 20.8.

[68] Matthew 10.41-42, cf. Mark 9.41.

[69] Matthew 20.1-16. Cf. Theissen/Merz 1998, 339ff. (GV = 1997, 305ff.) with reference to rabbinic parallels.

[70] On this, see Luz 2001, 524–38, esp. 527ff. (GV = 1985–2002, III: 138–56, esp. 142ff.); Theissen/Merz 1998, 340 (GV = 1997, 305); Avemarie 2002a.

[71] Luke 15.25-32; see chapter 15.

[72] Cf. Mark 10.31, note 59 above.

rejects every notion of *merit*.[73] However, in contrast to the entirely uncommon event in Matt 20.1-15, it recounts something that is a complete given. The Jerusalem Bible[74] speaks of "humble service":

> Which of you, with a servant ploughing or minding sheep, would say to him when he returned from the fields, 'Come and have our meal immediately? Would he not be more likely to say, 'Get my supper laid; make yourself tidy and wait on me while I eat and drink. You can eat and drink yourself afterwards'? Must he be grateful to the servant for doing what he was told? So with you: when you have done all you have been told to do, say, "We are merely servants: we have done no more than our duty."

Service in discipleship establishes no claim to merit and thanks; it is a taken-for-granted necessity. And yet, a chapter later, Luke can put a promise of overwhelming reward in the mouth of Jesus in relation to Peter: the follower will receive manifold reward.[75] However, it is basically only the reward that rests on God's grace.

14.4 The Judgment and the Separation

In the later prophetic-apocalyptic texts of the Old Testament the inner-historical conception of the "Day of YHWH" is changed into the conception of the end of the world, which brings the fates of humans to their divinely intended end.[76] At the end belongs the redemption of the people of God but also the judgment upon sinners from Israel and the nations. God is the *righteous judge* who concludes the history of humanity. Thus, in the last chapter of the book of Isaiah:[77]

> For by fire YHWH will hold judgment (with the whole earth)[78]
> . . . and by his sword with all flesh.

---

[73] Luke 17.7-10.

[74] A. Jones 1966, ad loc. Cf. Wansbrough 1985, 1718, which retains the heading "humble service."

[75] Luke 18.28-30: ὃς οὐχὶ μὴ [ἀπο]λάβῃ πολλαπλασίονα . . . ; cf. Mark 10.28-30 and Matt 19.27-29.

[76] On this, see Rad/Delling 1935, 948 (ET = 1964, 945–47); Soden/Bergman/Saebø 1982, 583 (ET = 1990, 28–30). Above all in Daniel there occurs for this terms such as *qeṣ* or *ʾaḥarît hay-yāmîm*.

[77] Isaiah 66.15a and 66.16b.

[78] V. 16 supplements with LXX: πᾶσα ἡ γῆ.

The book concludes with the portrayal of the punishment of the rebels:[79]

> For their worm shall not die and their fire shall not go out.
> They shall be an abhorrence to the whole world.

This text is taken up in Dan 12.2: Those who "sleep in the land of dust awake, the one to eternal life, the other to disgrace and eternal abhorrence." The fire of judgment in the Valley of Hinnom in the south of Jerusalem (Aramaic *gêhinnām*, Graecised γέεννα)[80] appears as eschatological place of punishment. For the Baptist's preaching of repentance the threat of the divine judgment of wrath and the "hell fire" had decisive significance; the baptism in the Jordan and the fruits of repentance were meant to preserve one from it.[81] The motif of judgment and punishment in various forms also occurs multiple times in the Synoptic Gospels, though with quite different emphases. Thus, we encounter it in the threat sayings against the Galilean places Chorazin and Bethsaida, which are marked out by Jesus' "deeds of power": "it will be more bearable for Tyre and Sidon in the judgment than for you," for they would have repented in the case of such healing miracles, and Capernaum, which was "exalted into heaven," "will descend into the kingdom of the dead." The place, which does not receive the disciples who are sent out, will suffer a worse fate on that day than Sodom and Gomorrah.[82] The queen of the South and the men of Nineveh will condemn "the men of this generation" in the judgment, for they reacted positively to Solomon's wisdom and Jonah's preaching of repentance, but in the person of Jesus "more than Solomon" and "more than Jonah" has come upon the scene.[83] Whoever rejects Jesus' preaching of the kingdom of God and his messianic activity will also be rejected in the impending judgment. These sharp sayings of Jesus point to a deep crisis already during his Galilean activity. He met with rejection and opposition from not a few of his compatriots, such as in his hometown and in the center that he chose on the northwest corner of the Lake of Gennesaret. This rejection came especially from the leading stratum. This may have prompted him at the end to take upon himself in a place-taking way the judgment for the guilt of his people, to walk the path of the servant of God, and to die at the Passover festival in Jerusalem.

---

[79] Isaiah 66.24.

[80] Jeremias 1964a (GV = 1933).

[81] Luke 3.7, 9, 17; Matt 3.7, 10, 12; see section 9.1.2.2 with note 59.

[82] Luke 10.13-15 = Matt 11.21-23; cf. Matt 11.24. On this, see section 12.2 with note 66 and section 16.1 with note 12. On this, see now Gregg 2005.

[83] Luke 11.31-32 = Matt 12.41-42.

Individual judgment paraeneses are characterized by a sharpness that gives offense. Thus, Mark has four *ṭôb* sayings, of which the first is directed against those who "cause one of these small ones who believe in me to stumble": it would be better for him if he were thrown into the sea with a millstone around the neck, i.e., he has fallen under God's judgment. The following saying exhorts one to rigorously separate from a body part that leads to sin, whether it be hand, foot, or eye. It would be better "to enter into (eternal) life" as a cripple than with one's body intact to be thrown "into Gehenna," i.e., "into the unquenchable fire." This dramatic appeal is underscored with a quotation from Isa 66.24 (LXX).[84] However, in terms of substance, this admonition basically expresses the same thing as Mark 8.36 in connection with the exhortation to suffering discipleship: "What does it profit a person to gain the whole world but forfeit his life?"[85] Participation in the kingdom of God means true life and missing it, eternal death. To be sure, it is telling that Mark speaks only once of γέεννα and its unquenchable fire, while it is mentioned by Matthew seven times in the mouth of Jesus and there are eight references to the fire of judgment.[86] Like Mark, Luke also shows conspicuous reserve in relation to this linguistic usage. Γέεννα appears in Luke 12.5, the fire of judgment occurs in a typical way twice in the concise proclamation of the Baptist, and, beyond this, as place of punishment in the kingdom of the dead (ᾅδης) very vividly in the parable of the rich man and poor Lazarus.[87] Typical of Matthew's tendency to multiply announcements of judgment is 8.12: "The sons of the kingdom will be thrown out into the outermost darkness. There will be weeping and gnashing of teeth there." We are dealing here with a formulaic linguistic usage, which Matthew also inserts into two parables.[88] The second sentence, with the formulation "weeping and gnashing of teeth," which, stemming from the sayings tradition, occurs only once in Luke[89] and

---

[84] Mark 9.42-48 = Matt 18.6-9, cf. Matt 5.29-30; Luke 17.1 formulates somewhat differently. Mark speaks twice of entering εἰς τὴν ζωήν and then εἰς τὴν βασιλείαν τοῦ θεοῦ. On the structure and meaning of the sayings, see section 12.2 with note 87. Mark is the only one who has the Isaiah quotation; cf., however, 2 Clem. 7.6 and Justin, *1 Apol.* 52.8; *Dial.* 130.2; 140.3. Matthew shortens, since he has an almost identical saying; Luke has only the warning against those who prepare stumbling blocks for "these little ones." He passes over the three sayings in Mark 9.43ff. because their drastic character does not fit in the work dedicated to Theophilus.

[85] Cf. Luke 9.25 = Matt 16.26; see note 49 above.

[86] Γέεννα: 5.22, 29-30; 10.28 (= Luke 12.5); 18.9; 23.15, 33; fire of judgment: 5.22; 7.19; 13.40, 42, 50; 18.8-9; 25.41.

[87] Baptist: Luke 3.9, 17; rich man: 16.23ff.

[88] Matthew 22.13; 25.30.

[89] Luke 13.28: in the context of the exclusion from the eschatological banquet in the kingdom of God.

which, in our judgment, Matthew has taken over from Luke, is used a total of six times[90] by the first evangelist as the conclusion of judgment parables. Precisely these parables, which are valued by him, have been elaborated by Matthew himself, usually beyond his *Vorlagen*, in which process his own contribution often covers over the inherited tradition. This applies, for example, to the parable of the tares and its interpretation,[91] to the parable of the net,[92] to the parable of the unforgiving servant,[93] and to the disruptive addition of the lacking wedding garment in the parable of the great supper, which has a completely different orientation.[94] This threat of judgment intensifies until the three great parousia parables in chapter 25, which conclude the teaching of the disciples prior to the actual passion. The ten virgins stand at the beginning in 25.1-13. Of these, five wise virgins provided for their lamps with sufficient oil, whereas five foolish ones did not. Surprised by the coming of the groom at midnight, the wise virgins can go to meet him for the wedding feast, whereas the foolish ones, who must first get oil and come too late, are shut out. The groom rejects the latter with the words "I do not know you." The evangelist concludes with the admonition to watchfulness. The parable of the talents follows in 25.14-30.[95] In this parable the "useless slave," who does not multiply the talent entrusted to him, is thrown out into the "outermost darkness." As the culmination there follows the picture of the world judgment in 25.31-46. Here the "Son of Man" and "King" on the "throne of glory" judges humanity, who are separated into "sheep" and "goats" according to their works—which remain hidden to themselves—toward "one of these least of these brothers" (25.40, 45) and thus carries out the final great separation: "and they will go, these to eternal punishment, but the righteous into eternal life." Here the theology of the evangelist, community tradition, and Jesus tradition have fused together into a indissoluble unity, with the Matthean tendency being predominant and exercising a fundamental influence upon the church's future picture of Jesus. That the coming Son of Man carries out a final separation already belonged to the content of the preaching of the Baptist and of

[90] Except for Matt 8.12; see also 13.42, 50; 22.13; 24.51; 25.30.

[91] Matthew 13.24-30, 36-43. See the end of section 12.3.

[92] Matthew 13.47-50.

[93] Matthew 18.23-25.

[94] Matthew 22.1-10 and 11-14 as Matthean addition; cf., by contrast, Luke 14.15-24.

[95] In the parallel version of Luke 19.11-27 it is only minas, i.e., six hundred grams (a talent is forty kilograms); Matthew intensifies the amount into the unrealistic; cf. also Matt 18.24: the debtor of ten thousand talents; on this, see note 115 below. Luke connects in 19.14, 27 the parable with an embassy of intractable citizens, who were punished; see the Jewish embassy to Augustus after the death of Herod, which attempts to hinder the appointment of Archelaus: Josephus, *Ant.* 17.300. On this, see the end of section 3.1.1 and the beginning of section 3.1.2.

the proclamation of Jesus himself, while Matthew admittedly identified the preaching of judgment of the Baptist and that of Jesus in terms of content.[96] The primitive community transfers the function of the judge to the exalted Christ. The judgment "according to works" becomes a firm component of the primitive Christian expectation all the way to Paul and John.[97] It is the necessary background and the presupposition of the message of radical grace, of the atonement effected by the death of Jesus, and of the love of the Father, who seeks out the sinner and wants to forgive him.

14.5 The Messianic Character of the Interpretation of the Will of God

Scholarship has gladly seen in the proclamation of Jesus an unbridgeable opposition between the eschatological-apocalyptic proclamation of the kingdom and his seemingly timeless ethical demand. Here, the "eschatological prophet" has been played off against the "wisdom teacher" with his ethical demands related to the present. A. Schweitzer attempted to balance out this opposition by means of his interim ethic theory.[98] This, however, is an incorrect interpretation. Precisely because God and his kingdom are now very near, indeed already present in the activity of Jesus—in his love for the lost and in judgment against the self-righteous—the concern is to bring to light again the original, actual will of God, which has been valid from the beginning[99] but was darkened through the power of sin and partly also through the Torah of Moses, which has been adjusted to the reign of sin. This is also the meaning of the *six antitheses* of the Sermon of the Mount in Matt 5.21-48. With the introduction "You have heard that it was said to the those of old . . . , but I say to you," the Matthean Jesus points out the difference between the commandments that Israel received on Sinai and his "messianic" Torah. While the antitheses have been configured by Matthew with great catechetical skill and with a climactic high point in 5.48: "You shall be perfect . . . ," in substance they nevertheless go back in large part to dominical tradition. An earlier form may be visible in the introduction to the Lukan Sermon on the Plain after the three beatitudes and woes: "But to you, those listening, I say: Love your enemies. . . ." The

---

[96] Luke 12.8-9 = Matt 10.32-33; Mark 8.38 = Luke 9.26 = Matt 16.27. On the Baptist and Jesus, see section 10.4.

[97] Second Corinthians 5.10; cf. Rom 2.16; 14.10ff.; Acts 10.42; 17.31; John 5.29; cf. also 15.6 and the last sentence of the Baptist speech in John 3.36.

[98] See section 13.3 with note 88.

[99] Mark 10.6: and the following quotation of Gen 1.27 and 2.24 LXX; cf. Matt 19.4-5 and 8. See also section 13.3 with notes 85–87.

closest parallel to this manner of speaking is the formulation "Amen, I say to you . . . ," which is especially frequent in Matthew.

The full, original obedience, which God had in mind since the creation of humanity, must now, since God's kingdom dawns, come into its own. Because God himself established the closest and deepest form of human community in the marriage of the first human couple, according to *the second antithesis*, committing adultery is not the first thing to transgress God's commandment from Sinai (Exod 2.14; Deut 5.18), but the lustful gaze upon another woman is already an act of adultery "in the heart." In hyperbolic radicality the Matthean Christ exhorts one to tear out the eye that prepares such an offense and to cut off the hand that leads one astray: *principiis obsta!*[100] In the *third antithesis* he prohibits a man from divorcing his wife, in accord with Deut 24.1, by means of a certificate of divorce, since he makes her into an adulteress through this—when she marries again. The only exception, which Matthew first allows to apply, is the infidelity of the wife.[101] According to the *fourth antithesis*, the Mosaic prohibition of making false oaths, which appears multiple times, is no longer adequate. One should not swear at all, for even the indirect invocation of God dishonors his name. Everything that exceeds the corroborating "yes, yes" or "no, no" has an evil origin.[102] James 5.12—"Let your yes be yes and your no be no"—probably contains an older, clearer version of this instruction. Under the banner of the kingdom of God and the fellowship with God and fellow humans that is bestowed through it, absolute truthfulness is required.

The appeal to the original will of God, for example in the double love command of the Torah,[103] does not exclude—its connection with the Golden Rule shows this—the appeal to rational insight. This is also shown by Luke 12.57: "Why do you not judge for yourself what is right?" Jesus' parables in particular—such as the good Samaritan, Luke 10.30-35, the rich man and poor Lazarus, Luke 16.19-31, the rich fool, Luke 12.16-21,

---

[100] On the antitheses, see Hengel 1999b, 267–73; Luz 1989, 273–351; 2007, 226–95 (GV = 2002, 324–416); Weder 1985, 98–155. On the second antithesis of Matt 5.27-30, cf. 18.8-9 = Mark 9.43-48. In Matthew this hyperbolic exhortation is so important that he has it twice. On the first human pair, see Gen 1.27; 2.18, 22-24; cf. Mark 10.7 parr.; Eph 5.31; see further also the *ṭôb* sayings at the end of section 12.2.

[101] Matt 5.32: παρεκτὸς λόγου πορνείας (cf. 19.9) is a Jewish Christian addition, which has grown from the community practice in the handling of Jesus' commandment in Mark 10.2-8 and attaches to the interpretation of Deut 24.1 through the school of Shammais: m. Giṭ. 9.10: "A man may divorce his wife only if he has found in her a disgraceful matter ('*ārwat dābār*)"; on this, see Bill. I: 312ff. On the first antithesis, see below. We have here an example how a commandment of Jesus is limited with casuistic justification.

[102] Matt 5.33-37.

[103] Lev 19.18; Deut 6.5; see section 14.2.

the tower construction and impending war, Luke 14.28-33, and the parable of the unrighteous steward,[104] which viewed superficially sounds very offensive—seek, after all, to explain and illustrate in a way that is drastic, practical, and evident to reason what is now God's will. And yet Jesus' demand has its validity and its meaning not from a generally available human experience and not from the mere demand of our "practical reason." It does not correspond to the virtue teaching of ancient philosophy nor does it know of a categorical imperative grounded by reason as a general "human law." Rather, it is grounded by Jesus' messianic authority and the dawning kingdom of God proclaimed by him. The second part of Lev 19.18—"You shall love your neighbor as yourself; *I am the Lord*"—must always be kept in mind. This means that through this his name is to be sanctified and his kingdom is to come! Only in this way is Jesus' partial criticism of the Torah to be explained. Because the love command presents the original and actual will of God, which is now proclaimed anew, vis-à-vis this command certain ritual individual stipulations or even the Sabbath command, if the situation requires it, can become secondary or even be annulled. When they oppose the active, concrete deed of love, they must give way. In this connection, Matthew has Jesus appeal twice to a prophetic saying: "I desire mercy and not sacrifice."[105]

Another example of this is Jesus' attack against *worry*, μεριμνᾶν.[106] After all, such worry presents only a form of fear for one's own existence. Since the expulsion of the first human couple from paradise, it is a basic human condition, which repeatedly misleads one to egoism and mercilessness. Instead of worry, what is required is thankful, cheerful trust. The lilies of the field and the ravens in Luke (or the birds under heaven in Matthew) are paradigms for this trust that is sure of the care of the heavenly Father. Worry and the concomitant egoistic striving for security are at bottom unbelief, indeed idolatry, which takes away honor from God: "No one can serve two lords; he will despise the one and love the other . . . you cannot serve God and Mammon."[107] The attachment to one's possessions proves to be a subtle kind of idolatry.[108] In other

---

[104] Luke 16.1-9: here, as the growth in v. 9 shows, an ethicizing change of meaning may have taken place. Originally, the concern, as in Matt 13.45-46 and 11.2, is with a rapidly decisive and therefore saving decision for God's kingdom.

[105] Hosea 6.6, quoted in Matt 9.13 and 12.7; on this, see Landmesser 2001, 186–87 index; see section 13.3 on the conflict over healing on the Sabbath.

[106] Luke 12.22ff. = Matt 6.25ff.

[107] Luke 16.13 = Matt 6.24. Μαμωνᾶς from Aramaic (*status emphaticus*) *māmônā'* "possessions, assets." On this, see Bauer/Aland/Aland 1988, 994. According to Rüger 1973, it was originally a Canaanite loanword with the meaning "nourishment, provisioning, reserves."

[108] Cf. Col 3.5; Eph 5.5; 1 Tim 6.10.

words: Only *one* can be Lord, the one who had grounded the love command with ^{a}*nî* ^{a}*dōnāy*, ἐγώ εἰμι κύριος, and only one single "worry" is demanded, the worry for the kingdom of God: "Seek his βασιλεία and all these things (about which you worry) will be added to you" (Luke 12.31). In Matt 6.33, the evangelist, in accordance with his theology, adds to βασιλεία "and his righteousness." To the command of "lack of worry" corresponds the fourth petition of the Lord's Prayer: "Give us today our bread for tomorrow."[109] The whole prayer, which Jesus teaches his disciples, is an expression of childlike trust in the Father, who knows what his children need before they ask (Matt 6.8), and who does not refuse them his good gifts (Matt 7.11 = Luke 11.3). Behind the whole Lord's Prayer stands the certainty of being heard (see chapter 15 with note 24).

The will of the God who draws near, which Jesus proclaims and which is connected with the good work of the creator (cf. Gen 1.31), means at the same time the nullification of the primordial disastrous fate in which the human being as a prisoner of evil has entangled himself from the beginning. The rejection of worry in connection with the reference to lilies and ravens is an expression of the removal of the curse after the fall.[110] When Jesus, in the sending out tradition, announces to the disciples: "Behold, I have given you power to walk on serpents and scorpions, and over all power of the enemy, and nothing will harm you," this puts an end to the power of the old serpent from Gen 3.15, and the messianic promises are thereby fulfilled.[111]

The threat of judgment in relation to the insult that injures the neighbor in the *first antithesis*, which goes far beyond the prohibition of killing in Gen 9.6 or the fifth commandment in Exod 20.13, and the nullification of the Old Testament "eye for an eye, tooth for a tooth" in the *fifth antithesis*,[112] in connection with the fundamental renunciation of violence and the demand for constant unconditional readiness for forgiveness and

---

[109] Matthew 6.11, cf. Did. 8.2; Luke 11.3 has replaced σήμερον with καθ᾿ ἡμέραν; cf. Luke 9.23; 16.19; 19.47; 22.53; Acts 2.46-47; 3.2 and elsewhere. The meaning of ἐπιού-σιος is uncertain; see Bauer/Aland/Aland 1988, 601; Blass/Debrunner/Rehkopf, § 123.1; Wolter 2016/2017, II: 92–94. A conceivable alternative would be "our necessary-for-life bread." Philonenko 2002, 76–86, refers to the daily gift of manna in Exod 16.4-5 (78) and advocates—in a similar way as Jeremias 1970, 199–200 (GV = 1979, 193–94)—an eschatological reference to the messianic meal. See, however, Luz 1989, 380–83; 2007, 319–22 (GV = 2002, 449–52), and the ninth petition of the Eighteen Benedictions.

[110] Genesis 3.16-19; on this, see Hengel 1999b, 280–82. On this, see 374.

[111] Luke 10.19; cf. Ps 91.13 and the reference to the messianic kingdom of peace in Isa 11.8-9; Hos 2.20.

[112] Matthew 5.21ff.; 5.38; cf. Exod 21.24; Lev 24.20; Deut 19.21 (against the false witness, who threatens the life of his comrade): "You shall practice no leniency, life for life, eye for eye, tooth for tooth, hand for hand, foot for foot."

reconciliation,[113] aim at an entirely new relationship to fellow human beings. Once and for all an end is put to the murderous evil spirit of Cain, who treacherously murdered his brother, and that of his descendent Lamech from Gen 4, who requited a minor injury with homicide and whose longing for revenge is insatiable.[114] In response to Peter's question of whether it was enough to forgive the brother who sins seven times, Jesus answers: "not seven times but seventy seven times" — as often as Lamech wanted to be avenged — and, according to the Matthean special material, he recounts after this the kingdom of God parable about the "unforgiving servant," who wanted to collect by force a small debt of a hundred denarii from a fellow slave, although his lord had forgiven him the immeasurable debt of ten thousand talents.[115] The one who sets himself up as a judge over his fellow human beings must also reckon on being judged by the same standard by God himself.[116] It belongs to the corrupt hypocritical nature of the human being to see the "splinter" in the eye of the other, but not perceive the "beam" in one's own eye.[117] Accordingly, in the fifth petition of the Lord's Prayer, the forgiveness that is asked for from the Father is inseparably connected with the forgiveness granted to the neighbor (Matt 6.12 = Luke 11.4). The near kingdom of God aims at the restitution of the original, beneficial, and good order of the creator, where a human being relates to his fellow human being as God in his love relates to him. Through this the human gains the freedom not only to love the enemy but also to renounce one's own right to retaliation and all counterviolence, extending to the paradoxical demand to make no resistance to the wrong that is done to oneself, such as in the fifth antithesis of Matt 5.38-42:

You have heard that it was said:
"An eye for an eye and a tooth for a tooth."[118]

---

[113] On forgiveness, see Luke 11.4 = Matt 6.12; Matt 6.14-15; 18.21-22, 35; cf. Mark 11.25. On reconciliation, see the double example that follows the first antithesis in Matt 5.23-26. Luke 12.58-59 recounts the second example in greater detail. Matthew could be dependent upon Luke here.

[114] Genesis 4.24: "If Cain is avenged sevenfold, then Lamech seventy-sevenfold." In connection with the anger of Cain against Abel, R. Akiba, according to Midrash Bereshit Rabbah 22.6 (Theodor/Albeck 1965, I: 210), stresses the *principiis obsta*: "At first sin is like a spider web but at the end it is like a ship's rope."

[115] Matthew 18.21-35 (special material). According to Josephus, *Ant.* 17.318–320, the yearly tax yield of the sons of Herod Archelaus, Antipas, and Philip was nine hundred talents. The high debts of the young Herod Agrippa, which threatened his friendship with Tiberius, amounted to ca. sixty talents: *Ant.* 18.158–165.

[116] Luke 6.37-38 = Matt 7.1-2; cf. Mark 4.24.

[117] Luke 6.41-42 = Matt 7.3-5.

[118] Exodus 21.24; Lev 24.20; Deut 19.21.

But I say to you:
Do not resist an evildoer,[119]
but whoever strikes you on the right cheek,
hold to him also the other,[120]
and to the one who wants to sue you and take your outer garment,
to him hand over also your undergarment.
And whoever wants to force you (to go) one mile,
go with him two.
To the one who asks from you, give,
And whoever wants to borrow from you, from him do not turn away.[121]

Whoever can renounce his right and its implementation, whoever is prepared to suffer rather than do wrong, is truly free, like the fatherly God and
Creator, "who makes his sun rise on the evil and on the good and makes
it rain on the righteous and the unrighteous" (Matt 5.45). Like the Good
Samaritan, he is therefore capable also of unconditional aid to others, even
if this involves personal danger.[122]

Paul, who is dependent in various ways on the teaching of Jesus in
his paraenesis, quotes as a concluding point of his paraenesis in Rom 12
the exhortation of Prov 25.21, which points in the same direction: "If
your enemy is hungry, feed him, if he is thirsty, give him something to
drink . . . ," and he adds as a final point: "Do not be overcome by evil but
overcome evil with good."[123] We must remember here that these sayings
of Jesus were spoken into an environment filled by hate against religious,
political, and social opponents. The love of the heavenly Father wants to
bring back lost human beings, to make them "God's children,"[124] which
means to change them fundamentally and renew them. We could therefore
place the phrase *"but seek his kingdom"* from Luke 12.31[125] as a motto

[119] Matthew 5.39: μὴ ἀντιστῆναι τῷ πονηρῷ.

[120] Cf. Lam 3.30; Isa 50.6. It is the conduct of the servant of God.

[121] Cf. Matt 6.31-32 = Luke 6.29-30. The shorter Lukan version may be the older
version.

[122] Cf. Luke 10.30-35; 15.20-32; 19.8; Mark 10.21 parr.

[123] Rom 12.20-21. This applies also to the relationship to the political powers, which
he addresses right afterward in 13.1-7, and to the paraenesis in 13.8ff. with the reference
to the love of neighbor as the fulfillment of the law, the quotation from the Decalogue and
from Lev 19.18.

[124] Matthew 5.45: ὅπως γένησθε υἱοὶ τοῦ πατρὸς ὑμῶν τοῦ ἐν οὐρανοῖς; cf.
Luke 6.35.

[125] As a conclusion to the collection of sayings on worry in Luke 12.22-31. To the
phrase τὴν βασιλείαν τοῦ θεοῦ Matt 6.33 adds the key phrase καὶ τὴν δικαιοσύνην
αὐτοῦ, which is important for him. Cf. 3.15; 5.6, 10, 20; 21.32. The term δικαιοσύνη is
completely lacking in Mark and Luke (except in the Benedictus in Luke 1.75). On this, see

over the whole eschatologically motivated ethical proclamation of Jesus. Through his fall and the expulsion from the garden of Eden, Adam lost his very home in the fellowship with God. Only trusting, obedient listening to Jesus' entirely extraordinary message, which transcends the existing prophetic imperative because with the kingdom of God it brings liberation and redemption, can regain this. Therefore, with good justification, we can also designate the "ethical preaching" of Jesus as "messianic."

Hengel 1999b, 249–54; Stuhlmacher 1965, 188–89 and on Jesus 240–57; Deines 2004, 441–46 and 710 index on Matt 6.33.

15

The Fatherly Love of God[1]

Jesus does not proclaim—as Marcion later claimed and as is repeated time and again, in particular in German Protestantism in various degrees up to the present—a new, unknown God, i.e., the God of love in contrast to an "Old Testament" God of justice and wrathful judgment. The God whose near kingdom he announced is the God of the old covenant. It is the God who created "heaven and earth," who, as Creator and Lord, is the Father already for Israel and is addressed as such by his children.[2] It is "the God of Abraham, Isaac, and Jacob," who, as the God of the fathers, is a God of the living and not of the dead and who with the coming of his kingdom calls the dead into life again, "for they all live to him."[3] Therefore, according to the witness of the prophet, with the dawning of the kingdom of God,

---

[1] Jeremias 1970, 61ff. (GV = 1979, 67ff.); Fitzmyer 1985.

[2] Genesis 1.1; 14.19; cf. Luke 10.21 = Matt 11.25: "Father, Lord of heaven and earth." Cf. Deut 32.6: "Is he not your Father and your Lord? Is it not he alone who created and prepared you?"; Isa 63.16-17: "But you are our Father. Abraham does not know us, and Israel wants to know nothing of us. You, YHWH, are our Father!" Cf. 64.7: "But now, YHWH, you are our Father!" See further God's accusation in Jer 3.4—"Do you not now cry out to me: my Father (*'ābî*)?"—and God's lament in Jer 3.19, 22: "I had thought: I want to regard you as a son . . . I thought: you will call me 'my Father' (*'ābî*). . . . Return, you renegade children, I will heal you from your disobedience." On Israel as God's firstborn son, see Exod 4.22; Jer 31.9. Hos 11.1 ("out of Egypt I have called my son") is related to the child Jesus as a fulfillment quotation in Matt 2.15.

[3] Mark 12.26-27; Luke 20.37-38. "Abraham, Isaac and Jacob and all the prophets" will "sit at table" (ἀνακλιθήσονται) as God's guests in the kingdom of God at the eschatological banquet, Luke 13.29. Salvation applies to Abraham's children, Luke 13.16; 19.9, including those who will be made into such: Matt 3.9; cf. also "Abraham's bosom" in Luke 16.22ff. After all, through Abraham all the nations of the earth are to be blessed, Gen 12.3, cf. Jer 4.2; Sir 44.21 (Hebrew) and Gal 3.8, 14; Acts 3.25. The promise begins to be fulfilled in Jesus' activity. The primitive Christian Gentile mission of the "Hellenists" is a consequence of this activity.

the people of God expect "a new heaven and a new earth."[4] For this reason, YHWH will "destroy death forever" and "wipe away the tears from every face."[5] Even though Jesus criticizes and adjusts the Torah of Moses in individual points and in certain situations, he certainly does not want to reject it fundamentally. Rather, we must assume that he usually kept it as a matter of course.[6] His concern is rather with letting the true will of God, which has been darkened by Israel's "hardness of heart,"[7] shine forth again in full power. The Torah as God's will is to become visible again in its original meaning, which accords with the good Creator and Lord of history. Jesus lives within the given framework of Jewish piety, taking it for granted. He wants neither to break out of his people nor to do away with the Torah. The Pharisees became his especially prominent opponents because they were his most intensive conversation partners in the controversy dialogues and because of all the Jewish "religious parties" they stood closest to him. After all, he presumably grew up in a family that was familiar with the Pharisaic form of piety.[8] On the other hand, it is quite certain that Jesus did not have a Pharisaic, scribal education. It is only with Paul—the former Pharisaic scribe—that we read "Christ is the end of the law for righteousness for everyone who believes."[9] And yet precisely the center, the heart of the proclamation of Jesus differs from other Jewish groups, even from that of the Baptist. It is not sufficient to emphasize only its theocentric character, which it has in common with others. Its proprium is the proclamation of the *love of God, the goodness of the Father*.

Jesus' messianic mission culminates neither in the announcement of the judgment nor in the call to repentance in the form of a "call to decision"—in both features he does not differ fundamentally from the Baptist—but rather in the announcement of the kingdom of God as the now already dawning deliverance of the lost and the joy over the salvation

---

[4] Isaiah 65.17; 66.22, cf. 51.6 and Rev 21.1; 2 Pet 3.13.

[5] Isaiah 25.8, cf. 11.9; Rev 21.4, 7.

[6] In contrast to Stephen and Jesus' law-strict brother James, who was stoned as a "breaker of the law" together with other Christians according to Josephus, *Ant.* 20.200, Jesus, apart from conflicts over the Sabbath (Mark 3.1-6 parr.), was not accused of not keeping the law, though the accusation was made that he dared to forgive sins and to receive sinners (Mark 2.7 parr. βλασφημεῖ, 2.16 parr.; Luke 7.48; cf. 7.34 par). On the charge due to βλασφημία at the interrogation by the Sanhedrin, see section 20.2.1 with note 33.

[7] Mark 10.5 = Matt 19.8: πρὸς τὴν σκληροκαρδίαν ὑμῶν; cf. Deut 10.16; Jer 4.4; Ezek 3.7 (LXX).

[8] Hengel/Deines 1996 (ET = 1995); Deines 1997; see also section 8.3 with notes 59–60.

[9] Romans 10.4; cf., by contrast, Matt 5.17-20, which sounds entirely different. To be sure, it refers not to the whole wording of the Torah but to its "messianic" interpretation in the Sermon on the Mount, which follows.

bestowed upon them through the love of the Father. Their "decision," their "repentance" is only possible because the heavenly Father already decided for them—i.e., in their favor. Through Jesus he wants to seek them out. This turn to the lost who have gone astray and to the outcasts among the Jewish people encounters opposition from the established piety. In this turn Jesus' consciousness of his messianic mission becomes especially clear: "I have not come to call the righteous but sinners."[10] It was the will (εὐδοκία) of the Father to grant his revelation through the Son to "the simple ones" (τοῖς νηπίοις).[11] In the three parables in Luke 15—two of them come from the special material of the evangelist[12]—he demonstrates the revelation of the love of the Father to the failures, hopeless, and lost, who were regarded as sinners in the public opinion: first in the double parable of the lost sheep and lost denarius and then in the great, almost novelistically developed parable of the lost son. In all three the narrative climax is not the finding or the repentance but rather, as J. Jeremias rightly stressed,[13] the joy over the finding—the joy of the Father over the homecoming of the lost children, so to speak: hence, Luke 15.7: "In the same way there will be joy in heaven over *one* sinner who repents, more than over ninety-nine righteous who need no repentance." This joy in heaven among the angels of God has its earthly and human counterpart in the overwhelming joy of the farmer who finds the treasure and of the merchant who finds the unique pearl and who sell all their possessions to buy them.[14]

While the scribes—according to Luke and Matthew—close down access to the kingdom of God through their demands that distort the will of God, Jesus opens it precisely for those who are excluded by the pious. While the scribes possess the key to it through the interpretation of the Torah, they do not enter themselves and hinder others from entering.[15]

---

[10] Mark 2.17 parr. Cf. the corresponding conclusion in 19.10, which is formulated by Luke, and on this Ezek 34.16: "I will seek the lost, lead back the scattered, bind up the broken, strengthen the sick."

[11] Luke 10.21 = Matt 11.25-26.

[12] Luke 15.8-10, 11-32. Vv. 3-7, the parable of the lost sheep, appear, with changed wording to some extent, in Matt 18.12-14 in the completely different context of community discipline. The Matthean version evinces the different, later situation of the evangelist. See also Gos. Thom. 107.

[13] Jeremias 1972, 128ff. (GV = 1998, 128ff.); cf. also section 10.3.

[14] Matthew 13.44ff. (special material). See the end of section 13.4 with note 100 and section 13.2 with note 29.

[15] Luke 11.52; expanded in the temporally later parallel of Matt 23.13. Vis-à-vis Luke 11.37-54 this polemic is increased in Matt 23 due to the special situation of the community between 90–100 CE in relation to Palestinian Judaism under Pharisaic-scribal leadership, which regained strength after the catastrophe of 70 CE. Cf. also Jesus' polemic against the tradition of the elders in Mark 7.1-13 = Matt 15.1-9.

Concretely, this opening occurs in the pronouncement of the forgiveness of guilt, i.e., of the nullification of the curse under which humans have stood ever since the fall. Here it becomes clear that the love of the Father precedes every human insight into one's own guilt. In the parable of the lost son the father sees the approaching wretched figure from afar, as if he had always been on the lookout for him, hurries to meet the one who is returning home, and then embraces and kisses him. Only now does the son confess: "Father, I have sinned against heaven and before you . . . I am no longer worthy to be called your son." However, the father commands his slaves: "Bring quickly the most valuable robe and clothe him with it, and put on him (as a sign of his newly granted dignity of son) a ring on the finger."[16] The acceptance is already evident before the confession of sin. God's prevenient love encounters the human first; it creates the condition for repentance and confession of guilt. Repentance becomes gift. The desperate decision of the son to return home is only a preliminary stage. He sets out for home out of a naked drive for self-preservation, so that he does not perish among the swine. That he will be received again as a son by the father is something that he cannot envisage. The older brother, who has always been obedient thus far and who is indignant at the feast of joy that is now beginning, is challenged by the father to let himself be overwhelmed by the joy over the return of the younger brother. The Father also does not withdraw his love from the older brother, who angrily protests out of an understandable human (indeed all too human) sense of justice. Nor does he let him remain outside: "Child, you are always with me, and everything that is mine is yours." He too should participate in the feast of joy.[17] No text of the Synoptic Gospels points out as clearly the way from Jesus to Paul as the parable of the lost son. This turning without precondition in connection with the joy that overcomes all opposition is what is decisive in this unique narrative. What oriental family head would have dared to act in such an unusual way? One need only think of the behavior of Herod toward his sons and the controversy between brothers among the Hasmoneans.

The chief tax collector Zacchaeus, who was small in stature, climbs, due to the large crowd that waits for Jesus, up a sycamore tree so that he, in his great curiosity, can see Jesus (Luke 19.1-10). Jesus spots him there, calls him down, and wants to stay at the house of this unpopular rich tax collector, despite the protest of the inhabitants of Jericho. The joy

---

[16] Luke 15.20-22. On this, see Rengstorf 1967b.

[17] Here one is reminded of the outrageous statement that Paul places at the end of his theological-soteriological argumentation in Romans: "God has shut up all in disobedience in order that he may have mercy on all" (11.32).

with which he receives Jesus (ὑπεδέξατο . . . χαίρων, v. 6) finds expression in a radical change of his life, which includes making restitution in a thoroughgoing manner (v. 8). Jesus, who, according to Luke, acts in the place of God, promises salvation to him and his family. After all, he too is a son of Abraham (v. 9). The task of the Son of Man, for which he is authorized by the Father, is to "seek and save the lost" (v. 10). It is no wonder that this Son of Man is reviled by his opponents as "friend of tax collectors and sinners" (Luke 7.34 = Matt 11.19). At the same time, it becomes understandable that the strict Matthew, who knew the Gospel of Luke and sometimes also made use of it, left aside this and related texts.

The concern is with unmerited caring also in the healing of the paralytic according to Mark, in which Jesus speaks forgiveness to the sick man without testing his worthiness, simply on the basis of faith, which manifested itself in the way he was brought by four others.[18] The same is true for the story of the woman who is a great sinner in Luke 7.36-50, where Jesus answers the protest of the Pharisee Simon, who takes offense at the fact that he lets his feet be anointed by a prostitute, with the parable of the two debtors. The one who was forgiven a great debt—without precondition—is capable of special love.[19] This means that love of God and of neighbor grow out of the joy of receiving a gift, out of gratitude—even more: out of the power of the love of God that changes the heart. In the Lord's Prayer, Luke 11.4, the petition for forgiveness grounds our readiness to forgive the brother, as in Matthew in the parable of the unforgiving servant,[20] in which the remission of an unimaginable financial debt of ten thousand talents stands at the beginning.

The experience of the all-encompassing love of God teaches humans complete trust, the *ᵃmûnāh* or πίστις[21] that moves mountains, and it manifests itself in the certainty that one's prayers are answered. The Lukan special material contains some examples of this. The prayer of the tax collector in the temple, who beats his breast and prays, "God be merciful to me a sinner," is a prayer of trust that God will be merciful to the sinner. Therefore "he went home justified" in contrast to the Pharisee.[22] A primitive Christian prayer paraenesis from this very Lukan special material encourages one to "pray at all times and not lose heart" and grounds this with several parables of Jesus. If an "unjust judge" who "neither fears God nor regards humans" reluctantly fulfills the wish of a widow who

---

[18] Mark 2.5 = Luke 5.20 = Matt 9.2: καὶ ἰδὼν ὁ Ἰησοῦς τὴν πίστιν αὐτῶν.

[19] Luke 7.40ff.

[20] Matthew 18.23-35; see note 115 in chapter 14.

[21] Mark 11.22; see section 18.4 with note 91.

[22] Luke 18.9-14. The word δεδικαιωμένος "justified (by God)," which is unique in the Gospels, is a 'Pauline' formulation in Luke.

constantly harasses him in order that he might give her justice so that she might leave him alone, how much more will God establish justice without delay for "his elect who call to him day and night." The Father does not leave in the lurch the assailed community of disciples who constantly pray for his intervention.[23] This is also made clear by the parable of the friend who asks at the completely opportune time of midnight, disturbing the sleep of the whole family (Luke 11.5ff.). Even if the one who is asked would not fulfill the request because it is his friend who stands before the door, he nevertheless does it because of his "pushiness" (ἀναίδεια). Precisely this "pushiness" in prayer is an expression of that complete trust in the fatherly goodness and care of God, which an essential basic component of Jesus' proclamation of the kingdom of God. Luke attaches the almost enthusiastic-sounding exhortation:

> Thus I say to you:
> Pray, and it will be given to you,
> seek, and you will find,
> knock and it will be given to you.

This is followed by another parable:

> But which father among you does his son ask for a fish, and instead of
> a fish will he give him a snake? Or he asks for an egg, and will he give
> him a scorpion? If you who are evil know how to give your children good
> gifts, how much more will the Father from heaven give the Holy Spirit to
> those who ask him?[24]

The Father certainly gives what his children need.

This finds expression most beautifully in the so-called Lord's Prayer, which begins with the trustful Father address, which Jesus taught his disciples, the intimate Aramaic "*Abba*," "dear Father," which was scarcely used as an address of God because of its familiarity. The common Palestinian Jewish formula was the formulation "Our Father in heaven" — attested since the beginning of the second century CE — which Matt 6.9 reintroduces

---

[23] Luke 18.1-8a (special material). Luke grounds this with the parousia, which is expected soon, and in v. 8b attaches the question of whether the Son of Man at his coming will still find such faith (πίστις, see section 16.2), which becomes visible in prayer, in the earthly community. On the prayer paraenesis, see Luke 21.36; Rom 12.12; 1 Thess 5.17; Phil 4.6; Col 4.2. The continuity with the Pauline paraenesis is obvious.

[24] Luke 11.5-13; cf. the more concise version in Matt 7.7-11. In 7.11 Matthew replaces the "Holy Spirit" of Luke 11.13 with a simple ἀγαθά "good things." John takes up the motif christologically in the Farewell Discourses: 14.13-14; 15.7; 16.24; cf. 1 John 3.22; 5.14.

into the Lord's Prayer in contrast to the older version of Luke 11.2. The simple vocative πάτεϱ in Luke 11.2 presupposes the simple "*Abba.*" The Matthean version "Our Father in heaven" more strongly expresses the distance again. We find the address "*Abba*" in the Aramaic original text—to be sure, in a context that is central for the evangelist—only once in the Gospels, namely in Mark 14.36, where the evangelist consciously has Jesus' prayer in Gethsemane begin with this word. However, it also lies behind the absolute ὁ πατήϱ or πάτεϱ in Matthew and Luke.[25] Even the Greek-speaking mission communities of Paul take over this Aramaic prayer-cry as a Spirit-effected expression of their assurance of faith.[26] The concern here is with the first word of the Lord's Prayer, which is also known to them.[27] What is peculiar here is that Jesus often speaks of "your Father" vis-à-vis the disciples but of "my Father" in relation to himself, whereas he never gathers together himself and the disciples with an "our Father."[28] Behind this probably stands the uniqueness of his relation to God and his special consciousness of his sonship (*Sohnesbewußtsein*), which could be designated as the "secret of his sonship" (*Sohnesgeheimnis*) and which is inseparably connected with his messianic sending. For the Synoptic Gospels the pronouncement of the voice from heaven at the baptism of Jesus—"You are my beloved Son, with you I am well pleased"—has the character of a commissioning of Jesus for his "messianic service."[29] Here the decisive difference between Jesus and the Baptist already becomes clear for them, which is then intensified further by the Fourth Evangelist. With the Lord's Prayer he teaches his disciples how they are to pray to the Father, because they are his children.

---

[25] Matthew 11.25; Luke 10.21; 11.2; 22.42; 23.34, 46.

[26] Romans 8.15; Gal 4.6.

[27] Jeremias 1966a; Philonenko 2002; Hengel 2004a, 173.

[28] ὁ πατὴϱ ὑμῶν: Mark 11.25; Luke 6.36; 12.30, 32; especially often in Matthew in the Sermon on the Mount: 5.16, 45, 48 (cf. Luke 6.36); 6.1, 14-15, 32; 7.11; but also 10.20, 29; 18.14; 23.9; see in addition ὁ πατὴϱ μου: 7.21; 10.32-33; 11.27 (= Luke 10.22); 15.13; 16.17; 18.10, 19, 35.

[29] Mark 1.11; Hengel 2004a and section 10.1 with note 11.

PART V
Jesus' Authority and Messianic Claim

16

The Prophetic-Messianic Miracle Worker[1]

In the earliest non-Christian mention of Jesus at all, the Testimonium Flavianum of Flavius Josephus, which arose ca. 90 CE, his "astonishing deeds," παράδοξα ἔργα, are emphasized as a special characteristic of this "messiah."[2] This judgment confirms the New Testament tradition.

EXCURSUS
The Miracle Stories

Traditionally the numerous variant rich seams in the four Gospels about the miraculous deeds of Jesus are assigned to different genres. In overview these include:

---

[1] Hengel/Hengel 1959; 1980 (= Hengel 2007b, 1–27); Pesch 1970; Theissen 1983 (GV = 1974); Hengel 1984a, 16ff. (ET = 1985b, 11ff.); Bultmann 1963, 218–44 (GV = 1995, 233–60); Twelftree 1993; 1999; 2017; Van Uytfanghe 2001; Meier 1994, 509–1038; Theissen/Merz 1998, 281–313 (GV = 1997, 256–83); Dunn 2003b, 667–96. On the concept of faith, see Roloff 1970, 141ff.; Betz/Grimm 1977.

[2] Josephus, *Ant.* 18.63: ἦν γὰρ (sc. Ἰησοῦς) παραδόξων ἔργων ποιητής. For the meaning of παράδοξος Rengstorf's Josephus concordance (Rengstorf 1973–1983, III: 288) provides the translation "unexpected, surprising, astonishing, unordinary, rare, strange, unbelievable, miraculous." These different nuances are heard here. On the meaning of the word, see also Bauer/Aland/Aland 1988, 1244–45. On the question of the Christian editing of the passage, see section 3.1.3 with note 82 and section 6.3 with note 58. As "so-called anointed one," which is not meant negatively, Josephus mentions Jesus in his note about the stoning of James, the brother of the Lord (*Ant.* 20.200: τὸν ἀδελφὸν Ἰησοῦ τοῦ λεγομένου Χριστοῦ).

1. Summaries (*Sammelberichte*)

With these notices the evangelists emphasize among other things that they cannot recount all of the healings of Jesus.[3] Their use in Mark served as a model for the others, for example (1) Mark 1.32ff. = Luke 4.40-41 = Matt 8.16; (2) Mark 1.39 = Matt 4.23-24 (cf. Matt 9.35); (3) Mark 3.10ff. = Luke 6.17ff. (cf. Matt 12.15-16); (4) Mark 6.55-56 = Matt 14.35-36. Beyond this, in Luke the women whom Jesus healed are mentioned by name in a short, historically valuable reference (8.2-3);[4] a general reference to the healing of sick people also appears in the question of the Baptist (Luke 7.21). In an exaggerating way, Matthew likes to add "all" sick and sicknesses to his Markan *Vorlage* (Matt 4.23-24; 8.16-17), and in 21.14, in contrast to Mark and Luke, he recounts healings in Jerusalem. John does not use any summaries, but the hyperbolic concluding verses of John 20.30 and 21.25 are reminiscent of them.

2. Healings and exorcisms

These form the majority of the miracle stories.[5] Mark is also foundational for the individual stories. Luke and Matthew follow him with their Synoptic parallel accounts, with Matthew usually shortening the stories:

(1) the possessed man in the synagogue: Mark 1.23-26 = Luke 4.33-35;
(2) the healing of Peter's mother-in-law: Mark 1.30-31 = Luke 4.38-39 = Matt 8.14-15;
(3) the leper: Mark 1.40-44 = Luke 5.12-14 = Matt 8.2-4;
(4) the paralytic: Mark 2.1-12 = Luke 5.17-26 = Matt 9.1-8;
(5) the man with the paralyzed hand: Mark 3.1-6 = Luke 6.6-11 = Matt 12.9-14;
(6) the Gerasene demoniac: Mark 5.1-20 = Luke 8.26-39 = Matt 8.28-34;
(7) the daughter of Jairus: Mark 5.21-24, 35-43 = Luke 8.40-42, 49-56 = Matt 9.18-19, 23-26;
(8) the woman with a flow of blood: Mark 5.25-34 = Luke 8.43-48 = Matt 9.20-22;
(9) the daughter of the Syrophoenician woman: Mark 7.24-30 = Matt 15.21-28;
(10) the deaf man with a speech impediment: Mark 7.31-37 = Matt 15.29-31;

---

[3] On this, see in more detail section 16.1; cf. also Meier 1994, 618.

[4] On this, cf. section 16.1; Aune 1980, 1524; Meier 1994, 618, 635 n. 7; Stuhlmacher 2018, 95ff. (GV = 1992, 81ff.); Wilckens 2002–2005, I/1: 139–63.

[5] Aune 1980, 1524, and Meier 1994, 618, 635 n. 7, count six exorcisms and seven healings (including the raisings of the dead), with Meier rightly pointing out that the traditional form-critical divisions fall short of the mark.

(11) the blind man at Bethsaida: Mark 8.22-26;

(12) the possessed boy: Mark 9.14-29 = Luke 9.37-43 = Matt 17.14-21;

(13) blind Bartimaeus: Mark 10.46-52 = Luke 18.35-43 = Matt 20.29-34 (cf. Matt 9.27-31);

Only in Luke and Matthew:

(14) the mute (Matthew: and blind) demoniac: Luke 11.14(-23) = Matt 12.22-23(-30);

In Lukan special material:

(15) the bent woman: Luke 13.10-17;

(16) the man with dropsy: Luke 14.1-6;

(17) the ten lepers: Luke 17.11-19;

(18) the ear of the high priest's servant: Luke 22.50-51.

Special material in John:

(19) the paralytic at the pool of Bethesda: John 5.1-9;

(20) the man born blind: John 9.

Material common to Luke, Matthew, and John:

(21) the healing from a distance of the slave of the centurion: Luke 7.1-10; Matt 8.5-13; of the son of a royal official: John 4.46b-54.

3. Raisings of the dead

From the Synoptic tradition we can adduce here the daughter of Jairus (see heading 2, number 7 above); Luke 7.11-16 (special material): the young man in Nain; further John 11 (special material): Lazarus.

4. Epiphany miracles

The walking on the sea can be classified here form-critically (Mark 6.45-52 = Matt 14.22-33 = John 6.16-21); further, the transfiguration (Mark 9.2-10; Luke 9.28-36; Matt 17.1-9). The Easter stories, too, are epiphany stories.

5. Gift miracles

The feeding of the four thousand (Mark 8.1-9 = Matt 15.32-38); the feeding of the five thousand occurs in all four Gospels (Mark 6.35-44; Luke 9.12-17; Matt 14.15-21; John 6.5-13). There are two variants of the miraculous catch of fish (Luke 5.1-11; John 21.1-11). The wine miracle in Cana (2.1-11) is Johannine special material. The coin in the fish's mouth (Matt 17.24-27) is Matthean special material.

6. Rescue miracles

The stilling of the storm can be designated as a rescue miracle (Mark 4.35-41; Luke 8.22-25; Matt 8.23-27); the rescue of the sinking Peter in Matt 14.28-33 (special material) can also be assigned here.

7. Punitive miracles

For this genre, which was popular in the Old Testament, early Judaism, and later in Christianity, there is only the example of the withered fig tree (Mark 11.12-14, 20-25 = Matt 21.18-22).

Thematically related to the miracle stories are the references to Jesus' fore-knowledge and to his superhuman knowledge of the hearts of others.[6] They also underline the portrayal of him as a messianic miracle worker:

Jesus perceives the thoughts of his opponents (Mark 2.8 = Luke 5.22 = Matt 9.4; Luke 11.17 = Matt 12.25), he announces the destruction of the temple (Mark 13.2 = Luke 19.43-44; 21.6, 20; Matt 23.38; 24.2); the "sign of Jonah" could also have originally referred to the destruction of Jerusalem.[7] The passion predictions, which are elaborated in the Gospels, have retained their original form in Luke 12.50; 13.33 and Mark 9.31a; 10.38-39 (cf. Mark 8.31; 10.33-34; Luke 9.22, 44; 17.25; 18.32-33; 24.7; Matt 16.21; 17.22-23; 20.18-19; 26.2; John 12.32-33). Mark already portrays the preparation of the entry into Jerusalem and the careful choice of the place for the last Pass-over meal as sovereign foreknowledge. The announcement of Peter's denial (Mark 14.30 = Luke 22.34 = Matt 26.34 = John 13.38) and the announce-ment of the betrayal by Judas Iscariot (Mark 14.18-21 = Luke 22.21-22 = Matt 26.21-24; John 6.64; 13.10-11, 21-27) are presumably not *vaticinia ex eventu*. We could also adduce the promise of martyrdom to the two sons of Zebedee (Mark 10.39-40 = Matt 20.23). The prediction of suffering to the disciples as well as their future fasting (Mark 2.20 parr.) are probably shaped by post-Easter experiences. This also applies to the Synoptic apocalypse in Mark 13.3-37 parr.[8]

John emphasizes the superhuman knowledge of Jesus most strongly; cf. 1.48: "before Philip called you, I saw you under the fig tree"; 2.4b: "my hour has not yet come"; 4.17-18 in relation to the Samaritan woman: "you have no husband"; 6.61: Jesus knows of his own accord the grumbling of the disciples; 11.14: Lazarus is already dead; 13.1, 3; 18.4: "Since Jesus knew everything that was coming upon him . . ."; cf. 19.28; he also announces mar-tyrdom to Peter (13.36; 21.18-19).

---

[6] Thus also Meier 1994, 618.

[7] Luke 11.29; Matt 12.39; 16.4; Liv. Pro. 10.8; cf. Schwemer 1995/1996, II: 78–82; Mittmann-Richert 2000, 170; on this, see section 16.1 with note 33.

[8] The authenticity of Mark 13.3-27 has now been vehemently defended by Pitre 2005, 231–53, 264–92, 264–92, 348–79.

16.1 The Healings of Jesus as Signs of His Messianic Authority

"By far the deepest impression Jesus made upon his contemporaries was as an exorcist and a healer." This sentence occurs not in a theological monograph but in the Jesus book of the ancient historian Michael Grant.[9] Relatively independently of one another, Mark, Luke, Matthew, and in his own way John testify to the fact that for the Galilean rural population Jesus' healing miracles possessed an even stronger appeal and attracted even greater attention than his preaching and yet also to the fact that the two cannot be separated. This applies first to the *summaries* of healings and exorcisms, which usually receive too little attention. They are not simply free redactional formations of the evangelists in the configuration of the "framework" of the Gospels, but go back as manifestations of a "collective memory" to kerygmatic summaries in primitive Christian missionary preaching, which were then paradigmatically illustrated in addition through concrete individual stories. This means that "summaries" and individual stories already stood alongside each other in the missionary preaching, which was based on oral tradition and belonged necessarily to the narrated "story of Jesus" from the beginning, with its wording being quite variable in detail.[10] The great extent to which we are standing on historically secure ground in the case of the healings—independent of the wording of the individual "miracle stories"—is shown by the conspicuous self-witness of Jesus, in which he points to his "deeds of power."[11] Thus in woe sayings about the Galilean places, which we have already mentioned multiple times:[12]

[9] Grant 1977, 31. Cf. note 2 above on the *Testimonium Flavianum*.

[10] Cf. Mark 1.32ff., 39 = Luke 4.40-41; Mark 3.10ff., cf. Luke 5.15; Mark 6.12-13, 56; on this, see the discussion of the summaries in the excursus above.

[11] δυνάμεις; Hebrew: gᵉbûrôt; Aramaic: gᵉbûrātā'. The word in the sense of "deed of power"/"miracle" in Mark 6.2, 5; 9.39; Luke 10.13; 19.37; Matt 7.22; 11.20-23; 13.54, 58; 14.2. Tellingly, John does not have it. He loves the hermeneutically considered term σημεῖον/σημεῖα, while the Synoptic Jesus rejects "signs" for his legitimation. Only the false messiahs and prophets do σημεῖα καὶ τέρατα, in order to lead the community astray (Mark 13.22 = Matt 24.24, cf. 2 Thess 2.9). It is a Septuagint formula. See also John 4.48. The term τέρας, which is familiar from the Septuagint, is completely lacking. We find this Old Testament formula all the more frequently in Acts and twice in Paul (Rom 15.19: ἐν δυνάμει σημείων καὶ τεράτων, ἐν δυνάμει πνεύματος θεοῦ, 2 Cor 12.12: He has done σημεῖα τοῦ ἀποστόλου in Corinth: σημείοις τε καὶ τέρασιν καὶ δυνάμεσιν). These "signs of an apostle" are an expression of the transference of the messianic authority of Jesus to the messengers of Jesus; see section 11.7. For the primitive community the deeds of Jesus are "incomparable" and at the same time "exemplary."

[12] Luke 10.13, 15 = Matt 11.21, 23a; see also section 12.2 with note 66.

Woe to you Chorazin,
Woe to you Bethsaida,
For if in Tyre and Sidon there had been *deeds of power*,
which happened among you,
they would have long sat in sackcloth and ashes
and would have repented.
And you, Capernaum, will you be exalted to heaven?
You shall be brought down to the underworld!

Matthew adds:

For if in Sodom there had been *deeds of power*,
which happened in you, it would exist until today.
But I say to you: it will be more tolerable for the land of Sodom on the day
of judgment than for you.[13]

Here an "enthusiastic" self-assessment of his δυνάμεις by Jesus becomes visible, which becomes comprehensible only through his preaching of the kingdom of God and of judgment.

The other key word concerns Jesus' "authority" and is related more strongly to his teaching. In the first appearance of Jesus according to Mark, the inhabitants of Capernaum, after the exorcism in the synagogue, were deeply impressed by his teaching, for he taught as "one having *authority*[14] and not as the scribes." Through the healing of the paralytic[15] Jesus emphasizes that "the Son of Man also has authority to forgive sins."[16] On the basis of his deed "all are astonished, praise God, and say: We have never seen such a thing." Jesus' "deeds of power" (δυνάμεις) and his message proclaimed in authority are closely related to each other. The deeds are a fundamental part of his announcement of the "kingdom of God that is in the process of realization."[17] In the sending out tradition it is Jesus himself who gives his disciples "authority" over unclean spirits, so that they, like

---

[13] Matthew 11.23-24; cf. Luke 10.12. On the key word "Sodom," see also Rev 11.8, related to Jerusalem. On the judgment, see the end of section 10.3.

[14] Mark 1.22: ὡς ἐξουσίαν ἔχων; cf. 1.27: διδαχὴ καινὴ κατ᾽ ἐξουσίαν, cf. Matt 7.29. Behind this stands Hebrew *rāšût*, Aramaic *rešûtā'*; see Jastrow 1903, II: 1449–50. On this, see the end of section 11.2 with note 46.

[15] Mark 2.1-12 = Luke 5.17-26 = Matt 9.1-8.

[16] Mark 2.10: ὅτι ἐξουσίαν ἔχει ὁ υἱὸς τοῦ ἀνθρώπου ἀφιέναι ἁμαρτίας ἐπὶ τῆς γῆς = Luke 5.24 = Matt 9.6. Cf. the choral conclusion of Matt 9.8: ἐδόξασαν τὸν θεὸν τὸν δόντα ἐξουσίαν τοιαύτην, i.e., the authority to heal and forgive sins.

[17] These relatively varied references to reactions of the onlookers of Jesus' miracles cannot simply be invalidated through the form-critical argument that here we are dealing with the narratively necessarily choral conclusion of the miracle story. These choral

he himself, perform exorcisms and heal the sick.[18] Such an authorization exceeds the ability of a prophet; it was for the evangelists a messianic act. Here too Jesus acts in the place of God.

The central eschatological significance of his deeds is emphasized through his answer to the *question of the Baptist*, which has already been quoted multiple times.[19] Luke has placed it after the paradigmatic Sermon on the Plain at the beginning of his collection of sayings of Jesus and inserted between them only the healing of the slave of the centurion of Capernaum and the raising of the young man of Nain, so that the question of the Baptist has been illustrated by at least two examples of Jesus' miraculous gift of healing and his ability to raise the dead.[20] He strengthens this impression through the insertion of a summary of Jesus' intensive healing activity at the time[21] when the messengers of the Baptist arrive. Jesus exhorts them: "Go and tell John what you have seen and heard" (Luke 7.22 = Matt 11.4). The "messianic–salvation-historical" grounding of his action becomes visible in his answer. It is a matter of the fulfillment of the Isaianic promises of the deaf hearing, the blind seeing, and the rising of the dead,[22] which find their summary and climax in Isa 61.1ff., where there is talk of the proclamation of the good news to the poor by the eschatological prophet "anointed by the Spirit." This πτωχοὶ εὐαγγελίζονται, in turn, refers back to the beginning of the Sermon on the Plain with the beatitude on the poor. From the Qumran text that was quoted in detail above it

---

conclusions are too different to simply be set aside historically through the reference to form criticism. They ultimately go back to the impact of the deeds of Jesus.

[18] Mark 6.7: ἐδίδου αὐτοῖς ἐξουσίαν τῶν πνευμάτων τῶν ἀκαθάρτων; 6.12-13. They proclaim repentance, cast out many demons, anoint many sick with oil and heal them. In the case of the anointing with oil we are dealing with a custom of the primitive Christian community; cf. James 5.14-15. Cf. also Mark 3.15; Luke 9.1; 10.19; Matt 10.3. By contrast, in Mark 11.28ff. parr. he refuses to answer the hierarchs' question about the origin of his ἐξουσία with respect to his activity in the temple.

[19] Luke 7.21-23; Matt 11.4-6; see section 10.5 and section 12.2 with notes 74–76.

[20] Luke 7.1-10, 11-18: The disciples of the Baptist proclaim to him in prison περὶ πάντων τούτων (v. 18).

[21] Luke 7.21: ἐν ἐκείνῃ τῇ ὥρᾳ ἐθεράπευσεν πολλοὺς ἀπὸ νόσων καὶ μαστίγων καὶ πνευμάτων πονηρῶν καὶ τυφλοῖς πολλοῖς ἐχαρίσατο βλέπειν. Luke, the "beloved physician" (Col 4.14), makes no distinction between bodily defects and possession. Jesus "heals" both. Θεραπεύειν appears five times in Mark, fourteen times in Luke, and sixteen times in Matthew. John has it, since he does not know of any summaries, only once in 5.10 as a participle. Luke has ἰᾶσθαι ten times, Matthew three times (once as a quotation of Isa 6.10), Mark only once, and John three times (once as a quotation of Isa 6.10). The healing terminology in the Gospels is almost as frequent as the terminology of proclamation and teaching.

[22] Luke 7.21-22 = Matt 11.4-5; on this, see Isa 26.19; 29.18; 35.5-6; 42.18.

becomes clear that messianic motifs are involved not only in the Christian interpretation but already in the Jewish expectation.[23]

We encounter there a *prophetic messiah image*, configured on the basis of Isa 61.1ff., which differs in a not insignificant way from the usual royal-militaristic image, which was largely regarded as the exclusive image up to now. In 11QMelch I 18, we already find a mysterious "Spirit-anointed" (*māšîᵃḥ ha-rûᵃḥ*), who is identical with the "bringer of good news" from Isa 52.7 and to whom the predicates from Isa 61.1-3 are related.[24] The Jewish messianology before 70 CE was richer than the Pharisaic-rabbinic messianology with its more strongly political conceptions, as they are found in Pss. Sol. 17 and later in the targums. In Qumran different Messiah figures are already known: the priestly Messiah as teacher, the sovereign "shoot of David" as war hero,[25] and the prophetic Messiah as Spirit-bearer. To these one can add from Dan 7.13 the mysterious figure of the "(son of) man."[26] Here overlaps were natural. Through these texts an entirely new light falls on the controversial question of the messiahship of Jesus.[27]

Luke already takes up this theme in Jesus' failed "inaugural sermon" in his hometown of Nazareth, where he has him interpret Isa 61.1 and 2: "The Spirit of the Lord is upon me, *because he has anointed me*. . . . Today this Scripture is fulfilled before your ears." Amazed at Jesus' "graceful words," the Nazarenes pose the counterquestion: "Is this not the son of Joseph?" Thereupon Jesus provokes his fellow citizens. He categorically refuses to perform the healings that he did in Capernaum also in his hometown and refers to the prophetic miracles of Elijah in the case of the Phoenican widow of Zarephath and the healing of the leprous Syrian Naaman by Elisha, i.e., deeds that took place for the hated pagan neighbors, a provocation that leads to the incensed Nazarenes wanting to throw him

---

[23] 4Q521; on this, see section 4.5 with note 201 and the end of section 10.4.

[24] On this, see Zimmermann 1998, 389–412.

[25] In contrast to the Pharisaic and rabbinic texts, the title "king" (*melek*), was avoided; he was called, following Ezekiel, only "prince" (*nāśî'*) and placed in rank behind the eschatological high priest. According to his coins, Bar Kokhba also took this title. See Zimmermann 1998, 46–127; Schürer 1973–1987, I: 544; Hengel 1996a, 349, and the end of section 17.1 below.

[26] The Son of Man of Dan 7.13 is not found in the preserved Qumran texts but could not have been completely unknown there since the book of Daniel was highly valued in Qumran and available in numerous exemplars in the library: 11QMelch I 18–19 quotes Dan 9.25 and Isa 52.7 with the "bringer of good news" in connection with the "Spirit-anointed." On the Son of Man problem, see section 17.4.1.

[27] Zimmermann 1998, 8ff.; 535 index, s.v. "Jesus Christus." Mark 13.22 = Matt 24.24 mentions ψευδόχριστοι and ψευδοπροφῆται in one breath almost as hendiadys. On the problem, see Schwemer 2001b, 165–230.

off a cliff. The passion is already foreshadowed here in Luke.[28] This Lukan beginning of the public activity of Jesus shows that the first Christian "historian" views Jesus, on the basis of Isa 61.1, as a "prophetic anointed one," who, like Elijah and Elisha, possesses the gift to perform miracles, a characteristic that recedes in the case of the Pharisaic royal Messiah. With this Luke has rightly grasped the special messianic character of the activity of Jesus. For him prophetic and royal Davidic Messiah do not form an opposition. This basically applies to all the evangelists, including John.[29]

Thus, for Luke and the other evangelists the eschatological proclamation of Jesus and the prophetic-messianic δυνάμεις (or in John σημεῖα) form an inseparable *unity* from the beginning. This also becomes visible in Jesus' answer to the Pharisees' warning about Herod Antipas' desire to kill Jesus according to Luke. Here Jesus' healing activity stands entirely in the foreground:

> Go and say to this fox: Behold, I am casting out demons and performing healings today and tomorrow. And on the third day I am completed. However, today and tomorrow I must wander. For it cannot be that a prophet would die outside of Jerusalem.[30]

This distinctive text in which Jesus is again designated—against post-Easter Christology—as a prophet proves how much his healing activity, grounded in various Isaiah texts, stood at the center of his activity. The

---

[28] Luke 4.16-30. The whole is an artificial Lukan composition, which already presages Jesus' way into the passion. On this, see Mittmann-Richert 2008. The motif of provocation and collective reaction is also found in the passion story in Luke 22.66ff. and in the martyrdom of Stephen in Acts 7. Luke is partly dependent on Mark 6.1-6, where the Nazarenes, deeply shocked (ἐξεπλήσσοντο), ask about Jesus' σοφία and δυνάμεις: "Is this not . . . the son of Mary?" and "they took offense at him (ἐσκανδαλίζοντο)"; cf. Luke 7.23 par. In addition, Luke has Jesus quote Mark 6.4 in his provoking speech: "No prophet is welcome in his hometown." Moreover, he has also incorporated older traditions of his own. We can no longer clearly separate pre-Lukan tradition and the evangelist's redaction. By contrast Matt 13.53-58 follows closely and shortens the Markan narrative. Here, he takes his orientation from the Peter student Mark. See section 6.4.3.

[29] See the end of section 17.1.

[30] Luke 13.32-33; on Jesus as messianic prophet, see Luke 4.18-27; 7.39 and above all 24.19-21. Here the "eschatological prophet" is joined with the messianic "redeemer." See also Mark 6.4; 8.28 parrs.; Matt 21.10-11; John 6.14-15 and the end of section 17.1. According to the verdict of the three Synoptics, it was especially Jesus' "deeds of power" that impressed the tetrarch: Mark 6.14: "John the Baptist has risen from the dead, therefore the (miraculous) powers (δυνάμεις) are at work through him" = Matt 14.2; cf. Luke 9.7. Herod hears of "everything that happened (through Jesus)" and is unsettled (διηπόρει). According to the Lukan account of the passion, "Herod hoped to see a sign (σημεῖον) from him" and urged him to this; Jesus, however, persistently kept silent (Luke 23.8-9).

people understood him initially as "eschatological prophet," who continued or, better, completed the work of the Baptist, though in an entirely different way. The boundary between this prophet and the Messiah was fluid.
However, Jesus clearly crossed it in the course of his activity. When Paul,
in Rom 15.8, says that Christ became "the servant of the circumcision"[31] to
fulfill the promises to the fathers, he may have especially had in mind this
part of the activity of Jesus, which was prefigured by the Isaianic promises and also included the "service" of the "servant of God." On the other
hand, Jesus, according to the witness of the Synoptic Gospels, decisively
rejected the exhortation to demonstrate his end-time prophetic-messianic
authority through a *legitimation sign*. According to Mark 8.11-12, the
Pharisees demanded from him "a sign from heaven." Jesus rejected this
categorically: "Why does this generation demand a sign? Amen, I say to
you: In no way will a sign be given to this generation!"[32] In the sayings
tradition[33] the answer runs as follows: To this "evil generation" "no sign
will be given except for the sign of Jonah," which refers to Jonah's preaching of repentance in Nineveh before the impending punitive judgment:
"For as Jonah became a sign to the inhabitants of Nineveh, so will the Son
of Man be to this generation." The pagan inhabitants of Nineveh spontaneously repent at Jonah's announcement of judgment. By contrast, the
present majority of his people, "this generation,"[34] does not heed Jesus's
message and refuses to repent. In a similar way to the woes against Chorazin, Bethsaida, and Capernaum, this saying points to a "crisis" during the
Galilean activity of Jesus.

The *crisis* is based not only on the opposition of the religious authorities and the threat from Herod Antipas and his henchmen. With respect
to his preaching of the dawning kingdom of God, Jesus probably also
had opponents among the simple population. The accusation against
these places becomes comprehensible only in this way. The opposition
in his hometown of Nazareth also points in this direction. Failures in
the healings may also have contributed to this, though these are not, of

[31] The phrase διάκονος γεγενῆσθαι περιτομῆς also evokes Jesus as "servant of
God"; cf. Mark 10.45 and Luke 22.27 ἐν μέσῳ ὑμῶν εἰμι ὡς ὁ διακονῶν; on this, see Matt
12.16-21 with the quotation from Isa 42.1-4, 9 and Acts 10.38, which alludes to Isa 61.1.

[32] Mark 8.11-12; in expanded form in Matt 16.1-4 (cf. Luke 12.54, 56). With the nega-
tion εἰ δοθήσεται Mark 8.12 contains a clear Hebraism: see Blass/Debrunner/Rehkopf
1984, 384–85 § 454.5, corresponding to the Hebrew negating *'im*; cf. Heb 3.11; 4.3, 5 with
the quotation from Ps 95(94).11 LXX.

[33] Luke 11.29-32; cf. Matt 12.38-42.

[34] Ἡ γενεὰ αὕτη is a dominical expression: Mark 8.12, 38; 13.30; Luke 7.31 = Matt
11.16 and elsewhere; see section 17.4.1.1. Cf. the interpretation of the sign of Jonah with
reference to the destruction in Jerusalem in Liv. Pro. 10.8. On this, see note 323 in chapter 3 and note 7 in the present chapter.

course, recounted by the evangelists. Instead, formulaically alluding to Old Testament promises, Matthew, already in Jesus' first appearance in Galilee, stresses that he "healed every sickness and every infirmity among the people."[35] That there were setbacks is shown by his failure in Nazareth according to Mark, where "he could do no deed of power,"[36] and the—unique—drastic warning against backsliding in the case of possessed persons, where the demon that has been cast out returns with seven others "and the last condition of that person is worse than the first was." Matthew adds and generalizes: "Thus it will happen with this evil generation." In reality, this is a graphically recounted example,[37] behind which exorcistic experiences may stand. The evangelists understandably tend to present the successes of Jesus as preacher and miracle worker, at least in part, in an exaggerated way and usually restrict the opposition to the leaders of the people. This may also be connected with the memory of the sovereignty of Jesus' activity.

In its eschatological enthusiasm inspired by the gift of the Spirit, *primitive Christianity* continued the claim to do "deeds of power" as Jesus himself, although the terminology changed to some extent. This is attested not only by the Synoptic sending out tradition, which ultimately goes back to an initiative of Jesus himself,[38] and by Acts, but also by Paul, who, in relation to the Romans who were unknown to him, self-confidently stresses that through him Christ "worked for the obedience of the Gentiles in word and deed by the power of signs and wonders, by the power of the Spirit of God."[39] As so often, here too an unmistakable continuity between Jesus' activity and the early community extending to the Pauline mission becomes visible. It should not be denied any longer.

As fulfillment of the prophetic promises in the present, the healing miracles of Jesus belong to the *present* aspect of his proclamation of the

[35] Matthew 4.23: θεραπεύων πᾶσαν νόσον καὶ πᾶσαν μαλακίαν ἐν τῷ λαῷ; cf. 9.35; 10.1; 12.15. In Matt 8.17 this is grounded with a *Reflexionszitat* (reflection citation) from Isa 53.4 (according to the MT). See also 53.3: εἰδὼς φέρειν μαλακίαν and Ps 103.3b (102.3 LXX): τὸν ἰώμενον πάσας τὰς νόσους σου; see further Exod 23.25: ἀποστρέψω μαλακίαν ἀφ᾽ ὑμῶν.

[36] Mark 6.5: οὐκ ἐδύνατο ἐκεῖ ποιῆσαι οὐδεμίαν δύναμιν; on this, see section 8.3 with note 71.

[37] Luke 11.24-26 = Matt 12.43-45.

[38] Mark 6.7-13 = Luke 9.1-6 = Matt 10.5ff.; cf. Luke 10.1ff.; see section 11.7.

[39] Romans 15.18-19; 2 Cor 12.12; see note 11 above; on this, see Theissen 1983, 282–83 (GV = 1974, 278–79). Paul's problem was that for his opponents in Corinth, who probably could appeal to Peter himself or his messengers, "these signs and wonders" were not enough because the latter showed themselves to be even more proficient therein. Cf. 2 Cor 11.4 on the proclamation of these messengers. On this, see Hengel 2010a, 76–77, 93 (GV = 2006b, 124–25, 152).

kingdom of God, with this presupposing—as shown especially by the exorcisms—a situation of conflict and a dualistic background. Gerd Theissen has fittingly described the subject matter:

> Satan has fallen from heaven (Lk 10.18); his kingdom is disintegrating (Mk 3.24-26), his house being plundered (3.27). The casting out of demons is the first sign of the arrival of the rule of God (Mt 12.28). The end of the negative has already come; the web of evil around this passing world has already been torn.[40]

Because such decisive signs occur already here and now, Jesus can largely forgo dualistic and apocalyptic pictures of the future. To be sure, we would not go on to say with Theissen: "The realization of the positive is still to come." Rather, as the contrast parables show, this has—even though it is inconspicuous, unrecognized, and met with hostility—already begun. When sick persons are healed, Satanic powers are conquered, sins are forgiven, hate and worry are overcome, and in the joy of liberation honor is given to the heavenly Father, then the "realization of the positive" is already at work for the one "who has ears to hear" and "eyes to see."[41] Jesus' message can, of course, also effect the opposite, hardening, and, as a consequence, God's judgment. This is shown already by his failure in his hometown, the reproaches against the Galilean places on the Lake of Gennesaret, and the polemic against this "evil and adulterous generation."[42] The evangelists, especially Mark, intensify this motif to the general hardening of the whole people, which, according to the quotation from Isa 6.9-10, is effected by God himself.[43] Later, John connects the hardening motif directly with the question of miracles: "Although he had performed so many signs before them, they did not believe in him, so that the word of the prophet Isaiah would be fulfilled, which he had said: 'Lord, who has believed our preaching . . . ?'"[44] Indeed, "they could not believe because Isaiah again had said: 'He has made their eyes blind and their heart hard, in

---

[40] Theissen 1983, 279 (GV = 1974, 276).

[41] Mark 4.9, 23; 7.16; 8.18; Matt 13.16 (= Luke 10.23) and elsewhere.

[42] Cf. Matt 12.45; 16.4; 17.17; Mark 8.38; Luke 9.41; 11.29 and elsewhere; see section 17.4.1.1.

[43] Mark 4.11-12: Jesus speaks in parables in order that (ἵνα) the "people may not understand and repent"; Matt 13.13 weakens and has ὅτι instead of ἵνα. See further Luke 8.10; Acts 28.26-27; and Mittmann-Richert 2008. On this, see also section 17.3.2 with notes 82–84.

[44] John 12.37-41; John quotes the word of the servant of God, Isa 53.1, and Isa 6.10.

order that they not see with the eyes and understand with the heart. . . .'"[45] For John, who, like Paul before him, thinks in a strictly predestinarian way, the signs of Jesus, which are especially astonishing precisely in his work, have an ambivalent, indeed a negative effect. The faith that is effected through them can be deceptive, a fact that Jesus perceives from the beginning.[46] Here we can see a broad later reflection on the connection between Jesus' activity and his external foundering on the unbelief of his compatriots in Galilee and in Jerusalem. The Markan "hardening theory"[47] belongs already in the context of the hostile reaction of his opponents—which was difficult to understand for the disciples and even more for the later community—to Jesus' prophetic-messianic activity, which led in the end to his way of suffering as "servant of God," to his being handed over to Pilate and to his execution.

16.2 Demand for Faith and Miracles

That Jesus himself reckoned with real θαυμάσια,[48] i.e., deeds that evoked extreme amazement, indeed—in conspicuously hyperbolic manner of expression—with what is in itself "impossible for human beings," is shown by his demand for *faith*—which was not yet oriented to the later church "kerygma" and also not directly to his message—in God's omnipotence, which he expresses with examples that contradict all experience and are almost offensive for his hearers.

Mark 11.22-23 has a distinctive saying follow the cursing of the fig tree:

---

[45] John 12.39-40 = Isa 6.10; cf. Rom 11.8. See also the end of section 16.2 and section 17.3.2 with notes 82–84.

[46] John 2.23-24; cf. 3.2; 4.48: Jesus' criticism; 6.2, 14, 26.

[47] Mark 4.10-12; see section 11.3 with note 64. See also section 17.3.2 with notes 82–84.

[48] Matthew 21.15: The opponents in the temple see τὰ θαυμάσια ἃ ἐποίησεν (Itala/Vulgata: *mirabilia*); on this, see Bauer/Aland/Aland 1988, 716–17. In the Septuagint the word occurs alongside the synonymous θαυμαστός ca. thirty times in the Psalms and then also in Sirach as translation of words based on the root *pl'*, which also appear frequently in the Qumran texts and refer to God's miracle and creation and (salvation-)history. We also find it frequently in Josephus and Philo. See also the multiple references to the θαυμάζειν at Jesus' deeds: Mark 5.20: καὶ πάντες ἐθαύμαζον, Luke 8.25: φοβηθέντες δὲ ἐθαύμασαν; 9.43; 11.14; 20.26; Matt 8.27; 9.33; 15.31; 21.20; John 7.15, 21.

Have faith in God. Amen, I say to you, whoever says to this mountain "be taken up and thrown into the sea" and does not doubt in his heart, but believes that what he says happens, it will happen for him.[49]

In Luke we find a small apothegm, in which the configuration comes from him. To the apostle's petition "Give us faith!" Jesus answers:

If you have faith as a mustard seed and you would say to this sycamore tree, be uprooted and planted in the sea, it would also obey you.[50]

Since the petition does not fit the saying and "the apostles" is a typically Lukan linguistic form, the saying in the source of Luke was probably unframed, and Luke transformed it out of a certain embarrassment into an apothegm.

A similar embarrassment in the interpretation of the "faith that moves mountains" occurs in the Gospel of Thomas, where the motif appears twice: "If two make peace with each other in the same house, (then) they will say to the mountain: 'move away,' and it will move," and "if you make the two one you will become sons of men," i.e., if you nullify the sexual differentiation between the sexes, the same miracle occurs. The saying about the faith that moves mountains, which is difficult to understand and even offensive due to its hyperbolic character, is domesticated in this gnosticizing late text via secondary moralization, which suppresses the decisive motif of faith.[51]

The intention of this enigmatic saying is grasped in a materially correct manner in Matt 17.20, which attaches it to the story of the healing of the possessed boy in Mark.[52] At the same time, due to its offensiveness, Mat-

---

[49] Cf. Matt 21.21: he intensifies and adds to the mountain also through the fig tree. First Cor 13.2 is dependent on this saying. Paul presupposes knowledge of it in Corinth.

[50] Luke 17.5-6. Cf. the planting of a tree as miracle of authentication through Eliezer b. Hyrcanus around 100 CE; see b. B. Meṣ. 59b. On this, see Fiebig 1911, 31ff. Cf. also Bill. II: 234. Connections to Jewish Christians were rumored for the charismatic Eliezer b. Hyrcanus; see Schäfer 2007, 42–51. There is an inner connection between the "faith like a mustard seed" and the parable of the kingdom of God (Luke 13.18-19 = Matt 13.31-32): that which is unthinkable and miraculous becomes possible; see section 13.2 with notes 50–51.

[51] Gospel of Thomas 48, 106. On the interpretation, see Ménard 1975, 149ff., 204–5. The second saying has an even stronger gnosticizing character.

[52] On this, see Matt 17.14-20 after the *Vorlage* Mark 9.14-28. Matthew 17.21 is a disruptive secondary parallel adoption from Mark 9.29. Matthew deletes this statement, probably because it does not correspond to his understanding of miracles. In 17.15 he provides the more exact "diagnosis": σεληνιάζεται. Luke 9.37-43 likewise deletes the Markan

thew deletes the striking dialogue of Jesus with the father from his Markan *Vorlage*.

> Because the disciples are helpless with regard to the sick child in Mark, the despairing father[53] turns directly to Jesus: "But if you can do something, help us, out of compassion for us." In response Jesus answers: "With respect to the 'if you can do something': *everything is possible for the one who believes*." After the moving answer of the Father: "Lord, I believe, help my unbelief!" Jesus performs the exorcism. The following question of the disciples to Jesus: "Why couldn't we cast it out?" then answers a problem of the exorcistic practice of the community: This kind of demons can be cast out "only through prayer."[54] "Faith" and "miracles" mutually condition each other.

Unbelief or doubt punishes itself by making miracles impossible, as in the case of the rejection of Jesus in Nazareth in Mark 6.5-6 or with the sinking Peter in Matt 14.31. That it is not the helpless father but Jesus himself who acts and helps is what is meant by the statement "everything is possible. . . ."[55]

Matthew, by contrast, places the difficult-to-understand saying about "faith as a mustard seed" in the mouth of Jesus as an answer to the question of the disciples. They could not cast out the demons because of their "little faith."[56]

> For Amen, I say to you, if you have faith as a mustard seed, you will say to this mountain: Move yourself from here to there, it will move, and nothing will be impossible for you.

---

dialogue and, in addition, also the question of the incapable disciples. He replaces the latter through the form-critically correct "fright" of the onlookers "at the greatness of God" (9.43). For Theophilus he wanted to avoid offensive stories as far as possible.

[53] Mark 9.22b.

[54] A great number of manuscripts add "and through fasting." This reading may be more original than the only slimly attested text in NA[27]; cf. THGNT, ad loc., which prints the longer reading. On the casting out of demons through prayer and fasting, see Liv. Pro. 4.3–4, 9, 12, 16. With εἰ μὴ ἐν προσευχῇ in Mark 9.29 a specific exorcistic "prayer formula" is certainly not intended but rather the persistent prayer in Spirit-effected authority, which is not given to everyone.

[55] Mark 9.23: πάντα δυνατὰ τῷ πιστεύοντι. On this, see Hofius 2004a, 136: "The emphasis lies on the statement that faith is given that which remains denied to unbelief: the miracle of divine help as the deed and gift of the one . . . who has the omnipotence of God at his disposal" (136).

[56] Matthew 17.20: διὰ τὴν ὀλιγοπιστίαν ὑμῶν. The accusation of being ὀλιγόπιστος probably goes back to Jesus but is typically Matthean; see notes 61–62 below.

The first evangelist has intentionally placed this saying at the end of the last healing miracle in Galilee and before the second passion prediction. From now on such a faith is demanded from the disciples. That this special form of a charismatic "miracle faith" is already well-known to Paul is shown by 1 Cor 13.2, where such a faith is not related to the kerygma and therefore is useless without love.[57] This "miracle faith" has its analogue in the affirmation that in prayer the faith that does not doubt may be certain of being answered.[58] The formula of salvation used by Jesus, "*Your faith has made you well*," which appears twice in Mark, three times in Luke, and once in Matthew, also belongs in this context.[59] The firm faith in the healing gift given to Jesus by God is to a certain extent the presupposition of miraculous healing. In the narrative of the two blind men who follow Jesus and ask for healing from him as Son of David in Matt 9.27-31—which is related to the two blind men of Jericho in Matt 20.29-34—Jesus first tests their faith: "Do you believe that I can (δύναμαι) do this?" They answer: "Yes, Lord." Only then does the healing saying follow: "'According to your faith may it happen to you,' and their eyes were opened." It is therefore only consistent when Jesus, due to the unbelief of his fellow citizens in Nazareth, "could (ἐδύνατο) do no miracle."[60]

The fact that the motif of faith is related not only to healings or to prayer but also stands behind the "impossible" demand not to worry is shown by Jesus' reference to the lilies of the field, which God clothes so gloriously, in relation to which there stands at the end the demand: "how much more you, *you of little faith*."[61] Matthew, who is also fond, after all, of repeating "dominical" expressions that sound archaic elsewhere, speaks of those "of little faith" four more times in analogous contexts of the legendary miracle tradition.[62] This probably occurs in Matthew because the word "of little faith" also appears as an accusation against Israel in the

---

[57] Cf. 1 Cor 12.9: ἑτέρῳ (δίδοται) πίστις ἐν τῷ αὐτῷ πνεύματι and Gal 5.22. Here too the charismatic "fruit of the Spirit," in which ἀγάπη occupies the first position and πίστις does not occur until the seventh, is not the faith that justifies the sinner.

[58] Mark 11.24 = Matt 21.22, cf. John 14.13-14; 15.7; 16.23.

[59] Mark 5.34: ἡ πίστις σου σέσωκέν σε = Luke 8.48 = Matt 9.22; Mark 10.52 = Luke 18.42, cf. Matt 9.28-29; see also Luke 17.19 and the "collective" faith of the men who bring the paralytic, Mark 2.5 = Luke 5.20 = Matt 9.2.

[60] Mark 6.5; see note 36 above. Memory of Jesus' activity and primitive Christian experiences of healing are combined in these texts.

[61] Luke 12.28 = Matt 6.30. The word ὀλιγόπιστοι refers to doubt in God's care and miraculous power. The word is a Christian neologism in Greek, but has a Jewish-Pharisaic background and occurs in the early rabbinic interpretation of the behavior of Israel at the Reed Sea and in the wandering in the wilderness; see Hengel 1999b, 281–82; on this, see Bill. I: 420–21. There it has the meaning of "persons who lack faith."

[62] Matthew 8.26; 14.31; 16.8; 17.20; cf. note 56 above.

Tannaitic exodus tradition in the context of the deliverance of the people of God at the Reed Sea in the miracle of the manna and the quail in the wilderness.[63] After all, in the liberating exodus from Egypt the concern was also with faith and the acknowledgment of God's rule.[64] Thus, with its Jewish-Palestinian background, the Synoptic "miracle tradition" is still entirely related to Jesus' proclamation of the kingdom of God. Basically, one could go one step further: the unbelief of the first human couple, who let themselves be deceived by the serpent into doubting God's beneficial instruction (Gen 3.1-7), is the origin of all evil. God's reign can realize itself without restriction only when trust in the omnipotence and goodness of the Father no longer knows any limits.

Jürgen Roloff has especially pointed to the fact that in the Synoptic tradition the "πίστις-motif shows itself to be largely free of characteristics of the community situation after Easter," for it lacks the connection to the post-Easter kerygma. In an investigation of the above-quoted central text of Mark 9.14-29 and its parallels he explains that "the historical motif of the contemplation of a characteristic feature of the earthly activity of Jesus (vv. 23-24) . . . does not (stand) in the way of the updating application (vv. 28-29)."[65]

The consciousness of the historical distance of the community to the activity of Jesus often emerges in a surprisingly clear manner both in Mark and in the sayings tradition. Even in the later Gospel of John it is one of the fundamental insights that while Jesus, through his "signs," temporarily encountered recognition, even "faith," among the crowds, this did not endure because the people, despite "so many signs," in accord with the hardening saying of Isa 6.9-10, "*could not believe.*"[66]

This ambivalent effect of Jesus' "deeds of power" goes back to an older aporia that was already visible in his activity, to the mystery of unbelief and the rejection that Jesus encountered, not only in his hometown of Nazareth and not only in Jerusalem, where his fate was fulfilled, but also in the Galilean places that stood at the center of his — short — activity.

---

[63] See Bill. I: 438.

[64] Exodus 14.31 LXX: Καὶ ἐπίστευσαν τῷ θεῷ καὶ Μωυσῇ τῷ θεράποντι αὐτοῦ; and at the end of the Song of Moses in 15.18: κύριος βασιλεύων τὸν αἰῶνα καὶ ἐπ' αἰῶνα καὶ ἔτι. On this, see section 13.1.

[65] Roloff 1970, 141–207 (quotations on 203, 205).

[66] John 12.37-40; cf. 2.23-24 and 4.48: "If you do not see signs and wonders, you do not believe!" Cf. also Mark 4.12 = Matt 13.14-15; Acts 28.26 and Rom 11.8. This includes the failure of the proclamation of the primitive community in Judaea: in the meaning of Isa 6.9-10, a text with which the offense and mystery of the unbelief of the own people could be explained, lies the root of the early Christian teaching of predestination in Paul and in his footsteps in John. See also the end of section 16.1.

The woes against them, which are found in Luke at the end of the mission discourse for the seventy-two disciples and before their return and the macarism on them,[67] confirm not only our judgment that the healing miracles of Jesus were a completely fundamental component of his proclamation of the kingdom of God that is in the process of realization; they also demonstrate his messianic claim, which surpasses everything that we know from his environment in terms of parallels, as well as his deep disappointment in relation to those places that he had sought out himself as the center of his activity, a disappointment that is the expression of a *crisis of his activity*.

These reproaches lose their meaning in the mouth of a later, Jewish Christian prophet, especially since every christological reference to the "exalted one" is lacking. They must therefore go back to Jesus himself, i.e., the one who performed these deeds of power speaks, and he does this also in the authority of the coming judge. No wonder that the one question arises time and again: τίς ἄρα οὗτός ἐστιν;[68] Who is this who can say and do such things?

16.3 On the Tradition-Historical and History-of-Religions Problem of the Miracles of Jesus

The *assurance*—despite all disappointments—of the victory, already visible and experienceable now, over the anti-God powers through healings and exorcisms as signs of the kingdom that is in the process of realization is a new feature in Judaism. At the same time, it becomes clear that the still popular category of the mere "prophet," "rabbi," or "wisdom teacher" is by no means adequate for understanding Jesus' activity and messianic claim, to say nothing of a "Jewish Socrates" or a "Galilean Cynic." The real Jesus can be coopted neither for the existential model of "one who calls to decision" nor for an enlightened, politically correct postmodern model. He stands before us as one who is relatively foreign and no less offensive today than he was in his own time.

To be sure, we know of a few "charismatics" and "miracle workers" from the Judaism of his time—which is more than we know from the contemporary Hellenistic world—above all the Galilean Hanina ben Dosa from the middle of the first century CE with his prayer healings and Honi the Circle-Drawer from the late Hasmonean period, who had a special reputation as one who prayed for rain. But they worked primarily through persistent prayer, and there is not a trace of an eschatological grounding

---

[67] Luke 10.13-15 = Matt 11.21-23. See section 14.4 with note 82.

[68] Mark 4.41: the question of the disciples after the stilling of the storm = Luke 8.25.

in their case. Their significance for understanding the miracles of Jesus should not be overestimated.[69]

Josephus, as an eyewitness, reports that a Jewish exorcist, in a dramatic-demonstrative manner, cast out demons in the presence of Vespasian with the help of magic practices that allegedly came from Solomon.[70] In the case of Jesus' own activity we hear nothing of prayer[71] or invocations but only the commanding word of healing or exorcism, the healing touch, and three times of the use of spittle, two of which are in Mark; in the case of the healing of the woman with a blood flow, who touches Jesus without his knowledge and is immediately healed, Jesus observes that "a power has gone out from him."[72] The two Markan stories in which Jesus heals with spittle are tellingly passed over by Luke and Matthew, and the latter has Jesus heal with only a word. The textual variants also show that this portrayal presented difficulties later. The event of the healing is portrayed in relatively great detail by Mark. With the blind man of Bethsaida it happens in stages. In the case of the man who is deaf and has a speech impediment, Mark includes the Aramaic command ἔφφαθα "be opened."[73] The concern is with the hearing of the sick man. As with the words "ṭālîtā qûm" in the raising of the daughter of Jairus, the word ἔφφαθα is not a ῥῆσις βαρβαρική, the secret, barbaric-incomprehensible language of the magician, for the Aramaic command is, after all, translated and is understandable in itself.[74] The evangelist and his tradition retained the word because with

---

[69] Thus, especially in Vermes 1973, 58–82: Jesus and charismatic Judaism, and here pp. 72–80 on Hanina b. Dosa. The later Hanina tradition of the Babylonian Talmud with its sometimes bizarre miracles is wholly legendary. For criticism of Vermes, see the careful work of M. Becker 2002. On the Jewish charismatics, see also section 3.1.1 with note 20. On the portrayal of the Old Testament models from Abraham and Moses to the prophets as miracle workers in the apocryphal and pseudepigraphical literature, see Koskenniemi 2005. Here the battle against the anti-God powers and thus exorcisms play a larger role than in the early Tannaitic literature.

[70] *Antiquities* 8.46–49: ἱστόρησα (46). On this, see Deines 2003.

[71] John 11.41-42 is the exception that proves the rule: the short prayer of thanks demonstrates the superfluousness of the prayer for a miracle. Mark 7.34 is a command and not a shout of prayer; Mark 9.29 refers to the experience of the community; cf. also Acts 9.40 (2 Kgs 4.33); James 5.14-16.

[72] Mark 7.33ff.; 8.23ff.; John 9.6-15. On the woman with a blood flow, see the vivid presentation in Mark 5.25-43 = Luke 8.43-56; Matt 9.20-22 radically shortens. This "physical" bestowal of power corresponds to the primitive Christian term δύναμις and appears later as a special charisma.

[73] Mark 7.34. On this, cf. Rüger 1984, 79; Beyer 1984, 130, 464, 673: Aramaic *'eppataḥ*, itpael of *pātaḥ*, with regressive assimilation of the *t* to the *p* in accord with numerous targumic attestations.

[74] The Old Syriac translation omits the Greek rendering and transcribes ἔφφαθα with *'ptḥ* philologically correctly. Swete 1927, 161.

it, as with other lexical Aramaicisms,[75] the concern was with the unique, wonder-working *word of Jesus*. In our view, we can indeed speak of *ipsissima verba* of Jesus in the case of the words *'eppataḥ* and *ṭālîtā' qûm*. The speculation that these are "magic words" of later Christian "healers" completely misjudges their significance.[76] According to Acts, healing at the "command"—now in the name—of Jesus continues in the primitive community.[77]

Certain motifs of the miracles of Jesus, such as an eschatology related to the present, exorcisms, healings, and a dualistic background, are at best encountered *cum grano salis* also in the community of Qumran, where in the worship service in the cultic fellowship with the angels heaven opens and they participate in the divine *malkût*.[78] In addition, we find psalms ascribed to David (or Solomon) there, which have the character of exorcistic rituals.[79] Exorcisms appear to have played no small role for the Essenes. Josephus also attests their gift of seeing into the future and the interpretation of dreams as well as medical-magical practices.[80] However, what becomes clear through these parallels is only the related religious milieu, in which the Pharisees before 70 CE probably also participated;[81] for, in contrast to the eschatologically motivated charismatic spontaneity of the healings of Jesus, which stand in the context of a popular movement triggered by him, in Qumran we encounter the institutions—solidified by long tradition—of an established religious group, in which the different spheres, i.e., the presence of salvation in the cult, the exorcistic rituals, and the eschatological overcoming of dualism, no longer stand in an inner, living connection. In the extant scrolls and fragments we find no real synthesis of this phenomenon as in the Gospels. Rather, what is ubiquitous there is the most extremely intensified demand for ritual purity, which excludes

---

[75] Mark 3.17; 14.36; 15.34.

[76] There were not so many girls raised prior to Mark in primitive Christianity that such Aramaic "magical" formulas could have been used meaningfully. Cf. also Meier 1994, 628, 759, and elsewhere.

[77] Acts 3.6; 9.34; 9.40 combines prayer and call; 14.9-10. In 1 Cor 12.9 and 28 Paul speaks of the charisma of healing. A problem was prepared by exorcists who, although they did not belong to the community themselves, healed in the name of Jesus: Mark 9.38-39; Acts 19.13. The reaction to it was ambivalent. Cf. also the sharp criticism of Christian miracle workers in Matt 7.22-23.

[78] Schwemer 1991a, 48, 53–54, and elsewhere; cf. already H.-W. Kuhn 1965.

[79] On this, see Eshel 2003; H. Lichtenberger 2003.

[80] Josephus, *Ant.*, 13.311; 15.373, 378; 17.346–347; *J.W.* 2.136, 159.

[81] On this, see the charismatics who stood near to Pharisaism, such as Honi and Hanina ben Dosa and the Pharisaic exorcists according to Luke 11.19 = Matt 12.27; cf. note 69 above.

the disabled and sick from entering the sanctuary,[82] and the rigorous observance of the law. Despite some points of contact, the Essenes are separated by a ditch from the Gospels and their accounts about Jesus' activity.

The form-critical approach with its ahistorical way of standardizing in the work of Rudolf Bultmann[83] led to a false appraisal and historical placement of the miracle stories. The compulsion to take forms and the firm stylistic elements in the healing stories are not primarily conditioned by the oral tradition and the creative shaping fantasy of the community but rather by the inner necessity of the subject matter that is to be narrated. The different stages of the report, the depiction of the sickness and the plight of the sick person, their encounter with the miracle worker, the event and demonstration of the healing, the portrayal of its effect in a choral conclusion at the end, belong with material necessity to the narrated "story," just as a modern account of a sick person must also be formed according to a specific given scheme, which precisely does not exclude its concrete relation to reality. To this one can add the fact that the healing accounts are not as uniform as form criticism claims.[84] Extraordinary events especially stick in one's memory, with their later reproduction in the narration admittedly tending toward exaggeration.

In his noteworthy article "Miracle in the New Testament" in the third edition of *Religion in Geschichte und Gegenwart*,[85] E. Käsemann emphasizes that

> more than other genres the New Testament miracle stories (reflect) the complicated path from the oral tradition to the redaction.

We can probably gladly affirm this statement, although we can admittedly hardly test the path of the pre-Markan tradition any longer with regard to different stages, and an extraordinary healing event in particular can stick very clearly in the memory for a lifetime. Here one need only read the memoirs of great physicians. Without a doubt Mark has given the miracles "the relatively greatest space with unmistakable joy in the telling,"[86] but there is reason for the "joy in the telling": the capability as healer

---

[82] 11QT 45.12–18.

[83] Bultmann 1963, 209–44 (GV = 1995, 223–60). On the style motifs, see Bultmann 1963, 220–26 (GV = 1995, 236–41). Bultmann had—in this he was a typical Neo-Kantian and student of Wilhelm Herrmann—a deep aversion to everything "miraculous"; the word "miracle" (*Mirakel*) is consistently used pejoratively for the miracles of Jesus; on this, see Herrmann 1903, 193ff. See also note 138 below.

[84] On this, see Hengel/Hengel 1959, 357.

[85] Käsemann 1962, 1836.

[86] Käsemann 1962, 1836.

and exorcist was a fundamental component of the activity of Jesus, and the narrative material of the Markan accounts surely played an important role also already for his guarantors of tradition, such as Peter.[87] The original event was not suppressed thereby. Luke and especially Matthew have sometimes rigorously shortened the accounts and created in this way more schematic, i.e., "stylistically more correct," miracle stories, which precisely do not present the more original form.[88] For this very reason they can be collected "only with difficulty under a common historical and material denominator." Here Käsemann rightly sees their "basic motif" in the eschatological manifestation, since Jesus already "understood them as announcements of the in-broken time of salvation."[89] "Time of salvation" and Messiah belong, however, together.

Moreover, in Mark a certain "biographical" interest becomes visible in a whole series of miracle stories. We would reckon to this, among other things, also concrete persons, such as the mother-in-law of Peter, Jairus and his daughter, and Bartimaeus;[90] place-names, such as Capernaum and Jericho in Mark (or Nain in Luke); and the previously mentioned Aramaic words. The "edifying and allegorizing contemporizing" did not yet suppress this interest.[91]

What is conspicuous in Mark is also the individual variety, which cannot be forced into a foreign form scheme. Typical of this is the aforementioned healing of the epileptic boy[92] or the Bartimaeus story,[93] which possesses a very distinctive character.[94] Accordingly, the Synoptic miracle tradition cannot be ascribed in general—indeed, not even primarily—to the difficult to define "Hellenistic community" and be placed under the no less fuzzy catchphrase *theios aner*, which does not, after all, conform

---

[87] It is no coincidence that Paul speaks of his own apostolic performance of miracles in the dispute with the effects of the Petrine mission in 2 Cor 12.12 and Rom 15.19. On this, see Hengel 2010a, 76–77, 93 (GV = 2006b, 124–25, 152). Cf. also Heb 2.4.

[88] The form-critical scheme has reversed itself here. Thus, from the tales regarded as secondary by M. Dibelius almost perfectly formed "paradigms" could arise; see Dibelius 1933, 34ff., 66ff.

[89] Käsemann 1962, 1836 (our emphasis).

[90] Mark 10.46: The half-Aramaic, half-Greek name is conspicuous and not an invention. On this, see Bill. II: 25. It is conspicuous that Mark translates the name as well as other Aramaic terms and formulas. John does the same. See the discussion of Mark 5.41 and 7.34 above with notes 73–76. Luke deletes the name, and Matthew makes from it two instances of two blind men: Luke 18.35; Matt 20.29ff.; cf. also 9.27ff., where the Matthean Jesus tests them first with respect to their faith.

[91] Roloff 1970, 115ff. (116).

[92] See section 16.2.

[93] Mark 10.46-52. It is first standardized by Matthew. See the start of section 18.1.

[94] Roloff 1970, 121ff.

to a clear ancient notion but was first developed about eighty years ago from sources that were predominantly Christian or at least pagan post-Christian.[95] As Hellenistic parallels of a miracle worker from the second half of the first century CE one could mention only to a very limited degree the Pythagorean Apollonius of Tyana, about whom we know very little historically, since the novel of Philostratus, which was completed about 220 CE, paints an ideal picture that is as far removed from the historical reality as later, apocryphal Jesus pictures of the second century are with regard to the man from Nazareth. In our view, Philostratus, who wrote his work at the instigation of the empress Julia Domna, knew the Gospels, as did Celsus before him, and it stands to reason to assume that he stylized his hero as an ideal picture of the true philosophical religion against the "superstition" of the Christians, which had spread in his time also among the educated and was confident of victory.[96] With the Syrian from Palestine who exorcised those who were moonstruck, Lucian (ca. 120–190) could also refer, in a parodying manner, to Christian exorcists in the style of Jesus. After all, Lucian probably knew of the "crucified sophist" from Palestine and the "new cult" founded by him.[97] This means that the portrayal of Jesus as a miracle worker in the Gospels is older than the sporadic "Hellenistic" parallels; indeed, the portrayal of them could already stand indirectly under Christian influence. The time of a Celsus, Lucian, and Philostratus is also the first heyday of the novelistic Christian Acts of apostles, which are overflowing with outlandish miracle stories.[98]

The great time of the "Hellenistic" miracle workers and magicians begins — literarily — only with the second and third century CE. The — pre-Christian — miraculous cures in the Asclepius sanctuaries, preserved on inscriptions, for example at Epidauros, have a different character. In the Hellenistic sphere the exceptional healings of Vespasian in Alexandria, attested to Tacitus by eyewitness accounts, come closest to the accounts of the Gospels.[99] In the first half of the first century CE we have — apart

---

[95] On this, see section 7.1 with note 19; cf. also note 1 in chapter 2.

[96] On this, see Koskenniemi 1994. Schirren 2005b has emphatically pointed to this.

[97] Lucian, *Philops*. 16. The scholiast suspects an allusion to Christ; cf. *Peregr.* 11, 13. On the "crucified sophist" and the καινὴ τελετή founded by him, see Schirren 2005a. On this, cf. 1 Cor 1.23-24.

[98] On this, see, for example, also the *mirabilia* of Phlegon of Tralles, FGrH 257, who (at the time of Hadrian) recounts in his chronicle, among other things, fulfilled predictions of Jesus: Hengel 2004c, 114ff.

[99] Tacitus, *Hist*. 4.81.3. At the time, since Tacitus writes the histories ca. 110 CE, i.e., about forty years after the events in Alexandria, there were still eyewitnesses alive, who under Trajan no longer had a reason to flatter the Flavian imperial house. It is about the same period of time that separates Mark from Jesus. On the eyewitnesses in Tacitus, see Byrskog 2000, 63–64.

from the legendary Apollonius (who more likely belongs in the second half)—practically no accounts of itinerant miracle workers in the Hellenistic-Roman East.[100] Only magicians practice their timeless business, although their great time—as shown by the magical papyri, which are strongly influenced by Judaism—also arrived only with the second and third century. Despite the later anti-Christian polemic, one should not classify Jesus among them.[101] Thus, the comparison with the Jewish and "Hellenistic" parallels shows that the miracle stories of the Gospels, which all arose, after all, in the first century, possess an astonishingly distinctive character both through their great number and through their content and that they precisely cannot be simply derived from their environment. They are a fundamental, indispensable component in the activity of Jesus as proclaimer of the kingdom of God, which is in the process of realization, and therefore they may not be pushed to the side as unimportant, because we find them disturbing today, in favor of the teacher of a higher morality or of the "one who calls to decision."

In the whole of ancient literature, including the Old Testament, where one could perhaps point at best to the Elijah and Elisha stories, which recount miraculous feedings, healings of sick persons, and two accounts of raisings of the dead and which have probably influenced the New Testament tradition,[102] there is not really any comparable collection of miracle stories that is tied to *one* person, as in the Gospels. This must also have historical foundations in the person of Jesus.

16.4 On the Evaluation of the Miracle Stories[103]

In contrast to the New Testament, which in the δυνάμεις of the Synoptics and the σημεῖα of the Fourth Gospel makes no distinction between the healings (or exorcisms) of Jesus and the so-called nature miracles, R. Bultmann[104] divides the Synoptic miracle stories into these two classes,

---

[100] On this, see Koskenniemi 1994, 207ff. (211–12).

[101] See note 40 in chapter 5 on Morton Smith and note 124 in the present chapter.

[102] Feedings: 1 Kgs 17.6; 19.5–8; 2 Kgs 4.1-7, 42-44: the nearest parallels to the feeding stories of the Gospels; healings of the sick: 1 Kgs 17.17-24; 2 Kgs 4.18-37; cf. 13.20-21. These "archaic" stories differ, although they have partly influenced the New Testament accounts, very fundamentally from those of the Gospels. The miracles ascribed to the prophets in the Lives of the Prophets are continuations of Old Testament impulses; on this, see Schwemer 1995/1996 I: 78–79; II: 388 index; on the Jewish "*Wirkungsgeschichte*" of the Old Testament miracle stories, see Koskenniemi 2005, on Elijah/Elisha, see 348 index; on the criticism of the "divine men" notion, see 3ff.

[103] On the discussion, cf. Wohlers/Riesner 2001.

[104] Bultmann 1963, 209ff., 215ff. (GV = 1995, 223ff., 230ff.). On pp. 231ff. (GV = 247ff.) he distinguishes in the case of the non-Christian miracles between (a) exorcisms of

a division which D. F. Strauss had already championed.[105] To be sure, this division is hardly adequate to the ancient understanding of miracle; rather, it introduces a modern distinction into the texts of the Gospels. Accordingly, in modern criticism healing miracles can sometimes still be regarded as historically possible as "psychosomatic" events, whereas "nature miracles" appear to be fundamentally impossible.[106] However, with this scheme one makes things too easy for oneself. It corresponds too much to our worldview and grasps the issues and problems of the Gospel narratives in an inadequate way or not at all. This applies also to the numerous pointers to Jesus' "miraculous" knowledge of people and hearts, his ability "to read thoughts," and above all his knowledge about future events, in which the passion predictions stand at the center.[107] Can one reject at the outset this knowledge, which transcends usual human possibilities? And what about the temptation story, the transfiguration story, the appearances of angels, which occur especially at the beginning and even more at the end of the Gospels, the heavenly voices, the extraordinary events at the death of Jesus, and, finally, the "miracle above all miracles," his resurrection? With the tradition about Jesus' activity and with primitive Christianity as such (including Paul) we enter into a miraculous, "mythical" world, which appears foreign to us and behind which stand experiences and expectations which are difficult to convey to us and which we cannot, however, simply deny and "demythologize," because through that we take away from ourselves the possibility of understanding them. The historian falls here into an aporia. He can draw upon Old Testament and history-of-religions parallels, refer to certain topoi, highlight contradictions and exaggerating motifs, and show in general the skepticism that is called for in relation to these phenomena; he cannot really explain these phenomena, which characterize to a large degree Jesus' activity and the whole of primitive Christianity. Despite all individual "attempts at explanation," they remain for him an ultimately unanswerable, open question.

---

demons, (b) other healings, (c) raisings from the dead, and (d) nature miracles. Throughout these distinctions are not conditioned form-critically but rather with reference to content.

[105] Strauss 1864, 425ff.

[106] On this, see, for example, the criticism of Kertelge 1970, 43: "The characterizing . . . as nature miracles . . . follows solely on the basis of the fact that the miraculous happening portrayed in them is perceived not in relation to humans but in relation to extrahuman phenomena of nature." Trocmé 1963, 37, even speaks of *actes violentes les lois naturelles*." Further references are provided in Bultmann/Theissen/Vielhauer 1971, 84. In correspondence with Jewish thinking, one should speak rather of "creation miracles." The word φύσις does not occur in the Gospels.

[107] On this, see the list at the end of the excursus at the start of this chapter with note 6.

A more fundamental difference arises from the different worldview and view of God. Palestinian Judaism and primitive Christianity do not know our modern concept of nature and the notion of unchangeable "laws of nature." Rather, the whole animate and inanimate world is God's creation and sphere of power. One often imagines that God rules the world through a hierarchy of angels who obey his command. A principle that runs through the Old and New Testaments is that "nothing is impossible" for him.[108] Theissen therefore avoids this distinction—which signals an aporia of the exegesis since the Enlightenment—between nature miracles and healing miracles and speaks of an "inventory of themes." To this he assigns exorcisms, therapies, epiphanies, rescue miracles, gift miracles, and norm miracles, with the themes sometimes merging into one another. The story of the healing of the woman in the synagogue, who was bent by a "spirit of sickness" for eighteen years, combines exorcism, therapy, and norm miracle and leads to a controversy dialogue.[109] Such an example supports our thesis that the miracle stories of the Gospels are more variable than is frequently assumed and often can be pressed only with difficulty into fixed schemes that satisfy our modern formalism. All these divisions are somewhat forced. The variety of the narrated phenomena can be grasped only to a limited degree thereby, even though the event of the miracle itself requires certain narratively fixed specifications, for example that the suffering must be identified and the success must be directly or indirectly recounted.[110]

Klaus Berger therefore denies that "miracle/miracle story" is a "genre designation" at all. For him it is only a "modern description of an ancient understanding of reality."[111] In the Gospels—we have already pointed this out—and in comparable Jewish texts, we find several terms that characterize the narrated events: deeds of power, signs, miraculous signs (δυνάμεις, σημεῖα, τέρατα).[112] The Greco-Roman world knows the "genre" θαυμάσια/ *mirabilia*: stories about events that move the hearers to "amazement"; accordingly, we can indeed speak of the "genre" of miracle story.

---

[108] Genesis 18.14; Jer 32.17, 27: "No miracle is too great for you." Cf. Mark 10.27 = Matt 19.26; Matt 17.20; Luke 1.37. The whole creation is unconditionally subjected to God's will. Only for this reason is the notion of "mountain-moving" faith in the sense of a radical trust in God conceivable.

[109] Luke 13.10-17 (special material).

[110] Hebrews 2.4 speaks of ποικίλαι δυνάμεις; see also the excursus at the start of this chapter.

[111] Berger 1984a, 305; cf. 305–18. See Berger 1984b, 1212–18; cf. 1214–15 on the criticism of Theissen and 1218 on the criticism of the genre miracle story.

[112] See section 16.1 with note 11.

With this, however, Berger points out the aporia—which we have already highlighted on several occasions—of the traditional form-critical perspective, though he continues to remain tied to it, since he also attempts again to make classifications and thus to establish questionable tradition-historical dependencies.[113] Either way the contingency of the recounted miraculous event—which in the ancient stories surely may often, indeed may usually, be based on fantastical fiction—is set aside in favor of a more or less artificial schematization. What is correct is the recognition that the Synoptic miracle stories deal "with very concrete situations of plight"[114] and usually involve a miracle for the benefit of a third party, with the exception of the cursing of the fig tree, behind which may stand a parable that has been transformed into a symbolic action:[115] apart from this one example, we seek in vain legitimation miracles, proof miracles,[116] self-help miracles, and punitive miracles, which are, after all, not infrequent in the Old Testament, for example in the Elijah tradition,[117] and are also found in the pagan environment and in later Christian tradition. The temptation story shows the negative evaluation of them. In this story the tempter presses Jesus to perform a miracle of self-help and proof but is firmly rejected. To this corresponds the rejection of the demand for a sign: Jesus refuses to legitimate himself.[118] Through this the original intention of the miracles becomes clear. They consistently aim to be *signs of the now dawning time of salvation*. In the later community this situation is changed again. The signs of the apostle are also meant there to serve his legitimation, and the divine punishment

[113] Berger 1984b, 1217, the questionable postulate "of a more Hellenistically characterized type" and of a "Jewish-Old Testament oriented one" in the case of raisings of the dead "within the Synoptic tradition." In the Hellenistic type the deliverer encounters the funeral procession, in the Old Testament type the raising occurs in the house. However, sick people usually die in the house, and strangers can meet dead people only by chance in the funeral procession. Berger does not say how he places the third possibility of the raising of the dead from the tomb.

[114] Theissen 1983, 81 (GV = 1974, 90). To be sure, we would not want to claim a priori that it must be a product of "narrative imagination" ("erzählende Phantasie").

[115] Mark 11.12-14, 20-21 = Matt 21.18-20: Matthew introduces a clear intensification of the miracle by making it happen immediately. From his version one could never infer the narratively more complicated and more original version of Mark. On the parable, see Luke 13.6-9.

[116] Cf. the rejection of miracles in Luke 4.9ff. = Matt 4.5ff.; Mark 8.11 = Luke 11.16; Matt 12.38-39; 16.1-4.

[117] Marcion in particular took offense at the punitive miracles of the Old Testament and ascribed them to the "just God." While Elijah caused fire to fall from heaven, Jesus forbids the disciples to request precisely this, and while Elisha causes the children who mock him to be killed by calling upon the righteous God, Jesus lets the children come to him: see Harnack 1960, *282 (no equivalent in Harnack 1990).

[118] See section 16.1 with note 32.

for the opponents plays no small role.[119] Apocryphal Gospels and Acts of apostles no longer know any inhibitions.

We must absolutely affirm, with Klaus Berger, that the miracle stories do not primarily aim to present only "symbolic actions,"[120] although they *also* possess symbolic character at least in part. Thus, the feeding stories point to the eschatological banquet and its festive joy, the healing of the blind to seeing with the eyes of Spirit-effected faith, the stilling of the storm to the saving of the assailed believer. However, the primitive Christian storytellers are concerned with more, namely with the concrete demonstration of God's saving power of creation in the person of Jesus, through which, in the midst of the time of the old world, the new, the kingdom of God, visibly makes its beginning for those with insight.[121] Early Christianity upheld the claim to the gift of miracle, though admittedly with varying intensity.[122]

What is peculiar is the fact that Jesus' ability to work "miracles" in the old world *was scarcely contested even by his opponents*. However, they were explained negatively, even during his lifetime, as a pact with the devil.[123] The later Jewish polemic and, independent of it, Celsus turn Jesus into a magician, who is said to have learned his magic arts in Egypt. This is continued in subsequent anti-Christian polemic.[124] In a dualistic world the miracle was precisely not unambiguous but *ambivalent*. Only for those who were ready for this insight was it regarded as a demonstration of God's power. After all, miracles could be the work of the devil, his demons, or deceptive illusion. Not only Moses[125] but also his opponents Jannes and

---

[119] Second Corinthians 12.12; Rom 15.19; cf. Acts 2.43; 5.12; cf. also Mark 16.17-18. Miraculous punitive actions: Luke 1.18-22; Acts 5.1-11; 12.23; 13.9-11; cf. 19.13-17; 1 Cor 5.4-5; 10.1-11.

[120] Berger 1984b, 1215, against Theissen 1983, 33ff. (GV = 1974, 43ff.): "symbolic actions"; cf. 264 (GV = 261): "collective symbolic actions in which a new way of life is opened up" (cf. 282–83, 287–90; GV = 279, 282, 285). In the conclusion on 300–302 (GV = 295ff.), Theissen attempts to intensify this interpretation: "They point to a revelation of the holy" (301; GV = 296).

[121] Berger 1984b, 1215: they are a "presentation of powerful religious experience, i.e., experience that reaches into the sphere of the bodily, in light of the person of Jesus. The termination of this kind of religious, charismatically brought about experience—and not modern scholarship—is the decisive hindrance in the understanding of miracle stories."

[122] See the excursus at the end of this chapter on the continued effect of the experience of miracles and the question of eyewitness testimony.

[123] See the Beelzebul accusation of the "scribes who had come from Jerusalem" in Mark 3.22-27; cf. Luke 11.15-23 = Matt 12.24-30; see section 10.5 with note 61. Cf. also the accusation that he is a possessed Samaritan in John 8.48.

[124] On this, see Cook 2000, 384 index, s.v. "Jesus as a magician" and "miracles"; Smith 1978.

[125] Gager 1972, 134–61.

Jambres in Egypt[126] were regarded among Jews, Christians, and Gentiles as great miracle workers and magicians, and according to the Synoptic apocalypse, shortly before the end, the eschatological deceiver is supposed to "perform great signs and miracles to . . . lead astray the elect."[127] Something similar is ascribed in an intensified manner to the Antichrist. As the eschatological instrument of Satan, he becomes the "deceiver of the world" *par excellence*.[128] Jews, Gentiles, and Christians mutually accused one another of magic and of deception effected by it, but they often did not call into question the reality of the miracle on the side of their opponent. Critical skeptics, such as Lucian in *Alexander the False Prophet*, became increasingly rare in late antiquity. This ambivalence emerges in sharpest form in the mocking of the crucified one: "He saved others; he cannot save himself. Let the Messiah, the king of Israel, come down from the cross in order that we may see and believe" (Mark 15.31-32). Celsus also poured out his mockery over the crucified one. Whoever dies so pitifully must be a godless deceiver (see note 73 in chapter 21).

Despite this ambivalence, which made questionable or at least restricted their use as a "proof" already in antiquity, miracles—alongside the proof from prophecy—play a not unimportant role among the apologists. The first apologist, Quadratus, at the time of Hadrian recounts that "even after the departure of the savior" those healed and raised by Jesus attested through their constant presence (ἀεὶ παρόντες) his deeds as "corresponding to the truth." Some are said to have lived until the time of the author.[129] This witness function of those healed by Jesus may indeed have a historical basis and may have been not without influence in Jewish Palestine. We find traces of it especially in Luke, John, and in Papias.[130]

According to Jerome, Porphyry said, "it is not a great thing to perform miracles," for "through magic arts" all sorts of miracles have occurred, for example through the Egyptian magicians against Moses, through

---

[126] They are mentioned in the New Testament in 2 Tim 3.8, in Pliny the Elder, *Nat.* 30.2.22, Apuleius, *Apol.* 90, in the Damascus Document V 17–19, in the Targums, and in rabbinic literature; portions of a Jewish pseudepigraphon about them are also preserved on papyrus; see Pietersma 1994.

[127] Mark 13.22 = Matt 24.24; cf. Mark 13.5-6 = Luke 21.8 = Matt 24.4-5 and note 11 above.

[128] Second Thessalonians 2.9-12; Rev 13.11-18; Did. 16.4: καὶ τότε φανήσεται ὁ κοσμοπλανὴς ὡς υἱὸς θεοῦ καὶ ποιήσει σημεῖα καὶ τέρατα; cf. Mart. Isa. 4.10.

[129] In Eusebius, *Hist. eccl.* 4.3.2; cf. Papias, frag. XI according to Philip of Side in Funk/Bihlmeyer 1924, 138 (translated and newly edited by Lindemann/Paulsen 1992, 298ff.).

[130] Luke 8.2-3; John 3.2; 4.45, 48; 6.14; 7.31; 9.8ff.; 11.45-46; Papias apud Eusebius, *Hist. eccl.* 3.39.8–9; cf. also Papias in note 129.

Apollonius of Tyana, and through Apuleius and others.[131] When he, for his part, questions the exorcism into the two thousand swine, it is not because he regards the story as impossible but because he was not willing to credit such a ridiculous-absurd misdeed to Christ, of whom he—in contrast to Celsus—does not have such a bad opinion.[132] In his *Life of Pythagoras*, the great Neoplatonist, who knew and sharply criticized the Gospels, as did his student Iamblichus after him even more strongly, made rich use of miraculous motifs on the basis of older traditions. In the intellectual controversies toward the end of the third and fourth century CE, such *Lives* must be understood, among other things, *also* as counterwritings against the Gospels.[133] This situation begins to change only with the radical criticism of miracles of the seventeenth century, paradigmatically in Spinoza's *Tractatus theologico-politicus*.[134] In his destruction of the picture of Jesus that predominated in the church, D. F. Strauss then had an especially easy time with the miracles of Jesus:

> There is little that is certain, and precisely with respect to the thing to which the church faith chiefly joins itself, the miraculous and super-human in the deeds and fates of Jesus, it is certain that it did not happen.[135]

He has particular contempt for "the story of the resurrection of Jesus." He can designate it, "taken historically," i.e., "comparing the immense effect of this faith with its absolute baselessness," only as "a world-wide deception."[136] On the other hand, he concedes that the "first class" of the miracles of Jesus, the healings of sick people, as "supposed miracle, though only in an entirely natural way, sometimes may really have been effected by Jesus."[137]

---

[131] Dodds 1985, 109; see Porphyry, *Christ.* (Harnack 1916, nr. 1, p. 46, frag. 4): *magicis artibus operati sunt quaedam signa non est autem grande facere signa; nam fecerunt signa et in Aegypto magi contra Moysen, fecit et Apollonius, fecit et Apuleius, et infinita signa fecerunt.*

[132] Porphyry, *Christ.* (Harnack 1916, 76–77, frag. 49).

[133] On this, see Van Uytfanghe 2001; Fauth 1987. This tendency continues in the later Neo-Platonic Lives.

[134] See Spinoza, *Tractatus theologico-politicus* (Gawlick/Niewöhner 1978, 190–227). On the prehistory, see Scholder 1990, esp. 138ff. on Spinoza (GV = 1966, 165ff.).

[135] Strauss 1864, 623–24.

[136] Strauss 1873, 83 (GV = 1872, 72–73).

[137] Strauss 1864, 425. On the concept of miracle in Strauss, see Hartlich/Sachs 1952, 140–46: his view of the "same law-conformity in everything that happens" (Strauss 1837, 87: "*der gleichen Gesetzmäßigkeit in allem Geschehen*") makes every "miracle" impossible. But is not precisely this materialistic-monistic determinism, where he finally landed, a typically modern superstition? Does it not overlook the fact that we humans are limited

For quite some time already, miracles had not been "the favorite child of faith" in liberal German Protestantism. Rather, they appeared—and this applies to this day—to have become "the most aggravating embarrassment of faith," which became visible in the Bultmann school in the fact that the term miracle (*Mirakel*) was readily used in a disparaging way,[138] without consideration of its original sense as θαυμάσιον, that which evokes extreme amazement and sometimes also dismay.[139] "Miracle" comes from *mirari*, which is synonymous with θαυμάζειν.

This deep aversion against everything miraculous had an impact on the judgment about our oldest source, Mark, and its historical value. The fact that the tendency toward "miraculous" embellishment grows in the progression of the tradition is shown by later apocryphal texts such as the fragment of the Gospel of Peter, the Infancy Gospel of Thomas, and the novelistic Acts of apostles. Moreover, it can hardly be doubted that the Synoptic Gospels already have a certain tendency toward the intensification of miraculous processes, although this—to the extent that we can test them through Synoptic comparison—is by no means very conspicuous. Matthew and Luke sometimes also omit embellishing characteristics. The tendency to narrative intensification is most prominent in the latest Gospel in the canon, in John, though he can also make critical statements in relation to miracles. A faith that is based only on them is without substance.[140]

The many legendary characteristics and miraculous stories cannot be adduced as an argument against the authorship of the oldest Gospels and the claim to eyewitness testimony. It is wrongheaded when, for example, Wellhausen, against Papias, fundamentally calls into question a connection between the author of the Gospel of Mark and Peter because the narrative of the calling of four disciples "is legendary and cannot go back

---

beings, have a field of vision that is subject to error, which in nature and history is capable only of limited knowledge of the "miracle" of God's creation and activity?

[138] See, for example, Bultmann 1984a, 36ff. (GV = 1948a, 48ff.). There he opposes the Pauline understanding of the resurrection in 1 Cor 15.3-8 as an "authenticating miracle."

[139] On Bultmann and his teacher Wilhelm Herrmann, see note 83 above. The θαυμάζειν (cf. Mark 5.20; Luke 11.14) can also be described as ἐκπλήσσεσθαι: Luke 9.43, cf. Mark 7.37. Mark uses this verb especially with respect to Jesus' teaching: 1.22; 6.2; 11.18.

[140] Typical cases are expansions: thus in the feeding of the five thousand "men" (= human beings) in Mark 6.44 in Matt 14.21 through the addition "without women and children" or in the walking on water story from Mark 6.45-52 in Matt 14.22-33. Through the failure of Peter and Jesus' critical question in 14.31 it receives a deeper theological significance. The word διστάζειν "to doubt" occurs only here and in Matt 28.17 within the New Testament. Cf. Mark 11.23 and Matt 17.20; Luke 17.6. On criticism of miracles, see John 2.23-24; 4.48; 6.14-15; 12.37; 20.29.

to Peter."[141] If the tradition of Mark is "obfuscated," then it is due to the conscious kerygmatic-narrative shaping, behind which stands the theological intention of the author. Whether his material "passed through the mouths of many people" before it came to the author remains an unprovable, indeed improbable assertion.[142] Here, Wellhausen overlooks the fact that in the Gospel tradition the intervals of time are far shorter than in the case of the Old Testament narrative material and that the decisive preachers and tradents were also authoritative teachers in the young mission communities.[143]

Eduard Meyer, who knew ancient history in its whole breadth better than the Old Testament scholar and orientalist, said this about the remarks of Wellhausen on this point:

> This judgment is completely incomprehensible to me.

To this he added

> when Wellhausen says further: "the miracle stories in the form in which they are presented in Mark oppose most of all the tracing back to the most intimate disciple," then this is actually a rationalistic failure to recognize the character of these stories and of the conceptual world out of which they grew. In the same way as they are told in Mark, believing eyewitnesses tell them in all times, not only in the Middle Ages and in the Orient but also in the Greek world.[144]

---

[141] Wellhausen 1987, 155.

[142] Wellhausen 1987, 155 (our emphasis). In that case one would have to ask approximately how many persons? After all, we have only a time of tradition of forty years. See note 99 above on Tacitus. In the Old Testament the situation was completely different. The claim that Peter "in his proclamation did not deliver lectures on the evangelical pericopes" and could not have brought them "in written form into to a series" creates a caricature. Peter *must* have told stories of Jesus. Otherwise the Gospel tradition, including the offensive miracle stories, would not have come to the west at all and the Gospels would not have arisen. See also section 6.4.1.

[143] See section 6.4.1 with note 142. For the Papias note, see section 6.4.1 with note 121.

[144] Meyer 1962, 159 n. 1 on Wellhausen 1911. Even if one does not share Meyer's speculations about a source of Peter and the twelve, one should nevertheless affirm his statement that "the tradition does not rest on community tradition but on very specific individualities" (160 n. 1), with Mark, for example, pointing "indeed to an individual emergence" against Dibelius' criticism of Meyer (Dibelius 1921, 232), as more recent scholarship shows. See notes 68–72 in chapter 5. On the problem of "miracles" and "eyewitness testimony," see the excursus below.

Beyond the examples of eyewitness accounts in the case of miraculous processes adduced by Meyer, we could also point to the phenomenon of the formation of legends during the lifetime of a hero, which is frequently attested from antiquity until the present. The companion, friend, and court historian Callisthenes recounts a "miraculous" passage of Alexander through a bay in Pamphylia, which Josephus already compares to Moses' passage through the Reed Sea.[145] Callisthenes recounts further that the priest of the Ammon oracle told Alexander that he was a "son of Zeus" and that the king before the battle of Gaugamela prayed for divine support, "if he descended from Zeus," support that he promptly obtained.

R. Merkelbach comments with respect to the Alexander legend:

> Legends arise, wherever we can observe them, simultaneously or right after the events.

Therefore, it was

> not at all surprising that the soldiers told such stories. The march of Alexander must have been an incredible adventure for them.[146]

> For many contemporaries and especially for his soldiers, Alexander (was) a mythical figure already during his lifetime. The presentations of the history of Alexander have largely obscured this. The genuine picture of the historical Alexander, however, also includes this mythical element.[147]

If here we insert "Jesus" for Alexander, "disciples" for his soldiers, and "critical Jesus research" for the history of Alexander, then we stand before a—still unrecognized—fundamental problem of New Testament

---

[145] FGrH 124 F 3: Strabo 14.3.9 (666–667); Arrian, *Anab.* 1.26.1–2. See Hengel 1984a, 17 n. 70 (1985b, 11, 124 n. 70). In *Ant.* 2.347–348 (trans. H. St. J. Thackeray, LCL, 317), Josephus comments cautiously and with consideration for educated Greco-Roman readers: "For my part, I have recounted each detail here told just as I found it in the sacred books. Nor let anyone marvel at the astonishing nature of the narrative nor doubt that it was given to men of old, innocent of crime, to find a road of salvation through the sea itself, whether by the will of God or maybe by accident." After this he refers to the story of Alexander. He concludes: "However on these matters everyone is welcome to his own opinion." Cf. *Ant.* 1.108. On this, see also Spinoza, *Tractatus theologico-politicus*, at the end of his chapter on miracles (Gawlick/Niewöhner 1978, 226).

[146] Merkelbach 1977, 61.

[147] Merkelbach 1977, 92.

scholarship. In our view, despite some advances,[148] the extremely controversial problem, legends or miracles and Jesus tradition, in the Gospels has indeed not yet been investigated in a satisfactory way. The contemporary formation of legends or eyewitness testimony and miracle stories cannot be explained adequately by form criticism and certainly not by a purely literary-rhetorical approach that wants to regard the stories as mere literary fiction. It is based above all on the historical figure of the hero and his effect.

EXCURSUS

The Continued Effect of the Experience of Miracles and the Question of Eyewitness Testimony

The problem of "miracle" and "eyewitness testimony" of contemporaries can be pursued in various ways from antiquity until the present. It belongs, among other things, to the special cases of an "oral history." We have already pointed to the witnesses, who still lived during his time, of the healings of Vespasian in Alexandria in 69 CE in Tacitus.[149] The Augustus legend recounts an appointed eyewitness testimony, where a *vir praetorius* is said to have testified under oath to the journey to heaven of the deified emperor.[150] In the second half of the second century CE, Lucian can parody this whole milieu by having unreliable eyewitnesses give accounts in *The Lover of Lies*, mocking the astonishingly rapid development of the legend of the fire death and journey to heaven of Peregrinus, and describing the success of a person admired as a thaumaturgist in *Alexander the False Prophet*. However, it is precisely his polemical and ironical accounts that show that there were not a few eyewitnesses of *mirabilia* and that these existed even among educated enemies of faith.[151]

---

[148] Meier 1994, 509–1038; Theissen 1983 (GV = 1974); Theissen/Merz 1998, 281–313 (GV = 1997, 256–83). By contrast, the work of Kollmann is flawed (see Kollmann 1996; 2002 and note 40 in chapter 5).

[149] See note 99 above.

[150] Seuetonius, *Aug.* 94–99 (97.1). As secretary to Hadrian Suetonius had access to the secret files. Livia is said to have bribed these eyewitnesses. Cf. also his contemporary Pliny the Younger, *Ep.* 7.27.12 (trans. Walsh 2006, 183), on the stories about *phantasmata*, which he believes, because he himself experienced such things: *Et haec quidem adfirmantibus credo; illud adfirmare aliis possum* ("These details are attested by other persons, and I believe them; but I can attest to others the truth of the story that follows").

[151] Lucian, *Philops.* 11ff.; *Peregr.* 39–41; *Alex.* Lucian had a certain knowledge of Christian tradition or of the Gospels and polemicized indirectly against them; see Hengel 2004c, 103.

The continuing effects of the Christian miracle tradition in the early church are attested in multiple and very different ways.[152] This applies despite the widespread view that in the time after the apostles, miracles "would no longer have been 'necessary.'"[153] Irenaeus wants to know about contemporary raisings of the dead.[154] Tertullian reports miraculous events during his time.[155] Origen also points to such events, which had become exceptions in comparison with the time of the apostles. According to him, the number of the signs of the Holy Spirit had decreased, but there were still "traces" of them "among some persons whose souls are purified by the Logos and by the deeds that correspond to him."[156] On the other hand, we also find in Origen a criticism of the overvaluation of miracles, since they have an ambivalent character.[157] As already indicated by his byname, special miracle traditions are connected with Origen's student Gregory Thaumaturgus[158] — including numerous, not very edifying punitive miracles — and with the earliest monks in Egypt, beginning with Athanasius' *Life of Anthony*. K. Heussi comments on them:

> It is completely impossible to unravel the emergence of the individual mira-
> cle stories that Athanasius has woven into his presentation. These . . . are . . .
> immensely important for understanding the activity of Anthony; nothing
> would be more wrong than to cut them out summarily with the critical knife.
> Athanasius by no means invented them. He drew . . . from the monastic
> tradition that had developed about Anthony. Thus, we can observe that these

---

[152] See now the overview in Van Uytfanghe 2001, esp. 1326ff.

[153] Van Uytfanghe 2001, 1326; cf. Van Uytfanghe 1981, 207–8.

[154] Irenaeus, *Haer.* 2.31.2 and 32.4 (= Eusebius, *Hist. eccl.* 5.7.2–5).

[155] Tertullian, *Scap.* 4. The Christian Proculus heals the emperor Septimius Severus through anointing with oil. The prayer of Christians effectively hinders water scarcity and drought. Cf. the miracle of rain in Marcus Aurelius' war against the Germans on account of the prayer of the Christian soldiers of the Melitene legion recounted in Eusebius, *Hist. eccl.* 5.5. Cf., however, Cassius Dio, *Hist. Rom.* 71.8: the miracle is said to go back to an Egyptian magician, and on this, in turn, the Christian epitomist Xiphilinus' criticism of the Roman historian regarding the cause of the rain miracle.

[156] Origen, *Cels.* 7.8; see also 1.2, 6, 46: effects of the Spirit attested through eyewitnesses in the present; 2.8 and *Hom. Jer.* 4.3. On the miracles of pagan philosophers, see *Cels.* 5.57.

[157] Origen, *Cels.* 3.33–38; Minucius Felix, *Oct.* 20.3–4, and on this Harnack 1981, I: 220ff., 226.

[158] Ca. 210–275 CE; cf. the *Life of Gregory Thaumaturgus* by Gregory of Nyssa (ca. 335–395), which is embellished in a strongly legendary manner (Heil 1990, 3–57). Gregory of Nyssa's grandmother was a student of Gregory Thaumaturgus. On this, see Crouzel 1983, 781–82: "In the case of the miracles that Gregory of Nyssa and others recount about G. *it is impossible to separate truth and fiction.* In any case, G. was a widely praised charismatic personality" (our emphasis).

miracles were told about him during the lifetime of Anthony. But we can only make speculations and estimations about the extent to which the individual stories are connected to a real experience of Anthony.[159]

To a large extent, such sentences could also be applied to the stories of the Gospels. This rich tradition continues from the fourth century with the Egyptian and Syrian-Palestinian monks and the great Cappadocians in Asia Minor.[160] In the last book of *The City of God*,[161] Augustine recounts numerous "miracles" which he either experienced himself or claims to have learned about from reliable sources. In response to the opponents' argument that the lack of miracles in the present shows the corresponding New Testament miracles to be doubtful he counters that many miracles have occurred also in his time, the eyewitnesses of which he knows or which are based on his own experiences, and it is only that these have largely remained unknown. To a larger extent they are connected with the relics of Stephen, which had been brought to Carthage not long before. He therefore prompted the collection of about seventy reports, which were read in the worship service, of which he comments on twenty-five. These reports, which go back in part to direct experience, are very different and interesting form-critically, but have never been made fruitful for the interpretation of the New Testament accounts, as is the case for the early church miracle tradition in general. Among others, they include three "raisings of the dead" of people who have just died; they, too, are, of course, legendarily embellished in part. This may go back already to the earliest eyewitnesses.[162] Sulpicius Severus (ca. 360–410 CE), a contemporary of Augustine, probably wrote his *Life of Martin of Tours* (316–397), which is brimming with miracles of every sort, right after his death. Two years earlier, in 395 CE, he had visited the saint. To be sure, he also recounts that doubts about the reality of these accounts arose in monastic circles of southern Gaul.[163] Around 593/594 CE Pope Gregory the Great (540–640) composed his *Dialogi de vita et miraculis patrum Italicorum* in four books. The second book contains the *Life of Benedict of Nursia* (d. 547), while the first and third books recount the stories of forty-nine saints of his time, who

[159] Heussi 1936, 86; cf. 171–78.

[160] On this, see Van Uytfanghe 2001, 1152ff. on Athanasius' *Life of Antony* (1186); 1202 on the *Historia monachorum in Aegypto*; 1206–7 on the *Historia Lausiaca*; see further 1182ff., 1187ff., 1195ff., 1199–1232.

[161] Augustine, *Civ.* 22.8.

[162] Augustine, *Civ.* 22.8: *nam etiam nunc fiunt miracula in eius nomine* . . . (8.1). On this, see Harnack 1910 (= 1980, 78–97).

[163] On this, see Frank 1975, II: 13ff., and Berschin 1986, 195ff.; Stancliffe 1983. His work gave the main impetus for the veneration of Martin. On this, see Van Uytfanghe 2001, 1262–70.

are mostly unknown. The belief in miracles of this work, which is structured in a literarily artistic way, can, to some extent, scarcely be outdone; Gregory constantly appeals to people who vouch for them.[164] Here too, despite the relative temporal proximity, legend and memory have inseparably fused together. Later, the Venerable Bede also frequently names contemporary eyewitnesses of miracles.[165] It is conspicuous that these peculiar stories are very multifaceted and are not forced to take a certain form. The whole complex deserves a detailed monographic investigation.

We could continue even longer in this milieu, which appears foreign to us today. The rural population in Galilee and also the disciples of Jesus were undoubtedly scarcely more critical than Augustine in North Africa or Sulpicius Severus in Gaul at the turn of the fourth to the fifth century, Gregory the Great in Italy in the sixth century, and Bede in Anglo-Saxon Northumbria at the turn from the seventh to the eighth century. The miracle stories and motifs of the Gospels were not a syncretistic or secondary product of the spread of Christianity in the pagan Hellenistic-Roman world. They belong from the very beginning to the proclamation of the primitive community and are rightly connected with the person of Jesus. Beginning with the first recounting, they may have been increasingly (in some cases massively; we can scarcely determine this in detail) intensified, reshaped, and adapted to the missionary situation. In terms of content they consistently have a Palestinian-Jewish character. Even the wine miracle of Cana need not be a direct import from the cult of Dionysus that made Jesus a competitor of Dionysus. In our view, it more likely comes from Galilean "Messiah haggada," which, for its part, had long since taken up Dionysian motifs.[166]

This line can easily be extended into the present. E. Meyer refers to his investigations on the Mormons. One could even more plausibly adduce the Eastern European Hasidim from the time of their founder Baal Shem Tov in the eighteenth century and above all the Roman canonization records and relatively contemporary figures of the nineteenth century such as Don Bosco, the orphan father of Turin, Jean-Marie Vianney, the

---

[164] Berschin 1986, I: 305–24: "One cannot dispute that the *Dialogi* are still problematic reading for many modern readers. Gregory portrays many miracles in a way that touches on magical notions" (307). A theological intent indeed stands behind this. See Manselli 1983, 948: "The saint is active as mediator and instrument, which through his prayer and his intercession expresses and effects even the intervention of God." Gregory "completed . . . his work as theologian and counselor of souls with a painting that is full of life" (949).

[165] See, for example, *Hist. Anglorum* 4.30–32; 5.1–12, and his *Vita Cuthberti* (PL 94.575–596). Bede was born in 672. Cuthbert died in 687.

[166] Hengel 1987b = 1995, 293–330 (GV = 2007b, 568–600).

pastor of Ars,[167] and the no less carefully reported "Blumhardtian stories," whose interpretation by Blumhardt himself is, of course, one-sided.[168] In the twentieth century one would need to mention the recently canonized Padre Pio. If one begins to search here, the examples are endless.

With this nothing is said yet about the "historicity" of "miracle stories" in the proper sense, i.e., about the "real happening" that underlies the stories. Often they are surely based on fiction, especially in the literary sphere, for example in the Acts of apostles or in the legends or biographies of saints. The religious taste of the masses seeks a pious sensational story. But there are also traditions that make one pause and think. After all, in itself the historical fact of the miracle can neither be proven nor explained. The concern is also not simply with a breaking of the laws of nature. This is a relatively modern notion. Ancient Judaism and early Christianity knew, as we have said, only God's "creation" and its reliable ordering, further its God-determined history and from this him as sovereign "creator," "preserver," "Lord," and "judge." It was decisive that the concern was with a happening that contradicted human experience and evoked general "amazement," precisely with a θαυμάσιον/*miraculum*, which could be ascribed only to a superhuman power, i.e., to God himself, "for whom all things are possible" (or to his adversaries). And this was (and is)—in the ambivalence of the process, which is difficult to control exactly—a matter of "apprehension" or interpretation, one could also say: of faith and of the understanding of reality connected with it. How does God's transcendence become an effectual reality in this world, and how does he act with us humans? In our context, the concern can, however, be only with the phenomenon of contemporary witness and eyewitness, with it always being necessary to take into account the consciousness of humans and of their respective time. In Galilee and in the primitive Christian communities rational criticism (in the modern sense) was certainly not very developed. But there too we should not simply presuppose an unrestrained belief in miracles and production of miracles. This occurs only in the semi-educated literary milieu of the novels about the apostles starting in the second half of the second century.

Today many are more prepared than in the nineteenth century, which in broad circles of the intellectual world up to the late D. F. Strauss was shaped by materialism à la Büchner's *Force and Matter*, to grant in principle miraculous healings to Jesus (which are attested relatively often in

---

[167] See the instructive—though on the whole entirely uncritical—compilation in Schamoni 1976, IX–X, and Schamoni 1968. See also the (liberal) church historian Nigg 1946, 354–91, on the pastor of Ars.

[168] See now Ising 2002.

the Gospels)—and perhaps also other "astonishing" processes, such as foresight and knowledge of human thoughts. Even the possibility that he brought back to life individual people who were critically ill and considered dead cannot be excluded. The well-known later parallels in Philostratus' *Life of Apollonius of Tyana* and Acts 20.9-10 and the examples of Augustine show that in antiquity one was not always so certain here. The account in Mark 5.35-43 about the twelve-year-old daughter of Jairus is—as 5.39 signals—told in an ambivalent way, and a similar judgment could be reached about the young man of Nain in Luke 7.11-17. This applies all the more to Acts 20.9-10. At that time burials took place on the day on which the person passed away. To be sure, the historicity of such stories can never be proven. However, whoever wants to regard all of them as mere fiction should at least try to justify this *sufficiently*.

The so-called "nature miracles"—which are even more enigmatic for us than the healings, which, for their part, can sometimes scarcely be separated from the exorcisms—are also ultimately connected with the deep impression made by the deeds and person of Jesus. We can only speculate about their starting point and the occasion of their development. Even a narrative such as the "stilling of the storm" in Mark 4.35-41 need not be based on mere fiction. In our view, it is too easy to regard such accounts in the earliest Gospel texts as free inventions. By contrast, it is understandable that they were developed and intensified in the—kerygmatically conditioned—continual telling of them.

We think that almost all of them have a concrete basis in the actions of Jesus and from there continued to take shape, whether under the influence of Old Testament motifs, such as the Elijah/Elisha miracles, thus, for example, in the feeding stories,[169] or whether through visionary experiences of the disciples, for instance in the transfiguration or the walking on the sea—we do not know. The transfer of motifs is also possible in individual cases. But we also should not—due to a false, "anti-miracle" apologetic and in order to obtain a modern Jesus—ascribe the miracle tradition as far away from him as possible to a temporally-spatially distant "Hellenistic community" but rather acknowledge that Jesus is at this point more foreign and uncanny than we enlightened Christians of the western world would like to believe. Presumably these features are better understood in the Third World. The understanding of ancient religious texts such as the Gospels is not furthered by rationalistic arrogance. The actual problem of such phenomena—which are extremely rare in our experience—is that they usually withdraw themselves from a simple rational explanation through their contingency. The "enlightened" person can only marvel (or

---

[169] See the end of section 16.3 with note 102.

"be irritated") at this; he cannot be compelled to a religious understanding. The ambivalence of "miracles," which we already encounter in antiquity, applies all the more today. To this one can add the fact that these phenomena are not restricted to the Christian faith but are also found in other religions—for example in Buddhism—and the fact that the danger of misuse is always connected with them.

Jesus himself, his disciples, and the Synoptic tradition understood these "deeds of power" as signs of the kingdom of God dawning with his activity and thus also as "messianic" signs. This continues—in intensified form—in the Johannine understanding of σημεῖον. Thus, not only Jesus' proclamation of the kingdom but also his "deeds" lead necessarily to the question of his "messianic" claim.

17

Prophet or Messiah?[1]

17.1 Jesus as the Messianic Prophet

In his short work *Die Erforschung der synoptischen Evangelien*,[2] R. Bultmann summarizes the result of his academic efforts with respect to Jesus' self-understanding and claim:

> To me . . . the necessary consequence of the analysis of his words appears to be

that Jesus did not

> regard himself to be the Messiah and . . . first became Messiah in the faith of the community. . . . In any case one sees clearly that Jesus did not appear with the claims that accompanied the Jewish view of the Messiah title. The correct characterization of his activity is that he was a *prophet*.

Thus far he follows William Wrede's theses,[3] which were admittedly formulated much more cautiously. Neither Wrede nor Bultmann had investigated in greater detail the diverse messianic expectations of Judaism at the turn of the age but started with the presupposition of a purely political image of the Messiah. Both were one-sidedly—today we could say

---

[1] Wrede 1971 (GV = 1969); Bultmann 2007, I: 26–32 (GV = 1984b, 26–34); Collins 1995; Zimmermann 1998; Hengel/Schwemer 2001; Hengel 1995, esp. 1–72; Dunn 2003b, 615–766. Cf. now also Allison 2010, 221–304; Deines 2012a; 2012b.

[2] Bultmann 1966, 49 (ET = 1934b, 71).

[3] In a letter to Harnack just two years before his early death, Wrede recanted his thesis of an unmessianic Jesus; see Rollmann/Zager 2001, 317, and Hengel/Schwemer 2001, IX, 19ff. with note 71 (ET = Hengel 1995, 17ff. with note 16). On Wrede's thesis, see sections 17.3.1–17.3.2.

inadequately—informed about the "Jewish views" that "were given with the title Messiah." This also applies to more recent investigations that have taken over the thesis of Wrede.[4] However, the sentences of the Marburg scholar that immediately follow stand in clear opposition to this view:

> To be sure, one may and must designate the movement that he ignited in the Jewish people as a *messianic movement*, for it was carried by the faith that the *messianic promises* are now fulfilled, that the kingdom of God is now dawning, and one already feels and sees its dawning in the mighty activity of Jesus and the flight of the evil spirits.[5]

Here the question arises: How can a figure who is firmly designated as nonmessianic and only as a "prophet" awaken "through his mighty activity" the impression of the "fulfillment of the messianic promises" and of the dawning of the kingdom of God and thereby ignite "a messianic movement," and yet himself strictly reject every "messianic claim"? And if the people saw in Jesus the fulfillment of "messianic promises" at work, should this not be connected with the fact that *he ultimately viewed himself as "fulfiller" of these very promises*? Or did he lead the people astray? Are not historical inconsistencies present here, which also make it impossible to distinguish in a meaningful way the eschatological "prophet" John from the "prophet" Jesus who followed him? Nevertheless, this contradictory view became widely established in German scholarship and partly also in American scholarship. Only Ernst Käsemann dared to contradict the head of the school at this point, when from the expression "But I say to you" of the antitheses of the Sermon on the Mount he inferred a "claim" that "far surpasses that of any rabbi or prophet," for

---

[4] A typical example is the habilitation thesis of Karrer 1990, which disdains what stands to reason and to some extent reaches very bizarre hypotheses in his derivation of the Messiah title. The texts of Qumran, whose significance he does not recognize, point, by contrast, in the right direction. See Zimmermann 1998, passim; Collins 1995, 209: "Jewish ideas of messianism were not uniform. There was a dominant notion of a Davidic messiah, as the king who would restore the kingdom of Israel. . . . There were also, however, minor messianic strands, which envisaged a priestly messiah, or an anointed prophet or a heavenly Son of Man. Christian messianism drew heavily on some of the minor strands (prophet, Son of Man)."

[5] Bultmann 1966, 49, our emphasis (ET = 1934b, 71–72); 2007, I: 26–32 (GV = 1984b, 26–34): Jesus' life and work were "unmessianic" (32; cf. 27; GV = 33; cf. 28). It "was not as a king but as a prophet and a rabbi [*sic*!] that Jesus appeared—and one, may add, as an exorcist" (27; GV = 28). But of what prophet was it said that Satan and the evil spirits had to give way before him? Would that not rather fit with a figure such as the archangel Michael (Rev 12)?

The only category *which does justice to his claim* (quite independently of whether he used it himself and required it of others) is that in which his disciples themselves place him—namely, *that of the Messiah.*[6]

Käsemann is surely to be affirmed in his claim that the question of whether and how far Jesus himself lay claim to *messianic titles* must be distinguished from the question of his *messianic claim*. It is not the titles which are decisive for the evaluation of his activity, but the *eschatological authority*—which is unmistakable and fundamentally intensified in comparison with contemporary authorities, who likewise appeared as eschatological teachers and prophets, such as the Teacher of Righteousness and above all John the Baptist. This means that in the first instance we need to ask not whether he designated himself as "the anointed one of God" (or let himself be designated as such) but whether he, going beyond the measure of a teacher and prophet, *acted* as such. It is also necessary to consider the larger bandwidth of the meanings of the term "the anointed one" attested by the Qumran texts, which is broader than what has previously been acknowledged and expressed at least as much an *eschatological function* given by God as it did a dignity. E. P. Sanders could be right when he begins his quest for Jesus with Jesus' *deeds* as signs of his intention,[7] though it is important to clarify that there is only an apparent opposition between deed and word, for the deed is also not wordless and the word can, as the healing accounts and the story of the stilling of the storm show, become a deed. Further, it would be necessary to ask whether through the verdict "prophet but not Messiah" a false opposition is established, which is one-sidedly oriented to the royal Messiah image of later rabbinic Judaism, where the Messiah appears to be primarily (but not exclusively) a politically active, royal-ruling figure and as a victorious warrior. We cannot presuppose in Judaism—at least in the prerabbinic period before 70 CE—a fixed "Messianic doctrine" and on such a dubious basis reject *a limine* the Synoptic reports about a messianic claim of Jesus.[8] For example, instead of the royal Messiah, the Samaritans, who acknowledged after all only the Pentateuch as Holy Scripture, expected the eschatological prophet as bringer of salvation on the basis of Deut 18.15, 18. This notion surfaces even in the Gospel of John. While the Johannine Baptist distances himself

---

[6] Käsemann 1964b, 38 (our emphasis; GV = Käsemann 1960/1964, I: 206). On this, cf. also Hengel/Schwemer 2001 (*Der messianische Anspruch Jesu*). The title of the book (The Messianic Claim of Jesus) was chosen on the basis of the quoted statement of E. Käsemann. On Jesus and the Baptist, see chapter 10.

[7] Sanders 1985, see 439 (index, s.v. "Intention") and 61 for the temple cleansing as the "surest starting point of our investigation."

[8] On this, see Hengel/Schwemer 2001; see now also Theissen 2003b, 28.

from it,[9] it is applied to Jesus by the people, while the Fourth Evangelist,[10] as Wayne Meeks has shown, presents Jesus, among other things, as the "prophet-king" characterized by Moses typology, who certainly as such absolutely surpasses and replaces Moses.[11]

By now we know that already in Qumran there was expectation, alongside the priestly and Davidic-royal anointed ones, of a prophetic anointed one in accordance with Deut 18 as well, and even the prophets, beginning with Moses, could be designated as "anointed ones." Prophetic and royal characteristics flowed into each other, as already in Isa 11.1ff. and Pss. Sol. 17/18. David, too, was, as exemplary bearer of the Spirit, king and prophet, and his psalms were, alongside Isaiah, the most important "prophetic" book in Qumran and in primitive Christianity. In Zech 9.9-10 the messianic king who enters Jerusalem is described as a humble ruler who brings peace.

In the text from 4Q521 quoted above, which is based on Isa 26; 35; 61 and Ps 146, it is, for example, disputed which "Messiah" is intended, with the salvific action of God and of his anointed one being connected with each other.[12] The question of the "messianic claim" of Jesus can therefore no longer be so easily dismissed, as sometimes still happens today, with a wave of the hand. This happened prematurely through Wrede, who after intensive study of the problem made a retraction, and it took place with far too much self-assurance and decisiveness through Bultmann and most of his students. Proceeding from the questionable alternative "prophet" or "Messiah" was an unacceptable simplification of the historical problem.

[9] John 1.21, 25: ὁ προφήτης, i.e., *the* eschatological prophet in the sense of Moses *redivivus*.

[10] John 6.14-15; cf. 7.40. The crowd asks after the feeding miracle: "Is this not truly the prophet who comes into the world" and then wants to seize him and make him king. Against Bultmann 1962, 158 n. 2 (ET = 1971, 213 n. 7; see, however, Jeremias 1926, 83), the eschatological prophet does, of course, have to do with the "Moses *redivivus*." Bultmann also errs in relation to John 1.21 when he (89; GV = 61) opines that the *interpretation* of the "prophet" from Deut 18.15, 18 as referring to the Messiah emerges only with Christianity: "In Judaism the expectation of the 'prophet' is not attested." All the more questionable is his speculation that we are dealing here with an expectation "in heretical and syncretistic circles," according to which, as in the Pseudo-Clementines (or with the Manichees), "the 'prophet' embodies himself in different figures . . . in the course of the generations" (GV = 61–62; cf. 1971, 90). The Jewish expectation of a messianic prophet according to Deut 18 is now also confirmed by the Qumran discoveries; see Zimmermann 1998, 379–87, on 4Q521; Collins 1995, 268 index, s.v. "Moses" and especially 112–22, 144–46. Schwemer 2001b, 208–17.

[11] Meeks 1967, 99; cf. 319–20.

[12] On this, see section 4.5 with note 201 and the end of section 10.5 with note 68. See also Zimmermann 1998, 379–88, and for the prophetic conceptions of the anointed in general, 312–417.

17.2 The I Sayings of Jesus[13]

Through his eschatological claim to bring the fulfillment of the Old Testament promises Jesus combined different aspects of contemporary Judaism. This was in its way unique. For precisely this reason he provoked that offense which brought him in the end to the cross. A necessary but not entirely natural homecoming to Judaism was promoted by the liberal neo-Protestant image of the unmessianic rabbi and prophet Jesus, whereas insightful Jewish scholars such as J. Klausner and D. Flusser did not doubt the messianic claim of Jesus. On the other hand, Protestant scholarship provided some Jewish scholars with arguments for interpreting Jesus as a mere "Pharisee of a special kind," which he was not.[14] For this he already lacked the interest in the halakah and its casuistry, which he in fact rejected. The distance of Jesus from the dominant contemporary Jewish groups, despite the indisputable fact that he was Jewish through and through, is visible precisely in the special form of his underivable messianic authority. This can be seen, for example, in the especially controversial sayings in which Jesus speaks of his messianic sending in the first person. Bultmann explained these words in general as secondary,[15] and most of his students followed him in this judgment. In them Jesus' sending is said to be summarized very generally merely in retrospect. By contrast, J. Jeremias has demonstrated, in our view convincingly, that the sayings introduced with ἦλθον, "I have come," followed by an infinitive, can sometimes simply mean in Aramaic texts "my task is . . . , I intend . . ."[16] The decisive question is whether these sayings really fit better in some later community situation or whether they cannot be more sensibly integrated into the overall context of the preaching of Jesus.

Mark 2.17: with two antithetical sayings Jesus rejects here the accusations of the Pharisees regarding his fellowship with sinners: "Those who are well do not need a physician but those who are sick. I have not come (this means: my task is not) to call righteous but sinners."[17] Here the concern is not with a later community situation—there the sinners and

---

[13] Bultmann 1963, 150–63 (GV = 1995, 161–76); Jeremias 1970, 250ff. (GV = 1979, 239ff.); Jeremias 1967b, 166–67.

[14] On this, see note 50 in chapter 5.

[15] Bultmann 1963, 155 (GV = 1995, 167).

[16] Jeremias 1967b, 166–67.

[17] Mark 2.17: οὐκ ἦλθον καλέσαι δικαίους ἀλλὰ ἁμαρτωλούς. Cf. Luke 5.31-32 = Matt 9.12-13, which also inserts the quotation from Hos 6.6 (cf. Matt 12.7). On the restraint of the Pharisaic *haberim* vis-à-vis the table fellowship with the *'ammê hā-'āreṣ*, see Bill. I: 498; see further the Cynic slogan ascribed to Diogenes in Klostermann 1971, 26–27, according to Stobaeus, *Flor.* 3.462.14.

even more so the tax collectors no longer stood at the center—but with an extremely controversial point in the activity of Jesus himself, since he breaks with the generally valid religious norm and therefore is defamed as "friend of tax collectors and sinners."[18] In the later Palestinian Jewish Christian community tax collectors and sinners were hardly highly appreciated any longer. The formula "Gentiles and tax collectors" again becomes an insult there.[19] Closely related to Mark 2.17 in terms of substance is Luke 19.10, where Luke, after the story of Zacchaeus, places in Jesus' mouth the saying "The Son of Man has come to seek and save what is lost." In this saying the same intention of Jesus finds expression.[20]

Luke 12.49-50 (special material): "I came to cast fire on the earth, and how I wish that it were already set on fire. I must be baptized with a baptism, and how impatient I am until it is finally accomplished." Related, but secondary, since it is no longer eschatologically conditioned, is Gos. Thom. 82: "The one who is near me is near the fire, the one who is far from me is far from the kingdom." In Luke Jesus interprets his own messianic commission to proclaim the kingdom. His message is to be active as a fire, which in the end even consumes him. To the fire as metaphor of judgment (and purification) corresponds water as symbol of death.[21] For Luke this saying is connected with the coming "stronger one" as "fire baptizer" in the preaching of John and with the pouring out of the Spirit at Pentecost.[22] The first is also an expression of God's presence, for the judging and purifying power of repentance and for the renewal of the sinful human being. According to the second half of the double saying of Luke 12.49-50 about the "fire baptism," Jesus reckons with his death, but still in an undefined way, in contrast to the passion predictions in Mark, which are more strongly developed as *vaticinia ex eventu*. The image of the death-baptism probably comes from the proclamation of the Baptist.[23] The emphasis on

[18] Luke 7.34 = Matt 11.19; cf. Mark 2.16 = Luke 5.30 = Matt 9.11; Luke 15.1.

[19] Matthew 18.17; cf. 5.46; 21.31-32: οἱ τελῶναι καὶ αἱ πόρναι.

[20] In John tax collectors no longer appear, and the term ἁμαρτωλός is applied only to Jesus in the controversy around the healing of the blind man in chapter 9. Tax collectors also play no role any longer in the epistles and in the later early Christian literature, including the apocryphal Gospels. The turning to "tax collectors and sinners" is also not a direct reference to the Gentile mission. Even in the apologists τελῶναι appears only once in Justin, *1 Apol.* 15.10, namely with a negative meaning as a quotation of Matt 5.46.

[21] Luke 24.32; cf. Jer 5.14; 23.29; Isa 10.17; 66.15; Deut 4.24; Ps 18.9 and elsewhere.

[22] Luke 3.16-17 = Matt 3.11-12; see section 13.6 with note 141; Acts 2.3, 19. On the metaphor, see Lang 1969 (GV = 1959); cf. Lang 1969, 944 (GV = 1959, 943.24): Luke 12.49 "comprehensively describes the mission of Jesus as a fulfillment of the promise of the Baptist." Cf. also Lang 1969, 935 (GV = 1959, 934.7): "fire is also a means of ritual purification."

[23] Cf. Mark 10.38-39; Luke 12.50 and the end of section 9.3.

Jesus' own inner struggle can scarcely be an invention of the community. And it is even more certain that one cannot ascribe the whole to a Christian prophetic saying. The reference to fire characterizes the immediate "messianic activity" of Jesus. In the mouth of a primitive Christian prophet the whole thing is meaningless.

Right after this double saying there follows another saying, which makes a no less provocative impression: "Do you believe that I have come to bring peace upon the earth, no, I say to you, but division!"[24] Jesus' message of the dawning kingdom brings in the first instance not external peace but unrest and division not only in Galilee and Jerusalem but right into the midst of families, between those who listen to Jesus and those who reject him. Matthew replaces the Lukan "division" (διαμερισμός) with "sword" (μάχαιρα), which could point to the increasing persecutions by the Roman rulership in his time between 90 and 100 CE under Domitian and Trajan. Moreover, in 10.35-36 he adds another ἦλθον saying and transforms Luke's allusion to the controversy in the family according to Mic 7.6 into a genuine quotation, which follows not the Septuagint but rather the Hebrew text.[25]

Luke 10.16 points to the sending out of the disciples in the authority of Jesus. The saying appears in variable form in all four Gospels: "Whoever hears you, hears me, and whoever rejects you, rejects me; but whoever rejects me, he rejects the one who sent me." Behind this stands the principle of the Semitic messenger that the sent one represents the sender himself.[26] The saying was quoted often and varied in diverse ways.[27] It is related in substance to Jesus' answer to the Baptist in Luke 7.23: "Blessed is the one who does not take offense at me." Whoever takes offense at Jesus, sins against God who sends him. Listening to Jesus and to his disciples is the opposite of the σκανδαλίζεσθαι, a listening to God himself.

The six antitheses that start in Matt 5.21, which are only found in Matthew, are especially controversial.[28] At best the form of the antitheses can be faintly heard in Luke 6.27, in the formula "But I say to you, to

---

[24] Luke 12.51 = Matt 10.34.

[25] The streamlined Matthean version need not point back to Q; rather, it is probably attributable to the evangelist. The introduction in 10.34 ἦλθον βαλεῖν . . . ἐπὶ τὴν γῆν could be formulated after Luke 12.49a. Matthew omits Luke 12.49b, 50 because a struggle of Jesus before Gethsemane is scarcely tolerable for him. See, by contrast, Luke 22.36-37.

[26] See section 11.7 with note 174 and m. Ber. 5.5; cf. Bill. III: 2 and Rengstorf 1933, 414–20 (ET = 1965, 413–19).

[27] Parallels (see Aland 2005, 149): Matt 10.40; Mark 9.37; John 12.44 and 13.20. It continues to have effects in Ign. *Eph.* 6.1; Did. 11.4 and Justin, *1 Apol.* 63.5.

[28] On this, see Hengel 1987c, 375ff. (= Hengel 1999b, 267ff.). See also section 14.5.

those listening,"[29] to which in Matthew the sixth antithesis about love of enemies corresponds. Even if this form cannot be directly traced back to Jesus, materially it brings to expression his unique eschatological authority, which fundamentally stands over that of Moses. His message contains as new "messianic Torah" the true will of the Father, which is valid for the kingdom of God and is not simply identical with the letter of the Torah from Sinai.[30]

The Amen sayings: The frequent "Amen, I say to you"[31] is a corroborating speech introduction, which, as Jeremias has shown,[32] has no analogies in Judaism. While there the responding *āmen* serves only as affirmation after the speech of another, Jesus uses it to introduce his very own authoritative sayings and to express their validity. The closest parallels are the sayings of revelation of the prophets: "Thus speaks YHWH" or "Saying of YHWH." In contrast to these sayings, however, Jesus no longer appeals to a word of God that has come to him but speaks in the authority of his own "divine immediacy" (*Gottesunmittelbarkeit*), which can only be called "messianic." Matthew, who imitates this and other formulaic expressions of the speech of Jesus, because he is still aware of their significance, has thirty-one uses of this language, Mark has thirteen, and the Greek Luke, who usually omits or translates Aramaic words and expressions, only six, often saying instead λέγω (γὰρ) ὑμῖν.[33] By comparison with the Synoptics John intensifies the introduction through doubling, using ἀμὴν ἀμὴν λέγω ὑμῖν twenty-five times. Even the Fourth Evangelist still knew of the uniqueness of this formula and wanted to outbid the Synoptics through the doubled ἀμὴν ἀμήν. This introductory formula may also stand behind the antitheses with their use of ἐγὼ δὲ λέγω ὑμῖν.[34] This means that this introduction communicates "a materially new thing, a consciousness of majesty that lays claim to divine authority." At the same time, it is an "unmistakable linguistic sign of the *ipsissima vox Jesu*."[35]

---

[29] Luke 6.27: ἀλλὰ ὑμῖν λέγω τοῖς ἀκούουσιν. . . .

[30] On the rabbinic parallel to the antithesis, see note 114 in chapter 14 and Hengel 1999b, 267–73. On Matthew's understanding of the Torah, see Deines 2004, passim.

[31] Ἀμὴν λέγω ὑμῖν (or once σοι).

[32] Jeremias 1966a, 148ff.

[33] Three times he replaces the ἀμήν with ἀληθῶς: Luke 9.27; 12.44; 21.3. He more frequently has simply λέγω (γὰρ) ὑμῖν: 7.9, 26, 28; 10.12, 24; 11.8, etc.

[34] Hengel 2002, 267–68.

[35] Jeremias 1966a, 148–51, quotation on 151. Berger 1970, 190, unjustifiably wanted to view it as a pre-Christian, Jewish-apocalyptic speech form and appealed for this to the long form (version A) of T. Ab. 8.7 and 20.2, which has clearly been reworked by Christians. In later Christian texts the formula is imitated time and again; see Berger 1970, 131–32. It is absurd to want to regard this formula as a "product of syncretism" (Berger 1970, 147).

These examples may suffice. In this context, we can leave to the side controversial sayings that are possibly secondary transformations, such as Matt 5.17, which expresses the evangelist's understanding of the law in connection with the Sermon on the Mount,[36] the invitation of the Savior (*Heilandsruf*) in Matt 11.28-30 (29),[37] and the ransom saying in Mark 10.45. But this last saying about the "service" of the Son of Man can indeed go back to Jesus. It concludes in Mark the discussion of the disciples before the arrival in Jerusalem and in our judgment belongs in the context of the Last Supper.[38] In all this it becomes clear that a fundamental stock of Jesus sayings characterizes his sending and special authority, i.e., the messianic task assigned to him by God, namely in such a way that he does not do what is expected by the religious leaders and what is acceptable to the majority of the people but rather the opposite:

1. He comes not as the one who confirms the righteous in their piety but as the one who brings salvation to the excluded and despised, whom God seeks to lead to repentance.

2. He does not bring tranquility, order, and prosperity; rather, God's kingdom, like the fire of judgment, is to run rampant, indeed, it will bring about division that extends into families.

3. His authority stands over the Torah of Moses, for he proclaims the eschatological, true and at the same time original will of God.

4. He speaks no longer only as a prophet but as one who stands in very direct connection to the Father and, authorized by him, can speak in his own name.

These sayings and forms of speech scarcely fit in the later situation and theology of the community. Rather, they express Jesus' unique claim, i.e., his messianic authority.

17.3 The Messianic Secret[39]

17.3.1 Wrede's Question Mark

William Wrede's small study *Das Messiasgeheimnis in den Evangelien* (ET = *The Messianic Secret*) became an important milestone in the

---

[36] On this, see now the fundamental work of Deines 2004.

[37] On this, see Hengel 2001c, 96–99 (ET = 1995, 87–89); Luz 2001, 170–76 (GV = 1985–2002, II: 216–24): "In Matthew Jesus calls in wisdom's stead" (ET = 172; GV = 218).

[38] On the inner connection with the Last Supper tradition, cf. Luke 22.27. On this, see the end of section 19.4. In our judgment, the story of the footwashing in John 13 has grown out of this tradition of the "serving" of Jesus in connection with the Last Supper.

[39] Räisänen 1990; cf. Dunn 2003b, 624–27 and elsewhere.

controversial quest for the historical Jesus.[40] Methodologically this book broke even more sharply with the older psychologizing Jesus research than the great work of Albert Schweitzer, which did not bear without reason the subtitle *Von Reimarus bis Wrede* (From Reimarus to Wrede) in its first edition.[41] In the same year as Wrede's book, Schweitzer's programmatic writing *Das Messianitäts- und Leidensgeheimnis. Eine Skizze des Lebens Jesu* (ET = *The Mystery of the Kingdom of God: The Secret of Jesus' Messiahship and Passion*) also appeared.[42] Wrede's study anticipated the methods of the later "redaction-critical" approach of inquiring about the theological intention of the author and one-sidedly determined the course of scholarship in the twentieth century, which had just begun, thereby creating a scholastic tradition, so to speak. Schweitzer's study, on the other hand, basically looked backward and through its psychologizing methods was itself still bound to the defects of the old life-of-Jesus scholarship of the nineteenth century. It followed the thread of the Markan narrative in a far too trusting way, as if one were dealing here with a continuous biography. And yet his conception points beyond Wrede's restrictive skepticism at the decisive point, namely in the fact that it dared to ask in a thoroughgoing way about the messianic self-consciousness of Jesus and the way of Jesus that was determined through this.[43] To be sure, Wrede was much

---

[40] Wrede 1969 [1901], with the subtitle: *Zugleich ein Beitrag zum Verständnis des Markusevangelium* (Or, a Contribution to the Understanding of the Gospel of Mark). For the English translation, see Wrede 1971. For critical interaction with Wrede, see also Hengel/Schwemer 2001, 257 index; Hengel 1995, 397 index.

[41] Schweitzer 1906; 1913² (ET = 2000).

[42] Schweitzer 1956 [1901] (ET = 1914). In a very thorough study B. Pitre has taken up again the concern of Schweitzer; see Pitre 2005, vii–viii, 10ff., 504ff. and elsewhere.

[43] Against Wrede he comes to the materially correct conclusion that the influence of the primitive Christian community faith upon the Synoptic accounts is much less far-reaching than scholars had previously tended to assume (Schweitzer 1956, ix; ET = 1914, 10). M. Dibelius also comes to this judgment in his review of Bultmann's *Geschichte der synoptischen Tradition*; see Dibelius 1922. Although Schweitzer, in the style of the old life-of-Jesus-writings, proposes an "eschatological and historical attempt at a solution" in place of the "modern-historical" one (1956, 13; cf. 1914, 83), he nevertheless places at the end of his small study an "outline of the life of Jesus," which is restricted "to the last months of his life" (1956, 98ff.; 1914, 253ff.). He presupposes an inner development of Jesus, and makes the narrative thread of Mark the basis of his work. As with some of his contemporaries, his goal corresponds wholly to the thinking that proceeded from the "hero cult" in the second half of the twentieth century, for example, with W. Bousset (on Bousset and Carlyle, see Verheule 1973, 373–75); Schweitzer wanted "*to depict the figure of Jesus in its overwhelming heroic greatness and to impress it upon the modern age and upon the modern theology*" (Schweitzer 1914, 274, Schweitzer's emphasis; GV = 1956, 109). This sentence also sheds light on the further life path of Schweitzer. He sets forth a portrait of Jesus that can still prove fascinating in many points today in light of its coherence and consistency. "With him it is not a question of *eschatological ethics*, rather is his world view

more cautious in his conclusions than the radical criticism that emanated from Bultmann and his school, which then quarreled again itself over how much was to be cleared away and over the theological significance of the Jesus question. In Wrede the concern, according to the first sentence of the preface, is in the first instance only with "the testing" of the "*Gospel tradition* of Jesus *as the Messiah.*" By contrast, he tables the question of Jesus' "messianic consciousness." Due to his premature death at the age of forty-seven on November 23, 1906, he was no longer able to write his "further studies on the subject."[44] Already at the end of his book on the messianic secret he expresses himself only with caution, especially since he knew that he contradicted the consensus of that time. Thus, in the concluding "Historical Elucidation" he states only:

> The question if Jesus considered himself as messiah at all and gave himself out as such has not been answered with assurance up till now.[45]

His own investigation leads then to the conclusion:

> *If* Jesus really did know he was Messiah and designate himself thus, then the genuine tradition is so much interwoven with later accretions, that it is not entirely easy to recognize.[46]

Although he advocates an "adoptionist Christology" effected by the resurrection visions, he does not seek to produce the counterevidence that Jesus possessed no messianic consciousness:

> We cannot decide here almost in passing, as it were, whether Jesus really considered himself to be the messiah. . . . It was my intention in these

---

an *ethical eschatology. As such it is modern*" (Schweitzer 1914, 256; GV = 1956, 100; emphasis added from the German version). Despite the dubiousness of his overall conception, which seeks to say more than we can know, there are valuable insights in his work that again merit more consideration than has been given to them previously.

[44] Wrede 1969, v (Wrede's emphasis; ET = Wrede 1971, 1). In his occupation with the historical problem of the messianic self-consciousness of Jesus, he appears to have changed his mind, perhaps under the influence of his friend Bousset. See his letter to Harnack in Rollmann/Zager 2001, 317, with note 61 in chapter 5 and notes 3 and 95 in the present chapter. Cf. also Schröter 2013, 104 n. 27 (GV = 2007, 115 n. 27).

[45] Wrede 1971, 209 (GV = 1969, 207).

[46] Wrede 1971, 209–10, Wrede's emphasis (GV = 1969, 208). One may gladly affirm the last part of the sentence. To be sure, his imitators know too much *negatively* about Jesus, i.e., what he surely must not have been and therefore also cannot have been.

remarks *to place a question mark* and thereby to indicate why I am not here attributing the view to Jesus himself.[47]

In order to place this question mark (out of which later scholars made an exclamation point), Wrede now admittedly also appealed to the thing for which he so mercilessly faulted his opponents, namely Jesus' psychology.

> The difficulty is simply shunted on to another line, *the psychological one*. . . . How can we imagine such certainty in the instance of Jesus . . . ? How can he know this, that is to say, how can he believe it firmly and with assurance? How, if he does no more than hope, can he have made an *explicit* messianic claim? And this he would no doubt in some sense have had to do if he is supposed to have pronounced his confession before the high priest and received the sentence of death as messiah.[48]

With this Wrede contradicts the prevailing opinion of the exegetes of his time, who do not want to allow "the yardstick of contemporary psychology . . . for a religious personality like Jesus."[49] In his concise remarks "on the Son of Man theme"[50] he also reaches again for the psychological argument, which he otherwise tends to reject. If one thinks it necessary to play Jesus psychology against Jesus psychology, then the foreign solution that has less to say to our everyday understanding is presumably to be preferred. We ought precisely not to transfer our normality onto him. Here, criticism is in danger of flipping over into a modern "enlightened" apologetic.[51] Today "critical portraits of Jesus" right down to *The Five Gospels*, Crossan, and Mack show this all too well.[52]

Wrede's actual sphere of argumentation is, however, the "psychology of the community." He believes, on the basis of his analysis of Mark, to be able to presuppose that the notion of "secret messiahship" in the case of Jesus, which dominates the Gospel of Mark, is "an idea of the community

---

[47] Wrede 1971, 223, modified (our emphasis; GV = 1969, 221).

[48] Wrede 1971, 222 (our emphasis; GV = 1969, 221).

[49] Wrede 1971, 222 (GV = 1969, 221).

[50] Wrede 1904b, 359–60: "The most important . . . argument for the assumption that Jesus did not use this self-designation appears to me to still be the impossibility of imagining in reality a manner of speaking as the Gospels assign to him." This manner of speaking in the third person "leads to caprice and is completely unnatural." What can a German professor around 1900 say about "caprice and what is unnatural" with respect to a messianic prophet from Jewish Galilee around 30 CE? On the philological problem, see Hampel 1990, 417 index, s.v. "Menschensohn/Umschreibung für 'ich,'" especially 160–67. See also the end of section 7.1.

[51] On the problem, see already Cadbury 1937.

[52] See note 53 in chapter 5 and note 159 in chapter 6.

which arose after the life of Jesus." According to Wrede, this idea could no longer have arisen if it were generally known "that Jesus had openly given himself out as messiah on earth."[53]

> Therefore, according to his logic, the messianic secret could have arisen only at a time "when as yet there was no knowledge of any messianic claim on the part of Jesus on earth." It is a "transitional idea"; it is to be explained "*as the after-effect of the view that the resurrection is the beginning of the messiahship at a time when the life of Jesus was already being filled materially with messianic content.*"[54] More cautiously Wrede designates these final considerations only "as an attempt" and not as "a proof that has removed every obscurity."[55] In our view, with this he has instead magnified the "obscurity."

In his reflections on the confession of Peter before Caesarea Philippi, Wrede also grants that "*proof* of unhistoricity is . . . not hereby achieved." The peculiar specification of place is even said to carry positive weight for its historicity. What is said to be decisive is rather the evaluation of the "other reports about Jesus' messianic claim. . . . As long as this has not been clarified, we do well to be reserved about our final judgment."[56] Unfortunately, his successors have no longer practiced such restraint, and have instead rejected the messianic claim of Jesus at the outset.

The work of Wrede was esteemed because of his incisive analyses, whereas the hypotheses of an unmessianic Jesus met with rejection from almost all known New Testament scholars of his time, even from such critical scholars as H. J. Holtzmann, A. Jülicher, J. Wellhausen, J. Weiss, P. Wernle, and H. von Soden. This also applies to his friend W. Bousset.[57] In the preface to the second edition of Wrede's short book on Paul, he points out that Wrede ended his work on the messianic secret

with a great question mark

---

[53] Wrede 1971, 227 (GV = 1969, 226).

[54] Wrede 1971, 229 (Wrede's emphasis; GV = 1969, 227, 228).

[55] Wrede 1969, 229 (ET = 1971, 230). He concludes the entire discussion (Wrede 1971, 211–30; 1969, 209–29) of the "Concealment of the Messiahship" up to the resurrection with the cautious statement "But this question ('*that Jesus actually did not give himself out as messiah*') cannot be fully worked out here."

[56] Wrede 1971, 240-241 (Wrede's emphasis; GV = 1969, 229). Bultmann makes the argumentation much easier for himself here; see notes 2 and 5 above.

[57] See the documentation in Hengel 2001d, 17–27 (ET = 15–26). He received applause especially from contemporary authors in whom a certain anti-Jewish emotion could be felt.

and that while Wrede himself was inclined to give a negative answer to the question of whether Jesus regarded himself as a Messiah, he

> was . . . much too cautious and conscientious to utter the answer no.

Moreover, he

> had not considered all the possibilities, nor thoroughly researched the broad area of the tradition of the sayings of the Lord. . . . He stopped at the halfway point.[58]

Bousset, the authority on Jewish apocalyptic, remained critical of Wrede's thesis of an unmessianic Jesus.[59] While he likewise expressed himself cautiously, he did not share Wrede's negative judgment,[60] but wanted to hold fast to Jesus' messianic claim. It came to prominence only with Bultmann. He later reached back to Wrede's thesis, adopted it without restriction,[61] indeed intensified it. This meant that the thesis largely established itself after World War II in Germany. Sometimes it even took a form even more radical than Wrede and Bultmann himself had advocated, for a large portion of his school, E. Käsemann, H. Conzelmann, P. Vielhauer, and others, also denied to Jesus all the Son of Man sayings. Today this view is advocated especially in connection with the thriving speculations about Q and the Gospel of Thomas in America.

17.3.2 Silence Commands and the Disciples' Incomprehension

Wrede concentrates on the Gospel of Mark in his work because in his day this oldest source was usually used as a biographical foundation for a presentation of Jesus in order to construct a psychological development of the

---

[58] Wrede 1907a, viii (= 1907c, viii).

[59] Bousset 1970, 32ff., 35, 39–40, 47 with notes 2, 35, 37–38 (GV = 1965, 2ff., 5, 9–10, 18 with notes 2, 35, 37–38).

[60] On this, see also Bousset 1904, 87–88 (ET = 1906, 172–73).

[61] Bultmann 1919/1920 (= 1967a, 1–10). His argumentation is extremely weak. Correspondingly, his *History of the Synoptic Tradition* classifies *from the outset* as inauthentic all the components in which a messianic consciousness could become visible: the prejudgment determines the "historical-critical" result. See also Bultmann 2007, I: 26–32 (GV = 1984b, 26–34), where he turns Wrede's hypothesis into a thesis that is certain for him: "It was no longer conceivable that Jesus' life was unmessianic . . . and so *the gospel account of his ministry was cast in the light of messianic faith*. The contradiction between this point of view and the traditional material finds expression in *the theory of the messianic secret*" (Bultmann 2007, I: 32, modified; emphasis added from Bultmann 1984b, 33).

messianic consciousness with regard to Jesus. It also formed the key to the understanding of Jesus for A. Schweitzer.

To be sure, Wrede summarized under the key phrase "messianic secret" very different things which can only be brought under the same heading in a relatively forced manner. Wrede investigated together motifs in Mark which are not, in fact, to be explained from a single root.

As a first motif Wrede mentions "the demons' recognition of the Messiah."[62] To be sure, in the case of the spectacular event of an exorcism, it stands to reason that through the presence of the healer or through his actions, the sick person falls into the most extreme excitement and expresses this with a shout. It is likewise understandable that this was explained as an expression of the demon in the possessed person, which recognizes the power of his opponent and defends itself. This need not yet all be understood "messianically." Texts such as Mark 9.20; 1.23ff.; and 1.34 are not part of the messianic secret already through the narrative itself but only through the broader context of the Gospel.

The recognition of the "messianic" dignity of Jesus by demons is found in only three texts. The first of these is Mark 1.23-25. Here Jesus is awarded the enigmatic title "the Holy One of God," which precisely does not correspond to an established "messianic doctrine."[63] Rather, we are dealing with a traditional scene. The second text, Mark 3.11-12, is a redactional summary, where the demons address Jesus with the title that characterizes the Christology of the Gospel: "You are the Son of God," upon which he energetically rebukes them, "in order that they not make him manifest."[64] Only here does the evangelist insert his understanding of the "messianic secret" in a clear way: Jesus' true dignity is not to become known through devilish powers for outsiders.[65]

Aside from this text, the connection between knowing and silence command could also be interpreted in such a way that Jesus does not want to receive any "confession" from the mouth of demons. Due to their

---

[62] Wrede 1971, 24 (GV = 1969, 23). Mark 1.24: οἶδά σε τίς εἶ, ὁ ἅγιος τοῦ θεοῦ. Cf. the summaries in 1.34–35; 3.11–12.

[63] Cf. Luke 4.34; cf. John 6.69. The designation ὁ ἅγιος τοῦ θεοῦ can refer to the high priest: Ps 106 (LXX 105).16; cf. Sir 45.6 and the golden headpiece of the high priest in Exod 28.36; 39.30 (LXX 36.37); further to the Nazarite in Judg 16.17 LXX Cod. B: ὅτι ἅγιος θεοῦ ἐγώ εἰμι, and only secondarily to the Davidic ruler: Ps 89 (LXX 88).36 according to LXX against MT. On "Jesus as the messianic high priest," see Schwemer 2001b, 226ff.

[64] Mark 3.12: πολλὰ ἐπετίμα αὐτοῖς ἵνα μὴ αὐτὸν φανερὸν ποήσωσιν.

[65] For Mark the title "Son of God" describes more than "Christos" and "Son of Man" the actual dignity of Jesus; see 1.1, 11; 9.7; 13.32; 14.61; 15.39. The whole Gospel is structured by it. Cf. also the twofold address of the devil to Jesus in Luke 4.3, 9 = Matt 4.3, 6: εἰ υἱὸς εἶ τοῦ θεοῦ.

"supernatural" knowledge the demons know and fear the "stronger one," who has power over them.[66]

In the third text, Mark 5.6ff., we have, in the case of the—pagan—demoniac of Gerasa, only the confession "Son of the Most High God."[67] The silence command is lacking. Jesus even enters into a discussion with the demon and commands the healed man to "proclaim what the Lord did for him" to his fellow citizens. This may be a subtle hint at the later Gentile mission by the evangelist.[68] It thus becomes clear that Mark, in two generally formulated texts—clearly in the graphic summary of Mark 3.10-12, and in strongly abbreviated form in 1.34, where the sense can be inferred only on the basis of 3.12—introduces into exorcism stories the motif of the "messianic secret" in the sense of the keeping secret of the dignity, but that these texts themselves vary far too much for one to bring them under a common denominator. Entirely independently of the Markan theory, the fact that the "messianic authority" of Jesus becomes visible in his exorcisms emerges from the sayings tradition with sayings such as Luke 11.20 or 10.18-20 and the interpretation of his person as the stronger one as well as from the saying about the messianic liberation of Isa 61.1-2.[69]

The silence commands to the demons must be distinguished fundamentally from the command to healed persons not to tell others about their healing, for in contrast to the former *there is no talk at all of Jesus' messianic dignity in the healings*. A total of three texts are in view here:

Mark 8.26 contains no silence command but only the exhortation to the healed person not to go back into the village of Bethsaida, from which Jesus had led him out. Only the secondary, strongly varying textual tradition adds a silence command to it as well.[70] In any case, the vividly recounted story falls out of the framework of the usual miracle stories, whose diversity in Mark is readily overlooked.

The *subject matter* occurs once in the healing of the leper in Mark 1.43-45, where Jesus follows the silence command with the atypical

---

[66] Cf. Mark 1.34b: "He did not allow the demons to speak, for they knew him"; Mark 1.24: "You have come to destroy us" and 5.7: "I adjure you by God: Do not torment me."

[67] On the address, cf. 1.24: here Mark uses a Septuagint formula. Θεὸς ὕψιστος was the official designation of the Jewish God vis-à-vis or by non-Jews. On this, see Hengel 2003a, 297ff. (GV = 1988, 544ff. and 687 index).

[68] The closest parallel, to which Wrede rightly refers (Wrede 1971, 32; GV = 1969, 30), is Acts 16.16ff. On this, see Avemarie 2003 (= 2013, 703–28); cf. also Acts 19.15 and section 16.3 with note 77.

[69] See section 16.1. On Jesus as the "stronger one," see Mark 3.27 = Matt 12.29; cf. Luke 11.21-22, but also Mark 1.7 = Luke 3.16 = Matt 3.11.

[70] The silence command is lacking in the best textual witnesses: ℵ, B, L, W, f¹ pc sy^s sa bo^pt.

instruction that the healed person should show himself to the priests.[71] We are dealing with an instruction that actually contradicts the sense of the silence command, for the fact that the healed man then proclaims the miraculous healing everywhere is a natural consequence and serves the dramatic intensification and contrast. Jesus can no longer come openly to Capernaum but must withdraw to an uninhabited place: "they came, however (adversative καί), to him from everywhere." It is similar to the healing of the deaf man with a speech impediment, which has a different narrative structure.[72] Jesus takes him away from the crowd and commands the healed man and his companions to tell nobody, but they proclaim it "all the more." In this way the choral conclusion, which alludes—like the εφφαθα in 7.34—to Isa 35.5,[73] is additionally reinforced.

By contrast, in Mark 5.35-43, the resurrection of the daughter of Jairus, Jesus explicitly commands the parents (and the three disciples), who are astonished, to keep the event secret. The following pragmatic command to give the girl something to eat underscores the reality of the miracle. In all three cases, the silence command has *expressis verbis* nothing to do with Jesus' *messianic* sending, which is not spoken of in the context, especially since the people, according to 6.14-15 and 8.28, already regard him as an especially authorized prophet. Certainly the separation of the deaf man with a speech impediment in 7.33 and the expulsion of the mourning women[74] are indeed sensible narrative features within the story. The miracle worker does not want to be disturbed in what he is doing. For Mark the silence command may effectively stress the contrast between Jesus' restraint and the present effect of the spread of his fame. The original meaning of the feature can still be inferred from 1.45. The miracle worker wanted to resist the influx of people, which was increasing with every healing, but had no success in this. Certainly the motif of him withdrawing into solitariness[75] has nothing to do with the messiah question. It is understandable in itself. In our view, the silence command in relation to healed people goes back to the memory of Jesus' activity. The fact that Mark uses it more for its narrative effect than for "dogmatic" reasons, which Wrede constantly imputes to him, is evident from the fact that he can forgo it in other healing

---

[71] Mark 1.44 = Luke 5.14 = Matt 8.4; cf. also Luke 17.14. In this way the priest becomes an "official" witness of the miraculous healing.

[72] Mark 7.32-37; according to 7.31, the healing probably takes place for Mark outside of Galilee in a Gentile region.

[73] Isaiah 35.5b: *tippātaḥnāh*, LXX: ἀκούσονται. See also section 16.3 with notes 73–74.

[74] Mark 5.40, cf. Peter in Acts 9.40.

[75] Mark 1.45b; cf. 1.12-13; 6.31-32, 46-47.

stories.[76] To keep Jesus free of a "messianic dogmatic," Wrede read much too much allegedly Markan "Messiah-dogmatic" into the second Gospel. Others have followed him in this. Mark, of course, always writes with a theological purpose, but he is also a highly gifted dramatic *narrator*. He *tells* "Jesus-stories" and does not compose a "theological treatise" about timeless truths but recounts what happened in space and time. Only one who takes him seriously as such a tradition-bound narrator[77] can also understand him as a "theologian."

Something similar applies to the "disciples' incomprehension," which, despite the fact that the disciples know who Jesus is, increases until the bitter end, i.e., until the betrayal of Judas, the sleeping in Gethsemane, the flight of the disciples, and the denial of Peter. It has *absolutely nothing* to do with the "messianic secret" in the sense of Wrede's theory that with this a balance was to be struck between the entirely unmessianic original Jesus tradition and a later portrait of Jesus that was painted over messianically. After all, according to Mark, the disciples already know Jesus' dignity before Peter's Messiah confession, which only declares their already gained conviction; for this reason, John moves the Messiah confession to the beginning scenes.[78]

Since Mark assumes that at least three of the first four disciples called in Mark 1.16ff. are present for the healings of Jesus,[79] he probably assumes that they regard him from the very beginning as the eschatological redeemer and Son of God. He presupposes a "development" in the biographical sense neither for Jesus nor for the disciples. In 2.10, 17, 19-20, 25-28, the Markan Jesus, entirely apart from the "confessions" of the demons, has said what is decisive christologically, namely in the presence of the disciples over against the opponents, who must reject Jesus' claim. Mark probably assumes that ὁ υἱὸς τοῦ ἀνθρώπου, Aramaic *bar 'enāšā'*, was a cipher that Jesus could use often as a self-designation because it was not yet a generally recognized designation for the Messiah, while presupposing, however, that the disciples knew what Jesus meant by this designation (see section 17.4.1 below).

[76] Cf. Mark 2.1-13; 3.1-5; 7.24-30; cf. also 8.22-25; 9.14-27; 10.46-52. The numerous summaries never mention general silence commands to the healed persons.

[77] He is also treated in this way by Luke and Matthew, who often follow him word for word. They know that the authority of Peter stood behind him.

[78] John 1.35-51; cf. Luke 5.8ff. (esp. v. 8) and 4.18ff., where he has Jesus point with a quotation from Isa 61.1-2 to his "Spirit-anointing" and the fulfillment of this promise. Mary (and Jesus' family?) are already in the know from the beginning. On the other hand, John and Luke, depending on the situation, can call Jesus prophet even after the revelation of his messiahship: John 4.44; 6.14; 7.40; 9.17; Luke 7.16, 39; 13.33; 24.19.

[79] In Mark 5.37 he takes only the chosen three, Peter, James, and John—note the sequence—with him; cf. 9.2; 14.33. Andrew appears, by contrast, only in the group of four in 13.3.

On the other hand, we receive the impression that Mark does not dismantle but rather *strengthens* the disciples' incomprehension or, better, the disciples' failure, despite their knowledge of Jesus' eschatological dignity, in the progression of his Gospel right through to the passion, just as the enmity of the religious leaders against Jesus already *increases* from chapter 2 onward.[80] In this way unique emphasis is placed on the end of Jesus. It is simultaneously the "salvation" and the climax of the "crisis" for Israel, which pertains to all without exception, disciples as well as opponents. The climax resides in what happens on Golgotha. There Jesus dies, forsaken by God and human beings.

Time and again consciously intended tensions and contradictions arise. Thus, after the appointment (or calling) of the twelve in 3.16-19, the disciples are the most intimate circle of his representatives and followers, who continuously surround him as a family, because they do the will of God.[81] According to 4.11, they are still the elected ones, to whom "the mystery of the kingdom of God is given," while "those outside," i.e., the crowd that is hardened according to Isa 6.9-10, receive only parables to hear as enigmatic sayings. In 4.34 the circle of the twelve is identified, entirely as a matter of course, with "his own disciples." To them alone he explains the true meaning of his enigmatic parables.

This — materially questionable — Markan "parable theory," which Wrede likewise wants to subsume under the "messianic secret," is in its present form a *theologoumenon* of the evangelist, which — like John 12.40; Acts 28.26-27; and Rom 11.8 — is meant to explain the offense of the unbelief of the people of God vis-à-vis its Messiah sent by God on the basis of Isa 6.9-10 as hardening by God. The "mystery of the kingdom of God" is made known only to the disciples, for whom Jesus unlocks his parables.[82] To the people, by contrast, he speaks in enigmatic speech "*in order that* . . . they hear and do not understand.*"[83] Therefore, they are not even able to believe his message. The unbelief of Israel is ultimately grounded in God's mystery and predestination. Precisely this theory — which really is now secondary — has nothing to do with an alleged unmessianic Jesus

---

[80] Mark 2.6-7; 3.6, 22.

[81] Mark 3.34-35: τοὺς περὶ αὐτὸν κύκλῳ καθημένους, cf. 4.10: οἱ περὶ αὐτὸν σὺν τοῖς δώδεκα.

[82] Mark 4.13, 34. See also note 66 in chapter 16 on unbelief and hardening on the basis of Isa 6.9-10.

[83] Mark 4.12; cf. Isa 6.10; see, however, the contradictory statement in 4.33: καθὼς ἠδύναντο ἀκούειν. On this, see the end of section 16.1 with notes 43–47. Isaiah 6.9-10 was a fundamental text for the primitive community, only comparable with Isa 53, the fourth servant song, which also speaks, after all, of the failure of the adherents of the servant of God.

and the actual Markan "messianic secret," which is in reality restricted to a very small number of texts.[84] Instead, it contradicts it.

The first reserved beginning of the criticism of the disciples is signaled for the first time through a question of Jesus in 4.13: "Do you not understand this parable? How then will you understand all the parables?" It continues in intensified form in 4.40; 6.52; 8.17 and reaches its first high point in the protest of Peter against the first passion prediction right after the Messiah confession and in Jesus' sharp rebuff of the disciple as Satan in 8.31-33. From then on the incomprehension is concentrated on Jesus' prediction of the passion (and resurrection)[85] and in a second line on the disciples' addiction to status,[86] with these two belonging together. Thus, the disciples become warning examples for the community, which also makes its confession to Jesus and yet in light of the expected final time of tribulation—the Roman Christian community at the time when Mark wrote his Gospel has the horrifying persecution under Nero in 64/65 only just behind it—stands in danger of denial and apostasy.[87] In this persecution the "cross-bearing" had already become a brutal reality.[88] Mark selected traditions that fit in this scheme, expansively developed them in some cases, for example in the individual passion predictions, and gave a narrative arrangement to the whole. However, concrete traditions, which go back to the circle of the disciples, and here especially to Peter, his most important source of tradition, usually stand behind this. These include, among other things, the Gethsemane scene,[89] the denial of Peter, and the question of the sons of Zebedee. Except for the Messiah confession of Caesarea Philippi, the enigmatic transfiguration story, and the predictions of the coming suffering of the Son of Man, these stories have no direct connection to the question of whether a "messianic" claim was connected already with the pre-Easter Jesus, which was contested by Wrede and especially by his successors. The fact that the disciples so frequently

---

[84] Räisänen 1973 (see also note 129 below); Räisänen 1990 hypothesizes that Mark took over the parable theory from the tradition and changed it in connection with the incomprehension of the disciples. In our view, he preceded in precisely the opposite manner. A direct connection is visible between Mark 4.10 and 13, and vv. 11-12 give the impression of a disturbing insertion; 4.33 also appears to be more original. V. 34, by contrast, is an addition that has become necessary through 4.11-12.

[85] Mark 9.10, 32; 10.32; 14.18-19, 27, 37, 40, 50, 68ff.

[86] Mark 9.5-6, 14ff., 33ff.; 10.35-45; 14.29.

[87] Mark 8.34-38; cf. 9.42-48; 13.12-13, 19; 14.38.

[88] See Tacitus, *Ann.* 15.44.4: *aut crucibus adfixi atque flammati* ("fixed to crosses and made flammable"; trans. Woodman 2004, 326). Hengel 1977a, 26. The much later Matthew already appears to know more traditions of this kind. See Matt 23.34 and 10.38, weakened in Luke 9.23.

[89] On this, see Feldmeier 1987.

make a rather bad impression in Mark is not a malevolent invention of later Christian authors but is connected with the deep impression made by the message of Jesus, which, after his death and resurrection, opened up the disciples' eyes to their failure and foolishness. They become "*justified sinners*," their speaker Peter above all others. Luke places this insight already in the confession of Peter at his calling.[90] In Mark these memories and impressions are paradigmatically and paraenetically formed. Later apocryphal Gospels and acts of apostles sketch a different picture here.

That the passion predictions that unpack the passion of Jesus are *vaticinia ex eventu* is also not in question. However, it is too *easy* to explain all the passion predictions of Jesus *a limine* as unhistorical. This assumes that he—after the execution of the Baptist—cluelessly journeyed to Jerusalem. This was surely not the case. After all, apart from the actual passion predictions in Mark, we have other texts that show themselves to be authentic through form and content, such as the sharply contoured, offensively phrased double saying in Luke 12.49-50 or, beyond this, Luke 13.33 and the whole Last Supper complex.[91] Would the later community have placed in Jesus' mouth such an unusual parabolic saying such as Luke 12.50 with the reference to his deep inner struggle? However, also in the case of the sayings about the suffering Son of Man in Mark, a *Grundform* could go back to Jesus himself.[92] Finally, Mark 12.1-9, which goes back to a real polemical parable of Jesus, must be mentioned here.[93]

The theories of Wrede and Schweitzer are diametrically different, and yet their error has the same root. Both believed that they could solve the controversial question of the messianic consciousness of Jesus through *one* comprehensive theory drawn from the Gospel of Mark. One thought that he had justified it, the other that he had refuted it. In reality neither the one nor the other is possible. The only possible approach to the historical reality lies in the interplay of numerous, rather different texts, from Mark and the sayings tradition, with the inclusion of four complexes: (a) the witnesses to the variety of the Jewish messianic expectations, which have

---

[90] Luke 5.8: ἔξελθε ἀπ' ἐμοῦ, ὅτι ἀνὴρ ἁμαρτωλός εἰμι. In John the sinful failure of the disciples is weakened. Thus, for example, the cowardly flight of the disciples is missing. Jesus protects them; see John 18.8: ἄφετε τούτους ὑπάγειν. In place of the sleeping and flight in Gethsemane comes the disciples' incomprehension in the farewell discourses, which is demonstrated by foolish speech and questions: 13.6-9, 36-38; 14.5, 8, 22; 16.17-18.

[91] One could also mention the following "wisdom saying" in Luke 13.34, 35a = Matt 23.37. Luke 13.35b appears to be a christological addition; cf. further Jesus' answer to the question of the sons of Zebedee in Mark 10.38-40 (on this, see section 11.3).

[92] On this, see Jeremias 1970, 277ff. (1979, 264ff.); Bayer 1986. See the end of section 17.4.1.

[93] On this, see Hengel 1968a; Bayer 1986, 90ff.; Snodgrass 1983; Kloppenborg 2006.

been significantly expanded by the Qumran texts; (b) the relationship of Jesus, presented above, to his "forerunner," the Baptist; (c) the accusation against Jesus and its Jerusalem prehistory since his entrance into the city; and (d) the question of the emergence of the earliest Christology and its development in the post-Easter circle of disciples, in which Jesus' word and deed were still directly vivid.[94] All four points were neglected by Wrede, and this is all the more true for his successors, i.e., for Rudolf Bultmann and the majority of his students. We must give great credit to Wrede that he himself, in contrast to his epigones, placed only a powerful question mark here and did not—as happened later in a historically less conscientious way—deny it with a categorical *quod non* but rather continued to reflect upon it, and, at the end, cautiously called his opinion into question again, as shown by his letter to Harnack.[95]

17.3.3 The Actual Messianic Secret

There remain the only two real "messianic secret texts" in the strict sense in Mark, the confession of Peter and the transfiguration story. Only in them does Jesus prohibit people from speaking about him as the Messiah–Son of Man.

Both stories are readily declared to be resurrection stories that have been brought into the Gospels. This speculation does not testify to the critical sense of its originators. In the case of the transfiguration story on the mountain of revelation neither Moses nor Elijah nor the voice from heaven,[96] nor the privileged disciples, nor the foolish behavior of Peter fits in a resurrection story. One needs a considerable amount of imagination to view it as such. After all, the resurrection appearances lead in the end to confessions of faith and the sending out of disciples and not to incomprehension and new failure. They can best be explained as a further development of a pre-Easter vision account. Visions turn up not only in the primitive community as a consequence of Easter but also already with Jesus and in the pre-Easter group of disciples. We refer here just to his baptism,[97] the temptation story, the walking on the sea, and to sayings such as Luke 10.18-19 and the words of the future revelation of the Son of Man in Luke 17.24. The apocalyptically colored enthusiasm of primitive Christianity begins with Jesus and continues in the primitive community

---

[94] On this, see Hengel/Schwemer 2001. Among others, Holtzmann 1901, 952–53, already emphasized points (c) and (d) in his substantial review of Wrede's book.

[95] See notes 3 and 44 above.

[96] It plays no role at all in the Easter tradition of the Gospels. Rather, the concern is with the seeing and the word of the risen one.

[97] See section 10.1.

as well as in Paul. After Pentecost, the community of disciples believed that it received the Spirit from him, the one exalted at the right hand of God, in whose fullness he himself had acted. We see little sense in emphasizing the significance of visions for the disciples after Easter (including multiple times in collective form), whilst rejecting them for the time of the fellowship with Jesus. Mark certainly formulated the text "This is my beloved Son, *listen to him*" with particular care theologically.[98] Following the confession of Peter, it represents the load-bearing center of the Gospel and directly picks up the voice of God at the baptism. Vis-à-vis the confession of Peter, in which what was already known to the disciples is only openly expressed for the first time, the voice from heaven introduces a genuine new revelation. Jesus, the Messiah of Israel, is also the Son who speaks in the place of God. This is why the disciples—and the whole Jesus community—should "listen to him," to him alone.[99] As is the case after the confession of Peter, a silence command also follows the voice of God. In itself it would indeed be plausible that Jesus prohibited the disciples to speak about visionary experiences. In the interpretation of Mark—we do not know in detail what tradition was available to him—the central messianic silence command in 9.9 signifies that the disciples really understood this revelation only after Easter, and this means especially the voice from heaven that commands them to listen *only* to the *Son of God*. Only through the encounter with the Risen One do they become established in their faith in Jesus as the *Son* who is inseparably connected with the Father.[100] As long as they did not become witnesses of the resurrection of the Son of Man and Son of God, they could not know what "resurrection from the dead" really meant,[101] even though every pious Jew of the time was familiar with texts such as Ezek 37.11-14; Isa 26.19; and Dan 12.2-3. Through Jesus' resurrection "the resurrection of the dead" becomes a living experience of the disciples and is no longer only shadowy apocalyptic knowledge. Behind Mark 9.10 and other texts of incomprehension may stand the general primitive Christian idea that the disciples received the Spirit only after the exaltation of Jesus and that the Spirit, as John stresses in the Paraclete sayings of the Farewell Discourses, disclosed the full secret of Jesus'

[98] Mark 9.7; cf. 1.1, 11; 15.39. See note 65 above.

[99] Mark 9.7: ἀκούετε αὐτοῦ. This advance in revelation is erased in Matt 16.16ff. through the detailed confession of Peter and Jesus' answer.

[100] Romans 1.3-4; cf. Acts 2.34-36; on this, see Hengel 1976b (GV = 1977b; 2006a, 74–145). Cf. also Luke 24.19-21 and on this Mittmann-Richert 2008, index.

[101] Mark 9.10. The saying stands in a certain opposition to 12.23, where the resurrection of the dead is simply presupposed as a generally known theologoumenon. In 9.10 we are dealing with a christologically grounded Markan hyperbole. In John, who knows Mark, this idea is taken up in a new form: 2.19, 22; 14.26; 20.9.

person, although Mark, if one ignores the saying of the Baptist,[102] does not speak *expressis verbis* of the post-Easter gift of the Spirit. Beyond this it becomes clear that for Mark the actual, solely adequate title of majesty of Jesus is not so much "Christos" but Son of God, which in his Gospel, in contrast to Son of Man (and Christos),[103] never appears in the mouth of Jesus, but is spoken to him twice by God himself, by the demons, by the high priest, and at the end by the Gentile centurion. In Mark 12.6ff. this occurs indirectly in the parable, and in 12.36-37 the title 'Kyrios' appears in connection with Ps 110.1 for the Messiah. The "messianology" of Mark is more multilayered and complicated than Wrede suspected. To this one can add the fact that Mark usually brackets out the post-Easter events more strongly than the later evangelists,[104] just as he does not, after all, mention resurrection appearances or "baptism in the name of Jesus."

The *confession of Peter in the villages of Caesarea Philippi*[105] and the following rebuke by Jesus cannot simply be traced back to Mark as the first author of a Christian Jesus novel or to mere "community forma-tion." Who is supposed to have "formed" this scene, which falls out of the framework in its details, later? Mark reworks here—as also otherwise in a theological considered manner and in dramatic form—important older tradition. No more than the transfiguration story is it "an Easter story pro-jected backward into Jesus' lifetime."[106] The very unusual specification of place "in the villages (or the region) of Caesarea Philippi," which presup-poses the historical and geographical content knowledge of the author or of his informant, already militates against that view. It concerns the capi-tal of the kingdom of Philip, the Hellenistic polis of Paneas, which Philip had renamed around 3 BCE in honor of Augustus. The city designation

---

[102] Mark 1.8. See the end of section 9.1.2.2 and section 22.2.2.

[103] Mark 9.41; 12.35.

[104] Exceptions are relatively clearly visible, such as Mark 2.20; 13.9ff.; 14.9.

[105] Mark 8.27-33; cf. Matt 16.13ff. Luke 9.18 omits the specification of place.

[106] Thus Bultmann 2007, I: 26–27, 45 (GV = 1984b, 27–28, 48); cf. Bultmann 1967a, 1–9. In Bultmann 1963, 257–59 (GV = 1995, 275–78) he speculates with regard to Mark 8.27-30 that "Matt 16.17-19 is the original conclusion to the story of the confession" and wanted "to reckon the whole narrative as an Easter story" (ET = 259; GV = 277). Matthew 16.17-19 is, already due to the mention of ἐκκλησία, a later formation. Bultmann entirely misses the fact that in Judaism *there was no fixed connection at all between resurrection and messiahship* and that the question of Jesus to the disciples (!) does not fit in an Easter story where the seeing is always followed by a spontaneous reaction from their side. In this point we can designate his—influential—hypothesis only as adventurous. Other specula-tions can be found in Bultmann/Theissen/Vielhauer 1971, 90–91. However, according to Mark 16.7, the seeing of the Lord is to take place in Galilee and not in such a peculiar location, as it is specified in 8.27.

Καισάρεια ἡ Φιλίππου also appears in Josephus[107] but then quickly disappears again. Agrippa II refounded the city after 54 CE and gave it the name Neronias. After the murder of Nero in 68 CE, it received—as attested by inscriptions, coins, and geographers—the official designation Καισ(άρεια) Σεβ(αστὴ) ἱερ(ὰ) καὶ ἄσυ(λος) ὑπὸ Πανείῳ, which is abbreviated as Καισάρεια Πανιάς. From the fourth century CE we find only the old name Πανεάς, which has endured until today (Banias). In talmudic literature we find already in the Mishnah only this name.[108] Due to the place-name, which was only in use for a short time, we must be dealing with an older tradition. By contrast, Bultmann's opinion that 8.27 belongs to the preceding story of the blind man of Bethsaida contradicts Markan style.[109] Conzelmann's view that "the motif of the 'retreat'" to Caesarea Philippi is "the messianic secret" likewise goes wide of the text. In Mark there is no talk of a "retreat." The specification of the goal is not motivated and cannot be explained "theologically." Only readers who understand the place in the way modern exegetes do could suspect a "retreat." In Rome, where the Gospel arose, nothing could be known of this. Rather, narratively Mark 8.27 forms a deep caesura in the Gospel. The crowd's opinion about Jesus corresponds entirely to the Jewish-Palestinian milieu and fits excellently in the context, whereas it would scarcely be understood by the Roman community. In 6.14-15 a similar tradition is artificially incorporated in order to create in the Gospel a transition to the strange story about the execution of the Baptist.[110] Conzelmann's further speculation is also wrongheaded:

---

[107] Josephus, *J.W.* 3.443; 7.23; *Ant.* 20.211; *Life* 74. Cf., by contrast, the simple form of the name in *J.W.* 2.168 = *Ant.* 18.28; *J.W.* 2.507ff.: Καισάρεια. Josephus has retained the designation ἡ Φιλίππου, which was known to him from the time of his youth (*ca. 38 CE), possibly due to his connection with the sovereign of the land Agrippa II, a great-grandson of Herod and great nephew of Philip, who was interested in the work of Josephus. By contrast, the predominantly Gentile population scarcely had an interest in the Jewish ruler Philip or the Herodians in general. Wrede noticed this uncommon specification of place; see section 17.31 with note 56.

[108] Schürer 1973–1987, II: 169–71; cf. Hölscher 1949; on the coins, see Rosenberger 1997, 38–47.

[109] The phrase καὶ (εἰσ/ἐξ)ῆλθεν with specification of place is a clear new beginning; cf. Mark 1.21; 2.1, 13; 3.1; 5.1; 6.1; 7.17; 9.33; 11.11-12; 14.26 and elsewhere. The phrase ἐν τῇ ὁδῷ appears for the first time here and from now on characterizes the itinerant situation of Jesus with his disciples (9.33; 10.17, 32), who had left Galilee. With the messianic confession the long journey to Jerusalem via Galilee (9.30) begins for Mark. Luke 9.51–19.27 greatly extends this time of itinerancy.

[110] See section 9.1.2.1.

The scene is not a story, but a piece of christological reflection given the form of a story. Peter utters the creed of the community.[111]

First, it is wrong to regard christological reflection and the historicity of a story fundamentally as oppositions in the Gospels, since in Mark basically all the stories of his "Gospel" are recounted on the basis of christological reflection. There are no "Christology-free zones" in his Gospel. Nevertheless, he remains a historical storyteller who is obligated to space and time. Secondly, the confession of Peter "You are the Messiah" is no longer "*the* confession of the community*" of the evangelist in Rome. For "Christos" had quite some time ago already become a name in the Greek-speaking community.[112] Paul already no longer uses it in a titular way.[113] Moreover, for Mark it is not so much the Christos title that is fundamental but "Son of God" and, alongside this, Kyrios. In this point the demons already know more than the disciples.[114] The fact that the confession was insufficient for "the community" is shown by the addition in Matt 16.16: "You are the Anointed One, *the Son of the living God.*" Luke too senses its incomplete character and adds "biblistically" from the Old Testament: "You are the Anointed *of God.*"[115]

To be sure, it is no longer possible to determine what Mark's *Vorlage* looked like. The silence command that follows is, together with 9.9, the only full attestation for the messianic secret. We may not identify it without further ado with the very differently motivated silence commands to the demons,[116] for—unlike what we find there—Jesus himself posed a ques-

---

[111] Conzelmann 1969, 130 (GV = 1967, 93: "*Die ganze Szene ist eine in Erzählung umgesetze christologische Reflexion. Petrus spricht das Bekenntnis der Gemeinde*"); cf. Conzelmann/Lindemann 1988, 323 (GV = 1985, 379): "The pericope contains no concrete, historical material but turns out to be a sort of creedal presentation in the form of a scene: that which the whole community believes."

[112] Cf. in Mark himself 1.1 and 9.41; see note 114 below.

[113] For Rome, cf. Rom 1.3-4; Heb 1.1ff.; 3.6, 14; 5.5 and elsewhere; on this, see 1 Clem. 36.4. Hengel/Schwemer 1998, 345, 348–49 (ET = 1997, 228–30); Hengel 2001d, 1–17 (ET = 1995, 1–15); Hengel 2002, 240–41.

[114] Cf. already Mark 1.1: ἀρχὴ τοῦ εὐαγγελίου Χριστοῦ υἱοῦ θεοῦ. As 1.1 and 9.41 show, for him "Christos" has already long become a personal name, even though the evangelist is very aware, of course, of its titular meaning and often makes use of it: 8.29; 12.35; 13.21; 14.61; 15.32; see also the early, supplementing reading in 1.34. The passion story can be understood only under this presupposition. On "Kyrios," see Mark 1.3; 5.19; 12.36-37; 13.20. On the demons, see Mark 3.11 and 5.7 and section 17.3.2 above.

[115] Luke 9.20. This applies all the more to John 6.69: "You are the Holy One of God." John 1.41 is also insufficient; 1.49 brings the necessary supplementation. In 20.31, by contrast, the emphasis lies, as in Matt 16.16, on "the Son of God."

[116] Thus Lührmann 1987, 146.

tion here.[117] He provoked this confession, which then followed from the mouth of his first disciple, for he wants to hear this confession from the mouth of the disciple, whereas the demons should not speak at all, let alone confess his divine dignity. While the following silence command vis-à-vis the disciples is formulated similarly to the commands to the healed persons, in those texts they are not to speak about their healing, with there being no talk at all about the eschatological dignity of Jesus, whereas here it reads "that they speak to nobody *about him*." The phrase "about him" is found only here.[118] In the context this meant "about him" in connection with his messianic dignity. They alone should already now recognize and understand him as the Messiah, who as the "servant of God" goes upon the way of suffering—but they do not do so.

To some extent Mark may have formulated the silence commands—which were differently motivated in terms of substance and which were certainly not all invented by Mark himself—in a similar way (though never identically) and placed them in a certain connection. In the silence command toward the disciples the most likely connection is with the summary that Mark writes about the casting out of demons in 3.11-12. In this text Mark provides the rationale "in order that they not make him manifest,"[119] which does not appear again in this form. We must distinguish here between Markan interpretation and the original tradition, where the motifs were still different.

We must also reject the speculation that the confession of Peter was originally followed in the pre-Markan tradition by 8.33, i.e., with the rebuke of Peter as "Satan," with the rationale that Jesus rejected the Messiah title. In that case, one would not only have to view the massive use of the title and name after Easter as a betrayal of Jesus' cause,[120] but Mark would also contradict himself through the taken-for-granted use of title and name.[121] A story in which Jesus provokes his disciples through an unmotivated question so that he can then rebuke the speaker of the disciples in the sharpest manner as Satan must appear senseless. Thus, this was surely not what was in his *Vorlage*. Behind all these attempts to expel the Messiah question from the activity of Jesus there appears to stand, rather,

---

[117] What the disciples "saw" according to Mark 9.2-8 and should not "relate further" also goes back to Jesus' initiative.

[118] Mark 8.30: ἵνα μηδενὶ λέγωσιν περὶ αὐτοῦ. This means that they should not correct the various opinions of the people. However, after this, his true dignity cannot remain hidden, as 10.46ff., the story of his entry into Jerusalem, and the question of the high priest show.

[119] Mark 3.12: ἵνα μὴ αὐτὸν φανερὸν ποιήσωσιν. See section 17.3.2.

[120] On this, see Hengel 2001d, 16–17 (ET = 1995, 14–15).

[121] Mark 1.1; 9.41; 12.35; 13.21; 14.61; 15.32.

the modern, indeed dogmatic wish that to the greatest extent possible the person of Jesus should not have anything to do with Jewish expectations about the Messiah, with this being understood in a one-sided, politically colored manner.[122]

Finally, in the evaluation of Wrede's critical analysis of Mark, which led via Bultmann and his students to a complete denial of the messiahship of Jesus, we must not overlook the fact that the Marburg New Testament scholar himself followed Wrede's positive explanation that with the messianic secret the primitive community or Mark wanted to overcome the offense of a historically unmessianic Jesus. Today there is only still agreement ion the negative verdict, whereas the patterns of interpretation diverge greatly from one another.

In 1939 Hans-Jürgen Ebeling already criticized Wrede's explanation of the Markan secrecy theory, in which he—under the banner of a purely kerygmatic interpretation of Mark that was far removed from history and determined by the dialectic theology of Bultmann—stressed that it does "not . . . arise from a reflection on historical conditions and events of Jesus' life," i.e., it does not seek to conceal the subsequently offensive historical circumstance of an unmessianic Jesus but rather explicates the fact that the earthly and the exalted Lord are one and the same and the fact that he gave his life into death for the salvation of all people. The messianic secret becomes the comprehensive secret of revelation, which the evangelist discloses in his work, which is oriented entirely toward the death of Jesus on the cross.[123]

Conzelmann also regards the messianic secret as a basic idea of Markan Christology. In his view, it expresses "the paradoxical character of revelation," that "the meaning of Jesus is not disclosed to the one merely seeing the miracles, rather it is faith that sees Jesus correctly from the vantage point of the cross and the resurrection."[124] But was the resurrection of Jesus for Mark and for the whole of Christianity not a "miracle," and are the "miracles" of Jesus not closely connected, precisely in Mark, with faith?[125] Is not the modern "fear of miracles" at work again in this thesis?

---

[122] On this, see Hengel/Schwemer 2001, 23ff., 34–45, 166–70 and 264 index, s.v. "Messiaserwartung" (ET = Hengel 1995, 20ff., 32–41, no equivalent).

[123] Ebeling 1939, 220–21.

[124] Conzelmann 1969, 139 (GV = Conzelmann 1967, 150); Conzelmann/Lindemann 1988, 220 (GV = 1985, 256ff.).

[125] See section 16.2. For Mark and his hearers, Jesus' sovereign foreknowledge, the solar eclipse on Passover, and the tearing of the temple curtain at the moment of Jesus' death are miracles of the Messiah and Son of God in connection with his *theologia crucis*.

To be sure, with these corrections the intention of the evangelist Mark is more appropriately grounded than in Wrede, but the origin of the motif is still not adequately explained, since Mark, in contrast to John, does not write a relatively freely configured "christological fiction,"[126] but intensively reworks older traditions, and also the silence commands in their different forms—this was already seen clearly by Wrede—were not simply invented by Mark, but stem from the tradition, whose Palestinian Jewish origin is palpable and which, in our view, goes back to Peter to a large extent.[127] Rather, Mark makes the various traditional historical motifs fruitful for his considered Christology and has shaped them—as all his material—accordingly. He has not simply invented them himself. They are too different in detail for this to be the case. If the silence commands were really a theological-novelistic new creation of Mark, then this would have taken place in a more uniform manner. They are ultimately grounded in Jesus' activity.

The fact that in the exorcisms the "demons" in the sick "had to be brought to silence" lies in the nature of the matter. As long as the sick person continued to shout he was not healed and the exorcism failed. The fact that time and again Jesus forbade healed people to proclaim their healing everywhere and that he withdrew into isolation at times is likewise understandable. He did not want to further stoke up the mass movement. Every successful physician must sometimes close his practice when it overflows, for the day has only twenty-four hours. This phenomenon has nothing to do with the Messiah question. Accordingly, from the texts on the "messianic secret" gathered by Wrede, which for the most part do not fit in this scheme, *no* argument against a "messianic claim" of Jesus can be deduced. At the end of his investigation, H.-J. Ebeling emphasizes:

> Thus, from the standpoint of our results, we are prohibited from taking a positive or negative position in the controversy of opinions about whether Jesus had a messianic consciousness. To be sure, Wrede's arguments for an unmessianic consciousness are not tenable, but the whole problem requires a far more extensive investigation and interpretation of the Gospel.[128]

---

[126] John does this at least in large portions of his work in the certainty of the inspiration through the risen one; see Hengel 1993a (ET = 1989a). On this cf. now also Frey 2018a; 2018b.

[127] Hengel 2008c, 120ff., 141ff. (ET = 2000b, 65ff., 78ff.); Hengel 2010a, 36–48 (GV = 2006b, 58–78).

[128] Ebeling 1939, 221 (our emphasis).

To this day this has, in our view, still not been satisfactorily carried out.[129] It would also burst the framework of our presentation. Conzelmann also rightly objects against Wrede (and *cum grano salis* against his teacher Bultmann):

> The materials reworked by Mark, especially the miracle stories, do not at all evince an unmessianic portrait of Jesus; even more, an unmessianic Jesus tradition does not exist at all.[130]

It is, however, then entirely incomprehensible how Conzelmann comes to an originally unmessianic Jesus, which is even more sharply maintained than in Wrede and Bultmann. When there is no "unmessianic Jesus tradition"[131] — a judgment that we readily affirm — how will he then so cleanly separate the "messianic" from the "unmessianic" so as to obtain a historically "purified," title-less portrait of Jesus? In that case, the radical, logical consequence would rather be for him to deny all pre-Easter tradition about Jesus and to declare the human Jesus to be an ungraspable phantom. But Conzelmann did not wish to be so radical. His large article in the third edition of *Religion in Geschichte und Gegenwart* (Conzelmann 1959; ET = 1973) contains many valuable, materially correct observations, even though he falls into irreconcilable contradictions through his denial of the messianic claim of Jesus.

17.4 The Problem of the Titles of Majesty

17.4.1 The Son of Man[132]

According to the Gospels (and we do not have another detailed source), the phrase "the Son of Man" (ὁ υἱὸς τοῦ ἀνθρώπου) belongs to the *ipsissima vox* Jesu,[133] one could also say: to his "very own language." It "is a

---

[129] See, however, Minette de Tillesse 1968; Räisänen 1973; 1990 (GV = 1976). To be sure, Räisänen's fundamental investigation of the problem goes astray in its results, for his historical attempts at solutions, which ascribe the invention of the messianic secret to Mark, who is said to have reacted to conflicts of his community with itinerant radicalism, are even more off target than the theses of Wrede.

[130] Conzelmann/Lindemann 1985, 257 (ET = Conzelmann/Lindemann 1988, 220).

[131] This "unmessianic portrait of Jesus" is found in the Jewish and pagan opponents, for example in Celsus and his Jewish authority, who misrepresent Jesus as a magician and deceiver who received his just punishment.

[132] Colpe 1972 (GV = 1969); Sjöberg 1955; Hahn 1969, 15ff. (GV = 1995, 13ff.); Jeremias 1970, 257ff. (GV = 1979, 245ff.); Hampel 1990; see now Horbury 1998a, 125–56; Dunn 2003b, 724–62. Cf. now also Deines 2012a, 92–94.

[133] On this, see section 12.1 and section 17.2 with note 35.

literal rendering, which is ambiguous, indeed unintelligible, in Greek,"[134] of the Aramaic definite *bar 'ᵉnāšā'* (בר [א]נשׁא).

> A connection to Dan 7.13 appears to be present from the beginning: "The New Testament ὁ υἱὸς τοῦ ἀνθρώπου must render the emphatic בר אנשׁא." Since this definite form of the singular[135] is uncommon in Aramaic (and is incomprehensible in Greek) "it can only mean: 'the (known from Dan 7.13) בר אנשׁ, the being called בר אנשׁא,' with the word בר אנשׁא, because it is a quotation, being retained. The expression בר אנשׁ is thus clear."[136]

That Jesus must have used this formula is evident not only from the fact that the expression ὁ υἱὸς τοῦ ἀνθρώπου, meaningless for a Greek, with double article as a translation of the Aramaic equivalent, occurs eighty-one times (!) in all four Gospels, with one exception (John 12.34) *always only in the mouth of Jesus*: in Mark fourteen times, in Luke twenty-five times, in Matthew thirty times, and in John twelve times.[137] Even if we cut out all parallel traditions, we still have thirty-eight individual attestations. While the other titles in the Synoptics appear only rarely or not at all in the mouth of Jesus, the phrase "Son of Man" appears there *only in sayings of Jesus*. Matthew, who has a feel for and fondness for dominical language, sometimes also introduces this formula—as with the "Amen, I say to you," the "kingdom of heaven," and "your (our) Father in heaven"—into the Markan, Lukan, and sayings *Vorlagen* of his Gospel. Seven attestations come from the texts common to Mark and Luke, and nine from their special material in each case.[138] Outside of the Gospels, we do not encounter the definite formula in the New Testament, with one exception in the heavenly vision of the martyr Stephen.[139]

---

[134] Colpe 1969, 406.10-11 (ET = 1972, 404). The indefinite *bar 'ᵉnāš* is translated in 1 En. 22.5 with ἄνθρωπος and in Dan 7.13 (LXX/Theodotion) with υἱὸς ἀνθρώπου and has the meaning "individual human being." On this, see Beyer 1984, 517–18.

[135] "The determinate plural בני אנשׁא occurs in Dan 2.38; 5.21. The determinate form אנשׁא has a generalizing . . . or collective sense" (Colpe 1969, 405.13–14; ET = Colpe 1972, 402).

[136] Beyer 1984, 518.

[137] In John there are two exceptions that prove the rule: in John 5.27, as in Dan 7.13 (*kᵉbar 'ᵉnāš*; LXX/Theodotion: ὡς υἱὸς ἀνθρώπου), the article is lacking: ὅτι υἱὸς ἀνθρώπου ἐστίν. This is a clear allusion to this text in Daniel; cf. Rev 1.13 and 14.14: ὅμοιον υἱὸν ἀνθρώπου. In John 12.34 it appears once in the mouth of the crowd, though as a reaction to a saying of Jesus.

[138] Hahn 1993.

[139] Acts 7.56: ἰδού θεωρῶ τοὺς οὐρανοὺς διηνοιγμένους καὶ τὸν υἱὸν τοῦ ἀνθρώπου ἐκ δεξιῶν ἑστῶτα τοῦ θεοῦ. Here the designation is connected in an idiosyncratic way with Ps 110.1. Cf. also the quotation with the indefinite form from Dan

Outside of the New Testament, it also occurs only at the margins, for example in the apocryphal James tradition, which has a Jewish Christian background.[140]

In Jewish sources "Son of Man" is not a generally acknowledged title before 70. The starting point in Dan 7.13 contains only a comparison, though in a text that was of central importance at the turn of the century. In the Parables of 1 Enoch,[141] similar formulations such as "Son of Man"—dependent on Dan 7.13—in various forms[142] are the cipher for an enigmatic human figure hidden in heaven since before times, who is also twice called the anointed one[143] and alongside this often the righteous one and the chosen one, whom God enthrones as eschatological judge and who is identified with Enoch at the end. The dating of the Parables is controversial, as is the question of the extent to which the human figure there has influenced the Gospels.[144]

Beyond this, the "(Son of) Man" is identified with the Messiah after 70 in Ezra; he appears very rarely in rabbinic texts, presumably because the Christians had appropriated this enigmatic figure from Dan 7.13.[145]

7.13 in John and Revelation (see note 137 above) and from Ps 8.5 in Heb 2.6. Only the very late Targum Psalm 8.5 has twice *bar nāšā'* for *ben 'ādām* and *'enôš*. Cf. also in Ps 80.18 the parallelism of *'iš yᵉmînekhā* and *ben 'ādām* (LXX ἄνδρα δεξιᾶς σου/τὸν υἱὸν ἀνθρώπου) and on this Ps 110.1; further related attestations in Horbury 1998a, 144–51, who refers, among other things, to Targum Ps 80.16 and 18 and to numerous examples of the messianic interpretation of ἄνθρωπος, *'iš*, *geber/gabrā*, and other terms.

[140] Cf. without the article Barn. 12.10; Ign. *Eph.* 20.2, both already in the style of the second century as juxtaposition to υἱὸς θεοῦ. On James, see the Gospel of Hebrews according to Jerome, *Vir. ill.* 2 (Aland 2005, 507), and in the Martyrdom of James according to Hegesippus apud Eusebius, *Hist. eccl.* 2.23.13; cf. Matt 26.64; on this, see Hengel 2002, 560–61. The shorter Latin version of Ascen. Isa. 11.1(2) also uses it for the earthly existence of Christ: *Et vidi simile filii hominis, et cum hominibus habitare in mundo* (Tisserant 1909, 203); this is also true for the Slavic version; on this, see Bettiolo 1995 (cf. Norelli 1995), 231, 315, 430. Mart. Ascen. Isa. is a Jewish Christian writing from the beginning of the second century and stands in firm Christian tradition.

[141] Chapters 37–71. They are only preserved in Ethiopic. In contrast to the other parts of 1 Enoch, no fragment of the Parables was found in Qumran. On this, see Sacchi 1980, 44ff.; Uhlig 1984. Cf. also Ign. *Eph.* 20.2.

[142] Gese 1977, 142 (ET = 1981, 157): "In 1 Enoch the son of man is still spoken of with greater terminological freedom." This stresses "the general human character of the figure" (142; ET = 157). In this Dan 7 is developed further and "presupposed even in the details" (142–43; ET = 157).

[143] First Enoch 48.10; 52.4. In the last text there is talk of the "rule of his anointed one." The influence of Isa 11.1-5 is also significant. See Gese 1981, 158 (GV = 1977, 143).

[144] The Parables presumably arose between the Parthian invasion in 40 BCE and the destruction of the temple. Theisohn 1975 hypothesizes only an influence on Matthew (see the index on Matt 19.28; 25.31).

[145] Fourth Ezra 13 is clearly dependent on Dan 7.2, 13; and Isa 11.4. On the Son of Man, see the additional parallels in Bill. I: 485ff., 957ff. On the rabbinic linguistic use

The formula is not found at Qumran, despite the variety of messianic conceptions and although the book of Daniel was already held in high esteem there.[146] The absence of a reference in Qumran and the relative rarity of the formula in the contemporary Jewish sources before 70 suggests that in the first century CE *bar 'ᵉnāšā'* was not, to be sure, a "messianic title" that was recognized by all as a matter of course, but that in certain groups it could nevertheless be understood as such on the basis of the interpretation of Dan 7.13.[147]

In our view, this whole state of affairs makes it extremely unlikely that the post-Easter community first placed this designation in the mouth of Jesus secondarily, especially since it is not used at all in the christological argumentation outside of the Gospels in the epistles or in the words of disciples or third parties. If "Son of Man" had been a generally used messianic title, one would have to expect it in the Gospels *also* in the mouths of the disciples and opponents, for example as a confession or in controversy dialogues. By contrast, in the Gospels it is conspicuous that with few exceptions, the title χριστός, anointed one, *never* appears in sayings of Jesus but is always brought to Jesus *from outside*, i.e., from followers and opponents, whereas "Son of Man" occurs *only* in the mouth of Jesus and also with *conspicuous frequency*. Moreover, in Mark "Son of Man" as a self-designation of Jesus does not fall under the messianic secret, perhaps because the evangelist still knew that it was *not a common* title for the Messiah, though it was probably on the way to becoming one.[148] From this two consequences can be drawn:

1. That Jesus used this formula *bar 'ᵉnāšā'*, i.e., "the human being," as a "messianic" cipher. The reference to Dan 7.13 already stood in the background. This belongs to the "secret of his person," which we cannot ultimately plumb. In our view, it is absurd to postulate that "the community" put in the mouth of Jesus in a massive way a formula that was still

---

of "the one of the clouds" or "the son of the clouds" for the Messiah from Dan 7.13, see Ego 1995, 29–32.

[146] Tov 1992, 96: fragments of five copies of Daniel. The book of Daniel, which arose in 165/164 BCE, must have quickly established itself as authoritative in Hasidic, and that means also Essene and Pharisaic circles. By contrast, it was rejected by the Sadducees.

[147] On this, see Bousset 1970, 40–45 (GV = 1965, 10–15). According to Bousset, "we will best be able to paraphrase and explain the strange and enigmatic designation . . . with the term 'the' (well known from Daniel's prophecy or from the apocalyptic tradition) 'Man'" (45; GV = 13). Horbury 1998a, 151: ". . . it may be said that messianic exegesis of Dan 7.13 probably arose not later than the early first century A. D., and possibly much earlier. . . . The messianic associations of the phrase would have been strengthened by a distinct, best comparable, pre-Christian messianic interpretation of words for 'man,' to be found in connection with biblical passages other than Dan 7.13."

[148] Cf. Horbury 1998a, 151–52.

not at all common as a messianic title and therefore unserviceable for the
christological proclamation, whereas the generally known title of Messiah, which soon became Jesus' name, was largely kept distant from him.
The Markan messianic secret would also become entirely unexplainable in
this way, for the "(Son of) Man" stands outside of this for the evangelist.

2. The cipher "Son of Man" or "Man" was apparently suitable neither
for the proclamation nor for the confession formulas, for it—in contrast to
the title "anointed one," *māšî'ḥ/mešîḥā'*/χριστός—did not clearly express
the nearness to God and the eschatological dignity of the exalted one in a
way that was clear and recognizable for all, since it was not already clearly
specified as a title by the Old Testament-Jewish tradition.

One could openly proclaim Jesus as Messiah, Son of God, and exalted
Lord, but not as the *bar 'enāšā'*, which was understandable only for the
circle of the initiated. When "Son of Man" nevertheless occurs very often
and only in the mouth of Jesus in the Synoptics and "Christos" appears
almost never, then this must point to an *original historical* situation, which
shows that in this point the "christological" tradition is more reliable than
is often assumed in critical scholarship. After all, the situation quickly
changed completely in the post-Easter community. There, in a very short
time *mešîḥā'*/χριστός became the decisive title for the exalted one and
then the second name of Jesus,[149] while Son of Man was retained only in
the Jesus tradition. There was still a memory of such old forms of the linguistic usage of Jesus. This is why we find "the Son of Man" only at the
margins in the christological argumentation of the Greek-speaking community, for example without the article as a quotation from Dan 7.13 and
Ps 8.5[150] or in Paul carried over as "last Adam" or as "man from heaven."[151]
In the vision of the accused Stephen in Acts 7.56 Luke places it in the
mouth of the first martyr, because he knows that this designation—after its
frequent use by Jesus himself—still played a role in the Jerusalem primitive community, whereas it did not do so any longer in the later mission
communities.[152] To be sure, the use by Jesus within the Synoptic Gospels
themselves is, in turn, mysterious, but we regard it as probable that precisely this enigmatic feature, which has led to continuous controversies

---

[149] On this, see Hengel 2002, 240–61; Hengel 2001d, 2ff., 8ff. (ET = 1995, 2ff., 7ff.).

[150] Cf. also Ps 80(LXX 79).16-18; Heb 2.6; Rev 1.13; 14.14; cf. John 5.27.

[151] First Corinthians 15.45, 47-48. Cf. Acts 17.31: God will judge the world ἐν ἀνδρὶ
ᾧ ὥρισεν. We regard it as possible that a reference to Adam in Gen 1–3 was hidden already
in the linguistic usage of Jesus; see note 164 below.

[152] In this "archaic" christological linguistic usage one could see a parallel to the
double use of παῖς (θεοῦ) in the speech of Peter in Acts 3.13, 26, in the prayer in Acts
4.27, 30, and then in old Jewish Christian prayers (1 Clem. 59.2–3; Did. 9.2–3; 10.2–3).

in the later explanation of the cipher until the present day, goes back to a differentiated linguistic usage of Jesus.

The investigation of V. Hampel comes to the conclusion that "the post-Easter community . . . under the influence of Dan 7.13-14 first (spoke) of the *coming* of the Son of Man" and Jesus in this "saying about the future majesty of the Son of Man"[153] referred originally to his own future revelation as Messiah.[154] The author thus finds four groups of Son of Man sayings in the usage of Jesus:

1. the sayings "about the future majesty of the Son of Man";
2. the sayings about his "present majesty";[155]
3. the sayings "about the present lowliness";[156]
4. the sayings about his suffering and his resurrection.[157]

According to him, the designation *bar 'ᵉnāšā'* was a cipher with which

Jesus very intentionally (takes) up an ambivalent enigmatic phrase in order to express his messianic self-understanding and his messianic commission in a way that was both concealing and suggestive. . . . Until his enthronement—i.e., his final legitimation by God himself, in connection with his worldwide public recognition as Messiah—he acts as Messiah *designatus* in Israel; and as such he designates himself בר אנשא.[158]

This means that Jesus characterized himself with it

as Messiah working in a hidden manner, who looks forward to . . . the revelation of his glory.

---

[153] Hampel 1990, 186–87. To be sure, in our view, with this the problem is simplified too much.

[154] According to Hampel, the concern is with Luke 11.30 = Matt 12.40; Luke 17.24 = Matt 24.27; Luke 17.26 = Matt 24.37 and Mark 14.62bα = Matt 26.64bα = Luke 22.69, which proved "(respectively at the core) to be authentic sayings of Jesus." The post-Easter secondary interpretation with reference to the coming of the Son of Man according to Dan 7.13-14 "took place due to a thoroughgoing primitive Christian updating of the authentic-dominical Son of Man sayings" (187). In our view, the connection to Dan 7.13 existed from the very beginning. It alone explains the distinctive linguistic usage.

[155] Mark 2.10, 28; Luke 19.10.

[156] Matthew 11.19 = Luke 7.34; Matt 8.19-20 = Luke 9.57-58.

[157] Mark 8.31 par.; 9.12b par.; 9.31 parr. and above all Mark 10.45.

[158] Hampel 1990, 371. On this, cf. Horbury 1998a, 151: "the range of meaning of the phrase allowed it to be both self-referential and messianic; in its aspects of opacity, which the hearer was invited to pierce, it resembled the parables."

Only through it does he become

> Messiah in power. Until then . . . his messianic claim . . . remains . . .
> ambivalent insofar as it has "faith and unbelief" as a consequence.

This more recent attempt at a solution is more successful than others at joining the various, seemingly opposing Synoptic Son of Man texts into a meaningful unity, without having to appeal too much to the constructive fantasy of the post-Easter community. Going beyond his assumptions, we must ask whether the connection between the self-designation *bar ᵉnāšā'* and Dan 7.13 was not already significant for Jesus.[159] He himself knew, of course, the book of Daniel, especially since for the book of Daniel the dawning of the kingdom of God plays the central role.[160] The use of the formula *bar ᵉnāšā'*/ὁ υἱὸς τοῦ ἀνθρώπου in the mouth of Jesus in the Synoptics points to an enigma, to a discrepancy, so to speak. On the one hand, we must assume that it was originally more likely a cipher and not a generally known messianic title. As such, Jesus used it to express his hidden dignity and authority as eschatological proclaimer of salvation, one could also say as Messiah *designatus*, and yet at the same time also his lowliness and his tribulation, at the end of which stood his execution.

On the other hand, the question of how Jesus imagined the consummation of the kingdom of God, its "coming in power,"[161] the day on which "the Son of Man is revealed"[162] is answered only in intimations, for precisely at this point the eschatological statements of his own proclamation and the disciples' expectations of the parousia of the crucified and exalted "Son of Man," i.e., the hope of the primitive community, are fused together in such a way that they can scarcely be separated. At the end of the Last Supper he expresses his certainty that God himself will bring about his

[159] Here one could also refer to the hidden "Son of Man" in the Parables of 1 Enoch; on this, see Sjöberg 1946; 1955; Colpe 1972, 423–29 (GV = 1969, 425–29); see also Otto 1954 (ET = 1938), which was once heatedly discussed. The noble review of Dibelius does greater justice to this work of the great history-of-religions scholar than R. Bultmann's scathing review (Bultmann 1937 = 2002, 328–53). See Dibelius 1935: "that here what is central in the message and work of Jesus is less explained than beheld, that it is securely integrated into the context of the history-of-religion development and on the basis of this context and an intuitive sympathy is—despite all doubtful interpretations—rightly beheld." See also Horbury in note 147 above.

[160] The trial of Jesus and the accusation because of his messianic claims are connected—among other things—also with his use of the Son of Man formula; see section 18.4 and section 20.2.2.

[161] Mark 9.1. See note 105 in chapter 13.

[162] Luke 17.30: κατὰ τὰ αὐτὰ ἔσται ᾗ ἡμέρᾳ ὁ υἱὸς τοῦ ἀνθρώπου ἀποκαλύπτεται; cf. 24.26.

kingdom, through and beyond the announced death, and yet indeed soon, and he, Jesus, will celebrate the messianic banquet there with the disciples in an entirely new way.[163] Here it is significant that Messiah hope and Son of Man expectation cannot be separated a priori. This is rightly stressed by Hartmut Gese:

> The tradition of the son of man . . . did not include a Messiah in addi-
> tion to the son of man, because the figure of the son of man involves a
> genuine transformation of the figure of the Davidic Messiah, and is not
> an addition to it. Therefore, if Jesus thought of himself as the Messiah,
> he must also have thought of himself as the future son of man.[164]

The saying about the eschatological judging function of the twelve disciples,[165] which follows the Passover meal in Luke, also points in this direction. Presumably Jesus already connected the dawning of the "kingdom of God in power" (Mark 9.1) with his revelation as "Son of Man" from heaven. The parables of the waiting slaves and householders and the waiting wise and foolish virgins also belong in this context, in which it is no longer possible to distinguish clearly between Jesus' own expectation and that of the earliest community.[166] The question of the time span between Jesus' sacrificial death and the coming of God's kingdom can be left open. The middle way between "thoroughgoing eschatology" and "realized eschatology" that W. G. Kümmel attempted to take may

---

[163] Mark 14.25 = Matt 26.29; cf. Luke 22.18. See section 13.2 with note 45.

[164] Gese 1981, 161, cf. 159–60 (GV = 1977, 146, cf. 144–45). It "expands and ele-vates" the national Davidic picture of the Messiah "so that it can encompass the entire mediatory function of divine revelation to mankind" (ET = 160; GV = 145). We could ask here whether the universal mediation of the "Son of Man" does not at the same time present a counterpicture to the disobedience of Adam and the universal fate connected with it. After all, the "kingdom of God that is in the process of realization" proclaimed by Jesus also restores the good creation of the heavenly Father disturbed by Adam's sin and turns the sinful human beings into God's children. The question concerns the extent to which—in a different form—primitive Christian, indeed dominical ideas ultimately stand behind the Pauline statement in Rom 5.12-21 and 1 Cor 15.21-22, 45-49. On this, see note 151 above. In that case, the formula "Son of Man" would be an expression for the true "human being in correspondence to God" (K. Barth), who opens the gates to paradise, i.e., brings about the kingdom of God.

[165] Luke 22.30; cf.—probably in dependence on Luke—Matt 19.28.

[166] Cf. Luke 12.35-48; Matt 24.42-51; 25.1-13; see section 17.4.1.2. On this, see also Kümmel 1961, 54–59 (GV = 1956, 47–52); on his expectation of an "interim period" between death and "parousia," see pp. 64–83 (GV = 58–76) and especially pp. 76ff. (GV = 69ff.) on Mark 14.25; cf. also Luke 13.35 par.; 17.22; 18.7-8. See further section 17.4.1.3 and the discussion of Jeremias' interpretation of Mark 9.31 there.

come closest to the reality here.[167] With his activity, Jesus proclaimed the dawning kingdom of God, described this with metaphors such as "life," "joy," and divine "glory" and with the conception of the eschatological banquet (see section 13.2), but did not specify a future date.[168] According to the sayings tradition, "the day of the Son of Man" comes in an entirely surprising manner and brings judgment and redemption.[169] We do not know whether or to what extent Jesus' "near expectation" changed under the impression of his "path of sacrifice" to Jerusalem. We cannot reconstruct a "systematic picture" of his near expectation that is without contradictions. However, one should not assume a complete nullification of the period of time until the "revelation of the Son of Man" expected by him. Otherwise, the disciples, who were after all the constant hearers of Jesus, would have acted differently after Easter. It would, however, be a violent coup if one were simply to make a general assignment of all the "apocalyptic" sayings of Jesus that belong in this context and are offensive to the modern "enlightened understanding" to the "community."

C. Colpe, following J. Jeremias, also posed the question of the connection between the person of Jesus and the future Son of Man figure:

> The apocalyptic Son of Man is a symbol of Jesus' assurance of perfecting.[170]

This means that there is a close, indissoluble connection between Jesus and the future figure, but a simple identification with Jesus' present activity is not permissible:

> If an identification is stated directly and explicitly, the dynamic element in the relation between the present and the future person is destroyed and the preaching loses its prophetic character.[171]

According to Colpe, in his distinction from Jesus and his connection with him, the future Son of Man initially remains enigmatically undetermined. This mystery is resolved only by the end event itself, i.e., for the disciples

---

[167] Kümmel 1956 (ET = 1961). See the introduction to the second edition (1956, 3; 1961, 7).

[168] Mark 13.32; cf. Luke 17.20-21; Matt 24.36.

[169] Luke 17.22-37 par.; on this, see section 17.4.1.2.

[170] Colpe 1972, 441 (GV = Colpe 1969, 443.23–24: "Der apokalyptische Menschensohn ist ein Symbol für Jesu Vollendungsgewißheit").

[171] Colpe 1972, 440 (GV = Colpe 1969, 442.30ff.: "Würde hier eine Identifikation direkt und ausdrücklich ausgesprochen, so würde die Dynamik in der Beziehung zwischen der gegenwärtigen und der zukünftigen Person aufgehoben und die Predigt ginge ihres prophetischen Charakters verlustig").

with the appearances of the crucified and risen one. By contrast, this—temporary—indeterminateness already speaks against the view that a post-Easter insertion into the Jesus proclamation took place here. The oldest version of the future revelation of the Son of Man, in which one can scarcely speak of a christological reshaping by the community, is available in the Lukan version.[172] The texts about his coming upon the clouds of heaven in Mark are already more strongly shaped by the primitive Christian hope, and in Matthew a further development can be observed, perhaps already under the influence of the Parables of 1 Enoch.[173]

The peculiar-enigmatic way in which Jesus designated himself as "(the Son of) Man" or spoke of the future revelation of the "Son of Man" is basically *a part of the true "messianic secret."* This is not restricted to the Gospel of Mark, and it also does not represent a mere construct of the post-Easter community that is meant to conceal an "unmessianic Jesus." Rather, it is a phenomenon behind which the *mystery of Jesus' person* stands. This, in turn, is most intimately connected with the *"mystery of the kingdom of God"*[174] and its presence, which is already active in Jesus' actions but is hidden to the outside until the "coming in power."[175]

17.4.1.1 The Sayings about the Present Activity of the Son of Man

Here Jesus uses the phrase to describe his own activity, i.e., instead of the first person singular. The sayings where "Son of Man" is used in this way express the special authority or afflicted situation of Jesus. The secret of Jesus' person comes especially to the fore in them, and they are basically connected with the I sayings, in which he expresses his "messianic sending": the "Son of Man" is sometimes interchangeable with the emphatic "I" of these sayings.[176]

---

[172] Luke 17.24-30; cf. Matt 24.27-39. On this, see Hengel 2002, 398–410. The question here is how far Matthew is *also* dependent on Luke.

[173] Theisohn 1975, index on Matt 19.28; 25.31. In Matt 25.31 "the Son of Man comes in his δόξα and is accompanied by all the angels," sits on the "θρόνος δόξης αὐτοῦ" and exercises judgment through separation. V. 34 calls him βασιλεύς; his βασιλεία is for those who are "blessed of the Father, prepared since the foundation of the world." This means that he acts as judge as God the Father himself and in his commission.

[174] Mark 4.11, cf. Luke 8.10 = Matt 13.11.

[175] Mark uses the phrase μυστήριον . . . τῆς βασιλείας τοῦ θεοῦ in 4.11 in connection with his hardening and parable theory. The subject matter, however, is given with the activity of Jesus in general. He therefore had to speak about the kingdom of God primarily in παραβολαί/ *mᵉšālîm*. On this, see section 12.3 with notes 126–29. The verbal agreement between Luke and Matthew against Mark is conspicuous: γνῶναι τὰ μυστήρια τῆς βασιλείας (plural). In the case of this and other minor agreements, Matthew is influenced by Luke. In the Synoptics the word μυστήριον appears only in these passages, which are dependent on Mark.

[176] Cf., for example, Matt 10.32-33 with the more original Luke 12.8-9; Mark 10.45 with Luke 22.27; Matt 5.11 and Luke 6.22. Decisions about the original form must be made on a case-by-case basis.

Six sayings are in view, two from Mark and four from the sayings tradition of Luke and Matthew. The first text is Mark 2.10[177] in the healing of the paralytic: ". . . in order that you may know that the Son of Man has authority on earth to forgive sins." The second text is Mark 2.28:[178] "The Son of Man is Lord over the Sabbath." Here it has been speculated that *bar 'enāšā'* originally meant the human being in general as "lord over the Sabbath." However, in the preceding controversy dialogue over the plucking of ears on the Sabbath, the climax of which is formed by our saying of Jesus, the concern is with the special—messianic—authority of Jesus, who compares himself with David, who in his flight from Saul ate from the holy bread of the presence, which was reserved for the priests, and also gave it to his companions.[179]

Luke 9.58 = Matt 8.20: "Foxes have holes and the birds of the air have nests, but the Son of Man has nowhere to lay his head." Jesus, who as itinerant teacher and proclaimer of the kingdom of God passes through Galilee and adjoining areas, has no fixed place of residence that belongs to him and must demand from his followers that they share the insecurity of his existence. This warning vis-à-vis a potential follower refers to the externally viewed uncertain existence of Jesus and should not be interpreted in an "existentialist," all-too-modern way as a reference to the "homelessness"[180] of the human being in general, since it thus loses its concrete meaning.

Luke 7.33-34 = Matt 11.18-19, from the speech about the Baptist:[181] "For John came, not eating or drinking, and it is said that he has a demon. The Son of Man eats and drinks and it is said: Behold, the glutton and wine-bibber. . . ." The saying makes sense only in the mouth of Jesus. Like Luke 9.58 par. it signals his afflicted situation. This saying, which, despite the great difference, connects the Baptist and Jesus but does not yet point to their violent death, does not fit in a post-Easter situation shaped by exaltation Christology. It thus runs counter to the later christological development, especially since John and Jesus appear here as representatives of

---

[177] The wording is almost identical in Luke 5.24 and Matt 9.6; cf. also the forgiveness of sins in relation to the sinful woman in Luke 7.46-50. On this, see section 13.2 with notes 34–36.

[178] Luke 6.5; Matt 12.8; cf. also Mark 3.1-6 parr.; Luke 13.10-16; 14.1-6; John 5.9ff.; 9.13ff.

[179] Mark 2.23-28 parr. Matthew expands in 12.5-6: the service of the priests also permits the profaning of the Sabbath.

[180] Thus Vielhauer 1965a, 123ff.

[181] See the end of section 10.7 and elsewhere.

divine "Wisdom," which is "justified" by her "children," i.e., their believing listeners.[182]

Luke 11.29-30: the answer to the demands for a sign: "This generation is an evil generation. It demands a sign, but no sign will be given
to it, except the sign of Jonah. For just as Jonah became a sign to the
Ninevites, so the Son of Man will be to this generation." The sign of Jonah
was his preaching in Nineveh. Jesus had precisely this in common with
the prophet. In response to the demand for a sign, Jesus therefore points
not—as in the question of the Baptist—to the efficacious healings of the
sick but to his public proclamation. Seeing signs does not change the heart
of a human being. Rather, like the Ninevites, the human being must hear
God's call to repentance and answer it in believing obedience.[183]

Luke 12.10 = Matt 12.32 is connected with the Beelzebul slander:
"Everyone who says a word against the Son of Man, it will be forgiven
him, but the one who speaks against the Holy Spirit, it will not be forgiven him." Even the slander of the person of Jesus will be forgiven; by
contrast, the one who interprets the activity of Jesus in the Spirit of God,
for example his exorcistic healings of sick persons, as deeds of the demon
prince Beelzebul excludes himself from salvation, because he opposes the
coming of God himself.

Behind this enigmatic linguistics usage, with which Jesus describes
his authority and his trials and hostilities, stands at the end of the day his
messianic secret. The true dignity and identity of the *bar 'ᵉnāšā'* are still
hidden and will become manifest only in the near future. There appears
here a similar dialectic to that between the present of the kingdom of
God in the activity of Jesus, which many fail to recognize, and its future
coming "in power."[184]

---

[182] Luke 7.35; cf. 10.21 par.; see Hengel 2001c, 87ff., 92, 99, 102 (ET = 1995, 79ff.,
83, 89, 92). In this context one would need to point to the close connection between wisdom and Son of Man in the Parables of 1 Enoch. On this, see Gese 1977, 143 (ET =
1981, 158): "To the nature of wisdom corresponds the most eminent bearer of wisdom."
Here lies a root of the later preexistence Christology, which still possesses entirely Old
Testament-Jewish features. A bridge to the Davidic Messiah is made by the emphasis on
the Spirit-effected, unique wisdom of the God-sent, righteous judge of Isa 11.1-16, a text
that also had an influence on the Son of Man of the Parables of 1 Enoch. On preexistence
Christology, cf. now also Deines 2012a, 100-113.

[183] Cf. Luke 16.29ff.; 11.28. On the "sign of Jonah" as his announcement of the
destruction of Jerusalem in Liv. Pro. 10.8, see Schwemer 1995/1996, II: 81ff. See also note
323 in chapter 3 and note 7 in chapter 16.

[184] Mark 9.1; see section 13.1.

17.4.1.2 The Sayings of the Coming Son of Man

This largest and most important group stands in a peculiar contrast, indeed in apparent opposition to the sayings about the earthly Son of Man. Jesus can speak about this figure seemingly as about a completely different, third person. Bultmann and his students, G. Bornkamm as well as Tödt and Hahn, believe that by this Jesus meant an apocalyptic, mythological figure who was distinct from him. Vielhauer, Käsemann, and Conzelmann regard it in general as a formation of the Palestinian community. In their view, Jesus used *bar 'ᵉnāšā'* neither for himself nor for an apocalyptic heavenly figure. Today, we find rather the opposite tendency to regard the apocalyptic sayings as secondary formations of the community and the sayings about the present Son of Man as dominical linguistic usage. For example, Mogens Müller assumes that the formula means "Jesus' circumlocution for 'I,'" namely as an expression of reverence, reserve, and humility," but thinks that this formula, despite Dan 7.13 and its interpretation in the Septuagint and in the Parables of 1 Enoch, does not allow one to infer a messianic consciousness. Moreover, he thinks that "all 'Son of Man' sayings that speak of Jesus' fate on the far side of the resurrection" must be understood as "creations of the primitive community."[185] Over against such hypotheses C. Colpe carried out pioneering work and, following his teacher Joachim Jeremias, carved out seven sayings in which the appearance of the eschatological Son of Man is announced and his function as judge is presented.[186] They can be traced back, at least in part, with some probability to Jesus.

Luke 17.24[187] = Matt 24.27, from the apocalyptic sayings tradition common to the two Gospels: "As lightning flashes from the rising of the sun and shines to the setting of the sun, so will it be with the Son of Man on that day." His sudden appearance with the now universally visible inbreaking of the kingdom of God makes him manifest to all and applies to all human beings. It brings judgment and redemption and stands in opposition to the zealot expectation of a Messiah hidden in the wilderness, who is to gather his followers there some day.[188] The Son of Man proves himself here to be the universal authorized representative of God.

---

[185] M. Müller 1984, 259. The author misses the fact that there is precisely not talk of the resurrection in these Son of Man sayings.

[186] Colpe 1972, 430ff. (GV = 1969, 433ff.).

[187] Cf. Luke 17.26, 30 = Matt 24.37, 39; Luke still speaks of the ἡμέρα; Matthew speaks in a Christianized way of the παρουσία of the Son of Man; cf. Paul in 1 Thess 2.19; 3.13; 4.15; 5.23.

[188] See Hengel 2002, 404ff. and note 291 in chapter 3.

This is supplemented by Luke 17.26ff. = Matt 24.37ff.: "And as in the days of Noah, so it will be with the Son of Man. They ate and drank, they married and were given in marriage, until the day when Noah entered the ark, and the flood came and destroyed them all. . . ." This means the Son of Man comes—thus probably already in the preaching of the Baptist[189]— unexpectedly, suddenly, and as judge of all human beings.

Analogous to this, the Markan apocalypse, Mark 13.26 stresses: ". . . then they will see the Son of Man in great power and glory." This coming of the Son of Man, which is visible to all, means, as already in Dan 7.13-14, 27, the consummation of the kingdom of God.[190] Since this is identical with the conferring of the kingdom upon the Son of Man or "the people of the holy ones of the Most High," one would also need to refer to Luke 22.29-30. It is no longer possible to distinguish cleanly between the expectation of Jesus and that of the community of disciples.

The individual saying of Luke 18.18 (special material) relates his coming to the messianic movement triggered by the Baptist and Jesus: "When the Son of Man comes, will he find faith upon the earth?" Interpreted with reference to the parable of the sower, this means: Will the sown seed bear fruit or perish? A related saying, which is formulated from the later standpoint of the evangelist, is Matt 24.12: "Because lawlessness proliferates, the love of many will grow cold."

Matt 10.23 belongs in the sending out tradition: "If they persecute you in this city, flee to another. For Amen I say to you, you will not finish going through the cities of Israel before the Son of Man comes!" Against the interpretation of the saying as a community formation, which is popular today, stands in the first instance the fact that it does not fit in the situation of the Palestinian community, for we have no indication of a systematic Jewish mission in Palestine from place to place, which was connected with constant persecutions. Moreover, it is unlikely that a primitive Christian prophetic saying, which was not fulfilled, was then transformed secondarily into a saying of Jesus and retained despite its nonfulfillment. By contrast, the saying fits in the sending out of the disciples by Jesus and was taken up into the sayings tradition because his authority stood behind it from the beginning.[191]

Luke 12.8-9[192] forms a bridge between the activity of Jesus and the coming Son of Man as judge:

[189] See section 9.1.2.2 with notes 37–38.

[190] Cf. Mark 8.38 and 9.1 = Matt 16.27-28 and 24.30.

[191] On the interpretation of the saying, see Künzi 1970. See especially its interpretation by A. Schweitzer, for whom the saying held special significance.

[192] Cf. Matt 10.32, which is clearly secondary vis-à-vis Luke and altered according to Matthean Christology. Matthew replaces ὁ υἱὸς τοῦ ἀνθρώπου with the first person and

But I say to you: everyone who confesses me before humans,
the Son of Man will also confess him before the angels of God.
But the one who denies me before humans
will also be denied before the angels of God.

Here it becomes clear how the behavior against Jesus draws after it as a consequence a corresponding reaction of the Son of Man in the judgment. It basically anticipates the decision of the judge.[193] The saying is closely related to the answer to the Baptist (Luke 7.23), which has been cited several times: "Blessed is the one who does not take offense at me."[194] Jesus distinguishes himself from all the prophets in the fact that he not only—as was already the case with the Baptist—appeared with the claim to bring the last exhortation to repentance before the coming of the Messiah–Son of Man, but also inseparably joined the coming salvation with the stance that was adopted toward his person and his action. With him message and person can no longer be separated. The decision against his activity and thus against him anticipates the decision of the coming judge.

With this we stand before the most important and most contested Son of Man saying, the answer of Jesus to the Messiah question in the hearing before the Sanhedrin, Mark 14.62, and somewhat divergently Luke 22.69. According to Mark, Jesus answers the question of the high priest— "Are you the Messiah, the Son of the Blessed?"—with a combination of quotes from Ps 110.1 and Dan 7:13: "I am (ἐγώ εἰμι), and you will see the Son of Man sitting at the right hand of the power and coming with the clouds of heaven." As a whole it is a judgment saying, which is directed against the judges of Jesus in the Sanhedrin. The accused points the accusers to the coming judge. The one exalted to the right hand of God and coming Messiah–Son of Man will judge them. In the Lukan version it is not the high priest but the Sanhedrin who asks. Jesus answers: "If I tell you, you will not believe, and if I ask you, you will not answer. From now on the Son of Man will sit at the right hand of the power of God."

"before the angels of God" with "before my Father in heaven." In the analogously formed sentence in Luke 12.9 = Matt 10.33 Matthew replaces the *passivum divinum* ἀπαρνηθή-σεται with the first person. The coming Son of Man as judge is identified with Christ as heavenly messianic king: Matt 25.31-46. Mark 8.38 has likewise been expanded secondarily and connected with a reference to the parousia (Mark 13.26-27). This Markan version is likewise taken up in Luke 9.26-27 as a doublet to 12.8-9, while the parallel in Matt 16.27 again contains the typically Matthean version of the idea of judgment.

[193] The phrase "before the angels of God" could point to the scene in Dan 7.10 with the myriads of angels and the heavenly court of justice.

[194] The highest intensification of this "denial before human beings" is Jesus' condemnation and handing over to Pilate. Mark 14.62 (see below) gives the answer to this.

Presumably neither the Markan version with its combination of quotations nor the Lukan version with the typical Lukan introduction ἀπὸ τοῦ νῦν, in which—corresponding to Lukan theology—the connection to the parousia recedes, contains the original answer of Jesus.[195] However, we are also not dealing with a free "community formation." Rather, what is significant is the content that is common to both: (1) that in the interrogation of Jesus, which ends with the handing over to Pilate, the Messiah question played the decisive role—we will need to discuss this in more detail in the trial of Jesus—and (2) that Jesus—in a provoking counterattack—answers the high priest with a reference to the Son of Man as exalted one and judge. His answer is sufficient for the Jewish authorities to hand Jesus over to Pilate as a messianic pretender. This means that Jesus—as in Luke 12.8—establishes a clear connection between himself and the Son of Man also in the trial, indeed, in it he reveals the messianic secret definitively and clearly.[196] His confession of his God-given task brings him to the cross.

17.4.1.3 The Sayings about the Suffering Son of Man[197]

The sayings about the "suffering Son of Man" are connected with those of the "present Son of Man." Here too the concern is with the human Jesus and specifically with the prediction of his future suffering. They form the salvation-historical bridge between the sayings of the present one and of the coming one. To be sure, this group of Son of Man sayings has a later secondarily developed character.

First, it is lacking in the sayings tradition and in the special material of Matthew and Luke and is found only in Mark.

Second, the seven or eight texts in Mark have a clear tie to the redactional structure of the Gospel. The first passion prediction appears in Mark 8.31 as Jesus' answer to Peter's messiah confession. Others follow in 9.12; 9.31; 10.33-34 and elsewhere until the Last Supper and the Gethsemane

---

[195] While the Lukan version may come from his special source, it is reworked by Luke.

[196] On this, see section 20.2.2 and Hengel/Schwemer 2001, 30–31, 64, 66, 149ff., 174, 207 (ET = Hengel 1995, 28–30, 58–60, no equivalent). The accusation of the high priestly leaders and Jesus' behavior also determined their action against the Jewish Christians extending to the stoning of James and other leading followers of Jesus around 62 CE. The claim that one could not know anything about the hearing of Jesus is misleading. The accusation against Jesus was on record and thus also present in the later accusations against Jewish Christians in Jerusalem. See Hengel/Schwemer 2019.

[197] Jeremias 1970, 276ff. (GV = 1979, 263ff.); Pesch 1984b, 47ff. on Mark 8.31ff.; Goppelt 1981, I: 187ff. (GV = Goppelt 1975/1978, I: 234ff.); Vielhauer 1965a, 55ff., 92ff.; Gese 1981, 160–66 (GV = 1977, 145–51); Bayer 1986; Pitre 2005, 381–454.

scene, Mark 14.21, 41.[198] They are meant to prepare for the passion as the climax of the Gospel.

Third, the predictions of the suffering Son of Man sketch out the passion of Jesus, to some extent even in its details. Not only his handing over (by God) to the members of the Sanhedrin and then to the Gentiles, i.e., to the Romans, his mocking and killing (10.33-34), but also the resurrection "after three days" is predicted. Here we are dealing with *vaticinia ex eventu*, with which Mark leads the reader to the passion of Jesus as the goal of his Gospel. In Matthew Jesus even refers twice to his crucifixion (20.19; 26.2).

Nevertheless, although the secondary influence here is evident, the question arises of whether a more original, simple form does not stand behind these sayings. This means that we must distinguish among the suffering sayings. After all, there are pointers to Jesus' way into the passion in diverse traditions of the Synoptic tradition[199] and not only in Mark. At least sayings such as Luke 7.34 (= Matt 11.19) and Luke 9.58 (= Matt 18.20)[200] point already to the agonizing struggle of the "present Son of Man."

Here, J. Jeremias has pointed out a possibility.[201] If one examines the sayings of the *suffering* Son of Man in Mark, Mark 9.31, where there is no elaboration, is striking: "The Son of Man will be handed over into the hands of human beings, and they will kill him, and having been killed, he will rise after three days."[202] This saying is not formulated by Mark himself. It can easily be translated into Aramaic as a wordplay and contains typical stylistic characteristics of the dominical *māšāl*. According to

---

[198] Cf. also Mark 9.12-13; 12.6-9; 14.1, 8, 11: the reference to the suffering of Jesus, which begins with 2.20 and 3.6, structures the design of the whole Gospel.

[199] See, for example, Luke 12.50; 13.33-34; 22.28: the πειρασμοί of Jesus; cf. also Mark 3.6 and 10.38-39 parr. On this, see section 11.3 with note 65.

[200] On this, cf. Luke 9.51; 12.49-50; 13.31-33; Mark 2.20; 3.6; 10.38-39, 45.

[201] Jeremias 1970, 281–86 (GV = 1979, 267–72).

[202] Mark 9.31: ὁ υἱὸς τοῦ ἀνθρώπου παραδίδοται εἰς χεῖρας ἀνθρώπων, καὶ ἀποκτενοῦσιν αὐτόν, καὶ ἀποκτανθεὶς μετὰ τρεῖς ἡμέρας ἀναστήσεται. On this, see Jeremias 1970, 285 (GV = 1979, 271). The unusual form speaks against the assumption that the phrase "after three days" is formulated *ex eventu*. Luke 9.22; 18.33 and Matt 16.21; 17.23; 20.19 turn this into the materially more accurate phrase "on the third day"; cf. 1 Cor 15.4. "Three days" means, by contrast, in the Semitic linguistic sphere "soon," since there is no equivalent to "several" or "some" there. Jeremias, idem, refers to C. H. Dodd, according to whom Jesus did not distinguish clearly between resurrection, parousia, consummation, or renewal of the temple, "but . . . all these expressions describe the triumph of God that is to follow soon" (Jeremias 1970, 285–86; GV = 1979, 271). See also Stuhlmacher 2018, 137–39, 147ff. (GV = Stuhlmacher 1992, 119–20, 127ff.) and Dunn 2003b, 801; see also section 22.1 with note 24.

Jeremias, the original form could have been: "*mitmesar*[203] *bar 'enašā līdē benē 'enāšā*," "God will (soon) hand over the human being (singular) into the hands of human beings (plural)." In a similar way as with the saying about the sin against the Spirit,[204] this is a riddling saying, which simultaneously conceals: The human being will—in the eschatological time of suffering—be handed over into the hands of his fellow human beings. The *passivum divinum* παραδίδοται in Mark could refer back to the analogous Aramaic *itmᵉsar* of the Targum of Isa 53.5b, because Jesus understood his way into suffering in analogy to the servant of God of Deutero-Isaiah.[205] Mark 10.45, the ransom saying, would also need to be mentioned here: "The Son of Man did not come to be served but to serve and to give his life as a ransom for many." This is a lowliness saying, which, in our view, belongs in the Last Supper tradition.[206] Thus, at bottom the sayings of the suffering Son of Man can be traced back to a special form of the sayings about the presence and lowliness of the Son of Man; in that case they would basically not be an independent group.

17.4.2 The Son of the Father[207]

On the basis of Old Testament–Semitic linguistic usage ancient Judaism was familiar with a diverse usage of the term "son" in the relationship to God. It was used for angels, for the Israelites as a collective, and also for individual pious and wise persons. Second Sam 7.14; Ps 2.7 and Ps 89.27-28 make possible a reference to the messianic king, which is illustrated by the messianic use of these texts in Qumran.[208] To be sure, the designation "son of God" for the Messiah is used only in individual cases and never in titular form. The question of whether Jesus used the title "Son (of God)" as a self-designation must remain open. While it plays a significant role in the earliest Synoptic tradition, in Mark, and in the

---

[203] Jeremias 1970, 282 (GV = Jeremias 1979, 268). According to Jeremias, the conspicuous present is to be translated, in correspondence to the Syriac Gospel texts, with a passive participle in the sense of a *passivum divinum*.

[204] Luke 12.10 = Matt 12.32.

[205] On the pre-Christian interpretation of Isa 53, see Hengel 1999b, 72–114; Stuhlmacher 2018, 138–40, 147–50 (GV = Stuhlmacher 1992, 120–21, 126–29); Stuhlmacher 2004 (GV = 1996); on Targum of Isaiah 53, see Ådna 2004.

[206] See note 66 in chapter 11 and note 75 in chapter 19.

[207] Hahn 1969, 279ff. (GV = 1995, 280ff.). Jeremias 1970, 56ff. (GV = 1979, 62ff.); Goppelt 1981, I: 162ff. (GV = 1975/1978, I: 210ff.); Schweizer 1969, 367ff., 380ff. (ET = 1972); Colpe 1983; Stuhlmacher 2018, 209–16 (GV = 1992, 184–90 and 413 index, s.v. "Sohn"); Hengel 1977b (ET = 1976b; 1986); 2004a.

[208] On this, see Zimmermann 1998, 153–70 and 540 index, s.v. "Sohn Gottes." On Israel as God's son, see chapter 15 with notes 1–2.

sayings tradition, and is for Mark the most important title, which structures the Gospel, it does not appear in the mouth of Jesus. Rather, it is found in Mark 1.11 at the baptism in the heavenly voice directed to Jesus himself and, similarly, in 9.7 at the transfiguration,[209] now addressed to the disciples, and in 3.11 and 5.7 in the mouth of exorcised demons; in 14.61 it is an explanatory addition to the title of Messiah in the question of the high priest, who uses a circumlocution for the name of God, and in 15.39 it constitutes the confession of the Gentile centurion.[210] Beyond this, we find it in the temptation story in Luke 4 and Matt 4 and secondarily in the expanded Matthean form of the confession of Peter.[211] The fact that it is lacking in the sayings of Jesus speaks for the age and quality of the sayings tradition.

The situation with the absolute use of ὁ υἱός, "the Son," is somewhat different. We find it in a decisive text in the sayings tradition, the revelatory saying in Luke 10.22 = Matt 11.27:

All things have been handed over to me by my Father,
and no one knows the son except the Father,
and no one knows the Father except the Son,
and anyone to whom the Son wishes to reveal him.

J. Jeremias has shown that an old saying of Jesus could indeed stand behind this four-liner. On the basis of the context, the "handing over" (παραδι-δόναι = *māsar/mᵉsar*) does not yet have the meaning of the conferring of the power of rulership as in Matt 28.18 but the meaning of "hand down" and means the knowledge of the revelation: My whole message comes from the Father; he has entrusted it to me, and therefore I alone really know him. In that case, the second and third lines do not give the ὁ υἱός the character of a title of majesty but refer in a comparison to the unique relationship of father and son.

All things have been entrusted to me by my Father,
and as only a father really knows his son,
so only a son knows his father.

---

[209] On the voice from heaven as a revelatory form, see P. Kuhn 1989.

[210] Mark 14.61: σὺ εἶ ὁ χριστὸς ὁ υἱὸς τοῦ εὐλογητοῦ . . . ; cf. Matt 26.63 as an adjuration under oath, almost identical in wording . . . τοῦ θεοῦ; Luke 22.67: εἰ σὺ εἶ ὁ χριστός, εἰπὸν ἡμῖν.

[211] Matthew 16.16; see section 17.3.3 with note 115.

But this parabolic saying would thus express Jesus' relationship to God, one may even say, his consciousness of sonship, together with his commission of revelation, and this means his messianic authority.[212] In this text we also encounter the root of the Johannine Christology in the sayings tradition.[213]

In the polemical parable about the wicked tenants, Mark 12.1-9, where the son sent by the father is killed by the tenants when he wants to collect the share of the yield, the son belongs in the source domain of the parable and is not used in the strict sense in a titular way.[214] To be sure, here too the source domain already expresses Jesus' messianic claim indirectly. By contrast, due to the unusual absolute use of "the Son," the enigmatic saying of Mark 13.32—"but concerning that day or hour no one knows, not even the angels in heaven nor even the Son, but only the Father"— could be, in its present form, a formation of the Greek-speaking community, in which the problem of the delay of the parousia is addressed. The possibility that it goes back, in an older form, to Jesus himself cannot, however, be excluded, since it expresses an offensive "lack," which fits poorly in the post-Easter exaltation Christology and transfer of power.[215]

Even though Jesus did not *expressis verbis* avail himself of the phrase "Son of God" as a title, his singular relationship to God, the use of "*Abba*" as an address to God, the distinction between "my Father" and "your Father," and his messianic commission nevertheless explain the fact that—as a complementary term to "Son of Man"—the title "Son of God" was very quickly applied to him after the resurrection event, indeed, the fact that this term became the central christological title for him in Mark. What is decisive is his relationship as Son to God as his Father. Here we strike upon the actual core, the heart of Jesus' messianic claim of revelation, which, in our view, is connected with the call experience at the baptism.[216]

The individual titles, which were applied to him very quickly in the primitive community, have interpretive significance. Jesus is the Son due to his unique bond to the Father and the divine dignity deduced from this after Easter. With a view to the fulfillment of the Old Testament promise

---

[212] Jeremias 1970, 68–74 (GV = 1979, 74–79); Hengel 2004a, 173, 178.

[213] Thus also Dunn 2003b, 718–19, 724.

[214] On the parable, see Hengel 1968a; Snodgrass 1983; Kloppenborg 2006. On the ζῆλος–φθόνος motif vis-à-vis the "son" and "heir" and the Joseph tradition, see Weihs 2003.

[215] Matt 28.18; 1 Cor 15.27 = Ps 8.7; Eph 1.20-22; Heb 2.5-8.

[216] See Hengel 2004a, 177–83. Tellingly, in Gal 1.16 and Acts 9.20 the conversion of Paul is connected with the Son of God title. It too belongs in the Christology of the primitive community. See Hengel 1977b (ET = 1976b; 1986).

to the people of God he bears the designation *māšī*ᵃ*ḥ*, anointed one. As the redeemer anointed by God, in his relationship to the world, he is the coming "(Son of) Man," and after Easter he is the "Lord," *mārēh*/κύϱιος for the community and for the world. The sonship describes his "nature" and the other titles rather his "functions." No one grasped this better than the Fourth Evangelist, for whom the absolute ὁ υἱός becomes the most frequent and also the central title.[217] Precisely the Johannine Christology has its ultimate root in Jesus' consciousness of sonship.

17.4.3 Jesus, the Messiah of Israel

Let us summarize the results:

According to the Synoptic tradition, which John also basically follows, the Messiah title was used by Jesus in only a few—probably secondary—places. While the cipher "Son of Man" (which is dependent on Dan 7.13), which he applied to himself in certain situations, describes his messianic sending, it initially has more of a concealing character. Therefore, despite the "messianic secret," Mark can put it in the mouth of Jesus from the beginning.

The fact that Jesus' claim is an eschatological and messianic claim, which fundamentally transcends that of the prophet qualitatively, because he brings the eschatological "fulfillment," becomes clear from the Synoptic texts, even apart from the question of titles. This becomes evident already from the investigation of Jesus' relationship to the Baptist and of his proclamation of "the kingdom of God that is in the process of realization," but also from his "deeds of power," which symbolically signal the victory over the power of evil and the restoration of the good creation of God. The sayings in which Jesus points to his sending in the first person are likewise to be understood on the basis of his special authority, and the passion story of the Gospels becomes understandable at all only under the presupposition of Jesus' messianic claim. This applies all the more to the rapid formation of Christology after Easter, which was, after all, created in its fundamental characteristics by the disciples who had constantly accompanied Jesus and heard him.

The Messiah *title* was also applied to Jesus from the outside. This happened first through the disciples, then through the wider circle of followers, and at the end through the opponents. Jesus, however, never rejected it. Indeed, he directly challenged the disciples to comment on this.

---

[217] ὁ υἱός appears a total of 17 times and corresponds to the even more frequent ὁ πατήϱ μου. In total υἱός appears 55 times in John and πατήϱ 137 times, usually in relation to Jesus and God.

Therefore, the disciples' and earliest community's confession of Jesus as God's "anointed one" is not based on an error. Rather, it is his messianic task given to him from the Father and his messianic claim that leads him into death. He interpreted the same in relation to the disciples in a way that was new and offensive to them by pointing to his violent fate in Jerusalem, which was expected by him. He rejected the opposition of Peter in the sharpest possible way. In the commission of the Father he walks upon the way of the servant of God.[218] In the tradition this event was connected with a stay outside of Galilee "in the villages of Caesarea Philippi," presumably because Jesus wanted to escape the hostility of Herod Antipas. The decision had to take place in Jerusalem. Mark recounts this event—as is also the case elsewhere in his Gospel—in such a concise and theologically stylized way that all psychologizing questions lead us astray. We *ought* to pursue the psychology neither of Jesus nor of the community (here the question would be: which community?) nor of Mark. As much as he resisted a psychologizing interpretation of Jesus, Wrede *wanted* to forgo neither the one nor the other.

Jesus himself could by no means appear with the open pronouncement "I am the Anointed One," for the Hebrew *qatil* formation *māšîₐḥ/ mᵉšîḥā'*, as well as the Greek verbal adjective χριστός, had passive meaning:[219] the χριστός θεοῦ is *the one anointed by God*. One could not—even if one knew oneself to be called into this eschatological function—reveal and proclaim oneself as "Anointed One." The claim ἐγώ εἰμι ὁ χριστός occurs only with false messiahs in the time of the final tribulation.[220] Rather, this revelation of the "Messiah" had to happen through God. In this sense Jesus speaks in the eschatological discourse in a concealing way of the "revelation of the Son of Man."[221] He proclaims the kingdom of God that is in the process of realization as Messiah *designatus*. Only with the coming of the kingdom "in power" will he be revealed to all as God's anointed one. A. Schweitzer is probably right in his claim that Jesus connected the hope in this coming toward the end of his activity with his way into death. Here Jesus' own messianic expectation of completion is fused with the hope of the community sparked off by the miracle of Easter. This could explain the

---

[218] Mark 8.31-33; cf. Mark 10.38-39, 45; 14.24, 27, 36; Luke 12.50; 22.19-20, 27-28.

[219] On this, see Seybold 1986, 52–53. The concern is with the "idea of a divinely initiated anointing." Cf. Hesse 1974, 498 (GV = 1973, 487.24): "Yahweh does the anointing at the marriage of an unnamed king in Ps 45:7."

[220] Matthew 24.5, cf. Mark 13.6; Luke 21.8; Mark 13.21 parr. On this, see Pitre 2005, 226–27, 327.

[221] Luke 17.30, cf. vv. 23-24 (Q). Cf. also, in a different way, Justin, *Dial.* 8.4.

fact that the disciples viewed his resurrection also as the beginning of the general resurrection (see note 7 in chapter 19).

Beyond this, Jesus could not publicly express his messianic claim with recourse to the Messiah title, because this would have immediately led to the most difficult political consequences. Here we strike upon a possible motif for the silence commands to the disciples. This would have—this is shown by the fate of the forerunner and by the trial in Jerusalem—put an end to his activity perhaps already in Galilee. After all, in the time between the death of Herod and the Bar Kokhba revolt, i.e., between 4 BCE and 132–136 CE, we have a multiplicity[222] of "messianic pretenders" of very different kinds, some with more political-royal and others with more prophetic character, and there were not only Jewish pretenders but also Samaritan ones. Unfortunately, we know almost nothing about their teaching and views. However, they all came very rapidly into conflict with their own religious authorities and even more so with the Roman authorities, and were violently done away with.[223] In Jewish Palestine, the title "anointed one" in the eschatological sense was always also an *emotive term, which could be politically (mis)understood*. The one who laid public claim to it had to reckon with state intervention. In the trial of Jesus the accusation of the high priest before Pilate led to his crucifixion as a political criminal. It is admittedly peculiar that, according to our sources, the Jewish Christians in the motherland were not persecuted any more by the Roman authorities at that time. They were probably aware from the beginning of the "pacifist" character of this eschatological movement, which fundamentally distinguished it from others.

If Jesus, through his messianic claim, came into proximity to such Jewish or Samaritan messianic pretenders, then to modern religious and ethical notions this appears rather offensive. Therefore, today—in a reversal of earlier situations—the denial of his messianic claim can indeed be understood as a form of modern apologetics in the interest of Jesus, which presents itself as "critical." An unmessianic ethical teacher of wisdom or the last herald of God's kingdom makes a more sympathetic, timeless, and therefore edifying impression than a stormy Messiah *designatus* seized by the Spirit of God in the turbulent Jewish Palestine around the turn of the era.

We know these Jewish eschatological charismatics and messianic pretenders only via the polemical perspective of their opponents, for example

---

[222] On this, see Hengel 1989c, 290–302 (GV = 1976c, 296–307); Hengel 1996a, 314ff., 358ff., 382ff.

[223] See the excursus on eschatological prophets in chapter 3; cf. Mark 13.6, 21 parr.; Hengel 1989c, 290–302 (GV = 1976c, 296–307).

through Josephus and to a lesser extent also through Christian authors. We know practically nothing about their teachings and their ways of life. If we possessed with regard to Jesus only the witnesses of Jewish and Gentile polemic, we would not obtain a more favorable picture of him. Luke does not shy away from a comparison to the eschatological prophets Theudas and Judas the Galilean, the most dangerous rebel of his time, by the Jewish school head Gamaliel I,[224] and his messenger Paul is placed in connection with the rebellious Egyptian prophet by the tribune of the fortress of Antonia. All these troublemakers failed miserably. Luke is astonishingly well informed here.[225] These comparisons show how primitive Christianity could be appraised by opponents and outside observers at that time. Historically they were surely incorrect. The "zealot Jesus," who has wandered like a ghost through scholarship time and again since Reimarus, is a false path. However, we should not fail to recognize the fact that his opponents, extending to the Jewish informant of Celsus, could (mis)interpret him in this way as a criminal rebel and deceiver of the people. The Gospels, especially Luke and John, have critically engaged with this false interpretation.[226] Moreover, Rom 13.1-8 and certain passages of Acts must, among others, be interpreted against this background. Features of the Jewish militaristic Messiah image surface later even in primitive Christian apocalyptic and continued to have an effect for a long time, especially in the millenialism of the Western church.[227] This much appears to be clear: the Jewish history of that time and the course of the trial of Jesus demonstrate that publicly appealing to one's own messianic claim with the use of the title was impossible also for political reasons. It is therefore understandable that Jesus had to prohibit his disciples from spreading his messiahship until the "revelation of the Son of Man." Thus, the complex "messianic secret" has very different aspects, *ultimately goes back to Jesus himself*, and is rooted in the secret of his person and his sending.

---

[224] Acts 5.36-37. The temporal placement of Theudas before Judas is an anachronism; cf. also 21.38; 24.5; Luke 23.2; John 10.8; 19.12; Mark 13.22 parr.

[225] Acts 5.36-37; 21.38; cf. Luke 20.20b; 23.2-4; Acts 17.7; John 11.48; 19.12; on the Egyptians, see Hengel 1989c, 230–33 (GV = 1976c, 236–38). On later Jewish polemic, see also Schäfer 2007.

[226] Mark 12.13-17 parr.; Luke 23.2; John 18.33-38.

[227] Revelation 19–20; cf. Hengel 1996a, 232ff. This line extends from Papias, Justin, and Irenaeus via Hippolytus, through to Victorinus of Pettau and Lactantius. Since Clement of Alexandria, Origen, Dionysius of Alexandria, and Eusebius, the East, under Platonic influence, has rejected these millennialist features and refused full canonical recognition to the book of Revelation.

Since the figure of the "eschatological redeemer" in the Judaism of the time could—already on account of its diversity, which was, among other things, conditioned by the plurality of the prophetic prophecies—have various manifestations, one should not appeal against Jesus' messianic claim to a contemporary "Jewish Messianic doctrine," which is said to contradict Jesus' behavior and proclamation, for such a clear "Messiah doctrine" did not exist at all in the manifoldness of the possibilities of that time. *It is solely Jesus' own activity in word and deed that determines what he understood by the "messianic liberator" (Isa 61.1-2).* He does this so impressively through his preaching of the kingdom, his healings, and his authoritative action in the place of God that the disciples recognized his sending as a "messianic" sending, and the Galilean flock of followers also hoped that he would bring the "messianic liberation."[228] By contrast, the argument advanced by the other side, namely that Jesus' assurance of God and God-like authority go far beyond the messianic statements of the Old Testament and that the Messiah title is therefore not admissible for him, prematurely reads the later christological development into the history of Jesus. However, we are not permitted to measure this by the high Christology of the later Christ hymns or of the Gospel of John,[229] let alone of the early church dogma. In appearing with the claim to be the messianic consummator, Jesus, through his activity for his followers and for the primitive community, interpreted the Old Testament promises in a new way that surpassed the previous understanding of them. The early church, from the beginning, consistently continued upon this path.

---

[228] Luke 24.21; Acts 1.6; cf. John 6.14-15; Mark 11.9-10 parr.

[229] Despite his unique emphasis on the divinity of Jesus, John consciously uses only the same designations for Jesus as the other Gospels. Χριστός as title and as name, also appears with the greatest frequency in the Fourth Gospel (John nineteen times, Matthew seventeen times, Luke twelve times, Mark seven times). The view that the Messiah title stands in opposition to the divine dignity of the incarnate Son of God and that one is therefore not permitted to ascribe a messianic claim to Jesus introduces a dogmatic prejudice into the texts. All four Gospels, and especially John, speak against this view.

PART VI
The Passion of Jesus

18

The Last Confrontation in Jerusalem[1]

18.1 The Entrance into Jerusalem

All the evangelists paint Jesus' entry into Jerusalem with messianic colors. This applies already to the earliest account in Mark, upon which all the others are dependent.[2] The Messiah motif occurs already in the preparatory story of the healing of the blind beggar Bartimaeus in Jericho. Here Mark has basically already nullified the messianic secret, for the blind man repeatedly calls out to Jesus, as he leaves Jericho with his disciples and many accompanying people: "Son of David, Jesus, have mercy on me." In this context, "Son of David" is a paraphrasing of "Messiah."[3] The healed man follows Jesus on the way to Jerusalem. For Mark the entire scene has fundamental significance. For the evangelist the blind man embodies the true Israel, which is healed from its blindness by the "Son of David" Jesus, confesses him as Messiah, and follows him on the way to the passion. The unusual form of the story, the address of Jesus with *rabbûnî*, and the Aramaic-Greek name point back, however, to a historical event.[4] By

---

[1] Schmidt 1919, 274ff.; Pesch 1984b (on Mark 11 and 12); Brown 1994; Theissen/ Merz 1998, 440–73 (GV = 1997, 387–414); Ådna 2000; Dunn 2003b, 765–824.

[2] Mark 11.1-10 = Luke 19.28-40 = Matt 21.1-9; cf. John 12.12-19, which presupposes knowledge of Mark (v. 14). Conspicuous is Luke 19.37, the praise of God by the "crowd of disciples" περὶ πασῶν ὧν εἶδον δυνάμεων, and John 12.17, the witness of the crowd that had been with him when he raised Lazarus.

[3] Mark 10.46-52 (47-48); on this, see note 90 in chapter 16. Luke 18.35-43 and Matt 20.29-34 simplify and omit the conspicuous name "Bartimaeus." Luke places the blind man before Jericho so that he can obtain space for the story of Zacchaeus in Jericho. Matthew speaks of two blind men, doubles the healing story (see 9.27-31), and adds—according to the majority of the manuscripts—a κύριε (20.30). For "Son of David," see section 8.4.

[4] On the name, see Ilan 2002, 18, 308; on the theological interpretation of the story, see Eckstein 1996: "Markus 10.46-52 als Schlüsseltext des Markusevangeliums". The Second Gospel has, to be sure, not a few of such key texts. On *rabbûnî*, which appears

connecting the healing of the blind man before Jericho with the conversion of the chief tax collector Zacchaeus, Luke creates a potent contrast: Jesus heals the poorest of the poor and fundamentally changes the life of the richest man in the place. This means that the Son of David effects salvation for all "children of Abraham," for "the Son of Man has come to seek and to save what is lost."[5]

The entry story itself[6] is shaped by the prophetic saying of Zech 9.9, which portrays the entrance of the messianic king of peace and is understood as its fulfillment:

Rejoice loudly, daughter of Zion, shout, daughter of Jerusalem!
Behold, your king is coming to you, righteous and victorious.
He is humble and rides upon a donkey,
on the foal of a she-donkey.

The messianic king brings peace not only to Israel but to the world. To be sure, Zech 9.9 is first quoted in the later texts in Matthew and John.[7] It is presupposed, however, by Mark and Luke. Beyond this, Jesus is also directly addressed by the crowd as βασιλεύς in Luke and John.[8] Matthew, by contrast, lets Jesus be acclaimed by the accompanying people as Son of David.[9] Mark restrains himself—accurately historically—with regard to these messianic acclamations. After the enigmatic procurement of the donkey foal as a riding animal,[10] "many spread their garments upon the way,[11] others cut branches, and those who went before and followed called out

---

elsewhere only in John 20.16 in the mouth of Mary Magdalene and can be understood as an intensification of *rabbî*, see Bauer/Aland/Aland 1988, 1467, and section 11.4. In rabbinic prayers *ribbôn-rabbôn* can be used as a designation for God.

[5] Luke 18.35–19.10; cf. 18.38-39; 19.9-10. Luke 19.10 takes the place of the statement of Mark 10.45. See also chapter 15 with note 10.

[6] Mark 11.1-10; Luke 9.28-40; John 12.12-19. See also note 60 below.

[7] Matthew 21.4-5, introduced as a "fulfillment quotation," and John 12.15.

[8] Luke 19.38 and John 12.13 in connection with Ps 118.25-26. In John the motif of the kingship of Jesus plays the greatest role in the passion story. In John the festival pilgrims and inhabitants of the city also come out to meet Jesus as one does a king (12.12-13, 18). On this, see the "official reception" (ἀπάντησις) of David in 2 Sam 19.12-16 after his return from the victory over Absalom and in 1 Thess 4.17 the "official reception" of the Kyrios at the parousia. Cf. Brunson 2003, 187–96.

[9] Matthew 21.9: ὡσαννὰ τῷ υἱῷ Δαυίδ and Ps 118.25-26. See Hengel 2004a, 164ff.

[10] Mark recounts it in a peculiarly shortened way. See also the preparation of the Passover meal in 14.12-16. In both cases instructions of Jesus obtain the character of a "miraculous foreknowledge of Jesus," Pesch 1984b, 179; and 181: "concrete features, which appear to reflect historical material, flow into the messianically stylized story."

[11] On this, see Pesch 1984b, 182: "The feature . . . appears to be based on recollection: it reflects the enthusiasm of the people accompanying Jesus."

'Hosanna! Blessed is the one who comes in the name of the Lord,'" a shout of reception from the—messianically interpreted—last Hallel psalm,[12] and adds: "Blessed be the coming kingdom of our father David, Hosanna in the highest."[13] According to Mark, Jesus is not yet directly acclaimed by his disciples and the festival pilgrims who accompanied him. Rather, they praise the kingdom of David, which was expected to come soon, i.e., the messianic kingdom of peace which Jesus was expected to establish. Zech 9.9, however, already stands clearly in the background in Mark.[14]

We cannot simply dismiss this striking narrative as a secondary christological construction. It does not fit in the conceptions of the later Christology with its powerful portrayals of the parousia.[15] Even less can it be derived as a whole from Old Testament texts.[16] Its graphic account, which presupposes a certain knowledge of the place,[17] still reflects concrete memory. In contrast to John, who recounts an official reception (*Einholung*) of Jesus by the Jerusalemites and the festival pilgrims gathered there, and to Matthew, who says that "the whole city was unsettled,"[18] Mark recounts only the behavior of the disciples and of the accompanying—presumably predominantly Galilean—festival pilgrims.[19] When R. Bultmann designates the second part of the story in Mark 11.7-10 as "legendary or at least strongly influenced by legend" and grounds this with the claim that "there can be no doubt about the messianic character of the animal,"[20] then we can disbelieve the first statement but readily

---

[12] Psalm 118.25-26; see also note 60 in chapter 19 on Mark 14.26.

[13] Mark 11.9-10. On the phrase ἐν τοῖς ὑψίστοις, see also Ps 148.1 LXX; Luke 2.14; 19.38.

[14] On this, see the Nathan oracle in 2 Sam 7.12-16; Luke 24.21; Acts 1.6.

[15] Cf. Mark 13.26-27 parr.; 8.38 parr.; Matt 25.31-32; 1 Thess 4.15ff.; Rev 19.11ff.

[16] Cf., for example, Gen 49.11; 1 Kgs 1.33, 40; 2 Kgs 9.13; Zech 14.4 or the context of 2 Sam 15.30-31.

[17] The placement of Bethphage before Bethany in Mark 11.1 should not be played against this. We do not know whether the street led via Bethany at that time. Mark mentions the last place to the east of Jerusalem probably only because it was significant for him as a place where Jesus stayed. Cf. Mark 11.1-2, 11-12; 14.3.

[18] Matthew 21.10. In response to the Jerusalemites' question "who is this?" the ὄχλοι answer "the prophet Jesus from Nazareth in Galilee." Prophet and Messiah are also not strictly distinguished for Matthew; see section 16.1 with notes 29–30.

[19] Mark 1.11; μαθηταί, 11.8: πολλοί/ἄλλοι, Luke 19.37: ἅπαν τὸ πλῆθος τῶν μαθητῶν; only with Matt 21.8-9 is the key word ὄχλος/ὄχλοι introduced. Mark speaks only in the Bartimaeus pericope in 10.46 of "his disciples and a sizeable crowd" as accompanying persons. Matthew presupposes that Jesus was still an unknown person in Jerusalem. Apparently he believed that the Markan Christology was historically accurate. According to John 12.18, by contrast, Jesus is well-known in Jerusalem. Therefore, the population comes to meet him.

[20] Bultmann 1963, 261, modified (GV = 1995, 281); on this, see also Hengel/Schwemer 2001, 60–61, 181 n. 80, 219ff. (ET = Hengel 1995, 55–56, no equivalent).

affirm the second one. His justification for its unhistorical character was that "the assumption that has to be made if we are to take the story as history, namely, that Jesus intended to fulfill the prophecy in Zech. 9.9 and that the crowd recognized the ass as the Messiah's beast of burden, is absurd." But this is determined by a far too enlightened Jesus psychology and his "dogma" of an unmessianic Jesus. How can we, as persons in the twentieth century, make judgments on the basis of our presuppositions about the intentions and actions of the Galilean and his followers? Why should the crowd of predominantly Galilean festival pilgrims, who knew a saying such as Zech 9.9 only too well, not have viewed Jesus as the fulfiller of messianic promises, or have acclaimed him with Ps 118.25-26 and other provocative shouts because they really expected that "he would redeem Israel and bring peace"?[21] And why should Jesus himself, in front of the temple and the holy city, which lay before him in all its splendor,[22] not have performed a—messianic—parabolic action, as he did previously with the appointment of the twelve and shortly thereafter in the cleansing of the temple and then at the Last Supper?

It is entirely possible, indeed probable, that Jesus, accompanied by disciples, had already previously frequented—like every pious Jew—major festivals in Jerusalem. According to John, he already went up to Jerusalem for the festival of booths in October of the previous year and two years earlier to the festival of Passover.[23] To be sure, it must remain questionable whether the conflict with his opponents already began at this festival of booths in Jerusalem a half year before the Passover of his death, dragged on to the festival of Hanukkah in December,[24] and already had the Messiah question (or the question of his divine sonship) at its center, as John recounts,[25] and, beyond this, whether Jesus was to be arrested[26] on multiple occasions for this reason and therefore withdrew into the land east of the Jordan.[27] Even Luke knows, in contrast to Mark/Matthew,[28] of more intimate contacts of Jesus with Judaea, but he nevertheless takes over the narrative thread of Mark.[29] On the other hand, the Markan account, on which

---

[21] Luke 24.19, 21; cf. Acts 1.6.

[22] Mark 13.1; Luke 21.5-6.

[23] John 2.13-22; 7.2ff.; cf., by contrast, 6.4 and section 11.1 with note 5.

[24] John 10.22.

[25] John 7.26-31, 40ff.; 9.22; 10.24; 11.27.

[26] John 7.32, 44-49; 10.39; 11.57.

[27] John 10.40ff.; after this he returns to Bethany for the resurrection of Lazarus in order to then withdraw due to his endangerment to a not identifiable "Ephraim near the wilderness" (11.54).

[28] Matthew 21.10—despite 4.25.

[29] Luke 4.44; 5.17; 6.17; 7.17; 23.5.

Luke and Matthew depend, appears to run in too much of a straight line. The prehistory of the last controversy in Jerusalem was more complicated, for Jesus was no longer a completely unknown person there due to earlier journeys. However, the Fourth Evangelist's tendency to fuse his high Christology with historical details has the consequence that it is no longer possible to distinguish between them. Therefore, plausible historical information about Jesus' activity can be obtained from John only in exceptional cases.[30] To us it appears certain that in his last journey into the holy city for the Passover of his death, Jesus himself pushed for a decision, indeed provoked the course of things, and that the Messiah question and at the end the sacrifice of his life stood at the center. Through this the account of the entry into Jerusalem obtains its special weight. Mark gives an account of this as the first; as is also often the case with him elsewhere, Petrine tradition probably stands behind this.

18.2 On the Chronology of the Last Days

In Mark 11.1–14.52, i.e., between the entry of Jesus and his arrest, the evangelist gives a dramatic account of the last conflict in Jerusalem, which is relatively clearly structured in a seemingly chronological way. The concern here is with a total of six days. On the first day Jesus enters, views the temple, and then spends the night in Bethany. On the next day the temple cleansing occurs, after which he then leaves the city (11.19) and returns again on the next morning (11.20, 27). The third day encompasses all the controversies and discourses about the question of authority until the end of the parousia discourse (13.37). On the fourth day follows, according to 14.1-2, the leaders' resolution to kill Jesus and the betrayal of Judas in 14.10-11. The anointing in Bethany at the house of Simon the leper (vv. 3-9), which is recounted between them, probably must also be placed on this day. According to 14.12ff., the preparations for the Passover meal, which is celebrated from the onset of the night, take place on the following, fifth day. Finally, Jesus is arrested in Gethsemane in the Passover night, and on the morning after it, on the sixth day, he is condemned and crucified. According to this timeline, the entry into the city took place on a Sunday and the crucifixion on a Friday.

While the Friday stands firm as the day of Jesus' death, since the day after his crucifixion is a Sabbath,[31] the Markan Christology of the last days

---

[30] On this, see the fundamental work of Dodd 1963, which itself still takes too much delight in hypotheses. On this point, cf. now also Frey 2018a; 2018b.

[31] Mark 16.1-2; Luke 23.54, 56; Matt 28.1; John 19.31 speaks of a "great Sabbath day," because this fell on the Passover festival; cf. 20.1, 19.

of Jesus proves, upon closer examination, to be questionable, at least in part, as K. L. Schmidt has shown.[32] Luke already no longer adheres to this schema but has general, extendable specifications of time without a counting of days.[33] However, the Markan account itself, with its emphasis on Bethany as a fixed point of support for Jesus and the reference to individual persons who apparently already know him from earlier visits and with his self-confident appearance and teaching in the temple,[34] suggests the hypothesis that Jesus had already visited Jerusalem on multiple occasions and that his opponents in the holy city also already knew him. He appears to have already stayed for some time in Jerusalem before the passion.[35] To be sure, it is even more impossible to obtain a clear chronology of the last days of Jesus from the complicated Johannine outline, which recounts multiple visits of Jesus in Jerusalem. Even the temple cleansing, which in itself fits excellently in the last controversy situation and later could also co-motivate the condemnation, is controversial, since John, in conscious opposition to Mark and Luke, places it at the beginning of the activity of Jesus (John 2.13-15). This occurs because of his Christology: Jesus himself as the embodiment of the presence of God is the true "temple" (John 2.21). At the beginning of his activity he must symbolically cleanse the temple in Jerusalem, which has degenerated into a "trading house" (John 2.16). Since, however, the Markan chronology of the last days is also not really reliable, we do not know exactly how long the last controversies in the capital lasted. After all, in John they last for months. According to John, the anointing in Bethany occurs before the entry into Jerusalem, and a large crowd has already come there to meet him.[36] His presentation is, to be sure, even less coherent than that of Mark. We have here, as so often, large gaps and uncertainties, which can no longer be clarified.

Probable, by contrast, is the concordant Synoptic account that Jesus was crucified on the festival of Passover, i.e., on Nisan 15, presumably

---

[32] Schmidt 1919, 274–303. See already Wellhausen 1909, 88; on the "day scheme" and on the chronology of the last days, see Ådna 2000, 191ff., 309–16; see also his attempt at a "reconstruction of the events" on pp. 328–33.

[33] Luke 20.1; 21.37-38; 22.1. By contrast, the whole early Christian tradition stands behind the nearness of the Passover festival.

[34] Cf. in Mark 14.3-6 the meal in Bethany "in the house of Simon the leper" and the nameless woman with the extremely expensive nard oil and John's strongly divergent version in 12.1-8. For Mark it belongs already to the opening of the passion story; on this, see the beginning of this section.

[35] Wellhausen 1909, 88: "Mark's attempt to press the stay into a week failed; the material resists the scheme of the six days, which is in itself somewhat uncertain, in which it is meant to be forced." Wellhausen points here to Mark 14.49: "a two-day teaching (11.15–12.28)" is not sufficient "to justify καθ' ἡμέραν."

[36] John 12.1-11. See note 52 in chapter 19.

in 30 CE.[37] The divergent Johannine day of Jesus' death on the day of preparation for the Passover, i.e., on Nisan 14, is christologically motivated again. Jesus is the "(Passover) lamb of God, who bears the sin of the world,"[38] he dies at the time when the Passover lambs are slaughtered in the temple.[39] By contrast, all the Gospels agree on the sequence of the weekdays: the Last Supper with the disciples takes place in the night of Thursday to Friday and the execution on Good Friday. Jesus rests in the tomb on the Sabbath. The empty tomb is discovered on Easter morning. This temporal sequence of the Gospels is clearly recognizable even in the references of Paul in 1 Corinthians.[40] However, in Mark, whom Luke and Matthew follow, several conflicts become visible, which prepare for the passion and which could, on the basis of their content, belong in the context of the last controversies in Jerusalem.[41]

18.3 The Temple Cleansing and the Question of Authority[42]

The only possibility for a historical perspective involves questioning the individual, paradigmatically compiled pericopes of Mark as our oldest witness for the days in Jerusalem and the passion with respect to their historical placement, the opponents of Jesus who appear there, and the special situation and examining the extent to which an inner connection with the trial of Jesus, which points back to the last controversies, becomes visible. Here too we must take into account the fact that the Markan narrative is very fragmentary and also theologically considered. This means that for the historical question only attempts at historical approximation are possible even in this temporally restricted space of several days. On the other hand, precisely here living memory must have remained preserved.

Since in the hearing before the Sanhedrin the temple question played a decisive role according to Mark 14.58 and Jesus' behavior in the temple also strengthened the leaders of the people's resolution to kill him in Mark

---

[37] The year 30 CE results from Luke 3.1 and the Pauline chronology in Gal 1.18 and 2.1 in connection with Acts 18.2 and the governorship of Gallio in Achaia in Acts 18.12ff. Cf. note 14 in chapter 11.

[38] John 1.29, 36; cf. Rev 5.6, 9.

[39] See section 19.4; cf. John 19.31-33, 36; cf. Exod 12.10, 46 LXX, and Hengel 2004d, 139ff.

[40] See 1 Cor 11.23 in connection with 15.3-4 and 5.6-8; see Hengel 2004d, 116ff.

[41] Cf. Mark 11.13–12.34; Luke 19.45–20.38; Matt 21.12–22.40.

[42] Eisler 1929/1930; Hengel 1971b, 15ff. (GV = 1970, 15ff. = 2007b, 227ff.); Roloff 1970, 89–110; Pesch 1984b, 189–202 (on Mark 11.12-21); Ådna 1999; 2000; Dunn 2003b, 636–40, 785–95.

11.18, it is, despite John 2, probably necessary to place the "temple cleansing" during these last days of Jesus in Jerusalem. If Jesus—which appears likely to us—went up to Jerusalem for the Passover of his death with a firm resolve to place the people and its leaders before a final decision for or against the kingdom of God (and thus for or against himself) and, if it was God's will,[43] to die for his people as the "servant of God," then precisely his provocative action in the temple fits excellently in this last appeal, indeed it is a decisive high point.

The second temple, which was expanded in a glorious way by Herod the Great from 20 BCE onward and was a Hellenistic construction of unheard-of splendor, was the religious center of the Judaism of the world of that time, the place that God had chosen as his place of residence upon Mount Zion.[44] For the three large pilgrimage festivals of Passover, Weeks, and Booths—and especially for Passover—not only great portions of the Jewish population of Palestine flocked together but also thousands of diaspora Jews from the Roman and Parthian empires came to Jerusalem.[45] Before 70 CE the holy city was probably among the greatest pilgrimage destinations in antiquity.[46] According to Josephus, this gathering of easily incited masses of people at the especially popular festival of Passover always brought with it the danger of political unrest.[47] After the death of his father Herod, Archelaus is said to have violently cleared the temple area through the use of his entire military force, after the people had initially driven out a whole cohort by throwing stones; three thousand Jews were said to have been killed in the process. Another mass protest took place at a Passover festival under the procurator Cumanus after 48 CE, when one of the Roman soldiers posted on the roofs of the porticos of the temple court provoked the crowd of pilgrims with an

---

[43] Cf. Mark 14.35-36 = Luke 22.42 = Matt 26.39; see also Mark 14.49 = Matt 26.54, 56.

[44] Hengel 1996a, 58; 1999b, 121–22, 140, 144ff.; Ådna 1999, 32–90. Netzer 2006, 137–78 and 442 index. On the temple construction, see also section 3.1.1 with notes 112–25.

[45] When Cestius Gallus, the governor of Syria, wants to occupy Lydda in the autumn of 66 CE, he finds the city abandoned by the Jewish population, for all have gone up, despite the dangers of war, to Jerusalem for the festival of booths: Josephus, *J.W.* 2.515; cf. also Luke 2.41-51 on the festival of Passover and Acts 21.16 for the festival of weeks.

[46] Hengel 1996a, 19–26, 472; Hengel 1999b, 135, 144, 174–75 on the Passover festival in 66 CE.

[47] Josephus, *J.W.* 1.88 (trans. H. St. J. Thackeray, LCL, 45): "it is on these festive occasions that sedition is most apt to break out." On Archelaus, see Josephus, *J.W.* 2.10–13 = *Ant.* 17.215–218; on Pilate, see Luke 13.1. On this, see chapter 1 with note 5 and section 3.1.3 with note 230.

obscene gesture. Cumanus deployed his troops against the protesters, which led to a mass panic.[48]

We can thus assume that the "temple cleansing" took place a relatively short time—perhaps only a few days—before the death of Jesus. According to Mark it took place one day after the entry into Jerusalem, in Luke and Matthew on the same day, right after his arrival.[49] It probably also played a significant role in the trial. Presumably this event provided the final impetus to arrest him. The temple question therefore stands at the beginning of the hearing.[50]

The account in Mark 11.15-17 is fundamental. In John 2.14-16 the whole is even more strongly elaborated. In the massive outer temple fore-court of the Gentiles, which represented in a way the marketplace of Jerusalem, the pilgrims from abroad had the possibility of exchanging their money for Tyrian didrachmas and tetradrachmas for sacrificial purposes, and especially for the Jewish temple tax of two drachmas. On the front these coins bore the head of the city god Melqart-Heracles, stylized as Alexander, and on the back the Ptolemaic eagle, the bird of Zeus. Even Roman denarii were not accepted. These silver coins with "idol images" apparently provoked no offense at the holy place, for they were the only coins in the East that from the reign of Herod to the year 66 CE did not diminish in silver content and thus in value. Here the financial advantage was stronger than the prohibition against images.[51]

Moreover, doves for the offering of the "small person" were sold there.[52] By contrast, according to rabbinic accounts, the sale of larger animals took place—contra John 2.15—outside of the temple area. Money changing and the sale of doves were necessary activities for the functioning of the cult. One may assume that the ruling high priestly families profited from the money changing and trade, especially the most powerful family of Annas, which supplied the high priest of that time Caiaphas,

---

[48] Josephus, *J.W.* 2.223–227 = *Ant.* 20.105–112; see section 3.1.5 with note 303. It is said that Cumanus initially admonished the crowd without success, μηδὲ στάσεις ἐξά-πτειν ἐν ἑορτῇ (109), cf. Mark 14.2 = Matt 26.5. On the key word στάσις, see Mark 15.7 and Acts 24.5. A violent action against Jews during a festival visit in Jerusalem is also reported for Pilate: see *J.W.* 2.175ff = *Ant.* 18.60ff. and Luke 13.1ff.; see also section 3.1.3 with note 230.

[49] Mark 11.11-12, 15-19; Luke 19.45-46; Matt 21.10-17.

[50] Mark 14.57-58 parr.; cf. also the accusation against Stephen in Acts 6.13-14.

[51] Ådna 2000, 252, 344–45, 384. Cf. also note 141 in chapter 3 and note 418 in chapter 13.

[52] Cf. Lev 5.11; 12.8; Luke 2.22-24.

the son-in-law of Annas. According to rabbinic accounts they possessed markets on the temple mount.[53]

Jesus most certainly did not — as R. Eisler[54] and others fantasize — storm the temple mount with his Galilean followers and drive out all the traders and money changers. This would certainly have led to the intervention of the Levite temple police as well as the Roman cohort that occupied the Antonia and watched the outer court from the roofs of the porticos[55] and have produced a great bloodbath. Josephus recounts several such violent actions of the occupying troops, precisely under Pilate.[56] Rather, the action of Jesus in the temple must be understood as a provocative and symbolic sign act. He may have overturned some money-changing tables and opened dove cages, while his disciples prevented deliveries of wares in the forecourt. We cannot reconstruct the event in detail. It need not have been more than a small tumult followed by a battle of words, so that the temple authorities (and the Romans) did not intervene in order not to increase this disturbance and to avoid the shedding of blood.[57] What is decisive in the account is the judgment saying. Mark 11.17 passes on a combination of quotations from Isa 56.7 and the temple discourse of Jer 7.11: "My house should be called a house of prayer, but you have made it into a den of robbers." The motif of the "house of prayer" (οἶκος προσευχῆς)[58] could go back to Jesus. In this context, Jesus probably also spoke the saying about the tearing down and building up of the temple, which was held against

---

[53] Bill. I: 850ff.; II: 570–571; Hengel 1989c, 211–12 with 212 n. 344 (GV = 1976c, 216–17 with 217 n. 1); cf. Ådna 1999, 74–75 with note 14, on the excavation of a workshop in which a scale with the inscription לבר קתרס was found and which had presumably belonged to the high priestly family Kathros (t. Menaḥ. 13.21; b. Pesaḥ. 57a); see further 91–95 on the high priesthood as "temple administration authorities."

[54] Eisler 1929/1930, II: 476ff., 513; on this, see Hengel 1989c, 216–17 (GV = 1976c, 221–22).

[55] See the incident under the procurator Cumanus at the Passover festival (see section 3.1.5 with note 303, and see the discussion above with note 48) and the riot against Paul at the festival of weeks in 57 CE in Acts 21.27-33, where the cohort above the steps that connected the Antonia with the courtyard quickly intervened and saved the life of Paul.

[56] See the discussion of Pilate in section 3.13 and notes 47–48 above.

[57] Mark 11.16: καὶ οὐκ ἤφιεν ἵνα τις διενέγκῃ σκεῦος διὰ τοῦ ἱεροῦ. This enigmatic short note, which is more of a pointer than an explanation, is omitted by Luke, who only provides a very short account, since he wants to avoid the accusation of rebellion, as well as by Matthew.

[58] Cf. Acts 2.42, 46; 3.1; 5.12, 20, 25, 42. According to Luke, the portico of Solomon in the eastern outer temple area became the place of assembling for prayer and of proclamation in the early primitive community. According to John 10.23, Jesus already taught there. For the teaching of Jesus in the temple in general, see Mark 12.35; 14.49 = Matt 26.55 = Luke 22.53; cf. Luke 19.47 (καθ' ἡμέραν); 20.1; 21.37; John 18.20.

him in the trial.[59] The goal of his symbolic parabolic action can be inferred from the concluding saying of the prophet Zechariah:[60] "There will no longer be a trader in the house of YHWH of the hosts on that day," i.e., the cleansing of the temple points symbolically to the dawning kingdom of God. A few verses earlier we read in Zech 14.9:

And YHWH will be king over the whole earth.
On that day YHWH is the only one
And his name the only one.

With the dawning of the kingdom of God, which Jesus wants to introduce with his activity, all sacrificial cult and thus all business activity, which profanes God's temple, becomes obsolete: Jesus' own atoning death may already cast its shadow here.[61] The profitable trade with sacrificial animals and money changing in the temple is against God's will.[62] According to Mark 11.27-33,[63] on the following day, Jesus' provocative action triggers the question of authority from the leaders of the people: "By what authority, in whose authority have you acted against the money changers and traders in the temple?"[64] With this question they indirectly ask about his messiahship. Jesus poses the counterquestion about the origin of the baptism of John the Baptist: "Did it come from heaven or from human beings?"[65] The leaders of the people refuse—due to fear of the crowds, who hold the Baptist high in honor as a martyr prophet—to answer, while Jesus leaves the question of authority unanswered. Here his own "messianic secret" shimmers through again clearly, i.e., the messianic claim that now surfaces plainly but is still not publicly explicit. He refuses to answer, just as he had already refused to perform a legitimation sign in Galilee.

---

[59] Mark 14.58; cf. Acts 6.14; see section 20.2.2.

[60] Zechariah 14.21; see Ådna 2000, 472 index, ad loc. The text has influenced, among others, John 2.16b. Cf. the discussion of Zech 9.9-10 at the beginning of this section.

[61] This context is emphasized especially by Ådna 2000, 425–30 and 500 index, s.v. "Sühne."

[62] Cf. also Mark 13.1-2 and 15.38.

[63] Cf. Luke 20.1-8 = Matt 21.23-27. Matthew agrees with Luke against Mark in five stylistic improvements of the Markan *Vorlage*. Apparently, he had looked at both Gospels; see λέγοντες, ἀποκριθεὶς, δέ, εἴπατε/εἴπητε and ἐάν δέ.

[64] Mark 11.28 = Luke 20.2 = Matt 21.23: ἐν ποιᾳ ἐξουσίᾳ. . . .

[65] Cf. Mark 11.30 = Luke 20.4 = Matt 21.25.

18.4 Polemical Dialogues in Jerusalem

In Mark we possess a series of additional controversy dialogues, which on the basis of their content belong to Jerusalem and most plausibly in this very last time. Mark has chosen them as examples in order thereby—as was already the case with the question of authority—to demonstrate at the same time the sovereign superiority of Jesus in controversy dialogues. For him this also belongs to the prophetic-messianic authority[66] of Jesus. At the end "no one dared to question him any longer," but "the great crowd, however, heard him gladly."[67] The evangelist has put together these scenes as examples; his narrative still reflects real memories of the last days in Jerusalem.

Thus he recounts a controversy dialogue with the Sadducees over the question of the resurrection,[68] for in Jerusalem the Sadducean priestly and lay nobility were at home and therefore most influential. They were politically dominant over the Sanhedrin and the city. They had less power in the open land outside of Jerusalem.[69] This applies all the more to Galilee, where we hear of Herodians, i.e., the partisans of Herod Antipas, in Mark, but do not find Sadducees.[70]

The controversy dialogue has no direct tie to the last controversy in Jerusalem but to an eschatological question that was debated by the "conservative" Sadducees and the "progressive" Pharisees. What is at issue is the reality of the hope in the resurrection of the dead. Mark 12.18 therefore introduces the story with the following words: "And there came to him the Sadducees who claim that there is no resurrection."[71] With an artificially constructed legal case based on the successive levirate marriage of seven

---

[66] Cf. Mark 1.22: ὡς ἐξουσίαν ἔχων καὶ οὐχ ὡς οἱ γραμματεῖς; see section 16.1 with note 14.

[67] Mark 12.34, 37.

[68] Mark 12.18-27 = Luke 20.27-40 = Matt 22.23-33. Cf. Meier 2001, 416–44, 468–87 and elsewhere.

[69] Cf. Schwankl 1987; on the Sadducees, see chapter 4 with notes 64–75.

[70] Mark 3.6; cf. 8.15. The powerful but numerically small group of the Sadducees was disempowered in the course of the Jewish revolt after 66 CE and met its end as a high priestly determined party through the destruction of the temple. The much later Matthew connects them—when they had lost all their power—with the Pharisees and also incorrectly places them in Galilee: 3.7; 16.1, 6, 11-12. Luke, who is fifteen to twenty years earlier than Matthew, is still better informed about them: Luke 20.27; Acts 4.1; 5.17; 23.6-8. John no longer mentions them at all and replaces them with the "high priests."

[71] Cf. Acts 4.2; 23.6-8. The controversy is also attested by Josephus and in the Talmud; see Bill. I: 885–86 and IV: 334–52 (344–45). On the resurrection in Judaism in general, see Bill. IV: 1166–98; cf. also Hengel 2001a.

brothers[72] they seek to lead the hope in the resurrection *ad absurdum.* Jesus rejects the question as foolish. Those who pose it "know neither the Scriptures nor the creative power of God." The one who revealed himself to Moses at the burning bush as "God of Abraham, Isaac, and Jacob" "is not God of the dead but of the living."[73] The patriarchs are not dead but live with regard to the promised resurrection of the dead. Jesus grounds this through a central text of the Torah, which the questioners must also acknowledge. The problem of the future husband of the woman, which they presented, becomes obsolete, for the "angel-like" risen ones in the presence of God no longer know the earthly form of marriage.[74] This argument is already encountered in the Pauline notion of the σῶμα πνευματικόν, which "corresponds to God and his heavenly world."[75] While it contradicts "commonly held views at the time of Jesus,"[76] it has a certain parallel in accounts of the appearances of the risen one.[77] The lack of any christological reference speaks for the age of the story—there is no allusion at all to the resurrection of Jesus. At the same time, it nevertheless reflects the resurrection conception of Jesus or of the primitive community, which is the presupposition for the earliest understanding of the resurrection of Jesus.

The Pharisees and Herodians' question about paying taxes to Caesar also points to Jerusalem.[78] It does not fit in Galilee, where taxes were paid to Herod Antipas and not directly to the emperor,[79] but rather fits best in the capital, with the goal of the questioner being—irrespective of how Jesus answered—to denounce him either before Pilate or before the people.[80] By

---

[72] Cf. Deut 25.5-10; Gen 38.8; Ruth 4.1-10.

[73] Exodus 3.6, 15-16; on this, see Bill. I: 892ff. Luke 20.38 adds fittingly: "for they all live to him."

[74] Mark 12.25; cf. Luke 20.36: ἰσάγγελοι γάρ εἰσιν καὶ υἱοί εἰσιν θεοῦ. Luke may make recourse here to a special source. With the eschatological consummation, the commandment of Gen 1.28 and the bitter consequences of 3.16; 4.1ff. are nullified.

[75] First Corinthians 15.40ff. (44); cf. Rom 8.11, 29.

[76] See Bill. I: 887–91 (889).

[77] Luke 24.31, 36; John 20.19. On the other hand, this does not exclude the "millennialist" realism of "eating" and "drinking," indeed of joyful "dancing" at the festive celebration (Luke 6.23; cf. 15.25) in the kingdom of God; see Mark 14.25; Luke 6.21; 14.15; Acts 10.41; Rev 19.9, etc. See also section 13.2 with notes 45–47.

[78] Mark 12.13-17 = Luke 20.20-26 = Matt 22.15-22. Luke speaks only of delegates of the "scribes and high priests" (20.19), who furtively watch Jesus but no longer want to question him themselves. In Matthew it is "disciples of the Pharisees" and "Herodians" (22.15-16) who question Jesus. On the subject matter, see Hengel 1989c, 127–40 (GV = 1976c, 132–45).

[79] Antipas, as a client ruler, was obligated only to the yearly payment of a certain tribute to the Romans and independently collected his own taxes. Jesus must have had a positive relationship to the tax farmers; see chapter 15.

[80] Mark 12.13b has simply ἵνα αὐτὸν ἀγρεύσωσιν λόγῳ "in order to catch him through a word." Luke explicates accurately: "so that they could hand him over to the

getting the questioners to show him a Roman silver denarius with the image and inscription of Tiberius, he exposes them. After all, the tax coin is the possession of the emperor, for it was minted with his name and image,[81] and the one who uses his coin and carries it around with them acknowledges this relation of ownership and thus also his rule. Extreme Zealots therefore refused even to touch the emperor's coins, which they regarded as idol images. They radically rejected as a matter of course every payment of taxes to Rome as a sign of slavery and idolatry.[82] After Jesus has convicted his opponents of not being serious with the question, since they carried Caesar's money around with them, he can give this unmasking answer: "Give back to Caesar what belongs to him, but to God what is God's!" The καί, which connects the two statements, must be understood adversatively. The emphasis lies on the second statement. For Jesus the emperor and his power are not a pressing problem. He is disempowered, since God himself stands before the door, indeed, is present in Jesus' person. All that matters is that his will now occurs in entire obedience. Jesus' answer could be formulated as follows: Give the coins with the image and inscription of Caesar back to him, and give yourselves, who are created according to God's image, wholly over to your creator. The second statement contains the same intention as the command to love God in the double love command, which Mark expresses a little later in 12.28ff. This last story is also an ideal scene, which due to the positive reaction of the scribe and through the narrative connection to the question of the Sadducees also belongs in Jerusalem.[83]

---

power and authority of the governor." In the accusation before Pilate in Luke 23.2 they accuse him of being a deceiver of the people, who forbids the payment of taxes to Caesar. In our view, Rom 13.7 presupposes the tax pericope. The zealot rejection of the payment of taxes to the Gentile ruler who lets himself be venerated as divine was also a certain temptation for primitive Christianity.

[81] On the coin legends under Tiberius, see Mattingly 1983, 120–45. The inscription was often *Ti(berius) Caesar Divi Aug(usti) f(ilius) Augustus*. It could vary in details. See also V. Taylor 1966, 479.

[82] Cf. Josephus, *Ant.* 18.4ff.; *J.W.* 2.118. Hengel 1989c, 190–96 (GV = 1976c, 195–201). In Judaea the Roman administration accommodated the Jewish prohibition of images insofar as the copper coins minted by the procurators did not bear an image of Caesar, as was already the case for the coins of the Hasmonean and Herodian rulers. Only in the case of the temple tax coin minted in Tyre was the revenue for the sanctuary more important than the prohibition of images. However, after 66 CE the insurgents immediately minted silver coins without human images with cult objects and political-religious fighting words.

[83] For Matt 22.34-40 a scribe who is evaluated positively has become intolerable. He therefore takes over from Luke 10.25 the νομικός as a tester of Jesus (Luke: ἐκπειράζων αὐτόν), Matt 22:35: ἐπηρώτησεν εἷς ἐξ αὐτῶν (of the Pharisees) νομικὸς πειράζων αὐτόν. Through the knowledge that Matthew, in addition to his Markan *Vorlage*, looked time and again at the Lukan text, the unresolvable problem of the 'minor agreements,' which has evoked a rich range of hypotheses, disappears. See section 6.4.2.

Moreover, to us it seems probable that the offensive parable of the merciful Samaritan in Luke 10.30ff., and the no less sharp parable of the Pharisee and tax collector in Luke 18.9ff., likewise belong in the Jerusalem polemical situation.[84] In the first of these parables, the Jewish nobility, the priest and the Levite, who were dominant in Jerusalem, are juxaposed in a negative way to the despised "heretic" and enemy of the people.[85] In the second there is a contrast between a tax collector and a Pharisee, the exploitative crook and the model pious person, during a visit to the Jerusalem temple. Both parables could have signified a provocation for the hearers of the leading strata. All the more they correspond to Jesus' message of the revelation of the love of the near God for the despised, excluded, and sinners, the "lost sheep of the house of Israel," which for him includes tax collectors and Samaritans. It is not birth and religious claim that counts now before God who justifies the sinner, but only the attitude of true repentance which leads to the confession "God be merciful to me a sinner,"[86] and the concrete deed of love.

The parable of the wicked tenants also points to a sharp conflict situation in Jerusalem itself. It is not, as is often claimed, a later allegorizing community formation but rather sheds light on the last controversy of Jesus.[87] As in the case of other parables, Jesus takes up here an — admittedly unusual but nevertheless not impossible — social situation from Palestinian daily life. A large estate owner has set up at considerable cost a vineyard and leased it out to landless renters for a fixed share in the yield. The owner has his place of residence in a distant city. He is not himself in position to personally collect his share after the vineyard produces the first harvest several years later but sends slaves. The tenants mistreat them and send them back with empty hands. This repeats itself. Finally, the owner sends his only son,[88] who — in contrast to the slaves who were previously sent — can validly represent him legally. To be sure, the tenants

---

[84] It may remain open whether it was during the last stay or during earlier ones. However, we regard it plausible that the last days constituted the original situation.

[85] Luke is — correctly in terms of history — especially interested in the Samaritans, in contrast to Matthew, who wants to keep Jesus away from them (10.5). On this, see Böhm 1999, 95–100, 239–60; see section 11.3. According to Josephus, *Ant.* 18.30, Samaritans, in ca. 9 CE, had defiled the whole temple in Jerusalem through bones of the dead, and in *J.W.* 2.232ff. = *Ant.* 20.118ff. conflicts arise between Jews and Samaritans because of the murder of Galilean festival pilgrims; on this, cf. Luke 9.52-56 (including the secondary expansion of the text, which could come from Marcion's Gospel; see note 68 in chapter 11).

[86] Luke 18.13; cf. Peter (5.8) and the lost son (15.21). Luke is, as a student of Paul, the evangelist of the justification of the ungodly (Rom 4.5). See the end of section 6.4.3.

[87] Mark 12.1-12 = Luke 20.9-19 = Matt 21.33-46; Gos. Thom. 65–66; cf. Luke 21.1-4; cf. Hengel 1968a; Snodgrass 1983; Kloppenborg 2006, 173–218, 219–77 (and passim).

[88] Mark 12.6: ἔτι ἕνα εἶχεν υἱὸν ἀγαπητόν.

calculate differently. For them he is the heir. If they kill him, the vineyard falls to them through acquisition by possession as land that has become without an owner. In that case, the point of the parable would then have to be deduced from its end. As the treacherous murder of the son by the tenants will have the certain intervention of the owner as a consequence, so the—intentional—killing of Jesus, the eschatological authorized representative of God, will bring forth judgment on the leaders who were responsible for it.[89] It connects therein the messianic secret with the announcement of his death and the reference to the judgment of God, a motif that surfaces again in the interrogation of Jesus before the high priest:

The stone which the builders rejected,
this has become the cornerstone.[90]

The parable is said to have provoked the opponents of Jesus to such a degree that they wanted to arrest him, but did not dare to do so out of fear of the people. It is peculiar that Mark no longer recounts any miracle stories in these last days of the controversies in Jerusalem. The only exception is the cursing of the fig tree, which, having perhaps grown out of a parable story, contains the character of a parabolic action that is meant to point to the judgment on the city and temple, but for Mark is also related to the "mountain-moving faith" and the certainty of one's prayers being answered.[91] At the end of this scene Mark places the story of Jesus' knowledge—which transcends human possibilities—about the gift of the poor widow, who, in contrast to the "many rich people," who "gave from their abundance," had put, with two λεπτά, all her possessions into the "offering box" of the temple.[92] This peculiar scene, which is out of the

---

[89] The parable probably concluded originally with the question "What will the lord of the vineyard do?" (Mark 12.9a). The hearers themselves could provide the answer.

[90] Mark 12.10-11 = Ps 118.22-23 LXX; cf. Luke 20.17; Acts 4.11; 1 Pet 2.4, 7.

[91] Mark 11.12-14, 20 = Matt 21.18-19; cf. the parable of the unfruitful fig tree in Luke 13.6-9. On faith and the answering of prayer, see Mark 11.22-24; cf. Matt 17.20 (see chapter 15 with note 21) and 7.7. Mark 11.25 also adds an admonition to be ready to forgive in connection with prayer; cf. Matt 5.23-24; 6.12; 18.35.

[92] Mark 12.41-44 = Luke 21.1-4. Matthew omits the story because of its apparent insignificance. The γαζοφυλάκιον is the treasure room of the temple (cf. Matt 27.6). Based on the context, it means here the offering boxes in this room; on this, see Bauer/Aland/Aland 1988, 300. Τὸ λεπτόν was the smallest copper coin. Mark explicates the two λεπτά with the Roman *quadrans*, one of the pointers to the emergence of the Gospel in Rome; cf. the explanation of the αὐλή, the palace of the prefect, with the Roman term "*praetorium*" in Mark 15.16. On the temple treasury room, see Bill. II: 37–41 (39ff.): Among the thirteen trumpet-like money containers there were six for voluntary gifts (t. Šeqal. 3.1ff.). The *lepton* corresponded to the *peruta*; a *quadrans* was a fourth of an *as*: Bill. II: 45.

ordinary in the Gospels, stands in contrast, on the one hand, to the accusation against the alleged greed of the scribes (12.40), who "devour the houses of widows," and points, on the other hand, to the Messiah's special Spirit-effected knowledge:

He will not judge according to appearance,
And he will not make judgments according to hearsay.
Rather, he judges the small in uprightness
and makes judgments with uprightness for the poor in the land.[93]

With this the evangelist transitions to the great eschatological prophecy about the fate of Jerusalem, the eschatological birth pains, and the coming of the Son of Man.

Right before this he has Jesus pose, with reference to Ps 110.1, the riddling question about the *relationship between son of David and Messiah*. If the Messiah is David's son, how can the divinely inspired composer of Psalms call him "(my) Lord"? This does not signify a contestation of Jesus' Davidic sonship,[94] but the Messiah is incomparably more than the scribes believe, namely the Kyrios, i.e., the Lord also of the royal founding father David. Jesus provides no solution to this question, which he, according to Mark, poses at the end of the controversy with the opponents. Rather, for the evangelist it is answered by the prophecy of the coming of the Son of Man[95] and above all by the passion and resurrection of Jesus. For the evangelist the Son of David Jesus is the Kyrios, the coming Son of Man, and the Son of God, whom the Spirit-filled king and prophet himself, looking ahead, designates as "my Lord." Mark has prepared for this question (and its implicit answer) through the ample use of the Kyrios (and Son) title for Jesus.[96] However, in contrast to John, the christological shaping in Mark has not yet largely suppressed the historical reality.

The fact that Mark—in complete contrast to John—no longer has any public miracles, such as healings, take place in Jerusalem may for him have the same reason as in the case of Jesus' failed appearance in Nazareth, where "he could do no deed of power."[97] The last healing, that

---

[93] Isaiah 11.3-4.

[94] On this, see note 106 in chapter 8.

[95] Mark 13.24ff.; cf. 8.38. On the christological significance of Ps 110.1 in primitive Christianity, see Hengel 1995, 119–26 (GV = 1993b, 119–22, 185–94; 2006a, 292–95, 358–67). It is the most frequently quoted Old Testament text in the New Testament.

[96] Mark 1.3; 5.19; 7.28; 11.3. Mark—and in his footsteps Luke and Matthew—could signal a knowledge of the preexistence of the Kyrios Jesus with texts such as 1.3, 11; 9.3-7; 12.6, 35-37. On this, see now Gathercole 2006; Rüggemeier 2017, 345–47.

[97] Mark 6.1-6(5); cf. Matt 13.58; see section 8.3 with notes 66–72.

of the blind Bartimaeus in Jericho, who already confesses Jesus as "Son of David" and "Lord" and, upon being healed, becomes his follower on the way to Jerusalem, has parabolic meaning. Only Matthew introduces in 21.14 the healing of several "blind and lame persons" in the temple. They inspire children to the acclamation "Hosanna to the Son of David" and bring about the protest of the "high priests and Pharisees." For Matthew the lack of healing miracles in Jerusalem probably appeared just as offensive as in the Markan note about Jesus' lack of success in Nazareth, which he likewise weakens. For Mark, the holy city, where Jesus, despite external successes,[98] is rejected and executed by the leaders of the people in the end, was no longer worthy of such "deeds of power."[99] After all, at the end stands the prophecy of the destruction of the temple in 13.1-2. The cursing of the fig tree and the parable of the tenants show clearly here the narrative tendency of the evangelist. In this way he powerfully traces the christological lines that already dominate the way of Jesus into the passion ever since the entry into Jerusalem in the older tradition. Here the most important line is the question of the messianic authority of Jesus.

This is different in John. Of the seven signs that are narrated in the Fourth Gospel only four occur in Galilee and three in or near Jerusalem. Beyond this, Jesus already does numerous spectacular signs in his first appearance in Jerusalem, which admittedly only encounter a superficial faith.[100] Moreover, the question of miracles is discussed especially in the polemical dialogues in Jerusalem.[101]

As addition, after the christological riddle of Ps 110.1 and the pericope of the poor widow in the temple treasure room, Mark introduces a very short *warning against the scribes*, more specifically against their addiction to honor and financial gain (Mark 12.38-40). This may be a key word connection to 12.28, 32, and 35, where only the key word γραμμα- τεῖς appears. As the religious leaders of Israel, they are, after the "high priests," the most important group in the Sanhedrin, and, next to the Pharisees, from which Mark rightly distinguishes them, they are already in

[98] Mark 12.34: "and no one dared to question him any longer"; 12.37: "the great crowd heard him gladly."

[99] It is completely different in John, where the emphasis is placed on the "signs" of Jesus in Jerusalem and in its vicinity: 2.23–3.2; 5.2-9; 9.1-7, 16; 10.41; chapter 11; 12.18, 37.

[100] The linking of signs and faith to Jesus' messiahship and divine sonship is much more strongly emphasized in John than in Mark, even though the signs do not awaken enduring faith among the crowds. See the texts referenced in notes 99 and 101 in this chapter.

[101] John 7.31; 9.16; 10.41; 11.47; 12.18, 37; cf. also 20.31 and the hyperbolic concluding saying in 21.25.

Galilee the sharpest opponents of Jesus. According to Mark 3.22, they come there from Jerusalem. By contrast, in Mark the Pharisees appear in Jerusalem only together with the Herodians in 12.13 in the tax question, and they are not mentioned at all in connection with the Sanhedrin. Mark is, in ca. 69/70 CE, still relatively well informed about the Jewish groups and party relations prior to the destruction of Jerusalem.[102] Ca. twenty to thirty years later, Matthew, in a changed situation, has reworked these three verses together with the traditional material from Luke and the sayings tradition as well as his own polemic, which has grown out of his situation, into the monumental chapter 23, which is decisive for the dating of his Gospel to between 90 and 100 CE.[103] The fact that Mark inserts these verses, which appear rather disruptive, may be connected to the last sentence right before the sharply contrasting narrative of the sacrifice of the poor widow and the Markan apocalypse in chapter 13: "They will receive an even stricter judgment."[104] In Mark, the last days of the conflict in Jerusalem simultaneously point to the judgment upon the ones who reject Jesus' messianic message, and this means his task given to him by God. For him, the Son of Man, whose coming as redeemer he portrays as the climax in 13.24-27, is at the end the just judge.[105] At the same time, the apocalyptic discourse of Mark 13, which is placed in Jesus' mouth, forms a bridge to the present of the evangelist through the reference to the post-Easter worldwide mission in 13.10 and through the admonition to the persecuted and afflicted church around 70 CE: "And you will be hated by all[106] for the sake of my name. But the one who endures to the end will be saved."[107]

---

[102] The same applies to Luke in contrast to the later Matthew and John.

[103] Hengel 2008c, 336ff. (ET = 2000b, 196ff.).

[104] Mark 12.40: οὗτοι λήμψονται περισσότερον κρίμα = Luke 20.47, cf. Matt 23.13.

[105] Mark 8.38; 13.26-27; 14.61-62. See section 17.4.1.2.

[106] Cf. John 15.18ff., which grounds this hatred of the world christologically. On this, see the accusation against the Christians in the Neronian persecution in Tacitus, *Ann.* 15.44.4: *odium humani generis convicti sunt* (they were convicted for their hatred of the human race); and the defense of the Christians, which accuses their persecutors of hatred: Diognetus 2.6; 5.14; 6.1, 7; Tertullian, *Apol.* 1.4; 2.3; 3.4ff.; 37.8; 46.4: the hatred against the Christians is hatred against the truth: Minucius Felix, *Oct.* 14.6; 31.8 etc. According to Hitchcock 1930; 1935, the hatred of the population against the Christians is also intended in Tacitus. This, however, is an incorrect interpretation. The accusation of hate was made by both sides. See also Tacitus, *Hist.* 5.5.1, against the Jews: *adversus omnes alios hostile odium* ("toward every other people they feel only hate and enmity"; trans. C. H. Moore, LCL, 183).

[107] Mark 13.13; cf. Luke 21.17-19 and Matt 24.9b, 13.

19

The Preparation of the Passion of Jesus[1]

19.1 The Historical and Theological Problem

The most attested report about Jesus of Nazareth in the first and second century CE is the fact that he was crucified. This statement already stands—paradoxically as a saving event—at the center of the Pauline missionary preaching. In the Babylonian Talmud[2] we find it as Baraita that Jesus was "hanged" on the eve of the Passover festival; we find the same assertion in ancient authors. Thus, in the middle of the second century CE, the satirist Lucian mocks the "crucified sophist," whom the dimwitted Christians worship.[3] For the Platonist Celsus[4] it is an unheard of provocation that the Christians demand: "Believe that this one is God's Son, although he was arrested in a dishonorable way and was executed in the most shameful form." The Neo-Platonist Porphyry[5] recounts an oracle of Apollo, which mocks the "empty deception" of the Christians, who "sing laments to a dead god, whom a rightly judging court condemned and whom a bad death destroyed in the best years through him being nailed onto the

---

[1] Blinzler 1969; Sherwin-White 1963; Hengel 1977a (= 1986, 93–185); Strobel 1980; Pesch 1984b; Betz 1982; Brown 1994; Hengel/Schwemer 2001, 45–63, 133–63 (ET = Hengel 1995, 41–58, no equivalent).

[2] b. Sanh. 43a. It is presupposed here that he was condemned by a Jewish court, stoned, and then "was hanged" according to Deut 21.23; cf. also R. Meir's parable of two twins and the "crucified king" in t. Sanh. 9.7. See further Tg. Esther 7.10, where the cross of Haman is designated as "teaching hall of Bar Pandera," i.e., of Jesus; on this, see Ego 1996, 125, 317ff. and Strack 1910, § 1 and 2 (pp. 18–19*); § 14 (p. 44*).

[3] Lucian, *Peregr.* 11, 13. Tacitus, *Ann.* 15.44.3 speaks only of the execution of Jesus by Pilate (*supplicio adfectus erat*), but he knows of course that he was crucified. When possible, Roman authors avoided the unrefined term "crucifixion." See Hengel 1977a, 37–38, 77–78.

[4] Origen, *Cels.* 6.10.

[5] In Augustine, *Civ.* 19.23.

cross." In addition, we would have to mention the mocking crucifix on the
Palatine from around 200 CE, which has a crucified person with a donkey
head and the inscription "Alexamenos worships god."[6]

At the same time, more thought and writing have been devoted to this
trial than to any other in the history of the world. The superabundance of
theories and hypotheses does not make its evaluation easier. The main
source is the relatively simple account of the Gospel of Mark in chapters 14 and 15, which can be illuminated at some points and with great
caution by the sometimes divergent accounts of Luke and John. While
these are based on their own tradition, the tradition usually displays secondary features vis-à-vis Mark. The additions of Matthew, who usually
follows Mark, who is an authority for him, are also almost always legendary in character.[7] Many questions will always remain open here, especially
since we know little about the criminal proceedings against provincials
(*peregrini*) in the empire. The most detailed sources on this are the letters of Pliny and the martyr acts on the trials of Christians.[8] An account
of the passion of Jesus was presumably available to the evangelist Mark
in written form before the composition of the Gospel, with it being possible indeed that he himself composed or shaped it at an earlier time. After
all, he himself comes from the Jerusalem primitive community. For him
the passion account was probably the starting point for the whole Gospel.
From the beginning a continuous story was recounted in it. Without such
an account Jesus could not have been proclaimed as the crucified Son of
God at all in the mission communities outside of the motherland.[9] The
age and scope of this preform are, of course, controversial. Rudolf Pesch
wanted to trace back this "primitive Gospel" with the passion story into

---

[6] From the imperial pagan educational establishment in Severian times, when the
Christians had already penetrated into the imperial household. On the donkey head, cf.,
for example, Tertullian, *Scap.* 4.5–6; an image can be found in Dinkler 1967, T. xiii, 33a.

[7] Cf. the saying about the twelve legions of angels in Matt 26.53, the suicide of Judas
in 27.3-10 (see note 190 in chapter 6), the wife of Pilate and the handwashing in 27.19, 24,
the resurrection of dead persons at the death of Jesus in 27.52, and the guarding of the tomb
in 27.62-66; 28.4, 11-15. Historically valuable are the name of the high priest *Caiaphas* in
Matt 26.57 (on this, cf., however, Luke 3.2; Acts 4.6; and John 11.49 and elsewhere; see
note 40 in chapter 20) and the name *Jesus* Barabbas in 27.16 (see note 28 in chapter 21).

[8] Mommsen 1955, 229–50: the criminal law pertaining to governors. On the trial of
Jesus, see pp. 240–41 n. 2: "Among the reports, which agree as a whole and in the main
are also historical, the purest appears to be that of Mark." See further Bickerman 1935;
Sherwin-White 1963, 13–23; 1985, 692–712.

[9] On this, see Hengel 2004d.

the time of the high priest Caiaphas, who was deposed in the autumn of 36 CE; this, however, is probably somewhat too bold of a venture.[10]

The age of the passion tradition emerges already from the tradition in 1 Cor 11.23ff., which is already known to Paul in a solidified form: "The Lord Jesus on the night in which he was betrayed (or handed over), took the bread, spoke the blessing, broke it, and said: This is my body (which is sacrificed) for you. . . ." It must be viewed together with 1 Cor 5.6-8, the reference to Jesus as the sacrificed Passover lamb and in relation to the Passover customs. Paul told the account which stands behind it to the Corinthians when he founded the community in 49/50 CE. He probably already came to know this after his conversion in Damascus and already disseminated it in his mission communities in Syria and Cilicia.[11] Here, living memory is still influential, indeed, Paul possesses "chronological" information, not only about the night of the handing over, but also about the resurrection of Jesus (from the tomb) on the third day (1 Cor 15.4).[12] Thus, the core of the Markan passion account goes back to eyewitnesses, and above all to Peter. One could forgo knowledge of the passion story neither in the worship service—this is shown by Paul's quotation in 1 Cor 11.23ff., by the Philippians hymn in 2.6ff., and by the later Passover homily of Melito of Sardis—nor in the missionary preaching, in which it was not only in Paul that the proclamation of the crucified one stood at the center.[13] For here the burning question had to be answered: How could Jesus be handed over by members of his own people, to whom he demonstrated his messianic authority in word and miracles,[14] to the Roman authorities and thus to crucifixion, i.e., the cursed death? Or, put differently, how could the Roman prefect Pilate condemn the unique "righteous one,"[15] Jesus of Nazareth, despite his innocence, as a common criminal to the most gruesome death known to Roman criminal justice? Thus, the passion story points from the beginning onward to the hardening theory of Mark and to the actual "messianic secret." The latter is completely unveiled through the passion of Jesus. Because from the beginning the primitive community

---

[10] Pesch 1984b, 1–27. He grounds this view, among other things, with the argument that Mark does not mention the name of the high priest, i.e., he presupposes it as generally known. Zuntz 1984b also wants to date Mark very early, to around 40 CE. See note 26 in chapter 7.

[11] Galatians 1.21.

[12] Hengel 2004d; 2001a. What is in view is the day of the discovery of the empty tomb by the women on Easter morning.

[13] First Corinthians 2.1ff.; Gal 3.1, 13; cf. Acts 2.23–24, 36; 5.30; 10.39; 13.28–29.

[14] Luke 24.19; Acts 2.22 etc.; Heb 2.4.

[15] Luke 23.47; Acts 3.14; 7.52; 22.14; Matt 27.19; 1 John 2.1: δίκαιος contains, on the basis of Isa 53.11, messianic meaning; cf. also Wis 2.12ff., 18ff.; 5.1–5.

had to provide information narratively about these questions and at the same time to offer theological explanation, the passion story was a central component of its message. Here, despite all legendary elaboration and christological shaping, Mark stands on historically secure ground. Certain "basic tendencies" become visible here, which were already determinative for the primitive community.

From the beginning there was a certain apologetic stance. It had to be stressed that with Jesus the worst judicial murder imaginable had taken place and that the blinded hierarchs of the Sanhedrin, the high priests, elders, and scribes, who handed over Jesus to Pilate, bore the true guilt. Pilate was not convinced of Jesus' guilt but was too weak and cowardly to resist their pressure. The proclamation of the crucified and risen Messiah and Son of God after Easter contains at least indirectly an accusation against the persons who were responsible for his death, i.e., the hierarchs in Jerusalem.[16] It is conspicuous here that—in contrast to John—in Mark and in Luke and Matthew, who are dependent on him, the key word Ἰουδαῖος is not used for the opponents and for the crowd. In Mark, one therefore cannot speak of a fundamental "anti-Jewish" stance in the passion story.[17] That his presentation is historically well founded emerges from the fact that Pilate and the later procurators, according to our sources, took no more action against the new messianic movement. They apparently did not regard it as politically dangerous. Roman rule had other, really threatening problems. During the next thirty-five years, the constant opponents remained the political and religious leadership in Jerusalem and here especially the clan of Annas.[18] For them the reasons for the execution of Jesus were upheld, for them the rejection of Jesus continued to have an effect in the enmity against the Jewish Christian community in Jerusalem.

To be sure, already before and in Mark, the most important "tendency" is the demonstration that the suffering of Jesus corresponds wholly to God's will and was predicted by the prophetic word of the Old Testament. This too applies to the whole of primitive Christianity. In 1 Cor 15.3 Paul quotes, following a Jerusalem tradition, as the gospel which he

---

[16] Cf., e.g., 1 Cor 2.8-9: the ἄρχοντες τοῦ αἰῶνος τούτου have crucified Jesus; see also Acts 4.10; 5.30. This accusation was made by the followers of Jesus from the beginning on and provoked a corresponding counterreaction. After the leading stratum in Jerusalem—understandably—rejected the new messianic movement, the opposition was then extended in later Christian polemic to the Jews in general, i.e., the leadership was identified with the people. See "polemical" statements such as 1 Thess 2.14ff. (the earliest letter of Paul around 50 CE); Acts 2.23; 3.13-14; 10.39; 13.27-28; Rev 11.8, etc.

[17] On this, see Schwemer 2001c, 133–63.

[18] See section 3.1.3 with notes 219–20 and section 19.2 below with notes 31–32. See further section 20.2.1.

"handed down" when he founded the community in Corinth that "Christ died for our sins *according to the Scriptures.*" When Jesus is arrested in Gethsemane, Mark has Jesus say in 14.49: "But this takes place in order that the Scriptures may be fulfilled." Here the psalms of suffering 22, 31, 69, and 118.22ff. were especially important, as well as, with a view to the soteriological interpretation of the death of Jesus, Isa 53,[19] and, beyond this, Zechariah texts such as 12.10-11 and 13.7. In the passion story in Mark, features that could be documented with the prophetic predictions of the Old Testament were often retained. The shameful death of the Messiah Jesus on the cross was a *skandalon*, which from the beginning had to be justified as God's will through an appeal to the Scriptures. In individual cases one would need to examine here whether Old Testament quotations directly had a history-forming influence. In our view, this happened much less than has been assumed by the hypercriticism. The passion story was not "spun out" of Old Testament texts without inhibition, but individual texts were connected with the memory of Jesus' passion.

To this can be added the paraenetic motifs. In obedience to God's will, Jesus went ahead of the community in his suffering. Christians should not fail like the disciples but follow their master, as he himself had demanded, and bear tribulation and persecution. After all, Mark emerged shortly after the Neronian persecution in Rome and has surely been influenced by the memory of this singular catastrophe. Here too we encounter a generally applicable primitive Christian motif, which was already fundamental for Paul.

Over everything stands the soteriological significance of Jesus' place-taking suffering, expressed in the high points of Mark 10.45 and above all 14.24: "This is my blood of the covenant, poured out for many." It is not their suffering discipleship that grounds the salvation of the disciples—here they fail rather—but Jesus' obedient way into death as suffering servant of God who gives his life for the many, i.e., inclusively for all. At the moment of Jesus' death the temple curtain is torn in two. The way in to the Holy of Holies, to God's saving presence, is opened through the atoning death of the Son of God for all human beings.[20]

---

[19] On this, see Hengel/Bailey 2004 (GV = Hengel 1996b; Hengel 1999b, 72–114); Stuhlmacher 2004 (GV = 1996); Hofius 2004b (GV = 1996); cf. Bellinger/Farmer 1996.

[20] Mark 15.38-39. The Roman centurion speaks representatively for all Gentiles. See Hengel 1981a, 33–75. Cf. also the Gethsemane prayer in Mark 14.35-36 and the self-surrender of Jesus in Mark 14.41-42, 48. John especially stresses that Jesus takes the way to the cross with complete unity of will with the Father; therefore he has to pass over the portrayal of the struggle of Jesus in Gethsemane.

J. Jeremias hypothesizes that there were probably two versions of the passion,[21] a long account, which contained the entry, the temple cleansing, and the question of authority, and then transitioned to the decision to kill Jesus and the crucifixion, and an even older short account, which begins with the arrest in 14.43ff. This is the actual passion story. We are inclined to a compromise. The temporally continuous narrative begins already with Mark 14.1, since it includes the Passover meal, in which the salvific significance of the death of Jesus stands at the center. The Markan account of the passion thus forms a relative unity. The different attempts to break it up via source criticism into different pieces cannot convince. An extreme position is advocated by E. Linnemann,[22] who wants to smash it into "twenty different original traditional units" and then nevertheless marvels at "the unity of this story in structure and character." More important than such source-critical attempts to isolate individual pieces or to scrape out a very concise "primitive account" (*Urbericht*) is the need to draw on the respective Jewish and Roman legal-historical materials for comparison and not only to work out the christological tendency of the account but also to illuminate the political-historical background of the trial. In our view, it is indeed possible that a more detailed—to some extent variable—account, which was delivered orally, originally stood behind the very concise Markan account.

19.2 The Opponents of Jesus:
Decision to Kill Jesus and Betrayal of Judas[23]

While Pharisees,[24] scribes with less frequency,[25] and also Herodians once in connection with Pharisees are prominent as opponents of Jesus in the Galilean activity in Mark,[26] this picture changes in Jerusalem. The first passion prediction in 8.31 already speaks of Jesus being condemned by the "elders, high priests, and scribes." This group of three, in which the "high

---

[21] Jeremias 1966c, 89–96 (GV = 1967a, 83–90).

[22] Linnemann 1970, 176. It is understandable that she later—influenced thereafter by a fundamentalist understanding of the Bible—radically renounced the "historical-critical method." Already in her earlier Marburg time she had never learned what "historical-philological" method really is. Cf. the compilation of the thirty-four (!) different attempts to reconstruct the pre-Markan passion story in Brown 1994, 1502–17.

[23] Jeremias 1969a, 147ff., 160ff., 222ff. (GV = 1969b, 166ff., 181ff., 252ff.); Lohse 1971a (GV = 1964); Schürer 1973–1987, II: 199ff., 227ff. (237ff.); Goodman 1987; Goodblatt 1994; Brown 1994; Hengel 2004d.

[24] Mark 2.16, 18, 24; 3.6; 7.1; 8.11.

[25] Mark 3.22; 7.1—there scribes from Jerusalem. In contrast to Matthew, he still distinguishes clearly between the two groups. See section 4.1.

[26] Mark 3.6; for Jerusalem, see 12.13.

priests" are usually mentioned first,[27] since they especially held political power in Jerusalem, has in view the parts from which the highest Jewish authority, the Sanhedrin, was composed, which consisted of seventy (or seventy-one) members under the chairmanship of the high priest. Its character before 70 CE is admittedly disputed in scholarship. Presumably this body was especially an instrument of ruling priestly families, especially of the overpowering clan of Annas.[28] They have been the actual opponents of Jesus since his entry into Jerusalem.[29] The Markan passion account is well informed with regard to the opponents of Jesus and the main responsibility of the high priests. In Mark, the passion of Jesus is dominated by a fundamental conflict of Jesus with the political-religious leaders in the holy city.

The ἀρχιερεῖς, the high priests, are the Sanhedrin members, who belonged to the leading priestly houses, in the first place to the house of Annas, and, beyond that, to that of Boethus, Phiabi, Kamithos, and others,[30] who constantly held the highest temple offices, such as that of the captain of the temple and temple treasurer, and who were so rich that they could also purchase in alternation the much sought-after office of high priest from the Roman prefects. Joseph, with the byname Caiaphas, the son-in-law of Annas (John 18.13), held this honor under Pilate. Of all the high priests between Herod and the destruction of the temple, he was in office the longest by far (from 18 to 36/37 CE).[31] This means that he must have developed a special ability to keep his office. The later high priests changed at times almost every year.[32]

The scribes (γραμματεῖς) may have been predominantly Pharisees[33] since the time of Queen Alexandra and of Herod, but were not restricted

---

[27] Cf. Mark 11.27; 14.43, 53; 15.1; in addition, only the "high priests and scribes" appear as the most important group: 10.33; 11.18; 14.1; cf. 15.31; often, however, only the high priests: 14.10; 15.3, 10-11; cf. 14.55: οἱ ἀρχιερεῖς καὶ ὅλον τὸ συνέδριον.

[28] Lohse 1971a (GV = 1964); Goodblatt 1994, 77–130; Goodman 1987, 110–16; see also index, s.v. "High Priest," "Sanhedrin," "The Problem of the Council before 70."

[29] Mark 11.18, 27; 14.1; 15.1 and elsewhere.

[30] Jeremias 1969a, 194 (GV = 1969b, 219): "Of the twenty-five illegitimate high priests of the Herodian-Roman epoch no fewer than twenty-two belonged to these four families" and on the whole 190–98 (GV = 215–23).

[31] On this, see section 3.1.3. On Caiaphas and the clan of Annas, see Hengel 1999b, 322–34; Schürer 1973–1987, II: 230 nr. 14; Horbury 1994a; Brown 1994, 409ff. and 1558 index, s.v. "Caiaphas"; see also the discussion of Caiaphas and Annas in chapter 3 with notes 273–74.

[32] Cf. the reference in John 11.49, 51, which assumes this later situation. On this, see Bill. I: 953 (Lev. Rab. 21) and II: 569 (y. Yoma 1.1.38c). A translation of the whole text can be found in Avemarie 1995, 14.

[33] Alexandra, the widow of the Sadducee-friendly Jannaeus, helped the Pharisees come to power after his death. After the conquering of Jerusalem in 37 BCE, Herod exercised

exclusively to this religious party. There were probably Sadducean and "neutral" scribes. They were the actual lawyers in this highest Jewish judicial authority. By contrast, the elders (γραμματεῖς) represented the lay aristocracy, i.e., the rich estate owners, heads of tribes, and merchants. Joseph of Arimathea, whom Mark designates as a "noble member of the council,"[34] may have belonged to them. Like most ethnic groups and cities in the Roman Empire, Palestinian Judaism had an aristocratic structure. This corresponded to traditional Roman politics, which consciously relied on representatives of the upper class in the provinces. The majority of the Sanhedrin belonged to the conservative party of the Sadducees dominated by the priests. The Pharisaic minority, by contrast, was focused rather on the common people and had the greater influence upon them, at least outside of Jerusalem.

The question is why the high priestly authorities in Jerusalem regarded Jesus as such a dangerous opponent that they had him arrested and handed over with such targeted accusations to Pilate that the latter had him nailed to the cross as a political criminal. R. Bultmann thought that we could understand "this execution (scarcely) as the inwardly necessary consequence of his activity"; "rather, it occurred on the basis of a misunderstanding of his activity as a political action." He connected with this the hypothesis that the entry of Jesus with his followers probably "appeared politically dangerous to the procurator." The "role of the Jewish authorities" can "no longer be determined, since the passion narrative is too thickly overgrown by legends. For the later Christians the Jews were the real enemies . . . ; thus, they also made them responsible for the *catastrophe of Jesus*."[35] To be sure, the whole New Testament tradition as well as Josephus attest that the initiative for the arrest of Jesus proceeded not from the Romans but from the highest Jewish authority, and it must have had its reasons for handing over an eschatological popular preacher and miracle worker, who was popular among large parts of the common people. It is often claimed that the main cause for the passion of Jesus lay in his criticism of the Jewish law.[36] This, however, was not so fundamental and clear that it would have been sufficient to lead to a sentencing. Moreover, the Romans showed no interest with regard to disputes among Jews regarding the law, and the

---

brutal vengeance on the Hasmonean-friendly Sadducees and initially favored the Pharisees and their scribal leaders. On this, see Deines 1997, 551–54; Hengel/Deines 1996, 425–32, 462–76 (ET = 1995, 29–35, 55–67). See section 4.3.2 and the excursus on the relationship of women to the religious parties at the end of section 4.4.

[34] Mark 15.43: εὐσχήμων βουλευτής. On his person, see section 21.3 with notes 92–95.

[35] Bultmann 1967a, 453. Bultmann 1966, 49–50 (Bultmann's emphasis; ET = 1934b, 72).

[36] On this, see Hengel 1978 (= 2007b, 352–74).

Jewish authority did not itself possess the right to execution. In order to be effective, the accusations against Jesus must have had a political character.[37] Stephen, against whom the accusation of polemic against the law and temple was made, was therefore killed, against the report of Luke, not on the basis of an ordinary trial before the Sanhedrin but fell victim to a tumultuous mob justice. Paul, too, almost suffered a similar fate.[38]

The reason for the execution of Jesus is clearly recorded in all four Gospels and dominates the entire presentation of the trial. The starting point is the titulus on the cross: "King of the Jews," ὁ βασιλεὺς τῶν Ἰουδαίων, which points to the *causa poenae*, the cause of the execution.[39] "King of the Jews" means, however, nothing but the translation of Jesus' messianic claim into the political language of the Romans, who understood this alone. The problem of the messiahship of Jesus runs like a red thread through the whole process, from the hearing before the Sanhedrin to the death of Jesus, indeed, it already becomes acute with the entry into Jerusalem. The leaders of the people apparently regarded the messianic claim of Jesus, which is connected with his proclamation of the dawning kingdom of God, and the criticism of the temple cult grounded by it as a threat to their own position of power, as an attack on their authority among the Jewish people, which was protected by the Roman power.

According to Josephus,[40] shortly before the outbreak of the Jewish War, the Jewish leaders had an ecstatic prophet, Jesus, son of Ananias, who continually called out threatening words against the temple, arrested and beaten up.[41] When this did not help, they handed him over to the procurator Albinus, who whipped him to the bone but then let him go again as an alleged madman. While threatening announcements against Jerusalem and the temple were already a reason for handing a person over to the Romans, they were not yet serious enough for an execution. After all, while a threatening word against the temple plays a role in the trial of

---

[37] Cf. Mark 12.13; Luke 23.2; John 18.33-38; 19.12 and the accusation that he is "king of the Jews" in Mark 15.2 parr.; cf., by contrast, the stance of the governor Gallio in Acts 18.14-15. Pilate may have been for himself of a similar opinion.

[38] Acts 7.54ff.; on this, see Hengel 2002, 1–67 (37–46); Acts 21.27ff. For the stoning of James, the brother of the Lord, with other Jewish Christians as lawbreakers during the absence of the procurator, see Josephus, *Ant.* 20.200ff.

[39] Mark 15.26: αἰτία = Matt 27.37; Luke 23.38; with the greatest detail—Ἰησοῦς ὁ Ναζωραῖος ὁ βασιλεὺς τῶν Ἰουδαίων—and in three languages in John 19.19 with a christological aim. The dignity of the crucified one is to become known to all the world. See note 68 in chapter 21.

[40] Josephus, *J.W.* 6.300ff.

[41] This means that one imposed on him the punishment of the thirty-nine blows according to Deut 25.3; cf. 2 Cor 11.24 and on this, Bill. III: 527ff.

Jesus (Mark 14.58), it was likewise not sufficient. Rather, it was the Messiah question that was decisive.

A special report in John has the Sanhedrin, after the raising of Lazarus, say: If "we let him go on like this, all will believe in him, and the Romans will come and take from us this (holy) place and (the rule over) the people!" Thereupon, the high priest Caiaphas gives the advice: "It is better that a person die for the people than that the whole people should perish."[42] While this is formulated according to Christian tradition, it nevertheless shows that in John the members of the Sanhedrin and its head regarded Jesus as a dangerous deceiver of the people,[43] who had to be rendered harmless. By contrast, according to Mark 14.1, the "high priests and scribes" made such a definitive decision only two days before the festival. This dating probably refers to the concrete carrying out of the plan and not to the fundamental desire to get rid of Jesus. It probably had already been in effect since the entry into Jerusalem or the temple cleansing, especially since the members of the Sanhedrin were concerned that the arrest not take place directly at the festival, lest there be a riot among people in the midst of the flood of festival pilgrims. Mark stresses multiple times that the prophetic-eschatological preacher from Galilee was popular among the common people and that one did not dare to make an open arrest out of consideration for the crowd.[44] The decisive impulse for active intervention was given by a disciple who belonged to the most intimate circle around Jesus, the "twelve," Judas Iscariot, and who offered to give Jesus in to their hands, upon which they promised to reward him with money.[45] He is always the last person in the different lists of the twelve.[46] He usually bears the stereotyped descriptor "who handed him over."[47] The byname

---

[42] John 11.48-51. The high priest is said to have spoken here on the basis of his prophetic charisma of his office. On this, see Bammel 1997, 133–39.

[43] On Jesus as a deceiver of the people, see Matt 27.63-64; John 7.12, 47; further attestations in Hengel 1981b, 40–42 (GV = 1968b 44–46; 2008b, 81–84).

[44] Mark 11.18; 12.12, 37; 14.1-2.

[45] Mark 14.10-11; cf. Luke 22.3-6 and Matt 26.14-16; on this, see Matt 27.3-10 (special material). The motif of payment may belong to primitive Christian polemic. John 12.6 (cf. 13.9) turns him into the manager of the money of the fellowship of disciples and into a thief.

[46] Mark 3.19; Matt 10.4; Luke 6.16: ὃς ἐγένετο προδότης, cf. Acts 1.17: κατηριθμημένος ἦν ἐν ἡμῖν. John 6.71 also mentions the name of his father Simon: τὸν Ἰούδαν Σίμωνος Ἰσκαριώτου. In that case, the byname could already have been that of his father. See also note 144 in chapter 11.

[47] Matthew 10.4: ὁ παραδοὺς αὐτόν. Cf. Matt 26.25; 27.3; John 6.71; 12.4; 18.2, 5; only Luke 6.16 calls him "betrayer"; cf. 22.3; Mark 3.19: ὃς καὶ παρέδωκεν αὐτόν, Acts 1.16: τοῦ γενομένου ὁδηγοῦ τοῖς συλλαβοῦσιν Ἰησοῦν; on this, see Hengel 2004d, 132ff.

Ἰσκαριωθ/Ἰσκαριώτης has nothing to do with the zealot Sicarii, as some scholars hypothesize,[48] but is probably a designation of origin: "the man from *Q^eriyyôt*," presumably a place in south Judaea, as in some manuscripts in John.[49] We cannot say more about the motive for the betrayal. The Gospel tradition mentions Satanic possession and greed; both are meant to explain the unexplainable. For unknown reasons he appears to have become deeply disappointed with regard to Jesus' behavior. The contestation of the historicity of the betrayal and the belonging of Judas to the circle of the twelve is absurd. For the primitive community the deed of Judas was a heavy burden and at the same time an enigma. It could only be explained as the devilish possession of the betrayer.[50] By contrast, the content of the betrayal is clear. The offer of Judas solves the problem of the leaders of the people, namely how they can, without causing a tumult at the festival, quickly and securely arrest Jesus and hand him over to the prefect. Since Judas appears as the guide for the police of the Sanhedrin and of the high priestly slaves on that Passover night in Gethsemane, he presumably betrays where Jesus—on the Passover night, in which one could not spend the night outside of the city area—was certainly to be found and arrested without causing a stir after the meal.

---

[48] On this, see Hengel 1989c, 47 n. 192; 328 n. 88 (GV = 1976c, 49 n. 3; 334 n. 4).

[49] Cf. Josh 15.25. The byname Ἰσκαριώθ (Mark 3.19; 14.10; Luke 6.16) would correspond to the form *'îš q^eriôt*, which is attested time and again in contemporary Hebrew; see Bill. I: 537–38. On the place, see John 6.71: in א*; Θ; f¹³; Sy^{hmg} and 12.4 in Codex D. This could be the original reading, which was then pushed out by the otherwise common Ἰσκαριώτου. In 6.71 and in other texts (Matt 10.4; Mark 3.19 etc.), Codex D and Itala have Σκαριωθ, a reading that some have interpreted as "Sicarii." On multiple occasions John has specifications of place that sound original. On this, see note 144 in chapter 11.

[50] Luke 22.3; John 13.27: the only time where the word σατανᾶς appears in John; cf. 13.2 and 6.70; only 17.12 calls him "son of perdition": υἱὸς τῆς ἀπωλείας. Second Thessalonians 2.3 gives the same designation to the Antichrist. By contrast, the newly discovered Gospel of Judas, which stems from Sethian Gnosticism and which Irenaeus mentions in *Haer.* 1.31.1, presents him in an entirely positive way. For an English translation of the Coptic text, see Ehrman/Pleše 2011, 389–411; Gathercole 2007, 61–113; Kasser/Meyer/Wurst 2007, 17–46. See also the essays by B. D. Ehrman, G. Wurst, and M. Meyer in Kasser/Meyer/Wurst 2007. A moral defamation was added later. According to John 12.6 he was—as already mentioned—a thief, who dishonestly managed the common moneybag; cf. 13.29. According to Mark 14.11 and Luke 22.5, the high priests promise him money. In Matt 26.15 Judas himself demands: "What will you give me, so that I hand him over to you." They offer him thirty silver coins, which he later attempts to give back in vain and then throws into the temple and hangs himself: Matt 27.3-10. The thirty pieces of silver are derived from Zech 11.13 in a reflection quotation. Acts 1.18-20 features an entirely divergent story about his death. Papias reports in a fantastic way (Frgm. III.2 in Funk/Bihlmeyer 1924, 136–37; Frgm. 6 in Körtner/Leutzsch 1998, 58–61). On the early church Judas tradition, see Bauer 1967b, 173–77, and Terbuyken 2001.

19.3 The Anointing at Bethany

Between the short note about the hierarchs' plans to kill Jesus (14.1) and the resolution of their aporia through Judas' offer to betray him (14.10-11) Mark inserts the story of an invitation of Jesus "in the house of Simon the Leper" in Bethany and recounts his anointing by an unknown woman (14.3-9). In this way he creates a sharp contrast to the murderous intentions of the hierarchs, which are then realized with the help of the betrayer from the most intimate circle of disciples. The otherwise unknown host belongs to the witnesses, who are often named in the ambit of the passion in Mark, such as Bartimaeus, Simon of Cyrene and his two sons, the Galilean women, and Joseph of Arimathea.

The woman breaks an alabaster vessel with costly nard oil over Jesus' head, so that—according to the elaborating portrayal of John, who is dependent on Mark here—"the house was filled with the aroma of the anointing oil" (12.3). The event provokes the indignation of some who are present over such waste. One could have better sold the nard oil for three hundred denarii—about a year's wages for a worker—and given the proceeds given to the poor. Jesus rejects such accusations:

> Leave her alone! . . . She has done a good deed to me. For you always have the poor with you, but you do not always have me.[51] She has anointed my body in advance for burial. Amen, I say to you: Wherever the Gospel is proclaimed in the whole world, what she has done will be told in memory of her.

This scene—which Matt 26.6-13 takes over in somewhat abbreviated form, whereas Luke omits it, because it is related in individual characteristics to his account of the woman who is a great sinner (Luke 7.36-50)—makes a bridge between a historical event and the present of the evangelist ca. forty years later. The unusual specification of name and place already shows that a historical event stands behind it. The story may, like broad parts of the Markan passion tradition, go back to Petrine tradition. As was already the case in Mark 13.10, it presupposes for the time of the evangelist the worldwide Gentile mission, in which the leading disciple also played a significant role. The pericope shows by way of example how in connection with the proclamation of the new message concrete stories of Jesus were

---

[51] Cf. at the beginning of the Gospel in Mark 2.20: "Days will come when the bridegroom is taken away from them." On Jesus' participation at banquets, see Mark 2.15ff. parr.; Luke 7.34 par. In contrast to the Baptist, he was not an ascetic.

told and interpreted in such a way that story and interpretation flowed into each other.

The Amen saying that the evangelist places in the mouth of Jesus—retrospectively—interprets the deed of the woman as anticipating the anointing of his corpse, which was no longer granted to him—the crucified one. The women who want to perform this service for him on Easter morning (Mark 16.1 = Luke 21.1) found the tomb empty. At the same time, the story prepares for the immediately following account of Jesus' Passover with his disciples, who, in the passion story that now begins, behave in such a completely different way than the woman. The orientation to the death of Jesus also stands at the center in this Last Supper.[52]

19.4 The Last Supper as Passover Meal[53]

The question of whether or not the Last Supper was a Passover meal is disputed in scholarship. By contrast, it is clear that Jesus' death took place on a Friday evening before a Sabbath. While the Synoptic tradition clearly identifies the Last Supper as a Passover meal on the night of Nisan 15, John explicitly stresses[54] that the day of the crucifixion of Jesus was already Nisan 14, i.e., the day of preparation for the Passover, so that Jesus died

[52] John 12.1-8 places the story of the anointing in Bethany before the entry into Jerusalem but after the leaders' resolution to kill Jesus on account of the raising of Lazarus (John 11.47-53), after which Jesus withdraws to a city Ephraim (11.54; see note 52 in chapter 10 and note 5 in chapter 11). Six days before the Passover festival he is said to come, despite continued danger to his life, to Bethany, where a meal was organized for him, in which Martha (the sister of Mary, 11.1-2) served the guests (cf. Luke 10.40), while her brother belonged to them (12.2). John identifies the woman, who is anonymous in Mark and Matthew, with Mary, and takes over verbatim motifs from both Mark 14.3-4, 6ff. and Luke 7.38, which show that he knows both accounts, with him intensifying these to some extent (12.3). He puts the criticism of this action in the mouth of Judas, "who was a thief and having charge of the common purse he used to pilfer what was put in" (12.6). Here the Synoptic comparison shows clearly the novelistic embellishing mode of operation of the Fourth Gospel, which usually makes it impossible to infer the historical reality that stands behind his presentation and to bring this into agreement with the Markan account. While the Lukan story of the great woman sinner at the invitation of Jesus by the Pharisee Simon (7.36, 40) could likewise be influenced by the Markan account, it goes back to an independent tradition.

[53] Jeremias 1966c (GV = 1967a); Schürmann 1968a; Gese 1981, 93–140 (GV = 1977, 85–128); Pesch 1978; 1991; Stuhlmacher 1987; 2018, 151–66 (GV = 1992, 131–43); Hofius 1993 (GV = 1988; 1989, 203–40); Brown 1994, 1364–73; Theissen/Merz 1998, 405–39 (GV = 1997, 359–86); Hofius 1998 (= 2000, 276–300); Dunn 2003b, 771–73; Hengel 2004d.

[54] John 18.28; 19.14: παρασκευὴ τοῦ πάσχα; cf. 19.31, 42. The change of date was required by the fact that Mark 15.42 speaks of the day of preparation for the Sabbath; cf. Luke 23.54 and Matt 27.62.

at the same time that the Passover lambs were slaughtered in the temple,
which were then consumed after the onset of night in meal fellowships
of at least ten people. The meal of Jesus in John 13, which introduces the
Farewell Discourses, appears as a festive, nighttime meal, beginning with
a footwashing, which is probably meant to symbolize baptism. Nevertheless, despite individual features which could point to a Passover meal,
it is consciously represented not as a Passover meal. It is typical for the
Fourth Evangelist that he places christological theory over historical reality and displaces the latter. Because Jesus is for John the Passover lamb, he
cannot have celebrated the Jewish Passover meal with his disciples. Paul
already says in 1 Cor 5.7: "Christ, our Passover lamb, has been slaughtered." He presupposes here the knowledge of the Passover customs in the
already predominantly "Gentile Christian" community in Corinth, and yet
probably because the Passover had been celebrated there in a distinctive,
"Christian" way. The Corinthians knew of it that "the night in which Jesus
was handed over" was the night of Passover. By contrast, John connects
the establishment of the Eucharist with the feeding of the five thousand,
which, according to him, took place at the time of Passover in Galilee one
year before the Passover of Jesus' death.[55]

In our view, J. Jeremias, in his fundamental monograph *Die Abendmahlsworte Jesu* (ET = *The Eucharistic Words of Jesus*),[56] convincingly
demonstrated that the Last Supper of Jesus was really a Passover meal.
From the numerous reasons that he adduces for this view, the most important are: (1) that the concern is with a festive meal of Jesus with his disciples during the night in the overcrowded city of Jerusalem at the time
of the festival in a prepared location. Nighttime meals were not otherwise common among the simple people. (2) Furthermore, it was a meal
in which one reclined at table on couches,[57] in other words a real festive
meal, in which (3) prior to the bread a dish[58] was passed around in which
one dipped herbs. (4) Moreover, at the Passover celebration, several cups
with wine, at least four according to the Mishnah, also for the poorest
people,[59] were passed around, and (5) interpretive words were spoken in
relation to the foods, which referred to the saving event of the exodus

---

[55] John 6.4 and the bread discourse in John 6.32-58. On the footwashing in John 13,
see Abramowski 2005. It could point to a special sacramental action of the Johannine
circle, which did not establish itself in the church. This "service" of Jesus picks up on the
saying in Luke 22.27. See note 74 below.

[56] Jeremias 1966c (GV = 1967a); see also Hengel 2004d, 141–54.

[57] Mark 14.15 = Luke 22.12; cf. John 13.23-25; 21.20. This table custom arose under
the influence of Hellenistic civilization.

[58] Fruit with dipping sauce and bitter herbs, even in John 13.26!

[59] Cf. Luke 22.17, 20.

from Egypt. This is said to correspond to Jesus' "words of institution."
Another significant feature was (6) the striking up of the Hallel psalms
at the end,[60] which found their conclusion with Ps 118. Under the influence of the messianically interpreted saying of Ps 118.26: "Blessed be the
one who comes in the name of the Lord" is, there emerged a little later,
in connection with Dan 7.13, the prayer cry of the primitive community
"our Lord, come!" (μαράνα θά), which was called out especially at the
end of the primitive Christian celebrations of the Lord's Supper.[61] When
(7) Jesus, according to the testimony of Paul in 1 Cor 11.24ff., exhorts the
participants in the meal to celebrate it "in memory of me" and in doing
so "to proclaim the death of the Lord," then here the remembrance of the
suffering and death of Jesus has basically taken the place of the recounting
remembrance of the Jewish "gospel," the exodus from Egypt.[62] The fact
that a reference to the Passover is no longer made in the meal words of
Jesus handed down by Paul and Mark is connected to the fact that the sacrificial death and resurrection of Jesus replaced the Passover sacrifice and
the exodus event, i.e., the fact that the definitive, concluding saving event
displaced the Old Testament-Jewish type. The fact that the exodus could
also continue to play a role is shown by the Passover homily of Melito of
Sardis in the second half of the second century. Moreover, at a relatively
early point the Lord's Supper was celebrated on a weekly basis (or even
more frequently), whereas the Passover meal was celebrated only once
per year. For this reason, there was no longer room within the framework
of the words of institutions, which was what especially mattered, for a
direct reference to the Passover tradition. Finally, (8) it was the festival
night—in which all Jerusalem reverberated, of which it was said that its
sound "shattered the roofs" and in which the revelers, made weary by
extraordinary wine consumption, fell asleep at the end[63]—on which Jesus
could be arrested without risk, if one only knew where he was staying
after the Passover meal.[64] A violent attack by the festival pilgrims from

---

[60] With 14.26: καὶ ὑμνήσαντες ἐξῆλθον = Matt 26.30. The conspicuous Markan
note is grounded in a sensible way only by the Passover meal. By contrast, Luke 22.24-
38 features a small farewell discourse. The Synoptic accounts of the Passover meal are
important Jewish sources for the celebration of the meal before the rabbinic tradition in the
Mishnah and Tosefta of the tractate Pesaḥim.

[61] First Corinthians 16.22; Did 10.6; cf. Rev 22.20 and 1 Cor 11.26: ἄχρι οὗ ἔλθῃ. On
this, see Hengel 2004a, 161–71.

[62] On this, cf. the exhortation to remember in Exod 12.14: καὶ ἔσται ἡ ἡμέρα ὑμῖν
αὕτη μνημόσυνον, and 13.3.

[63] Hengel 2004d, 151. Cf. m. Pesaḥ. 10.8; y. Pesaḥ. 10.8, 37d: it is sometimes assumed
that all fell asleep. In that case, no one would continue to eat.

[64] Mark correspondingly recounts the sleeping of the disciples in Gethsemane: 14.37,
40-41.

the land, for example from Galilee, was precisely not to be feared on this night. They were occupied with other things. On the day of preparation for the Passover festival, where the cleansing of the house from leaven already began during the night before and the city was full of unrest and tense expectation, the situation looked very different.

Jesus thus held the Passover meal among the circle of the twelve in his last night. The betrayer still participated in the meal and left the circle of disciples after it—in John, while the meal was still going on.[65] The words of institution: "this is my body" and the word of the blood of the covenant, whose original form can no longer be clearly reconstructed since it is different in Mark 14.24[66] and 1 Cor 11.25,[67] were probably spoken as interpretive words in relation to the bread and the cup, the bread word at the blessing of the bread before the actual main meal and the cup word perhaps over the third cup after the meal.[68] We are dealing with a "messianic" parabolic action of Jesus, with which he gives the fruit of his impending sacrificial death, the new covenant with the Father in heaven, to the disciples and, beyond them, to all.[69] We have already encountered such "messianic parabolic actions" of Jesus on multiple occasions. Apparently, Jesus' understanding of his own way into suffering concentrated on this point of self-sacrifice. The connection to the atoning self-giving of the servant of God in Isa 53.12 probably played the decisive role here. It was joined by the reference to the covenant sacrifice of Moses in Exod 24, which was followed by the vision of God and the eating and drinking of the elders of Israel before God.[70] Presumably Jesus wanted, through the sacrifice of

[65] John 13.21-30. The realistic-symbolic ἦν δὲ νύξ has a counterpart in the phrase "the night in which (Jesus) was handed over" in 1 Cor 11.23.

[66] Mark 14.24: τοῦτό ἐστιν τὸ αἷμά μου τῆς διαθήκης τὸ ἐκχυννόμενον ὑπὲρ πολλῶν: "This is my blood of the covenant, which is poured out for many."

[67] First Corinthians 11.25: τοῦτο τὸ ποτήριον ἡ καινὴ διαθήκη ἐστὶν ἐν τῷ ἐμῷ αἵματι: "This cup is the new covenant through my blood." See also 1 Cor 10.16: "The cup of blessing (τὸ ποτήριον τῆς εὐλογίας), to which we speak the blessing, is it not fellowship with the blood of Christ (οὐχὶ κοινωνία ἐστὶν τοῦ αἵματος τοῦ Χριστοῦ)?" Cf. Ps 116.13: "The cup of salvation."

[68] Cf. 1 Cor 11.25: μετὰ τὸ δειπνῆσαι.

[69] Mark 14.24: ὑπὲρ πολλῶν. Mark 10.45: λύτρον ἀντὶ πολλῶν, cf. 1 Tim 2.6: ὁ δοὺς ἑαυτὸν ἀντίλυτρον ὑπὲρ πάντων. The saying belongs in the context of the Last Supper; cf. Luke 22.27c. Luke 22.19-20, which combines the Pauline words of institution with the Markan account and his own tradition, adds to the bread saying (in a manner similar to Paul in 1 Cor 11.24) a ὑπὲρ ὑμῶν διδόμενον and replaces the inclusive τὸ ἐκχυννόμενον ὑπὲρ πολλῶν (cf. Isa 53.12) of Mark with a τὸ ὑπὲρ ὑμῶν ἐκχυννόμενον. In Luke Jesus' giving of himself is related to the community.

[70] Exodus 24.8: "After this Moses took the blood and sprinkled it on the people and said: This is the blood of the covenant, which YHWH has made with you." On the vision of God and on the eating and drinking, see Exod 24.10-11.

his own life understood as atonement, to break through the power of sin and the hardening in Israel, which hindered the advent of the kingdom of God. Mark follows the words of institution with an Amen saying, which expresses Jesus' eschatological assurance of the consummation. He will no longer drink from the fruit of the vine "until I drink it anew in the kingdom of God."[71] Here we strike upon historical bedrock. As a community formation this saying is meaningless. It also makes clear the originally eschatological orientation of the Lord's Supper. The Passover meal of Jesus and the self-giving of the Messiah as servant of God expressed in it point to the coming kingdom of God and the revelation of the Son of Man that are expected to come soon. In this saying Jesus appears as the master of table and host in the future kingdom. This nighttime meal is at the same time a forward look to the expected eschatological meal.[72] This parabolic action may have been followed by table conversations, which John expands and completely reconfigures.[73] Luke 22.24ff. also recounts, among other things, such a conversation about the service of Jesus and of the disciples:

> But a dispute arose among them as to which of them was the greatest. But he said to them: The kings of the Gentiles rule over them, and those who exercise power let themselves be called benefactors. But not so you, but let the one who is greater among you become as the smaller and the leader as a serving slave. . . . I am in your midst as a serving slave.[74]

The ransom saying in Mark 10.45 stands in a similar context, though there admittedly before the entry into Jerusalem as the conclusion to the public teaching of Jesus:

> The Son of Man did not come to be served but to serve and to give his life as a ransom for many.

---

[71] Mark 14.25. Here an allusion is also made to Exod 24.11. In Luke 22.15-18 the motif of the oath of renunciation is sounded in vv. 15-16 in relation to the Passover meal. On this, see Schwemer 2004, 201 n. 59; 213–14. On Jesus' future expectation, see section 13.2.

[72] On the eschatological meal with respect to Jesus, see section 17.4.1 with note 163.

[73] Luke 22.23-38; John 13-17. Cf. also the eschatological ἄχρι οὗ ἔλθῃ in 1 Cor 11.26, and, further, Rev 19.9 and Luke 14.15.

[74] Luke 22.27: ἐγὼ δὲ ἐν μέσῳ ὑμῶν εἰμι ὡς ὁ διακονῶν. It is a typically Lukan reserved parallel to Mark 10.45. For the context of the dispute of the disciples and Jesus' answer, see Mark 10.41ff. = Matt 20.24ff. John, who knows Luke, expresses this service through the ὑπόδειγμα (13.15) of the footwashing. In Luke too it may hint at the "service of the servant of God" and thus the atoning death of Jesus. On this, see Mittmann-Richert 2008. See further the doubling of the ὑπὲρ ὑμῶν in 22.19-20; cf. note 69 above and Rom 15.8.

It is also preceded there by a dispute among the disciples over rank. Jesus could have expressed himself in this way at the Last Supper. It supports the authenticity of this saying that it points back to an Aramaic foundation.[75] This saying about the service of Jesus through his atoning death could be regarded as the legacy of Jesus to his disciples.

In John, by contrast, the footwashing before the meal points first, through the motif of cleansing (13.8-11), indirectly to baptism and, second, to the service of the disciples among one another (13.14-17). After the designation of the betrayer, with the motif of the new commandment of love (13.34), he resumes this motif and develops from there the centerpiece of his theology in the following Farewell Discourses. Here Jesus reveals himself as the preexistent Son of the Father who through voluntary atoning suffering goes to meet his glorification before those who belong to him and promises to them the sending of the Spirit-Paraclete, who will open up to them in the first place the right understanding of his message. It is precisely from this that the Fourth Evangelist gains his far-reaching freedom vis-à-vis the historical reality.[76]

---

[75] Cf. the Hellenized version in 1 Tim 2.6; see note 69 above. On the whole, see in detail Stuhlmacher 2018, 139ff., 146–66 (GV = 1992, 120ff., 129–43).

[76] Frey 1997–2000, III: 104–5. See now also Frey 2018a; 2018b.

20

Gethsemane, Arrest, and Interrogation of Jesus

20.1 Gethsemane and Arrest[1]

After the singing of the Hallel psalms (Mark 14.26), which concludes the Passover meal, Jesus leaves Jerusalem with his disciples, crosses the Kidron Valley in the east of the city below the temple,[2] and seeks out a garden with the name Gethsemane, which was located at the foot of the Mount of Olives.[3] Mark recounts a prayer struggle, in which Jesus finds his most intimate disciples, Peter, James, and John[4] — whom he, separate from the others, took with him — sleeping three times. They leave Jesus alone in his trial. It is no accident that Mark here, in the only prayer that he hands down, has the intimate address to God "*'Abbā'*" appear in his mouth.[5] He knows how to consciously place his emphases. According to Mark, for Jesus the way into suffering was indeed not a matter of course;

---

[1] Mark 14.32-52 = Luke 22.39-53 = Matt 26.36-56; John 18.1-12. Cf. Feldmeier 1987; Brown 1994, I: 246–52.

[2] John 18.1 with local knowledge ἐξῆλθεν . . . πέραν τοῦ χειμάρρου τοῦ Κεδρὼν ὅπου ἦν κῆπος, cf. 2 Sam 15.23; 1 Kgs 15.13 and elsewhere (LXX).

[3] Mark 14.32: Γεθσημανι (cf. Matt 26.36), "oil press" = *gat šᵉmînî* (or "oil valley," *gê' šᵉmînî*); see Bauer/Aland/Aland 1988, 307. According to Luke 22.39 Jesus goes, according to his custom, to the Mount of Olives, followed by his disciples. He thus replaces an unusual Aramaic designation with a place specification that is common to him. Instead of Golgotha, in 23.33 he writes Κρανίον "skull."

[4] On this group of three, see Mark 5.37 parr.; 9.2 parr. Cf. also 3.16-17 and 13.3, supplemented by Andrew, the brother of Simon Peter; see section 11.6 with note 126.

[5] Mark 14.36. According to 14.39 he repeats the prayer: προσηύξατο τὸν αὐτὸν λόγον. Cf. Rom 8.15 and Gal 4.6; see the end of section 13.2 and Hengel 2004a. Cf. the closeness to the third petition of the Lord's prayer: Mark 14.36: οὐ τί ἐγὼ θέλω ἀλλὰ τί σύ. Matt 6.10b: γενηθήτω τὸ θέλημά σου. This prayer form is older than the First Gospel; see also Luke 22.42: μὴ τὸ θέλημά μου ἀλλὰ τὸ σὸν γινέσθω. On Mark 15.34 = Ps 22.2, see note 82 in chapter 21. Here, the question is whether the Aramaic cry of Jesus is to be understood as a prayer.

he too had to fight through to it. After all, the possibility of fleeing in the night would have still been open to him. He does not use this possibility, but he accepts the way assigned to him by the Father. The picture of the troubled Jesus in Gethsemane is certainly not a later invention of the community, but goes back to painful recollection, in our view, again by Peter himself, who later did not conceal his and the disciples' failure. John omitted the whole scene because of its offensiveness. It fits neither in his Christology, according to which Jesus in a completely free decision goes into death sovereignly and directly, nor in his picture of Jesus' relationship to his disciples.[6] In a special tradition of the Lukan text, which is already handed down in Justin but is missing from many early manuscripts, Jesus' "prayer struggle" (ἐν ἀγωνίᾳ) is vividly elaborated.[7] The struggle of Jesus contradicts all later Christian martyr ideology and is bitterly mocked by Celsus. Julian the Apostate finds the whole scene to be "pitiful" (ἄθλιος).[8] Heb 5.7-8 knows the same tradition. No ancient hero behaves in this way. Here Mark has connected concrete memory of a real event and theological interpretation in an artful way.

The betrayer led the police of the Sanhedrin or the temple guard, reinforced by slaves from the high priestly families, especially of Annas and Caiaphas, to the place where Jesus was spending the night. A larger group of people is in view. It reckons with resistance and is armed.[9] The disciple of Jesus had agreed on a sign,[10] so that his group could identify with certainty and arrest the searched for person in the darkness. They were interested only in him. Thus, he greets the master with the address "Rabbi" and a kiss, "the one whom I will kiss, seize him and lead him away securely,"[11] and no one else is arrested—which is, however,

[6] A weak intimation of his being troubled is preserved only in John 12.27. Cf. also John 10.11, 17-18; 15.13.

[7] Luke 22.43-44: An "angel from heaven strengthens him," and in his prayer struggle "his sweat falls like drops of blood onto the earth"; on this, see Metzger 1975, 177. On the expanded text, see Justin, *Dial.* 103.8, ℵ D L Θ Ψ f¹ 𝔐 lat syᶜ and others. Bauer 1967b, 171, regards a deletion due to its offensiveness as more likely: "How does Jesus look if he needs strengthening by an angel!" "The orthodox Christians thus felt compelled to get rid of the pericope, which was suited for causing harm." See also Tuckett 2002. The scene is said to correspond to "Luke's literary strategy of presenting Jesus and Paul in similar ways" (144).

[8] Origen, *Cels.* 2.9–10, 24, 70; on this, see Cook 2000, 49–50, 297–98; on Julian, see p. 297 n. 130.

[9] Mark 14.43: ὄχλος μετὰ μαχαιρῶν καὶ ξύλων. Cf. V. 48: "as against a robber you have come out against me . . ." = Matt 26.47, 55. See also the slave of the high priest, Mark 14.47 parr.

[10] Mark 14.44: σύσσημον; on this, see Bauer/Aland/Aland 1988, 1585; Matt 26.48: σημεῖον.

[11] Mark 14.44-45 = Matt 26.48-49; cf. Luke 22.48.

indeed an pointer to the historicity of the scene. John also omits this. It is too offensive for him. Judas, who is possessed by the devil, "the son of perdition,"[12] is no longer permitted to kiss the master. John also deletes the flight of the disciples.[13] Jesus, who according to Mark 14.42 and John 18.4 went to meet the captors, made it easy for them. He lets himself be arrested without resistance. One person from the group of disciples, surprised, attempts to resist, and cuts off the ear of a high priestly slave with his short sword.[14] The legend embellished this. In John 18.10, it is Peter who struck a blow. John also knows the name of the slave, Malchus.[15] In Luke 22.49ff., the persons accompanying Jesus (οἱ περὶ αὐτόν) still ask: "Lord, should we strike with the sword?" One of them does and strikes the right ear of the slave, after which Jesus heals the injured man. Matt 26.52[16] uses the incident for an admonishing saying of Jesus: "put the sword in its place, for all who reach for the sword will die by the sword." In order that "the Scripture may be fulfilled," "this had to happen in this way." Therefore, Jesus deliberately does not make use of divine help.[17] The sword-strike episode especially stimulated the narrative and interpretive zeal of the evangelist. This tendency to novelistic and paraenetic expansion can be observed in the whole passion story from Luke to the Gospel of Peter.[18] Here too the simple Markan account shows itself to be the most reliable.

This applies to another point: contrary to John's portrayal, there were no Roman troops at the arrest. In addition to the "slaves of the high priests and Pharisees," John also speaks of a cohort[19] under the command of a tri-

---

[12] John 17.12; on this, see note 50 in chapter 19.

[13] Mark 14.50 is concise and precise: καὶ ἀφέντες αὐτὸν ἔφυγον πάντες. See, by contrast, Jesus' advocacy for them in John 18.8 as the fulfillment of earlier promises.

[14] Mark 14.47, cf. Luke 22.49-51; Matt 26.51-54; John 18.10-11. On the "short sword" (μάχαιρα), see Plümacher 1991 (GV = 1981); cf. also the enigmatic eschatological saying about the swords in Luke 22.36, 38.

[15] The name occurs especially among Arabians and Nabataeans; see Ilan 2002, 390–91. The concern could be with a non-Jewish slave. Perhaps this special detail rests on tradition after all.

[16] Cf. Rev 13.10. The saying is directed against Jewish Zealotism, which lived on after 70 CE and led to the Bar Kokhba revolt in 132 CE. See also John 18.36.

[17] Matt 26.53-54. The saying about the "more than twelve legions of angels," which the Father could send at his request, also fends off the accusation of the complete power-lessness of the Son of God. On this, see Celsus' informant in Cook 2000, 149–50, and the mocking scene discussed at the end of section 21.1; cf. Ps 91.11-12 and the quotation of this verse in the temptation story (Matt 4.6 = Luke 4.10-11); on this, see also John 18.36b.

[18] On this, see Bauer 1967b, 169–243.

[19] John 18.3, 12: σπεῖρα, in the case of auxiliary cohorts of ca. six hundred men. They come with "lanterns, torches, and weapons."

bune.[20] In the case of intervention by Roman soldiers there would certainly
have been bloodshed: for this we have enough examples in Josephus. The
presentation of the Fourth Gospel increases the opponents of Jesus according to the motto "the more enemies, the more honor" in a dramatic scene.[21]
Due to Jesus' self-identification "I am he," the whole army draws back
and falls to the ground. Only after a second exhortation and the rebuke
of Peter do they dare to arrest Jesus and bind him. Thus, the presentation
of John has the divine dignity of Jesus become apparent already at the
arrest—presumably also in response to a pagan defamation in the style of
Celsus. In reality the quick arrest of Jesus by the Jewish police authorities
in the Passover night was not a great problem. The disciples flee without
offering further resistance: "and all left him and fled."[22] Only Peter constitutes an exception and follows "from a distance" into the inner courtyard
of the high priestly palace and waits with the servants, who have gathered
around the fire to see how things develop. This whole portrayal is based
on Petrine tradition. Ever since the church fathers, the strange young man
in Mark 14.51-52 (special material), who leaves behind his undergarment
and flees naked, has presented exegetes with an insoluble riddle. We must
assume that Mark presupposes that his hearers and readers still understood
the event, indeed, he must have had "a personal interest" in this event or in
this person.[23] Of all the hypotheses, a hidden reference to the evangelist or

---

[20] John 18.12: χιλίαρχος. The occupying Roman troops in Judaea consisted at the
core only of five auxiliary cohorts of ca. six hundred men each. It had the character of a
police troop rather than a powerful garrison. See section 3.1.3 with note 214. Acts 21.31ff.;
22.24ff.; 23.10-30 portrays in detail the behavior of the χιλίαρχος and commander in the
fortress Antonia, Claudius Lysias, who saves the life of Paul.

[21] John 18.2-12.

[22] Mark 14.50. John omits the flight. Instead Jesus stands protectively before the disciples in 18.8: "if you seek me, let these go."

[23] Wohlenberg 1910, 360; with reference to the hypotheses of the fathers, see also
Zahn 1907, 217, which references the material parallel in Eusebius, *Hist. eccl.* 6.40.7. See
further Lagrange 1966, 367–68: "De toute façon elle provient d'une tradition personelle
de Marc." Similarly, Wellhausen 1909, 122: "The teller must have been in the know."
Lohmeyer 1963, 324: This "meaningless" scene is meant "to call to mind an eyewitness
of the arrest of Jesus," and this only makes sense if one still knew who he was. To be sure,
Brown 1994, I: 294–304, rejects with the greatest sharpness every attempt at identification
"with a real person" as "imaginative flights of fancy" (299), but interpretations of him as "a
symbolic figure" (299ff.) or his own allegorical-edifying proposal are even more 'fanciful.'
The reference to Amos 2.16 (11) is just as little helpful as the relation to the—in our view,
forged—Secret Gospel of Mark, in which the forger shows a very special "personal interest" precisely in this scene (295). How should the first hearers have read such eccentricities
out of the text? Bauckham 2017, 197–200, regards the identification as "redundant," since
Papias emphasizes that the author of the Second Gospel was not a personal disciple and
hearer of Jesus.

to an anonymous eyewitness, who was still known to the evangelist, still appears most plausible.[24]

In the case of an intervention of the Roman cohort, it would hardly have been comprehensible why Jesus was not immediately led to the praetorium of the prefect, but first taken to the high priestly palace,[25] which was presumably located on the eastern descent of the western hill above the Tyropoeon Valley facing the temple. This means, however, that the arrest of Jesus was not initiated by the Roman authorities but by the Jewish leaders and took place with the help of the temple police. What mattered to the hierarchs was to arrest Jesus alone and to avoid any further shedding of blood, for this would have only made them hated in the eyes of many festival pilgrims. The closest parallel is the prophet of doom Jesus son of Ananias. He too was first arrested by the Jewish authorities and punished with beatings and was brought before the procurator Albinus only when the members of the Sanhedrin had accomplished nothing.[26]

20.2 Jesus' Hearing before the Sanhedrin

20.2.1 The Clan of Annas and the Jewish Capital Punishment Jurisdiction[27]

After the transformation of Judaea into a Roman province until King Agrippa I took power, i.e., 6–41 CE, the high priestly office was—with the agreement of the respective prefect, of course—with two very brief exceptions in the hands of the family of Annas. Annas, son of Sethi, the family head, was high priest between 6 and 15 CE. Josephus stresses that his five sons also held the high priestly office,[28] which was possible only through the favor of the ruling power. Also after his time of office, he was

---

[24] This view is often advocated in the older exegesis. See B. Weiss 1901, 222–23; Zahn 1907, 248–50; V. Taylor 1966, 561–62. Bauckham 2017, 197–201, hypothesizes an eyewitness whom the evangelist does not name out of consideration.

[25] Mark 14.54: ἡ αὐλὴ τοῦ ἀρχιερέως; John 18.13: πρὸς Ἄνναν πρῶτον, v. 24: πρὸς Καϊάφαν τὸν ἀρχιερέα.

[26] Josephus, *J.W.* 6.300–309; see section 3.1.7 with note 433 and section 20.2.2 with note 50.

[27] Jeremias 1969a, 382 index, s.v. "high priest," and 381 index, s.v. "Caiaphas" (GV = 1969b, 421 index, s.v. "Hohepriester," and 422 index, s.v. "Kaiaphas"); Sherwin-White 1963, ch. 1–2; Schürer 1973–1987, I: 368–69; II: 199ff., 218ff.; Blinzler 1969, 129ff., 216–44; Betz 1982, 568ff.; Brown 1994; Theissen/Merz 1998, 455–65 (GV = 1997, 399–407); Hengel 1999b, 322–44.

[28] Josephus, *Ant.* 20.197–198. See the list of high priests in Schürer 1973–1987, II: 229–32, with Caiaphas under nr. 14. Twenty-six names are listed there between Herod (40–4 BCE) and 65 CE.

the *éminence grise* who pulled the strings in the background. His son-in-law[29] Joseph Caiaphas had the longest time in office by far, between 18 and 37 CE. He must have had a very good relationship with Pilate, since he was in office during the entire rule (26–36 CE) of the prefect. The family of Annas thus controlled what happened in the temple, indeed in Jerusalem. Through the trade of sacrificial animals and the changing of money they received a lot of revenue, which they could use, in turn, to secure their hegemony. The issuance of the high priestly vestments, which were kept by the Romans in the fortress of Antonia,[30] presumably had to be obtained from the prefects each year with new payments. In total Josephus mentions only seven high priests between 6 and 41 CE, five of whom come from the clan of Annas. Later the high priest changed more rapidly. Altogether we know the names of eighteen high priests during the time of the prefects or procurators between 6 and 70 CE, of whom seven came from the family of Annas.

It is very likely that the action against Jesus proceeded from the officiating high priest and his father-in-law. In John 11.49-50 the decisive word against Jesus is spoken by Caiaphas himself.[31] In the Sanhedrin, the Pharisees, represented by a number of scribes, were only a minority, but they too would have predominantly been opponents of the Galilean messianic pretender Jesus and his message. The criminal law that was in force in the Sanhedrin was not yet the pharisaic-rabbinic, as it finds expression after 200 CE in the tractate Sanhedrin of the Mishnah, but the priestly Sadducean, concerning which Josephus emphasizes that it was stricter than the Pharisaic.[32] The reason for this was that the judicial decisions of the Sadducees were made according to the letter of the Torah, and they rejected the oral halakah of the Pharisees, which alleviated the criminal law. We do not know any details about the Sadducean criminal law. The often repeated objection that in cases involving the death penalty, the Sanhedrin, according to the Mishnah tractate Sanhedrin, was not permitted to have nightly sessions, is thus just as invalid as the view that the confession of Jesus in Mark 14.62 does not constitute blasphemy, with the rationale that, according to later Pharisaic opinion, only the pronouncement of the forbidden name of God YHWH, i.e., the tetragrammaton, may be

---

[29] We learn this fact only through John 18.13. This also explains why he is mentioned together with Annas, e.g., in Luke 3.2 (cf. Acts 4.6). On his person, see Hengel 1999b, 322–34. See also Horbury 1994a.

[30] cf. Josephus, *Ant.* 18.90, 95; 20.12.

[31] On this, see section 19.2 with note 42.

[32] Josephus, *Ant.* 20.199.

prosecuted as blasephemy with death.[33] After the excesses of the Jewish War in 66–70 CE and especially of the Bar Kokhba revolt in 132–136 CE, the rabbinic teachers endeavored to limit the possibility of applying the death penalty, with their right to capital punishment being largely academically abstract, especially since the governor had the last word. Since we do not know the more severe Sadducean criminal law, we can say nothing further about the possibility or impossibility and the legality of an assembly of the council in the second half of the Passover night.

After the transformation of Judaea into a Roman province in 6 CE, a Roman prefect[34] from the equestrian class replaced the Jewish king or ethnarch, i.e., Herod and his son Archelaus. This equestrian prefect usually had to manage unruly peripheral provinces. They usually came from the military track and did not stem from the Senate nobility. Their main task was to maintain Roman rule in the province with military-police measures. The right to sentence someone to death and to carry it out, which the king previously held, now passed to the prefects. Regarding such restrictions of the local right to capital punishment we possess some reports from the Greek cities of Cyrenaica at the time of Augustus.[35] The local courts continued to be responsible for less severe cases. The prefect,[36] as the highest Roman official, could of course take cases for himself as he wished. In the proceedings against Paul, who was accused of defiling the temple, the procurators Felix and Festus were forced to make a decision since Paul was said to be a Roman citizen. It remains controversial whether the Sanhedrin in Jerusalem, as the highest judicial court, possessed the right to sentence people to death, which the prefect would then have to confirm before the sentence was carried out, or whether from the outset all capital cases had to be transferred to the prefect and with regard to a crime worthy

---

[33] See Bill. I: 1008ff.; Blinzler 1969, 216–29; Bock 1998; according to Josephus, *Ag. Ap.* 2.194, the abuse of the high priest represented a form of blasphemy, which had to be punished with death; see Schwemer 2001c, 150 n. 82; see note 57 below.

[34] This was the official title according to the Pilate inscription from Caesarea (see note 94 in chapter 3) in analogy to the equestrian *praefectus* of Egypt, who was also appointed by the emperor. The title was *procurator* only from the time of Claudius, who sent freedmen to Judaea for the first time. We therefore find this designation in Tacitus. Cf. *Ann.* 15.44.3 (incorrectly with regard to Pilate) and 12.54.4 (rightly for Felix and Cumanus). Luke and Matthew mostly give Pilate, Felix, and Festus the title ἡγεμών: Luke 20.20; cf. 3.1: ἡγεμονεύοντος Ποντίου Πιλάτου τῆς Ἰουδαίας, Matt 27.2 and elsewhere; Acts 23.24; 24.1 and elsewhere. For the provincial governor with senatorial rank Luke otherwise has ἀνθύπατος: Acts 13.7-8; 18.12; cf., however, 1 Pet 2.14 and Luke 2.2.

[35] Sherwin-White 1963, 2, 5, 15–17 and elsewhere; see 199 index; text of the edicts 7/6 BCE and 4 CE in Ehrenberg/Jones 1949, 139–43 nr. 311.

[36] Cf. Acts 23.33ff.; 24.1–27.32. On this, see further section 21.1.1.

of death only accusations before him could be made. Presumably the latter was the case.

John 18.12ff. probably contains a correction of the Markan account in 14.53ff. that must be taken seriously. According to John, Jesus, after his arrest, was not immediately led before the Sanhedrin, but first (πρὸς Ἄνναν πρῶτον) taken to a nightly hearing before the especially influential Annas. This probably bridged the period of time that was needed to inform the members of the council of Jesus' arrest and gather them, as far as they were within reach and could be addressed at all during the Passover night. Accordingly, in John the denial of Peter occurs in the palace of Annas (18.15-18, 25-27). From the hearing he recounts only a dramatic episode. The high priest asks Jesus about his disciples and his teaching. Jesus answers that he has publicly "taught in synagogue and in the temple where all the Jews come together" (John 18.20; see also Mark 14.49); he can therefore ask the hearers. Due to this frank answer one of the attendants of the court strikes Jesus in the face: "Do you thus answer the high priest?" Jesus defends himself: "If I have spoken wrongly, bear witness about the wrong, but if I have spoken rightly, why do you strike me?" (18.19-23). With this realistic scene John expresses the sovereignty of Jesus vis-à-vis the high priest. At the same time, he replaces the disgraceful mocking scene of the Synoptics. The Johannine Jesus forfeits nothing of his majesty in it.

By contrast, Mark reports plerophorically that *all* the high priests, elders, and scribes came together and "the high priests and the whole Sanhedrin were seeking testimony against Jesus in order to kill him."[37] In reality, we do not know anything in detail about the extent and exact composition of the council in the Passover night.[38] It was presumably ruled predominantly by the partisans of Annas and Caiaphas. The distinction between a mere hearing and a formal court session is also difficult due to the partly divergent accounts of the Gospels. After all, even if no real sentence of death was issued,[39] for them to hand him over to the prefect the resolution of a council concerning the points of accusation was

---

[37] Mark 14.53, 55.

[38] On this, cf. Josephus, *Ant.* 20.200: After the death of Festus, while the new procurator Albinus travels, Annas II calls together a "juridical council" (καθίζει συνέδριον) in order to have James, the brother of the Lord, and other Jewish Christians condemned to death through stoning. Luke 22.66 (cf. Acts 22.5) speaks of the πρεσβυτέριον and uses there συνέδριον in the sense of "advisory council." John has the key word only in 11.47 in the same sense as Luke and Josephus.

[39] Thus Luke 22.66–23.1 and John 18.19-24, 28. In Mark there is also no talk of a clear legally executed sentence of death. Mark 14.64 reproduces in the first instance only a "general opinion": τί ὑμῖν φαίνεται. The unanimous judgment: ἔνοχον εἶναι θανάτου could be translated: "He has merited death." See Schwemer 2001c, 151ff.

nevertheless necessary in order to give this weight. One had to be in agreement about which crime Jesus could be charged with before the prefect. The grounded accusation that Jesus was a messianic pretender and agitator practically amounted to a sentence of death.

This concluding resolution presumably occurred after the hearing before Annas not too long before the break of day before Caiaphas. Mark probably joins together two events, which John rightly separates, namely hearing and resolution, into one, and upgrades the council to "the whole Sanhedrin." He does not mention the name of the high priest who conducted the proceedings. Caiaphas occurs first in Matthew and John. In Luke he is also, together with Annas, not unknown.[40] During the hearing[41] before Annas, the council presumably came together before Caiaphas. While John only recounts that Jesus, after the interrogation by Annas, was led to Caiaphas and then from there to Pilate in the Praetorium,[42] Mark and Matthew provide a more detailed portrayal of the proceedings before the officiating high priest, whereas Luke, in his shorter account, omits the role of the high priest entirely and has Jesus be confronted in the early morning directly with the members of the council of the "high priests and scribes." Here he presumably follows in his passion story a source of his own in addition to Mark.[43] In John one has the impression that he presupposes the Markan account and at the same time seeks to correct or supplement it. Luke also consciously deviates from the Markan account, while Matthew, supplemented by legendary expansions, follows it faithfully.

20.2.2 The Account of the Proceedings

The purpose of the proceeding before the Sanhedrin was to find points of accusation against Jesus, which would justify handing him over to Pilate in connection with a charge that was worthy of death—and this meant at

---

[40] Matt 26.57; John 18.24; Luke 3.2 and Acts 4.6 mention the two names of Annas and Caiaphas next to each other. Otherwise, Luke usually speaks in the plural of ἀρχιερεῖς. The singular appears only in Luke 22.50, 54: the "house of the high priest."

[41] According to Mark and Matthew, the proceedings drag on into the night. According to Luke 22.66, the "assembly of the elders" occurs only at the break of day. He probably presupposes here the usual ancient legal convention of the court session in the early morning.

[42] John 18.24, 28.

[43] In Luke 22.54 Jesus is led into "the house of the high priest," where Peter denies him. According to 22.66-71, the "council of elders of the people" (τὸ πρεσβυτέριον τοῦ λαοῦ) assembles at daybreak, and they lead him into their "council" (εἰς τὸ συνέδριον αὐτῶν) and collectively ask Jesus the Messiah question. In response to Jesus' Messiah confession, they again react together. They do not need any other witness. What Jesus himself says is sufficient to accuse him before Pilate.

the same time a political one. The messianic pretender from Galilee who appeared dangerous—and he alone—had to be rendered harmless. This resoluteness is understandable. They regarded him as a danger for their own dominant position, for the temple, and for the holy city, indeed for the whole Jewish population of the province of Judaea.[44]

Mark emphasizes two themes here. First, he highlights the saying against the temple:[45] "I will tear down this temple, which is made with hands, and in three days build another, which is not made with hands." It is spoken by witnesses who for the evangelist are false witnesses, since their witness does not agree in detail. The witnesses had, as often in ancient law, the role of the accuser. This feature of the dissonance in the questioning of witnesses could in particular—against the tendency of Mark, who speaks of false witnesses—be a pointer to the fact that there was an attempt in a relatively fair procedure to get to the bottom of the truth. The questioning of witnesses had to be made separately, and the stipulations about this were, at least according to rabbinic law, strict.[46] According to John 2.19, Jesus spoke such a temple saying in connection with the cleansing of the temple. One should probably interpret it originally as a messianic polemical saying: the dawning of the kingdom of God signifies the end of the continually misused temple in Jerusalem and its cult.[47] The Johannine version formulates the saying as an imperative: "Tear down this temple and in three days I will raise it up" and interprets this in a post-Easter manner as a reference to Jesus' death and resurrection. It can hardly be doubted that Jesus spoke a comparably critical saying about the temple. It also plays a role in the proceedings against Stephen, where Luke introduces it. Stephen is to have said: "Jesus the Nazarene will destroy this place."[48] The later community probably regarded the death of Jesus in Mark 15.37 as the sign of the fulfillment of this threat saying, expressed through the tearing of the curtain in 15.38; this means that the Holy of Holies has opened itself. Through Jesus' death the temple and its sacrificial cult have become obsolete. The Holy of Holies as the place of the presence of God is

---

[44] John 11.47-50; cf. 19.12; Mark 12.13ff.; Luke 23.2.

[45] Mark 14.58.

[46] On this, see Bill. I: 1001–3: "if the two witnesses contradict themselves . . . then their witness was invalid." See also Susanna and the false accusation of the two elders, which is unmasked by Daniel (Dan 13.51ff.); see further the two early Pharisaic teachers Yehuda b. Tabai and Simeon b. Shetach on the impartiality in the administration of justice and the thoroughness of the (separated) hearing of witnesses in m. ʾAbot 1.8–9.

[47] Cf. already Mark 11.17 as well as 13.1-2. On this, cf. Ådna 2000, 381–87; see further 482 index on Mark 11.17. See the end of section 18.3.

[48] Acts 6.14. By contrast, Luke omits this whole temple question in the account of the proceedings and brings it in later as a—false—accusation in relation to Stephen. In his love for the temple he regards such a saying in the mouth of Jesus to be inappropriate.

profaned and no longer exists. The crucified and risen one mediates access to God and his heavenly sanctuary and thus to eschatological salvation.[49]

Apparently, however, this saying about the temple and Jerusalem was just as inadequate for a handing over and accusation before Pilate as was the case later with the ecstatic prophecy of Jesus, son of Ananias, against the temple and Jerusalem, who for this very thing was, after all, not condemned to death but rather flogged and set free again by the procurator.[50] As O. Betz has shown,[51] behind the temple saying probably stands the messianically interpreted Nathan prophecy in 2 Sam 7.13-14, where it is said of David's and God's son, i.e., according to Jewish exegesis, of the Messiah: "He will build a house for my name, and I will establish the throne of his kingdom forever. I will be to him a father, and he will be to me a son." This means, however, that in this hearing the concern is ultimately with the messiahship of Jesus. The "new temple" embodies the perfect presence of God and fellowship with God mediated through the Messiah in the eschatological "true Israel."

The second theme which Mark emphasizes is that it is only consistent that the high priest finally, in Mark in dramatic form,[52] poses as the last possibility the messianic question "Are you the anointed one, the Son of the Blessed?"[53] Jesus answers with a clear "I am he" (ἐγώ εἰμι)[54] and with the judgment saying "you (the members of the Sanhedrin) will see the Son of Man at the right hand of the Power and coming with the clouds of heaven."[55] The original form of this answer, which is based on a linking

---

[49] Cf. the key word προσαγωγή: Eph 2.18; 3.12; Rom 5.2 and esp. Heb 4.16, etc. Later Jewish Christians in Palestine and Syria, the so-called "Ebionites," also rejected the sacrificial cult. This aversion is probably older and could apply to at least parts of the Jewish Christianity in Jerusalem already in the first century CE. See Strecker 1959, 495.

[50] See section 3.1.7 with note 33 and section 19.2 with notes 40–41.

[51] Betz 1991, 101–5; see also Betz 1987, 154ff.; Schwemer 2001c, 144ff.

[52] Mark 14.61-62; Matt 26.63-64, which is dependent on Mark.

[53] Mark 14.61: Σὺ εἶ ὁ χριστὸς ὁ υἱὸς τοῦ εὐλογητοῦ; Note the periphrasis of the name of God with ὁ εὐλογητός, *hab-bārûkh* or *ham-mebôrākh* (m. Ber. 7.3). Matthew 26.63 turns the question of the high priest into an adjuration: ἐξορκίζω σε κατὰ τοῦ θεοῦ. Through this Jesus' answer receives "the meaning of an explanation under oath," Bill. I: 1006.

[54] The answers in Matt 26.64 and Luke 22.70 are also to be understood as unequivocally positive. In our view, this also applies to the answers in relation to Pilate; see section 21.1.2.

[55] Mark 14.62 = Matt 26.64. The Lukan version (22.66-71) differs significantly and is clearly secondary vis-à-vis the Markan version. Luke has the members of the Sanhedrin ask twice: first whether he is the Messiah (v. 67) and then about his divine sonship (v. 70). In Jesus' answer to the first question he restricts himself to the future exaltation of the Son of Man "at the right hand of God" and omits the seeing and coming on the clouds of heaven, i.e., he eliminates the apocalyptic future statement of Dan 7.13 and relates Jesus' statement

of Ps 110.1 and Dan 7.13, can just as little be reconstructed in detail as the words of institution at the Last Supper. It is, however, also not simply a free "christological construction" of the evangelist. The two texts, Ps 110.1 and Dan 7.13, were related to each other in the Jerusalem primitive community already at a very early date. They are fundamental for the earliest Christology. The one exalted to the right hand of God is the one who comes as judge and savior.[56] A self-statement of Jesus about his identity with the coming Son of Man–judge that went in this direction and at at the same time unveiled the messianic secret probably provoked the verdict against him or the resolution to hand him over. Such an authoritative saying may have appeared blasphemous to the members of the Sanhedrin, for example because of the sitting at the right hand of God or because of the "disobedience" vis-à-vis the high priest;[57] however (against Mark and Matthew and with Luke and John), a formal sentence of death due to blasphemy was not issued by the council.

In the further course of the hearing the "blasphemy" no longer plays a role at all. The concern is only with what is suddenly now a question about a politically interpreted Messiah, whether Jesus is the "king of the Jews." The prefect was not interested in questions of the law and the temple.[58] As the basis of the hearing against Jesus before the Sanhedrin A. Strobel[59] points to texts of the Torah such as Deut 13.6ff. and 17.8ff., which speak of the condemnation of the deceiver and of false prophets who lead the people to apostasy. This would correspond to the later Jewish accusations in b. Sanh. 43a, in Justin, and in Celsus.[60] Vis-à-vis the prefect, by contrast, the political accusation was made that Jesus wanted to be "king of the Jews." This

---

to the resurrection. In response to the second question he answers: ὑμεῖς λέγετε ὅτι ἐγώ εἰμι (Luke 22.70). With this the eschatological edge is taken from Jesus' confession.

[56] The motif of seeing the coming one is already found in the sayings tradition (Luke 13.35 = Matt 23.39) in connection with Ps 118.26; cf. 1 John 3.2; Rev 1.7; Barn 7.9–10; on this, see section 19.4.

[57] In our view, Jesus could have pointed to Ps 110.1 and his messianic significance already in the controversy dialogues in Jerusalem in Mark 12.35-37. See chapter 18 with note 95. For the question of blasphemy, see Bock 1998 and Schwemer 2001c, 149ff. on the blasphemy against the high priest with references to the relevant attestations in Josephus, *Ant.* 13.293–296; *Ag. Ap.* 2.187, 194, 217.

[58] Cf. Gallio in Corinth in Acts 18.14-15; Pilate in John 18.31: "take him and judge him according to your law"; 19.6.

[59] Strobel 1980, 81ff.

[60] On Jesus as "deceiver of the people," see Hengel 1981b, 40–42 (GV = 1968b, 44–45; 2007b, 81–82); cf. Matt 27.63-64: πλάνος/πλάνη; John 7.12: πλανᾷ τὸν ὄχλον and 7.47; see further Justin, *Dial.* 69.7: λαοπλάνος; 108.2: Ἰησοῦ τινος Γαλιλαίου πλάνου . . . ; Origen, *Cels.* 1.68ff.: ταῦτα θεομισοῦς ἦν τινος καὶ μοχθηροῦ γόητος (71); Cf. also Cook 2000, 35–39. In b. Sanh. 43a Jesus is condemned by the Jewish court to stoning and hanging of the corpse "because he practiced magic, deceived, and led Israel astray (to idolatry)." On this, see Schäfer 2007, 63–74.

reinterpretation ensured a securely effective accusation, compelling the prefect, according to human judgment, to impose a death sentence. The much-disputed nightly session of the high priestly council with preceeding hearing and following resolution to hand him over was necessary because, according to Roman legal convention, court was held in the morning at daybreak and Jesus had to be handed over at this time to the prefect.[61]

Against the historicity of the account about the hearing before the high priest and his council it is often objected that one could know nothing about this, since no eyewitnesses from the followers of Jesus were present. Apart from the question of the "noble councillor" Joseph of Arimathea[62] and the fact that Peter had dared to proceed into the lion's den, i.e., into the court of the high priestly palace,[63] the execution of Jesus at the Passover festival in 30 CE was surely the conversation of the day in Jerusalem and over the further course of the festival.[64] One could also point to the unnamed disciple in John 18.15, who got Peter access into the inner courtyard.[65] Moreover, it is significant that the accusations against Jesus as a criminal deceiver of the people and his handing over to the Roman judiciary were constantly present in the next thirty years until the stoning of his brother James together with other Jewish Christians as "lawbreakers" in ca. 62 CE at the instigation of Annas II.[66] In order to justify themselves, the clan of Annas and the members of the Sanhedrin had to ground his handing over and execution time and again as just and necessary: Jesus was, as a messianic pretender, also a false prophet, deceiver of the people, and blasphemer. The document of indictment and the resolution to hand him over were available in the high priestly archive, and their content probably also played a role in the multiple actions of the members of the Sanhedrin, of King Agrippa I, and of Annas II against the Jewish Christians in Jerusalem. The persecution "of the communities in Judaea," which Paul mentions in First Thessalonians 2.14-15, received its ultimate justification through the accusation of the Sanhedrin against Jesus, the deceiver of the people.[67] The Jewish Christians could appear as criminals to their opponents in the hierarchy because their master had already been

---

[61] Blinzler 1969, 255, with reference to Sherwin-White.

[62] Mark 15.43: εὐσχήμων βουλευτὴς; see note 92 in chapter 21.

[63] Are we to think that Peter and with him the whole community did not have had a burning interest in these events also after Easter?

[64] Luke 24.18; cf. Acts 2.22; 10.37.

[65] On this, see Hengel 1993a, 322 (ET = 1989a, 132); see also below.

[66] Josephus, *Ant.* 20.200ff.; see section 3.1.5 with notes 344–46.

[67] The grounding of the controversial statement of 1 Thess 2.15 also presumably lies here: καὶ τόν κύριον ἀποκτεινάντων Ἰησοῦν καὶ τούς προφήτας; cf. Luke 13.34 = Matt 23.37. On this, see Schwemer 2005.

one. The Stephen story shows how points of accusation against Jesus were transferred to Christians. The execution of Jesus is also connected with the condemnation of his disciples in b. Sanh. 43a.

It is plausible that Jesus, after the resolution was made, was struck and mocked as a messianic false prophet[68] by his guards—the police of the Sanhedrin or the high priestly slaves. His claim is satirized.[69] In ancient judicial practice it would be strange if this had not been the case. It is all the more certain that we stand upon historical ground in the case of the denial of Peter in the courtyard of the high priestly palace before the cock crow which announced the morning. Like the Gethsemane story, it probably goes back to Peter himself. Mark has integrated this episode in a narratively skilled way into the interrogation scene and thus pointed out a sharp contrast between the confession of Jesus and the failure of the leading disciple.[70] In our view it is absurd to regard this as a later community polemic against Peter due to his inconstancy. It is possible—thus John—that an unnamed disciple,[71] who was known to the high priest, got Peter access to the courtyard of the palace. This information may go back to a tradent to whom we also owe other motifs and local traditions in the Johannine passion story that are to be taken seriously, for example, the footwashing, the Kidron Valley, the hearing before Annas, the reference to the place of the condemnation of Jesus, and others.[72] We believe that the author of the Fourth Gospel, who is himself from Jerusalem, while being so free with regard to historical questions elsewhere, has, despite all tendencies to "christologically intensify" the events, brought in good individual traditions at multiple points here.

[68] Mark 14.65; Luke 22.63 and—also influenced by Luke—Matt 26.67.

[69] See Schwemer 2001c, 153–54.

[70] Luke 22.60-61 intensifies the drama of the story: while Peter is still speaking, the cock crows, "and the Lord turned and looked at Peter."

[71] John 18.15ff. He could be identical with the Beloved Disciple. The concern may be with the later author of the Fourth Gospel, the Presbyter John. On this, see Hengel 1993a, 215–16, 309, 314, 321–325 (ET = 1989a, 78–79, 124–35). See also note 65 above.

[72] John 19.13: Λιθόστρωτον/Γαββαθα: presumably a place plastered with stones on the eastern side of the palace of Herod turned toward the city in the western part of the city. On the historicity of Johannine tradition, see Hengel 1999b, 293–334.

21

The Crucified Messiah

21.1 The Hearing before Pilate

21.1.1 The Handing over to the Prefect and the Trial[1]

Right at daybreak the members of the Sanhedrin handed over Jesus to Pilate with the accusation that he was a messianic agitator[2] and thus also a rebel against Roman rule,[3] presumably with a short, written accusation, which was based on a resolution of the council. In this way the case became for the prefect a capital case from the outset in which it was a matter of life or death. The disputed phrase συμβούλιον ποιήσαντες[4] is not a reference to a second, special morning session of the Sanhedrin, nor does it point to a simpler form of the older passion story. Rather, it is simply a redactional connection to Mark 14.65 and means in this context: "they made a resolution (namely, to hand over Jesus to Pilate)." After all, Jesus, son of Ananias, whom we have mentioned multiple times, was similarly handed over to Albinus as troublemaker after a preceding court session

---

[1] Bickerman 1935 = 1986, 82–138. This fundamental study deserves greater attention. See the postscript of the great Jewish author shortly before his death on p. 138: "Les exégètes recueillent avec soin de mon article les données qui confirment, ou semblent confirmer, leurs vues personnelles, et négligent ce qu'infirme leurs hypotheses, mais on évite de comprendre la leçon de méthode." See esp. his judgment on Mark (pp. 104–5) in comparison with Luke and Matthew, which agrees with the judgment of Mommsen (see note 8 in chapter 19). See further Sherwin-White 1963, 1–47, 186ff., 194ff.; Blinzler 1969, 245–83; Dunn 2003b, 628–34, 765–824; Schwemer 2001c, 154–57.

[2] Mark 15.1 = Matt 27.1; cf. Luke 22.66–23.1; John 18.28.

[3] Luke 23.2; cf. John 18.29-37; 19.12; Acts 17.7.

[4] Mark 15.1: συμβούλιον ποιήσαντες. The reading συμβούλιον ἑτοιμάσαντες correctly interprets it in the sense of "to make a resolution"; see Metzger 1975, 117: a Latinism, Vulg.: *consilium facientes*, Vetus Lat.: *consilium fecerunt*. On the word meaning, see Bauer/Aland/Aland 1988, 1552.

with hearing and punitive beating.[5] Thus, the handing over with written accusation introduced the trial before the prefect. During the great festival, when he visited Jerusalem, he probably did not have his headquarters, as some have hypothesized, in the fortress of Antonia or in the Hasmonean palace, but in the strongly fortified Herodian castle in the northwest of the city. The praetorium, the casern of part of the occupying cohorts and of other troops that he had brought from Caesarea, was there.[6] When Pilate arrived in Jerusalem, presumably accompanied by a cohort, is unknown to us, as is the duration of his stay. It could have been very short.

The *imperium* given to the prefect by the emperor encompassed in the province entrusted to him the highest military legal and financial position, i.e., he held there in the place of the emperor the highest power to govern. In relation to the provincials, the *peregrini*, his legal authority was practically unrestricted. He could issue sentences of death against them already on the basis of his commission to uphold public order, his simple policing power (*coercitio*).[7] There was no fixed arrangement for trials. He largely had a free hand here.

In contrast to this stood the more detailed *cognitio* trial procedure, which was applied, for example, to Roman citizens and therefore also to Paul.[8] Here the presupposition was a proper accusation by an accuser, who had to bring the criminal to court or, if he was already in prison, to appear personally and publicly support the written accusation. As in Jewish law there was no "state prosecutor" in Roman law. Even in cases of official crimes it usually depended on private accusers. In the most difficult cases the judge consulted with a *consilium* of associate judges of his choosing. Unfortunately, we possess only very few descriptions of trial proceedings in the provinces against provincials. The later trials of Christians are especially instructive, for example the letter of Pliny the Younger to Trajan and Trajan's answer (*Ep.* 10.96, 97), and the martyr acts starting with the martyrdom of Polycarp in Smyrna. In the case of *peregrini* the prefect could decide relatively quickly due to his policing power. In clear contrast to this stands the roughly five-year trial of Paul, who was a Roman citizen,

---

[5] Josephus, *J.W.* 6.302–305: οἱ ἄρχοντες . . . ἀνάγουσιν αὐτὸν ἐπὶ τὸν παρὰ Ῥωμαίοις ἔπαρχον (303). See section 3.1.7 with note 433, section 20.2.2 with note 50, and section 21.1 with note 26.

[6] Mark 15.16 = Matt 27.27; John 18.28, 33. On this, see Dormeyer 2001.

[7] Thus, Trajan to Pliny (*Ep.* 10.78): *si qui autem se contra disciplinam meam gesserint statim coerceantur* ("If some offend against my order, they should be punished immediately").

[8] Acts 22.25ff.; 23.16-35; 24–26. Sherwin-White 1963, 13–30, 48–70; Barrett 1994/1998, II: 1047ff., 1075, 1088–74; Tajra 1989.

appealed to Caesar, and was transferred to Rome![9] After the procurator Felix had protracted the trial and his successor Festus wanted to move it to Jerusalem, Paul appealed to Caesar. After consulting with his council, Festus granted this appeal.[10]

By contrast, a decision about the accusation against Jesus was made relatively quickly without consultation with associates and other legal efforts. The trial took place in the relatively free form of a *cognitio extra ordinem*[11] with written accusation, oral hearing of the accused and the accusers, and concluding judgment. In complete contrast to the political trials among modern dictators, it was usually public, i.e., conducted before the eyes of observers. The accusers presented their *delatio*, and the prefect functioned as an individual judge—thus Pilate against the *peregrinus* Jesus—but could also draw on an advisory council. The accused had to defend himself. If he remained silent, this could amount to a confession of guilt. If he confessed, then he already passed the sentence on himself: *confessus pro iudicato habetur*, "the one who confesses is treated as condemned."[12] This principle goes back as far as the law of the Twelve Tables. The judgment was made in individual proceedings, i.e., without *consilium, secundum arbitrium iudicantis*,[13] "according to the discretion

---

[9] Ca. 50–62. The trial against Paul extended from about two and a half years before the festival of weeks in 57 CE to the autumn of 59 CE in Caesarea and continued, after the arrival of the accused in Rome in the spring of 60 CE, for another two years. It remains controversial whether the apostle was then executed or whether he initially got free, traveled to Spain (Rom 15.24), and was only then beheaded in connection with the Neronic persecution, which is more likely in our judgment. See 1 Clem. 5.4–7; Dionysius of Corinth in ca. 170 CE: Peter and Paul are said to have suffered martyrdom at the same time in Italy, apud Eusebius, *Hist. eccl.* 2.25.8; Mur. frag. 38–39. Mark 13.10; 14.9 par presumably already presupposes knowledge of this (Hengel/Schwemer 1998, 403 n. 1660; ET = 1997, 267, 476 n. 1373). On this, see now Schnabel 2002, 1216ff. The long duration of the trial is an argument for the view that Luke speaks the truth with respect to the Roman citizenship of Paul. Through the judicial murder by Annas and the Sanhedrin called together by him of James, the brother of the Lord, and of a larger number of Jewish Christians (Josephus, *Ant.* 20.200ff.), which led to the sharp protest of the new procurator Albinus, the negotiation position of the Jerusalem authorities was greatly weakened also in the trial against Paul in Rome (ca. 61/62 CE). In our view, Paul was therefore released after the two years of Acts 28.30. He was able to continue to preach ἀκωλύτως (v. 31).

[10] Acts 25.12: συλλαλήσας μετὰ τοῦ συμβουλίου. In 26.30 he consults with "those who were sitting with" (συγκαθήμενοι), who include King Agrippa II and his sister Berenice.

[11] The form of this *cognitio* was very free; "it eludes every scientific presentation. Its nature is legalized formlessness": Mommsen 1955, 340.

[12] Cf. Sallust, *Bell. Cat.* 52.36; *Dig.* 42.2.3 and others; further attestations in Luz 2005, 495 (GV = 1985–2002, IV: 270 n. 29): "If one was a *confessus*, a formal declaration of guilt on the part of the judge was no longer necessary."

[13] Sherwin-White 1963, 17–18, 20–22.

of the judge." There was no appeal, and the verdict was usually enforced immediately; longer terms of imprisonment were rare. Here the fundamental difference from the trial against Paul becomes evident. The life of a provincial from the lower class was not worth much. To be sure, with the conservative legal and administrative praxis of the Romans it was possible that consideration was sometimes shown for special legal traditions of the respective provinces and their cities and people groups, insofar as these did not stand in the way of Roman interests. Only very wealthy and influential provincials who had good relations with Rome had the chance, against the prefect and his legal decisions, to make an accusation before the governor in Syria who was over him or before the emperor himself. The threat of the high priests and their group in John 19.12 could be understood against this background: "If you release him, you are no friend of Caesar . . . ," but it is hardly historical. Thus, the Samaritans later instituted proceedings against Pilate after the bloodbath at Mount Gerizim caused by him, after which he was promptly recalled by Tiberius in 36 CE.[14] But behind this stood leading men of a whole people group (ἔθνος) and not an individual person. With the trial of Jesus, the situation was completely different. He was a simple Galilean craftsman without influence,[15] while a decision against the politically accented accusations of the leaders of the people could become uncomfortable for Pilate. The Roman administration of justice in the provinces as in Rome itself was a class justice to a pronounced degree.

21.1.2 The Accusation and Condemnation[16]

Jesus was brought before Pilate by the leaders of the people. The public trial took place on the side of the palace of Herod that faced the city right after sunrise. For the Gospels it is self-evidently conducted in Greek, which was the predominant language of communication in the east of the Roman Empire. Jesus' mother tongue was Aramaic, but he, as well as some of his disciples, probably spoke a nonliterary Greek. Apparently, Jesus affirmed the decisive question of Pilate: "Are you the king of the Jews?" The disputed phrase σὺ λέγεις must be understood in the sense of "You say it" and not as a rejecting, materially meaningless "This is what you say!"[17] With this, he had made, in the eyes of the prefect, a

---

[14] Josephus, *Ant.* 18.85–89.

[15] His great impact on the common people was detrimental rather than helpful to him.

[16] Waldstein 1964, 41–44.

[17] Cf. Jesus' answer before the high priest in Mark 14.62: ἐγώ εἰμι, which Matthew interprets with a positive σὺ εἶπας (26.64); cf. also Luke 22.70 and John 18.37: σὺ λέγεις ὅτι βασιλεύς εἰμι, who knows and interprets Mark and Luke. After all, according to John,

confession, for the decisive accusation point was the charge that Jesus claimed to be the "king of the Jews," that is, the Messiah. *From beginning to end the Messiah question was the fundamental question of the trial.* The high priests had formulated the accusation politically for the prefect: Jesus appeared with the claim to be the "king of the Jews." This was high treason (*perduellio*) and sedition (*seditio*) against the rule or majesty of the Roman people and of the emperor (*maiestas populi Romani et principis*) and at the same time an endangerment of the peace in the province. In itself "king of the Jews" was not a christological title in Judaism or in early Christianity and is definitely not based on a later "dogmatic invention" of the community. On the contrary, by introducing this designation because of the historical circumstances, Mark rather makes the Christians suspicious. In the turbulent times of the Roman rule between Pompey and the destruction of Jerusalem, 63 BCE and 70 CE, too many Jewish agitators of very different origins had made "kingly" and thus sometimes also "messianic" claims.[18] The formulation of the accusation came rather from the leaders of the people, and Jesus, according to the Synoptics, did not contradict it but kept silent in relation to further accusations, after he had given a positive answer to the question of Pilate: "Are you the king of the Jews?"; an uncommon behavior in a capital trial, which amazed the prefect.[19] Only John recounts—against all historical probability—a detailed theological dialogue between Jesus and Pilate in the praetorium, i.e., not in public and without witnesses,[20] in which precisely this political accusation against Jesus is rejected: "My kingdom is not from this world; if my kingdom were from this world, my servants would fight for me."[21] While this saying, which is revolutionary for the ancient understanding of religion, is formulated in the style of Johannine theology, it makes visible the problem that was at hand.

Pilate appears to have honestly grappled with this strange prisoner, from whom nothing could be drawn out. The accusers hardly had proof

---

Jesus has control over a βασιλεία (18.36). The "good confession," which Jesus, according to 1 Tim 6.13, "testified" before Pilate could refer to Jesus' answer. On the language of Jesus, see section 12.1.

[18] Cf. Matt 2.2ff.; Acts 17.7; John 19.12. Hengel 1989c, 290–302 (GV = 1976c, 296–307); Hengel 2001d, 52–55 (ET = 1995, 47–51); see further the end of section 3.1.1 and the excursus on eschatological prophets in chapter 3.

[19] Mark 15.5: ὥστε θαυμάζειν τὸν Πιλᾶτον, intensified in Matt 27.14; cf. Justin, *Dial.* 102.5 and already the question of the high priest in relation to the silent Jesus in Mark 14.60-61. This realistic feature cannot be derived simply from Isa 53.7.

[20] John 18.33; 19.9, 13. According to John, the conversation was conducted under four eyes. The high priestly accusers remained outside so as not to defile themselves: 18.28.

[21] John 18.36: ἡ βασιλεία ἡ ἐμὴ οὐκ ἔστιν ἐκ τοῦ κόσμου τούτου; cf. Hengel 2007b, 408–29.

of violent rebellion against Roman rule.[22] On the other hand, the silence of Jesus could be evaluated as *pertinacia* and *obstinatio*, as obdurateness, and this also means as an acknowledgment of guilt.[23]

Especially controversial is the Barabbas episode.[24] In our view, it must have a historical background, for there is not a sufficient motive for subsequently inventing and incorporating it. The release of a prisoner at the festival of Passover, the festival of clemency,[25] due to the petition of the people could be an old Jewish legal custom from the time of the Hasmonean and Herodian rulers, which the prefect continued as legal successor. The Romans placed value on the preservation of old legal customs. We have a parallel on an Egyptian papyrus to such a release of a guilty person due to a petition of the people.[26]

Roman legal custom was familiar with the possibility of the *venia*, a pardon in the sense of a release from deserved punishment. In general, in antiquity the *vox populi* had no little influence on the course of trials—which took place, after all, in public. Influencing the judge through shouts etc. was common, and not every bearer of power had the strength of character to resist the demands of the crowd, especially if the city aristocracy stood behind it.[27]

In this context, a group of the Jerusalem population appears to have intervened in the course of the trial, namely in support of a (Jesus)

---

[22] Apart from Jesus' action in the "temple cleansing." Pilate may also have possessed his own information about this contrary Galilean. It is peculiar that he no longer takes action against the Jesus movement later. Apparently, in comparison with other Jewish groups, he regarded it as harmless.

[23] In his letter to Trajan (*Ep.* 10.96.3), Pliny also stresses the *pertinaciam . . . et inflexibilem obstinationem* of the Christians, who must be punished because they refuse to sacrifice to the gods and to swear by the genius of the emperor. On this, see Sherwin-White 1985, 699, 784.

[24] Mark 15.6-15. It is handed down in all the Gospels: Luke 23.13-25; Matt 27.15-26; John 18.39-40.

[25] Cf. Exod 12.13, 27: *pāsaḥ* = σκεπάζειν: *psḥ* in Qal "pass over," "spare," "cover," "protect."

[26] Cf. Blinzler 1969, 303: an accused person had innocent persons arrested contrary to the law, i.e., had made himself guilty of usurpation of office and deprivation of liberty. The prefect, however, refrained from punishing him and followed the petition of the crowd: "You would have deserved a flogging . . . but I will give you to the crowd" (cf. John 19.1; Luke 23.16). Cf. also Deissmann 1923, 230 (Pap. Florentinus 61; 85 CE); on this, see Waldstein 1964, 41–44. According to Josephus, when Archelaus took office, the crowd demanded not only the reduction of taxes but also the release of the prisoners locked up by Herod: *Ant.* 17.204–205. Archelaus sought to please the crowd and yielded. Later they demanded the punishment of those who were favored by Herod: *Ant.* 17.207, cf. *J.W.* 2.4, 7.

[27] Cf. Hadrian's edict to Minucius Fundanus, the governor of the province of Asia, in Justin, *1 Apol.* 68.8; on this, see Hengel 1996a: 376 n. 68–69; Codex justin. 9.47.12: *Vanae voces populi non sunt audiendae*.

Barabbas, who had been arrested with others in a tumult[28] in which a murder took place. It could also be a case of "went with—arrested with." Here we probably strike upon the old and far-reaching opposition between the urban population in Jerusalem and the province. Most of the Jerusalemites adopted an understandably reserved stance toward Jews from the province, and all the more toward those from remote, rustic Galilee and the eschatological-messianic movements that came from there.[29] The prosperity of the city and its role as world-famous pilgrim destination depended on the preservation of the Pax Romana. All troubles of a political religious sort meant a direct threat. The most dangerous Jewish rebel between the transformation of Judaea into a Roman province in the outbreak of the Jewish War (6–66 CE), Judas, had the byname "the Galilean." In the Synoptics Peter is addressed as a follower of Jesus in the high priestly palace because he is a "Galilean." In its beginnings the Jesus movement was especially a Galilean phenomenon.[30] With the influence of the high priestly leaders of the people, especially the family of Annas, in the capital it was easy for them to influence the action of the crowd (ὄχλος) portrayed in Mark 15.8ff. It was sufficient if one brought together before the praetorium a larger number of economic dependents and clients on the morning of the Passover festival and if the family and friends of Jesus Barabbas assembled because they regarded him as innocent. Due to a certain tendency of Mark (and to an even greater degree of all later portrayers of the process) to exonerate Pilate and blame the leaders of the people (or since Matthew and John "the Jews"), one could of course reckon with the possibility that Barabbas and Jesus were not presented to the crowd for selection but there was a direct petition for the release of Barabbas. But since Pilate is presented by Josephus[31] and Philo[32] as an enemy of Jews, stubborn and inflexible, it is also conceivable that, in the case of this silent prisoner, who was so pointedly charged with the most serious crimes

---

[28] Mark 15.7 speaks of στάσις and στασιασταί, but does not yet designate Barabbas himself as a murderer. This first occurs in Luke 23.19. In John 18.40 he becomes a "robber" (λῃστής). Matthew 27.16-17 calls him a "notorious prisoner" (δέσμος ἐπίσημος). His first name, Jesus, is handed down in some manuscripts twice (Θ, f¹, 700* pc sy^s, Or^mss), which is presumably the original reading. On this, see Metzger 1975, 67–68.

[29] This opposition then becomes visible especially after the outbreak of the Jewish War before the actual siege. In the end, the moderate urban population was subjected to the radical groups from Galilee, Idumaea, and the Jewish hinterland. *J.W.* 4.369–373, 377–378, 383.

[30] See sections 8.1 and 11.1–2; Hengel 1989c, 56ff., 76ff., 476 index, s.v. "Galileans and Galilee" (GV = 57ff., 79ff., 469 index, s.v. "Galiläa/Galiläer"); Mark 14.70: ἀληθῶς ἐξ αὐτῶν εἶ, καὶ γὰρ Γαλιλαῖος εἶ. Cf. Luke 22.59; Matt 26.73 has the addition ἡ λαλιά σου δῆλόν σε ποιεῖ.

[31] Josephus, *Ant.* 18.55–62, 85–89.

[32] Philo, *Legat.* 299–305. See also note 228 in chapter 1.

against the state by the leaders of the people, for the purpose of irritating the high priests, he initially did not comply with their wishes and—also as a mocking of the people and its leaders—offered to release to them the "king of the Jews," this wretched, ill-treated figure. In the end, in this matter, which was unclear to him, the prefect took the way of least resistance. He released Barabbas and condemned Jesus to the only possible punishment in view of the severity of the accusations, crucifixion. He needed no grand act to do so, but only three words, for example: *ibis in crucem!* In his letter to Trajan, Pliny remarks very concisely: *perseverantes duci iussi*, "the Christians who persist (after being questioned and warned two or three times), I order to be led away (to execution)."[33] Presumably two "robbers" were also condemned in the same trial to death on the cross at the same time as Jesus.[34]

21.1.3 Flogging and Mocking[35]

Corresponding to the condemnation, Mark describes without form in terse shortness: "And he handed over Jesus so that he might be flogged and crucified."[36] This means the accused is handed over to the execution squad of the soldiers. In Matt 27.19 and John 19.13 Pilate makes his judgment in an official way from his judgment seat.[37] John also specifies the place of the pronouncement of judgment and calls it Λιθόστρωτον, an elevated place that is probably covered with marble plates on which the judgment platform stood.[38] To be sure, the flogging and the associated mocking

---

[33] Pliny the Younger, *Ep.* 10.96.3. Cf. Williams 1990, 71, 140; Walsh 2006, 278.

[34] Mark 15.27 = Matt 27.38; see section 21.2 with note 71.

[35] Blinzler 1969, 321–36, 345–46; Brown 1994, I: 862–77; Schwemer 2001c, 161–62.

[36] Mark 15.15: καὶ παρέδωκεν τὸν Ἰησοῦν φραγελλώσας ἵνα σταυρωθῇ. John 19.16 could be misunderstood to mean that he handed over Jesus not to the soldiers but to his Jewish opponents for execution: παρέδωκεν αὐτὸν αὐτοῖς; see, however, 19.19, 23, 26: the *titulus* of Pilate and the (Roman) soldiers; Luke 23.24 is different: παρέδωκεν τῷ θελήματι αὐτῶν, which means "he surrendered Jesus to their will." Gos. Pet. 2–5 has an extreme distortion. There Herod has Jesus led away to crucifixion against the will of Pilate: ἔδωκεν τῷ λαῷ, namely—with John—on the day of preparation for Passover. The motif of the handwashing (Matt 27.24-25) is also intensified in Gos. Pet. 1. Herod and the Jewish opponents refuse the same. Through this the Gospel of Peter shows itself to be a later shoddy work from the middle of the second century, in which the anti-Jewish stance leads to a complete distortion of the tradition. It presupposes throughout the older, "canonical" Gospels.

[37] βῆμα; see Bauer/Aland/Aland 1988, 280. Properly it means "stand," and, derived from this, it means the elevated judgment seat: Acts 18.12, 16-17; 25.6, 10, 17; 2 Cor 5.10; Rom 14.10.

[38] John 19.13. He also mentions the Aramaic name Γαββαθά, probably in Aramaic "the hill" (*gabbᵃtā*). See Görg 1988, 719, and Dormeyer 2001, "For a plastered, public

of Jesus are reported in two contradictory versions in Mark 15.15-20a and John 19.1-5.

In Mark the flogging is the punishment that commonly accompanies the sentence of death in Roman criminal law and occurs after its announcement and before the execution (15.15). Thus, Mark Antony had the last Jewish priest king from the family of the Hasmoneans, Antigonus, executed with the axe in 37 BCE in Antioch at the urging of Herod. Before his execution, he was fastened to a pole (σταυρός) and flogged. Cassius Dio explicitly adds that no king had previously suffered such shameful treatment from the Romans.[39] Shortly before the outbreak of the Jewish War the procurator Gessius Florus, in the context of his plundering of parts of Jerusalem, had numerous Jews imprisoned, flogged, and crucified. He condemned to death also members of the aristocracy, who were Roman citizens, even members of the equestrian class, and had them publicly flogged before his judgment seat and nailed to the cross.[40] Thus, the event, as Mark reports it, corresponded to Roman custom in Judaea.

In John, by contrast, the flogging appears as an action during the hearing. Here it appears to be a special punishment due to the policing power of the prefect with the goal of "teaching Jesus a lesson" and then releasing him again after the flogging. The bloodily flogged Jesus is presented to the people: "Here is the man"—in a depreciating sense.[41] For John, of course, the scene contains a profound christological deeper meaning. The offer of the prefect in Luke 23.16 must be understood similarly: "I will release him after the flogging." The procurator Albinus proceeded in the same way with the prophet of doom Jesus son of Ananias, whom we have already mentioned on multiple occasions. He had him flogged before the leaders of the people until the bones showed. The tortured one gave no answer to the question of the procurator but continued to utter his woe sayings over Jerusalem without interruption. Albinus saw that he was only a madman and released him.[42] It is possible that Pilate initially wanted to treat Jesus in a similar way, since he did not really trust the accusations of the leaders

---

place, on which the judgment platform with the judgment seat was is established, the plateau of the palace of Herod more likely comes into consideration."

[39] Cassius Dio 49.22.6. Previously, Jugurtha had already been strangled in the Carcer Mamertinus: Volkmann 1979.

[40] Josephus, *J.W.* 2.306, 308: ἄνδρας ἱππικοῦ τάγματος μαστιγῶσαί τε πρὸ τοῦ βήματος καὶ σταυρῷ προσηλῶσαι. He could permit himself such a violation because his wife was friends with Poppaea, the wife of Nero, and he had received this office through the advocacy of Poppaea. Even Agrippa II did not dare to protest his despotic rule, which helped to trigger the Jewish War, according to Josephus; cf. *J.W.* 2.342–343; *Ant.* 20.252, 257. See also section 3.1.7 with note 380.

[41] John 19.5: ἰδοὺ ὁ ἄνθρωπος.

[42] Josephus, *J.W.* 6.300–309: καταγνοὺς μανίαν ὁ Ἀλβῖνος ἀπέλυσεν αὐτόν (305).

of the people. The course of things in Mark, however, is clear and there-fore probably also more original. John could have taken up the motif from Luke 23.16 and elaborated it.

The flogging took place in the casern[43] and was followed by the mock-ing. It must be understood as a cruel amusement of the soldiers and had an anti-Jewish character. The Roman occupying troops in Judaea were not legionaries and Roman citizens but rather auxiliary troops, who had been recruited since the times of Herod from the Hellenistic-Syrian urban popu-lation of Palestine, who hated the Jews. The so-called Sebasteans from the Herodian military colony Sebaste, the former Samaria, and from Caesarea were especially feared. The execution of a supposed king of the Jews gave them an opportunity to let off steam.[44] According to Mark, the whole cohort came together in the Herodian castle for this raw spectacle. The closest parallel is the mocking of a half-crazy person, Carabas, as supposed king of the Jews at a visit of Herod Agrippa I, who had just been appointed king by Caligula, in Alexandria by the rabble of the city in 38 CE.[45] This too was an anti-Jewish excess.

Such mocking scenes had their model in the ancient theater farce, the mime, which was quite vulgar. The so-called "crown of thorns" is, in real-ity, a crown of thistles or other prickly plants. It signifies a parody of the golden crown which oriental kings and dignitaries wore. The red soldier cloak corresponds to the royal purple and the reed to the ruler's scepter.[46]

---

[43] Mark 15.16-20 = Matt 27.27-31a. Luke indicates the possibility of flogging only in 23.16. He omits the mocking entirely. Presumably he does not want to confront the noble Theophilus with this scene. With this the reference to the soldiers also falls away. Only in 23.47 is the centurion who commanded the execution mentioned. Despite 4.6, the presen-tation of Luke shows a conspicuous, relatively positive stance toward Roman rule, which also continues in Acts.

[44] Among other things, after the death of King Agrippa I (Josephus, *Ant.* 19.356ff., 361, 364ff.), they mocked the dead king and his family in an obscene way and are said to have been punished for this by being moved to Pontus (on the Black Sea). Their unbridled actions were later one of the causes of the outbreak of the Jewish War. Cf. also the incident at the Passover festival under Cumanus (*Ant.* 20.108), which was understood as an insult to God and led to a protest of the people gathered in the temple area. See section 3.1.4 with note 284 and section 3.1.5 with notes 302–3.

[45] According to Philo, *Flacc.* 36–39; on this, see Schürer 1973–1987, I: 390; Van der Horst 2003, 130–31. The rabble paid homage to Carabas, who had been decked out as "king," with the Aramaic exclamation "Μαρίν," "our Lord"; cf. 1 Cor 16.22.

[46] Matt 27.28, 31: χλαμὺς κοκκίνη. Mark 15.17, 20 speaks in an exaggerating way of "purple." See Bauer/Aland/Aland 1988, 1760. On the "royal mime" in relation to Carabas and the mime character of the mocking of Jesus, see Wüst 1932, 1751–52. The Christians and their trials were also mocked later in the mime. Thus, the mocking crucifix on the Pala-tine with the donkey head probably points to a mime representation. On the later mocking of Christ and the Christians in the mime, see Reich 2005, 80–89.

Thus, the theme of mocking is determined by the accusation and signifies a travesty of the accused and at the same time a mocking of the messianic expectation of the Jews in general. Thus, the mocking of the blood-soaked flogged man as king of the Jews—"hail, king of the Jews"[47]—corresponded well to the taste of the anti-Jewish soldiers. This motif of anti-Judaism also explains the fact that the mocking in the casern became known in the city. This was taken care of by the soldiers themselves, for every nationally conscious Jew must have felt affected and insulted by this event.

21.2 The Walk to the Place of Execution and Crucifixion[48]

The punishment of crucifixion was first used by the Persians and then adopted by Alexander the Great and the Hellenistic rulers. As early as the capture of Tyre, Alexander had two thousand captured Phoenicians crucified on the shore of the sea in view of the destroyed city.[49] Via the Carthaginians in Carthage this—most cruel—ancient death penalty came to the Romans. They usually applied it only to the lowest strata of the people, slaves and provincials, and also only for serious crimes such as highway robbery, murder, and especially crimes against the state—i.e., for every sort of "upheaval." The crucified slave and robber is a relatively common motif in ancient entertainment literature, for example in novels and in satire. Roman citizens and members of the upper class were in principle not permitted to be crucified, though Roman governors did not always adhere to this. In his famous speech against Verres, the unscrupulous governor of Sicily, who had crucified a Roman citizen in this way, Cicero calls crucifixion a *crudelissimum taeterrimumque supplicium*, the cruelest and most hideous manner of execution;[50] on multiple occasions it is also simply designated as *servile supplicium*, as slave punishment.[51] It had probably been known in Judaea since the time of the Persians.

Jewish kings from the high priestly family of the Hasmoneans also used it. Thus, Alexander Jannaeus allegedly had eight hundred Pharisees crucified in Jerusalem while he feasted with his concubines.[52] Under the

---

[47] Mark 15.18: χαῖρε, βασιλεῦ τῶν Ἰουδαίων = Matt 27.29.

[48] Hengel 1977a (= 1986, 93–185); Kuhn 1982. On crucifixion in Jewish Palestine by Jews, see Hengel 1984c, 27–36. Cf. now also Cook 2019.

[49] Q. Curtius Rufus, *Hist. Alex.* 4.4.17; see Hengel 1977a, 73.

[50] *Verr.* 2.5.165. Hengel 1977a, 8, 33ff., 39ff.

[51] Hengel 1977a, 51ff.

[52] Josephus, *J.W.* 1.96–98; *Ant.* 13.380–381. The report goes back to Nicolaus of Damascus. The number is probably exaggerated. An older biblical example is the high

Hasmoneans it was apparently, as indicated by the Temple Scroll, the punishment for traitors and defectors:[53]

> If a man passes on information about his people, and he betrays his people to a foreign people and does evil against his people, then you shall hang him on a tree, so that he dies. . . . Cursed by God and by humans are those hanged on a tree.[54]

Under Roman rule it was often used in the turbulent Judaea as a political deterrent, so that rabbinic and probably already the preceding Jewish-Pharisaic criminal law rejected crucifixion, since it was regarded as the punishment of "the regime" (*malkût*). Among other things, the governor Quintilius Varus, due to the unrests that broke out after the death of Herod in 4 BCE, is said to have crucified two thousand agitators around Jerusalem.[55] In 1968, around Mount Scopus near Jerusalem, the skeleton of a Jewish crucified man from the Roman period was found in an ossuary. The nail passed through both heel bones; it was nailed very twistedly into the cross. He was about twenty-seven / twenty-eight years old. He is also proof of the fact that a person crucified by the Romans in Judaea could receive an ordinary burial.[56]

The cross consisted of a pole rammed into the earth and the crossbeam. The condemned person, who had to carry the crossbeam (*patibulum*) himself to the place of execution, was first nailed or fastened with both hands to the crossbeam and then lifted up on the pole. The nailing on was probably the worst. Together with the flogging it led more quickly to death through the loss of blood.[57] There were two forms. The *crux commissa* resembled a T, the *crux immissa* our cross. The height varied greatly. The feet were often only a few centimeters above the ground. The cross usually had a small seat to support oneself on, the so-called *sedile*. In this horrific situation the crucified persons could remain alive for the whole day if they were strong in stature, until they died through the heat, loss of

---

"pole" (ξύλον), which Haman intended for Mordecai (Est 5.14) and on which he (7.9-10) and his sons (9.13-14) were hanged. Cf. Hengel 1984c.

[53] 11QT 64.6ff. (= 11Q19); cf. 4QpNah frag. 3–4 I, 7–8; Hengel 1977a, 84–85; H.-W. Kuhn 1995.

[54] A reversal and expansion of Deut 21.22-23.

[55] Josephus, *J.W.* 2.75; cf. As. Mos. 6.9.

[56] Tzaferis 1985. The ossuaries were for the second burial of the bones of a dead person after his decay.

[57] On the nail wounds, see Luke 24.39; John 20.25, 27; cf. Col 2.14 and 1.20: διὰ τοῦ αἵματος τοῦ σταυροῦ αὐτοῦ, on this, see Hengel 1977a, 31–32. Crucifixion (with preceeding flogging) was, in contrast to a view that is often advocated today, anything but a "bloodless" manner of death.

blood, and especially through circulatory collapse as the consequence of complete lack of movement. Josephus recounts that after Jerusalem was conquered, he discovered near Tekoa, among a large number of crucified Jewish prisoners, three former friends who were still alive. Titus permitted them to be taken down from the cross. Despite medical treatment, only one survived.[58]

The place of execution, Golgotha,[59] was presumably a small hill, which had the form of a skull. It was located directly to the north of the main wall within an old quarry in an area that was incorporated by Herod Agrippa I into the city area through the so-called third wall at the beginning of the forties. It was thus very close to the city.[60] The Christian place tradition appears to have maintained itself. Hadrian already erected at the Christian crucifixion and tomb site a pagan temple complex for Venus, the main Roman goddess, and Constantine then built the so-called Church of the Holy Sepulchre. If the place tradition had developed at a later time, the place would certainly have been sought outside of the third wall of Agrippa. This presumably corresponds to what is today the northern wall of the old city.[61]

The straightforward, relatively simple account of Mark has the greatest claim to have retained the historical process of the crucifixion of Jesus. Matthew often follows him word for word because for him the text of the student of Peter is based on reliable tradition. When he supplements, he does so for theological reasons, for example in the peculiar reference to the earthquake and the opening of tombs in Matt 27.51-53: The death of Jesus has opened the gates of the underworld. Luke likewise follows Mark in part, but features some distinctive sayings of Jesus, which point to a special source, for example, his saying to the lamenting women of Jerusalem (Luke 23.27-31); the petition for the forgiveness of his murderers, who "do not know what they do" (23.34), which is lacking in the older textual witnesses and was perhaps omitted because of its offensiveness; and the exchange of words with the two men crucified with Jesus, in which Jesus promises the insightful one that he will be received into paradise, the place of the blessed dead (23.39-43). While John presupposes the text of

---

[58] Josephus, *Life* 420.

[59] Derived from Aramaic *gôlgôltā'*, Hebrew *gulgolet*, "skull"; see Gesenius 1987, 215: "Something round, therefore skull . . . head"; on this, see Rüger 1984, 78; Beyer 1984, 544.

[60] John 19.20: ἐγγὺς ἦν ὁ τόπος τῆς πόλεως ὅπου ἐσταυρώθη ὁ Ἰησοῦς. Here we again have an example of accurate place information in the Fourth Gospel. See note 144 in chapter 11.

[61] On the location and Golgotha tradition, see Jeremias 1926; Riesner 1988, 71–72; J. E. Taylor 1998.

Mark and Luke and sometimes has contact with them, he largely presents the events in his own distinctive way.

Jesus' journey to the place of execution was not very long. He probably went from the Herodian castle to the Garden Gate in the north wall and from there outside to the nearby hill of execution. As is also attested otherwise in antiquity, the condemned person had to carry the crossbeam, the *patibulum*, himself. The fact that his clothes were put on him again after the flogging and mocking[62] is probably to be explained with reference to the fact that nakedness was strongly frowned upon among Jews; in addition, the soldiers who were carrying out the execution were meant to receive them as spoils. That he could no longer carry the beam the short way could be connected with the large loss of blood from the flogging. A diaspora Jew who came from outside of the city, Simon of Cyrene, was compelled by soldiers to carry the crossbeam in his place.[63] The fact that Mark—entirely against Jewish custom—mentions his two sons Alexander and Rufus instead of his father's name indicates that these two sons were known in the Roman community in which Mark wrote. John contradicts this portrayal and stresses in 19.17: "and he carried the cross himself." For him Jesus needed no help from another on the way to the execution. This contradiction with the Synoptics shows that, as so often in John, Christology has covered over the historical event.[64] On a bilingual tomb inscription in the Kidron Valley, the name Alexander, son of Simon, has been discovered with the Hebrew addition *qrnyt*, which probably means "from Cyrene."[65]

After the place of execution was reached, Jesus was offered wine mixed with myrrh. According to early Jewish sources, this occurred as a labor of love, in order to daze the condemned ones and mitigate their torment.[66] This wine is said to have been donated by the rich women in Jerusalem. Jesus rejects this gift. A tablet was very likely already carried in front of the march of the guards, upon which the capital crime, the *causa poenae*, was recorded as a general deterrent. Thus, in 177 CE, in the persecution of Christians in Lyon, the Christian Attalus was led around

---

[62] Mark 15.20 = Matt 27.31.

[63] Mark 15.21: he could, as a returnee from the diaspora, have lived in or near Jerusalem. On Jews and Jewish Christians from Cyrene, see Acts 2.10; 6.9; 11.20; 13.1. On the large Jewish diaspora in Cyrenaica, see Schürer 1973–1987, I: 512, 529–32; III: 60–62.

[64] This applies, among other things, also to the date of Jesus' death. See section 19.4.

[65] Avigad 1962, 9; cf. Ilan 2002, 258 nr. 27. In Rom 16.13 a Rufus as ἐκλεκτὸς ἐν κυρίῳ and his mother appear, whom Paul must have known personally.

[66] Bill. I: 1037.

with such a tablet in the amphitheater: *"Hic est Attalus Christianus."*[67] This tablet was then affixed to the cross itself in the crucifixion. The longer the criminal's struggle with death lasted and the more observers read the tablet, the greater its intended effect was. John 19.20 explicitly stresses: "Many Jews read this inscription." Its content, according to Mark ὁ βασιλεὺς τῶν Ἰουδαίων, "the king of the Jews,"[68] signifies a public mocking of all Jews, as was already the case with the mocking of Jesus after the flogging in the praetorium. Such mocking is indeed plausible for the execution squad and for Pilate.[69] The whole event is not a later Christian invention. "King of the Jews" was never a Christian title of majesty for Jesus.[70]

The political character of the execution of Jesus also becomes clear from the fact that two other condemned persons were crucified with him, who are called λῃσταί in Mark 15.27.[71] Behind these "robbers" one could perhaps see zealot rebels, Jewish guerilla fighters. Josephus consistently designates the Jewish insurgents since the time of Herod in a stereotypical way as λῃσταί.[72]

The mocking of Jesus by individual opponents may also have its historical occasion. According to the Synoptics, they are related again to his messianic claim, which dominates, after all, the whole passion story. It is instructive in Mark that in contrast to the accusation before Pilate and the inscription on the *titulus*, Jesus is addressed as *Messias crucifixus*: "If

---

[67] Eusebius, *Hist. eccl.* 5.1.44. For other examples, see Hengel 2001d, 52ff. (ET = 1995, 47ff.). The tablet could also be placed around the neck of the criminal. Mark does not yet say anything about the fastening of the "inscribed tablet" (15.26: ἐπιγραφή). Luke 23.38 has a simple ἐπ' αὐτῷ. John 19.19 has ἐπὶ τοῦ σταυροῦ. Only according to Matthew is it fastened over the head of Jesus (ἐπάνω τῆς κεφαλῆς αὐτοῦ). This would presuppose a *crux immissa*.

[68] Mark 15.26 has the simplest form. Matthew 27.37 adds the name Ἰησοῦς. Luke 23.38 is identical to Mark in substance: ὁ βασιλεὺς τῶν Ἰουδαίων οὗτος. John 19.19-20 has not only the longest version but also the indication that the τίτλος (lat.: *titulus*) was written in three languages "Hebrew (= Aramaic), Latin, and Greek." With this he probably seeks to signal the universal significance of Jesus.

[69] This is also the explanation for the scene in John 19.21-22 with the objection of the high priests to the *titulus* ordered by Pilate and the refusal to change the text by the prefect.

[70] We have a series of ancient parallels to such notifications of the *causa poenae* in the case of criminals, also before a crucifixion. See Blinzler 1969, 367ff., and Hengel 2001d, 52ff. (ET = 1995, 47ff.).

[71] This is also the case for Matt 27.38.

[72] Cf. Hengel 1989c, 24–46 and 465 index, s.v. λῃστής/-αί (GV = 1976c, 25–46 and 484 index, s.v. λῃστής/-αί). Luke 23.33b speaks of "criminals" (κακοῦργοι). John 19.18 mentions only "two others." In 18.40 he designates Barabbas as λῃστής. Perhaps the two persons are identical with the στασιασταί mentioned in Mark 15.7. See note 28 above. From a legal perspective all insurgents, who were not regarded as official enemies (*hostes*), were *latrones* in Roman eyes, i.e., λῃσταί.

he is the anointed one (χριστός), the king of Israel, then let him come down from the cross, so that we may see and believe." The mocking leaders of the people do not use the formulation of the *causa poenae* but the Jewish "salvation-historical" terminology. The mocking motif appears in the psalm of suffering 22 and yet also elsewhere in Old Testament texts, especially in the Psalms.[73] As eyewitnesses at the crucifixion, in addition to Simon of Cyrene, there is mention of the numerous Galilean women who had accompanied Jesus and the disciples to Jerusalem. They watched the execution "from afar." Mark mentions three of them by name, Mary Magdalene, Mary, the mother of James the small and of Joses, and Salome,[74] according to Matthew the mother of the Zebedaids.[75] Influenced by the psalms of suffering, Luke places "all his acquaintances" before the Galilean women here.[76] Only John 19.25ff. introduces, perhaps building on Luke, the enigmatic Beloved Disciple, the mother of Jesus, her nameless sister, Mary the (wife?) of Clopas, and Mary Magdalene as witnesses in the immediate vicinity of the cross.[77]

Mark 15.25 and 33-34 connect the crucifixion with an hour scheme. According to it, the crucifixion itself takes place at the third hour, i.e., at 9 in the morning. From the sixth to the ninth hour a darkness covers the land. The death of Jesus then takes place around the ninth hour, about 3 in

---

[73] Mark 15.32 (29-32). On the motif, see esp. Ps 22.7-9; on the "shaking of the head," see also Ps 109.25; cf. 44.15; Jer 18.16 and Lam 2.15ff.; see further Isa 53.3-4. Matthew 27.39-43 strengthens the motif of the "suffering righteous one" with a quotation from Ps 22.9 but omits the key word χριστός (cf., by contrast, Matt 27.17 in the mouth of Pilate [!]: Ἰησοῦν τὸν λεγόμενον Χριστόν; on the formulation, cf. Josephus, *Ant.* 20.200). Luke 23.35 abbreviates greatly, while strengthening the Messiah motif: ὁ χριστὸς τοῦ θεοῦ ὁ ἐκλεκτός. John completely omits the mocking as inappropriate in relation to Jesus' divine dignity. A stronger argument is the complete helplessness of Jesus against it in the Jew of Celsus (Origen, *Cels.* 2.55), a text which presupposes Mark 15.31b = Matt 27.42a: "while he lived, he did not help himself," in contrast to Dionysius, who avenged himself on Pentheus in the *Bacchae* of Euripides.

[74] Mark 15.20: ἀπὸ μακρόθεν θεωροῦσαι, cf. 16.1. On the women and their names, see Bauckham 2002, 234ff., 298–304 and elsewhere.

[75] Matt 27.56; cf. 20.20.

[76] Mark 15.40 = Matt 27.55; Luke 23.49: πάντες οἱ γνωστοί: cf. Ps 31(LXX 30).12; 38(37).12; 88(87).12.

[77] John 19.25: εἰστήκεισαν δὲ παρὰ τῷ σταυρῷ τοῦ Ἰησοῦ. . . . The number of the women is not entirely clear. There may be four women, for the fact that the mother of Jesus and her sister have the same name is unlikely. On the problem, see Schnackenburg 1982, 321ff.: "The close relatives are introduced first, then there follows two other women with the name Mary, who are distinguished by additions" (322). Miriam/Mary was by far the most common name for women in Jewish Palestine; see Ilan 2002, 9, 242, 248: ca. 48 percent of the women mentioned in the sources bear this name. On Clopas, cf. Luke 24.18. According to Hegesippus (Eusebius, *Hist. eccl.* 3.11), "Clopas was the brother of Joseph."

the afternoon. Luke makes a solar eclipse out of this.[78] The third and ninth hours were the times of the tamid offering in the temple and of prayer.[79] John makes a correction: according to him, Jesus is only condemned by Pilate later, around the sixth hour, i.e., about 12 pm. In his Gospel the trial has lasted much longer because of the dialogue.[80] In reality, in the case of Jesus Pilate made a "short trial." After all, the two other criminals were also condemned in addition to him. In any case, the death of Jesus occurred relatively early, some time before the onset of darkness, i.e., before the beginning of the Sabbath, so that he could be taken down from the cross before it and put in a nearby tomb (John 19.41).

Luke and John omit both the Aramaic cry of prayer reported by Mark in 15.34 and its interpretation in relation to Elijah in 15.35-36 because they contradict their view of the dignity of the dying of Jesus. They are, however, old tradition and go back to the earliest Palestinian community. In our view, there is no good reason to doubt their historicity. By contrast, other events such as the great three-hour darkness, the tearing of the temple curtain, and the witness of the centurion are more likely legendary in character, while having fundamental theological significance for Mark. The cry of Jesus ελωι ελωι λεμα σαβαχθανι, "My God, my God, why have you forsaken me?" is the beginning of Ps 22. It is unusual that it is given in Aramaic, since the language used for psalms and prayers in the synagogue and temple was Hebrew. It is probably necessary to assume for this an early popular psalm targum.[81] We are dealing here with an original motif.[82] It expresses his last, deepest desolation of Jesus, whose life

---

[78] Luke 23.45: τοῦ ἡλίου ἐκλιπόντος. Phlegon of Tralles at the time of Hadrian is said to have pointed to the same. A solar eclipse at the time of the Passover festival, i.e., of the full moon, was an astronomically impossible event. On this, see Hengel 2004c, 110–11. Cf. also Wolter 2016/2017, II: 530–31.

[79] On the prayer at three times, see Dan 6.11, 14; Ps 55.18. On the prayer times, see Bill. I: 297 n. 1: "In general we can probably probably assume that the morning prayer was carried out around 9 in the morning, the mincha prayer around 3 in the afternoon." For prayer at the sixth hour, see Acts 10.9 and Bill. II: 696–702.

[80] On John, see 19.14: "On the day of preparation for the festival of Passover, around the sixth hour." John probably mentions this time because on the day of preparation for the Passover festival the evening Tamid offering was slaughtered already at 12:30 pm; see Bill. II: 698. In that case, Jesus would have been crucified roughly at this time. Otherwise John has no more specifications of time. In him, too, the death of Jesus occurs relatively quickly: 19.33.

[81] The known targums on the Hagiographa are very late. We have, however, pre-Christian targums on Job and Leviticus from Qumran: 4QtgJob (157); 11QtgJob (10); 4QtgLev (156). Presumably, such a targum also existed for the Psalter.

[82] The quotation in Greek transcription is phonetically unobjectionable. As a Palestinian Jew, the evangelist Mark understood Aramaic. See Rüger 1984, 73–84 (78–79). On the significance of Ps 22 for the passion story, see Gese 1974; on Jesus' words on the cross, see Schwemer 1998; Schwemer 2001c, 143, 156 n. 109.

appears to come to an end in unspeakable torments under the mocking of the bystanders in seemingly complete God-forsakenness. Jesus dies in the tribulation of the remoteness from God that already dominates the Gethsemane scene.[83] This cry was misunderstood by a portion of the bystanders in such a way that it was regarded as a cry of the dying one for Elijah, the proven helper in distress, who aids the individual pious person in a miraculous way.[84] This leads to the attempt of someone to give him sour wine (ὄξος), the drink of the poor and of soldiers, to drink.[85] For Mark the death of Jesus with a second loud cry[86] simultaneously signifies the end of the temple cult as an event of atonement. The curtain of the temple tears, i.e., the temple has lost its function as place of atonement for Israel, for in the death of the Son of God, the sufficient sacrifice for all human beings has taken place.[87] For Mark, the confession of the centurion who commands the execution squad at the death of Jesus: "Truly, this human being was God's Son"[88] corresponds to the completely valid confession of the later Gentile Christian community and has an inner connection to the tearing of the curtain. Luke, by contrast, weakens it: "Truly, this human being was righteous." This sounds more plausible for Theophilus: the execution of Jesus was a judicial murder.[89] Luke has already introduced the lamenting crowd with the women in Jesus' walk to the cross (23.27-31) and correspondingly concludes the dramatic scene with a reference to the deep

---

[83] Feldmeier 1987, passim.

[84] Mark 15.35. Cf. Schwemer 1998, 14–15. It could also be another mocking of the messianic claim of Jesus: Elijah should come and take Jesus down from the cross and anoint him, see Justin, *Dial.* 8.3: he is unknown and powerless μέχρις ἂν ἐλθὼν Ἡλίας καὶ φανερὸν πᾶσι ποιήσῃ.

[85] Mark 15.36 = Matt 27.48-49. The scene is lacking in Luke. John 19.28-29, by contrast, recounts a real giving of something to drink as a reaction to the "διψῶ" of Jesus: for John it has anti-docetic character.

[86] Mark 15.37: ἀφεὶς φωνὴν μεγάλην ἐξέπνευσεν, similarly Matt 27.50: πάλιν κράξας φωνῇ μεγάλῃ ἀφῆκεν τὸ πνεῦμα. This cry is interpreted in Luke 23.46 via Ps 31.6 and in John 19.30 via the cry τετέλεσται. On this, see Schwemer 1998, 23-27 and Hengel 1989b, 279, 284ff. (= 2007b, 633, 638ff.): John 19.30 contains an allusion to Gen 2.1-2. The work of "new creation" is "finished" with the death of Jesus. The Sabbath rest (19.31) now begins in the tomb.

[87] Mark 10.45; 14.24.

[88] Mark 15.39: ἀληθῶς οὗτος ὁ ἄνθρωπος υἱὸς θεοῦ ἦν. In Matt 27.54 this becomes the confession of the whole team of guards in response to an earthquake, which has been added.

[89] Luke 23.47-49. δίκαιος is, to be sure, also a predicate of the servant of God according to Isa 53.11: *yaṣdîq ṣaddîq 'abdî lārabbîm*. On this, see Mittmann-Richert 2008. An Old Latin manuscript (g[1]) and the oldest Syriac textual witnesses (sy[s.c]) add a reference to the destruction of Jerusalem: *dicentes: vae nobis quae facta sunt hodie propter peccata nostra appropinquavit enim desolatio Hierusalem.* This could be an addition from the Diatessaron.

dismay of the observers: they beat their breasts before they return home (23.48). The author—who writes only a few years after the destruction of Jerusalem and, still being deeply moved by this event, writes about it in the greatest detail of all the evangelists—establishes in this way a connection between the crucifixion of Jesus and the catastrophe of the year 70 CE.[90]

21.3 The Entombment[91]

On the basis of Deut 21.22-23, according to Jewish law, the *tālûy*, the person who is stoned and thereafter hanged, whose corpse was hanged on a tree as a sign of the divine curse, is not permitted to remain "on the wood" overnight but must be taken down and buried before the onset of darkness. This specification was applied in New Testament times also to persons who died on a cross. Through the intervention of a "noble councillor,"[92] Joseph of Arimathea,[93] who presumably belonged to the lay nobility and was perhaps a member of the Sanhedrin, secures a proper burial for Jesus. Mark does not characterize him directly as a disciple of Jesus, but he is said to be one "who was waiting for the kingdom of God,"[94] i.e., for Mark he belonged to those Jews who had been impressed by the eschatological preaching of the Baptist and of Jesus. He could be called a sympathizer of Jesus.[95] According to the "ideal" law of the Mishnah, there were

[90] Hengel 2008c, 324–31 (ET = 2000b, 189–94). In his passion story, Luke must have used a "special source," which corresponds more to his theology than the Markan portrayal. It is probably based, at least in part, on older tradition. As in the birth story in Luke 1 and 2, Luke's own shaping and original source cannot be separated here. Perhaps, what is in view is his own older notes, which could go back in part to eyewitness reports.

[91] Blinzler 1969, 387ff.; Pesch 1984b, 509–19; Brown 1994, II: 1240–41; Hengel 2001a; Dunn 2003b, 781ff.

[92] Mark 15.43: εὐσχήμων βουλευτής. Matthew 27.57 turns him into a "rich man" (cf. Isa 53.9 LXX). For this he omits the "councillor" and designates him as a disciple of Jesus (ἐμαθητεύθη τῷ Ἰησοῦ). A Jewish "councillor," which means in his time a rabbinic "Sanhedrist," is for him not capable of such a deed. In a similar way he changes the "leader of a synagogue" in Mark 5.22, 35 into an ἄρχων (Matt 9.18, 23) and deletes Jesus' positive judgment on the scribe in Mark 12.28, 34. In Matt 22.35 this scribe becomes a νομικός who tests Jesus, in dependence on Luke 10.25. Luke 23.50-51 supplements the βουλευτής with the predicate "good and upright" and stresses that he had not agreed with the "resolution and deed" of the Sanhedrin. For John Joseph appears as a "secret disciple of Jesus out of fear for the Jews," who buries the corpse together with Nicodemus (19.38-39). The Markan version is the most original.

[93] Probably Ramatayim, 1 Sam 1.1, a small city ca. thirty kilometers northwest of Jerusalem; see Görg 1991, 167.

[94] Mark 15.43: καὶ αὐτὸς ἦν προσδεχόμενος τὴν βασιλείαν τοῦ θεοῦ.

[95] The role of Joseph of Arimathea also suggests that Jesus was no longer an unknown person in Jerusalem already prior to the Passover of his death and, as was also the case in

two special burial places for criminals, for sinners should not be placed together with the righteous.[96] There is no reason to relate this text to Jesus. After all, Jesus was not condemned and executed by a Jewish court but by the Romans. The control over his corpse was solely in the hands of the prefect. With his crucifixion the hierarchs had achieved their goal.

Roman law was familiar—as a punishment that accompanied execution—with the refusal of any honoring of the dead, which included proper burial. The corpses of the Christians who were tortured to death in the arena in Lyon in 177 CE were guarded for six days and finally burned, and their ashes were thrown in the Rhone.[97] The one who removed the corpse of an executed person without authorization had to reckon with punishment.[98] The release was left solely to the discretion of the authority that had decreed the sentence of death, i.e., in the case of Jesus, to the discretion of Pilate.[99] We have, however, numerous witnesses for the fact that the petition for the release of the corpse of executed persons was granted in a generous way. Above all, Augustus usually gave a positive answer to such petitions of relatives. With the later emperors this was almost the rule.[100] It is thus understandable that Joseph of Arimathea "dared" to turn to Pilate[101] and that the prefect granted the petition of this influential man, presumably on account of the usual financial incentive.[102] Perhaps we may view this feature as an indication that Pilate did not consider the guilt of Jesus to be very weighty. After all, according to all that we know, in contrast

---

Bethany, had a certain number of followers or sympathizers. Therefore, a little later the community of disciples could find a foothold in Jerusalem.

[96] m. Sanh. 6.7c. Corresponding to the four types of execution stipulated in Mishnah Sanhedrin, there was a grave "for stoned persons and burned persons and a different one for beheaded persons and strangled persons" (i.e., for the four Jewish types of execution). "When the flesh had decayed, the bones were gathered buried in their place," i.e., in the family tomb. At the same time, the relatives were to express their agreement with witnesses (accusers) and judges. An outer mourning was forbidden to them. See Krauss 1933, 204–5. Here, we are largely dealing with an unrealistic construction, which cannot be related to the burial of Jesus; cf. Josephus, *J.W.* 4.317 and *Ant.* 4.202; 5.44; Bill. I: 1049. Blinzler 1969, 390–91. On the burial of Jesus, see also Hengel 2001a, 129–38.

[97] Eusebius, *Hist. eccl.* 5.1.62; cf. Mart. Pol. 17.2: The release of the corpse is prevented so that the Christians do not honor the martyrs instead of the crucified one.

[98] See the novella in Petronius, *Sat.* 111–112, about the military guarding of a crucified criminal whose corpse is stolen by his family.

[99] It belonged to the *arbitrium iudicantis*; see section 21.1.1 with note 13.

[100] Blinzler 1969, 385–86. Dig. 48.24.3: *corpora animadversorum quibuslibet petentibus ad sepulturam danda sunt.*

[101] Mark 15.43 portrays this in a way that is true to the situation: τολμήσας εἰσῆλθεν πρὸς τόν Πιλᾶτον καί ἠτήσατο τὸ σῶμα τοῦ Ἰησοῦ. In the case of a political criminal, the step of the petitioner was not entirely without risk.

[102] Philo, *Legat.* 302 mentions in the first position of his vices the δωροδοκία (i.e., capability of being bribed), then ὕβρεις and ἁρπαγαί.

to the clan of Annas and Caiaphas, he did not further harass the followers of Jesus in the following six years of his time in office. This lack of information about the oppression of the new messianic movement in Palestine by the Roman authorities applies—according to our knowledge—to the whole first century CE.[103] Joseph caused the burial to be carried out in a rock tomb which was shut with a roll stone and was located, according to John, in a garden near the place of execution. This too could preserve one of those valuable place specifications that are typical for John.[104]

Doubt about the entombment tradition is unfounded. The assumption that the corpse of Jesus was thrown in a mass grave has no basis in the sources. The bones of the crucified Jonathan, son of Ezekiel (?), discovered at Mount Scopus in 1968, were also gathered after the first burial in the usual way in a family ossuary, and in this traces of an anointing of the bones with oil (after the second burial) were even still visible, as the women wanted to do to the corpse of Jesus.[105] The fact that from the beginning the entombment of Jesus was not an insignificant feature is evident from 1 Cor 15.3-4, where the formula "that Christ died for our sins according to the Scriptures" is followed by the phrase "and that he was buried." We are not dealing here with a superfluous formula. It constitutes the bridge between the death of Jesus and the confession of his resurrection.[106]

With this the story of Jesus appeared to be concluded once and for all, for Pilate and the Jewish leaders but also for the disciples who had fled, who probably stayed hidden in Jerusalem,[107] since, after all, the women had likewise continued to remain in Jerusalem. The day of Jesus' death on the first day of the Passover festival was followed by a Sabbath,[108] which

---

[103] The first execution of Christians by the Romans in Palestine of which we know is the execution of the second bishop of Jerusalem, Symeon, son of Clopas, allegedly a cousin of Jesus, who was crucified under the governor Atticus at the time of Trajan (after 98 CE): Hegesippus according to Eusebius, *Hist. eccl.* 3.11, 32.

[104] Mark 15.46 = Matt 27.60 = Luke 23.53; cf. John 19.41. According to Matthew, it was the personal tomb of Joseph. According to Mark, Luke, and John, it was new, i.e., no dead person had been placed in the tomb. In Gos. Pet. 23–24, Herod releases the corpse and the burial takes place "in his own tomb," which is called the Garden of Joseph. The dependence upon John is obvious. It also becomes clear here how the tradition grows. On the other hand, a firm place tradition appears to be present from the beginning. On the tomb of Jesus, see Biddle 1998.

[105] Mark 16.1; cf. Luke 23.56 and 24.1. See section 22.1.

[106] On this, see Hengel 2001a. The phrase καὶ ὅτι ἐτάφη underlines in the same way the reality of the death of Jesus and the reality of his "resurrection from the grave." See section 22.1.

[107] Cf., for example, John 20.19; Gos. Pet. 14.

[108] John 19.31 speaks of a "great Sabbath," since it fell, according to the Johannine chronology, on the first day of the festival of weeks, the day after the Passover night; cf. also Mart. Pol. 8.1; 21.1.

held special weight due to the festival of unleavened bread and on which all activities were prohibited in the holy city. The women's visit to the tomb in the early morning of the first day after the Sabbath in order to make up the anointing that had been left undone in the overly hurried entombment on the evening of the Sabbath was a final labor of love, a consequence of their inner bond with the failed messianic prophet Jesus of Nazareth. What happened, of course, was entirely different.

PART VII
The Testimony to the Resurrection of Jesus

22

The Testimony to the Resurrection of Jesus[1]

The primitive community knew from the beginning that God raised the crucified Messiah Jesus "from the dead."[2] After the catastrophe of Golgotha, the flight of the disciples, and the apparent end of their hopes, this confession points to a radical change that is, according to human judgment, entirely unexpected. It leads to a new beginning, to the emergence of the church, and forms its basis today. In what follows, our interest is not one-sidedly with the confession of Jesus as the risen one but more with the emergence of this confession, i.e., we must ask about the phenomenon of the resurrection event, which is still historically graspable for us.

We basically have three quite different kinds of pointers to this event: the resurrection confessions, the stories of the empty tomb, and—as the decisive statements—the reports of the appearances of the risen one before eyewitnesses. The confessions occur in concise form especially in the New Testament letters and in Acts, whereas the stories of the empty tomb and the appearances are found at the end of the four Gospels, at the beginning of Acts, and in a confession-like short report (as our oldest and most important witness) in 1 Cor 15.3-8. In relation to them we find ourselves in a difficult position, for in these formally disparate witnesses we are always

---

[1] Grass 1962; Rengstorf 1967a; Campenhausen 1966; K. Lehmann 1968; Kremer 1967; 1973; Pesch 1973a; 1973b; Kasper 1973; Schelkle 1973; Stuhlmacher 1973; Hengel 1973 = 2006a, 52–73; Kasper 1977, 124–62 (GV = 1974, 145–88); Theissen/Merz 1998, 474–511 (GV = 1997, 415–46). Cf. the contributions of Chester 2001; Schwemer 2001a; 2010; Hengel 2001a; Eckstein 2003. Cf. the annotated bibliography, which considers only English-language literature, in Charlesworth/Elledge 2006, 233–40.

[2] The formulaic expression ἐγείρειν ἐκ νεκρῶν (more rarely also ἀνιστάναι) occurs in almost all the writings of the New Testament about thirty times, chiefly in relation to the resurrection of Christ and most frequently in Paul. Cf. Eckstein 2003, 232ff. The resurrection statements can point both to God as acting subject and to Jesus (or Christ, Kyrios, Son of God).

dealing at the same time with statements of faith, which largely elude the objectifying grasp of the observer and appear foreign to our world which we define in the technical terms of the natural sciences. As was already the case in the quest for the human being Jesus of Nazareth, here it is all the more true that we can speak only of attempts to draw near.

22.1 The Oldest Witness: 1 Cor 15.3-8[3]

This witness, which is one of the most frequently discussed and most controversial texts of the New Testament, goes back in terms of content to the beginnings of the primitive community in Jerusalem. All three forms of references to the resurrection are combined in it:

(a) the two-membered christological confession of the atoning death of Christ and his resurrection by God, i.e., the so-called formula of faith;
(b) the reference to the tomb of Jesus;
(c) a concise listing of the appearances of the risen one.

The concern in 1 Cor 15.3-8 is with Jesus' death, burial, resurrection on the third day, and with the fact that he was seen by many, in statements of extreme, unadorned brevity. The fact that such reported confessional statements are formulated at all is grounded in the fact that the resurrection of Jesus could not be proclaimed as a pure testimony of faith without reference to a real event. Rather, there was a need to emphasize at the same time the eyewitness testimony of those to whom the risen one had appeared, who saw him and thus, according to the opinion of the earliest communities, really perceived him. For the persons involved the confession was based on real, indeed, from their perspective, one must say *objective events*, which were kept in memory and testified to. For the primitive Christian missionary preaching no confession of faith in the resurrection of Jesus was possible without reference to the eyewitness testimony. Paul therefore consciously lists the witnesses just as Luke 1.2 speaks later of "eyewitnesses and servants of the word,"[4] who passed on the Jesus tradition; for the eyewitness testimony led in the case of the persons involved

---

[3] Schrage 2001, 10–108; Hengel 2001a; Schwemer 2007.

[4] Heb 2.3 is similar; see note 36 in chapter 1 and section 6.41 with note 130; cf. also Paul himself in 1 Cor 9.1 and 15.8. In terms of substance, Luke is completely correct with the reference—which is often criticized by theologians—to eyewitness testimony in Acts 1.22; 2.32; 3.15; 5.32; 10.41; cf. 26.16. John 20.29 (cf. 17.20); 1 Pet 1.8 refer to the situation of later generations. On this, see Hengel 2012b (GV = 2007a); Bauckham 2017, 114ff. and elsewhere. Cf. also Hengel 2005.

to the proclamation of what was seen and really experienced. With the confession of Peter and John before the leaders of the people in Acts 4.20—"we cannot keep silent about what we have seen and heard"—Luke reproduces a primitive Christian consensus.[5] Paul himself confesses in 1 Cor 9.1: "Am I not an apostle, have I not see Jesus, our Lord?" In primitive Christianity, lived history as "salvation history" and proclaimed message of salvation are indivisibly joined to a unity.

When Paul, in ca. 49/50 CE, founded the community in Corinth just twenty years after the Passover of Jesus' death, he taught there newly gained Christians "among the first points"[6] precisely the confession which he quotes in 1 Cor 15 and which, in addition to the salvation event of the death and resurrection of Jesus, also lists the first eyewitnesses. At the same time, he designates this confession-like historical report as εὐαγγέλιον. We could designate these three verses as an important crystallized core of the later Gospel writing. In so doing Paul surely also provided narrative elaboration on these confession-like statements. Without such elaboration they would not have been comprehensible at all to Corinthian Jewish and Gentile Christians. This means that here Paul identifies an event in space and time that is real for him, which at the same time bursts the human experience of space and time, as publicly proclaimed message of salvation, as "kerygma."[7] The fundamental opposition between experienceable history and kerygma as "pure word event," which has been stressed recently, did not exist in this way for earliest Christianity. As the Gospel according to Mark must be understood as a kerygmatically shaped historical account,[8] so too the Pauline-primitive Christian formula of 1 Cor 15.3ff. must be understood for the apostle and his mission communities as a confession with historical content and only as such as εὐαγγέλιον.

The listing of the resurrection witnesses in 1 Cor 15.3-8 is admittedly not completely uniform. A fashioned confession is probably present only in vv. 3-5:

---

[5] Acts 4.20: οὐ δυνάμεθα . . . ἡμεῖς ἃ εἴδαμεν καὶ ἠκούσαμεν μὴ λαλεῖν. Cf. the instruction of the risen one to Saul/Paul according to the third report of Luke in Acts 26.16: ἀλλὰ ἀνάστηθι καὶ στῆθι ἐπὶ τοὺς πόδας σου· εἰς τοῦτο γὰρ ὤφθην σοι, προχειρί-σασθαί σε ὑπηρέτην καὶ μάρτυρα ὧν τε εἶδές με ὧν τε ὀφθήσομαί σοι. Cf. already Luke 19.37 the praise of the disciples at the entry into Jerusalem περὶ πασῶν . . . ὧν εἶδον δυνάμεων.

[6] First Corinthians 15.3: παρέδωκα . . . ἐν πρώτοις.

[7] On the term in Paul, which is almost interchangeable with "gospel," see Rom 16.25; 1 Cor 1.21; 2.4; 15.14 and 2 Tim 4.17; Tit 1.3. Correspondingly, the verb κηρύσσειν comes close to εὐαγγελίζεσθαι.

[8] On the Gospel as narration of the "salvation event," cf. Mark 1.1: ἀρχὴ τοῦ εὐαγ-γελίου Ἰησοῦ Χριστοῦ . . . and on this, 14.9. See Hengel 2008c, 158–96 (ET = 2000b, 90–115).

that Christ *died* for our sins according to the Scriptures
and that he was *buried*
and that he was *raised* on the third day according to the Scriptures
and that he *appeared* to Cephas,
then to the twelve.[9]

It recounts an event which the men whom Paul names experienced and testified to and which, in addition, was theologically interpreted and confessed as an eschatological saving event in the formulas "for our sins" and "according to the Scriptures." What interests us is the specifications about concrete events contained in it. Here a reference is made in the first line to the death of the Messiah. In this pre-Pauline formula, Christos has not yet been smoothed down to a personal name but expresses the messianic dignity of the crucified one. The statement of the death of Christ, which is widespread in Acts and in the letters of the New Testament, is founded, among other things, on the memory that Jesus was crucified because of his messianic claim as "king of the Jews."[10] Through the resurrection God had proven true his messianic claim—which appeared to be refuted by the crucifixion—in an entirely unexpected, unfathomable way.

The second statement, "that he was buried" (ὅτι ἐτάφη), is often misinterpreted. It does not simply underline in a banal way the reality of the death of Jesus, as is often claimed, for this was not yet doubted at the time of Paul. This did not occur until fifty–sixty years later in the Johannine corpus and in Ignatius through the so-called docetists. This statement emphasizes in the first place that Jesus not only died but—what was not entirely self-evident for one who was executed as a criminal—was placed in a tomb. Paul also refers to Christ being buried in Rom 6.4.[11] A meaningless empty phrase had no place in such a "confession." In antiquity, criminals were sometimes left to the "vultures and dogs" for "burial."[12] Thus,

---

[9] First Corinthians 15.3-5:

ὅτι Χριστὸς ἀπέθανεν ὑπὲρ τῶν ἁμαρτιῶν ἡμῶν κατὰ τὰς γραφάς.
καὶ ὅτι ἐτάφη
καὶ ὅτι ἐγήγερται τῇ ἡμέρᾳ τῇ τρίτῃ κατὰ τὰς γραφὰς
καὶ ὅτι ὤφθη Κηφᾷ
εἶτα τοῖς δώδεκα.

[10] Hengel 2002, 240–61. On the "dying formulas" in connection with Χριστός, see Rom 5.6, 8; 6.9; 14.9, 15; 1 Cor 8.11. See the end of section 21.3 and note 34 below.

[11] Cf. also Col 2.12; Acts 13.29. Outside of the Gospels these are the only references. See Hengel 2001a, 136ff. On the denial of the humanity and thus also of the death of Jesus by the docetists, see Hengel 1993a, 176–201 (ET = 1989a, 59–72).

[12] Cf. Homer, *Il.* 22.350–354: Achilles refuses burial to the dying Hector. Even if his father wanted to counterbalance his corpse with gold, "the dogs and birds will tear you

the still living memory of the burial of Jesus stands behind it. After all, the event lay only a short time in the past. Another controversial question is whether knowledge about the discovery of the empty tomb is implicitly presupposed in the phrase "and that he was buried." In our view, this too is the case and means that with the phrase "that he was buried" more was being communicated than simply the real death of Jesus. Rather, it speaks at least as much to the radical contrast between entombment and resurrection and thus to the reality of the following resurrection statements. In Palestinian Judaism and to some extent also in the diaspora, rising from the dead was understood very concretely as the leaving of the grave through God's miracle. Behind this stands the eschatological hope of the restitution of all Israel in the kingdom of God through the resurrection of the dead following prophetic texts such as Ezek 37.1-28, Isa 26.19, and especially Dan 12.2-3, 13.[13] The formula says: The risen one, who appeared to the disciples, is the one who was buried. Here we must consider the fact that Paul, in 1 Cor 15, fights for the reality of the Christian hope in the resurrection against the typical Greek contestation of the bodily resurrection in Corinth. To be sure, in 15.49ff., he says "that flesh and blood cannot inherit the kingdom of God" but rather needs transformation into the image of the exalted Lord, which awaits all believers at the parousia.[14] But this is not a confirmation of the Greek radical devaluation of the body and not a restriction of the resurrection to a purely spiritual event, for in v. 51 it is stated clearly that while not all die, "we will all be changed" (πάντες δὲ ἀλλαγησόμεθα). This means that body and soul will not be separated. The body is not rejected as "prison" or "tomb of the soul"[15] as in Platonism but changed: the "fleshly body" (σῶμα σαρκικόν) becomes a "spiritual body" (σῶμα πνευματικόν), which corresponds to God's holiness; this applies to those who have fallen asleep and to those who are alive. The primitive community apparently interpreted the resurrection of Jesus from the beginning as a transformation of the corpse. According to Jesus' controversy with the Sadducees in Mark 12.18-27, those who are resurrected through God's creative power will be "as the angels in heaven" and thus

---

apart." On this, see Hengel 1982a, 17–20. According to a verse inscription from Caria, a slave who had murdered his master was crucified "as food for the birds and wild animals." Hengel 1977a, 76. See also the guarding of the corpse of a crucified robber in Petronius, *Sat.* 11.5ff., which was meant to hinder a burial: Hengel 1977a, 48.

[13] See Hengel 2001a, 150–72.

[14] Cf. also Rom 8.29-30; Phil 3.20-21; Back 2002, 161–84.

[15] On this, see Schweizer 1971, 1028 (GV = 1964, 1028.35ff.): "Thus the σῶμα is felt to be the σῆμα of the soul . . . , an evil in which man is trapped . . . and which is thus to be despised and avoided as much as possible."

not know of marriage any longer,[16] i.e., the concern is with transformation as "new creation" amidst preservation of personal bodily identity.

According to the primitive Christian accounts, the risen one can "appear" suddenly and become invisible, go through closed doors, and yet, on the other hand, he can be touched, indeed can even consume food.[17] For Palestinian Jews of a Pharisaic character—and Paul was a former Pharisee—the resurrection was only imaginable as a *bodily resurrection from the grave*. It is wrongheaded when it is stressed time and again that the stories of the empty tomb are late legends without exception, with the rationale that it is not spoken of in the oldest confession of 1 Cor 15.3ff. In the conciseness of the confession statements we must assume that the statement "that he was buried" with the following statement "he was raised on the third day" together imply the tradition of the empty tomb, with the reference to burial admittedly still being ambiguous when taken on its own. The fact that the women, who play the decisive role in the Gospels' accounts of Easter morning, are completely absent from this entire list is connected with the fact that according to Jewish law, they had no witness function and therefore would be out of place in a proof through witnesses;[18] indeed it is connected with the fact that the testimony of women was regarded as questionable. In itself it is unlikely that only men saw appearances of the risen one. Nevertheless, Paul passes over the women for this reason. Celsus still has his Jewish informant mock: "Who then has seen this? A crazy woman, as you say. . . ."[19] Thus, when Paul says nothing *expressis verbis* about the empty tomb and the women, this does not prove that he knew nothing about them and that these traditions were based on late legends. The narrative confession is also silent about other "fundamental facts," for example that Jesus was crucified and that his execution in Jerusalem took place at the festival of Passover.

Scarcely less controversial is the dating "raised *on the third day*." Among other things, it has been objected against this dating—which, in our view, can be explained best by the discovery of the empty tomb by the women on Easter morning, i.e., on the third day after the death

---

[16] Mark 12.25: ἀλλ' εἰσὶν ὡς ἄγγελοι ἐν τοῖς οὐρανοῖς = Matt 22.30; cf. Luke 20.36: ἰσάγγελοι . . . καὶ υἱοί εἰσιν θεοῦ. See section 18.4 with note 74.

[17] Luke 24.15, 31, 40ff.; Matt 28.9, 16ff.; John 20.14ff., 19ff., 24-29; cf. 1 John 1.1. See section 22.2.2 with notes 100–101. On this, cf. Schwemer 2004.

[18] Bill. III: 558–60; cf. 217, 251. The basis is Sifre Deut. 190: "Men and not women"; m. Šebu. 4.1–2: "The oath of witnesses applies in the case of men but not of women." On individual exceptions, see m. ʿEd. 1.2; m. Yebam. 15.2–3. See Ilan 1999, 53.

[19] Origen, *Cels.* 2.55: τίς τοῦτο εἶδε; Γυνὴ πάροιστρος, ὥς φατε. This refers to John 20.11-18, cf. Matt 28.8-10.

of Jesus—that this detail was "spun out"[20] of a scriptural proof, namely Hos 6.1-2. There, it says: "Come, let us return to YHWH, for he has torn us and will heal us . . . , he will revive us after two days, on the third day he causes us to rise, that we may live before him." Against this hypothesis stands not only the collective reference to sinful Israel which has fallen away from God—the whole is a prayer of repentance, which fits badly with the crucified Messiah—but also the fact that this text is quoted neither in the New Testament nor in the whole of the second century. It is only with Tertullian, after 200 CE, that it is adduced as a proof from Scripture.[21] The motif of the resurrection on the third day is too firmly and frequently anchored in the most diverse strata of the tradition[22] to be regarded as a late invention from Scripture. The early emphasis on the first day of the week in the primitive community also shows that concrete memory stands behind this specification.[23] For the community this historical experience was connected with the special meaning of the "third day" as a "short period of time" in Old Testament texts.[24] The first appearances certainly did not take place only quite some time after the death of Jesus, for example with a temporal distance of weeks or months in Galilee. We find visions of people who have died on multiple occasions in Judaism.[25] What is "without analogy" is for the primitive community the appearance of the one who has been raised bodily from the grave before many witnesses.

---

[20] On the term, see Conzelmann 1965, 7 (= 1974, 137); Conzelmann 1967, 52 (ET = 1969, 66).

[21] Tertullian, *Marc.* 4.43.1, as prophecy of the women and their service on Sunday morning. Cf. also Ps.-Tertullian, *Adv. Jud.* 13.23. On this, see Hengel 2001a, 132ff., and the discussion of the whole problem there. The text may have already played a role in primitive Christianity, but the resurrection of Jesus "on the third day" cannot simply be derived from it. On Hos 6.2, see in detail K. Lehmann 1968, 205–30. Among other things Lehmann points (182–85) to the enigmatic temporal specification in Luke 13.32: τῇ τρίτῃ (ἡμέρᾳ) τελειοῦμαι.

[22] Luke 9.22; 13.32; Acts 10.40 and elsewhere. In addition, we also have the statement of the resurrection "after three days": Mark 8.31; 9.31; 10.34; John 2.19-20 in the temporal sense of within a short period of time.

[23] Cf. 1 Cor 16.2; Acts 20.7; Rev 1.10. See section 22.1.1 with note 73 below.

[24] Genesis 22.4; 31.22; 34.25; 40.20; 42.18; Exod 19.11, 15-16; Lev 7.17-18; Num 19.12, 19; Josh 9.17; Judg 20.30 etc. On this, see K. Lehmann 1968, 159–316. On the symbolic meaning of the third day, see Gese 1981, 164 (GV = 1977, 148). The formula expresses the direct connection with the crucifixion.

[25] Cf., e.g., 1 Sam 28.3-25; see also Josephus, *Ant.* 6.332–336; 2 Macc 15.12-16. See further Luke 16.19-31. In the parable of the rich man and poor Lazarus, the brothers of the rich man would not repent if Lazarus appeared to them as one who had risen from the dead. Cf. the elaboration in John 11. See Frey 1997–2000, III: 423–24. The appearance of the dead in a dream is widespread in Jewish texts: Josephus, *Ant.* 17.349–353: Glaphyra's deceased first husband Alexander, son of Herod I, appears to her shortly before she dies. Rabbinic attestations can be found in Bill. II: 228ff. on Luke 16.24 and 233 on Luke 16.30.

Presumably only the mention of *Cephas* and the twelve belonged to the original formula. The other witnesses were joined to it later or were added by Paul. Cephas, from Aramaic *kêfa'*, rock, Greek Πέτρος, was the Aramaic byname that Jesus had given to Simon.[26] The disciple, who already played a central role in the most intimate circle around Jesus, was the leading figure in the primitive community in Jerusalem until he had to hand over the leadership function to James, the brother of the Lord,[27] due to the persecution under Agrippa I, and with this became—despite the division of the spheres of mission in Gal 2.7—a competitor of the Pauline mission between Asia Minor and Rome. We owe considerable portions of the Gospel tradition to him. It is no accident that he always occupies the first position in the lists of disciples in the Gospels. We have no detailed narrative of this first appearance to Peter. However, the concise, almost confession-like formulation with which the eleven gathered in Jerusalem receive the returning Emmaus disciples in Luke shows that the knowledge of this remained alive: "The Lord has truly risen and has appeared to Simon." Here too we are dealing with an old formula.[28]

Cephas-Peter is followed by the "twelve,"[29] i.e., the more intimate circle of disciples that was already gathered by Jesus, which expressed his claim on the twelve-tribe people. It is possible that Simon-Cephas called this circle together again on the basis of the first appearance to him. The "twelve" go back to the call of the earthly Jesus and were not constituted for the first time by the appearances of the risen one. The betrayer Judas had already belonged to it until Jesus' last night. The fact that Paul speaks of the "twelve" and not—as would have been historically exact—of the "eleven" is conditioned by the fact that "the twelve" was an established term[30] and the eleven had been quickly supplemented again through the

---

[26] Mark 3.16; see section 11.6 with notes 145–49. It is conspicuous that Paul usually uses the Aramaic name, which occurs eight times, in relation to his Greek-speaking communities. The only exception is in Gal 2.7-8. On the person of Cephas and the significance of his name, see Hengel 2010a (GV = 2006b). In our view, the name should more likely be translated with "rock" than with "stone." The wordplay πέτρος—πέτρα in Matt 16.18 may very well go back to the primitive community, for example to the Hellenists.

[27] Acts 12.1-17; cf. the sequence of the three pillars with James at the head in Gal 2.9. The persecution probably took place at the Passover festival in 43 CE. See section 3.1.4 with notes 270–72.

[28] Cf. Luke 24.34: ὄντως ἠγέρθη ὁ κύριος καὶ ὤφθη Σίμωνι. On this, see section 22.2.2 and Eckstein 2003, 152ff. On the emphatic, front-placed ὄντως, see Luke 23.47; Mark 11.32; John 8.36; 1 Cor 14.25. It gives the formula the character of a confession.

[29] First Corinthians 15.5: εἶτα τοῖς δώδεκα.

[30] Cf. Gos. Pet. 59: ἡμεῖς δὲ οἱ δώδεκα μαθηταὶ τοῦ κυρίου ἐκλαίομεν καὶ ἐλυπούμεθα ("But we, the twelve disciples of the Lord, wept and grieved"; trans. Ehrman/Pleše 2011, 387). See further Justin, *Dial.* 42.1. One could point to the designation—which

election of Matthias.[31] It is also significant that Paul can presuppose that the Corinthians know who these twelve are. He must, as with Cephas-Peter, also have spoken about them[32] when he explained this formula to the Corinthians at the founding of the community. According to 1 Cor 1.12, Cephas-Peter appears to have visited Corinth himself later. The community there knew much more about him and the other resurrection witnesses than we do.

The *age of this foundational formula* is controversial. While J. Jeremias[33] hypothesizes an Aramaic *Urform* in Jerusalem, H. Conzelmann,[34] among others, postulates that the confession emerged first in Antioch, for which there is no indication. In any case, the content of the foundational formula points back to the primitive community. In it there is not yet talk of the institutional church but only of the first Palestinian witnesses. The controversial but insoluble question of an Aramaic *Urform* is immaterial, for Greek was also spoken in Jerusalem. The text probably arose where Cephas and the twelve were active: in the Jewish capital. Paul became acquainted with it shortly after his conversion in ca. 33 CE, presumably in Damascus, where he was baptized and received into the community.[35] After all, following his call, he immediately became a missionary in Nabataean Arabia and traveled to Jerusalem about three years later to get to know the first resurrection witness, Peter-Cephas.[36] It is plausible that

---

can be documented since Justin—"the seventy" for the translators of the Septuagint, although there were seventy-two according to the original tradition. See Hengel 1999b, 335–42; cf. also Luke 10.1 and the *varia lectio* 72. By contrast, the canonical evangelists consistently have οἱ ἕνδεκα: cf. Luke 24.9, 33; Acts 1.26; 2.14; Matt 28.16; Mark 16.14. According to John 20.19ff., Jesus initially appears to only ten disciples, since Thomas is absent.

[31] Acts 1.15ff.; on this, cf. also John 20.24: Thomas is εἷς ἐκ τῶν δώδεκα, although only eleven disciples remain. See also Gos. Pet. 59 (on the Greek text, see note 30 above): "we, the twelve disciples." On the twelve as apostles, see the following discussion in this section.

[32] Cf. 1 Cor 9.5; Gal 1.17, 19.

[33] Jeremias 1966c, 101–5 (GV = 1967a, 95–98); 1966b; 1969c.

[34] Conzelmann 1965 (= 1974, 131–41); he is followed by Vielhauer 1965b, 57–61 (= 1965a, 180–84); Güttgemanns 1968. For the discussion, see Schrage 2001, 21–25. He regards an emergence in Jerusalem as possible. The dispute is focused especially on the question of whether the meaning "messiah" still shines through in χριστός. This is certainly still the case in the pre-Pauline dying formula. In Greek Χριστός was completely unusual as a name or title of a person. The messianic meaning of Χριστός did not completely disappear in a short time: see Hengel 2002, 240–61 (250–51). Rather, it remained alive in the whole of primitive Christianity.

[35] Galatians 1.17: Among the τοὺς πρὸ ἐμοῦ ἀποστόλους the "twelve" are the core group.

[36] According to Gal 1.18 he stays for fifteen days with Peter; see Hengel/Schwemer 1998, 229–36 (ET = 1997, 144–50).

this formula goes back to the Hellenists who were driven out of Jerusalem, who for their mission needed a concise summary of the kerygma, which they mediated to the newly converted Christians as an "iron ration."

Paul *supplemented* the fundamental formula of 1 Cor 15.3-5 with *additional specifications of witnesses*, probably at the latest during his time as a missionary in Cilicia and Syria.[37] The great number of witnesses is meant to reinforce the proclamation of the risen one through the argument that an illusion, a self-deception of an individual or a group, is impossible, for the number of the witnesses is overwhelming; moreover, they are also very different in character. For Paul the certainty of his faith did not depend on this number—after all, he had seen the Lord himself—but for the mission communities founded by him a reliable list of witnesses was necessary. The fourfold εἶτα or ἔπειτα from the twelve via the five hundred until James and "all the apostles" is in itself to be understood temporally, but not in the sense of a strict chronology; thus, it is not, for example, said that the appearance before ἀπόστολοι πάντες must have happened at one time and prior to the appearance before the five hundred brothers.[38] Rather, the concern is probably with a larger number of appearances, for those who are specified with "all the apostles" were more numerous than "the twelve." Luke is the first to reduce the apostles to the circle of the twelve. Their scope remains uncertain and was probably also contested already early on. Peter, James, and the rest of the eleven certainly belonged to it.[39] By contrast, in the case of the five hundred a shared seeing is stressed by the emphatic ἐφάπαξ. It is also uncertain whether the whole list is exhaustive. Paul need not have listed all the witnesses known to him here. At the end he places himself in the series of eyewitnesses. To be sure, he clearly demarcates himself from the previous appearances—chronologically as well—through the emphatic "but last of all he appeared also to me as to one untimely born."[40] As the last by far he is a controversial special case and as such an example of the free, electing grace of God.

The majority of the "*more than five hundred brothers*" mentioned in 1 Cor 15.6, to whom the risen one appeared in a shared vision, were still

---

[37] Galatians 1.19ff.: ca. 36–48 CE. The first supplementations presumably go back already to the informants from whom he received the tradition. After all, as a persecutor in Jerusalem he was probably already confronted with the claims of the followers of Jesus.

[38] Thus, the two Emmaus disciples could, for example, be assigned to this group or also Barnabas; see 1 Cor 9.5-7.

[39] Cf. 1 Cor 9.1ff. The apostleship of Paul, by contrast, was not generally recognized. On this, see Frey 2004, passim.

[40] First Corinthians 15.8: ἔσχατον δὲ πάντων ὡσπερεὶ τῷ ἐκτρώματι ὤφθη κἀμοί. On the unusual expression ἔκτρωμα, see Spicq 1978, I: 237ff. Paul expresses with this the unusual character and suddenness of his life turn to faith and to apostleship (239).

alive twenty years later at the time of the founding of the community in Corinth, though some had "fallen asleep," which also means that Paul is well informed about the details of the founding event in Palestine. He could indeed also have written an "Acts of the Apostles." Impulses toward this are present in his letters.[41] But his task was a different one. We do not know where and in what manner this greatest of all Christophanies occurred. We can assume that women also belonged to it and that it was scarcely an assembly of men alone. The term "brother" points to the fact that the Christophany occurred in the midst of the members of the primitive community, i.e., the church in *statu nascendi*. At the same time, it is the only relatively reliable larger number from the history of the primitive church. The numbers at the beginning of Acts — 120 (10 × 12) at the election of Matthias before Pentecost, the three thousand at Pentecost, and the five thousand a little later[42] — have only limited historical value.[43] We do not even know whether this appearance occurred in Galilee or in Jerusalem. Since Paul knew the Jerusalem community better, we are inclined to assume the latter. Since C. H. Weisse, in 1838, via A. von Harnack, E. von Dobschütz, and K. Holl through to J. Jeremias, this appearance before the five hundred has been brought into connection with the account of Pentecost in Acts 2.[44] This remains an unprovable postulate: the only *tertium comparationis* would be the mass event. Against this view it has been rightly objected that the Pentecost story in Acts 2 speaks not of a Christophany but of the Spirit-effected Easter witness of the disciples, especially of Peter, that the numbers that are specified diverge completely, and that in Paul the bestowal of the Spirit is connected to baptism and not to an Easter appearance.[45] This example simultaneously shows how little we know about the history of primitive Christianity.

A peculiarity is the appearance before James, the brother of the Lord, in 1 Cor 15.7. For he, in a similar way as Paul, had not previously been a follower of Jesus, but rather had probably adopted a critical stance toward his brother.[46] We find a reflex of this Christophany before James,

---

[41] Galatians 1 and 2; 1 Cor 9.1ff.; 15.4ff., 11; Rom 15.18ff.

[42] Acts 1.15; 2.41; 4.4. See Hengel/Schwemer 2019.

[43] The number of the "ten thousand" (μυριάδες, Acts 21.20) Jewish Christians in Jerusalem is also surely exaggerated.

[44] Texts in Hoffmann 1988, 35–36; Harnack 1988, 94; cf. Gilmour 1988 (= 1981); supporting and opposing opinions also in Schrage 2001, 55–56 with note 198. Cf. Wilckens 2002–2005, I/2: 127–28: an appearance in Galilee is probably in view.

[45] See the objections of Kremer 1973, 233–38.

[46] John 7.2-5; cf. Mark 3.21, 31ff., and section 8.3. See also Hengel 1999b, 549–82 (560–61).

the brother of the Lord, in the apocryphal Gospel of the Hebrews, which emerged in the first half of the second century:[47]

> But when the Lord had given the linen cloth to the servant of the priest, he went and appeared to James. For James had taken a vow not to eat bread from the time he drank the cup of the Lord until he should see him raised from among those who sleep (trans. Ehrman/Pleše 2011, 219).

When he appeared to him, the risen one is to have said:

> "Bring a table and bread." . . . He took the bread and blessed it, broke it, gave it to James the Just, and said to him: "My brother, eat your bread. For the Son of Man is risen from among those who sleep" (trans. Ehrman/Pleše 2011, 219).

Here we encounter James as the recipient of the first appearance of Jesus. The eucharistic meal scene displays a certain kinship with the account about the Emmaus disciples who recognize Jesus in the breaking of bread. This story is probably intended to ground the priority of James over Peter in the later Jewish Christian community.[48]

The statement "and appeared" (καὶ ὤφθη) of Paul in 1 Cor 15.3-8 has a broad Old Testament prehistory and is sometimes understood as an expression of the legitimation of the person in question by the risen one. One should not, however, claim that the verb ὤφθη expresses only this legitimation.[49] Paul's statement about his own vision of Christ already contradicts this view. Nor does it describe a mere coming to faith. Rather, as shown by the constant εἶτα/ἔπειτα, the concern is with events that can be fixed chronologically. They are concrete experiences, whose last witness, separated from all others temporally (ἔσχατον . . . πάντων), is Paul himself. With him the series of resurrection witnesses is concluded. Paul intends, as foreign as it may seem to us, a real "optic" seeing of the risen one, who is recognized as the crucified Jesus. If the concern were

---

[47] Cf. Aland 2005, 507; Ehrman/Pleše 2011, 218–19. Preserved through Jerome, *Vir. ill.* 2; cf. on the parallels, Klijn 1988, 4011; see further Klauck 2003a, 42–43 (GV = 2002, 61-62).

[48] Cf. also Gos. Thom. 12; Schwemer 2004, 221ff., and Hengel 2010a, 9 (GV = 2006b, 13).

[49] On this, see Eckstein 2003, 166ff.: "Neither in the Old Testament texts nor in the New Testament attestations is the concern with a 'legitimation formula' that is used in an exclusively technical way to ground the authority of a person without reference to the appearance in the actual sense" (167–68). It is an appearance that mediates authority. On this, see in detail below.

with a mere legitimation and a purely spiritual, inward "seeing of faith," then it would be hard to understand why those who came to faith later could not also appeal in the same way to a "he appeared also to me" (ὤφθη κἀμοί).[50] For Paul and all the more for the witnesses before him the concern was with real "Christophanies," irrespective of how we attempt to explain these phenomena today.

To be sure, Paul, in 1 Cor 15.3-9 and 1 Cor 9.1, has a different concept of apostleship from Luke, who, except for Acts 14.4, 14, withholds this title from Paul (and Barnabas).[51] However, in the fundamental question of the temporal and personal limitation of the resurrection appearances Luke is—despite all the large differences between them—united with Paul.[52] To be sure, there is a significant difference in the fact that Luke, according to Acts 1.3, restricts this limited time of the resurrection appearances to *forty days*, while Paul presupposes a longer period of time. For his call vision we must assume a larger distance vis-à-vis those mentioned previously. A later tradition, which is preserved, among others, in Irenaeus and in the Ascension of Isaiah,[53] speaks of a duration of eighteen months, during which the risen one stood in connection with his disciples. Harnack hypothesized that this was precisely the period of time until the conversion of Paul. With a view to what is presented in Acts 1–8, eighteen months seems too short to us, and we hypothesize a conversion of Paul rather in 33 CE. Certainty cannot be obtained here.

The Lukan restriction to the forty days of the fellowship of the risen one with his disciples and its conclusion through the "ascension" is oriented to Old Testament models—Moses at Sinai—and is aimed against speculative efforts to extend the time of revelation of the risen one too far.[54] Numerous gnostic writings of the second and third centuries were presented as secret revelations of the risen one after Easter. Just as Luke restricts the apostles to the twelve, so he reduces the period of the fellowship

---

[50] On this later problem, see John 20.29; 1 John 3.2; 1 Pet 1.8; cf. 2 Cor 5.7.

[51] Hengel/Schwemer 1998, 45–46, 333, 358 (ET = 1997, 25–26, 218–19, 235).

[52] In Acts 10.41, in the speech before Cornelius, Luke has Peter stress that Jesus appeared "not to the whole people but (only) to the witnesses previously determined by God, i.e., to us."

[53] Ascension of Isaiah 9.16: 545 days; Bauer 1967b, 266; in addition, we can now add the Apocryphon of James from Nag Hammadi (NHC I 2 p. 2): 550 days; on this, see Riesner 1994, 56–65; Hengel/Schwemer 1998, 47–48 (ET = 1997, 27).

[54] That the "ascension" (as well as the "forty-day period of time") "(is) first a product of Luke, as is well known"—thus, Schrage 2001, 59 n. 218, cannot be proven. In our view, it more likely goes back to Jerusalem tradition. Cf. the forty-day period in Jesus' temptation in the wilderness (see section 10.2) and in the rapture of Ezra (4 Ezra 14.23) and Baruch (2 Bar. 76.4) as a time of the perfect instruction of the people. The contradiction to Paul is, however, obvious.

with the risen one as a time of revelation to the forty days. By contrast, Paul has a broader concept of apostleship. This is shown by the last two members of the series of witnesses: "all the apostles" and he himself, the last of all and at the same time the "least among the apostles, who is not worthy to be called an apostle," because he "persecuted the community of God."[55] This means that for him and his communities—in contrast to Luke, Matt 10.2, Rev 21.4, and probably already Mark 6.30—the "apostles" are not yet identical with the twelve disciples called by Jesus. The ἀπόστολοι πάντες of 1 Cor 15.7 describe a broader circle of proclaimers, in which the "twelve" form the center but is by no means restricted to them and which is constituted by the fact that the risen one appeared to them all and they received their sending from him. Therefore, Paul can confront his opponents, who can test his apostleship, with the argument: "Am I not an apostle? Have I not seen our Lord Jesus?"[56]

In the case of "all the apostles" it need not have been *one* vision at the same point in time. Rather, we can assume that Paul summarized here a series of events. The scope of this circle, which receives its authority through the appearance of the risen one, must remain open. Paul sees himself as belonging to the circle, albeit as an outsider, the last in time, and the lowest in rank, while knowing that his claim was contested in Jerusalem, at least by some.[57] In Gal 1.17 he stresses that he, after his conversion in or near Damascus, did not "go up to Jerusalem to the apostles before me (πρὸ ἐμοῦ)," but traveled to (Nabataean) Arabia. A trace of this broader circle is perhaps still visible in Rom 16.7, where he mentions Junia (presumably a woman) and Andronicus, "his fellow prisoners," who "are famous among the apostles" and who became Christians before him (πρὸ ἐμοῦ).[58] Barnabas and perhaps even the seven leading Hellenists in Acts 6 also could have included themselves in it.[59] Even Luke calls Barnabas

---

[55] First Corinthians 15.9. On the concept of apostle in Paul and Luke, see Frey 2004, 126ff., 144ff., 149ff.

[56] First Corinthians 9.1: οὐκ εἰμὶ ἀπόστολος; οὐχ Ἰησοῦν τὸν κύριον ἡμῶν ἑόρακα. . . .

[57] Cf. 1 Cor 9.2: "If I am not an apostle to others (for example in Jerusalem), I am, nevertheless, to you. For you are the seal of my apostleship in the Lord," because he had founded the community in Corinth. On this, see Hengel 2010a, 111–16 (GV = 2006b, 180–89).

[58] It could, of course, also be the case that they possessed special honor in the circle of apostles as non-apostles. We also do not know whether the wives of the "apostles," who accompanied their husbands on journeys (1 Cor 9.5), participated in the apostolic title. Cf. Hengel 2010a, 129–30 (GV = 2006b, 211).

[59] Acts 21.8 calls Philip "εὐαγγελιστὴς . . . ἐκ τῶν ἑπτά," from the circle of the "seven" mentioned in Acts 6.5. The titles ἀπόστολος and εὐαγγελιστής are related in substance. They are missionary proclaimers of the gospel. Cf. later Eph 4.11; 2 Tim 4.5.

and Paul "apostles" in Acts 14.4, 14 on the first missionary journey—by the back door, so to speak.[60] For them it is decisive that they have received a *sending commission* from the Lord. Therefore, they bear the title "messengers of Jesus Christ," ἀπόστολοι Ἰησοῦ Χριστοῦ, on which Paul himself—as shown by the openings of 1 and 2 Corinthians, Galatians, and Romans—places the greatest value. The uncertainty in the interpretation is evident in the fact that Origen later postulates[61] that the ἀπόστολοι πάντες of 1 Cor 15.7 are identical to the seventy from Luke 10.1.

It is an impressive and at the same time very diverse listing of witnesses, which Paul summarizes in 1 Cor 15.3-8 under the key word ὤφθη plus a person in the dative. It is also clear that here Paul wishes to recount isolatable, concrete events that are separated by place and time and that the named witnesses are meant to vouch for the truth of these events. Nevertheless, the meaning of ὤφθη plus a person in the dative is not always completely clear. In the Septuagint, this relatively frequent formula "and the Lord appeared to so and so"[62] points not only to a theophany of YHWH but also to the *word of revelation* connected to it. Even if one rejects the thesis that the concern in 1 Cor 15 is exclusively with a legitimation formula, in which the concrete "seeing" no longer plays a role,[63] it initially remains open what kind of seeing is intended here. Paul can describe the first appearance to Peter-Cephas and the other appearances as well as his own vision of Christ before Damascus with ὤφθη plus the dative. In this respect he stands in a certain contradiction to the Lukan account, which, in the appearance of Jesus before the eleven in Luke 24.39, has Jesus say: "See my hands and my feet, that it is I myself. Touch me and see, for a spirit does not have flesh and bones." When the disciples remain unbelieving, he eats a piece of cooked fish before their eyes (24.42-43). The risen one demonstrates his corporality in a similar manner before

---

Perhaps εὐαγγελιστής was meant to replace ἀπόστολος later, when the apostle title was not continued. It could, however, not establish itself. Not it but the "elders" and later the bishops take the place of the "apostles."

[60] See the discussion above. Luke knows about this conflict and represents the more narrow Jerusalem view here in Acts 1ff. In that case, Acts 14.4, 14 appears as a conscious compromise.

[61] Origen, *Cels.* 2.65; cf. Theophylact, PG 124, 755.

[62] καὶ ὤφθη κύριος τῷ ... (or the like), see Gen 12.7; 17.1; cf. 18.1; 22.14; 26.2, 24; 35.9; 48.3; Exod 3.2; Judg 6.12; 1 Kgs 3.5; 9.2, as a translation of *rāʾāh* in the niphal. On this, see Eckstein 2003, 167ff.: "As much as the moment of 'seeing' is emphasized already through the word pair ὀφθῆναί τινι/ὁρᾶν, so clearly are the Old Testament appearance formulas already connected with a *word revelation*. . . . They are perceived as *visions* and as *auditions*" (169, Eckstein's emphasis).

[63] See note 49 above. On the diverse interpretations of ὤφθη, see Schrage 2001, 43–51; Stuhlmacher 2018, 196–98 (GV = 1992, 172–73).

Thomas (John 20.27). At the same time, he can go through closed doors, and suddenly appear and disappear. The transfigured corporality of the risen one can scarcely be portrayed in a more graphic and mysterious way. By contrast, according to Luke, the appearance of Christ to Paul on the way to Damascus is a heavenly vision.[64] A light shines from heaven, brighter than the sun, and he hears a voice: "Saul, Saul, why do you persecute me?" The hearing or seeing the light remain restricted to Paul; his companions perceive it only partially. In this point the vision accounts in Acts 9.3ff.; 22.6ff.; and 26.13ff., which deviate from each other in part, are relatively similar.[65] In 9.7 the companions see nothing and only hear, whereas in 22.9 they see only the light and hear nothing. With Paul it is completely different. According to 1 Cor 9.1, which interprets the ὤφθη κἀμοί of 15.8, he is an apostle because he has seen (ἑόρακα) the Lord. However, when he lists the ὀπτασίαι καὶ ἀποκαλύψεις κυρίου in 2 Cor 12.1ff., the vision before Damascus is precisely not included. It has a completely distinctive character: Paul insists on a real seeing. He distinguishes this call experience—which he describes in Gal 1.15-16 and 2 Cor 4.6 as a divine act of revelation that with respect to its content includes a "hearing"—from later visions and ecstatic experiences.[66] Thus, a comparison of Paul and Luke reveals differing presentations and evaluations of the appearances of the risen one. At a later time there is a tendency to portray these in a more graphic way, which continues in the apocryphal Gospels. In the Gospel of the Hebrews, which has already been quoted, Jesus hands over the linen corpse cloth to the slave of the high priest as evidence. In the Gospel of Peter,[67] the guards of the tomb and their captain see how two angels open the tomb and Christ ascends with them to heaven, and they report it to Pilate. Behind these later developments stand anti-docetic and apologetic tendencies. There was a desire to refute the accusation that the disciples had been deceived by a specter[68] and to counter objections such as those raised by the enemy of Christianity Celsus around 170: "If Jesus had really wanted to prove his divine power he would have had to appear

---

[64] Acts 26.19: οὐράνιος ὀπτασία; cf. v. 13: οὐρανόθεν . . . φῶς and the portrayal of the vision that follows.

[65] On the three accounts of Luke, see Hengel/Schwemer 1998, 63–71 (ET = 1997, 38–50), and Schwemer 2007. Perhaps Luke signals through this contradiction that diverse versions of it were in circulation.

[66] Cf. also Gal 2.2; Acts 18.9; 22.17, 21; 23.11; cf. 16.9; 27.23.

[67] Gospel of Peter 35ff. (around 140–150 CE); see also Eusebius, *Hist. eccl.* 6.12.2–6; Hengel 2008c, 22ff. (ET = 2000b, 12ff.); Klauck 2003a, 82–88 (GV = Klauck 2002, 110–18).

[68] Cf. already Luke 24.39: "a spirit does not have flesh and bones" and Ign. *Smyrn.* 3.2. See note 100 below.

to his enemies and to the judge, in fact—to all."[69] These tendencies do not yet become visible in the oldest account of Paul in 1 Cor 15.3ff.

Through his reference to the great number of the eyewitnesses Paul fortifies a primitive Christian fundamental confession, which in varied form, alongside the formula "Christ died for us," represents the oldest New Testament confession of all: "God raised Jesus from the dead."[70] Behind this stands the old Jewish prayer formula from the second Berakah of the Eighteen Benedictions: God is the *meḥayyeh ham-metîm*, "the one who raises the dead."[71] Here, we must consider that James, the brother of the Lord, and Paul were, after all, overcome and led to faith through the appearance of the Lord. Paul mentions no witnesses who did not come to faith.

22.2 The Empty Tomb and the Appearances of the Risen One

22.2.1 The Burial Accounts[72]

Thus far we have attempted to infer the community-founding resurrection event from the confession of the resurrection in 1 Cor 15.3-8 and the witnesses mentioned there. It rests on memory and personal contacts. Since, however, it is only listed and not actually narrated, its interpretation must remain contested.

The more detailed appearance accounts of the first, third, and fourth Gospels (Matt 28; Luke 24; John 20–21) not only diverge very significantly from one another, but were also first committed to writing about two generations later, between 75 and 100 CE. The older Gospel of Mark (ca. 69/70 CE), by contrast, provides only the account of the visit of the women to the tomb in Mark 16.1-8 and a reference to the appearances in Galilee only indirectly in the command of the angel in 16.7: "there you will see him." In these later stories there is also a considerable distance from the listing of the witnesses in 1 Cor 15. We can speak only of punctiliar agreements. The Gospels recount fewer appearances, but sometimes

---

[69] Origen, *Cels.* 2.63.

[70] It appears both as a statement in the active, e.g., Rom 10.9: καὶ πιστεύσῃς . . . ὅτι ὁ θεὸς [scil. Ἰησοῦν] ἤγειρεν ἐκ νεκρῶν; cf. 1 Cor 15.15; 1 Thess 1.10; Acts 3.15; 4.10; 10.40; 13.30; as *passivum divinum*, e.g., Rom 6.4, 9; 7.4; 8.34; 1 Cor 15.4, 12, 17; 2 Tim 2.8; and especially as a participial specification of God: Rom 4.24: τοῖς πιστεύσουσιν ἐπὶ τὸν ἐγείραντα Ἰησοῦν . . . ἐκ νεκρῶν, cf. Rom 8.11; 2 Cor 4.14; Gal 1.1; Eph 1.20; Col 2.12; 1 Pet 1.21. See also the overview in Eckstein 2003, 232–37.

[71] Cf. Elbogen 1995, 44; Sysling 1996, 1–2.

[72] Campenhausen 1966; Hengel 1963; Schenke 1968; Broer 1972; Pesch 1984b, 519–43; Hengel 2001a; Dunn 2003b, 828ff.; Schwemer 2010.

elaborate them powerfully. Nevertheless, it would be premature to characterize these stories fundamentally as historically worthless. Legends can also contain historical points of reference. They were not developed from nothing. We have already referred to two such points of agreement, namely the ὅτι ἐτάφη and the date of the third day. According to Mark 16.2ff., the women come in the early morning of the first day of the week (λίαν πρωὶ τῇ μίᾳ τῶν σαββάτων), i.e., on our Sunday, and, on the third day after the crucifixion, find the tomb open. This day is already emphasized in 1 Cor 16.2. According to Acts 20.7, the Pauline mission community in Troas assembles on the Sunday to break bread at night. In Rev 1.10 it already bears the name κυριακὴ ἡμέρα, as is also the case in the Didache, in Ignatius, and in the Gospel of Peter.[73] The day obtains significance for the worship service through the fact that the community believed that on it, namely still during the night, before the break of day, the resurrection of the Lord took place, since the women found the tomb empty.[74] Only in later accounts such as Matt 28.2 (ca. 90–100 CE), where the descent of an angel, who rolls away the stone, is portrayed, and then in a graphic way in the Gospel of Peter around 150, where resurrection and ascension are portrayed dramatically, did anyone dare to describe the miraculous event directly.[75] It was recognized from the beginning that the event itself had to remain a mystery. In the stories of the finding of the empty tomb and the appearances of the risen one, the concern could not be with a presentation that was as objective and neutral as possible. Rather, they recount the shock and joy of the witnesses, which overcame all resistance, for example their previous despondency. But doubts were also not concealed.[76] According to the first accounts, the risen one appeared only to those who were close to him and effected faith. The event is observed by outsiders only in the later accounts, in Matthew, in the Gospel of the Hebrews, and in the Gospel of Peter. According to Matthew, the guards

[73] Didache 14.1; Ign. *Magn.* 9.1; Gos. Pet. 35, 50. The pagan designation ἡ ἡλίου ἡμέρα appears for the first time in Justin, *1 Apol.* 67.3, i.e., the Sunday as day of the worship service, since ἡ κυριακὴ ἡμέρα was out of place in an apology addressed to the emperor and Gentiles; for in inscriptions and papyri the adjective κυριακός usually meant "imperial."

[74] After all, according to the Jewish reckoning of time, the day begins on the preceding evening with the setting of the sun (cf. Gen 1.5). Therefore, the church celebrates the night from Saturday to Sunday as the night of the resurrection.

[75] See Schneemelcher 1991/1992, 179–87 (GV = 1990, 180–88); Ehrman/Pleše 2011, 371–87. It already presupposes all four Gospels; see Hengel 2008c, 22–23, 107, 137–38, 192, 202–3 (ET = 2000b, 12–13, 59, 76, 113, 119); Klauck 2003a, 82–88 (GV = Klauck 2002, 110–18).

[76] Luke 24.11, 37; Matt 28.17: οἱ δὲ ἐδίστασαν, John 20.25. On the topic of doubt in the New Testament, cf. now Schliesser forthcoming.

of the tomb fall as dead men. In the Gospel of the Hebrews, Jesus gives the tomb linen to the slave of the high priest. In the Gospel of Peter, the centurion and the guards at the tomb recount in detail the marvelous things that they saw.[77] Here we are dealing with—understandable—apologetics, in Matthew, for example, in response to the Jewish accusation that the corpse of Jesus was stolen by the disciples.[78] In reality the emphasis on the third day, which we already encounter in the old confession of 1 Cor 15.4, occurred due to the women's discovery of the empty tomb on Easter morning.

By comparison to these tendencies, which became increasingly graphic, *the oldest account in Mark 16.1-8* is markedly sparse, indeed sometimes objectionably so, as is already the case for the passion story in Mark. If we view the angel in the tomb narrative in Mark 16.5-7 as the *angelus interpres*, who is necessary for the theological interpretation, then what remains is only the report that the women visited the tomb on the first day of the week after the Sabbath of the Passover festival in order to anoint the corpse of Jesus, but to their amazement found it empty. In the case of the angel figure himself we must take note of the fact that he points the women away from the tomb: "He has risen and is not here." The tradition may already oppose the beginnings of a cultic veneration of the tomb of Jesus in the community in Jerusalem. Moreover, it is conspicuous that the original conclusion of Mark in 16.8—"They went out (of the rock tomb) and fled from the tomb, for trembling and fright had taken hold of them; and they said nothing to anyone, for they were afraid"—stands in irreconcilable opposition to the instruction of the *angelus interpres*: "Go and tell the disciples and Peter that he is going before you to Galilee. There you will see him. . . ."[79] To be sure, it is not entirely certain whether Mark intended to conclude his work with 16.8. Perhaps the original conclusion was lost very early on or perhaps he was hindered from really concluding his account. We can, however, only take the existing form as our point of departure. The Gospel as it has been preserved for us concludes with the blatant disobedience of the women, who were the first ones to receive

---

[77] Matthew 28.4; cf. vv. 11-15: their report to the high priests, the bribing of them by the high priests, and the emergence of the rumor that the disciples stole the body; Gospel of the Hebrews apud Jerome, *Vir. ill.* 2 (see Aland 2005, 507; Ehrman/Pleše 2011, 216–21); Gos. Pet. 35–49 features a story that is embellished in a fantastical manner.

[78] Matthew 28.11-15; Gos. Pet. 45–49; Justin, *Dial.* 108.2; Tertullian, *Spect.* 30.5–6, and the Toledot Yeshu. See Hengel 2001a, 179–80.

[79] Mark 16.7 = Matt 28.7. In Mark 14.28 = Matt 26.32 Jesus himself says that he will go before the disciples to Galilee. In Matt 28.10 the risen one himself tells the women to announce this to the disciples. In Matt 28.16-17 they go onto the mountain, where Jesus had commanded them to go and where he appears to them.

the message of the resurrection and yet did not obey it but rather fled in panicked fear and kept silent. Mark 16.1-8 is not a late legend, as is claimed time and again, but rather has a historical point of departure—the discovery of the empty tomb by the women and their frightened flight. The later evangelists all found the concluding verse of the Gospel offensive and changed it accordingly. Luke has the women, after their return from the tomb, immediately tell "the eleven and the rest" about their experience, without them believing it. After this, he says that Peter visited the tomb and marveled.[80] In Matt 28.8 the "trembling and fright" of Mark 16.8 becomes a "fear and great joy," and the women also obediently hurry to bring the good news to the disciples. Because a work that bore the title "Gospel" must not conclude with the statement "for they were afraid," two supplementing texts were added to Mark as a conclusion. The second later conclusion, which is very short,[81] has the women—despite the preceding v. 8—"announce without delay (συντόμως) to the circle around Peter everything that was commanded to them (by the angel)." After this, it says that Jesus himself sent them into the whole world with the "message of salvation." The story recounted by Mark in 16.1-8, which is theologically considered and yet simply told, is wholly unsuited to be an apologetic legend that is meant to undergird the fact of the resurrection in a historicizing manner. The more detailed, first Markan conclusion in 16.9-20 was added relatively quickly in the first decades of the second century. It is a cento from the other three Gospels, mixed with material which we are familiar with in part from Papias.[82]

Thus, Mark 16.8 shows that the empty tomb, taken on its own, could not furnish proof for the resurrection—on the contrary, it produced "fear and fright." The women failed in relation to him, as the disciples did when he was arrested in Gethsemane (Mark 14.50). The words "they fled" appear

---

[80] Luke 24.1-12. In Luke 24.23-24 there are multiple disciples who confirm the women's account. Although it is lacking in D, Luke 24.12 is original. John 20.1-10 is dependent on it. There it is Mary Magdalene alone who finds the tomb empty, and prompted by her statement that the corpse of the Lord has been taken away, Peter and the Beloved Disciple hurry in a race to the tomb. John presupposes Mark and Luke and seeks to correct older accounts with his version. The pointer that Peter alone (Luke 24.12) or the Beloved Disciple and Peter (John 20.5ff.) saw the linen cloths there is meant to stress the reality of the resurrection and indirectly reject the accusation that the body was stolen. On Luke 24.12, see Neirynck 2002. Contrary to the hypothesis of Ehrman 1993, 133, 255, the text is not an anti-docetic interpolation.

[81] See NA[27], 147 (L Ψ 099 0122 579 etc.).

[82] On Mark 16.9-20 and its many variants, see now in detail Kelhoffer 2000. This longer conclusion may be attested already by Justin and certainly by Irenaeus and Tertullian: see NA[27], 148–49.

in both cases.[83] This ambivalence applies even to the story of Luke, which goes further. The Emmaus disciples, who have heard of the discovery of the empty tomb and of the women's vision of angels, nevertheless wander home in despair.[84] After all, the "apostles" had not believed the report of the women and regarded it as foolish nonsense.[85] It lacks precisely the compelling probative force. Therefore, Paul, in 1 Cor 15.3-4, could forgo the reference to the empty tomb. Moreover, it would have burst the framework of his confession. What the community knew via recounting need not be mentioned again in a concise confession.

22.2.2 Narratives about Christophanies

By contrast, as already mentioned, the decisive church-founding Christophany before Cephas-Peter (1 Cor 15.5) is strangely not recounted to us in the Gospels. Only in Luke 24.34 do we have a small reference to it, though it is formulated as fundamental "good news." The assembled eleven testify to the Emmaus disciples: "The Lord has truly (ὄντως) risen and has appeared to Simon." The ὤφθη Σίμωνι in Luke corresponds to the ὤφθη Κηφᾷ in 1 Cor 15.5.[86] It is only the appearance of Jesus that grants certainty and brings an end to the astonishment over what has happened at the empty tomb.[87]

On the other hand, we have several admittedly quite different stories about appearances before the "eleven," which correspond to the "twelve" in Paul in 1 Cor 15.5. Apparently, for the later community tradition, the appearance of Jesus before the group of the eleven was the actually constitutive Christophany, which was even more important than the first appearance to Peter. This is connected with the Jewish understanding of testimony, which required at least two or three witnesses for the testimony to an event. The testimony of a single person was inadequate.[88] To be sure, while Luke and John have this fundamental appearance occur before the

---

[83] ἔφυγον. Cf. Gos. Pet. 57: φοβηθεῖσαι ἔφυγον. On the conclusion of the Gospel in 16.8 (ἐφοβοῦντο γάρ), see Van der Horst 1972; Denyer 2006.

[84] Luke 24.13-27. On this, see also the discussion below.

[85] Luke 24.11: λῆρος; cf. Mark 16.11: they did not believe Mary Magdalene, to whom Jesus appeared as the first (John 20.14, 18).

[86] See section 22.1 with note 28. The ὄντως gives the statement the character of a confession. On Luke 24.33-34, cf. Ign. *Smyrn.* 3.2. Here the risen one comes πρὸς τοὺς περί Πέτρον, i.e., the circle of the eleven is defined by Peter; cf. Mark 1.36 and Mark 16.9, the short secondary Markan ending (NA²⁷, 147): the women proclaim this περὶ τὸν Πέτρον.

[87] Luke 24.12 on Peter: θαυμάζων τὸ γεγονός. John says only of the Beloved Disciple that he "saw and believed" (εἶδεν καὶ ἐπίστευσεν) at the empty tomb (20.8). With this John consciously outbids the accounts of the older Gospels.

[88] Deuteronomy 17.6; 19.15; cf. Matt 18.16; 2 Cor 13.1; 1 Tim 5.19.

circle of disciples in *Jerusalem*, Matthew, building on Mark, places it on a mountain in *Galilee*.[89] Another Christophany before seven disciples, in which Peter and the Beloved Disciple are at the center, occurs in the subsequently added chapter John 21 in connection with a catch of fish on the Lake of Gennesaret, again in Galilee.[90] Entirely anomalous is the old narrative of the two disciples who journey from Jerusalem to Emmaus, sixty stadia or ca. eleven kilometers northwest of Jerusalem, which is artfully developed by Luke.[91] According to Hegesippus, one of the travelers, Cleopas, was a brother of Joseph, i.e., an uncle of Jesus. This narrative, in which the risen one overcomes the misunderstanding and blindness—one could also say "the hardening"—of the two disciples shows that Jesus also had followers in Judaea. As with Mary Magdalene in John 20.14 and with the catch of fish at the Lake of Gennesaret in John 21.4ff., here in Luke 24.16 it is peculiar that the risen Jesus is initially not recognized.[92]

The contradiction in the localization of the appearances is also conspicuous. In conscious opposition to his Markan *Vorlage*, Luke stresses that they all occurred in the sphere of Jerusalem, for, according to him, the risen one commands the disciples "not to depart from Jerusalem."[93] In Mark and Matthew, by contrast, the women are sent away from the tomb with the promise that the risen one will go before the disciples to Galilee; not until there would they see him.[94] John initially follows the Jerusalem tradition with two appearances with an interval of seven days on the evening of the first day of the week.[95] However, in the added chapter he has a Christophany in Galilee on the Sea of Tiberias, which is recounted in

---

[89] Matthew 28.16; cf. 28.7, 10 and 26.32 = Mark 16.7 and 14.28.

[90] Cf. also Gos. Pet. 58ff.: only after the end of the festival of weeks do the twelve (!) disciples sorrowfully return home. Peter, his brother Andrew, and Levi, the son of Alphaeus (Mark 2.14), prepare for a catch of fish, then the text breaks off. In a similar way to John 21, this was presumably followed by a recounting of the first appearance of Jesus. Peter speaks here—a typical sign of an apocryphon that presupposes the four Gospels—in the first person.

[91] The location of the place is disputed. On this, see Schwemer 2001a, 100–101. The concern is with a village (Luke 24.13, 28: κώμη) Emmaus and not with the city Emmaus, which was about twenty-three kilometers away as the crow flies and was the capital of a Roman toparchy.

[92] Luke 24.13-35. On Cleopas/Clopas, cf. John 19.25: Κλωπᾶ, and Hegesippus according to Eusebius, *Hist. eccl.* 3.11; 3.32.4ff. His son Symeon is said to have been the successor to James, the brother of the Lord, as bishop of Jerusalem. On this, see Schwemer 2001a, 105–7. On their incomprehension, see Luke 24.25ff. For the theological interpretation, see Mittmann-Richert 2008.

[93] Acts 1.4; cf. Luke 24.49ff. Luke exercises clear criticism of his Markan *Vorlage* here.

[94] Mark 16.7 = Matt 28.7.

[95] John 20.19, 26.

detail.[96] Conversely, Matthew knows of only one appearance before the disciples in Galilee on the mountain of revelation, though, according to him, the women who visit the tomb already encounter the risen one in Jerusalem when they are returning from the tomb and do homage to him.[97] This contradiction between the appearances in Jerusalem and Galilee can be resolved neither in the sense of Luke nor of Mark. Here, two contrary claims collide with each other, presumably those of the communities in Galilee and those of the Jerusalem community. Matthew and John, the two latest Gospels, attempt, each in a different way, to mediate between them. It is common to them, however, that the first appearance in Jerusalem took place before *women*. Apparently, Christophanies took place in both places. We can only ask where this happened first. Here the Markan account, as the oldest, may reproduce the original circumstance. In that case, the first vision before Peter and the one that followed before the eleven would have taken place in Galilee, whereas the appearances before James and "all the apostles" would have occurred in or near Jerusalem. Against his Markan *Vorlage*, Luke, in his narrative, would then have brought together to a day and a night events that were originally separate in time and place. That he does not shy away from such apparent contradictions can be seen in the fact that in the Gospel he has the ascension take place right after the night of the appearance (24.50-51), whereas in Acts 1.3 he speaks of forty days "with many proofs,"[98] i.e., appearances and conversations until his departure from the disciples. In Acts 10.41 he even has Peter say: "We have eaten and drunk with him," i.e., celebrated the Eucharist with him.[99]

[96] John 21.1-23. The temporal specification remains unspecific: μετὰ ταῦτα. John recounts a total of four appearances. See also 20.14ff., 19ff., 24ff.

[97] Matthew 28.9-10. Jesus greets them with χαίρετε. They grasp his feet and throw themselves before him (προσεκύνησαν); cf. the eleven disciples in 28.17: ἰδόντες αὐτὸν προσεκύνησαν. This προσκυνεῖν before Jesus is typically Matthean. Cf., however, also Luke 24.52 at the parting of Jesus.

[98] Acts 1.3: οἷς παρέστησεν ἑαυτὸν ζῶντα . . . ἐν πολλοῖς τεκμηρίοις. Luke presumably understood the "ascension" not as an event that is dated at different times but as the respective translations into heaven of the risen and exalted one who from his heavenly doxa appeared on earth. To be sure, Luke 24.50 with the preceding speech of Jesus initially appears to be the final parting of Jesus from his disciples, which concludes the Gospel in a meaningful way. In that case, Acts 1.1ff. could be viewed as a correction. On the problem, see Zwiep 2001; on Luke 24.26, the entering of Jesus into his heavenly doxa before the appearance before the disciples, see Schwemer 2001a, 108.

[99] Cf. also the use of συναλιζόμενος in Acts 1.4, which is uncertain in its translation. It can mean "eat together" and "come together." On this, see Schwemer 2004, 203–8. Ignatius, *To the Smyrneans* 3.3 also stresses—for anti-docetic reasons—that Jesus "after the resurrection ate and drank with them (the disciples)": ὡς σαρκικός, καίπερ πνευματικῶς ἡνωμένος τῷ πατρί ("as in the flesh, although spiritually united to the Father").

The apologetic and anti-docetic characteristics of the presentation of the Christophanies in Luke, Matthew, and John prohibit us in principle from making any adequate statements about the manner of the appearances, let alone about the bodiliness of Jesus. In the oldest pointers, the "that" and not the "how" stands at the center, even though concrete conceptions about the "how" were formed from the beginning. This is already shown by the lack of a portrayal of the first appearance to Peter. More accounts were presumably in circulation, from which Luke, Matthew, and John each feature a theologically processed selection. Here it is instructive for the Gospel accounts that the bodiliness is, on the one hand, portrayed as real,[100] and yet at the same time as mysterious and not fixable. The risen one comes and disappears, even through closed doors. Mary Magdalene is prohibited from touching him, i.e., she should not detain Jesus, who has not yet ascended to his Father; disbelieving Thomas is exhorted to put his hands in the wounds. The Emmaus disciples, Mary Magdalene, and the seven disciples at the catch of fish initially do not recognize Jesus.[101] All these texts have something undetermined about them, which conceals the view of the appearances and allows them their mystery. Against the view of most scholars today, in addition to the tradition of the discovery of the empty tomb by *women* on Easter morning, we regard the account of the first appearance of Jesus to the women in Jerusalem as oldest tradition. In different forms, it is independently handed down to us in Matt 28.9-10 and John 20.11ff.[102] In Matt 28.8-10 there are—as is often the case in Matthew—two witnesses, Mary Magdalene and "the other Mary."[103] In John it is only Mary Magdalene. With her it is conspicuous that she—like Peter—is mentioned in the first position in different lists of women in the Gospels.[104] Her rank may be connected with the fact that she, like Peter, was the recipient of the first appearance of Jesus. To be sure, her vision could make no impression in Jewish Palestine. Reference

[100] Especially graphic in the anti-docetic sense is the special tradition in Ign. *Smyrn.* 3.2, where the risen one exhorts those gathered around Peter: "Touch me and see that I am no bodiless specter. And immediately they touched him and believed, since they were closely united with his flesh and spirit." Cf. Luke 24.39, as well as Mark 6.49 and Matt 14.26.

[101] Luke 24.15-16, 30-31; John 20.14-16; 21.4ff.

[102] Cf. also Mark 16.9, which is dependent on John 20.14, 18 and Luke 8.2. See Hengel 1963.

[103] Cf. Matt 28.1 and 27.61; according to 27.56, it is Mary, the mother of James and Joseph; cf. Mark 15.40 and on this Bauckham 2002, 257–310. On "twoness" in Matthew, see 4.18, 21; 8.28; 9.27; 20.30; and 21.1, which is dependent on Mark.

[104] Mark 15.40, 47; 16.1; Luke 8.2-3; 24.10; Matt 27.56, 61; 28.1. The only exception is John 19.25. There she appears at the end of the list after the mother of Jesus, her sister, and Mary the wife (?) of Clopas as the only one who did not belong to the relatives of Jesus among the circle of women.

has already been made to Celsus' mocking of her first vision.[105] It is therefore more than understandable when the women are absent as resurrection
witnesses elsewhere.[106] With the five hundred brothers of 1 Cor 15.6 the
concern is also probably not with an exclusive assembly of men, indeed
even among the ἀπόστολοι πάντες individual women could have been
included. In the Synoptics, the women receive from the *angelus interpres* the commission to announce the resurrection of Jesus to the disciples.
While they keep silent in Mark out of fear, in Luke they carry out the command but encounter unbelief. In Matthew and John the instruction of the
risen one even contains the conspicuous phrasing that they are to proclaim
the good news "to my brothers." This calls to mind the Pauline designation
of the Son of God as the "first born among many brothers" (Rom 8.29).
This means that in the eschatological consummation, believers, as children of God, are to participate in the glory of the exalted Jesus, who was
understood from the beginning as the "first born from the resurrection."[107]
Mary Magdalene appears as the first person, who, in a similar way to Paul,
can confess before the disciples: "I have seen the Lord" (ἑώρακα τὸν
κύριον, John 20.18; 1 Cor 9.1).

Amidst all the differences, the diverse narratives as well as the list in
Paul have a fundamental point in common. *Alongside the seeing there is
always the spoken word*, the audition, usually *as a sending by the risen
one*. According to Paul, the Christophany means calling into the office and
commission of the apostle, of the "emissary of Jesus Christ."[108] In the only
Christophany before the disciples in Matthew, in 28.16ff., the risen one
gives the eleven a universal missionary command: "Go and make disciples
of all nations. . . ." In a completely different form—not on a mountain
in Galilee but in a house in Jerusalem, behind closed doors, but related

---

[105] See section 22.19 with note 21. The Jewish tradition also recounted it in a disparaging way. Among other things, she was identified with the mother of Jesus. "Magdala" was
translated as "plaiter of hair"; see Strack 1910, § 9, 12–13, 34ff.; on this, see now Schäfer
2007, 18, 150 (notes 11, 22): also in the rabbinic literature she is additionally identified
with the woman who is a great sinner in Luke 7.36-50, whose long, unbound hair identifies
her as a prostitute; cf. Schäfer 2007, 99.

[106] In Luke 24.9-12 her witness is sharply devalued. Peter has to verify it and is amazed
but not convinced. Cf. John 20.1-10, where she reports only about the corpse that has disappeared and Peter and the Beloved Disciple rush there. See section 22.2.1 with note 80.

[107] Matthew 28.10: ὑπάγετε ἀπαγγείλατε τοῖς ἀδελφοῖς μου; John 20.17 on Mary
Magdalene: "πορεύου πρὸς τοὺς ἀδελφούς μου and say to them: I am ascending to my
Father and to your Father. . . ." The brotherhood between Jesus and the disciples becomes
visible in the resurrection. On the phrase πρωτότοκος (ἐκ) τῶν νεκρῶν, see Col 1.18;
Rev 1.5, cf. also 1 Cor 15.23.

[108] First Corinthians 9.1ff.; 15.7; 1.1: κλητὸς ἀπόστολος Χριστοῦ Ἰησοῦ, cf. Rom
1.1; 2 Cor 1.1; Gal 1.1, 16ff.

in substance—in John 20.21-22 the risen one says: "As the Father has sent me, I send you!" While he says this, he breathes on them and says to them: "Receive the Holy *Spirit*." Sending into the world for mission and gift of the Spirit mutually condition each other. To be sure, in Matthew, due to his specific theology, the place of the Spirit is taken by the didactic proclamation of the message of Jesus and the obedience to his commands, which is the presupposition of true discipleship.[109] In Luke, too, sending and Spirit are related to each other, at the end of the farewell discourse of the risen one, for example. In his name the disciples are to "proclaim repentance for the forgiveness of sins to all nations," and he himself will send to them for this purpose "the promise of the Father." Therefore, they are to remain in Jerusalem until they are "equipped with power from on high." The prediction at the beginning of Acts corresponds to this: "You will receive the power of the Holy Spirit, who comes on you, and you will be my witnesses in Jerusalem, in all Judaea and Samaria and unto the end of the earth."[110] To be sure, that which is a unity in John, i.e., the appearance of the risen one, the sending, and the reception of the Spirit, falls apart temporally in Luke. According to him, the disciples, before the eyes of the people in Jerusalem, do not receive the Spirit until ten days after the ascension of Jesus at the so-called festival of weeks, i.e., seven weeks after the Passover festival.[111] In all these accounts one sees clearly that the form of the presentation could differ greatly in accord with the diverse theologies of the respective evangelists, but that the "that" of the sending by the risen one is nevertheless clear and can already be derived from the oldest pre-Pauline tradition and from Paul's concept of apostleship. This means that the resurrection event cannot and does not aim to be understood simply as a mere fact in the modern sense, as a historically secure and demonstrable fact that is detached from believing obedience. Whoever approaches the witness of the sources with this intention will misunderstand them. If at

---

[109] Matthew 28.20. Cf. also the two secondary endings of Mark, 16.15ff. and the short form after v. 8 (see section 22.2.1 with note 81 above). After 16.14, Codex W introduces a late small dialogue among the disciples, who defend themselves, and Jesus about the power of the evil one and its overcoming by the death of Jesus, the so-called "Freer-Logion." On this, see Kelhoffer 2000, 2 n. 5 and 528 index.

[110] Luke 24.47ff.; Acts 1.8. This is retrospectively formulated by Luke under the presupposition of the Pauline (and later also the Petrine) mission to the nations. In Mark this instruction is incorporated into the prediction of Jesus in 13.10 and 14.9 (= Matt 26.13). In Mark 13.11 the conferment of the Spirit is reduced to the situation of persecution. Initially the primitive community understood the commission of the risen one as a sending to their own people; cf. Matt 10.5-6 and the Lukan preaching of Peter in Acts 2–5 (e.g., 3.25-26). The phrase Ἰουδαίῳ τε πρῶτον (Rom 1.16) basically applies to the whole of Christianity in the first century.

[111] Acts 2.1-41. See Hengel/Schwemer 2019.

all, then it is at this point that faith and reality must not be separated. In our day in particular, the resurrection witnesses—as much as, indeed even more than, the cross, which can still be idealized as the sign of the martyrdom of a benefactor of humanity—are at the same time an offense and foolishness for those who disdain the insight and the venture of faith.[112]

Given this, with all due caution we want to attempt to bring the different statements and accounts into a temporal-spatial connection. Due to the state of our sources, the whole remains—at least in part—a hypothetical attempt.

1. Early on Easter morning the women find the tomb open and empty and flee frightened, Mark 16.1-4, 8.
2. Mary Magdalene returns and has the first appearance of the risen one (John 20.11ff.; cf. Matt 28.9-10). However, the disciples do not believe her (Luke 24.11). They now have—since the corpse of Jesus has disappeared—all the more reason to depart quickly for Galilee.
3. The tradition now splits. According to Mark, Matthew, and the Gospel of Peter, the disciples returned to Galilee. In that case, the first appearance to Peter occurred there and after that the appearance to the circle of the twelve. By contrast, according to Luke and John, this occurred on the evening of Easter day in Jerusalem. Competing traditions of the communities in Galilee and Jerusalem probably stand behind these contradictory traditions. To us the Galilean tradition appears to be more original. The placement of the first vision of Peter in Galilee could explain why Luke 24.34 does not provide a more detailed account of it. Later, due to the leading position of the community in Jerusalem, one had an interest in concentrating all the decisive Christophanies on the first resurrection day, which became, after all, the "day of the Lord" in the church, and in the one location of Jerusalem, which, according to Jewish-primitive Christian belief, was the center of the world. There God himself had chosen Zion as his place of residence, there Christ was crucified, and there he was expected to come again (Acts 1.11; Rom 11.26). The Markan Galilee tradition probably goes back to Petrine tradition. It is confirmed by John 21 and the last preserved verses of the Gospel of Peter.
4. We can only speculate about the place and time of the appearances before James, the five hundred brothers, and all the apostles. If it is not, in fact, connected with Pentecost, the event with the

---

[112] See the verdict of D. F. Strauss in section 16.4 with notes 135–37.

five hundred could have taken place in Galilee. By contrast, the Christophanies of James, the brother of Jesus (thus in the Gospel of Hebrews), and of (the majority of) "all the apostles" should more likely be placed in Jerusalem and its surroundings (Luke 24.13-32). This could be one of the reasons why James received the leadership role in the community later in Jerusalem. In any case, after the first visions in Galilee, the disciples returned to Jerusalem so that at the next festival—the festival of weeks, fifty days after Passover,[113] when numerous Jewish pilgrims gathered and when Jesus' death on the preceding Passover festival was still in direct memory—they could proclaim before their own people the resurrection of the Messiah Jesus, who appeared to them as the one exalted to God, and call them to repentance. It is thus very probable that Christophanies occurred also in and around Jerusalem, especially since Galilee no longer played a role in subsequent early Christian history—at least in the sources that have been preserved for us—and Jerusalem quickly became the center of the primitive community.[114]

5. The conversion of Paul, which is identical with his calling, occurred at most three years after the resurrection event. Harnack and others hypothesize that the temporal specification of eighteen months, which occurs in later—especially Gnostic—sources, refers to the period up to the conversion of the apostle to the Gentiles.[115] This seems to be too short a period of time to us. Paul himself points to a clear temporal distance of his vision from the earlier Christophanies.[116] At the same time, he designates himself as the last person to see the risen one. This means that the appearances of the risen one as a community-founding event must be clearly distinguished from later visions of Christ[117] both in the number of the persons involved and thereby called and in their temporal framework.

---

[113] Thus the name ἡ ἡμέρα τῆς πεντεκοστῆς for the Jewish festival of weeks in Acts 2.1. The Latin translation takes over the Greek word, and from this arose the English designation "Pentecost" and the German designation "Pfingsten."

[114] For the rapid receding of Galilee, see Hengel/Schwemer 1998, 51–56 (ET = 1997, 30–33). Galilee is no longer mentioned in the New Testament epistolary literature or in the Apostolic Fathers.

[115] Riesner 1994, 56–65. See section 22.1 with note 53.

[116] First Corinthians 15.8-9. This applies also to the narrative of Acts, which presupposes a fairly long development in chapters 2–8. On this, see Hengel/Schwemer 1998, 46ff. (ET = 1997, 26ff.).

[117] Cf. 2 Cor 12.1ff.; Acts 18.9; 22.17ff.; Rev 1ff.

What is conspicuous is the diversity—which almost appears contradictory—of the resurrection witnesses in Paul, in the four Gospels, and in Acts, which opposes every form of harmonization. Even Tatian's Diatessaron refrained here from such an attempt and instead recounted the presentations of the Gospels in succession. On the other side stands the restraint in the reporting, which differs from the apocryphal Gospel-like revelation literature of the second century. After all, it would have been natural to develop numerous encounters of the disciples with the risen and exalted Lord in a fanciful way. By contrast, the focus of all four Gospels is on the activity of the earthly Jesus, even though the glory of the exalted one becomes increasingly visible in him—especially in the Fourth Gospel (John 1.14).[118] The high point of their presentation remains the passion of Jesus, though it is illuminated by his resurrection. We can only measure from a distance the extent to which the Easter events shook the disciples and changed their lives. The constitution of the primitive community in the power of the Spirit, looking to their Lord who is now exalted to God and retrospectively looking at his earthly activity, is the miracle of Easter that is visible to us and that continues to have effects today.

---

[118] On this topic, see now Frey 2018a, esp. chapter 7; 2018b.

Retrospect and Prospect

In retrospect,[1] our thesis is confirmed that the fragmentary character of the sources preserved for us, as well as the independence of mind of the four Evangelists in the selection of the traditional material and in its shaping and arrangement—one could also say their theological intent—makes impossible a presentation of Jesus that is really satisfying to our modern "historical curiosity." We cannot set forth a self-contained picture or joined-up history of him. However, as we have repeatedly stressed, what is possible are concrete attempts to approach the historical reality. In other words, based on their approach, the Gospels especially aim to be viewed as foundational documents of faith in Jesus—one could also say, as the most important deposit of the "apostolic witness" about Jesus. As such a witness they also possess, of course, a clearly visible historical foundation, which is based on living memory of the activity and fate of Jesus and as such could be retold.

In the same way, the presentation of Judaism at the time of Jesus suffers from the chance character and fragmentary nature of the sources and from the partisan and apologetic tendencies and rhetorical aims of our main author Josephus, who also always follows his own goals in his works. While the fortuitous discovery of the Dead Sea Scrolls has immensely expanded our knowledge about the rich Jewish religious thought in the ca. 230 years between the Maccabean period and the destruction of Jerusalem, it has also raised many new questions that we cannot adequately answer. One of the most impressive aspects here is the diversity of the Jewish expectations for bringers of salvation, which can no longer be restricted to the "anointed" ruler from the lineage of David. The figure of Jesus must also be painted into this context and at the same time withdraws from it again through his unmistakable uniqueness. Three aspects appear fundamental to us for the craftsman from Galilean Nazareth.

First, there is his proclamation of the "kingdom of God that is in the process of realization" in word and deed and the concomitant message of the love of the heavenly Father, who wants to bring home his lost creatures.

---

[1] For another retrospective on this volume by Martin Hengel, see Hengel 2010c (= Hengel 2013). Cf. also the responses to Hengel/Schwemer 2007 in Breytenbach/Frey 2013.

Second, there is his messianic claim, which runs through his activity. It clearly distinguishes him from the last prophetic herald, John the Baptist, and finds completion in his giving of his life as the servant of God on the cross and in the miracle of his resurrection, which must remain a mystery when viewed from a purely historical perspective.

Third, there is the calling of disciples into discipleship, whom he, instructed by him, sent out as his emissaries and who, despite their incomprehension and failure, after Easter not only proclaimed him as the Messiah and Son of God exalted to God but also retold his message and his fate and in this way preserved for coming generations his history and his words as εὐαγγέλιον, as "the message of salvation." Paradoxically, it is his eschatological claim and his way determined by it that grounds and carries forward the history of the church.

Accordingly, we believe not only that the human being Jesus indispensably belongs in a history of early Christianity but also that there is continuity that can be demonstrated in many points between Jesus' activity in word and deed and the proclamation of the primitive church, which includes the apostle to the Gentiles, Paul, who did not belong to Jesus' circle of disciples. Time and again, we have attempted to point out such continuities. After all, the Gospels, as a fundamental part of the apostolic proclamation, turn Jesus' message, activity, and way into their own content. Despite various transformations, they preserve—we have tried to make this clear—an abundance of genuine memory. There need not be a "wide ugly ditch" between the Jewish Christian primitive community and the later Gentile Christian mission communities. If that had been the case, the message of Jesus would never have reached the Greek-speaking non-Jews as "gospel."

In conclusion, we wish to make this continuity clear with an example:

What the Apostle Paul, about twenty-six years after the Passover of Jesus' death, confessed as ultimate assurance in relation to the community in Rome, which was unknown to him, already applied to the faith of the primitive community and was ultimately based on Jesus' messianic proclamation of the kingdom of God: "For I am sure that neither death nor life, nor angels nor powers, nor things present nor things to come . . . nor any other created thing can separate us from the love of God, which is in Christ Jesus, our Lord."[2] Jesus already teaches this assurance of salvation, which is based entirely on grace, in his parables, and he has established it for all human beings through his way as the servant of God.

---

[2] Romans 8.38-39.

Bibliography

Finding a Work in the Bibliography

In the English translation, works have been referenced in two different ways. First, a small number of works have been referenced using abbreviations, which are explained below. Second, most literature has been referenced by author date, e.g., Hengel 1988. If necessary, works from the same year have been distinguished through the addition of a letter, e.g., Schwemer 1991a and 1991b. While the bibliography sometimes includes earlier publication dates in square brackets, e.g., Bousset 1965 [1913], this information is not included in the body of the translation, e.g., Bousset 1965.

(1) Abbreviations

The abbreviations used in this work are primarily based on the list of abbreviations in the *Theologische Realenzyklopädie*, compiled by S. M. Schwertner (Berlin: Walter de Gruyter, 1992). For the English version we have also consulted the *IATG3—Internationales Abkürzungsverzeichnis für Theologie und Grenzgebiete*, compiled by S. M. Schwertner (Berlin: Walter de Gruyter, 2014) and the second edition of the SBL Handbook of Style (Atlanta: SBL, 2014).

For the text and bibliography, special note should be made of the following abbreviations, some of which differ from the conventions adopted in the aforementioned works.

AE *L'Année épigraphique*
ANRW *Aufstieg und Niedergang der römischen Welt*. Edited by H. Temporini and W. Haase. Berlin, 1972ff.
Bill. Strack, H. L., and P. Billerbeck. *Kommentar zum Neuen Testament*

aus Talmud und Midrasch. Vols. 1–4. Munich: Beck, 1922–1928 (also cited as Strack/Billerbeck 1922; 1924; 1926; 1928).

BNP　*Brill's New Pauly, Antiquity*. Edited by Hubert Cancik and Helmut Schneider. Leiden: Brill, 2002–2010.

ChW　*Christliche Welt*

CIJ　*Corpus Inscriptionum Judaicarum*. Edited by JeanBaptiste Frey. 2 vols. Rome: Pontifical Biblical Institute, 1936–1952.

CPJ　*Corpus Papyrorum Judaicarum*. Edited by V. Tcherikover and A. Fuks. Cambridge, Mass.: Harvard University Press, 1957–1964.

DJD　Discoveries in the Judaean Desert

DNP　*Der Neue Pauly: Enyklopädie der Antike*. Edited by Hubert Cancik and Helmut Schneider. Stuttgart: Metzler, 1996–2003.

EDNT　*Exegetical Dictionary of the New Testament*. Edited by H. R. Balz and G. Schneider. Grand Rapids: Eerdmans, 1990–1993.

EWNT　*Exegetisches Wörterbuch zum Neuen Testament*. Edited by H. R. Balz and G. Schneider. Stuttgart: Kohlhammer, 1980–1983.

FGrH　*Die Fragmente der griechischen Historiker*. Edited by F. Jacoby.

GGA　*Göttingische gelehrte Anzeigen*

JNSL　*Journal of Northwest Semitic Languages*

KP　*Der Kleine Pauly*. Edited by K. Ziegler. Stuttgart: Metzler, 1964–1975.

LCL　Loeb Classical Library.

LSJ　Liddell, H. G., R. Scott, and H. S. Jones. 1996. *A Greek-English Lexicon*. 9th ed. Oxford: Clarendon Press.

NA[26]　*Novum Testamentum Graece*. 26th ed. Edited by K. Aland, M. Black, C.M. Martini, B. Metzger, and A. Wikgren. Stuttgart: Deutsche Bibelgesellschaft, 1979.

NA[27]　*Novum Testamentum Graece*. 27th ed. Edited by B. Aland, J. Karavidopoulos, C. M. Martini, and B. M. Metzger. Stuttgart: Deutsche Bibelgesellschaft, 2001.

NBL　*Neues Bibel-Lexikon*. Edited by M. Görg and B. Lang. Zürich: Benzinger, 1991-2001.

OGIS　Orientalis Graeci inscriptions selectae

OTP　*The Old Testament Pseudepigrapha*. Edited by J. H. Charlesworth. 2 vols. Garden City, N.Y.: Doubleday, 1983–1985.

PG　Patrologia Graeca. Edited by J. P. Migne. 162 vols. Paris: Migne, 1857–1886.

PRE　*Paullys Real-Encyclopädie der classischen Alterthumswissenschaft*

PW　*Paullys Real-Encyclopädie der classischen Alterthumswissenschaft*. New ed. G. Wissowa.

RAC　*Reallexikon für Antike und Christentum*

RGG¹   *Religion in Geschichte und Gegenwart.* 3rd ed. Edited by F. M. Schiele and L. Zscharnack. Tübingen: Mohr, 1902–1913.

RGG³   *Religion in Geschichte und Gegenwart.* 3rd ed. Edited by K. Galling. Tübingen: Mohr, 1957–1962.

RGG⁴   *Religion in Geschichte und Gegenwart.* 4th ed. Edited by H. D. Betz et al. Tübingen: Mohr, 1998–2007.

RPP   *Religion Past and Present.* Edited by H. D. Betz et al. Leiden: Brill, 2006-2013.

SEG   Supplementum epigraphicum graecum

TDNT   *Theological Dictionary of the New Testament.* Edited by G. Kittel and G. Friedrich. Grand Rapids: Eerdmans, 1964–1976.

TDOT   *Theological Dictionary of the Old Testament.* Edited by G. J. Botterweck and H. Ringgren. Grand Rapids: Eerdmans, 1974–2006.

THGNT   *The Greek New Testament, Produced at Tyndale House, Cambridge.* Edited by D. Jongkind and P. Williams. Crossway, 2017.

ThWAT   *Theologisches Wörterbuch zum Alten Testament.* Edited by G. J. Botterweck and H. Ringgren. Stuttgart: Kohlhammer, 1973–2001.

ThWNT   *Theologisches Wörterbuch zum Neuen Testament.* Edited by G. Kittel and G. Friedrich. Stuttgart: Kohlhammer, 1932–1979.

TRE   *Theologische Realenzyklopädie.* Edited by Gerhard Krause and Gerhard Müller. Berlin: Walter de Gruyter, 1977–2004.

ZNThG   *Zeitschrift für neuere Theologiegeschichte*

(2) Literature

Abramowski, L. 2005. "Die Geschichte von der Fußwaschung (Joh 13)." *ZThK* 102: 176–203.

Adam, A., and C. Burchard. 1972 [1961]. *Antike Berichte über die Essener.* Berlin: Walter de Gruyter.

Ådna, J. 1999. *Jerusalem Tempel und Tempelmarkt im 1. Jh. n. Chr.* ADPV 25. Wiesbaden: Harrassowitz.

———. 2000. *Jesu Stellung zum Tempel.* WUNT 2/119. Tübingen: Mohr.

———. 2004. "Servant of Isaiah 53 as Triumphant and Interceding Messiah." Pages 189–224 in *The Suffering Servant: Isaiah 53 in Jewish and Christian Scriptures.* Edited by B. Janowski and P. Stuhlmacher. Translated by D. P. Bailey. Grand Rapids: Eerdmans.

Aland, B., J. Karavidopoulos, C. M. Martini, and B. M. Metzger, eds. 2001. *Novum Testamentum Graece.* 27th ed. Stuttgart: Deutsche Bibelgesellschaft.

Aland, K. 1983. *Vollständige Konkordanz zum griechischen Neuen Testament: Unter Zugrundelegung aller modernen kritischen Textausgaben und des Textus receptus.* Berlin: Walter de Gruyter.

———. 2005. *Synopsis Quattuor Evangeliorum.* 15th ed. Stuttgart: Deutsche Bibelgesellschaft.

Albani, M. 1997. "Der 364-Tage-Kalender in der gegenwärtigen Forschung." Pages 79–126 in *Studies in the Book of Jubilees*. Edited by M. Albani, J. Frey, and A. Lange. Tübingen: Mohr.

Albertz, R. 1997. *Religionsgeschichte Israels in alttestamentlicher Zeit.* 2 vols. GAT 8,2. Göttingen: Vandenhoeck & Ruprecht.

Alexander, L. 1993. *The Preface to Luke's Gospel: Literary Convention and Social Context in Luke 1:1-4 and Acts 1:1.* MSSNTS 78. Cambridge: Cambridge University Press.

Alexander, P. S. 1991. "Orality in Pharisaic-Rabbinic Judaism at the Turn of the Eras." Pages 159–84 in *Jesus and the Oral Gospel Tradition*. Edited by H. Wansbrough. Sheffield: JSOT.

Alföldy, G. 1999. "Pontius Pilatus und das Tiberieum von Caesarea Maritima." *SCI* 18: 85–108.

Alkier, S. 1993. *Urchristentum: Zur Geschichte und Theologie einer exegetischen Disziplin.* BHTh 83. Tübingen: Mohr.

———. 2000. "Frühkatholizismus (Begriff)." Page 402 in *RGG⁴* 3.

———. 2008. "Early Catholicism." Page 230 in *RPP* 4.

Allison, D. 2010. *Constructing Jesus: Memory, Imagination, and History.* Grand Rapids: Baker Academic.

Alt, A. 1953. "Galiläische Probleme." Pages 363–455 in *Kleine Schriften zur Geschichte des Volkes Israel*. Vol. 2. Munich: Beck.

Althaus, P. 1959. *The So-Called Kerygma and the Historical Jesus*. Translated by D. L. Cairns. Edinburgh: Oliver and Boyd.

———. 1963. *Das sogenannte Kerygma und der historische Jesus*. BFChTh 48. Gütersloh: Gütersloher.

Arav, R. 1999. "New Testament Archaeology and the Case of Bethsaida." Pages 75–99 in *Das Ende der Tage und die Gegenwart des Heils: Festschrift H.-W. Kuhn zum 65. Geburtstag*. Leiden: Brill.

Arnim, J. de, ed. 1962. *Dionis Prusaensis quem vocant Chrysostomum quae extant omnia.* 2 vols. Berlin: Weidemann.

Asín y Palacios, M. 1919/1926. "Logia et Agrapha Domini Jesu." *PO* 13.3 and 19.4: 347–431 and 528–624.

Aufhauser, J. B. 1925. *Antike Jesus-Zeugnisse.* 2nd ed. KlT 126. Bonn: Weber.

Augstein, R. 1971. *Jesus Menschensohn.* Gütersloh: Bertelsmann.

———. 1977. *Jesus, Son of Man.* Translated by H. Young. New York: Urizen Books.

———. 1999. *Jesus Menschensohn.* Hamburg: Hoffmann & Campe.

Aune, D. E. 1980. "Magic in Early Christianity." Pages 1470–1557 in *ANRW* II 23/2.

———. 1991. "Oral Tradition and the Aphorisms of Jesus." Pages 211–65 in *Jesus and the Oral Gospel Tradition*. Edited by H. Wansbrough. Sheffield: JSOT.

Aurelius, E. 2001. "Gottesvolk und Außenseiter: Eine geheime Beziehung Lukas-Matthäus." *NTS* 47: 428–41.

Avemarie, F. 1995. *Yoma. Versöhnungstag.* ÜTY 2/4. Tübingen: Mohr.

———. 1996. *Tora und Leben.* TSAJ 55. Tübingen: Mohr.

———. 2002a. "Das Gleichnis von den Arbeitern im Weinberg (Mt 20,1-15)— eine soziale Utopie?" *EvTh* 62: 272–87.

———. 2002b. *Die Tauferzählungen in der Apostelgeschichte: Theologie und Geschichte.* WUNT 139. Tübingen: Mohr.

———. 2003. "Warum treibt Paulus einen Dämon aus, der die Wahrheit sagt?" Pages 550–76 in *Die Dämonen.* Edited by A. Lange, H. Lichtenberger, and K. F. D. Römheld. Tübingen: Mohr.

———. 2013. *Neues Testament und frührabbinisches Judentum: Gesammelte Aufsätze.* Edited by J. Frey and A. Standhartinger. Tübingen: Mohr.

Aviam, M. 2018. "The Synagogue." Pages 127–34 in *Magdala of Galilee: A Jewish City in the Hellenistic and Roman Period.* Edited by R. Bauckham. Waco: Baylor University Press.

Aviam, M., and R. Bauckham. 2018. "The Synagogue Stone." Pages 135-60 in *Magdala of Galilee: A Jewish City in the Hellenistic and Roman Period.* Edited by R. Bauckham. Waco: Baylor University Press.

Avigad, N. 1962. "A Depository of Inscribed Ossuaries in the Kidron Valley." *IEJ* 12: 1–12.

———. 1967. "Aramaic Inscriptions in the Tomb of Jason." *IEJ* 17: 101–11.

Avi-Yonah, M. 1962. "A List of Priestly Courses from Caesarea." *IEJ* 12: 137–39.

Baasland, E. 1992. *Theologie und Methode: Eine historiographische Analyse der Frühschriften Bultmanns.* Zürich: Brockhaus.

Bacher, W. 1890. *Die Aggada der Tannaiten.* Vol. 2. Strasbourg: Trübner.

———. 1903. *Die Aggada der Tannaiten.* Vol. 1. 2nd ed. Strasbourg: Trübner.

Back, F. 2002. *Verwandlung durch Offenbarung bei Paulus.* WUNT 2/153. Tübingen: Mohr.

Backhaus, K. 1991. *Die "Jüngerkreise" des Täufers Johannes.* PaThSt 19. Paderborn: Schöningh.

———. 2006. Review of E. M. Becker (ed.), *Die antike Historiographie und die Anfänge der christlichen Geschichtsschreibung.* *ThR* 102: 32.

Bader, R. 1940. *Der ΑΛΗΘΗΣ ΛΟΓΟΣ des Kelsos.* Stuttgart: Kohlhammer.

Bahat, D. 1999. "The Herodian Temple." Pages 38–58 in *The Cambridge History of Judaism.* Vol. 3. Edited by W. Horbury, W. D. Davies, and J. Sturdy. Cambridge: Cambridge University Press.

Baldensperger, W. 1892 [1888]. *Das Selbstbewußtsein Jesu im Lichte der messianischen Hoffnungen seiner Zeit.* 2nd ed. Strasbourg: Heitz.

Baltz, H. 1982. "παρατηρέω." Page 82 in *EWNT* 3.

———. 1994. "παρατηρέω." Page 35 in *EDNT* 3.

Bammel, E. 1986. *Judaica: Kleine Schriften I.* WUNT 37. Tübingen: Mohr.

———. 1997. *Judaica et Paulina.* WUNT 91. Tübingen: Mohr.

Bardet, S. 2002. *Le Testimonium Flavianum: Examen historique, considérations historiographiques.* Paris: Cerf.

Barrett, C. K. 1994/1998. *The Acts of the Apostles.* 2 vols. ICC. London: T&T Clark.

Barth, K. 1922. *Der Römerbrief.* Munich: Kaiser.

———. 1947. *Die protestantische Theologie im 19. Jahrhundert: Ihre Vorgeschichte und ihre Geschichte.* Zürich: Evangelischer.

———. 1953 [1933]. *The Epistle to the Romans.* Translated by E. C. Hoskyns. London: Oxford University Press.

——. 2001. *Protestant Theology in the Nineteenth Century*. Translated by B. Cozens and J. Bowden. London: SCM.

Bauckham, R. 1990. *Jude and the Relatives of Jesus in the Early Church*. Edinburgh: T&T Clark.

——, ed. 1998. *The Gospel for All Christians: Rethinking the Gospel Audiences*. Grand Rapids: Eerdmans.

——. 2002. *Gospel Women: Studies of the Named Women in the Gospels*. Grand Rapids: Eerdmans.

——. 2017 [2006]. *Jesus and the Eyewitnesses: The Gospels as Eyewitness Testimony*. 2nd ed. Grand Rapids: Eerdmans.

Bauer, W. 1927. "Jesus der Galiläer." Pages 16–34 in *Festgabe für A. Jülicher*. Tübingen: Mohr (= Bauer 1967a, 91–108).

——. 1933. *Das Johannesevangelium*. 3rd ed. HNT 6. Tübingen: Mohr.

——. 1967a. *Aufsätze und kleine Schriften*. Edited by G. Strecker. Tübingen: Mohr.

——. 1967b [1909]. *Das Leben Jesu im Zeitalter der neutestamentlichen Apokryphen*. Darmstadt: Wissenschaftliche Buchgesellschaft.

Bauer, W., K. Aland, and B. Aland. 1988. *Griechisch-deutsches Wörterbuch zu den Schriften des Neuen Testaments und der frühchristlichen Literatur*. 6th ed. Berlin: Walter de Gruyter.

Bauer, W., and M. Hornschuh. 1964. "Das Apostelbild in der altchristlichen Überlieferung." Pages 11–41 in *Neutestamentliche Apokryphen in deutscher Übersetzung*. Vol. 2. 3rd ed. Edited by E. Hennecke and W. Schneemelcher. Tübingen: Mohr.

——. 1966. "The Picture of the Apostle in Early Christian Tradition." Pages 35–87 in *The New Testament Apocrypha*. Vol. 2. Edited by E. Hennecke and W. Schneemelcher. Philadelphia: Westminster.

Baum, A. D. 2004. "Bildhaftigkeit als Gedächtnishilfe in der synoptischen Tradition." *JThBeitr* 35: 4–16.

Baumstark, A. 1922. *Geschichte der syrischen Literatur*. Bonn: Marcus & Weber.

Bayer, H. F. 1986. *Jesus' Predictions of Vindication and Resurrection: The Provenance, Meaning and Correlation of the Synoptic Predictions*. WUNT 2/20. Tübingen: Mohr.

Becker, E.-M. 2006. *Das Markus-Evangelium im Rahmen antiker Historiographie*. WUNT 194. Tübingen: Mohr.

Becker, H.-J. 1990. *Auf der Kathedra des Mose: Rabbinisch-theologisches Denken und anti-rabbinische Polemik in Matthäus 23,1-12*. ANTZ 4. Berlin: Institut Kirche und Judentum.

Becker, J. 1972. *Johannes der Täufer und Jesus von Nazareth*. Neukirchen: Neukirchener.

——. 1993. *Das Urchristentum als gegliederte Epoche*. SBS 155. Stuttgart: Katholisches Bibelwerk.

Becker, M. 2002. *Wunder und Wundertäter im frührabbinischen Judentum*. WUNT 2/114. Tübingen: Mohr.

Bellinger, W. H., Jr., and W. R. Farmer, eds. 1996. *Jesus and the Suffering Servant*. Harrisburg, Pa.: Trinity Press.

Benoit, P., J. T. Milik, and R. de Vaux. 1961. *Les grottes de Murabba'at*. DJD IIa. Oxford: Clarendon Press.

Berger, K. 1970. *Die Amen-Worte Jesu: Eine Untersuchung zum Problem der Legitimation in apokalyptischer Rede*. BZNW 39. Berlin: Walter de Gruyter.

———. 1984a. *Formgeschichte des Neuen Testaments*. Heidelberg: Quelle & Meyer.

———. 1984b. "Hellenistische Gattungen im Neuen Testament." Pages 1031–1432 and 1831–85 in *ANRW* II 25/2.

———. 1997. *Im Anfang war Johannes: Datierung und Theologie des vierten Evangeliums* Stuttgart: Quell.

Berschin, W. 1986. *Biographie und Epochenstil im lateinischen Mittelalter*. QULPU 8. Stuttgart: Hiersemann.

Best, E. 1985. "Mark's Preservation of the Tradition." Pages 119–33 in *The Interpretation of Mark*. Edited by W. Telford. Philadelphia: Fortress.

Bethge, H.-G. 2005. "Appendix I: Das Thomasevangelium." Pages 517–46 in *Synopsis Quattuor Evangeliorum*. Edited by K. Aland. Stuttgart: Deutsche Bibelgesellschaft.

Bettiolo, P., ed. 1995. *Ascensio Isaiae: Textus*. CChr.SA 7. Turnhout: Brepols.

Betz, O. 1982. "Probleme des Prozesses Jesu." Pages 565–647 in *ANRW* II 25/1.

———. 1987. *Jesus der Messias Israel*. WUNT 1987. Tübingen: Mohr.

———. 1990. *Jesus, der Herr der Kirche*. WUNT 52. Tübingen: Mohr.

———. 1991. *Was wissen wir von Jesus: Der Messias im Licht von Qumran*. Wuppertal: Brockhaus.

Betz, O., and W. Grimm. 1977. *Wesen und Wirklichkeit der Wunder Jesu*. ANTI 2. Frankfurt: Lang.

Beyer, K. 1984. *Die aramaischen Texte vom Toten Meer samt den Inschriften aus Palästina, dem Testament Levis aus der Kairoer Genisa, der Fastenrolle und den alten talmudischen Zitaten*. Göttingen: Vandenhoeck & Ruprecht.

———. 1994. *Die aramaischen Texte vom Toten Meer: Ergänzungsband*. Göttingen: Vandenhoeck & Ruprecht.

Beyschlag, K. 1974. *Simon Magus und die christliche Gnosis*. WUNT 16. Tübingen: Mohr.

Beyschlag, W. 1893. *Das Leben Jesu*. Vol. 1. 3rd ed. Halle: Strien.

———. 1897. *Das Leben Jesu*. Vol. 2. 2nd ed. Halle: Strien.

Bickerman, E. 1935. "Utilitas crucis: Observations sur les récits du procès de Jésus dans les Evangiles canoniques." *RHR* 112: 170–241 (= Bickerman 1986, 82–138).

———. 1937. *Der Gott der Makkabäer*. Berlin: Schocken.

———. 1986. *Studies in Jewish and Christian History*. Part 3. AGAJU 9. Leiden: Brill.

Biddle, M. 1998. *Das Grab Christi: Neutestamentliche Quellen, historische und archäologische Forschungen, überraschende Erkenntnisse*. Gießen: Brunnen.

Black, M. 1967. *An Aramaic Approach to the Gospels and Acts*. 3rd ed. Oxford: Clarendon Press.

Blanc, C., ed. 1992. *Commentaire sur Saint Jean*. SC 157. Paris: Cerf.

Blass, F., A. Debrunner, and F. Rehkopf. 1984. *Grammatik des neutestamentlichen Griechisch*. 16th ed. Göttingen: Vandenhoeck & Ruprecht.

Bleicken, J. 1999. *Augustus*. 3rd ed. Berlin: Fest.

———. 2016. *Augustus: A Biography*. Translated by A. Bell. London: Penguin.

Blinzler, J. 1967. *Die Brüder und Schwestern Jesu*. SBS 21. Stuttgart: Katholisches Bibelwerk.

———. 1969 [1950]. *Der Prozess Jesu*. 4th ed. Regensburg: Pustet.

Böcher, O. 1988. "Johannes der Täufer." Pages 172–81 in *TRE* 17.

Bock, D. L. 1998. *Blasphemy and Exaltation in Judaism and the Final Examination of Jesus*. WUNT 2/106. Tübingen: Mohr.

Bockmuehl, M. 1994. *This Jesus: Martyr, Lord, Messiah*. Edinburgh: T&T Clark.

———. 2010. *The Remembered Peter*. Tübingen: Mohr.

———. 2017. *Ancient Apocryphal Gospels*. Louisville: Westminster John Knox.

Boffo, L. 1994. *Iscrizioni greche e latine per lo studio della Bibbia*. BSSTB 9. Brescia: Paideia Editrice.

Böhm, M. 1999. *Samarien und die Samaritai bei Lukas*. WUNT 2/111. Tübingen: Mohr.

Bösen, W. 1998 [1985]. *Galiläa—Lebensraum und Wirkungsfeld Jesu*. 2nd ed. Freiburg: Herder.

Botermann, H. 1996. *Das Judenedikt des Kaisers Claudius*. Hermes.E 71. Stuttgart: Steiner.

Böttrich, C. 2001. *Petrus. Fischer, Fels und Funktionär*. BG 2. Leipzig: Evangelische Verlagsanstalt.

Bousset, W. 1892. *Jesu Predigt in ihrem Gegensatz zum Judentum*. Göttingen: Vandenhoeck & Ruprecht.

———. 1904. *Jesus*. RV 1. Ser. 2/3. Halle an der Saale: Gebauer-Schwetschke.

———. 1906. *Jesus*. Translated by J. P. Trevelyan. New York: Putnam's Sons.

———. 1965 [1913]. *Kyrios Christos: Geschichte des Christusglaubens von den Anfängen bis Irenäus*. 5th ed. Göttingen: Vandenhoeck & Ruprecht.

———. 1970. *Kyrios Christos: A History of the Belief in Christ from the Beginnings of Christianity to Irenaeus*. Translated by J. E. Steely. Nashville, Tenn.: Abingdon Press.

Boustan, R. 2005. *From Martyr to Mystic*. TSAJ 112. Tübingen: Mohr.

Bovon, F. 1996. *Das Evangelium nach Lukas (Lk 9,51–14,35)*. EKK 3/2. Zürich: Benzinger.

———. 2013. *Luke 2: A Commentary on the Gospel of Luke 9:51–19:27*. Translated by D. S. Deer. Edited by H. Koester. Minneapolis: Fortress.

Bowden, J. 1988. *Jesus: The Unanswered Questions*. London: SCM.

Brandon, S. G. F. 1967. *Jesus and the Zealots*. New York: Scribner.

Breytenbach, C., and J. Frey, eds. 2013. *Reflections on the Early Christian History of Religion. Erwägungen zur frühchristlichen Religionsgeschichte*. Leiden: Brill.

Bringmann, K. 2005. *Geschichte der Juden im Altertum*. Stuttgart: Klett-Cotta.

Brock, S. P. 2004. "Syrische christliche Literatur." Pages 2002–5 in *RGG⁴* 7.

———. 2012. "Syrian Christian Literature." Pages 444–46 in *RPP* 12.

Brockelmann, C. 1928. *Lexicon Syriacum*. 2nd ed. Halle: Niemeyer.

Broer, I. 1972. *Die Urgemeinde und das Grab Jesu: Eine Analyse der Grable-gungsgeschichte im Neuen Testament.* StANT 31. Munich: Kösel.

Brook, G., et al. 1996. *Qumran Cave 4. XVII: Parabiblical Texts, Part 3.* DJD 22. Oxford: Clarendon Press.

Broscio, G. 1998. "Julius Africanus." Pages 408–9 in *Lexikon der antiken christlichen Literatur.* Edited by S. Döpp and W. Geerlings. Freiburg: Herder.

Broshi, M. 1999. "The Archaeology of Palestine 63 BCE–CE 70." Pages 1–37 in *The Cambridge History of Judaism.* Vol. 3. Edited by W. Horbury, W. D. Davies, and J. Sturdy. Cambridge: Cambridge University Press.

Brown, R. E. 1966/1970. *The Gospel According to John.* 2 vols. New York: Doubleday.

———. 1994. *The Death of the Messiah: From Gethsemane to the Grave; A Commentary on the Passion Narratives in the Four Gospels.* 2 vols. New York: Doubleday.

Bruneau, P. 1982. "'Les Israélites de Délos' et la juiverie délienne." *BCH* 106: 465–504.

Brunson, A. C. 2003. *Psalm 118 in the Gospel of John: An Intertextual Study of the New Exodus Pattern in the Theology of John.* WUNT 2/158. Tübingen: Mohr.

Bühner, J.-A. 1983. "Jesus und die antike Magie." *EvTh* 43: 156–75.

Bultmann, R. 1919/1920. "Die Frage nach dem messianischen Bewußtsein Jesu und das Petrus-Bekenntnis." *ZNW* 19: 165–74 (= Bultmann 1967a, 1–10).

———. 1921. *Geschichte der Synoptischen Tradition.* FRLANT 29. Göttingen: Vandenhoeck & Ruprecht.

———. 1925. "Die Bedeutung der neuerschlossenen mandäischen und man-ichäischen Quellen für das Verständnis des Johannesevangeliums." *ZNW* 24: 100–46.

———. 1931. *Geschichte der Synoptischen Tradition.* 2nd ed. FRLANT 29. Göttingen: Vandenhoeck & Ruprecht.

———. 1933–1965. *Glauben und Verstehen: Gesammelte Aufsätze.* Tübingen: Mohr.

———. 1934a. Review of H. Lietzmann, *Geschichte der Alten Kirche*, Bd. I. *ZKG* 53: 624–30 (= Bultmann 2002, 293–99).

———. 1934b. "The Study of the Synoptic Gospels." Pages 11–76 in *Form Criticism: A New Method of New Testament Research.* Edited and trans-lated by F. C. Grant. Chicago: Willett, Clark & Company.

———. 1937. Review of R. Otto, *Reich Gottes und Menschensohn.* *ThR NF* 9: 1–35 (= Bultmann 2002, 328–53).

———. 1939. Review of H. Lietzmann, *Geschichte der Alten Kirche, Bd. II.* *ZKG* 58: 260–66 (= Bultmann 2002, 377–384).

———. 1948a. "Neues Testament und Mythologie." Pages 15–53 in *Kerygma und Mythos.* Vol. 1. Edited by H.-W. Bartsch. Hamburg: Herbert Reich.

———. 1948b. "Zu J. Schniewinds Thesen, das Problem der Entmythologisier-ung betreffend." Pages 135–53 in *Kerygma und Mythos.* Edited by H.-W. Bartsch. Hamburg: Reich.

———. 1950. *Das Evangelium des Johannes*. 11st ed. KEK 2. Göttingen: Vandenhoeck & Ruprecht.

———. 1952. *Das Urchristentum*. 2nd ed. Zürich: Artemis.

———. 1956. *Primitive Christianity in Its Contemporary Setting*. Translated by R. Fuller. Philadelphia: Fortress.

———. 1961. "A Reply to the Theses of J. Schniewind." Pages 102–23 in *Kerygma and Myth: A Theological Debate*. Edited by H.-W. Bartsch. Translated by R. H. Fuller. New York: Harper & Row.

———. 1962. *Das Evangelium des Johannes*. 17th ed. KEK. Göttingen: Vandenhoeck & Ruprecht.

———. 1963. *The History of the Synoptic Tradition*. Translated by J. Marsh. New York: Harper & Row.

———. 1964. "The Primitive Christian Kerygma and the Historical Jesus." Pages 15–42 in *The Historical Jesus and the Kerygmatic Christ: Essays on the New Quest for the Historical Jesus*. Translated and edited by C. E. Braaten and R. A. Harrisville. Nashville, Tenn.: Abingdon Press.

———. 1965. *Das Verhältnis der urchristlichen Christusbotschaft zum historischen Jesus*. Vol. 3. SHAW.PH 3 1960. Heidelberg: Winter.

———. 1966 [1925]. *Die Erforschung der synoptischen Evangelien*. 5th ed. Berlin: Töpelmann.

———. 1967a. *Exegetica. Aufsätze zur Erforschung des Neuen Testaments*. Edited by E. Dinkler. Tübingen: Mohr.

———. 1967b. "Das Verhältnis der urchristlichen Christusbotschaft zum historischen Jesus." Pages 445–69 in *Exegetica. Aufsätze zur Erforschung des Neuen Testaments*. Edited by E. Dinkler. Tübingen: Mohr.

———. 1971. *The Gospel According to John*. New York: Doubleday.

———. 1984a. "New Testament and Mythology." Pages 1–43 in *New Testament and Mythology*. Selected, edited, and translated by S. M. Ogden. Philadelphia: Fortress.

———. 1984b [1948–1953]. *Theologie des Neuen Testaments*. Edited by O. Merk. 9th ed. Tübingen: Mohr.

———. 1995. *Die Geschichte der synoptischen Tradition*. 10th ed. FRLANT 29. Göttingen: Vandenhoeck & Ruprecht.

———. 2002. *Theologie als Kritik: Ausgewählte Rezensionen und Forschungsberichte*. Edited by M. Dreher and K. W. Müller. Tübingen: Mohr.

———. 2007. *Theology of the New Testament*, vols. 1 and 2. Translated by K. Grobel. Waco: Baylor University Press.

Bultmann, R., G. Theissen, and P. Vielhauer. 1971. *Die Geschichte der synoptischen Tradition: Ergänzungsheft*. 4th ed. Göttingen: Vandenhoeck & Ruprecht.

Burchard, C. 2000. *Der Jakobusbrief*. HNT 15/I. Tübingen: Mohr.

Burke, T., ed. 2013. *Ancient Gospel or Modern Forgery? The Secret Gospel of Mark in Debate: Proceedings from the 2011 York University Christian Apocrypha Symposium*. Eugene: Cascade Books.

Burney, C. F. 1925. *The Poetry of Our Lord: An Examination of the Formal Elements of Hebrew Poetry in the Discourses of Jesus Christ*. Oxford: Clarendon Press.

Byrskog, S. 2000. *Story as History—History as Story: The Gospel Tradition in the Context of Ancient Oral History*. WUNT 123. Tübingen: Mohr.

———. 2005. "Das Lernen der Jesusgeschichte nach der synoptischen Evangelien." Pages 191–209 in *Religiöses Lernen in der biblischen, frühjüdischen und frühchristlichen Überlieferung*. Edited by B. Ego and S. Byrskog. WUNT 180. Tübingen: Mohr.

Bystrina, I. 1991. "Das Erbe des Schamanismus in Palästina." Pages 181–213 in *Hungrige Geister und rastlose Seelen: Texte zur Schaminismusforschung*. Edited by M. Kuper. Berlin: Reimer.

Cadbury, H. J. 1937. *The Peril of Modernizing Jesus*. New York: Macmillan.

Campenhausen, H. Freiherr von. 1966. *Der Ablauf der Osterereignisse und das leere Grab*. 3rd ed. SHAW.PH. Heidelberg: Winter.

Camponovo, O. 1984. *Königtum, Königsherrschaft und Reich Gottes in den frühjüdischen Schriften*. OBO 58. Göttingen: Vandenhoeck & Ruprecht.

Cancik, H. 1984. "Bios und Logos: Formgeschichtliche Untersuchungen zu Lukians 'Leben des Demonax.'" Pages 115–30 in *Markus-Philologie*. WUNT 33. Tübingen: Mohr.

Cardauns, B., ed. 1976. *M. Terentius Varo: Antiquitates Rerum Divinarum*. Teil I: *Die Fragmente*. AAWLM.L. Wiesbaden: Steiner.

Carleton Paget, J. N. 1999. "Jewish Christianity." Pages 731–75 in *The Cambridge History of Judaism*. Vol. 3. Edited by W. Horbury, W. D. Davies, and J. Sturdy. Cambridge: Cambridge University Press.

———. 2017. "Das 'Gottesreich' als eschatologisches Konzept: Johannes Weiß und Albert Schweitzer." Pages 55–65 in *Jesus Handbuch*. Edited by J. Schröter and C. Jacobi. Tübingen: Mohr.

Carlson, S. C. 2005. *The Gospel Hoax: Morton Smith's Invention of Secret Mark*. Waco: Baylor University Press.

Casey, M. 1998. *Aramaic Sources of Mark's Gospel*. MSSNTS 102. Cambridge: Cambridge University Press.

———. 2002. *An Aramaic Approach to Q: Sources for the Gospels of Matthew and Luke*. MSSNTS 122. Cambridge: Cambridge University Press.

Chadwick, H. 1950. "The Silence of Bishops in Ignatius." *HThR* 43: 169–72.

———. 2001. *The Church in Ancient Society*. Oxford: Oxford University Press.

Chamberlain, H. S. 1899. *Die Grundlagen des 19. Jahrhunderts*. 2 vols. Munich: Bruckmann.

Chancey, M. A. 2002. *The Myth of a Gentile Galilee*. MSSNTS 118. Cambridge: Cambridge University Press.

———. 2005. *Greco-Roman Culture and the Galilee of Jesus*. MSSNTS 134. Cambridge: Cambridge University Press.

Charlesworth, J. H. 1988. *Jesus within Judaism: New Light from Exciting Archaeological Discoveries*. New York: Doubleday.

Charlesworth, J. H., and C. D. Elledge, eds. 2006. *Resurrection: The Origins and Future of a Biblical Doctrine*. New York: T&T Clark.

Charlesworth, J. H., and C. Newsom, eds. 1999. *The Dead Sea Scrolls*. Vol. 4B. Tübingen: Mohr.

Chester, A. 2001. "Resurrection and Transformation." Pages 47–77 in *Auferstehung—Resurrection*. Edited by F. Avemarie and H. Lichtenberger. Tübingen: Mohr.

Chilton, B. 1984. *A Galilean Rabbi and His Bible: Jesus's Use of the Interpreted Scripture of His Time*. Wilmington, Del.: Michael Glazier.

Claussen, C. 2002. *Versammlung, Gemeinde, Synagogue: Das hellenistisch-jüdische Umfeld der frühchristlichen Gemeinden.* SUNT 27. Göttingen: Vandenhoeck & Ruprecht.

Collins, J. J. 1995. *The Scepter and the Star.* New York: Doubleday.

Colpe, C. 1969. "ὁ υἱὸς τοῦ ἀνθρώπου." Pages 403–81 in *ThWNT* 8.

———. 1972. "ὁ υἱὸς τοῦ ἀνθρώπου." Pages 400–77 in *TDNT* 8.

———. 1983. "Gottessohn." Pages 19–58 in *RAC* 12.

———. 1990. *Das Siegel der Propheten.* ANTZ 3. Berlin: Institut Kirche und Judentum.

Conzelmann, H. 1959. "Jesus Christus." Pages 619–53 in *RGG³* 3.

———. 1965. "Zur Analyse der Bekenntnisformel 1 Cor. 15:3-5." *EvTh* 25: 1–11.

———. 1967. *Grundriß der Theologie des Neuen Testament.* Munich: Kaiser.

———. 1969. *An Outline of the Theology of the New Testament.* Translated by J. Bowden. London: SCM.

———. 1971 [1969]. *Geschichte des Urchristentums.* 2nd ed. GNT 5. Göttingen: Vandenhoeck & Ruprecht.

———. 1973a. *Jesus: The Classic Article from RGG Expanded and Updated.* Edited by J. Reumann. Philadelphia: Fortress.

———. 1973b. *History of Primitive Christianity.* Translated by J. E. Steely. Nashville, Tenn.: Abingdon Press.

———. 1974. *Theologie als Schriftauslegung.* BEvTh 65. Munich: Kaiser.

———. 1997. *Grundriß der Theologie des Neuen Testament.* 6th ed. Revised by A. Lindemann. Tübingen: Mohr.

Conzelmann, H., and A. Lindemann. 1975. *Arbeitsbuch zum Neuen Testament.* Tübingen: Mohr.

———. 1985. *Arbeitsbuch zum Neuen Testament.* 8th ed. Tübingen: Mohr.

———. 1988. *Interpreting the New Testament: An Introduction to the Principles and Methods of N.T. Exegesis.* Translated by S. S. Schatzmann. Peabody, Mass.: Hendrickson.

———. 2000. *Arbeitsbuch zum Neuen Testament.* Tübingen: Mohr.

Cook, J. G. 2000. *The Interpretation of the New Testament in Greco-Roman Paganism.* STAC 3. Tübingen: Mohr.

———. 2019. *Crucifixion in the Mediterranean World.* 2nd ed. WUNT 327. Tübingen: Mohr.

Cotton, H. M. 1999. "Some Aspects of the Roman Administration of Judaea/Syria-Palestina." Pages 75–91 in *Lokale Autonomie und römische Ordnungsmacht in den kaiserlichen Provinzen vom 1. bis 3. Jahrhundert.* Edited by W. Eck. Schriften des historischen Kollegs. Kolloquien 42. Munich: Oldenbourg.

Crossan, J. D. 1988. *The Cross That Spoke: The Origins of the Passion Narrative.* San Francisco: Harper & Row.

———. 1991. *The Historical Jesus: The Life of a Mediterranean Jewish Peasant.* San Francisco: HarperSanFrancisco.

Crouzel, H. 1983. "Gregor I (der Wundertäter)." Pages 779–93 in *RAC* 12.

Cureton, W. 1855. *Spicilegium Syriacum.* London: Rivingtons.

Dalman, G. 1898. *Die Worte Jesu.* Leipzig: Hinrichs.

———. 1902. *The Words of Jesus*. Translated by D. M. Kay. Edinburgh: T&T Clark.

———. 1922. *Jesus-Jeschua: Die drei Sprachen Jesu; Jesus in der Synagoge, auf dem Berge, beim Passahmahl, am Kreuz*. Leipzig: Hinrichs.

———. 1928–1942. *Arbeit und Sitte in Palästina*. 7 vols. Gütersloh: Bertelsmann.

———. 1930 [1898]. *Die Worte Jesu*. 2nd ed. Leipzig: Hinrichs.

———. 1965 [²1930]. *Die Worte Jesu: Mit Berücksichtigung des nachkanonischen jüdischen Schrifttums und der aramaischen Sprache*. Darmstadt: Wissenschaftliche Buchgesellschaft.

———. 1967 [1919]. *Orte und Wege Jesu*. 4th ed. BFChTh 2/1. Darmstadt: Wissenschaftliche Buchgesellschaft.

———. 2001. *Arbeit und Sitte in Palästina*. Vol. 8. Berlin: Walter de Gruyter.

Davies, W. D., and D. C. Allison. 1988/1991/1998. *A Critical and Exegetical Commentary on the Gospel According to Saint Matthew*. 3 vols. Edinburgh: T&T Clark.

Deines, R. 1993. *Jüdische Steingefäße und pharisäische Frömmigkeit*. WUNT 2/52. Tübingen: Mohr.

———. 1997. *Die Pharisäer: Ihr Verständnis im Spiegel der christlichen und jüdischen Forschung seit Wellhausen und Graetz*. WUNT 101. Tübingen: Mohr.

———. 2000. "Pharisäer." Pages 740–43 in *DNP* 9 (ET = Deines 2007b).

———. 2001a. "The Pharisees between 'Judaisms' and 'Common Judaism.'" Pages 443–504 in *Justification and Variegated Nomism*. Vol. I: *The Complexities of Second Temple Judaism*. Edited by D. A. Carson, P. T. O'Brien, and M. A. Seifrid. Grand Rapids: Eerdmans.

———. 2001b. "Sadduzäer." Pages 1204–6 in *DNP* 10 (ET = Deines 2008).

———. 2003. "Josephus, Salomo und die von Gott verliehene τέχνη." Pages 365–94 in *Die Dämonen*. Edited by A. Lange, H. Lichtenberger, and K. F. D. Römheld. Tübingen: Mohr.

———. 2004. *Die Gerechtigkeit der Tora im Reich des Messias: Mt 5,13-20 als Schlüsseltext der matthäischen Theologie*. WUNT 177. Tübingen: Mohr.

———. 2007a. "Jesus der Galiläer: Traditionsgeschichte und Genese eines antisemitschen Konstrukts bei Walter Grundmann." Pages 45–134 in *Walter Grundmann: Ein Neutestamentler im Dritten Reich*. Edited by R. Deines, V. Leppin, and K.-W. Niebuhr. 21 AKTh. Leipzig: Evangelische Verlagsanstalt.

———. 2007b. "Martin Hengel: A Life in the Service of Christology (trans. W. Coppins and S. Zahl)." *Tyndale Bulletin* 58: 25–42.

———. 2007c. "Pharisaei, Pharisees." Pages 923–27 in *New Pauly: Brill's Encyclopedia of the Ancient World*. Vol. 10. Edited by H. Cancik, H. Schneider, and M. Landfester. Boston: Brill (GV = Deines 2000).

———. 2008. "Sadducees." Pages 858–59 in *BNP* 12.

———. 2012a. "Christology between Pre-existence, Incarnation and Messianic Self-understanding." Pages 75–116 in *Earliest Christian History: History, Literature, and Theology; Essays from the Tyndale Fellowship in Honor of Martin Hengel.* Edited by M. F. Bird and J. Maston. WUNT 2/320. Tübingen: Mohr.

———. 2012b. "Martin Hengel: Christology in Service of the Church." Pages 33–72 in *Earliest Christian History: History, Literature, and Theology; Essays from the Tyndale Fellowship in Honor of Martin Hengel.* Edited by M. F. Bird and J. Maston. WUNT 2/320. Tübingen: Mohr.

———. 2017. *Jakobus: Im Schatten des Größeren.* Biblischen Gestalten 30. Leipzig: Evangelische Verlagsanstalt.

Deissmann, A. 1923. *Licht vom Osten.* 4th ed. Tübingen Mohr.

den Boer, W. 1965. *Scriptorum paganorum I–IV Saec: De Christianis Testimonia.* 2nd ed. Textus Minores II. Leiden: Brill.

Denis, A. M. 1970. *Introduction aux Pseudépigraphes Grecs d'Ancien Testament.* SVTP 1. Leiden: Brill.

Denyer, N. 2006. "Mark 16:8 and Plato, Protagoras 328D." *TynB* 57: 149–50.

Des Places, E., and M. Forrat, eds. 1986. *Eusebius: Contra Hiéroclès.* SC 333. Paris: Cerf.

Dexinger, F. 1992. "Der Ursprung der Samaritaner im Spiegel der frühen Quellen." Pages 67–140 in *Die Samaritaner.* Edited by F. Dexinger and R. Pummer. WdF 604. Darmstadt: Wissenschaftliche Buchgesellschaft.

Dibelius, M. 1919. *Formgeschichte des Evangeliums.* Tübingen: Mohr.

———. 1921. Review of E. Meyer, *Ursprung und Anfänge des Christentums.* *DLZ* 42: 225–235.

———. 1922. Review of R. Bultmann, *Geschichte der synoptischen Tradition,* 1st ed. 1921. *DLZ* 43 [7/8]: 128–34.

———. 1932. Review of R. Bultmann, *Geschichte der synoptischen Tradition,* 2nd ed. 1931. *DLZ* 53 [NF 3]: 1105–11.

———. 1933. *Formgeschichte des Evangeliums.* 2nd ed. Tübingen: Mohr (ET = Dibelius 1971).

———. 1935. Review of R. Otto, *Reich Gottes und Menschensohn.* *GGA* 1935/197: 209–21.

———. 1971. *From Tradition to Gospel.* Translated from the revised 2nd ed. of *Die Formgeschichte des Evangeliums* in collaboration with the author by B. L. Woolf. London: James Clarke.

Dihle, A. 1962. *Die Goldene Regel.* SAW 7. Göttingen: Vandenhoeck & Ruprecht.

———. 1981. "Goldene Regel." Pages 930–40 in *RAC* 11.

———. 2001. "Prosarhythmus." Pages 433–37 in *DNP* 10.

———. 2008. "Prose Rhythm." Pages 39–44 in *BNP* 12.

Dinkler, E. 1967. *Signum Crucis: Aufsätze zum Neuen Testament und zur Christlichen Archäologie.* Tübingen: Mohr.

Dobschütz, E. von. 1928. "Matthäus als Rabbi und Katechet." *ZNW* 27: 338–48.

———. 1980. "Matthäus als Rabbi und Katechet." Pages 52–64 in *Das Matthäusevangelium.* Edited by J. Lang. WdF 525. Darmstadt: Wissenschaftliche Buchgesellschaft.

Dochhorn, J. 2005. *Die Apokalypse des Mose.* TSAJ 106. Tübingen: Mohr.

Dodd, C. H. 1963. *Historical Tradition in the Fourth Gospel.* Cambridge: Cambridge University Press.

Dodds, E. R. 1985. *Heiden und Christen in einem Zeitalter der Angst.* Frankfurt am Main: Suhrkamp.

Doering, L. 1999. *Schabbat.* TSAJ 78. Tübingen: Mohr.

Döring, K. 1984. "Der Sokrates des Aischines von Sphettos und die Frage nach dem historischen Sokrates." *Hermes* 112: 16–30.

Dormeyer, D. 1993. *Das Neue Testament im Rahmen der antiken Literaturgeschichte. Eine Einführung.* Darmstadt: Wissenschaftliche Buchgesellschaft.

———. 2001. "Prätorium." Pages 163–64 in *NBL* 3.

Downing, F. G. 1992. *Cynics and Christian Origins.* Edinburgh: T&T Clark.

Drews, A. 1909. *Die Christusmythe.* Jena: Diederichs.

Droysen, J. G. 1972 [1932]. *Historik.* Edited by R. Hübner. 7th ed. Darmstadt: Wissenschaftliche Buchgesellschaft.

Dschulnigg, P. 1986. *Sprache, Redaktion und Intention des Markus-Evangelium.* 2nd ed. SBB 11. Stuttgart: Katholisches Bibelwerk.

Dungan, D. L. 1971. *The Sayings of Jesus in the Churches of Paul.* Philadelphia: Fortress.

Dunn, J. D. G. 2003a. "Altering the Default Setting: Re-envisaging the Early Transmission of the Jesus Tradition." *NTS* 49: 139–75.

———. 2003b. *Jesus Remembered.* CM 1. Grand Rapids, Mich.: Eerdmans.

Dupuis, C. F. 1794. *Origine de tous les cultes.* Paris: Chasseriau.

———. 1984. *The Origin of All Religious Worship.* New York: Garland.

Ebeling, H. J. 1939. *Das Messiasgehemnis und die Botschaft des Marcus-Evangelisten.* Berlin: Töpelmann.

Eck, W. 2001. "Praefectus." Pages 241–49 in *DNP* 10.

———. 2003. "Vespasianus." Pages 126 in *DNP* 12,2.

———. 2007. "Praefectus praetorio." Pages 757–63 in *BNP* 11.

———. 2010. "Vespasianus." Pages 334–38 in *BNP* 15.

Eck, W., A. Caballos, and F. F. Gómez. 1996. *Das Senatus consultum de Cn. Pisone patre.* Vestigia 48. Munich: Beck.

Eckstein, H.-J. 1996. "Markus 10.46-52 als Schlüsseltext des Markusevangeliums." *ZNW* 87: 30–50.

———. 2003. "Die Wirklichkeit der Auferstehung Jesu." Pages 157–77 in *Der aus Glauben Gerechte wird leben: Beiträge zur Theologie des Neuen Testament.* Beiträge zum Verstehen der Bibel 5. Münster: Lit.

Edwards, C., ed. 2000. *Suetonius: Lives of the Caesars.* Translated with an introduction and notes by C. Edwards. Oxford: Oxford University Press.

Ego, B. 1991. "Gottes Weltherrschaft und die Einzigkeit seines Namens: Eine Untersuchung zur Rezeption der Königsmetapher in der Mekhilta de R Yishma'el." Pages 257–83 in *Königsherrschaft Gottes und himmlischer Kult.* Edited by M. Hengel and A. M. Schwemer. WUNT 55. Tübingen: Mohr.

———. 1995. "Daniel und die Rabbinen." *Judaica* 51: 18–32.

———. 1996. *Targum Scheni zu Esther.* TSAJ. Tübingen: Mohr.

Ehrenberg, V., and A. H. M. Jones, eds. 1949. *Documents Illustrating the Reigns of Augustus and Tiberius.* 2nd ed. Oxford: Clarendon Press.

Ehrman, B. D. 1993. *The Orthodox Corruption of Scripture: The Effect of Early Christological Controversies on the Text of the New Testament.* Oxford: Oxford University Press.

——. 2003. *Lost Christianities: The Battles for Scripture and the Faiths We Never Knew*. Oxford: Oxford University Press.

Ehrman, B. D., and Z. Pleše. 2011. *The Apocryphal Gospels: Texts and Translations*. Oxford: Oxford University Press.

Eisler, R. 1929/1930. *ΙΗΣΟΥΣ ΒΑΣΙΛΕΥΣ ΟΥ ΒΑΣΙΛΕΥΣΑΣ*. Heidelberg: Winter.

Elbogen, I. 1995 [³1931]. *Der jüdische Gottesdienst in seiner geschichtlichen Entwicklung*. Olms Paperbacks 30. Hildesheim: Olms.

Elledge, C. D. 2006a. *Life after Death in Early Judaism*. WUNT 208. Tübingen: Mohr.

——. 2006b. "Resurrection of the Dead: Exploring Our Earliest Evidence Today." Pages 22–52 in *Resurrection: The Origin and Future of a Biblical Doctrine*. Edited by J. H. Charlesworth and C. D. Elledge. New York: T&T Clark.

——. 2006c. "The Resurrection Passages in the Testaments of the Twelve Patriarchs." Pages 79–103 in *Resurrection: The Origin and Future of a Biblical Doctrine*. Edited by J. H. Charlesworth and C. D. Elledge. New York: T&T Clark.

Epstein, I., ed. 1938. *The Babylonian Talmud: Seder Mo'ed in Four Volumes. II*. Translated into English with notes, glossary, and indices under the editorship of Rabbi Dr. I. Epstein. London: Soccino Press.

Erlemann, K. 1999. *Gleichnisauslegung: Ein Lehr- und Arbeitsbuch*. UTB 2093. Tübingen: Francke.

Ernst, J. 1989a. *Johannes der Täufer*. BZNW 53. Berlin: Walter de Gruyter.

——. 1989b. "War Jesus ein Schuler Johannes' des Täufers?" Pages 13–33 in *Vom Urchristentum zu Jesus: Festschrift J. Gnilka*. Freiburg-im-Breisgau: Herder.

Eshel, E. 2003. "Genres of Magical Texts in the Dead Sea Scrolls." Pages 395–415 in *Die Dämonen*. Edited by A. Lange, H. Lichtenberger, and K. F. D. Römheld. Tübingen: Mohr.

Eshel, E., H. Eshel, and A. Yardeni. 1992. "A Qumran Composition Containing Part of Ps. 154 and a Prayer for the Welfare of King Jonathan and His Kingdom." *IEJ* 42: 199–229.

Falk, H. 1985. *Jesus the Pharisee: A New Look at the Jewishness of Jesus*. New York: Paulist Press.

Fascher, E. 1924. *Die formgeschichtliche Methode*. BZNW 2. Gießen: Töppelman.

Fauth, W. 1987. "Pythagoras, Jesus von Nazareth und der Helios-Apollon des Julianus Apostata: Zu einigen Eigentümlichkeiten der spätantiken Pythagoras-Aretalogie im Vergleich mit der thaumasiologischen Tradition der Evangelien." *ZNW* 78: 26–48.

Feldman, L. H., ed. 1965. *Josephus: Jewish Antiquities, Books XVII–XX*. Vol. 9. LCL. Cambridge, Mass.: Harvard University Press.

——. 1984. *Josephus in Modern Scholarship (1937–1980)*. Berlin: Walter de Gruyter.

Feldmeier, R. 1987. *Die Krisis des Gottessohnes*. WUNT 2/21. Tübingen: Mohr.

Fiebig, P. 1904. *Altjüdische Gleichnisse und die Gleichnisse Jesu*. Tübingen: Mohr.

———. 1911. *Jüdische Wundergeschichten des neutestamentlichen Zeitalters.* Tübingen: Mohr.

———. 1912. *Die Gleichnisreden Jesu im Lichte der rabbinischen Gleichnisse des neutestamentlichen Zeitalters.* Tübingen: Mohr.

———. 1929. *Rabbinische Gleichnisse.* Leipzig: Hinrichs.

Fieger, S. M. 1991. *Das Thomas-evangelium: Einleitung, Kommentar und Systematik.* NTA NF 22. Münster: Aschendorff.

Field, F. 1875. *Origenis Hexapla.* 2 vols. Oxford: Clarendon Press.

Figueras, P. 1983. *Decorated Jewish Ossuaries.* Leiden: Brill.

Fischer, B., ed. 1983. *Vulgata.* Vol. 1. 3rd ed. Stuttgart: Deutsche Bibelgesellschaft.

Fischer, M. 2001. "Kapharnaum." Pages 43–56 in *RAC* 20.

Fitzer, G. 1964. "σφραγίς κτλ." Pages 939–54 in *ThWNT* 7.

———. 1971. "σφραγίς κτλ." Pages 939–53 in *TDNT* 7.

Fitzmyer, J. A. 1971. *Essays on the Semitic Background of the New Testament.* London: Chapman.

———. 1979. *A Wandering Aramean: Collected Aramaic Essays.* Missoula, Mont.: Scholars Press.

———. 1985. "Abba and Jesus's Relation to God." Pages 15–38 in *À cause de l'évangile: Festschrift Jacques Dupont.* LeDiv 123. Paris: Cerf.

———. 1997. *The Semitic Background of the New Testament: Combined Edition of Essays on the Semitic Background of the New Testament and A Wandering Aramean; Collected Aramaic Essays.* 2 vols. Grand Rapids: Eerdmans.

Fjärstedt, B. 1974. *Synoptic Tradition in 1 Corinthians: Themes and Clusters of Theme Words in 1 Corinthians 1–4 and 9.* Uppsala: Rotobeckman.

Flusser, D. 1981. "Pharisäer, Sadduzäer und Essener im Pescher Nahum." Pages 121–66 in *Qumran.* Edited by K. E. Grözinger. WdF 410. Darmstadt: Wissenschaftliche Buchgesellschaft.

———. 1986. "'The House of David' on an Ossuary." *Israel Museum Journal* 5: 37–40.

Foerster, W. 1924. *Herr ist Jesus.* NTF 2/1. Gütersloh: Bertelsmann.

———. 1938. "Κύριος κτλ." Pages 1083–95 in *ThWNT* 3.

———. 1966. "Κύριος κτλ." Pages 1086–95 in *TDNT* 3.

Frank, K. S., ed. 1975. *Frühes Mönchtum im Abendland.* Vol. 2. Zürich: Artemis.

Frey, J. 1993. "Erwägungen zum Verhältnis der Johannesapokalypse zu den übrigen Schriften im Corpus Johanneum." Pages 326–429 in *M. Hengel, Die johanneische Frage: Eine Lösungsversuch.* Tübingen: Mohr.

———. 1997–2000. *Die johanneische Eschatologie I–III.* WUNT 96, 110, 117. Tübingen: Mohr.

———. 1999. "Temple and Rival Temple—The Cases of Elephantine, Mt. Gerizim, and Leontopolis." Pages 171–203 in *Gemeinde ohne Tempel.* Edited by B. Ego, A. Lange, and P. Pilhofer. Tübingen: Mohr.

———. 2002. "Der historische Jesus und der Christus der Evangelien." Pages 273–336 in *Der historische Jesus: Tendenzen und Perspektiven der gegenwärtigen Forschung.* Edited by J. Schröter and R. Brucker. BZNW 114. Berlin: Walter de Gruyter.

———. 2003. "Die Scholien nach dem 'judischen Evangelium' und das sogenannte Nazoräerevangelium." *ZNW* 94: 122–37.

———. 2004. "Apostelbegriff, Apostelamt und Apostolizität: Neutestamentliche Perspektiven zur Frage nach der 'Apostolizität' der Kirche." Pages 91–188 in *Das kirchliche Amt in apostolischer Nachfolge*. Vol. I: *Grundlagen und Grundfragen*. Edited by T. Schneider and G. Wenz. Dialog der Kirchen 12. Göttingen: Vandenhoeck & Ruprecht.

———. 2005. "Paulus und die Apostel." Pages 197–227 in *Biographie und Persönlichkeit des Paulus*. Edited by E.-M. Becker and P. Pilhofer 187. Tübingen: Mohr.

———. 2012. "Martin Hengel as Theological Teacher (trans. V. Adrian)." Pages 15–32 in *Earliest Christian History: History, Literature and Theology; Essays from the Tyndale Fellowship in Honor of Martin Hengel*. Edited by M. F. Bird and J. Maston. WUNT 2/320. Tübingen: Mohr.

———. 2013. "Das vierte Evangelium auf dem Hintergrund der älteren Evangelientradition. Zum Problem: Johannes und die Synoptiker." Pages 239–94 in *Die Herrlichkeit des Gekreuzigten: Studien zu den Johanneischen Schriften*. Vol. 1. Edited by J. Schlegel. WUNT 307. Tübingen: Mohr.

———. 2015. "Das Corpus Johanneum und die Apokalypse des Johannes: Die Johanneslegende, die Probleme der johanneischen Verfasserschaft und die Frage der Pseudonymität der Apokalypse." Pages 71–133 in *Poetik und Intertextualität der Apokalypse*. Edited by S. Alkier, T. Hieke, T. Nicklas, and M. Sommer. WUNT 346. Tübingen: Mohr.

———. 2016. "Das Vaterunser im Horizont antik-jüdischen Betens unter besonderer Berücksichtigung der Textfunde vom Toten Meer." Pages 1–24 in *Das Vaterunser in seinen antiken Kontexten: Zum Gedenken an Eduard Lohse*. Edited by F. Wilk. FRLANT 266. Göttingen: Vandenhoeck & Ruprecht.

———. 2018a. *The Glory of the Crucified One*. Translated by W. Coppins and C. Heilig. Edited by W. Coppins and S. Gathercole. BMSEC 6. Waco: Baylor University Press.

———. 2018b. *Theology and History in the Fourth Gospel*. Waco: Baylor University Press.

Freyne, S. 1980. *Galilee from Alexander the Great to Hadrian 323 BCE to 135 CE: A Study of Second Temple Judaism*. Wilmington, Del.: Michael Glazier.

———. 1988. *Galilee, Jesus and the Gospels: Literary Approaches and Historical Investigations*. Philadelphia: Fortress.

———. 1998 [1980]. *Galilee: From Alexander the Great to Hadrian 323 BCE to 135 CE; A Study of Second Temple Judaism*. Edinburgh: T&T Clark.

———. 2000. *Galilee and Gospel: Collected Essays*. WUNT 125. Tübingen: Mohr.

———. 2001. "The Geography of Restoration: Galilee–Jerusalem Relations in Early Jewish and Christian Experience." *NTS* 47: 289–311.

———. 2006. "Galilee and Judaea in the First Century." Pages 37–51 in *The Cambridge History of Christianity*. Vol. 1: *Origins to Constantine*. Edited by M. M. Mitchell and F. M. Young. Cambridge: Cambridge University Press.

———. 2007. "Galilean Studies: Old Issues and New Questions." Pages 13–29 in *Religion, Ethnicity and Identity in Ancient Galilee*. Edited by J. Zangenberg, H. W. Attridge, and D. B. Martin. Tübingen: Mohr.

Froehlich, K. 1996. "Petrus II. Alte Kirche." Pages 273–78 in *TRE* 26.

Fuchs, S. E. 1965. *Zur Frage nach dem historischen Jesus: Gesammelte Aufsätze*. Vol. 2. 2nd ed. Tübingen: Mohr.

Funk, F. X. von. 1964. *Didascalia et Constitutiones apostolorum*. Paderborn: Schoeningh.

Funk, F. X., and K. Bihlmeyer. 1924. *Die apostolische Väter*. Tübingen: Mohr.

Funk, K. 1907. "Untersuchungen über die lukianische Vita Demonactis." *Philol. Suppl.* 10: 558–674.

Funk, R. W. 1996. *Honest to Jesus: Jesus for a New Millennium*. San Francisco: HarperSanFrancisco.

Funk, R. W., and A. J. Dewey. 2015. *The Gospel of Jesus: According to the Jesus Seminar*. 2nd ed. Salem, Ore.: Polebridge.

Funk, R. W., R. W. Hoover, and the Jesus Seminar, eds. 1997 [1993]. *The Five Gospels: What Did Jesus Really Say? The Search for the Authentic Words of Jesus*. San Francisco: HarperCollins.

Funk, R. W., and the Jesus Seminar. 1998. *The Acts of Jesus: What Did Jesus Really Do?* San Francisco: HarperSanFrancisco.

———. 1999. *The Gospel of Jesus: According to the Jesus Seminar*. Santa Rosa, Calif.: Polebridge.

Gabba, E. 1999. "The Social, Economic and Political History of Palestine 63 BCE–CE 70." Pages 94–167 in *The Cambridge History of Judaism*. Vol. 3. Edited by W. Horbury, W. D. Davies, and J. Sturdy. Cambridge: Cambridge University Press.

Gager, J. G. 1972. *Moses in Greco-Roman Paganism*. JBL.MS 16. Nashville, Tenn.: Abingdon Press.

García Martínez, F., and E. J. C. Tigchelaar. 1997/1998. *The Dead Sea Scrolls Study Edition*. 2 vols. Leiden: Brill.

García Martínez, F., and A. S. van der Woude. 1989/1990. "A 'Groningen'-Hypothesis of Qumran Origins and Early History." *RdQ* 14: 521–41.

Gathercole, S. 2006. *The Preexistent Son: Recovering the Christologies of Matthew, Mark, and Luke*. Grand Rapids: Eerdmans.

———. 2007. *The Gospel of Judas: Rewriting Early Christianity*. Oxford: Oxford University press.

———. 2012. *The Composition of the Gospel of Thomas: Original Language and Influences*. SNTSMS 151. Cambridge: Cambridge University Press.

———. 2014. *The Gospel of Thomas: Introduction and Commentary*. TENTS 11. Leiden: Brill.

———. 2018. "The Alleged Anonymity of the Canonical Gospels." *JTS* 69: 447–76.

Gawlick, G., and F. Niewöhner, eds. 1978. *B. Spinoza: Opera; Lateinisch-Deutsch*. Vol. 1. Darmstadt: Wissenschaftliche Buchgesellschaft.

Georges, K. E. 2003. *Ausführliches lateinisch-deutsches und deutsch-lateinisches Handwörterbuch*. 2 vols. 8th ed. Darmstadt: Wissenschaftliche Buchgesellschaft.

Gerber, C. 1997. *Ein Bild des Judentums für Nichtjuden von Flavius Josephus: Untersuchungen zu seiner Schrift Contra Apionem.* AGJU 40. Leiden: Brill.

Gerber, W. E. 1966. "See Genezareth." Pages 1754–55 in *Biblisch-historisches Handwörterbuch.* Vol. 3. Edited by B. Reicke and L. Rost. Göttingen: Vandenhoeck & Ruprecht.

Gerhardsson, B. 1988. "The Narrative Meshalim in the Synoptic Gospels." *NTS* 34: 339–42.

———. 1991. "Illuminating the Kingdom." Pages 266–304 in *Jesus and the Oral Gospel Tradition.* Edited by H. Wansbrough. Sheffield: JSOT.

Gese, H. 1974. "Ps 22 und das Neue Testament: Der älteste Bericht vom Tode Jesu und das Herrenmahl." Pages 180–201 in *Vom Sinai zum Zion: Alttestamentliche Beiträge zur biblischen Theologie.* Munich: Kaiser.

———. 1977. *Zur biblische Theologie: Altestamentliche Vorträge.* BEvTh 78. Munich: Kaiser.

———. 1981. *Essays on Biblical Theology.* Minneapolis: Augsburg.

———. 1991. "Die dreifache Gestaltwerdung des Alten Testaments." Pages 1–28 in *Alttestamentliche Studien.* Tübingen: Mohr.

———. 1996. "Zur Komposition des Koheletbuches." Pages 69–98 in *Geschichte–Tradition–Reflexion: Festschrift für Martin Hengel.* Vol. 1: *Judentum.* Edited by H. Cancik, H. Lichtenberger, and P. Schäfer. Tübingen: Mohr.

Gesenius, W. 1987. *Hebräisches und aramäisches Handwörterbuch über das Alte Testament.* 18th ed. Berlin: Springer.

Gigon, O. 1979. *Sokrates: Sein Bild in Dichtung und Geschichte.* 2nd ed. Sammlung Dalp 41. Bern: Francke.

Gilmour, S. M. 1981. "The Christophany to More than 500 Brethren." *JBL* 80: 248–52.

———. 1988. "The Christophany to More than 500 Brethren." Pages 133–38 in *Zur neutestamentlichen Überlieferung von der Auferstehung Jesu.* Edited by P. Hoffmann. WdF 522. Darmstadt: Wissenschaftliche Buchgesellschaft.

Gnilka, J. 1978/1979. *Evangelium nach Markus.* 2 vols. EKK 2. Zürich: Einsiedeln.

———. 1990. *Jesus von Nazaret: Botschaft und Geschichte.* HThK Suppl. III. Freiburg im Breisgau: Herder.

Gogarten, F. 1948. *Die Verkündigung Jesu Christi.* Heidelberg: L. Schneider.

Goodacre, M. 2002. *The Case Against Q: Studies in Markan Priority and the Synoptic Problem.* Harrisburg, Pa.: Trinity Press International.

———. 2012. *Thomas and the Gospels: The Case for Thomas' Familiarity with the Synoptics.* Grand Rapids: Eerdmans.

Goodblatt, D. 1994. *The Monarchic Principle: Studies in Jewish Self-Government in Antiquity.* TSAJ 38. Tübingen: Mohr.

Goodman, M. 1987. *The Ruling Class of Judaea: Origins of the Jewish Revolt A.D. 60–70.* Cambridge: Cambridge University Press.

Goodrich, R. J. 2015. *Sulpicius Severus: The Complete Works.* Introduction, translation, and notes by R. J. Goodrich. New York: Newman Press.

Goppelt, L. 1975/1978. *Theologie des Neuen Testaments*. Edited by J. Roloff. 2 vols. Göttingen: Vandenhoeck & Ruprecht.

———. 1981. *Theology of the New Testament*. Translated by J. E. Alsup. Edited by J. Roloff. 2 vols. Grand Rapids: Eerdmans.

Görg, M. 1988. "Gabbata." Page 719 in *NBL* 1.

———. 1991. "Arimathäa." Page 167 in *NBL* 1.

Grant, M. 1977. *Jesus of Nazareth*. London: Regel.

Grappe, C. 2001. *Le Royaume de Dieu: Avant, avec et après Jésus*. Geneva: Labor et Fides.

———. 2004. "Le repas de Dieu de l'autel à la table dans le judaïsme." Pages 95–102 in *Le Repas de Dieu—Das Mahl Gottes*. Edited by C. Grappe. Tübingen: Mohr.

Grass, H. 1962. *Ostergeschehen und Osterberichte*. 2nd ed. Göttingen: Vandenhoeck & Ruprecht.

Grässer, E. 2001 [1979]. *Forschungen zur Apostelgeschichte*. WUNT 137. Tübingen: Mohr.

———. 2002. *Der zweite Brief an die Korinther, Kapitel 1,1–7,16*. ÖTK 8/1. Gütersloh: Gutersloher.

Gregg, B. H. 2005. *The Historical Jesus and the Final Judgment Sayings in Q*. WUNT 2/207. Tübingen: Mohr.

Grelot, P. 1984. "L'arrière-plan araméen du 'Pater.'" *RB* 91: 531–56.

Gressmann, H. 1929. "Die Aufgaben der Wissenschaft des nachbiblischen Judentums." *ZAW* 43: 1–32.

Grundmann, W. 1941. *Jesus der Galiläer und das Judentum*. 2nd ed. Leipzig: Wigand.

———. 1973. "χρίω κτλ." Pages 482–85, 518–76 in *ThWNT* 9.

———. 1974. "χρίω κτλ A: General Usage." Pages 493–96 in *TDNT* 9.

Gunkel, H. 1903. *Zum religionsgeschichtlichen Verständnis des Neuen Testaments*. FRLANT 1. Göttingen: Vandenhoeck & Ruprecht.

Güttgemanns, E. 1968. "Χριστός in 1. Kor. 15, 3b—Titel oder Eigenname?" *EvTh* 28: 533–54.

———. 1970. *Offene Fragen zur Formgeschichte des Evangeliums*. BEvTh 54. Munich: Kaiser.

———. 1979. *Candid Questions Concerning Gospel Form Criticism: A Methodological Sketch of the Fundamental Problematics of Form and Redaction Criticism*. Translated by W. G. Doty. Pittsburgh: Pickwick.

Haelst, J. v. 1978. *Catalogue des papyrus littéraires Juifs et Chrétiens*. Paris: Publications de la Sorbonne.

Hagner, D. A. 1973. *The Use of the Old and New Testaments in Clement of Rome*. NT.S 34. Leiden: Brill.

Hahn, F. 1969. *The Titles of Jesus in Christology: Their History in Early Christianity*. Translated by H. Knight and G. Ogg. New York: World.

———. 1978. "Das Problem des Frühkatholizismus." *EvTh* 38: 340–57.

———. 1993. "υἱός." Pages 381–92 in *EDNT* 3.

———. 1995 [1965]. *Christologische Hoheitstitel: Ihre Geschichte im frühen Christentum*. 5th ed. FRLANT 83. Göttingen: Vandenhoeck & Ruprecht.

———. 2002. *Theologie des Neuen Testaments*. Vol. 1: *Die Vielfalt des Neuen Testament*. Tübingen: Mohr.

Hampel, V. 1990. *Menschensohn und historischer Jesus*. Neukirchen-Vluyn: Neukirchener.

Harnack, A. von. 1874. *De Apellis gnosi monarchica: Commentatio historica*. Leipzig: Bidder.

———. 1900. "Probabilia über die Adresse und den Verfasser der Hebräerbriefs." *ZNW* 1: 16–41.

———. 1906. *Lukas der Arzt: Der Verfasser des dritten Evangeliums und der Apostelgeschichte*. Leipzig: Hinrichs.

———. 1907. *Sprüche und Reden Jesu*. Leipzig: Hinrichs.

———. 1908. *Apostelgeschichte*. Leipzig: Hinrichs.

———. 1909. *Lehrbuch der Dogmengeschichte*. Vol. 1. Tübingen: Mohr.

———. 1910. "Das Problem des zweiten Thessalonicherbriefs." *SB*: 100–25 (= Harnack 1980, 78–97).

———, ed. 1916. *Porpyrius: 'Gegen die Christen.' 15 Bücher. Zeugnisse, Fragmente und Referate*. APAW.PH 1916, 1. Berlin: Königlich Akademie der Wissenschaften.

———. 1960 [1923/1924]. *Marcion: Das Evangelium vom fremden Gott; Eine Monographie zur Geschichte der Grundlegung der katholischen Kirche*. Neue Studien zu Marcion. Darmstadt: Wissenschaftliche Buchgesellschaft.

———. 1980. *Kleine Schriften zur Alten Kirche*. Vol. 1: *Berliner Akademieschriften 1890–1907*. Edited by J. Dummer. Opuscula IX/1. Leipzig: Zentralantiquariat der Deutschen Demokratischen Republik.

———. 1981 [⁴1924]. *Die Mission und Ausbreitung des Christentums in den ersten drei Jahrhunderten*. Wiesbaden: VMA.

———. 1988. "Die Verklärungsgeschichte Jesu, der Bericht des Paulus (1 Cor 15.3ff.) und die Beiden Christusvisionen des Petrus." Pages 89–117 in *Zur neutestamentliche Überlieferung von der Auferstehung Jesu*. Edited by P. Hoffmann. WdF 522. Darmstadt: Wissenschaftliche Buchgesellschaft.

———. 1990. *Marcion: The Gospel of the Alien God*. Translated by J. E. Steely and L. D. Bierma. Durham, N.C.: Labyrinth Press.

Harnisch, W. 1995. *Die Gleichniserzählungen Jesu: Eine hermeneutische Einführung*. UTB 1343. Göttingen: Vandenhoeck & Ruprecht.

Harrington, D. J. 1983. "The Jewishness of Jesus." *Bible Review* 3: 33–41.

———. 1987. "The Jewishness of Jesus: Facing Some Problems." *CBQ* 49: 1–13.

Hartin, P. J. 1991. *James and the Q Sayings of Jesus*. JSNT.S 74. Sheffield: JSOT.

Hartlich, C., and W. Sachs. 1952. *Der Ursprung des Mythosbegriffs in der modernen Bibelwissenschaft*. Tübingen: Mohr.

Hase, K. von 1891. *Geschichte Jesu: Nach akademischen Vorlesungen*. 2nd ed. Gesammelte Werke 4. Leipzig: Breitkopf & Härtel.

Hausrath, A. 1908. *Jesus und die neutestamentlichen Schriftsteller*. Berlin: Grote.

Häusser, D. 2006. *Christusbekenntnis und Jesusüberlieferung bei Paulus*. WUNT 2/210. Tübingen: Mohr.

Heckel, T. K. 1999. *Vom Evangelium des Markus zum viergestaltigen Evange-lium.* WUNT 120. Tübingen: Mohr.

Heckel, U. 2002. *Der Segen im Neuen Testament.* WUNT 150. Tübingen: Mohr.

Heil, G., ed. 1990. *Gregorii Nysseni Opera.* Vol. 10,1. Leiden: Brill.

Heinemann, J. 1977. *Prayer in the Talmud: Forms and Patterns.* Studia Juda-ica 9. Berlin: Walter de Gruyter.

Heitmüller, W. 1912. "Jesus Christus." Pages 359–61 in *RGG*[1] 3.

———. 1913. *Jesus.* Tübingen: Mohr.

Hellegouarc'h, J. 1982. *Velleius Paterculus, Histoire Romaine.* Tome I, livre i; Tome II, livre ii. Collection Budé. Paris: Les Belles Lettres.

Helm, R., ed. 1977. *Apuleius: Verteidigungsrede; Blütenlese.* Berlin: Akademie.

Hengel, M. 1963. "Maria Magdalena und die Frauen als Zeugen." Pages 243–56 in *Abraham unser Vater: Festschrift Otto Michel.* Edited by O. Betz, M. Hengel, and P. Schmidt. Leiden: Brill (= Hengel 2007b, 28–39).

———. 1968a. "Das Gleichnis von den Weingärtnern Mc 12,1-12 im Lichte der Zenonpapyri und der rabbinischen Gleichnisse." *ZNW* 59: 1–39 (= Hengel 2007b, 139–76).

———. 1968b. *Nachfolge und Charisma.* BZNW 34. Berlin: Walter de Gruyter (Revised and expanded in Hengel 2007b, 40–138).

———. 1969. "Mc 7,3 πυγμῇ: Die Geschichte einer exegetische Aporie und der Versuch einer Lösung." *ZNW* 60: 182–98.

———. 1970. *War Jesus Revolutionär?.* CwH 110. Stuttgart: Calver.

———. 1971/1972. "Die Ursprünge der christlichen Mission." *NTS* 18: 13–38.

———. 1971a. "Kerygma oder Geschichte? Zur Problematik einer falschen Alternative in der Synoptikerforschung aufgezeigt an Hand einiger neuer Monographien." *ThQ* 151: 323–36 (= Hengel 2007b, 289–305).

———. 1971b. *Was Jesus a Revolutionist?* Translated by W. Klassen. Philadel-phia: Fortress.

———. 1972a. "Augstein und der Menschensohn." *EvKomm* 5/11: 666–70.

———. 1972b. "Christologie und Chronologie." Pages 43–67 in *Neues Testa-ment und Geschichte: Historisches Geschehen und Deutung im Neuen Testament; Festschrift für Oscar Cullmann zum 70. Geburtstag.* Edited by H. Baltensweiler and B. Reicke. Zürich: Theologischer Verlag (= Hen-gel 2006a, 27–51).

———. 1973. "Ist der Osterglaube noch zu retten?" *ThQ* 153: 252–69 (= Hen-gel 2006a, 52–73).

———. 1976a. *Juden, Griechen und Barbaren.* SBS 76. Stuttgart: Katholisches Bibelwerk.

———. 1976b. *The Son of God: The Origin of Christology and the History of Jewish-Hellenistic Religion.* Translated by J. Bowden. Minneapolis: Fortress.

———. 1976c. *Die Zeloten: Untersuchungen zur jüdischen Freiheitsbewe-gung in der Zeit von Herodes I. bis 70 n. Chr.* 2nd ed. AGAJU 1. Leiden: Brill.

———. 1977a. *Crucifixion in the Ancient World and the Folly of the Message of the Cross.* Philadelphia: Fortress (= Hengel 1986, 93–185).

——. 1977b. *Der Sohn Gottes: Die Entstehung der Christologie und die jüdisch-hellenistische Religionsgeschichte.* 2nd ed. Tübingen: Mohr (= Hengel 2006a, 74–145).

——. 1978. "Jesus und die Tora." *ThBeitr* 9: 152–72.

——. 1980a. *Acts and the History of Earliest Christianity.* Translated by J. Bowden. Minneapolis: Fortress.

——. 1980b. "Hymnus und Christologie." Pages 1–23 in *Wort in der Zeit: Festgabe für Karl Heinrich Rengstorf zum 75. Geburtstag.* Edited by W. Haubeck and M. Bachmann. Leiden: Brill (= Hengel 2006a, 185–204).

——. 1980c. *Jews, Greeks, and Barbarians.* Translated by J. Bowden. London: SBL.

——. 1981a. *The Atonement: A Study of the Origins of the Doctrine in the New Testament.* London: SCM.

——. 1981b. *The Charismatic Leader and His Followers.* New York: Crossroad.

——. 1981c. "Das Ende aller Politik: Die Bergpredigt in der aktuellen Diskussion." *EK* 14: 686–90.

——. 1982a. *Achilleus in Jerusalem.* SHAW.PH. Heidelberg: Winter.

——. 1982b. "Die Stadt auf dem Berge." *EK* 15: 19–22.

——. 1983a. "Der Historiker Lukas und die Geographie Palästinas in der Apostelgeschichte." *ZDPV* 99: 147–83.

——. 1983b. "Probleme des Markusevangelium." Pages 221–66 in *Das Evangelium und die Evangelien.* Edited by P. Stuhlmacher. WUNT 28. Tübingen: Mohr (= Hengel 2007b, 430–77).

——. 1983c. *Between Jesus and Paul: Studies in the History of Earliest Christianity.* Translated by J. Bowden. London: SCM.

——. 1984a. "Entstehungszeit und Situation des Markusevangelium." Pages 1–45 in *Markus-Philologie: Historische, literargeschichtliche und stilistische Untersuchungen zum zweiten Evangelium.* Edited by H. Cancik. Tübingen: Mohr (= Hengel 2007b, 478–525).

——. 1984b. *Evangelienüberschriften.* SHAW.PH 3. Heidelberg: C. Winter.

——. 1984c. *Rabbinische Legende und frühpharisäische Geschichte: Schimeon b. Schetach und die achtzig Hexen von Askalon.* AHAW.Ph 2/1984. Heidelberg: Winter.

——. 1984d. *Zur urchristlichen Geschichtsschreibung.* 2nd ed. Stuttgart: Calwer.

——. 1985a. "Jakobus der Herrenbruder—der erste 'Papst'?" Pages 71–104 in *Glaube und Eschatologie: Festschrift Werner G. Kümmel.* Edited by E. Grässer and O. Merk. Tübingen: Mohr (= Hengel 2002, 549–82).

——. 1985b. *Studies in the Gospel of Mark.* London: SCM.

——. 1986. *The Cross of the Son of God.* Translated by J. Bowden. London: SCM.

——. 1987a. "Das Christuslied im frühesten Gottesdienst." Pages 357–404 in *Weisheit Gottes—Weisheit der Welt. Festschrift für Joseph Kardinal Ratzinger zum 60. Geburtstag.* Vol. 1. Edited by W. Baier. St. Otilien: EOS (= Hengel 2006a, 205–58).

———. 1987b. "The Interpretation of the Wine Miracle at Cana: John 2:1-11." Pages 83–112 in *The Glory of Christ in the New Testament: In Memory of G. B. Caird.* Edited by L. D. Hurst and N. T. Wright. Oxford: Clarendon Press (= Hengel 1995, 293–330).

———. 1987c. "Zur matthäischen Bergpredigt und ihrem jüdischen Hintergrund." *ThR* 52: 327–400 (= Hengel 1999b, 219–92).

———. 1988. *Judentum und Hellenismus: Studien zu iherer Begegnung unter besonderer Berücksichtigung Palästinas bis zur Mitte des 2. Jh.s v.Chr.* 3rd ed. WUNT 10. Tübingen: Mohr.

———. 1989a. *The Johannine Question.* Translated by J. Bowden. London: SCM.

———. 1989b. "Die Schriftauslegung des 4. Evangeliums auf dem Hintergrund der urchristlichen Exegese." *JBTh* 4: 249–89 (= Hengel 2007b, 601–43).

———. 1989c. *The Zealots: Investigations into the Jewish Freedom Movement in the Period from Herod I until 70 A.D.* Translated by D. Smith. Edinburgh: T&T Clark.

———. 1991a. *The Pre-Christian Paul.* Translated by J. Bowden. London: SCM.

———. 1991b. "Der vorchristliche Paulus." Pages 177–293 in *Paulus und das antike Judentum: Tübingen–Durham–Symposium im Gedenken an den 50. Todestag Adolf Schlatters (19. Mai 1938).* Edited by M. Hengel and U. Heckel. WUNT 58. Tübingen: Mohr (= Hengel 2002, 68–184).

———. 1993a. *Die johanneische Frage: Ein Lösungsversuch; Mit einem Beitrag zur Apokalypse von J. Frey.* WUNT 67. Tübingen: Mohr.

———. 1993b. "'Setze dich zu meiner Rechten!' Die inthronisation Christi zur Rechten Gottes und Psalm 110,1." Pages 108–94 in *Le Trône de Dieu—Der Thron Gottes.* Edited by M. Philonenko. WUNT 69. Tübingen: Mohr (= Hengel 2006a, 281–367).

———. 1995. *Studies in Early Christology.* Edinburgh: T&T Clark.

———. 1996a. *Judaica et Hellenistica: Kleine Schriften I.* WUNT 90. Tübingen: Mohr.

———. 1996b. "Zur Wirkungsgeschichte von Jes 53 in vorchristlicher Zeit." Pages 49–91 in *Der Leidende Gottesknecht.* Edited by B. Janowski and P. Stuhlmacher. FAT 14. Tübingen: Mohr.

———. 1997a. "Der Finger und die Herrschaft Gottes in Lk 11,20." Pages 87–106 in *La Main de Dieu—Die Hand Gottes.* Edited by R. Kieffer and J. Bergman. Tübingen: Mohr.

———. 1997b. "Die Urspünge der Gnosis und das Urchristentum." Pages 190–223 in *Evangelium—Schriftauslegung—Kirche: Festschrift für Peter Stuhlmacher zum 65. Geburtstag.* Edited by J. Ådna, S. J. Hafemann, and O. Hofius. Göttingen: Vandenhoeck & Ruprecht (= Hengel 2008a, 549–93; ET = Hengel 2012a).

———. 1999a. "Das Johannesevangelium als Quelle für die Geschichte des antiken Judentum." Pages 292–334 in *Judaica, Hellenistica et Christiana: Kleine Schriften II.* WUNT 109. Tübingen: Mohr.

————. 1999b. *Judaica, Hellenistica et Christiana: Kleine Schriften II*. WUNT 109. Tübingen: Mohr.

————. 2000a. "Die 'auserwählte Herrin,' die 'Braut,' die 'Mutter' und die 'Gottesstadt.'" Pages 260–63 in *La Cité de Dieu—Die Stadt Gottes*. Edited by M. Hengel, S. Mittmann, and A. M. Schwemer. WUNT 129. Tübingen: Mohr.

————. 2000b. *The Four Gospels and the One Gospel of Jesus Christ: An Investigation of the Collection and Origin of the Canonical Gospels*. Translated by J. Bowden. London: SCM.

————. 2001a. "Das Begräbnis Jesu bei Paulus und die leibliche Auferstehung aus dem Grabe." Pages 119–83 in *Auferstehung—Resurrection: The Fourth Durham–Tübingen Research Symposium; Resurrection, Transfiguration and Exaltation in Old Testament, Ancient Judaism and Early Christianity, Tübingen, September 1999*. Edited by F. Avemarie and H. Lichtenberger. Tübingen: Mohr (= Hengel 2006a, 386–450).

————. 2001b. "Ein Blick zurück im Zorn: Rudolf Augsteins 'Jesus Menschensohn.'" *ThBeitr* 32: 158–63.

————. 2001c. "Jesus als messianischer Lehrer der Weisheit und die Anfänge der Christologie." Pages 81–131 in *Der messianische Anspruch Jesu und die Anfänge der Christologie*. Edited by M. Hengel and A. M. Schwemer. Tübingen: Mohr (ET = Hengel 1995, 73–117).

————. 2001d. "Jesus der Messias Israels." Pages 1–80 in *Der messianische Anspruch Jesu und die Anfänge der Christologie: Vier Studien*. Edited by M. Hengel and A. M. Schwemer. WUNT 138. Tübingen: Mohr (ET = Hengel 1995, 1–72).

————. 2001e. "Judaism and Hellenism Revisited." Pages 6–37 in *Hellenism in the Land of Israel*. Edited by J. J. Collins and G. Sterling. Notre Dame, Ind.: University of Notre Dame Press.

————. 2001f. "Der Jude Paulus und sein Volk." *ThR* 66: 338–68.

————. 2002. *Paulus und Jakobus: Kleine Schriften III*. WUNT 141. Tübingen: Mohr.

————. 2003a. *Judaism and Hellenism: Studies in Their Encounter in Palestine during the Early Hellenistic Period*. Translated by J. Bowden. Eugene, OR: Wipf and Stock.

————. 2003b. "Les manuscrits de Qumrân et les origines chrétiennes." *CRAI* 4: 1435–45 (GV = Hengel 2008a; ET = Hengel 2012d).

————. 2003c. "'Salvation History': The Truth of Scripture and Modern Theology." Pages 229–44 in *Reading Texts, Seeking Wisdom*. Edited by D. F. Ford and G. N. Stanton. London: SCM.

————. 2004a. "Abba, Maranatha, Hosanna und die Anfänge der Christologie." Pages 145–83 in *Denkwürdiges Geheimnis: Beiträge zur Gotteslehre; Festschrift Eberhard Jüngel*. Edited by I. U. Dalfert, J. Fischer, and H.-P. Großhans. Tübingen: Mohr (= Hengel 2006a, 496–534).

————. 2004b. "Elias Bickermann: Erinnerungen an einen großen Althistoriker aus St. Petersburg." *Hyperboreus Studia Classica* 10: 171–77.

————. 2004c. "Die ersten nichtchristlichen Leser der Evangelien." Pages 99–117 in *Beim Wort nehmen—die Schrift als Zentrum für kirchliches*

Reden und Gestalten: F. Mildenberger zum 75. Geburtstag. Edited by M. Krug. Stuttgart: Kohlhammer (= Hengel 2007b, 702–25).

———. 2004d. "'Das Mahl in der Nacht, in der Jesus ausgeliefert wurde' (1 Kor 11,23)." Pages 115–60 in *Le Repas de Dieu—Das Mahl Gottes.* Edited by C. Grappe. WUNT 169. Tübingen: Mohr.

———. 2005. "Eye-witness Memory and the Writing of the Gospels (trans. W. Coppins)." Pages 70–96 in *The Written Gospel.* Edited by M. Bockmuehl and D. Hagner. Cambridge: Cambridge University Press.

———. 2006a. *Studien zur Christologie: Kleine Schriften IV.* Tübingen: Mohr.

———. 2006b. *Der unterschätzte Petrus: Zwei Studien.* Tübingen: Mohr (ET = Hengel 2010a).

———. 2007a. "Der Lukasprolog, seine Augenzeugen: Die Apostel, Petrus und die Frauen." Pages 195–242 in *Memory in the Bible and Antiquity: The Fifth Durham–Tübingen Research Symposium (Durham, September 2004).* Edited by S. C. Barton. WUNT 212. Tübingen: Mohr (= Hengel 2008b, 242–97; ET = Hengel 2012b).

———. 2007b. *Jesus und die Evangelien: Kleine Schriften V.* WUNT 211. Tübingen: Mohr.

———. 2008a. "Qumran und das frühe Christentum." Pages 488–96 in *Studien zum Urchristentum: Kleine Schriften VI.* WUNT 234. Tübingen: Mohr.

———. 2008b. *Studien zum Urchristentum: Kleine Schriften VI.* Tübingen: Mohr.

———. 2008c. *Die vier Evangelien und das eine Evangelium von Jesus Christus.* WUNT 224. Tübingen: Mohr.

———. 2009. "Heilsgeschichte." Pages 3–34 in *Heil und Geschichte: Die Geschichtsbezogenheit des Heils und das Problem der Heilsgeschichte in der biblischen Tradition und in der theologischen Deutung.* Edited by J. Frey, S. Krauter, and H. Lichtenberger. Tübingen: Mohr.

———. 2010a. *Saint Peter: The Underestimated Apostle.* Translated by T. H. Trapp. Grand Rapids: Eerdmans (GV = Hengel 2006b).

———. 2010b. *Theologische, historische, und biographische Skizzen: Kleine Schriften VII.* Edited by C.-J. Thornton. WUNT 253. Tübingen: Mohr.

———. 2010c. "Zur historischen Rückfrage nach Jesus von Nazareth: Überlegungen nach der Fertigstellung eines Jesusbuch." Pages 1–29 in *Gespräch über Jesus. Papst Benedikt XVI. im Dialog mit Martin Hengel, Peter Stuhlmacher und seinen Schülern in Castelgandolfo 2008.* Edited by P. Kuhn. Tübingen: Mohr.

———. 2011. *Die Zeloten: Untersuchungen zur jüdischen Freiheitsbewegung in der Zeit von Herodes I. bis 70 n. Chr.* Edited by R. Deines and C.-J. Thornton. 3rd ed. Tübingen: Mohr.

———. 2012a. "The Earliest Roots of Gnosticism and Early Christianity (trans. T. H. Trapp)." Pages 473–521 in *Earliest Christian History: History, Literature, and Theology; Essays from the Tyndale Fellowship in Honor of Martin Hengel.* Edited by M. F. Bird and J. Maston. WUNT 2/320. Tübingen: Mohr.

———. 2012b. "The Lukan Prologue and Its Eyewitnesses: The Apostles, Peter, and the Women (trans. N. Moore)." Pages 533–87 in *Earliest Christian History: History, Literature, and Theology; Essays from the Tyndale Fellowship in Honor of Martin Hengel*. Edited by M. F. Bird and J. Maston. WUNT 2/320. Tübingen: Mohr (GV = 2007a; 2008b, 242–97).

———. 2012c. "Paul and the Torah (trans. W. Coppins)." Pages 625–34 in *Earliest Christian History: History, Literature, and Theology; Essays from the Tyndale Fellowship in Honor of Martin Hengel*. Edited by M. F. Bird and J. Maston. WUNT 2/320. Tübingen: Mohr.

———. 2012d. "Qumran and Early Christianity (trans. L. Kierspel)." Pages 523–31 in *Earliest Christian History: History, Literature, and Theology; Essays from the Tyndale Fellowship in Honor of Martin Hengel*. Edited by M. F. Bird and J. Maston. WUNT 2/320. Tübingen: Mohr.

———. 2012e. "A Young Discipline in Crisis (trans. W. Coppins)." Pages 459–71 in *Earliest Christian History: History, Literature, and Theology; Essays from the Tyndale Fellowship in Honor of Martin Hengel*. Edited by M. F. Bird and J. Maston. WUNT 2/320. Tübingen: Mohr.

———. 2013. "Zur historische Rückfrage nach Jesus von Nazareth: Überlegungen nach der Fertigstellung eines Jesusbuch." Pages 29–46 in *Reflections on the Early Christian History of Religion. Erwägungen zur frühchristlichen Religionsgeschichte*. Edited by C. Breytenbach and J. Frey. Leiden: Brill.

Hengel, M., with D. P. Bailey. 2004. "The Effective History of Isaiah 53 in the Pre-Christian Period." Pages 75–146 in *The Suffering Servant: Isaiah 53 in Jewish and Christian Sources*. Edited by B. Janowski and P. Stuhlmacher. Translated by D. P. Bailey. Grand Rapids: Eerdmans.

Hengel, M., and R. Deines. 1996. "E. P. Sanders' 'Common Judaism,' Jesus und die Pharisäer." Pages 392–479 in *Judaica et Hellenistica: Kleine Schriften I*. Edited by M. Hengel. WUNT 90. Tübingen: Mohr.

Hengel, M., and R. Hengel. 1959. "Die Heilungen Jesu und medizinisches Denken." Pages 351–61 in *Medicus Viator: Fragen und Gedanken am Wege Richard Siebecks: Eine Festgabe seiner Freunde und Schüler zum 75. Geburtstag*. Edited by P. Christian and D. Rössler. Tübingen: Mohr.

———. 1980. "Die Heilungen Jesu und medizinisches Denken." Pages 338–73 in *Der Wunderbegriff im Neuen Testament*. Edited by A. Suhl. WdF. Darmstadt: Wissenschaftliche Buchgesellschaft.

Hengel, M., and A. M. Schwemer, eds. 1991. *Königsherrschaft Gottes und himmlischer Kult im Judentum, Urchristentum und in der hellenistischen Welt*. WUNT 55. Tübingen: Mohr.

———. 1997. *Paul between Damascus and Antioch: The Unknown Years*. Translated by J. Bowden. London: SCM.

———. 1998. *Paulus zwischen Damaskus und Antiochien: Die unbekannten Jahre des Apostles*. Tübingen: Mohr.

———. 2001. *Der messianische Anspruch Jesu und die Anfänge der Christologie: Vier Studien*. WUNT 138. Tübingen: Mohr.

———. 2007. *Jesus und das Judentum.* Vol. 1 of *Geschichte des frühen Christentums.* Tübingen: Mohr.

———. 2019. *Die Urgemeinde und das Judenchristentum.* Vol. 2 of *Geschichte des frühen Christentums.* Tübingen: Mohr.

Henige, D. P. 1982. *Oral Historiography.* London: Longman.

Henrichs, A., and L. Koenen, eds. 1988. *Der Kölner Mani-Kodex.* Papyrologica Coloniensia 14. Opladen: Westdeutscher.

Herrenbrück, F. 1990. *Jesus und die Zöllner.* WUNT 2/41. Tübingen: Mohr.

Herrmann, W. 1903. *Der Verkehr des Christen mit Gott.* 4th ed. Stuttgart: Cotta.

Hesse, F. 1973. "χρίω κτλ." Pages 485–500 in *ThWNT* 9.

———. 1974. "χρίω κτλ." Pages 496–509 in *TDNT* 9.

Heucke, C. 1997. "Arrianos." Pages 28–29 in *DNP* 2.

———. 2003. "Arrianus." Pages 26–28 in *BNP* 2.

Heussi, K. 1936. *Der Ursprung des Mönchtums.* Tübingen: Mohr.

Hezser, C. 1990. *Lohnmetaphorik und Arbeitswelt in Mt 20,1-16. Das Gleichnis von den Arbeitern im Weinberg im Rahmen rabbinischer Lohngleichnisse.* NTOA 15. Göttingen: Vandenhoeck & Ruprecht.

Hill, C. E. 1998. "What Papias Said about John (and Luke). A 'New' Papian Fragment." *JThS* 49: 582–629.

———. 2006. *The Johannine Corpus in the Early Church.* Oxford: Oxford University Press.

Himmelfarb, M. 2002. "The Mother of the Messiah in Talmud Yerushalmi and Sefer Zerubbabel." Pages 369–89 in *The Talmud Yerushalmi and Graeco-Roman Culture.* Vol. 3. Edited by P. Schäfer. TSAJ 93. Tübingen: Mohr.

Hirsch, E. 1939. *Das Wesen des Christentums.* Weimar: Deutsche Christen.

Hitchcock, F. R. M. 1930. "The Charges against the Christians in Tacitus." *CQR* 103: 300–16.

———. 1935. "A Note on Tacitus Annals XV, 44." *Hermanthena* 49: 184–88.

Höcker, C. 1996. "Ara Pacis Augustae." Pages 941–43 in *DNP* 1.

———. 2002. "Ara Pacis Augustae." Pages 951–53 in *BNP* 1.

Hoehner, H. W. 1972. *Herod Antipas.* Cambridge: Cambridge University Press.

Hoffmann, P. 1988. "Die historisch-kritische Osterdiskussion von H. S. Reimarus bis zum Beginn des 20. Jahrhunderts." Pages 15–67 in *Zur neutestamentliche Überlieferung von der Auferstehung Jesu.* Edited by P. Hoffmann. Darmstadt: Wissenschaftliche Buchgesellschaft.

Hofius, O. 1978. "Agrapha." Pages 103–10 in *TRE* 2.

———. 1988. "Herrenmahl und Herrenmahlparadosis: Erwagungen zu 1Kor 11.23b-25." *ZThK*: 371–408 (= Hofius 1989, 203–40; ET = Hofius 1993).

———. 1989. *Paulusstudien.* WUNT 51. Tübingen: Mohr.

———. 1991. "Isolated Sayings of the Lord." Pages 88–91 in *New Testament Apocrypha.* Vol. 1. Edited by W. Schneemelcher and R. M. Wilson. English translation edited by R. M. Wilson. Revised edition. Louisville: Westminster John Knox.

———. 1993. "The Lord's Supper and the Lord's Supper Tradition: Reflections on 1 Corinthians 11:23b-25." Pages 75–115 in *One Loaf, One Cup:*

Ecumenical Studies of 1 Cor. 11 and Other Eucharistic Texts: The Cambridge Conference on the Eucharist, August 1988. Edited by O. Knoch and B. F. Meyer. Macon, Ga.: Mercer University Press.

———. 1996. "Das vierte Gottesknechtlied in den Briefen des Neuen Testaments." Pages 107–27 in *Der leidende Gottesknecht: Jesaja 53 und seine Wirkungsgeschichte.* Edited by B. Janowski and P. Stuhlmacher. Tübingen: Mohr.

———. 1998. "'Für euch gegeben zur Vergebung der Sünden': Vom Sinn des Heiligen Abendmahls." *ZThK* 95: 313–37 (= Hofius 2000, 276–300).

———. 2000. *Neutestamentliche Studien.* WUNT 132. Tübingen: Mohr.

———. 2004a. "Die Allmacht des Sohnes Gottes und das Gebet des Glaubens." *ZThK* 101: 117–37.

———. 2004b. "The Fourth Servant Song in the New Testament Letters." Pages 163–88 in *The Suffering Servant: Isaiah 53 in Jewish and Christian Scriptures.* Edited by B. Janowski and P. Stuhlmacher. Translated by D. P. Bailey. Grand Rapids: Eerdmans.

———. 2012. "A.I.1. Außerkanonische Herrenworte." Pages 184–89 in *Antike christliche Apokryphen in deutscher Übersetzung.* Vol. 1.1–2. *Evangelien und Verwandtes.* Edited by C. Markschies and J. Schröter. Tübingen: Mohr.

Holl, K., M. Bergermann, and C.-F. Collatz, eds. 2013. *Epiphanius I: Ancoratus und Panarion Haer. 1–33.* Edited by Karl Holl. Second, expanded edition edited by M. Bergermann and C.-F. Collatz. Vol. 1/1. GCS NF 10/10. Berlin: Walter de Gruyter.

Holladay, C. R. 1983. *Fragments from Hellenistic Jewish Authors.* Vol. 1: *Historians.* Texts and Translations 10. Pseudepigrapha Series 10, 20. Chico, Calif.: Scholars Press.

———. 2005. *A Critical Introduction to the New Testament: Interpreting the Message and Meaning of Jesus Christ.* Nashville, Tenn.: Abingdon Press.

Holmes, M. W. 2002. *Apostolic Fathers: Greek Texts and English Translations.* 2nd ed. Grand Rapids: Baker Books.

Hölscher, G. 1949. "Panias." Pages 594–600 in *PW* 18.

Holtzmann, H. J. 1901. Review of W. Wrede, *Das Messiasgeheimnis in den Evangelien. GGA* 1901/12: 948–60.

———. 1907. *Das messianische Bewußtsein Jesu.* Tübingen: Mohr.

Horbury, W. 1991. "Herod's Temple and 'Herod's Days.'" Pages 103–49 in *Templum Amicitiae: Essays on the Second Temple Presented to Ernst Bammel.* Edited by W. Horbury. JSNT.S 48. Sheffield: JSOT.

———. 1994a. "The 'Caiaphas' Ossuaries and Joseph Caiaphas." *PEQ* 126: 33–48.

———. 1994b. "Jewish Inscriptions and Jewish Literature in Egypt." Pages 9–43 in *Studies in Early Jewish Epigraphy.* Edited by J. W. van Henten and P. W. van der Horst. Leiden: Brill.

———. 1996. "The Beginnings of the Jewish Revolt under Trajan." Pages 283–304 in *Geschichte–Tradition–Reflexion: Festschrift für Martin Hengel.* Vol. 1: *Judentum.* Edited by H. Cancik, H. Lichtenberger, and P. Schäfer. Tübingen: Mohr.

———. 1998a. *Jewish Messianism and the Cult of Christ.* London: SCM.

———. 1998b. *Jews and Christians in Contact and Controversy.* Edinburgh: T&T Clark.

———. 1999. "Der Tempel bei Vergil und im herodianischen Judentum." Pages 149–68 in *Gemeinde ohne Tempel: Community without Temple.* Edited by B. Ego. WUNT 118. Tübingen: Mohr.

———. 2003. *Messianism among Jews and Christians: Biblical and Historical Studies.* Edinburgh: T&T Clark.

Horbury, W., and D. Noy. 1992. *Jewish Inscriptions of Graeco-Roman Egypt.* Cambridge: Cambridge University Press.

Huggins, R. V. 1992. "Matthean Posteriority: A Preliminary Proposal." *NT* 34: 1–22.

Hurst, D., and M. Adriaen, eds. 1969. *S. Hieronymi Presbyteri Opera: Pars I, Opera exegetica. 7, Commentariorum in Matheum libri IV.* Turnhout: Brepols.

Hurtado, L. W. 2003. *Lord Jesus Christ: Devotion to Jesus in Earliest Christianity.* Grand Rapids: Eerdmans.

Hüttenmeister, F. G. 1998. *Sota.* ÜTY 3/2. Tübingen: Mohr.

Ilan, T. 1992. "'Man Born of Woman . . .' (Job 14,1): The Phenomenon of Men Bearing Metronymes at the Time of Jesus." *NT* 34: 23–45.

———. 1996. "Josephus and Nicolaus on Women." Pages 221–62 in *Geschichte—Tradition—Reflexion: Festschrift für Martin Hengel.* Vol. 1: *Judentum.* Edited by H. Cancik, H. Lichtenberger, and P. Schäfer. Tübingen: Mohr.

———. 1999. *Integrating Women into Second Temple History.* TSAJ 76. Tübingen: Mohr.

———. 2002. *Lexicon of Jewish Names in Late Antiquity.* Vol. 1. TSAJ 91. Tübingen: Mohr.

———. 2006. *Silencing the Queen.* TSAJ 115. Tübingen: Mohr.

Instone-Brewer, D. 1992. *Techniques and Assumptions in Jewish Exegesis before 70 CE.* TSAJ 30. Tübingen: Mohr.

Ising, D. 2002. *Johann Christoph Blumhardt: Leben und Werk.* Göttingen: Vandenhoeck & Ruprecht.

Isser, S. 1999. "The Samaritans and Their Sects." Pages 569–95 in *The Cambridge History of Judaism.* Vol. 3. Edited by W. Horbury, W. D. Davies, and J. Sturdy. Cambridge: Cambridge University Press.

Janowski, B. 1982. *Sühne als Heilsgeschehen: Studien zur Sühnetheologie der Priesterschrift und zur Wurzel KPR im Alten Orient und im Alten Testament.* WMANT 55. Neukirchen-Vluyn: Neukirchener.

———. 1989. "Das Königtum Gottes in den Psalmen." *ZThK* 86: 389–454.

———. 1997. *Stellvertretung: Altestamentliche Studien zu einem theologischen Grundbegriff.* SBS 165. Stuttgart: Katholisches Bibelwerk.

Jastrow, M. 1903. *A Dictionary of the Targumim, the Talmud Babli and Yerushalmi, and the Midrashic Literature.* 2 vols. New York: Putnam.

Jenks, G. C. 1991. *The Origins and Early Development of the Antichrist Myth.* BZNW 59. Berlin: Walter de Gruyter.

Jensen, M. H. 2006. *Herod Antipas in Galilee: The Literary and Archaeo-logical Sources on the Reign of Herod Antipas and its Socio-Economic Impact on Galilee*. WUNT 2/215. Tübingen: Mohr.

Jeremias, G. 1963. *Der Lehrer der Gerechtigkeit*. StUNT 2. Göttingen: Van-denhoeck & Ruprecht.

Jeremias, J. 1926. *Golgotha*. Leipzig: Pfeiffer.

———. 1933. "γέεννα." Pages 655–56 in *ThWNT* 1.

———. 1935. "Ἠλ(ε)ίας." Pages 930–43 in *ThWNT* 2.

———. 1942. "Μωϋσῆς." Pages 852–78 in *ThWNT* 4.

———. 1964a. "γέεννα." Pages 657–58 in *TDNT* 1.

———. 1964b. "Ἠλ(ε)ίας." Pages 928–41 in *TDNT* 2.

———. 1965. *Unbekannte Jesusworte*. 4th ed. Gütersloh: Mohn.

———. 1966a. *Abba: Studien zur neutestamentlichen Theologie und Zeitge-schichte*. Göttingen: Vandenhoeck & Ruprecht.

———. 1966b. "Artikelloses Christos: Zur Ursprache von I Kor. XV 3b-5." *ZNW* 57: 211–15.

———. 1966c. *The Eucharistic Words of Jesus*. Translated by N. Perrin. New York: Charles Scribner's Sons.

———. 1967a. *Die Abendmahlsworte Jesu*. 4th ed. Göttingen: Vandenhoeck & Ruprecht.

———. 1967b. "Die älteste Schicht der Menschensohn-Logien." *ZNW* 58: 159–72.

———. 1967c. "Μωϋσῆς." Pages 848–73 in *TDNT* 4.

———. 1969a. *Jerusalem in the Time of Jesus*. Trans. F. H. and C. H. Cave. London: SCM.

———. 1969b. *Jerusalem zur Zeit Jesu*. 3rd ed. Göttingen: Vandenhoeck & Ruprecht.

———. 1969c. "Nochmals: Artikelloses Christos in I Kor 15,3." *ZNW* 60: 214–19.

———. 1970. *New Testament Theology: The Proclamation of Jesus*. Trans-lated by J. Bowden. New York: Scribner.

———. 1972. *The Parables of Jesus*. Translated by S. H. Hooke. 3rd ed. London: SCM.

———. 1979 [1971]. *Neutestamentliche Theologie*. 3rd ed. Gütersloh: Mohn.

———. 1998 [1947]. *Die Gleichnisse Jesu*. 11st ed. Göttingen: Vandenhoeck & Ruprecht.

———. 2002. *Jesus and the Message of the New Testament*. Edited by K. C. Hanson. Minneapolis: Fortress.

Jones, A., ed. 1966. *The Jerusalem Bible*. Garden City, N.Y.: Doubleday.

Jones, F. S. 1995. *An Ancient Jewish Christian Source on the History of Christianity: Pseudo-Clementine Recognitions 1.27–71*. Atlanta: Schol-ars Press.

Jülicher, A. 1906. *Neue Linien in der Kritik der evangelischen Überlieferung*. Gießen: Töpelmann.

———. 1979. *Die Gleichnisreden Jesu*. Zwei Teile in einem Band. Darmstadt: Wissenschaftliche Buchgesellschaft.

Jülicher, A., and E. Fascher. 1931. *Einleitung in das Neue Testament.* 7th ed. Tübingen: Mohr.

Jüngel, E. 1979 [1962]. *Paulus und Jesus: Eine Untersuchung zur Präzisierung der Frage nach dem Ursprung der Christologie.* 5th ed. HUTh 2. Tübingen: Mohr.

Kähler, M. 1882. *Der sogenannte historische Jesus und der geschichtliche, biblische Christus: Vortrag auf der Wuppertaler Pastoralkonferenz.* Leipzig: Deichert.

———. 1896. *Der sogenannte historische Jesus und der geschichtliche, biblische Christus: Vortrag auf der Wuppertaler Pastoralkonferenz.* 2nd ed. Leipzig: Deichert.

———. 1953. *Der sogenannte historische Jesus und der geschichtliche, biblische Christus: Vortrag auf der Wuppertaler Pastoralkonferenz.* Edited by E. Wolf. Munich: Kaiser.

———. 1988. *The So-Called Historical Jesus and the Historic Biblical Christ.* Translated, edited, and with an introduction by Carl E. Braaten. Philadelphia: Fortress.

Kampen, J. 1988. *The Hasideans and the Origin of Pharisaism: A Study in 1 and 2 Maccabees.* SCSt 24. Atlanta: Scholars Press.

Karrer, M. 1990. *Der Gesalbte: Die Grundlagen des Christustitels.* Göttingen: Vandenhoeck & Ruprecht.

Käsemann, E. 1954. "Das Problem des historischen Jesus." *ZThK* 51: 125–53.

———. 1960/1964. *Exegetische Versuche und Besinnungen.* 2 vols. Göttingen: Vandenhoeck & Ruprecht.

———. 1962. "Wunder im Neuen Testament." Pages 1835–37 in *RGG³* 6.

———. 1964a [1954]. "Das Problem des historischen Jesus." Pages 187–214 in *Exegetische Versuche und Besinnungen.* Vol. 1. Göttingen: Vandenhoeck & Ruprecht.

———. 1964b [1954]. "The Problem of the Historical Jesus." Pages 15–47 in *Essays on New Testament Themes.* Translated by W. J. Montague. SBT 41. London: SCM.

———. 1964c. "An Apologia for Primitive Christian Eschatology." Pages 169–95 in *Essays on the New Testament.* Translated by W. J. Montague. London: SCM.

———. 1969a. "Blind Alleys in the 'Jesus of History' Controversy." Pages 23–65 in *New Testament Questions of Today.* Translated by W. J. Montague. Philadelphia: Fortress.

———. 1969b [1968]. *Jesus Means Freedom.* Translated by F. Clarke. Philadelphia: Fortress Press.

———. 1969c. "Paul and Early Catholicim." Pages 236–51 in *New Testament Questions of Today.* Translated by W. J. Montague. Philadelphia: Fortress.

———. 1972 [1968]. *Der Ruf der Freiheit.* 5th ed. Tübingen: Mohr.

Kasher, A. 1990. *Jews and Hellenistic Cities in Eretz Israel.* TSAJ 21. Tübingen: Mohr.

Kasper, W. 1973. "Der Glaube an die Auferstehung Jesu vor dem Forum historischer Kritik." *ThQ* 153: 229–41.

———. 1974. *Jesus der Christus.* Mainz: Matthias Grünewald.

————. 1977. *Jesus the Christ*. Translated by V. Green. New York: Paulist Press.

Kasser, R., M. M. Meyer, and G. Wurst, eds. 2007. *The Gospel of Judas*. Washington, D.C.: National Geographic.

Keel, O., M. Küchler, and C. Uehlinger, eds. 1982. *Orte und Landschaften der Bibel*. Vol. 2. Zürich: Benzinger.

Kehne, P. 2000. "Pax." Pages 454–55 in *DNP* 9.

————. 2007. "Pax." Pages 657–59 in *BNP* 10.

Kelhoffer, J. A. 2000. *Miracle and Mission: The Authentication of Missionaries and Their Message in the Longer Ending of Mark*. WUNT 2/112. Tübingen: Mohr.

————. 2005. *The Diet of John the Baptist*. WUNT 2/176. Tübingen: Mohr.

Kertelge, K. 1970. *Die Wunder Jesu im Markusevangelium*. SANT 23. Munich: Kösel.

Kittel, G. 1935. "ἔρημος." Pages 654–57 in *ThWNT* 2.

————. 1964. "ἔρημος." Pages 657–60 in *TDNT* 2.

Klauck, H.-J. 1986 [1978]. *Allegorie und Allegorese in synoptischen Gleichnistexten*. 2nd ed. NTA NF 13. Munich: Aschendorff.

————. 1989. "Güttergemeinschaft in der klassichen Antike, in Qumran und im Neuen Testament." Pages 69–100 in *Gemeinde—Amt—Sakrament*. Würzburg: Echter.

————. 1992. "Gleichnis." Pages 853 in *NBL* 1.

————. 1994. "Adolf Jülicher—Leben, Werk und Wirkung." Pages 181–211 in *Alte Welt und neuer Glaube*. NTOA. Göttingen: Vandenhoeck & Ruprecht.

————. 1997. *Vorspiel im Himmel? Erzähltechnik und Theologie im Markusprolog*. BThSt 32. Neukirchen-Vluyn: Neukirchener.

————. 2000. *Dion von Prusa: Olympische Rede oder über die erste Erkenntnis Gottes*. SAPERE 2. Darmstadt: Wissenschaftliche Buchgesellschaft.

————. 2002. *Apokryphe Evangelien: Eine Einführung*. Stuttgart: Katholisches Bibelwerk.

————. 2003a. *Apocryphal Gospels: An Introduction*. Translated by B. McNeil. London: T&T Clark International.

————. 2003b. *Religion und Gesellschaft im frühen Christentum: Neutestamentliche Studien*. WUNT 152. Tübingen: Mohr.

————. 2005. *Apocryphe Apostelakten: Eine Einführung*. Stuttgart: Katholisches Bibelwerk.

————. 2008. *The Apocryphal Acts of the Apostles: An Introduction*. Translated by B. McNeil. Waco: Baylor University Press.

Klausner, J. 1945. *Jesus of Nazareth: His Life, Times, and Teaching*. New York: Macmillan.

————. 1952. *Jesus von Nazareth*. 3rd ed. Jerusalem: Jewish Publishing House.

Klein, G. 1961. *Die zwölf Apostel: Ursprung und Gehalt einer Idee*. Göttingen: Vandenhoeck & Ruprecht.

Klein, W. 2004. "Schamane/Schamanin/Schamanismus." Pages 864–65 in *RGG⁴* 7.

————. 2012. "Shamanism." Pages 671–72 in *RPP* 11.

Klijn, A. F. J. 1988. "Das Hebräer- und das Nazoräerevangelium." Pages 3997–4033 in *ANRW* II 25/5.

Kloppenborg, J. S. 2006. *The Tenants in the Vineyard: Ideology, Economics, and Agrarian Conflict in Jewish Palestine.* WUNT 195. Tübingen: Mohr.

Kloppenborg Verbin, J. S. 2000. "Dating Theodotus (CIJ II 1404)." *JJS* 51: 243–80.

Klostermann, E., ed. 1904. *Das Onomastikon der biblischen Ortsnamen.* GCS 11,1. Leipzig: Hinrichs.

———. 1971. *Das Markusevangelium.* 5th ed. HNT 3. Tübingen: Mohr.

Knopf, R. 1905. *Das nachapostolische Zeitalter: Geschichte der christlichen Gemeinden vom Beginn der Flavierdynastie bis zum Ende Hadrians.* Tübingen: Mohr.

Koch, K. 1977. "חָטָא chāṭā'." Pages 857–70 in *ThWAT* 2.

———. 1980. "חָטָא chāṭā'." Pages 309–19 in *TDOT* 4.

Koester, H. 1957. *Synoptische Überlieferung bei den Apostolischen Vätern.* TU 65. Berlin: Akademie.

———. 1990. *Ancient Christian Gospels.* London: SCM.

Köhler, L., W. Baumgartner, J. J. Stamm, and Z. Ben-Ḥayyim, eds. 2004. *Hebräisches und aramäisches Lexikon zum Alten Testament.* 3rd ed. Leiden: Brill.

Köhler, W.-D. 1987. *Die Rezeption des Matthäusevangeliums in der Zeit vor Irenäus.* WUNT 2/24. Tübingen: Mohr.

Kokkinos, N. 1989. "Crucifixion in A. D. 36: The Keystone for Dating the Birth of Jesus." Pages 133–63 in *Chronos, Kairos, Christos: Nativity and Chronological Studies Presented to Jack Finegan.* Edited by J. Vardaman and E. M. Yamauchi. Winona Lake, Ind.: Eisenbrauns.

———. 1998. *The Herodian Dynasty: Origins, Role in Society and Eclipse.* JSPE.S 30. Sheffield: Sheffield Academic Press.

Kollmann, B. 1996. *Jesus und die Christen als Wundertäter.* FRLANT 170. Göttingen.

———. 2002. *Neutestamentliche Wundergeschichten.* Stuttgart: Kohlhammer.

Körtner, U. H. J., and M. Leutzsch, eds. 1998. *Papiasfragmente, Hirt des Hermas.* SUC III. Darmstadt: Wissenschaftliche Buchgesellschaft.

Koskenniemi, E. 1994. *Apollonios von Tyana in der neutestamentlichen Exegese.* WUNT 2/61. Tübingen: Mohr.

———. 2005. *The Old Testament Miracle-Workers in Early Judaism.* WUNT 2/206. Tübingen: Mohr.

Krauss, S. 1933. *Die Mischna: Text, Übersetzung und ausführliche Erklärung.* Gießen: Töpelmann.

———. 1964 [1899]. *Griechische und lateinische Lehnwörter in Talmud, Midrash und Targum.* Hildesheim: Olms.

———. 1977 [1902]. *Das Leben Jesu nach jüdischen Quellen.* Hildesheim: Olms.

Kremer, J. 1967. *Das älteste Zeugnis von der Auferstehung Jesu.* 2nd ed. SBS 17. Stuttgart: Katholisches Bibelwerk.

———. 1973. *Pfingstbericht und Pfingstgeschehen.* SBS 63/64. Stuttgart: Katholisches Bibelwerk.

Krüger, T. 2000. *Kohelet (Prediger)*. BKAT XIX. Neukirchen-Vluyn: Neukirchener.

Küchler, M. 1979. *Frühjüdische Weisheitstraditionen: Zum Fortgang weisheitlichen Denkens im Bereich des frühjüdischen Jahweglaubens*. Freiburg, Switzerland: Universitätsverlag.

Kuhn, H.-W. 1965. *Enderwartung und gegenwärtiges Heil*. StUNT 4. Göttingen: Vandenhoeck & Ruprecht.

———. 1982. "Die Kreuzesstrafe während der frühen Kaiserzeit." Pages 648–793 in *ANRW* II 25/1.

———. 1995. "Kreuzigung." Pages 548–49 in *NBL* 2.

Kuhn, P. 1989. *Offenbarungsstimmen im antiken Judentum*. TSAJ 20. Tübingen: Mohr.

Kuhn, T. K. 2001. "Strauß, David Friedrich (1808–1874)." Pages 241–46 in *TRE* 32.

Kümmel, W. G. 1956. *Verheißung und Erfüllung*. 3rd ed. AThANT 6. Zürich: Zwingli.

———. 1961. *Promise and Fulfillment*. Translated by D. M. Barton. London: SCM Press.

———. 1970. *Das Neue Testament: Geschichte der Erforschung seiner Probleme*. 2nd ed. Freiburg: Alber.

———. 1972. *The New Testament: The History of the Investigation of Its Problems*. Translated by S. M. Gilmour and H. C. Kee. Nashville, Tenn.: Abingdon Press.

———. 1975. *Introduction to the New Testament*. Translated by H. C. Kee. Revised edition. Nashville, Tenn.: Abingdon Press.

———. 1983. *Einleitung in das Neue Testament*. 21st ed. Heidelberg: Quelle & Meyer.

Künzi, M. 1970. *Das Naherwartungslogion Mt 10,23*. BGBE 9. Tübingen: Mohr.

Kupisch, K. 1957. "Berlin." Page 1058 in *RGG³* 1.

Lagrange, M.-J. 1966. *Évangile selon Saint Marc*. 9th ed. Paris: J. Gabalda.

Landau, T. 2006. *Out-Heroding Herod: Josephus, Rhetoric and the Herod Narratives*. AJEC (AGAJU) 63. Leiden: Brill.

Landmesser, C. 2001. *Jüngerberufung und Zuwendung zu Gott*. WUNT 133. Tübingen: Mohr.

Lane Fox, R. 1973. *Alexander the Great*. London: Lane.

———. 2006. *Alexander the Great*. London: Penguin.

Lang, F. 1959. "πῦρ κτλ." Pages 927–53 in *ThWNT* 6.

———. 1969. "πῦρ κτλ." Pages 928–52 in *TDNT* 6.

Lang, F. G. 1978. "'Über Sidon mitten ins Gebiet der Dekapolis': Geographie und Theologie in Markus 7,31." *ZDPV* 94: 145–60.

Lattimore, S. 1998. *Thucydides: The Peloponnesian War*. Translated, with introduction, notes, and glossary by Steven Lattimore. Indianapolis: Hackett.

Lehmann, K. 1968. *Auferweckt am dritten Tag nach der Schrift*. QD 38. Freiburg: Herder.

Lehmann, M. 1970. *Synoptische Quellenanalyse und die Frage nach dem historischen Jesus.* BZNW 38. Berlin: Walter de Gruyter.

Lehnardt, A. 2002. *Qaddish: Untersuchungen zur Entstehung und Rezeption eines rabbinischen Gebetes.* TSAJ 87. Tübingen: Mohr.

Lehnardt, T. 1991. "Der Gott der Welt ist unser König: Zur Vorstellung von der Königsherrschaft Gottes im Schema und seinen Benedictionen." Pages 285–308 in *Königsherrschaft Gottes und himmlischer Kult.* Edited by M. Hengel and A. M. Schwemer. WUNT 55. Tübingen: Mohr.

Leith, M. J. W. 1997. *Wadi Daliyeh I.* DJD XXIV. Oxford: Clarendon Press.

Leloir, L., ed. 1966. *Ephrem de Nisibe, Commentaire de l'Évangile concordant ou Diatessaron.* SC 121. Paris: Cerf.

Lemcio, E. E. 1991. *The Past of Jesus in the Gospels.* Cambridge: Cambridge University Press.

Lencman (Lenzmann), J. A. 1974 [1973]. *Wie das Christentum entstand.* Wuppertal: Peter Hammer.

Lentzen-Deis, F. 1974. "Kriterien für die historische Beurteilung der Jesusüberlieferung in den Evangelien." Pages 78–117 in *Rückfrage nach Jesus.* Edited by K. Kertelge. QD 63. Freiburg im Breisgau: Herder.

Levy, S. J. 1867. *Chaldäisches Wörterbuch über die Targumim.* Leipzig: Baumgärtner.

Lichtenberger, A. 1999. *Die Baupolitik Herodes des Großen.* Wiesbaden: Harrassowitz.

———. 2003. *Kulte und Kultur der Dekapolis.* ADPV 29. Wiesbaden: Harrassowitz.

Lichtenberger, H. 1987. "Täufergemeinden und frühchristliche Täuferpolemik." *ZThK* 84: 36–57.

———. 2001. "Auferstehung in den Qumranfunden." Pages 79–91 in *Auferstehung—Resurrection.* Edited by F. Avemarie and H. Lichtenberger 135. Tübingen: Mohr.

———. 2003. "Ps 91 und die Exorzismen in 11QPsApa." Pages 416–21 in *Die Dämonen.* Edited by A. Lange, H. Lichtenberger, and K. F. D. Römheld. Tübingen: Mohr.

———, ed. 2013. *Martin Hengels "Zeloten": Ihre Bedeutung im Licht von fünfzig Jahren Forschungsgeschichte. Mit einem Geleitwort von Roland Deines.* Tübingen: Mohr.

Lichtenberger, H., and A. Lange. 1997. "Qumran." Pages 45–79 in *TRE* 28.

Liddell, H. G., R. Scott, and H. S. Jones. 1996. *A Greek-English Lexicon.* 9th ed. Oxford: Clarendon Press.

Lietzmann, H. 1927. *Petrus und Paulus in Rom: Liturgische und archäologische Studien.* 2nd ed. AKG 1. Berlin: Walter de Gruyter.

———. 1928. *An die Römer.* HNT 8. Tübingen: Mohr.

———. 1999. *Geschichte der Alten Kirche.* Mit einem Vorwort von C. Markschies. 4./5. Auflage in einem Band. De Gruyter Studienbuch. Berlin: Walter de Gruyter.

Limbeck, M. 1995. "Judas." Pages 243–44 in *NBL* 2.

Lindemann, A., and H. Paulsen. 1992. *Die apostolischen Väter: Griechisch-deutsche Parallelausgabe.* Tübingen: Mohr.

Lindeskog, G. 1973 [1938]. *Die Jesusfrage im neuzeitlichen Judentum*. Darmstadt: Wissenschaftliche Buchgesellschaft.

———. 1986. *Das jüdisch-christliche Problem*. Stockholm: Almqvist & Wiksell.

Linnemann, E. 1970. *Studien zur Passionsgeschichte*. FRLANT 102. Göttingen: Vandenhoeck & Ruprecht.

Lipiński, E. 1993. "שָׂנֵא śanēʾ." Pages 828–39 in *ThWAT* 7.

———. 2004. "שָׂנֵא śanēʾ." Pages 164–74 in *TDOT* 14.

Lipsius, R. A. 1976 [1883–1890]. *Die apocryphen Apostelgeschichten und Apostellegenden: Ein Beitrag zur altchristlichen Literaturgeschichte und zu einer zusammenfassenden Darstellung der neutestamentlichen Apokryphen*. Vol. 1–2/1.2 and Supplement. Amsterdam: APA-Philo.

Lohmeyer, E. 1963. *Das Evangelium des Markus*. 16th ed. KEK 1/2. Göttingen: Vandenhoeck & Ruprecht.

Löhr, H. 2003. *Studien zum frühchristlichen und frühjüdischen Gebet: Untersuchungen zu 1 Clem 59 bis 61 in seinem literarischen, historischen und theologischen Kontext*. WUNT 160. Tübingen: Mohr.

Löhr, W. A. 1996. *Basilides und seine Schule: Eine Studie zur Theologie- und Kirchengeschichte des zweiten Jahrhunderts*. WUNT 83. Tübingen: Mohr.

Lohse, E. 1959. "ῥαββί." Pages 962–66 in *ThWNT* 6.

———. 1964. "συνέδριον." Pages 858–69 in *ThWNT* 7.

———. 1968. "ῥαββί." Pages 961–65 in *TDNT* 6.

———. 1971a. "συνέδριον." Pages 862–70 in *TDNT* 7.

———. 1971b. *Die Texte aus Qumran*. 2nd ed. Darmstadt: Wissenschaftliche Buchgesellschaft.

Loofs, F. 1916. *Wer war Jesus Christus*. Halle: Niemeyer.

Lüdemann, G. 1980. *Paulus, der Heidenapostel*. Vol. 1: *Studien zur Chronologie*. FRLANT 123. Göttingen: Vandenhoeck & Ruprecht.

———. 2000a. *Jesus after 2000 Years: What He Really Said and Did*. Translated by J. Bowden. London: SCM.

———. 2000b. *Jesus nach 2000 Jahren*. Lüneburg: Klampen.

———. 2000c. "Das Urchristentum." *ThR* 65: 121–79, 285–349.

Lührmann, D. 1987. *Das Markusevangelium*. HNT 3. Tübingen: Mohr.

———, ed. 2000. *Fragmente apokryph gewordener Evangelien in griechischer und lateinischer Sprache*. MThSt 59. Marburg: Elwert.

Luz, U. 1985–2002. *Das Evangelium nach Matthäus*. 4 vols. EKK 1. Neukirchen-Vluyn: Neukirchener.

———. 1989. *Matthew 1–7: A Continental Commentary*. Translated by W. C. Linss. Minneapolis: Fortress.

———. 2001. *Matthew 8–20*. Translated by J. E. Crouch. Edited by H. Koester. Hermeneia. Minneapolis: Fortress.

———. 2002 [1985]. *Das Evangelium nach Matthäus (Matt 1–7)*. 5th ed. EKK 1/1. Zürich: Benzinger.

———. 2005. *Matthew 21–28: A Commentary*. Translated by J. E. Crouch. Edited by H. Koester. Hermeneia. Minneapolis: Fortress.

———. 2007. *Matthew 1–7: A Commentary*. Translated by J. E. Crouch. Edited by H. Koester. Hermeneia. Minneapolis: Fortress.

Mack, B. L. 1993. *The Lost Gospel: The Book of Q and Christian Origins.* San Francisco: HarperSanFrancisco.

Magen, Y. 2000. "Mount Gerizim—A Temple City." *Qadmoniot* 120: 74–118.

Maier, G. 1971. *Mensch und freier Wille.* WUNT 12. Tübingen: Mohr.

Maier, J. 1978a. *Jesus von Nazareth in der talmudischen Überlieferung.* EdF 82. Darmstadt: Wissenschaftliche Buchgesellschaft.

———. 1978b. *Die Tempelrolle vom Toten Meer.* UTB 829. Munich: Reinhardt.

———. 1988. *Das Judentum: Von der biblischen Zeit bis zur Moderne.* 3rd ed. Munich: Kindler.

———. 1995–1996. *Die Qumran-Essener: Die Texte von Toten Meer.* 3 vols. Munich: Reinhardt.

———. 1997. *Die Tempelrolle vom Toten Meer.* 3rd revised and expanded edition. UTB 829. Munich: Reinhardt.

Manselli, R. 1983. "Gregor I (Gregor der Große)." Pages 930–51 in *RAC* 12.

Manson, T. W. 1963. *The Teachings of Jesus.* Cambridge: Cambridge University Press.

Mara, M. G. 1973. *Évangile de Pierre.* SC 201. Paris: Cerf.

Markschies, C. 1992. *Valentinus Gnosticus? Untersuchungen zur valentinianischen Gnosis mit einem Kommentar zu den Fragmenten Valentins.* WUNT 65. Tübingen: Mohr.

———. 2001. "Adolf von Harnack als Neutestamentler." Pages 365–95 in *Adolf von Harnack, Theologe, Historiker, Wissenschaftspolitiker.* Edited by K. Nowak and O. G. Oehler. Göttingen: Vandenhoeck & Ruprecht.

———. 2007. *Kaiserzeitliche christliche Theologie und ihre Institutionen.* Tübingen: Mohr.

———. 2015. *Christian Theology and Its Institutions in the Early Roman Empire: Prolegomena to a History of Early Christian Theology.* Translated by W. Coppins. Edited by W. Coppins and S. Gathercole. BMSEC 3. Waco: Baylor University Press.

Markschies, C., and J. Schröter, eds. 2012. *Antike christliche Apokryphen in deutscher Übersetzung.* Vol. I: *Evangelien und Verwandtes (in zwei Teilbänden).* Tübingen: Mohr.

Mason, S., ed. 1999ff. *Flavius Josephus: Translation and Commentary.* 10 vols. Leiden: Brill.

———. 2000. *Flavius Josephus und das Neue Testament.* UTB 2130. Tübingen: Francke.

———, ed. 2001. *Flavius Josephus: Translation and Commentary.* Vol. 9: *Life of Josephus.* Leiden: Brill.

———. 2003. *Josephus and the New Testament.* 2nd ed. Peabody, Mass.: Hendrickson.

———. 2017. "Jüdische Quellen: Flavius Josephus." Pages 165–71 in *Jesus Handbuch.* Edited by J. Schröter and C. Jacobi. Tübingen: Mohr.

Massaux, É. *Influence de l'Évangile de saint Matthieu sur la littérature chrétienne avant saint Irénée.* Louvain: Publications universitaires de Louvain, 1950.

Mattingly, H. 1983. *Coins of the Roman Empire in the British Museum*. Vol. 1: *Augustus to Vitellius*. London: British Museum.

Meeks, W. A. 1967. *The Prophet-King: Moses-Traditions and the Johannine Christology*. NT.S. Leiden: Brill.

Mehlhausen, J. 1980. "Bauer Bruno." Pages 314–17 in *TRE* 5.

———. 1998. "Bruno Bauer." Pages 1167–68 in *RGG⁴* 1.

———. 2007. "Bauer, Bruno." Pages 643–44 in *RPP* 2.

Meier, J. P. 1991. *A Marginal Jew: Rethinking the Historical Jesus*. Vol. 1: *The Roots of the Problem and the Person*. ABRL. New York: Doubleday.

———. 1994. *A Marginal Jew: Rethinking the Historical Jesus*. Vol. 2: *Mentor, Message, and Miracles*. ABRL. New York: Doubleday.

———. 2001. *A Marginal Jew: Rethinking the Historical Jesus*. Vol. 3: *Companions and Competitors*. ABRL. New York: Doubleday.

———. 2009. *A Marginal Jew: Rethinking the Historical Jesus*. Vol. 4: *Law and Love*. ABRL. New Haven: Yale University Press.

———. 2016. *A Marginal Jew: Rethinking the Historical Jesus*. Vol. 5: *Probing the Authenticity of the Parables*. ABRL. New Haven: Yale University Press.

Ménard, J.-É. 1975. *L'Évangile selon Thomas*. NHS 5. Leiden: Brill.

Merchal, G. P. 1988. "Memoria, Fama, Mos Maiorum." Pages 291–320 in *Vergangenheit in mündlicher Überlieferung*. Edited by J. von Ungern-Sternberg and H. Reinau. Stuttgart: Teubner.

Merkel, H. 1971. *Die Widerspüche zwischen den Evangelien: Ihre polemische und apologetische Behandlung in der Alten Kirche bis Augustin*. WUNT. Tübingen: Mohr.

———. 1974. "Auf den Spuren des Urmarkus: Ein neuer Fund und seine Beurteilung." *ZThK* 71: 123–44.

———. 1978. *Die Pluralität der Evangelien als theologisches und exegetisches Problem in der Alten Kirche*. TC 3. Bern: Lang.

———. 1990. "Anhang: Das 'geheime Evangelium' nach Markus." Pages 89–92 in *Neutestamentliche Apokryphen in deutscher Übersetzung*. Vol. 1. 6th ed. Edited by W. Schneemelcher. Tübingen: Mohr.

———. 1991. "Die Gottesherrschaft in der Verkündigung Jesu." Pages 119–61 in *Königsherrschaft Gottes und himmlischer Kult im Judentum, Urchristentum und in der hellenistischen Welt*. Edited by M. Hengel and A. M. Schwemer. WUNT 55. Tübingen: Mohr.

———. 2005. "Der Lehrer Paulus und seine Schüler." Pages 235–52 in *Religiöses Lernen in der biblischen, frühjüdischen und frühchristlichen Überlieferung*. Edited by B. Ego and S. Byrskog. WUNT 180. Tübingen: Mohr.

Merkelbach, R. 1977. *Die Quellen des griechischen Alexanderromans*. Munich: Beck.

Merklein, H. 1989. *Jesu Botschaft von der Gottesherrschaft: Eine Skizze*. 3rd ed. SBS 111. Stuttgart: Katholisches Bibelwerk.

Merz, A., and T. Tieleman, eds. 2012. *The Letter of Mara bar Sarapion in Context: Proceedings of the Symposium Held at Utrecht University, 10–12. December 2009*. Leiden: Brill.

Meshorer, Y. 1967. *Jewish Coins of the Second Temple Period*. Tel-Aviv: Am Hassefer.

——. 1982. *Ancient Jewish Coinage.* 2 vols. Dix Hills, N.Y.: Amphora Books.

——. 1990–1991. "Ancient Jewish Coinage. Addendum I." *INJ* 11: 104–32.

Meshorer, Y., and S. Qedar. 1991. *The Coinage of Samaria in the Fourth Century B.C.E.* Jerusalem: Numismatics Fine Arts International.

Metzger, B. M. 1975. *A Textual Commentary on the Greek New Testament.* Corrected edition. Stuttgart: United Bible Societies.

Meyer, E. 1921. *Ursprung und Anfänge des Christentums.* Vol. 1: *Die Evangelien.* 1–3rd ed. Stuttgart: Cotta.

——. 1962. *Ursprung und Anfänge des Christentums.* Vol. 1: *Die Evangelien.* Reprint of the 4th and 5th edition. Darmstadt: Wissenschaftliche Buchgesellschaft.

Meyers, C. L., and E. M. Meyers. 1997. "Sepphoris." Pages 527–36 in *Oxford Encyclopedia of Archaeology in the Near East.* Vol. 4. Edited by E. M. Meyers. Oxford: Oxford University Press.

Meynet, R. 1998. *Rhetorical Analysis: An Introduction to Biblical Rhetoric.* JSOT.S 256. Sheffield: JSOT.

Michel, O. 1942. "μικρός κτλ." Pages 650–61 in *ThWNT* 4.

——. 1955. "Der 'historische Jesus' und das theologische Gewißheitsproblem." *EvTh* 15: 349–63 (= Michel 1986, 135–147).

——. 1967. "μικρός κτλ." Pages 650–56 in *TDNT* 4.

——. 1986. *Dienst am Wort: Gesammelte Aufsätze.* Neukirchen-Vluyn: Neukirchener.

Michel, O., and O. Bauernfeind. 1962. *Flavius Josephus: De Bello Judaico; Der jüdische Krieg, I–III.* 2nd ed. Munich: Kösel.

Mildenberg, L. 1984. *The Coinage of the Bar Kochba War.* Aarau: Sauerländer.

——. 1998. "Schekel-Fragen." Pages 170–75 in *Vestigia Leonis: Studien zur antiken Numismatik Israels, Palästinas und der östlichen Mittelmeerwelt.* Edited by U. Hübner and E.-A. Knauf. Göttingen: Vandenhoeck & Ruprecht.

Millar, F. 1990. "Reflections on the Trial of Jesus." Pages 355–81 in *A Tribute to Geza Vermes.* Edited by P. R. Davies and R. T. White. Sheffield: JSOT.

——. 1993. *The Roman Near East, 31 BC–AD 337.* Cambridge, Mass.: Harvard University Press.

Milson, D. 2007. *Art and Architecture of the Synagogue in Late Antique Palestine.* AJEC (AGAJU) 64. Leiden: Brill.

Minette de Tillesse, G. 1968. *Le secret messianique dans l'Evangile de Marc.* Paris: Cerf.

Mittmann, S. 2000. "Tobia, Sanballat und die persische Provinz Juda." *JNSL* 26/2: 1–50.

Mittmann-Richert, U. 1996. *Magnifikat und Benediktus: Die frühen Zeugnisse der judenchristlichen Tradition von der Geburt des Messias.* WUNT 2/90. Tübingen: Mohr.

——. 2000. *Einführung zu den historischen und legendarischen Erzählungen.* JSHRZ VI, 1/1. Gütersloh: Gütersloher.

——. 2008. *Der Sühnetod des Gottesknechts: Jesaja 53 im Lukasevangelium.* WUNT 220. Tübingen: Mohr.

Möllendorf, P. von., ed. 2000. *Hermotimos oder Lohnt es sich Philosophie zu studieren?* TzF 74. Darmstadt: Wissenschaftliche Buchgesellschaft.

Mommsen, T. 1843. *Ad legem de scribis et viatoribus et de auctoritate commentationes duae.* Kiliae: Mohr.

——. 1955 [1899]. *Römisches Strafrecht.* Berlin: Akademie.

Morgenthaler, R. 1958. *Statistik des neutestamentlichen Wortschatzes.* Zürich: Gotthelf.

Mosshammer, A. A., ed. 1984. *Syncellus, Georgius: Ecloga chronographica.* Berlin: Walter de Gruyter.

Mournet, T. C. 2005. *Oral Tradition and Literary Dependency.* WUNT 2/195. Tübingen: Mohr.

Müller, K. W. 1991. "König und Vater." Pages 21–43 in *Königsherrschaft Gottes und himmlischer Kult im Judentum, Urchristentum und in der hellenistischen Welt.* Edited by M. Hengel and A. M. Schwemer. WUNT 55. Tübingen: Mohr.

Müller, M. 1984. *Der Ausdruck "Menschensohn" in den Evangelien: Voraussetzungen und Bedeutung.* Leiden: Brill.

Mussner, F. 1974. "Methodologie der Frage nach dem historischen Jesus." Pages 118–47 in *Rückfrage nach Jesus.* Edited by K. Kertelge. QD 63. Freiburg im Breisgau: Herder.

——. 1987. "Das 'Unjudentum' in Jesus und die Entstehung der Christologie." Pages 137–39 in *Die Kraft der Wurzel: Judentum—Jesus—Kirche.* Freiburg im Breisgau: Herder.

Mutschler, B. 2006. *Das Corpus Johanneum bei Irenäus von Lyon: Studien und Kommentar zum dritten Buch von Adversus haereses.* WUNT 189. Tübingen: Mohr.

Na'aman, N. 2004. "Samaria." Pages 816–18 in *RGG⁴* 7.

——. 2012. "Samaria." Pages 426–27 in *RPP* 11.

Nagel, T. 2000. *Die Rezeption des Johannesevangeliums im 2. Jahrhundert: Studien zur vorirenäischen Aneignung und Auslegung des vierten Evangeliums in christlicher und christlich-gnostischer Literatur.* ABG 2. Leipzig: Evangelische Verlagsanstalt.

Naveh, J., and Y. Magen. 1997. "Aramaic and Hebrew Inscriptions of the Second-Century BCE at Mount Gerizim." *'Atiqot* 32: 9*–17*.

Neirynck, F. 1988. *The Double Tradition Passages in Greek.* Leuven: Peeters.

——. 2002. "Luke 24.12: An Anti-Docetic Interpretation?" Pages 145–58 in *New Testament Textual Criticism and Exegesis: Festschrift for Joël Delobel.* Edited by A. Denaux. BEThL 161. Leuven: Peeters.

Netzer, E. 1999. "A Synagogue from the Hasmonean Period Recently Exposed in the Western Plain of Jericho." *IEJ* 49: 203–21.

——. 2006. *Architecture of Herod, the Great Builder.* TSAJ 117. Tübingen: Mohr.

Netzer, E., and Z. Weiss. 1994. *Zippori.* Jerusalem: Israel Exploration Society.

Neugebauer, F. 1962. "Geistsprüche und Jesuslogien." *ZNW* 53: 218–28.

——. 1972. *Jesus der Menschensohn: Ein Beitrag zur Klärung der Wege historischer Wahrheitsfindung im Bereich der Evangelien.* AzTh I. Stuttgart: Calwer.

——. 1986. *Jesu Versuchung: Wegentscheidung am Anfang.* Tübingen: Mohr.

Neusner, J. 1971. *The Rabbinic Tradition about the Pharisees before 70.* Leiden: Brill.

———. 1988. *The Mishnah: A New Translation*. New Haven: Yale University Press.

———. 2002. *The Tosefta: Translated from the Hebrew with a New Introduction*. 2 vols. Peabody: Hendrickson.

Newsom, C. 1985. *Songs of the Sabbath Sacrifice: A Critical Edition*. HSS 27. Atlanta: Scholars Press.

Nigg, W. 1946. *Große Heilige*. Zürich: Artemis.

Nissen, A. 1974. *Gott und der Nächste im antiken Judentum*. WUNT 15. Tübingen: Mohr.

Nock, A. D. 1933. *Conversion: The Old and the New in Religion from Alexander the Great to Augustine*. London: Oxford University Press.

Norden, E. 1958. *Die antike Kunstprosa: Vom VI. Jahrhundert v. Chr. bis in die Zeit der Renaissance*. 5th ed. Darmstadt: Wissenschaftliche Buchgesellschaft.

Norelli, E. 1995. *Ascensio Isaiae: Commentarius*. CChr.SA 8. Turnhout: Brepols.

Nowak, K. 2001. *Schleiermacher*. UTB 2215. Göttingen: Vandenhoeck & Ruprecht.

Noy, D. 1995. *Jewish Inscriptions of Western Europe*. Vol. 2: *The City of Rome*. Cambridge: Cambridge University Press.

Oberlinner, L. 1975. *Historische Überlieferung und christologische Aussage: Zur Frage der "Bruder" Jesu in der Synopse*. FzB 19. Stuttgart: Katholisches Bibelwerk.

Oepke, A. 1933. "βάπτω κτλ." Pages 527–44 in *ThWNT* 1.

———. 1964. "βάπτω κτλ." Pages 529–46 in *TDNT* 1.

Öhler, M. 1997. *Elia im Neuen Testament*. BZNW 88. Berlin: Walter de Gruyter.

Ostmeyer, K.-H. 2005. "Armenhaus und Räuberhöhle? Galiläa zur Zeit Jesu." *ZNW* 96: 147–70.

Otto, R. 1938. *The Kingdom of God and the Son of Man: A Study in the History of Religions*. Translated by F. V. Filson and B. Lee-Woolf. London: Lutterworth.

———. 1954 [1933]. *Reich Gottes und Menschensohn. Ein religionsgeschichtlicher Vergleich*. Munich: Beck.

Overbeck, F. 1963 [1919]. *Christentum und Kultur: Gedanken und Anmerkungen zur modernen Theologie*. Edited by C. A. Bernoulli. Darmstadt: Wissenschaftliche Buchgesellschaft.

Paret, R. 1957. *Mohammed und der Koran*. UB 32. Stuttgart: Kohlhammer.

Park, J. S. 2000. *Conceptions of Afterlife in Jewish Inscriptions*. WUNT 2/121. Tübingen: Mohr.

Paschen, W. 1970. *Rein und Unrein: Untersuchungen zur biblischen Wortgeschichte*. StANT 24. Munich: Kösel.

Perler, O., ed. 1966. *Méliton de Sardes: Sur la Pâque*. SC 123. Paris: Cerf.

Pesch, R. 1970. *Jesu ureigene Taten?* QD 52. Freiburg: Herder.

———. 1973a. "Entstehung des Glaubens an die Auferstehung Jesu." *ThQ* 153: 201–28.

———. 1973b. "Stellungnahme zu den Diskussionsbeiträgen." *ThQ* 153: 270–83.

———. 1978. *Das Abendmahl und Jesu Todesverständnis*. Freiburg im Breisgau: Herder.

———. 1983. "Das Evangelium in Jerusalem: Mk 14,12-26 als ältestes Überlieferungsgut der Urgemeinde." Pages 113–55 in *Das Evangelium und die Evangelien: Vorträge vom Tübinger Symposium 1982*. Edited by P. Stuhlmacher. WUNT 28. Tübingen: Mohr.

———. 1984a. *Das Markusevangelium*. Vol. 1: *Kommentar zu Kap. 1,1–8,26*. 4th ed. HThKNT 2/1. Freiburg im Breslau: Herder.

———. 1984b. *Das Markusevangelium*. Vol. 2: *Kommentar zu Kap. 8,27–16,20*. 3rd ed. HThKNT 2/2. Freiburg im Breslau: Herder.

———. 1991. "The Gospel in Jerusalem: Mark 14:12-26 as the Oldest Tradition of the Early Church." Pages 106–48 in *The Gospel and the Gospels*. Edited by P. Stuhlmacher. Grand Rapids: Eerdmans.

Petersen, W. 2001. *Zur Eigenart des Matthäus: Untersuchung zur Rhetorik in der Bergpredigt*. Osnabrücker Studien zur Jüdischen und Christlichen Bibel 2. Osnabrück: Rasch.

Peterson, E. 1959. "The 'Taufe' im Acherusischen See." Pages 310–32 in *Frühkirche, Judentum und Gnosis*. Rome: Herder.

Philonenko, M. 2002. *Das Vaterunser*. UTB 2312. Tübingen: Mohr.

Pietersma, A. 1994. *The Apocryphon of Jannes and Jambres the Magicians: P. Chester Beatty XVI (with New editions of Papyrus Vindobonensis Greek inv. 29456 + 29828 verso and British Library Cotton Tiberius B. v f. 87)*. Leiden: Brill.

Pitre, B. 2005. *Jesus, the Tribulation, and the End of the Exile*. WUNT 2/204. Tübingen: Mohr.

Plümacher, E. 1981. "μάχαιρα." Pages 978–80 in *EWNT* 2.

———. 1991. "μάχαιρα." Pages 397–98 in *EDNT* 2.

Preuschen, E. 1905. *Antilegomena*. Gießen: Töpelmann.

Prieur, A. 1996. *Die Verkündigung der Gottesherrschaft: Exegetische Studien zum lukanischen Verständnis von βασιλεία τοῦ θεοῦ*. WUNT 2/89. Tübingen: Mohr.

Procksch, O., and K.-G. Kuhn. 1933. "ἅγιος κτλ." Pages 87–116 in *ThWNT* 1.

———. 1964. "ἅγιος κτλ." Pages 88–115 in *TDNT* 1.

Prostmeier, F.-R. 1998. "Papiscus von Ariston." Pages 51–52 in *Lexikon der antiken christlichen Literatur*. Edited by S. Döpp and W. Geerlings. Herder: Freiburg.

———. 1999. *Der Barnabasbrief*. KAV 8. Göttingen: Vandenhoeck & Ruprecht.

Prümm, K. 1972. *Gnosis an der Wurzel des Christentums? Grundlagenkritik des Entmythologisierung*. Salzburg: Müller.

Pucci Ben Zeev, M. 1998. *Jewish Rights in the Roman World*. TSAJ 74. Tübingen: Mohr.

Puech, E. 1983. "Inscriptions Funeraires Palestiniennes: Tombeau de Jason et Ossuaires." *RB* 90: 481–533.

Pummer, R. 2002. *Early Christian Authors on Samaritans and Samaritanism: Texts, Translations and Commentary*. TSAJ 92. Tübingen: Mohr.

Qimron, E., and J. Strugnell. 1994. *Qumran Cave 4*. Vol. 5: *Miqṣat Maʿase Ha-Torah*. DJD X. Oxford: Clarendon Press.

Rad, G. von., and G. Delling. 1935. "ἡμέρα." Pages 945–56 in *ThWNT* 2.

———. 1964. "ἡμέρα." Pages 943–47 in *TDNT* 2.

Rahmani, L. Y. 1994. *A Catalogue of Jewish Ossuaries in the Collections of the State of Israel.* Jerusalem: Israel Antiquities Authority.

Räisänen, H. 1973. *Die Parabeltheorie im Markusevangelium.* Schriften der Finnischen Exegetischen Gesellschaft 26. Helsinki: Finnische Exegetische Gesellschaft.

———. 1976. *Das 'Messiasgeheimnis' im Markusevangelium: Ein redaktionskritischer Versuch.* Helsinki: Finnische Exegetische Gesellschaft.

———. 1990. *The "Messianic Secret" in Mark's Gospel.* Translated by C. M. Tuckett. Edinburgh: T&T Clark.

Rajak, T. 2001. "Josephus." Pages 585–87 in *RGG⁴* 4.

———. 2010. "Josephus, Flavius." Pages 41–42 in *RPP* 7.

Rauer, M., ed. 1959. *Origenes Werke.* Vol. 9: *Die Homilien zu Lukas in der Übersetzung des Hieronymus und die griechischen Reste der Homilien und des Lukas-Kommentars.* 2nd ed. GCS 49. Berlin: Akademie.

Reed, J. L. 2000. *Archaeology and the Galilean Jesus: A Re-examination of the Evidence.* Harrisburg, Pa.: Trinity Press International.

Reich, H. 2005 [1903]. *Der Mimus.* Hildesheim: Olms.

Reiser, M. 1990. *Die Gerichtspredigt Jesu.* NTA NF 23. Münster: Aschendorff.

———. 1997. *Jesus and Judgment.* Translated by L. M. Maloney. Minneapolis: Fortress.

———. 2000. "Numismatik und Neues Testament." *Bib.* 81: 457–88.

———. 2001a. "Von Caesarea nach Malta: Literarischer Charakter und historische Glaubwürdigkeit von Act 27." Pages 49–74 in *Das Ende Des Paulus.* Edited by F. W. Horn. BZNW 106. Berlin: Walter de Gruyter.

———. 2001b. *Sprache und literarische Formen des Neuen Testaments: Eine Einführung.* UTB 2197. Paderborn: Schöningh.

Rengstorf, K. H. 1933. "ἀποστέλλω κτλ." Pages 397–448 in *ThWNT* 1.

———. 1959. "Ἰορδάνης." Pages 608–23 in *ThWNT* 6.

———. 1965. "ἀποστέλλω κτλ." Pages 398–447 in *TDNT* 1.

———. 1967a. *Die Auferstehung Jesu.* 6th ed. Witten: Luther.

———. 1967b. *Die Re-Investitur des Verlorenen Sohnes in der Gleichniserzählung Jesu Luk. 15,11-32.* VAFLNW.G 137. Cologne: Westdeutscher.

———. 1968. "Ἰορδάνης." Pages 608–23 in *TDNT* 6.

———, ed. 1973–1983. *A Complete Concordance to Flavius Josephus.* Leiden: Brill.

Resch, A. 1906. *Agrapha: Ausserkanonische Schriftfragmente.* 2nd ed. Leipzig: Hinrichs.

Riesner, R. 1988. *Jesus als Lehrer: Eine Untersuchung zum Ursprung der Evangelienüberlieferung.* WUNT 2/7. Tübingen: Mohr.

———. 1994. *Die Frühzeit des Apostels Paulus: Studien zur Chronologie, Missionsstrategie und Theologie.* Tübingen: Mohr.

———. 1997. "Paulus und die Jesus-Überlieferung." Pages 347–65 in *Evangelium—Schriftauslegung—Kirche: Festschrift für Peter Stuhlmacher.* Edited by J. Ådna. Göttingen: Vandenhoeck & Ruprecht.

———. 1998. *Essener und Urgemeinde in Jerusalem.* 2nd ed. Gießen: Brunnen.

Robinson, C. A. J. 1953/1963. *The History of Alexander the Great*. 2 vols. Providence, R.I.: Brown University Press.

Robinson, J. A. T. 1985. *The Priority of John*. London: SCM.

Robinson, J. M. 1959. *A New Quest of the Historical Jesus*. London: SCM.

———. 1971. "LOGOI SOPHON: Zur Gattung der Spruchquelle Q." Pages 70–106 in *Entwicklungslinien durch die Welt des frühen Christentums*. Edited by H. Köster and J. M. Robinson. Tübingen: Mohr.

———, ed. 1988. *The Nag Hammadi Library in English*. Translated and introduced by members of the Coptic Gnostic Library Project. Leiden: Brill.

Robinson, J. M., P. Hoffmann, and J. S. Kloppenborg. 2000. *The Critical Edition of Q: Synopsis Including the Gospels of Matthew and Luke, Mark and Thomas with English, German, and French Translations of Q and Thomas*. Leuven: Peeters.

Robinson, J. M., L. Vaage, and J. Daniels. 1985. *Pap. Q*. Claremont: Institute for Antiquity and Christianity.

Roller, D. W. 1998. *The Building Program of Herod the Great*. Berkeley: University of California Press.

Rollmann, H., and W. Zager. 2001. "Unveröffentlichte Briefe William Wredes zur Problematisierung des messianischen Selbstverständnisses Jesu." *ZNThG* 8: 274–322.

Roloff, J. 1969. "Das Markusevangelium als Geschichtsdarstellung." *EvTh* 29: 73–93.

———. 1970. *Das Kerygma und der irdische Jesus: Historische Motive in den Jesus-Erzählungen der Evangelien*. 2nd ed. Göttingen: Vandenhoeck & Ruprecht.

Rose, C. 2003. "Gleichnis." Page 450 in *Calwer Bibellexikon*. Vol. 1. Edited by O. Betz and W. Grimm. Stuttgart: Calwer.

Rosenberger, M. 1977. *City Coins of Palestine*. Vol. 3. Jerusalem: Rosenberger.

Rubenstein, R. L. 1972. *My Brother Paul*. New York: Harper & Row.

Rudolph, K. 1999. "The Baptist Sects." Pages 471–500 in *The Cambridge History of Judaism*. Vol. 3. Edited by W. Horbury, W. D. Davies, and J. Sturdy. Cambridge: Cambridge University Press.

Rüger, H. P. 1973. "Μαμωνᾶς." *ZNW* 64: 127–31.

———. 1978. "Aramäisch II: Im Neuen Testament." Pages 602–10 in *TRE* 3.

———. 1981. "ΝΑΖΑΡΕΘ / ΝΑΖΑΡΑ ΝΑΖΑΡΗΝΟΣ / ΝΑΖΩΡΑΙΟΣ." *ZNW* 72: 257–63.

———. 1984. "Die lexikalischen Aramaismen im Markusevangelium." Pages 73–84 in *Markus-Philologie: Historische, literargeschichtliche und stilistische Untersuchungen zum zweiten Evangelium*. Edited by H. Cancik. Tübingen: Mohr.

Rüggemeier, J. 2017. *Poetik der markinischen Christologie. Eine kognitiv-narratologische Exegese*. WUNT 2/458. Tübingen: Mohr.

Rusam, D. 2004. "Sah Jesus wirklich den Satan vom Himmel fallen (Lk 10,18)? Auf der Suche nach einem neuen Differenzkriterium." *NTS* 50: 87–105.

Sacchi, P. 1980. "Henoch-gestalt/Henochbuch." Pages 42–59 in *TRE* 15.

Saldarini, A. J. 2000 [1989]. *Pharisees, Scribes and Sadducees in Palestinian Society*. Edinburgh: T&T Clark.

Sallmann, K. 2001. "Suetonius." Pages 1084–88 in *DNP* 11.

———. 2008. "Suetonius 2." Pages 918–22 in *BNP* 13.

Sanders, E. P. 1969. *The Tendencies of the Synoptic Tradition*. Cambridge: Cambridge University Press.

———. 1985. *Jesus and Judaism*. Philadelphia: Fortress.

———. 1993. *The Historical Figure of Jesus*. London: Allen Lane.

Sato, M. 1988. *Q und Prophetie*. WUNT 2/29. Tübingen: Mohr.

Schadewaldt, M. 1982. "Wolfgang Schadewaldt." *ThBeitr* 13: 198–200.

———. 1985. "Wolfgang Schadewaldt." Pages 85–88 in *Studies in the Gospel of Mark*, by Martin Hengel. Translated by J. Bowden. Philadelphia: Fortress.

Schadewaldt, W. 1982. "Die Zuverlässigkeit der synoptischen Tradition." *ThBeitr* 13: 201–23.

———. 1985. "The Reliability of the Synoptic Tradition." Pages 89–113 in *Studies in the Gospel of Mark*, by Martin Hengel. Translated by J. Bowden. Philadelphia: Fortress.

Schaeder, H. H. 1942. "Ναζαρηνός." Pages 879–84 in *ThWNT* 4.

———. 1967. "Ναζαρηνός." Pages 874–79 in *TDNT* 4.

Schäfer, P. 1981. *Der Bar-Kochba-Aufstand*. TSAJ 1. Tübingen: Mohr.

———. 2007. *Jesus in the Talmud*. Princeton: Princeton University Press.

Schalit, A. 2001. *König Herodes: Der Mann und sein Werk*. 2nd ed. Berlin: Walter de Gruyter.

Schaller, B. 1998. "Paralipomena Jeremiou." Pages 661–777 in *Historische und legendarische Erzählungen*. Edited by B. Schaller and W. G. Kümmel. JSHRZ 1/8. Gütersloh: Gütersloher.

Schamoni, W. 1968. *Auferweckungen vom Tode: Aus den Heiligsprechungsakten übersetzt*. Self-published.

———. 1976. *Wunder sind Tatsachen: Eine Dokumentation aus den Heiligsprechungsakten*. 4th ed. Würzburg: Naumann.

Schaper, J. 1995. *Eschatology in the Greek Psalter*. WUNT 2/76. Tübingen: Mohr.

———. 1999. "The Pharisees." Pages 402–27 in *The Cambridge History of Judaism*. Vol. 3. Edited by W. Horbury, W. D. Davies, and J. Sturdy. Cambridge: Cambridge University Press.

———. 2000. *Priester und Leviten im achämenidischen Juda*. FAT 31. Tübingen: Mohr.

Schattner-Rieser, U. 2015. "Das Aramäische zur Zeit Jesu, 'ABBA!' und das Vaterunser. Reflexionen zur Muttersprache Jesu anhand der Texte von Qumran und der frühen Targumim." Pages 81–144 in *Jesus, Paulus und die Texte vom Toten Meer*. Edited by J. Frey and E. E. Popkes. WUNT 2/390. Tübingen: Mohr.

Schechter, S. 1887. *Abot de-Rabbi Nathan*. Vienna: Lippe.

Scheck, T. P., ed. 2008. *Jerome: Commentary on Matthew*. Edited and translated by T. P. Scheck. Washington, D.C.: Catholic University of America Press.

Schelkle, K. H. 1973. "Schöpfung des Glaubens." *ThQ* 153: 242–43.

Schenke, H.-M., H.-G. Bethge, and U. U. Kaiser, eds. 2001/2003. *Nag Hammadi Deutsch*. 2 vols. GCS NF 8/12. Berlin: Walter de Gruyter.

Schenke, L. 1968. *Auferstehungsverkündigung und leeres Grab*. SBS 33. Stuttgart: Katholisches Bibelwerk.

Schiffman, L. H. 1999. "The Qumran Community's Withdrawal from the Jerusalem Temple." Pages 267–84 in *Gemeinde ohne Tempel*. Edited by B. Ego, A. Lange, and P. Pilhofer. WUNT 118. Tübingen: Mohr.

Schirren, T. 2005a. "Lukian über die καινὴ τελετή der Christen (*De morte Peregrini* 11)." *Ph*. 149: 354–59.

———. 2005b. *Philosophos Bios: Die antike Philosophenbiographie als symbolische Form*. BKAW 2/115. Heidelberg: Winter.

Schlatter, A. 1905. *Atheistische Methoden in der Theologie*. BFChTh 9. Gütersloh: Bertelsmann.

———. 1969. *Zur Theologie des Neuen Testaments und zur Dogmatik: Kleine Schriften*. ThB 41. Munich: Kaiser.

———. 1995. "Adolf Schlatter on Atheistic Methods in Theology (translated by D. R. Bauer)." Pages 211–25 in *W. Neuer, Adolf Schlatter: A Biography of Germany's Premier Biblical Theologian*. Translated by R. W. Yarbrough. Grand Rapids: Baker Books.

Schleiermacher, F. D. E. 1864. *Das Leben Jesu*. Berlin: Reimer.

———. 1975. *The Life of Jesus*. Translated by S. M. Gilmour. Edited by J. C. Verheyden. Minneapolis: Fortress.

Schlichting, G. 1982. *Ein jüdisches Leben Jesu*. WUNT 24. Tübingen: Mohr.

Schliesser, B. Forthcoming. *Zweifel: Studien zum Phänomen des Zweifels im frühen Christentum*. WUNT. Tübingen: Mohr Siebeck.

Schmid, J. 1958. "Christusmythe." Pages 1182–83 in *Lexikon für Theologie und Kirche*. 2nd ed. Vol. 2. Edited by J. Höfer and K. Rahner. Freiburg im Breisgau: Herder.

Schmidt, K. L. 1919. *Der Rahmen der Geschichte Jesu: Literarkritische Untersuchungen zur älteste Jesusüberlieferung*. Berlin: Trowitzsch.

———. 1921. "Eduard Meyer und die Evangelienforschung." *ChW* 35/7: 114–20.

———. 1923. "Die Stellung der Evangelien in der allgemeinen Literaturgeschichte." Pages 50–134 in *Eucharisterion: Festschrift für Hermann Gunkel zum 60. Geburtstag*. Vol. 2. Edited by H. Schmidt. Göttingen: Vandenhoeck & Ruprecht.

———. 1981. *Neues Testament—Judentum—Kirche: Kleine Schriften*. ThB 69. Munich: Kaiser.

———. 2002. *The Place of the Gospels in the General History of Literature*. Translated by B. R. McCane. Columbia: University of South Carolina Press.

Schmiedel, P. W. 1901. "Gospels." Pages 1761–891 in *Encyclopedia Biblica*. Vol. 2. Edited by T. K. Cheyne. London: Black.

Schmithals, W. 1961. *Das kirchliche Apostelamt*. FRLANT 79. Göttingen: Vandenhoeck & Ruprecht.

———. 1963. *Paulus und Jakobus*. FRLANT 85. Göttingen: Vandenhoeck & Ruprecht.

Schnabel, E. J. 2002. *Urchristliche Mission*. Wuppertal: Brockhaus.

Schnackenburg, R. 1965. *Gottes Herrschaft und Reich: Eine biblisch-theologische Studie*. Freiburg: Herder.

———. 1982. *Das Johannesevangelium III*. 4th ed. HThK IV/3. Freiburg: Herder.

Schneemelcher, W. 1981. *Das Urchristentum*. UB 336. Stuttgart: Kohlhammer.

———. 1987. *Neutestamentliche Apokryphen in deutscher Übersetzung*. Vol. 1. Tübingen: Mohr.

———, ed. 1990. *Neutestamentliche Apokryphen*. Vol. 1: *Evangelien*. 6th ed. Tübingen: Mohr.

———, ed. 1991/1992. *New Testament Apocrypha*. 2 vols. Cambridge: Clarke.

———, ed. 1999. *Neutestamentliche Apokryphen*. Vol. 2: *Apostolisches, Apokalypsen und Verwandtes*. 6th ed. Tübingen: Mohr.

Schneider, J. 1962. "Der Beitrag der Urgemeinde zur Jesusüberlieferung im Lichte der neuesten Forschung." *ThLZ* 87: 401–12.

Schnelle, U. 1998. *The History and Theology of the New Testament Writings*. Translated by E. M. Boring. Minneapolis: Fortress.

———. 2002. *Einleitung in das Neue Testament*. Göttingen: Vandenhoeck & Ruprecht.

Scholder, K. 1966. *Ursprünge und Probleme der Bibelkritik im 17. Jahrhundert: Ein Beitrag zur Entstehung der historisch-kritischen Theologie*. Munich: Kaiser.

———. 1990. *The Birth of Modern Critical Theology*. Translated by J. Bowden. London: SCM.

Scholz, H. 1899. "Der gegenwärtigen Stand der Forschung über den dogmatischen Christus und den historischen Jesus." *ThR* 2: 169–81, 211–24.

Schrage, W. 1964. *Das Verhältnis des Thomas-Evangeliums zur synoptischen Tradition und zu den koptischen Evangelienübersetzungen*. BZNW 29. Berlin: Walter de Gruyter.

———. 1982. *Ethik des Neuen Testaments*. GNT 4. Göttingen: Vandenhoeck & Ruprecht.

———. 1988. *The Ethics of the New Testament*. Translated by D. E. Green. Edinburgh: T&T Clark.

———. 2001. *Der erste Brief an die Korinther: 1 Kor 15,1–16,24*. Vol. 4. Neukirchen-Vluyn: Neukirchener.

Schreiner, J. 1984. *Das 4. Buch Esra*. JSHRZ V/4. Gütersloh: Gütersloher.

Schreiner, S. 2004. "Das Festmahl der Gerechten in mittelalterlicher jüdischer Überlieferung." Pages 343–76 in *Le Repas de Dieu—Das Mahl Gottes*. Edited by C. Grappe. Tübingen: Mohr.

Schremer, A. 1997. "The Name of the Boethusians." *JJS* 48: 290–99.

Schröder, B. 1996. *Die 'väterlichen Gesetze': Flavius Josephus als Vermittler von Halachah an Griechen und Römer*. TSAJ 53. Tübingen: Mohr.

Schröter, J. 1997. *Erinnerung an Jesu Worte: Studien zur Rezeption der Logienüberlieferung in Markus, Q und Thomas*. WMANT 76. Neukirchen-Vluyn: Neukirchener.

——. 2004. "Anfänge der Jesusüberlieferung: Überlieferungsgeschichtliche Beobachtungen zu einem Bereich urchristlicher Theologiegeschichte." *NTS* 50: 53–76.

——. 2007. *Von Jesus zum Neuen Testament: Studien zur urchristlichen Theologiegeschichte und zur Entstehung des neutestamentlichen Kanons.* WUNT 204. Tübingen: Mohr.

——. 2013. *From Jesus to the New Testament.* Translated by W. Coppins. Edited by W. Coppins and S. Gathercole. BMSEC 1. Waco: Baylor University Press.

——. 2014. *Jesus of Nazareth: Jew from Galilee, Savior of the World.* Translated by W. Coppins and S. B. Pounds. Waco: Baylor University Press.

Schulte, H. 1997. "Reimarus, Hermann Samuel (1694–1768)." Pages 470–73 in *TRE* 28.

Schulz, S. 1976. *Die Mitte der Schrift: Der Frühkatholizismus im Neuen Testament als Herausforderung an den Protestantismus.* Stuttgart: Kreuz.

Schürer, E. 1973–1987. *The History of the Jewish People in the Age of Jesus Christ (175 BC–AD 135).* 3 vols. A new English version revised and edited by G. Vermes, F. Millar, and M. Black. Edinburgh: Clark.

Schürmann, H. 1968a. *Der Paschamahlbericht Lk 22,(7-14.)15-18.* 2nd ed. Munich: Aschendorf.

——. 1968b. "Die vorösterliche Anfänge der Logientradition." Pages 39–65 in *Traditionsgeschichtliche Untersuchungen zu den synoptischen Evangelien.* Düsseldorf: Patmos.

——. 1983. *Gottes Reich—Jesu Geschenk.* Freiburg: Herder.

——. 1984. *Das Lukasevangelium.* Vol. 1. 3rd ed. HThK 3/1. Freiburg: Herder.

Schwankl, O. 1987. *Die Sadduzäerfrage (Mk 12,18-27 parr).* BBB 66. Frankfurt am Main: Athenäum.

Schwartz, D. R. 1990. *Agrippa I: The Last King of Judaea.* TSAJ 23. Tübingen: Mohr.

——. 1992. *Studies in the Jewish Background of Christianity.* WUNT 60. Tübingen: Mohr.

Schweitzer, A. 1906. *Geschichte der Leben-Jesu-Forschung: Von Reimarus bis Wrede.* Tübingen: Mohr.

——. 1913. *Geschichte der Leben-Jesu-Forschung.* 2nd ed. Tübingen: Mohr.

——. 1914. *The Mystery of the Kingdom of God: The Secret of Jesus' Messiahship and Passion.* Translated by W. Lowrie. London: A. & C. Black.

——. 1956 [1901]. *Das Messianitäts- und Leidensgeheimnis: Eine Skizze des Lebens Jesu.* 3rd ed. Tübingen: Mohr.

——. 1967. *Reich Gottes und Christentum.* Edited by U. Neuenschwander. Tübingen: Mohr.

——. 1968. *The Kingdom of God and Primitive Christianity.* Translated by L. A. Garrard. Edited by U. Neuenschwander. London: Black.

——. 1998. *Straßburger Vorlesungen.* Edited by E. Grässer and J. Zürcher. Munich: Beck.

———. 2000. *The Quest of the Historical Jesus*. First complete edition. Translated by W. Montgomery, J. R. Coates, S. Cupitt, and J. Bowden. London: SCM.

Schweizer, E. 1964. "σῶμα." Pages 1024–91 in *ThWNT* 7.

———. 1969. "υἱὸς κτλ." Pages 364–95 in *ThWNT* 8.

———. 1971. "σῶμα." Pages 1024–94 in *TDNT* 7.

———. 1972. "υἱὸς κτλ." Pages 363–92 in *TDNT* 8.

Schwemer, A. M. 1991a. "Gott als König und seine Königsherrschaft in den Sabbatlieder aus Qumran." Pages 45–118 in *Königsherrschaft Gottes und himmlischer Kult*. Edited by M. Hengel and A. M. Schwemer. WUNT 55. Tübingen: Mohr.

———. 1991b. "Irdischer und himmlischer König: Beobachtungen zur sogenannten David-Apokalypse in Hekhalot Rabbati §§ 122–126." Pages 309–59 in *Königsherrschaft Gottes und himmlischer Kult im Judentum, Urchristentum und in der hellenistischen Welt*. Edited by M. Hengel and A. M. Schwemer. WUNT 55. Tübingen: Mohr.

———. 1994. "Elija als Araber: Die haggadischen Motive in der Legende vom Messias Menahem bin Hiskija (yBer 2,4 5a; EkhaR 1,16 § 51) im Vergleich mit den Elija- und Elischa-Legenden der Vitae Prophetarum." Pages 108–57 in *Die Heiden: Juden, Christen und das Problem des Fremden*. Edited by R. Feldmeier and U. Heckel. Tübingen: Mohr.

———. 1995/1996. *Studien zu den frühjudischen Prophetenlegenden*. 2 vols. TSAJ 49–50. Tübingen: Mohr.

———. 1997. *Vitae Prophetarum*. JSHRZ 1/7. Gutersloh: Mohn.

———. 1998. "Jesu letzte Worte am Kreuz (Mk 15,34; Lk 23,46; Joh 19,28ff)." *ThBeitr* 29: 5–29.

———. 2001a. "Der Auferstandene und die Emmausjünger." Pages 95–117 in *Auferstehung—Resurrection: The Fourth Durham–Tübingen Research Symposium; Resurrection, Transfiguration and Exaltation in Old Testament, Ancient Judaism and Early Christianity*. Edited by F. Avemarie and H. Lichtenberger. WUNT 135. Tübingen: Mohr.

———. 2001b. "Jesus Christus als Prophet, König und Priester." Pages 165–230 in *Der messianische Anspruch Jesu und die Anfänge der Christologie: Vier Studien*. Edited by M. Hengel and A. M. Schwemer. WUNT 138. Tübingen: Mohr.

———. 2001c. "Die Passion des Messias nach Markus." Pages 133–63 in *Der messianische Anspruch Jesu und die Anfänge der Christologie: Vier Studien*. Edited by M. Hengel and A. M. Schwemer. WUNT 138. Tübingen: Mohr.

———. 2004. "Das Problem der Mahlgemeinschaft mit dem Auferstandenen." Pages 187–226 in *Das Problem der Mahlgemeinschaft mit dem Auferstandenen*. Edited by C. Grappe. WUNT 169. Tübingen: Mohr.

———. 2005. "Verfolger und Verfolgte bei Paulus: Die Auswirkungen der Verfolgung durch Agrippa I. auf die paulinische Mission." Pages 169–91 in *Biographie und Persönlichkeit des Paulus*. Edited by E.-M. Becker and P. Pilhofer. Tübingen: Mohr.

————. 2007. "Erinnerung und Legende: Die Berufung des Paulus und ihre Darstellung in der Apostelgeschichte." Pages 277–98 in *Memory in the Bible and Antiquity: The Fifth Durham–Tübingen Research Symposium (Durham, September 2004)*. Edited by S. C. Barton. WUNT 212. Tübingen: Mohr.

————. 2009. "Das Kommen der Königsherrschaft Gottes in Lk 17,20f." Pages 107–38 in *Le Jour de Dieu—Der Tag Gottes. 5. Colloque Strasbourg—Tübingen—Uppsala 11–3 Septembre 2006*. Edited by A. Hultgård and S. Norin. Tübingen: Mohr.

————. 2010. "Die Frauen am leeren Grab und die Auferstehung Jesu—Markus 16,1–8." Pages 137–48 in *Der rätselhafte Gott: Gottesdienste zu unbequemen Bibeltexten*. Edited by H.-H. Auel. Dienst am Wort. Die Reihe für Gemeindedienst und Gemeindearbeit 126. Göttingen: Vandenhoeck & Ruprecht.

————. 2011. "Der jüdische Aufstand in der Diaspora unter Trajan (115–117 n.Chr.)." *BN.NF* 148: 85–100.

————. 2013. "Die 'Eiferer' Elia und Pinchas und ihre Identifikation." Pages 21–80 in *Martin Hengels "Zeloten": Ihre Bedeutung im Licht von fünfzig Jahren Forschungsgeschichte*. Edited by H. Lichtenberger. Tübingen: Mohr.

————. 2016. "Agrippa I.—sein Tod als 'Gottesfeind' bei Josephus und Lukas." Pages 147–73 in *L'adversaire de Dieu—Der Widersacher Gottes, 6. Symposium, Strasburg, Tübingen, Uppsala, 27.–29. Juni 2013*. Edited by M. Tilly, M. Morgenstern, V. Drecoll, and H. Stoppel. WUNT 364. Tübingen: Mohr.

Seeberg, R. 1918. "Die Herkunft der Mutter Jesu." Pages 13–24 in *Theologische Festschrift für G. Nathanael Bonwetsch zu seinem siebzigsten Geburtstage*. Edited by H. Achelis. Leipzig: Deichert.

Segal, A. 1986. *Rebecca's Children: Judaism and Christianity in the Roman World*. Cambridge, Mass.: Harvard University Press.

Segert, S. 1984. "Semitic Poetic Structures in the New Testament." Pages 1433–62 in *ANRW* II 25/2.

Seybold, K. 1984. "melek." Pages 926–56 in *ThWAT* 4.

————. 1986. "mšh." Pages 46–59 in *ThWAT* 5.

————. 2000. "Dalmanutha (8:10)." *ZDPV* 116: 42–48.

————. 2003a. "Poesie, I.1 Altes Testament." Pages 1416–18 in *RGG⁴* 6.

————. 2003b. *Poetik der Psalmen: Poetologische Studien zum Alten Testament*. Vol. 1. Stuttgart: Kohlhammer.

————. 2011. "Poetry. I.1. Old Testament." Pages 182–84 in *RPP* 10.

Seybold, K., and H.-J. Fabry. 1997. "*melek*." Pages 346–75 in *TDOT*.

Sherwin-White, A. N. 1963. *Roman Society and Roman Law in the New Testament*. Oxford: Clarendon Press.

————. 1985. *The Letters of Pliny*. 2nd ed. Oxford: Oxford University Press.

Siegert, F. 1980. *Drei hellenistisch-jüdische Predigten*. Vol. 1. WUNT 20. Tübingen: Mohr.

————. 1992. *Drei hellenistisch-jüdische Predigten*. Vol. 2. WUNT 61. Tübingen: Mohr.

———. 2001. *Josephus. Aus meinem Leben (Vita).* Kritische Ausgabe, Übersetzung und Kommentar von Folker Siegert in Verbindung mit Heinz Schreckenberg und Manuel Vogel. Tübingen: Mohr.

Sjöberg, E. 1946. *Der Menschensohn im äthiopischen Henochbuch.* SHVL 41. Lund: Gleerup.

———. 1955. *Der verborgene Menschensohn in den Evangelien.* SHVL 53. Lund: Gleerup.

Smith, M. 1973. *Clement of Alexandria and a Secret Gospel of Mark.* Cambridge, Mass.: Harvard University Press.

———. 1978. *Jesus the Magician.* New York: Harper & Row.

Snodgrass, K. 1983. *The Parable of the Wicked Tenants.* WUNT 27. Tübingen: Mohr.

Soden, W. von, J. Bergman, and M. Saebø. 1982. "jôm, jômām, jôm JHWH." Pages 559–86 in *ThWAT* 3.

———. 1990. "yôm, yômām, yôm YHWH." Pages 7–32 in *TDOT* 6.

Soggin, J. A. 1972. "Ephraim." Pages 420–21 in *Biblisch-historisches Handwörterbuch.* Vol. 1. Edited by B. Reicke and L. Rost. Göttingen: Vandenhoeck & Ruprecht.

Sokoloff, M. 2002. *A Dictionary of Jewish Palestinian Aramaic.* Ramat-Gan: Bar Ilan University Press.

Spicq, C. 1978. *Notes de lexicographie néo-testamentaire.* 2 vols. OBO 22.1–2. Fribourg: Éditions universitaires.

Stancliffe, C. 1983. *St. Martin and His Hagiographer: History and Miracle in Sulpicius Severus.* Oxford: Clarendon Press.

Stanton, G. N. 1974. *Jesus of Nazareth in New Testament Preaching.* Cambridge: Cambridge University Press.

Steck, O. H. 1991. *Der Abschluß der Prophetie im Alten Testament.* BThSt 17. Neukirchen-Vluyn: Neukirchener.

Stemberger, G. 1991. *Pharisäer, Sadduzäer, Essener.* SBS 144. Stuttgart: Katholisches Bibelwerk.

———. 1992. *Einleitung in Talmud und Midrasch.* 8th ed. Munich: Beck.

———. 1999. "The Sadducees—Their History and Doctrine." Pages 428–43 in *The Cambridge History of Judaism.* Vol. 3. Edited by W. Horbury, W. D. Davies, and J. Sturdy. Cambridge: Cambridge University Press.

Stern, E., and Y. Magen. 2002. "Archaeological Evidence for the First Stage of the Samaritan Temple on Mount Gerizim." *IEJ* 52: 49–57.

Stern, M. 1976–1984. *Greek and Latin Authors on Jews and Judaism.* 3 vols. Jerusalem: Israel Academy of Sciences and Humanities.

———. 1987. "Aspects of Jewish Society: The Priesthood and Other Classes." Pages 561–630 in *The Jewish People in the First Century.* Edited by S. Safrai and M. Stern. CRINT 1/2. Assen: Van Gorcum.

Stettler, H. 1998. *Die Christologie der Pastoralbriefe.* WUNT 2/105. Tübingen: Mohr.

Steudel, A. 1994. *The Midrasch zur Eschatologie aus der Qumrangemeinde (4QMidrEschat^{a,b}).* STDJ XIII. Leiden: Brill.

———. 2001. *Die Texte aus Qumran.* Vol. 2. Darmstadt: Wissenschaftliche Buchgesellschaft.

Strack, H. L. 1910. *Jesus, die Häretiker und die Christen: Nach den ältesten jüdischen Angaben; Texte, Übersetzungen und Erläuterungen.* SIJB 37. Leipzig: Hinrichs.

Strack, H. L., and P. Billerbeck. 1922. *Kommentar zum Neuen Testament aus Talmud und Midrasch.* Vol. 1: *Matthäus.* Munich: Beck.

———. 1924. *Kommentar zum Neuen Testament aus Talmud und Midrasch.* Vol. 2: *Markus, Lukas, Johannes, Apostelgeschichte.* Munich: Beck.

———. 1926. *Kommentar zum Neuen Testament aus Talmud und Midrasch.* Vol. 3: *Briefe, Apokalypse.* Munich: Beck.

———. 1928. *Kommentar zum Neuen Testament aus Talmud und Midrasch.* Vol. 4: *Exkurse und Indices.* Munich: Beck.

Strack, H. L., and G. Stemberger. 1996. *Introduction to the Talmud and Midrash.* Translated and edited by M. Bockmuehl. 2nd ed. Minneapolis: Fortress.

Strauss, D. F. 1835/36. *Das Leben Jesu kritisch bearbeitet.* 2 vols. Tübingen: Osiander.

———. 1837. *Das Leben Jesu kritisch bearbeitet.* Vol. 1. 2nd ed. Tübingen: Osiander.

———. 1838/1839. *Das Leben Jesu.* 2 vols. 3rd ed. Tübingen: Osiander.

———. 1864. *Das Leben Jesu für das deutsche Volk bearbeitet.* 2nd ed. Leipzig: Brockhaus.

———. 1865. *Der Christus des Glaubens und der Jesus der Geschichte: Eine Kritik des Schleiermacher'schen Lebens Jesu.* Berlin: Duncker.

———. 1872. *Der alte und der neue Glaube.* Leipzig: Hirzel.

———. 1873. *The Old and the New Faith: A Confession.* Translated by M. Blind. London: Asher.

———. 1892. *The Life of Jesus Critically Examined.* 2nd ed. Translated from the 4 German edition by George Eliot. London: Sonnenschein.

———. 1977. *The Christ of Faith and the Jesus of History: A Critique of Schleiermacher's Life of Jesus.* Translated by L. E. Keck. Philadelphia: Fortress.

Strecker, G. 1959. "Ebioniten." Pages 487–500 in *RAC* 4.

———. 1969. "Die historische und theologische Problematik der Jesusfrage." *EvTh* 29: 453–76.

———. 1979. *Eschaton und Historie. Aufsätze.* Göttingen: Vandenhoeck & Ruprecht.

———. 1984. *Die Bergpredigt.* Göttingen: Vandenhoeck & Ruprecht.

Strickert, F. 2002. "The First Woman to Be Portrayed on a Jewish Coin." *JSJ* 33: 65–91.

Strobel, A. 1980. *Die Stunde der Wahrheit: Untersuchungen zum Strafverfahren gegen Jesus.* WUNT 21. Tübingen: Mohr.

Stuhlmacher, P. 1965. *Gerechtigkeit Gottes bei Paulus.* Göttingen: Vandenhoeck & Ruprecht.

———. 1973. "Kritischer müßten mir die Historisch-Kritischen sein!" *ThQ* 153: 244–51.

———, ed. 1983. *Das Evangelium und die Evangelien: Vorträge vom Tübinger Symposium 1982.* WUNT 28. Tübingen: Mohr.

———. 1987. "Das neutestamentliche Zeugnis vom Herrenmahl." *ZThK* 84: 1–35.

———, ed. 1991. *The Gospel and the Gospels*. Grand Rapids: Eerdmans.

———. 1992. *Biblische Theologie des Neuen Testaments*. Vol. 1: *Grundlegung: Von Jesus zu Paulus*. Göttingen: Vandenhoeck & Ruprecht.

———. 1996. "Jes 53 in den Evangelien und in der Apostelgeschichte." Pages 93–105 in *Der leidende Gottesknecht*. Edited by B. Janowski and P. Stuhlmacher. FAT 14. Tübingen: Mohr.

———. 1999. *Biblische Theologie des Neuen Testaments*. Vol. 2: *Von der Paulusschule bis zur Johannesoffenbarung*. Göttingen: Vandenhoeck & Ruprecht.

———. 2004. "Isaiah 53 in the Gospels and Acts." Pages 147–62 in *The Suffering Servant: Isaiah 53 in Jewish and Christian Scriptures*. Translated by D. P. Bailey. Edited by B. Janowski and P. Stuhlmacher. Grand Rapids: Eerdmans.

———. 2018. *Biblical Theology of the New Testament*. Translated and edited by D. P. Bailey. Grand Rapids: Eerdmans.

Sullivan, R. D. 1978. "Papyri Reflecting the Eastern Dynastic Network." Pages 908–38 in *ANRW* II 8.

Swete, S. H. B. 1927. *The Gospel According to St. Mark*. 3rd ed. London: Macmillan.

Sysling, H. 1996. *Tehiyyat Ha-Metim*. TSAJ 57. Tübingen: Mohr.

Tajra, H. W. 1989. *The Trial of St. Paul*. WUNT 2/35. Tübingen: Mohr.

Talmon, S. 1997. "A Masada Fragment of Samaritan Origin." *IEJ* 47: 220–32.

Taylor, J. E. 1997. *The Immerser: John the Baptist within Second Temple Judaism*. Grand Rapids: Eerdmans.

———. 1998. "Golgotha." *NTS* 44: 180–203.

Taylor, V. 1966. *The Gospel According to St. Mark*. 2nd ed. London: Macmillan.

Terbuyken, P. 2001. "Judas Iskariot." Pages 140–60 in *RAC* 19.

Theisohn, J. 1975. *Der auserwählte Richter: Untersuchungen zum traditions geschichtlichem Ort der Menschensohngestalt der Bilderreden des Äthiopischen Henoch*. StUNT 12. Göttingen: Vandenhoeck & Ruprecht.

Theissen, G. 1974. *Urchristliche Wundergeschichten: Ein Beitrag zur formgeschichtlichen Erforschung der synoptischen Evangelien*. StNT 8. Gütersloh: Gütersloher.

———. 1983. *The Miracle Stories of the Early Christian Tradition*. Translated by F. McDonagh. Minneapolis: Fortress.

———. 1989a. "Gewaltverzicht und Feindesliebe (Mt 5,38-48/Lk 6,27-38) und deren sozialgeschichtlicher Hintergrund." Pages 160–97 in *Studien zur Soziologie des Urchristentums*. 3rd ed. WUNT 19. Tübingen: Mohr.

———. 1989b. *Lokalkolorit und Zeitgeschichte in den Evangelien: Ein Beitrag zur Geschichte der synoptischen Tradition*. NTOA 8. Göttingen: Vandenhoeck & Ruprecht.

———. 1992. *The Gospels in Context: Social and Political History in the Synoptic Tradition*. Translated by L. M. Maloney. Edinburgh: T&T Clark.

———. 2003a. "Historische Skepsis und Jesusforschung; Oder: Meine Versuche über Lessings garstigen breiten Graben zu springen." Pages 327–63 in *Jesus als historische Gestalt: Beiträge zur Jesusforschung*. Edited by A. Merz. Göttingen: Vandenhoeck & Ruprecht.

———. 2003b. *Jesus als historische Gestalt: Beiträge zur Jesusforschung*. Edited by A. Merz. FRLANT 202. Göttingen: Vandenhoeck & Ruprecht.

———. 2004. *Die Jesusbewegung: Sozialgeschichte einer Revolution der Werte*. Gütersloh: Gütersloher.

Theissen, G., and A. Merz. 1997 [1996]. *Der historische Jesus: Ein Lehrbuch*. 2nd ed. Göttingen: Vandenhoeck & Ruprecht.

———. 1998. *The Historical Jesus: A Comprehensive Guide*. Translated by J. Bowden. Minneapolis: Fortress.

Theissen, G., and D. Winter. 1997. *Die Kriterienfrage in der Jesusforschung: Vom Differenzkriterium zum Plausibilitätskriterium*. NTOA 34. Freiburg: Universitätsverlag.

———. 2002. *The Quest for the Plausible Jesus: The Question of Criteria*. Translated by E. M. Boring. Louisville: Westminster John Knox.

Theobald, M. 2002. *Herrenworte im Johannes-Evangelium*. HBS 34. Freiburg im Breslau: Herder.

Theodor, J., and C. Albeck. 1965. *Midrash Bereshit Rabba*. Vol. 1. Jerusalem: Wahrmann.

Thoma, C., S. Lauer, and H. Ernst. 1986–1996. *Die Gleichnisse der Rabbinen*. Bern: Lang.

Thomas, J. 1935. *Le mouvement baptiste en Palestine et Syrie*. Gembloux: Duculot.

Thornton, C.-J. 1991. *Der Zeuge des Zeugen: Lukas als Historiker der Paulusreisen*. WUNT 56. Tübingen: Mohr.

Thyen, H. 2005. *Das Johannesevangelium*. HNT 6. Tübingen: Mohr.

Tilly, M. 1994. *Johannes der Täufer und die Biographie der Propheten: Die synoptische Täuferüberlieferung und das jüdische Prophetenbild zur Zeit des Täufers*. BWANT 137. Stuttgart: Kohlhammer.

Tisserant, E. 1909. *Ascensión d'Isaie*. Paris: Letouzey et Ane.

Tov, E. 1992. "The Unpublished Texts from Cave 4 and 11." *BA* 55: 94–103.

———. 1996. "The Socio-Religious Background of the Paleo-Hebrew Biblical Texts Found at Qumran." Pages 353–74 in *Geschichte—Tradition—Reflexion: Festschrift für Martin Hengel*. Vol. 1: *Judentum*. Edited by H. Cancik, H. Lichtenberger, and P. Schäfer. Tübingen: Mohr.

Trilling, W. 1966. *Fragen zur Geschlichtlichkeit Jesu*. Düsseldorf: Patmos.

Trocmé, E. 1963. *La formation de l'Évangile selon Marc*. EHPhR 57. Paris: Presses Universitaires de France.

———. 1971. *Jésus de Nazareth, vu par les témoins de sa vie*. Paris: Delachaux et Niestlé.

———. 1973. *Jesus and His Contemporaries*. Translated by R. A. Wilson. London: SCM.

Tuckett, C. M. 2002. "Luke 22,43-44: The 'Agony' in the Garden and Luke's Gospel." Pages 131–44 in *New Testament Textual Criticism and Exegesis: Festschrift for Joël Delobel*. Edited by A. Denaux. BEThL 161. Leuven: Peeters.

Twelftree, G. H. 1993. *Jesus the Exorcist: A Contribution to the Study of the Historical Jesus.* Peabody: Hendrickson.

———. 1999. *Jesus the Miracle Worker: A Historical and Theological Study.* Downers Grove, Ill.: Intervarsity.

———, ed. 2017. *The Nature Miracles of Jesus: Problems, Perspectives, and Prospects.* Eugene, Ore.: Cascade Books.

Tzaferis, V. 1985. "Crucifixion—The Archaeological Evidence: Remains of a Jewish Victim of Crucifixion Found in Jerusalem." *BAR* 2: 44–53.

Uhlig, S. 1984. *Das äthiopische Henochbuch.* JSHRZ V/6. Gütersloh: Mohn.

Ungern-Sternberg, J. von, and H. Reinau, eds. 1988. *Vergangenheit in mündlicher Überlieferung.* Colloquium Rauricum 1. Stuttgart: Teubner.

van der Horst, P. W. 1972. "Can a Book End with a ΓΑΡ? A Note on Mark XVI,8." *JThS* 23: 121–24.

———. 1997. "'The Finger of God.'" Pages 89–103 in *Sayings of Jesus: Canonical and Non-Canonical; Festschrift Tjitze Baarda.* Edited by W. L. Petersen, J. S. Vos, and H. J. de Jonge. NT.S 89. Leiden: Brill.

———. 2003. *Philo's Flaccus: The First Pogrom.* Philo of Alexandria Commentary Series 2. Leiden: Brill.

———. 2006. *Jews and Christians in their Greco-Roman Context.* WUNT 196. Tübingen: Mohr.

VanderKam, J. C. 1981. "2 Macc 6:7a and Calendrical Change in Jerusalem." *JSJ* 12: 52–74.

———. 2010. *Dead Sea Scrolls Today.* Revised edition. Grand Rapids: Eerdmans.

Vansina, J. 1985. *Oral Tradition as History.* Madison: University of Wisconsin Press.

van Uytfanghe, M. 1981. "La controverse biblique et patristique autour du miracle et ses répercussions sur l'hagiographie dans l'Antiquité tardive et le haut Moyen Âge." Pages 205–33 in *Hagiographie: Cultures et sociétés* Paris: University of Paris Press.

———. 2001. "Biographie II (spirituelle)." Pages 1088–1364 in *RAC Suppl.* 1.

van Voorst, R. E. 2001. *Jesus Outside the New Testament.* Grand Rapids: Eerdmans.

Veltri, G. 2003. "Philo." Pages 1286–88 in *RGG⁴* 6.

———. 2011. "Philo of Alexandria." Pages 51–52 in *RPP* 10.

Verheule, A. E. 1973. *Wilhelm Bousset: Leben und Werk.* Amsterdam: Bolland.

Vermes, G. 1973. *Jesus the Jew: A Historian's Reading of the Gospels.* London: Collins.

———. 1993. *Jesus der Jude: Ein Historiker liest die Evangelien.* Neukirchen-Vluyn: Neukirchener.

Vielhauer, P. 1965a. *Aufsätze zum Neuen Testament.* TB 31. Munich: Kaiser.

———. 1965b. "Ein Weg zur neutestamentlicher Christologie: Prüfung der Thesen Ferdinand Hahns." *EvTh* 25: 24–75.

———. 1975. *Geschichte der urchristlichen Literatur.* Berlin: Walter de Gruyter.

Volkmann, H. 1969. *Res gestae Divi Augusti.* 3rd ed. Berlin: Walter de Gruyter.

———. 1979. "Iurgurtha." Pages 1513–14 in *KP* 2.

Volney, C. F. 1791. *Les ruines, ou, Méditations sur les révolutions des empires*. Paris: Desenne.

———. 1796. *The Ruins, or A Survey of the Revolutions of Empires*. New York: Davis.

———. 1828. *Volney's Ruins, or, Meditations on the Revolutions of Empires*. Translated by J. Barlow. New York: Dixon and Sickles.

Vouga, F. 1994. *Geschichte des frühen Christentums*. UTB 1733. Tübingen: Francke.

Wacholder, B. Z. 1962. *Nicolaus of Damascus*. UCPH 75. Berkeley, Calif.: University of California Press.

Waldstein, W. 1964. *Untersuchungen zum römischen Begnadigungsrecht*. Commentationes Aenipontanae XVIII. Innsbruck: Wagner.

Walsh, P. G. 2006. *Pliny the Younger: Complete Letters*. Translated with an introduction and notes by P. G. Walsh. Oxford: Oxford University Press.

Walzer, R. 1949. *Galen on Jews and Christians*. London: Oxford University Press.

Wandrey, I. 1998. "Josephos." Pages 1088–91 in *DNP* 5.

———. 2005. "Iosephus 4." Pages 920–22 in *BNP* 6.

Wansbrough, H., ed. 1985. *The New Jerusalem Bible*. New York: Doubleday.

Webb, R. L. 1991. *John the Baptizer and Prophet*. JSNT.S 62. Sheffield Sheffield Academic Press.

Weber, E. 1974. *Augustus, Meine Taten/Res Gestae Divi Augusti*. 2nd ed. Munich: Heimeran.

Wedderburn, A. J. M. 2004. *A History of the First Christians*. London: T&T Clark International.

Weder, H. 1985. *Die "Rede der Reden": Eine Auslegung der Bergpredigt heute*. Zürich: Theologischer Verlag.

Weihs, A. 2003. *Jesus und das Schicksal der Propheten*. BThSt 61. Neukirchen-Vluyn Neukirchener.

Weiss, B. 1882. *Das Leben Jesu*. 2 vols. Berlin: Hertz.

———. 1885. *Lehrbuch der Biblischen Theologie des Neuen Testaments*. Berlin: Hertz.

———. 1901. *Die Evangelien des Markus und Lukas*. 9th ed. KEK 1,2. Göttingen: Vandenhoeck & Ruprecht.

———. 1927. *Aus neunzig Lebensjahren 1827–1918*. Edited by H. Weiss. Leipzig: Koehler & Amelang.

Weiss, J. 1892. *Die Predigt Jesu vom Reiche Gottes*. Göttingen: Vandenhoeck & Ruprecht.

———. 1900. *Die Predigt Jesu vom Reiche Gottes*. 2nd ed. Göttingen: Vandenhoeck & Ruprecht.

———. 1964. *Die Predigt Jesu vom Reich Gottes*. Edited by F. Hahn. 3rd ed. Göttingen: Vandenhoeck & Ruprecht.

———. 1971. *Jesus' Proclamation of the Kingdom of God*. Translated, edited, and with an introduction by R. H. Hiers and D. L. Holland. London: SCM.

Weissenrieder, A. 2003. *Images of Illness in the Gospel of Luke*. WUNT 2/164. Tübingen: Mohr.

Wellhausen, J. 1908. *Das Evangelium Johannis*. Berlin: Reimer.

———. 1909. *Das Evangelium Marci*. Berlin: Reimer (Reprinted in Wellhausen 1987, 321–457).

———. 1911. *Einleitung in die drei ersten Evangelien*. Berlin: Reimer (reprinted in Wellhausen 1987).

———. 1987. *Evangelienkommentare*. Berlin: Walter de Gruyter.

Wells, G. A. 1986. *Did Jesus Exist?* 2nd ed. London: Pemberton.

Wenham, D. 1995. *Paul—Follower of Jesus or Founder of Christianity?* Grand Rapids: Eerdmans.

Westermann, C. 1964. *Grundformen prophetischer Rede*. 2nd ed. BEvTh 31. Munich: Kaiser.

———. 1991. *Basic Forms of Prophetic Speech*. Translated by G. M. Tucker. Louisville: Westminster John Knox.

Wifstrand, A. 2005. *Epochs and Styles*. Edited by L. Rydbeck and S. E. Porter. WUNT 179. Tübingen: Mohr.

Wilckens, U. 2002–2005. *Theologie des Neuen Testaments*. Vol. 1. Neukirchen-Vluyn: Neukirchener.

Wilke, C. G. 1838. *Der Urevangelist oder kritische Untersuchung über das Verwandtschaftsverhältnis der ersten drei Evangelien*. Dresden: Fleischer.

Williams, W., ed. 1990. *Pliny: Correspondence with Trajan from Bithynia (Epistles X)*. Translated, with introduction and commentary, by Wayne Williams. Warnister, England: Aris & Phillips.

Windisch, H. 1929/1930. "Das Problem der Geschtlichtlichkeit Jesu: Die außerchristlichen Zeugnisse." *ThR NF* 1: 266–88; 2: 207–52.

Wink, W. 1968. *John the Baptist in the Gospel Tradition*. MSSNTS 7. Cambridge: Cambridge University Press.

Winkelmann, F. 2002. "Iulius Africanus." Pages 508–18 in *RAC* 19.

Wirk, R. 1988. "Vergangenheit in mündlicher Überlieferung: Einige Aspekte Neuerer Geschichte." Pages 331–34 in *Vergangenheit in mündlicher Überlieferung: Colloquium Rauricum 1. Stuttgart: Teubner*. Edited by J. von Ungern-Sternberg and H. Reinau. Stuttgart: Teubner.

Wirth, G. 1964. "Arrianos." Pages 605–6 in *KP* 1.

Wischmeyer, O. 1999. "Herrschen als Dienen—Mk 10,41-45." *ZNW* 90: 28–44.

Wohlenberg, G. 1910. *Das Evangelium des Markus*. KNT 2. Leipzig: Deichert.

Wohlers, M., and R. Riesner. 2001. "Kontroverse." *ZNT* 7: 48–58.

Wolter, M. 2016/2017. *The Gospel According to Luke*. Translated by W. Coppins and C. Heilig. Edited by W. Coppins and S. Gathercole. 2 vols. BMSEC 4–5. Waco: Baylor University Press.

Wolters, A. 1996. *The Copper Scroll: Overview, Text and Translation*. Sheffield: Sheffield Academic Press.

Woodman, A. J., ed. 2004. *Tacitus: The Annals*. Translated with an introduction and notes by A. J. Woodman. Indianapolis: Hackett.

Wrede, W. 1904a. *Jesus*. Vol. 1. RV 1, Series 2/3. Halle: Gebauer-Schwetke.

———. 1904b. "Zum Thema 'Menschensohn.'" *ZNW* 5: 359–60.

———. 1907a. *Paulus*. 2nd ed. Tübingen: Mohr.

———. 1907b. "Die Predigt Jesu vom Reiche Gottes (1884)." Pages 84–126 in *Vorträge und Studien*. Edited by A. Wrede. Tübingen: Mohr.

———. 1907c. *Vorträge und Studien*. Edited by A. Wrede. Tübingen: Mohr.

———. 1969 [1901]. *Das Messiasgeheimnis in den Evangelien. Zugleich ein Beitrag zum Verständnis des Markusevangeliums*. 4th ed. Göttingen: Vandenhoeck & Ruprecht.

———. 1971. *The Messianic Secret*. Translated by J. C. G. Greig. Cambridge: Clarke.

Wright, W. C., ed. 1922. *Lives of the Sophists*. LCL 134. London: Heinemann.

Wucherpfennig, A. 2002. *Heracleon Philologus: Gnostische Johannesexegese im zweiten Jahrhundert*. WUNT 142. Tübingen: Mohr.

Wüst, E. 1932. "Mimos." Pages 1727–63 in *PRE* 15.2.

Zahn, T. von. 1900. "Brüder und Vettern Jesu." Pages 225–363 in *Forschungen zur Geschichte des neutestamentlichen Kanons*. Vol. 6. Leipzig: Hinrichs.

———. 1906. *Einleitung in das Neue Testament*. Vol. 1. 3rd ed. Leipzig: Deichert.

———. 1907. *Einleitung in das Neue Testament*. Vol. 2. Leipzig: Deichert.

———. 1920. *Das Evangelium des Lucas*. 3rd/4th ed. KNT 3. Leipzig: Deichert.

———. 1922. *Das Evangelium nach Matthäus*. 4th ed. Leipzig: Deichert.

———. 1924. *Einleitung in das Neue Testament*. Leipzig: Deichert (reprint of Zahn 1906 and Zahn 1907).

Zahn-Harnack, A. 1951. *Adolf von Harnack*. 2nd ed. Berlin: Walter de Gruyter.

Zangenberg, J. 2001. "Samaritaner." Pages 2–4 in *DNP* 11.

———. 2008. "Samaritans." Pages 916–18 in *BNP* 12.

Zeller, D. 2004. "Jesu weisheitliche Ethik." Pages 193–215 in *Jesus von Nazaret—Spuren und Konturen*. Edited by L. Schenke. Stuttgart: Kohlhammer.

Ziegler, T. 1908. *David Friedrich Strauß*. 2 vols. Strasbourg: Trübner.

Zimmermann, J. 1998. *Messianische Texte aus Qumran*. WUNT 2/104. Tübingen: Mohr.

Zuckermandel, M. S. 1880. *Die Tosefta nach den Erfurter und Wiener Handschriften*. Pasewalk: Meier.

Zuntz, G. 1984a. "Ein Heide las das Markusevangelium." Pages 205–22 in *Markus-Philologie: Historische, literargeschichtliche und stilistische Untersuchungen zum zweiten Evangelium*. Edited by H. Cancik. WUNT 33. Tübingen: Mohr.

———. 1984b. "Wann wurde das Evangelium Marci geschrieben?" Pages 47–71 in *Markus-Philologie*. Edited by H. Cancik. Tübingen: Mohr.

Zwiep, A. W. 2001. "Assumptus est in caelum: Rapture and Heavenly Exaltation in Early Judaism and Luke-Acts." Pages 323–49 in *Auferstehung—Resurrection*. Edited by F. Avemarie and H. Lichtenberger. WUNT 135. Tübingen: Mohr.

Index of Ancient Sources

IX. Rabbinic Writings

1. Mishnah, Tosefta, Talmud and Extra-Canonical Tractates

Index of Authors